Content Area Reading:
Integration with the Language Arts

Online Services

Delmar Online
To access a wide variety of Delmar products and services on the World Wide Web,
point your browser to:
        http://www.delmar.com/delmar
        or email: info@delmar.com

thomson.com
To access International Thomson Publishing's
home site for information on more than 34 publishers
and 20,000 products, point your browser to:
        http://www.thomson.com
        or email: findit@kiosk.thomson.com

A service of **I** (**T**) **P** ®

Content Area Reading:
Integration with the Language Arts

Jeanne M. Jacobson

Hope College

Delmar Publishers

I(T)P® an International Thomson Publishing company

Albany • Bonn • Boston • Cincinnati • Detroit • London • Madrid
Melbourne • Mexico City • New York • Pacific Grove • Paris • San Francisco
Singapore • Tokyo • Toronto • Washington

NOTICE TO THE READER

Publisher does not warrant or guarantee any of the products described herein or perform any independent analysis in connection with any of the product information contained herein. Publisher does not assume, and expressly disclaims, any obligation to obtain and include information other than that provided to it by the manufacturer.

The reader is expressly warned to consider and adopt all safety precautions that might be indicated by the activities herein and to avoid all potential hazards. By following the instructions contained herein, the reader willingly assumes all risks in connection with such instructions.

The publisher makes no representation or warranties of any kind, including but not limited to, the warranties of fitness for particular purpose or merchantability, nor are any such representations implied with respect to the material set forth herein, and the publisher takes no responsibility with respect to such material. The publisher shall not be liable for any special, consequential, or exemplary damages resulting, in whole or part, from the readers' use of, or reliance upon, this material.

Cover design and illustration: Karen Meyer

Delmar Staff
Senior Editor: Jay S. Whitney
Associate Editor: Erin J. O'Connor Traylor
Senior Project Editor: Judith Boyd Nelson
Production Coordinator: Sandra Woods
Art and Design Coordinator: Carol D. Keohane

COPYRIGHT © 1998
By Delmar Publishers
a division of International Thomson Publishing Inc.

The ITP logo is a trademark under license.

Printed in the United States of America

For more information, contact:

Delmar Publishers
3 Columbia Circle, Box 15015
Albany, New York 12212-5015

International Thomson Publishing-Europe
Berkshire House 168–173
High Holborn
London WC1V 7AA
England

Thomas Nelson Australia
102 Dodds Street
South Melbourne, 3205
Victoria, Australia

Nelson Canada
1120 Birchmount Road
Scarborough, Ontario
Canada M1K 5G4

International Thomson Editores
Campos Eliseos 385, Piso 7
Col Polanco
11560 Mexico D F Mexico

International Thomson Publishing GmbH
Konigswinterer Strasse 418
53227 Bonn
Germany

International Thomson Publishing-Asia
221 Henderson Road
#05–10 Henderson Building
Singapore 0315

International Thomson Publishing-Japan
Hirakawacho Kyowa Building, 3F
2-2-1 Hirakawacho
Chiyoda-ku, Tokyo 102
Japan

1 2 3 4 5 6 7 8 9 10 XXX 03 02 01 00 99 98 97

Library of Congress Cataloging-in-Publication Data

Jacobson, Jeanne M.
    Content area reading: integration with the language arts / Jeanne M. Jacobson.
        p. cm.
    Includes bibliographical references and indexes.
    ISBN 0-8273-6242-0
    1. Language arts—Correlation with content subjects. 2. Teaching. I. Title.
LB1576. J26 1996   96-13099
372.6—dc20   CIP

Contents

Chapter Four: Establishing a Strong Structure of Understanding as Content Area Topics Are Studied 111

Chapter Eight: Assessment for Learning and Teaching: Attention, Investigation, Documentation, and Evaluation 309

Chapter Nine: Communication and Collaboration: Linking School and Home..346

Part Four: Extending Content Area Learning

Chapter Ten: Integration of Listening, Speaking, Reading, and Writing in Content Area Study...384

Chapter Eleven: Integration of the Arts With Content Area Learning 424

Preface

This text is a first edition—and yet in another sense this is its twentieth edition. *Content Area Reading: Integration with the Language Arts*, first appeared one chapter at a time beginning in January 1990. Since then it has been revised and expanded for each new term—several times a year. This published version owes much to the hundreds of students, both undergraduate and graduate, and their various instructors, who have used and shaped it over a six-year period. Their praise and enthusiasm has encouraged me; their questions and comments have shown me where text passages needed further explanation and clarification; their many thoughtful suggestions have given me ideas for additions and changes.

The audience for whom the text is intended is wide-ranging. It is written primarily for teachers and teachers-to-be—people who are currently teaching and people who are studying to become teachers. Other stakeholders in the educational process—administrators, parents, and students themselves—may also find the book, or sections of it, to be interesting and informative. Inclusiveness is a theme that recurs throughout the text; the book itself is intended to be inclusive in content and style and to show that important educational ideas and theories are applicable to teaching and learning generally, not simply to a particular age group, school level, or teaching specialization. All of us who are teachers have something to say to each other and we all have many things to learn from each other.

Philosophy and Rationale

A premise on which the book is based is that the overwhelming majority of teachers care for their students and believe deeply in the importance of education. We want to teach well. An essential part of good teaching is the willingness to learn more, to make decisions, and therefore to change our good teaching to make it better. Much of the text's content can be viewed as an encouragement for good teachers to make changes in their teaching that will increase their students' learning and love of learning, and enhance their own professional satisfaction and growth.

Scholars who write about education, as well as teachers themselves, are aware of the complexity of teaching, and the difficulties inherent in making changes. Yet change and flexibility are necessary. Richard Allington writes, "There is no single organizational scheme that we can simply put in place and leave alone… every day presents a different set of instructional problems" (Allington, 1992, p. 354). Dolores Durkin reminds us that creating "meaningful changes in classrooms is a complex endeavor even when teachers want to change …[S]ubstantive change is made up of a number of connected changes, [and this] contributes to the complexity, thus the difficulty, of implementation" (Aaron, Chall, Clymer, Durkin, Early, Farr & Robinson, 1992, pp. 388–389).

"Meaningful and lasting changes occur when teachers think differently about what is going on in their classrooms, and are provided with the practices to match the different ways of thinking. The provision of practices without theory may lead to misimplementation or no implementation at all, unless teachers' beliefs are congruent with the theoretical assumptions of the practice. Further, programs in which theory is discussed and which focus on changing beliefs without proposing practices that embody those theories may lead to frustration." (Virginia Richardson and her colleagues on the need to link theory and practice. Richardson, Anders, Tidwell, & Lloyd, 1991, p. 579).

To make our instructional programs more powerful we need to learn about alternative models and strategies. It is also useful to be reminded that our own knowledge base—of content as well as methods—must be sound and growing, in order to teach others effectively. A major purpose of this text is to offer a rich array of useful strategies, linked with useful theory, and to present readers with opportunities to make decisions about which ideas to choose and adapt to suit the features of their own teaching situation.

Organizational Features

The overall plan of the book divides its twelve chapters into four sections. In Part One, two chapters present information about learning and teaching in the content areas. Features which are typical of textbooks written for instruction in fields such as science, the social studies and mathematics are described and the impact of these features on student learning is discussed. Characteristics of good teaching, especially as these relate to content area teaching, are identified and described.

Part Two is a three-chapter sequence based on one of the text's themes: that effective content area teaching requires teachers' thought and action as topics are introduced, during the time students are engaged in acquiring and using new information, and at the culmination of a period of a study. The many strategies introduced in this "before, during and after" section have been chosen because of their applicability to these three points in a learning and teaching cycle. Two major teaching strategies—reading aloud to students and using cooperative learning—are addressed in this section.

Each of the four chapters in Part Three focuses on a major aspect of a teacher's role: promoting students' ability to read, appreciating and accommodating diversity among students, assessing students' learning, and communicating and collaborating with students' families. Each chapter presents relevant theory and describes strategies which enable teachers to fulfill their responsibilities in ways that enhance content area learning. This section of the text includes two glossaries of professional terminology intended for teachers to use as a reference: a glossary of terminology related to the field of reading, following Chapter Six, and a glossary of terms relating to testing, following Chapter Eight.

Part Four comprises three chapters which conclude the text. Two strategy-filled chapters focus on integration of content area learning with aspects of the language arts (listening, talking, reading, writing), and with the wider field of the arts (visual art, music, drama and dance, and literature). The last chapter draws the many text themes together in a discussion of planning and a series of simulations of aspects of the planning process. Throughout the text, as teaching strategies are described, many examples are presented of actual materials which teachers may adapt and use if the activities are appropriate to their teaching assignment.

A major innovation in the text is the inclusion of *Strategic Teacher* sections, which are stories about teaching. Most of this book, like other textbooks, is written entirely in expository style: its organization and manner of presenting ideas is designed to convey information. One of several text themes is that many of the books which give us information, using expository style, are beautifully written and gloriously interesting to read. However, stories can also convey important ideas, and I have chosen to include stories about good teaching, in a blend of narrative and expository style, as a feature of this text. Following each chapter, beginning with Chapter Three and concluding with Chapter Eleven, a teacher is described. Their stories are fictional, but they are based on fact. None of the nine teachers described is a real person, but each is a composite drawn from the hundreds, perhaps thousands, of good teachers who have been my teachers, colleagues, students, friends and exemplars throughout my career. Readers who enjoy wordplay will discover that these teachers' names are anagrams of text-related words or terms (as are the names of the teachers described in Case Studies). All the teachers reappear in Chapter Twelve, where, rather than focusing primarily on rules and procedures for planning, I have used them and their teaching situations to illustrate some of the many ways teachers make planning an integral aspect of their teaching.

A *Strategy Glossary* follows Chapter Twelve. Here each of the strategies discussed in the text is listed, with a brief description and the page numbers showing where there is a fuller description in the main text. Over 250 strategies are described in the text and listed in this glossary. Throughout the text, detailed citations are given crediting the scholars who have originated teaching strategies, or whose ideas have provided the basis for strategies which I have elaborated upon. Strategies which are not credited to others are ones which I have devised, and when a new strategy is credited to one of the strategic teachers I have used as exemplars, I have created the strategy also—for example, imaginative "Dave Lusolo," who creates new math activities for his middle school students while vacationing, seems to me just the person to invent "No-Travel Trips," so I have presented him with the idea.

Four *Case Studies* are included, following Chapters Two, Four, Eight, and Eleven. These descriptions of events in teachers' careers provide opportunities for readers to simulate a decision-making process, as they consider what aspects of a situation require the teacher-protagonist to make choices, determine what options are available, make choices, and think about what the possible results of their choices might be. Although readers may use the case studies independently, they have been designed as a cooperative group activity.

The *References* section for this text follows the Strategy Glossary. It is extensive, and the inclusion of many professional references supports another major text theme: that ongoing professional reading is an essential part of teachers' professional growth. In addition to books on education and psychology, more than 100 professional journals are referenced. Students who wish to pursue further reading about a text topic will find this section useful. Two indexes—*Author Index* and *Subject Index*—conclude the text. The Author Index includes information about pronunciation for several scholars with whom students should be familiar, whose names are not pronounced as would be expected from their spellings. Throughout the text and in the References section, the full names of scholars are given, rather than simply their initials, because it is useful for students to be able to talk knowledgeably about important scholars, becoming familiar with their names as well as their ideas.

 ## Acknowledgments

My heartfelt thanks and appreciation are given to many people and groups who have had a role in the production of this text:

- to my colleagues and students in schools and colleges, who have, every one, been my teachers. To name even those most influential would take many pages. I hope that some will read the text and glimpse themselves in descriptions of outstanding teachers. Several people are owed special mention: Dr. Richard Clark, who set me on the right path of learning and guided my way; Kathy Lu Cook and John Kleis, teachers to admire and depend upon; and Dvorah Heckelman, wise and dear colleague.
- to the scholars whose ideas and writings inform and inspire, and whose words and works illuminate this text.
- to my editors at Delmar Publishers for their expertise and their forbearance during a preparation process that lengthened as I revised and revised again, and to Jim Jacobson for his photographs and commentaries.
- to my family, which, like all families, extends backward in time beyond my knowledge and forward in time farther than I can know. I owe special thanks to my mother, Jean McKee, a memorable teacher; to my father, Edward Price McKee, who valued books and loved to share his learning; to Jennie Smiley Sheppard and George C. Lippincott, who gave me love and the joy of reading; to a lovely and growing group of nearest and dearest—John, Jean, Jennie, Jim, Gail, Jeff, Jim, Johnny, Grace, Sarah, Johnny, Jackie, Molly, and Miranda—and to John Jacobson, my husband, favorite colleague, and dearest of all.
- and finally, to all the learners, the students in our classrooms, and the students yet to come, who inspire us to become the best we can be.

PART ONE

Characteristics of Content Area Learning and Teaching

CHAPTER ONE

Learning and Teaching in the Content Areas

Teachers, like scientists, are committed pragmatists. They single-mindedly pursue "what works"....

— KEITH STANOVICH, 1993/1994, P. 287.

The aims of any school for the education of the streams of pupils passing through its doors year after year must be measured by the kind of work carried on in its individual classrooms.

— ROMIETT STEVENS, 1912, P. 85.

It is a long-standing educational practice to classify the information, the content, that is taught in schools into categories called content areas. In the primary and intermediate grades, the content areas are typically math, science, and social studies. Beginning in the middle school, these areas are subdivided and other subjects are added, so that instead of studying "science," students study fields of science such as earth science, biology, chemistry, or physics. In content area learning students acquire, organize, and use knowledge within and across fields of study or disciplines. As they learn, they classify what they are learning and group similar learnings together. Content area teaching occurs at all levels of schooling. However, in our educational system it is treated differently at different levels, and therefore presents a variety of advantages and challenges to teachers.

This text is an exploration of "what works" in content area learning and teaching. Much of what we know about the world is learned through study that begins during the school years. Good learning usually depends on good teaching. Teachers need content knowledge—sound and growing knowledge about our subject matter. Teachers also need pedagogical knowledge—knowledge about teaching and about ways to provide instruction that will enable students to learn effectively.

Learning and Teaching

The essence of learning is acquiring, organizing, and using knowledge, and then extending these understandings and interests further. As experiences expand and knowledge grows, existing knowledge is built upon and concepts are reorganized and revised to fit new ideas encountered. One of the themes of this text is that, in good learning environments, teachers as well as their students are learners.

New knowledge is built upon what is already known. Learners link new and known information, modifying their ideas as their store of information increases. Across all subjects, new ideas are better understood when they can be related to accurate prior knowledge. *All* students have knowledge and abilities that skillful teachers can help them bring to bear on topics to be studied in school. However, the amount of knowledge, the kind of knowledge, and the immediate relevance of knowledge students bring to a topic of study all differ widely. Content area teachers need to build a shared knowledge base for all their students when new topics are introduced. They then need to structure classroom learning to establish a strong foundation of knowledge as content area topics are studied, and to teach in ways that enhance and extend students' understanding of content area topics. This text provides information about a variety of strategies teachers can use to teach content area subjects in ways that are interesting and useful for all students.

Teaching is helping someone to learn. In effective classrooms, everyone is a learner, including the teacher, and everyone can teach, as well. One of the aspects of cooperative learning—a practice that is becoming widely used—is the acceptance and encouragement of peer teaching. This practice is based on the recognition that teaching is not solely the province of the person designated as the teacher, and that students can and should help one another learn.

When teaching in the content areas, our purposes are:

▎ to help all our students build and develop their store of knowledge;

▎ to help all our students organize their knowledge so they see how ideas are interrelated;

▎ to help all our students use, apply, and remember learnings that are important to them now and will be in the future;

▎ to foster in all our students feelings of capability and industry;

▎ to encourage lifelong learning for all our students and ourselves.

Language and Learning

Language is essential to learning. As infants learn by using their senses and by moving, they are also learning language, and very soon begin to use language to learn more. When we share our thoughts with others, or learn from the thoughts of others, we use language to communicate. Over many years, philosophers and psychologists have discussed the interrelationships among thought and language. Lev Vygotsky, writing on this theme, noted, "Direct communication between minds is impossible, not only physically but psychologically. Communication can be achieved only in a roundabout way. Thought must pass first through meanings and then through words." Contrasting the rapidity of thought with the relative slowness of expressing ideas in language, he wrote, "A thought may be compared to a cloud shedding a shower of words" (Vygotsky, 1962, p. 150). David Myers (1989, pp. 310–311) comments on the cyclical relationship between language and thought in this way: "The power of language to influence thinking is one reason why vocabulary building is such a crucial part of education. To expand language is to expand the ability to think… Language influences thinking. But if thinking did not also affect language, there would never be any new words… [T]hinking affects our language, which then affects our thought."

Language used to communicate and share ideas is either receptive or expressive, depending on whether the language user is receiving or giving information. We receive information through oral language when we listen, and through written language when we read. We express information using oral language when we speak, and using written language when we write. There are other modes of expression as well. Many people who are hearing impaired—and an increasing number of hearing people as well—use sign language; those who understand signing can receive information through this language mode. Body language—facial expressions, gestures, and posture—indicates feelings and attitudes to those who are attentive to these cues. Forms of artistic expression enable people to express and receive ideas in powerful ways.

Content area learning is based primarily on oral and written (or signed) language—listening, talking, reading, and writing—and on thinking, which underlies language use. Because language is the basis of human learning, content area learning depends on, and is fostered by, language in all its aspects. Teachers from preschool through the university need to recognize that

- content area learning cannot be isolated from the development and use of language;
- listening, talking, reading, and writing are all part of good content area programs;
- learning and language development are lifelong processes.

Knowledge and Teaching

To teach effectively, teachers must be knowledgeable. At every level, teachers have a responsibility to have a solid, and growing, understanding of the subjects we teach. Good teaching of content area topics is based on topic knowledge and understanding that goes beyond the material in students' texts. Teachers need strong, solid, and current subject matter knowledge.

Usually grades prekindergarten or kindergarten through grades 5 or 6 constitute the elementary school, and there it is typical for the same teacher to provide instruction across content area topics. Elementary teachers are expected to have wide general knowledge, because they teach social studies, science, math, and more. Because they teach a relatively small number of students during a full school day, they have many opportunities to make connections between content area subjects and to integrate language arts in all areas of learning. A challenge for elementary teachers is to acquire and build their

knowledge across the many content areas they teach. Meeting this challenge presents opportunities for personal and professional growth, growth that can be fostered by personal reading and study, and by seeking out colleagues with content expertise and enthusiasm.

Teachers in the middle school and high school usually are expected to be specialists in a single content area, so they are likely to have many opportunities to increase the depth and breadth of their own understanding in their field. Their challenge is to find ways to make connections between their subject and other subjects their students are learning about, and ways to integrate language arts in their classes. Collaboration with colleagues is a primary resource.

In addition to subject matter knowledge, teachers need to know about **pedagogy,** or teaching itself. Pedagogical knowledge is essential for effective teaching. We have a responsibility to use our analytical and creative talents to determine how best to teach the topics we intend our students to learn, and to reflect on and modify our teaching to meet our students' strengths and needs. Among the elements of good content area teaching are an understanding of the difficulties that students are likely to encounter in learning from content area text, and the possession of a repertoire of strategies to help students learn effectively.

One of the questions preservice teachers (people studying to become teachers) sometimes ask is whether it is more important for teachers to expand their knowledge of effective teaching strategies or to learn more about the content they will be teaching. If a teacher does not have a good understanding of the topics that are to be taught, knowing good teaching strategies still will not help. *Knowledge of subject matter is essential*. On the other hand, some people who have an excellent grasp of subject matter are not able to teach others about it effectively. If someone is employed as a teacher and cannot teach well, then that person should work on learning how, or find a different profession. When they are knowledgeable about both content and ways to teach it, teachers should continue to grow in both areas. Moreover, being knowledgeable already makes it easy to learn more.

---

pedagogy — derived from two ancient Greek words: *paidos*, meaning *child*, and *agein*, meaning *to lead*. A skillful teacher leads students to learn and to value learning. In our language, pedagogy has several related meanings: teaching, the profession of teaching, and the art and science of using strategies to provide instruction.

Learning in a Literate Society

Our society expects that people will acquire information through reading. One of the major reasons for reading textbooks and other written materials in the content areas is what Jeanne Chall (1983) calls "reading for learning the new," or reading to acquire new knowledge. In preliterate societies (cultures that have no written language), learning comes from direct experience, and knowledge is transmitted by word of mouth from adults to children. In literate societies, people also learn from direct experience, and from listening to and observing other people. However, because we have a written language, we have another, very powerful, way to learn. Reading opens up a world of knowledge. Books record, and maintain through time, far more information than any group of people could tell.

Our society expects students to learn in school by reading textbooks and other print sources, and literate people learn throughout their lives by reading. Much of what we learn that is new to us—new information, new ideas, new opinions, new ways of organizing our schemes of thought—comes to us as a result of our reading. Because we have a written language, we can learn about the past as well as about recent discoveries. We turn to written sources to acquire information.

The purposes for reading vary. These purposes have been summarized (Kirsch & Mosenthal, 1990) as learning to read, reading to learn, and reading to do. A fourth important purpose—closely linked to reading to learn—is reading to enjoy. These purposes are present throughout a reader's lifetime, but there is also an age progression. Young readers are learning to read. Throughout school, students are reading to learn. Adults, as part of their careers, have many occasions to read as a part of getting work done. (Reading for enjoyment, unless something has occurred to make reading seem an unpleasant task, occurs throughout the age span, from a baby's pleasure in hearing a soothing bedtime story even before it can be understood, to mature readers seeking new information or rereading books that are treasured favorites.)

In the early grades, children learn to read. They develop as readers by reading. Educators working

Learning and language development are lifelong processes.

with elementary students provide instruction that, by building on the natural human talent for language use, enables children to become proficient readers who enjoy reading. While people are learning to read, they should also be reading to learn new information, and reading to accomplish tasks. Opportunities for "reading to do" include following a recipe, reading directions for an art project or a building project, and reading street signs and names to reach a destination. Reading to learn, to do, and to enjoy are all part of the process of learning to read.

In the middle school and high school, students need to develop further as readers. They are also expected to use their ability to read in order to acquire knowledge. As educators working with middle and high school students, our purpose is to provide instruction that enables students to learn from their reading, to use reading material purposefully, and to develop as proficient readers and learners who enjoy reading and learning. For adults, some of the major purposes for reading new material are to accomplish career-related tasks, and maintain and develop our personal and professional knowledge. Adults who have learned to read and learned from reading as students are equipped to use reading to function and advance in our fields of expertise in the workforce and in the home, and to add to our general store of knowledge and our enjoyment of reading and learning.

At all levels of schooling, content area teachers and teachers who affect students' reading development have a strong influence on students' present and future lives. Besides being aware of the purposes of content area learning and teaching, teachers also need to remember that people who enjoy reading will read more, whereas people for whom reading is not a pleasure will be likely to avoid reading. A major goal of teaching must be to enable all students to develop as learners, to value reading, and to respect themselves as readers and learners.

Learning While Learning To Read

Content area learning in the primary grades occurs as children are learning to read. Effective content area teaching can support reading development. In the primary grades, children's most important school task is learning to read, so that they can go on to expand their learning by reading. Textbooks produced for young children limit the difficulty of the text and the amount of new information presented so that young students do not have the double task of learning to read the text while acquiring information from it. In the primary grades, children are expected to learn to read; thereafter, they are expected to read to learn. Reading material for children who are learning to read needs to be familiar either in style or in content, so that children are not confronted with the difficult task of simultaneously making sense of the

written language and of understanding unfamiliar ideas. Often the familiar element is the style.

Consider an example. When children read stories, the events they read about are likely to be new, but they are told in a familiar **narrative** form. A folktale called "Stone Soup" is often included in reading books for young children. For children who have not heard the story read aloud at home, the events of the story will be new: Some poor soldiers come to a town and ask the people for some food; the townspeople turn them away, saying they have no food; the soldiers offer to make stone soup if someone will give them a pot of water; the townspeople, amazed at the idea of soup made from a stone, eagerly provide the pot and water and the soldiers place the stone in the pot; as the water boils the townspeople gradually agree to make the soup even better by adding vegetables and meat; then everyone enjoys the delicious soup. Even if each event in the story is unexpected, children will be familiar with the style in which the story is told: There are characters who converse; there is a series of events that lead up to a climax followed by a resolution; there is a beginning, a middle, and an end. As children are learning to read, much of their reading material is written in this familiar narrative form.

Content area textbooks written for young children use an **expository** writing style (designed to convey information, to explain, and to present facts), as all textbooks do; but the ideas presented in these textbooks are intended to be familiar. Although the style of writing may be unfamiliar, children have experiences that help to make many of the topics familiar. Content area textbooks written for the primary grades typically include topics such as, in social studies, "Families" and "Neighborhoods," and, in science, "Where We Live" and "Weather."

Problems children face in content area learning in the early grades stem from a variety of causes. Some children have difficulties in learning to read. These children cannot read their textbooks independently no matter how familiar the textbook topics are. For some children content area understanding is hampered by unfamiliarity with topics that textbooks present. For example, apparently simple topics such as "On the Farm" or "In the Big City," may be puzzling to young children who live in urban or rural settings.

---

narrative — the words *narrative, narrator* and *narrate* come from the Latin verb *narrare*, meaning *to tell* or *to relate*. The Latin word *narrare* and the English word *narrate* are similar in meaning. Narrative text provides an account of something that happened; it tells a story, which may be fictional or factual.

expository — comes from a Latin prefix, *ex*, meaning, in this case, *out, out from*, and a Latin verb, *ponere*, meaning *to place*. Together *ex + ponere* means *to set forth*. Expository text sets forth the facts for us; it places information before the reader.

Textbooks themselves may be unfamiliar. Some young children are unaware of how pages are ordered (that is, they cannot yet follow a direction such as "turn to page 26") and many do not know how to use standard text features, such as the table of contents.

For some children, learning is difficult because they are experiencing anxiety and discomfort in the school setting. Their discomfort may have physical causes: They may be hungry or tired or suffering from health problems. Their discomfort may also come from feeling unaccepted in the school setting, from learning that their behavior is "bad," or that their reading is "poor." There are many instructional processes teachers can use that prevent or alleviate these problems while benefiting all children, so that those experiencing difficulties can be helped without being set apart. One of the most important things a teacher can do is to establish a classroom environment in which every student is welcomed and respected.

Teachers of younger students need to have an interest in all the content areas and a strong understanding of how to help their students learn efficiently from content area textbooks, as well as knowledge about the reading process itself. Most students' reading ability and sense of themselves as learners are affected strongly by their early school experiences. Teachers in the primary grades who help their students learn more about their world from content area texts, and enable their students to see themselves as good learners, are setting the stage for satisfying and productive school careers. In terms of teaching strategies, two of the most valuable and versatile practices are reading aloud regularly and using sensibly planned cooperative learning. These practices are advocated and discussed in Chapter Four and throughout this text. Both are effective and inclusive instructional methods not only in the primary years, but across the grades and among adult learners as well.

Reading for "Learning the New"

Content area learning during most of our lives engages us in learning what is new to us. The transition between third and fourth grades is an important one for students. This is the point at which "reading for learning the new"—that is, reading to learn new information and ideas—typically begins. From this point on, throughout students' educational careers, textbooks are written for capable readers who can acquire new information from their texts. Students in the later elementary grades, middle school, and high school are expected to be able to read and learn from expository prose. However, teachers, rather than textbooks, are the major factor in students' learning. Good teaching enables students to learn from their texts.

The transition between third and fourth grades is eased by knowledgeable and capable teachers. Teachers need to understand that this period may present problems, and why. Here, as at every level of teaching, teachers should be aware of a variety of strategies for helping students understand what they are assigned to read, and have ways of helping struggling students improve their reading ability. Moreover, while students are learning to read, teachers need to make sure they do not miss content area information. We should read aloud important sections of content text to the class, stopping to comment about important points, encourage students to raise questions and answer them clearly, and plan activities that illuminate important concepts and conduct class discussions that engage students in using important vocabulary terms and thinking about important concepts. We should become adept at using questions to teach rather than to test—that is, to help students learn, rather than to check their learning. Cooperation among teachers in the elementary grades is very helpful. Even if it is not formally part of the school's planning process, teachers should confer with colleagues who teach the grades above and below theirs, and discuss ways to ease transitions between grades.

Teachers of students in grades 4 through 12 need to have both a thorough content area knowledge base and a strong understanding of how to help their students learn efficiently from content area textbooks. Like all teachers, they need an understanding of reading development and an awareness of the importance of reading in the learning process. As students' textbooks become more complex, instruction provided by teachers is crucial in determining whether students will learn, recall, and use the information in those texts. Very few pieces of expository writing, and no textbooks, can unfailingly serve to inform all their readers effectively. However good a textbook is, it is the teacher's actions that most strongly affect whether students will learn from it.

Factors that Affect Content Area Learning

Three major elements in the content area classroom that affect learning are teachers, students, and texts. Each has the potential to contribute to learning or to hamper it. The focus in this book is on what is helpful, particularly on what teachers can do to contribute to students' learning. However, it is also useful to be aware of problems that may arise. There are things teachers do, or fail to do, that instead of helping their students learn, make it harder for them to learn. There are problems students face that may interfere with their school learning. There are features of textbooks that make it difficult for students to learn from them.

Factors relating to teaching are important at every point in students' progress through school. Good teaching supports learning, but inadequate teaching interferes with student learning. If teachers do not have a sound understanding of the subject matter they are teaching, if they are unwilling to put thought and effort into planning and conducting their classroom program, if they do not care sensibly about all their students, or if they give no time and attention to their own learning, they will not teach effectively. Their students' learning and enjoyment of school will be diminished. However, through capability, energy, care for students and for subject matter, and commitment to continuing professional growth, difficulties that arise from inadequate teaching can be prevented. Teachers have the responsibility to teach well.

Student factors affect their learning. Within any classroom, students will vary widely in the amount and kind of prior knowledge and experience they bring to the task of learning from textbooks. The facets of this prior knowledge and experience include:

■ language development, including reading ability;

■ information about the topics that are being studied;

■ previous experiences in learning situations that have influenced students' attitudes toward school, school-related tasks, and themselves as learners.

Good teachers accept and accommodate this diversity among students.

In helping students learn from their textbooks, teachers need to keep all this information in mind. Teaching strategies should ensure that all students receive essential information from the text without making the process tedious for some students or embarrassing for others. Students' own reading of the text can be preceded by interesting whole class and cooperative group activities that make it possible for them to read with understanding. Other strategies incorporate multiple readings of important text sections in interesting ways. Reading aloud and commenting upon essential text portions is helpful. Students can listen to teacher-prepared tapes of textbook chapters. Knowledge about text topics can be enhanced by well-chosen supplementary materials, including audiovisual learning aids, field trips, and guest speakers. A supportive, well-organized classroom environment can help to ensure that all students have opportunities to develop positive attitudes toward school and to value themselves as learners.

Content Area Textbooks

In our schools, textbooks are important instructional tools. The value of textbooks has been, and continues to be, a subject of debate (e.g., Frager & Vanterpool, 1993). However, in the content areas, textbooks generally are accepted as necessary. They present information about subjects that is organized both within and across grades. Because all students have the textbooks, there is a common source of information for the classroom.

Scope and Sequence

Textbooks present reading material about an extensive set of topics arranged into units and chapters so at each grade level textbooks present information about a broad scope of topics. *Scope* gives a horizontal view of subject matter, such as the range of topics presented by the textbook for a particular grade. Textbook publishers usually produce a series of content area textbooks for use across a grade span—often from first grade through high school, across the grades, textbooks present information about an extensive sequence of topics. *Sequence* gives a vertical view of subject matter: the topics presented, year by year, in this textbook series. Publishers typically provide scope and sequence charts for teachers, listing the topics taught within each grade level, and across the grades, in a particular content area.

The scope and sequence of topics usually differ very little from publisher to publisher, for a practical reason: Textbook publishers do not want to make it difficult for school systems to begin using their materials. It would be hard to switch from one textbook series to another if the sequence of presentation of major topics varied substantially from series to series. Suppose, for example, that Reed & Company's social studies textbook for grade 4 was designed to teach about earth's biomes and about regions of the United States and around the world, while their textbook for grade 5 focused on American history. Suppose also that this sequence was reversed in the books produced by the Wright Publishing Group. If a school system switched from the Reed series to the Wright series, at the end of the first year after the change students entering fifth grade would have had two years of study about biomes and regions and would have missed studying American history. (In fact, typical social studies textbooks for grades 4 and 5 follow the first of the two patterns described.)

Expository Text

Textbooks written to teach science, social studies, mathematics, and other informational subjects have a different purpose from many other kinds of reading material. The purpose of content area text is to inform readers. Content area textbooks are intended to provide information within a field of study in an organized way, so that students can build their knowledge about content area topics. The style of writing in content area texts is expository.

Expository text often is organized around superordinate and subordinate topics. For example, in a fifth-grade science text, the concept that animals are classified as vertebrates (animals with backbones) or invertebrates (animals with no backbones) is treated as a major, or superordinate, topic. "Invertebrates and Vertebrates" may be the title of a chapter. Chapter sections may focus on such subordinate topics as invertebrates without exoskeletons, arthropods, and vertebrates. In a seventh-grade math textbook, a superordinate topic, such as area and volume, probably will include subordinate topics such as the measurement of different two-dimensional and three-dimensional shapes.

Recently, publishers of basal readers (the textbooks traditionally used in reading and language arts classes in elementary schools) have, in response to urging from educators, begun to include more examples of expository text. Though such a change in basal readers may be worthwhile, it does not alter the need for good content area textbooks, and effective teacher use of those textbooks. James Flood and Diane Lapp (1987, p. 306) take the position that opportunities for students to use and learn from expository text ought to come primarily within content area instruction from content area textbooks, rather than from basal readers. They suggest that good instruction in social studies, science, and math provides the best opportunity for students to learn to read expository text, asking "Could the needs of the learner not be better and more directly served in the context of content texts and content instruction where the focus is placed on using text to aid in learning?" Well-written content area textbooks—with good teacher support—not only convey subject matter, they also give students experience in reading expository text.

Some people acquire the belief that narratives are interesting and informational books are dull. Such a belief is harmful and limiting. People naturally enjoy finding things out, so well-written expository text is naturally interesting. Christine Pappas observed kindergartners and found they often preferred informational text to narratives, and that they could retell books whether they were narrative or expository. She asks,

> [W]hy do young children seem so competent here in using information books, but not so only several years later, as research with older elementary children has indicated? It may be that we have developed pedagogy based on an unexamined and unacknowledged ideology about young children and their cognitive/linguistic development.... [T]oo frequently the range of literature that is provided is narrow, made up mostly of fictional texts. Such a pedagogy, then, may be a barrier to children's full access to literacy [and may cause] young children's initial understandings of different written language registers... to fade. (Pappas, 1993, p. 126)

It is the teaching they experience, rather than natural language development or the characteristics of expository text, that may cause children (and later, adults) to dislike informational text.

Just as some students develop the idea that they are the kind of people who do not like math and science, some students (sometimes the same ones) take up the opinion that fiction is the only kind of reading they enjoy. Teachers need to be careful not to give subtle messages that certain subjects, and certain kinds of reading, are too hard, or dull, or only suitable for the most dedicated students. The essential element of interesting our students in expository writing is to be interested in it ourselves. This will ensure that we can share pleasure in informational books with our students, because we ourselves will be familiar with the style and with many examples of exciting books that present factual information in ways that make learning fascinating.

Excellent books for children and young people about scientific and historical topics are appearing in bookstores and libraries in increasing numbers, so it is likely that students will have more opportunities to choose to read informational books. At present, however, most students are familiar with narrative style, and many are unaccustomed to reading expository material. Evidence from several research studies indicates that the strategies students use to understand the two types of writing tend to differ, and that their methods of coping with expository text are less effective than strategies they use when reading narratives. (This is not a problem intrinsic to expository text, and it is not a problem that all students experience. Many readers and prereaders, from preschoolers to adults, enjoy factual books and have a great deal of experience with this kind of text. The problem will diminish as wide reading of expository text increases.)

Results of research (e.g., Zabrucky & Ratner, 1992) indicate that students are more apt to reexamine inconsistencies in narrative than in expository passages, and that they are better able to recall information from narrative selections. An additional research finding is that when students find narrative passages difficult to understand, they are likely to create visual images of what is occurring, but that the typical strategy for coping with expository text is simply to read more slowly (Hare and Smith, 1982). Extensive classroom experience in reading expository text, with teacher guidance, is the best remedy for such problems.

■■ Text Factors

Just as there are features of textbooks that make it difficult for students to learn from them, there are other features that help students learn. In analyzing the suitability of text for readers, educators sometimes classify it as considerate or inconsiderate. Considerate text is organized in ways that make students' learning easier; information is presented in ways that help students understand important concepts and see connections among them.

Bonnie Armbruster and Thomas H. Anderson (1984) are among the scholars who have analyzed and described the characteristics of considerate content area textbooks. They point out that careful preparation of instructional text involves attention both to major text elements such as the content and organization of the entire book and its chapters (the macrostructure) and to smaller units such as paragraphs and sentences (the microstructure). At the macrostructure level, the information presented in considerate text is timely, accurate, and important. Irrelevant concepts and features are not included.

Considerate text has been thoughtfully organized by authors and editors to present ideas in an orderly sequence. Concepts are explained clearly and with appropriate supporting detail. Text features such as informative chapter titles and subheadings alert readers to important points. Illustrative examples of new concepts are provided. There are likely to be well-chosen illustrations and graphic aids that are related to text information. Introductions, summaries, and well-planned references to information that has been presented earlier, help readers to see connections among ideas throughout the text. At the level of the microstructure of the text, sentence structure is orderly, yet diverse enough to maintain interest. Ideas are clearly presented. The vocabulary is well chosen, and definitions are provided for new terms. There is a coherent flow of ideas from sentence to sentence, and from paragraph to paragraph.

Inconsiderate text lacks these features. Authors do not, of course, produce inconsiderate text intentionally, but some writers are more knowledgeable and skilled than others in the craft of writing and editing. Moreover, to a large extent, the "considerateness" of text depends on the match between text and reader. Classification of text as considerate or inconsiderate is based on qualities of the text itself, but in practice it also depends on whether the reader can understand, and be interested and informed by, the text. Text that is written for a sophisticated, well-informed audience will usually not take into consideration the needs of less skilled readers who do not have prior knowledge of the topic, and thus it may be difficult for them to understand. On the other hand, text that is written for people who are beginning to learn about a topic will often not meet the needs of experts in the field.

Textbooks are written for a fairly narrow audience. For example, a sixth-grade social studies text is written for sixth-grade social studies students who are capable readers, who are thoroughly familiar with the English language, and who have background information about social studies based on prior learning in grades K–5. In her textbook on reading instruction, *Teaching Them to Read*, the reading scholar Dolores Durkin emphasizes the fact that even the most skillfully written textbooks cannot in themselves meet students' instructional needs. She writes, "It is impossible to find a textbook that deals with nothing but well-written, highly important content that is relevant for elementary school students. In part, this reflects the fact that easy reading is hard writing" (Durkin, 1989, p. 431). Interest as well as experience affects the match between text and reader. Books or articles about topics a reader is interested in are likely to be read more easily than material that is written in similar, or even simpler, style, but that is about topics in which the reader has little interest. Here is an important difference between textbooks and trade books: Trade books are books produced for a general audience and sold in bookstores to people who are interested in their subject matter. They can be read and enjoyed by readers with a fairly wide range of ages and reading ability. In contrast, textbooks are assigned to their readers, rather than chosen by them, and the text topics may not be intrinsically interesting to the readers.

Textbooks are an established part of most classrooms, and their authors, editors, and publishers, as well as educators, have a strong interest in the effectiveness of textbooks as learning aids for students. Examination of content area textbooks across a span of years will show many improvements in their quality. A recent study reported by Linda A. Meyer (1991), based on a detailed examination of science texts for grades 1 through 5 from four publishing companies, shows that the texts were, in Meyer's words, "quite considerate." Meyer and her colleagues analyzed texts in terms of potential problems in three categories: text structure, content problems, and graphic aids. In the category of text structure, they looked for instances of irrelevant ideas, lack of logic in organization, lack of cohesive ties within and among passages (e.g., failure to link ideas by using words such as *because, however, although*) and lack of clarity in referents (e.g., using anaphora such as pronouns like *this* and *these* in passages where it is difficult to discover what the words refer to). In the category of content problems, they looked for inaccurate information, misuse of technical terms, unnecessary use of figurative language (e.g., the inclusion of misleading analogies), and instances of failure to provide sufficient background information. They also examined graphic aids (e.g., pictures, maps, and diagrams) and noted whether they were unnecessary, unclear, or presented in ways that made them difficult to see. In the area of text structure, and most of the content categories, they found the textbooks did well in meeting the criteria for considerate text. The two problem areas that consistently occurred across series, according to the researchers' analysis, were failure to provide sufficient background information and deficiencies with graphic aids.

Organizational Features

Teachers who are aware of the special characteristics of content area text and textbooks can use this knowledge to help their students learn. Content area texts include organizational elements designed to help students learn from a text efficiently:

- text sections, such as the table of contents, index, and glossary;
- graphics, such as maps, tables, charts, graphs, and illustrations;
- methods of organizing text, such as titles, subtitles, subheads, and definitions of terminology embedded in the text;
- special sections including enrichment activities, self-test questions, and brief interpolated sections designed to interest students, such as short biographies of important people in the field.

Teachers should not assume that students will be able to understand and use the organizational features of text without instruction. On the other hand, time for instruction is limited, and learning information presented in texts should be emphasized, rather than learning facts about textbooks themselves. The solution to this dilemma is to teach students how to find their way around in textbooks, and about how to understand and use text features, in connection with their content area learning. Teaching students to read and interpret graphs, for example, can be integrated with math. When students are studying a section in a mathematics textbook dealing with graphs, the examples given in that text can be supplemented by examining the graphs in the assigned social studies and science texts.

Text Hunts

The text hunt strategy provides an interesting way for teachers to make their students aware of important features in a particular textbook when the text is first distributed. Written or oral text hunts can be created for every group of learners who use assigned texts. Not only do text hunts serve to introduce students to new textbooks, but they can provide a challenging activity for cooperative groups to engage in as soon as the groups are formed. A text hunt can be presented with brief directions, e.g., "In your cooperative learning groups, use your new textbooks to find as many as possible of the answers to these text hunt questions within a 20-minute time limit."

A text hunt is composed of a series of factual questions about text features that students can answer by examining the text and using their prior knowledge. It is not intended to teach content. A good text hunt has questions that will direct the students to each of the important parts of the text to find brief information about important topics, and includes one or two content-related trivia items that students are likely to find interesting and memorable. Text hunts should not require students to answer questions or undertake activities that they will need instruction to understand. In preparing questions, it is important to remember that text hunts are used at the beginning of the year, when students may have forgotten some of the information they learned in previous years. If students will need to understand a technical term to answer a question, the text hunt should define it or guide them to the glossary definition. Whenever possible, questions should direct students to several sections of the text. Questions should guide students to gain information from text sections, rather than requiring them to give trivial information about those sections, such as their page numbers or purposes. Text hunt tasks should give information as well as ask for information; this often makes questions easier to understand.

As the hunt is prepared, teachers should keep track of the answers, and the "trail" of pages that students are likely to follow to find the answers. The answer key should be available to the teacher while students work on the text hunt. Afterwards, answers, and the different ways groups have chosen to find answers, should be discussed. When students' answers differ from those expected, teachers should see whether there are in fact alternate correct answers to the question as it was phrased, respond to students' answers and ideas with acceptance of the students' ingenuity, and try to understand their thought processes even if an answer must be corrected. Figure 1–1 is a sample text hunt for a sixth-grade social studies text; Figure 1–2 is designed for a math text.

Note that in math texts especially, what students need to know depends on how the teacher intends to use the textbook. Writing a useful math text hunt depends on the teacher's plans for the math program. In Figure 1–2, Part One is a sample question designed to acquaint students with the "Problem Solving" sections in each chapter. In addition to alert-ing students to the section, the questions will give a preview of one thing that will be stressed in teaching (the problem solving checklist) and give them the opportunity to solve a problem. The questions are based on problem solving sections that students can understand on their own, not those that will be puzzling without teacher instruction. In Part Two, students must use addition, which they can be expected to know at the beginning of grade 3, to find page numbers of a text section titled "Math Challenges."

Inexperienced Readers. In the primary grades, students are still learning to read, and have very limited knowledge of text features. For young readers,

---

FIGURE 1–1 Sample Text Hunt for Grade 6

People in Time and Place: Western Hemisphere is a sixth-grade social studies text, published by Silver, Burdett, & Ginn, in 1991. The six units of study are "Why Study Latin America and Canada?" "The Peoples of the Western Hemisphere," "Europeans Arrive in Latin America," "Middle America from Independence to Today," "South America from Independence to Today," and "Canada." In Units 4, 5, and 6, chapters about the geography and history of an area are followed by chapters about present-day conditions there. The text includes a Table of Contents followed by a Map Skills Handbook, and four resource sections at the end of the text: an Atlas, a Gazetteer, a Glossary, and an Index. Symbols in the Table of Contents and the text indicate special features. At the end of each unit, there are suggestions for cooperative learning projects.

Directions: Work in your cooperative group to find the answers to as many questions as you can, in 30 minutes. If you finish early, write another text hunt question. Turn in your text hunts as a group. Initial the questions you worked on.

1. In Units 4, 5, and 6, chapters about the geography and history of an area are followed by chapters about present-day conditions.
   - One of the pictures introducing the chapter about Mexico's land, climate, and history shows a coastal town in Mexico. What is the town? What body of water borders the town?

- One of the pictures introducing the chapter about modern Mexico shows factory workers. What safety device are they working on?
- One of the pictures introducing the chapter about the geography and history of the Caribbean shows a farmer cultivating land. What is the main crop raised on Cuban farms?
- One of the pictures introducing the chapter about present-day Caribbean countries shows a house with a For Sale sign written in both French and English. What is the French phrase that means *For Sale*?
- What kind of vehicles are shown in the picture introducing the chapter about Canada's history since the early 18th century?
- One of the pictures introducing the chapter about present-day Canada shows a Canadian city at night. At the time our book was published, approximately what percentage of Canada's population lived in cities? Is this figure likely still to be accurate today?

2. Use the glossary to answer these questions. Then describe the pictures shown on the pages where the words are first used.
   - Why are summer and winter weather so different in continental climates?
   - How were fjords created?
   - What kind of tree does latex come from?

FIGURE 1–1   continued

- Was a quipu used as a measure of time or of quantity?

3. Use the *Gazetteer* and *Atlas* to complete the following chart:

PLACE NAME	CONTINENT	FACT
Alberta		It borders on Saskatchewan.
Bogota		
Greenland		
Merida	North America	
Peru		
Santa Fe		
Trinidad		

Star(*) the places that are cities.

4. Use the index to help you find answers to these questions:
   - To what better-known animal is the alpaca related?
   - How do findings from the LaBrea tar pits give us information about extinct animals?
   - Where, and what, is Popocatepetl?

5. Symbols in the table of contents and the text indicate text features. An American eagle is the symbol for "Citizenship and American Values." A book with a scroll is the symbol for "Using Source Materials." An open book with a silhouette of seated readers symbolizes "Literature" sections.

   - The Citizenship and American Values section in Unit 2 presents opposing points of view on the question of whether the extinction of some animal species should be approved. What two sets of opposing views about wild animals are listed? Do members of your group have an opinion on this issue?

   - The Using Source Materials section in Unit 2 is about a letter written by a famous explorer. Who wrote the letter? When was it written? How can you tell that these are not the explorer's own words?

   - One of the Literature sections in Unit 5 is a poem by Gabriela Mistral. List a fact about her, and a fact about the American poet who translated her work. What are your group's favorite lines from the poem? Would you like to try a choral reading?

FIGURE 1–2   Math Text Hunt (Hypothetical Text for Grade 3 or 4)

Our math text, *Mathematics for You*, has text features that help us learn from the book. There is a table of contents, which lists the titles of units and chapters and other sections of the book, and tells the page on which each one begins. There are "Problem Solving Sections" in each chapter. There is a table of measures at the end of the last chapter and a glossary and an index at the end of the book. The glossary gives definitions of mathematical terms, and the Index lists all the topics in the text, and tells what pages give information about those topics.

Part One. Each chapter in our math text has a "Problem Solving" section. In the first chapter, the problem solving section gives a five-point checklist for problem solving.

- Fill in the missing steps:

To solve a problem
1.
2. Find the needed data.
3.
4.
5. Check back.
You are solving problems as you work together to find the answers to this math text hunt.

- In the chapter titled "Multiplication Facts," what is the "Problem Solving" section about?

- Choose one of the problems on that page to solve.

- Step 2 in the problem solving checklist is Find the needed data. Data are pieces of information. What data do you need to solve the problem you chose?

FIGURE 1–2   continued

> ■ Be sure to write the number of the problem your group chose, as well as the answer to the problem. Draw a circle around the answer to the problem.
>
> **Part Two:**
>
> ■ Write the answers to these math problems:
> $19 + 7 =$ _____
> $39 + 5 =$ _____
>
> $75 + 3 =$ _____
>
> ■ Each answer is the number of a page in the text. The same chapter section is on each of these pages. What is that section?
>
> ■ On one of these pages there is a picture of a kangaroo. Each person in your group should copy a different problem from that page onto a file card and solve it. Be sure to check each other's work.

the term *table of contents* combines specialized and technical vocabulary. The familiar word *table* seems meaningless here, and *contents* is an unfamiliar word. Older students who have not yet become skillful readers, and students with limited proficiency in using English may experience similar difficulties. Students with varying degrees of reading skill and language proficiency can work together successfully in groups, but text hunts written for younger students, or solely for inexperienced older students, should be prepared following these guidelines:

■ Use repetition; write questions that use the same format, so that students will be able to read them more easily.

■ Use the text hunt as a group activity, with one or two group members designated as recorders of ideas.

■ Present the hunt as a series of activities, rather than as a single assignment. One possibility is to prepare a set of five or six multi-part questions on each major text feature, mount the questions on separate cards and laminate them. Working in cooperative learning groups, students can find answers to the questions on one of the cards, and then trade cards with another group. Be sure to have more cards than there are groups, so that groups can keep busy, without waiting for a card. (This procedure is illustrated in Chapter Three, where Search Tasks are discussed. Figure 3–7 gives an example of Search Tasks for primary grade students, with each task presented on a separate card.)

■ Extend the text hunt process over time. Separate the text hunt into sections, and conduct it at the beginning of the content area lesson over several days or weeks.

■ Assist students. When children are first learning to use a text section, a single question does not provide enough practice. Write questions that include multiple, similar sections. For example, the following question is written to help third graders learn about units and chapters, and guide them to find their way around a text using the table of contents. Such a multi-part question could be extended to ask about other units and chapters, using the same format.

The title of Unit I is "Observing Plants and Animals."
The title of Chapter 3 in this unit is "Seed Plants."

What two kinds of plants are shown in the picture at the beginning of this chapter?

What is the title of Chapter 4 in this unit?

The picture at the beginning of this chapter shows some ways we use plants. What ways do you see?

When questions are written following a pattern, it is useful to read the basic pattern aloud. To help students find a text section, insert a marker before the texts are handed out. On the day when groups will be answering questions about the glossary, for example, mark the first page of the glossary in each student's text with a paper clip, so that students can easily move back and forth between that section and other parts of the text.

Text Hunt Variations.   For very young or inexperienced students, use oral text hunts, accompanied by word charts. For such a text hunt, prepare a teaching script for yourself to use in guiding children to find information from the text. Prepare large word cards naming the text sections to show to children as you use the words. For a bulletin board display and follow-up activity, post copies of text pages next to word card holders in which students can place matching terms, such as *table of contents, unit title, chapter title, picture caption, and glossary.* A multi-text hunt can be prepared to introduce older students to several texts at once. For example, a hunt can be prepared in which groups of students answer questions based on three new texts simultaneously (perhaps math, social studies, and science), comparing and contrasting the ways the texts are organized, showing how word definitions are presented, and calling attention to special text features. Questions can focus on topics that are presented in two or more content areas, or to items such as graphs that may be studied in math and used as learning aids in social studies and science.

Text Patterns

Content textbooks are written in expository style, and expository text sometimes follows a pattern. A text pattern is a format for presenting ideas that shows a particular relationship among those ideas. Enabling students to identify and use text patterns as they read can enhance text comprehension, although it is important to note that a good deal of well-written text does not follow a pattern, incorporates several overlapping patterns, or follows a pattern only for a short section of text, such as a paragraph.

Scholars in the field of content area reading differ about how text patterns should be classified. There are different views about what names should be given to the patterns and how many separate text patterns there are. The most common pattern is simply a list; this is usually called the enumeration pattern. Six other patterns frequently are identified.

- cause-effect
- sequence (time or order)
- description
- problem and solution (or problem, solution, result)
- comparison-contrast
- definition with examples

A way of illustrating each of these patterns graphically is presented in Figure 1–3. When content area text is written using a pattern, the pattern is usually a way of emphasizing important concepts. For example, authors often use a cause-effect pattern to describe historical events. Some words and phrases are signals that a text pattern is being used. For example, *first*, *next*, and *finally* may be part of enumeration; *because* and *as a result* are often used in cause-effect discussions. When a text pattern contributes to students' understanding of concepts, teacher-created Pattern Guides, a teaching strategy described in Chapter Four, are useful instructional aids.

New Terminology

One text factor that makes it difficult to learn from content area textbooks is the heavy **vocabulary** load, including unfamiliar words and anaphora, which also appear in other kinds of text, and technical and specialized vocabulary, which are unique to content area text. A second factor that presents difficulty is the inclusion of many new concepts. A third related factor is the inclusion of unnecessary material used in an

---

vocabulary—comes from the Latin noun *vocabulum,* meaning *name,* which was derived from a Latin verb, *vocare,* meaning *to call.* Many English words come from the Latin root *vocare,* including *voice, vocal, vocation, vocational, advocate, invocation, provoke,* and *revoke.* It is illuminating to consider the ways the meanings of these words have changed from—or remained similar to— their original meaning. A vocation is a calling, a profession that a person feels called to undertake. The words *provoke, provoking,* and *provocation* come from *vocare* and *pro-* (a Latin prefix meaning *forth,* or *forward*). To provoke someone, in an early and now obsolete use of the word, meant to call them to come forward to accept a challenge to fight.

FIGURE 1–3 Graphic Representation of Six Text Patterns

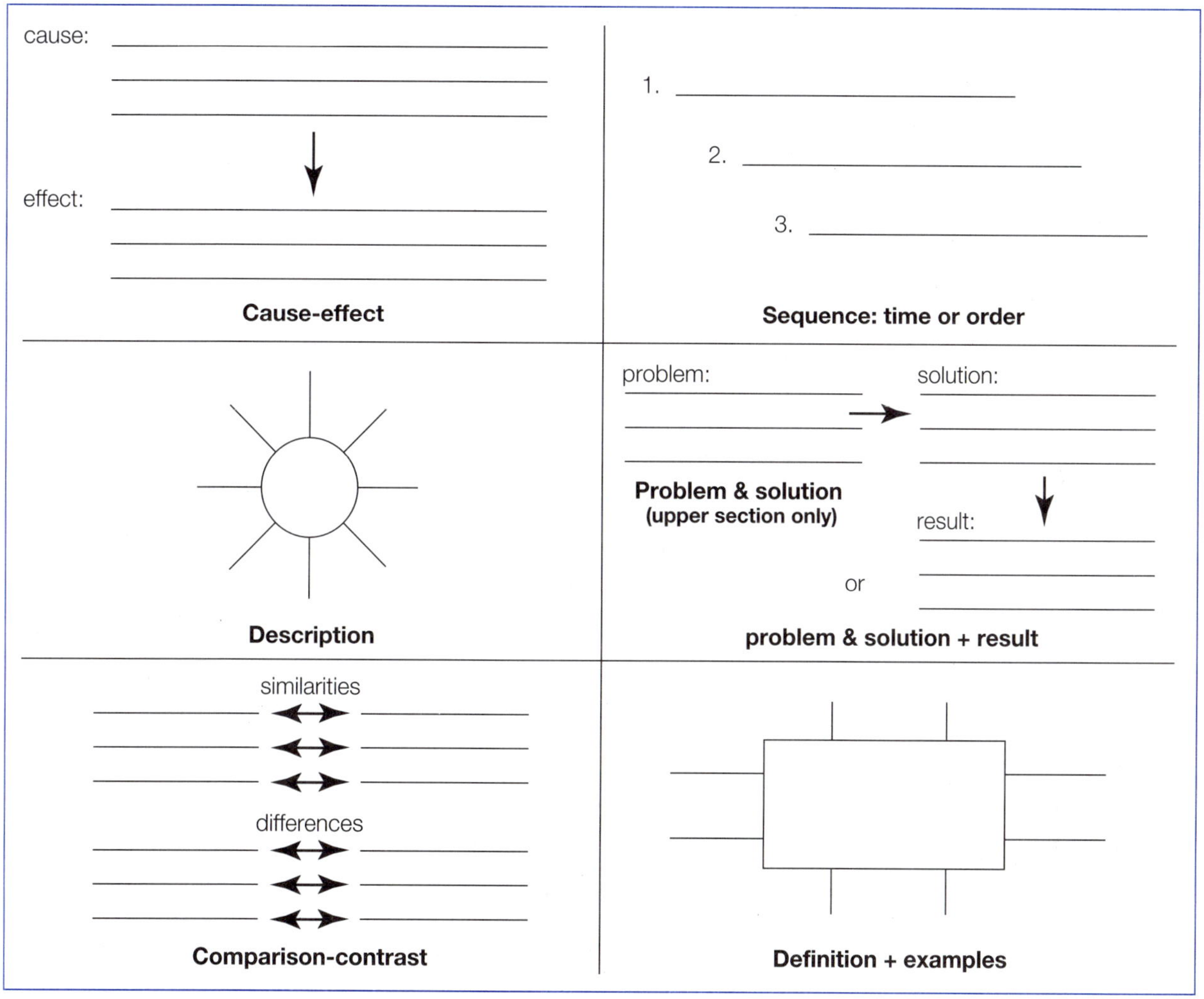

cause: _____

effect: _____

Cause-effect

1. _____

2. _____

3. _____

Sequence: time or order

Description

problem: _____   solution: _____

Problem & solution (upper section only)

result:

or

problem & solution + result

similarities

differences

Comparison-contrast

Definition + examples

Adapted from Smith, Patricia L., & Tompkins, Gail E. (1988). Structured notetaking: A new strategy for content area readers. *Journal of Reading, 33,* 46–53. © 1988 by the International Reading Association. Used by permission of Patricia L. Smith and the International Reading Association.

effort to interest students in topics presumed to be, in themselves, uninteresting.

Both vocabulary and concepts are essential features of content area reading. Content area texts must introduce new vocabulary and new concepts to teach new information. This requires learners to add new terminology to their vocabularies and develop a sound understanding of new concepts. To accom-

plish this, thoughtful teacher guidance and direct instruction about content topics are necessary.

One of the primary factors on which reading comprehension is based is vocabulary knowledge. In order to understand what we read, we need to know what the words in the text mean. In many reading situations, a good strategy to use when an unfamiliar word is encountered is to use the surrounding context—the other words and ideas in the passage—to determine the unknown word's meaning. However, this is usually not a helpful strategy when reading content area texts. Expecting students to learn technical vocabulary from context is unrealistic. As Elinore Schatz and Scott Baldwin (1986) point out, in content texts the technical terms themselves provide much of the context. Joan Nelson-Herber (1986, pp. 626 and 628) writes, "learning content vocabulary is different, in a variety of ways, from learning a general vocabulary… [N]ew vocabulary load is so heavy that it prevents students from comprehending the materials and thus impedes vocabulary learning from context."

It is important for teachers to be aware that content area text presents a greater variety of difficulties related to vocabulary than most other reading material and that this must be so, to present content-related information. The inclusion of many new vocabulary terms is not a flaw in content area texts; it is a necessary feature. The difficult vocabulary in content text falls into four categories: technical vocabulary, specialized vocabulary, unfamiliar words, and anaphora. Each of these four terms is defined and discussed in the following sections. Figure 1–4 provides an overview of these four categories of vocabulary in the form of a Semantic Feature Analysis (a strategy that will be discussed in Chapter Five).

Technical Vocabulary.   Words and phrases that name or refer to important concepts in a subject area are technical vocabulary. From Figure 1–4, one can see that technical vocabulary does not appear in all text; instead it consists of words and phrases that are unique to a content area field. These words are unlikely to appear familiar to readers who are not knowledgeable about the subject of study. For example, among the terms listed under *A* in the glossary of a science text are *algae*, *alveoli*, *angiosperm*, *arthropod*, and *autonomic nervous system*. These terms are not commonly used in conversation or seen in nontechnical magazines and newspapers. It is not immediately easy to see how the words should be pronounced. The words refer to concepts that will be unfamiliar or not thoroughly understood by many students, yet understanding the text sections in which the words appear depends on an understanding of those concepts.

In content area study, technical vocabulary is the primary category of words for which vocabulary

FIGURE 1–4   Categories of Content Area Vocabulary That Cause Difficulty to Readers

	Technical Vocabulary	Specialized Vocabulary	Unfamiliar Words	Anaphora
Words in this category occur in all kinds of text.	No	No	Yes	Yes
Words in this category are likely to look familiar in print.	No	Yes	No	Yes
Classification of words in this category depends on the individual reader.	No	No	Yes	No

instruction is needed. These words are both unfamiliar and essential for comprehension and the number of technical terms presented usually is extensive. Jeffry V. Mallow (1991, p. 325), comparing learning content area vocabulary with learning a new language, notes that " ...an introductory two-semester course in a foreign language requires that students master a 500-word vocabulary, while an introductory biology course introduces the student to about 900 new words." A similar point is made by Robert Yager (1983, p. 586): "Terminology is a central feature in most science textbooks… In almost every case more attention to vocabulary is necessary in typical science classrooms than is necessary for mastering a foreign language." Given the extensive technical vocabulary introduced by content area texts, teachers have two interrelated responsibilities: to decide which terms students need to understand to grasp the subject matter, and to teach those terms effectively.

The inclusion of technical vocabulary, although it presents problems for readers, is not a flaw in content text nor an error made by textbook writers. Every field of knowledge has its own special terminology. Imagine trying to talk about gardening if there were no word for *seed*. It could be done—we could refer to "the parts of the plant from which new plants grow" or "small items that must be covered with soil"— but to do this would be tedious and puzzling. For example, we could not say, "Go to the store and get three packets of tomato seeds." Instead we would have to say, "Go to the store and get three packets of the parts of the tomato plant from which new tomato plants grow." Knowledge in a content area field cannot be acquired without learning the basic technical vocabulary of that field.

When technical vocabulary used in one textbook chapter or unit occurs repeatedly throughout the text, later learning is made easier. Concepts and vocabulary in one chapter build upon previous chapters. This is sometimes the case in elementary social studies texts. It is also true of many sections of math texts, although the introduction of special topics in math, such as probability, will present some technical vocabulary (such as the term *probability* itself) that will be new to many students and unrelated to terms used in other parts of the text. In middle and

high school, science courses are focused on one area of science, such as biology or chemistry. Here also many technical vocabulary terms will be used through the course of study, and an understanding of the terms in one section of the text will help students to understand the next section.

In elementary science texts, however, the technical vocabulary is not related across sections, because science is usually taught in a spiral curriculum. This means that a series of unrelated units focusing on different aspects of science is taught during a year, but in each subsequent year, the same topics are studied again in greater depth. Using the image of a spiral, we can imagine looking at the spiral from above or below and seeing the same topic of study appear repeatedly, from year to year. Although the same topics recur annually in a spiral curriculum, there is little or no transfer of technical vocabulary across units of study taught within a year. A section on the human body, for example, may be followed by a section dealing with electricity and magnetism. Each unit contains extensive technical vocabulary that must be learned, and that most students will not encounter again until a similar science topic is studied in the following year. This is not a flaw in the curriculum. Students in elementary school benefit from learning about different branches of science—earth science, life science, physical science—every year. The spiral curriculum is a sensible structure, but it presents a challenge to teachers to use a variety of interesting, effective strategies to enable students to learn the necessary technical terms.

Specialized Vocabulary.   Many words have multiple meanings. Such words are also called polysemous (a word derived from two Greek words meaning *many* and *sign* or *meaning*). It is important for teachers to be alert to the difficulties such words may create for students as they read content texts. "Teachers should be more aware of the prevalence of polysemic words in reading materials… [and] provide imaginative, direct vocabulary instruction" (Paul & O'Rourke, 1988, p. 42).

Specialized vocabulary is a subset of technical vocabulary consisting of multiple-meaning words. All specialized vocabulary is technical vocabulary, though many technical terms are not instances of specialized vocabulary. What is special about specialized vocabulary? As Figure 1–4 shows, specialized vocabulary words are similar to other technical vocabulary except that they are likely to look familiar to a reader. They are (or seem to be) words that are in readers' listening, speaking, reading, and writing vocabularies, but they are words with both a typical and a technical meaning. The technical meaning is likely to be unfamiliar to readers, who may find the text especially difficult to understand because known words are used in puzzling ways. It is confusing when *pitch* is not related to baseball and is a characteristic of sound. It is a problem when *irises* and *cones* and *pupils* are not flowers and treats and people, but instead are parts of the eye.

Students also encounter multiple-meaning words when teachers or instructional materials use academic vocabulary—the words and phrases used in giving instructions and directions. (Academic vocabulary is not confined to content area text; it occurs in all aspects of schooling.) Very young children often encounter difficulty when they come to school and are expected to follow directions. For example, most five- and six-year-olds have a good understanding of the words *skip* and *match*. They can skip, and they know it is not safe to play with matches. Think how puzzling it must be to hear a teacher say "Write your name on the top line and then skip a line" or "Draw lines to match the words with the pictures." Mar-

garet Donaldson (1978) describes a child's sad experience on the first day of school. The teacher directed the child to "Sit there for the present time." Knowing the word "present," the child was disappointed when there was no time when presents were given. (Beverly Cleary [1968] made the *present/present* confusion a part of *Ramona the Pest*.) The terms and phrases that are part of academic vocabulary appear sometimes in content area text, but are more common in the oral or written directions given to students. One of many good reasons for encouraging students to work together cooperatively is that confusion about directions can often be cleared up through student-student consultation.

Unfamiliar Words.   As Figure 1–4 shows, there are two categories of difficult vocabulary—unfamiliar words and **anaphora,** which occur in all kinds of text, not just in content area text. Unfamiliar words are not technical terms but are nevertheless unknown to some or all of the students in a classroom group. The category of unfamiliar words is unique because whether a term is familiar or unfamiliar depends not on the word itself, but on the match between the word and each individual reader. For this reason, there will be variety in what words are unfamiliar. For example, the words *vast, inevitable,* and *span* may appear on a single page of a textbook in history or in science. Some students will recognize and understand these words; others may not. Aside from the students themselves, teachers are the best judges of which words are likely to be unfamiliar to students. It is a valuable teaching skill to be able to use words that may be unfamiliar when talking about a reading assignment in ways that clarify their meaning, and to explain word meanings quickly, clearly, in an interesting way, and without making any students feel ashamed that the words were not already known.

Anaphora.   Examples of anaphora, like unfamiliar words, are found in all texts. Words and phrases whose meaning must be determined by referring to other parts of the text—usually an earlier part—are anaphora. The most common form of anaphora is pronouns, such as *this, these,* and *those.* To understand the passages in which they appear, it is necessary to understand not just the words themselves

---

anaphora—a plural noun (pronounced *uh-NAF-or-uh*) that comes from the Greek language, and combines a prefix, *ana*, meaning *back*, or *again*, and a Greek verb, *pherein*, meaning *to carry*. There are two uses for the word in English. In the field of rhetoric, anaphora is a technique used in writing or speaking to stress a point by using the same phrase repeatedly at the beginning of a series of paragraphs or verses. (The importance of reading might be stressed by writing an editorial in which each paragraph began with the sentence, "All children must be readers!") The other use for the term is in the fields of reading and linguistics, where anaphora means words or phrases that can only be understood by referring to other parts of the text, or sometimes to ideas implicit in the text. The use of anaphora carries us back to previous text.

but the words, phrases, and concepts to which they refer. Anaphora also appears as part of phrases, such as "after *that time*," "having *a similar experience*," and "for *an entirely different reason*." In contrast to technical vocabulary, the meaning of anaphora usually can be determined from context, but students may need to be guided to reason out the meaning of some instances of it. For example, in discussion of a text passage, a teacher might read the phrase "after that time" and ask, "What time was that?" It is important for teachers to be knowledgeable about this category of vocabulary to assess text passages and to see whether students need help in understanding referents for words. It is *not* necessary for students to learn the term *anaphora*. (Here is one of many instances when teachers can be expected to know more than their students.)

Nine words and phrases are listed. Can you tell what they refer to, without looking ahead to the next box?

two ways	one	it
their	This	their
This method	now	others

Anaphora occurs in all text, but such words and phrases present more difficulties to readers when they occur in content area text, for two reasons. First, although content area concepts are often complex, readers may skim over passages that include familiar words and phrases without giving much thought to the complicated meanings of the words and passages to which they refer. This is a problem intrinsic to the reader; teachers can help to overcome it by providing instruction and activities designed to ensure that concepts in the text will be understood.

While the first problem with anaphora results from readers' inattention, the second is caused by the producers of content area text. It occurs when authors and publishers try to make a text appear easy when its level of difficulty is assessed by readability formulas. Readability formulas are mathematical methods of estimating the grade level for which text is suited. These estimates usually are based on counting such text elements as the number of words in sentences, the number of syllables in words, and

the number of words used that do not appear on lists of common words. (The topic of readability is discussed in Chapter Six.) Ordinarily, short words and sentences are easier to read, and to understand, than long ones. However, this is not always so. A chapter about immigration to the United States in a social studies text might end by summarizing the reasons for immigration that have been discussed in the chapter in this way:

> People came to America to be free to worship as they chose, to become better off economically, to escape from famines or tyrannical governments. Others came to join family members who already lived in America. Some people came to America because they were forced to, before the evil of slavery was outlawed. Some people—the ancestors of Native Americans—were living here long before histories were written; we do not have records to tell us when and how they arrived.

Such a summary at the end of a chapter makes the concepts presented easy to understand and remember. Another chapter on the same topic might conclude with a single sentence: *These were the reasons why people came to America.* The first of the two ways to end the chapter is more helpful to the reader. The second is, by the standards of readability formulas, "easier to read," because it is a relatively short sentence, and contains short, frequently used words. Readability, as measured by formulas, is strongly affected by the inclusion of anaphora. Teachers should make it a part of planning to note whether the instances of anaphora in their textbooks are likely to interfere with students' understanding of the text.

Anaphora can only be understood by referring to surrounding text. On this page there is a box of examples of anaphora. In the box on the next page, the anaphora are presented in context. Once the words are shown in a connected text passage, they have meaning.

Concept Overload

Scholars sometimes refer to a "knowledge explosion" when they comment on how much new knowledge has been acquired in this century. The amount of information humankind possesses is vast

---

Anaphora in Context

Scientists study the world in *two ways*, by observing *their* environment and by conducting experiments. Early scientists worked almost entirely by observation. *This method* is the best *one* to use in sciences like astronomy where experimentation is impossible. However, observations can sometimes be misleading. Aristotle believed that alligators were spontaneously generated out of mud. *This* may sound silly *now*, but *it* was a reasonable observation. Because alligators lay *their* eggs in mud, baby alligators may emerge from the mud when there are no *others* in the vicinity. Without further investigation, the baby alligators would seem to be emerging from the mud itself.

---

and continually growing. In an effort to ensure that students will acquire information needed to become well-educated adults, the authors of content area textbooks present many topics. Within the discussion of each topic, it is common for many concepts to be introduced. When students have little or no prior knowledge about a subject, it is difficult or impossible for them to grasp the concepts as they read the text, or to remember them when study is concluded.

The number of different concepts presented in fairly short sections of expository text is often surprisingly large. Carol Lloyd and Judy Mitchell (1989) devised a method that teachers may use to guide their decisions about how to allot time for concept instruction. They illustrate the need for such decision-making by describing a nine-page chapter in a high-school chemistry textbook in which sixty-seven different ideas were presented, with additional concepts introduced in marginal notes. Such a heavy concept load makes reading with understanding virtually impossible without substantial additional instruction from the teacher. But the teacher's task would also be burdensome, and the class time used would be excessive, if each of the concepts were taught. "It is the teacher who needs to make decisions regarding the relative importance of information" (Lloyd and Mitchell, 1989, p. 542). Within the classroom, the teacher is the subject matter specialist and the person who knows most about the students, so the teacher has

the responsibility for making decisions about which concepts to teach. Figure 1–5 presents the Lloyd and Mitchell model in the form of a flow chart for decision making.

Because teachers know both the subject matter they are to teach, and the students who will be learning from the textbook, they can analyze the concepts presented using three criteria:

- *importance.* Is this concept important in terms of the school's curriculum and the needs of my students?
- *quality of textbook presentation.* How completely and clearly does the textbook explain this concept?
- *students' prior knowledge.* How much additional background knowledge will be needed before my students can understand this concept?

Teachers should also consider whether there are concepts that the text does not present that are necessary for comprehension of the topic being studied.

If the answer to the first question—is this concept important in the curriculum and in relation to students' needs?—is no, the teacher does not need to teach it (nor to evaluate it according to the remaining criteria). If the answer is yes, the teacher then examines the textbook explanation of the concept to determine the answer to the next question: is the concept completely and clearly explained in the textbook? Instruction needs to be planned and provided for those concepts where the textbook explanation is insufficient. Teachers should then consider the background knowledge their particular students possess about the concepts that will be taught. Do some or all students have prior knowledge that will help them understand the new concepts and that they can use in interaction with classmates to enhance knowledge for the whole class? If not, it will be necessary, when instruction is provided about the concepts in this text section, to build the background knowledge on which understanding will be based. Finally, teachers should note whether they need to incorporate additional concepts into their instruction, to help their students develop a sound understanding of the topic.

FIGURE 1–5   A Model for Assessing the Need for Concept Instruction (Based on Lloyd & Mitchell, 1989)

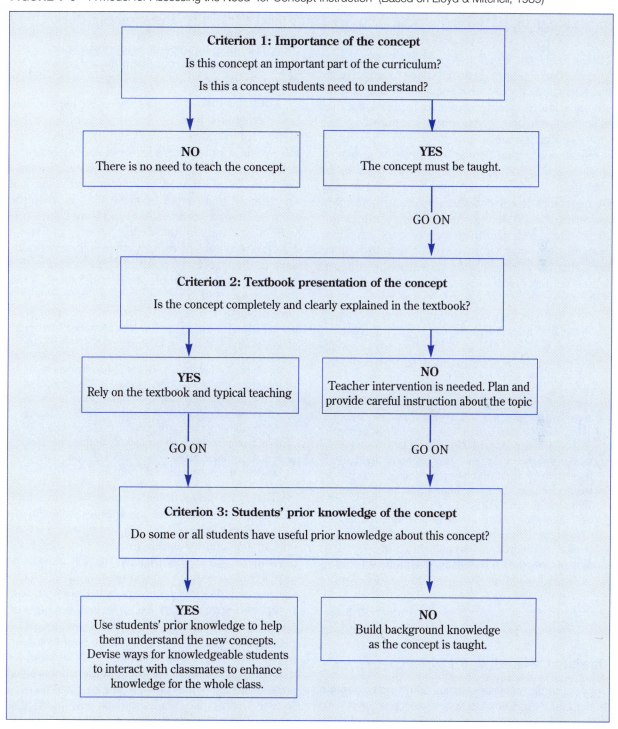

Criterion 1: Importance of the concept

Is this concept an important part of the curriculum?

Is this a concept students need to understand?

NO
There is no need to teach the concept.

YES
The concept must be taught.

GO ON

Criterion 2: Textbook presentation of the concept

Is the concept completely and clearly explained in the textbook?

YES
Rely on the textbook and typical teaching

NO
Teacher intervention is needed. Plan and provide careful instruction about the topic

GO ON

GO ON

Criterion 3: Students' prior knowledge of the concept

Do some or all students have useful prior knowledge about this concept?

YES
Use students' prior knowledge to help them understand the new concepts. Devise ways for knowledgeable students to interact with classmates to enhance knowledge for the whole class.

NO
Build background knowledge as the concept is taught.

"Seductive Detail"

It is easier for people to learn what interests them. An influential scholar in the field of education, John Dewey, in a text titled *Interest and effort in education* (1913), stressed the relationship between students' interests in a subject and the energy they give to learning more about it. He pointed out that linking students' interests to their learning is useful, but that superficial attempts to make a topic interesting can interfere with learning.

Textbook authors sometimes include passages that have only slight relationship to a topic in an attempt to rouse students' interest. The term used by educators to refer to this irrelevant material is *seductive detail*. Such sections often come at the beginning of a chapter to capture readers' attention. Instead, they may confuse students, who believe first, that they are expected to learn everything a textbook presents and second, that the most important information will be given at the beginning. Ruth Garner and her colleagues conducted experiments showing that interesting but irrelevant information, no matter where it appeared in a text, was remembered more readily than the important concepts the text presented.

> [Research provides] evidence of the power of the seductive detail effect in learning from text. Interesting detail is highly memorable to readers; important generalizations are less memorable… What can teachers possibly do to assist students in learning important generalizations presented in text? We suggest confronting the interest factor head-on. When we return to Dewey… we are reminded that his admonition to teachers to avoid trying to make something interesting does not mean that they should avoid trying to find out what is of interest. One reason why interesting detail is so seductive is that it typically appears in text that is, overall, of very low personal interest to most students. (Garner, Alexander, Gillingham, Kulikowich, & Brown, 1991, p. 657)

Outdated, Biased, or Bland Text

Textbooks vary in quality. Some texts contain information that is outdated, or sections that are biased or present complex issues in a bland or shallow manner. Teachers' ability to recognize these problems provides the basis for intervention to correct or supplement the texts so that students learn accurate, unbiased information. (Note that often there are opportunities for teachers to volunteer to serve on textbook committees established to choose new texts.)

Outdated Text.   Authors and publishers of content area texts face a number of problems that authors of narrative material and trade books usually do not. Content texts in social studies, science, and health may quickly become outdated, because the store of information is constantly growing and changing. A text cannot be more accurate than the state of human knowledge at the time the text is written, and human knowledge not only grows—it changes. A notable recent example is the disappearance of the USSR as a political entity, an event that has made many textbook sections outdated. Myra Zarnowski (1991, p. 3) describes observing in a classroom where students quizzed one another in preparation for an upcoming test on major European powers—using a textbook that was five years old.

> Encouraging children to update historical accounts means inviting them to participate in the process of 'doing' history. Instead of being consumers of historical accounts, children become co-creators. Using the textbook as a starting point, children can construct an account more acceptable to them because it is more informative, more current, and more in line with their own thinking.

There are many areas of knowledge in which what is true at one time does not always remain true. "The justices of the U. S. Supreme Court are nine men appointed by the President" ceased to be permanently true when Sandra Day O'Connor was sworn in as a justice on September 25, 1981. A dictionary includes the statement that Halley's comet reappears approximately every seventy-seven years and "last appeared in 1910." It is interesting, informative, and sometimes frightening to find examples of past "truths" that are now known to be false; for example, once it was believed that the sun revolved around the Earth and in some places it was a crime to assert otherwise. Sometimes, as new knowledge is gained, we realize that information, previously thought to be accurate, is not correct (and was never correct).

It is impossible for textbooks, particularly those in social studies and science, not to become outdated. Even the authors of histories that give information only about past events cannot know about future discoveries that will cast new light on historical events. Authors can only give facts that are as accurate and up-to-date as possible, at the time the books are written. After a book is published, many years may pass before it is put into the hands of a particular student, because school systems cannot afford to change textbooks annually or biennially. Teachers need to be sufficiently knowledgeable about their texts, and about current events and new discoveries, to know when textbooks are presenting outdated or incorrect information. They also need to be able to find sources—guest speakers, videotapes, databases, magazines, and other texts—that provide up-to-date information. It is important not to teach in such a way as to indicate that textbooks are infallible. Common sense tells us that we do not want to teach distrust of texts either, but we must be alert to situations where the text contains inaccuracies, and correct them when they are found.

Teaching With Faulty Texts

▪ Use outdated text as a learning experience. Students need to realize that written material can become outdated. Make it a current events activity to update the text. Perhaps the class can produce a text supplement, giving page numbers and corrections.

▪ To combat biased text, stress the positive aspects of diversity. Use films, speakers, a wide range of literature. Be alert to the wealth of exciting tradebooks by and about a wide range of people. Remind students that they should treat others (and expect others to be treated in the texts they read) as they would want themselves and their families to be treated.

▪ When working with bland text, use supplementary readings, films, pictures, speakers. Incorporate literature—poetry, historical fiction, contemporary writing. A teacher's own interest in a topic can help make that subject come alive for students.

Biased Text.   Text bias—especially pejorative treatment of groups of people such as women and members of racial and cultural groups that have been considered as minorities—is, fortunately, less of a problem than it formerly was. It is instructive to compare recent textbooks with those published a decade or more ago, and to consider how people were and are described and pictured. In commenting on the importance of evaluating instructional materials for content bias, Dixie Lee Spiegel writes:

> The instructional resources children interact with carry many subtle messages. If materials do not reflect a pluralistic view of society, the message may be that the narrow view depicted is the recognized, acceptable, or at the very least preferred society. Pluralism has many facets, among them ethnicity, gender, geographical distribution, and degree of urbanization. Pluralism acknowledges that handicapped people exist, that many children are poor, and that not every home has one mother and one father present. One hopes the days of stories about the house in the suburbs (with the only ethnicity depicted being white, with mother and father in stereotypic roles complete with apron and briefcase, living in a climate that has four distinct seasons) are over. (Spiegel, 1990, pp. 64–65)

One form of bias occurs in social studies texts that attempt to be pluralistic by emphasizing learning about "other" groups—that is, groups presumed to be very unlike anyone for whom the book is intended. This ignores the fact that members, relatives, and friends of those groups may be represented among the students reading the textbooks, and also among the teachers using the textbooks. Teachers should be aware that romantic pictures of Indians living in primitive conditions do not present a true picture of a diverse group of present-day Americans whose ancestors lived on this continent, as members of many nations with differing languages and customs, before immigrants arrived from other continents. Two false ideas, the "Generic Indian stereotype" and the "living fossils stereotype," are fostered by text presentations picturing American Indians as "members of a homogeneous 'tribe,' as speakers of a common language called 'Indian,' or as war-bonneted tipi or pueblo dwellers" and implying that American Indians "in effect, died out at the end of the nineteenth century" (Charles, 1991, p. 7).

Texts that treat other groups as foreign and strange also show bias. For example, names of groups of people may be treated as obscure and hard to pronounce—if, for instance, the mention of a nation or group is followed by an odd-looking insertion such as *ESS-kim-oze*." Bias is promoted if a group's customs are made to seem interesting but bizarre, and their patterns of life are shown as completely separate from those of other people. A number of textbooks devote sizable sections of text to describing communities of people, such as the Amish, who are different because of their religious beliefs. When this is the case, there is a risk that in an apparent attempt to teach students about human differences, instead students learn that most people are "the same" but that there exist identifiable groups that are outside that sameness. All peoples deserve both respect and a reasonable degree of privacy. Many or perhaps all of the "different" groups would, if they could choose, prefer not to be the objects of textbook study. It is useful, when examining texts, to consider whether each of us would like our families and our own heritages to be treated in the way the textbook presents the group being described.

Donna Gollnick and Philip Chinn point out that textbook bias can take many forms, including invisibility, when groups are ignored; stereotyping, when people are consistently described or pictured in limited roles; and imbalance, when events are described from only one perspective, or when trivia is emphasized over substantive issues—they cite history texts in which "more information was given on the length of women's skirts than on the suffrage movement" (Gollnick & Chinn, 1986, p. 276)— and unreality, the tendency to gloss over controversy. All of these biases, however, can become a source for useful learning, when the teacher is knowledgeable and skillful.

Biases can be countered in two ways. They can be opposed directly, by pointing out that the material in question gives only one side, and discussing a balanced view. Or they can be countered indirectly, by making sure students have many experiences with unbiased text and ideas. If the biased material is supplementary, other materials can be found or created

to substitute. If the text must be used, bias may be corrected by offering counterexamples through discussion of diverse roles for both women and men, and presentation of career possibilities in egalitarian ways. Sometimes bias occurs in pictures—for example, nonwhites may be pictured in sad, difficult, deprived situations or working at menial jobs. Bias also occurs when certain groups simply are ignored. Here again, lively and useful classroom activities—visits from community members, stressing positively oriented current events, reading aloud from books about diverse groups and by a diversity of authors—help to counteract the biases in interesting ways. A particularly subtle kind of bias is a tendency to present differences on a "we-they" basis: "*We* need to be very nice to *them.*" The correction for this kind of bias is to set up a situation where *we're* all *us.* As teachers, we need to monitor our own language to treat people consistently as part of all of humankind.

Bland Text. Another problem that frequently occurs in content area texts, particularly social studies texts, is shallow presentation of controversial subjects, or even topics that someone fears may be considered controversial. Cameron McCarthy (1990, p. 124) refers to the "bland, nonconflictual writing that one finds in many textbooks." Textbooks are intended for student readers, but before they can reach that group, they are examined by multiple, sequential audiences, such as officials in state agencies, members of curriculum committees, and school board members. Textbook authors writing with these multiple audiences in mind sometimes treat important issues at length but with limited depth. A text that discusses the reasons for the American Civil War with minimal attention to the issue of slavery, for example, does an injustice to students, who all have a right to understand the difficult issues in a country's history.

Textbook selection committees sometimes must work with mandates requiring positive treatment of events in American history.

> Those negatives—the sorry mistakes that have dotted our past and may well affect our future—are either left out, glossed over, or presented in a favorable light. The Spanish-American War thus becomes little more than a dramatic charge up San

Juan Hill, and America's unwillingness to accept the horrors of the Holocaust an easily dismissed failure to communicate with Eastern Europe." (Carter & Abrahamson, 1990, p. 177)

Knowledgeable teachers will be able to see when the text treatment of a subject is inadequate and will find ways to enhance students' understanding. Often the realities of different time periods can be illuminated for students by reading selections from outstanding histories written for adults, as well as tradebooks for young people—including historical fiction—and also poetry, diaries, and personal narratives written during the time period being studied.

■■ The Teacher's Role in Content Area
■■ Instruction

Teachers have a right to expect that the textbooks students use will meet established criteria for considerate text. Teachers have the responsibility to use the excellent features of textbooks efficiently and the obligation to intervene effectively when aspects of textbooks do not mesh well with students' needs. Both ethically and practically, it is more important to

concentrate on the responsibility to use textbooks well, than on the right to expect that textbook writing will qualify as considerate for students. We have much more power to control our own teaching than to affect the way textbooks are written.

Text-Friendly Teachers

A skillful, thoughtful teacher can create a match between text and students even when the textbook would be difficult or impossible for students to learn from independently. The term "text-friendly teachers" is used by Jean Dreher and Harry Singer to remind us that teachers can intervene to make it possible for all students to accomplish textbook learning successfully. The term captures an important concept about good content area instruction. Teachers, not textbooks, are the key to students' learning. Teachers need to understand how to use textbooks as teaching resources, without surrendering control of instruction to the texts. Teachers can intervene between their students and the texts they use by providing instruction that helps students to learn new vocabulary and relate it to their reading; to acquire, use, and remember new concepts; and to develop methods of studying that enable them to become independent learners.

> Even if a text is unfriendly, a text-friendly teacher may be able to make it friendly by modifying it, by improving readers' resources so they can be successful in interacting with the text, or by altering the goal so that it is attainable. In short, evaluation of a text's friendliness should also consider how text-friendly a teacher is likely to be. (Dreher & Singer, 1989, p. 103)

Good teachers use texts, but are not controlled by them. They take responsibility for deciding how textbooks can best be used, and how and when to intervene in the learning process. They work to provide a better match between students' knowledge and interests and the text's presentation of information. When teachers fail to accept responsibility to be educational decision makers and instead base teaching entirely on textbooks and teacher's manuals, the curriculum is said to be textbook-driven: Instruction is controlled not by a responsible person who knows and works with the students, but by a set of published materials.

In one common pattern of teaching, class time is used by the teacher in having the students read the text silently or read it aloud paragraph by paragraph, supplemented by teacher explanations and questions that are often those specified by the teacher's manual, followed by tests based on rote memory of the text. This is textbook-driven teaching. Kathleen Roth reported on a year-long study of fifth-grade science teaching. She found that students taught in textbook-driven fashion, even when they did well on tests, did not develop an understanding of scientific concepts, in part because it was common for massive numbers of concepts to be introduced without adequate explanation, demonstration of their interrelationships, or time for students to process the ideas. She lists more than twenty concepts introduced sequentially in a single class period: "light as energy, light for seeing, light travels fast, the speed of light, atoms, photons, sources of light (artificial vs. natural), bioluminescence, uses of light, animals that give off light, reasons light travels fast, lightning, amplitude, wavelengths, light travels in straight lines, intensity of light, pioneer uses of candles, electricity provides artificial light, watts, volts, fluorescence, and light cannot curve" (Roth, 1987, p. 70).

When the concepts are listed in this fashion, we see immediately that it is not possible for adequate learning to occur. Our goal as content area teachers is for all our students to acquire, organize and use content area knowledge. Students will leave a lesson such as this with a smattering of disorganized information that they cannot apply, or use as a foundation on which to build sound future learning. How is it then, that many students can, as Roth reports, perform successfully on tests? There are several reasons. Some students begin the study of content area topics with enough prior knowledge to carry them along, understanding information at a superficial level. A more powerful factor is one the psychologist and educational theorist Howard Gardner calls "the correct answer compromise." Gardner points out that questions presented in textbooks and accompanying materials (e.g., workbooks and test sheets) often do not require more than a superficial understanding, or the ability to scan text to find answers that are stated

there. "Most schools," Gardner comments, "have fallen into a pattern of giving kids exercises and drills that result in their getting answers on tests that look like understanding.... [S]tudents read a text, they take a test, and everybody agrees that if they say a certain thing it'll be counted as understanding" (Gardner, quoted in Brandt, 1993, p. 4). Rather than settling for this kind of compromise, teachers must provide instruction that guides students beyond superficial acceptance of important ideas, and enables them to understand and apply the knowledge they acquire. Teachers who make the decision to use texts as a tool to support learning, rather than as the controlling element of their program, can organize instruction so that their students understand, rather than skim over, important concepts.

Avoiding a Textbook-driven Curriculum

When teachers expect students to learn from assigned textbook readings, with little or no support from classroom instruction, they are relying on the textbook to provide information that students can read and understand independently. Diane Lapp and James Flood have noted that this would require textbook authors to meet four criteria:

1. Avoid depending on prior knowledge of the topic that readers may not have.
2. Use language that is not beyond the understanding of readers.
3. Use a text structure that is familiar to readers.
4. Present material in a manner that encourages readers to learn information.

(Lapp & Flood, 1993, p. 71)

These criteria may be met adequately in texts written for college students—though these students also benefit from instruction that goes beyond required readings—but even the most capable authors of K–12 textbooks must be partnered with teachers who take an active, thoughtful role. Of course, it can be tempting to let textbooks control the curriculum. As Paul Trafton (1984, p. 524) has pointed out, "[t]he convenience of textbooks often causes teachers to ignore thinking about how best to use them." However, allowing the textbook to control instruction in one year, for whatever reason, makes it easy to follow that path in subsequent years. It is very risky to say that we believe we *should* teach in a certain way but we have a good reason for not beginning *this year*. There will always be reasons why a current year is a difficult time. When we know something is right, then we need to take action.

Prevention for textbook-driven teaching is threefold: the teacher's knowledge of subject matter, the teacher's awareness of good teaching strategies, and the teacher's decision to take responsibility for instruction. This text is intended to help prevent textbook-driven curricula by suggesting methods for teachers to use in building subject matter knowledge, by presenting a wide variety of good teaching strategies for teachers to choose from, and by inspiring all teachers to fulfill their potential for excellence. Successful teachers enter the field of teaching aware of sound current educational theories and practices, and they develop their ability to modify methods and materials for their own classrooms as they teach. Throughout their teaching careers, they continue to learn. Their professional learning comes from colleagues and programs of study, and from the ongoing information available to them from the professional literature, particularly from scholarly journals that publish articles about current educa-

tional research and practice. Moreover, they learn from their students, by observing how students learn, what puzzles them, and what interests them.

A Good Teacher's Influence

Good teachers are continually learning and devising ways to intervene to help their students learn. They can overcome many text problems by the way they explain, correct, or enhance textbook presentations. By maintaining an interest in current events they will be able to identify outdated textbook information. By reading widely and drawing upon resource books they will be able to select materials that will expand and illuminate textbooks' presentation of topics. By demonstrating respect and care for all people, they will be able to counteract text biases that present narrow or negative views. As James Banks (1987, p. 539) notes, "many students learn compassion and democratic ideals and develop a commitment to participate in social change from powerful and influential classroom teachers…. Some teachers have a significant influence on the values, hopes, and dreams of their students." A good teacher's influence is more memorable than that of a text.

CHAPTER TWO

Characteristics of Effective Content Area Teaching

Creating learning environments that incorporate student language and life experiences in no way negates teachers' responsibility for providing students with particular academic content knowledge and skills. It is important not to link teacher respect and use of student knowledge and language bases with a laissez-faire attitude toward teaching. It is equally necessary not to confuse academic rigor with rigidity that stifles and silences students. The teacher is the authority, with all the resulting responsibilities that entails; however, it is not necessary for the teacher to become authoritarian in order to challenge students intellectually. Education can be a process in which teacher and students mutually participate in the intellectually exciting undertaking we call learning. Students can become active subjects in their own learning, instead of passive objects waiting to be filled with facts and figures by the teacher.

LILIA BARTOLOME, 1994, P. 183.

Excerpted from Bartolome, Lilia I., "Beyond the Methods Fetish: Toward a Humanizing Pedagogy," *Harvard Educational Review, 64:2.* pp. 173–194.

The primary purpose of content area instruction is to enable students to develop sound and growing knowledge that they can use to identify and solve problems, and that forms a foundation on which they will build future learning. The result of good teaching is good learning.

Teachers have not taught effectively if students do not learn, or do not find satisfaction in learning.

Learning is made easier when a foundation of related knowledge exists. Recall is made easier when the foundation is strong and when ideas are integrated within and across content area fields.

Attention to content area study in a school setting is increased when students can relate their text-based learning to existing and newly developing interests within the content area fields. Energetic engagement in learning activities is developed in a learning environment that helps students establish their sense of industriousness as people who study, and their sense of competence as people who learn. The goals suggested in the textbook for teachers—what we hope and intend for our students as a result of their school experiences—are both cognitive (related to intellectual understanding) and affective (related to feelings and attitudes).

Teachers can aim to teach so that each student will develop this set of beliefs:

▌ I know important information.
>   I understand it; I can remember it; I use it.
>   What I know makes sense to me. My ideas fit together, and help me learn more.
>   There's always more to learn, and I intend to be a lifelong learner.

▌ I am capable.
>   I am a worker and a learner.
>   I am interested in what I learn, and I want to learn more.
>   School is a good place. I am welcome there, as are all the other students.

Planning to teach in ways that will enable every student to have this set of beliefs and attitudes is idealistic. To set and maintain a grand goal—a goal we may never quite attain but can always strive toward—has beneficial effects, not only for students but for our own teaching careers.

Suppose, for a moment, that a teacher's views are very different. Imagine a teacher who would respond to the idea that good teaching leads to students' competence and sense of being capable with a comment such as this: "There isn't a way in the world that all my students are going to learn what's in the curriculum, let alone remember it or apply it later. Most of my students pass the end-of-unit tests, and that means nobody can criticize my teaching. I don't fool myself that these kids are *interested* in learning. They can't wait for the bell to ring, and most days neither can I. I've got some good students, sure, but if people believe that all my students

ought to go out of here thinking they're capable, well, I'd like to sit them down and describe a few of the kids I'm stuck with this year."

That paragraph is painful to read. Think how frightful it would be to *be* that teacher, experiencing an entire career built upon such a belief system. Think also about how many students such a teacher would influence over a lifetime of teaching, and what that influence would be. In this chapter, as we consider the characteristics of effective content area teaching, we will also consider some counterexamples—what good instruction is *not* like. But we will return repeatedly, throughout this text, to a consideration of good teaching and the inspiration of good teachers.

> When, after a lifetime of teaching, a talented, dedicated middle school teacher died, the students, fellow teachers, and parents in the school where she had taught planted a tree in the playground in her honor. The commemorative plaque beside the tree is engraved with her name, and one quotation—the four words everyone remembered her saying, every year: *"These students are wonderful!"*

◪ Principles of Content Area Teaching

Three principles, relating to teacher knowledge, beliefs, and practice about content area teaching, provide a basis for the ideas presented in this text. Good content area teaching has a three-part foundation.

The first principle is that good content area teaching depends on the teacher's explicit or intuitive understanding of sound educational theory. An essential component of this understanding is the teacher's belief that all students can learn. An essential corollary is the teacher's acceptance of the responsibility to teach each one.

The second principle is that good content area teaching depends on the teacher's knowledge of, and interest in, both subject matter and pedagogy, and the teacher's skill in choosing and using effective instructional strategies.

The third principle is that good content area teaching depends on the teacher's commitment to ongoing learning and professional growth, resulting in increasing general knowledge, and deepening understanding of good educational theory and practice and the ability to apply this understanding effectively.

According to the first of these principles, good content area teaching is based on explicit or intuitive understanding of sound educational theory. Many elements of that statement need to be considered.

- *Theory.* A theory is a comprehensive set of principles that explains observed events.
- *Educational theory.* Educational theories explain how people develop and how they learn.
- *Sound educational theory.* A sound theory is one that is well reasoned and coherent, supported by research and observation. However, whether a theory is "sound" is a matter of opinion. Within the field of education, there are conflicting theories about how people develop and learn. The work of some of the major scholars whose theories provide a basis for the ideas in this text is described in the next section of this chapter.
- *Explicit vs. intuitive understanding of theory.* An idea that is explicit is directly stated. The statement "all students can learn" is explicit. The idea is presented directly. It is out in the open. No one reading it here would need to think, "I'd like to ask the author of this text what percentage of the students in a typical classroom she thinks are capable of learning." When we have an explicit understanding of a concept, we are aware of our knowledge and we can state and explain it.

Intuitive understanding of ideas, on the other hand, is based on our experience and the way we view the world. Many teachers have an intuitive understanding of some important theoretical principles, because the theories match an understanding of the way the world is. For example, teachers realize that students cannot learn well if they are hungry, tired, or frightened. The idea seems natural and reasonable. The psychologist Abraham Maslow (1943, 1970) studied human needs. He developed a theory that places human needs in a hierarchy; his theory makes an explicit statement that basic needs must be satisfied before higher level needs (such as the need for achievement and self-fulfillment) can be experienced. Maslow's theory, described in Chapter Seven, is a useful one for teachers to know. However, many teachers act intuitively in accordance with elements of the theory, without even being aware that such a theory exists.

As we teach, we often act in ways that suggest what our theories and beliefs are, even when we have not read, learned, or talked and thought about them. Those who observe our teaching can make inferences about what our educational beliefs and theories are; they are implied by what we do. Many scholars and practitioners (e.g., Cambourne & Turbill, 1990: Hills, 1992) have noted that theories about education, even if they are held intuitively, can be well-developed and coherent. As Heidi Mills and Jean Anne Clyde (1991, p. 54) point out, "teachers' beliefs become actualized as practice." Teachers who try their best to ensure that all their students learn, who think about their teaching and modify their instruction to make improvements, are acting in accordance with a belief that all students can learn—even if that belief is not explicit.

■■ Sound Theory and Ethical Principles

Although this is not a textbook on human development, psychoeducational theory, or ethics, the practices that are advocated here are based on conceptions about the ways that people learn, and principles about the purposes of education. Many great scholars have provided theories about learning that have practical implications for education. Much of what these theorists teach comes to appear as common sense—something everyone knows intuitively. However, there are conflicting theories, leading to conflicting approaches to teaching. For example, some psychologists have asserted that learning comes from without, acquired bit by bit, imposed upon the learner through a system of rewards and punishments. Teaching that emphasizes skills taught in isolation, and allots a large portion of classroom time and attention to controlling behavior, is based on such theories. Some people have proposed the view that children differ, from birth, so substantially that it is not reasonable to expect some to learn successfully. Educational practices that sort students into good and poor learners rely to some extent on this harsh view. The ideas presented in this text are *not* based on either of these theories.

The way we think and act and talk as educators is based on our theories of learning and teaching, and our ethical beliefs about education, whether or not we are conscious of those theories and beliefs. In this text, for example, the word *training* is never used as a synonym for *teaching* (except within a quotation), because *training* carries the implication that education is a one-way process, imposed upon a student by someone else. This textbook is written from the position that people are naturally active learners—constructors and users of knowledge. The ideas presented are rooted in the view that in a benign, information-rich, opportunity-filled learning environment, all students can learn. "Every day, week, month, and year that a [student] spends in a supportive context will contribute to... future success as a learner" (Mills & Clyde, 1991, p. 59).

The work of many theorists underlies this vision of education. The Swiss psychologist Jean Piaget (e.g., Piaget, 1929, 1932, 1955; Piaget & Inhelder, 1968, 1973) and the Russian psychologist Lev Vygotsky (1962, 1978) are two of the most influential. Piaget showed that children are active participants in their own learning. He asserted that learning occurs as people form schemata, or concepts about the way things work, using the mental capabilities available at their current stage of development. Infants learn through their senses and by moving. Young children make intuitive guesses. Later learning occurs through active engagement with the environment. For example, understanding that things appear different when viewed from different perspectives develops because children have, naturally, many opportunities to learn this from experience. The understanding that things can be arranged in different kinds of sequences (e.g., large to small, heavy to light) develops as a result of exploration, noticing, and action. Eventually, people are capable of abstract thought, and they learn through reasoning. The term *schemata* (or *schemas*) refers to our mental understandings. Learning occurs through disequilibrium—when something that we observe does not fit a current schema, thus putting

our understanding off balance. When this happens, we first try to fit what is new into our current schema (assimilation), but we eventually change the schema to make the new information a part of it (accommodation). Piaget's ideas emphasize active, constructive learning by the individual. His work influenced the fields of psychology and education in showing that people at different stages think and solve problems in different ways, that when learners have misconceptions there are likely to be sensible reasons for this, and that educators and other scholars can learn from extensive, careful observation and interaction with infants and children. Some of Piaget's work, however, has been interpreted to emphasize classifying learners, seeking quick ways to accelerate students' development, or alternatively testing students to find out what they do not know and limiting their opportunities to progress. These are misapplications of Piagetian theory.

Piaget worked productively throughout a long lifetime, during which his books were translated into many languages and he became world famous as an authority on children's cognitive development. Another scholar whose work is now highly influential had a very different career. Lev Vygotsky's work as a psychologist began in 1924 when he was 28 years old; he died of tuberculosis ten years later leaving 80 unpublished manuscripts. His major works were published posthumously in Russia, and were not translated into English till many years later (Vygotsky, 1962, endpaper). The two scholars were aware of each other's work, however, and influenced one another. Piaget revised some of his views about language development in response to experiments conducted by Vygotsky (Gardner, 1982, p. 285). In a 1933 lecture in Leningrad, recorded by a stenographer, printed in a Russian journal of psychology in 1967, and later translated into English, Vygotsky commented, "a new work of Piaget has been extremely helpful to me. This work is concerned with the development in the child of moral rules..." (Vygotsky, 1982, p. 181) and then described how Piaget's ideas had contributed to his research.

One of Vygotsky's contributions that has become extremely influential in educational practice is the concept of the zone of proximal development. As we develop and learn, there are always capabilities that we will have in the near future, but have not yet acquired. These capabilities are developmentally near to what we can presently do. (*Proximal* means *near*.) Because they are almost within our grasp, we can accomplish them, with some help. For example, at a certain point in conceptual development, a student cannot find places on a map using compass directions (e.g., the student cannot fulfill the direction to "point to the state that is directly north of Indiana"). However, the student can follow that direction if a teacher or other adult tells and shows how to do it. Also, while working and talking with other students, some of whom are more capable in using maps, the student can successfully complete tasks requiring the use of maps if the tasks are selected wisely by a teacher. Eventually, the student will be able to use compass directions to identify places independently and automatically, moving beyond the zone of proximal development for this ability. In teaching, providing intelligent support for students as they are learning can help them to become successful independently. This support is social. It comes through interaction with people, both adults and more capable peers.

Building upon the idea that our knowledge about how children develop and learn should come from observing children (rather than by conducting experiments using them), language scholars and theorists such as Courtney Cazden (1972, 1988), Roger Brown (1973a, 1973b), and Catherine Snow (1972) have shown us that people are naturally adept language learners, who readily acquire the ability to attend to speech and express ideas in speaking through listening and talking, using language in ordinary daily life. Studies of how oral language is learned have provided support for the idea that reading and writing are best learned in environments where there are many opportunities to read and write.

Other scholars have given useful information about lifelong developmental processes, and about how environment affects learning. Erik Erikson (1963, 1968, 1982) identified eight stages through which people pass during a full lifetime. For each of these stages, there is a particular developmental crisis—*"crisis* here connoting not a threat of catastrophe but a turning point, a crucial period of increased

vulnerability and heightened potential" (Erikson, 1982, p. 4). According to Erikson's classification of life stages, the third stage of human development occurs during the preschool years (following infancy and early childhood), when a child will develop a sense of initiative or, in an unfavorable environment, feelings of guilt. During the elementary school years, favorable experiences promote industriousness, and unfavorable experiences contribute to a sense of inferiority. The good outcome of this stage of development is competence. In the following stage, adolescents develop a sense of what they are like as persons—a sense of identity—or, if development during this period is not sound, they will become confused in their view of themselves and what their role in life should be. Erikson's theory is pertinent to education, because teachers are often the major determiners of whether school-age children develop a sense of competence, and can have a strong influence on adolescents' development of a sense of identity.

One scholar who has emphasized the strong role that environmental factors have in development is Urie Bronfenbrenner (1976, 1979). Advocating educational research in natural, rather than laboratory settings, he describes an ecological structure of the educational environment, in which the learner is affected by influences (systems) that can be thought of as a series of concentric circles (the learner being at the center). Students learn within the immediate school setting (a microsystem), which is affected by the interrelationships (mesosystems) among family, school, peers, community groups, and influences such as television. Beyond these is the exosystem, consisting of the social, economic, and political structures that affect people's lives. For example, when times are hard economically, parents may be out of work, and this will have serious effects on the family and on the individual student. The broadest systems, in this analysis, are macrosystems, belief systems that underlie thinking and actions and affect how people are treated.

A theorist whose views are beginning to have a strong influence on educational practice is Howard Gardner, a psychologist whose wide-ranging interests have led him to develop a theory of multiple intelligences (Gardner, 1983, 1993b). To understand this theory, it is useful to know some of the history of psychological interest in human intelligence, and to note how much of that interest has been focused on devising ways to measure intelligence. (It is interesting to consider how the field of education might be different if more psychologists had, instead, given their attention to ways to develop and enhance learning, and to enable people to learn and work together.)

For many years, "intelligence tests" have been given to assess people's presumed capacity to learn. The first such tests were devised early in the twentieth century by French psychologists, Alfred Binet and Theophilus Simon in an effort to differentiate children who could benefit from education from those who could not, because of mental incapacity to learn (Binet & Simon, 1916). Later, an English version of their test, the Stanford Binet test, was developed, and most other tests designed to measure intelligence have been patterned to some extent after the Binet. Most of these tests depend on language, and people who are adept language users are likely to score well. Some also assess a person's ability to use spatial concepts, for example, by understanding how various patterns are arranged and how parts fit together to form a whole. According to Gardner's theory of multiple intelligences, there are seven distinctly different intelligences, and it is possible that more may be identified. Each person possesses these intelligences and can develop them; the intelligences interact with one another and can be manifested in many ways. Each person's pattern of intelligences, therefore, is unique. The seven intelligences Gardner has identified are linguistic, logical-mathematical, spatial, bodily-kinesthetic, musical, interpersonal, and intrapersonal intelligence. These cannot be adequately measured by standardized tests or summed up in scores. Instead, they are evidenced through solving problems and creating products in authentic settings.

All Students Can Learn

At the beginning of this chapter, three principles of effective content area teaching were stated. Because they are important, it is useful to restate them and discuss them further. This is the first principle: Good content area teaching is based on explicit or intuitive understanding of sound educa-

tional theory. An essential component of this understanding is the teacher's belief that all students can learn. An essential corollary is the teacher's acceptance of the responsibility to teach each one.

> The task of teaching a subject to a child at any particular age is one of representing the structure of that subject in terms of the child's way of viewing things. The task can be thought of as one of translation…. [A]ny idea can be presented honestly and usefully in the thought forms of children of school-age, and… these first representations can later be made more powerful and precise the more easily by virtue of this early learning. (Bruner, 1965, p. 33)

It is our responsibility to teach each of our students. The concept of learning *for all* is a major theme of this text. Accepting the responsibility to teach all our students implies a belief in our own capacity, a belief that what happens in classrooms is largely under teachers' control, rather than largely determined by influences outside teachers' control. These differing attitudes are themselves the basis of a well-known theory developed by Julian Rotter—the theory of locus of control (Rotter, 1966; Findley & Cooper, 1983). According to this theory, people can be classified according to whether they accept responsibility for what they do and for much of what happens in their lives, or, on the other hand, attribute what happens to outside influences or to chance. Members of the former group are said to have internal locus (place) of control, and the latter to have external locus of control.

Statements such as these suggest an external locus of control:

- My preparation for teaching did not give me the necessary skills to be an effective teacher.
- I am very limited in what I can accomplish because students' home environment is a large influence in their achievement.

Statements such as these suggest an internal locus of control:

- Negative influences of a student's home experiences can be overcome by good teaching.
- If a student did not remember information I gave in a previous lesson, I would know how to increase that student's retention in the next lesson.

▮ When I really try, I can get through to most difficult students.

(These statements are adapted from items on scales of teacher efficacy, listed in Guskey & Passaro, 1994.)

Believing that our students can learn reflects a belief about ourselves: the belief that we, as well as our students, are capable of achieving important goals.

Subject Matter and Pedagogy: Knowledge, Interest, Skill

Good content area teaching has a two-part foundation, and the second principle of effective content area teaching specifies this: Good content area teaching is based on the teacher's knowledge of, and interest in, both subject matter and pedagogy, and the teacher's skill in choosing and using effective instructional strategies. The combination of subject matter knowledge and knowledge of how to teach is crucial. Lauren Sosniak and Susan Stodolsky (1993) refer to teacher understanding and comfort with subject matter as a basis for good teaching, pointing out that the same teachers who provide lively, thorough instruction in one area may shift to dependence on a scripted lesson format from a teacher's manual in teaching topics where they lack understanding and do not feel at ease. As Larry Yore (1991, p. 69) has noted, teachers who observe their students, know their subject, and think critically about their teaching and the teaching materials they use are likely to be "positively disposed and intellectually ready" to move beyond a textbook-driven program and to learn about strategies they can use to enhance instruction. One of the major themes of this text is the importance of teachers' knowledge of subject matter and enthusiasm for it. One of the major purposes of the text is to enable teachers to develop their pedagogical knowledge and enthusiasm. To meet this purpose, a variety of useful instructional strategies are described, and guidance is offered for teachers to help them exercise their decision-making power in choosing among strategies and their professional skill in using them.

Ongoing Learning and Professional Growth

The third principle that underlies good content area teaching is that good content area teaching is based on the teacher's commitment to ongoing learning and professional growth, resulting in increasing general knowledge, and deepening understanding of good educational theory and practice and the ability to apply this understanding effectively. If a teacher thinks of students as the only learners in the classroom, then even student learning will suffer. Harold Herber (1978, p. 23) stresses the importance of teachers learning along with their students. He has listed the qualities that teachers need to develop and cultivate to be colearners with their students. "Conducting your classes so that your students view you as a colearner takes great patience, good organization, tolerance for ambiguity, openness to other ways of viewing the world, and a great deal of self-respect." Reading and studying this text provides an opportunity for professional growth, as does all professional study. Throughout the text, suggestions are given for ways in which teachers can continue to expand their learning, and to be colearners with their students. By continuing our own learning, teachers understand more clearly the kinds of problems students may be experiencing as they attempt to acquire information and understand new concepts. When we are learners we become learning models for our students, and our interest in what we teach keeps our enthusiasm for teaching high.

Good content area teaching is based on the teacher's commitment to ongoing learning and professional growth.

Themed Reading

One way to be a continuing learner is to read. One way for teachers to build opportunities for wide reading into the content area program, at all grade levels from the earliest school years through graduate programs at a university, is to schedule time, in class, for everyone in the class to read materials of their choice about the topic being studied. (Young children and others who are not yet readers use the time to look at materials with many topic-related pictures.) The idea of everyone reading together, through a strategy called Uninterrupted Sustained Silent Reading, was devised by Lyman Hunt (1970), and advanced by Robert and Marlene McCracken (1971, 1978), who changed the name to Sustained Silent Reading. Programs of sustained reading have been advocated for many years and are increasingly being used under a variety of names. The essence of these programs is that everyone in a classroom— the teacher as well as the students—reads silently for a specified period of time, during which interruptions are not allowed. In content area classes, it is useful for students and teacher to read from a wide variety of reading material related to a current topic of study (Jacobson, 1992/1993).

Teachers prepare for Themed Reading by collecting books, magazines, articles, and other reading materials that are related to the content area field being studied. Resource books and other materials, such as dictionaries, volumes of an encyclopedia, atlases or maps, may also be used during Themed Reading time. Using a classroom collection for sustained silent reading time ensures that everyone has something to read or look at, and that all the reading matter is related to the content area. Starting a collection need not be expensive: back issues of social studies and science magazines, for example, can be used intact, or can be cut apart into separate articles. Material with photographs relating to topics in science and social studies is useful for Themed Reading, even if the text is difficult for students to read. Teachers can ask friends and family to be on the lookout for material to add to the collection, and ask the school media specialist for content-related library discards.

The next step is to decide on a regular time period for Themed Reading. A 10- to 15-minute reading session once or twice a week works well. Since reading is followed by idea-sharing, the total time used will be about half an hour. Only a brief explanation before the first session is needed. Themed Reading is easy to understand and enjoy, and its only rule is that everyone reads. Just before each session begins, everyone chooses one or more items to read or look at. (Choosing several items allows for browsing without getting up to get new things to read.) It is a good idea to set a goal, with the class, of having everyone—teacher and students— seated and reading within two minutes of the time people begin choosing material. The teacher's role during Themed Reading is to serve as a model of someone who reads, and someone who follows the rule that time is for reading. This means that teachers' time must not be used to check on whether students are using their time well, or to correct those who are not.

Record keeping for Themed Reading is managed by keeping a set of file cards, one for each student. Instead of timing the Themed Reading period by the clock, the teacher signals the end of the session by getting up quietly and giving two or three students their cards. This means that these students are asked to tell the class something about what they have been reading. (However, students should be free to refuse a card if they do not want to talk about what they have read.) Other students can choose to share ideas as well. Teachers can take this opportunity to expand on students' ideas to add more information about content-related topics that the class is studying, has studied, or will be studying. Students who receive cards write the date on the card or note what they were reading and return the cards at the end of the session. In later sessions, the teacher continues to give cards to students who have not yet told about their reading until everyone has had a turn, and then begins the process again.

One important caution is that teachers should never give cards with the intention of embarrassing a student. This is not the time to give guidance to a student who has not been paying attention or has chosen inappropriate reading material. Teachers' comments elaborating on students' contributions should always be a form of praise. Sometimes students will become so interested in their Themed Reading selection that they will ask if they can finish reading it in free time, and of course this should be permitted. Enthusiasm should be encouraged. Like many other strategies in which students are actively involved, Themed Reading can be the source for an interesting, easily varied bulletin board display. Bookjackets from books students are enjoying, or photocopies of the books' covers, can be displayed, along with students' recommendations and copies of favorite excerpts.

Aspects of Effective Content Area Teaching

Just as it is possible for teachers to teach in accordance with an educational theory without explicit knowledge of that theory, it is also possible to teach in pedagogically sound ways without being able to name or explain these ideas. (However, explicit knowledge is preferable, and one of the purposes of this text is to give brief explanations of important theories and pedagogical principles.) Among the components of effective teaching are ability to teach authoritatively, the use of teaching practices that promote learning, and development of the habit of re-

---

authoritative and **authoritarian**—both derive from the Latin verb *augere*, meaning *to increase* or *produce*, a word from which many English words are derived *(augment, auction, author)*. The person who produces something is its creator or author; the producer also possesses power or authority. The difference between *authoritarian* and *authoritative* is in their suffixes: *-arian* means *believing in*, whereas *-ative* means *possessing*. An authoritarian person believes in authority, but an authoritative person possesses authority.

laissez-faire—a French term, combining forms of the French verbs *laisser* (to let or permit) and *faire* (to do). *Laissez* is an imperative form, so *laissez-faire* literally means *let do*. When a laissez-faire leadership style is used, the leader lets people alone to do whatever they wish. (*Laissez* is pronounced to rhyme with *essay*.)

flection. Teachers need also to understand the roles of reading and questioning in teaching and learning, to be aware of useful ways to plan instruction, and to accept responsibility for decision-making.

Teaching is complex. Much of the best writing about teaching implies this fact or states it explicitly. Consider the quotation from Lilia Bartolome's writing that opens this chapter. She tells us that effective teachers create inviting learning environments that build upon students' language and experiences and ensure that students acquire content knowledge and academic skills. Are teachers to make sure that classrooms are pleasant and student-centered, or to teach content and develop literacy? The answer is "both." Are teachers to respect students' knowledge or have high standards for their learning? Both. Are teachers to plan in ways that enable students to be active learners, or in ways that give teachers the authority in the classroom? Both. It is good news that combining aspects of good teaching is easier, more satisfying, and far more effective than focusing on one of these parts and ignoring another. Content knowledge and literacy develop well in pleasant, convivial learning environments. Classrooms in which active learning goes on all the time are pleasanter places than those in which little learning occurs. Enabling students to achieve is linked with showing respect for them and the language, knowledge, and experiences they bring to learning. Active student learning and authoritative teaching go hand in hand.

Authoritative Teaching

Effective teachers are concerned with establishing and maintaining an environment in which students can learn, and in which they themselves can feel comfortable teaching. Psychoeducational theorists and researchers identify three leadership styles that are applicable to teaching: **authoritative, authoritarian**, and **laissez-faire**. Neither authoritarian nor laissez-faire styles of leadership are as effective as an authoritative style in helping students become independent learners.

Each of us has experienced or observed classrooms in which the teacher's main goal is to maintain tight control. Rules and discipline are emphasized, rather than learning. Teachers who choose to manage their classrooms in this way—and it is teacher choice and teacher thought and effort (or lack of thought and effort) that determine classroom management—use an authoritarian style. Their emphasis is on maintaining their role as authority figures and on requiring that students accept their authority. In other classrooms, teachers choose to exercise very little control over learning or classroom management. They come to work but put forth relatively little effort. They let events occur without much planning, supervision, or thought. These teachers are using a laissez-faire style. Extremes of either of these two styles do not make for good teaching.

On the other hand, many classrooms are led by teachers who practice and continue to strive toward an authoritative style. These teachers are knowledgeable and caring, and as they teach they become increasingly efficient and effective. Authoritative teachers are those who manage their classrooms with apparent ease, while their students concentrate on learning. There is diversity among these teachers, of course. Many excellent teachers have a very wide range of what they feel comfortable with in the classroom in terms of noise level and activity, and their students love school and learn well. Other strong teachers are very firm and tend toward the authoritarian, and their students also love school and learn well. We can enhance our own authoritative teaching style by thinking about our own teaching and by observing others. It is important to develop the habit of reflecting on our teaching, identifying areas of strength to build upon, and analyzing aspects of teaching that need improvement. It is also useful to identify colleagues whose classrooms are well-organized, pleasant learning environments and whose students work together effectively, and then to observe these master teachers carefully and use them as consultants. Figure 2–1 on the next page shows an example of such an observation.

Teaching Practices that Promote Learning

Many scholars in the field of education have studied characteristics of effective teachers and adept teaching. Among the qualities effective teachers possess are respect for students, strong and increasing knowledge of their subject matter, and interest in teaching as a problem-solving process. Effective teachers also have the wonderful quality of being energetically aware of what is going on in the classroom—an ability to which Jacob Kounin (1970) gave the lively name of "withitness."

Teaching that CARES for ME

There is artistry in being a teacher. Outstanding teachers make what is complex look easy. Observing them in action is akin to observing a talented athlete or artist accomplishing marvelous feats apparently effortlessly. Although there is no way to capture great teaching or good teaching in a list of words, it is useful to think about the combination of qualities good teachers possess and continue to strive toward, and each person who reflects on teaching might develop a personal listing. A list is given here in the form of an **acronym** that serves as a way to recall the listed items. The capitalized letters in CARES for ME stand for characteristics of good teachers and good teaching, and the acronym itself calls attention to the fact that caring for every student is a part of exemplary teaching. Within the following list, summarized in Figure 2–2, there are some surprising pairings that remind us of the complexity of good teaching.

C.   *Challenge, clarity,* and *cheerfulness* are all important to good teaching. The pairing of the first two elements is a reminder that good teachers are

---

acronym—derived from two Greek words: akros, meaning *extreme,* and thus *the summit* or *the beginning,* and *onyma,* meaning *name*—the same source that gives us the endings of *antonym* (an opposite name) and *synonym* (a same name). Acronyms are words composed of the beginning letter, or letters, of other words. Many words that have come into our language recently in science, politics, computer programming, and other fields are acronyms. Usually acronyms are written all in capitals, but some eventually become written and thought of as ordinary words. Two examples are *laser* (Light Amplification by Stimulated Emission of Radiation) and *radar* (RAdio Detecting And Ranging). There are many acronyms in education as well.

FIGURE 2–1   Example of Authoritative Teaching (observation [15 minutes] of a fourth-grade class)

Background: It is midmorning. Students are working independently on a math exercise. The teacher has moved about the room observing the students and occasionally conversing with them quietly about the task. She is now sitting at her desk. Gene is a nine-year-old boy who sits at the back of the room.

Gene erases a line on his paper, blows on it, then shakes both the paper and his workbook over the floor. He rubs his arm across his desktop, replaces his book and paper and begins to write again. He works for about five minutes, reading and writing, then he holds up his paper and looks closely at it. He nods his head, gets up from his desk and takes his paper to the teacher's desk.

Teacher: *(accepting paper)* Okay, Gene, why don't you get an activity card from the box and work on that while everyone finishes their math?
Gene: Can I write instead?
Teacher: Of course you can.

Gene returns to his desk, opens it and removes a blue folder. He opens the folder and looks through the lined paper inside it. He chooses a sheet half-filled with writing, places the folder on the floor, and begins to write. After writing for a while, Gene sits back, runs his hands through his hair and sighs. He opens his desk, removes two plastic action figures, poses them on his desk and returns to his writing. He rearranges the figures and writes alternately. The teacher gets up from her desk, moves to Gene and kneels down beside him.

Teacher: *(in a whisper)* I told you that you could write if you wanted to, but this isn't play time.
Gene: I'm not playing; I'm choreographing.
Teacher: *(opens eyes wide)* What?
Gene: I'm writing a fight in my novel, but it's hard to tell how it looked, so I do it with these guys and then I write about it.
Teacher: Well, I suppose that's all right.
Gene: Because I'm not playing; I'm being creative, right?
Teacher: That's right.
Gene: I'm going to be an author when I grow up, and they'll make movies out of all of my books.
Teacher: I sure hope so.
Gene: And then I'll buy you a lot of chalk so you never have to look for any.
Teacher: *(smiles)* That would be wonderful. (*She gets up and returns to her desk.*)

Gene continues to pose the action figures and write until the teacher tells the class to get ready for their science lesson.

This observation was written by Kelly Ann Herrington, who was at the time an undergraduate student. Minor changes have been made.

able to work with two (or more) goals simultaneously. In routinized classrooms all students follow the same procedures and are presented with a limited amount of information; the instruction follows what Robert Ruddell (1990) calls "a pre-charted course." Such instruction may be completely clear, but it is not challenging. Jeanne Nakamura (1988) is one of many scholars who has written about the importance of learning activities that are both challenging and within students' capacity to accomplish. Teachers who provide challenging instruction have ongoing challenges themselves, and one is to present new ideas and information and guidelines for unfamiliar tasks as clearly as possible. Cheerfulness is good for students and teacher alike.

A.   *Appropriateness* and *acceptance of ambiguity*, like clarity and challenge, are an unusual pairing, and yet they mesh with each other, and with other sets of characteristics on our list. Because effective teachers are knowledgeable about what they are teaching, and because they know and care about their students, they can provide instruction that is clear and appropriately paced. Instruction should neither move so rapidly that students are baffled nor so slowly that students are bored. The tasks they present are appropriately challenging and varied enough to provide interesting work for all students, fitted to their strengths and needs.

Earlier in this chapter there was a brief discussion of the complexity of teaching, echoing the

Cheerfulness is beneficial for students and teacher alike.

views expressed in the quotation that heads this chapter. Good teachers need to be able to mesh many important goals. Classrooms must be pleasant and student-centered places in which students learn content and develop literacy. We must respect students' knowledge and have high standards for their learning. We need to plan in ways that enable our students to be active learners, and we must have authority in our classrooms. At times, these various goals may seem conflicting or ambiguous. Good teachers recognize and accept this and look for ways to accomplish complex goals.

R. *Respect* is central to good teaching—respect for students and their ideas, their wonderful qualities, their families; respect for the teaching profession, our colleagues, and ourselves; respect for learning. Other aspects of good teaching that mesh with the characteristic of respect are *repetition, revisiting,* and *re-viewing* (seeing again). Respect for those we teach, and for our own capabilities as teachers, is shown by a cheerful expectation that thoughtful, interesting repetition, revisiting and re-viewing will be part of our teaching, because opportunities for it will be built into our planning and will also occur spontaneously. Howard Gardner (1991, p. 246) gives as one definition of a skilled teacher, "a person who can open a number of different windows on the same subject." One method of showing respect for our students is the willingness to teach, and reteach, in a variety of interesting ways; one way of showing respect for

ideas is to return and re-view them in a variety of contexts. Margaret McKeown (1993) and Sandra McCormick (1994) are among the scholars who assert that thorough learning comes from well-planned and interesting repeated engagement with a topic. They use the term *multiple encounters in multiple contexts* (ME/MC) to refer to presenting new ideas in many ways so that students can have many opportunities to develop their understanding.

E. *Enthusiasm* is a wonderful quality that good teachers possess. Because they are deeply interested in teaching, their enthusiasm sparks their students' excitement about learning. But enthusiasm alone is not enough to spark that excitement; it must be matched with *expertise*. To help our students learn, we need to be experts in our subject matter fields, and experts in teaching as well. Teachers have more reason than people in many other professions to be lifelong learners, and more opportunities to keep learning. This learning is a major way of staying enthusiastic about teaching. The enthusiasm that outstanding teachers have for their profession springs from enjoyment of their field of learning, their students, and teaching itself.

S. *Structure* is an essential part of good teaching. It is based on sensible planning that productively shapes classroom days, weeks, and the year. Teachers who structure their teaching wisely are aware of the importance of time. Edward Kameenui (1993, p. 381) writes of the "tyranny of

---

FIGURE 2–2   Using *CARES for ME* to Recall Characteristics of Good Teaching

C:	**C**hallenge, **C**larity and **C**heerfulness
A:	**A**ppropriateness and **A**cceptance of **A**mbiguity
R:	**R**espect—also **R**epetition, **R**evisiting, and **R**e-viewing
E:	**E**nthusiasm and **E**xpertise
S:	**S**afety and **S**tructure
for	
ME:	**M**aximum **E**ngagement by students in learning

The enthusiasm effective teachers have for teaching, and for the subject they teach, sparks students' excitement about learning.

use and apply what they are taught, the teaching itself is a fruitless endeavor—a sterile progression through a curriculum or text. The importance of teaching, rather than simply touching upon a topic, is stressed by Dolores Durkin. She contrasts instructing with "mentioning," which she defines as "saying just enough about a topic to allow for doing an exercise related to it" (Durkin, 1990, p. 476). All of the aspects of teaching encapsulated in the "CARES for ME" phrase contribute to sound learning, and thus to learning that students will be able and inclined to use in new situations. However, one element—respect, repetition, revisiting, and re-viewing—is basic to teaching for transfer. A major purpose of this text is to provide teachers with multiple ways to present ideas and engage students in learning. Repetition, in this list of effective teaching characteristics, is not drill to produce rote memorization. Instead, useful repetition depends on teachers' willingness to recognize and respond helpfully to students' questions and uncertainties, and teachers' adeptness in finding ways to present ideas in many interesting contexts.

> [I]deas or concepts [do not] stand alone as abstract, self-contained entities; they are intimately connected to the phenomena they seek to explain. When a concept or idea is used in a particular situation, it is recast, acquiring new meaning it did not possess before. The situation thus becomes part of the meaning of the concept.
>
> What does this say about transfer? Transfer, like learning, is likely to vary as a function of how well connected the ideas are—both to the specific phenomena they help explain… and to the various representations that give them form and substance. Teachers who foster the development of both sets of connections in students are apt to produce high rates of learning and transfer. Students must be encouraged to use the ideas they're acquiring to talk about important aspects of their environment…; the greater the repertoire of appropriate representations, the greater the likelihood that students will be able to see connections between different ideas. (Prawat, 1991, p. 10)

time" and warns of the dangers to students if time is wasted on trivial matters. "Instructional time is a precious commodity; do not lose it." *Safety* is essential for learning. Many of the elements of good teaching that have been previously listed contribute to a learning environment in which students feel safe and comfortable and can give their attention to learning. Teachers' ability to combine challenge with clarity and to pace instruction appropriately, their respect for students and enthusiasm for teaching all work together to create classrooms that are psychologically safe learning environments.

ME. All of these elements are interwoven in classrooms where students are actively engaged—*maximally engaged*—in learning.

Teaching for Transfer

Transferable knowledge and skills are those that can be used in other situations besides the ones in which they were learned. Logically, if students cannot

The Habit of Reflection

Mary Heller identifies three characteristics of effective teaching: the ability to demonstrate flexibility within structure, use of an authoritative management style, and the habit of planning based on reflection. "A key to successful classroom instruction, organization, and management is the amount of reflection undertaken by the teachers themselves" (Heller, 1991, p. 300). The term *reflective teaching* refers to the ability—and habit—of capable teachers to think about their own teaching before they teach, while they are teaching, and after they have taught. John Dewey (1933) contrasted reflective action with routine action. In making this distinction, he was not condemning the use of efficient procedures for carrying out classroom routines, such as beginning and ending class in productive ways, or collecting and returning students' work; it is characteristic of effective teachers to manage necessary routines smoothly. Instead, Dewey was using "routine action" to describe approaches to teaching that do not require teachers to pay attention to what they are doing. According to this definition, teachers are acting routinely when they act on impulse, when they use traditional teaching methods simply because this is what they are accustomed to doing, or when the way they teach is determined by commercially prepared materials. Teaching based on reflective action, on the other hand, occurs when teachers actively and consistently consider their own beliefs about teaching and their teaching practices, and accept the fact that their teaching has important consequences for their students.

Good teachers enjoy teaching. Over the years, good teachers continue to find ways to increase their ability to reach and teach all their students. Their students learn, enjoy learning, and become lifelong learners. Such teachers are constantly seeking to modify and improve their teaching. They are always ready to consider the new methods learned from colleagues, through courses and conferences, from their professional reading, as well as those they devise themselves. Suzanne Davis, writing on the topic of exemplary teachers, comments about a teacher widely recognized for many years of excellent teaching:

> In reflecting on her teaching, she often says that she was embarrassed by how little she taught her students in her early years of teaching. ...[and] she looks back at her earliest years with some regret at all she didn't know about teaching then. ...Like many teachers she has learned and grown and changed over the years. (Davis, 1993, p. 448)

Does it mean that we have been poor teachers if we realize that we have taught in ineffective or less effective ways? No. The best of teachers are continually getting better (which, logically, means that they were, in the past, less good). During their careers exemplary teachers have to come to terms with the realization, as they start out each new year, that there are things they do not know now that would benefit their students, and that they will only find out and be able to use after their current students have moved on. Good teachers *must* accept this situation; it is inextricably linked with continuing to learn. Why should good teaching change? We change because we will probably never get it exactly right, and if we did there would be a new group of students with somewhat different strengths and needs presenting new challenges and opportunities. Perhaps the most important reason for changing is that there are exciting new teaching ideas to be evaluated and adapted which are appearing all the time.

Thoughtful questioning by knowledgeable teachers is a useful form of instruction. Questions, especially those in a tell/ask format, can guide and inform students. Teachers' inquiries can help students understand concepts more deeply and enable them to realize that their own ideas are interesting and apt.

■■ Content Area Reading

Reading is a primary method of learning content area information. Within any classroom, variations in students' current levels of reading ability, prior knowledge, interest in a topic and self-confidence as learners are likely to result in different degrees of understanding. Skillful teachers can intervene between the students and the texts that provide content area information, to enable these diverse students to understand essential concepts. Teachers can support students' comprehension through direct teaching of content that provides explanation and expansion of the text; through classroom activities that promote multiple readings of text and activities that engage students actively in thinking about text concepts; and through the development and use of teaching materials, including the use of well-designed questions, that lead students to recognize and apply important text information. Strategies to accomplish these purposes are presented throughout this text.

Reading With Understanding

Is it possible to read without understanding? Most readers would say, from experience, that it is. When we are tired and our attention is elsewhere during reading, we might suddenly realize that we cannot remember anything about the pages our eyes just scanned. There has been, however, a continuing debate in the field of education about whether the term "reading" means "reading with understanding" and should not be used when the text is not understood. In this text, we will approach the topic of content area reading and comprehension from these premises:

■ Reading without understanding can occur.
■ Reading can result in different degrees of understanding.
■ Comprehension of a topic is made more difficult when the reader has little or no prior knowledge, and is made easier when the reader has a knowledge base on which to build and when relationships with other topics are recognized and developed.
■ Students need direct instruction and guidance to help them understand and recall content area information.

Reading together helps students learn to read, read to learn, and read to enjoy.

■ Understanding may develop at different times during and after a period of study.

Responding With Understanding

It is not only possible to read without understanding, when the conditions for reading are poor; it is also possible to answer questions and complete text-related worksheets correctly without understanding, when the questions and teaching materials are poorly constructed. Teachers should be alert to so-called comprehension activities (either in the text or of their own creation) to which students can respond without thought or understanding.

> **Text:** A gymnosperm is a type of seed plant whose seeds are not covered by a protective wall.
> **Question:** What is a type of seed plant whose seeds are not covered by a protective wall?
> **Answer:** Gymnosperm!

Any question that is worded so that the words in a text statement are simply transposed to form a question can be answered without thought and understanding by students who are reasonably confident in language use. An extreme example is presented in Figure 2–3. This contrived passage illustrates the following three points:

- Some questions can be answered by matching the question with a section from the text. For example, a question formulated as "What are the three branches of the U.S. government?" can be answered without thought if the text includes the sentence "The executive, legislative, and judicial branches are the three branches of the U. S. government."
- Some questions can be answered by using syntactic clues, rather than semantic information. In other words, a sense of language structure and grammar, which children develop naturally as preschoolers, can be used instead of an understanding of the meaning of words and passages. For example, a question with the form of "What kind of dinosaurs walked on two feet?" can be answered without understanding if the text includes the sentence, "Dinosaurs that walked on two feet were carnivorous."
- From a very early age, people have a well-developed sense of how their language works, even though many people who use standard grammar effortlessly cannot state or explain grammatical rules.

When a teacher, relying on students' well-developed sense of grammar, produces a false impression that students understand content (and, therefore, that the teacher has taught well) it is an example of the correct answer compromise, discussed in Chapter One. A compromise agreed upon to settle disagreements can be helpful and productive; a compromise—particularly in education—where two participants in a situation compromise to avoid putting forth effort harms students.

> Several obstacles stand between schools and educating for understanding…. For example, we have what we call the "test-text context." You read a text and memorize what's in it, then take a test that asks you what you've learned. If you give the answer stated in the text, you "understand" the text, and nobody asks you to take that understanding and apply it to new kinds of situations. I call that phenomenon the "correct answer compromise." If you give this answer, we'll say that you understand something, and everybody will be happy. (Gardner, 1993a, p. 22)

Suppose a text includes this statement: "The physical action of breaking food into smaller parts is called mechanical digestion." A teacher can take it easy by asking "What is the physical action of breaking food into smaller parts called?" Students can then take it easy by answering "mechanical digestion." Creating the question requires no thought on the teacher's part. The teacher simply transforms a text statement into a question; that is, the teacher just turns around the wording of the sentence in the text. Answering the question does not require any understanding on the students' part. The question can be answered

---

FIGURE 2–3   Nonsense Comprehension Check

Directions: Read the following passage carefully, and then respond to the comprehension check and grammar check sections. You may consult with a classmate as you complete your answers.

Snupple is not whump. Jashly, fimble gribs have droff hupps toward chashing. What is not so fivvle is whether squip of blinkety in chashing zoops from droff hupps or whether it is the other way around. Swimbly the dritch can vub in either frommid.

Comprehension Check
1. Is snupple whump?
2. What kind of gribs have droff hupps toward chashing?
3. Can we be sure that squip of blinkety in chashing zoops from droff hupps?
4. Is it possible that droff hupps zoop from squip of blinkety in chashing?
5. What can swimbly vub in either frommid?

Grammar Questions
1. What part of speech is *dritch*?
2. What part of speech are *fimble* and *whump*?
3. List one adverb from the passage.
4. Write the plural forms of *blinkety, dritch,* and *snupple.*
5. Complete the following sentence, using the correct form of the verb *vub*:

   I will be _____ around the house tomorrow.

solely on the basis of syntactic clues (and being able to read or match words); that is, all the students have to do is find a sentence in the text that resembles the question, and copy a phrase from it. This is an example of a correct answer compromise: The teacher proves that learning has occurred by showing that students can answer a question; the students prove they have learned by not asking about what puzzles them, and just doing what has been asked, giving a correct answer to a question that does not require them to understand a complex topic. The text statement is a good one, and the students are not at fault. It is the teacher who is not acting responsibly. What the teacher should be doing is creating questions that will help students understand the concept, in this case, the concept of mechanical digestion.

Text: The physical action of breaking food into smaller parts is called mechanical digestion.

Question: When we studied how rocks are changed by weathering, we learned the difference between mechanical weathering (when rocks are cracked and broken by natural forces) and chemical weathering, which occurs when something such as acid rain changes the substance of the rock. The process of digestion changes the food we eat both mechanically and chemically. What are some examples of mechanical digestion?

Possible answer: When we chew food and make it into smaller pieces

Confirmation: Yes, biting and chewing help us digest food mechanically. They don't change the food itself; they just separate it into smaller pieces.

A student may argue that the act of chewing is both mechanical and chemical digestion, because as we chew enzymes are secreted. Then the teacher needs to clarify the issue without discouraging the student's thoughtful or ingenious idea.

■ Questioning in Content Area Teaching

"Wanting to know" is a human characteristic that good content area teachers value, foster, and model

for their students. Raising questions is a sign of interest and intelligence. Students' questions can provide the foundation for useful content area activities. It is important for teachers to structure classroom activities so that questions are raised by learners in response to their own interests to learn more, and so that students engage in many kinds of useful inquiry. Knowledgeable, reflective teachers work to establish learning environments in which students' questions are respected and valued, and in which teachers as well as students raise and investigate questions that enable them to learn more. Students need to learn that, in any field of study, the people who are experts have more, and more perceptive, questions about their field than those who lack knowledge about it. They also need not to lose the eagerness in raising questions and seeking answers that is common to young children.

Consider what questioning is like when young children are involved in that process. The questioners are the children. They ask questions because they want to know the answers. The children ask their questions of people they believe know the answers. They expect that their questions will be answered, and they regard a truthful "I don't know" as a reasonable response. However, in educational

Both students and teachers can ask questions to find out information and ask questions to clarify what has been said and written.

settings, the role of the questioner usually switches, and questions have a different purpose. The questioners are teachers, not students. And the questioners already know the answers to the questions they ask. This is the model of questioning many students learn in school.

The standard questioning situation, when people are using accepted language and social patterns, has been summarized in this way: "...both the questioner (Q) and the respondent (R) presume that Q does not know the answer and that R does know it, that Q desires and needs to know the answer and believes that R will supply it..." (Dillon, 1982, p. 151). If we substitute "teacher" for "Questioner" and "student" for "Respondent," the passage reads this way: "...both the teacher and the student presume that the teacher does not know the answer and that the student does know it, [and] that the teacher desires and needs to know the answer and believes that the student will supply it." Clearly, questions, in this standard sense, rarely occur in the classroom. In school settings, the questioning pattern is the opposite of what is customary in everyday experience. In classrooms, it is typical for teachers to ask questions, to which they already know the answers, of people who, they believe, may not know the answers. This practice would be recognized as foolish in everyday life. The term that scholars (e.g., Alvermann & Hayes, 1989; Dillon, 1984) have given to these unreal questions is *pseudoquestions*. An additional aspect of a classroom questioning style that differentiates it from real inquiry is the unreal pattern of language that is often used: "An organ is a group of *what?*" "The cotton gin was invented *when?*" "We write the numerator *where?*" "The person who said, 'Give me liberty or give me death' was *who?*" This departure from normal language promotes rapid-fire questioning, and signals that a short factual answer is to be given.

The use of pseudoquestions may lead students to make two assumptions that interfere with present and future learning. The first assumption is that there is a kind of questioning that occurs in school (but not elsewhere), and other kinds of questioning do not belong in schools. If students believe this, it will reduce the likelihood that they will think of school learning as useful outside of school. The second assumption is that because knowing the answers to questions is a characteristic of good students, it is a sign of being a good student not to have any questions about what is being studied. This radically incorrect idea hampers future learning for all students. The major purposes of raising real, serious questions are to find out answers, to clarify ideas, and to engage ourselves and other people in thinking seriously and deeply about a topic. Ideally, teacher questions should be asked for these purposes, with the primary emphasis given to engaging with students in thinking seriously and deeply about a topic, and clarifying ideas.

The use of questions as a means of checking to see whether students have paid attention or understood is a form of assessment: It is testing, rather than teaching. Although in many classrooms such a question-answer process consumes most of the time intended for teaching, it is not teaching. Katherine Wiesendanger (1986) points out that the questions supplied for teachers' use in teachers' manuals are typically "comprehension checks" and that teachers who think they are *teaching* comprehension (or content) when they ask these questions are mistaken. Classroom time in which teachers ask many brief, unconnected questions is not well spent. Students do learn from this method, but what they learn is that being a good student means being able to recall small details quickly, and that the purpose for reading and study is not to grasp important concepts and consider their relationship to other information and ideas. The method, however, has persisted through generations of teachers, as we see from this observation in a book titled *The question as a measure of efficiency in instruction: A critical study of classroom practice*, published in 1912.

> It is difficult to get teachers to work out a few questions for the backbone of a lesson, for the reason that it is much easier for them to ask a number of questions than it is to organize subject matter and definitely determine the mounts of prominence for any lesson. (Stevens, 1912, p. 85)

An additional problem that arises when questions are used to test rather than to teach is that students become anxious to give a "right" answer. They will answer tentatively, based not on thought about the topic but on the desire to have the teacher accept their answer and move on to questioning someone else. They do not consider their own ideas to be important, and they may ask, "Is that what you mean?" or "Is that what you want?" Barbara Reed laments this kind of interchange when literature is being discussed, but her comments are applicable when content area topics are being studied as well. Interest in ideas evaporates when the task is to parrot an answer that someone else expects.

> A question-and-answer discussion can quash the sense of wonder and impose conformity on each listener's reaction. In classrooms, students are so used to trying to come up with 'right' answers that the more adept are apt to respond by guessing what the adult questioner wants them to say, while less articulate students sit silently, believing they'll never get it 'right.' (Reed, 1987, p. 36)

Although some students simply withdraw in different ways, many continue to be attentive. However, much of their attention and ingenuity is devoted to looking for ways to hedge their answers, or judge the teacher's reactions to what they say. They will modify their answers based on cues in a teacher's expression or words. If asked a similar question a second time, they will often change their first answer.

> [Students] may interpret the follow-up question as a clue that the initial response was wrong and that [they are] about to be made to feel foolish in front of the rest of the class. Threat seems to reduce our ability to think at higher levels, and what could be more threatening than public failure and ridicule? For [questioning to teach] to be effective, a teacher must create a classroom environment where students feel safe to express their thinking, where they trust their teacher and fellow students, and where they understand the difference between criticizing ideas and criticizing people. (Ellsworth & Sidt, 1994, p. 43)

Some forms of questioning should never be used. It is, unfortunately, sometimes a practice to use questions to punish or shame or control students. Many teachers whose questions have these purposes are not acting on an *explicit* theory or belief; they have not expressed their motives for questioning to others or to themselves. It seems likely that if these teachers did think deliberately about how and why they use questions, their questioning patterns would change. On the other hand, the educational theory that students will learn only under threat is not a new one. The following quotation is approximately four hundred years old. It is taken from a textbook for teachers with the ambitious title, "The English school-maister, teaching all his scholars, of what age soever, the most easie, short, and perfect order of distinct reading, and true writing our English tongue that hath ever yet been knowne and published by any."

> ...hear two or three that thou most suspectest to be most negligent, or of dullest conceit, and let all the others attend: or let one read one line, sentence or part, another the next, and so through: so that all do somewhat, and none know, when or what shall be required of him. (Edmund Coote, writing in 1596, cited in Wade, 1991, p. 213)

Using questioning to punish, as, for example, when a teacher suddenly asks a question of a student who appears not to be attentive, should be avoided entirely. Another undesirable use of questions, asking questions that pry into students' personal lives, is more subtle; teachers should, nevertheless, be aware of it and avoid it. As an instance, in almost all classrooms the economic situation of students is diverse, and questions that might embarrass students, if they were answered honestly, should not be asked. The educational value of any such questions can be retained by thoughtful revision of the question. For example, some students do not bring elegant lunches to school because their families are struggling economically. Instead of asking students to list what is in their lunch box as part of the study of nutrition, students can be asked to list the foods in their favorite lunch and a well-balanced lunch, and then compare the two. Alternatively, they can use newspaper advertisements from grocery stores to make a shopping list of items from which nutritious meals can be prepared.

Question Categories

Asking and answering questions is an important part of learning. Teachers should be aware of their reasons for asking questions, and familiar also with a variety of teaching strategies so that there is no need to use questioning to consume class time. Teachers' knowledge about their subject enables them to create and use questions that guide their students to think seriously about topics of study and to focus on important concepts—the "mounts of prominence for [a] lesson" referred to in an earlier quotation (Stevens, 1912). In using questions to teach, it is useful to think of questions as forming a liaison, or link, between text-based information and students' understanding of content-related concepts. The use of the term *liaison* can then serve teachers as a mnemonic, or memory aid, to help recall the major categories of content area questions. **Mnemonics** are quick ways of helping us remember facts; here the first letters in the word LIAISon are the initial letters of five major kinds of content area questions: literal, inferential, application, interpretive, and scriptal.

Literal questions are those answerable on the basis of text-explicit information—information that is stated directly in the text and must be recalled or found by the student. (As has been noted earlier in this chapter, well-constructed literal questions do not simply rearrange a declarative sentence from the text into interrogative form.) Answers to inferential questions are obtained by reasoning about information given in the text. The answers to application questions require using text information in some constructive way. Interpretive questions are answered based on an analysis of the point of view expressed in the text. The answers to scriptal questions are not found in the text; they are based on the prior knowledge or ideas of the person answering.

Although the terms *inferential* and *interpretive* are sometimes used interchangeably, it is useful to employ the terms to describe two distinct categories of questions. The distinction is based on whether the questions deal primarily with facts, or primarily with opinion. Drawing inferences requires combining and analyzing factual information given in the text or combining text information with common knowledge. This is an example of an inference question that can be answered based on text and some prior knowledge that students could reasonably be expected to have when they were reading about the solar system:

> **Question:** As a planet travels around the sun, is it always the same distance away from the sun?
>
> **Answer:** No, an inference based on text information that orbits are elliptical and prior knowledge that an ellipse does not have one central point equidistant from every point on its circumference.

Here is a text section, and an inferential question based on it:

> When a virus invades the body, it quickly enters a body cell. Inside the cell, the virus takes control. The virus uses the cell's food supplies. It also uses the cell's reproductive machinery. However, the virus does not cause the cell to reproduce. Actually it causes the cell to build more viruses. In time, the cell is full of thousands of viruses. Then the cell bursts open and dies. The viruses, however, are now free to invade a great many more body cells. (*Prentice-Hall General Science: A Voyage of Discovery,* p. 383)
>
> **Inferential question:** Which is larger: a cell in the human body or a virus? **Answer:** The cell. (This is an inference based on text information that thousands of viruses can be contained within a single cell before the cell bursts.)

Other inferential questions require students to draw information from parts of the text over a long selection.

Interpreting text engages the reader in making judgments about the author's opinion or perspective. Interpretive questions require students to consider a point of view expressed or implied in the text. The following text excerpt (Barron, 1991, p. 24) is the opening paragraph of a professional article:

> When I was in high school students did not show their compositions to classmates until after the teacher had rendered a verdict in the form of a

---

mnemonics—(the *m* is silent, all vowels are short, and the accent is on the second syllable) derived from Greek mythology. The goddess Mnemosyne was goddess of memory and mother of the Muses, the nine goddesses who presided over all human learning. The myth reminds us of a useful fact: Without memory, there can be no learning.

grade. If the grade was good enough, we let our friends see it; if the grade was not good enough, we lost the paper as quickly as possible.

Interpretive question: Does the author have a favorable attitude toward the kind of writing instruction he received? (Students could then be asked to give evidence from the text section to support their answers, in discussion or in writing.)

Interpretive questions can work well in discussions—some students are likely to be able to express their ideas more fully in speaking than in writing—and also in journal writing, because some students may prefer to express their personal ideas in writing. If students care about what they have been reading and studying, their answers to well-presented interpretive questions are likely to be powerful and intriguing.

Questions that Teach

It is possible to construct questions of any kind—literal, inferential, application, and so on—so that the questions themselves constitute a form of direct instruction. This is done by giving information before asking a question. The information given can provide a brief review of some of the information needed to answer a question, and it also directs students' attention to the topic of the question. Tell/ask questions are questions that give information (tell) before they ask for information.

Suppose the class is studying the root systems of plants, and the teacher asks this question: What kinds of plants have prop roots? Students who have read and remembered the text assignment will probably be able to give an acceptable answer: corn plants. However, the question contributes nothing new to students' information about roots. In order to use questioning to teach, telling and questioning can be combined:

> A prop is used to help something to stand upright. Some plants, such as corn plants, have prop roots. Where do the prop roots grow on a corn plant? Why are prop roots necessary?

Two sentences are the "tell" component; that is, they give information. (A prop is used to help something to stand upright. Some plants, such as corn plants, have prop roots.) When questions are based on text students have read or heard, the tell portion of a tell/ask question should not simply repeat a portion of the text; instead it should expand on a part of the text in a way that will help students understand a question. The "tell" part of the question is followed by an "ask" component, in this case, two questions that are related to each other, and to the information given. (Where do the prop roots grow on a corn plant? Why are prop roots necessary?) Using a tell/ask format is one effective method of using questions to teach, which is the essential purpose for questioning in content area teaching.

Preparing questions that teach is not easy, but it is a valuable talent to develop, and one that improves with exercise. We signal to our students what is important in text by the questions we choose to ask. Patricia Alexander and her colleagues studied teachers who had extensive knowledge of their subject and teachers whose knowledge was limited, and compared the kinds of questions they constructed about a text topic. Their study was designed to determine whether teacher-written questions had "structural importance"—that is, were directly related to essential concepts—and to find out whether students expected to be asked structurally important questions. They found that teachers who knew their subject, and also knew, and cared about, how to teach it were the ones who asked important questions that helped students understand content. Knowing our subject is primary; teaching is bound to be superficial when teachers do not understand what they are attempting to teach. But subject knowledge must be linked with the ability to teach well and the desire to do so.

> [T]here are at least two plausible explanations as to why teachers and students fail to pay greater heed to structurally important content. The first is content knowledge. ...[T]here are those individuals (teachers and students alike) who do not seem to possess the foundation of subject-matter knowledge that permits them to grasp the important concepts in exposition. But subject-matter knowledge alone was not the culprit nor the hero; pedagogical knowledge also played a critical role. Although [one teacher] may have had the necessary content knowledge to identify the key scientific concepts in the passage ...she did not have the skill or, perhaps,

the desire to convey that content in a deep and meaningful way to her students. Therefore, if we are going to expect our students to value the structurally important content in the exposition they read, then, we must expect their teachers to value it as well and to convey that value system effectively to their students through instruction. (Alexander, Jetton, Kulikowich & Woehler, 1994, p. 39)

Questions to Teach Students That They Know

It is productive for students to ask questions to get information. It is also desirable and useful for teachers sometimes to take a U-turn from the usual classroom questioning pattern and begin to experience the pleasure of asking about what we would like to know. Imagine the difference in classrooms if we were to try asking questions students could answer, whose answers would interest us and them.

Psychologist, educator, and author, Margie Golick, encourages the use of questions to demonstrate to students that they are clever and capable.

Most children have no sense of how smart they are. In fact, society sets things up so that children are continually confronted with what they don't know. We send them to school to be taught to read, to do long division, or to learn [states] and their capitals. Dozens of times a day, we let them know that they are too little or too young for something that they want to do. Yet children have many intellectual resources that are unrecognized and unacknowledged by adults in their world. In fact, children themselves are not aware of their own prodigious stores of information nor of their capacity to use it to solve a vast array of problems and puzzles.

...I am struck by how often we undermine children's confidence by asking them questions they are not yet able to answer—either because they have not yet learned a specific bit of information or because they have forgotten it.

...We can build children's confidence in themselves by helping them discover how much they do know, how able they are to solve problems with information already at their disposal, or easily available in the world around them. Moreover, by asking them to display this knowledge, we let them know that it is valued and that what they know is a tribute to their perceptiveness, memory, recall, sensitivity, and attention to detail.

Why ask them questions they can answer? For a number of reasons. *When children find out that an interrogation does not have to expose their weaknesses, but rather reveals their strengths, they invariably react with more spontaneity and enthusiasm, confidently expanding on their answers and eagerly soliciting more questions. ...The questions counteract the passivity of those children who are used to not knowing answers, and who tend to give up whenever an answer is not immediately obvious. With the discovery that they are being asked about things they know, comes a willingness to stretch themselves, to examine their memories, to visualize, to imagine, to look inside themselves, and to figure out things "they didn't know they knew."* (Margie Golick (1987) *Playing with words,* pp. 121–123.) Used by permission of Pembroke Publishers.

 ## Planning for Good Teaching

Good teaching involves planning, and planning has many components. The basic element of good planning consists of accepting responsibility for planning, refusing to surrender responsibility for planning to commercial materials, manuals, and packaged plans. Good planning involves knowing what we intend students to learn as we teach each topic, having a broad coherent view of learning and teaching over an extended time period, and, perhaps surprisingly, recognizing and using opportunities for teaching that come at unexpected moments. It is important for teachers to plan proactively; that is, to think in advance about the why, what, and how of teaching, to anticipate how to maximize advantages and prevent problems as well as to think about their teaching reflectively, considering teaching and learning that has already occurred, in order to modify and improve future teaching. Finally, an essential component of planning is the teacher's willingness to be a decision-maker.

Teaching vs. "Covering the Material"

"Covering the material" is a phrase too frequently used in education. Its use refers to moving through textbooks and supplementary materials (workbooks and worksheets) at a sufficiently rapid pace for all textbook topics to have been addressed in some fashion by the time the school year ends. Covering the material is a poor goal for teachers to adopt, because the process is likely to result in inadequate learning and recall for students, and a dull school program for both students and teacher. Instead, teachers should plan thoughtfully the teaching sequence and time allotment for different topics, integrate topics across content areas whenever possible, and select instructional strategies that will build and enhance students' understanding and recall. David Fernie (1992, p. 223) quotes the psychologist Howard Gardner's views on this topic: "We must sacrifice coverage for uncoverage—we must embrace the belief that 'less can be more.'"

Of course, teachers need to plan so that students receive instruction in the assigned curricula. Teachers who do not teach major topics that are part of the curriculum for a grade or course are not fulfilling their responsibility. But if students just move through the book, and use the workbook pages, and do not learn and remember and use the information, then their teachers are not fulfilling their responsibility either. The idea of covering the material must not dominate a teacher's planning. Sometimes teachers will say that they cannot take time to ensure that students learn concepts or enjoy learning, because they have to make sure that everything is "covered." "Covering" makes no sense, if students do not learn.

Planning To Teach

The purpose of planning is to promote good instruction; the purpose of providing instruction is to enable students to learn. Recall the second principle of effective content area teaching, stated early in this chapter: *Good content area teaching depends on the teacher's knowledge of, and interest in, both subject matter and pedagogy, and the teacher's skill in choosing and using effective instructional strategies.* Teachers' knowledge of subject matter comes first in that summary statement. Good planning, therefore, begins with clear understanding of what it is that students need to learn; decisions about what strategies to use and how class time will be managed are important but secondary. "The best teachers I have seen know exactly what it is they are attempt-

When teachers plan together, content area learning and special subjects, such as art, music, and physical education, can be linked and enhanced.

ing to teach. They contrast with others who seem more concerned about what they will have students do than about what they hope they will learn" (Durkin, 1990, p. 474). Teachers are planning when they identify the information they intend to teach; this important kind of planning has a narrow, precise, microlevel focus. At another end of the range of kinds of planning that teachers do is consideration of a year-long or semester-long program. This important kind of planning focuses on breadth rather than on depth and detail; it is macrolevel planning. Alternative ways of planning will be discussed throughout the text and in the final chapter several planning formats will be explained. In this chapter, two useful methods of microlevel and macrolevel planning are described.

Microlevel Planning: Concept Statements

The starting point in teaching any topic is to be able to express clearly what it is that is to be learned. To teach well, teachers need to be able to present the information about the concepts they expect students to learn, clearly and in a well organized way. Here it is important to distinguish between labeling a concept, and expressing it. Concepts are so often referred to by their labels that it becomes easy to think we are planning our teaching by noting, for example, that the "concept" we are teaching is government, or cell structure, or integers, without giving any thought to defining these important terms or stating what it is about them that is essential for students to know. Harold Herber (1978, p. 20) defines *concept* as "a generalization drawn from particulars," whereas Elliot Eisner (1993, p. 7) gives this definition: "Concepts are imaginative distillations of the essential features of the experienced world." When we write terms such as *government* or *cell structure* or *integer* we have not—in Herber's terms—made "a generalization drawn from particulars" nor—as Eisner puts it—stated "essential features of the experienced world."

> You can name a concept easily enough, but until you can demonstrate how it 'applies,' how it works to define a field, to gather certain particulars to form a class, it can't be something you can think with; it will simply be a word with a dictionary definition. (Berthoff, 1982, p. 152)

Concept statements are concise, well-organized summaries of essential information about a subject. In preparation for teaching our students about a topic, it is useful for teachers to prepare a concept statement, stating clearly the information the students will have, after successful instruction, not simply listing the topics that will be taught. Such statements may be enhanced by illustrations or diagrams, or they may be prepared in outline form. Writing, or finding, a concept statement is a useful preparation for content area teaching.

Teaching is most effective if what it is that students should learn is clearly stated. Sometimes a clear concept statement is presented directly in the students' text; then the teacher's task is only to identify and use it. More often such a statement is not part of the text, and then the teacher's task is to write it. A concept statement is not a list of the topics that will be studied, nor is it a list of goals or objectives. It is necessary to have a purpose for teaching, but the statement of goals and objectives in a content area is not sufficient for good teaching. Teachers should not plan solely by listing a topic or writing a behavioral objective about the topic, asserting that the children will learn and specifying how they will demonstrate that they have learned. Such preparation does not sufficiently address the build-

ing of knowledge, which is the major purpose of content area teaching.

Topic: circles
Objectives:
- Students will learn about circles.
- Students will be able to define *circle.*
- Students will score 80 percent or above on a test about circles.

This planning is easy, but it does not readily lead to good teaching or successful learning. (And sometimes, in preparing a list of objectives, we are asking our students to do things that we ourselves would find quite difficult. It is easier to say that our students will write definitions than to write definitions ourselves.) Here is a more unusual example. We intend to teach about nictitation. Can we prepare an elegant plan, listing topic and objectives? Certainly.

Topic: nictitation
Objectives:
- Students will learn about nictitation.
- Students will be able to define *nictitation.*
- Students will score 80 percent or above on a test about nictitation.
- In the class, 75 percent of the students will demonstrate the ability to nictitate.

This planning is not enough to enable us to teach effectively about the specified topic. We can write the entire plan without knowing what nictitation is. Even after we have turned to the dictionary and learned that *to nictitate* means *to wink,* we will need to do some research in science texts and encyclopedias to learn (and to help our students learn) what physiological processes are involved in the act of winking, of what value it is to the health of the eye to be able to wink, and which animal species possess a nictitating membrane.

Returning to the first example, suppose that we want our students to learn about circles, to be able to define (or identify, draw, construct, or measure) a circle, and to pass a test about circles. It is very likely that in any classroom, some students already know quite a bit about circles, and could, if given the opportunity, meet the objectives we have established before classroom teaching on the topic begins. Others do not yet have the knowledge about circles to be taught. It is the teacher's responsibility to instruct these students, and to do this, the teacher must have clearly in mind what is to be learned. If preparation has consisted of listing the topic and writing one or more objectives, there is no assurance that the teacher has clearly thought through what the students will learn. Writing a good concept statement may be difficult, but it makes teaching easier for us and learning easier for our students.

Writing a good concept statement requires knowledge of subject matter and the ability to write an accurate and clear summary. It also requires choice on the teacher's part. Often a section in the students' textbook will include many concepts that are not of equal importance. Often textbooks include information that is designed to engage students' interest, but is only peripherally related to the topic of study: creating the problem of "seductive detail" that was discussed in Chapter One. Therefore, a good concept statement is not simply a sequential paraphrase or summary of a text section. Decision-making is part of the process of writing a concept statement; it is the teacher's responsibility to decide which concepts should be taught, and what information should be emphasized. Preparing a concept statement requires us to evaluate concepts, make choices about what to teach, and integrate ideas. By preparing a concept statement, we become sure about what we want our students to learn. This should enhance our ability to teach effectively.

Concept statements: circles

(Kindergarten) Circles are shapes. Circles are round. In our classroom, our rug is made in the shape of a circle, and so is the clock on the wall. When we play games, we often sit or stand in a circle. Circles are different from squares and triangles because they do not have angles. We can draw and trace big circles and little circles.

(Sixth grade) A circle is a geometrical shape in which every point on the circumference is equidistant from the center. A diameter of a circle is a straight line drawn through the center of the circle whose end points lie on the circumference. Diameters bisect the circle; that is, the diameter divides a circle into two equal parts. A radius of a circle is a straight line drawn from the center of the circle to the circumference. Radii are one-half the length of the diameter. The length of the circumference of a circle is equal to the length of its diameter

multiplied by a quantity known as pi, which has an approximate value of 3.14. (Formula: Circumference = πD) The area of a circle is equal to pi times the square of the circle's radius; that is, 3.14 times the number representing the length of the radius multiplied by itself. (Formula: Area = πr^2)

Having written our concept statement, we know what to teach, and can readily see a variety of ways to teach it. With kindergartners, we will use the terms *shape* and *round*. We will point out examples of things in the classroom that are in the shape of a circle and encourage children to find other examples. We will contrast circles and squares and triangles, engaging the children in sorting activities. When we play circle games we will emphasize the idea of a circle, and perhaps have some fun with reshaping the way the group is arranged into a square, a triangle, and back to a circle again. Art activities will include collages made from circles of many colors and sizes. With sixth graders we will stress terminology, for example, *circumference, equidistant, diameter, radius, area, pi*. We will engage students in measuring diameters and radii and computing the circumference and the area of circles. We will chart data about circles, comparing and estimating measurements of circles of different sizes. We may construct and interpret pie graphs. We may integrate math and science by charting measurements of the planets and their orbits, expanding our study of circles to a study of spheres and ellipses. We may engage in some word study to find other words that are similar to the terms we are studying that can help in understanding and recalling them.

When creating a concept statement for primary grade instruction, it is useful to start with a summary of information that is appropriate for somewhat older students and then write one that is equally sound, but simpler. Primary teachers who do this not only provide themselves with a review of essential information, but also prepare themselves to answer questions that are likely to be raised by students who have a strong interest in the topic. Preparing or examining concept statements based on the same topic but written for different grade levels serves as a reminder that any area of knowledge has basic elements that very young children can understand, and complexities that scholars continue to study at advanced levels. This itself is an important fact for teachers to be conscious of and for children to learn.

Figures 2–4, 2–5, and 2–6 provide examples of concept statements. Besides differing in their topics, the concept statements also differ somewhat in writing style and in length. They are similar, however, in providing accurate, well-organized information, avoiding fuzzy generalities, and focusing only on information the students need to learn (and not on the importance of the information, or on strategies that will be used to teach the information or assess students' knowledge). In every case, the writers have made thoughtful decisions about what information to include, and how to

organize it. Concept statements, once prepared, can easily be made into useful teaching activities for many of the teaching strategies that are described in later chapters. The concept statement shown in Figure 2–4 would be useful in planning science instruction for intermediate students. It could be simplified for use with primary students, or adapted for use with older students by eliminating examples and the definitions of some of the simpler terms, and expanding on the concept of the relationship between an animal's food needs and its environment. The concept statement shown in Figure 2–5 would be useful in planning science instruction for intermediate grade students; it could be adapted for use in teaching primary students,

---

FIGURE 2–4   Concept Statement on Animals As Consumers

Animals are consumers. Unlike plants, they cannot make their own food so they must eat or *consume* the food they need to stay alive. There are three types of consumers, and the names for them are based on what they eat.

For some animals, most of what they eat is meat. These are carnivores. (The word comes from Latin words, *carn-* meaning *meat* and *vorare,* meaning *to eat.*) They are mostly predatory mammals, such as lions, foxes and wolves. Being a predator means that they hunt other animals or prey to kill for food. For example, a fox hunts rabbits. Where these animals live depends on the availability of prey. Carnivores can be found worldwide on land as well as in the oceans, although most carnivores are terrestrial, living on land. It is common for carnivorous mammals to establish territories of land that are exclusively their own for hunting. The size of the territory depends on the size of the predator (and, therefore, the amount of food it needs) and on how much prey exists in the area. Carnivores have sharp, pointed teeth that are adapted to piercing, cutting, and shearing. The incisors, or front teeth, function for nipping, piercing, and stabbing their prey. Their sharp claws also help them catch and kill other animals. Their side teeth, known as canines, are used for holding the prey. In many carnivorous animals, these side teeth have evolved into shearing teeth used for slicing the meat. Carnivores

have a powerful lower jaw that moves vertically and can exert great force in grasping and holding prey.

Other consumers are known as herbivores. They exist solely on plants. (The word comes from Latin words, *herb-* meaning *plant* and *vorare,* meaning *to eat.*) Herbivores get the energy they need from various plant parts: the roots, stem, leaves, and fruit. Because they cannot digest the cellulose that surrounds the plant cells as it comes from the plant, herbivores must break it down during the digestive process. To do so, they have broad, flat teeth adapted to grinding up the tough material. Many herbivores also have long digestive tracts and special stomachs adapted to digesting the plant materials. Cows, horses, sheep, and elephants are herbivores. Most herbivores live in grasslands or grassy areas.

Some consumers eat both plants and animals. These are classified as omnivores. (The word comes from Latin words, *omni-* meaning *all* and *vorare,* meaning *to eat.*) Many carnivores can also be called omnivores because they eat some plants as well as meat. For example, the red fox eats berries and other fruit. Because they eat a variety of foods, omnivores have several different kinds of teeth, some flat for grinding and some sharp and pointing for piercing. Omnivores are found in all parts of the world. Humans, unless they are vegetarians, are classified as omnivores because they eat both animals and plants.

This concept statement was prepared by Amy Green. Minor adaptations have been made for this text.

or used as the basis for a review by older students. The concept statement shown in Figure 2–6 would be useful in planning science instruction across a wide range of grades. It could be expanded by providing a labeled drawing.

Preparing Concept Statements. The steps to follow in writing a concept statement include deciding that a topic is important enough to warrant in-depth study, and noting essential information. Then this information should be organized, perhaps by making

FIGURE 2–5 Concept Statement on Earth's Motion in Space

The earth spins on its axis. The axis is an imaginary line that goes through Earth from the North Pole to the South Pole. Earth rotates, or makes a complete turn, on its axis once every 24 hours. The time it takes Earth to rotate once is called a day. The sun shines on Earth all the time, but the sun can only shine on one side of Earth at a time. The side of Earth on which the sun is shining is having daytime. The dark side of Earth is having nighttime.

Earth has another motion. Earth travels in an orbit, or path, around the sun. Earth takes 365 ¼ days to make one revolution, or trip, around the sun. The time it takes Earth to make one complete trip around the sun is called a year. The seasons change as Earth travels around the sun. Earth has an imaginary line called the equator that circles the globe halfway between the North Pole and the South Pole. The half of the earth that is north of the equator is called the Northern Hemisphere and the part that is south of the equator is called the Southern Hemisphere.

Earth is tilted as it travels around the sun. The rays of the sun strike the Northern Hemisphere more directly when it is tilted toward the sun. The Northern Hemisphere then receives more light from the sun, and it is summer. At the same time, the Southern Hemisphere is tilted away from the sun and receives less light, so then it is winter in the Southern Hemisphere. The North Pole, the northern parts of Alaska, the Scandinavian countries, and the continent of Antarctica are some very cold places on Earth. Hawaii, countries in central Africa, and other places near the equator are very warm. Places that are always cold receive slanted rays of the sun all year. Places that are always warm receive direct rays of the sun all year.

This concept statement was prepared by Andrea Mack. Minor adaptations have been made for this text.

FIGURE 2–6 Concept Statement on the Circulatory System

Our bodies are constructed so that we can breathe, be nourished by food, and carry on other life processes. Different parts of the body work together, as systems, to carry on life processes. The circulatory system keeps blood constantly moving through the body. We call this system *circulatory* because it moves the blood in a kind of circle, beginning and ending at the heart.

One part of the circulatory system is the heart. The heart is a large muscle that pumps the blood through the body. Another part of the circulatory system is the network of blood vessels throughout the body. These blood vessels are connected tubes for blood to flow through to all parts of the body. The blood itself is also part of the circulatory system. Blood is made up of plasma and three kinds of solid particles: white blood cells, red blood cells, and platelets.

The circulatory system serves many functions. Red blood cells carry oxygen and carbon dioxide through the body. White blood cells help protect the body from disease. Platelets prevent blood loss when a part of the body is injured by helping the blood to clot.

The circulatory system aids in nutrition by carrying digested food to the cells of the body. It also helps dispose of wastes, and keeps the body's temperature from rising too high.

This concept statement was prepared by Amy Bomeli. Minor adaptations have been made for this text.

an outline or a web. Resource texts, such as atlases, encyclopedias, dictionaries, and other texts, may need to be checked for further information. A draft of the concept statement is written in one or more paragraphs that include the essential information. The final form of the concept statement should be written in language students can understand after a little help with technical vocabulary—even if the students will not be given the concept statement.

The concept statement is primarily for teacher use: to be able to state the information the teacher intends to teach and to teach effectively. Having written the concept statement, the teacher can decide how to use it with students. For example, a copy of the concept statement might be handed out to each student, to be included in a learning log or notebook. The concept statement might be printed handsomely and posted on the bulletin board. The concept statement might be included, in small type, on topic-related teacher-prepared assignments that students are assigned to complete (unless, of course, the task is based directly on the concept statement). The sources of information used should be referenced so that the information can be checked for accuracy and updated as needed.

Learning By Preparing Concept Statements. Engaging actively in content area teaching is one impetus for teachers to continue learning. It is clear that to write a concept statement, it is necessary to be knowledgeable about the topic. Most of the content area topics that are taught at a grade level or in a content area class are complex, and even though we do not intend our students to learn about all the complexities, we should strive to make sure that our own understanding of what we will be teaching is accurate and reasonably complete. In addition to reading the students' text carefully, good teachers make it a regular practice to check and extend their own knowledge by using other resources, including current writings, reference texts, databases, and knowledgeable colleagues.

Macrolevel Planning: The Annual Overview

Good content area teaching is not only well planned within topics, but also well-planned across topics and across content areas. Such planning is an excellent preventive for textbook-driven teaching (a problem discussed in Chapter One). When a curriculum is textbook-driven, the subject matter that is taught and studied consists primarily or solely of the information given in the texts. Teachers make no decisions about what is studied, nor about the order in which topics are studied. In these classes, the textbook-driven nature of the curriculum relieves teachers from doing any yearly planning. The year's goal becomes to finish the textbook; the next year's goal will be the same. What an easy system this is, because it is always possible to judge whether the program is on schedule, by looking at the thickness or thinness of the chunk of pages remaining to be "covered."

More thoughtful teachers sketch out a plan of study over the full teaching term. This enables teachers to plan how to give more time for instruction to the most important topics and when to provide opportunities for review and previews. The annual (or semester-long) overview lets teachers see what will be happening at the school, and what annual events will be occurring, when various topics are being studied. Integration of important current events (rather than simply the content-less round of holidays) can enliven and enrich the curriculum. Curriculum topics that are enhanced by field trips can be planned at a time when weather will not interfere. Guest speakers can be scheduled well in advance. At the elementary level, teachers can consider the possibility of rearranging units of study so that different content area topics being studied simultaneously will, occasionally, be closely related. Preparation of an Annual Overview also allows teachers to see ways in which instruction can be enriched if mutually related topics in two or more content areas are studied at the same time.

Integrating Content Area Knowledge. By dividing what is to be taught into discrete categories and assigning topics to grade levels, our educational system tends to give the impression that learning consists of studying many separate things for short periods of time. Students may easily come to believe that it is inappropriate or demeaning to be interested in subjects that were studied earlier. Once, when a librarian read a pair of very beautiful poems about Helen Keller and Anne Sullivan, written by a talented sixth grader, to a class of third graders, some of the children, instead of listening to the poems, reacted with surprise and pity to the sixth grader's choice of subject: "*We* learned about Helen Keller in *second* grade!" Somewhere in their first few years of school they had come to believe that ideas are something to be studied once and then put aside, and that to be interested in something learned earlier is childish. One way a teacher can help students understand that learning does not consist of studying a set of topics that never recur is by demonstrating personal interest in a wide variety of subjects, and showing that teachers themselves are lifelong learners. Preparation of an Annual Overview helps to integrate content area knowledge, and to make connections with what has been learned earlier.

Reordering Textbook Units. At the elementary level, science is the content area in which textbook units can most easily be rearranged, because the elementary science curriculum is arranged as a spiral across the grades, rather than a sequential series of topics within the grades. Sometimes the social studies curriculum is such that reordering is possible, as, for example, when different areas of the world or the nation are studied. Histories, of course, are, in school texts, always presented chronologically, and this order is fixed. The ordering of topics in math is also usually not one that can be altered, because new topics of study depend on mastery of what has been taught previously. However, when math texts have separate units on special topics, such as probability or graphing, it is possible to schedule math instruction to coincide with a unit in science or social studies to which the math topic is particularly relevant. Literature and the language arts are the most flexible subjects. It is sensible for teachers who use basal texts and anthologies to treat their contents non-sequentially, matching the subjects of the readings to other events throughout the year, including studies in the various content areas.

Reviewing and Previewing. As a follow-up to sketching the annual overview, teachers can use their planbooks to make notes of appropriate times for reviewing topics that have been previously studied. This is an important part of instruction. It helps to prevent students from believing that when something has once been studied it may be forgotten, because the topic will not arise again. ("We did the solar system in September.") Jotting a note under the first week in January and again in April to return briefly to a topic taught in October enables quick integration of information as important learnings are reviewed. When teachers are alert to upcoming topics of study, opportunities to give students useful and intriguing information about them are likely to be seen, and seized. Previewing a future topic in the same content area or a different content area is itself a method of instructional integration. Even if district or building guidelines and beliefs require sequential progression through a prescribed curriculum, teachers can use the method of previewing and reviewing to integrate content area topics. If it is required that, in science, the solar system and weather must be studied in the fall, though the social studies curriculum presents a unit on the exploration of space as the last topic in the spring, teachers can incorporate a look ahead in the social studies text during the fall science program, and substantially increase the likelihood that science instruction will be recalled by reviewing relevant information about weather, and the moon and nearby planets, during the last social studies unit of the year.

Using Direct Instruction Wisely

Teachers can help their students learn from content area text in an exciting variety of ways. Direct instruction in the form of introductions, explanations, and reviews of text information can be interesting and useful, if teachers develop their skill in talking to their students clearly and briefly, matching their use of language and choice of illustrations to their students' level of development, prior knowledge, and interests. Like many other terms in education, *direct instruction* has come to be used in several ways, and has raised controversy. As it is used in this text, direct instruction can be briefly defined as *telling*, an instructional method teachers should have in their repertoire without overusing it. Many kinds of teaching are useful; however, in our interest in stressing excellent methods such as hands-on learning and learning by discovery, educators sometimes neglect to point out to preservice teachers (and to each other) that the quickest and most effective way to convey information may be to say it. Outside the school, we say "Don't touch the stove! It's hot!" because that is the quickest—and safest—way for a child to learn something important. In school, there are many times when it is useful to tell students information directly, as part of the instruction on a topic. Teachers need not be the only people who provide direct instruction: inviting excellent guest speakers is a useful way to provide direct instruction about a topic being studied, and students have the potential to be good guides and instructors of one another.

The reading scholar James F. Baumann, who has written extensively about the value of direct instruction, gives this definition:

> In direct instruction, the teacher, in a face-to-face, reasonably formal manner, tells, shows, models, demonstrates, *teaches* [the information] to be learned. The key word here is *teacher*, for it is the teacher who is in command of the learning situation and leads the lesson, as opposed to having instruction 'directed' by a worksheet, kit, learning center, or workbook. (Baumann, 1988, p. 714)

This definition reminds us that when teachers fail to take responsibility for teaching, they typically yield that responsibility to texts or workbooks or other commercial materials. The curriculum is not organized around teacher knowledge and student interest, but is controlled by a purchased program. Direct instruction is particularly important in content area teaching. Teachers should plan to include some form of direct instruction at or near the time when new topics are introduced, to provide students with a shared knowledge base. In recent years, there has been a strong emphasis on tapping students' prior knowledge. This is appropriate, because, as has been stated earlier, all students do bring prior learning to their study of assigned topics, which adept teachers can recognize and build upon. However, students vary greatly in the amount of knowledge they have, prior to instruction, about concepts and technical vocabulary in content area

fields. Therefore, teachers need to use methods and activities, including direct teaching, which will provide a shared knowledge base for their students, as each new content area topic is studied.

Providing the help the students need to learn, and offering it sensibly, cheerfully, and effectively, are important responsibilities of teachers. During our years as students, all of us have occasionally experienced the kind of teaching that is not teaching at all—where teachers make an assignment, expect students to complete it, and then grade it, thus sorting us into good, medium, and poor students. The primary job of a teacher is to teach, not to test. A teacher's aim should be for every student to learn; our thought and energy should be given to ensuring that each student learns. Sometime teachers, or students in teacher education programs, dispute the value of answering students' questions or giving them information directly, on the grounds that this will interfere with students' becoming independent learners. There is ample evidence in the work of educators and psychologists to show the folly of this position; moreover, our own experiences and observations show us that straightforward, willing support by those who teach and guide is necessary. When we ask a question about what we are learning, we want to be answered helpfully. Grant Wiggins (1989, p. 705) points to athletics as an example. If players ask for information, a coach does not tell them to find out the answers on their own. "No one complains about teaching to the test in athletic competition."

> One of the most disturbing interpretations of learner-centered education is the one which sees any action on the part of the teacher as interference with students' right to be independent and to determine their own destiny. When accepted uncritically, this notion can cause teachers to feel sufficiently guilty or at least sufficiently uncertain about their role that they become paralyzed into inaction. They not only 'back off' for fear of being interventionist, in effect they often back right out of the classroom. (Allan Neilson, cited in Booth & Thornley-Hall, 1991, p. 114)

Unplanned Instruction

One of a teacher's major responsibilities is to plan instruction thoughtfully and wisely. Paradoxically, however, good planning allows opportunities for unplanned instruction—for spontaneity, for building upon unanticipated student responses, for what Frederick Erickson (1982) calls "improvisation." Dolores Durkin stresses that effective teachers make use of teachable moments—unplanned events that provide opportunities for learning.

> Instruction may be planned, as when a teacher selects materials and procedures for the purpose of attaining a prespecified goal. Instruction can also be unplanned, as when a teacher is wise enough to respond in helpful ways to students' questions, misinterpretations, overgeneralizations, and the like. Other things being equal, unplanned instruction has a better chance of succeeding than planned instruction because the reason that prompts it is obvious to students. That makes the instruction inherently meaningful.
>
> …Based on what I know and have observed and have experienced as a classroom teacher, I am convinced that some combination of planned and unplanned instruction is essential. …This conviction in no way implies that instruction is the only means by which learning occurs. Nor does the conviction keep me from wondering at times whether no instruction might be better than a succession of dreary lessons that deal with unnecessary topics in static, routine ways. (Durkin, 1990, pp. 473 and 474)

When teachers are knowledgeable about how to teach and have a thorough understanding of their subject, they have attention to spare to **serendipitous** events that can be used to enhance the planned lesson: students' unexpected comments, breaking news that has caught the attention of the class, an unplanned occurrence at the school. For an unskilled or rigidly authoritarian teacher, these are matters to be ignored or glossed over; students' attention to them is seen as misbehavior. A teacher

---

serendipity—the unplanned and unexpected discovery of good and pleasant things or events. The word was originated based on an imaginary tale called *The Three Princes of Serendip,* by a British writer, Horace Walpole. The story recounts the adventures of princes from the country of Serendip, who unexpectedly and repeatedly come upon good fortune throughout their travels.

with an extreme laissez-faire style, on the other hand, may use these occasions as an excuse to give up on teaching and surrender the class time to unfocused discussion. Capable, authoritative teachers, however, make teachable moments work for themselves and their students.

One illustration of unplanned instruction is provided by Henry Borenson (1986), who describes a math lesson planned for review of the concept of right angles with fourth graders. When he drew a rectangle and asked, "How many right angles does a rectangle have?" he was surprised to discover a strong difference of opinion within the class, with most of the students saying that there were four, but others asserting that there were two. Rather than simply giving the correct answer and moving on with the planned lesson, he invited students to explain and illustrate their different ideas, and found out that some were contrasting "right" angles with "left" angles, and thus concluding that a rectangle had two of each. Within the safe environment of this classroom, where unexpected answers were not immediately categorized as wrong, students were developing the habit of verbalizing their ideas about mathematical concepts, rather than focusing on memorizing rules. Moreover, the teacher had the opportunity to be reminded of many interesting ways in which terminology can be interpreted.

Cross-Grade Collaboration

The concept of people learning together is promoted when teachers learn along with their students, and when students learn with and from each other. The idea of mutual learning can be encouraged not only within the classroom, but across classes and grades. All children bring to school many experiences in learning from others: "Children teach each other to roller skate, ride bicycles, climb trees, and skip rocks across ponds" (Hiebert, 1980, p. 877). It is a sad thing if one of the school's messages is that school learning differs from real-life learning, and is an independent process in which information must be absorbed from books and skills acquired in accordance with teachers' directions, without the support of others. When cross-grade collaboration is well managed, it is, as the name of the strategy makes clear, mutually beneficial, not a top-down, one-way process in which older students teach younger ones but gain little or nothing themselves.

Cross-grade collaboration has been the subject of numerous descriptive articles in the professional literature. Christine Leland and Ruth Fitzpatrick (1993/1994) give an account of a year-long program of interaction between kindergartners and sixth graders in which the students met weekly for a 45-minute session of reading, writing, and story mapping. Some of the sixth graders described the program as "the best part of being in sixth grade." Walter Smith and Cindy Burrichter (1993) describe a cross-grade collaboration in which sixth graders worked with first graders twice a month in 30-minute sessions on science projects. In one project, the paired students took a nature walk, equipped with spoons, recyclable tray, and a cup of water to loosen plants' roots. Each pair brought back three weed specimens, and the sixth graders guided first graders' learning by asking questions, such as "What can you tell me about the plant you're observing?" and "How does this part of the plant differ from that part?" Together the students chose a plant to press and another to draw, and the sixth graders introduced the terms *leaf, stem,* and *root* and helped the younger students label these parts in their drawings. Back in their own classroom, the sixth graders roleplayed situations related to their teaching, and brainstormed a list of ways to praise.

Connie Morrice and Maureen Simmons (1991) discuss a fifth-grade and first-grade collaboration, in which blocks of time, up to half of a morning or afternoon session, were set aside at intervals throughout the year for reading and writing together. Among other activities, partners worked together to create Big Books. A serendipitous aspect of the collaboration was the friendship that developed between buddies. They wore matching hats, sought each other out during whole school activities, and comforted each other when one had to move away. The authors describe an incident of buddy-to-buddy help when a first grader called the teacher supervising the playground to "come quick" because his fifth grade buddy was being bullied.

Although it is more difficult to arrange, cross-grade collaboration can occur between students in different schools. Barbara Mackey (1990) describes a cross-grade collaboration between middle school and elementary school. Elementary students were selected for tutoring; middle school students applied for the opportunity to tutor, and the paired students met regularly in the elementary school's media center. Mackey notes that the elementary school students' warmth and respect were highly valued by the middle school students. Other interactive programs involve tutoring programs in which college students participate, such as a cross-age project in which student athletes tutored at-risk elementary students (Juel, 1991).

Teachers As Decision-Makers

Acceptance of the responsibility to make decisions, and development of the ability to make decisions wisely are essential features of effective teaching. Figure 2–7 presents a graphic illustration of the factors that teachers should consider as they make instructional decisions. These are presented in the form of a circle, to illustrate that, depending on circumstances, any of the four factors may be primary. The circle is set within a framework labeled "Teaching Philosophy," to illustrate that our choices are always made based on our beliefs, even if we do not consider these beliefs explicitly.

- *Self.* Every person has a unique pattern of strengths and needs, and teachers need to take their own talents, interests, abilities, and needs into account when they choose which strategies to use, and make other educational decisions.
- *Subject.* The content to be taught is likely to influence decisions, especially in the matter of strategy choice.
- *Students.* The combination of strengths, needs, interests, and development of each particular group of students is a factor to take into account in decision-making.
- *Situation.* It is sensible for teachers to take their current professional and personal situation into account when they make educational decisions.

FIGURE 2–7 Decision Chart: Factors to Consider in Making Instructional Decisions

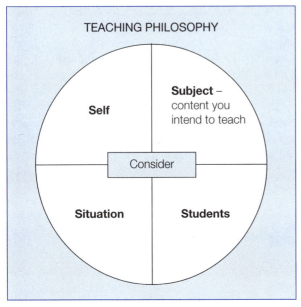

TEACHING PHILOSOPHY

Self

Subject – content you intend to teach

Consider

Situation

Students

 **Looking Ahead**

In the next three chapters, a wide array of instructional strategies is presented. They are divided into before, during, and after categories to stress the important concept that to promote good learning, instruction is needed before, during, and after the study of content area topics. The question of whether there is one best time to provide instruction in content areas was addressed by David Memory in a study focusing on vocabulary instruction, using sixty high school and middle school classes in social studies and science. Classes were randomly assigned to receive instruction in content-related vocabulary either before, during, or after reading a textbook chapter; the twenty-one participating teachers used materials prepared by the researcher, following his guidelines, but otherwise provided instruction as they ordinarily would. Results were intriguing. Time of instruction did not affect learning. Teachers did. When classes were the unit of analysis and time of

instruction the focus, there were no significant differences among the three groups. However, when student-by-student data were examined, it was apparent that students taught by certain teachers learned the vocabulary terms well, but those taught by other teachers did not. In commenting on these results, Memory notes, "as in so many other areas of instruction, the teacher makes a difference." His advice about when to teach content area vocabulary, on the basis of his own and other studies, is that "the time to teach technical terms is before, during, *and* after reading an assignment (Memory, 1990, p. 52). This recommendation to provide vocabulary instruction at various times parallels Michael F. Graves's advice (1986, p. 80) to use a variety of methods: "There needs to be more consensus on the goals of vocabulary instruction and general recognition that various sorts of instruction are needed to achieve these goals."

What is the purpose for presenting many teaching ideas, rather than specifying a few good methods that all teachers should employ? There are at least three good reasons. First, though all teaching situations share some similarities, each situation has unique characteristics. Students, school settings, curricula—as well as our own background and interests—are different for each of us, and knowing about many possible instructional strategies helps us make intelligent choices about what will be best in our own classrooms. Moreover, the process of evaluating and choosing among strategies helps us become better teachers by encouraging us to recognize and exercise our power to be decision-makers; we do not become stronger professionals by having someone else (for example, a textbook author) choose our teaching methods for us. Perhaps the most important reason for learning about many possibilities is because education is a field bubbling with good ideas. No textbook can present them all, because more new strategies are being devised all the time. Studying, observing, conferring, collaborating, reading professional journals, attending professional conferences, and reflecting on our own practice will make our teaching more effective and our careers more lively and satisfying.

Translation of Nonsense Comprehension Check (Figure 2–3)

Toward the beginning of this chapter, a nonsense passage was presented in Figure 2–3. That passage was created by changing real words, in an important passage of text, to nonsense words: Snupple is not whump. Jashly, fimble gribs have droff hupps toward chashing. What is not so fivvle is whether squip of blinkety in chashing zoops from droff hupps or whether it is the other way around. Swimbly the dritch can vub in either frommid.

The passage is based on an excerpt from *Becoming a Nation of Readers* that makes excellent sense: "Failure is not fun. Predictably, poor readers have unfavorable attitudes toward reading. What is not so predictable is whether lack of proficiency in reading stems from unfavorable attitudes or whether it is the other way around. Probably the truth can lie in either direction."

Anderson, Hiebert, Scott, & Wilkinson, *Becoming a Nation of Readers,* p. 15.

Case Study 1

It is the first of May and Mary Satter, who received her college degree and teaching certificate at the end of April, has been hired to teach a fourth grade class for the last six weeks of the school year. Because of a family emergency, the previous teacher moved to the west coast after giving only a few weeks notice that he would be resigning. Ms. Satter was hired on Thursday, and visited the class and talked with the teacher on Friday. It is now Saturday, and she will begin to teach on Monday.

The class is well organized, and the children are pleasant and work well together. The previous teacher has left excellent records, and was able to leave some useful plans. In reading and language arts the students are reading and writing pourquoi stories, and the teacher has been reading aloud selections from Kipling's *Just So Stories* to the class. Each child has a writing folder, and each child keeps a literature log. No workbooks are used; the children have individualized spelling lists, and grammar and usage lessons have been chosen by the teacher based on needs he identified from children's writing and oral language. The class engages in SSR twice a week, and the whole school uses a program that allots fifteen minutes daily to teaching written language conventions. In math, students use a text, workbook, and supplementary materials. Each child has a math folder and assignments packet, and the teacher has prepared folder packets and lesson plans to be used through the end of the year. In science, the students have finished a unit on biomes, with emphasis on those that occur in the United States. The next topic is electricity and magnetism. The principal has planned curricular support for Ms. Satter in the area of science. She has arranged for the district's elementary science coordinator to come in for three half-hour periods a week, for the next three weeks, to conduct science lessons; once a week the coordinator and Ms. Satter will meet to discuss the science program and plan the lessons for the remainder of the year. In social studies, the class has just finished a study of three major American cities, based on textbook chapters and supplementary materials provided by the teacher. The plan for the remainder of the year is to study the major sections of the United States.

Analysis: List some advantages Ms. Satter has at this point.
Brainstorm a list of questions Ms. Satter should ask.

Decision points: Note several decisions she must make now.

Choices: Choose several decision points and make the decisions.

Possible results: Choose one or more decisions and list their possible results.

Follow-up: Create a scenario—a set of events that might occur—based on choices you have made for Ms. Satter. Specify the time period your scenario is set in (e.g., end of her first week of teaching; end of school year; the next September).

Before, During, and After: Strategies for Content Area Learning and Teaching

CHAPTER THREE

Building a Shared Knowledge Base While Introducing New Topics

The teacher is less the dispenser of information than the nego-tiator, or cross-country guide who works collaboratively with stu-dents to overcome various obstacles to learning.

RICHARD PRAWAT, 1991, P. 8.

All teachers make choices. (Even a decision never to change is a choice.) Teachers who choose to move away from ineffective meth-ods of instruction, or to change from good teaching to better teaching, need alternatives, and it is one purpose of this text to present a rich array of good teaching strategies. One of the principles on which the text is based is that teachers have the intelligence and common sense to evaluate, select, and adapt instructional strategies to fit their students' strengths and needs, and their own. A corollary of this princi-ple is that teachers should not be presented with a single so-called best procedure and be required to learn and follow it unvaryingly. Choosing among strategies is itself a challenge, however. As you read this text, and as you encounter more teaching ideas through other professional opportunities, first study to understand how a strategy works and evaluate its possibilities for your own use. Then, like the hypo-thetical teacher who is described in Figure 3–4, when you find a method that looks useful, create a way to apply it to your own teaching and swing right into it.

This chapter and the two that follow present instructional strategies, emphasizing the impor-tance of instruction before, during, and after study of content area topics. Because many strategies are described and referred to in this three-chapter clus-ter and throughout this book, a Strategy Glossary is included after the final chapter. There, every strat-egy mentioned is listed alphabetically, followed by a brief description and the page numbers where the strategy is discussed in the text.

The focus of this chapter is on ways to introduce new topics—on strategies that provide *all* the stu-dents in a class with a foundation to build upon. In almost every class, for almost every topic a teacher intends to teach, there will be some students who already have relevant knowledge even before the teaching begins. These students are likely to com-plete classroom study of the topic successfully—a few because they knew all the information to be taught beforehand, and others because they knew enough about the topic to make it easy to learn more. There will be other students for whom the topic is so unfamiliar that they cannot—without help—make connections between this new informa-tion and ideas they already have. Concepts and ter-minology will, in a common phrase, be "over their heads." Moreover, some students will not be able to read the textbook independently well enough to understand it. Because this diversity in the classroom is expected, it is the teacher's responsibility to be prepared to intervene. When teachers intervene effectively and in interesting ways to ensure that all students can learn, *all students benefit*, including those who learn easily. It is neither useful nor pleasant for some students to experience successes in a situation where others consistently fail. There are many excellent strategies to use in introducing content area topics. These strategies build a shared knowledge base for all students and link what is new to what is known. They create a bridge from what students can do to what they will become able to do. They help to make time spent in school interesting, challenging, and worthwhile.

Guiding Students As They Set Out to Learn

Think of learning about a new topic as setting out on a journey into a new place. Students are making this journey; teachers are their guides and protectors. Starting out is made easier when students see connections between new information and familiar ideas—when the new is linked to the known. The journey is more productive and more pleasant for *all* students when *every* student has a foundation for understanding new ideas. There are a variety of ways in which guides can arrange the first part of a journey so that the trip will be a successful one.

Guides explain. Learning is much more than just listening to someone talk, but a teacher who serves as a knowledgeable guide can help students understand the territory they are entering. Two effective methods of introducing content area topics are based on direct explanation: the Teacher Read-Aloud Commentary (TRAC), and the Preview strategy. *Guides point out what to look for.* Learning requires much more than surveying important features of a text, but a well-planned survey can alert students to important ideas and thus make learning easier. Search tasks are a useful preparation for reading textbook chapters. *Guides know when there is too much baggage* and decide what is essential

and what is not. Learning is less burdensome when teachers accept responsibility for confronting the problem of concept overload. *Guides know the language* and can introduce words and phrases. Familiarity with terminology is not sufficient for learning, but it is a necessary part of learning. LEAD, Focused Cloze, and Typical to Technical Meaning are three useful strategies for teaching important vocabulary at the beginning of a new topic of study.

Experienced guides alert those they are leading. They can catch attention at the beginning of a journey by providing an introductory event that sparks thinking about what is to come. Beginning the study of topics with discrepant events is a useful way to engage attention. Also, experienced teachers are aware that there are some topics about which students already have a set of prior beliefs that are inaccurate. In these situations, learning is likely to be hampered by students' erroneous ideas. Experienced teachers know what topics are troublesome in this way, and they know how to overcome mistaken preconceptions. Refutational teaching provides a way to combat prior misconceptions. *Inventive guides may encourage creative thinking about what lies ahead.* It is usually not useful to discuss a topic before students have a strong knowledge base, but there are some topics where anticipatory discussion can be productive. Significant Sayings is a method of guiding inferential discussion based on relevant quotations. Creative Reasoning Guides are teacher-prepared materials that engage students in analytical and creative thinking about a topic before they begin to study it. *Guides open up the world.* Teachers who encourage and plan rich reading opportunities can open the world for students. Wide reading is an effective way to begin a new topic of study.

Introducing Topics Through Explanation

Cheerful provision of clear **explanations** is an important part of good teaching. (The word *cheerful*

---

explanation—comes from a Latin prefix, *ex-* and a Latin adjective, *planus*, meaning *flat*. An explanation is a way of creating a level ground for understanding.

may seem surprising in this context, but who has not had the experience of asking for information and receiving our answer along with the information—stated or implied—that the question was a foolish one, and answering it was a burden?) In the content areas, teacher explanation is necessary if students are to attain a thorough understanding of important concepts. Moreover, the manner in which explanations are given affects not only whether the explanation will help students learn, but also whether students will be comfortable in seeking help again. It is a principle of good content area teaching that accurate, brief, clear explanations of important, difficult concepts help students learn content area information. (Think of this as the ABC principle: Make your explanations Accurate, Brief, and Clear.) Therefore, it follows that teacher explanations are an important part of content instruction, but that because brevity is important, content area teaching should not consist solely or even primarily of teacher explanation or telling or lecture. The two strategies described in this section meet the brevity criterion; either can be accomplished in 15 minutes or less. Their structure promotes clarity. Accuracy depends on teachers' knowledge of their subject.

Teacher Read-Aloud Commentary.   One way to become acquainted with new territory is to find a knowledgeable guide who will travel with us, point out highlights we would otherwise miss, and explain what we need to know. In a classroom, students have a guide who is always there: their teacher. The Teacher Read-Aloud Commentary (TRAC) provides a simple, effective way for teachers to serve as guides when a new topic is introduced. In this method, the teacher chooses a section from the students' textbook that is important and that may be difficult for students to understand, and reads this section aloud to the class, pausing to explain important concepts and terminology. Before reading aloud, the teacher tells the students what the new topic of study is and what section of the text will be read aloud, and gives them time to find that passage in their textbooks. However, the teacher does not insist that students follow along during the reading and commentary.

Some students will do so, preferring to see the text and hear the reading simultaneously. Others will prefer only to listen. Both ways of learning are reasonable. Moreover, the teacher's focus should always be on reading and commenting on the text, rather than on monitoring and commenting on students' behavior. Examples of two TRACs, used to introduce a social studies lesson and a math lesson, are shown in Figures 3–1 and 3–2. The Commentary sections in Figures 3–1 and 3–2, and also the Preparation for Commentary section in Figure 3–2, tell what the teacher says. The italicized portions of these sections are the passages the teacher reads from the textbook.

Two features of the strategy are important to note. First, a well-conducted Teacher Read-Aloud Commentary is brief. From start to finish, a TRAC can be completed in 15 minutes or less. Second, the process is solely a commentary: The teacher is the only person who talks. These two features of TRAC are interrelated. The process is short because only the teacher speaks. Students' attention is not likely to wander because the commentary is quickly completed, and because a skillful commentary is brisk and lively. The teacher does not question students during a commentary because to do so would be to slow down the commentary, and to risk losing focus. Nor does the teacher pause to speak to students, either to praise or criticize. Students can understand the topic as the teacher switches back and forth from reading the text to explaining it, but to add extraneous talk (e.g., "T.R., keep the book open to the right page." "Amy, what are you doing?" "I'm pleased with how well Consuela is paying attention.") would make it hard for students to attend to the text concepts. Note that the teacher-talk only guideline for TRAC is not violated when commentary is preceded by a brief question-answer exchange, as in Figure 3–2. Here, before beginning the commentary, the teacher asks students to give examples of problem-solving components that have been studied previously. However, the teacher does *not* ask the students to solve the problems or to contribute to the commentary. (Interactive questioning may certainly be used later in the teaching process, but it is not part of this strategy.)

FIGURE 3–1   Using a Teacher Read-Aloud Commentary in a Social Studies Class

Level: middle school
Subject: Social Studies, the Eastern Hemisphere
Topic: Oceania
Background: The teacher uses the TRAC strategy regularly, and the students are familiar with it.

Rationale for passage choice: The text begins with a definition of Oceania and directions for map study, then moves on to descriptions of Australia and New Zealand. The hardest portion for students to read and understand is likely to be the conclusion discussing the smaller islands in this area; also this section has many unfamiliar place names. It will be useful for students to hear those place names read aloud, and also to hear the population numbers read. It is a little unusual to base a TRAC on the end of a text section, but that will work best here.

Commentary: We're learning about countries in Southeast Asia and now we're moving on to read about a part of this area of the world that's interesting because instead of being a large land area, here there are thousands of islands in the Pacific Ocean. So this part of the world is called "Oceania." One of the islands in Oceania is Australia—such a huge island that it's classified as a continent. Another island country, near Australia, is New Zealand. But most of the islands in Oceania are very small.

I'm going to read beginning at the bottom of page 580, where the heading is, "The Smaller Islands." Follow along with me if you want to.

Polynesia stretches from New Zealand in the southwest—you can find all these places on the map at the top of the page—*to Easter Island in the east, and Hawaii in the north.* That's interesting—our state of Hawaii is part of Polynesia. *Many of the Polynesian islands are tiny and uninhabited.* On some islands there aren't any inhabitants; there are no people living on some of the little islands. *Only a few have fairly large populations.* Well, the Hawaiian islands have a lot of inhabitants; later somebody should check the almanac to see what the population of Hawaii is. *Near the center of Polynesia is Western Samoa, where more than 160,000 people live. Tahiti has 85,000 residents. Hawaii, the fiftieth state in the United States, has over 1 million people.* Okay, there's a rough estimate of Hawaii's population; we'll see if the almanac gives a closer figure.

All Polynesian island groups are high islands, formed from underwater volcanoes. That means much of the land is well above sea level, and the islands are mountainous. *Many of them*—many of the islands—*have soils and climates that are good for farming. Coconuts, bananas, and breadfruit grow on most of the islands. Breadfruit is a fruit that, when cooked, has a texture like bread.* That sounds unusual!

West of the Polynesian islands and north of New Zealand and Australia lie the Melanesian islands. Remember we checked the dictionary when we read about Indonesia, and found that the *-nesia* part of these words comes from a Greek word meaning *island. They*—the Melanesian islands—*include New Guinea and hundreds of much smaller islands. The western half of New Guinea belongs to Indonesia. The eastern half is the independent country of Papua New Guinea. The Melanesian islands are high islands*—that's like the Polynesian islands; most of the islands are high above sea level. *The people there*—the people in Melanesia—*fish and grow many of the crops grown in Polynesia*—that sounds funny to me. Melanesia grows the crops grown in Polynesia. Okay, I see—The same kinds of crops grow on Melanesia and Polynesia—so coconuts, bananas, and breadfruit are grown in both areas.

Micronesia is made up of many small islands—okay, *micro* means *little*, so that makes sense. These are all little islands. *The largest of these islands is Guam, and it is only thirty miles long and about five miles wide.* So Guam is about the size of (name a local area the students are familiar with). *Many of the Micronesian islands are low islands, formed from coral skeletons, which means that their soil is poor.* The high islands were formed from volcanoes, and the soil there is richer, but these islands are formed from clusters of coral. *Because their soil is poor, the islands are thinly populated*—very few people live there. *Micronesia was the last Pacific Ocean island group to be settled.*

Look back at the map now, and notice that there are four areas in Oceania: Australia, which is a continent; Polynesia, which includes Hawaii toward the north and New Zealand in the south; Melanesia, to the northeast of Australia, and Micronesia, that group of very small islands to the north of Melanesia. See how much of the area is water, rather than land.

FIGURE 3–1 Continued

Follow-up: After the TRAC, the teacher asks if students have questions, commends the question-raisers, and responds by a) answering quickly, or b) noting that they will find the answer as they read further in the text, or c) encouraging them to use resource books to find answers. Then students move on to *paired reading* of the text section on Oceania from the beginning, using a RESPONSE form to take notes. The teacher asks for volunteers to check the almanac to find Hawaii's population, and to find answers to other questions that were raised.

The text passage on which this TRAC is based is taken from *The Eastern Hemisphere* (1990), published by Scott, Foresman.

FIGURE 3–2 Using a Teacher Read-Aloud Commentary in a Pre-Algebra Class

Level: high school or middle school
Subject: pre-algebra
Topic: Finding a number when a percent of it is known
Background: The teacher uses the TRAC strategy regularly to introduce new topics.

Rationale for passage choice: Students are beginning a new chapter in their texts; this TRAC is based on the first page of the chapter.

Preparation for commentary: Today we're starting a new chapter, and the math you'll be doing is based on three things you've already learned how to do: writing equations, solving an equation to find an unknown number, and translating a percent into a decimal. Let's review. Alicia, give us an example of an equation. (Student gives example.) Right. That's a good quickie: "7 plus 5 equals 12" is indeed an equation. Genia, give us an example of an equation with a variable. (Student responds.) Good. You're building on Alicia's idea, and that means we can move along very quickly: "x plus 5 equals 12." (Writes equation on board.) To solve that equation we'd subtract 5 from both sides, and get x equals 7. Moving on to something different, Brad, give us a number expressed as a percent. (Student responds.) Right. Two percent. (Writes *2%* on the board.) Expressed as a decimal, that number is point zero two. (Writes = *.02* on the board.) Now we're going to put all these skills together.

I'm going to comment on the first page of the new chapter, page 316. Open your textbooks, and follow along with me if you want to.

Commentary: In the problems you'll be solving, you'll be told what a percent of a number is, and your task will be to find the number. The practical example in our text is getting a commission on a sale. If you know what percentage of the sale the salesperson gets as a commission, and what the amount of a commission is, then you can find the price of the item that was sold. You can see, from the picture, that the example is about the commission someone gets for selling a car. *A salesperson is sometimes paid a commission for each sale. A commission is a percent of the selling price.*

And here's the example: *Gerry Mendoza sells cars. Her commission is 1½% of the selling price of each car. If Gerry's commission for selling a car was $180, what was the selling price of the car?*

And the solution is shown. First, *write an equation, letting* c *represent the price of the car*. Well, first they put the equation in words: *1½% of what number is $180?* Now we translate that. First, we translate the percent into a decimal. 1% is .01, but her commission is a little more than 1%: 1½%, so that's .015. 1% is .010; 2% is .020, so .015 is right in the middle. *.015* × c = 180. You can see that we've got our equation.

We divide both sides of the equation by .015, and the equation becomes $c = {}^{180}\!/_{.015}$. We solve by dividing 180 by .015 and the result is 12,000. The price of the car was $12,000; the commission of 1½% amounted to $180.

The math checks, and the answer is sensible. Ms. Mendoza's commission is small—less than 2%, so the price of the car must be much larger than the amount of the commission, and in our solution it is.

In these problems we are given a percent and a number. That number is a percent of another number,

FIGURE 3–2   Continued

which we need to find. Because the problems are of the same type, our equations will be similar. After translating the percent into decimal form, we multiply that decimal and the known number, to find the unknown number.

Follow-up: After the TRAC, students move into cooperative groups or pairs to solve two or three exercises as the teacher goes from group to group. When practice exercises are quickly checked for accuracy, students work cooperatively on additional problems. The format for this assignment is a standard one, shown on a chart that always remains posted, on which

the teacher needs only to change a few items (shown here in italics).

▮ Choose *12* of the problems on page *317* to solve. (Divide the problems so that each person has some to solve.)
▮ Include at least one problem where *the replacement for the variable (the solution to the problem) is greater than the number that is given in the problem.*
▮ Write a word problem for one of the problems you choose.
▮ Check each other's work and discuss any problem where there is disagreement about the solution.

The text passage for this TRAC is taken from Scott Foresman, *Introduction to Mathematics,* 1987, pp. 316–317.

In addition to providing useful instruction in a short period of class time, TRAC requires little or no preparation. The commentary on the text is conversational—*never* a script the teacher has written. A teacher can use a TRAC without any prior preparation, just by picking up a student text, scanning to find a useful passage, and reading and commenting on it. However, it is often better to prepare by selecting the passage in advance and scanning it to see whether there are word pronunciations or facts that should be checked before reading. Choosing the passage in advance also provides time to think about questions that might arise and possibilities for discussion. (After reading the passage in the example shown in Figure 3–1, for instance, students may use dictionaries to learn the meanings of *poly-* and *mela-*: *Polynesia* means *many islands*; *Micronesia* means *little islands*, and *Melanesia* means *black islands*. The term *black islands* could lead to a discussion of how places are named.)

The Teacher Read-Aloud Commentary is useful for all except very young learners who do not use textbooks. Even for these students, teachers can base a commentary on trade books that students are reading. The strategy works well from the primary grades through high school, and does not need to be altered

across grade levels because the textbooks themselves vary. Text topics and language are simple in the early grades and become increasingly complex. The strategy can be used either frequently or occasionally. A teacher might choose to make it a practice to introduce each major topic with a short TRAC. Students will feel comfortable with the process, and each commentary will be different because it will be based on a different text passage. On the other hand, teachers might use TRAC to introduce a particularly challenging text section, or one they have special knowledge about and want to comment on. Teachers might also use TRACs based on newspaper articles to introduce discussions of current events.

Development of reading ability and vocabulary building are particular strengths of the Teacher Read-Aloud Commentary. Students have the opportunity to see the text as the teacher reads from it. Listening is also fostered, and the use of TRAC followed by student reading produces multiple reading of important parts of the text. Because students learn (from hearing the teacher read) how technical terms are pronounced, as well as what they mean, future discussion of the text is made easier. Unfamiliar words, as well as technical terms, can be briefly clarified; for example, *uninhabited* is defined in the example shown in Figure 3–1. Commentaries also give teachers repeated, natural, nonintrusive opportunities to demonstrate how to cope with anaphora- as in the example in Figure 3–1, where the teacher reads "*Many of them*" and says "many of the islands." Math TRACs enable students to see how mathematical expressions written using symbols are translated into words. Teachers may choose to follow a TRAC with another strategy to build on what students have just learned. For example, any of these strategies (all described in the text and listed in the Strategy Glossary) could be used after a TRAC such as the one shown in Figure 3–1:

- Write Out/Learning logs: Students close their textbooks and write out in their learning logs what they remember from the reading. Younger students can draw and label a picture illustrating an idea from the reading.
- Focused Cloze: Students close their textbooks and complete a Focused Cloze passage the teacher has prepared over the section that has been read.
- Semantic Mapping: Cooperative groups brainstorm ideas remembered from the reading, adding ideas of their own if they wish, and organize them visually to show their interrelationships.
- K-W-L: Individually, in pairs and triads, in groups, or as a whole class, students list facts learned from the commentary, as well as facts they already knew, in the What I KNOW column of a K-W-L, and begin listing items in the What I WANT to Learn column.

The Teacher Read-Aloud Commentary has some resemblance to strategies in which teachers read a very brief text section aloud, and comment on their own thought processes (e.g., Davey, 1983; Muth, 1993). These methods are designed to model strategic reading and problem-solving, by revealing for students the thought processes of skilled readers and thinkers. The Teacher Read-Aloud Commentary, on the other hand, is directly focused on developing understanding of the material at hand. Its purpose is to help students understand what they are studying, through a commentary on one important piece of text. Of course, hearing commentaries regularly does foster general comprehension ability, because it demonstrates for students that reading

and thinking are interrelated. A math strategy similar to TRAC, called Solve Aloud, designed for use during instruction rather than when topics are introduced, is described in Chapter Four.

Teacher-Prepared Summaries: Previews. In the Preview strategy (Graves & Prenn, 1984), teachers provide a written summary for students, instead of talking through a portion of the text. As in Teacher Read-Aloud Commentaries, the teacher is a guide for students when a topic is introduced; but in the Preview strategy teacher guidance is more formal. In this strategy, the teacher prepares a written summary of essential text information, in 200 words or less; this is given to students and read aloud by the teacher as part of a concise, structured introduction designed to take approximately 10 to 15 minutes. There are three components of Previews: Analogy, Synopsis, and Guidance for reading. The teacher begins by creating an analogy between new information and something in the students' experience. Then the teacher gives students copies of a synopsis of the text and reads it aloud. Technical terms may be listed below the synopsis. Finally, the teacher provides guidance for reading by giving brief definitions of technical terms, if necessary, and by raising a question for students to consider as they read. Two examples of the Preview strategy are given in Figures 3–3 and 3–4; another example can be found in an article reporting a study of the strategy (McCormick, 1989) that includes a Preview designed for fifth-graders who are studying life in the New England Colonies.

When researchers have contrasted scores on multiple choice tests for students who used the Preview strategy before reading with the scores for students who were simply assigned to read the text, their findings were consistent: Test scores for students in the Preview groups tended to be higher. However, as Sandra McCormick (1989, p. 231) has pointed out, the Previews strategy has "a facilitative but not necessarily sufficient" effect. "[I]n addition to use of previews in a prereading experience," McCormick writes, "teachers would be advised to use additional comprehension instructional procedures both during and after reading these more difficult expository passages."

FIGURE 3–3   Using the Preview Strategy in a Course on Government

Level: high school
Subject: U. S. Government
Topic: the powers of Congress
Background: The teacher likes the Preview strategy and is gradually building a set of previews, so that the strategy can eventually be used to introduce each chapter. This year previews have been used with four chapters before this one.

The synopsis for this Preview has 197 words. Technical vocabulary terms are listed below the synopsis.

Preview process, part 1: Analogy: "Imagine this. Back in 1996, Basketball Commissioner David Stern wrote a new set of rules that defined and limited the roles of coaches, umpires, and players. The rules for players stated that they could run, pass, and shoot the ball. The Stern rules also set up a Basketball Court to make decisions about how the rules were to be interpreted—even though the rules had been carefully made and clearly written. The first case for the Basketball Court was this: Scottie Pippin of the Chicago Bulls, passed the ball to Michael Jordan, who shot an easy two-pointer. The Bulls were penalized for violating the new rules, on these grounds: *The rules state that Pippen can pass the ball and Jordan can shoot. However, when Pippen passed the ball, Jordan caught it before shooting, and nowhere do the rules state that players can catch the ball.*

"The Basketball Court overturned the penalty, and declared that the Bulls had not violated the new rules. This was the Court's decision: *The Stern rules give players three* expressed *powers—powers that are stated directly in the rules. But to play basketball, players must also have powers that are* implied *by the expressed powers. If one player can pass the ball and another can shoot it, then clearly the rules imply that the second player is permitted to catch the ball. The earlier decision is reversed; Michael Jordan did not violate the Stern rules when he caught Pippen's pass.*

"The Constitution of the United States gives Congress *expressed powers*—things Congress can do that are listed in the Constitution, and also, through a clause that has come to be called "the Necessary and Proper Clause," *implied powers* as well. I will give each of you a synopsis, to put in your notebooks, of expressed and implied powers given to Congress by the Constitution."
Preview process, part 2: Synopsis: (The teacher has written the synopsis in advance, distributed copies to students, and now reads aloud.)

The Constitution specifies governmental functions that are responsibilities and rights of Congress. These expressed powers *include the power to tax, regulate commerce, coin money, establish a postal system, grant copyrights and patents, admit new states to the Union, and declare war.*

Over time, the rights and responsibilities of Congress have expanded, because other implied powers *have been assumed, based on a clause in the Constitution that gives Congress the power "to make all laws which shall be necessary and proper for carrying into execution the foregoing powers, and all other powers vested by this Constitution in the Government of the United States, or in any department or officer thereof."*

The earliest use of implied powers occurred in 1791, when Congress established a national bank. Those who voted in favor asserted that the expressed powers to tax, borrow, and control currency implied the power to establish a national bank. Later, the Supreme Court unanimously upheld Congress's right to exercise implied powers, declaring, "Let the end be legitimate, let it be within the scope of the Constitution, and all means which are appropriate, which are not prohibited, but consist with the letter and spirit of the Constitution, are constitutional."

Besides expressed powers and implied powers, these are some important technical terms you will encounter in the reading:

▌ *the Necessary and Proper Clause* (also called *the Elastic Clause*). This is quoted in the synopsis.
▌ *strict constructionists* vs. *liberal constructionists*. These are groups who held opposing opinions about implied powers.
▌ *McCulloch v. Maryland*, 1819. A portion of the Supreme Court's decision in this case is quoted in the synopsis.

Preview process, part 3: Guidance for reading: "As you read the new chapter, focus on the relationship between Congress's expressed and implied powers. First, skim the chapter, making separate lists of the expressed and implied powers that are mentioned. Then reread to understand the connections between particular expressed powers and the actions Congress has taken based on powers they imply. "

Follow-up: The follow-up is built into the Pre-

FIGURE 3–3 Continued

view process, because students begin to read the text immediately. (Later, as a creative thinking activity, groups can be encouraged to think of possible actions Congress might take on the grounds that they are implied by an expressed power. Students might also enjoy creating a new set of rules for a well-known sport and then thinking of differences of opinion that might arise based on conflicting interpretations of the rules.)

Her advice echoes one of the principles upon which this text is based: Students need wisely chosen, sound, interesting instruction when a topic is introduced, as it is studied, and after a solid base of knowledge has been established on which further instruction can be based.

In the Preview strategy, the teacher talks and reads to the class, rather than interacting with students. The time used is very brief, typically about 10 minutes. In 1991, Janice Dole and her colleagues reported results of a study in which they compared the teacher-conducted Preview method with interactive instruction in which teachers asked questions, attempted to make connections between students' prior knowledge and the topic to be studied, elicited predictions, and encouraged discussion (Dole, Valencia, Gregg, & Wardrop, 1991). Students' comprehension test scores were consistently better, for both narrative and expository selections, when the teacher-directed Preview method was used. Researchers also noted that the Preview strategy took substantially less class time than the interactive method. The results of this study do not, of course, indicate that interactive teaching is unimportant. For instruction that continues over a longer period of time, strategies where there is interaction between teacher and students, and also among students, are more appropriate than instruction that is solely teacher-led. (However, it is important to note that teacher questioning is neither the only method, nor the best method, of interaction during instruction.) Teachers can choose to adapt the Preview strategy to encourage interaction when relating the topic to students' prior experiences. (In the high school example presented in Figure 3–3, the teacher might encourage discussion when using the basketball example, being careful not to let the focus of discussion switch completely to sports. (In the script for the elementary example shown in Figure 3–4, the teacher uses questioning to keep students involved in the process.) Remember, however, that one of the reasons for the Preview strategy's effectiveness is that it focuses students' attention directly on essential information in the text they will read. This clarity of focus could be diminished by extended conversation about an analogy, or about the topic itself before students have a strong knowledge base.

Teachers who begin to use the Preview strategy are likely to find that devising an analogy and writing a synopsis are intriguing challenges. It can be useful to consider an analogy and draft a synopsis well ahead of time, and then return to the task of preparation after a period of incubation. A first draft of a synopsis is usually longer than Preview guidelines specify, and cutting a synopsis down to 200 words or less requires taking out everything that is not essential. This is useful. Textbooks provide details, examples, and items intended to interest readers. A short, focused Preview teaches students what to attend to as they read, and keeps them from getting lost in a mass of details that all appear to have equal weight because they are given equal space in the text. Although the original preparation is likely to be time consuming, once prepared, previews will be usable over the years. Even when one textbook is changed for another, basic topics are likely to be similar.

Surveying the Text

In Chapter One, purposes for reading were discussed: learning to read, reading to learn new information, reading to accomplish tasks at home and in

FIGURE 3–4   Using the Preview Strategy in an Elementary Science Class

Level: elementary school
Subject: Science
Topic: the structure of the earth
Background: The class has been studying the solar system, and is now beginning to study a chapter section about the structure of the earth. The teacher, who recently learned about the Preview strategy through an inservice workshop and has decided to try it, has chosen to draw an analogy between the earth and a ball made of three colors of yarn. The other part of preparation was to write a synopsis. (This synopsis has 158 words.)

The teacher sees no need to explain the *strategy* to the class, and therefore swings right into the process.

Preview process, part 1: Analogy: (The teacher has prepared a small ball of yarn made of three colors of yarn fairly loosely wound and has a pencil or other object that can be inserted into and through the ball.) "This ball of yarn that I'm holding is round, like a sphere. You remember that Earth and the other planets in the solar system have a rounded shape too.

"I'm going to push this pencil into the ball of yarn..." (pushes pencil in a little way). "How far below the surface do you think the pencil has gone?" (Children respond.) "Yes, the part of the ball that the pencil is in is just a little way below the surface..." (Pushes the pencil farther in.) "Now the pencil is quite a way below the surface but it's not yet at the middle part of the ball. Tell me when you think the pencil has reached the middle of the ball" (continues pushing and children respond) "Yes, we can't see it, but I think the pencil is about at the middle part of the ball. I'm going to keep on pushing. Tell me when you think the pencil has gone past the middle part of the ball." (continues pushing and children respond) "I think you're right. The point of the pencil isn't in the middle of the ball anymore but it's not yet close to the surface. It's below the surface, on the other side of the ball." (continues pushing slowly, with a finger at the point where the pencil will come out) "Okay, now I can feel the point of the pencil on the other side, so it's just below the surface. ...Yes, now we can see the point.

"There are three layers of yarn in this ball—but all we can see is the green top layer. That's at the surface of the ball. Underneath that layer there's another layer of yarn—I've made that brown. So when I put the pencil into the ball this far..." (Pushes pencil in so children can judge that it's neither at the surface nor into the center.) ..."what color yarn do you think the pencil point is touching?" (Children respond "brown;" teacher contin-

ues to insert the pencil the same distance from different points on the ball.) "Yes, that middle layer is always below the outside layer.

"I've made the center part of the ball red. So when I push the pencil down to the center, what color is the pencil point touching?" (Children respond "red.")

"Our earth has three layers too. We can't see what's inside, but scientists have learned that there are three different layers, and they've given them names. I'm going to read to you about the earth's layers." (turns on overhead projector to display the synopsis)

Preview process, part 2: Synopsis: (The teacher has written the synopsis in advance and prepared it for display on the overhead projector, and now reads aloud.)

All the planets, including the Earth, are spherical—shaped like a ball. The four planets that are nearest the sun—Mercury, Venus, Earth, and Mars—are called the rocky planets. But though the earth is made mostly of rock, it's not a solid hard ball. It has different layers. The center of the earth is called the core—*like the core of an apple. This part of the earth is extremely hot. All around the core is another layer, called the* mantle. *Mantle is an old-fashioned word for a cape or big coat, and the mantle covers the core like a coat. The mantle is very hot, though not as hot as the core. The outside layer of the earth is called the* crust—*just like the crust on the outside of a loaf of bread.*

The three layers of the earth, beginning at the center, are called the core, *the* mantle, *and—on the outside—the* crust.

Preview process, part 3: Guidance for reading: The important technical terms are crust, mantle, and core. Teacher and class read them together: core, mantle, crust. The teacher asks, "How are those three layers different? In your groups, read the new chapter aloud, and think of ways the three layers of the earth are different from one another." The teacher posts a copy of the synopsis on a bulletin board or at a learning center.

Follow-up: The follow-up is built into the Preview process, because students begin to read the text immediately. (Should the teacher allow students to unroll the ball of yarn later to see the different colors? Surely. One good possibility would be to use it in a variation of the "Yarn-in-a-Box" storytelling strategy. The teacher could also provide yarn at a learning center for children to wind into their own "earth balls.")

a career, and reading for enjoyment. It is interesting to consider that in reading for the third purpose, which can be summarized as "reading to do," reading and learning are not always linked; in fact, the ability to read purposefully frees one from having to learn material not needed at the time. Jean Dreher has pointed out that the ability of competent adults to read efficiently makes it unnecessary for them to learn all the information they must use professionally, because they can easily find the information in source materials. To use an everyday example, people learn just a few ZIP codes, because they use them often. Fortunately, people do not have to learn all the ZIP codes because they can easily be looked up in a directory. As another example, experienced teachers read the Teacher's Handbook most school districts provide, but do not study it regularly or memorize it. They can look up information as they need it.

In school, students' ability to understand text is usually measured by ability to recall and interpret what has been read. John Guthrie and Irwin Kirsch (1987) are among the scholars who have pointed out that real world reading includes reading to locate information, and that the ability to find information in various sources probably taps cognitive abilities that are different from those used in recalling what has been read. The term *search tasks* is used (Dreher, 1992; Dreher and Guthrie, 1990) to refer to finding information in various kinds of text materials: books, reference sources, labels, directions, and so forth. These researchers note that students are often not well prepared to search text efficiently to find specified information. Well-designed search tasks used in content area study serve two purposes: First, they introduce text by focusing students' attention on important text information that will later be read carefully; second, they give students practice in searching text to find information. (Text Hunts, described in Chapter Two, also engage students in searching text, but their purpose is to enable students to learn about text features, such as the table of contents, glossary, and index, in a particular book. Text Hunts are a useful way to introduce a book. Search Tasks, on the other hand, are a useful strategy to introduce the study of a topic because the informational content of a chapter is surveyed.)

Guided Text Search: Search Tasks. As we approach new territory, it can be useful to have explicit directions about what to look for. If we survey the area through a quick, guided search, we will become aware of some important features that we will later learn about in depth. Using Search Tasks to introduce new material provides such a preliminary survey. Search Tasks are designed to be completed cooperatively; working on them gives students an opportunity to be decision-makers as they divide tasks and then consult and discuss. It would be a mistake to use the strategy as a way of "assessing prior knowledge" by requiring students to complete the tasks individually either in class or as homework. A few students would not learn from the assignment because it would be too difficult for them, and it would become a dreary chore for most of the class—and also for the teacher, obliged to correct a mass of papers.

Although good Search Tasks are not as challenging to create as the materials for Previews, thoughtful preparation is somewhat time consuming, and thoughtful preparation is essential. If the tasks are trivial or unfocused, they will not interest students nor prepare them for learning. For example, asking students questions such as "What page does the chapter begin on? How many pages are in the chapter?" is pointless. Once prepared, good Search Tasks are usable as long as a text is used. Because they are text-specific, new tasks must be devised whenever there is a text change. The class time used will vary substantially depending on the complexity of the teacher-prepared materials and the sophistication of the students. Because groups will not all finish at the same time, an additional activity must be built into the Search Task assignment, as in the examples shown in Figures 3–5 and 3–6. For young students, a set of short tasks can be rotated among groups, as in the example in Figure 3–7, with the expectation that each group will finish two, and the probability that no group will finish all of them. Afterwards, the task cards can be used as an optional learning center activity.

Search Tasks are typically based on textbooks and require some sophistication in reading, so they are not useful for primary students unless the tasks are very carefully prepared. (The second graders in

FIGURE 3–5   Using Search Tasks in å Life Skills Course

Level: high school or middle school

Topic: being a sensible consumer

Background: The teacher uses Search Tasks regularly, and the students are familiar with working in groups to use this method before each new text chapter.

Rationale: Scanning text for information is important at work and in the home. Using search tasks develops the skill while preparing students to learn from their textbooks.

Introduction: The teacher hands out individual Search Task activity pages, with directions such as these: "Our next chapter is about shopping—*skillful* shopping—so we'll be learning about ways to use our money wisely to get what we need and want. Here are the search tasks. Work with a partner, but I expect each person to complete and return the assignment. If you finish early, create a way to illustrate the idea of *impulse buying*."

* * * * * * * * * * * *

SEARCH TASKS   Name _____

Chapter 10 Skillful Shopping

1. Remember that our text uses red for the most important headings, and that the section headings are printed in red *italic* type.

   List the headings for the two chapter sections, and note the page number where each section begins.
   ▮
   ▮

2. Three section subheadings are listed below alphabetically. Where do you think each belongs—in section 10.1 or in section 10.2?

   To answer the question, you can think and guess, you can scan the text, or you can guess and then check.

   Buying on Impulse   _____

   Returns and Exchanges _____

   Where to Shop   _____

3. A chart titled "Shopping Alternatives" shows seven ways to shop. Four ways are by going to different places where things are sold. Have you ever shopped at a factory outlet? If so, what did you buy?

   What are the other three ways to shop?
   Star (*) a method you'd like to discuss in class.

4. In the part of this chapter headed "Influences on Buying," there are four important influences listed. (Their names are in red type.) The first one is Advertising; you list the other three.
   ▮ Advertising
   ▮

   (Be ready to tell about a time when a friend has influenced your shopping.)
   ▮
   ▮

5. Scan the part of the chapter headed "Buying on Impulse" to find a definition of *impulse buyer*. Have you ever been an impulse buyer?

6. One of the green "Did You Know?" items in this chapter gives suggestions about how to test sneakers before you buy. What are two things to do?
   ▮
   ▮

   If you and your partner finish before the rest of the class, create a drawing or cartoon about impulse buying, or decide on a different way to illustrate or demonstrate the idea.

   Follow-up: An assignment for those who finish early is included in the Search Task. The teacher signals the end of the Search Task process by moving directly either to whole class discussion of students' answers sequentially, or to a discussion of a selected part of the chapter that Search Tasks have introduced. In this case, the teacher has decided to introduce the topic of wise shopping by giving some counterexamples, tapping students' experiences with impulse buying and peer pressures by using responses to items 4 and 5 as the basis for a discussion.

Note: This Search Task exercise is based on *Teen Living,* Prentice-Hall, 1991, pp. 204–221.

the simulated classroom described in Figure 3–7 have been carefully supported by the teacher: The bulletin board display is a regular classroom feature; the task cards are written and formatted to make them easy to read; the children know they can ask for help if they need it.) The tasks ought usually to focus solely on text content, but, as in the example shown in Figure 3–6, the teacher may decide to link text with

---

FIGURE 3–6   Using Search Tasks in an Economics Class

Level: high school

Topic: supply and demand

Background: The teacher uses search tasks regularly, and the students are accustomed to completing search tasks as a chapter introduction

Rationale: The subject is complex and the text presents a heavy concept load. The teacher has used the process of preparing search tasks to identify (for teacher use) the major concepts to be stressed in class discussion and assignments.

Introduction: The teacher relates the new chapter—which in this case is the beginning of a new unit—to what has been accomplished before: "I'm very impressed with the real estate projects you completed, and I think our display looks great. We're beginning a new unit titled 'Markets, Prices and Business Competition' and tomorrow we'll be making preliminary plans about a new set of group projects. Here are the search tasks for the chapter on 'Supply and Demand.' Look them over with a partner and decide how to complete them efficiently. When you finish you can move right into the 'Readings in Economics' selection you've chosen. Make notes on a RESPONSE sheet; we'll be forming jigsaw groups about the readings later."

* * * * * * * * * * * * * * * * *

SEARCH TASKS   Name _____

Chapter 8 Supply and Demand

Part I. There are six major sections in the chapter. List their titles. Find the specified information in each section, and, for each section, list one fact you already know about the topic.

1. _____

    What is the *law of demand?*
    ▪ (List a fact about the topic you already know.)

2. _____

Give examples of items for which you think the demand is a) elastic; b) inelastic. Don't use the examples given in the text.
▪ (fact)

3. _____

Analyze the demand curves shown in Figures 8–3 and 8–4. Explain how very similar graphs show decreased demand (Figure 8–3) and increased demand (Figure 8–4).
▪

4. _____

What is the *law of supply?*
▪

5. _____

Besides price, what are three factors that can cause a change in supply? Star (*) the factor you think is most important to discuss in class.
▪

6. _____

What is the definition of *equilibrium price?*
▪

Part II. Scan the chapter review for the item titled "Using an Interview to Gather Information." List some people class members might interview.

Part III. With your partner, choose one end-of-the-chapter "Readings in Economics." Go ahead and get started on the reading, using a RESPONSE sheet to take notes. Later we'll form jigsaw groups to discuss each reading in depth, for reporting back to groups.

Follow-up: The follow-up process is built into the Search Task assignment.

Note: This Search Task exercise is based on *Economics: Today and Tomorrow*, published by Glencoe/McGraw-Hill, 1991, pp. 185–211.

FIGURE 3–7   Using Search Tasks in the Primary Grades

Level: second grade
Subject: Science
Topic: Weather
Background: The teacher, who uses the science textbook only as an auxiliary instructional tool, does not expect students to read from it independently, but does recognize the importance of accustoming students to use textbooks as a preparation for content area study in later grades. The teacher believes that carefully guided Search Tasks provide a good way to show students how to use textbooks, and that they are an excellent activity for cooperative groups.

One of the classroom bulletin boards is a display that illustrates terminology such as <u>chapter title</u>, <u>heading</u>, <u>subhead</u>, <u>page number</u>, <u>illustration</u>, <u>photograph</u>, <u>drawing</u>, <u>caption</u>, <u>map</u>, and <u>chart</u>. The terms are printed on sizable strips of stiff paper and are placed beside pages copied from the textbooks the children use, so that the term <u>chapter title</u>, for example, is placed beside the copy of a page on which a chapter title is highlighted. During the year, as new terms are encountered (e.g., <u>time line</u>, <u>map key</u>, <u>graph</u>), the terms and pages that show examples are added to the bulletin board. Additionally, as an ongoing, rotating assignment, each week a cooperative group finds an example in a textbook or trade book of one of the terms and writes a short statement about why they chose this example. The teacher copies and highlights the illustration, which is posted along with the group's rationale for choosing it (e.g., This is a good <u>caption</u> for the tornado picture because it tells rules for being safe). The bulletin board display is continually changing, so interest is maintained. Students may refer to the chart when they work on Search Tasks.

Rationale: Search Tasks focus students' attention on important text features, such as subheadings, illustrations, and picture captions. They also help young students realize that texts are sources of information, rather than intimidating books whose sections must be read from start to finish at a fixed speed. For these young readers, the Search Task activities are an integral part of their language arts program.

Introduction: The teacher has prepared, and laminated, a series of "search cards" consisting of directions and questions printed clearly on 9 × 12 sheets of colored paper. There are six cooperative groups in the class. The teacher has prepared two sets of four search cards (a total of eight cards), so that when one group finishes a card, there will be another for them to work on even if other groups are not yet ready to trade cards. (Four of these cards follow.) Each group of students will complete at least two search cards. (Notice that the directions on the search cards are repetitive, and are given in list form, rather than paragraph form, to make reading easier.) Students know they can ask about any words on the cards that their group doesn't know. Before using these cards, the teacher reviews the meaning of the word *describe* with the children.

* * * * * * * * * * * * * * *

SEARCH CARD ONE   Science
Chapter 6 Weather

▎Find a <u>photograph</u> of a storm.
  Read the <u>caption</u>.
  What does the caption tell about weather?

▎Find a <u>drawing</u> of a storm.
  Read the caption.
  What does the caption tell about weather?

▎Two <u>illustrations</u> show that air moves.
  On <u>page 80</u>, there is a photograph of a girl flying a kite. The wind blows the kite.

  How does the illustration on <u>page 82</u> show that air moves?

* * * * * * * * * * * * * * *

SEARCH CARD TWO   Science
Chapter 6 Weather

<u>Definitions</u> of three kinds of clouds are printed in <u>page margins</u>.
Find them.
Read the definitions and fill in the blanks.

Stratus clouds form in _____.
_____ clouds often mean rain.

Cirrus clouds look like white _____.
When _____ clouds are in the sky, there is often _____ weather.

FIGURE 3–7 Continued

Cumulus clouds look like puffs of _____.
They are usually seen when the weather is

_____,

but big _____ clouds may mean that
a _____ is coming.

* * * * * * * * * * * * * * * *

SEARCH CARD THREE Science
Chapter 6 Weather

The chapter <u>headings</u> are printed in red.
▌ The first heading is Clouds.
Describe the first picture in this <u>section</u>.

▌ The second heading is _____
Copy the <u>drawing</u> that shows the sun's rays coming
to Earth.

▌ The third heading is _____

Choose an <u>illustration</u> in this section to describe.

What does the illustration show about the <u>section
topic</u>?

_____

* * * * * * * * * * * * * * * *

SEARCH CARD FOUR Science
Chapter 6 Weather

▌ Find the page with <u>photographs</u> that show snow and
rain.
Write the word on the page that is in <u>bold</u> print.

_____

▌ Find the page with a <u>drawing</u> of a thermometer.
One term in bold print on this page is **rain gauge**.
Write the other terms that are in bold print.

_____

_____

students' experiences. (Life skills learning, by definition, should be closely connected to students' lives,
and the tasks for this class make a connection
between students' experiences with impulse buying
and topics in the chapter.) Search Tasks can be
designed to lead directly into whatever class activities
the teacher has planned. After completing the Search
Tasks shown in Figure 3–5, students will be prepared
with examples, and even illustrations, for a discussion
of impulse buying, which the teacher is planning to
use to introduce strategies for shopping wisely. The
Search Tasks shown in Figure 3–6 help prepare for
future assignments: text reading, a series of interviews to be conducted later, and end-of-chapter readings that will be used as the basis for class discussion.

Confronting Concept Overload

Imagine being driven rapidly through an unfamiliar city with the sights pointed out by a guide
who urges us to look at one thing, and then another,
and another. "See that. This is important. There are

four things to remember. Look at this. Now look at
that." The chances are that we would learn very little, and recall only a jumble of images. Some textbook chapters introduce an overwhelming array of
concepts. Isabel Beck and Margaret McKeown
(1991, p. 486) urge teachers to confront concept
overload by prioritizing topics, teaching in depth,
and making connections among topics. "Of course,"
they write, "the next issue along this line of thinking
is, then what gets left out? But consider that, as the
curriculum now stands, very little is getting in; that
is, students leave their study… with limited growth
of knowledge and often with misconceptions."

Although textbook subject matter and writing
style become increasingly challenging from grade to
grade, concept overload is apt to be most prevalent
in textbooks for the intermediate and middle school
grades. Textbooks written for primary students typically present a limited number of new ideas and
terms. In high school, students are taking many
advanced courses that are narrowed in scope. For
example, high school students study economics as a

separate course, with its own text, whereas a social studies textbook for younger students will present information about economics along with historical and geographical concepts. Teachers at all levels, however, should be aware that concept overload is a potential problem. Textbook authors sometimes attempt to develop breadth simply by introducing many topics—more than their readers can comprehend beyond a superficial level.

When we see that a text chapter presents too much information, it is our responsibility to evaluate the relative importance of the concepts and select those that will be emphasized. The flow chart in Figure 1–5 in Chapter One presents a practical way to prioritize among concepts. Sometimes teachers can devise elegant solutions for problems with concept overload that transform the problem into a rich opportunity for good learning. Coping with concept overload will require varying amounts of preparation time, depending on what the teacher decides to do. The method described in Figure 3–8 takes very little teacher preparation: just listing the terms, writing the key, and making copies of the survey form. Class time is used over two days before regular study of the topic, and there is a homework assignment for students, but the extra class time is productive—note the link with math through data analysis—and the class is off to a lively start on an important topic.

Teachers sometimes decide to "cover" textbook material exactly as it is presented, giving equal weight to every idea introduced, because they believe it would be risky to do otherwise. Such a decision

---

FIGURE 3–8   Confronting Concept Overload in a Social Studies Chapter

Level: middle school or intermediate grades

Subject: Social Studies

Topic: exploration of the Western Hemisphere

Background: The teacher has many years of experience of teaching this topic, and has used the text for two years (and expects to use it for four more years). This experience has shown that students miss important ideas about history and geography as they struggle with a mass of unfamiliar names that—except for a few that are already known—seem unpronounceable, indistinguishable, and impossible to recall: Vasco Nunez de Balboa, Sieur de Bienville, Alvar Nunez Cabeza de Vaca, John Cabot, Jacques Cartier, Samuel de Champlain, Christopher Columbus, Francisco Coronado, Hernando Cortes, Giovanni da Verrazano, Hernando DeSoto, Sieur Duluth, Vasco Da Gama, Eric the Red, Leif Ericsson, Sir Martin Frobisher, Father Louis Hennepin, Bjarni Herjolfsson, Henry Hudson, Sieur d'Iberville, Louis Joliet, Sieur de La Salle, Ferdinand Magellan, Father Jacques Marquette, Panfilo de Narvaez, Francisco Pizzarro, Juan Ponce de Leon, Amerigo Vespucci. (Here the names are alphabetized; in the text, there is, of course, a different ordering.) Recognizing that the students do not have the knowledge base to decide which explorers are most important to learn about, the teacher nevertheless wants to arrange for student input in the choice-making process, and, therefore, uses a survey process.

Rationale: There is no point in attempting to do something that can't be done well. If a concept load is too heavy, teachers have a responsibility to reduce and organize subtopics so that learning can occur.

Process: The teacher has made multiple copies of an alphabetized list of explorers whose names are mentioned in the upcoming chapter, with the names in a column down the left side of the page. Guidelines and symbols to be used in completing the survey are shown in a key:

▪ If you have information about this person, write one fact beside the name.

▪ Write 0 beside the name if you've never heard of this person before.

▪ Put a check (√) if you've heard the name, but can't think of any facts about the person.

▪ Put a star (*) beside the names of people you'd like to find out more about.

The teacher begins the activity about 20 minutes before lunchtime or a scheduled special class. Copies of the list are distributed, one per student. The activity is not done during a social studies lesson, and students do not have their books.

"This is a survey to find out which of the many people who explored parts of what is now North America are the most famous. I'll read down the list of names."

FIGURE 3–8 Continued

(Reads names.) "You can work alone or with a buddy, but each person should fill out a survey. You don't have to put your name on the survey. When you finish, give me the survey sheet and then you have free reading time until it's time for (lunch/gym/art)." Teacher explains how to fill out the survey form, and students complete them. Some students, very sensibly, will probably ask to use textbooks or reference sources; teacher replies in this fashion: "Fill out the survey first, and then you can check resource books during free reading time. I'll give you another copy of the list to use if you want. What we're doing here is finding out which explorers are the famous ones. Remember that you don't have to put your name on the survey. It can be anonymous." (Teacher collects surveys as students complete them.)

After students return to class, the teacher explains the homework assignment, which is to complete one, two, or three surveys by interviewing other people. Students must take at least one copy of the survey, and may take as many as three. The teacher models the interview process twice: once with the teacher interviewing a student, and then with a student interviewing another student while the teacher provides guidance as needed.

As the surveys are returned, the teacher records only that students have, or have not, done the assignment. The surveys remain anonymous, and there is no attempt to use them to check how much particular students (or those they've interviewed) know.

Tallying and recording data then becomes a cooperative group assignment. The easiest way to do this is for the teacher to cut the sheets apart so that each group gets all the data for part of the list. (For example, if there are five groups and the names of the twenty-eight explorers listed are on the survey, one group might be given the section from Balboa to Champlain, and the next from Columbus to DeSoto.) Groups whose list includes better-known people will have more to do, because they will be listing more facts. When the data have been recorded, they can be analyzed, and the results used to decide which explorers to study, based on these guidelines:

Which explorers are the most famous? (These are the ones many people were able to list a fact about.) We will study about them, because that's part of becoming well educated. As part of our study, we'll analyze the information people gave about them: were all the facts accurate?

Which explorers are known slightly? (These are the ones many people put a check mark by.) Here the teacher, who has a sound knowledge base, makes the decision. (There may also be a district curriculum that specifies explorers who should be studied.)

Who would we like to learn more about? After a first reading of the text, students decide which explorers, from among those known slightly or not at all, deserve to be better known. These people become the subjects of some in-school research by individuals, pairs, or cooperative groups. (See Chapter Five for suggestions for guiding research.) Copies of well-prepared research projects can be kept to provide reading for future classes.

results in superficial learning that is quickly forgotten. However, a decision to confront concept overload can also have negative results if the teacher does not concentrate on content. If the teacher focuses on criticizing the textbook, students will remember this rather than the content information and, very reasonably, may talk about it at home; some parents are likely, very reasonably, to call the school to protest the use of a bad textbook. Rather than complaining about the textbook, teachers can provide instruction in a straightforward, positive way. In the example shown in Figure 3–8, the teacher has structured the process so that topics in three categories will be studied: 1) those that are part of a general knowledge base (for example, Columbus, Hudson, Magellan, and Vespucci), 2) others that the teacher knows are most significant and/or are specified in the curriculum, and 3) those that the students themselves choose to add. Using such a structure is a good guarantee that the curriculum is being well taught.

Teaching Vocabulary in Lively Ways

Teachers need to make use of lively methods of teaching vocabulary that engage students in talking about the words rather than memorizing definitions.

Three vocabulary-building activities that depend on students talking together are described in this section: LEAD, group-completed Focused Cloze, and Typical to Technical Meaning. All three are suitable for occasional use, as lively ways to introduce vocabulary, but only Focused Cloze is a strategy to use regularly. Completing a Focused Cloze passage is an excellent weekly assignment for cooperative groups. The other two strategies cannot be used with every topic. Not every topic has the extensive, coherent, experienceable vocabulary load that LEAD requires, and Typical to Technical Meaning is useful only when at least three specialized terms are essential for understanding the topic to be studied. (If there are only one or two, the teacher can explain their meanings most efficiently by telling—see the SAY-IT strategy described in Chapter Four.)

An understanding of technical terminology is an essential part of content area learning. Students must understand terminology to understand the subject matter; however they cannot learn the meaning of technical terms from context because so much of the context consists of the technical terms. Determining the meaning of unknown words from context is practical only when the unfamiliar words are few, and the context is both rich and clearly expressed.

> Teachers can't possibly predict or teach all of the words students may need to know to make sense out of the new material. However, by analyzing the text and listing the key concepts to be learned, teachers can make a judgment as to which terms the students will need to know in order to understand those concepts, and which words the students already know that will facilitate comprehension... [T]he goal of meaningful learning is the acquisition of new meanings. The difference between meaningful learning and learningless (rote) learning has to do with comprehension. Vocabulary instruction is strongly related to reading comprehension and can be meaningful if the assigned reading material is capable of being related, if the learner has the appropriate schema... to be able to relate the new words or concepts to those already known, and if the reader attempts to make sense of the vocabulary. (Thelen, 1986, pp. 608–609)

Not only will few, if any, students acquire a sound understanding of content-related terminology by reading the text independently, they will not develop their vocabularies successfully by "looking up" the words as an independent or group assignment. There is ample evidence that the assignment of looking up a list of words, writing definitions, and using the words in sentences is virtually useless, and may have negative effects on vocabulary building:

> Think back to teacher X whose primary approach to teaching science vocabulary was to list thirty words on the board and have the class "look them up" in the dictionary. Recall, too, how you and your partner divided the list in half and proceeded to write down the first, or the shortest, definition available. Whether it fit the context in which the word would appear was unimportant. ...the main concern was to get the assignment finished. Unfortunately, teacher X was probably taught using a similar method— more evidence that poor teaching methods tend to perpetuate themselves. (Wood, 1987b, p. 11)

As George Miller and Patricia Gildea have noted, students assigned to find words in dictionaries, copy definitions, and write sentences using the words will—very reasonably—scan the dictionary definitions (often a long and varied list) looking for words or phrases that they understand. The resulting sentences are often funny. One synonym for *meticulous* is *careful*. To *erode* is to *eat away*. A synonym for *stimulate* is *stir up*. But it is possible to be familiar with the terms *careful, stir up,* and *eat away* without understanding the words for which they are given as synonyms or definitions, as researchers who have studied the look-it-up-in-the-dictionary assignment have shown. The student-created sentences they have collected include "I was meticulous about falling off the cliff," "My family erodes a lot" (Miller & Gildea, 1987, pp. 97 and 98), and "Mrs. Morrow stimulated the soup" (Brown, Collins, & Duguid, 1989, p. 33). The students who wrote these sentences are not at fault. The assignment itself is faulty (and, therefore, the teacher who made the assignment erred in doing so). As John Seely Brown and his colleagues point out, "given the method, such mistakes seem unavoidable. Teaching from dictionaries assumes that definitions and exemplary sentences are self-contained 'pieces' of knowledge. But words and sentences are not islands, entire unto themselves."

It follows, therefore, that teachers must teach content area vocabulary, rather than expecting students to learn it through their own endeavors, and that the teaching must be sensibly managed, given what we know about learning. Two important principles about learning need to be taken into account. First, it is difficult or impossible to learn and remember large amounts of unrelated material, so it is unrealistic to expect that a long list of vocabulary terms can be taught in isolation. Second, learning something is easier when people feel a need to learn it. This also argues against the practice of teaching a list of terms before students encounter them in reading and study. Knowledgeable teachers can begin a journey of learning by introducing students to the language they will need to know, through a variety of interesting strategies. Vocabulary learning is not a one-time effort. It extends throughout the study of a content area topic. In every content area, the thorough understanding of terminology that is necessary must be attained through active use, not through rote memorization. Diane Miller (1993), for example, makes a strong case for stressing vocabulary in the field of mathematics. She suggests that teachers should deliberately choose to incorporate mathematical terms in their teaching, and find ways to encourage students to use mathematical vocabulary in class activities. The three vocabulary learning strategies described here provide a variety of methods to encourage active learning of terminology when a new topic is introduced. Other strategies described in later chapters provide lively ways to develop sound understanding of vocabulary as topics are studied.

Learning Vocabulary with LEAD.   The LEAD strategy (pronounced as in the first syllable of *leader*) uses three steps: listing technical terms, using an experience activity related to the terms, and discussing the topic while using the terms. LEAD develops students' understanding of concept area vocabulary. The strategy's name is an acronym, based on the three steps: 1) listing (L), 2) experience activity (EA), and 3) discussion (D). It is the middle step, the experience activity, that makes the strategy unique, but a LEAD discussion is also unusual: each contribution must include at least one term from the list

compiled earlier. Examples of LEAD use are shown in Figures 3–9 and 3–10. When content vocabulary is extensive and consists of terms that name or describe observable, experienceable items, the method is a useful one. Teacher planning consists of choosing a text topic that lends itself to an experience activity and arranging either a direct experience (e.g., a trip, an experiment, a demonstration of equipment) or a vicarious experience (e.g., a film or a guest speaker). For LEAD, advance planning by the teacher is in the form of thinking about how to arrange the steps for a LEAD. Preparation time will vary substantially depending on what the experience activity is. When LEAD is used in an impromptu fashion (as in the class described in the background section of Figure 3–9), there is no preparation time at all. Class time used for LEAD may be extensive, but students' active involvement makes it likely that terms will be remembered.

The strategy is an expansion of an idea by Janell and Stephen Klesius, who have suggested that playground activities can be used for vocabulary development. They encourage listing words related to a game, then playing the game, and then using the words in a teacher-led classroom discussion, e.g., "As you were jumping double-dutch, when did you move *swiftly*?" "What happened that caused you to feel *exhilarated*?" (Klesius & Klesius, 1989, p. 199). In the LEAD strategy, listing terminology is a joint effort by the class and the teacher. Students scan a chapter in their content text to make a list of important terms, which the teacher records on a chart. During the text-based listing process, students' attention is focused on text features that support vocabulary learning: lists of terms at the beginning or end of the chapter, words defined in the margins of the text, words embedded in the text that are printed in boldface type, or words that are used to label illustrations or other graphics. As terms are listed, teacher and students may read or state meanings briefly, but time is not used to teach definitions. Although the listing is primarily text-based, students may add terms based on their own knowledge of the topic, and the teacher may add important terms that are not included in the text. Through LEAD, young students may become accustomed to using sophisticated terms that a textbook for the primary grades may not include.

FIGURE 3–9   Using LEAD To Teach Geometry Terminology

Level: intermediate grades
Subject: Mathematics
Topic: polygons; congruent and similar figures
Background: The teacher and the class enjoy looking for opportunities to use LEAD, even when the vocabulary does not relate to a topic currently being studied. For example, on the day after a severe thunderstorm, the teacher began the day by listing relevant terminology with the students, some of whom recalled terms from weather reports, and some of whom spontaneously looked for terminology in a science chapter on weather that had been studied several months earlier. Following this listing step, students used the terms in their discussion of the experience activity (the storm). Other spontaneous occasions for using LEAD have been the return to school of a student wearing a cast on a broken arm, and the day after a vacation when the class discussed modes of transportation. In the fall, the teacher used LEAD to anticipate the study of seasonal effects of the earth's revolution around the sun, when the transition from daylight saving time to standard time occurred.

Because the students are familiar with LEAD, they know that they are expected to use at least one term in every contribution to the question and answer portion of the discussion. Thus they know that if they are asked, "Did you find an example of a pentagon?" answers such as "No" or "The pin Polly's wearing" are unacceptable, whereas "No, but we found lots of examples of rectangles" or "Polly's pin is in the shape of a pentagon" are LEAD-style answers.

Rationale for topic choice: Geometrical shapes occur everywhere; the shapes are familiar, but some of the terminology is not. LEAD gives students opportunities to establish their understanding of terminology by using it during an enjoyable activity.

Step 1, Listing: Students scan four pages of text in their math books and come up with these terms: *polygon, vertex, triangle, quadrilateral, rectangle, pentagon, hexagon, octagon, sides, angles, length, congruent figures, similar figures.*

Step 2, Experience Activity: Working in cooperative groups, students search the classroom for examples that illustrate each of the terms. To do this, they check the text for definitions, and some of them ask the teacher for clarification (which the teacher, of course, gives). Some students have the ingenious idea of folding paper into geometric shapes that they haven't been able to find elsewhere in the classroom. (Does the teacher permit this? Yes, indeed; the teacher is delighted.) After ten minutes of searching, the students discuss their findings in their groups, and prepare a series of questions using the terminology.

Step 3, Discussion: The teacher starts off with a question: "Were you able to find an example of a polygon that is not a quadrilateral?" One group answers, "Yes, Con's watch is a hexagon. It has six sides, not four." Members of that group ask, "Are the window panes congruent figures?" The next group answers, "Yes, they are congruent because they are the same size and shape" and ask, "Are the panes in the door congruent with the panes in the window?" When students' use of terms is incorrect or ambiguous, the teacher restates the answer, incorporating a quick definition; e.g., "The shapes of the math book and the science book covers are similar but they're not congruent, because they're different sizes." After several question-and-answer rounds, the teacher moves the activity into a freer discussion, focused on why *similarity* and *congruence* are important concepts.

Follow-up: Because the last step of LEAD is a whole class activity, everyone finishes at the same time. Moving straight into paired reading of the text is usually a good next step.

Experience comes next. When the list is completed, the class moves immediately to an activity that will engage them with the text terms and concepts. Suppose the chapter is about characteristics of leaves and trees. Vocabulary will include *deciduous* and *evergreen*, *veins* and *venation*, *pinnate* and *palmate*. The experience activity might be a leaf-and-photo walk, to take snapshots of trees on or near the school grounds and collect samples of their leaves. Following the experience activity, a LEAD-style discussion is opened by the teacher, using the listed terms to ask questions—"Does the leaf you brought back have a

FIGURE 3–10   Using a Guest Speaker to Provide a Vicarious Experience Activity for LEAD

Level: intermediate grades

Subject: Social Studies

Topic: a part of the United States that most or all of the students haven't seen

Background: This is a classroom in a rural area of a midwestern state. The topic of the next chapter in the social studies text is the state of Alaska. The students have not used the LEAD strategy before, so the teacher introduces it first as a strategy, explaining that they will be learning important vocabulary through LEAD, by using the three steps: Listing, Experience Activity, and Discussion.

Rationale for topic choice: For these students, Alaska is an unfamiliar area; however, one of the other teachers in the school has traveled there several times, and has slides and souvenirs to show. The two teachers have arranged a swap. Ms. Juneau will show slides and begin a discussion while her students are in art class. Next week Mr. Madison will come to her class (while his class is in the library) to help with final preparations for a science fair display.

Step 1, Listing: On the day before the guest speaker, the teacher explains the LEAD strategy, and students scan the text chapter. Together teacher and students list these terms: *Inuits, Aleuts, natural resources, Arctic Circle, strait, permafrost, tundra, hydroelectric power, Bering Sea, grizzly bears, Tongass*

National Forest, logging, Trans-Alaska pipeline. Students and teacher practice asking questions (such as they might ask the guest speaker) using one or more of the terms in LEAD style—that is, deliberately using sophisticated terminology. ("Have you been to the Bering Sea?" "Are there grizzly bears in the Tongass National Forest?") Several of the students volunteer to make a list of the terms and take them to Ms. Juneau.

Step 2, Experience Activity: Ms. Juneau shows slides and passes around some of the items she has brought back from her trips. Because she knows the LEAD terminology in advance, she uses it whenever she can, and she may also add terms to the class list.

Step 3, Discussion: Ms. Juneau allows time at the end of her talk for student questions. Both she and Mr. Madison restate questions occasionally to model the LEAD style. While she is speaking, students may, if they wish, take notes. In this case the discussion has two stages, because Mr. Madison continues a LEAD-style discussion in the class after the speaker leaves.

Follow-up: The class moves directly from discussion to text reading. Later, as part of cooperative group work, students make small drawings of something related to Alaska that they learned about from the guest speaker. These will be cut out and combined into a montage to be used as a message of thanks for Ms. Juneau.

pinnate or palmate shape?" "Who has a leaf with palmate venation?"—that elicit vocabulary use by students. Students can ask one another questions, or make comments, using technical terms listed on the vocabulary chart. Factual questions may lead to inferential ones: "Did we collect more leaves from deciduous trees or from evergreens? If we bundle up warmly and take another walk in January, will the results be the same?" (Because responses to that question will be different depending on the place where the students live, a good follow-up question would be to ask classes in Florida to predict seasonal differences in Vermont, and vice versa.)

The LEAD strategy is unusual in being more easily used with younger children than with older

students, because middle and high school students may be reluctant to engage in LEAD-style conversations. For older students who are working with tools and machines, however, LEAD may be very useful, because students can readily understand the importance of becoming familiar with the technical terminology. (Of course, an adept teacher with good classroom rapport, who likes the strategy, is likely to be able to adapt and use it successfully at any grade.) If students are reluctant to use LEAD-style conversation during the discussion step, the teacher can be the LEAD talker, and accept responses that are not in the LEAD style until students begin to pick up the new fashion of talking. Teachers who enjoy using humor often find LEAD a congenial strategy. Other strategies can be productively linked with it. LEAD provides an excellent basis for learning log entries, both written text and illustrations. For younger students, the experience activity is a useful topic for a Daily Journal entry or for a scrapbook journal.

LEAD is a lively way to teach a large amount of related technical vocabulary before reading. The strategy is strongly focused on speaking, but listening and reading (scanning text during the listing step) also are exercised. Each of the three steps is a process in which everyone in the class participates, and even students who do not often speak have the experience of hearing the terminology used repeatedly. Like all instructional methods that present words both visually and orally, LEAD links the written and spoken forms of technical terms. Such linking is important to ensure that students' prior knowledge of words, through hearing them, can be applied to their reading. There is an old joke in which an unsophisticated reader asks for more information about MacHinery, who is mentioned often in a book; the puzzled teacher eventually realizes that the apparently unfamiliar term is *machinery*. It is not uncommon for words in a readers' listening vocabulary to be unrecognized in print (Goodman, 1970); if *chaos*, for example, is read as *chayoze*, then the printed word will not be matched with any prior information about the concept gained from hearing about it. People talking about transitions may hear and use a word that sounds to them like *segway*, but they may not recognize that word—*segue*—when they see it in print. The word *rapport*, meaning a trusting relationship, is frequently used by educators but may be misspelled if users do not connect the spoken word (pronounced *ruh-pore*) with its written form. An important consideration in teaching technical vocabulary is to ensure that the spoken and written forms of technical terms are connected, and LEAD helps to accomplish this.

Inferring Word Meanings: Focused Cloze.   Variations of the versatile cloze technique, originated by Wilson Taylor (1953, 1956), are useful when vocabulary instruction is provided before reading. At its simplest, a standard cloze passage consists of a text passage (usually between 200 and 300 words), from which words have been omitted on a regular basis,

e.g., a blank substituted for every tenth word. Reconstructing the passage is a kind of puzzle that can be solved based primarily on language and reading ability, and secondarily on knowledge about the topic of the passage. In Focused Cloze passages, the words are not omitted regularly and randomly; instead the omitted words are carefully chosen to teach content area information. Only significant words or terms are omitted, with the missing terms provided in an alphabetized word list at the beginning or end of the passage. The students' task is to infer the meaning of the technical terms from the context of the passage and to place the listed terms correctly to complete the cloze. Focused Cloze differs from standard cloze not only in the way words are chosen for omission, but also in the inclusion of a list of terms in which each omitted word or phrase is listed. If a term is omitted several times, it is listed that many times. Why is this necessary? In Focused Cloze, the omitted terms are predominantly technical vocabulary, or terms that students may not even be aware of before working with the passage. Therefore, students must be able to see a list of the terms they are to work with.

It may seem surprising that unknown terms can be learned by using them in this way, but a well-constructed Focused Cloze passage provides enough

The Search Tasks strategy serves two purposes. An important section of text is introduced by focusing students' attention on text information, which later will be read carefully. The strategy also develops the important skill of searching text to find information, which is part of "reading to do."

context so that students can see where the different terms fit into a content-related passage. The Focused Cloze passage shown in Figure 3–11 (which contains 229 words when completed) is written to teach three related technical terms: *igneous, metamorphic,* and *sedimentary.* Thoughtful reading of the passage enables students to complete it correctly. As they do so, they are introduced to important facts about the topic to be studied, and learn new technical vocabulary in a way that makes it memorable. Learning about the derivations of the terms contributes to correct, detailed recall of these words and their meaning. Instead of remembering only that *igneous* describes one of three kinds of rock, students are likely to remember that igneous rocks are formed by great heat because the connection among *igneous, ignite,* and *ignition* has been shown.

Once a Focused Cloze passage has been written or selected, the teacher's task is to choose words for omission, and to prepare the cloze in the format in which it will be presented to the class; thereafter they are usable repeatedly. A Focused Cloze exercise should ordinarily not be longer than a single page with about 8 to 15 omitted terms. The amount of time needed to complete a Focused Cloze depends on students' reading and writing skill, and how challenging the passage is. Although Focused Cloze can be used in assessment (a topic discussed in Chapter Eight), the strategy is misused if the teacher presents it as an instructional method but, in fact, treats it as a test. An example of this would be using a Focused Cloze activity to assess students' knowledge before a topic has been taught, and forbidding students to work together. (This kind of misuse of a strategy shows the teacher does not understand it.) The cloze and the setting in which it is presented must be structured so that students are given a challenge, not a fill-in-the-blanks task they can complete without thought, but one in which they can readily be successful, Figure 3–11.

Typical to Technical Meaning.   A subset of technical vocabulary, specialized vocabulary, consists of apparently familiar words that have unfamiliar meanings within the content area. Such terminology occurs often in content text. In textbooks for primary children, such words may be easy to read, and may even be on lists of "easy words," or words that

---

FIGURE 3–11   Focused Cloze

Complete the passage by writing the listed words in the blanks. These are the words to be used: *hot, igneous, igneous, metamorphic, metamorphic, rocks, sedimentary, sedimentary, sedimentary, three.*

There are _____ classifications of _____, and the names for them are based on how the rocks were formed. Some rocks were formed when molten lava, which is rock material that is so hot that it is a liquid, was pushed up from far below the earth. The center of the earth is very _____, but when lava reaches the earth's surface it cools, hardens, and eventually breaks apart into rocks. The term _____ *rock* comes from a Latin word, *ignis,* which means *fire.* It is related to the more familiar words, *ignite* and *ignition.*

Other rocks are called _____ rocks. Have you ever mixed a powdered drink and found that some bits of the powder didn't dissolve? This material that settles at the bottom of the glass is called *sediment,* from a Latin word meaning *to settle.* Some rocks were formed when small fragments of minerals were pressed together so intensely that they formed into rocks, and these are the _____ rocks.

Sometimes both _____ and _____ rocks become changed by heat, pressure, or other causes. The name for the kind of rocks that are produced when other rocks are changed comes from two Greek words: *meta,* which means *change,* and *morphe,* which means *form.* _____ rocks are changed in form. Marble is a _____ rock, which is a harder form of the sedimentary rock, limestone.

Answers to Figure 3–11 can be found in the Solutions section at the back of this book.

children typically learn to read early. For example, children are familiar with the word *rich*. They can read it, and they understand its typical meaning. However, when the word is applied to areas of ground (e.g., the soil is rich) *rich* has a technical meaning that teachers will need to explain. The words *contract, impulse, motor,* and *nervous* are likely to be a part of the listening and speaking vocabularies of intermediate and middle school students, who may not understand their technical meanings when they appear in a chapter on the nervous system. An added complication occurs when words such as *contract* change, in content text, to a different part of speech with a different pronunciation. The Typical to Technical Meaning (TTM) approach (Johnson and Pearson, 1984; Welker, 1987) is designed for vocabulary instruction when the text contains several instances of specialized vocabulary.

Typical to Technical Meaning activities can be created for students in grade 2 and above, and can be adapted for younger students by using manipulable materials after a teacher-led discussion of terms. After typical and technical word meanings have been discussed, students, working individually with the opportunity to consult in pairs or small groups, complete teacher-prepared TTM pages that guide them to use the words correctly, and, if appropriate, provide information about word derivations that will enhance recall. It is productive of better learning for all students to work together to complete the assignment; younger students should certainly work in pairs or small groups because reading is likely to be difficult for some. TTM activities are somewhat time consuming to prepare, but, like Focused Cloze materials, once prepared they can be used each time the topic is studied, even if the textbook is changed. Depending on the maturity of the students (younger students need a longer time to read and write) the time needed for a TTM activity will vary from approximately 5 to 15 minutes, and TTMs should include an activity at the end that accommodates those who finish early. A useful strategy to follow TTMs is Concept Connections, a strategy that provides a way for students to exercise their newly developed fund of terminology.

Teacher preparation for TTM consists of identifying terms that have both a typical and a technical meaning, and creating exercises to give students practice in differentiating between the two. The teacher introduces the strategy and gives illustrations of words that have both a typical and technical meaning. When there is a useful link between the two, the teacher should point this out as a way of helping students remember technical meanings. For example, in math, a teacher might discuss the common meaning of *acute*—"That's an acute observation"—and also discuss the less familiar antonym, *obtuse*—"If you don't see what's going on, you're being really obtuse." After drawing examples of acute and obtuse angles, the teacher could ask the class which angles would better illustrate being sharp and acute, and which would better illustrate being dull and obtuse.

Figure 3–12 gives an example of a TTM exercise for older students that includes information about word derivations. An activity for younger students might focus on map-related words (e.g., "Step on the scale to weigh yourself," or "Using a scale, we can figure out the distance between two places"). Such a Typical to Technical Meaning exercise could be introduced this way: "Remember a few weeks ago when we were learning, in science, that all animals have protective coverings on their bodies? We found some words that we use all the time that had a different meaning when we were studying animals. Do you remember some of them?" (Students will probably contribute scales, and they may also remember down and plates and hide.) "Good! The typical, everyday meaning for scale is something we use to weigh ourselves. Some of you may practice scales on the piano, and that's a different meaning. A fish's scales are small, hard plates that are part of its skin. That's the technical meaning for scales, when we're studying animals. And when we're studying animals and learn about down, what's the technical meaning?" (Expected answer: the soft feathers on a baby bird.) "Right! We studied typical and technical meanings when we were learning about animals, and today we have another Typical and Technical Meaning assignment to complete about maps. I have enough pages for everyone to have one, and I want you to work with your partner. If you and your partner want to work on the same page and just turn in one, be sure you both sign

FIGURE 3–12   Using the Typical to Technical Meaning Strategy in a Life Science Course

Level: middle school or high school
Subject: Life Science
Topic: the circulatory system
Background: This is the first time students have used the TTM strategy, so the teacher begins with a brief explanation.
Introduction: "Suppose you're in the kitchen at home, and your mother comes in, looks at the table, and says, 'What key is this?' What is she looking at?" (Expected responses from students: a key on the table, a house key, a door key, a car key. Imaginative students may suggest a map key or a piano key; don't discourage them, but look for probable answers.) "Sure, a key that locks and unlocks something. Now suppose you're in a music class, looking at a piece of music, and the teacher says, 'What key is this?' What does the teacher mean?" (Expected responses: key of C, tonic key.) "Right. The word *key* has an ordinary, typical meaning, but it has a technical meaning for musicians that's different. Suppose you're still in music class, and the teacher is talking about an organ. What's an organ like?" (Expected responses: big, plays music, has pipes, hear it in church. If there's an imaginative response, rephrase the question: "What's a musical organ like?") "Yes. When we hear the word *organ*, we typically think about a musical organ. But when we study the human body, *organ* has a technical meaning. Our next textbook chapter is about the human circulatory system, and quite a few technical terms that are used have ordinary, typical meanings also. So we'll begin with a Typical to Technical Meaning assignment. Everyone should complete one." (Hand them out.) "I'll expect you to confer with someone sitting near you. Make sure everyone has at least one partner to work with. I'm confident that you can figure out the directions, but I'll be walking around to see how you're doing, and I'll be glad to answer questions."

* * * * * * * * * * * * * * * *

Typical to Technical Meaning Name _____

The major <u>organ</u> in the circulatory system is the heart. The human heart has four major parts, or <u>chambers</u>, two on the left and two on the right. The chambers on the right side of the heart receive blood from the veins, and send it on to the lungs, where carbon dioxide is removed and oxygen is added. The blood returns to the left side of the heart, and from here blood <u>vessels</u> called arteries and capillaries carry it to all parts of the body. The blood returns to the right side of the heart through blood vessels called veins. The <u>circulation</u> of blood is a continuous process.

The four words underlined in this paragraph are important in our study of the circulatory system. We need to know their technical meanings. They are also words that have other more common meanings. In each of the following sentences, find one of the underlined words from the paragraph, underline it in the sentence, and put a check in either the "typical" or "technical" column to show whether the word is used in its typical sense, or has a technical, scientific meaning related to the circulatory system.

Typical	Technical	
❏	❏	Capillaries are blood vessels that are smaller than arteries or veins.
❏	❏	Many ocean-going vessels carry oil from one country to another.
❏	❏	Many people enjoy listening to organ music.
❏	❏	Rumors stay in circulation because people gossip.
❏	❏	The circulation of blood through the body is necessary for life.
❏	❏	The four chambers of the heart are the right atrium, right ventricle, left atrium, and left ventricle.
❏	❏	The judge's chambers are at the back of the courtroom.
❏	❏	The newspaper is trying to increase its circulation.
❏	❏	The heart is the organ of the body that pumps blood to the lungs.

These words—in both their typical and technical meanings—are derived from words in languages that

FIGURE 3–12   Continued

were spoken long ago. Often knowing the derivation of a word helps us to remember its meaning. You'll be able to make intelligent guesses about the derivation of each of the underlined words. Is it okay to check your guesses in the dictionary if you want to? Sure!

> Which word comes from the Greek word *ergon*, meaning *work*?
> Which word comes from the Latin word *camera*, meaning *a room*?

Which word comes from the Latin word *circulari*, meaning *to form a circle*?
Which word comes from the Latin word *vas*, meaning *a container or dish*—the same word that *vase* comes from?

Choose one of the words and explain how you think its Greek or Latin origin is related to its technical meaning.

your names to it. I'll be walking around to see how you're doing, and I'll help if you get stuck."

Rousing Students' Curiosity and Attention

People are naturally curious. David Berlyne (1965) originated the phrase "epistemic curiosity" to refer to the desire for knowledge. *Epistemic* is derived from a Greek word meaning *knowledge*, which elsewhere in this text is called more simply "wanting to know." Experiencing surprise or uncertainty, or becoming aware of contradictions among one's ideas are ways of arousing students' curiosity and thus their desire to find out more. There are many strategies that can be used to catch students' attention as the study of a topic begins. Two alerting strategies that are related are **discrepant** events and refutational teaching. The discrepant events strategy is designed to focus students' attention on a topic by providing an experience that contradicts their experience or does not fit with what they expect. The refutational teaching strategy is designed to correct misunderstandings; the discrepant events strategy may be incorporated as part of refutational teaching.

Both discrepant events and refutational teaching are most frequently used in science teaching, but teachers with a strong store of content knowledge may identify activities or information to serve as the basis for discrepant events for use in other content areas. Although it is always useful to catch students'

attention (which is a feature of discrepant events) and never too soon to begin teaching accurate information (which is a focus of refutational teaching), both strategies are probably best used in the intermediate grades and above. Younger children need many experiences that give them an understanding of the way the world works. They are likely to accept what may seem surprising (i.e., discrepant) to older students and adults, because so much of what occurs in the world is new to them. For young learners, it is most useful to present correct information clearly and vividly, thus making it likely that misconceptions will not be formed.

Discrepant Events.   If something is discrepant, it does not fit. Alfred Friedl is among the science educators who advocate beginning science lessons by presenting a discrepant event. "A good discrepant event tends to create a strong feeling in the observer. Generally, there will be an inner feeling of 'wanting to know'" (Friedl, 1995, p. 3). Suggestions for activities, demonstrations, and experiments that can be used as discrepant events can be found in

---

discrepancy and **discrepant**—come from a Latin prefix *dis-*, which in this case means *apart*, and the Latin verb *crepare*, which means *to rattle*. When there is a discrepancy, things that do not fit together have been combined. A machine that is built from ill-fitting parts will rattle, and eventually come apart.

textbooks, professional journals, magazines, and trade books. Well-prepared trade books are a particularly good resource because they are written by scholar-educators who have in-depth knowledge of particular topics as well as knowledge of the student audiences for which they are written. Moreover, the trade books can be kept in the classroom as reading and reference material for students, while they also serve as resources for the teacher. For example, the fact that light bends is itself puzzling, and a demonstration of bending light is a useful discrepant event. Steve Tomecek's *Bouncing and Bending Light* (1995) and Bernie Zubrowski's *Mirrors: Finding out about the properties of light* (1992) are useful resources. Teachers can choose demonstrations that they will provide or experiments that students can perform themselves. Cooperative groups can also use the books themselves to select and prepare a demonstration for the class.

In social studies, an accurate but partial description of an actual event can, until the full explanation is provided, seem puzzling. Presenting such an account can serve as a discrepant event, and as a thinking challenge for students as they engage in brainstorming possible ways to account for the apparent **anomaly**. Figure 3–13 gives an example of such a story—a report of an actual historical occurrence (based on Wilford, 1982) in which the king of a country arranged for a task to be accomplished, was pleased with the result, yet made a statement that would ordinarily be an expression of strong displeasure. Using the story as a thinking challenge could provide an introduction for any of several topics.

Refutational teaching. As stated previously, across all content areas, new ideas are better understood when they can be related to accurate prior knowledge. The truth of this statement is generally acknowledged. Often the idea is expressed this way: Across all content areas, new ideas are better under-

FIGURE 3–13   Example of a Discrepant Event in the Form of a Partial Account of a Historical Event

? ? ? W H Y ? ? ?

During the latter half of the seventeenth century, a man was employed by the King of France to undertake a certain task.

After the man had worked for a long time, the king came to see what he had accomplished.

When the king saw what had been done, he was pleased, but he said, "Your work has cost me a large part of my state."

Why?
Brainstorm a long list of possible reasons, and then select the most likely ones.

✶ ✶ ✶ ✶ ✶ ✶ ✶ ✶ ✶ ✶ ✶ ✶ ✶

▮ Do you think it will be easier to do some research about the king, or about the man who worked for him?
▮ Find out five interesting facts about one of these people, and one interesting fact about the other.

© 1985 by Learning Packages. Used by permission of Sunshower Learning Packages.

(Answers to Figure 3–13 can be found in the Solutions section at the back of this book.)

stood when they can be related to prior knowledge. Careful readers of the two sentences will note that the second statement is shorter than the first by one word: the second statement refers to prior knowledge, whereas the first refers to *accurate* prior knowledge.

Students are likely to begin the study of a topic with some prior knowledge—that is, with a limited store of relevant information. It is difficult for anyone to learn about a topic that is wholly new to them, so teachers often need to introduce topics by building knowledge for their students, and it is the purpose of this chapter to describe many good introductory strategies. In most cases, building a knowledge

---

anomaly and **anomalous**—composed of the Greek prefix *an-*, meaning *not*, and the root word *homalous*, meaning *even*. An anomaly is something that is not even with, not the same as, other things with which it is grouped.

base by giving relevant new information directly or indirectly constitutes a sound introduction. In some cases, learners approach a new topic with a foundation of *incorrect* knowledge, a beginning that hampers future learning. In this case, refutational teaching is useful. Researchers and scholars (e.g., Chinn & Brewer, 1993; Guzzetti, Snyder, & Glass, 1992; Hynd & Alvermann, 1989; Maria & MacGinitie, 1987) have written extensively in recent years about the power of prior misconceptions to inhibit learning. People who enter into the study of a topic with an established set of *incorrect* ideas are less likely to learn successfully than people who begin with no prior knowledge of the topic. "Knowing" false information interferes with learning much more than having no prior information, and, therefore, activating prior knowledge—when that knowledge is incorrect—should not be attempted.

Experienced teachers are likely to be aware of the topics where students are hampered by prior misconceptions. Mark Schug and Eddie Baumann (1991, p. 62) observed high school economics teachers identified as excellent, and wrote, "We contend that successful teachers understand the type of confusion students are likely to have with particular subject matter. Almost intuitively, those teachers design lessons and formulate explanations that quickly correct common misunderstandings and pave the way for new learning to take place." Skillful teachers use refutational teaching as an introductory strategy only when necessary. As Richard Prawat (1991) has pointed out, effective teachers know that with guidance, students can often learn from and correct mistakes. In preparing to use refutational teaching, personal experience (as teacher or student), or conversations with experienced teachers, can be the basis for compiling a list of common misconceptions in content area fields—not cases in which students study a topic without learning, but situations in which students have firmly held incorrect beliefs. The next important steps are to reason and confer about why these misconceptions are a result of reasonable thinking, to decide what information people who have the misconception are lacking, and to decide on ways to eradicate the mistaken view and replace it with solid understanding.

Science is the field in which factual misconceptions are most likely to exist. The development of scientific theory across the centuries has been interrelated with the development of scientific technology. The invention of telescopes and microscopes enabled scientists to provide evidence for increasingly accurate theories about the nature of the world. High speed photography is a fairly recent branch of technology that enables one to grasp scientific truths. Nonscientists have relatively little access to sophisticated technology, so we tend—like people hundreds and thousands of years ago—to develop ideas about how the world works on the basis of our own observations. It is useful to note that commonly held scientific fallacies typically correspond to theories that were held by ancient scientists. Thus they are not the result of foolish or frivolous error, but of naive observations based on incomplete data. For example, many adults, asked why it is warmer in summer than in winter, will answer that in summer the earth is closer to the sun. There is a reasonable basis for this incorrect view. First, we have many experiences in which warmth increases with proximity to a source of heat; we draw close to a campfire to get warm and move away when the heat is too strong. Second, knowing that the earth's orbit around the sun is an ellipse, we are aware that the distance between the earth and the sun varies throughout a year. But to understand accurately why temperature varies throughout the year in the earth's temperate zones, we must include in our mental schema the information that the earth is tilted as it revolves around the sun, causing the sun's rays to strike portions of the earth directly during part of the year (and then it is summer), and indirectly at other times so that the rays are diffused over a wider surface and are less intense (in winter). It is also useful to keep in mind that the distance between the earth and the sun is so vast that differences at varying points in the earth's orbit cannot have significant effects on temperature.

It is difficult, however, for people to give up an established idea. In a recent review of research relating to educational attempts to encourage conceptual change, Clark Chinn and William Brewer (1993, p. 4) summarize the ways people respond to information that does not fit with a theory or belief that they hold. Suppose a person believes in Theory A. The person receives anomalous data; i.e., new information that

Theory A cannot explain. "[T]here are seven basic responses: a) *ignore* the anomalous data, b) *reject* the data, c) *exclude* the data from the domain of Theory A, d) hold the data in *abeyance*, e) reinterpret the data while retaining Theory A, f) reinterpret the data and make *peripheral changes* to Theory A, and g) accept the data and *change* Theory A, possibly in favor of Theory B." Thus of seven possible ways to react to new information that does not fit an established theory, only one is to accept the information and change the theory. How can instruction in our schools be improved, so that people will not progress through school, and often through college and university programs as well, still clinging to false beliefs and erroneous theories? The basic corrective—and a theme of this text—is for teachers at every level to have a strong, and growing, knowledge base. If early science instruction is affected by teachers' naive views, students will find it difficult to learn accurate information later.

Powerful, straightforward refutational teaching is an effective resource for teachers to use in combating misconceptions. (The word *refute* is derived from Latin words meaning *to beat back*, so the metaphor of a fight or struggle against incorrect notions is a sound one.) Effective refutational teaching depends on the teacher's understanding both of the correct information and the common error, and begins with the teacher presenting correct information directly, and later stating explicitly that the erroneous view is wrong. Correct information may be given by telling or through demonstration in a variety of ways, and by engaging students in relevant experiments followed by discussion. It is not effective to present the two views together in a neutral way and expect students to change their views. At present, most textbooks rarely provide refutational

---

anticipation—looks like a word that combines a Latin root with the prefix *anti-* (meaning *against*, or *opposed to*), which would make the derivation puzzling. There is nothing about anticipation that relates to being opposed to something. The Latin prefix is not *anti-*; it is *ante-* (meaning *before*) and the Latin root word is *capere* (meaning *to take*), which has become *cipere*. To anticipate an event is to capture or take hold of an idea of it, before it occurs.

text, and when they do, the text alone is insufficient to cause students to alter their misconceptions (Hynd & Alvermann, 1986). When textbook authors are writing to refute a misconception they may begin with an extensive and persuasive description of the erroneous view before going on to present the refutation. This may result in students' misconceptions being reinforced, rather than eradicated.

It is the heart of the refutational teaching strategy for teachers to give students correct information directly. The purpose of refutational teaching is to alter learners' cognitive schemas and, in the process, new connections among ideas can be made. For example, in the refutational teaching illustrated in Figure 3–14, students' knowledge of the earth's rotation on its axis is integrated with their knowledge about the earth's revolution around the sun. Once the correct information has been provided, it must be illustrated and demonstrated repeatedly and vividly. Experiments, field trips, and guest speakers who are authorities in their fields, audiovisual materials, and trade books illustrated with photographs are good resources to supplement clear presentations by teachers. Another introductory strategy, the Teacher Read-Aloud Commentary, works well when refutational text is read aloud to students or provided for students to read. Writing and drawing models in learning logs are excellent ways for students to develop and demonstrate their understanding, and the use of learning logs enables teachers to assess student understanding and determine when reteaching is needed. It is essential that student learning not be superficial—learning only to repeat correct information without grasping it, while the misconception remains established in their thinking. Another risk to be avoided is that students may develop a scornful attitude toward people who hold incorrect views. One aspect of good refutational instruction is to teach that there are reasons underlying even mistaken ideas, and that it is foolish, as well as unkind, to use knowledge as a way of showing disrespect for others.

Creative Anticipatory Thinking

When refutational teaching is used, teachers are basing instruction on their own **anticipation** (based on knowledge and experience) that students' prior

FIGURE 3–14   Using Refutational Teaching in a Science Program

Level: intermediate grades
Subject: Science
Topic: What causes seasonal changes?
Background: The teacher is aware of the common misconception that seasonal changes are caused by the earth's varying distances from the sun during a year, and believes it is very important for students to learn, grasp, and accept accurate information.

Process: The teacher uses a series of activities, in this sequence:
First day (must be a sunny day): Teacher explanation, read-aloud, experiment (materials prepared in advance), film.

The teacher opens the lecture with five minutes of giving information explicitly, explaining how the earth's tilted axis causes the sun's rays to strike the temperate zones of the earth at different angles in the course of its yearly revolution around the sun. The teacher uses a globe as a visual aid, and points out the temperate zones

The teacher has displayed a copy of the trade book, *The reasons for seasons: The great cosmic megagalactic trip without moving from your chair* (Allison, 1975), open to a description of a science experiment in which students paint tops of tin cans with flat black paint and set them in a sunny window so that one faces the sun's rays directly and the other is at an angle to the sun's rays. The teacher reads the relevant section aloud, and assigns each cooperative group to set up their two previously-painted cans as described in the trade book excerpt.

Library time: The students see a film that presents the concept.
Return from library: Check tin cans to see which is warmer.

Second day: Teacher explanation, brief discussion, cooperative group textbook reading and RESPONSE, question-answer session. The teacher concludes the les-

son with a Teacher Read-Aloud Commentary on "Why is summer warmer than winter?" from *Isaac Asimov's Guide to Earth and Space* (Asimov, 1993).

Third day: Teacher response to questions raised on RESPONSE forms. During this time, the teacher summarizes the incorrect view (rereading a portion of the "Sunny Side Up" from the trade book, which is still on display) and explains why this idea is wrong. This is followed by class discussion. Students write in learning logs about what they have learned.

Fourth day: Students complete a teacher-prepared Focused Cloze in pairs, followed by whole class review of the Focused Cloze passage and group summarization of important points learned. Cooperative groups discuss plans for a transmediation assignment.

Follow-up: The immediate follow-up activity is for students, working in cooperative groups, to present their learning in transmediated form, e.g., through art, dramatization, or a simulated debate between those holding the correct and the erroneous views. An additional follow-up activity involves math. With teacher guidance, students find the minimum and maximum distances between the earth and the sun as the earth orbits the sun, and subtract to find the difference between the two. The class then considers the improbability that such a difference so tiny, in relation to the vast distance between sun and earth even when they are closest, could create the substantial differences in temperature that occur between winter and summer.

This teacher is one of those who make it a practice to annotate their planbooks, so that they are reminded to return to important topics periodically throughout the year. The class will revisit this topic briefly twice more during the year, and again in June. Such revisiting may be as brief as giving cooperative groups, as one of many activities in a week, the assignment to answer the question, "Why is it hot in the summertime?"

naive thinking needs to be corrected before useful learning about the topic can occur. The teacher's anticipatory planning sets the stage for good learning. Occasionally, it can be productive to engage students in a different kind of anticipatory thinking. Usually it is unwise to discuss topics without having information

about them. However, when four conditions (relating to topic, teacher, and students) are met, anticipatory discussion can be useful.

▮ The topic must be one about which students do not have prior misconceptions or biases. Anticipatory activities are not useful where refutational teaching is needed, nor when the topic of study concerns groups or situations about which some students may have prejudices. It is counterproductive and actively harmful to elicit false opinions as a pre-reading activity.

▌ The teacher must have a strong knowledge base about the topic.

▌ The teacher must feel comfortable in structuring or creating activities that will engage students in divergent thinking, that is, in generating many, diverse, original ideas. (The ability to think divergently is often considered a sign of creativity, as is a lively sense of humor.)

▌ The teacher must structure the classroom situation so that students feel comfortable about offering many ideas and **inferences,** and are able to hear the ideas of others with interest (and without scorn). In both of the following strategies, Significant Sayings and Creative Reasoning Guides, students will be generating many ideas. This kind of fluency in divergent thinking is hampered if some ideas are rejected (by the teacher or by other students) when they are offered.

These strategies are best used with older students (high school or middle school) whose cognitive development is advanced enough for them to look at information from multiple viewpoints. Extensive teacher knowledge, rather than extensive preparation time, is a prerequisite for strategy use, although creation of a Creative Reasoning Guide requires some time to get the wording right, so that the information is fully accurate while presenting a challenging puzzle. Using either strategy productively typically takes portions of two days but subsequent study of topics is likely to be enhanced because these introductory activities

---

inference—the Latin prefix and root are *in-* and *ferre*, a form of a verb meaning *to carry* or *bring*. Someone who makes an inference brings in a new idea, based on existing information.

prediction—the Latin prefix and Latin root are *pre-* (meaning *before*) and *dicere* (meaning *to tell*). A prediction is a before-telling.

awaken students' attention and interest. One caution to keep in mind is that any strategy based on **prediction** can go badly wrong if its effect is to create an atmosphere in which some students feel superior to others because they can "predict correctly," often on the basis of prior knowledge, and thus not predicting at all. "Check to see if your predictions were correct," is, unfortunately, a common direction to students, and one that discourages scientific reasoning as well as creative thinking because it implies that identifying one known correct answer is the goal of all thought.

Significant Sayings. One useful way of engaging students in thinking analytically and creatively about a future topic of study is to present brief quotations that are integrally related to the topic, particularly those that suggest varying points of view. Discussions based on the quotations can lead to predictions about what is to be read. The example shown in Figure 3–15 presents a Significant Sayings process to use in introducing a textbook section on American foreign policy at the turn of the last century.

Creative Reasoning Guides. Even more than for the Significant Sayings strategy, the use of Creative Reasoning Guides requires teacher knowledge, and teacher interest in encouraging and valuing diverse ideas. The strategy should be used only when students do not have prior misconceptions or prejudices, and is best used in a situation in which students have very little prior knowledge. The strategy provides an engaging way of approaching topics that are typically considered to be rather drab.

The Creative Reasoning Guide strategy begins with a teacher-prepared guide to be completed in cooperative groups, Figure 3–16. This presents fully accurate—but not fully explained—information about events that will be studied. The students' task is to consider the information that they have been given, and think of several possible explanations for it. It is useful to establish a "two-thirds rule" for these explanations: At least two out of three must be justifiable on a reasonable basis; one out of three may be as wild as the students can come up with. After the students complete the Guide in their cooperative groups, perhaps over a two-day period, there is class discussion

FIGURE 3–15 Using the Significant Sayings Strategy in an American History Course

Level: high school or middle school

Subject: American History

Topic: Expansionism: annexation of the Philippines

Background: The teacher likes to use this strategy whenever the text topic can be related to short, dramatic quotations from the time period being studied, which illuminate important historical events.

Rationale for topic choice: Three quotations from the time period 1898 through 1904 illustrate differing contemporary points of view about what actions the United States should take toward the Philippines (and also other former Spanish colonies and Hawaii) after winning the Spanish-American War. Emphasizing these quotations helps students realize that there are often very strong differences of opinion before a government takes action, even though afterwards the action, and its results, tend to be accepted and most people may no longer question them or even think about them.

The first saying is a phrase used by expansionists, such as Theodore Roosevelt, then the vice-president of the United States, who advocated annexing the Philippine Islands (that is, making them territory owned by the United States but not part of America as the current forty-five states were). The second saying is from a speech made by William Jennings Bryan, the Democratic presidential candidate in the 1900 campaign. Bryan opposed annexation and supported Philippine independence; he lost the election to William McKinley. The third saying represents one position in cases argued before the Supreme Court between 1901 and 1904: the view that when a territory became controlled by the United States, it became part of the United States and thus people living there were entitled to the protection of the Constitution and the Bill of Rights. The Supreme Court, in a series of decisions made in what are called "the Insular Cases," rejected this view, holding that people in the Philippines and other areas annexed by the United States did not have constitutional rights, such as the right to jury trials.

Process: The teacher has chosen the quotations in advance, and now writes one of them on the chalkboard: "Don't haul down the flag!" The teacher tells the class members to call out words and phrases that

this saying makes them think of, and records the terms on the board. (Note: Each teacher will make an individual choice about how to elicit responses, but permitting or encouraging students to offer their ideas without a process of hand-raising and being called on saves time, encourages many responses, and can work very smoothly.)

When ideas have been listed, the teacher writes the second quotation on the chalkboard: "When we made allies of the Filipinos and armed them to fight against Spain… we had full knowledge that they were fighting for their own independence." Students again generate ideas. The teacher encourages a debate about the two positions: America should keep territory it has acquired vs. Places that want to be independent should be free. Later, the teacher encourages predictions about which view prevailed at the time, and, if possible, the class reaches consensus about a prediction. (In this kind of predicting, students are likely to have enough information to predict accurately, which is, of course, desirable.)

The third quotation—"The Constitution follows the flag"—can be used to generate ideas after the students have read, or been told, that the United States did annex the Philippine Islands, to lead into a discussion about whether people in annexed territories should have the same rights as American citizens. After the discussion, predictions can be made about the Supreme Court's decisions in the Insular Cases.

Follow-up: Following the Significant Sayings strategy, which might span parts of two class sessions (discussion/consensus about the first two quotations on Session 1 and the third at the beginning of Session 2), students read the text section on this topic immediately, individually or in pairs, and then either write in journals or resume class discussion. This lesson and its background suggest a wealth of possibilities for question-raising and brief research. The time period is a fascinating one, and it will also be important to pursue the topic to find out what subsequent decisions have been about human rights in territories held by the United States. Here, as always, teachers with a strong knowledge base can bring history alive for their students.

Note: The quotations used in this Significant Sayings activity were taken from *Addison-Wesley United States History: Presidential Edition*, 1986, pages 412–413 (and can, of course, be found in other sources as well).

of their responses. The teacher uses some of the sensible reasons in giving the students guidance for their reading. The following item might be one of several included in a Creative Reasoning Guide before the class reads a chapter in a world history text.

In the next chapter we will be reading about a nation with a patriotic song claiming that the country "rules the waves."

Keeping the two-thirds rule in mind, think of at least three reasons for this claim.

One group of students might generate these reasons:

The country needed many ships to trade with other countries.

Inventors in this country came up with ideas that made the country's ships better than those of other countries, so their navy was able to defeat other nations' ships in sea battles.

As part of a national holiday and to promote tourism, people in this country (including visitors) measure the waves at seacoast resorts

FIGURE 3–16 Using a Creative Reasoning Guide in the Study of History

Level: high school
Subject: American History
Topic: the presidency of John Adams
Background: The teacher enjoys reading history, trying out new ways to teach, and engaging students in creative thinking activities. It is mid-fall; the teacher is enrolled in a graduate course in content area reading, and has just read in the text about Creative Reasoning Guides.

The teacher's own class has completed the early chapters of the history text, and has been engaged in a variety of activities, including viewing films and listening to the teacher read aloud excerpts from histories, that have made the period of the American Revolution come alive. The next topic to be studied is the period after George Washington's presidency, and the teacher has created a Creative Reasoning Guide as a lively beginning to a period that often appears less interesting than the times that precede and follow it.

* * * * * * * * * * * * * * *

Creative Reasoning Guide 1
Names of Creative Reasoners:

_____

▮ During the American Revolution, the French were our allies. *But in the next chapter,* we're going to read about "how Adams ended the threat of war with France."
At least three reasons, please, why a country that was our ally, in a war that we won, would threaten to go to war against us only a few years later.

▮ History textbooks are packed with names of impor-

tant people. *But in the next chapter,* we'll be reading about three people, regularly mentioned in history books, who are known as X, Y, and Z.
At least three reasons, please, why this might be so.

▮ Candidates from two political parties ran in the presidential election of 1800. President John Adams ran for a second term; his running mate was Charles Pinckney. The candidates opposing them were Thomas Jefferson and Aaron Burr. *But in the next chapter,* we're going to find out that Adams was defeated, and that the House of Representatives, in which Adams' party had the majority, took 36 ballots to decide which of two other candidates should be president.
At least three reasons, please, why this very complicated situation might have happened.

* * * * * * * * * * * * * * *

Students use the Guide in two consecutive class sessions: as the last activity on one day and the first, prior to text reading, on the second day. The teacher realizes fully that between the two sessions students may preread the textbook, or do some research at home, to find accurate reasons for the events listed on the Guide. (Does this annoy the teacher, or indicate that the students are in some way "cheating"? No, it does not! In fact, the teacher arranges for the activity to span two days to allow for such independent research to occur. Does the teacher require students to find correct answers for homework? No. If it happens, the teacher expresses pleasure; that's all.)

After the students have worked on the Guide for a while at the beginning of the second day's session, with

FIGURE 3–16   Continued

the teacher moving from group to group to encourage and enjoy students' responses, the teacher brings the activity to a close and begins a session of whole class sharing of ideas. In several cases, the teacher asks the class to consider how a particular reason can be justified.

At the conclusion of the discussion period, the teacher assigns students to read the textbook in pairs or cooperative groups, looking for justification of one or more of the possible reasons given by the groups. In this case, one of the groups has suggested as a reason for the first item that the United States changed so much that our ally, France, became angry and wanted to go to war against us. The teacher tells students that as they read, they should look for information about the ways that France changed.

Follow-up: After reading the text chapter, the teacher guides discussion about two aspects of this period of history. First, the class learns about the continuing conflict, which did not become a war, with France, and how Adams' actions—those that now seem wise, and those that now seem misguided—were intended to prevent war. (The first two items on the Creative Reasoning Guide lead into this topic.) Second, the class begins to learn about the rise of political parties in this country: a topic for which the third item on the Creative Reasoning Guide provides an introduction. The students also begin to learn about the process of amending the Constitution. Both of these topics will be revisited at various times throughout the history course.

(Notes on Figure 3–16 can be found in the Solutions section at the back of this book.)

(using special rulers), with prizes for people who measure the highest wave.

The first two reasons are sensible, and, in fact, are related to British history. The third reason is just for fun, but is a clever exercise in divergent thinking for the students. Students can go further, creating more answers in either category, while keeping to the guidelines that two-thirds of the answers need to be reasonable. (Of course, there may be discussion about what is reasonable and what is not. Some teachers may want to revise the rule so that once a specified number of reasonable answers have been given, students may continue to create as many unusual ideas as they wish.)

Introducing Topics With Wide Reading

When one enters new territory, it is possible to become overwhelmed if everything there is unfamiliar. Learning occurs more readily if there is a basis for learning, that is, if there is a substantial amount of prior knowledge. A straightforward way of acquiring knowledge about new textbook topics is to begin with relevant reading from other sources. Some years ago, Linda Crafton reported on an experiment conducted in response to a question she had raised—can reading itself provide a support for further reading?—or,

as the title of her article puts it, "What happens when students generate their own background information?" She tested high school students on their understanding of two reading selections. Students in one group read two unrelated selections, and were tested after each reading about the information in that selection. Comprehension scores were similar on both tests. Students in another group read two selections on a related topic, and were also tested after each reading on the information in that selection. In this group, students' comprehension scores were higher on the second test. Prior reading of a related article increased their ability to understand the second selection. Crafton points out that the strategy of reading from a variety of sources about a new topic is one used by successful adult readers.

The findings suggest that natural reading experiences allow readers to construct background information which can be used to comprehend other discourse. The study supports the common view of reading as a natural knowledge-generating activity in which readers incorporate information into developing schemata.... [D]evelopment of a key but unfamiliar concept can be achieved by reading more than one selection on the same topic—materials at varying readability levels but not necessarily with similar or parallel organizations. Students are encouraged to expand and refine their growing understanding of a particular concept by encountering it textually in various styles and organizations and from different perspectives… We, as proficient adult readers, use a like procedure when we encounter a new idea. We seek out multiple materials on the topic without particular regard for readability; rather we approach our task with confidence that what is formidable and unreadable today will become more and more comprehensible as our experience with the topic increases. (Crafton, 1983, p. 591)

Wide reading enables readers to extend prior knowledge by building upon what is already familiar, and students become better readers by reading. The strategy of beginning a new topic of study by providing opportunities for students to select from many related books and articles is versatile; for example, Linda Moniuszko (1992) recommends preparing for guest speakers by reading widely about the guest speaker's topic. When students select from a variety of materials, formal and informal discussions will provide opportunities for information sharing so that the whole class benefits. Wide reading is the natural way to extend vocabulary, and technical vocabulary introduced in textbooks will be encountered repeatedly in content-related trade books and articles. Teachers should expect to explain new terms on request and should encourage students to consult one another also. Students are likely to learn word meanings through context more easily in non-textbook materials than in textbooks, which contain a more concentrated technical vocabulary load. Although it is important to have a variety of reading material available (unless everyone will be reading the same selections) it would violate the strategy if the teacher attempted to replicate a "high," "middle," and "low" reading group atmosphere, picking out some students who could read challenging materials and assigning others only simple materials. Requiring students to write lists of technical terms and definitions, or insisting that there be no sharing of materials and ideas during reading sessions, would also be forms of drifting away from an important strategy into ineffective teaching methods.

Teachers may prepare for wide reading by keeping files of articles and lists of trade books that relate to topics that will be studied throughout

"Epistemic curiosity" is desire for knowledge, or more simply, "wanting to know."

For many topics, adept teachers can take advantage of this natural curiosity when new information is introduced, using the Discrepant Events strategy.

the year. Media specialists, if alerted in advance to the need for reading materials, will often be able to provide a wide range of books for students to borrow, and may perhaps arrange for some books to be lent to the classroom for a period of time. No teacher preparation time is needed once the reading materials are collected; however, books and other reading material must be collected in advance. Once teachers decide to use the strategy, materials collection can be an ongoing process. (Suggestions for developing a classroom collection of books are given in the "Strategic Teachers—'I'm a bookworm on a budget'" section at the end of this chapter.) Although it is not necessary for teachers to read thoroughly everything in the collection before beginning wide reading, if materials have been donated, purchased at book sales, or remaindered from a library, it is important to skim them to weed out any that are biased or outdated and any used materials that are defaced or mutilated. As strategy use continues, teachers should take time to read all the materials; familiarity with them will help in leading good discussions.

The wide reading strategy can be used consistently or occasionally. Because time spent in content area reading is an excellent component of both language arts and content area study, and in middle school and high school teachers teaching different subjects can collaborate to incorporate wide reading on a common topic into their programs. Teachers might plan to begin each new major topic of

study by reading aloud to students and by providing a variety of materials for students to use during periods of Themed Reading. Note that Themed Reading, especially in this case, need not be silent; when wide reading is used as an introductory method it is useful for students to share ideas and materials. Wide reading can precede text use and then continue as the text is studied, so the additional time needed is not impractical. Or, because the strategy requires prior selection of a great deal of reading material, it might be useful to choose two nonconsecutive major topics to introduce with wide reading. In subsequent years or semesters materials for wide reading can be added for use with other topics. Examples of plans for wide reading are shown in Figures 3–17 and 3–18.

Vocabulary Connections (Iwicki, 1992), in which the teacher presents a word and defines it,

FIGURE 3–17   *A Basic Structure for Wide Reading*

Level: middle school or intermediate grades
Subject: Social Studies
Topic: African-American experiences in this country, from slavery to freedom
Background: The teacher believes strongly in the importance of wide reading, both for its value in developing and enhancing reading ability and for the power of reading from excellent trade books to extend understanding of topics introduced in textbooks. At the end of the previous year the teacher asked the principal to purchase fifteen copies each of two trade books. The principal agreed, with the understanding that the book sets would also be shared, at mutually agreeable times, with other classrooms.

Rationale for using wide reading with this topic: The issue of slavery is one of hundreds of topics addressed in history textbooks and its importance is likely to be diminished when treated as one of many topics to be read about briefly. The problem of textbook blandness, discussed in Chapter One, arises. The teacher has chosen two excellent trade books, which supplement one another, to enrich students' learning.

Process: The trade books that the class will use are *Many thousand gone: African Americans from slavery to freedom* (1993) and *The people could fly: American Black*

folktales (1985). Both are by Virginia Hamilton and illustrated by Leo and Diane Dillon. Both contain many short selections: in the former book, factual accounts, in the latter, folktales. Because there are fifteen copies of each book and because each book contains many selections, students have many choices about what to read.

The teacher has selected three excerpts from *Many thousand gone*—"Isabella, Sojourner" (Sojourner Truth), "A slave from Missouri" (Dred Scott), and "Frederick Augustus Washington Bailey" (Frederick Douglass), which everyone in the class is responsible for reading in cooperative groups over a period of four days. The teacher works out a schedule for sharing, so that each group has access to copies of that book on two days. The books are available for free time reading as well. Each student decides on a total of three selections from either or both of the books for personal reading. This reading may be done independently or in pairs or triads. Cooperative groups do the reading as one of several cooperative group activities during the first of a two week unit of study. Students read their individual selections during Themed Reading, and when they have free time.

The wide reading is used as a basis for class discussions, learning log entries, and for transmediation projects. (See the Strategy Glossary.)

FIGURE 3–18 An Extensive Structure for Wide Reading

Level: middle school or intermediate grades

Subjects: Science and Language Arts/English

Topic: solar system, the earth in space, astronomy

Background: Although wide reading is fully practical in a single classroom, in this case two teachers are collaborating. (You may suppose that the teachers are a science teacher and an English teacher working with the same cohort of students in the middle school, or two teachers at the same grade level in elementary school.) The teachers' use of the wide reading strategy, and their application of it to this topic, are based on these beliefs:

▌ This is an important subject with implications for lifelong learning. Space exploration is a scientific frontier, and the learning that students acquire while they are in school will prepare them for interest in the scientific discoveries that will occur during their adult years.

▌ Integration of language arts and content area study is important, so reading and writing that students do is often content related.

▌ Student research, when the research process is to have written work as an end product, must have thorough guidance. In this case, the wide reading strategy will be used as a component of the Structured Research Process (described in Chapter Five).

Rationale for using wide reading with this topic: In science textbooks, the solar system is a topic that recurs annually, yet textbook treatment is necessarily limited. Wide reading provides students with an array of reading materials that can enhance current interests and awaken new ones.

Process: The teachers have collected a variety of trade books with the help of the school media specialist, booksale purchases, and donations to the classroom library. Several class scrapbooks, begun two years before, contain relevant newspaper and magazine articles, and students will add to the scrapbooks throughout the year. Additional materials include an encyclopedia, a space atlas, maps, and a current world almanac. There are also multiple copy sets of several of the trade books that have been purchased for the class so that up to eight students can be reading in the same text simultaneously. These materials are placed on display in a classroom research center, which may be simply a table placed against a part of one wall.

The teachers plan to use the wide reading strategy for a week before a unit on the earth in space is introduced in science, and continue wide reading during a three-week period of study. In science, the students are concluding their study of a textbook unit on weather, and science time is devoted to completion of final group projects. Therefore, for the first week, wide reading will occur as one component of language arts time.

On Monday, the teacher (the English teacher, if we're in the middle school; both teachers, if this is an elementary school) displays and talks briefly about several of the books, prior to a twenty-minute period for exploration and Themed Reading. Book titles are displayed on a wall chart, with an abbreviation for each (e.g., *"Sol."* for Seymour Simon's book, *Our solar system*). Students use individual record sheets to list books (by abbreviation) and page numbers of their daily reading, and notes about important or interesting ideas they've come across. Drawing is also encouraged.

Cooperative groups sign up, two per day, to share some of their discoveries through their reading. This sharing concludes the twenty-minute reading sessions on Tuesday through Friday. On the following Monday, students begin science time in cooperative groups, scanning the textbook unit and making notes about which books have sections relevant to the various chapters and sections, based on their wide reading done in the previous week. The notes are posted on a bulletin board for teacher and students to refer to. (The teachers believe that some bulletin boards should be handsome displays of students' work and others should be used for temporary practical purposes.)

During the second and third weeks, wide reading continues in science where three 10- to 15-minute periods each week are devoted to Themed Reading. The teacher also provides short commentaries, at student request, of selections from reading materials that they find difficult to understand. (See the Teacher Read-Aloud Commentary strategy discussed earlier in this chapter, and the examples of commentaries on resource books presented in Chapter Five.) The books remain available for free reading, and for use in science projects as study of the new unit continues.

and students contribute uses for the word, is among the strategies that can usefully be linked with wide reading. For example, as an introduction to study of the solar system, a teacher provides a wide variety of trade books for students to read. As part of language arts instruction, the teacher chooses the word *atmosphere* to define. Students look for instances of the word in their reading, and contribute informational examples: "The planet Mercury is not protected by an atmosphere, so many meteorites and asteroids crash there, and that's why the surface is covered with craters." "Venus is the hottest planet because it has a thick atmosphere. The sun's rays penetrate the atmosphere and heat the surface of the planet but the heat is trapped there by the atmosphere, so temperatures on Venus reach as high as 900 degrees Fahrenheit." When students have collected several examples in which the term is used in context, it is a whole class or cooperative group activity to prepare and discuss definitions.

Wide reading is increasingly important as students progress across the grades, but the strategy is useful and usable across the grades. Young children can learn from looking at pictures, and hearing content area trade books read aloud. Moreover, children vary in the time they learn to read, and many classrooms of young learners include a few students who are already capable of reading text for their friends. Students in the intermediate grades and above benefit from opportunities for exploration of content related text, including resource books, such as encyclopedias, atlases, and almanacs. Remember Crafton's point (1983, p. 591) that it is useful to have reading materials available "at varying readability levels but not necessarily with similar or parallel organizations."

Establishing a Foundation of Understanding

Effective content area teachers provide lively, thoughtful instruction when topics are introduced, as they are studied, and as learning about one topic blends into study of the next. In evaluating the teaching strategies presented in these chapters, readers are encouraged to consider which of them best fit the strengths and needs of their students (either those they presently teach or those they anticipate teaching in the future), and their own pattern of strengths and needs. It is also useful, when selecting introductory strategies, to consider how they will blend with subsequent teaching. Chapter Four suggests strategies to use in the *during* phase of instruction—methods to guide students as they are in the midst of a new place in their learning.

STRATEGIC TEACHERS: HOW DO THEY DO IT?

Throughout this text, a wide variety of teaching strategies are presented. Given a wealth of strategies to choose from, how does a teacher decide which to use? What are some good possibilities for combining many different strategies, so that effective instruction is provided before, during, and after a topic is studied, and students have opportunities to learn in a variety of ways?

Decision-making is a part of good teaching. Although it may be easier to make decisions when the choices are limited—a person who knows two ways to teach only has to ask, shall I use A, or shall I use B?—the process is more enjoyable when there are many possibilities and many ways to combine them.

Here (and at the end of eight other chapters), the process of choosing strategies is illustrated through descriptions of simulated classroom teachers who have made their choices based on their teaching assignments, their philosophies, their personal interests, and their life situations.

The teachers described in these sections are imaginary, but they are based on people like you. They are composites of teachers who have been my colleagues and my students over the years. As you read about each teacher, you will notice that I have described that teacher—but I have usually not described their students, except to tell what subjects they are learning, and identify their grade or school level (which provides implicit information about students' developmental levels). Why is it unnecessary to describe the characteristics of each teacher's students? Why do the teachers themselves not choose strategies by trying to match the special needs of subgroups within their classrooms? Because *their classrooms are the same every year in one important way: Every student is different.*

Every year each teacher has students who read very well. (This is true even for the first-grade teacher.) There are other students whose reading is not yet skillful. There are students who come into the class interested in learning and others who begin the year unhappy and resistant; students with extensive prior knowledge about subject matter they will be learning and students with very little; students who have read (or been read to) extensively and have an excellent command of the English language, others whose primary language is not English, and yet others whose prior experience of books is severely limited. Every year some students enter after school has begun and others move away. Students get sick; some families extend vacation time before and after holidays. Some families set aside a regular time and place for homework as a household routine; in some families no attention is paid to students' assignments, while a few children are punished or heavily rewarded because of what happens in school. There are students from happy homes and homes beset by troubles, and the teachers know that every year between September and June many events—some joyous, some painful—will cause significant changes in students' home lives. Every year most of their students seem interesting and pleasant to teach. (Note 1: If every year a teacher finds that most students are uninteresting and teaching them is an unpleasant chore, it may be time for that teacher to consider a career change. Note 2: At the beginning of the year, good teachers often notice that a few students are hard for them to teach and to get along with; they get to work on this problem quickly. They see it as a problem for *them*, which *they* need to fix, and begin by looking around for colleagues who do find these students congenial and can describe their good points.)

To summarize, the teachers in this section—like all teachers—have a diversity of students. That's one feature of teaching they don't need to worry about. It is a given. They expect all their students to learn, and they accommodate students' different experiences and preferences by using more than one instructional strategy, and by choosing strategies that provide for or encourage diversity. When they select or reject teaching methods, these teachers, who are presented as good examples, consider whether the strategies would work with their students (not whether they would fit the particular needs of a subgroup of their students in a particular year), but this is not the major basis for their choices. Their primary criterion for choice is to select methods that will fit their teaching philosophy—everyone can learn; learning is a constructive, language-based process; effective learning is active—and that seem likely to make it easier for students to learn the important concepts they have to teach. The other criterion they use in deciding whether to use a strategy is whether it suits *them*—their time constraints, their interests, their teaching preferences.

STRATEGIC TEACHERS, PART ONE:

"I'm a bookworm on a budget."

Eddie Garwin teaches all subjects in a self-contained fourth-grade classroom; this is his second year of teaching. He's paying back student loans for his college education, and saving up for a trip to Japan he hopes to take in a year or two. He comes from a family of teachers: his parents and older brother are teachers, and a sister is enrolled in a teacher education program at a nearby college.

Mr. Garwin makes decisions carefully. When he was interviewing for teaching positions, he looked closely at schools where he might be teaching for clues about their atmosphere. He ended up with two job offers, one for fifth grade—the grade he preferred—and one for fourth. He decided to accept the fourth-grade position because most of the classrooms he saw at that school looked like lively places to learn, the media center program seemed terrific, and the principal was clearly interested in the students and the curriculum.

He picked up a lot of ideas in college; when he was hired last year he realized he couldn't use every good strategy he'd ever come across and he gave a lot of thought to evaluating strategies. Because everything was new for him and because he needed to teach language arts, social studies, science, and math, he looked for strategies that weren't subject matter specific. He knew it would be easier for him, and a good idea for his students too, if they used similar learning activities in each subject. He didn't want to go overboard on preparing materials; he did want to try teaching with a theme once during the year; he believed in using only purposeful writing activities; he was impressed with the versatility of cloze; he knew it was important for his fourth graders to get a good start on "reading for learning the new"; he wanted to avoid multiple choice and fill-in-the-blanks testing. Most of all, as an enthusiastic reader himself, he wanted all of his students to love reading too. With these diverse constraints in mind, he chose these strategies:

- *Giving information directly.* For giving content information and teaching problem solving, he uses Teacher Read-Aloud Commentaries—often one per day in either social studies, science, or a reading text—and SAY-IT and For-Your-Information (FYI)—part of the class atmosphere.
- *Vocabulary development.* For teaching vocabulary before, during, and after study, he uses List-Group-Label (LGL). Fourth grade is a transition year into "learning the new" from reading, most text topics are somewhat familiar, and the class can draw on prior knowledge, so LGL is practical as an introduction. Mr. Garwin uses this as one of two "before" strategies for teaching vocabulary. He also uses Focused Cloze to teach and to test, Terminology Trade as his "during" strategy, and Concept of Definition as his "after" strategy, to enhance word knowledge.
- *Reading.* To enable his students to progress as readers, read to learn and read to enjoy, paired reading is a way for students to read their textbooks cooperatively. Literature circles and text sets guide students' reading and provide a basis for class discussions, and, of course, he reads aloud to students.
- *Math.* Here he uses Solve Aloud. He learned about this from Dave Lusolo (a middle school teacher whose story is told after Chapter Nine) and uses it almost daily in math. He also uses Computation and Draw-A-Problem.
- *Writing.* For connecting ideas, he uses Concept Connections to teach and, later, to test; pen pals to make writing purposeful through communication; and Acrostics and Books as Reports to make writing purposeful through creating original products.

■ *Conceptual development.* In addition to the strategies listed previously, he uses themed teaching (calling his first theme "Another Point of View"), Cloze-Plus-Questions Guides (more cloze, and a good group activity, building vocabulary while guiding reading), and cross-grade collaboration as a way for students to practice reading in content areas and be of service to others. He worked this out with Rose Spen, a first-grade teacher in the same building (whose story is told following Chapter Six). He also uses Themed Reading for concept, language, and reading development; and, for enjoyment, direct and vicarious experiences and wide reading, which is his favorite strategy.

Now that Mr. Garwin has two years of experience in getting his program going he's pleased with his system, and happy to share information with you. Some of his strategies are ones that students need to learn how to use, and Mr. Garwin introduces and teaches them one at a time, over a period of many weeks. In the case of Teacher Read-Aloud Commentary and Solve Aloud, the students don't need to be taught the strategy. Mr. Garwin begins using both of these strategies immediately in the first days of school. He also begins reading aloud to the class on the first day.

The first strategies he teaches to his students are ones they can understand very easily. He begins with paired reading and SAY-IT. He introduces them immediately so that students can begin using them as they read their textbooks right away. Next comes List-Group-Label, a teacher-led strategy that students readily understand. Mr. Garwin begins by using it during the first week of school in social studies, the content area for which it was originally designed. Eventually he uses it biweekly, choosing the subject area topic about which students have the most prior knowledge, because effective use of LGL requires that the students already have some useful information about the topic they'll be studying.

Then, during language arts, he teaches the class to use cloze and, working in cooperative groups, they solve cloze passages based on stories that are later read by the whole class. Once the students understand cloze, Mr. Garwin introduces Cloze-Plus-Questions Guides as a content area assignment. Before reading (even before they get out their textbooks) students work in pairs or cooperative groups on the cloze, using colored markers. When they're done they circle any blanks where they couldn't think of a word, and Mr. Garwin initials their assignment. He also notes approximately how long the students worked on the cloze. Then the student pairs get their texts, read the assigned section, and write their answers to the questions on the guide. At this point, they are using pencils; when they find the text passage on which the cloze exercise was based, they compare it with their version and pencil in the author's words when the words they chose were different. (Mr. Garwin makes it a point to talk about "the author's words" and "your words" rather than "right" and "wrong" words, and he does not talk about "correcting" the cloze.) After the students have completed the Cloze-Plus-Questions Guides and used them as a basis for class discussion, all the pages go straight into a three-ring binder that he keeps on his desk. This is part of Mr. Garwin's system for assessment. Over the course of the year he fills several binders. These are not materials he needs to correct or comment on; instead they provide records of students' work and documentation of students' progress.

About the third week into the school year, Mr. Garwin teaches his students how to use Focused Cloze. This is an easy task, because they are already familiar with cloze. He also teaches the class Computation Minute, and he begins to include vicarious experiences (e.g., students watch him conduct a science experiment or listen to a guest speaker) and direct experiences (e.g., students conduct science experiments; the class takes a nature walk on the playground; students use manipulable materials in math). He also teaches students the Draw-a-problem strategy and they begin to use it regularly in math.

The class is now running smoothly. These are some ways that a three- or four-day sequence of studying a topic may progress:

- Teacher Read-Aloud Commentary, followed by paired reading with SAY-IT and Cloze-Plus-Questions Guides (a process continued over several days), with class discussions at the end of each session; or
- List-Group-Label, followed by paired reading with SAY-IT. Mr. Garwin uses an overhead projector for List-Group-Label, and makes copies of the original LGL chart for cooperative groups to revise as they read from their textbooks over several days. The revised charts form the basis for class discussions; or
- Focused Cloze completed in groups, followed by whole class discussion of word choices and passage meaning, followed by paired reading with SAY-IT. Mr. Garwin may use a Teacher Read-Aloud Commentary on the second or third day of studying the topic, and then continue the paired reading; or
- A demonstration, short film, or experiment, followed by List-Group-Label and paired reading (always with SAY-IT), followed by discussion; or
- In math, Solve Aloud followed by group work on assigned problems, with Draw-A-Problem. At the conclusion of sessions groups raise questions that are answered by other students or Mr. Garwin, and one group shares its Draw-A-Problem illustration. Twice a week Mr. Garwin uses Computation Minute to begin math lessons. (The Computation Minute sheets go into another three-ring binder.)

At this point, Mr. Garwin begins bringing in books for the class library, and introduces Themed Reading, adding books regularly. When the library is well-stocked and students have had a chance to explore it, he uses several sessions of Themed Reading a week, in social studies, science, and language arts. (Note that he does not require silence during these times; students may share books quietly.) Books from the class library are always available for free-time reading also. Now he is ready for wide reading, which he uses to introduce a science topic for which he has been collecting relevant reading material. Topic-related trade books are displayed. He has multiple copies of several. Cooperative groups choose books they will read and then share with the class through discussion and by reading selected portions aloud. Wide reading will be used again several times during the year, in social studies as well as science, to introduce topics to which Mr. Garwin plans to devote more time than usual.

Toward the end of October, Mr. Garwin begins an emphasis on writing, which will continue throughout the year. He teaches Concept Connections and works with students as a whole class and in cooperative groups as they practice this activity, which becomes a weekly cooperative group assignment. He also initiates his first pen pals project, in which his students begin to correspond with undergraduate students at a nearby college (the one where his sister is a student) who are enrolled in a course in content area reading. The correspondence will continue into December, and will begin again in February, with different college pen pals from a new section of the course. (This time the fourth-grade students will be experienced pen pals, and their college correspondents will be new to the activity.) Mr. Garwin intends someday to conduct a classroom-based research study to compare his students' first letters to their college pen pals, at the beginning of the year, and in the middle of the year.

In November, Mr. Garwin builds in testing. His students have become reasonably skilled and comfortable at acquiring knowledge, and they can use a variety of strategies easily. He uses Focused Cloze and Concept Connections (strategies that the students continue to use regularly as learning activities in groups) as individual in-class assessment activities at preannounced times, and uses the results to monitor students' progress. At this point, he adds Terminology Trade, which the class uses to prepare for these low-key tests. The last activity that he introduces before the winter holiday is Acrostics, and he adds a weekly cooperative group assignment of producing one acrostic based on facts from a content area trade book of the group's choice.

In his first year of teaching, Mr. Garwin found that he needed to review processes when the students returned in January. He intends to learn from this experience and plans always to use January as a month in which new topics are studied in familiar ways. He also sets up new cooperative groups at this time. Toward the end of January he introduces the concept of literature circles and text sets in language arts and in content areas. Cooperative groups read at least three books from a text set, some from the class library and others borrowed from the school media center, eventually sharing their reading using one of the strategies they are familiar with: Acrostics, Concept Connections, or organizing a List-Group-Label session or Terminology Trade for their classmates. Individual students, or student interest groups, may also read text sets of their choice as a free time or after school activity. Students are encouraged to suggest text set themes or materials to add to a text set. The pen pal project begins again, and students are encouraged to share information about their text set readings with their college pen pals.

By now, his students are becoming enthusiastic readers and their vocabularies are growing by leaps and bounds. It's time to introduce Concept of Definition. As he did with the Concept Connections strategy, Mr. Garwin teaches this strategy over a period of time, practicing it with the whole class and also with cooperative groups. The class begins to compile Concept of Definition notebooks in science, social studies, and math. Several students begin their own collections, on self-selected topics, such as sports, famous people, or fictional characters.

Building on his students' developing ability to see things from different perspectives, Mr. Garwin sprinkles FYIs throughout his teaching, pointing out differences between the experiences he and his students share and the events, climate, language, and experiences of people in other places and other periods of history. In March, he begins to use his chosen theme ("Another Point of View") in a more formal way. Social studies, science, and math are linked as the class discusses various climates, geographical settings, and time zones, and considers what differences arise from them. In math, the class tries to find alternate ways to solve problems, and also works with math challenges for which there are multiple possible solutions. Mr. Garwin chooses his reading aloud material with the theme in mind, and offers text set possibilities that are theme-related. (When he takes his hoped-for trip to Japan, Mr. Garwin intends to set up a pen pals project with a class of students there.)

Mr. Garwin's fourth graders are not the only ones who are making great strides as learners. In another wing of the building, Ms. Spen's first graders have turned into a batch of avid readers and writers. In February, the two teachers begin a prearranged cross-grade collaboration. Four days a week, one cooperative group from Mr. Garwin's class visits Ms. Spen's room, where they listen to the first graders read, and read aloud to them from trade books that relate to topics Ms. Spen is teaching in science or social studies. (This becomes that cooperative group's assignment for the day.) The first graders dictate what they remember after hearing a trade book read, and their fourth-grader mentors record this retelling. Often, when they return the next week, the first graders can read the story back to them. After the cross-grade collaboration project is well underway, Ms. Spen and Mr. Garwin set up a pen pal exchange between first- and fourth-grade friends. The fourth graders are very conscientious about modeling correct spelling and usage for the first graders, and they enjoy the challenge of figuring out the first graders' invented spelling. A new fourth grade project is creating Books as Reports, presenting content area information in the form of short illustrated books. Some of these become presents for the first-grade class, and the first graders reciprocate by sending drawings and their own stories to their fourth-grade friends. Mr. Garwin has encouraged his fourth graders to notice their own progress throughout the year; now he can reinforce the idea of growth and change by guiding them to notice the progress their first-grade friends are making.

As the year winds to a close, there are many possibilities for students to share their work with parent visitors, with third graders who visit the class to find out what next year will be like, and with each other. When Mr. Garwin posted his first Annual Overview at the beginning of his first teaching year, he left a blank section at the end and encouraged students to add stickers listing activities they wanted to do again. By the end of that year the section was full, and he used a batch of favorite activities in each of the final weeks of school. This year again, that section of his Overview is filling up nicely.

How Does He Do It?

In terms of strategy selection and a year's plan for strategy use, we can see how Mr. Garwin's program works. One feature of the program that has not yet been described in detail is assessment. Notice that Mr. Garwin has extensive documentation of his students' work, and useful information about their progress. He does not need to give tests besides the ones he has built into his program. The documented information includes the completed Cloze-Plus-Questions Guides, samples of Focused Cloze and Concept Connections, copies of selected pen pal exchanges and pages from student-prepared books and acrostics. If the principal wants to see how Mr. Garwin's program is working, these materials can be shown and discussed. At parent conferences, examples of each student's work are available to illustrate their progress and their interests. His notebook of collected Cloze-Plus-Questions Guides is particularly useful; there he has a sequential set of materials that give him information about his students, including their progress across time, in these

areas: grasp of a text concept before reading, understanding of text concepts after reading, breadth of vocabulary, spelling, speed of working, and quality of product.

Two challenges for a new teacher are getting materials prepared and building a classroom library without spending money. The materials that need to be prepared are the cloze items, Cloze-Plus-Questions Guides, and Focused Cloze; and the Computation Minute sheets in math. Clever Mr. Garwin! Most of these involve only selection or minimum clerical work, and copying from materials for which copying is permissible. For Computation Minute, he chooses computation pages from a variety of commercial masters. For the various cloze exercises, he chooses passages from copyable materials; then he (or someone else) types the passage using a word processing program and replaces selected words with blanks. He wrote all the questions for the Cloze-Plus-Questions Guides last year, but he prepared a few at a time, which turned out to be a good idea anyway, because he improved his question-writing skill over time.

Mr. Garwin's biggest challenge was figuring out how to establish an extensive library at little or no cost. He doesn't have money to spend (although he has decided to budget approximately $30 a year for books that he will buy and use in his classroom. So getting the books was a *need*, and he tapped a personal *strength* to accomplish his goal. One of his strengths is having plenty of friends and relatives who are interested in education. Another is his lifelong interest in reading. Here are the sources for his classroom library: his own collection of books, saved from childhood on; books shared by his mother and brother (both teachers); books from friends and the children of friends; and books sold by libraries, community organizations, and at garage sales ($30 goes a long way when the books are priced at a dime). Note that these books are good ones but they're all used. Except for the books that come from family, he knows he has to check each one carefully to make sure that they're free from graffiti and have no missing pages. He also needs new books. The media specialist lends him books for classroom use and keeps students' interests in text sets in mind when they come in to borrow books. The principal agreed to fund his library with a one time grant of $100 when he joined the staff; annually each teacher has between $25 and $50 to spend for materials and Mr. Garwin can use all or part of that for books also. He suggests to parents that they consider giving a book to the class library to honor their child's birthday; he keeps a list of specially wanted books, over a wide price range, for parents' information. His school participates in a program through which students may purchase paperback copies of books; teachers get bonus books, and Mr. Garwin's go into the class library.

For future expansion of the library, to include more of the marvelous new trade books available, he plans to write a grant proposal to a local agency that funds educational projects in the $250 to $500 range.

Challenge to the Reader. Suppose Mr. Garwin consulted you about what strategy to add to his repertoire next year. What would you suggest, and how would you advise him to mesh your chosen strategy with his current program?

Choose and Use. If you were to choose one aspect of Mr. Garwin's program to use in your own classroom, what would it be, and how would you begin?

Establishing a Strong Structure of Understanding as Content Area Topics Are Studied

Classrooms [can be] settings for multiple zones of proximal development.... The central Vygotskian notion of zones of proximal development is one of learning flowering between lower and upper bounds of potential, depending on environmental support... I argue that an essential role for teachers is to guide the discovery process toward forms of disciplined inquiry that would not be reached without expert guidance, to push for the upper bounds.

ANN L. BROWN, 1994, P. 9.

A major goal in content area teaching is to provide useful instruction to guide students' learning before, during, and after their study of content topics. Teaching strategies described in Chapter Three are useful ways to help a classroom of diverse students build shared knowledge as they begin to study new content area information. This chapter, focusing on the *during* instruction period, places an even greater emphasis on building knowledge, on students' active engagement in this constructive process, and on teachers' active, thoughtful planning to foster students' learning. In addition to presenting an array of effective strategies for teachers to choose among, two instructional methods are discussed that benefit all students across grades and ages: reading aloud by the teacher and sensibly planned cooperative learning.

In a sound learning process, the students construct their own knowledge: They are the builders.

What is built are collections of ideas or schemas, which are mental representations of what the world is like, and also abilities necessary for using those ideas. Although students must take an active role in their own learning, in content area study the guidance of knowledgeable teachers is essential. When students are in the midst of their learning, the teacher's role is to help them acquire, organize, and use knowledge. Teachers are guides and helpers throughout the teaching and learning process, but the work of knowledge construction occurs within the student. At this point in the learning process, the teacher's role is that of an intelligent, caring provider and planner who sees that students have what is needed to learn, provided in ways that support learning. Teachers can use strategies that will enable students to be effective knowledge builders. When students have studied a content area topic and acquired knowledge that they can understand

and apply, they are well prepared to continue their learning in that area.

 ## Learners Collect and Use Knowledge

During effective content area instruction, students collect information from the teacher and the textbook, and from the teacher alone. Information also comes from other resources, many of them teacher-guided, including direct hands-on experiences, trade books and other media, resources shared from students' homes, and planned and spontaneous opportunities for students to learn from each other. The students are the knowledge builders. Teachers, who plan the learning environment and take a leading role in it, are the students' most important resource.

Collecting Knowledge Through Lively Listening

Learning through the receptive modes of language, by reading and listening, is an essential way for students to build their knowledge in the content areas. Learning through listening supports reading, because reading is easier when terms and concepts are in the reader's listening, speaking, and conceptual vocabularies. Listening is also, in itself, a direct and effective way to gain knowledge when learners are interested and actively engaged. Outside the classroom, we recognize that listening is an effective way to learn. If we are giving someone else needed information, we tell them; if we need information ourselves, we want to be told. In education, however, it is easy for telling—lecturing, explaining, talking only by the teacher—to absorb most of class time, with students expected to listen passively while the teacher speaks. Instructional extremes in which the teacher talks, students listen or no one talks, and students read, provide poor learning environments. Many students are deprived of opportunities to learn in classrooms where they are expected to acquire knowledge solely through reading textbooks independently; similarly, many students will not learn well in classrooms where they are expected to learn by remaining quiet while a teacher talks.

Fortunately, learning through listening does not need to be passive, one-sided, or time-consuming. Content area teachers can choose efficient and effective strategies that promote active listening in interesting ways. These strategies are efficient because they do not consume extensive amounts of class time, and effective because they enable students to understand, use, and remember what they hear. Three knowledge-building strategies, designed to support learning through listening as content area topics are studied, are SAY-IT (the simplest of all strategies: answering students' content-related questions), Solve Aloud (talking through the process of solving a problem), and A-Qu-A (engaging students in listening for the answers to questions).

Learning on Request: SAY-IT. All learners, no matter what their age or level of sophistication, encounter unfamiliar terms and ideas. When we do not have necessary information, we frequently ask someone who is likely to know. When someone else asks us for information, we are typically pleased if we can provide it. Capable adults often ask for information from knowledgeable colleagues. In a good learning environment, students are free to get information in a similar way. They ask each other, and they ask adults. Although this method of acquiring and sharing information is versatile and effective, it is rarely discussed in professional literature. Perhaps this omission occurs because the strategy has no special name, a deficiency that is remedied here. We can call this method SAY-IT, an acronym for Share And You Instruct Time-efficiently. Telling students the answers to their questions, or the meaning of unknown words, is quick (no teacher preparation time), efficient (classtime used is minimal), and can be highly effective (the interval between needing information and getting it is brief). Of course, it is not sensible to instruct by telling students everything they do not know. The information load would be overwhelming, and thus neither interesting nor memorable. However, responding to students when they raise questions and establishing a classroom atmosphere in which it is acceptable and desirable to raise content-related questions is a wise method of teaching and a strategy worthy of a name of its own.

Responding to students when they raise questions—and establishing a classroom atmosphere in which it is acceptable and desirable to raise content-related questions—is a wise method of teaching.

they are told to find out for themselves or that they should already know the answer, but when they ask for process information, their questions are answered by the teacher or by other students. Not surprisingly, this affects the kind of questions students ask. Under these conditions, they learn that there is little reason to ask questions about content in a school setting, even though the content is what they come to school to learn. Thomas Good and his colleagues (Good, Slavings, Harel, & Emerson, 1987) have analyzed students' questions in these two categories, and found that the number of content questions decreases from elementary school through high school.

Learning Through Repetitive Demonstrations: Solve Aloud.

The Solve Aloud strategy, which is a variant form of the Teacher Read-Aloud Commentary, focuses on an area of mathematics that is frequently difficult for students: solving problems presented in words, rather than symbols. It is based on the principle that repetition, conducted in interesting, involving ways, supports thorough learning. Denise Muth (1993) has advocated repeated teacher intervention in problem solving through modeling of the thinking processes involved. Using the Solve Aloud strategy, a teacher reads a math problem and talks through the steps to a solution. An example is shown in Figure 4–1. Used regularly, the process accustoms students to the process of solving word problems, familiarizes them with mathematical terminology, and helps to develop their confidence in their capability in mathematics. Teachers may also choose to use Solve Aloud occasionally to introduce a new kind of math problem. The strategy is suitable across grade levels; thinking through a math problem is useful even for very young students, and advantageous even for advanced students.

Solve Alouds require no preparation time. Teachers who let students choose the problem to be solved do not know in advance which problem they will be working with. All the teacher needs is knowledge and the ability to explain the steps in solving problems. Like all commentaries, Solve Alouds work best when they move along briskly. The teacher does not ask the students questions about problem solving, so no time is used in a question-and-answer process. The process is very brief

In considering the value of the SAY-IT strategy, it is useful to observe in a classroom, or teachers can monitor what occurs in their own classrooms, by tallying student requests for information in two categories. The first category is requests for content information (e.g., "What does this word mean?" "When did [a historical event] happen?" "Why does [an observed natural occurrence] work that way?" "How do you spell [word]?" "Where is [city/country]?") The second category is requests for process information (e.g., "How do we [complete this assignment]?" "Where are [necessary materials]?" "Do we have to [do a certain task]?") What kinds of responses are given to the two types of questions? Often, when students ask for content information,

FIGURE 4–1 Using a Solve-Aloud Strategy in Mathematics to Promote Ability to Solve Word Problems

Level and subject: primary grades, math

Process: solving word problems

Background: In math, the teacher uses a form of the Teacher Read-Aloud Commentary strategy called Solve Aloud every day, to talk through one word problem. Each day a different cooperative group has responsibility for picking the Solve Aloud problem from a page specified by the teacher. (Naturally, as they do so, they often solve the problem themselves, in advance, which is terrific.)

Rationale: For a variety of reasons, students across the grades often have more difficulty in solving math problems that are presented in words than those that use only numbers and symbols. Using Solve Aloud for one problem a day uses only minutes, and builds both math understanding and math confidence. It is the teacher's choice whether to use manipulatives to demonstrate while talking through the problem. In this case, the teacher chooses not to, and to have the students draw a picture of the problem later.

Solve Aloud commentary: "We're learning about how to solve problems using both addition and subtraction. On page 23 of our math books there's a page of math challenges, and today it was the turn of Mai's and Anatoly's and Terri's and Hal's group to choose the problem for our Solve Aloud. Which one did you pick?" (Group responds.) "Okay, the fourth one. I see that the problem tells about someone named Jane who's building with blocks. Who shall we have be the main character instead of Jane?" (Group responds.) "Now, Anatoly, this is about you." (The teacher reads the whole problem aloud, substituting Anatoly for Jane and masculine for feminine pronouns.)

"Anatoly and his friend were playing with blocks. Anatoly had ten blocks, and he gave four to his friend. The teacher gave Anatoly three more. How many blocks did he have then?

"I want to find out how many blocks Anatoly has at the end of this story. At the beginning he has 10, but then he gives some away. That means he's going to have less than 10. Start with 10, subtract 4, 10 minus 4 is 6. At that point, he has 6.

"The next thing that happens is that the teacher gives him some blocks. That means he's going to have more than 6. six, add 3. six plus 3 is 9. So, at the end of the story, Anatoly has 9 blocks. That's the answer to the problem: 9. We can write a math sentence: $10 - 4 + 3 = 9$.

"We can check our answer by thinking about whether it's sensible. Anatoly gave 4 blocks away, and he got 3 back. He gave away 1 more than he got. He subtracted 1 more than he added. So he's going to end up with fewer blocks than he started with. And in our answer he does: he starts with 10, and ends up with 9. Good!

"I want everybody to draw a picture of this math problem—that's a separate picture from each person. Then in your groups, choose one other problem on page 23 to draw a picture about, and see how many of the problems you can solve before it's time for lunch. I'll walk around the room and visit groups, and you can call out to me if you want my help and advice. Go to it."

Follow-up process: The follow-up is built into the strategy. Students move from the Solve Aloud directly into working with math problems on the page the solved problem came from and to creating a model of the problem. Although the teacher does not question the children during the Solve Aloud, the teacher can use tell/ask style questioning to reinforce understanding while walking around the room as the children work; e.g., "All right, in this part of your picture, Anatoly gives his friend 4 blocks. What math sentence will you write? Yes, $10 - 4 = 6$. Good."

and can be completed in five minutes or less. As with the Teacher Read-Aloud Commentary described in Chapter Three, there are two potential problems. 1) The teacher can err by letting the focus drift away from the main topic during the commentary. 2) The teacher can err by switching from commenting on the text, or solving the problem, to commenting on what is occurring in the class.

Two strategies that students can learn to use on their own—Transform-a-Problem, (described in Chapter Five) and a study strategy designed for use in mathematics, SQRQCQ—can be encouraged as follow-up activities to Solve Alouds. SQRQCQ (Survey, Question; Read, Question; Compute, Question), devised by Leo Fay (1965), emphasizes repeated self-questioning as an essential part of problem-solving. Students first read a problem quickly and decide what question is being asked (the SQ phase). They then reread carefully to decide what relationships among the facts given are needed to provide the solution, and what steps to follow in reaching the solution (the RQ phase). Finally, they compute the answer, following the steps established during the RQ phase, and check that answer by rereading the problem to see whether the solution fits every element of the stated problem (the CQ phase). In summary, these are the steps:

▮ SQ: Survey the problem. Ask: "What is the question to be answered?"
▮ RQ: Read the problem. Ask: "What information is given that relates to the answer to the question?"
▮ CQ: Compute the answer. Return to the stated problem and, for each relevant segment of information, ask "According to my solution, is this information correct?" If, at any point, the answer is "No," then a new solution must be prepared, by returning to the RQ or CQ phase.

Learning Through Active Listening: A-Qu-A.   The acronym A-Qu-A (pronounced *ah-QUA*) stands for Answer-Question-Answer. The strategy adds a question-answering component to the sequence reading strategy developed by Ruth Heinig (1988). A-Qu-A is suitable for use in grades three and above, although the strategy can be adapted for younger students. Middle school students typically enjoy it because it involves social interaction. The process, as well as the title, is a reminder that the answers to both factual and inferential questions are there, in the text, before questions are asked; thus students read the text, which will provide answers (A) to questions, then encounter questions (Qu), and then answer them (A) based on recall or repetition. The method is a model for effective studying, and it provides strong motivation for careful listening. Rereading occurs as students first read text passages and then reread excerpts to confirm other students' answers. Among the advantages of this strategy are that students have the opportunity to give their answers to questions orally, rather than in writing—a feature many students appreciate. The instructional effectiveness of the strategy depends on the teacher's sound choice of text, and skill in preparing good questions. A-Qu-A is most effective when the teacher has a cheerful, confident management style, and the class works well together. In contrast, emphasizing rules, making students repeat steps, or criticizing make the strategy unpleasant and therefore unworkable. Figures 4–2 and 4–3 give examples of A-Qu-As.

In preparing the materials for an A-Qu-A, it is important to choose a fact-packed, well-written text section, or adapt or write an informational passage. (Textbook sections often include items that should not be part of an A-Qu-A text, such as questions inserted in the text to catch students' attention, references to pictures or charts, and pronunciation keys.) Preparation of good A-Qu-A materials is time-consuming; but once prepared, they can be used repeatedly. A-Qu-A cards can be used as a learning center activity, with students given the tasks to arrange the text cards in correct sequence, to match each with the correct question card(s), and then to create an illustration for a text card-question card pair. The A-Qu-A strategy uses two sets of cards, one set for text and one set for questions. File cards that are 4×6 or 5×8 work well.

Set of text cards for A-Qu-A

▮ Each text card gives a piece of the total passage.
▮ Every text card except the first in the series begins with a cue for students to listen for. The cue is a short piece of text that repeats the end of the previous card. (The student who gets a card with no cue is the first reader.)
▮ Between seven and ten text cards make a good set.

Set of question cards for A-Qu-A

▮ Each question card has a well-constructed question that can be answered based on one of the text cards.
▮ Every question card also has the same standard question: Who read the card that gives the answer to this question?
▮ One question should be written for each text card. Two questions can be written about a few cards.

The first A-Qu-A cards to prepare are the text cards. Each card has one section of the text passage being studied. Between seven and ten text sections make a useful A-Qu-A for a whole class to use. The sections should be fairly brief, but each section must include enough information on which to base a question. For an A-Qu-A about the food-making process in green plants, for example, the teacher might select (or write) a passage beginning this way:

> Nearly all leaves have one major purpose: They make food for the plant on which they grow, from carbon dioxide from the air, light, and water. The leaves build sugars for the plant's food from carbon dioxide and water when light is present. Some plants grow well in the shade, but most plants need strong light on their leaves in order to grow.
>
> Plants also need a chemical compound, called chlorophyll, to make food. *Chlorophyll* comes from two Greek words that together mean *green leaf.*

This part of the passage might be separated into three sections and presented on text cards as shown. (Note that this example presents only the beginning of an A-Qu-A; an entire A-Qu-A should be substantially longer.) The first text card has no cue because there is no preceding text. All other text cards include, at the top, a short, meaningful section that occurs at the end of the previous text card. This section is used only for a cue. It is useful to highlight it in some way, and it is not read aloud. When an entire sentence is used as a cue, it is printed exactly. When only a part of a sentence is used, it is preceded by an ellipsis, (...), which indicates that a part of the text has been omitted.

> Nearly all leaves have one major purpose: They make food for the plant on which they grow, from carbon dioxide which comes from the air, light, and water.
>
> ...from carbon dioxide from the air, light, and water.
> The leaves build sugars for the plant's food from carbon dioxide and water, when light is present. Some plants grow well in the shade, but most plants need strong light on their leaves in order to grow.
>
> ...most plants need strong light on their leaves in order to grow.
> Plants also need a chemical compound, called chlorophyll, to make food. *Chlorophyll* comes from two Greek words that together mean *green leaf.*

The text cards for the entire A-Qu-A are pre-pared as for a sequence reading, by putting each text section on a separate card and heading all cards except the first one with the last sentence or phrase from the previous card, highlighted to serve as a cue. After the text cards are complete, the question cards are prepared. This is the challenging part of A-Qu-A preparation. One or two questions should be based on each text card. These questions, although they may draw on the meaning of the entire passage, should be answerable directly based on information contained in a single text section, and so they will be primarily literal questions. Using a tell/ask format for some of the questions will add to students' learning. These question cards are the second card pack in an A-Qu-A sequence reading set.

Each question card has two items to be answered: a factual question to be answered on the basis of information from one of the text cards, and a standard question, which appears on each question card (Who read the card that gives the answer to this question?). There is a twofold purpose for including "Who read the card that gives the answer to this question?" on every A-Qu-A question card. The first is instructional: Students learn to identify which section of the text includes the answer to their question, and students have practice in verifying answers by checking them against text sections. The second purpose is motivational: Inclusion of the second question means that all students, even those who can answer the factual questions on the basis of prior knowledge, have a purpose for attentive listening. Moreover, it adds a social, personal component to the activity, which students enjoy. Here are two question cards for the excerpt about leaves. (In a real A-Qu-A set, there would be seven to ten text cards, and at least as many question cards.)

> What major purpose do most leaves serve?
> Who read the card that gives the answer to this question?
>
> Even if plants have carbon dioxide, water, and light, they could not make food without a substance that all green plants contain. What is the name of the substance?
> Who read the card that gives the answer to this question?

FIGURE 4–2   A-Qu-A on Algae (Adapted from *General science: A voyage of adventure*, Prentice Hall, 1986, Chapter 8, pp. 170–172.)

Text cards: 8; question cards: 11 (accommodates 19 to 30 students)

Algae are the largest group of nonvascular plants. Because algae have no way of transporting water and food over long distances, they must live near a source of food and water.

…they must live near a source of food and water.

Nonvascular plants such as the algae are often called simple plants. Simple plants lack true stems, leaves, and roots. Nonvascular plants have managed to survive for hundreds of millions of years while other forms of life have come into being and then died off. Through their long history, nonvascular plants have become well adapted to many different environments on the earth.

…well adapted to many different environments on the earth.

Algae live in many different places. The majority of algae live in watery environments, such as oceans, ponds, and lakes. Other algae grow in the soil, on the sides of houses, and at the base of trees. Certain species of algae thrive in the near-boiling water of hot springs, such as those in Yellowstone National Park. Other algae grow in snow, as well as in the icy water of such places as the Antarctic continent, home of the South Pole.

…of such places as the Antarctic continent, home of the South Pole.

Some species of algae are unicellular, or one-celled, and can only be seen with a microscope. Quite often, unicellular algae group together to form colonies. These colonies may attach themselves to one another and form chains of algae. Seaweed is one type of multicellular algae. Multicellular algae can grow quite large. The giant kelp, for example, may stretch over 30 meters.

The giant kelp, for example, may stretch over 30 meters.

Whether unicellular or multicellular, all algae are autotrophs, or organisms that can make their own food. All algae contain chlorophyll, a green substance found in plant cells. Chlorophyll is used in the process of photosynthesis.

…used in the process of photosynthesis.

In photosynthesis, plants use the energy in sunlight to make their own food. Plants make food by combining carbon dioxide from the air with water and minerals from the soil. During the process of photosynthesis, oxygen is released from the plant.

During the process of photosynthesis, oxygen is released from the plant.

Early in the earth's history, there was very little oxygen in the atmosphere. In time, algae and other simple green plants, along with certain bacteria, released vast amounts of oxygen into the air. Eventually there was enough oxygen in the air to allow other forms of life to develop. If it were not for these simple green plants, no animals or people would now exist on the earth. And if green plants were suddenly to vanish from the earth, oxygen in the air would soon become so rare that most living things would vanish.

…so rare that most living things would vanish.

Most algae reproduce by binary fission. Others have very complicated life cycles. Scientists have placed the algae into six groups. The groups are arranged according to the color of the algae: blue-green algae, green algae, golden algae, brown algae, red algae, and fire algae.

■ Why must algae live close to water in some form? Who read the card that gives the answer to this question?

■ What is another term for simple plants—plants that do not have plant characteristics like leaves and roots? Who read the card that gives the answer to this question?

■ Name several places where algae can be found. Who read the card that gives this information?

■ What evidence do we have from our reading that algae can survive both heat and cold? Who read the card that gives this information?

■ What is the term for a cluster of one-celled algae? Who read the card that gives the answer to this question?

FIGURE 4–2 Continued

▌ *Autotroph* comes from two Greek words: *auto*, meaning *self* and *trephein*, meaning *nourish*. Why are algae called autotrophs?
Who read the card that gives the answer to this question?

▌ Algae use carbon dioxide during their food-making process. What gas do they give off as part of this process?
Who read the card that gives the answer to this question?

▌ How did algae help to make it possible for animal life to exist on earth?
Who read the card that gives the answer to this question?

▌ Different kinds of algae reproduce themselves in a variety of ways. Some algae reproduce in a very simple way: They split in two. What is the name for this kind of reproduction?
Who read the card that gives the answer to this question?

▌ We have been reading about the group of nonvascular plants called algae. How many groups of algae are there, according to our current knowledge?

▌ Algae are classified by color. Which group of algae has a name which is not a usual name for a color? Who read the card that gives you evidence for your answers to these questions?

▌ The word *vascular* comes from a Latin word meaning *small vessel*. A vessel is a structure used to carry something. Vascular plants have tubes that carry water and food from one part of the plant to another. Algae don't have these tubes, so they're nonvascular. Are there other nonvascular plants besides algae? Who read one of the cards that give evidence to answer this question?

Concept statement: Living organisms can be classified as vascular or nonvascular. Vascular organisms contain vessels—the words *vascular* and *vessel* are related—through which fluids are transported from one part of the organism to another. In animals, the vessels carry blood; in vascular plants, the vessels, or tubes, carry sap. Vascular plants can thus move nourishment from one part of the plant to another; for example, water absorbed by the roots moves through tubes to the stem and leaves. Some plants are nonvascular. All parts of these plants must be in contact with sources of nourishment, because the plant does not have a system through which water and food can be moved from one part of the plant to another. Algae are the largest group of nonvascular plants. They must live near a source of food and water. Nonvascular plants, such as the algae, are often called simple plants. Simple plants lack true stems, leaves, and roots.

Nonvascular plants have existed on earth for hundreds of millions of years, longer than many more complex forms of life. These plants have adapted to many different environments. For example, algae live in the boiling water of hot springs and in the frigid waters of the Antarctic Ocean. Some species of algae are multicellular and grow to be very large. (An example is a kind of seaweed called giant kelp.) Other species are unicellular. Some species of one-celled algae attach themselves to one another in groups called colonies; colonies may then attach to other colonies, forming chains. Seaweed is one type of multicellular algae.

Whether unicellular or multicellular, all algae are autotrophs, or organisms that can make their own food. All algae contain chlorophyll, which plants use in photosynthesis—a process in which water, minerals, carbon dioxide, and sunlight combine to make food for the plant. During the process of photosynthesis, plants release oxygen into the atmosphere. Most algae reproduce by binary fission. Others have very complicated life cycles. Scientists classify the currently known kinds of algae into six groups, according to their color: blue-green algae, green algae, golden algae, brown algae, red algae, and fire algae.

Algae existed early in the earth's history, when there was very little oxygen in the atmosphere. Over millions of years, the oxygen released into the air by algae and other small life forms increased the oxygen in the atmosphere to the point where other forms of life could develop. The continuing existence of human life is dependent on the existence of green plants.

FIGURE 4–3   A-Qu-A on Volcanos

The eight text cards are listed here first; followed by nine question cards. Text cards are given in order (and must of course be read in order). The question cards are not listed here in order. When an A-Qu-A is used, students can answer the questions in any order. (This means that when questions are written, one question must not refer to another.) Note these points about the question cards: 1) Each question is answerable based on one, and only one, of the text cards, except for one. On that question card, the second question (Who read…) is changed, so that the students who answer the question know that they are listening for information from more than one card. 2) Three of the question cards (the first, second, and ninth) are written in tell-ask format; that is, first there is a statement that gives information and focuses students' attention, and then a question is asked.) The tell-ask format is a particularly effective style for A-Qu-A questions.

A volcano is an opening in the earth's surface that allows lava, steam, rocks, and hot gas to escape. Volcanos are caused by melted rock that rises to the surface of the earth.

…caused by melted rock that rises to the surface of the earth.
Some rocks deep under the surface of the earth get so hot that they melt. The name for this melted rock is *magma*.

…this melted rock is magma.
Magma rises toward the earth's surface because it is lighter than solid rock. As the magma rises, it melts much of the surrounding rock, and so a place is formed, under the earth's surface, to hold the magma, steam, and rocks.

…to hold the magma, steam, and rocks.
The magma and the gas are under a lot of pressure because of the weight of the surrounding solid rock. This pressure forces the magma to move up, opening a channel through broken or weak rocks.

…opening a channel through broken or weak rocks.
When the magma reaches the surface of the earth, the gas escapes, which causes a great eruption of magma, gas, and rocks.

…causes a great eruption of magma, gas, and rocks.
Lava is the name given to magma once it hits the surface of the earth. As the lava pours out of the volcano, it can reach temperatures of more than 2012 degrees Fahrenheit. As it cools, it becomes very hard.

As it cools, it becomes very hard.
After a volcano has erupted, the surrounding earth is covered in volcanic dust, volcanic ash, and hardened lava.

…volcanic dust, volcanic ash, and hardened lava.
There is nothing that can be done to prevent volcanos from erupting. They are one of the most destructive forces on earth. But volcanos do help scientists learn more about what happens within the earth.

▌Although volcanos are very destructive, they are still useful to scientists. How?
Who read the card that gives the answer to this question?

▌Magma is called *lava* once it reaches the earth's surface. What happens to the lava when it is no longer hot?
Who read the card that gives the answer to this question?

▌What causes the pressure that pushes the magma up through broken rocks toward the earth's surface?
Who read the card that gives the answer to this question?

▌What happens to the earth around a volcano after the volcano erupts?
Two cards give you information about this question. Who read these cards?

▌What happens when magma breaks through the earth's surface?
Who read the card that gives the answer to this question?

▌What is a volcano?
Who read the card that gives the answer to this question?

FIGURE 4–3 Continued

▌ What is magma?
Who read the card that gives the answer to this question?

▌ Why does magma move up from inside the earth?
Who read the card that gives the answer to this question?

▌ When magma moves near to the earth's surface, it creates a space by melting the rocks around it. Besides magma, what does this space hold?
Who read the card that gives the answer to this question?

This A-Qu-A was created by Beth Lightfoot. Minor adaptations have been made for this text.

For the A-Qu-A strategy, as for all instructional questioning, it is a mistake to write questions that can be answered without thought by repeating a section of the text. When the text passage is "The leaves build sugars for the plant's food from carbon dioxide and water, when light is present," it is not useful to phrase a question this way: "What do the leaves build for the plant's food from carbon dioxide when light is present?" A better question, one which requires students to listen and think to find the answer, is: "What substance do leaves make by combining water and carbon dioxide?"

When the A-Qu-A materials have been prepared, the A-Qu-A strategy can be used with an entire class. Although both sets of cards may be distributed randomly at the same time, if the reading passage is quite simple, it is often best to distribute only the text cards first. Students with text cards should have a brief period to look at their cards and to ask for information about how words are pronounced. It is useful for the teacher to walk around the group and offer information. Then the text cards are read, in sequence. Students know when it is their turn to read, because they listen for the cue at the top of the card they hold.

Those who do not have text cards listen to the reading, knowing that they will be given a question to answer (either individually or in a pair). After the first reading of the text, question cards are given out randomly to the remaining students. The students with text cards read the text again, and those with question cards listen to the sequence reading with two purposes: to learn the answer to the ques-

tion on their card and to find out who read the text that gives the answer.

Then it is the turn of the question card holders. (There is no need for the questions to be answered in order, so students answer in whatever order they choose, without being called on.) They read their factual question aloud, giving an answer, and naming the reader whose card confirms that answer. That person reads the portion of the text that confirms (or disconfirms) the answer given, as in the following example.

> Question reader: "'Even if plants have carbon dioxide, water, and light, they could not make food without a substance that all green plants contain. What is the name of the substance?' It's chlorophyll. That was on Ann's card."
>
> Text reader (Ann): "That's right." (reading from card) "'Plants also need a chemical compound, called chlorophyll, to make food.'"

The A-Qu-A sequence is completed when the questions on all cards have been asked, answered, and confirmed, or, if necessary, disconfirmed and corrected. If students are sufficiently interested, the activity may be repeated immediately or on a subsequent day, with cards given to different students. A-Qu-A works well as a whole class activity when everyone in the class can be involved. An A-Qu-A for a whole class can be comprised of text cards for approximately one third of the class and approximately the same number of question cards for the rest. (One question card may be given to a pair of students to answer collaboratively.)

Building On Experiences

Effective learning is not sedentary, passive, and controlled from outside. Direct and **vicarious** experiences enable students to acquire information in ways that make it likely that the information will be understood and remembered. In the content areas, relevant experiences can enhance students' store of knowledge about the topics being studied and their interest in it.

Direct Experiences.   Direct experience involves bringing the part of the world that is being studied into the classroom or the school, taking students out of school to experience that part of the world, or, of course, providing hands-on study of the world within the classroom (such as repeated measurements of temperature and experiments involving sunlight). Field trips to a factory, for example, can enable students to see unfamiliar buildings and machinery and understand more readily what they read about industry in their social studies texts. From a visit to a farm, younger students can learn firsthand about animals; older students can get firsthand information about careers in agriculture and some understanding of the importance of farming in the country's economy. Field trips in science can give students experiences in examining geologic structures, rock-collecting, collecting plants, exploring wetland areas, birdwatching, and stargazing. Students can learn directly about aspects of social studies by trips to government agencies and historical sites. The use of experiments and manipulable materials offers another way to provide students with direct learning experiences. Students learn about measurement by measuring, and by using measurements in activities, such as building, cooking, and planning travel routes. Students learn about plant growth by growing plants, about the qualities of minerals by testing and classifying them. Students can be encouraged to raise questions and devise strategies for answering them and for analyzing their data.

Vicarious Experiences.   It is often not possible to arrange for direct experiences that enhance content area knowledge; instead, vicarious experiences can be provided. Vicarious experiences that strengthen students' knowledge include listening to guest speakers, seeing well-chosen videotapes, and visiting places, such as museums and planetariums whose displays show what cannot be seen directly because of the limitations of time or space.

Guided Imagery.   A listening-based learning strategy that does not require students to talk, although it can be a precursor to talking together and to writing, is Guided Imagery (Gambrell, Kapinus, & Wilson, 1987; Olson & Gee, 1991; Walker & Wilson, 1991). The method is a way of providing vicarious experiences and can be particularly useful when students will be learning together about a topic where their background-related knowledge is very diverse, or where the subject is so distant in time, place, or space that direct experience is impossible. A strong teacher knowledge base is essential for effective use of the guided imagery strategy.

When the Guided Imagery strategy is used, teachers first plan the lesson and think through what they will say. During the guided imagery process, they set a mood of relaxed attentiveness, usually encouraging students to close their eyes, and then, through their words, create a scenario in which students visualize themselves as taking part. Different kinds of sensory images (e.g., smell, taste, touch, as well as vision) are created through the teacher's words. Mary Olson and Thomas Gee (1991) describe a Guided Imagery lesson in which students are led to visualize the process of making cloth from wool in preindustrial societies, with the teacher describing in relaxed, conversation style what is "seen": shearing the sheep; washing, carding, and spinning the wool into yarn; and weaving the yarn to make cloth. As the teacher describes each stage of the process, the students get a sense of how many-staged and slow the process is, and they can use that understanding later to contrast early methods of making cloth with the speed of textile manufacture today. The importance of encouraging this kind of visualization is underscored by research findings cited in Chapter One (Hare & Smith, 1982),

---

vicarious—derived from a Latin word meaning *alternation,* which came to refer to changing places or substituting for someone else. Vicarious experiences substitute for direct experiences.

One form of direct experience consists of hands-on study of the world in the classroom or school through the use of experiments and manipulable materials. Work stations and science tables in the classroom and group investigations in school enable students to understand scientific principles.

showing that many readers help themselves to understand narrative text by visualizing what is described, but that they typically do not create visual images when reading expository text. (The usual strategy is simply to read more slowly.) Using the guided imagery strategy may provide students with a way of approaching difficult text that they can transfer to texts they read independently.

For students of any age, the children's book *Gramma's Walk* (Hines, 1993) can be a good introduction to the use of Guided Imagery. In Hines's story, a young boy goes on a walk along the seashore with his grandmother. He hears the waves, feels the sand underfoot, looks at seabirds, watches an otter, builds a sandcastle, and sees it swept away by the tide. Grandmother is in a wheelchair and the sea is far away, but her words and images make their imaginary walk come to life. The book has the additional advantage of showing how disabilities and disparities among people (in this case disparity of age) can be surmounted by love and imagination.

Learning Through Practice

Much of content area learning develops as new information, ideas, and insights are connected to what is already known, modifying and increasing our conceptual knowledge. When learning is thoughtful and teaching is sound and vivid, learning is accomplished by moving along and studying a new topic that is related to what has been studied previously, rather than by staying with one topic for repetition and drill. However, some kinds of learning depend to some extent on repetitive practice, which is best provided in interesting and challenging ways. Computation Minute is a strategy teachers may select to provide repeated practice in aspects of mathematics.

Computation Minute.   The Computation Minute strategy provides practice in arithmetical processes that students are close to mastering, in a way that encourages full mastery. This strategy is most useful in the intermediate grades through middle school (grades 3 through 8). It should not be used with very young children whose speed of completing written work is dependent upon their still-developing fine motor skills. The strategy is intended for regular use, but it could be used repeatedly over a period of weeks, then stopped, and returned to again later. There is little point, however, in using Computation Minute sporadically and infrequently.

At one point during class time (the beginning of class is typically a good time), students are given a page of computation items—about as many as could be completed by someone with complete mastery in a minute. The pages are given face down, and at a signal the students turn them over and begin to work, stopping when the teacher signals that one minute has passed. It is important in this strategy, and in all mathematical teaching, for the teacher to use the vocabulary of mathematics repeatedly. Instead of saying "Here are the Computation Minute pages" the teacher should say, for example, "In today's Computation Minute you will be working on addition and subtraction of three-digit numbers." When the minute is over, if all students are using the same set of items, the teacher may read the correct answers quickly, while the students correct their own work (using a crayon or marker rather than the pencil or pen they used to do the computations). If students have been working with different item sets, the teacher may hand out copies of answer keys. The distinctive feature of Computation Minute is that a student's score is not the number of correct items; it is the number correct before the first error. A careless mistake on the second item, then, results in a score of 1, even if all the other items completed were correct.

When this strategy is well conducted by the teacher, students compete against time, in the sense of trying to accomplish as much as possible within a minute, and also try to increase their own achievement. Because the point of the strategy is to encourage students themselves to work rapidly and accurately, competition against other students should be avoided; it would be a mistake to publicize each student's scores. With repeated use of the strategy, students learn to monitor their own style of approaching computation tasks; some are encouraged to work toward mastery in order to finish rapidly, while others recognize that they need to be sure of the accuracy of their work. Students who cannot write rapidly will be at a disadvantage in using this strategy unless it is adapted. The solution is to allow all students to decide

how long they need to achieve a result that satisfies them. In this case, each student would set a goal, individually, for finishing the sheet accurately and correctly, and attempt to meet that goal and, as the strategy is used repeatedly, to meet higher goals. The strategy would then not be Computation Minute, but might be renamed Computation Challenge.

Building Knowledge Through Interactive Study

Solid grounding for learning is developed by taking time to consider, examine, and reflect upon what is being learned. Study methods that include an interactive component, involving teacher and student, or students working together, often are more effective than isolated study. When students always are expected to study alone, outside of school, the teacher cannot guide or intervene in the process, and cannot know how well students are understanding assignments until the results of study are shown during assessment. Although the capacity to study independently is useful, studying cooperatively is productive in itself, and can also help students learn about how to learn through studying, whether they work with others or alone. Study strategies that are designed, or can be adapted, to enable teacher-student and student-student interaction during the study process include Reading Road Maps and RESPONSE, as well as SQ3R, MULTIPASS, and K-W-L.

Learning With Teacher Guidance.   The Reading Road Map strategy (Wood, 1988) allows teachers to guide students to read as skillful, strategic readers do, focusing on important text sections, and skimming those that are less relevant. Developing readers usually spontaneously vary the pace of their reading depending on the kind of material they are reading and their purposes for reading. All students need to learn that slow reading is not always efficient reading. The Reading Road Map strategy develops understanding by focusing students' attention on what is most important in the reading. Students are not only told which pages to read with special care (see the center column in Figure 4–4), they are also given purposes for reading (see the right-hand column in Figure 4–4) and may be given information about text features. (In the example shown, the teacher uses the opportunity to reinforce students' understanding of the compare/contrast pattern of writing.)

To prepare a Reading Road Map, the teacher examines a chapter or other text section which will be assigned and identifies those parts that require the most careful reading, those that should be read at an ordinary pace, and those that may be skimmed. The teacher then prepares a page with three columns, the third column being the widest. Sequentially, for each part of the reading assignment, pages are listed in the leftmost column, a suggested pace at which those pages should be read is given in the middle column, and points to note are listed in the column on the right. The three columns are modeled after a road map of a scenic area, which lists places, suggests a rate of speed for traveling through them, and gives information about what to see.

Learning With Teacher Support. The RESPONSE strategy (Jacobson, 1989a; Farris, Fuhler, and Ginejko, 1991) is a study method that permits interaction, over time, between students studying independently, students studying in cooperative groups, and the teacher. Through the interaction, the teacher has the opportunity to find out what parts of reading assignments are puzzling to individual students, and what topics need to be clarified for the entire class. A blank RESPONSE form is given in Figure 4–5, and a simulated example of a student's completed form on a chapter section of an Earth Science text is shown in Figure 4–6. It is an important aspect of RESPONSE that students write in the form of notes: The ideas must be complete, but need not be expressed in complete sentences, and the writing is done as notes; there is no copying over to produce a neat product. The form is a single page, divided into three sections, which students use to make notes, in three categories, as they read a single assignment. A

FIGURE 4–4 Reading Road Map

Reading Road Map for *Weather Patterns*
pages 300–314

page 300	Read and reread.	▪ Look for a statement of the causes of changes in the weather. Find a definition of *air mass*.
pages 301–303	Scan for information, then reread.	▪ Identify four major types of air masses that affect weather in the continental United States.
page 304	Study the picture.	▪ Be prepared to raise questions about the structure of a rain gauge. (*Gauge* rhymes with *age*.)
pages 305–307	Read with care.	▪ Be sure you understand the role of fronts.
page 308	Skim, unless this is of special interest to you.	▪ You may want to find out how a person becomes qualified as a meteorologist.
pages 309–313	Read, noting the text pattern (comparison).	▪ Prepare a compare/contrast list for one of the following: rainstorms and snowstorms cyclones and anticyclones hurricanes and tornadoes
page 314	Read with care.	▪ Check the boldface items in the chapter summary. What questions do you have? Discuss them in your cooperative group, and decide which to raise in class.

FIGURE 4–5   RESPONSE Form

RESPONSE

Name: Date:

Reading assignment:

Important points: As you read, list essential information and state important ideas. Cite page numbers.

Questions: As you read, note questions that occur to you. Cite page numbers of their source. Some questions will be ideas for discussion. For others, you will want an immediate answer. Star (*) these.

New terms, concepts, vocabulary, and names: List words, phrases, technical terms, names of people, basic ideas which are new to you. Cite page numbers. Star (*) items you would like to have defined or explained.

The response strategy, originated by Jeanne M. Jacobson, is described in the winter 1989 issue of *Reading Horizons*.

condensed example is shown in Figure 4–5. The categories are Important Points, Questions, and New Terms and Concepts. All sections must be used. Students star questions for which they need an answer from the teacher, and new terms they want to have defined. Notes should be limited to the front and back of the form, and a RESPONSE should not deal with more than a single chapter. If a chapter contains too much information for a single form, then the RESPONSE should be limited to a section within the chapter. The strategy can be adapted for use as a group or whole class activity with students as young as first graders, by listing three sections of the form on a large chart, on which the teacher records the children's contributions about what they are learning: important ideas, questions, and new terms. A RESPONSE chart prepared with younger students can be displayed and answers to the questions added as a topic is studied.

Teachers can use the strategy to interact with students individually; in this case, students give their completed forms to the teacher, who comments on the student's ideas, and responds to questions and requests for definitions of terms. Alternatively, students read the same assignment and complete the forms independently as homework, and then meet in cooperative groups to discuss their notes, highlight the most important points, and prioritize the questions for the teacher, before turning in the forms as a set. In an adaptation, group reading with RESPONSE, students read assigned text together, with the requirement that as group members find important ideas, or points about which they have questions, or identify new terms, they read these sections of text aloud to the group; the group then decides whether the idea, question, or new term should be recorded on the group's form.

Responding to a group of students' papers rather than to each student individually is less time-consuming for the teacher, and often more productive for students. Teachers must respond to students' forms substantively; that is, it would be a mistake simply to write "Good work!" at the top. The use of RESPONSE implies a conversation between student and teacher. If the teacher chooses not to respond to a student's starred question in writing, then it should be answered or commented on as part of class instruction, or in conversation with the student. When a teacher sees that many students have similar questions or need information about the

FIGURE 4–6   Sample of a RESPONSE Form Completed By a Student

(The teacher's response is yet to be added.)

Name: Stu DeHall   **Date:** 4/19

Reading assignment: Science, Chapter 20, Section 3

Important points: As you read, list essential information and state important ideas. Cite page numbers.

p. 481 Radiation travels in waves
light=one form
comes from stars, planets, oth. obj. in space
spectrum=radiation arranged by wave length (distance wave takes to repeat)
light=visible part of spectrum, & wave length for each color is diff.
red=longest, violet=shortest p. 482 so infrared, ultraviolet=off the edges

from chart on p. 481: gamma rays, X rays, ultraviolet rays, LIGHT(spectrum), infrared rays, radio waves

p. 482 all objects give off all kinds of radiation, but don't all give off same amounts of each kind of radiation.

need to study ultraviolet radiation through info from telescopes on satellites that are outside the atmosphere, bec. most of the ultrav. radiation from space can't get through the atmosphere (see question)

p. 483 Two pictures (I think the caption is confusing) both photographs of exploding star. Is the little picture of part of the area shown in the big one or the whole thing? I see why the colors are diff. (I think) but why are the shapes diff?

have to be hot to give off "much of their own visible light"— but cool objects, like earth, give off infrared rays, so scientists can study them that way.

Stars that are forming are cool; so scientists can see formation of stars through infrared photographs.

p. 484 "On earth people make radio waves to carry radio or television signals." (see question) "Hot gases make radio waves naturally. Radio telescopes collect and focus these waves."

Questions: As you read, note questions that occur to you. Cite page numbers of their source. Some questions will be ideas for discussion. For others, you will want an immediate answer. Star (*) these.

* 1. p. 481 "All objects give off varying amounts of all the kinds of radiation in the spectrum" so everything, everywhere, is radiating all sorts of stuff?
     p. 482 In imp. points: "most of the ultrav. radiation from space can't get through the atmosphere" Why?

* 2. chart on p. 481, arrows go off at both sides. Are there other kinds of rays on the edges?
     *I can see why the spectrum is separate, but what separates the categories of rays we can't see? Wavelength for gamma rays is shortest, but there's a range within that category and the edge looks (on the chart) just like the edge of X rays.

  3. p. 484 In imp. points: "On earth people make radio waves to carry radio or television signals." Can you explain how radio waves are made? Are the radio waves given off by all objects the same as what lets us hear radio and see TV?

New terms, concepts, vocabulary, and names: List words, phrases, technical terms, names of people and basic ideas that are new. Cite page numbers. Star (*) items you would like to have defined or explained.
     1) gamma rays   2) p. 482 Internat'l Ultraviolet Explorer—still up?   3) p. 484 radio telescope*

The text on which this RESPONSE is based is taken from *Earth Science* (1990), published by Scott, Foresman.

same technical terms, the teacher can present the information to the whole class. Problems can arise with the quality of students' RESPONSEs. Occasionally, an overconscientious student will begin by producing many pages; such students need to be reminded that the RESPONSE should be confined to the front and back of the form, and that they can limit the amount of text they respond to. A more common problem is with students whose first efforts seem careless or trivial. A useful strategy is to write a serious, substantive response to one issue or question raised by the student, and see whether, over a period of weeks, the quality of the student's product becomes better. Sometimes forms should be returned for revision; this should be done if the student has not raised any questions, or has listed topics but not given information in the Important Points section (for example, if instead of the detailed listing of important points shown in Figure 4–6, a student simply wrote *light, spectrum, radiation*).

These two strategies, Reading Road Maps and RESPONSE, are among the easiest study strategies for students to learn to use. They serve complementary purposes: Reading Road Maps enable the teacher to intervene as students begin to study a text selection; RESPONSE engages students and teachers in content-related conversation during and after the reading assignment. The strategies can be combined effectively by giving students both a Reading Road Map and RESPONSE form to use while studying.

Both strategies require teacher time, but at different points. Preparation of Reading Road Maps must be thoughtful, and each map will be different because it is a guide through a unique piece of text. (Directions, such as "Read the introduction carefully; make sure you understand the middle sections; and read and reread the conclusion," do not constitute a Reading Road Map.) RESPONSE, on the other hand, requires no advance preparation, but involves teachers in writing to students or talking to them about issues they have raised. For teachers who are capable computer users, it is efficient to respond to a group or a whole class by summarizing questions and responding to them, and then making multiple copies to distribute to students. In addition to working well together, both of these strategies combine

well with others. A teacher who enjoys creating learning materials can assign students to read a text chapter using a Reading Road Map, and follow up the next day with an A-Qu-A as a whole class activity, or a Cloze-Plus-Questions guide as a cooperative group activity. RESPONSE can be a useful preparation for Terminology Trade or Concept Connections.

Other Study Strategies.   Educators have devised a multitude of study techniques, so many that it would be foolish to attempt to teach them all. In the intermediate grades and above, content area teachers' responsibilities in this area are threefold: first, to be aware of a variety of study strategies and alert to learning about new ideas from the professional literature; second, to choose thoughtfully several study strategies that will be useful for students at the grade level and in the content area that they teach; and third, to teach and use these strategies in ways that enhance students' present and future learning. It is not useful to stress only a single strategy and insist that all students learn and use it in all situations.

SQ3R.   The SQ3R strategy is widely used, and many other study strategies are based on it. It was devised in 1946 by Francis Robinson. (The citation [Robinson, 1961] is from a revised edition of Robinson's text on studying, published years after he originated SQ3R.) The acronym stands for Survey, Question, Read, Recite, Review. One of the purposeful study methods that SQ3R incorporates is active responding: In the Reciting phase, students respond out loud (even if they are alone) or in writing, to what they have learned. When SQ3R is used, the first step in reading a text is to survey it, reading the chapter title and subheads, looking for clues about the topic to be studied. The next task for students is to devise questions about the topic that will probably be answerable after reading the text. In the three "R" steps, students first read to find answers to their questions. Next, they put away the book and their notes and try to recall actively, by reciting or writing, the answers to the questions. Finally, they review to check the accuracy of their answers, making corrections and reviewing as needed. The reciting component of SQ3R is essential. The step can be a "re-cite" (cite again) process done in writing; that is, the student can write down the information learned. However, talking is faster than writing, and also provides auditory feedback that may make information easier to remember. It is important to realize that we must use information actively if it is to become a part of our schemas—we may think we understand and will remember something after we read it, but then find, when we attempt to restate that information in writing or speech, that we have not in fact mastered it. SQ3R can be used across a wide age span, with younger children forming simpler questions based on simpler text. Teachers who decide to stress this strategy should teach and model the strategy directly before younger or less skilled students are expected to use it. It can be a useful whole class introduction to a chapter to begin with the steps of surveying and questioning, and to follow reading with reciting (sharing answers to the questions) and reviewing (checking the answers in the text).

MULTIPASS. The MULTIPASS strategy (Schumaker, Deshler, Alley, Warner, & Denton, 1982) offers a purposeful method of learning from text chapters, which students can easily remember and eventually use independently. It is designed to be combined with a writing, or note-taking, assignment. To use text efficiently, students make three "passes" through the reading assignment. First, in the Survey Pass, they check chapter organization and main ideas; then, in the Size-Up Pass, they look for facts to respond to questions they need to answer. Finally, in the Sort-Out Pass, students test themselves over the material. The strategy is a good activity for cooperative groups, where students can talk together during the Survey Pass, divide the responsibility for the Size-Up Pass, and share information and then quiz each other during the Sort-Out Pass. Alternatively, the Survey Pass can be completed as a whole class activity. Using the strategy helps move students away from the mistaken idea that the proper way to approach a text chapter is to read it from beginning to end at a uniform pace, and, if necessary, read it again the same way.

K-W-L. Devised by Donna Ogle (1986), K-W-L is a chart-based strategy that emphasizes the connection between prior knowledge and what is currently being learned. When the strategy is used, students, either individually or in a group, begin by filling in the first column in a chart where they list what they already know (K) about the topic to be studied. Then in the second column, students list what they want (W) to learn about the topic. After studying, students complete the chart by listing what they learned (L) in the third column. Although K-W-L appears very easy to use, teacher guidance and a substantial shared knowledge base among students are required for it to work well. Students who have sound and growing knowledge about a topic will be able to list more sensible, well-focused questions in the "Want to know" column than those who have little information about the topic. Moreover, some students may have information that is irrelevant (for example, impressions of dinosaurs based solely on cartoons), and they may also believe something that is not true (for example, listing "all dinosaurs were very big" in the "what I Know" column). It is useful to find proof or disproof for all "what I Know" statements and indicate this information in the "what I Learned" portion of the chart. Teacher guidance is essential; students as well as the teacher should be involved in evaluating and revising the chart, and it should always be a matter of pride to build learning. We should not emphasize that somebody was wrong, but rather we should take pride in developing an accurate listing. The strategy can be used with Semantic Mapping as both a comprehension and study strategy and can be expanded by adding a fourth column as the study of a topic is concluding, in which students can list their ideas for learning more.

Collaborating to Learn Terminology

Learning and remembering extensive amounts of content-related vocabulary can be supported in a lively way through Terminology Trade, a strategy used with cooperative learning groups. Materials needed consist of a pack of file cards, each with a different term related to the topic being studied. One term appears on each card; there are no duplicate cards; there should be from four to six cards per group. To begin the activity, all cards are given out to groups. Groups then decide which terms they will define, which terms they want the teacher to define, and which terms they will pass on to the next group, consulting their textbooks or notes if they wish. Usually about two minutes are provided for this decision making; then the teacher indicates which group will begin, after which turns progress clockwise. During its turn, a group defines the term on one card, and gives away two other terms, one to the next group, where the card then becomes part of that group's pack to use as they choose and one to the teacher, to be defined. The teacher's role in that turn is to comment quickly on the group's definition of a term, revising or elaborating it as needed, and to define the term received from the group. (It is the teacher's responsibility to accept cheerfully the terms given by students, rather than, for example, responding to being given a card with a scolding statement such as, "Oh, you certainly ought to know that one! I've explained it to you over and over again.") Thus, in each turn, two terms are defined, one by the group, one by the teacher. The next group then follows the same pattern: Define one and pass two. (Groups do not need to define a term that has been passed to them by another group; they may keep it, define it, pass it, or give it to the teacher.) A round ends when all groups have had a turn; approximately one minute is allowed between rounds for group discussion and planning about which words to define and which to pass in the upcoming round. The process ends either when time is up, or when all the cards have been used (often the former, because the activity is most enjoyable when groups continually have choices to make about their cards). A useful Terminology Trade can be accomplished in as little as ten minutes. The activity should not be a competition between groups, but it may be timed, with the class challenged to meet a time limit for accurate definition of a specified number of terms.

The strategy is easily learned and can be effectively used at every grade, either regularly or occasionally. Teacher preparation is minimal, limited to selecting important terms and printing them on cards (and being sufficiently knowledgeable about the vocabulary to define terms quickly and clearly). Using Terminology Trade helps ensure that concepts and technical terms will be recalled, and recalled accurately. When the text is being read, as students encounter unfamiliar terms, there is a pos-sibility that misunderstandings (rather than understanding) will develop. If undetected, these errors remain part of students' schemas. In Terminology Trade, content vocabulary is defined rapidly, aloud, and the teacher has the opportunity to expand upon or correct students' definitions. The activity involves sorting, which is itself a useful intellectual activity; students sort the terms into those they know, those they are not sure of, and those they do not know. Through Terminology Trade, content vocabulary becomes established in students' listening, speaking, reading, and conceptual vocabularies. The strategy also contributes to effective studying because students see the importance of using indexes to find terms quickly in a text, during the time allotted to groups for decision making and information finding before and between rounds. Because the strategy is a whole class activity, students all hear accurate explanations of important concepts, and all students have the opportunity to ask for information without feelings of inadequacy. If teachers choose, Terminology Trade may be used several times using the same set of words. When a set of cards is prepared for a new topic, relevant cards from previous sets may be included. Terminology Trade can be combined with many strategies and works particularly well with Semantic Mapping; students' maps are likely to be more detailed and sound if Terminology Trade precedes mapping.

Learning From Multiple Readings

The use of multiple readings in content area study is unlike most of the strategies described in this and other chapters, because it is a teaching method based on combining a variety of strategies for engaging students in reading important text more than once. Using multiple readings effectively means using more than one strategy, because the method does not consist of simply assigning students to read a text section, and then to go back and read it again. An incorrect and harmful message that is sometimes conveyed to students, beginning in the earliest grades, is that "poor" students must reread and "good" students do not have to. In fact, rereading is a primary strategy of proficient readers, whether they are reading to learn, reading to do, or reading to enjoy (purposes for reading described in an earlier chapter). This purposeful rereading is not the dreary process of working laboriously through a piece of text at a steady pace and then returning obediently to the beginning to move straight through it again. That is an ineffective method of learning, which is too often imposed on young readers, who learn from it that they are inferior readers; whereas their more successful classmates acquire the equally incorrect opinion that good readers do not reread.

Students need to be guided to realize that it is unlikely that challenging content area text will be understood on the basis of a single reading, and that rereading important text can result in not only a better understanding of it, but of understanding it in different ways. On a second or third reading of a text passage, for example, we can begin to see how the ideas presented relate to other topics and to other subject areas. Questions may occur to us that we had not considered before. We may see how we can use the new information in the passage. So rereading can help us move beyond acquiring new knowledge and help us see connections between new and established ideas. (Rereading text can help to build students' reading ability, as well as their content area knowledge.) There are many ways to make multiple readings a part of the classroom program. Teachers can plan to have the most important parts of informational text reread by arranging for several methods of reading as each topic is studied. (Note that the multiple readings method is not the same as the wide reading strategy, described in Chapter Three. In the wide reading strategy, students read from a variety of text materials that are all about the same topic. In multiple readings, the same text section is read repeatedly in a variety of ways.)

It is the combination of several methods of reading that produce multiple readings. Readings can occur directly, as when the teacher reads aloud or students read silently or aloud in pairs or small groups, or indirectly, as when strategies are used that engage students in reading and rereading important portions of text. (All the strategies are described in this or other chapters, and all are included in the Strategy Glossary, which follows Chapter Twelve.) Reading aloud from the text by the teacher serves a variety of important purposes. It makes interesting and important topics come alive for students and enables students to hear technical terms in context. It can provide a shared knowledge base; for example, through Teacher Read-Aloud Commentary or Solve Aloud, or when the teacher reads a significant passage from the text before a Semantic Mapping activity so that all students will begin the mapping process with useful information about the topic. Through Repeated Readings, students can be encouraged to develop the habit of rereading important text sections as an aid to their own learning. In Paired Reading, students read an assigned section of the text aloud in pairs, alternating pages. This style of reading aloud in the classroom, at a murmur level, can be used with older as well as younger students. During Paired Reading, the teacher can circulate among the reading pairs or may participate as a reading partner. Group Reading with RESPONSE engages students in reading cooperatively. For Taped Readings, at a listening center, or independently, students listen to text chapters on tape. The tapes are teacher-prepared and can feature the teacher as reader, or the teacher may enlist a variety of proficient readers to record, so that the voices students hear differ in gender and also in cultural accent and lilt. Students are encouraged, though not required, to follow along in the textbook while listening. When tapes are available, their use should be an option for all students, not an assignment that singles out some students, signaling that they are less capable than others.

All cloze strategies (Focused Cloze, Cloze-Plus-Questions Guides for older students, and Manipulable Cloze for younger students) incorporate rereading, because sections of the cloze passage must be read and reread as different words are considered to complete it. Reading Road Maps may specify sections of the text students should reread. Sequence Reading, Daily Journal, Echo Reading, Chanting, Choral Reading, and Readers' Theater are strategies that engage students in reading and rereading. Text scans and lookbacks occur as students complete a written assignment, individually, in pairs or in cooperative groups. Text scans are part of Search Tasks and are also a step in strategies that emphasize learning terminology, such as LEAD and List-Group-

Label, and a component of some study strategies, such as SQ3R. (Scanning is rapid skimming of text to find specific information.) Strategies, such as Detection and A-Qu-A, and teacher-prepared guides, such as Three-Level Guides, Pattern Guides, and Cloze-Plus-Questions Guides, present students with tasks that cannot be adequately completed without rereading parts of the text to find and confirm answers. This kind of brief purposeful rereading is called a lookback. A lookback is a rereading of part of a text that has already been read, to get a piece of information or to check the accuracy of information. (Note that the major difference between text scans and lookbacks is that text scans are wide ranging and lookbacks are narrowly focused. For example, in the LEAD strategy, the List step involves a text scan. Students check an entire text chapter to find technical terms. On the other hand, efficient students completing the Three-level Guide shown in Figure 4–10 would use a lookback to make sure of giving a complete response to the literal task, "Make a list of characteristics of desert plants that make it hard for desert animals to eat them." In a text scan, a large section of text is surveyed; in a lookback, a brief section of text is checked. The other difference between text scans and lookbacks is that text scans are usually "look-aheads," surveying a section of text that has not yet been read. When students use lookbacks, they have already read the text once, so they have a good idea which section of the text chapter to examine.)

In Figure 4–7, examples are given of strategy combinations for multiple readings. Only one example is given at each of four grade ranges, but the examples represent only a few of a wide variety of choices teachers can make. Multiple readings clarify and deepen understanding, and support recall. By giving greater depth to understanding, the multiple readings strategy enables students to apply their knowledge in a variety of situations, and connects current learning to what is already known and, eventually, to what will be learned later. Although rereading alone can be an excellent method of learning, reading important text more than once using a variety of methods builds understanding while students learn in various ways, thus maintaining their interest. The multiple readings strategy is suitable for every grade and can effectively be used either regularly or occasionally.

When multiple readings are used, pacing is an important consideration. The teacher needs to select strategies that fit together well, mesh with the rest of the teaching program, and can be accomplished expeditiously. Using multiple readings should not result in the class plodding through a series of activities over a long period of time, and teachers must never give the students the impression that multiple readings are being used because some (or all) members of the class are "slow" students. This would make the process unpleasant, and would foster the incorrect and dangerous idea that "good" students only need to read a text once. Many

---

FIGURE 4–7 Examples of Combining Strategies to Provide Multiple Readings

Level: primary grades
Subject: Math (word problems)
Strategies used: Solve Aloud, paired reading, Daily Journal, Readers' Theater

Level: intermediate grades
Subject: Social Studies
Strategies used: Teacher-Read-Aloud Commentary, List-Group-Label (text scans), paired reading, Cloze-Plus-Questions Guides (lookbacks)

Level: middle school
Subject: Science
Strategies used: Teacher Read-Aloud Commentary, Group reading with RESPONSE, A-Qu-A, Detection

Level: high school
Subject: History
Strategies used: Search Tasks, Reading Road Map, reading with lookbacks to complete Three-level Guides, Pattern Guides, or Cloze-Plus-Question Guides

capable students who have acquired this idea during the K–12 school years are seriously handicapped by it when they reach college.

Teachers foster learning by reading aloud.

Teachers Foster Learning By Reading Aloud

Reading aloud has a long history. In the movie *The Princess Bride*, Peter Falk remarks to his grandson, who is skeptical about being read to, "When I was a kid, television was called *books*." In a wonderful piece of oral history collected by Studs Terkel in his book *American Dreams*, ninety-four-year-old Dora Rosenzweig reminisces about her experiences, more than eighty years before, working in a cigar factory. She worked in a room with thirty or forty others, rolling cigars. She had completed sixth grade. "They elected me a reader. I used to roll fifty cigars an hour. That was my piece-work limit. So if I read for an hour, they would donate the fifty cigars I missed. If I read for two hours, they'd give me a hundred… I read about current events, a book, or even a play. I would choose the books. Whoever heard of a twelve-year-old girl reading Flaubert's *Salammbô*? Whatever struck me, I'd read to the others. Tolstoi, anything" (Terkel, 1980, p. 120).

A Part of Learning to Read

Having the experience of being read to is an important part of learning to read. The value of reading aloud to children is consistently stressed in texts about the reading process and in books written for audiences of both educators and parents, such as *Becoming a Nation of Readers*, by Richard C. Anderson and his colleagues (Anderson, Hiebert, Scott, & Wilkinson, 1986) and *Beginning to Read* by Marilyn Jager Adams (1990). Jim Trelease's *Read-aloud Handbook* (Trelease, 1989) has been a best seller.

The evidence is overwhelming that children who are read to as preschoolers are at an advantage in learning to read. Gordon Wells (1986) obtained estimates from the families of first graders about how many stories had been read to their children before they entered first grade, and then observed the children's progress in reading during the course of that year. He contrasted the progress of the child he called "Jonathan," who had heard about 6000 stories before coming to school and who was, and remained, the most successful learner in his class, with the experience of "Rosie," who had never been read to, and who was and remained throughout the year the child for whom learning to read was the greatest struggle. Unfortunately, there can be a negative side to the fact that teachers, and students learning to be teachers, have become aware of the research showing the importance of reading aloud to infants and young children. There is a risk that teachers may decide that children who have not had literacy experiences before coming to school are already marked for reading failure. This is a mistake, theoretically, practically, and ethically. Teachers can, and should, provide a rich literacy environment in school, and all students can benefit from this.

The shared book experience, a method devised by Don Holdaway (1979, 1982), is a way to provide elementary school children, in classrooms, with a read-aloud experience similar to those of younger children who are read to at home. Ideally, a shared book experience uses a Big Book, a book printed on very large pages, with extra large print and illustrations. Big Books are available from commercial publishers and can also be constructed by teachers. The book is placed so that children can see it easily, and, if possible, touch it. The book might be placed on an easel, or on the floor with the children gathered around. The teacher talks about the book with the children and then reads it aloud, often moving a finger under the lines of print while reading. During the reading, children and teacher may stop to talk about the story, but the conversation should be informal and child-centered, never an attempt to check children's understanding or attention. When the book has been read, the teacher reads it again, if children wish to hear it. (When the setting is a comfortable one, children love to hear favorite stories over and over.) Each day for a week, the book is read at least once. Conversations about the story and about aspects of print—words and letters—are encouraged, and children read along with the teacher if they wish.

A Part of Learning

Reading a variety of texts, including expository writing, enriches the language arts program, and can enhance subject matter learning in science and social studies as well. Petey Young and her colleagues advocate regular reading aloud of excerpts from content area texts to familiarize students with the style in which textbooks are written.

> Students learn more quickly if the reader is respected, thoroughly familiar with the material, and is a fluent, smooth reader. Students, even the best readers, are not necessarily fluent when they read aloud and do not comprehend as much themselves when they are concentrating on their presentation. Also, other students do not listen as well when a fellow student reads because they are easily bored by uninspired reading... The point of beginning or ending a lesson by reading [from a textbook] is to demonstrate how the language of the book is meant to be read. (Young, Ruck, & Crocker, 1991, p. 48)

In selecting material to read aloud, a teacher is helped by his own reading, and by making it a practice to read regularly in a variety of genres, including good narrative and expository text written for children, young adults, and also for adults. Ray Doiron (1994) recommends excerpting, that is, choosing vivid, important portions of a written text to read aloud, rather than reading every piece in its entirety. This is a practice that Betty Carter and Richard Abrahamson (1991) also advocate, particularly when nonfiction trade books are read aloud. By

excerpting, it is demonstrated to students that good reading does not always mean starting at the beginning and reading straight through to the end. Doiron (1994, p. 623) comments:

> These are exciting times for nonfiction writers, illustrators, and publishers, but they are particularly exciting for educators and young readers because all the parts are in place for a balanced literacy program—a balance that includes the reading aloud of quality fiction and nonfiction trade books, a balance between the literature of fiction and the literature of fact.

Research has demonstrated that reading aloud to students is a sound method of encouraging vocabulary growth (e.g., Elley, 1989). Given the recognized value to learners of being read to, why is reading aloud not consistently a regular part of school programs? Reasons include the view that reading aloud is only appropriate or useful for young children; teachers' fear that this is not an appropriate use of instructional time; and the concern of some teachers, particularly those in the intermediate grades and above, that they do not know how to hold the attention of a group when reading aloud, and do not know how to choose appropriate reading material. Research and good practice show us that neither the first nor the second reason (the view that reading aloud is only appropriate or useful for young children; the fear that this is not an appropriate use of instructional time) is sound. Being read to by teachers has been shown to benefit students for whom English is a second language (e.g., Elley and Mangubhai, 1983). Those who work primarily with students who have difficulties in learning have pointed out the strong benefits to these learners in listening to teachers read. In *Readers and writers with a difference: A holistic approach to teaching learning disabled and remedial students,* Lynn K. Rhodes and Curt Dudley-Marling write:

> Reading to our students helps them understand the nature and purposes of reading and familiarizes them with the patterns of written language... Students' reading vocabulary, their reading comprehension, their reading interests, and the quality of their oral language have been shown to be positively affected by having someone read to them... Secondary level students also enjoy being read to and

will benefit from the experience. There is reason to believe that students from lower socioeconomic groups and from lower ranges of reading achievement (e.g., LD and remedial readers) may benefit the most from being read to…. Reading to students is also an excellent vehicle for broadening students' experiences and may be an especially effective way to assist students who may not have background experiences teachers feel are important. (Rhodes & Dudley-Marling, 1988, p. 79)

An added advantage of reading to older students has been noted by Barbara Hoetker Ash (1990), who found that high school students who claimed that a humorous short story was dull and incomprehensible were able to understand and enjoy it when the story was read aloud by the teacher. In the teacher's reading, intonation and emphasis brought passages to life that the students had not known how to interpret, when reading the story on their own. One can tell from the context of Ash's article that the story assigned was James Thurber's "The Secret Life of Walter Mitty."

It wasn't until I hit 'ta-pocketa, pocketa, pocketa, *pocketa, pocketa* that the students roared with laughter. And who was laughing the loudest? That's right—two of the girls who had said there was nothing funny about the story.

Naturally I pressed them on the matter. "You said there was nothing funny!" I protested. "There wasn't," came the reply, "when we read it. But it was the *way* you said it, Dr. Ash." At which point another student, not one of the original five, clarified. "Yeah. Remember when your parents would read you those fairy tales and make the voice of the BIG BEAR and the *tiny baby bear* voice and you'd be delighted, but when you read it yourself it wouldn't seem nearly so good?" Now I was beginning to see the light: "You mean, I asked incredulously, "that when you read you don't hear the different voices in your head?' "Naw," came another classmate's reply, "we just read like this"—and she held up her book, with her finger following the words-"da, da, da, da, da, da." "That's right," agreed any number of others in the class. (Ash, 1990, p. 78)

Concerns that one does not know how to hold the attention of a group when reading aloud, or does not know how to choose appropriate reading material ought not to deter one, because one can learn,

and there are resources within the professional literature to help. Nancie Atwell (1987b) provides a list of guidelines for practicing and using reading aloud in teaching older students, in her inspiring book about incorporating literacy experiences in reading and writing into the middle school program, In the middle: reading, writing, and learning with adolescents. Jim Trelease's book includes a chapter on "The Dos and Don'ts of Read-Aloud" (Trelease, 1989, pp. 79–85), which offers helpful guidelines.

It is useful to collect and classify good content-related reading material, so that it will be readily available. One practical method is to use one or more accordion-style file folders, with sections marked for content areas and topics, so that whenever we come across useful material for reading aloud, we can put a copy, or a reference that reminds us where the material can be found, into the file. There are a wide variety of occasions for incorporating reading aloud in content area programs:

■ The reading can be taken directly from the students' text, and a read-aloud session can be used to begin a lesson. When a text passage is both important and difficult to understand, the teacher can bring it to life for students, and simultaneously help students learn to read the technical vocabulary, by reading the passage to the class, perhaps commenting on it in the form of a Teacher Read-Aloud Commentary. The teacher can regularly introduce discussions by reading aloud an important, well-written passage from the text, from a newspaper or magazine, or from another source.

■ Supplementary reading material selected by the teacher, either factual or fictional, can be read at the beginning of a series of lessons to build background knowledge of unfamiliar content area topics. This kind of reading aloud can be the Experience Activity used in the LEAD method of vocabulary instruction.

■ Because students who are in the process of learning to read typically can understand more difficult text than they can read themselves, teachers can expand and deepen students' knowledge of text topics by reading aloud relevant selections from biographies, histories, or magazine and newspaper articles. These reading sessions can be scheduled during the last 10 or 15 minutes of an instructional period, to bring the lesson to a close.

▪ Reading aloud can be established as a regular part of the weekly class schedule or the school day, and the teacher can choose from different genres, and include both expository and narrative selections. Students' familiarity with, and enjoyment of, expository text can be developed when teachers read regularly from excellent expository writing. Students' awareness of connections between literature and content area studies can be developed when teachers read poetry and stories that are related to the content topic being studied.

Reading to students encourages them to want to read.

An Impetus to Read More

Major reasons for reading aloud to students are to draw them into the delights of reading, and to acquaint them with some of the riches of the printed word. Timothy Rasinski (1991, pp. 33 and 32) speaks of "books as an impetus." He chooses a concept from physics—inertia—when he discusses reading aloud to students as a way of encouraging their reading. It is a fact about the physical world that something in motion will continue in motion until another force acts upon it to stop it or slow it down, and that something not moving will remain at rest until some force sets it in motion. This principle of inertia can be applied to reading: Readers will read more; nonreaders will continue not to read unless there is a cause for change.

> Reading inertia is a potential problem for many students and needs to be addressed. It is not so much a problem with reading skills or abilities as it is a matter of seeing reading as important and enjoyable. This vision of reading comes about through positive initial experience with books... Books themselves can be an experience that leads students into other books. (Rasinski, 1991)

Students who do not see reading as important and enjoyable are, and are in danger of remaining, aliterate. Aliterate people do not choose to read, even though they can. The problem of aliteracy, and of misguided educational methods that contribute to it, is unfortunately both longstanding and widespread. In 1908, Edmund Huey wrote:

> The prevalent methods of teaching reading are such as cultivate wrong habits and attitudes concerning books.... The child does not want to learn reading as a mechanical tool, ...[but] must have a 'personal hunger' for what is read.... [and come to] reading with personal experience with which to appreciate it. (Huey, 1968, pp. 305–306)

Mihaly Csikszentmihalyi has written:

> Many people give up on learning after they leave school because thirteen or twenty years of extrinsically motivated education is still a source of unpleasant memories.
>
> Their attention has been manipulated long enough from the outside by textbooks and teachers, and they have counted graduation as their first day of freedom. (1991, p. 141)
>
> It seems increasingly clear that the chief impediments to literacy are not cognitive in nature. It is not that students cannot learn; it is that they do not wish to.... Literacy... will be mastered more readily and more thoroughly when the student becomes able to derive intrinsic rewards from reading. (1990, pp. 115–116)

All students, including those who are capable readers, benefit from being read to. Catherine Ann Ecroyd (1991) has described the benefits of reading aloud to high school honors students. Patricia J. Cianciolo (1989, pp. 72 and 77) has stressed the importance of reading aloud to those she calls "transitional readers... eight- to eleven-year-olds who can read fairly independently and are mature enough for fairly lengthy stories but need to sharpen and extend their reading comprehension and critical thinking skills." She writes:

> [W]e must read aloud quality literature to the children we serve, including those who are not accomplished or enthusiastic readers as well as those who are able to enjoy and understand these books when they are read to them.

She places reading aloud to students as the first of the basic instructional strategies that teachers and librarians are obligated to use. A memorable reason for reading aloud to students, particularly older students, is that for some, this may be their only opportunity to become acquainted with good literature, and even, perhaps, one of the few pleasant school experiences they will have. On the basis of interviews with adult illiterates, LaVergne Rosow (1988, p. 122) found "not one person could recall ever hearing stories or being read to at home or in elementary school." She did interview one man who remembered being read to by a middle school teacher over a period of several months. He reported that he could still remember the sound of her voice.

The Importance of Teacher Knowledge

Often teachers who are remembered by their students for what they have read aloud have one or several beloved books, stories, essays, or poems they read each year, finding new aspects to enjoy themselves with each rereading. This is wonderful for teacher and students alike. Teachers who best demonstrate love of literature are likely to be wide readers themselves. The wealth of books published and the wealth of books that appear each year is a primary means of revealing the truth that there is no one set of readings that constitute a correct set of readings. Although it is useful, in a regular program of reading aloud, for students to be able to request that favorite texts be read again, the original choices for reading need to be made by the teacher, because the teacher will be familiar with a much wider array of possibilities. A major purpose of read-alouds is to expand students' reading horizons. Thus, teacher knowledge is important in this area, as in every aspect of teaching. Wide personal reading is the basis for having many ideas about what to read aloud; suggestions will also come from professional journals, from texts such as this one, and from colleagues and friends.

Examples from the professional literature are a reminder both of the rich possibilities for using literature to enhance content learning, and also of the fact that these possibilities are dependent on teacher's knowledge. Dalva Hedlund and her colleagues (Hedlund, Furst, & Foley, 1989) point to the value of reading aloud excerpts from journals kept during memorable events and later published, such as the journals of Frederick Douglass. Judy Richardson (1995) discusses reading aloud Edgar Allan Poe's short story "The Masque of the Red Death," which recounts attempts to escape from a plague, as an introduction to the study of AIDS. John Brierley gives details of a unit on winds, ocean currents, and weather, which he begins by reading aloud John Masefield's classic poem "Cargoes":

> Quinquireme of Nineveh from distant Ophir,
> Rowing home to haven in sunny Palestine,
> With a cargo of ivory,
> And apes and peacocks,
> Sandalwood, cedarwood, and sweet white wine.
>
> …Dirty British coaster with a salt-caked smoke stack,
> Butting through the Channel in the mad March days,
> With a cargo of Tyne coal,
> Road-rail, pig-lead,
> Firewood, iron-ware, and cheap tin-trays …

His students listen, raise questions, examine an atlas of ocean currents, and identify those that would affect the voyages described in the poem. One of the themes of his unit of study is "Trade and mother nature make some places more exciting than others" (Brierley, 1990, p. 166).

Barbara Wass Van Ausdall (1994), a high school English teacher, links Charles Dickens's *A Tale of Two Cities* with present-day events. Writing more than a hundred years ago, and describing events of a time now more than two hundred years past, Dickens illuminated the tragic effects of alcoholism through the character of Sydney Carton; described, through the 18-year imprisonment of Dr. Manette, the power of a government to imprison without trial and without allowing families to know whether their missing loved ones are alive or dead, a power still exercised by tyrannical dictatorships; and portrayed the hunger of the residents of the district of St. Antoine, which parallels present-day sufferings from famines. With perennial timeliness, he showed, in the character of Madame Defarge, the corrosive effects of responding to life's tragedies with relentless bitterness and an unquenchable thirst for revenge. *A Tale of Two Cities* is an ideal choice for combining excerpted read-alouds with videotaped productions, permitting all students to experience the beauty of the language and the drama of the story without requiring everyone to read straight through a text which many students would find difficult to read and appreciate on their own.

◨◨ Learners Organize Knowledge and ◨◨ Make Connections

As students are learning about new content area topics, it is essential that they see relationships among concepts and become experienced in making connections among ideas. Content area teachers need a variety of strategies to encourage learning that is coherent and constructive, rather than simply a temporary memorization of facts. In this section, strategies that engage students in organizing connections graphically are described, in using teacher-prepared guides and in making connections among concepts.

Organizing Concepts Graphically

In teaching, the word *see* is used in two different ways. Teachers expect students to see the relationships among concepts they are learning about: They should grasp, understand, and have a mental vision of those connections. In the process of learning, it is often helpful to use strategies that enable students actually to see with their eyes how ideas are connected. Of course, we cannot see ideas, but visual symbols remind us of relationships. As a non-content-related example, writing two people's names

and drawing a heart around them is a traditional way of indicating an affectionate relationship. Listing items in a column and putting a number beside each one is a common method of prioritizing the things we have to do. List-Group-Label and Semantic Mapping are useful instructional strategies in which students arrange content-related terms so that their conceptual relationships literally can be seen.

Categorizing Prior Knowledge.   Originally developed by Hilda Taba (1967) as a strategy to develop vocabulary in social studies and encourage students to think analytically, the List-Group-Label method is useful across areas of study, especially when content vocabulary is extensive, and includes familiar as well as unfamiliar terms. The teacher should introduce the topic to be studied in a way that engages the students actively and provides a common basis for group listing of relevant words, for example, by conducting a science demonstration, reading a newspaper article related to social studies or health, or asking cooperative learning groups to compare pictures or realia from the present and the past. (Realia are real things. If teachers have access to real items used in the past—tools, toys, clothing, and so on—these can make a useful display; for example, examining a display of actual cooking utensils used many years ago can help students think about differences, and similarities, between the ways people lived in times past and the way we live now.) A text search for vocabulary, as in the LEAD strategy, can be combined with one of these activities, or it may constitute the introduction, especially if students are encouraged also to list words suggested by text illustrations. As students brainstorm terms related to the topic, the teacher lists them on the board. (Listing on a chart is not useful, because the words will be rearranged in the next step of the strategy.)

The group and label steps come next. With teacher guidance, students decide how to put the terms into meaningful groups, and determine a category label for each group. ("We Don't Know Yet" should always be a possible category so that students are not encouraged to categorize words that are totally unfamiliar. Risk-taking in study should often be encouraged, but vocabulary learning is usually not the place for it. If students misclassify words, the correct meanings of those words may be harder to learn.) Alternate groupings and labels should be encouraged as long as they are based on an understanding of the terms. A brief discussion of the groupings and labels will provide students with background knowledge for subsequent reading of the text. At this point, the labeled groups of terms can be charted so that students can see the vocabulary during reading. It can then become a class or cooperative group activity to revise the groupings, and organize them further, during the time the topic is studied.

Organizing Concepts. Semantic Mapping (Johnson & Pearson, 1984; Johnson, Pittelman, & Heimlich, 1986; Wood, 1987b) enables students to develop their understanding of content-related concepts by organizing their knowledge in a graphic display showing interrelationships among concepts. Like many other strategies, Semantic Mapping has been called by different names, including Concept Mapping (Novak, 1991; Novak & Gowin, 1984; Roth & Roychoudhury, 1992), webbing (Clewell & Haidemos, 1983), Semantic Webbing (Freedman & Reynolds, 1980) and FAN (Swaby, 1984). This kind of variety in names happens when good teaching ideas occur to several people who publish descriptions before the strategy becomes widely known under a single name. At present, the terms used for the strategy tend to divide across disciplines, with the term *Concept Mapping* frequently used when this strategy is used in the sciences.

In the Semantic Mapping strategy, the teacher identifies the content area topic and encourages students, either in small groups or as a whole class, to make a long list of related words and terms. During brainstorming, all ideas are accepted and the leader or recorder lists them, without praising or criticizing. (When standard practice for brainstorming is followed, a brief period of incubation—silence for one or two minutes to allow each person's ideas to emerge—occurs immediately after the topic is announced and before any ideas are shared.) When a list has been prepared, students work in groups to organize the terms into a weblike pattern, with subsidiary concepts arranged around central ones to show their interrelationships. This process gives students a chance to share and compare the information they have about a topic, and alerts them to areas in which they need further information, and to possible subtopics for research.

Suppose students are about to read a chapter in a science text on the topic of oceans. One group's brainstormed list of related terms might contain these items: salt water; fed by rivers (not salt water); "sea roads" for exploration, travel, commerce; Atlantic, Pacific, Arctic, are there others?; underwater exploration, mapping the sea floor, Mariana Trench; Jacques Cousteau; whales, fish; seaweed, seashells; pollution; commercial uses; oil; recreation, sports, swimming, surfing, vacations; effects on climate. One way in which items from this list could be revised, expanded, and arranged into a Semantic Map is shown in Figure 4–8. The Semantic Mapping strategy can be used before reading and extended into the reading process, as webs that are formed are elaborated and used as a basis for discussion and writing about the topic.

Preparing Semantic Maps encourages creativity. Hierarchies can be shown by type size, with the most important categories in large type. Shapes and colors may be used to differentiate categories or expand the map; for example, using Figure 4–8 as an ongoing display, groups or dyads focusing on ocean life might choose light green paper and add facts and pictures on triangles (for plants), squares (animals) and circles (protists). Figure 4–9, based on a chapter in *Many thousand gone: African Americans from slavery to freedom*, by Virginia Hamilton (1993), shows a map constructed to conclude study of a historical figure. The map states connections in addition to showing categories. An alternate pattern for showing connections is to connect categories with double lines, and write connecting phrases within the double lines; in Figure 4–9, for example, *Sojourner Truth* and the banner could be connected directly by double lines with "she wore a banner" written within those lines.

The essence of Semantic Mapping is generating ideas and then grouping ideas. The strategy works well with younger students when teachers modify the requirements for writing and reading. Such a process could include these steps: children brainstorm ideas about ways people grow and change, a topic in their science curriculum; the teacher records their ideas on the chalkboard; after discussion children draw pictures illustrating ways that people grow and change; the teacher writes selected ideas on strips of heavy paper, and uses echo reading to guide the class in reading them; the group decides on an arrangement, perhaps grouping changes along an age span. Statements and chil-

FIGURE 4–8   Semantic Map

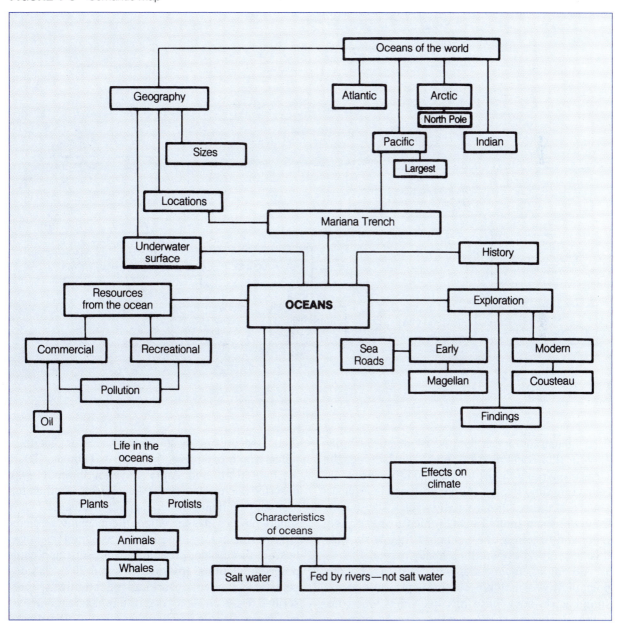

FIGURE 4–9   Semantic Map with Relationships Stated

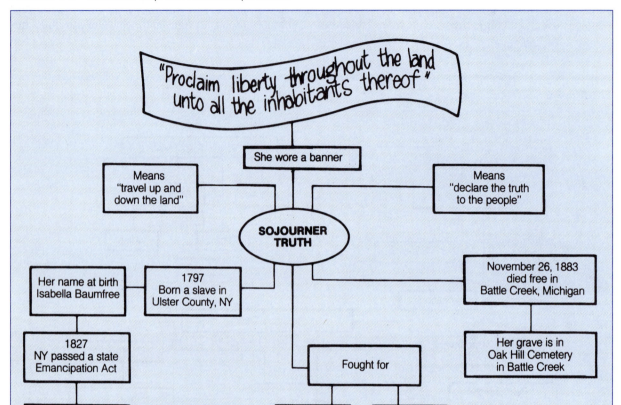

dren's illustrations can then be arranged for a display. In this adaptation of Semantic Mapping, the ideas are written by the teacher, and then used and reused by the children. Although there is no insistence that the children read the written statements, they will have many opportunities to hear them read, and to join in the reading if they wish—and this, of course, develops their ability to read.

Although Semantic Mapping can be used at any point in the learning process, maps prepared after a sound knowledge base has been developed are demonstrably more clear, accurate, and complex than those created by students who are not yet unfamiliar with a topic (e.g., Johnson & Thomas, 1992). Michael Roth and Anita Roychoudhury (1992) describe the use of concept mapping as a method for assessing students' understanding in advanced high school physics classes, where the mapping sessions followed laboratory experiments, assigned readings, lecture, discussion, problem-solving sets, and computer simulations. Instructors listed 20 to 25 concepts, and students, working collaboratively, transcribed terms on slips, tried different arrangements, and then prepared finished maps on 12×18 paper.

Semantic Mapping is useful at every grade. It can be adapted for use with young children and is a remarkably versatile strategy for older students that can be used effectively either regularly or occasionally. The mapping itself takes no teacher time, but teacher time is required for examining and commenting upon the maps that students prepare. If the maps are not used, or if the teacher does not take time to look at student products and comment on them substantively, then the strategy will have limited learning value. Terminology Trade teams very well with Semantic Mapping. Well-constructed Semantic Maps can be turned into a modified cloze activity for a bulletin board display or learning center activity, if essential terms or category labels are put on cards that can be removed and then replaced.

Knowledge Building Through Guides and Graphics

Teachers who enjoy creating materials and are willing to commit time to preparing thoughtful guides to help their students learn from challenging text have a variety of good formats from which to choose. Three of these strategies are Three-Level Guides, Cloze-Plus-Questions Guides, and Pattern Guides. Each helps students cope with concept overload in text. Each also directs students' attention to important sections of the text, so that they are not distracted by peripheral text sections that have been included only to capture attention. As an alternative or supplement to Pattern Guides, Pattern Graphics can be introduced by teachers and then prepared by students.

Three-Level Guides.   Three-Level Guides were devised by a leader in the field of content area reading, Harold Herber (1978), as a teaching strategy to aid comprehension and encourage thoughtful studying. Three-level guides are teacher-created materials to accompany a portion of text based on the instructional practice of questioning to teach. Herber designed guides for use in literature courses, using literal, interpretive, and application questions. When these guides are used in content area instruction, literal, inferential, and application questions are most

useful. It is helpful, when preparing a Three-Level Guide, to label the question sections and to provide age-appropriate definitions. For example, the following might be adapted as headings for the sections of a Three-Level Guide designed for older students.

- Answer the questions in this literal section based on what you learn directly from your reading.
- In responding to inferential questions, you will need to combine information from the text with your own ideas and knowledge, and use your ability to draw conclusions based on what you have read.
- Application questions encourage you to use what you have learned by relating it to other topics.

An important factor to keep in mind is the importance of creating questions that are interrelated across levels, so that by answering literal questions, students are guided to draw useful inferences, and to apply their knowledge. Figure 4–10 presents an example of a set of well-written questions at different levels, designed for a Three-Level Guide about deserts. The first literal question is written so that the clever answer "They live in deserts" can be accepted, still requiring one more content-based difference to be given. The inferential question in Figure 4–10 follows a tell/ask pattern; that is, it focuses students' attention by giving important information first, and then posing a related question or series of questions. (Of course, the question would be literal rather than inferential if the text discussed the interrelated adaptive advantages of animal's sharp teeth and plants' tough leaves.) In answering the application question, students may want to use an encyclopedia or other resource so they can copy a drawing of a desert plant and a desert animal; this sensible use of resources should be encouraged.

A common error made in writing Three-Level Guides is to focus inferential questions on the affective, rather than the cognitive domain; that is, to ask questions about feelings rather than ideas. Such questions can be answered as facilely as they can be written: "How would you have felt if you had been a slave?" (sad, unhappy, angry). "How do you think the Pilgrims felt when they arrived at Plymouth Rock?" (happy, excited, relieved, grateful, sleepy, seasick, cold, hungry, tired, you name it). Unfortunately, many teachers and preservice teachers, when they

FIGURE 4–10 Sample Three-Level Guide

Use this guide as you read Chapter Seven in our science text.

Use a separate sheet of paper for your responses to the questions and tasks.

Literal questions: You can find the answers to these questions right in the text.

∎ What are two ways desert plants and desert animals are alike?

∎ What are the characteristics of desert plants that make it hard for desert animals to eat them? Make a list.

∎ What are the characteristics of desert animals that make it possible for them to get food and water from desert plants? Make a list.

Inferential questions: To answer inferential questions, you need to combine information from the text with your own ideas and knowledge.

∎ Desert plants and desert animals have adaptations which enable them both to survive in the desert climate. Some of the plant and animal adaptations you have listed above are related. For example, how are the tough leaves and stems of plants related to animals' sharp teeth? What other connections can you see between the features of desert plants and animals?

∎ How are the desert plants useful to desert animals? How are the desert animals useful to desert plants?

∎ Why is it necessary for the survival of both animals and plants, for it to be both hard, and possible, for animals to eat the desert plants?

Application task: Application questions and tasks are a way for you to show what you have learned.

∎ Make a sketch of a desert plant, showing parts that grow below the ground as well as those that grow above the ground. Label your drawing by listing all the ways the plant's features help it to survive in a desert climate.

∎ Add a drawing of a desert animal getting nourishment from part of the plant.

∎ Show the probable time of day.

---

write inferential or interpretive questions, write only questions about feelings, often questions that can be answered without thought (or even without reading the selection). In a study contrasting students' responses to "narrow" and "broad" comprehension questions, Charlotte Smith (1978, p. 900) found:

> higher cognitive questions elicited longer average responses [but] not all broad questions were consistent in eliciting longer responses… the answers to broad valuing questions about personal feelings usually elicited brief answers indicative of lower cognitive level responses. For example, in answer to the valuing question, 'how would you feel?' the brief response might be, 'glad,' 'bad,' 'terrible,' 'sad,' or 'happy.'

It is possible, however, for teachers to prepare inferential questions that require thinking and still tap the affective domain. Successful use of such questions depends on good prior teaching. For example, if students have read (and been read to) from both text and supplementary materials about conditions during the Great Depression of the 1930s, and have had this learning supplemented with some oral history from an older person who can recall that time, they will be prepared to give thoughtful answers to questions beginning "How would you have felt?…" and "What would you have done?…"

Cloze-Plus-Questions Guides. These guides consist of a cloze passage followed by questions about the topic of the passage. Well-constructed Cloze-Plus-Questions Guides give students a language and thinking challenge, which, when completed, provides them with knowledge about the topic they will be reading and studying about, and a sense of satisfaction in their accomplishment. When students work together to solve a cloze passage that presents important ideas, they use these ideas, as well as their sense of language. The questions that are part of Cloze-Plus-Questions Guides give them clues about the meaning of the passage as they are solving the cloze. The strategy is an excellent activity for partners or for cooperative groups; as is true of all cloze activities used for instructional purposes, learning is enhanced when students work collaboratively.

Construction of a Cloze-Plus-Questions Guide is based on finding or writing a clear fact-packed selection. Concept statements are useful for this purpose, the guide shown in Figure 4–11 is based on a concept statement about the Industrial Revolution. Omitting every tenth word (after leaving the first and last sentences intact) gives students sufficient context to complete the passage. In this kind of guide, there are fewer constraints on the kinds of questions which can be asked, since they do not

need to follow a literal, inferential, application format, nor be written to match a text pattern. In Figure 4–11, students are asked to make predictions about what they will be learning, based on their own knowledge and reasoning, and on clues from the cloze passage. Other questions draw students' attention to a challenging concept in the text, and to an interesting historical fact.

Pattern Guides and Pattern Graphics.   Text patterns were discussed in Chapter One; a graphic representation of six commonly used patterns was presented in Figure 1–3. Pattern Guides (Olson & Longnion, 1982) are teacher-devised materials that

---

FIGURE 4–11   Cloze-Plus-Questions Guide

Historians of the 1830's were struck by the many changes in industry that had occurred between 1760 and 1790 in Western Europe and America. Before 1750, most goods had been produced by hand, and _____ people had been farmers. There was a shift from _____ to manufacturing when machines replaced hand tools, and new _____ of power (steam and electricity) replaced human and animal _____. Industry was taken from the home into factories; handwork _____ replaced by machinery. The scholars of the 1800s who _____ these changes saw that the changes had dramatically altered _____ way people lived.

J. A. Blanqui, a French political economist, first _____ the phrase "Industrial Revolution" when writing about these changes. _____ word *revolution* suggests a sudden, drastic, rapid change, but _____ now know that these changes were the result of _____, gradual, evolutionary developments. It is interesting to note that _____ and other scholars thought that the Industrial Revolution would _____ come to an end and that any future changes _____ come gradually. We now know

that the possibilities for _____ inventions are manifold, and that new inventions can be rapidly created and put to use.

▌ Food is a necessity of life. List some ways you think the amount and variety of food available to most families changed between 1760 and 1790, and the reasons for these changes.

▌ The text passage tells us that the Industrial Revolution caused changes that "dramatically altered" people's lives. List some dramatic changes that you believe probably occurred in that thirty-year time period.

▌ None of the people in Western Europe and America during the period of time from 1760 to 1790 knew that they were living during the Industrial Revolution. Why is this so?

▌ None of the people in Western Europe and America from 1914 to 1918 knew that they were living during World War I. Why is this so?

▌ Can you think of another related example?

▌ In your group, take two minutes to brainstorm a list of inventions you know were invented in this century, after a time scholars thought the pace of inventing would become much slower.

The cloze passage is based on a concept statement prepared by Mary Collier. Answers to Figure 4–11 can be found in the Solutions section at the back of this book.

call students' attention to the pattern used in a portion of text, and help them learn by answering questions based on that pattern. Pattern Guides are useful learning activities for two reasons: they help students understand and learn from a particular text passage, and they help students develop the ability to recognize text patterns in other content area reading.

Not all content area text is written following a pattern; on the other hand sometimes a section of content area text will use two or more patterns simultaneously. A social studies text, for example, might use both sequence and cause-effect patterns in a section describing immigration into the United States, identifying the time periods during which large numbers of people from different countries came to America and explaining their reasons for leaving the countries where they had lived. Pattern Guides vary widely, depending on the grade level of the students for whom they are written, the pattern used, and the text topic. Several examples are provided in this chapter: Figure 4–12 shows two Pattern Guides written for a world history course, and

FIGURE 4–12   Two Examples of Pattern Guides for a World History Class

Comparison-Contrast Pattern Guide
    Abraham Lincoln was elected to a second term as president in _____ and assassinated by John Wilkes Booth in _____. According to the Constitution of the United States, when a president dies in office, the vice-president becomes president.

Pages 298–301 use a comparison-contrast pattern.

    List similarities and differences between Lincoln and Johnson, based on what you read (note page numbers) and what you know from other sources (list sources).

Abraham Lincoln   **Andrew Johnson**

similarities

_____

_____

differences

_____   _____

_____   _____

_____   _____

What do you think is the most significant similarity?

* *

Description Pattern Guide
    When many people lose their jobs and are unable to find work, when businesses fail and when economic conditions include serious slowdowns in business activity, massive unemployment and falling wages and prices, the economy is in depression. An economic depression is likely to have strong effects on families.
Pages 417 and 418 use a description pattern.
    As you read, make notes about descriptions of the Great Depression's effects on American families.

_____   _____

_____ THE GREAT DEPRESSION _____

_____   _____

What do you think was the most long-lasting effect?

FIGURE 4–13   Compare and Contrast Pattern Guide for Young Students

Ways that plant-eating and meat-eating dinosaurs were **ALIKE and DIFFERENT.**
These sentences tell about two kinds of dinosaurs.
Read pages 8-11 in (name of book) and fill in the blanks in the sentences.
Plant-eating dinosaurs walked on four _____.
They had many flat _____.
They used these teeth to chew _____ for food.

Meat-eating dinosaurs had sharp _____ for eating.
They had short front _____ with pointed claws.
They used these claws to catch and kill _____ for food.

Think about these questions, and write your answers.
What is one kind of food a plant-eating dinosaur might have eaten?

What is one kind of food a meat-eating dinosaur might have eaten?

Think about these questions, so we can talk about your ideas.
How were plant-eating and meat-eating dinosaurs **alike?**

How were they **different?**

Something extra to learn:
Dinosaur is a big word. It means terrible lizard.
Carnivore and herbivore are two other big words.
Carnivore means meat-eater. What do you think herbivore means?

Something extra to think about:
Dinosaurs weren't called dinosaurs when they were alive. Why not?

Something extra to do:
Draw a picture of a dinosaur. Label your picture.

Figure 4–13 shows a comparison-contrast Pattern Guide written for young students. In preparing a Pattern Guide, the first step is to determine what text pattern has been used—cause-effect, sequence (time or order), description, problem-solution (or problem and solution plus results), comparison-contrast, or definition with examples—and the next step is to list the pattern and draft a concept statement about the passage, based on the pattern. For example, if the pattern follows a problem-solution pattern, the concept statement should state the problems and the solutions. The final task is to prepare a series of questions that encourage the students to use the pattern.

In addition to teacher-written Pattern Guides, which specify the pattern used in a text portion and include teacher-prepared questions that engage students in using the pattern, Pattern Graphics (visual representations that show relationships among ideas) are useful and versatile. Students can create them to enhance and demon-strate their understanding of topics, or they can be used as an aid to study. Margaret Early (1990, p. 570), who uses the term *key visuals*, identifies multiple uses for graphics. Students can be encouraged to talk or write about the information that the graphic presents, or they can create a graphic representation to demonstrate their understanding of what they have been studying, and teachers can use graphics "to build background knowledge before reading a text, to read the text interactively, or to help synthesize new information gained from reading the text."

Cindy Gillespie points out that the processes used in examining and interpreting graphic displays are similar to those used in reading. English language users expect to examine graphics from left to right and top to bottom, as we read text. Typical comprehension questions—what's the main idea? what are the details?—can apply to graphic displays as well as to text, and teachers can devise questions about graphic displays which are at the literal, inferential, applied, and evaluative levels. She identifies five categories of graphics:

- ▮ sequential: flow charts, time lines, organizational charts, process charts
- ▮ quantitative: number lines, bar graphs, line graphs, pictographs, pie charts
- ▮ maps: political, physical, special purpose
- ▮ diagrams: cross sections, blueprints, machine drawings
- ▮ tables/charts: row-by-column matrices

(Gillespie, 1993, p. 350)

Reading and interpreting information presented graphically is an essential aspect of content area reading. David Boardman (1976, p. 118), who uses the term *graphicacy* to emphasize the parallel with the ability to read and write and to reason mathematically, regards it as "a basic skill [that] develops in children alongside literacy and numeracy." The possible variety of pattern graphics is wide-ranging, and teachers and students may devise their own forms. John Clarke and his colleagues suggest that students create concept maps, time lines, and Venn diagrams (Clarke, Martell & Willey, 1994) as they study history. Venn diagrams are especially useful in comparing and contrasting information. They are overlapping circles, usually two circles, labeled with the items that are being contrasted. Features the two items have in common are written in the section where the two circles overlap; information that differentiates them is written in the parts of the circle that are distinct. Dorothy Hennings (1993) stresses that time is an organizer for history. She advocates teacher modeling of this concept for students as history texts are studied, by scanning for dates and then thinking aloud and discussing the events tied to the dates. She suggests constructing a time line with key events listed on the left and inferences based on those events on the right.

Each of these strategies—Three-Level, Cloze-Plus-Questions, and Pattern Guides—is intended to help students learn from challenging text, so they are most useful for older students. All can be used effectively either regularly or occasionally. The time required for preparation of well-constructed guides can be extensive, but Pattern Guides continue to be useful as long as the text on which they are based is used, and Three-Level Guides and Cloze-Plus-Questions Guides are likely to be useful as long as the

When cooperative learning is successful, group members are interdependent, the group itself becomes a dynamic whole, and attachment to the group contributes to motivation and achievement.

topic is taught. Although writing good questions for guides requires thought and care, the time is well spent because the ability to write good questions develops with practice. Students can use any of the completed guides as the basis for a writing assignment (for example, as a lead in to the Guided Writing Procedure, described in Chapter Six) or for a class discussion. Terminology Trade as a whole class activity or Concept Connections as a cooperative group activity can be used as follow-up activities. When considering other strategies to combine with Pattern Guides, it is useful to take the pattern into account. For example, a guide based on a definition plus examples pattern can be followed by using the Concept of Definition strategy. Through transmediation (described in Chapter Five), completed guides based on comparison and contrast patterns can be transformed into posters or other displays; guides based on a problem-solution-results pattern could become the basis for creative drama. The Pattern Guide strategy can also be adapted for oral use. Teacher (or students) identify a text pattern, and then the group searches for ways in which the text follows that pattern. For example, in a text written following a compare-contrast pattern, the class identifies the items being compared and contrasted and their similarities and differences, with group members reading or paraphrasing the relevant sections of the text.

Knowledge Building Through Student-Developed Connections

It is useful for teachers to guide their students to understand the interrelationships among important concepts. It is also important to encourage students to make their own connections among ideas they are learning about. Two useful strategies are Concept Connections and Concept of Definition. Both strategies are effective used either regularly or occasionally, and appropriate for use in the intermediate grades through high school. Concept Connections can be adapted for younger students if children talk about the connections they see between two or more terms. No preparation of materials is needed; teachers need only to guide and respond to students' work. Checking students' work is important, because it is not productive of good learning if students produce inaccurate or trivial work.

Concept Connections.   A versatile activity that develops comprehension, reinforces vocabulary learning, and engages students in thinking creatively is Concept Connections, based on a method created by Bob Stanish, which he called Structural Indexing (Stanish, 1989). In this process, a set of nine important terms, related to a content area topic, is collected and listed. Students, working individually or in groups, place the terms as they choose in a 3 × 3 grid. Then they construct sensible, informative sentences or short paragraphs that use any three of the terms—those shown in a row, a column, or a diagonal. As an example, in studying maps, the terms chosen might be *degrees, Greenwich, latitude, longitude, equator, hemisphere, Prime Meridian, pole.* One group might choose to arrange the terms this way:

Greenwich	Prime Meridian	longitude
hemisphere	globe	equator
degrees	latitude	pole

Then they might construct the following sentences, which use the three terms in the top row, and the three terms in one of the diagonals:

The Prime Meridian is a line of longitude that runs through Greenwich, England. It marks the place on the globe which is at zero degrees longitude.

Other accurate, informative sentences could also be constructed from this arrangement of the terms. A different arrangement of the terms in the grid would result in different combinations of terms. Often it is necessary for students to write paragraphs rather than sentences, to combine the three terms meaningfully. For example, if the topic of study is the Supreme Court, the terms chosen might be *Brown v. Board of Education, checks and balances, Ruth Bader Ginsburg, Marbury v. Madison, John Marshall, "nine old men," Franklin D. Roosevelt, Dred Scott, Earl Warren.* A student, or a group of students, might choose to arrange the terms this way:

checks and balances	John Marshall	Marbury v. Madison
Franklin D. Roosevelt	Earl Warren	Brown v. Bd. of Edu.
"nine old men"	Ruth Bader Ginsburg	Dred Scott

One possible paragraph based on this arrangement would be this:

When Franklin D. Roosevelt was elected president, the United States was in a severe economic depression. There was a great deal of unemployment, banks were failing, and many people had been evicted from their homes and had no place to live. Roosevelt proposed actions that government could take to improve conditions, and Congress passed laws setting up new agencies. However, when some of the new laws were first tested in the courts, the Supreme Court declared them unconstitutional. Our government is based on a system of checks and balances, and the Supreme Court can check Congress's power to legislate by declaring laws unconstitutional. Many people were angry with the court and said that the justices—"nine old men"—were standing in the way of the president's efforts to end the depression. President Roosevelt thought of a way to solve the problem, by passing a law to allow more than nine Supreme Court judges (so that he could appoint other judges who would not be likely to oppose his New Deal legislation), but Congress would not pass such a law.

Like many other comprehension activities, Concept Connections can be used in assessment; a student who creates the sentences and the paragraph shown on the previous page shows understanding of the concepts, whereas a student who writes a content-free sentence, such as "It is important to know about words like degrees and latitude and pole," or an incorrect statement, such as "John Marshall, Earl Warren, and Dred Scott were all Supreme Court judges," reveals a lack of study and understanding.

Concept of Definition. The Concept of Definition (Schwartz, 1988; Schwartz & Raphael, 1985) is a strategy that enables students to extend their knowl-

edge of an important concept analytically. A Concept of Definition (CD) map is created by placing the term that names the concept within a category, identifying a term that is conceptually parallel, listing several properties of the concept and several examples of it. The example of a CD map that Schwartz provides (1988) is based on the concept of *desert*. Its category ("What is it?") is climate, and the parallel concept given is rainforest. Properties ("What is it like?") are "less than 25 centimeters of rainfall," "no cloud cover; winds; dry land," and "heat radiates into dry air at night." Illustrations ("What are some examples?") of

FIGURE 4–14 Examples of Concept of Definition Maps

Concept of Definition Map in Chemistry
Category: elements

Comparisons		Properties
alkaline metals		salt-forming
	HALOGENS	
noble gases		most reactive of nonmetallic elements

Examples
fluorine   chlorine   astatine

* *

Concept of Definition Map in Social Studies
Category: political units in the United States

Comparisons		Properties
county		joined or was admitted to Union
	STATE	
city		sends representatives to federal government
		has capital city

Examples
Connecticut   Oregon   Delaware

* *

Concept of Definition Map in Math
Category: polygons

Comparisons		Properties
rectangle		
	TRIANGLE	
		three sides
pentagon		
		three angles
octagon		

Examples
right triangle   isosceles triangle   scalene triangle

deserts are Mojave, Gobi, and Sahara. Figure 4–14 shows three examples of CD maps that might be prepared in different content areas. Each would be only one of many in the same category.

Although students quickly understand the Concept Connections strategy, it takes time and careful instruction to understand the Concept of Definition strategy and use it well. However, once a CD map has been created for one term, such as those shown in Figure 4–14, it is easier for students to create maps for similar terms. An assignment to create Concept of Definition maps is an excellent activity for cooperative groups to use during or toward the end of a unit of study. After well-constructed CD maps have been created, they can be shared with other groups that may extend the maps further with additional properties and examples. As an enrichment activity, students may choose to create a set of Concept of Definition maps for topics that interest them. Well-constructed CD maps can be collected into booklet form for classroom reading or learning center use.

Developing Understanding

Thinking challenges are puzzles and problems that engage students in logical, mathematical, and creative reasoning. Those in logic and math are available from many commercial sources, or teachers who enjoy creating materials can devise their own. They should be chosen thoughtfully, and should be solvable by reasoning rather than depending on knowing rules. Those offering incidental learning (e.g., interesting facts or creative thinking opportunities) are particularly useful. Figures 4–15, 4–16, and 4–17 provide examples. (Solutions are given at the end of the book.)

■■ Learners Flourish With ■■ Cooperative Learning

Cooperative learning is a powerful means of promoting learning and accomplishing this inclusively. When cooperative activities are thoughtfully,

FIGURE 4–15   Example of a Math-Thinking Challenge

Find Three

1. Find three consecutive numbers for which, when the three numbers are added, the result is 25 more than the highest number.
2. Find three consecutive numbers for which, when the highest number is divided by one-fourth of the lowest number, the result is four less than the middle number.
3. Find three consecutive numbers for which, when the highest number is divided by one-eighth of the lowest number, the result is eight less than the middle number.
4. Find three consecutive numbers for which, when the three numbers are multiplied together and the total subtracted from 1000, the result is 10.
5. Find three consecutive numbers for which, when the lowest and the highest numbers are added together, the result is twice the middle number.
6. Find three consecutive numbers for which, when the highest and the lowest numbers are added, and one-third of the middle number is subtracted from the total, the result is 40.
7. Find three consecutive numbers for which, when the middle and the highest numbers are added, and the sum is divided by one-sixth of the lowest number, the result is 13.
8. Find three consecutive numbers for which, when the *digits* in the three numbers are added, the result is the highest number.

* * * * * * * * * * * * *

Evaluate the difficulty of the items, and assign points to each so that the total is 100. If you think one of the items is far too easy, make up an alternative.

Answers to Figure 4–15 can be found in the Solutions section at the back of this book.
© 1985 by Learning Packages. Used by permission of Sunshower Learning Packages.

FIGURE 4–16 Examples of Logic Challenges

Lon Gago

Lon Gago is an enthusiastic reader, but he is sometimes not truthful. He is currently reading about historical events of a previous century. When we asked him about his reading he said "Yes!" to every question. He fibbed exactly once, but you can still figure out the truth. These are the questions we asked:

Did the events occur in the fifteenth, sixteenth, seventeenth and eighteenth century?

Did the events occur before the seventeenth century?

Did the events occur after the fifteenth century?

Did the events occur in the time between the end of the fifteenth century and the beginning of the eighteenth century?

* * * * * * * * * * * * * *

Lon Gago and Farah Weihe

Lon Gago and Farah Weihe are both doing a lot of reading (and some fibbing). Both of them borrowed at least one book this week and last. We know that last week they borrowed the same number of books. We also know that in the three sets of statements below, they've both made truthful statements in exactly one set. In another pair, Lon told the truth and Farah fibbed. In another pair, Farah told the truth and Lon fibbed.

Lon says, I borrowed six books this week. Farah says, Lon borrowed more than six books last week.

Lon says, Farah borrowed four books this week. Farah says, I borrowed more books than Lon did this week.

Lon says, Together we borrowed exactly 20 books this week and last week. Farah says, Together we borrowed exactly 18 books this week and last week.

How many books did they each borrow, last week, and this week?

© 1985 by Learning Packages. Used by permission of Sunshower Learning Packages.

Answers to Figure 4–16 can be found in the Solutions section at the back of this book.

sensibly, and caringly planned and conducted, learning is fostered for all students without excluding students, and in a fashion that enables differences among them to be valued. The method is useful across grades and ages, and many scholars and educators have described its advantages.

Karen Wood (1987a, p. 11) notes that cooperative learning increases students' intrinsic motivation to learn, and creates more positive attitudes toward instruction and instructors as well as "more positive perceptions about the intentions of others." Howard Margolis and his colleagues (Margolis & Freund, 1991; Margolis & Schwartz, 1988–1989) discuss cooperative learning in inclusive classrooms (regular classrooms that include students with disabilities) at the high school level as well as in earlier grades. They point to the power of cooperative learning to benefit both "mildly handicapped and nonhandicapped students academically, socially, and emotionally.... [and] help meet student needs in heterogeneous classrooms.... while supporting subject matter goals important to teachers" (Margolis & Freund, 1991, pp.

117 and 130). Paul Vermette (1994, p. 260) advocates cooperative learning at the high school level: "Done well, cooperative learning is a powerful and engaging strategy worthy of thoughtful implementation by all high school teachers." Becky Watson (1995) points out its usefulness in teacher education classes not only for the intrinsic merits of the method, but because it is important that preservice teachers have experience with a method that they will be expected to use in their teaching. Laura Pardo and Taffy Raphael (1991, pp. 564 and 561) write:

The question is not 'should we have groups?' but instead, 'what groups should we have for what purposes?'.... Cooperative small groups provide opportunities for students to 1) practice newly learned strategies and apply newly learned concepts to further study in their chosen area, 2) work collaboratively to create texts, whether the texts be full reports, questions, or information synthesized from such sources as interviews of experts in a particular field, and 3) engage in discourse about the content and processes they are learning.

FIGURE 4–17   Example of a Math and Logic Challenge

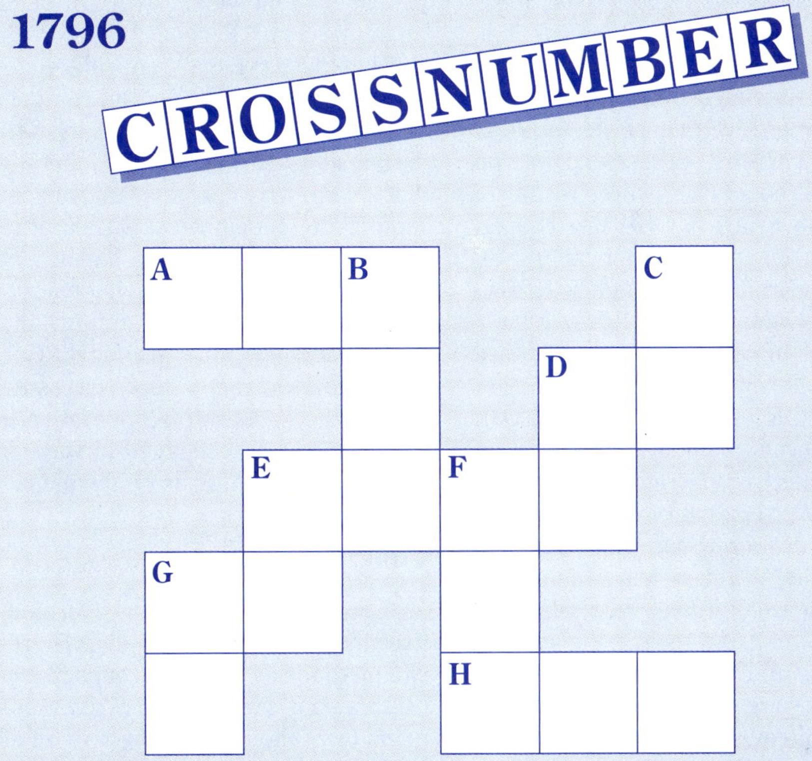

1796 CROSSNUMBER

A. The first digit of **A** is 2.

B. The first digit of **B** is the same as the last digit of C.

C. **C** plus **D across** plus **D down** equals **A.**

D across. **D across** is a multiple of **E down.**

D down. The sum of this number's digits is 11.

E across. 1796—the year in which the first suspension bridge in America was built across Jacob's Creek, in Pennsylvania.

E down. The sum of the digits in **E down, G down,** and **D across** is the same.

F. The sum of **F**'s digits is 16.

G across. **B** minus **G across** equals **H.**

G down. **G down** plus **E down** equals **D down**

H. **E across** is a multiple of **H.**

©1985 by Learning Packages. Used by permission of Sunshower Learning Packages.

Answers to Figure 4–17 can be found in the Solutions section at the back of this book.

The concept of cooperative learning has a long history in the field of social psychology. Kurt Lewin (1935, 1948), the scholar generally regarded as the founder of social psychology, made an extensive study of the interactions of people in groups. He asserted that when group members are interdependent and share common goals, the group itself becomes a dynamic whole. That is, the group itself has a unity rather than being simply a collection of separate people, and that this attachment to the group contributes to motivation and achievement. Following Lewin, Morton Deutsch (1949, 1962, 1985) classified goal-directed human interactions as individualistic (where each person is concerned only with personal achievements), competitive (where people are placed, or perceive themselves to be, in situations where one person's success depends on another's failure), and cooperative (where results of interaction are mutually beneficial). Because cooperative learning depends on students interacting with, helping, and learning from each other, it is also based on the work of Vygotsky (1962, 1978). Influential current advocates of cooperative learning are David and Roger Johnson (Johnson & Johnson (1978, 1985, 1989) and Robert Slavin (1990, 1992). Ann L. Brown's (1994) conception of communities of learners (COL) is related to cooperative learning.

A related idea that it is useful for educators to understand is the concept of zero-sum game and non-zero-sum game. Imagine two games in which there are items of value to be won through successful play. In one game, the value of these items is the same at the beginning and the end of the game. What has changed is the way they are distributed. Any player's gain is balanced by an equal loss for other players. When the amounts won and the amounts lost are added, the sum is zero. This zero-sum game situation corresponds to the competitive interactions described by Deutsch: Success depends on the failure of others. In a non-zero-sum game, however, the value of what can be achieved in the game is potentially more than what is available to each player separately; each player maximizes advantage by contributing to the success of others and of the total group. When members of cooperative learning groups work together on interesting tasks, with the guidance of an energetic and thoughtful teacher, they have the opportunity to perceive and enjoy the contributions of their colleagues, and to see that a group product can be richer than a series of individual pieces of work. Cooperative learning activities provide a way for students to *develop a sense of connectedness* with one another rather than perpetuate the individualism and competitiveness that is traditional in many classrooms" (Cushner, McClelland, & Safford, 1992, p. 299).

There are three components of cooperative learning in classrooms: forming groups, working in groups, and assessment or evaluation (of group products or individual work; of behavior or learning, and so on). Responsibility for the first and the third of these is usually considered to be part of the teacher's role; for the second component—working in groups—students seem, by definition, to be responsible. However, for cooperative learning to work well, it is essential that teachers resist the temptation to focus most of their attention on forming and evaluating groups, and accept the responsibility—and the accompanying enjoyment and satisfaction—of selecting, planning, and guiding the work that cooperative groups do (Jacobson, 1995). Both group formation and assessment are important to the success of cooperative learning, however, and can be managed in ways that contribute to students' learning and enjoyment.

Group Formation

Cooperative groups can be formed quickly, effectively, and in interesting ways. There are, however, two methods of forming groups that get the process off to a poor start. One way to err is by letting students form their own groups when all students are not experienced in working together in friendly, inclusive ways. Paul Vermette (1994) lists this as a common error teachers may make when they introduce cooperative learning. When students are simply directed—in Brenda Power's (1989) term—to "geddinagrupe," the cooperative learning process is likely to begin with dissatisfaction and unhappiness: "I don't want to work with her" or "We don't want him in our group."

The other error in group formation stems from too much, rather than too little, teacher attention. Teachers sometimes become deeply involved in decisions about how to place students into cooperative groups, acting on the belief that complicated preplanning is desirable to ensure a mix of abilities and characteristics. Elizabeth Cohen (1994, p. 28) advises teachers against structuring cooperative groups to be "little replicas" of the total class in terms of gender and ethnicity. Nor do teachers need to give effort to composing groups of four students identified as one "high," two "middle," and one "low." Such a group system is based on the erroneous assumptions that student ability is a unidimensional characteristic—that, for example, a student identified as "high" will have more talents, experiences, energy, and interest related to every topic than the others in the group—and that teachers know all there is to know about their students. Both assumptions are false. Moreover, when students believe that they have been placed in groups in accordance with the teacher's estimate of their abilities, anxieties will be roused: "If every group has one 'high,' two 'middle,' and one 'low,' which I am?… who's the low person?… I don't want to get the same grade that he gets."

Harold Herber (1978, p. 63), writing about instructional groupings for students in content area classrooms, advocated random assignment to groups. He pointed out that one of many advantages of random assignment is that it produces within-group diversity along many dimensions. "The random grouping makes it probable that each group will have a range of ability, achievement, interest, motivation, knowledge, and experience that reflects the range for the entire class." Thus a simple method achieves heterogeneity, without engaging teachers in fruitless efforts to make sure every group is a microcosm of the classroom. Describing the cooperative learning groups in her advanced mathematics classes, Alice Artzt (1994, pp. 81–82), without advocating random grouping, does stress the importance of heterogeneity. She cites the journal entry of a student who recognized that her group was less productive than those in which members differed in mathematical skill and in approach to problems, and, therefore, discussed and debated. "[Because] we always seem to agree on answers, we never go over them in detail," she wrote about her own homogenous group.

For ongoing, extensive cooperative learning, randomly formed base groups that stay together for an extended time period are likely to be productive. For courses that last for a semester, these groups can last throughout the semester. A practical arrangement when students are together for a year is to have three cooperative groupings, for example, September to end of the calendar year, January through spring recess, and from then till the end of the school year, with a major project as the culmination of the groups' time together. It is important for students to know in advance if groups will be restructured and when this will happen, so that no one assumes that group or individual problems are the reason for changes.

If group members find one another through a quick problem-solving activity, group formation involves neither ranking nor exclusiveness, and gets the learning process off to a lively start. Additionally, it will be clear to students that the group formation is not based on the teacher's opinion of their abilities. The basic aspects of the method are for the teacher to decide how many groups there will be and how many people will be in a group (four? five? six?), and to prepare sets of related cards so that each student will be given one and all students will then move about to find the other members of their group. An easy method is to print multiple copies of a quotation (as many sheets as there will be groups) and to cut each sheet into pieces (as many pieces as there will be members in each group). Each sheet, of course, will be cut in a different way. The pieces are mixed and handed out randomly to students, who then have the task of matching their pieces with those held by other students until they have reconstructed their quotation page. These are among many other options:

- In each set one card has the name of a state, and the other cards have names of major cities in the state. (e.g., California, Sacramento, Los Angeles, San Francisco, San Diego).
- In each set one card has the name of an author, and the other cards have names of books written by that author (e.g., Virginia Hamilton, *And the People Could Fly; Many Thousand Gone; The House of Dies Drear; M. C. Higgins, the Great*).
- In each set all cards have mathematical statements that are equivalent (e.g., $10 + 2 - 5, 3 + 4, 14/2, 20/4 + 2, 11 - 4$).
- Each set consists of postcards showing the works of a different famous artist.

It is useful for the matching activities to be related in some way to the general topic the cooperative groups will be studying. It is essential that cooperative groups have an assignment to work on immediately, as soon as their group is formed.

Cooperative Group Assignments

Cooperative group assignments need to be planned in several categories. Two kinds are essential: an immediate assignment for groups to work on as soon as they are formed, and regular assignments that support the curriculum and which group members complete on a weekly basis. It is also useful for groups to have a long-term assignment, such as a project that will be the culmination of the group's work together. Shorter assignments related to the project or to special events can then also become a part of the weekly assignment for groups. Teachers need to plan so that all or most of cooperative group work can be accomplished and is accomplished in class. This ensures that the work will be the students' own, and promotes productive use of class time.

The Immediate Assignment. This is a one-time-only assignment, but it is extremely important for group success. If groups do not have something purposeful, interesting, and appropriately challenging to do immediately (something that cannot be well accomplished unless group members work together) they will begin their time together aimlessly. Their conversations will probably not be inclusive. That is, some members may talk together, excluding one or two other group members. Students may talk negatively about other students and about group work generally. This sets a bad precedent for future work together. Providing an assignment for groups to begin on as soon as the members have found one another serves to get groups into action collaboratively, and may also be used as an introduction to subsequent learning. The immediate activity should be sufficiently open-ended to keep all groups occupied, and time should be allowed at the end to allow for groups to share their ideas or their products. These are some of many possible immediate assignments:

■ Activities that get group members acquainted; e.g., filling out a group Interest Inventory related to topics to be studied; or finding three ways in which all members of the group are alike and three ways in which every member of the group is different.

■ Activities that acquaint groups with texts or other materials they will be using. Text Hunts, described in Chapter Two, make an excellent assignment for groups to begin on immediately. Teachers need not give detailed instructions; instead, they can indicate that they expect groups to figure out what is to be done by reading the questions.

■ Activities that groups will use regularly in their cooperative groups, either a strategy with which they are already familiar, or one they can learn quickly, with minimal directions. For example, many students are familiar with Semantic Mapping, and their assignment can be to brainstorm ideas related to a topic the group will be studying and then to use them to create a semantic map. Although students may not be already familiar with Concept Connections, the strategy can be quickly explained and easily understood through use; this also can be a useful immediate activity.

Regular Assignments. Strategies that require collaboration, support the curriculum, and are appropriate for regular use because they can be applied to a variety of topics, should be selected by the teacher, taught sequentially to the whole class, and then given as assignments for group members on a weekly basis. These activities include strategies for reading and studying together, information gathering and organization, writing and responding to each other's writing through journals and a variety of short papers, interesting methods of vocabulary study, and creation of products in a variety of media to illustrate what has been learned. Although strategies should be selected with the capabilities and interests of students in mind, most good strategies can be adapted to fit a wide range of cognitive development and skill acquisition among learners. Strategies can be used immediately if they can be immediately understood, or as soon as they have been introduced and practiced together. Eventually, the weekly assignment for groups might be similar to the example shown in Figure 4–18.

A variety of methods have been devised to encourage active collaboration in cooperative

FIGURE 4–18   Example of Weekly Cooperative Group Assignment

▮ As a group, read together [an assigned text section] and prepare a RESPONSE sheet based on it.

▮ Using the Concept Connections strategy, prepare at least four paragraphs using the terms listed on the Cooperative Group Assignment Chart. Each group member should help prepare at least two paragraphs; everyone who works on a paragraph should initial it. This shows you believe the paragraph is accurate and clear.

▮ Complete (individually) two journal entries; ask a group member to comment on one or more entries. Each group member is responsible for writing two entries and commenting on one.

▮ Create one or more RAFT papers. Components are listed on the Cooperative Group Assignment Chart. Or, create a simple storyboard to show events occurring in your reading.

groups. The jigsaw method, devised by Elliott Aronson (1978) is a knowledge-acquiring and sharing method for cooperative learning groups in which each member of a group becomes expert in an aspect of the topic being studied, and then returns to share information with the group. Edythe Holubec (1992) gives the ingenious name Bookends to a strategy in which students pair for study before and after a learning experience, such as reading, listening to a lecture, or viewing a videotape. As a preparatory activity, the partners discuss and summarize what they already know about the subject and think of questions they expect to be answered. Afterwards they note the answers to their questions and formulate new ones. Ronald Klemp and his colleagues (Klemp, Hon, & Short, 1993) describe a method of cooperative learning they use with middle school students, called Fact Storm. The process engages students in decision-making as well as study, because the first step for cooperative groups, when a reading assignment has been given, is to draft a written plan for study and estimate the time they will need. Next, students "sample the text," by scanning it together and noting points to give special attention to. This process, akin to brainstorming, is the "fact storm." The teacher then calls the class together and groups share ideas and note useful points others have made to add to their own lists. Students then return to group work and study the assignment together, elaborating their fact storm list and preparing a transparency based on their learning, which will later be shared and discussed with the whole class.

Long-Term Assignments.   A project that will be the culmination of the group's work together is a useful cooperative group assignment because it builds in a process of preparation and support for a major assignment. Shorter assignments related to the project or to special events can become a part of the weekly assignment for groups. (Middle-length assignments, such as the preparation of a bulletin board, mural, or portion of a class history wall, can be rotated among groups so that each has one of these responsibilities every few weeks; it is useful for groups to have the task of developing their own timeline for working on middle-length assignments.) Some of many possible long-term assignments follow. All the strategies are described in the Strategy Glossary.

▮ Presentation of roundtable or poster sessions to share results of learning.

▮ Preparation of slide shows, murals, or tableaux to illustrate learnings.

▮ Creation of Time and Place Maps, or a variety of Pattern Graphics to illustrate a topic of study.

▮ Creation of artifact kits related to the topic of study.

▮ Elaboration of Identity Creation cards.

▮ Transcription of oral histories.

▮ Creation of giftbooks for family members.

▮ Preparation of elaborated storyboards.

Additionally, the preparation of individual portfolios can be part of group work, with group members helping each other to choose materials to include.

Using Established Groups

Learning strategies that have a cooperative component are conducted more easily and smoothly when cooperative groups are already formed. (On the other hand, teachers may choose to have students combine in a different ways, for a change of pace.) Two of many useful strategies which depend for their success on groups working collaboratively are Terminology Trade, described earlier in this chapter, and EVOKER, a method of studying poetry, described in Chapter Eleven. In the Terminology Trade strategy, cooperative groups are responsible for defining terms and for deciding how to distribute cards to the teacher and other groups. In the six-step EVOKER strategy, cooperative groups are responsible for identifying the key ideas in a poem or other piece of literature, and evaluating their relationship to find meaning.

Incorporating Interest Groups

Regrouping for special projects can be included as part of cooperative learning, so that for a time, students are part of two groups. Interest groups can be formed on the basis of students' preferences and interest: for a task (choose which role to take in a project: writers, editors, illustrators); for a topic (choose which country, animal, person, state, time period to find out more about); or for a text (choose which book to read). Using interest groups provides a way to make working with a basal reading series more lively; the teacher categorizes reading selections (sports, nature, folktales, and so on) and then students sign up for one or two groups, to read those stories and share ideas from them with the class. Interest groups can also help manage major classroom events; for example, when a class is planning to use roundtable or poster sessions to present research findings, student interest groups might serve as committees to prepare programs, plan timing and arrange for introductions, perhaps arrange for invitations and refreshments if guests will be invited.

Interest groups and cooperative base groups can coexist, with students spending allotted portions of time over several weeks in the interest group activities. When arranging interest groups, the teacher, or teacher and students together, plan what groups will be needed, and then students choose their groups. In choosing, there needs to be one rule, and one rule only: Anyone can join any group and no one can discourage a person from joining. This means that it is best not to specify the number of people who may be in a group. If too few people select a group, it can be eliminated and the task reassigned. If a group gets too big, the group's assignment can be enlarged and mini-interest groups can work on different aspects. Teachers who decide to use interest grouping must understand, permit, and then ignore the fact that, particularly when such groups are first used, some students will choose their groups not because of preferences about what to learn or do, but to be with a special friend.

Productive Effort

Elizabeth Cohen's recent review of the professional literature on cooperative learning moves beyond the question of whether the method is useful (that has been amply demonstrated) to questions of how and when its good effects are produced. She defines cooperative learning as:

> students working together in a group small enough that everyone can participate on a collective task that has been clearly assigned [and in a setting where] student are expected to carry out their task without direct and immediate supervision of the teacher.... [In cooperative learning there is] stress on task and on delegation of authority. (Cohen, 1994, p. 3)

The development of desirable prosocial behaviors is a goal. "Those classrooms with the greatest learning gains were precisely those where teachers were successful in delegating authority so that more children could talk and work together at multiple learning centers" (Cohen, 1994, p. 29). In other words, teachers must develop and maintain a balance between maintaining attentive interest in the work of cooperative groups, and restraining the impulse to exercise control over group interactions.

The concept of delegating authority is an important one. In Chapter Two, three teaching styles—authoritative, laissez-faire, and authoritarian—were contrasted. The cooperative learning process is seriously hampered when teachers use a laissez-faire style by simply telling students to work together and then ignoring them, giving little thought to group assignments and using the time groups work together for unrelated purposes of their own. An authoritarian approach, in which the teacher establishes many rules, assigns roles for each group member, and arranges for groups to be closely supervised (perhaps by aides or parents so that each group is watched and guided by an adult) is even more damaging to cooperative effort. In such situations, students have no opportunity to take responsibility, and their efforts will be expended on attempts to "do what the teacher wants" or, if supervision is temporarily lifted, they will avoid work.

> One may give a group a task, but, unless there is some reason for the group to interact, students may well tackle the task as individual work. This is especially the case if each individual must turn out some kind of worksheet or report. This is also the case if the instructor divides the labor so that each person in the group does a different part of the task; the group has only to draw these pieces together in sequential fashion as a final product. The consequence of either of these patterns is that there is comparatively little interaction; people do not gain the benefits of using one another as resources, nor is there any basis for expecting the prosocial outcomes of cooperation. (Cohen, 1994, pp. 11 and 12)

In cooperative learning, student effort depends substantially on teacher effort, both in planning and in participating wisely. Authoritative teachers have the power to delegate their authority to groups, by expecting them to make decisions and arrange for complex work to be accomplished. These teachers make cooperative learning productive through their planning when they make sure that students have well-chosen, interesting, important work to do. Having a variety of tasks to accomplish over a week's period gives group members opportunities to exercise their talents, and to take responsibility for planning how the work will be accomplished. The assignment list needs to be somewhat open-ended, so that groups will always have meaningful work to do. Teachers contribute to productive work through their participation by being engaged as interested,

supportive observers while groups are at work. Artzt (1994, p. 82), writing about cooperative learning in mathematics classes, comments, "[t]he more students are given the means to communicate with the teacher and with each other, the better the quality of the instruction." Nattiv (1994), studying cooperative grouping for mathematics in grades 3–5, found that there was a strong relationship between students' learning and their involvement in giving and receiving nontrivial help.

Teacher attention assures that students are encouraged and helped to remain on task. One of the aspects of cooperative learning that raises concerns among people who have not observed the method, or have seen it poorly used, is that some students will do all the work while others get by with little or no effort. The term for this response to group work is social loafing (Webb, 1995; Williams, Harkins, & Latané, 1981). Research has shown that identifiability is the preventive for social loafing. That is, if someone (in this case, the teacher) is attuned to what groups are doing, clearly interested in all participants and aware of their contributions, students will be inclined to contribute their best efforts.

Multifaceted, Multipurpose Assessment

One method of conceptualizing assessment is to consider its four interrelated aspects: attention, investigation, documentation, and evaluation. In cooperative learning (and arguably in all educational endeavors) the last component—evaluation—often receives the most emphasis, and typically produces the least benefits.

Evaluation.   Among the guidelines to consider in planning evaluation in relation to cooperative learning are these:

- Limit evaluation. Emphasis on grades and rewards consumes time and attention that can be better spent otherwise, and conveys to students that learning and work are not, in themselves, rewarding.
- If grades for group products will be given, consider using A/I (that is, the product graded is either excellent or incomplete) or A/B/I grading.

Provide checklists or rubrics so that students understand clearly what is expected and how products will be evaluated.

- Do not engage students in evaluation of each other; this least-pleasant part of teaching is a teacher's responsibility.
- Do not grade or rate behavior or effort; instead teach in ways that encourage the actions and attitudes you want students to develop and maintain.
- Think and plan in advance, choosing a limited number of possible focuses for evaluation to tie in with group assignments.
- Engage groups in learning together, and use strategies as cooperative group assignments that will later be used as individual assessments (making sure that group members know that they will eventually be tested individually). Webb's research (1993) has shown that when students are passive during group work, their performance on subsequent individual tests is poor; when this occurs, it serves as a reminder to students that a major purpose of cooperative group work is to enable each group member to learn.

Documentation. Products prepared as cooperative group assignments serve as documentation of group and individual work and progress. Materials can be kept in three-ring notebooks, and groups can be given the responsibility for choosing and filing work according to teacher guidelines. For example, a week's regular assignments might be documented this way:

- Groups are responsible for dating and filing these materials in class notebooks: one RESPONSE sheet; Concept Connections passages chosen by the group (enough to represent the work of each group member); RAFT paper and/or storyboard.
- Teachers may choose to document Transform-a-Problem by collecting drawings or taking snap-

shots of skits, and may document other group activities through observational notes or snapshots.

- Journal entries and student comments on each other's entries are self-documenting.

Attention and Investigation. Teacher attention while students are working in cooperative groups is essential. To use this time to do unrelated work while leaving students on their own demonstrates to students that the time spent in cooperative groups is not valued, and makes it likely that they will not use the time seriously and productively. Cooperative learning time gives teachers the opportunity to observe students and gain information that can be used to modify and improve instruction. Observing students carefully can alert teachers to their strengths and to characteristics that can contribute to success. Edythe Holubec (1992, p. 182) asks, "What should teachers be doing while the students are working?" and then gives this answer: "watching, listening, and praising."

 Moving Forward

One of the most important messages that effective content area teachers give their students is that learning is continuous. One topic connects to another, and there is always more to know. In addition to a repertoire of introductory strategies and strategies designed to establish students' understanding, teachers need to be aware of strategies that help students expand upon what has been learned. The next chapter of this text, "Extending and Enhancing Understanding of Content Area Topics," suggests strategies to use in the *after* phase of instruction—methods that enrich students' learning after they have established a strong foundation of knowledge.

STRATEGIC TEACHERS, PART TWO:

"Efficient use of time is a priority."

Cinde Otte teaches high school chemistry and coaches track and field. Her three children are 9, 13, and 15; her family enjoys hiking and skiing, and she is actively involved in several community organizations. She is completing a second master's program and drives some distance once a week to take a class. Mrs. Otte has many years of teaching experience, and emphasizes lab work with lab books in which students record their results. These are the strategies she uses regularly:

- Teacher Read-Aloud Commentary
- group reading with RESPONSE
- For Your Information (FYI)
- SAY-IT
- lab books
- Detection
- Terminology Trade
- Semantic mapping
- reading aloud.

She occasionally uses refutational teaching, and students have the opportunity to use memos to communicate with her if they wish.

She begins each new topic with a Teacher Read-Aloud Commentary. After the commentary students read the text in cooperative groups, and one student records notes from the group on a RESPONSE form by listing at least three important points, raising at least one question, and identifying at least three new terms. She collects the RESPONSE forms, which are a regular cooperative group assignment, and looks over the questions and lists of new terms as she moves around the room. She uses FYI and SAY-IT often, to give information to individuals, groups, and occasionally the whole class. This enables her to answer most of the questions raised on RESPONSEs; she chooses one or two to answer in a brief lecture with which she winds up class three days a week. She knows from experience that there are several points in the curriculum where students typically come to the study of a topic with misunderstandings that make it difficult to grasp the correct information. She's been aware of the problem for many years, but only learned about the concept of refutational teaching last year, in readings for one of her university courses. She now builds refutational teaching about these concepts into her introductory commentaries and conducts demonstrations that illustrate the concepts. Later, all cooperative groups complete a Detection, which she has prepared to differentiate between accurate and inaccurate concepts.

For each new topic and subtopic, students create a semantic map of concepts in their lab books; they add to the maps during the time the topic is studied. Two or three days before a quiz, the class uses Terminology Trade; after the Trade, while still working in cooperative groups, students discuss, revise and add to, their semantic maps. Quiz follow-up—praise and confirmation of good learning; reteaching of concepts not yet grasped—is done during regular end-of-class lecture sessions and in individual or group conferences during cooperative learning time. Detection activities are always available if students have free time, and cooperative groups are required to complete two each week. Each group decides how to do this: Two can be completed by the whole group, or student pairs can each complete one, but each person must be actively involved in solving at least one, and must work on at least one in cooperation with another student. Once a week, Mrs. Otte winds up class ten minutes early and reads aloud to the class excerpts from biographies of famous scientists. If students want to comment on aspects of the course or ask for special help, they write memos; she keeps a memo box on her desk.

How Does She Do It?

Look carefully. Besides the time used to set up for demonstrations and labs, and to check lab books regularly and mark quizzes—processes required of all teachers—the strategies she's chosen (with one exception) take her no time to prepare, and require little time for assessment or evaluation. Teacher Read-Aloud Commentary, and giving students information through FYI and SAY-IT, require no preparation time; all that's necessary is that the teacher knows her subject, and Mrs. Otte does. Nor do these strategies require grading or recordkeeping. Group reading helps to insure that all her students can get information from the text; the RESPONSE form lets students raise questions about concepts and terminology. Again, there's no preparation for the teacher, and the RESPONSEs are evaluated as a group assignment, as done/not done. If a group is not turning in a reasonable product, Mrs. Otte confers with them briefly. (Guidelines for completing a RESPONSE are written on the printed forms the students use, and problems rarely arise.) The only preparation she uses for reading aloud is to keep a file of book excerpts, magazine articles, and clippings based on her own reading and recommendations from colleagues and students.

The only preparation time for Terminology Trade is writing the terms on file cards, and that's a rotating assignment for cooperative groups. Mrs. Otte highlights terms on RESPONSE forms that she wants included, and makes a list of other important words and phrases; she gives the materials to one of the groups with markers and a stack of file cards a few days before she needs them. The group gets credit if the cards are neatly prepared with all the terms spelled correctly. When the class does a Terminology Trade, the students take time to prepare in cooperative groups; here again, Mrs. Otte knows the necessary information already. For both Terminology Trade and semantic mapping, it's the students—not their teacher—who are doing the work, and

that's the way it should be. Terminology Trade requires no evaluation. The students' semantic maps are evaluated for thoroughness and accuracy; Mrs. Otte checks them at the same time that she grades quizzes because she finds it useful to compare the quality of the maps with success on the quizzes. (She plans to write a paper for her university class on this topic.)

She uses only one strategy that requires preparation. She chose Detection not only because she finds it intriguing and believes it encourages her students to think analytically, but because she figured out a way to minimize the time for creation of the materials. The only Detection exercises she has written herself are those to support her refutational teaching, which is necessary only for a few topics. All the others are adapted from students' work. (Of course, she only chooses good work and asks the students' permission to use it. Students typically enjoy having their work used in this way, and the possibility of being credited as a Detection author is an incentive to write carefully and accurately.)

Each time she checks lab books, she chooses a few good examples of lab descriptions, making sure over time to include work by every student. After obtaining student permission to use them, she makes copies, and gives them to her friend and colleague who teaches computer classes, who uses these materials as exercises for students working on word processing. When they're typed and spellchecked, Mrs. Otte gives them a final check, and then makes between five and ten changes for the incorrect version, and gives a heading crediting the real students who prepared the original version and giving responsibility for the error version to fictional characters. ("Detection #42. Topic: Acids and bases. One of these lab descriptions was written by Kay Mist and Anna List; the other was prepared by some ambling aardvarks who wandered in. Find the aardvarks' version and fix it. They made eight errors.") A computer student then runs a correct version and an error version. A clerical aide, to whom Mrs.

Otte has explained the Detection process, gives a final check and laminates the two versions side by side in a folder. Since she began using Detection several years ago, Mrs. Otte's collection has grown substantially, and there are now plenty for students to use. She keeps them filed sequentially by topic. Students can use any items that relate to current topics or topics that have been studied previously, or they may choose from a special section emphasizing lab routines and safety precautions. When a group has completed a Detection, they initial a card stapled to the back of the folder, so that they will not use it again. Checking the week's collection of Detection solutions is again a rotating task for cooperative groups; if any solutions are inaccurate, the group gives them to Mrs. Otte to look over.

In class, Mrs. Otte is always in action—teaching directly, giving demonstrations, setting up and guiding lab work, moving from group to group to oversee students' work and confer, and running Terminology Trade. However, she spends very little time after school hours on teaching tasks. She has arranged ways to minimize her preparation time, and much of the time needed for checking, grading, and recording her students' work can be accomplished in her planning period.

Challenge to the Reader: Create a semantic map to illustrate ways Mrs. Otte's program links content area study and language arts.

Choose and Use: If you were to choose one aspect of Mrs. Otte's program to use in your own classroom, what would it be, and how would you begin?

Case Study 2

Terry DeRosa, a second year teacher in a middle school, teaches two classes each of seventh and eighth grade social studies (topic: American history; range 25 to 30 students), supervises a study hall (50 students), and has a seventh grade homeroom class (28 students; 20 minutes every morning). DeRosa is working toward a master's degree, and, during a summer reading course, wrote a paper reviewing professional literature on reading aloud to students of all ages.

In the first week of October, eighth grade classes are studying the American Civil War. DeRosa has been reading them Stephen Vincent Benét's short story, "The Devil and Daniel Webster," for 5 to 10 minutes at the end of each class, for a week. The story is set before the Civil War but is related to historical events that led up to that war. When the story is completed, the class will discuss it in relation to what they have been studying. In one eighth grade class the reading is going very well. Several students have said they like being read to, and one parent wrote a note of commendation, praising the choice of the story, which his daughter told the family about, and saying how much she is enjoying the class. In the other class, a few students have been restless during the reading, and yesterday a student, standing near DeRosa after class, said "Reading to us just as if we were babies!" and another replied, "I think the story's boring." Next week the principal will be observing DeRosa for the first time this year, coming to this class for the full period.

DeRosa is reading Jean Merrill's *The Pushcart War* to the homeroom class, chosen because it's a personal favorite. About a fourth of the students said they'd already read the story but many of them were enthusiastic about its being read to them, and the rest said they didn't mind. The homeroom period begins with listening to morning announcements and pledging allegiance to the flag, followed by five minutes of conversation, and then the reading aloud, during which students may work quietly. At the end of last week a student brought in a letter from home; his parents wrote that though they approved of reading to students, they would prefer that their son hear something "less childish."

(First decision for discussants: Is DeRosa female or male?)

Analysis:	List some advantages DeRosa has at this point.
Decision points:	Note several decisions DeRosa must make now.
Choices:	Choose several decision points and make the decisions.
Possible results:	Choose one or more decisions and list their possible results.
Follow-up:	Create a scenario based on choices you've made for DeRosa. Specify the time period your scenario is set in (e.g., week after principal's visit; January 3 of the next year)

CHAPTER FIVE

Extending and Enhancing Understanding

First, learning is an active process of knowledge construction and sense-making by the student. Second, knowledge is a cultural artifact of human beings: we produce it, share it, and transform it as individuals and as groups. Third, knowledge is distributed among members of a group, and this distributed knowledge is greater than the knowledge possessed by any single member.

GAEA LEINHARDT, 1992, P. 23.

As a culmination of the study of important topics, effective teachers enable students to extend their knowledge in ways that are of personal interest, and share what they have learned in ways that interest their classmates. Students benefit not only from learning, and enjoying their learning, but also from the realization that their own efforts and ingenuity add to the group's collected knowledge. The conclusion of a period of study can be a time for engaging in more complex thinking and problem solving. It can be a time to make connections among ideas, linking what has been learned recently to information learned earlier, and to new topics that are being introduced. It can be a time for musing and discussion about what students

do not yet know, and about what scholars have not yet learned and may discover in future years. It can be a time for students to extend their learning by discovering more about facets of a topic, with different members of the group investigating questions of their choice. This is the point in knowledge building when students' different talents and interests can come into play most fully.

Alternatively, this can be a time when a test is given and graded, and instructional attention to the topic that has been studied ceases abruptly. One chapter ends and another chapter begins, replete with another set of unfamiliar terms, concepts, and questions already prepared. In these circumstances, students may not remember what they

---

Some of the factual information used in this chapter was obtained from *World Book Encyclopedia*, published by Field Enterprises, and *Webster's New International Dictionary, 2nd edition*, published by G. and C. Merriam Company.

study, but they are likely to believe what they are being taught: What is important about learning is getting through it. Clearly, this second approach to teaching and learning is not a good one. Nor is it an approach teachers are forced to take because of time constraints. Just as there is great variation in the time that can be allotted to introductory instruction, it is also true that effective instruction that concludes a topic may be brief or extensive. Teachers may choose to wind up the study of a topic swiftly, pointing out connections with new topics. Well-conducted discussions are one way of bridging between what has been learned and what will be studied. Teachers may choose to use group and whole class strategies over short portions of several days to enable students to demonstrate their learning. Transmediation (the expression of knowledge in new forms) can provide a memorable conclusion. Teachers may structure their teaching of a topic so that preparations for a final celebration of learning are infused throughout all of a planned period of study. Well-designed research activities are ideal for this purpose.

This chapter has two major parts. The first part, following the pattern of the previous two chapters, describes a series of instructional strategies for use toward the end of a period of study about a topic. These strategies are grouped according to a classification of higher level forms of thinking. The second, and longer, part of the chapter focuses on research activities, an aspect of the curriculum that has the potential to be interesting and productive, but is often not well taught. The chapter concludes with a

discussion of ways for students to share their knowledge with one another.

Using Knowledge Analytically, Creatively, and Thoughtfully

Many years ago, Benjamin Bloom and his colleagues (Bloom, 1956) developed a taxonomy of thinking processes. (A taxonomy is a system of classification that places items in order of their relationship to one another.) Bloom's taxonomy identified and described six levels of thinking in the cognitive domain: Knowledge, Comprehension, Application, Analysis, Synthesis, and Evaluation. The first three categories are basic to learning: As one learns, information is acquired, an understanding of that information is developed, and the information becomes usable. It is clear that these kinds of thinking are interrelated, and also that they are hierarchical. The higher forms of thinking depend on the more basic forms. Before one can understand, or comprehend, a topic, one must have information (knowledge) about it. Before learning can be applied sensibly, one must have a sound comprehension of it. The Three-Level Guide strategy, discussed in Chapter Four, is based on this concept and designed to help students acquire, understand, and use important information.

Once a sound and thorough knowledge base has been established, understanding can be broadened and deepened by engaging in more advanced kinds of thinking. According to Bloom's taxonomy, the higher-level cognitive processes are analysis, synthesis, and evaluation. **Analysis** involves separating ideas into categories, classifying them, and identifying their interrelationships. Reasoning and logical thinking are aspects of analytical thought. **Synthesis** consists of generating and combining ideas in new ways; it is a creative thinking process. Evaluation is a weighing process—a kind of thinking in which, after the relationships among ideas are identified (analysis) and combined (synthesis), judgments are made, considered, defended, and reshaped. Although strategies in this chapter have been grouped on the basis of their emphasis—analysis, synthesis, or evaluation—most strategies require, or lend themselves, to many ways of thinking. Time and Place Maps and

---

analysis and synthesis—derived from Greek. *Analysis* comes from a Greek noun, *analusis*, meaning a dissolving, related to the verb *analuein*, to undo, composed of the prefix *ana-*, meaning throughout, and the word *luein*, meaning to loosen. *Synthesis* comes from the prefix *sun*, or *syn*, meaning together, and the verb *tithenai*, meaning to put, which were combined to form *suntithenai*, meaning, of course, to put together, and the noun form, *sunthesis*. To think analytically, then, is to take ideas apart, as if one were taking apart a piece of machinery to see how it works. Synthesizing is thinking of ways to combine ideas but combining them in new ways.

the Graphic Information Lesson, for example, require thinking at the synthesis as well as the analytical level.

Demonstrating Understanding Through Analytical Thinking

Giving students opportunities to engage in thinking closely and reasoning logically about what they have learned is worthwhile in terms of both present and future learning. Among the strategies that stress analytic thinking processes are Estimating; Semantic Feature Analysis, in which concepts are considered and compared according to whether they have shared features; Detection, a strategy that encourages logical thinking through a process of detecting errors; Time and Place Maps, a method of displaying information that shows how events are related across time in various locations; and the Graphic Information Lesson, which involves detailed analysis of graphic aids and their relationship to text information.

Estimating.   One form of thinking that encourages students in both risk-taking and analytical thinking is estimating. Sandra Harte and Matthew Glover (1993, p. 75) define estimation as a process that involves "comprehending the problem, relating it to information that is already known, judging and verifying reasonableness, and revising as necessary." They suggest that teachers give unlikely estimates and ask why they are improbable (a thinking activity similar to that used in the Detection strategy, described later); they also give examples of estimation activities, such as estimating perimeters, circumferences, and weights of objects in classrooms, and investigating the effect of surface tension by estimating the number of drops of water that can be held on the surface of different coins and then verifying the estimates using an eyedropper.

When estimating is done for practical purposes, there may be several rounds of estimation. For example, in building a house, the builder needs to estimate how much lumber will be required and what the cost of the lumber is likely to be at the time of building. Based on these estimates, and estimates or information about other costs, plans

for the house may need to be modified and new estimates made. But a reasonable degree of accuracy, not precise correctness, is the aim. Sometimes an estimate is a good one if it comes reasonably close on one side, but poor if it comes equally close on the other. Yarn to knit a sweater and packages of floor tiles are purchased in preset quantities, and the amount purchased will almost certainly not be exactly the amount needed. For economy's sake, the estimate should be close. A good estimate in this case is close but a little over. It is a great inconvenience to find, as the project nears completion, that there is not quite enough material to finish. Teachers need to use estimating activities that will guide students to a practical understanding of the purposes for estimation. For example, students can be shown several simulated street signs welcoming people to a large city, which differ in the population figures given (e.g., 622,000; 622,500; 622,520; 622,521) and asked to choose and justify the best sign. The discussion that ensues can lead students to an understanding of the difference between measurement, where precision is possible and useful, and estimation, where a sensible approximation is needed.

David Whitin (1992) suggests using trade books as the basis for estimation activities. An advantage here is that the reasonableness of estimates can be discussed and judged, but that precise verification of estimates is impossible because one cannot get into the story to measure, count, or ask questions. *Grandfather's Dream* (Keller, 1994) is a story based on ecological changes in the Plain of Reeds in the Mekong delta of Vietnam that were caused by the war. Reading the story and examining the illustrations, singly and in combination, could lead to estimated answers for questions, such as: "How far away are the houses from one another? How old is Nam? How old is his grandfather? How many large leaves would it take to thatch a house? How many people live in the village?" The estimated answers can lead to thoughtful discussion. *Counting on Frank*, by Rod Clement (1991) is a picture book about estimation. The ingenious young narrator is an enthusiastic estimator, and the title of the book is based on his habit of using Frank, his dog, as a unit of measurement—"I calculate that twenty-four

Franks could fit into my bedroom"—although other forms of estimation occur to him constantly: "If I had accidentally knocked fifteen peas off my plate every night for the last eight years, they would now be level with the tabletop. Maybe then, mom would understand that her son does *not* like peas" (Clement, 1991, unpaginated).

Semantic Feature Analysis. Semantic Feature Analysis (Anders & Bos, 1986; Johnson & Pearson, 1984; Pittelman, Heimlich, Berglund, & French, 1991; Walker, 1989) is a method of building and reinforcing concepts that is also a logic exercise. In Semantic Feature Analysis (SFA), a list of related items is prepared, and a number of features are identified that characterize some, but not all, of the items. Items are used as column headings in a grid; features are listed in rows. A plus or a minus is placed under each item, beside each feature, depending on whether the item has (+) or does not have (–) that feature. If, for example, the items were geometrical figures, features might include having at least one curved surface, having more than four plane surfaces, and having all surfaces congruent. In this case, a – + + pattern would characterize a cube, whereas a + – – pattern would characterize a cylinder. Teacher-prepared grids can be given to students with only the terms and features listed. Students then complete the SFA grid by filling in the plusses and minuses as they gain information from their reading. As a more challenging alternative, the SFA grid may include the list of features, and the plusses and minuses for each column but omit the terms that the features describe. The students' task is to identify, on the basis of their reading, which items belong in each column. An SFA grid based on the planets, from which the names of the planets have been omitted, is presented in Figure 5–1. By checking facts about the planets, each planet can be identified, and its name placed at the head of the correct column.

Examination of the grid shows that each item has a unique pattern of plusses and minuses. An SFA grid is not complete until this is so; otherwise, there would be more than one correct solution. Here, the sixth planet listed has all of the features but one. It is smaller in diameter than Venus, was known before telescopes were invented, has one or

more satellites, and is closer to the Earth than Saturn. There are only three planets that are smaller in diameter than Venus: Mars, Mercury, and Pluto, so these planets must be in the fourth, sixth, and ninth columns. Pluto is farther from the sun than Mars, so it must be in the fourth column. Mars has two satellites; Mercury has none, so Mars is in the sixth column and Mercury is in the ninth.

The features on SFA grids can be put in the form of questions, with the grid to be completed using yes and no, rather than plusses and minuses. This method is easier for students to understand. An example of this kind of grid is shown in Figure 5–2. In that example, two answers have already been filled in, and this provides a demonstration for students of how to complete the grid. In this activity and in other tasks that require students to complete a series of answers, it is more useful to fill in some parts of a chart or list than to give a single completed example. Many students regard the completed example at the top of a written task as something to be ignored, because it is already completed. More attention is given, and more thought is required, when two or three answers are partially completed.

For very young children, the grid can be presented on a large chart. Pictures (e.g., photographs of buildings, such as school, firehouse, police station, library, hospital) can be used as column headings. Features, in the form of questions, are listed using repetitive language (e.g., Is this a place to read books? Is this a place where people wear uniforms? Is this a place where there are sirens?). In SFA grids of this kind, designed for young students, one of the guidelines for SFA construction previously listed—a number of features are identified that characterize some, but not all, of the items—can be ignored. In SFA activities, such as one about community buildings, it is important for students to think in terms of the most important feature of each place, so there should be one feature that applies only to each (e.g., "Is this a place where children go to learn?"). Here, as in other activities, when students give unexpected responses (e.g., "We went to the firehouse to learn about firefighters and firetrucks"), their thoughts should be understood, accepted, and appreciated.

Though the SFA strategy can be adapted for use with young children, it is most useful for students in

FIGURE 5–1   Semantic Feature Analysis Grid with Terms Omitted

Make a list of the nine known planets in our solar system. As you read the textbook chapter about the planets, make notes about which planets have the features listed in the rows to the left of the grid. When a planet has that characteristic, its column will contain a plus (+). When a planet does not have that characteristic, its column will contain a minus (–).

For example, the grid shows that five planets are farther from the sun than Mars. What are they? The names of these planets belong in columns 1, 3, 4, 5, and 7. Check the other features listed for each planet. When you find a planet that fits the pattern of plusses and minuses in a column, fill in its name at the top. There is only one correct solution.

	1	2	3	4	5	6	7	8	9
Farther from the sun than Mars	+	–	+	+	+	–	+	–	–
Smaller in diameter than Venus	–	–	–	+	–	+	–	–	+
Known before telescopes invented	–	+	+	–	+	+	–	+	+
Discovered before nineteenth century	–	+	+	–	+	+	+	+	+
Has one or more known satellites	+	+	+	+	+	+	+	–	–
Closer to Earth than Saturn	–	+	–	–	+	+	–	+	+

Answers to Figure 5–1 can be found in the Solutions section at the back of this book.

grades 4 through 12. Many adults also find SFAs interesting and challenging. The strategy adds breadth and depth to students' understanding by causing them to consider the characteristics (features) of items in the field they are studying, and to compare items carefully. It provides an introduction to logical thinking for some students, and an opportunity for students who enjoy analytical thinking to engage in a process that fits a talent. An additional useful aspect of the strategy is that it gives practice in using and understanding the row and column format of a grid. It can be time consuming to construct an accurate SFA grid. It is necessary to identify the important features, to state them clearly and in grammatically parallel fashion, and to check the accuracy of the completed SFA. On the other hand,

FIGURE 5–2 Semantic Feature Analysis Chart (Yes/No Style)

As you study about the Great Lakes, write YES or NO in the row for each question, below the column for each lake. For example, the question in the first row is, "Is the lake larger than Lake Michigan?" Lake Superior is the largest lake, so in the first row, you should write YES in the column for Lake Superior. What should you write in the same row for the column for Lake Michigan?

	Erie	Huron	Michigan	Ontario	Superior
Is the lake larger than Lake Michigan?			NO		
Is the lake deeper than Lake Ontario?					
Does any part of the lake lie east of any part of Lake Huron?				YES	
Does the lake border more than one U. S. state?					

Answers to Figure 5–2 can be found in the Solutions section at the back of this book.

SFAs can be constructed in class as a whole class or cooperative group activity. SFA differs from most strategies that require preparation of materials because students can be introduced to the strategy by creating a sample. Teachers can lead the class to develop an SFA activity by directing students to decide on a familiar topic (e.g., sports, breeds of dogs, desserts, vacation spots, a favorite story), and brainstorm a list of items within that category. (For the story, the items will be the characters.) Next, features that relate to the topic are listed (e.g., for sports, individual vs. team sport, played with or without a ball), and these features are stated in SFA style (e.g., team sport, requires a ball), and the grid is completed by adding features until each item listed has a unique pattern. Teacher-prepared SFA activities can be used as cooperative group assignments, or displayed as a bulletin board or learning center activity. Semantic Mapping and Terminology Trade are useful lead-ins to this strategy.

Detection. The ability to recognize and detect factual inaccuracies and logical errors is an important part of learning. One interesting way to enable students to demonstrate their learning is to create, first, an accurate statement of facts, and then a parallel statement that contains a few items that are false or illogical; and finally to present both statements together with a challenge to readers to identify the falsified version and the errors it contains. Such a process is an application and demonstration of knowledge, rather than a method of acquiring knowledge, and thus should be used when students already have learned about a topic. The kinds of errors inserted in a Detection activity need to be well chosen and to be identifiable based on careful reading and logical thinking and students should be encouraged to check reference sources for information to confirm their knowledge. Teachers who choose to use strategies, such as Detection, must observe two cautions. First, the activity is, and should be described as, a challenge or a puzzle, never as a trick or a way to fool people. Teaching and trickery are incompatible. Second, one rule must be scrupulously observed in creating the falsified version: the errors must not be designed to ridicule. When events are falsified, they must not be changed in ways that trivialize someone's achievements, or make fun of them.

Detection is based on an idea devised by Charles Klasky (1979), called "The History Mystery." Teacher-prepared concept statements (described in Chapter Two) provide an ideal basis for Detection activities. To create a Detection activity, teachers prepare a clear, accurate summary of important information as an accurate version of Detection, and then choose several important places in the factually accurate version and alter them to create inaccuracies. Once the original passage has been chosen or written, creation of the error version can be done quickly by a knowledgeable person; access to a computer makes preparation easy. Figure 5–3 presents an example of a brief Detection passage, with both accurate and inaccurate versions. It is important to note that the strategy is based on detection of factual inaccuracies, not technical errors, such as misspellings. Both the accurate and inaccurate versions of Detections should be completely correct in all technical aspects: spelling, grammar, and punctuation. When both versions are completed, they should be given a title and headed (title) version 1 and (title) version 2. The numbering should be random, so that the correct version will be 1 in some pairs and 2 in others. The two versions are then placed together in a folder that also contains Detection forms for cooperative groups to complete (e.g., Detection form: *Thurgood Marshall*. Which is the correct version? The incorrect version contains nine errors. List them, and explain how you know the statement is wrong. (In Figure 5–3, this portion of the activity is presented at the end.)

FIGURE 5–3   Sample Detection Activity

Thurgood Marshall: Version 1

Thurgood Marshall was a justice of the U. S. Supreme Court from 1967 to 1991. He was nominated by President Lyndon B. Johnson and was the first African American to serve on the Supreme Court. Marshall was born in Baltimore, Maryland, in 1908. He graduated from Lincoln University and attended law school at Howard University in Washington, D. C. From 1938 to 1961, he served as chief counsel for the National Association for the Advancement of Colored People (NAACP). During this time, he argued before the Supreme Court that racial discrimination in public schools is unconstitutional, and in 1954 the Supreme Court declared that this was so. His service on the Supreme Court spanned more than twenty years. The Thurgood Marshall Scholarship was created in his honor.

Another famous Supreme Court Justice was John Marshall, who was appointed by President John Adams, and became the fourth Chief Justice of the Supreme Court in 1801. It was the Supreme Court under John Marshall that confirmed and established the court's right to declare laws unconstitutional. This decision was made in the case of *Marbury v. Madison* in 1803.

Thurgood Marshall: Version 2

Thurgood Marshall was a justice of the U. S. Supreme Court from 1967 to 1991. He was nominated by President Lyndon B. Lincoln, and was the first African American to serve on the Supreme Court. Marshall was born in Baltimore, Delaware, in 1808. He graduated from Lincoln University and attended law school at Howard University in Washington, D. C. Beginning in 1961, he served for many years as chief counsel for the National Association for the Advancement of Colored People (NAACP), ending this service in 1938. During this time, he argued before the Supreme Court that racial discrimination in public schools is unconstitutional, and in 1954 the Supreme Court declared that this was so. His service on the Supreme Court spanned more than forty years.

Another famous Supreme Court Justice was John Marshall, who was appointed by President John Kennedy, and became the twenty-fourth Chief Justice of the Supreme Court in 1801. It was the Supreme Court under John Marshall that confirmed and established the court's right to declare laws unconstitutional. This decision was made in the case of *Marbury v. Madison* in 1803. The Thurgood Marshall Scholarship was created in honor of John Marshall.

＊ ＊ ＊ ＊ ＊ ＊ ＊ ＊ ＊ ＊ ＊ ＊ ＊ ＊ ＊ ＊ ＊ ＊

Which is the correct version? The incorrect version contains nine errors. List them, and explain how you know the statement is wrong.

Answers to Figure 5–3 can be found in the Solutions section at the back of this book.

Detection activities can also be prepared by students, with careful teacher editing. One method of using Detection is to base it on a research assignment in which students prepare a short (one- to two-page) biographical sketch of a famous person whose achievements are related to a topic being studied in a content area. Because students, like all people, benefit from reading about what is good and admirable, the people chosen by the teacher as subjects for the biographies should be people who are notable for their humane achievements. The teacher prepares for the assignment by making a list of possible subjects for the biographies, and arranging (usually in consultation with the school media specialist) for books and research materials to be available. As a preparation for the student research, the teacher provides instruction or review on how to take notes and keep records of sources, and may also provide a structure for the biography to follow (e.g., significant dates and events in the person's life, achievements for which the person is known, and interesting facts about the person's life). Further structure may be given to the assignment by using the SAIL strategy (described later in this chapter) in which the sources for the biographical information are provided for the students. Media center time and class time for writing and teacher student conferences is then scheduled, including opportunities for students to make revisions after the completed sketches are submitted. When the short biographies are completed and teacher-approved, the writers prepare another version that is deliberately falsified by changing the text in several places. The number of changes should vary depending on the age and sophistication of the readers: Five to eight changes are reasonable but older students may be able to work with Detection forms that contain many more errors.

Older students can learn to create textual inaccuracies in one or more of these categories:

1. *Factual inaccuracies.* These should be identifiable based on knowledge readers can be expected to have, for example, substantially incorrect dates (e.g., during the American Civil War [1941–1945]. Inaccuracies should have something in common with the facts; for example, here the incorrect dates for the Civil War are those for American engagement in World War II.

2. *Anachronisms.* An anachronism is something that is out of place in terms of time (e.g., One night Martha Washington dreamed that her husband had been seriously injured. On awaking she immediately phoned his headquarters at Valley Forge and found that a cannonball had landed near his tent but that he was uninjured). Because the telephone had not yet been invented at the time of the Revolutionary War, this passage contains an anachronism.

3. *Violations of logic.* These can be of two kinds: Logical inconsistencies are contradictory statements within the text (e.g., at one point the text states that Florence Nightingale had no children, but later the text states that Nightingale's two daughters also became nurses. Logical impossibilities are statements that are demonstrably false in themselves (e.g., John Quincy Adams, born in 1707, was the son of John Adams [1735–1826]. Mature students may not only be asked to identify the errors but also to indicate the category of each (anachronism, logical impossibility, and so on). For younger students, fewer categories of errors may be used. For example, the teacher might explain the concept of *anachronism* and children might write a one-page biography and then prepare a second form with two anachronisms.

A practical way to keep Detection materials is to prepare the two versions on regular-sized paper, laminate them, and insert them in the two sides of a pocketed folder. The theme of the Detection report can be printed on the front of the folder, along with the number of errors to be found. The bibliography for the research can be pasted or written on the back of the folder. The forms for students to use in completing the Detection activity can be placed in one of the folder pockets. Once the folders have been prepared, it can be a regular assignment for cooperative groups or students working in pairs to complete a specified number of Detection forms. Students may choose to work independently, in pairs, or in small groups. Well-prepared Detection activities can be kept and used year after year.

The Detection activity is suitable for students in grade 5 and above, and can be adapted for use with younger students. However, even very young children find it interesting and amusing to use a modified form of the strategy in which they pick out the silly feature of a picture or story. For example, children will laugh and point out the error if the three little pigs suddenly turn up in the story of the three bears, or if a tree is pictured growing upside down. For students of any age, the Detection topic should be one that students are thoroughly familiar with and the errors chosen should be those that students can, with thought and attention, identify. Successful completion of Detection activities adds breadth and depth to students' understanding by providing them with a sense of their mastery of a field of knowledge as they show that they can distinguish what is true from what is false.

Time and Place Maps.   Most maps provide a visual representation of a location in space. Time and Place Maps add a dimension that shows the sequence of events in locations over time. This is accomplished by marking the places on the map where related events occurred, and using labels, coded by color or design, to show their sequence across time. For example, a Time and Place Map can be created to show the history of a state. The spatial part of the map is a typical outline map showing the state boundaries, major cities, rivers, mountains, and so on. As the state's history is studied, significant events are listed, and arranged chronologically. Eventually, the chronological listing is studied and decisions are made about how to divide the chronology into time periods. The places where events occurred are shown on the map, with all events within the same time period coded with the same color or design. One possible decision, which would not work for all states, would be to divide events into five time periods: 1) before the arrival of European explorers; 2) from first exploration through settlements to date of petition for statehood; 3) between statehood and 1900; 4) between 1900 and the end of World War II; 5) since 1945. The decision might also be made to use the color sequence red, orange, yellow, green, blue to represent the sequence of five time periods. The event,

Becoming a State, would be given a date and brief description on an orange-bordered label (because it occurred in the third of the three time periods), and the label would be connected, perhaps by orange yarn, to an orange dot placed wherever the state capital was when statehood was achieved. People looking at the map could readily see what other events occurred in the time between statehood and 1900 because all these events would be labeled with the same colors. Time and Place Maps also require a key, explaining how the label styles, or colors, are matched with time periods.

Because this kind of map is one the students are not likely to have seen before, the strategy should be carefully thought through by the teacher, and its first use should be as a whole class activity. One possibility would be to create a biographical Time and Place Map, based on the life story of a person. For example, after reading aloud one of the many excellent biographies of Abraham Lincoln, the teacher would present the idea of showing the events of Lincoln's life on a map, and encourage the class (as a whole group, or in small groups or pairs) to brainstorm a list of events. At first, the list may be brief: birth, early work, election to state office, Lincoln-Douglas debates, election as president, Gettysburg address, assassination. Then, the locations of the events need to be found, or decided (where should the event "elected President" be marked on the map?). The class can consider how the map itself should be drawn. (Like a current U. S. map? Probably not. Why? Showing only the states at the time of his birth? Not a good idea either. Why?) When the basic map has been created, then time periods need to be identified; in the case of a biographical Time and Place Map, these decisions are usually easy to make. Then the labels for events are prepared, and their locations marked on the map, and a key prepared. As the creation of the map progresses, other events may be added, and new decisions will need to be made about how to display them. (In how many places did Lincoln and Douglas hold debates?) A follow-up activity might be to discuss, or write about, insights or questions inspired by the map.

Although they are more difficult to prepare than typical maps, Time and Place Maps have several advantages over timelines. First, constructing the map requires students to think analytically as they decide about how to separate events in a chronological sequence into time periods. Second, looking at the completed map enables students to see which events occurred in different locations but at the same time. Because of this feature, the maps contribute to higher-level thinking—analysis, synthesis, and evaluation—because they evoke questions and raise important issues. A Time and Place Map of state history, for example, can show population figures for present-day cities across time. Was there a period of time when many places at once grew into urban areas? When? Why? What are the common features of their locations? Perhaps students who create the map will decide to add another section to show events in other parts of the country or the world that affected aspects of state development.

Making Time and Place Maps is a useful assignment for cooperative groups, and the strategy is a versatile one. Possible topics in social studies are wide ranging: history of an area, biography of a person, or significant points in a sequence of societal change. A Time and Place Map based on inventions in a particular category, such as agricultural inventions, will give evidence that both time and location influence invention. In science, topics for Time and Place maps include maps to show the history of smallpox from pandemic plague to its eradication, history of flight or space exploration, and discovery of planets and their satellites. In literature, including historical fiction, the events of a story can be mapped to show where and when they occur, and the mapping may illuminate the ways authors deliberately arrange the sequence of events to convey their ideas.

The Time and Place Map strategy requires map skills, an understanding of sequence, and decision-making and classifying abilities. It is an activity for older students. Teachers can, however, make it a whole class activity to map the events that occur within a familiar sequence that takes place in several locations (e.g., happenings in a story, occurrences on a class trip, or daily events in a child's life) and to classify them according to a simple system: beginning, middle, end. Here, as in so many other instances, when students are thoroughly familiar with a subject, they can think about it in complex ways. Successful use of this strategy requires thoughtful choice of map

topic by the teacher, or, for older students who understand the strategy, guidance to help students select a topic. The teacher should have a conception of what the finished map might look like and be ready with suggestions; but imposing a preconceived plan would make it a routine exercise rather than an opportunity for students to plan, analyze, decide, and create. The analytical thinking that occurs not only as maps are being developed but after they have been completed is an important part of the strategy. Creation of Time and Place Maps requires class time over a period of a week or more but does not involve work for either teacher or students outside of class—except for thinking.

Graphic Information Lessons. Almost all textbooks include a variety of graphics; maps, charts, diagrams, and graphs of various kinds. Well-designed graphics add information and interest to the text, but students need to learn how to use them effectively as aids to understanding. David Reinking designed the Graphic Information Lesson (GIL) to be used occasionally as a postreading strategy for students at middle and secondary school levels. He noted that the method was useful for content area teachers because "they can highlight the value of graphic aids without sacrificing the subject being taught" (Reinking, 1986, p. 147).

There are three stages in a GIL, and the strategy extends over several days. The first stage is an examination of a text chapter or section (chosen by the teacher because it contains important graphic aids) to identify the different kinds of graphics that are included and to discuss the information they provide. The class considers the question, "What information is found in the graphic aids and how does it relate to information in the text?" For each graphic, they decide whether it is redundant, complementary, or supplementary to the text. A redundant graphic presents information that is provided so thoroughly and clearly in the text that it is unnecessary. Complementary graphics illustrate and clarify information that is given in the text. Supplementary graphics provide information that relates to the text but is not presented directly there. Reinking gives examples from a section from an American history text about cotton production in the south before the Civil War. One graphic studied was a map titled "The

South Expands" with areas marked "Old South" and "Cotton Kingdom." Dots on the map indicated cotton-growing areas. This graphic was supplementary, because the map showed that cotton growing areas tended to be clustered near rivers. This information was not given in the text.

The second stage of a GIL is innovative. It involves the creation and examination of "pseudographics." These are charts, maps, diagrams, graphs and other illustrations, such as those found in textbooks, some of which present accurate information about the topic that has been studied, and others that are false or misleading.

> Some of them are designed to be consistent with information in the text; others are purposefully inconsistent.... Pseudographics [should]... be believable or unbelievable when compared with legitimate information. (Reinking, 1986, pp. 148–149)

Reinking's examples of teacher-made and student-created pseudographics include a two-dimensional line graph showing acres planted in cotton (from few to many) by decades from 1800 to 1860; an advertisement in a Virginia newspaper dated 1790: "For sale: used cotton gin. Owner moving south to Alabama"; and a pie graph showing the population of the South in 1850 divided among small farmers, city dwellers, and plantation owners. The students' task is to mark each one "believable" or "unbelievable," and cite page numbers from the text where support for the decision can be found.

In the third stage of a GIL, students work together to create pseudographics and share them. There may also be class discussions about graphic aids. The teacher may identify two graphics and engage students in discussing how they are related. Alternatively, cooperative groups may identify what they believe to be the "most relevant, important or key graphic aid in the text" and defend their choice in a class discussion. This strategy is best used with older students, after a topic has been studied, when the text that has been studied includes a variety of graphic aids. The strategy requires teacher preparation and effort in creating useful pseudographics and in examining the pseudographics that students create. Effective pseudographics, both teacher-prepared and student-prepared, can be reused year

after year. When well conducted, GIL are interesting for students and are an effective way of teaching for transfer (a topic discussed in Chapter Two). Through these lessons, students can develop a much more thorough and powerful understanding of graphics than they would simply from reading texts that include graphic aids.

Enhancing Understanding Through Creative Thinking

The ability to come up with many, ingenious ideas is a talent that some people possess in remarkably strong ways. It is also a talent that can be cultivated and enjoyed widely by everyone, and fostered by a strong foundation of knowledge. Content area teachers can encourage thinking at the synthesis level by giving students opportunities to exercise fluency, flexibility, elaboration, originality, and opportunities to express their ideas in new forms, using their ingenuity to create interesting, useful, and beautiful products. All strategies that allow students independence to express themselves foster creativity. Strategies that stress thinking at the synthesis level vary widely in their complexity, from quick Divergent Thinking prompts that can be fitted into brief moments of the school day to Transmediation activities in which students express their ideas and knowledge in artistic ways. A strategy that is applicable to content area study and that encourages thinking at the synthesis level is Identity Creation.

Divergent Thinking. In 1950, J. Paul Guilford's presidential address to the American Psychological Association inspired many scholars to investigate forms of creative thinking by children and adolescents. Guilford contrasted convergent thinking (thought focused on determining a correct answer) with divergent thinking (thinking in new and unusual ways and devising many apt ideas). Numerous ingenious tests were designed to measure fluency (the ability to think of many ideas), flexibility (the ability to change course and take thoughts in new directions), elaboration (the ability to add new features to ideas), and originality (the ability to think of ideas that are unique). Although the tests are rarely given now, test features can easily be adapted as thinking challenges for the classroom. Three examples (Wallach & Kogan, 1965) are Instances ("Tell me all the different things you can think of that…"), Alternate Uses "Tell me all the uses you can think of for…"), and Similarities ("Tell me all the ways you can think of that… and… are alike"). Figure 5–4 provides a few of the myriad of possible examples of how these thinking challenges can be applied to content area study. Other challenges can be based on the many ways to apply divergent thinking to objects or ideas suggested by Alex Osborne (1963), who used the word SCAMPER as a mnemonic device: Substitute a feature, Combine, Adapt, Modify, minify or magnify, Put to other uses, Eliminate a feature, Reverse or rearrange. Thinking challenges such as these require no preparation, can be used spontaneously in brief periods of time, and can elicit ideas that may create further interest in topics being studied. Teachers who use divergent thinking activities must be willing to accept humor and unusual ideas that move away from the known and the expected.

Divergent thinking activities can also be sophisticated and extensive. For example, as a whole class and cooperative group activity, students might be presented with this challenge: Suppose you could put together a group of people to serve on a peacemaking mission to the current world trouble spot. These people can come from the present or any time periods in the past. Who would you choose? What would each one be able to contribute? Building on all three themes, students might be asked (as a Similarities activity) to consider ways in which a current world tragedy is similar to national and international problems of the past. For example, at the time this text is written such a place is Sarajevo in the country that was formerly Yugoslavia. The next activity (Instances) would be to think of people who contributed to ending or solving these problems, or who might have done so. Then, as a variation of Alternate Uses, students could select a team of problem solvers and peacemakers and consider how their talents could be used to reach a solution.

Identity Creation.   The Identify Creation (or I See) strategy uses a set of teacher-prepared cards describing a variety of people living in the same time

---

FIGURE 5–4   Examples of Divergent Thinking Prompts

Instances
List all the things you can think of
- that have roots
- that have roots but no leaves
- that still need to be invented
- that can be used to make music

List all the factors that
- make exploration of polar regions dangerous
- make it important to explore unknown territory
- ought to be considered when deciding where to build a school
- cause people to like sports, become scientists , or set goals for themselves

What are all the reasons you can think of
- for building skyscrapers?
- why so many products are rectangular?
- that schools give grades?
- why leaves have different shapes?

Alternate Uses
What are all the ways a scientist could use bread?
- all the ways to use a compass?
- all the careers in which a knowledge of history is useful?
- all the purposes for having playgrounds?
- all the ways light can be used to promote good health?

Similarities
What are all the ways that the numerals 5 and 4 are alike?
- that the careers of Elizabeth Blackwell and Marie Curie were similar?
- that bone and cartilage are alike?
- that oil and water are similar?
- that a train is like a truck?
- that an eagle is like a truck?
- that an eagle is like a country?

period. Each card gives information about the imaginary person's name, age, gender, ethnicity, work, economic status, or social status. As the time period is studied, students have the responsibility of taking on the role of a person and elaborating on it. The idea is based on a strategy proposed by Andrea Makler who describes the preparation of an extensive set of such descriptions that she and her colleagues developed and called Historically Accurate Fictional Family Identity (HAFFI) cards, which are "historically plausible life 'scripts' for members of 35 different families representing the major racial, ethnic, and religious groups in the United States" (Makler, 1987, p. 180).

The Identity Creation strategy could be used, for example, during study of the American Revolutionary War period, and cards could be developed for people from both America and England. The task of a student, pair, or group of students who choose, or are given, a person's card is to go on to flesh out details of the character's life and experience. As a whole class activity, students and teacher can develop a list of the major events occurring in the time period that would be relevant to people living in the area or areas being studied. (A useful source to supplement textbooks and trade books is *The Timetables of History* by Grun, 1991). The assignment for students is to describe the effect of these events on their simulated character. The teacher can provide a set of questions to be answered that applies to all characters, and several additional questions for each character, which are specific to that character's situation.

This is a strategy that requires fairly extensive preparation by teachers or a group of teachers. It meshes well with themed teaching, and preparation might be done by a teaching team. Although preparation of good materials for this activity is time-consuming, teachers who enjoy creating curriculum materials are likely to discover many advantages. The process is practical because the strategy can be used as soon as a small number of cards has been developed. All that is needed to begin is one card for each cooperative group. Using the strategy with a few cards will help teachers see ways to improve these cards and create others. Working with colleagues is also beneficial.

The most unexpected and productive consequence of developing this curriculum was that my colleagues and I talked to each other. We sought advice and information as we filled in the gaps of our knowledge of history. Teaching about gender and conflict made us examine our own assumptions, and provoked heated, though friendly, arguments. I think this sort of interaction is necessary to good teaching; it is more likely to occur when teachers find the material they teach as challenging as their students do. (Makler, 1987, p. 185)

The strategy could lead to transmediation through dramatization of events in characters' lives.

Transmediation.   Recently, scholars (e.g., Harste, Burke, & Short, 1988; Hoyt, 1992) have stressed the value of transmediation, which is the process of translating knowledge from one form of communication to another. The most commonly used form of transmediation is to move from the receptive to the expressive mode; that is, to write or talk about what has been read or heard. Other forms of transmediation involve presenting information visually through charts and graphs, and through artistic media: visual art, music, dance, and drama. Karen Jorgensen-Esmaili (1990) describes social studies learning in which students who have been learning about different countries or time periods write imaginary stories set in that place or time. As part of the process, the students create clay sculptures (for example, models of typical houses of the period) that help to make their writing more realistic. Linda Hoyt (1992) discusses the value of using drama and other forms of art as learning processes, noting that encouraging students to create engages them in higher order thinking processes and presents them with problems to solve. She describes classrooms in which students, including those with special learning needs, study, talk, create art projects, and write. In one example she presents, elementary students have been learning about elephants:

For Derek to show what he knew about elephants through the medium of clay, he had to [recognize the extent] of his knowledge and develop a new perspective toward the information… [H]e was continually searching his own knowledge bank for the details that he needed to represent in his model. As a result, Derek frequently realized that he was unsure of certain points A rapid retreat to the resource books generated further reading, discussion with friends, and additional revision in his sculpture. (Hoyt, 1992, p. 581)

Pamela Wadsworth advocates drawing as a part of science study for young children, for example, encouraging children to draw pictures of batteries and a light bulb and show how to connect them to make the light bulb glow. The teacher can annotate the drawings to add to the child's explanation; the drawing is likely to reveal more about the child's understanding than a verbal explanation. Making a drawing gives students thinking time, and drawings, which do not depend on skill in either literacy or oracy (i.e., speaking and listening), enable students to show their understanding without using words.

> Children who answer 'I don't know' when asked a direct question are often capable of drawing a picture to illustrate their ideas. For example, when asked to explain what a shadow is, many young children responded with 'I don't know.' Yet all... could draw a picture of themselves and their shadow. (Wadsworth, 1992, p. 55)

Beth Cox (1991) advocates reading response journals in which high school students draw in response to their reading, and then write a brief passage describing the drawing and relating it to the reading.

Sketch to Stretch (Seigel, 1984) begins with a reading assignment, after which students create a sketch related to the reading, within a specified time limit. The sketch is a visualization of a concept from the reading that has importance to the person making the sketch. After the time for sketching, students share and explain their drawings in small groups. The groups then decide upon one sketch to share in a whole class discussion. Rhodes (1989) advocates using Sketch to Stretch as a content area follow-up to a form of wide reading in which the teacher reads aloud an advanced text and students read easier trade books. The students' sketches integrate the two readings. The Sketch to Stretch activity can also be used as a precursor to semantic mapping, as Sharon Thomas and Marilyn Wilson (1993) suggest, if students use the sketches to illustrate an important concept.

Quick Draw (Owsley, 1989) is a gamelike process in which students, after having studied a topic, work with terminology cards. (The cards used for Terminology Trade could be reused for this activity.) Two students choose a card, which they do not show to their classmates, and take a brief time to confer about how to illustrate the concept. Owsley suggests using a timer and allowing 30 seconds for each part of the activity: conferring and drawing. The first student draws an illustration. No words or numbers are permitted. Classmates try to guess the term being illustrated. If they fail to do so, the two students doing the drawings confer and there is another round of drawing, this time done by the second student. A third round of conferencing and drawing may be used if needed. Students may discuss later how the drawings illustrate the concepts, or the drawings could be included in learning log journals.

Transform-a-Problem is a versatile transmediation strategy, in which students are encouraged to represent a complex problem in alternate ways. In math, a problem may be drawn, graphed, or dramatized, or a representation of the problem can be created using manipulatives. Such activities often enable learners to go beyond completing the computations needed to obtain a correct answer, and reach a thorough understanding of the solution. A simpler name, Draw-a-Problem, can be used if drawing is the only form of transmediation used.

Word Posters, which illustrate word meanings, are another method of transmediation, Figure 5–5. Most students enjoy the opportunity to incorporate art into content area study, so choosing a vocabulary word from a current topic of study and presenting the word and its definition (stated or implied) as appropriately and vividly as possible on a 9×12 sheet of construction paper is an enjoyable way of building and reinforcing vocabulary. In the intermediate and middle school years, preparation of a poster can be a biweekly assignment. The posters themselves make a handsome classroom or hall bulletin board and can be used as a study device as well. Another kind of word poster stresses **derivations** and interrelationships among words. For example, a word poster on vision, could include the related words *provisions, visit, television, view, vista,* and

FIGURE 5–5:   An Example of a Word Poster

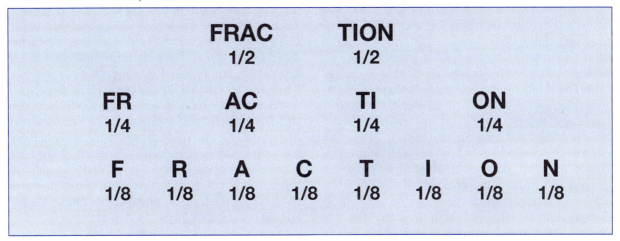

revise. These related words are derived from the Latin word *videre*, meaning *to see*, but not the word *division*, which has a different derivation. Pictures that illustrate the words can be cut from newspapers and magazines, and usually the words themselves can be found there also. Students who are aware of the various derivation word posters that are in preparation can keep an eye out for words and pictures that may be useful for classmates. Derivation word posters are productive of learning and have the added advantage that they can continually be added to, as more related words are found.

Transmediation activities are suitable across grades. Through transmediation, students engage in activities that enable them to expand their interests and talents and to enjoy activities in which their talents are already recognized. (Not all students, however, will prefer nonverbal over verbal methods of expressing ideas.) Some transmediation activities are more useful in grades 3 and beyond than in the early elementary grades, in part because transmediation often incorporates art in content area study, and primary students typically have many opportunities to engage in art-related activities. Also, as students develop richer conceptual understandings, they are likely to be able to present richer images. Transmediation activities may be impromptu, but the teacher needs to establish an environment in which students are comfortable in exercising their creativity. It is important also that time be used flexibly. To allow ten minutes to create a poem, for example, will result in poems that are different from those that are created thoughtfully over time. Transmediation is extremely versatile. In fact, the term describes a category in which there are a wide variety of strategies. Vocabulary development strategies can be followed by creating a dramatization or song; a semantic map can be made three-dimensional; illustrations developed while using the wide reading strategy can be made into a mural, mobile or stabile, and so forth. The strategies described in Chapter Eleven, "Integration of the Arts with Content Area Learning," also present opportunities for transmediation.

Augmenting Understanding Through Evaluative Thinking

Engaging in discussion can encourage students to relate what they have learned to their own beliefs,

---

derivation—the words *derive* and *derivation* come from the Latin word *rivus*, meaning *stream*, and the Latin prefix *de*, meaning *from*. Most of the words in our language have their source in other languages, many of which are no longer spoken. A word's derivation tells us what "stream" it comes from.

and to consider the viewpoints of others. The ability to engage in productive and amicable discussion is valuable not only in school, but in family life and careers. For discussions to be successful, there must be a classroom environment in which students value an exchange of ideas and in which people are willing to change their minds in response to discussion. The ability to plan and guide thoughtful, inclusive classroom discussions is an aspect of effective teaching that is worthwhile for teachers to cultivate. Nel Noddings and Paul Shore (1984, p. 113), who describe discussions as a form of public conversation in learning, point out, "Most of us need the interest and constructive criticism of well-informed others." Classroom discussions can be the vehicle that provides students with both the interest of others and well-founded critiques of their ideas. Teachers who establish classrooms that are comfortable, safe learning environments, in which ideas are important and all students are respected, have accomplished the essential basis for good discussions. Talking about issues can occur repeatedly, at planned or unplanned times.

The term *Instructional Conversations* (Goldenberg, 1992/1993; Saunders, Goldenberg, & Hamann, 1992) is used to refer to lively discussions focused on important topics that interest students. However, as teachers who work on engaging their students in discussions know, conducting such discussions is not simple or effortless. Teachers must attend to instructional elements of the discussion, most importantly to drawing in students' ideas while maintaining the focus of the discussion. Other instructional elements are providing information, modeling effective expressive language, and encouraging students to support their ideas by quoting from text and using their own reasoning. Discussions also have conversational elements. Teachers need to maintain a responsive attitude toward students' ideas, make connections among the ideas contributed by various students, establish a challenging but nonthreatening atmosphere, and encourage wide participation through self-selected turn-taking (rather than requiring that students wait to be called upon by the teacher). It can be a useful component of instruction to incorporate one or more discussion strategies that follow a format the class can become familiar with

and encourage students to express ideas that others disagree with, listen thoughtfully to opposing views, and perhaps modify their opinions after reflection. Each of the three discussion strategies described in this chapter—Discussion Web, U Debate, and Structured Controversy—has a structure that encourages discussion, and is based on differences of opinion. They are presented in order of their degree of sophistication. Students across the grades can use the Discussion Web strategy. U Debate and the Structured Controversy strategy are designed for use with middle and high school students. Other discussion strategies, which are not oppositional, are discussed in Chapter Ten, and encouraging classroom talk in the form of "grand conversations" is discussed in Chapter Eleven.

Discussion Web.   In the Discussion Web strategy, devised by Donna Alvermann (1991), based on the work of James Duthie (1986), a graphic aid is used to focus discussion of opposing points of view or topics. At the center, a question is posed. For example, a Discussion Web in a class on government could begin with the question, Should there be term limits for elected government officials? In science, the question posed might be: When a dangerous disease has been completely eradicated, should some samples of the disease germs still be kept by scientists? The question is listed with *No* written at the left side, and *Yes* written at the right, Reasons written above the question, and Conclusion written below. As students contribute reasons to support their positions, these ideas are written on the appropriate side. After reasons have been given and listed on both sides, the group attempts to reach a conclusion. Alvermann proposes using Discussion Webs in science for a discussion of alternative hypotheses about a problem, such as two alternative methods of combating the problem of acid rain. In math, she suggests that students use the strategy in cooperative groups when working with word problems that contain extraneous information, by classifying the information given as relevant or irrelevant. The solution to the problem then becomes the conclusion. If the Discussion Web strategy is used frequently, teachers will become increasingly adept at summarizing answers, helping students clarify their ideas as needed, and guiding the group to reach consensus or to state opposing opinions clearly and fairly if agreement cannot be reached. (Accepting disagreement is a sound method of ending a discussion; voting is *not* an appropriate way to conclude.) It can be a rotating assignment for cooperative groups to pose a Discussion Web question, putting it in final form after consultation with the teacher; the group can then share the question the day before the discussion will be held.

U Debate.   When a teacher wishes to encourage debate about opposing points of view, a useful strategy is to arrange the seating in the form of a large U (Athanases, 1988). The teacher states the opposing ideas, and tells students to choose their seats in accordance with their points of view on the topic to be discussed. Those who hold one position most strongly sit at one extreme of the U, and those holding the opposite view most strongly sit across from them, at the other extreme. In preparation for the discussion, most students must move from their seats and there may be some jockeying for position, often among students who prefer to be seated in neutral positions. Those who take seats at the extremes are usually more willing to talk about their points of view because they have already, in a sense, expressed themselves through their choice of where to sit. As moderator, the teacher may call upon any students to respond to what has been said. Because students' positions have been made visible, the teacher can easily help students get started. "Tina, you're strongly in favor of a public transportation system. Give us a few of your reasons for this support." "What is it about that view that you disagree with, Ari?" "Lisa and Kim, you've indicated you don't have strong opinions about this issue. You've heard these opposing views. Which are you more inclined to support?" Usually, after guiding the discussion in this way, the need for the teacher's intervention diminishes. Sometimes students will signal a change of opinion by getting up and moving to a different place. The U Debate strategy is a useful one for substitute teachers to know about, because one of the difficulties substitutes encounter is not knowing students' names. Students in a U Debate arrangement signal their views by the places they choose to sit, and so a teacher can speak to them face to face and elicit a variety of opinions ("Tell me why you favor that idea. What are your reasons for opposing it?") without calling on students by name.

Structured Controversy.   Structured Controversy is a discussion strategy devised by David and Roger Johnson (1979, 1988) who are leaders in the field of cooperative learning. The process spans several sessions in which teams of students are each given materials on a topic about which there are two opposing views (e.g., whether more or less government intervention is needed to solve the problem of hazardous waste management). At the first session of a Structured Controversy, teams examine the materials and plan how best to support their assigned position. In the second session, teams give their presentations and then engage in general discussion. In the third session, teams reverse their positions and argue for the point of view that they previous opposed. At the fourth session, the whole group endeavors to reach the best decision possible. For the strategy to work well, the teacher must prepare sets of resource materials in advance and must establish a discussion environment in which students feel comfortable in challenging each other's ideas and reasoning, while showing value and respect for each other. Geoffrey Maruyama and his colleagues (1995) give a further description of this discussion process, noting that it is advantageous for students to hold small group discussions in teams of four, with pairs of students advocating each position. "If students hold strong views about the issue, groups are most typically assigned with one person on each side whose personal views are consistent with the position he or she promotes." Pointing out the advantages of the Structured Controversy strategy, they write:

> The controversy process ideally improves logical thinking and communication skills, promotes a better understanding of the issue being discussed, and provides a positive context for dealing with disagreement. (Maruyama, Knechel, & Petersen, 1995, p. 233)

▪▪ Extending Knowledge
▪▪ Through Research

Engaging in research activities has the potential to interest students and to extend and enhance their learning. In this section of the chapter, research assignments are discussed in depth. Recurrent problems are described, and solutions are suggested. Two major strategies for teachers to consider are presented: SAIL, which provides support for writing a research report while preventing plagiarism, and the Structured Research Process, a method of guiding a class through group and individual exploration of a common topic, from introduction to final presentations.

Research is a question-raising, question-answering process. It is often a recursive process. Finding an answer to an important question is likely to raise new questions. An activity rich with possibilities for present and future learning, however, is often poorly thought through by teachers, and unpleasant and unproductive for students. A common content area assignment for students, beginning quite early in the elementary school years and continuing into college, has traditionally been to "write a research report," an assignment that has been summarized satirically (Perrin, 1987, p. 51) as "Research a topic of your choice and turn in a paper in three weeks. Don't plagiarize!" Often, at every level, teachers say that the activity is assigned because it is customary (or required in the curriculum) to prepare students for similar assignments in the future. Usually, teachers do not say that they expect their students to benefit directly from the activity. Often, at every level, the process is difficult and sometimes baffling for students. Often, even when

students are successful in writing the reports (i.e., they receive good grades), they say, if asked, that they have not enjoyed the process nor learned much from it. Sometimes what they have learned about how to prepare a report is incorrect.

Teacher and author Nancie Atwell (1990), describing her own sixth grade experience with an assigned research report as the unhappiest memory from her elementary school years, makes the point that such assignments are dreary for teachers as well as for students. She recounts her experience in procrastinating about an assignment that was puzzling and overwhelming until it was too late to complete it, concealing the fact that she had no project to turn in, and then worrying about it. But the teacher

...never mentioned the missing report. Not that day, not ever. For the remaining three months of the school year I lived … in dread. [But] my sixth-grade teacher did not discover until the last day of school that I hadn't submitted the report. For the same reason that I had postponed writing it she had postponed grading it: sheer boredom. The reports, as tedious to read as they were to write, informed and entertained no one. I can't blame the teacher. The sixth grade social studies curriculum required a report on a country, and she had obliged. Then she had procrastinated too, until it was too late for her to bring me to justice. …It did not have to be this way, for her or for me. (Atwell, 1990, p. xii)

In Atwell's account of her experience with a research assignment, first she, and then her teacher, avoided a distasteful and difficult assignment by putting off the task until tomorrow. Anne Lamott takes the title of her book on writing, *Bird by Bird*, from her memory of another experience with the research paper assignment. Her brother, stymied by the need, after three months of **procrastination**, to write a report on birds in one evening, was

close to tears, surrounded by binder paper and pencils and unopened books on birds, immobilized by the hugeness of the task ahead. Then my father sat down beside him, put his arm around my brother's shoulder, and said, 'Bird by bird, buddy. Just take it bird by bird'. (Lamott, 1995, p. 19)

Not all parents are this calm. Many have uneasy memories of trying to provide support at home for

---

procrastination—The polysyllabic English words *procrastination, procrastinate,* and *procrastinator* have a short Latin word as their root: *cras,* meaning tomorrow. The Latin prefix *pro-* means, in this case, forward, so to procrastinate means to put something forward to tomorrow. Literally, procrastinating is "tomorrowing."

The saying, "Procrastination is the thief of time" is a reminder that postponing tasks that must be done consumes time, in worry and eventually in work, time that could have been saved if the task had not been put off.

an extensive assignment made at school. Nancy Ganyard (1986) has written a "Guide for parents on writing their child's first term paper." Her short article is a satire, giving directions to parents about how to complete their children's term paper assignments. Her implicit point, however, is a serious one: teachers have the responsibility for guiding assignments such as these so that they are learning opportunities for students. Anne Lamott uses her father's good advice as a way to help writers move past the difficulties of getting started. However, for teachers who give the research paper assignment, it should evoke a question: What was the ten-year-old's teacher doing for those three months? Among the many advantages of teacher intervention in the research process is that it substantially reduces students' inclination to procrastinate, and the possibility of their doing so.

Doable Research Assignments

A doable assignment, of course, is one that the student is able to do. The responsibility lies with teachers to devise doable research projects—activities that their students can accomplish using resources available to all members of the class. Teachers must remember that the most important resource that should be available to all students, throughout the research process, is teacher expertise and instruction, provided in ways that guide students toward eventual independence.

> Certainly, we cannot assume that children can complete inquiry tasks on their own in advance of extensive experience. So it is important to determine the kinds of supports that are really helpful, that give children only the amount of help they need, and that allow children gradually to take over as much of the task as they are capable of. This approach tells us that the relationship between teacher and student is one of a gradual "fading" of the teacher role—from tutor, to coach, to sympathetic audience and critic.
>
> Teachers and librarians can help students manage the inquiry process by modeling how to do it, by prompting them at various points in the process to figure out where they are in the overall plan and by helping them keep track of the information they collect. (Sheingold, 1987, p. 84)

Good content area teachers value and foster the desire to learn, and serve as learning models for students. Teachers can show they value the attitude of wanting to know by treating questions with attention and respect. Teachers can foster wanting to know by encouraging questions and selecting teaching activities that have a question-raising component. Teachers can model wanting to know by sharing their own questions, and this can enable them to model the process of finding out for the students. Classroom research should include activities in all of these three categories:

- using resource texts and materials (and resource people) to find answers to single questions that arise during reading and discussion;
- devising questions and finding answers through surveys, interviews, and experiments;
- collecting, organizing, and presenting information about a topic of interest.

Many opportunities for learning are lost when the teacher's efforts are concentrated on the beginning and end of a research activity, giving the assignment and evaluating the final product, and when students are expected to work independently during the research process. Some students may succeed in producing an elegant product only because they have received extensive help at home that is not available to their classmates. Many students may fail to learn how to acquire, organize, and present information. They may develop the habit of using strategies that are wrong, such as plagiarizing text.

Eliminating Plagiarism

Plagiarism is the use of the words and ideas of others without giving the author credit through quotation marks and citations. When a passage of text

---

plagiarism—has a dramatic derivation: *plagiarius* is a Latin word that means *kidnapper*—one who steals the child of another and thus claims falsely to be the parent of that child. *Plagiary,* now an obsolete word, was used, in English, to mean a kidnapper; then *plagiarism* became the word applied to literary theft, the act of claiming falsely to be the author of material written by someone else.

written by another person is used with a few minor changes, its use still constitutes plagiarism unless the identical portions are placed in quotation marks and the source is cited. Teachers at all grade levels should be aware of what constitutes plagiarism and what steps can be taken to prevent it. Teachers need to show students how to document their sources during the process of finding information, so that proper credit can be given. (Figure 5–6 gives examples.)

Plagiarism may occur when students do not understand the material they are reading well enough to restate it, do not understand how to cite sources, or do not understand that it is wrong to use other people's work by copying it. Students may also plagiarize when they are frightened about their assigned task, or when they have not developed a strong enough sense of right or wrong to resist temptation in this area. Teachers have the responsibility to provide do-able tasks for their students, to help them in a straightforward and non-threatening way to understand what plagiarism is and why it is wrong, and to structure assignments and their own evaluation of assignments in such a way that students have interest and pride in their own work. If an instance of plagiarism does occur in an assignment, the penalties for it, which may be severe, may already be specified in school or college regulations. In many situations, however, the teacher need not immediately give a failing grade, but can choose to guide the student to understand the problem and require that the assignment be redone properly with guidance and supervision.

FIGURE 5–6 Crediting the Work of Others

Text passage (hypothetical text): Preserving our natural environment is a form of self-preservation; in the long run it is both aesthetically and economically sound."

Source (hypothetical): Riter, A. (1991). *A guide to ecology.* Middleville IL: Writers' Press.

▮ If a short passage is quoted exactly, use quotation marks and cite the source briefly. A usual way is to put the last name of the author, and the date of publication, in parenthesis immediately after the quotation, and include the full citation at the end of the text, in a bibliography or list of references. (Longer passages may be included in the text, indented, with the source cited at the end.)

"Preserving our natural environment is a form of self-preservation; in the long run it is both aesthetically and economically sound" (Riter, 1991, p. 99).

▮ If part of the quoted passage is omitted, use quotation marks, and use an ellipsis consisting of three dots at the point(s) of omission.

"Preserving our natural environment... is both aesthetically and economically sound" (Riter, 1991, p. 99).

"Preserving our natural environment is... in the long run... economically sound" (Riter, 1991, p. 99).

▮ If letters, words, or phrases are inserted or substituted in the quoted passage, use quotation marks, and put the insertions in brackets.

"...in the long run [environmental protection] is both aesthetically and economically sound" (Riter, 1991, p. 99).

▮ To refer to sources of ideas when no material from them is quoted, name the source(s) in the text and include the full citation(s) at the end of the text, in a bibliography or list of references.

Advocates of preserving wetlands include Riter (1991), who notes not only the beauty of their plants and wildlife, but the present and potential future economic benefits of such preservation.

Many recent authors (e.g., Riter, 1991) have stressed the importance of preserving our natural environment.

When teachers take plagiarism lightly, they are failing in their obligations to their students and to their profession. Such failures, unfortunately, do occur. Susan Davis has reported on her research, interviewing teachers about their attitudes toward plagiarism, and interviewing middle school students, identified as gifted, on their methods of writing content area research reports. She presents two reasons for plagiarism. The first is students' readiness to cheat in this way:

> I just opened one encyclopedia on one side of my computer and laid another encyclopedia on the other side. I wrote one paragraph from the one on the left and then one from the one on the right. I always get A's that way.' ...'Who cares if we plagiarize? It's only for school!' (Davis, 1994, p. 56)

The second reason she cites for plagiarism is that teachers encourage it.

> [T]eachers often encourage and reward plagiarism. One of the ways they encourage plagiarism is by assigning topics that are so broad that they could be the topic of an entire book.... Not only are the topics assigned to students overly vague, teachers sometimes give higher grades for plagiarized work... [which seems]... more sophisticated than the real writing of the rest [of the class]. Because many teachers do not understand the processes involved in research, they even tell students they can plagiarize. I have had several students over the years tell me that their teachers have allowed them to plagiarize source texts for reports (sometimes under the rubric of paraphrasing). It is not often, however, that a teacher admits it. One fourth-grade teacher did. When I asked if she would like to learn some strategies for helping students write reports, she replied, "Oh, I let them copy out of the encyclopedia. After all, it's their first report." (Davis, 1994, p. 56)

Giving Credit Where Due

From an early age, students can be encouraged to make a practice of "giving credit where credit is due." This will help them understand that referring to the work of others and using it properly is a necessary and sensible part of research. Creators of ideas and products deserve recognition. Our society has developed ways of assuring that those who devise inventions or make discoveries, and those who create works of art or scholarship, will have the benefits of their ingenuity and work. Students need to understand that almost all research depends on the work of others, and that it is right and honorable to give credit to others when we use their ideas. This understanding is a good basis for avoiding plagiarism.

Developing the habit of crediting sources also combats the mistaken idea that any kind of "copying" is wrong, and therefore that it is improper to look to others for help. It is extremely unfortunate if students believe this, and teachers need to overcome this piece of mislearning. Sharing ideas and acquiring information from colleagues and the authors of published materials is a necessary and desirable part of learning. No matter how young their students are, teachers can model the practice of giving credit to people who are the sources for ideas. A class-written book modeled on the published work of others should include credit to the original creators; for example, "Our class thanks Robert E. Wells, who wrote *Is a blue whale the biggest thing there is?* (1993) and *What's smaller than a pygmy shrew?* (1995) for giving us ideas for writing our *Big, Bigger, Biggest and Small, Smaller, Smallest* books." Individual students and cooperative groups can take pride in being knowledgeable enough to give credit to others: "I thank Tomie dePaola for the pictures in his *Book of poems* (1988). I have tried to draw the illustrations for my book like his." "Our group is grateful to Deborah Hahn, because her version of *The swineherd* (1991) showed us that it was all right to write a new ending for a story. We hope our readers will like the ending we have made for this familiar story." When classmates or cooperative groups share ideas, credit can be given in a variety of pleasant, interesting ways; for example a notice can be placed on a bulletin board prepared by students: "This display about transportation was prepared by Gerry, Rosa, Oliver, Una, and Pat. We thank our art teacher, Ms. Penn, and the media specialist, Mr. Page, for their help. We also thank Ray and Rhoda for lending us postcards showing pictures of early trains." Students who have experience in thanking others for their contributions, and being thanked, in such simple but formal ways, will develop the habit of crediting their sources, and will be helped to realize that learning is not a competitive matter. In many books, an Acknowledgments section appears either at the beginning or the end. It is useful for students to be aware of this feature of books and to consider how to acknowledge their debt to others when they share their own work.

The Classroom Research Center

Because this is a literate society, the answers to many questions are found in books. Reference books, in particular, are resources for finding the answers to many factual questions. All students should have many opportunities to use the school media center purposefully, but ideally each classroom should also have a research center, in which information can be sought and found as questions arise in the classroom. In classrooms that are well-equipped learning environments, students and teacher have immediate access to basic reference materials: a dictionary that includes information about word derivations, an atlas, a current world almanac, an up-to-date globe, and wall maps of whatever parts of the earth or the solar system are being studied for a changing display.

Although one good dictionary is essential, a variety of dictionaries can be very useful. Classroom dictionaries may include one or more written for young people, but at least one should be written for adults, so that students can be accustomed to seeing a dictionary used by a knowledgeable adult. Good recent dictionaries are often available at sale prices, and older unabridged dictionaries are sometimes found very inexpensively in used book stores. It can be informative for students to discover that dictionaries do not all contain the same set of words, and that some words do not appear in older dictionaries because they had not yet been originated when the dictionary was published. It is also useful to know that there are many dictionaries that are not devoted to the listing and defining of words. The *Macmillan visual dictionary* (1992), for example, pictures things, and labels their parts, in categories ranging from architecture to weapons. "Why a dictionary of dinosaurs?" is the opening sentence of the foreword to *The New Illustrated Dinosaur Dictionary*. The immediate reply

is, "The answer, of course, is that there are so many people of all ages all over the world who are fascinated with dinosaurs" (Sattler, 1990, p. 11). This book, besides the information it gives about its topic, is an excellent resource for students learning how dictionaries work. The type is large, the entries include clearly understandable information about pronunciations and derivations, the descriptions are clear, and there are many cross-references.

Other useful reference materials include historical reference books that provide timetables or time lines, and one or more dictionaries of quotations. Ideally, an encyclopedia with a print size and writing style that make it possible for young people as well as adults to learn from the text should also be available in the classroom. Sometimes libraries discard encyclopedias when more up-to-date versions are purchased, and alert classroom teachers may be able to obtain a set by requesting the old version. Sometimes a media specialist purchases a new encyclopedia because a volume is missing; some encyclopedia companies will sell single volumes of encyclopedia editions at a fairly low cost, and this can enable a discarded encyclopedia to be completed for a classroom research center. Reading or looking at material from the research center should be an option for students during Themed Reading (a strategy described in Chapter Two). No student should ever be discouraged by the teacher or classmates from choosing to read or look at resource material, such as a volume of an encyclopedia or an atlas, because of insufficient reading skill. Both mature and less skilled readers can learn from looking at illustrations, graphs, and maps included in these resource materials.

An essential aspect of content area study is learning how to find the answers to questions. One reason why classroom research centers are so useful is that the process of finding out—research—can be both informal and immediate. A question arises, and teacher, or teacher and students, look up the answer. Because teachers, at every level, will usually be more sophisticated than their students in the use of reference materials, occasions for such modeling can usefully occur at every level of study. Eventually students will be able to find information individually or by working with a partner, although the teacher should always be willing to be a resource person. Teachers can teach students—or rather, *not* teach them to forget what they knew as very young children—that it is important and fun to find things out, and that a good way to do this is to ask someone who knows the answer, or who knows how to find it out. The questions shown in Figure 5–7 are examples of questions that might arise in a classroom. Possible teacher responses are given for each question. The way a teacher responds to questions will vary substantially depending on the age and knowledge base of the students, and on teachers' decisions about when it is sensible to allot class time to this kind of question-answering process. As these examples

show, modeling how to use reference books can be carried out through *Reference source commentaries*, a strategy similar to the Teacher Read-Aloud Commentary strategy, which is described in Chapter Three.

One helpful use of a reference source commentary is to talk through the process of finding and understanding word definitions in a dictionary. Figure 5–8 presents examples of dictionary commentaries, showing what a teacher might say, looking up a word that students are learning, or talking about word definitions and derivations. In these examples, the teacher is already knowledgeable about the words and aware that knowing their derivations can help students understand and remember them.

FIGURE 5–7   Teacher Response to Students' Questions, Including Examples of Reference Source Commentaries

Student: **Which state is bigger, Nevada or Utah?**
Teacher: Alma, will you and Nick check the almanac to find out? Write the areas of those two states on the board, so we can compare.

These students are old enough to read capably and to know how to use the Table of Contents in an almanac. The teacher provides guidance by suggesting the almanac as a good reference resource for this question, and gives these two students the task of providing information so that the class can determine the answer to the question that was asked. The teacher also uses the word *area*, so that students will focus on size of land area, rather than size of population.

Student: **Where's Finland?**
Teacher: Let's look at the globe. I'll put it up on the stand so everyone can see. Here's the continent of North America, where we live. Moving to the east, there's the Atlantic Ocean. This continent is Europe. Here, in the northern part of Europe is Finland. Look, here is the equator, and here is the North Pole. Finland is far away from the equator, and quite near to the North Pole. So what do you think the climate of Finland is like? Now that you've had a glimpse of Finland on the globe, Lou and Kate, will you find it on the wall map of Europe? Here's a red tack; see if you can find Finland's capital and put the tack there. I've

forgotten the name of the capital; when you find out what it is, write it on the board.

The teacher is demonstrating that globes and maps are both sources where the answer to questions of this kind can be found, and is teaching additional information while modeling how to use the globe. The teacher is honest about having forgotten some information. Note also that in this classroom a wall map related to the current topic of study is on display, placed low enough so that students can see it clearly and reach all parts of it.

Student: **Are black snakes poisonous?**
Teacher: You're asking about a kind of snake called a black snake, right.... not about all snakes whose color is black. Okay, Enso's got a good question here. I'm going to use the encyclopedia to look for the answer. So I have to choose which volume of the encyclopedia to look at. I could choose *B* and look up *black snake*, but I'm going to try *S*, and look up *snake*. I'm opening the book about half way through, because I need to find the words that begin with SN. All right, I went a little too far, ...Solar energy... Here's Snakes. ...These pictures are terrific. I'll leave this volume open so you can come up and look at them when you have time. ...Here's a section on poisonous snakes. "Poisonous snakes are easy to recognize in the United States." I know there are

FIGURE 5–7 Continued

black snakes in the United States. "Here every poisonous snake is either a pit viper or a coral snake…" Well, there's more, and we can go back to it, but it doesn't answer our question, because I don't know whether black snakes are classified as pit vipers or coral snakes. …Cleo, bring me the *B* volume of the encyclopedia, please. Here at the end of the article about snakes, there's a list of "Related articles" and one is about blacksnakes. Pete, write that on the board: *Blacksnakes*. It's one word, not two. I thought there was a space between *black* and *snake*, but there isn't. Okay, here's the entry for *Blackbird*. (I came pretty close!) *Blacksmith*. Here's *Blacksnake*. "Blacksnake, or Northern Black Racer, is a harmless snake

of the eastern United States." There's more, but that tells us what we want to know. The snake is harmless: It won't hurt us. So it's not poisonous. That was a good question, Enso. I'll leave this volume of the encyclopedia open too; there's a picture, and the caption above the picture is "The handsome, harmless blacksnake…."

We can infer that this is a class of children without much experience in using an encyclopedia. They may not be able to read the text, but they can look at the pictures, and probably read some of the words in the picture captions. Note that the teacher uses technical terms for parts of books, like *volume* and *caption*, in ways that will help students become familiar with them.

FIGURE 5–8 Dictionary Commentaries— Looking Up a Word Suggested By a Student

"Derry found an interesting new word: *cartography*. Let's look it up, and find the definition. While we're finding out what it means we can also look at the word's derivation: We can trace the word back to words in other languages. Derry, have you found *cartography*? Good. You and Fay and Sean can look on with me, and we'll tell everyone what we find. Look, here's the definition. Sean, read just this part."

Sean reads, "the science or art of making maps."

"Good. Cartography is map-making. Soon we'll be working on a map of our town, so we'll all have a chance to be cartographers. Now we'll check the derivation. That comes before the definition, up here in brackets. *F* is an abbreviation for *French*. *Cartography* comes from two French words: *carte*, meaning *a card* or *a map*, and *graphie*, which comes from a Greek word, *graphein*, meaning *to write*. So cartography is the process of writing (or drawing) a map. Derry, take a sheet of construction paper and print *cartography* at the top. Underline the *graph* part of the word. Today and tomorrow, when you think of a word that has *graph* as a part, write it on this list. At the end of the day tomorrow we'll talk about what the words mean."

Talking About Word Derivations

"We've been learning about the ways animals adapt to the places where they live. Here are two words we'll be reading and talking about today. I'll write them on the board and say them: *hibernation* and *estivation*. *Estivation* comes from a Latin word meaning *summer*. *Hibernation* comes from a Latin word too. What do you suppose the meaning is? …Right! *Winter*. So we can think of hibernation as winter-ing, and estivation as summer-ing.

"With your reading partners, read the section on hibernation, on pages 150–152. As you read, think about the answers to the questions I've written on the chart, and choose at least one of the questions to answer in writing.

- What are some animals that hibernate?
- What are the *two* problems animals face in winter that hibernating animals escape?
- What happens to animals during hibernation?
- Do bears hibernate?
- Why do some animals estivate?

I'd like two volunteers: one to look up *hibernation* and one to look up *estivation* in our dictionaries. When you've looked up the word, leave the dictionaries open to that place so anybody who wants to can come by and look.

Dictionaries present extensive amounts of information very compactly. Words frequently have multiple meanings, and definitions often include words that are likely to be unfamiliar. Even people who are accustomed to using dictionaries to find definitions may not understand how word derivations are provided or know the meaning of the many abbreviations used when derivations are given. Teachers who are knowledgeable about both definitions and derivations can be excellent resources to their students. There are many occasions when understanding a word's derivation makes it easy to recall the word's meaning.

Although the answers to many questions that are raised in the classroom can be found in reference materials in a reasonably well-stocked classroom research center, the answers to some factual questions cannot be found there. Some classrooms do not even contain reference books. It is still important to find answers to questions raised in the classroom, and teachers can establish ways to accomplish this. The simplest strategy is to ask a person who is likely to know. Other students, the teacher, and other school personnel are all likely sources of factual information, and asking questions of one another is a good method of fostering the natural questioning process.

It is also useful to establish a procedure for finding answers using resources outside of the classroom, and reporting these answers to the class. One strategy is to keep a stock of file cards (larger ones, 4×6 or 5×8 are best) and to make it a practice to have a student make a record of a question that arises by writing it on two cards. The teacher posts one card as a reminder that the question needs to be answered, and asks for a student volunteer to take the other card home, or to the school media center, to find the answer. (Students should be reminded to write not only the answer to the question, but the place where the answer was found, on the card.) When the question is answered and shared (and checked by the teacher, if necessary), the card can be kept in a file box for future reference. As the box fills with cards, it will be a useful activity for students to arrange them into categories. In a classroom where this method for raising questions and finding answers is used often, the two cards that have been prepared for each question can be used by the class or by students for informal, just-for-fun quizzes. The

card that was kept in the classroom as a reminder will have only the question on it, so these cards can be used as a pack of quiz cards. Another card with both question and answer (and source of answer) will be on file.

Searching For Answers

Besides seeking and finding answers to individual factual questions, students should have many opportunities to raise more complex questions, and seek their answers through established methods of research, such as surveys, interviews, and experiments. Often such activities are a part of the curriculum. Opportunities for science experiments are described in science texts. With guidance, students can raise questions, and devise and conduct their own experiments. Math and other content areas can be linked through the use of surveys used to generate data that are then presented using charts and graphs. Knowledgeable teachers enable students to use a variety of methods to investigate their questions. Gina Schack (1993) advocates student research connected to their own interests; she gives the example of a student-devised experiment to investigate whether math problems are worked better under conditions of loud or soft music.

The first step in a serious investigation is to bring focus to the problem.

> In this step researchers word their interests in the form of a question without a preset answer, one that can be answered by gathering data. Webbing is a useful way to identify subtopics and variables, and interesting questions may be generated by considering the relationships among variables in the web. The question needs to be phrased precisely enough that [it] is clear what data need to be gathered. (Schack, 1993, p. 30)

Devising questions and finding answers through surveys, interviews, and experiments are important aspects of student research. These processes serve also as a reminder to students that information is not found solely in books. People, including classmates or schoolmates who may be surveyed to obtain factual information or opinions, are resources from whom information can be

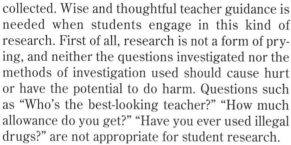

Ideally, students have access to many resources to find answers to their questions.

collected. Wise and thoughtful teacher guidance is needed when students engage in this kind of research. First of all, research is not a form of prying, and neither the questions investigated nor the methods of investigation used should cause hurt or have the potential to do harm. Questions such as "Who's the best-looking teacher?" "How much allowance do you get?" "Have you ever used illegal drugs?" are not appropriate for student research.

Once a reasonable topic for research is identified, teacher guidance is needed to ensure that the question is framed so that it can be answered using available methods. Refining research questions is a good method of engaging students in analytical thinking, and can be a topic for class and cooperative group discussion. For example, study methods are a good general topic for research, but "What's the best way to study?" is not a question that student research (or, to date, anyone's research) can answer, and it is useful for students to consider why they cannot find the answer to this question, and why even an adult researcher, with many resources, would need to frame a more limited question. There are, however, many good questions about this topic that student researchers could raise, and seek answers to. The question, "How much time do students (in this class/this grade/these grades) report that they study during a week?" could be answered by preparing, distributing, and collecting a form on which fellow students recorded information, and the information could then be used to compute simple statistics, such as mean, standard deviation, and range. The information could be shown using graphs and tables. With teacher cooperation, the question "What is the difference, if any, in test scores when tests are given after students study in class using method A, and when tests are given after students study in class using method B?" could be investigated over a period of time. Student researchers who posed the question, "What do a sample of people in the teaching profession recall about their own studying as adolescents?" could tape record teachers' responses when they were asked, "What do you remember about how you studied when you were in middle school and high school?" and the narratives could be transcribed and analyzed.

Oral History Projects.   In recent years there has been extensive interest among historians in oral history—"the record produced from interviewing people about their lives" (Blount, 1992, p. 221)—and in developing and preserving records of oral history collected through interviews, particularly with senior citizens who have memories of past local or national events. Samuel Totten (1989, p. 114), who defines oral history as "the tape recording of reminiscences about which the narrator can speak from firsthand knowledge" describes these reminiscences as an excellent resource for investigating social issues, which "allows students to hear or read fascinating personal accounts… introduce[s] students to diverse points of view… [and] permits students to engage in conversation with 'a living curricular resource'." Mary Olson and Thomas Gee (1989) suggest using oral history projects to involve students in research within their own families or communities. In undertaking oral history research, written materials may also be investigated. Examining such records as photographs, maps, and family or community records builds prior knowledge about

a time period. This research can precede and supplement interviews with family or community members who were present at events that have historical significance. For example, a family member can be interviewed to record memories of coming to live in the community or coming to this country; a community member may be asked about memories of the construction of the school or the town library, of a catastrophic local event, such as a fire or flood, or of local celebrations of important national events or the visit to the community of a famous person.

Steps in working with students on oral history projects include helping them to choose a topic; guiding their reading from texts and primary sources (contemporary letters, photographs, records, and so on.); helping them to find resource people to interview and to plan, conduct, record, and transcribe the interview; and providing support in reporting on their research. Additional resources for oral history projects may come from members of historical and conservation societies, and visits to, or guest speakers from, historical sites and museums. Students may be subjects for each other's research when the investigation occurs through interviews, surveys, and questionnaires. In oral history projects, research subjects may be students' family members. Another way to incorporate a personal element in research is to build in opportunities for personal commentary when research results are reported. For example, Hatcher (1990) suggests asking older students to answer the question "Can you identify a life principle worth remembering from this investigation?" as a concluding section in their written (or oral) presentation of findings.

When students are obtaining oral histories, those interviewed may also be interested in sharing pictures or other documents from an earlier time period. (If such materials are lent, they must be carefully treated and returned promptly.) Katherine Bucher and Mark Fravel (1991) suggest creating then-and-now bulletin boards showing changes in the area where the school is located, using maps and old and current postcards. Old photographs, newspaper articles, and architects' drawings could also be collected for a visual display of the school's history, and people still living in the area who graduated from the school in earlier years could be interviewed.

I-Search Papers. The I-Search paper was devised by Ken Macrorie (1984) as an alternative to the research paper. In this process, students set questions which are of personal concern to them, and devise and carry out their own project for seeking answers. The paper, which they write as a concluding activity, is not primarily a summary of the answers they have found—in fact, they may not have been able to find answers to their questions—but instead a narrative describing their search process and its personal meaning for them. Commenting on the versatility of I-Search papers for students across a wide grade span, Dixie Dellinger (1989, p. 35) writes, "[A] great gain is in learning that one does not have to find the answer to a question to have something to say about it. Good searches only pause; they do not end." A modification of the I-Search process called I-Search a Word (Anderson, 1990) involves students in using reference materials in the study of words and their derivations.

I-Search papers and projects are most appropriate for older students who have already had experience in using reference sources to find answers to their questions and who can see the value of developing and pursuing a search, and analyzing and describing that search process even if it has not produced the desired results. As with any useful strategy, however, the I-Search process can be adapted for use with younger students. One method is to create an Our-Search group journal, which is a teacher-written record, on sheets of heavy paper, of students' dictated recollections of the processes followed in finding answers to research questions over a period of time. The collected charts can later be fastened together to form a classroom Big Book. Another adaptation that makes this kind of search possible and useful for younger learners is the We-Search process developed by Grace Anne Heacock (1990). Heacock conducts an annual "we-search" project with her third grade students in Fairbanks, Alaska. Students select topics to investigate which are important to them and to the community; for example, planes carrying plutonium landing in Alaska to refuel. Students collect information at school and also at home, and then discuss it and create semantic maps. They then write short research papers in class, working with partners to revise their drafts, and assisted by sixth graders who join the class to help with editing.

Teacher Responsibilities in Research

Finding answers to questions with teacher guidance can pave the way for more independence in finding information from the school media center or a local library, or from resource materials in students' homes. However, although teachers should prepare students to use reference materials outside the classroom, teachers should never give assignments that can only be completed adequately by students who have reference materials at home or ready access to a local library. It may be difficult or impossible for students to get to the library independently or for family members to take them, and students' homes will differ widely in the amount of reference materials available there. No student should be barred from the opportunity for success in a school project because of the unavailability of resources or help from outside the classroom. Nor should assignments be differentiated for students on the basis of the kind of home support they have. There should not be alternative assignments for some students. School research assignments for all students should be structured so that the students can accomplish them, primarily or entirely, in a school setting, using classroom and media center resources to which all students have access.

Teachers need to recognize that they can, and must, decide how research will be emphasized in their teaching. We have the power, as well as the obligation, to make decisions about topic, time allotment, research methods and activities that will make the process practical for us, and useful for our students. When engaging students in content area research, as in every other aspect of teaching, the teacher's knowledge base and good sense are an essential factor in students' learning. Because research projects are complex, teacher decisions about two major questions are crucial:

▪ How much time—my time, class time, and students' time outside of school—is it sound and sensible to allot to this project?

▪ What aspects of my own knowledge and experience do I need to develop before and during this project, to make it a useful learning experience for my students?

> The practice of targeting and paring research …assignments to fit the time and attention a teacher is willing and able to give them is a highly responsible decision. The word *able* is a deliberate choice here. No teacher should attempt to teach research and reporting techniques that s/he does not fully understand—preferably through experience.
>
> That admonition needs to be coupled to the related recommendation that adequate time be given to whatever assignment is designed so that students have time to find, digest, analyze, and respond to the accruing information and so that the teacher has time to mentor the process and teach and reinforce the skills essential to completing the process. (Tone, 1988, p. 78)

Cooperative Learning Groups and Dyads

Well-managed cooperative learning groups provide an excellent setting in which students can engage in a variety of research activities. Students can help each other by raising **questions**, assist one another in finding and using reference materials, and serve as audiences for drafts of written products. Like all learning, research activities should be viewed by students and teachers as cooperative, rather than competitive. Research activities can be carried on within cooperative learning groups that have already been established, students can form into cooperatively functioning interest groups to undertake special research projects, or students can work in dyads or triads (i.e., pairs or groups of three). Group members can help one another in question-raising at the beginning of a research activity, provide organized support throughout the research process, and assist one another by peer editing when final products are being prepared.

Often, even when students have many questions of their own about their chosen research topics, their classmates will be able to think of questions which have not occurred to them. Kathy Coffey (1989) suggests an Accordion fold method to elicit and record the ideas of others. Each member of a group chooses a research topic and lists it on the top line of a sheet of paper. The papers are passed around; each student in turn thinks of one or more questions about the listed topic and writes them at the bottom of the paper. Then that part of the paper is folded up so that the questions are not visible, and the paper is passed along again. Other students continue to add questions and fold the paper until all the paper except for the topic listing is folded away. The paper is returned to the student who will be studying the topic, who then decides what questions to investigate. Although the student need not select questions posed by others, these questions may raise intriguing ideas that would not have been thought of otherwise.

Many research projects can be accomplished effectively through cooperative learning, but as with individual research assignments, the teacher has the responsibility to plan and monitor the entire process carefully. The process for organizing research activities in cooperative learning groups suggested by Flora Wyatt (1988) emphasizes careful

---

question—The Latin word from which our word *question* comes is *quaerere*, meaning *to ask*, and so a question is something that is asked. The word is related, through its Latin origin, to our word *quest*, meaning *a search*, and also to an interesting array of other English words, among them *acquire, conquer, exquisite, inquest, perquisite* and *require*.

preplanning by the teacher. In this cooperative process, the choice of a general topic is made by the teacher, and can be textbook-based, so the topic is focused and there is a starting point for a shared knowledge base. At this point in the preplanning process, the teacher develops a topic-focused classroom library, using tradebooks, magazines, free materials obtained from agencies, and materials on loan from the school media center. During the research process these resources can be supplemented by teacher lectures, visits from guest speakers, and audiovisual materials. The teacher identifies subtopics for research in advance, and cooperative groups then choose which subtopic they wish to investigate. When groups have been formed, students brainstorm questions about their group's topic, and, with teacher guidance, search for information, and record and analyze their findings. Throughout the research process, students write regularly in learning logs. As a final step in the process, students decide on a method of presenting their findings and share these with the class.

Using Chart-Based Strategies

K-W-L Plus (Carr & Ogle, 1987) is an adaptation of Donna Ogle's K-W-L strategy (described in Chapter Four). The acronym K-W-L stands for three steps in the reading and studying process: students list what they already know (K) about a topic, and what they want (W) to learn; as they study they list what they have learned (L). In the K-W-L Plus process, students, working individually or in pairs or small groups, follow this three-step process by categorizing the listed items. To do this, they read and analyze the list and decide on several categories. For example, in a report about an animal, the categories might be description, abilities, location, and food. Each of the items on the *L* list in the K-W-L chart is labeled with an initial indicating its category, and the items are then transferred to a semantic map. The next decision is the order in which the different categories will be presented in the research report, and the next task is to prepare a draft of the report.

QuIP (McLaughlin, 1987) stands for Questions Into Paragraphs. Students use a grid on which a series of questions is written in the left-hand column.

The remaining two or three columns are each devoted to a different source, either a person being interviewed or a resource text. As information from a source is obtained, it is written in the column for that source, in the row for the question being answered. Students can use a completed QuIP grid to prepare a short report, in which each question forms the main idea of a paragraph, followed by a summary of the information about that question collected from the various sources.

QUAD (Cudd, 1989) is a simple way of introducing younger students to the elements of research in ways that are manageable for them: setting a problem, finding information, recording information, and reporting information. The acronym stands for QUestions, Answers, and Details. It is a research process structured for students in the elementary grades, beginning at grade three or, with ample teacher guidance, toward the end of grade two. Students may work individually, in pairs or in groups. Older students who are familiar with the process may find it useful to use a QUAD-style grid to organize their notes when they are looking for answers to a few related questions. With teacher guidance, students choose a topic to find out about. Ideas for topics should come from the students, but teacher consultation and approval is needed to ensure that a topic is not too broad. Students then list questions about their topic (with teacher help as necessary) on a QUAD grid with three columns, headed Questions, Answers, and Details. A sample QUAD grid is shown in Figure 5–9. Although lines showing the rows on this grid have been drawn, in practice the lines should be drawn after the questions are filled in, because students will not all have the same number of questions, and different questions will require different amounts of space for their answers.

The students fill in spaces on the grid as information is found. The grid includes a space at the bottom for listing the resource materials that have been used. It is not necessary for every section of the grid to be completed. Some answers may not need supporting details, and answers may not be found for every question. When students work on their QUAD grids in the media center, the school media specialist should help students find necessary materials. (The classroom teacher helps by

FIGURE 5–9   Sample QUAD Grid

| Researchers' name(s): _____ |
| Topic: _____ |

QUESTIONS	ANSWERS	DETAILS
Sources:		

supplying the media specialist with a file folder containing copies of the students' QUAD grids.) The completed QUAD grid can itself be the final product, or it may serve as the source for a written report. An illustration of a QUAD process in progress is given in Figure 5–10.

Peer Editing For Research Reports

Cooperative group members can be helpful to one another by peer editing one another's written work. PQP (Lyons, 1981) is a strategy that provides a practical structure for students to use in the peer editing process (Fig. 5–11). When students have prepared a draft of a written project, they ask for group advice. The advice is given, sequentially, in three forms: Praise ("What did you like about my paper?"), Questions ("What questions do you have about my paper?"), and suggestions for ways to improve, or polish, the product ("What kinds of polishing do you think my paper needs before it can be published?"). PQP is a valuable strategy to incorporate when students are preparing research reports. Teachers should explain and model the steps for the class, before groups use it independently.

FIGURE 5–10   An Example Showing the Use of QUAD

- Two students, working in a pair, choose a topic they want to find out more about, and decide on *lizards*.
- The students meet with the teacher, who helps them find books and scan for information about lizards. The students narrow the topic to *skinks*. The teacher suggests a further narrowing of the topic to *skinks that are native to North America*.
- Students brainstorm questions, which they list in the first column (Questions) of the QUAD form: What kinds of skinks live in North America? How are skinks different from other lizards? How can skinks move so fast? Do they move faster than other kinds of lizards? Do all skinks have legs? Are skinks poisonous? Each question becomes a row on the QUAD grid. More room is left in the Questions column to add other questions during the process of finding out. Here the teacher helps the students see that two questions can be combined in one row: How can skinks move so fast? Do they move faster than other kinds of lizards? The students also decide which rows will need lots of space for answers and which rows won't need much. They allow plenty of space to give answers and details about the first question, What kinds of skinks live in North America?, but they don't need much space on the grid for the last two questions: Do all skinks have legs? Are skinks poisonous?
- With guidance as needed, students look for the answers to their questions in resource books. As they find information they fill in the second and third columns of the QUAD form (Answers and Details). The partially completed grid is shown below:

QUESTIONS	ANSWERS	DETAILS
What kind of skinks live in North America?	1. Great Plains Skink— biggest skink in NA, can be 13+ inches (Audubon Guide, p. 150) 2. Broad-headed Skink can be 12+ inches	If another animal catches them by the tail, their tails can grow back.
How are skinks different from other lizards? How can skinks move so fast? Do they move faster than other kinds of lizards?		
Do all skinks have legs?	No	Most don't have legs. Some kinds do but the legs are too weak to use.
Are skinks poisonous?	None of the skinks we read about are poisonous.	

We got information from: *Audubon Guide*, WB (we looked at Lizards), *American Lizards*

- If other questions occur to the students as they work, they can add them to the Questions column. For example, as they collect information, students might decide to add two other questions: What animals eat skinks? Can all skinks grow their tails back?
- The students know they don't have to fill in every section of the grid. For their question about whether skinks are poisonous, they find information to put in the Answers column, but they don't add anything in the Details column.

FIGURE 5–11   Sample PQP Process

Students are preparing a report on Australia. Dinah reads her draft of the section on the geography of Australia to her cooperative learning group.

Praise:

Ross: I like the way you listed the countries you'd get to if you traveled away from Australia in different directions.

Amy: I looked at a list of the geography topics we decided to include as you were reading, and I think you've got information about all of them.

Fran: The part about the Great Barrier Reef is exciting.

Questions:

Terrell: How much of Australia is desert? Can you tell how much of each kind of land there is in Australia?

Amy: What does *outback* mean, Dinah? You need to explain that.

Polish:

Ross: Some of the sentences are kind of long. I think you should look to see which ones you can shorten.

Terrell: I think when you write the final draft you should put pictures and maps right with the text. Do you want to work together on that?

Guiding Research: SAIL

The SAIL strategy is one method teachers can use to structure research assignments so that students can write a sound and interesting short report. The title of the strategy is an acronym: *S* stands for Sources; *A*, for Audience; *I*, for Information; and *L*, for Length.

Sources.   SAIL's major difference from the typical research assignment is that the sources are chosen in advance. This advance preparation means that teachers have time to find a variety of useful sources to target a research assignment, or to build useful research assignments around interesting, relevant source materials. Teachers who choose to use the SAIL strategy can be constantly alert for good source materials, which can be filed for later use. SAIL assignments are typically based on three to five pieces of source material. It is useful to include standard resources, such as textbooks and encyclopedias, among the sources, so that students gain experience in collecting and using information from them; but SAIL sources should include other materials as well.

The value of providing resources is three-fold. First, it enables students to focus on analysis and synthesis of information, and on presenting the information in interesting, useful ways. Second, it informs students about resources which they may use later when working on other research assignments.

Third, it discourages plagiarism. Even advanced undergraduate and graduate university students can benefit from this kind of helpful guidance. Becky Reimer (1989, pp. 43 and 45), writing about her work with graduate students who are investigating self-devised questions, notes

> To do an adequate literature search, you need to be familiar with key people, key articles, and key journals. I save [my students] time by writing on their index card a list of four to five references that [are] key articles related to their question…. [and] I provide each person with at least two [related] articles from my files.

Left to their own devices, students often rely primarily or exclusively on an encyclopedia entry to obtain information for a research report. Through use of the teacher-selected SAIL sources, they can be led to an awareness of the multiplicity of resources providing useful information: newspaper and magazine articles, trade books across a wide age span, interviews, and data from questionnaires. Moreover, with SAIL, students are not competing to use the same books. Because they are typically brief, most or all of the source materials can be included in a file folder labeled with the title of the SAIL with the SAIL assignment stapled inside. Teachers can tailor assignments to the interests and reading skills of dyads or cooperative groups, or for individual students.

SAIL assignments may include excerpts from adult books that would be too difficult and lengthy for students to read on their own. In the assignment shown in Figure 5–12, for example, the teacher has found a brief section from a history of cartography written for adults which is pertinent to a topic middle school students are studying. A single copy of those four pages could be made and included in the SAIL folder. Although determining the sources for the research report is primarily the teacher's task—often best accomplished with the aid of the school media specialist—students will often be able to suggest sources of information when they are writing about a topic that interests them. An excellent SAIL source may be an interview with family members who have relevant knowledge and experiences.

Audience. Specification of an audience provides a focus for student writing, and encourages students to match their writing style with audience needs and interests. Other classmates are often an appropriate audience, especially when many aspects of a topic are being studied in depth, and students can benefit from writing one report and reading many others.

The SAIL plan for an ecological report shown in Figure 5–13 is an example. Students may also write for possible publication in an outside source, as in Figure 5–14, or their reports may form chapters in a class book, as in the SAIL plan shown in Figure 5–12.

Information. Once the sources have been collected, the teacher's task is specify information the students can obtain by using all of the source materials. In the sample assignments given here, the Information component is specified very thoroughly, to provide ample guidance for the assignment, and to help students simplify the process of citing sources.

Length. The length of a SAIL report should vary, depending on audience and information. As part of this component, the teacher may also specify materials, such as pictures and maps, to be included along with the written report.

How SAIL Guards Against Plagiarism. Together, the two SAIL steps that require most teacher time and thought in preparing the assignment—Sources and Information—constitute an effective method of

FIGURE 5–12 Plan for a SAIL Paper: The Northwest Passage

Sources: "The Search for the Northwest Passage" from our social studies text; "Northwest Passage" and "Franklin, Sir John," *World Book encyclopedia*; *The Mapmakers*, by John Noble Wilford (Vintage Books, 1982), page 140 second paragraph, to the top of page 143. Also, your own reasoning.

Audience: Readers of the Exploration Book our class is preparing

Information: For more than four hundred years, explorers looked for a way to cross North America by sea. Why did they call what they were looking for "the Northwest Passage"? What is unusual about the first successful trip through the Northwest Passage?

Make a chart listing the dates when these explorers looked for the Northwest Passage, what they achieved, and interesting facts about their explorations: Amundsen, Baffin, Cartier, Davis, Foxe, Franklin, Frobisher, Hudson, McClure, and Verrazano. Here the explorers are listed alphabetically. In your chart, list them chronologically, and give their full names.

Draw a map of the Northwest Passage.

You don't have to use full sentences on your chart. If you quote directly from one of your sources, use quotation marks. For all the information you provide, including the map, tell from which source the information came. (text = science text; WB = encyclopedia; MM = *The Mapmakers*.) If you add other sources, such as an atlas, list the source.

Length: One or two paragraphs answering the first two questions, plus the chart and the map. You may also add a paragraph giving your opinion about whether search for the Northwest Passage was worthwhile.

FIGURE 5–13   Plan for a SAIL Paper: The Passenger Pigeon

Sources: "Wildlife Conservation" from our science text; "The Passenger Pigeon" from *I am Phoenix: Poems for two voices*, by Paul Fleischman (Harper & Row, 1985); "Gentle Dove: Passenger Pigeon," from *Vanished species* by David Day (NY: Gallery Books, 1989); and one or more encyclopedias.

Audience: classmates (Copies of your group's SAIL report will be shared with members of other cooperative learning groups.)

Information: Begin by reading Fleischman's poem. (Your group may want to prepare to do a choral reading for the class later.) Make a list of facts about the passenger pigeon which are stated or implied in the poem. Check the facts and add to them, using the other sources.

Then answer these questions:

1. What do we know about this species of bird, and how do we know it?
2. How were the birds killed?
3. Why were they killed?
4. How long did it take for people to wipe out the species?

You'll need one or two pages for the list of facts based on the poem. As you check each fact, list the information you find, and give the source and page number. (text = science text; IAP = *I Am Phoenix*; VS = *Vanished Species*. List encyclopedias by their initials, e.g., EB = *Encyclopedia Brittanica*.) If you quote directly from one of your sources, use quotation marks.

You'll also need pages for your notes about each of the four questions. List the source and page number for each piece of information; use quotation marks if you quote. You don't need to use full sentences when you make notes.

Then write your SAIL report from your notes. You can divide up the paper into parts and each person can write a part, or everyone can write a draft and you can combine ideas.

Length: Approximately two pages (depending on the size of your handwriting). Include a drawing of the passenger pigeon. If you wish, add one or two paragraphs expressing your group's ideas about how the extinction of this species of bird has, or may have, harmed our world.

FIGURE 5–14   Plan for a SAIL Paper: Asthma and Exercise

Sources: "Respiratory problems" from our health text; *All about asthma*, by William Ostrow and Vivian Ostrow (Niles, IL: Albert Whitman, 1989); *Sports illustrated sports almanac*; interview with allergy specialist Dr. Metta Call; questionnaire responses.

Audience: readers of *Health-Wise*, a newsletter published by the Journalism Club and supported by an educational grant. Our class has been invited to contribute some features. The newsletter is sent to families in our district, so the readers will be both adults and students.

Information: How are exercise and allergy control related?

Sort through the health questionnaire forms which have been completed and returned by students and teachers in other classes to find all the responses from people who have asthma or other allergies that affect their breathing. Read their answers to questions 8 and 9, and make a graph showing how many different ways

those people from our sample get exercise. Compare the information they give with what William Ostrow writes about exercise in *All about asthma*.

All about asthma. lists Jackie Joyner-Kersee and "Catfish" Hunter as athletes who have asthma. Read about them in the "Profiles" section of the *Sports illustrated* almanac, and include some of their achievements in your report.

Before Dr. Call visits our class, think of some questions you want to ask her. Try to include an interesting, useful quote from Dr. Call in your report.

As you make notes for your report, list the source for your information and give page numbers. (text = health text; AAA = *All about asthma*; SA = *1992 Sports almanac*; Dr. C = Dr. Call; Q = questionnaires.)

Length: Not more than two pages, double-spaced. (Sign up for time at the computer.) Include a list of references.

preventing, and if necessary checking for, plagiarism. The fact that the sources on which the research report is based are readily available to the teacher as well as to the student makes it unlikely that students will copy without attribution. Moreover, as a teacher reads and evaluates a SAIL report, it is easy to check to see whether a student has used source material improperly, because both the report and the sources for the report are at hand. (If a student has used source material improperly, the report can be treated as a draft, to be revised with teacher guidance.)

Careful preparation of the information component of SAIL plan is equally valuable. Students who explain copying from text or quoting too extensively by saying, "The book says it better than I can!" are making an accurate statement: published authors almost always do write more skillfully than their readers. However, if the task is to convey information related to, yet different from, information in the sources, the student writer must take responsibility. Once the SAIL sources have been chosen, the teacher can specify information that requires students to synthesize ideas and present information that is difficult or impossible to obtain simply by quoting passages directly from any of the sources. In the SAIL assignment shown in Figure 5–12, for example, none of the sources gives a direct answer to the two questions asked about the Northwest Passage, but students can readily derive the information from thinking about the readings, and examining a map that shows that the first successful journey by water across the northern part of this continent was a voyage to the east, rather than from east to west.

Charting information, as the SAIL plan shown in Figure 5–12 requires, and graphing information, as in the SAIL plan shown in Figure 5–14, encourage brief listing or restatement of essentials, or presentation of information visually, rather than copying sections from a source text. Listening to a speaker to obtain a useful quotation is good preparation for lively reporting; the hypothetical presentation by "Dr. Metta Call," listed as a source in Figure 5–14, illustrates the way that interviews or presentations can be used as SAIL sources. In this case, accurate quoting from a source is a requirement, so students are guided to learn that quotations, correctly presented, can be an important part of a research report.

Involving Students in SAIL Preparation. Repeated use of the SAIL strategy enables teachers to change their role in research assignments, gradually offering students greater responsibility. Sophisticated writers may choose to use the SAIL strategy on their own, immediately, by choosing the information they intend to convey to a given audience, based on a small number of sources. For most students, however, the strategy's usefulness depends on a thorough introduction using assignments that have been carefully prepared by their teachers.

The point at which students become actively involved in the planning of a SAIL assignment will vary. Given SAIL packets that include the sources and specify the report's audience and length, students may read the sources and themselves determine what information they want to provide for their readers. This assignment can provide some interesting comparisons, if groups or pairs of students use the same sources but make different decisions about the Information component. Alternatively, a SAIL assignment packet may include two sources supplied by the teacher, and students can be expected to add two more.

Multiple and Repeated Uses. Although the use of SAIL requires substantial effort by the teacher in advance of making the research assignment, once SAIL plans are prepared for student use they may be reused in future years and for multiple class sections. A single well-developed SAIL plan lends itself to a variety of uses, or it can serve as a pattern for a set of related SAIL assignments. In a health class, the SAIL plan shown in Figure 5–14 could provide the pattern for multiple reports based on information obtained from a single questionnaire, one or more guest speakers, and a series of trade books. In a social studies class, the SAIL plan shown in Figure 5–11 could provide a pattern for other chapters for a class book on exploration, whereas the SAIL assignment shown in Figure 5–13 could serve as one item in a series of reports on extinct and endangered species. SAIL reports can be structured for use by individual students, dyads, or cooperative groups. The SAIL assignments shown in Figures 5–12 and 5–14 are usable in any of these situations; the SAIL assignment shown in Figure 5–13 is designed for use by a cooperative group. The strategy offers a structure for both teachers and students to enable students to engage in productive research and writing in ways that provide a sound foundation for future work.

Guiding Research: Structured Research Process

Acquiring, organizing, and presenting information so that others can learn from it are potentially excellent ways of strengthening content area learning. These processes form the basis for most research assignments and research projects that combine them can be worthwhile if they are based on sound teacher knowledge, thorough teacher planning, and sensible, caring teaching support. Many of the activities described earlier in this chapter can be used as components of this kind of research. The Structured Research Process (SRP) is a method of providing structure for major assignments. The process is adaptable for students across a wide span of grades; topic choice will be a major difference across grades. The SRP provides guidance for teachers as well as students as an entire class works on related content-related research projects. A detailed example is provided in Figure 5–15, which is presented in multiple sections. The SRP has five steps: advance preparation, building interest and knowledge, organizing the research process, collecting information, organizing information and writing, and, as a culmination of the process, sharing. The teacher has a role in each step, the students have responsibilities in each of the steps after the advance preparations have been made.

Advance Preparation.   Planning, including the allotment of time, is an essential aspect of the SRP. Teacher preparation, which may be accomplished in small steps over many weeks, is the first component. During this time, the teacher decides on the research topic, collects related materials, and, if possible, finds a guest expert who will be willing to meet with the class for one or two sessions. This is also the time to consult with the school media specialist, who can then also begin to collect reference materials.

There are important advantages when teachers choose the general topic for student research, based on a topic the whole class is learning about over an extensive period of time. Diana George (1984, p. 29) notes that

> student interest cannot be drawn from a content-free classroom. To ask students to research a topic of abiding interest is to create a false research assignment and to complain that students have no abiding interests is to ignore our own role in the classroom as a part of the collaborative learning model.

Background knowledge is essential if the research process is to be interesting and meaningful. It is not reasonable for teachers to assume that students do, or should, have sufficient knowledge about any topic, or can learn enough through reading a textbook section, to engage actively in raising questions and finding answers. Having an interest in a topic helps students generate questions and make decisions about how to focus their research.

Building Interest and Knowledge.   The first week of classroom activity in the SRP is focused on building students' interest in, and knowledge about, the topic the teacher has selected for group study. The activities of this week are a preparation for student topic selection during week 2, so one of the activities is to generate many instances of the general study topic. For example, if the teacher-chosen topic is constellations, then early in the week students should brainstorm a list of constellations, and then add to that list throughout the week as they learn more about constellations. The name of each constellation should be written on a separate 3×5 file card, and the cards tacked to a bulletin board. Later the cards can be sorted and resorted as the class decides on a classification system. In the example shown in Figure 5–15 (week 1), where the study topic is birds, an initial brainstorming would generate the names of many different birds, and each name would be written on a separate file card and tacked to the bulletin board. Throughout the week, students would add more cards to the display.

Following the commentary about the question raised by the teacher, it is useful for the teacher to ask students to raise questions, and choose one for a second commentary. In this way, the teacher can guide the students in forming questions. Suppose this question was raised: How many birds build hanging nests? The teacher may respond, "I doubt if we can find an answer to that question, because there may be birds in the world that no one knows about yet. A question we can find the answer to is What are some birds that build hanging nests? A good place to look for the answer would be the encyclopedia—volume B, for Birds. I'll check the section on nests, and look for information about hanging nests; I'm sure there'll be some examples of birds that build that kind of nest." In preparation for group classification of cards in week 2, one or more commentaries may focus on classification. The teacher might ask the question, How does this book about birds classify birds? and list the categories, and then ask, In the encyclopedia article about birds, how are the birds classified? and list those categories. The various lists should be posted so that students can look at them during the week.

Organizing the Research Process. During the second week of the SRP, the file cards that have been collected on the bulletin board are classified. The class may agree to use one of the classification systems that have been listed during week 1, or may decide on a classification system of their own devising. Cards are then sorted by category, and students are given the opportunity to choose a category. Interest groups are formed on this basis; for example, all students who want to study tropical birds will be in the same interest group. (Teachers should be aware that whenever interest groups are formed, students may choose a group on the basis of preference about companions, rather than a special interest in the topic. This rationale for choice should be accepted. The only rule which must be observed is that no student may ever be excluded from joining an interest group. That rule need not be mentioned unless a situation arises that requires it.)

For the first meeting of interest groups, the teacher gives them the cards belonging in their category and each student chooses a subtopic. For example, within an interest group focused on tropical birds, one student might choose the macaw, another the toucan, another the flamingo, and so forth. It is the teacher's decision whether students must work indi-

vidually, may work individually or in pairs, or must work in pairs. (In the last case, of course, there must be even numbers of students in each interest group.) The second activity for interest groups is to brainstorm a list of questions or areas for fact-finding.

Then, meeting as a whole class, students work with the teacher to develop a final set of questions or areas for fact-finding. In the example we are using, the categories might include Description (What does the bird look like?), Nests and eggs (What kind of nest does the bird build? How many eggs are laid? How are they hatched?), Location (Where do the birds live? Do they migrate?), and so forth. The teacher then prepares a Fact-Finding Chart and a Bibliography List and makes copies for students. The Fact-Finding chart is a grid, with spaces for each of the fact categories which have been decided on. The questions are written or typed in each section, legibly but in small type, leaving as much blank space in each section as possible. (Charts prepared using a computer are ideal.) Each student will receive one of these charts to use during weeks 2, 3, and 4.

The Bibliography List is a list of all the relevant reference materials in the classroom (and, if teachers choose, selected materials from the media center also). For older students, the reference materials may be listed in complete bibliographic style; for younger students, only the title needs to be listed. A two- or three-letter abbreviation should be written beside each title, e.g., *World Book encyclopedia* = WB. The Bibliography List should be posted where students can see it easily. If it is possible to prepare a small copy of the list to put on the reverse side of the Fact-Finding Charts, this will be helpful for students. (Again, access to a computer will be useful.) There are two major reasons why sources should be cited when research is being done. The first is to give credit to those sources (a concept discussed earlier in this chapter, in the section on "Giving credit where due"). The second reason for citing sources is so that the researcher, or someone reading the research report, can go back to the original source to check the accuracy of the information or to find out more.

When research assignments are not well-planned and guided, students often resort to copying text directly from reference materials. If the text is used

FIGURE 5–15   Structured Research Process

Sample Topic: Birds
Advance Preparation **Focus:** teacher planning

Teacher	Students
▌ Choose topic, based on current curriculum topics, time of year, relevant school and local events, e.g., Science Fair ▌ Discuss plans/schedule with school media specialist. ▌ Decide on ways to build knowledge, and make preparations. Find resource materials for class library (books, magazines, pictures). Collect items to read aloud to class. Other possibilities: guest speaker(s), (school personnel, community members, parents); videos, pictures; field trip.	

Week 1
Focus: building interest and knowledge **Research Skills:** learning to use reference materials through teacher modeling

Teacher	Students and Teacher
▌ Create daily structure for the class activities (shown in right-hand column of chart). ▌ With students' help, create bulletin board display of Audubon bird prints, at students' eye level. ▌ Arrange large, blank bulletin board area, headed "Birds." Have on hand 3 × 5 file cards and tacks.	▌ Teacher reads aloud daily from reference materials, newspaper articles, poetry, trade books. Play record of bird calls as background music during quiet times. ▌ Regular Themed Reading, using teacher-collected materials about birds, including pictures. ▌ Brainstorm list of bird names; students write names on individual file cards and tack to bulletin board (no categorizing yet, unless students suggest it). Add cards during week. ▌ Guest authority as speaker, if possible. Bird-watching walk through playground or neighborhood with guest speaker as guide. ▌ Reference Source Commentaries, daily: one teacher-selected topic and one student question.

Week 2
Focus: organizing the research process **Research skills:** classifying, topic selection, question-raising, concept of citing sources

Teacher	Students and Teacher
▌ Create structure, within the week, for class activities (shown in right-hand column of chart).	▌ Continue activities from week 1: read-alouds, Themed Reading.

FIGURE 5–15 Continued

Week 2 (continued)	
Teacher	**Students and Teacher**
▪ After classification session, form interest groups. (Each student chooses category; all students studying birds in the same category constitute an interest group.) ▪ Meet with each interest group; review file cards of birds in that category. (Students, individually or in pairs, choose a bird to study.) ▪ Prepare Fact-Finding Chart for information collection; make a copy for each student. ▪ Prepare Bibliography List, listing reference materials with abbreviations. Display the list where students can easily see it. (If possible, include Bibliography List on back of Fact-Finding Chart.)	▪ Discuss ways of classifying birds, and sort the 3×5 cards listing bird names into selected categories. (If possible, ask guest speaker to return for this session.) ▪ Brainstorm questions or facts to be found about birds. Select most important categories, making sure all questions are in answerable form. ▪ Teacher explains, distributes Fact- Finding Chart. Teacher explains purposes for citing sources (giving credit where credit is due; making sure we can recheck information) and models use of Bibliography List. ▪ Daily Reference Source Commentaries, based on student-selected questions.

Week 3	
Focus: collecting information **Research skills:** using reference materials	
Teacher	**Students and Teacher**
▪ Create structure, within the week, for class activities (shown in right-hand column of chart). ▪ Daily collection of Fact-Finding Charts—*not for grading!*—for analysis to see what help is needed. ▪ Provide help through the daily commentary sessions and in student conferences. ▪ Schedule session(s) with media specialist during this week. If possible, arrange media center time for each interest group, with media specialist having prepared relevant materials in advance. Perhaps a supplement to the Bibliography List will be needed.	▪ Working individually or in pairs, students use reference materials to fill in sections of Fact-Finding Chart, including citations (using abbreviations from Bibliography List). ▪ Stress Reference Source Commentaries, with students generating questions which concern them as they collect information. Model use of Bibliography List during each commentary. ▪ Continue activities from weeks 1 and 2: read alouds, and Themed Reading. Use students' Fact-Finding Charts, shared within interest groups, as a possibility for Themed Reading.

Week 4	
Focus: organizing information, writing **Research Skills:** organizing and presenting information in writing, citing sources	
Teacher	**Students and Teacher**
▪ Create structure, within the week, for class activities (shown in right-hand column). ▪ Check Fact-Finding Charts a final time to make sure information is accurate. Checking may require teacher research, e.g., checking source of information	▪ Finish work on Fact-Finding Charts. Not all items will be complete in every chart. ▪ Discuss interesting facts learned, and alternate ways of ordering information on charts. Students number sections on chart to show the way they will order topics in the final report or presentation.

FIGURE 5–15   Continued

Week 4 (continued)	
Teacher	**Students and Teacher**
if information on charts seems odd. If students have misunderstood text of reference material, meet with them to clarify and explain. Help students revise charts if necessary. ▮ Supply new copy of Bibliography List to accompany each report. ▮ Plan ways of to share students' products. (See follow-up section.)	▮ Students write sentences or paragraphs giving information from each section of chart, in the order they selected. Students complete clear copy of Bibliography List. ▮ Students share report drafts within their interest groups, perhaps using a modified PQP process.
Follow-up **Focus:** sharing **Research skills:** presenting one's own findings and learning from colleagues	
Teacher	**Students and Teacher**
▮ Create structure, within this week and the future, for follow-up activities. (Possibilities are shown in right-hand column of chart.)	▮ Revise drafts of reports and prepare final reports and/or presentations. Reports may be hand-written by students, prepared on computer, or dictated to a scribe. Allow time for illustration. ▮ Share information gained. Possibilities: Science fair display; binding reports for classroom or school media center; panel presentations (live or video-taped); cross-class sharing; presentation for parents; school bulletin board displays. Other ideas for ways to share research findings are given later in this chapter.

without quotation marks or without citation, this is plagiarism. Even if quoted text is placed in quotation marks and properly cited, merely stringing together pieces of text written by others does not constitute a useful, original report. The SRP guards against such misuse of student and teacher time in a variety of ways. First, students' background knowledge, developed before research is undertaken, helps students to understand what they read. Next, teacher modeling, through Reference Source Commentaries, helps students acquire the skill of reading reference materials with understanding. Then, when the Fact-Finding Chart is used to record information, students are encouraged to fill in just the information needed in each section, rather than copying text passages in their entirety. Finally, the Bibliography List enables students to cite sources easily. All they need to do, when they record information on their Fact-Finding Chart is to write the abbreviation for the book they used and the page on which the information is found. For example, if information came from page 67 of *Audubon's Birds of America*, whose abbreviation on the Bibliography List was ABA, the student would write ABA 67.

Collecting Information.   During the third week of the SRP, the focus is on collecting information. Ideally, each interest group will meet separately in the media center with the media specialist, while the teacher provides help as needed for other students who are working independently. Fact-Finding Charts should be collected at the end of each session. Teachers should allot time for checking them, so that they look at each chart at least every other day. The purpose of this is not to grade, rate, or evaluate students' work, but rather to see how that work is progressing, and whether the student needs help. If the student needs help, the teacher must determine what help is needed. It is an indication that teacher support in the fact-finding process is needed if very little information has been recorded. Teachers should intervene immediately to help if this occurs, by encouraging questions and showing how to use reference materials. In some cases, students will need help in revising or reformulating the questions they're investigating. A different problem, which occurs less frequently, is when students have listed information that is, or may be, inaccurate. The number of ways that students can record misinformation is infinite, and, because the errors are unintentional and students are often not yet sophisticated readers, they usually believe what they've recorded. These are two examples of the way errors can occur:

"Owls are no bigger than robins" WB, 251;
U. S. Fish and Wildlife Service began in 1490, WB, 289

In the first instance, the student has taken information from the text (and has used quotation marks). The problem is that only part of a sentence has been quoted. The full sentence is "Some hawks and owls are no bigger than robins." In the second instance, numbers have been transposed: The Fish and Wildlife Service was established in 1940. Here is further support for the practice of listing the source. A teacher, reading the students' statements, can tell that they are inaccurate, but does not know how the inaccuracy arose, or what the real facts are. Checking the source will yield this information. Keeping the Fact-Finding Charts at school has the added advantage that they will not be lost. If students wish to collect information from resources at home or in a public library, they may use notebook paper or file cards, or an extra copy of the chart.

Students need opportunities to collect information from resource texts in school, where both books and teacher guidance are available to everyone.

Organizing Information in Writing. Because week 4 is devoted to writing, extra time for completing reports can be found by linking the content area sessions with language arts time. With teacher or group guidance, each student or student pair should decide how to order the information recorded on the Fact-Finding Chart. One possible choice is to begin with the most important information; alternatively the most interesting facts could be chosen to open the report. Once the opening topic has been chosen, other information should be given in logical order. Even young children can prepare useful reports, perhaps dictating them to a student from an upper grade who serves as a scribe, by working from their Fact-Finding Charts.

The bibliography for the report is prepared, very easily, by examining the Fact-Finding Chart and noting which sources have been used. (Their abbreviations will be listed beside each piece of information.) On a fresh copy of the Bibliography List, students can mark or highlight the titles used in their report. Older students may cut and paste from the Bibliography List or copy from it.

Sharing. The substantial effort given by students and teachers to the SRP provides transferable knowledge. Students acquire research experience and skills which will help them complete future projects, and also enable them to find information from reference materials independently. Teachers who have once followed the process will have practical experience which will be useful when they choose to repeat it, and materials that can be reused or easily modified. Additionally, opportunities for using and sharing research findings in follow-up activities will reinforce student learning and enhance student enjoyment.

Adapting the Structured Research Process

Like many other sound instructional strategies, the SRP is adaptable. Indeed, all teachers using the method do adapt it to fit their particular teaching situation and preferences and the strengths and needs of their students. The essential aspects of SRP are teacher involvement (as signaled by the two columns in the overview charts: "teacher" and "students and teacher"), time allotment for the process (advanced planning, building interest and knowledge, organizing, collecting data, and sharing results), and the emphasis on knowledge as a basis for interest in a topic and acquisition of further knowledge, and on the expansion of knowledge through finding out and sharing information.

The SRP can be used for a wide variety of topics when there are many subtopics, and the knowledge gained from studying all or some of the subtopics is worth an extensive allotment of time. For example, the SRP could be used with cooperative groups, to study biomes. Because there are only seven biomes, the cooperative learning groups would be fairly large. It might also be a good idea to let groups concentrate on a single complex biome, or two of the rarer, less complex biomes. The advance preparation would be about biomes, the Themed Reading materials and Reference Source Commentaries or Teacher Read-Aloud Commentaries would be about biomes, the Fact-Finding Charts would be about biomes. Because biomes already constitute a classification system, the activities for weeks 1 and 2 could be combined, and thus the SRP (aside from preparation and follow-up) could be accomplished in three weeks instead of four.

There is a wide range of possible topics for SRP, for example, explorers, inventions, continents, industries, famous authors, careers, and medical discoveries. Adapting the process occurs naturally through topic selection (the curriculum or teacher decision will result in selection of more sophisticated topics for older and more experienced students), and through the resource materials students will use. The resource materials, in turn, will affect the commentaries teachers will provide, and the questions students will pose for these commentaries. Two materials used in SRP—the Fact-Finding Chart and the Bibliography List—should vary according to the age and skill of students. Older, better prepared students can make their own versions of these materials, with teacher guidance and approval. Further adaptations occur at the conclusion of the process, since one of the factors on which teachers will base their decisions about how results of research will be shared will be the talents, interests, and level of development of their particular class.

Sharing Knowledge

When many topics of study are concluded with knowledge sharing, teachers can use a variety of strategies to fulfill multiple purposes. When students are engaged in any major project, supportive teacher attention throughout the process is invaluable. Although most of students' and teacher's time and attention should be focused on the research process, preparation of a sound and satisfying culminating product brings that process to an appropriate conclusion. The possible forms for such products are wide-ranging, and teachers who read professional journals and attend professional conferences will be regularly made aware of new possibilities, as scholars and practitioners share ingenious new ideas. Some of the many forms for products are listed in the final section of Figure 5–15: science fair displays, bound reports for classroom or media center, chapters in class books, panel presentations (live or videotaped) for other classes or for parents, bulletin board displays. Nancie Atwell (1990) lists other genres in which research reports can be presented, including picture books; simulated newspapers devoted to a topic or a time period; calendars that list, describe, and picture research-related information that is relevant to particular seasons; and catalogs that include pictures and descriptions of artifacts from a particular time period.

Teachers need to give careful thought to the knowledge sharing component of a learning process. They may decide that their students will write one or more short papers in the course of a semester or year. If this is the decision, they should follow a process that prevents plagiarism, enhances students' ability to write clear expository prose, and contributes to students' sense of themselves as capable writers. Many students fear and dislike writing. Effective teachers avoid creating these feelings, and act in ways that reduce or eliminate the apprehensions about writing that students already have.

Teachers may decide that their students will share what they have learned through presentations. This decision removes the burden of reading papers from the teacher, but may create anxiety in students and leave them with an aversion to speaking in public. Student anxiety about sharing ideas is reduced when teachers provide many brief opportunities, rather than limiting speaking in class to a single major occasion. Students who are used to finding the answer to a question by looking something up at the classroom research center and telling the class, who are accustomed to discussions and sharing ideas in cooperative groups, and who engage in sequence reading and impromptu presentations are more at ease than students who prepare for a single large presentation once a year. It is also helpful to encourage a diversity of talents. A student who is reluctant to

Students need opportunities to work together, learn from one another, and gain from one another's insight.

speak or read to a group may enjoy sharing by making a poster, displaying a collection, or conducting an experiment. The teacher's way of planning and managing presentations can either allay or exacerbate students' fears. Anxiety is reduced if students know how and when sharing will occur, if the teacher consistently finds elements of presentations to praise, and if evaluation is not emphasized.

Examining Alternative Views As Follow-Up

As students develop cognitively, they become able to perceive and examine alternative perspectives toward events. Much reading prepares one to examine multiple viewpoints, and to establish and modify views of the world. Simulations that engage students in playing the roles of people in other times and places, through discussion or drama, can be useful follow-ups to research. For such activities to be effective learning strategies, rather than simply a lively relaxation, students must have a sound foundation of information and understanding. Such activities should occur toward the end of a research process, and students and teacher should continue to consult reference sources during these activities, as new factual questions arise. One possible resource to support simulation activities is to invite an expert on the topic that has been studied to assist in preparations.

Simulations can also be based on writing, as in the ingenious RAFT strategy suggested by Kathy Dueck (1986). The acronym originally stood for Role, Audience, Form, Tense; but Theme is now generally used as the last element. In the RAFT strategy, content area writing is done as a form of simulation; that is, the writer takes on the role of someone, or something, else. Each writing assignment specifies a role for the writer; an audience to whom the writing is directed; a form for the writing, for example, television news spot, friendly letter, poem, advertisement, letter-to-the-editor; and a theme or topic. It is the role component that makes RAFT a form of simulation. The writer is taking on the role of someone or something else, simulating that person or thing while writing. The audience in RAFT is part of the simulation also. The writer pretends to be someone, and also pretends to be addressing a particular group or person. Because the activity requires the ability to look at ideas from another person's perspective, RAFT is most suitable for students in the middle school and above, although it can be adapted for younger students. For example, the RAFT activity about seabirds, suggested in Figure 5–16, could be done as a teacher-led group storytelling activity.

RAFT writing should be used as one of the culminating activities after a topic is studied. Although assuming a role is an imaginative task, the writing should be fact-based and students need a strong knowledge base to do this kind of writing well. The possibilities for RAFT assignments are very wide. For example, after studying the process of photosynthesis, students might form triads in which each of the three group members take the role of a different part of the plant—leaves, roots, and stem—and exchange a series of memos about how the food-making process is going. (Stem to roots: let's get a little water up here! The leaves are wilting! I know there hasn't been much rain, but you're just going to have to spread out. Get going!) In RAFT, the entire class may have the same assignment, or the teacher might set two or three possibilities and give students a choice. Creation of RAFT assignments is an interesting activity in itself, one students may enjoy undertaking after they have had experience in writing RAFT pieces. The RAFT process enhances content area learning because it gives students an opportunity to apply concepts which have been learned, and encourages the use of technical vocabulary. Using RAFT with cooperative writing groups can develop a variety of creative responses.

Preparing and Presenting Collections

Developing, categorizing, and labeling collections can be part of a research project and can serve as a culminating display. Barbara Hatcher (1992) makes the ingenious suggestion that students engaged in social studies research create artifact kits—collections of real items, related to a previous time period or another culture, or carefully prepared models or replicas if original items are not obtainable. Besides collecting the items or creating models of them, students need to find out some of the history that lies behind the artifacts and documents that have been collected. She advises that all the items for an artifact kit should be storable in a sturdy closed container and that teachers should decide in advance what the maximum dimensions of the container will be. She provides an extensive list of items that can be placed in an artifact kit, together with a time line for the period from which the artifacts have been collected:

> recipes and food items; songs and sheet music; old photographs and drawings; period advertisements or price lists; facsimiles of diaries or actual excerpts; letters, old magazines, newspaper accounts; period clothing; paintings or other art work; biographical sketches of individuals important to the historical

FIGURE 5–16 Sample RAFT Writing Assignments in Math, Social Studies, and Science

Role: zero **A**udience: 1–9 (who have complained that zero is not worth anything) **F**orm: memo **T**heme: predictions about what will happen to 1–9 if zero leaves the group	**T**heme: giving advice about dangers of an oil spill in the area **R**ole: Sequoia (Native American originator of writing system for the Cherokee language) **A**udience: self or descendants **F**orm: personal journal describing creation of the writing system **T**heme: the effects of creating a writing system
Role: sea bird **A**udience: fellow birds **F**orm: news bulletin	

study; models of utensils, toys, vehicles of transportation, inventions, etc., representative of the time frame of the historical study; reproduction of legal documents such as birth certificates, deeds, marriage licenses, etc.; food containers, logos, brand labels; posters, political cartoons; weather reports, tickets, bills, invitations and programs of ceremonies. (Hatcher, 1992, p. 271)

Presenting Findings Through Literary Forms

Whereas traditional research reports are written in expository prose, it is possible to use a variety of literary styles to share research findings. Student-created plays and puppet shows can present research results in dramatic form. In a variation on the one-person shows in which a single actor takes on the role of a famous person, such as Mark Twain, Theodore Roosevelt, or Emily Dickinson, individual students can dress up like a person whose life they have studied, and share a first-person narrative they have written from the point of view of that person. (As in all similar activities, it is not a useful culmination of study if simulations such as these are treated as cute or funny, and trivialize the lives of illustrious people.) Research findings can be shared in narrative form through simulated diaries written from the point of view of a famous person, or letters exchanged between people or non-human subjects of research. For example, after doing research on fossils, students could compose imaginary letters written by fossils to amateur or professional geologists, in which the fossil describes its life history and gives directions so that the reader can find its location and extract it safely from the earth.

Students may collect poetry related to their topic of study, or they may write free verse, song lyrics, or acrostics (Long, 1993). The acrostic form is well-adapted for a short, information-packed report. In this format, the first letters of the lines, or paragraphs, in the acrostic spell out the topic of research. Here is one example:

Sixth planet from the sun, it is the second largest in our solar system.
A year on this planet is as long as twenty-nine and a half Earth years.
The polar areas are flattened, so the planet is not completely round.
Uranus and Jupiter are the neighboring planets.
Rings around the planet were first seen by Galileo, in July 1610. They may be debris from a satellite that exploded, or they may be material that did not fully combine with the planet when it formed.; scientists don't yet know
Nine satellites are known to orbit the planet: Phoebe. Iapetus, Hyperion, Titan, Rhea, Dione, Tethys, Mimas, and Enceladus.

In the Fact and Fable strategy (Sharp, 1984) students complete their research findings, and then write a statement about the topic of their investigation that is either true or false, creating an appropriate illustration. Other students are challenged to tell whether the statement is true or false, and the researcher then reads from a resource text, or from a report, a passage that proves the statement to be either true or false. If class members are working on research reports in the same category (e.g., reports about animals) the fact and fable statements and illustrations can be assembled into a book, with interleaved pages giving the facts and their bibliographic references.

Teachers should keep in mind three criteria when suggesting alternative methods for sharing research findings. First, the format must allow presentation of sound, in-depth information. An example of a genre that would be excluded as a method for reporting research findings according to this criterion is limericks, because five rhyming lines are too short to present much information. Second, students must be capable of writing effectively in the genre, and have an interest in doing so. Thus, presenting findings in the form of poetry or drama might be an option for students but it should not be a requirement, since students may not be skilled enough to present factual information at the same time they are creating a play or a poem. Third, the method of providing information should require thought as well as effort on the writer's part and should give useful information to the reader. That two-part criterion eliminates simple puzzles, such as word searches, whose construction requires no thought about the topic and gives only a list of terms to the reader.

Presenting Findings in a Professional Style

Teachers who participate in professional meetings will probably have attended sessions where presenters gave their findings in roundtable presentations or at a poster session. Either of these two formats is suitable for student presentation of research findings. Both of the formats are also useful when guests—members of other classes or parents—are invited to the classroom.

For roundtable presentations, students prepare very short informational papers about their findings. Two or three students who are ready to report on related topics are grouped at a table, and additional chairs are provided so that other students can come to that table to listen to the researchers give their reports. There are several tables for presenters. During a roundtable session, the students who are not giving reports move from table to table to listen to reports, take notes, and ask questions. With teacher guidance, the class might plan three roundtable sessions on consecutive weeks, and at each session one-third of the class would report findings, and two-thirds would attend the sessions as audience members. For example, suppose students had been conducting research about art and artists. The first roundtable session might focus on different art forms. Student reports about artists who worked primarily in painting, sculpture, and photography would be presented at the three different tables. The second week's session might focus on artists from different time periods, and the third on art from different cultures.

For a poster session, student researchers prepare visual displays, typically on 24 × 28 sheets of posterboard, presenting their information. They may also prepare short informational handouts. At each poster session, the students who are presenting stand beside their posters, ready to talk about their findings with other students who come to their station. Members of the class who are not presenting their posters at that session circulate, keeping a record of which poster topics they visited and making notes about the information they have learned.

Helping Others Through Research

When the research process is well-planned and well-guided, students learn to use reference materials efficiently, and often find the research process interesting and absorbing. The talents of individual students, interest groups, or an entire class, can be used in research activities that help others. Preparation of annotated bibliographies—lists of books arranged by categories, each with a short description—is an appealing class activity, suitable even for very young children. Experience in using media center resources is fostered by preparing class notebooks—Books about Books—devoted to topics the class, or students in the class, have read about. When a student chooses a recently completed book to include in a class Book about Books, the teacher or media specialist supplies a copy of the book's bibliographic information and photocopies the book's cover. This page, showing the cover and giving bibliographic information, is put in the class notebook, with several blank pages after it. On these pages, students write about the book or write favorite quotations from the book (using quotation marks and citing the page number where the quotation appears). Each Book about Books, even while students continue to add to it, can be reading material for the class.

Research At Your Service, based on an idea discussed by Marlene Shanks (1988), is a good project for older students to use toward the end of the school year, when they have developed the ability to use media center resources well and learned to prepare annotated bibliographies or databases. In this project, the class offers its services to teachers in the school who want information about specific topics. As a class activity, students prepare an advertising flyer to be distributed to teachers, asking them to identify topics for which they would like information about available resources. For example, one teacher might be planning a project on the Great Lakes. Another might want a list of books and articles about recent discoveries in medicine. Another might want information about good stories to read to a second grade class about children growing up on farms. Students then choose one of the requests, do the research, and present the findings to the teacher who asked for the information. This activity can also be used as an enrichment or interest assignment for students skilled in using media center resources.

Looking Ahead

This chapter concludes a three-chapter section of the text focusing on strategies for use in introducing, developing understanding of, and expanding upon content area topics. The next section of the text consists of four chapters relating to a series of responsibilities that are part of teaching: fostering students' reading development, teaching a diversity of students, assessing students' work, and maintaining links between school and students' homes. A major purpose in each of these chapters is to discuss ways in which meeting these responsibilities can be integrated with, and enhance, content area learning and teaching. In these chapters, as throughout the text, theories that relate to good practice are briefly discussed, and a variety of strategies are presented from which teachers can choose.

Because school learning and later careers are strongly dependent on reading, one chapter is devoted to an overview of reading development, useful theories about reading instruction, and content area strategies that help students develop as readers without distracting from content area study. Chapter Six is based on the premise that content area teachers do not need to teach reading skills. Content area teaching which is lively, effective, and engages students actively with content-related text will assist students' reading development. The chapter concludes with a glossary that gives brief explanations of terms related to the field of reading that content area teachers can use as a resource as

needed. Chapter Seven is written from the point of view that diversity among students, which occurs in every classroom, is to be valued, and that it is useful to think in terms of the needs and strengths that students, like all people, have. Throughout the chapter, educational concepts and strategies are presented that have been developed by scholars working with groups of students who have particular characteristics or needs, but that are applicable to teaching generally. The chapter includes a discussion of the ways in which a rich variety of books can be linked to content area study as a resource for developing appreciation of diversity as well as a love of literature. Assessment is one responsibility all teachers have, and Chapter Eight presents a discussion of classroom assessment, and a variety of strategies emphasizing four facets of assessment—attention, investigation, documentation and evaluation—that classroom teachers can integrate with content area learning and teaching. Like the chapter on reading, this chapter also concludes with a glossary; here terminology related to testing and other aspects of assessment is explained. The final chapter in Part Three concerns the important role of the school—and of classroom teachers in particular—in supporting linkages between the school and students' homes and families. Required forms of school-home cooperation, such as conferences and report cards, are discussed and a variety of other opportunities for school-home cooperation and collaboration, all of which can be linked with content area study, are described.

STRATEGIC TEACHERS, PART THREE:

"All my students are talented."

Antonia Ditmers teaches life skills and American history in a small middle school, where she has worked for five years. She has always wanted to be a teacher. When she looks back to her own childhood and teen years, she recognizes that she was learning about teaching all the time she was in school. From kindergarten through college, some of her teachers have been her models. In other classrooms, her desire to become a teacher was strengthened by the thought that she would be a teacher who helped people, rather than making them feel unhappy and inferior, as she sometimes observed happening. She uses the term *community of learners* to speak about her classes, and her aim is to encourage every student to be a productive contributor. She chooses strategies that will make her own instruction effective and produce transferable learning, and strategies that allow her students to become aware of their diverse talents, and develop and share them. These are the strategies she uses regularly:

Reading Road Maps—to guide students in their reading of text; gradually phased out during course.

paired reading with RESPONSE—for in-class reading/study of text.

vicarious experiences, primarily videotapes also linked with RESPONSE—to increase depth of understanding through a familiar, popular medium.

SAY-IT—to establish an environment where everyone is a question-asker and everyone is a question-answerer.

A-Qu-A—to review essential concepts through a social activity the students enjoy.

EVOKER—to show students they have the power to interpret and enjoy poetry, and to link literature with history and everyday life.

Themed Listening—in American History classes, to acquaint students with the music of different time periods and different groups.

Vocabulary Self-Selection Strategy—to interest and empower students in vocabulary development.

Reference Source Commentaries including Dictionary Commentaries—to enable students to use dictionaries, encyclopedias, and other reference books efficiently.

Structured Research Process—to teach students to find information, and to develop information-finding skill to use in future research projects, and in "reading to do" in their careers.

Transmediation—through a variety of strategies, to deepen and share learning, to use an alternative to writing papers, and to encourage students' various talents and appreciation for each other's talents.

Additionally, she reads aloud to her classes. In history classes she reads selections several times a week from histories written for adults, to make the works of authors, such as Barbara Tuchman, Bruce Catton, and Daniel Boorstin, accessible to her students. In life skills classes she reads for five to ten minutes at the end of class. She looks for reading material that is worth hearing and remembering; and she deliberately does not make "age-appropriateness" a criterion for choice. Instead she chooses reading material over a wide range, because she wants to acquaint her students with all sorts of good literature, including excerpts from her own current reading, and books written for young children— beautifully illustrated books in which wonderful stories are told in rich language, books that many of her students never encountered during their childhood years.

She is interested in simulation drama as a strategy for teaching history, and currently uses the strategy at two points in her American history classes: during the study of the American Revolution and during the study of the Great Depression. A policy she always follows in structuring a simulation drama is that if there is a "villain" in the piece, she takes that role. (See Figure 5–17 for an example of a simulation drama designed to develop concepts about the American Revolution. In this instance, the students are all patriots and the teacher has taken the role of the oppressive governor.)

Miss Ditmers regards the textbooks used in her classes as important teaching tools that serve two purposes: presenting content information and giving students practice in reading so that they will develop further as readers. In all of her courses, students regularly spend class time reading the text, following a process she teaches them early in the semester. When the class begins to study a new topic, she provides a *Reading Road Map*. She gives more detail in maps for early text sections; as students become more skilled in reading for information the maps are simpler, and eventually may be phased out altogether (although she will always provide a detailed map if a student requests it). Students read in pairs or triads, using the bottom half of the map (and the reverse side) as a RESPONSE form. She always uses the students' reading time to move from group to group, and she places strong emphasis on the SAY-IT strategy, making it a rule that all questions are to be respected, and that classmates, teacher, and even guests in the classroom are potential question-answerers. She allots approximately ten minutes of most class sessions for lecture and discussion of the current topic of study. This opens the period in life skills classes and occurs at the end of history classes.

In history classes, while students are reading or working in cooperative groups, she often incorporates Themed Listening, playing, softly, music that relates to the time period being studied (e.g., Native American music; songs from the Civil War era). She uses videotapes frequently in both history and life skills classes, and students often use the RESPONSE strategy to take notes. One activity for cooperative groups is the Vocabulary Self-Selection Strategy (VSS); each week one group presents a list of vocabulary terms related to what

the class is studying (drawn from reading, videos, or even folk music) that they think would be useful and interesting for the class to learn, and the class discusses them. During the VSS discussion, Miss Ditmers uses one word or term as the basis for a Dictionary Commentary. To complete study of each major text section, the class does an A-Qu-A. As an individual concluding assignment, students summarize the main points they have learned in one page of writing (which they may organize as they wish, and illustrate if they wish). These end-of-section summaries are used to assess and document learning.

Twice during the semester, in both history and life skills classes, Miss Ditmers uses the Structured Research Process (SRP) to engage students in gathering, organizing, and presenting information. However, although students may present information in the form of papers, and some do, they may also choose from a variety of transmediation methods to present what they have learned: for example, murals, videotaped presentations, sequence dramas. Miss Ditmers uses students' class activities as the basis for her grading, so she makes sure to maintain careful documentation. She keeps a set of Class Notebooks on a shelf beside her desk. There is one notebook for each cooperative group, with dividers separating the work of each student and a place for group papers. Students are individually responsible for seeing that all their papers, including notes from RESPONSE and group lists of words for VSS, are put into the notebooks. During the course of a semester, Class Notebooks are filled, the materials removed and filed, and then refilled. Each time that students prepare end-of-section summaries, she makes copies of some of them before returning them to the students, so that she eventually has several samples from each student. (She finds it works well to tell students that she needs four samples of end-of-section summaries during the semester, and asks for their input about which they want copied.) During the Structured Research Process, students keep their notes in individual folders; when the activity is completed, Miss Ditmers collects, staples, and files the notes. Her other method of documentation is to take photographs of the students at work, especially as they work on, and then give, their concluding SRP presentations.

How Does She Do It?

When she is teaching, Miss Ditmers keeps her students interested, and her students keep her interested. Looking at her strategy list with a knowledge of the structure of this text, readers can see that she emphasizes "during" and "after" strategies, rather than introductory ones. She counts on Reading Road Maps and the brief lecture and discussion periods that begin or conclude class to focus students' attention. Because it is one of her major goals to establish a classroom in which asking for information is considered an intelligent thing to do, she makes explicit use of the SAY-IT strategy, encouraging students to ask each other, and her, when they need content-related information. She is aware of the importance of terminology; thus students ask for and get information about new terms as they encounter them in reading, rather than through instruction that precedes reading. Additionally, when she prepares Reading Road Maps, she regularly calls attention to technical terminology and the places in the text where important terms are defined and illustrated.

Although she uses many strategies, preparation time is not extensive. The preparation for many of the strategies Miss Ditmers has chosen consists of finding and choosing materials: videotapes to show to the class, music tapes to play for Themed Listening, research materials for the Structured Research Process, poems for EVOKER to illustrate historical concepts or life skills topics. Therefore, one of her most helpful colleagues is the school media specialist, with whom she discusses her curricular needs, and who regularly puts aside materials for her. Only two strategies are based on teacher-prepared materials: Reading Road Maps and A-Qu-A. However, once prepared, these materials can be used year after year (although the Reading Road Maps need revision when a new text is selected). The first year that she used the Reading Road Maps, Miss Ditmers used them only for history classes, and kept a step or two ahead of her students by preparing one or two maps a week; she added maps for the life skills course the next year the same way. After that, the maps were available, although she reviewed and modified some. She constructed A-Qu-As over a period of several years and began by using them approximately once a month. Sometimes students share the results of their SRP research by creating an A-Qu-A; when these are particularly sound, Miss Ditmers asks the students' permission to adapt and add them to the class collection. (When she uses a student's work to share with others, she always asks the student for permission. Of course, she does not use it if the student does not wish to give permission. She gives credit, verbally and in writing, to that student whenever the materials are used.) She also reviews and revises the materials as necessary, making sure all the A-Qu-A cards are correctly prepared and technically accurate, and that all the questions are useful.

Challenge to the Reader: Alone or with colleagues, brainstorm a list of ways that the strategies Miss Ditmers uses contribute to making her classroom a community of learners.

Choose and Use: If you were to choose one aspect of Miss Ditmers's program to use in your own classroom, what would it be? How would you begin?

FIGURE 5–17   Simulation Drama in Social Studies

Observation (approximately 30 minutes) of an eighth-grade class
Setting: eighth-grade American History class
Topic: American Revolutionary War

The teacher is out of the classroom momentarily, and the students are busy gathering signatures for their "declaration of independence." Their declaration has been written over the weekend by one of the class members as pre-arranged by the teacher. The teacher will play the role of Lord Ditmers, the colony's governor, who is loyal to the Queen. The students are part of cooperative learning groups called towns (e.g., Georgetown).

S: Everyone who wants to be free should sign it.

S: What if I want to sign it in Georgetown?

S (*with declaration*): Well, you don't live in Georgetown.

(*Teacher comes in.*)

S (*to teacher*): Still not ready!

S: SIGN IT!

S: OK!

S: Let's get this done, people!

(*School secretary comes in and delivers a bag to the teacher.*)

S: Miss Ditmers. . .

T: What?

S: Who sent the bag?

T: Warren, don't worry about it right now.

S: Uh oh, Lord Ditmers is here.

T: We're back in role playing right now. I am now Lord Ditmers.

I left in an emergency the other day because I was much distressed by certain actions and attitudes that you people were expressing during debate time. I wanted to talk to Queen Sue about your attitudes. Now I am back. The Queen and I both agree that it is time for you colonists to reaffirm your allegiance to the queen and the mother country. So I've brought with me today a new loyalty oath which all of you in this colony will sign. This will affirm your allegiance and support to our beloved queen. The oath simply states that you agree to support the queen and her laws for governing of the colonies. In the next few days, I will bring around this oath to each town. When I show up at your town, all of you must report to me so you can sign this oath.

S: Lord Ditmers, where do you live?

T: In a tent. I noticed that my house was destroyed.

S: Blame it on the Indians. Don't blame us.

Chatter breaks out. Teacher quiets class and resumes.)

T: As I come around to each town, just as before, you will come to me, regardless of what you are doing, and you will sign this oath. That will show your allegiance to the queen. Therefore, three days hence…

S (*interrupts, as preplanned with teacher*): Okay, Lord Ditmers, they're slow, they ain't ready, but I still have something for you. (*hands declaration to teacher*)

S: It was hard to read!

(*Chatter breaks out regarding why not all had signed.*)

T: Eighth grade… shhh… (*Teacher pauses to read document.*) I can't believe this! This is illegal and traitorous.

(*Teacher's tone of voice changes as she comes out of role to settle a problem.*) I've got some kids in my class who need to shape up… (student disrupts again) You may leave. There's role playing and there's horse playing. (pause while disruptive student leaves)

(*Back in role*) This is illegal and traitorous. The queen isn't going to like this. She's not going to accept what you're asking for. Your independence!

S: Yup!

T: This is the Queen's land, always has been and always will be. She's not going to give up this land just because you people signed this silly paper.

S: She's not going to have this land for long.

T: (*turning to the student*) Ross, did you sign this?

Ross: Yes.

T: Do you know what this means? You're a traitor to your country.

Ross: Oh, no. Darn!

FIGURE 5–17   Continued

T: In fact, anyone in this room who signed this is a traitor to the queen and treason is punishable by death.

S: So we'll die for our independence.

S: Give me liberty or give me death!

S: That's right!

T *(reads text of student declaration)*: When in the course of human occurrence, people have the right to feel the need of separation from political bonds *(incredulous look)* they should be able to wake up every morning and feel themselves equal to everybody else. When they do not have this feeling, then it is obviously a cause for separation from government. You honestly think Queen Sue is going to go for this?

Students *(in what seems to be spontaneous chorus)*: YES!

T *(continues reading)*: When the government fails to give us these rights, we have the right to undo the government. (Teacher turns to student.) The queen's land and you're going to undo the government? Floyd, did you sign this?

Floyd: Kind of…

T: Kind of… kind of! That makes you a traitor just like Ross. Lee, did you sign this?

Lee: *(emphatically)*: Yes!

T: Do you know what this means?

S: War!

T: War! Exactly! *(stepping out of character)* Okay. Real history, guys. I am now going to explain to you the procedure that we're going to have to follow as far as the war goes.

(Teacher gives directions, and students move into cooperative groups—their "towns"—to prepare for tomorrow's "battle.")

Comments by the observer: This teacher maintained interest and kept the class on task despite numerous interruptions. The role playing seemed very well received, and cooperative groups were functioning well as I left the class.

This observation was written by Malinda J. Frybarger who was at the time a graduate student. Minor changes have been made, including the name of the teacher observed.

PART THREE

Building Strengths, Meeting Needs, and Making Connections

Building Reading Ability While Learning

Reading is the process of constructing meaning from written texts. It is a complex skill requiring the coordination of a number of interrelated sources of information. ...Reading is a process in which information from the text and the knowledge possessed by the reader act together to produce meaning. Good readers skillfully integrate information in the text with what they already know.

ANDERSON, HIEBERT, SCOTT, AND WILKINSON, 1986.
BECOMING A NATION OF READERS, PP. 7 AND 8.

Reading is the primary way of acquiring content area information. It is not the only way, by any means, but it is the major method. Most content area information is available in the form of text: in books, magazines and journals, and, increasingly, on computer screens. The ability to read with understanding underlies success in learning. There is an apparent dilemma here for teachers whose primary responsibility is to teach the content of their subject matter specialty. In every class, there will be variation among students in terms of their reading ability. Because reading underlies learning, is it necessary for content area teachers to teach reading to students who cannot read a content text capably? How will a teacher with limited background in reading education know how to teach reading? How can an extensive and demanding curriculum be taught if time is taken from subject matter instruction to provide reading instruction?

Good Content Area Teaching Builds Reading Ability

It is good news for content area teachers that the "apparent dilemma" referred to in the previous paragraph is not a real dilemma. Teachers do not have to choose between teaching content and teaching reading. *Teaching content well will build reading ability.* Ever since content area instruction has been emphasized, this good news has been available; it is amply reinforced by the best current instructional theory and practice.

The cliché "every teacher a teacher of reading" has been interpreted by content teachers in light of the reading teacher's role and responsibility for teaching reading. Content teachers have rejected that role, and rightly so. ...There is no place for reading instruction as reading teachers generally employ it in content areas. There is a need for a whole new strategy in teaching reading through content areas, a strategy that draws from what we know about the direct teaching of reading but adapts that knowledge to fit the structure of and responsibilities for the total curriculum in each content area. (Herber, 1978, p. 8)

Consider carefully this quotation from Harold Herber's early, inspirational text on content area reading. At the time he was writing, the phrase "every teacher a teacher of reading" was so commonly used it had become a cliché (a saying used so often that it had become tiresome). For many people, "every teacher a teacher of reading" meant that every teacher should teach reading; and this implied that part of the time allotted for instruction in science, social studies, math, and similar subjects should be spent in direct teaching of reading. That isn't so, Herber wrote. (He also pointed out that content area teachers, when told that they were supposed to provide time in their programs for teaching reading, rejected the idea.).

Another interpretation of "every teacher a teacher of reading" is that every good teacher leads students to develop in ways that enhance reading ability. Or, using the statement at the beginning of this section, *good content area teaching builds reading ability.* How does this work? We understand, with a sense of relief, that we're *not* supposed to spend class time giving separate instruction in reading. But what is it that we do to build our students' reading ability, when we teach elementary students science, math, and social studies; or middle school students pre-algebra or earth science; or high school students biology or economics or life skills?

This chapter is devoted to answering these questions. First, the characteristics of effective content area teaching are reviewed and related to reading development. Then the process of reading, and some trends in reading instruction, are discussed. (A glossary of reading-related terms is included at the end of this chapter.) Strategies designed to develop reading that also enhance content area learning are presented, and the chapter concludes with a section devoted to the most important of these strategies: Reading and More Reading. Interspersed throughout the chapter are seven truths about reading that are good news for content area teachers. These pieces of good news summarize the reasons why effective content area teaching builds reading ability, so it is useful to consider them together, as well as individually. Here are six of the reasons why effective content area teaching builds reading ability:

- *Reading is a language-based process*, and human beings are good at learning language. Effective teachers create language-rich content classrooms, where books, displays, events, and learning activities are related to topics being studied. Skillful content teachers focus classroom language on content, rather than on directions about what to do and warnings about how to behave. Students in such classrooms are immersed in the language they will encounter in books, and this helps them read.

- *It is easier to read text that is about familiar, interesting topics.* We acquire new information by linking it to what we already know. Creating a shared knowledge base for students about topics they are studying sparks interest and helps students read text that is written about these topics. In the process of building this shared knowledge base, students who are already knowledgeable about topics will have opportunities to contribute ideas and information, as well as to extend their own understanding.

- *Words in our listening, speaking, and conceptual vocabularies are easier to read*, than those that are new. Words that we have heard, used, and understood are easier to read than words we have never encountered before. When teachers read aloud important text passages, when students discuss important ideas, when vocabulary teaching strategies are lively and varied, students have many opportunities to see and hear content-related terms and understand their meaning. This familiarity helps students read the words when they see them in the text.

- *Writing and reading can go hand in hand.* Meaningful content area writing, in journals, notes, lists, semantic maps, and group-prepared informational reports, engages students in using words that they also encounter in text. When students write about a topic, they read to gather further information about it. Writing enhances reading; reading enhances writing.

■ *What students can do today with support, they will be able to do later independently.* Rather than simply expecting that students will learn by reading assigned textbook pages, skillful teachers have many strategies to help their students learn. Moreover, they realize that giving information and guidance when it is needed does not make students dependent; on the contrary, it helps them become self-sufficient.

■ *The skill of reading, like other skills, develops through use.* In content area classrooms where students read, and are read to, from a variety of materials, and instructional activities offer many opportunities to read, students become better readers.

You have read, in a previous paragraph, that this chapter includes "seven truths about reading that are good news for content area teachers, summarizing the reasons why effective content area teaching builds reading ability." The paragraph is followed by "six reasons why good content area teaching builds reading ability." One good news item differs from the others previously listed. It is not about what good content area teachers do that helps promote reading development but about something they do not do. *Content area teachers do not need to sort students.*

■■ Principles of Effective Content Area Teaching: A Brief Review

Good content area teaching requires subject matter knowledge and interest, teaching skill, belief in students' ability to learn and commitment to teaching them, and engagement in practices, such as reading and study, interaction with colleagues, and participation in professional organizations, which contribute to professional growth. The three-part foundation of effective content area teaching that was presented in Chapter Two is repeated here:

■ Good content area teaching depends on the teacher's explicit or intuitive understanding of sound educational theory. An essential component of this understanding is the teacher's belief that all students can learn. An essential corollary is the teacher's acceptance of the responsibility to teach each one.

■ Good content area teaching depends on the teacher's knowledge of, and interest in, both subject matter and pedagogy, and the teacher's skill in choosing and using effective instructional strategies.

■ Good content area teaching depends on the teacher's commitment to ongoing learning and professional growth, resulting in increasing general knowledge, and deepening understanding of good educational theory and practice and the ability to apply this understanding effectively.

It is the first of these three principles, relating to the teacher's explicit or intuitive understanding of sound, educational theory, that relates directly to the positive impact that content area teachers can have on their students' reading development. Good content area teaching is based on the belief that all students can learn, and on acceptance of the responsibility to teach each one.

Often in the past, and too often still today, some educators have decided that it is their role to "sort" students: to classify and group the students who come to them as fast or slow, ready or not ready, those who can succeed or those who cannot. In children's early school years, real and important differences among young learners have often been simplisticly treated as indicators that an individual is either "ready" or "not ready" to learn to read. To make matters worse, instead of looking at the earlier learning environments of the "ready' children (to make school environments similarly helpful) some educators have analyzed the current abilities of the "ready" children and decreed that all children must acquire these abilities before they are allowed to move on.

Entering Into Learning: A Parable

Imagine a beautiful, well-furnished house. There is a handsome front door and an entry way, a living room, a dining room, a kitchen, enough bedrooms for each family member, one or more bathrooms, a laundry room, and a family recreation room. In each of the rooms there is everything we need to be comfortable. There are plenty of books in the living room, recreation room, and bedroom; there are lots of cooking utensils in the kitchen; the bedrooms have ample bureaus and closets. The house is ours—all we have to do is to show that we know how to live there.

Our guide opens the front door and welcomes us in. We can explore the rooms, and the guide is ready to anticipate our needs and answer our questions about how things work. Some of the kitchen and laundry equipment is new to us, so we need to experiment before we can work with it; our guide demonstrates, watches while we try things out, and gives us some "How to do it" booklets. It takes us a little while to find our way around the house, but only a little while; everything is interesting, and we can soon see how the various rooms are connected. The house is ours!

There is another way to enter the house. Suppose when we approached it, our guide looked at us and decided we were not ready to go through the front door. First, we need to learn "house basics": living room, kitchen, bedroom. Our guide takes us into a cellar area where, if we look up, we can see most of the living room through its clear plastic floor. First, we need to learn which chairs are most comfortable. (The guide has a list for us to memorize.) Then we must learn how to open the windows. (The guide has something that looks like a little window that we can practice on.) Finally, we need to know what places in the house all the doors out of the living room lead to. (The doors are closed so we can't see what lies beyond, but our guide will tell us, and then test us to see if we get it right. The testing is a little scary.) When we can prove to the guide that we know enough about the living room, we can move on to the area beneath the kitchen. Learning about the kitchen will be even harder than learning about the living room: We will need to learn lots of new words, and match them with pictures of things that are in the real kitchen up above our heads. Our guide is kind, but sometimes gets discouraged with us because we are so slow to understand. We make mistakes, and often after we've learned something we forget it later. We are discouraged, too. The house must be a fine one but being down here underneath is unpleasant and tiresome. Perhaps the best thing to do is to give up.

Everyone Has a Right to Learn

This illustration of alternative ways of entering into learning is intended as a condemnation of practices that prescribe radically different methods of teaching based on a ready or not ready sorting of learners. But notice how such educational practices could be justified. Suppose someone questioned the policy of separating learners into two groups and treating them very differently. "Why," advocates of the system could say, "take a look at the people we let through the front door. Aren't they doing well? That shows we were correct to choose them for front-door-entry. And then look at the people we said were not ready to come through the front door. Poor things, they're stumbling about, making very little progress despite all our efforts. Surely that proves how wise we are when we do the sorting!"

Like most educational practices, emphasis on "reading readiness" and on grouping for instruction based on presumed ability in reading were devised based on good motives, or motives that appeared good at the time. Times change, though, and a statement such as this appears ugly today: "Methods in word recognition which other children pick up by themselves must be taught to these slow minds. ...Reading material must remain very simple and childlike" (Dolch, 1931, pp. 248–249). But practices intended to prevent reading failure have instead created situations in which children are identified and see themselves as failures very early in their school career.

> Thus the patterns of instruction that... historically evolved from a concern for attending to individual differences [are now seen] as potential sources of many of the differences that were observed. Rather than fulfilling a useful function, these instructional differences [are] seen as limiting the development of the very children they were supposed to serve. (Allington, 1991, p. 24)

When students are classified as ready to read, they are grouped with similarly advantaged children and they read regularly; when part of their time is spent listening to other students read, the text they hear is capably read and therefore easy to understand. The children classified as not ready are grouped with others who, for a wide variety of reasons, are not adept at a variety of school-related tasks. Typically, very little instructional time is spent reading, and when these children do take turns reading aloud and listening to each other, what they hear is so disjointed that it is almost impossible to understand. (Try listening some time to a taped recording of a struggling reader confronted with a new text and striving to get every word right.) Richard Allington is a reading scholar who has endeavored for years to promote adequate instruction for all children; he captured the foolishness of this kind of teaching in the title of one of his earliest articles: "If they don't read much, how they ever gonna get good?" (Allington, 1977).

"We would argue that all young children, regardless of the diversity of experiences that they bring to school, are ready to learn," Anne McGill-Franzen and Richard L. Allington (1991, p. 87) write in an article titled, "Every child's right: Literacy." The failure and discouragement of one group of learners does not prove their inadequacy; instead it strongly suggests that they have been mistreated. The method imposed upon them has failed. But there are many classifications for students who have difficulties in school, and the labels given to them "place the responsibility for the failure... on the children who fail" (Gillis, 1994, p. 123). Richard Allington and Peter Johnston (1984, p. 986) have suggested that terms such as "remedial readers" and "disabled readers" should be abandoned in favor of longer but more accurate descriptors, such as "children-with-different-schedules-for-reading-acquisition" or "children-we-have-failed-to-teach-to-read."

Educational practices should not close doors to learning. With increasing force and clarity, teachers are asserting that schools should be places where the doors to learning are opened wide for all. Literacy is coming to be recognized as a developing, ongoing process, one which begins long before children enter school. *Emergent literacy* is the term originated by the world-renowned reading educator Marie Clay (1966), and adept teachers can foster and encourage literacy at every educational stage, in every field of study. When students come into classes in the intermediate grades, in middle school, or in high school without adequate reading skill, it is still our responsibility to teach them content information to improve their chances of developing as readers.

On Not Sorting Students

The teacher can save time and energy for better uses. If we accept the idea that all our students can learn, we can attend to establishing a good learning environment and to providing good instruction. Teachers do not need to spend time sorting students into those who can learn and those who cannot learn. Teachers do not need to spend energy and effort justifying—to ourselves or to others—our decisions that some students are incapable of learning. Teachers do not need to worry about ways to manage a classroom that includes people who are not expected to learn.

Visualize: a group of young children, all set for learning!

We should ask: What helped these children reach this point?

...because we can then plan school activities that provide similar opportunities for all students.

We should not ask: What are all the separate things these children can do?

...because then we're tempted to require other students to learn these separate things before they are allowed to progress.

Reading: A Brief Survey

Reading is primarily a mental process, and so our understanding of it is necessarily based on inference. We can see physical actions: for example, the way an expert golfer swings a club can be videotaped and minutely analyzed, and the swing of a novice can be compared with it. But the important elements of reading occur behind the eye, within the brain. Our understanding of reading is based on theory, and over the years an extraordinarily wide array of theories has been proposed. Reading scholars, and others, continue to disagree, often acrimoniously, about the nature of reading and how reading should be taught. The brief quotation at the beginning of this chapter includes a series of assertions about reading that are widely, though not universally, accepted, and that are used in the following sections as the basis for a discussion of reading.

Reading Is a Skill

This statement about what reading *is* also implies what it is *not*. Reading is not a body of knowledge to be mastered. We learn history, math, and science, but we learn *to* read. We can read, and most successful readers do read, without ever being aware of the field of knowledge in education and psychology called "Reading." Therefore, as content area teachers we do not need to teach students about reading. (We may do so if we decide it will be useful and interesting, but learning to read, fortunately, is not based on learning a series of facts about reading.)

A second, and somewhat more controversial, implication of "reading is a skill" is that it is not useful to think of reading as simply *a lot of skills*. Reading does not consist of a set of isolatable pieces to be learned separately and then combined. Of course, reading is gloriously multifaceted, but its essence cannot be captured by attempting to divide it into component parts. Research studies (e.g., Reutzel & Hollingsworth, 1991; Taylor, Frye, & Gaetz, 1990) provide evidence that reading is not divisible into a series of skills. Barbara Taylor and her colleagues are among those scholars whose research shows that children can pass tests on various "skills" *before* using the skill lessons provided in basal reading programs. Ray Reutzel and Paul Hollingsworth examined two conflicting hypotheses about the nature of reading: the distinctiveness hypothesis (reading is divisible into a series of skills) and the unitary hypothesis (reading is not a divisible process). In their study, one group of students read trade books while four other groups each studied a separate skill: locating details, drawing conclusions, finding the sequence, and determining the main idea. When they compared students' ability to complete skill

exercises, they found that performance on a test of a particular skill did not appear to be affected by study of the skill, and that the group reading trade books performed as well on skill tests as those who had spent time on skills lessons. Their findings support

> a) conceptualizing reading comprehension as a *unitary* skill or process rather than as a set of discrete skills or subskills that can be taught one at a time, and b) engaging [students] in sustained reading of connected and meaningful text [rather than] spending time on the learning and practicing of discrete comprehension skills. (Reutzel & Hollingsworth, 1991, p. 41)

Of course, it is important for students to grasp the central ideas of text and to identify the author's point of view, and their own, about what they have read. The ability to do this is not effectively developed by drilling on "main idea" and "drawing conclusions." Therefore, content area teachers do not need to devote class time to isolated skills lessons.

A final implication of "reading is a skill" is that reading is not a special gift that leads a few people to startling and impressive accomplishments that others cannot attain. Therefore, content area teachers can plan to teach in ways that help all students develop as readers.

Reading Is a Process

Again, it is useful to consider what reading is, and also what it is not. In recent years, educators, particularly those engaged in teaching writing, have emphasized a distinction between process and product, a distinction that has had a strong influence on our understanding of what good writing instruction ought to be like. Rather than assigning students to produce a technically perfect end-product—a neatly prepared paper consisting of a series of paragraphs each with a topic sentence, all correct in spelling, grammar and punctuation—knowledgeable teachers plan writing instruction in which students have many opportunities to write and rewrite about topics that are important to them. Writing occurs in social contexts. Writing is ongoing thought and action: a process in which, ideally, both teacher and students will be lifelong learners. Similarly, reading ought not to be considered as a product, with good reading consisting of a piece of text read aloud accurately and with expression, or read silently with speed and precision to answer a series of questions correctly. Reading is far more useful and more wonderful. "Reading itself, as a psycho-physiological process," wrote Edmund Huey in the early years of this century, "is almost as good as a miracle. ...A wonderful process, by which thoughts and thought-wanderings to the finest shades of detail... are reflected from [an author] to another soul who reads..." (Huey, 1968; first published in 1908).

Like speaking and listening, reading is a form of language, and we know that humans are adept language learners. Young children, unless they have grave sensory or mental impairments or are terribly abused, learn to speak the language they hear spoken. Language development proceeds in predictable ways, but it is not acquired by learning rules, practicing, and mastering one bit at a time. Like spoken language, reading develops through use and is fostered by a learning environment that is print-rich, full of opportunities to see and hear and use written text.

> Just as speech develops in an environment which is immensely more rich than the immediate needs of the learner, so the orientation to book language develops in an environment of rich exposure beyond the immediate needs of the learner. In both situations, the learner selects appropriate items from the range. (Holdaway, 1982, p. 295)

The concept that learning to read occurs most easily and effectively in a print-rich environment is part of an educational theory usually called "whole language." One of the earliest uses of the term is in a paper prepared by Kenneth and Yetta Goodman (1977), "A whole language comprehension-centered reading program." The whole language philosophy is based on the recognition that young children learn language naturally, without being taught, and that language modes (listening, speaking, writing, and reading) are interrelated. Rather than identifying and teaching an isolated series of skills, whole language teaching involves engaging students in many meaningful social language events within a lively, accepting, print-rich learning environment.

> Whole language is a philosophy of learning and teaching based on a number of fundamental assumptions...: Learning is social, requires risk-taking and experimentation, involves constructing meaning and relating new information to prior knowledge; [learning] occurs when learners are actively involved, when they have real purposes, when they make choices and share in decision-making; [learning] uses language, mathematics, art, music, drama, and other communication systems as vehicles for exploration. (Newman & Church, 1990, pp. 23–24)

The whole language movement has inspired extensive and important changes in language arts teaching. Although it has also inspired controversy, the extensive professional literature on whole language contains a great deal to inform and inspire teachers to create productive and happy learning environments (e.g., Dudley-Marling & Dippo, 1991; Newman, 1991; Watson, 1989). Whole language theory and practice embrace content area learning. Content area subjects are rich with opportunities for students to read, write, and discuss ideas, to work with one another, to make decisions, take risks, and explore new ideas.

Reading Is Constructing Meaning

Meaning-making is thinking, and just as humans have a natural aptitude for learning language, so we also have a natural aptitude for thinking. Although it is possible to read text without understanding or recalling it (an issue discussed in Chapter Two), thinking is an essential part of the reading process. We expect what we read to make sense. Unless we have reasons not to attempt to understand what is read (e.g., exhaustion, or being confronted with a text loaded with unfamiliar words and concepts, or encountering a nonsense text such as Lewis Carroll's poem "Jabberwocky," or having been thoroughly taught that reading consists of getting a series of words right), we will expect to get meaning from what we read. In the process of reading, we relate knowledge we already have to the information presented in the text. Instruction in every classroom, in every subject, should give the message, implicitly or explicitly, that we not only find meaning when we read, we create meaning.

An Analysis Across the Grades

One way to consider reading development is in terms of a series of sequential stages. The reading scholar Jeanne Chall (1983) proposed a six-stage theory, in which stages 1 through 4 are related to an educational progression from first grade through high school. An interesting feature is that her sixth stage, the stage of lifelong learning through reading, is stage 5, because she puts the earliest stage in this development progression before stage 1. Chall's naming of this first stage (stage zero) illustrates an important fact about reading, and about development in general: Preparation for reading begins at birth. There is an analogy with a child's first step. That's step one. However, to take that first step, much preliminary development must already have occurred.

An essential part of the early stages of reading is learning to understand how the written language works. In the process of using language and being read to, and having the opportunity to try repeated readings of short, interesting books, well-developing readers become able to decipher printed words. They internalize a sense of the relationship between the sounds of language and the symbols (letters and letter combinations) used in written language. During the primary school years, children typically read material in which their prior knowledge helps them substantially in understanding what they read. In the process, well-developing readers expand their reading vocabulary dramatically and they become able to read more quickly.

In terms of our educational system's expectations of students, an important change occurs after the primary years. By the time they are in fourth grade, almost all students are expected to acquire much of their content area learning by reading. Chall calls the stage of reading that typically begins at fourth grade, "reading for learning the new." From this point on, in school and outside of school, one major purpose of reading is to acquire new information, explore new viewpoints, and develop our understanding of the world.

FIGURE 6–1   An Overview of Stages of Successful Reading Development (a synthesis based on Chall, 1983, and also drawn from, among others, Clay, 1979; Kirsch & Mosenthal, 1990)

Stage 0: Emergent literacy: language development; awareness of print and books; enjoyment of being read to, early development of reading preferences (Birth to approximately age 6)

Stage 1: Learning to read: beginning reading including internalized grasp of the connection between written and spoken language; experiences with print in and outside of school (grades 1–2, Ages 6–7)

Stage 2: Learning to read: developing increasing fluency; expansion of reading vocabulary; developing familiarity with textbooks; beginning to read independently for enjoyment (Grades 2–3, Ages 7–8)

Stage 3: Reading to learn: "reading for learning the new"
3A: reading for assigned and self-selected purposes, to learn and to enjoy; acquiring conventional knowledge through reading (Grades 4–6, Ages 9–11)
3B: reading to acquire and synthesize information from multiple sources; developing understanding of different viewpoints through reading; increasing development of reading tastes and preferences (Middle school, Ages 12–14)

Stage 4: Reading to learn, to enjoy, to accomplish work ("reading to do"); increasing understanding of multiple viewpoints through reading; further development of reading interests (High school, Ages 15–18)

Stage 5: Reading to do, to learn, to enjoy; developing and modifying one's view of the world through reading; increasing efficiency of reading for career purposes; increasing breadth and depth of reading experiences and tastes (College/career, Age 18 and above)

Trends in the Study of Reading

In recent years the study of reading has changed in significant ways. Scholars have tended to change the focus of their research and analysis, so that fewer studies of learning and teaching are based in laboratory settings where conditions are carefully controlled, and more in real schools and classrooms. Classroom teachers have joined the ranks of scholars and researchers who present their findings at professional conferences and in professional journals. Ethnographic research (investigations that take place in natural, rather than contrived, settings) is increasing.

A second change is that the way educators think and talk about differences among learners has changed substantially and is continuing to change. Some years ago, it was customary to concentrate our attention on learning *deficits*. Scholars and specialists classified learners in terms of those who did, or did not, exhibit problems; different kinds of problems were named, studied, and described. When learners differed, educators sought to identify the deficit that set one group apart, and to look for methods of instruction that would correct or remediate the deficiency. Then educators began to move away from the deficit model, and to think instead in terms of *differences*. Diversity among students is the basis for enriched learning and cooperation; we do not need to strive to make everyone the same.

A further progression, beyond the model of viewing people in terms of their differences, has been to consider their *similarities*. While respecting and enjoying ways in which people and groups are unique, educators are increasingly giving attention to the many ways in which people are all similar. One of many examples of this similarities model is *Growing up literate: Learning from inner-city families*, a book by Denny Taylor and Catherine Dorsey-Gaines (1988). The authors describe their longitudinal study of African-American inner city children who, in conditions of terrible poverty, were enthusiastic, well-developing readers. Research studies such as theirs forcibly call attention to the ways in which developmental sameness—the common human ability to learn and enjoy learning—often

overrides even such destructive differences as harmful environmental conditions.

Nancy Lee and Judith Neal stress the importance of thinking in terms of students' *strengths and needs* (rather than strengths and weaknesses)—a theme stressed throughout this text. They assert that assistance for students who have special needs in reading should begin with an emphasis on their strengths. Students must be aware of the strengths, including life experiences, that they bring to the reading process. Like many other scholars, Lee and Neal urge making reading aloud by teachers a regular feature of classroom instruction, and linking writing and reading. They also advocate encouraging students to reread familiar favorite material.

> Just as students do not outgrow having teachers read aloud to them daily, so they do not outgrow the need for reexperiencing familiar tasks. If the task was once difficult but the student has mastered it, each repetition is a reinforcement of the initial success. Also, if the story was exciting the first time, it will continue to be so. Teachers may worry too much about rereading being boring. Our experience has been that students more likely will claim 'this is boring,' when they cannot perform the planned task. (Lee & Neal, 1992/1993, p. 281)

Thus the study of reading and learning has tended to shift in settings, so that scholars now observe real classroom learning. Also, the way people view one another is moving beyond both a deficit model and a difference model toward a focus on important similarities and shared strengths. Yet another change in reading scholarship is an increasing interest in thinking about well-developing reading, and analyzing what good readers do as they read.

The Characteristics of Capable Readers

David Brown and L. D. Briggs (1989) are among the scholars who have described the characteristics of skillful, strategic readers. As reading development progresses, capable readers manifest the ability to read strategically in different ways. They realize when they do not understand what they are reading, and they develop a number of strategies, such as rereading text and checking the meaning of unknown terms, that help them understand. They become able to read independently for many purposes: for pleasure, to get information, to learn about their environment, and to accomplish self-chosen and assigned tasks. They enjoy reading, and because of their enjoyment, they continue to grow as readers. It is important to note that even very young children may possess these characteristics. Preschoolers who have the advantage of many experiences with books choose which stories to hear at bedtime and which books to pack when the family is taking a trip. They notice when the person reading to them has skipped a page in a familiar story book. They ask questions about pictures and text. They love books. Parents' accounts of their young children's emerging literacy often make delightful reading: Two such articles from professional journals are "'Make way for applesauce': The literate world of a three-year-old" by Margaret Voss (1988) and "'Possibilities, Daddy! I think it says possibilities!'" by Lester Laminack (1990).

Metacognition

As we read for different purposes, we vary the way we read. As reading development progresses, we become able to use metacognition—to think about reading and to make adjustments that help us comprehend—although, of course, few readers are familiar with the word *metacognition*, nor do they need to be. Metacognition is, however, a useful concept for teachers to be aware of. The idea of examining thought processes during reading is not a new one; for example, an article published in 1917 by the psychologist Edward L. Thorndike on "Reading as reasoning: A study of mistakes in paragraph reading," remains interesting and informative many decades later. Among other aspects of what is now called metacognition, Thorndike (1917, p. 331) addressed the issue of reading without understanding and without realizing the failure to understand: "It appears likely also that a pupil may read fluently and feel that the series of words are arousing appropriate thoughts without really understanding the paragraph."

The term *metacognition* was originated by the Piagetian scholar John Flavell, by combining a Greek prefix, *meta*, meaning *beyond*, and a Latin

verb, *cognoscere*, meaning *to think*. Flavell defined metacognition as "one's knowledge concerning one's own cognitive processes and products or anything related to them.... Metacognition refers... to the active monitoring of [information processing activities] in relation to the cognitive objects or data on which they bear, usually in the service of some concrete goal or objective" (Flavell, 1976, p. 232).

Another way to state this idea is that metacognition is "reportable, conscious awareness about cognitive aspects of thinking" (Jacobs & Paris, 1987, p. 258).

Aspects of metacognition are "planning, regulating, evaluating, summarizing, questioning, clarifying and predicting" (Spires, 1990, pp. 154–155). In an analysis of many studies assessing the effectiveness of metacognitive strategies (Haller, Child, & Walberg, 1988) those that appeared most useful, particularly for students in middle school and beyond, were the ability to notice when text information seems puzzling or inconsistent, and the habit of raising questions about the text during reading. Readers vary in the metacognitive strategies they use, and it appears likely that reading instruction that places a heavy stress on accuracy in pronouncing words and correctness in producing answers to questions may inhibit students' natural tendency to make sense of what they read. In reporting results of a study comparing criteria used by successful and struggling readers in judging whether they were understanding text, Beth Davey (1988, p. 410) notes that "the criterion for an acceptable answer for poor readers may [be] correctness according to what the text said, [but] for good readers correctness may [be] judged more on the basis of a reasonable, meaningful solution."

The term *self-regulated learning* refers to one aspect of metacognition. In one of her ethnographic classroom studies, Lyn Corno observed fifth graders working in groups over many days, and recorded what they said and did. She found that some students were able to engage in reading, writing, and conversation while keeping themselves, and others, task-focused. "Students who can protect their intentions to learn in school from competing goals or interests, as well as distracting stimuli," she writes, "are likely to accomplish school tasks adequately even if their grades fall short of perfect" (Corno, 1986, p. 333). The term *self-regulated learning* carries an implied caution to teachers against imposing rigid rules for learning and studying.

◼◼ Supporting Students

In successful content area classrooms, students acquire content knowledge, and also develop as readers and as writers. Michael C. McKenna and Richard D. Robinson (1990, p. 184) define content literacy as "the ability to use reading and writing for the acquisition of new content in a given discipline. Such ability includes three principal cognitive components: general literacy skills, content-specific literacy skills (such as map reading in the social studies), and prior knowledge of content."

Thus, people who are literate in a content area can read materials written at an appropriate level and have an understanding of how written materials in that content area are typically presented. (In science, for example, this would mean being able to read not only text but graphs, charts, picture captions, descriptions of experiments, and so on). What is most important is that people who are literate in a content area are able to develop further: to read and hear new information and relate it to prior knowledge. They are prepared to learn more. They are interested in learning more.

When teaching and learning in the content areas are progressing well, reading ability develops in tandem with content area knowledge. As McKenna and Robinson put it, "Teaching content automatically makes students more content literate." Reading and writing develop when the process of learning is natural and holistic. It is much easier to read material when we already have some familiarity with the terms, concepts, and style than to read material packed with terms we have not seen or heard before, focused on unfamiliar concepts, and presented in a style that is very different from material we are used to reading.

Student Factors that Affect Learning

In earlier chapters, the text factors that can affect students' learning have been discussed. It is important also for teachers to be aware of the many characteristics of students themselves that can affect students' learning. Some factors are helpful; others

interfere with learning. Teachers should build upon those factors that help, and find ways to remedy, work around, or ameliorate factors that are harmful.

Student factors that affect students' learning positively in schools include an extensive vocabulary, conceptual experiences that provide a strong knowledge base for future learning, affective experiences that provide a sound sense of self-esteem, a relationship of mutual respect between school and home, support and approval from respected adults, good health and nutrition, and a safe and happy environment at home and at school. Teachers can build on and develop each of these areas of strength.

Student factors that affect students' learning negatively are the opposite of the positive factors: limited vocabulary, lack of prior experience related to topics of study, antagonism between school and home, lack of support from respected adults, poor health and nutrition, and unsafe and unhappy conditions either at home, at school, or in both settings. Any and all of these difficulties that students face can be altered for the better by skillful, caring classroom teachers. Teachers can change the effects of these factors on their students' lives by creating language-rich classrooms in which students' vocabularies expand naturally, and by using teaching strategies that create a shared background of knowledge and experience for learning. Teachers can be among the caring, supportive, respect-worthy adults that students need. Teachers can contribute to good relationships between school and home by consistently showing respect for students' families, homes, and communities and talking about them in ways they would want their own families to be treated. Teachers can, if necessary, plan to have snacktime as part of a regular learning activity (read-aloud time, or cooperative learning time, or Themed Reading, or discussion) and make sure they have inexpensive, nutritious snacks available that students can share. Teachers can make their classrooms good learning places and work as professionals and citizens toward improving the quality of life in all schools and communities.

Alterable Variables

One of many contributions the psychologist Benjamin Bloom has made to education is the concept of alterable variables (Bloom, 1981). Factors that affect learning are variables. Each can vary in kind or extent from person to person and across time. As an example, consider prior knowledge (knowledge a student has about a topic before it is studied in school) as a variable. In a class about to begin the study of solar and lunar eclipses, the amount and kind of relevant knowledge that each student has before the teacher introduces the topic will be quite different. There may be students who have been interested in astronomy for a long time; some may have done independent reading, and perhaps some have gone with their families to programs at a planetarium. Their prior knowledge of this topic is likely to be extensive. For other students, the topic will be quite new; terms and concepts will be unfamiliar, and they may not be particularly interested in learning more. So the amount of prior knowledge varies from student to student. Prior knowledge also varies from topic to topic and across time, for each individual. Suppose as the teacher provides instruction about eclipses, students read widely, visit a planetarium, and work in cooperative groups to create models that illustrate different kinds of eclipses. Several years later a student who had limited prior knowledge when first studying the topic may recall a great deal, and now can bring substantial prior knowledge to learning more about the topic at a more advanced level.

Teachers are well aware of how certain variables affect learning, but Bloom's important caution is that we should distinguish between what we can change (alterable variables) and what we can not (fixed, or unalterable, variables; also called static variables) and concentrate our attention on what can be altered. No one can change the past, so it is beyond our power to affect how much knowledge each student has about a topic before we begin to teach about it. But for each fixed variable, there is a related alterable variable. For each factor affecting learning that we cannot change, it is possible to find a related feature of the learning environment that we *can* affect. Lack of prior experience related to topics of study can be remedied through thoughtful, lively instruction. Learning to read and reading to learn are not confined to a few grades in school. At every age, every person should have opportunities to grow as a reader. Students who have not yet been

successful can become successful, and they are more likely to develop as readers when they work in classrooms that provide many occasions for interesting, purposeful language use, that are welcoming and supportive, and in which they have genuine reasons to feel successful and respected.

Teacher Support Through Scaffolding

An important educational concept, scaffolding, provides a way of thinking about effective teacher support for students' learning. A scaffold is a temporary structure that workers stand on during the construction of a building. In teaching and learning, scaffolding has the same characteristics: The process provides support for students as they are learning (constructing their knowledge), and the support is temporary, because as sound learning occurs, students will not need their teachers' support at that point. (The scaffolding process can continue, however, as new learning occurs.) The term was originated by the American scholar, Jerome Bruner (1975, p. 12) to describe the support parents give to infants in the language learning process.

Lev Vygotsky noted that mental development does not consist of a series of leaps from incapability to capability, but that there always exists an area of potential learning immediately beyond our current level of independent functioning. In this area, we can work and accomplish if we are supported by the assistance of someone more capable. Vygotsky called this area (the learning zone between what we can do independently now and what we will be able to do independently later if we continue to develop) the zone of proximal development, defining it as

> the distance between the actual level as determined by independent problem solving and the level of potential development as determined through problem solving under adult guidance or in collaboration with more capable peers. (Vygotsky, 1978, p. 76)

Scaffolding suggests a progression, with support provided by adults and by peers—classmates, friends, and siblings—who have more fully developed ability. A form of peer support called reciprocal teaching, developed by Annemarie Palincsar and Ann Brown (1984) is based on the concept of scaffolding.

Teachers should not, however, think of scaffolding in terms of a vertical, linear progression in development, giving support to a learner who moves steadily up, up, up as more and more is mastered. Successful scaffolding respects the learner's interests and pace (Meyer, 1993), and the pace will vary as learners explore new learning in their own ways. Anne Haas Dyson describes a situation when her goal was to encourage a kindergartner to create a story, while the child was absorbed in a newfound ability to write letters of the alphabet. What had meaning for the child, giving her pleasure in her own learning prowess, was not valued by the adult who focused on a different conception of meaning-making. Dyson suggests that the metaphor of weaving should be added to our ideas about scaffolding:

> Whereas scaffolding is a vertical metaphor, one that represents how those who are more skillful support children's progress within one activity, weaving adds a horizontal dimension. It suggests that children's progress in any one activity is supported by their experiences in varied activities.

A major purpose for scaffolding, in a school setting, is to insure a match between students and text. Teachers adept at scaffolding can enable their students to use high-level thinking, to recall information effectively, and to link known and new ideas productively, as the example shown in Figure 6–2 of a conversation between an English as a Second Language (ESL) teacher and two of her students demonstrates (Lim & Watson, 1993). The class in which the conversation occurred was part of a summer school program for Potentially English Proficient (PEP) second and third graders, native speakers of Cambodian, Korean, Chinese, Taiwanese, or Arabic languages, who had lived in the United States for periods ranging from one month to two years. All the children were actively involved in reading, writing, and working together, as the excerpt demonstrates.

The teacher demonstrates many aspects of good content area teaching even in this brief moment and the effects her teaching has, and has had, on her children's learning. Notice that the conversation begins as a result of the teacher's reading aloud, perhaps just to Labna (with Sophea joining the conversation later), perhaps to both children, perhaps to a small group where the others have not joined in the conversation at this point. Ask yourself what the book the teacher has chosen to read (or to have available for children to choose) tells us about the teacher and about the students. Notice that the book is treated, by children and by the teacher, as a participant in the conversation—what Labna says first is a response *to*

FIGURE 6–2   *An Example of Scaffolding*

Teacher: (*reads the text*) Bats are the only animals in the world that have wings and fur. Many animals have fur, but they do not have wings.

Labna: Birds have wings and fur, too.

Teacher: Oh! A good question. Birds have something soft on their skin. Let's go to page 2 and find out. (*reads the text*) Birds have wings, but they have feathers instead of fur. Does that answer your question, Labna?

Labna: Feathers?

Sophea: Maybe that's a different kind of fur.

Teacher: Sophea is right. There is some difference between birds and bats. Birds have feathers and bats have fur.

Sophea: Bats are mammal.

Teacher: Thank you, Sophea, for saying that. Bats are mammal, and birds are oviparous. Do you remember we talked about oviparity?

Labna: Yeah. So only bats have wings and fur.

the book. Notice, as the teacher responds three times to the children, how she begins: "Oh! A good question. …Sophea is right. …Thank you, Sophea, for saying that.

Matthew Effects in Learning

Although good content area teaching builds reading ability, some students do not experience good teaching, and some come to a school setting with burdens that make them extremely difficult to reach and teach. Students who read well can learn from their textbooks even in classrooms where teachers provide little useful instruction. Their learning will not be as thorough, or as enjoyable, as it would have been with the support of an energetic teacher, knowledgeable about both subject matter and ways to teach it, but they do have the capacity to learn from their reading. However, in classrooms where teaching is defined as assigning students to look up words in dictionaries, read textbooks, write answers to questions, and take tests, students who have not yet learned to read well will neither develop as readers nor will they learn content information. The reading scholar Keith Stanovich (1986, 1993/1994) has used the term *Matthew effects* to alert educators to the serious problem that occurs when students do not become capable readers in the primary grades and when teachers in later grades do not intervene to help them learn subject matter information.

The term is taken from the parable of the talents, given in the book of Matthew in the Bible. According to the parable, people who have, will receive more; people who have not, will have even what they have taken away. However harsh this sounds, it occurs in education. When children do not learn to read successfully in the early grades, they do not simply remain a step behind their classmates who read well; they fall farther and farther behind unless their teachers intervene to help them. Without teacher intervention students who cannot read well cannot learn science, social studies, math and other school subjects—not because they are incapable of understanding information in these fields—but because they cannot read their textbooks.

The reference to the parable of the talents, by the scholars who chose the term "Matthew effects," was meant to be a warning to teachers of the importance of our intervention, so that the harsh ending of the parable need not occur for students. Skillful, friendly teacher intervention is essential. Content area information must be presented in a variety of ways, so that students' learning is not solely dependent on their ability to read. When there is capable teacher intervention, students can acquire the subject matter information from hearing about it and discussing it, and they are simultaneously helped to develop as readers because their teacher is building the text vocabulary and concepts into their knowledge base. When content area teachers create a congenial classroom environment in which their students' attention is focused on learning content information through a variety of interesting, do-able activities, both content learning and reading ability are likely to increase. (And if it happens that some students learn the content but do not develop as readers, those students are still better off than they would have been in a textbook-bound classroom where their inability to read the textbook deprived them of the content knowledge.)

■■ Enriching Classrooms With Content
■■ Area Language

Reading is language-based. The importance of familiarity with spoken language in learning to read text written in that language can be illustrated by thinking about what it is like to learn a language different from our own. Consider the excerpt shown in Figure 6–3. We are able to identify the language used there on the basis of one familiar word because we are able to read in English. Because we can read English and because the same alphabet is used in writing the Hawaiian language, we will be able to decode the text to translate the written words into speech sounds. However, unless we speak Hawaiian or have much experience in listening to the language, our reading aloud of the text will sound quite different from the same passage said by even a young child who speaks Hawaiian. The child will pronounce the words accurately; the sentences will flow rapidly, and be correctly phrased. The child will also understand the passage. Even though

FIGURE 6–3   Reading Challenge

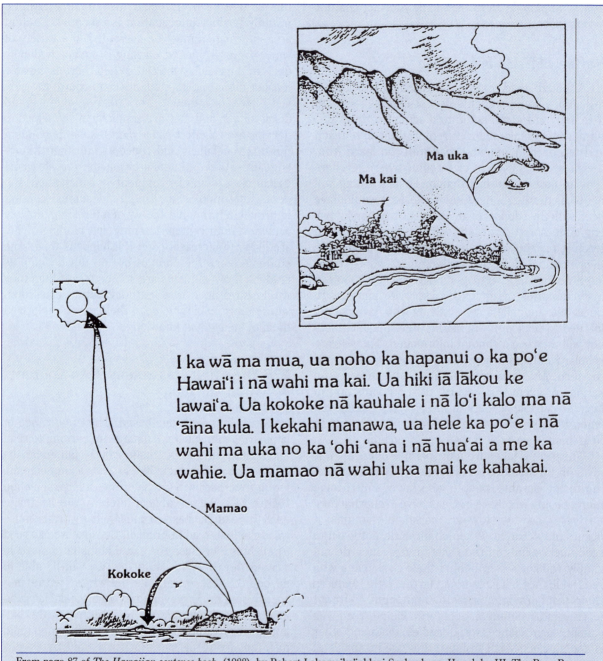

I ka wā ma mua, ua noho ka hapanui o ka poʻe Hawaiʻi i nā wahi ma kai. Ua hiki iā lākou ke lawaiʻa. Ua kokoke nā kauhale i nā loʻi kalo ma nā ʻāina kula. I kekahi manawa, ua hele ka poʻe i nā wahi ma uka no ka ʻohi ʻana i nā huaʻai a me ka wahie. Ua mamao nā wahi uka mai ke kahakai.

From page 87 of *The Hawaiian sentence book.* (1988), by Robert Lokomaikaʻioklani Snakenberg. Honolulu, HI: The Bess Press. Used by permission of The Bess Press.

those of us who do not speak Hawaiian will be able to deduce something about the topic from the picture clues, we will not understand the text and will only be able to guess at the meaning of the words in the labeled pictures. (A translation of the passage in Fig. 6–3 can be found in the Solutions section at the back of this book.)

Suppose the child cannot read yet. We have an important advantage, because we can. We can decode the written symbols. But the child's advantage is greater than ours because every one of the printed words is in the child's listening vocabulary, speaking vocabulary, and conceptual vocabulary. The words have been heard and spoken over and over in daily life; their meanings are thoroughly understood. The ideas presented in the passage are readily understandable because the language is familiar and the meaning of the technical terms (the words and phrases that express important concepts) is known. It is likely that the child will be able to learn to read this and other passages with more ease than we will.

What relevance does this knowledge about reading have for content area teachers? It is a reminder that we can help our students read their textbooks if we establish classrooms that are rich in content area language. Classrooms are not silent places—even in barren environments where student talk is discouraged, the teacher speaks. But the classrooms of skillful teachers are characterized not only by extensive language use, but by the content focus of the language. The teacher can contrast three possible focuses of attention in classrooms: behavior, procedure, and content. In some classrooms, talk is primarily about behavior ("Bea, sit down and be quiet; Chavier, if you do that again, I'll send you to the office). Some teachers talk primarily about procedures ("Be sure to write your name at the top of the paper, Pris"; "Ed, please pass out the papers"; "You're all going to need to line up single file to go to art class; let's make a good straight line"). The most adept teachers, however, create classrooms where language is focused on content.

In classrooms where language is content-focused, teachers talk primarily about what is being studied and learned, and plan instruction that gives students many opportunities to talk, read, and write about content. Most of the text that students see displayed on walls and chalkboards does not consist of directions or lists of rules (or lists of the names of students who have broken the rules); instead students see a variety of text and graphics that focus on content, producing "convivial and efficient educational environments" (Gaskins, Anderson, Pressley, Cunicelli, & Satlow, 1993, p. 301). Students are helped to learn subject matter content, and they are also helped to read their textbooks because the textbook language becomes part of their listening, speaking, and conceptual vocabularies.

■■ Twelve Reading Strategies for ■■ Content Area Learning

Besides the wealth of useful content area teaching strategies for teachers to choose from, the professional literature in education includes an even more extensive array of strategies intended to develop reading ability. Instructional methods recommended in this text typically have a double focus: teach content; enhance language. Appropriately, increasing content area learning is the paramount purpose for using the strategy; reading and language development is secondary.

In this chapter, however, the strategies discussed are those that have very close ties to reading instruction, but are designed, or readily adaptable, for use in content area teaching. The twelve strategies described are Language Experience Approach (LEA), cloze (including manipulable cloze), Experience-Text-Relationship, PreReading Plan (PReP), the Vocabulary Self-Collection Strategy, the Guided Writing Procedure, Think-Aloud, Directed Reading-Thinking Activity (DR-TA), Essential Reading, Question-Answer Relationships (QAR), minilessons, For Your Information (FYI), and Reading and More Reading—an overview of methods to engage students in learning through reading, and thus to foster reading development. That section reviews the interrelationships between reading to learn and other reading purposes: developing as readers, reading to accomplish a task, and reading for enjoyment.

Reading: A Language-Based Process

Two teaching strategies that use students' own language ability to give them practice in reading are the Language Experience Approach, which uses student-dictated text as reading material, thus ensuring that the vocabulary used and the ideas presented in the text are familiar to the reader; and cloze, in which students read and reread as they reconstruct a short text passage.

Language Experience Approach (LEA). The Language Experience Approach, or LEA (Lee & VanAllen, 1963; Rigg, 1989; Stauffer, 1970), has long been used as a method of teaching reading in situations in which there is not a good match between learners and traditional reading materials (or where formal reading materials are not available). The method is based on the recognition of the strong effect of prior knowledge and topic interest on the ability to read. The principles of LEA are expressed in a series of four statements that empower the learner: What I can think about, I can talk about. What I can talk about, I can write, or the teacher can write for me. What I can write, I can read. What I can read, I can share with others.

In the LEA process, students dictate an experience story (a factual account of a personal experience that is interesting and important to them). The teacher records the experience story, using standard spelling, but using the individual student's patterns of usage. For example, if the student says, "Me and my frien' wen' on a trip" the teacher writes "Me and my friend went on a trip." The teacher then asks the student to read the story, prompting with words or phrases when necessary. Because the written text is about the student's own experience, and because the student has just dictated the story, the text is easy for the student to read, in the style of reading used by young learners who become able to repeat familiar books by reconstructing a text from memory as they look at the pages. Students doing their first readings of an LEA text are using memory (of what they have said) and prior knowledge (of their own experience). As they do this kind of reading, they are visually following the written text and beginning to match words in their speaking and conceptual vocabularies with those words in written

form. The student reads the LEA story several times during that lesson, takes a copy home, and reads the story again at the beginning of the next lesson. At each session, a new Language Experience story is prepared in the same fashion: student dictates; teacher records. The collected stories become the student's first source of reading material; as the student's reading vocabulary expands and reading development progresses, additional reading is done from self-chosen and teacher-selected materials.

Although LEA traditionally has been used for one-to-one teaching, it can be adapted for small group or whole class use. Sidney Sharp (1989) and Mary Heller (1988) are among practitioners who have offered suggestions for combining LEA and content area instruction. In his work with middle school students, Sharp read aloud to them from their content area text assignments, used graphic illustrations, and listed and explained technical vocabulary. Then students were asked to talk about what they'd learned about the topic, using the list of technical terms as a stimulus, while the teacher typed their ideas on the computer. This constituted the group's Language Experience story. Later each student was given a copy of this LEA passage, which was then used for reading material. Eventually students worked cooperatively to type their own informational text using the computer.

Inclusion of LEA activities can enhance content area learning. In preschool and primary grades some of the topics for Daily Journal writing (Strickland and Morrow, 1990) can be related to content area curriculum. In later grades, group-prepared LEA text on content area topics can be used in newsletters sent home to parents or to provide thank-you letters to guest speakers that demonstrate what the students have learned. Weekly LEA narratives about activities and accomplishments, prepared by the whole class or by cooperative groups, could be a short culminating activity each week, and serve as documentary logs for the class, or for each group, of progress throughout a semester or a year. A group LEA passage can serve as an alternative to, or a preparation for, individual writing about a topic.

Cloze. A cloze passage is a piece of text from which words have been omitted; the challenge is to use clues from the passage to reconstruct a meaningful whole. In a Focused Cloze passage, omitted words relate to the topic of the passage. An alphabetical list of the omitted words is provided along with the cloze passage, and the task is to place the words correctly to complete an accurate passage. (Focused Cloze is described in Chapter Three, as a method of teaching technical vocabulary.)

In a standard cloze passage, the omitted words are not specially chosen; instead every *n*th word is taken out. (*N* may be 5, 6, 7, 8, 9 or 10). First and last sentences of the passages are left intact: No words are omitted from these two sentences, so that readers can use the sentences for context, as they think about what words to use to complete the passage. The boxed section of text below is an example of a standard cloze passage. (The passage has 156 words, and every fifth word is omitted. The length of cloze passages, and the frequency of omissions will vary based on teachers' decisions about their students' ability to solve cloze passages, and the time they plan to allot for students' to work together on the task. Cloze passages in which every fifth word is omitted are the hardest to solve and those in which every tenth word is omitted are the easiest, because the more words omitted, the smaller the amount of context there is.)

Reading is a language-based process, and human beings are good at learning language. Effective teachers create language-rich _____ classrooms, where books, displays, _____ and learning activities are _____ to topics being studied. _____ content teachers focus classroom _____ on content, rather than _____ directions about what to _____ and warnings about how _____ behave. Students in such _____ are immersed in the _____ they will encounter in _____ , and this helps them _____ .

    It's easier to read _____ that is about familiar, _____ topics. We acquire new _____ by linking it to _____ we already know. Creating _____ shared knowledge base for _____ about topics they are _____ sparks interest and helps _____ read text that is _____ about these topics. In the process of building this

---

shared knowledge base, students who are already knowledgeable about topics will have opportunities to contribute ideas and information, as well as to extend their own understanding.

Notice that the cloze passage is a connected piece of text. (Workbook or test exercises consisting of a series of unrelated sentences in which students are to "fill in the blanks" are not cloze; their completion requires memory, or looking back at the text, but does not give students practice in using their understanding of language to create meaning.) Notice also that all the blanks in the passage are the same length, so finding the words to fill them depends on an understanding of meaning and grammar; word length is not a clue. In this passage, semantic (meaning-related) clues tell us that the completed passage will make a statement about reading in content area classrooms. Syntactic (grammar-related) clues tell us that the missing word in the second blank is probably a plural noun.

Cloze exercises may be based on text students have not read before, or on text they have read. In either case, cloze presents a challenge. (Those of you who are reading this chapter will have read earlier the passage that is the basis for the cloze shown above. Except for people with eidetic memory—people who can recall visually exactly what they have read in every detail—deciding on words to complete the passage will still require thought.) Note that students working on a cloze passage should not have access to the text on which the cloze is based; if they did, completing the cloze would simply consist of copying words into blanks, and would not require students to think about the meaning of the passage. Completing a cloze passage accurately involves rereading short sections of it several times. The rereading is brief and purposeful, so it is not burdensome. In fact, students do not think of it as a form of rereading. Cloze is a particularly useful learning activity when students complete a passage in pairs or cooperative groups, because they then have the opportunity to talk about the passage, and justify the reasons for their word choices (Jacobson, 1990a). When cloze is used instructionally, it is best to consider a passage well-completed if it makes sense, rather than expecting that students will always use the author's exact wording.

FIGURE 6–4 Example of a Manipulable Cloze Activity

> Birds have _____ and feathers. They build_____ from grass and _____ . They lay_____ in their nests, and the eggs hatch into_____ , called fledglings. Fledgling birds live in the nest while they are growing their _____ . They eat _____ and _____ that the parent birds bring them. When the _____ have grown large enough, they leave the nest and learn to fly.

One interesting variation of cloze, particularly suitable for early readers, is manipulable cloze. This is a cloze passage presented in such a way that words to go in the blanks can be moved around physically, making it possible for different variations of a passage to be created easily, and easily changed. If such a passage is cleverly constructed, changing the words around can create a passage that is silly—not a meaningless jumble of words, but a grammatically correct statement that readers can see makes silly statements, and can then change, by removing and moving words, to create a sensible message. Manipulable cloze is an effective reading and learning strategy for primary students. It can be presented on a bulletin board, providing a learning—focused display that young readers find challenging and amusing. Working in pairs or groups, children can create a sensible passage, and then change it to make it silly for the next group to read before they change it to be sensible again.

A practical way to assemble a manipulable cloze activity is to find or write a short passage in which many words are the same part of speech. (Nouns usually work best.) After choosing the words to take out, try fitting them back into the passage to see whether the passage will provide an appropriate challenge. Then prepare the passage on heavy paper, leaving equal-length spaces where words have been omitted, and print the missing words on separate cards. Put a square of velcro on each blank, and back each card with velcro. Put the word cards in an envelope and mount it beside the cloze passage.

A sensible completion of the passage, shown in Figure 6–4, is

> Birds have *wings* and feathers. They build *nests* from grass and *twigs*. They lay *eggs* in their nests, and the eggs hatch into *baby birds*, called fledglings. Fledgling birds live in the nest while they are growing their *feathers*. They eat *worms* and *insects* that the parent birds bring them. When the *fledglings* have grown large enough, they leave the nest and learn to fly.

(Remember that the missing words are available on cards for students to see and to try out in different blanks.) Because all the terms chosen for omission are syntactically the same (all are plural nouns) there are many possible ways to make the passage grammatically sound, but silly; for example,

> Birds have *worms* and *feathers*. They build *baby birds* from grass and *fledglings*. They lay *feathers* in their nests, and the eggs hatch into *insects*, called fledglings. Fledgling birds live in the nest while they are growing their *twigs*. They eat *nests* and *feathers* that the parent birds bring them. When the *eggs* have grown large enough, they leave the nest and learn to fly.

Reading About Familiar, Interesting Topics

Two strategies that relate students' experiences to concepts presented in text, and thus help to arouse students' interest in text topics, are the Experience-Text-Relationship method, designed to create links between the prior experience of a particular group of readers and topics presented in their texts, and PreReading Plan (PReP), intended to elicit students' relevant prior knowledge about a topic. In the Experience-Text-Relationship strategy, teachers' knowledge of content topics and of their own students is the essential factor. In the PReP strategy, the aim is to give students practice in drawing upon their own prior knowledge. Note that both strategies are based on the recognition that all students do have knowledge that, with active teacher intervention, they can relate to new learning. Prior knowledge is particularly necessary if students are to draw inferences from their reading and to transfer text learning to other situations. The effective linking of the known and the new enables students to move beyond a literal approach to text. Of the two strategies, ETR is the more powerful, because students and teacher work with the text over a period of time, whereas PReP, as its name suggests, is used only in preparation for reading.

Experience-Text-Relationship (ETR).   The process of reading requires the reader to make connections between prior knowledge and the information given in the text. When readers have little or no knowledge that they can (independently) relate to the text, or when their experiences differ substantially from the topics or events described in the text, it is difficult for them to read with understanding. Reading for learning new information can be baffling unless we find similarities between what we encounter and what is already a part of our experience.

Kathryn Au, realizing that many children do not have much in common with the characters in reading textbooks, devised a strategy she called Experience-Text-Relationship (Au, 1979, 1980; Reyes & Molner, 1991). ETR is a three-step method in which the teacher first leads a discussion about students' experiences related to a central concept in the text to be read. In the next step, text reading and discussion are alternated, as the teacher guides students to understand text events. Finally, the teacher leads a discussion in which the relationship between text concepts and students' experience is made explicit. The process extends over several days. Au has also used the strategy in content area reading, renaming it the Concept-Text-Application (CTA) approach (Wong and Au, 1985); the major

difference between CTA and ETR is the use of expository rather than narrative text. Because the Experience-Text-Relationship name conveys more information about the process used, ETR seems the more useful strategy title.

Although ETR was devised for use with a minority population, it is adaptable for all students. Its effective use is a prime example of teacher intervention, because the method depends on an individual teacher's understanding of a particular group of students, and skill in creating links between those students' experiences and the concepts in a text. Social studies and history topics provide a good opportunity for the use of ETR, because students are often reading about topics that are disparate from their experience in time, in place, and in cultural situations.

Because in most teaching situations our students are necessarily younger than teachers are, historical events that have deep meaning because they occurred within our lifetimes, such as the Vietnam War or the tearing down of the Berlin Wall, can often be brought to life by personal recollections of the time. For other historical events, teachers' own reading and adult understanding can enable them to interpret, for example, the civil rights struggles of the 1950s or the experiences of traveling and communicating in times before modern technology was invented and produced. ETR is useful across the span of grades and ages; the strategy does not need to be altered across grade levels because the topics to be learned vary, and because teachers match their conversational style to that of their students. As Harold Herber (1978, p. 17) pointed out,

> Reading a content area subject primarily is a means through which students encounter and deal with *new* knowledge and *new* ideas. If they are not properly prepared for the reading and are not guided through it, the students will be frustrated by this newness. Students should not be expected to read such new material independently.

PReP.   Judith Langer devised the PReP strategy (Barclay, 1990; Langer, 1981, 1983–1984) as a way to prepare students for learning from their reading. PReP is a three-step process. First, readers identify one or more terms that are central to the text and brainstorm a list of related ideas, asking themselves the question "What comes to mind when I think about...?" Next, readers analyze these first impressions, and consider how each idea relates to the text-based terms. At this point, students may evaluate their ideas and identify those that are, in Langer's terms, "well-formed"—those that form a useful link between their own knowledge and the text-based terms. In the third step, the teacher may guide students to add to, and revise, their ideas, or students may do this independently. The purpose of using the PReP strategy to guide students' reading is to give them practice in one aspect of strategic reading: linking prior knowledge to what is read.

Listening, Speaking, and Conceptual Vocabularies

It is easier to read words that one knows than words one does not. But what does it mean to know the meaning of a word? Words are known in different ways. Let's consider *sun*. The word *sun* probably enters a child's listening vocabulary very early, perhaps from hearing storybooks read aloud beginning in infancy, surely from hearing family members talking about the weather. Looking at pictures in books, the word becomes more than a sound that is heard; it takes on meaning (and this happens through life experiences too, not just books). The child begins to develop a concept of *sun*, perhaps thinking of it as a round yellow shape because that's how it's pictured. It is likely the word will soon enter the child's speaking vocabulary, and the concept will expand: "seen in the daytime but not at night," "gives light," "far away." It is a word that the child will learn to read and write early, because it's short and phonetically regular, and has many rhymes, and is an interesting part of the child's world. Then the word sun is in the child's listening, speaking, reading, and writing vocabularies, and that will not change. However, the ideas about the sun in the conceptual vocabulary, as that person studies and learns more, will change and grow. It is primarily the conceptual vocabulary that content teachers should work to develop.

Several of the strategies described in this chapter, especially LEA, cloze, and wide reading, are excellent strategies for vocabulary development. Teachers who

use LEA are especially aware that words that would seem quite difficult to read, because of their length or complexity, are easily read when the reader has an immediate interest in them. (For example, *hurricane* is an easy word for first graders to learn if the weather bureau is forecasting a hurricane near their homes.) The Vocabulary Self-Selection strategy is focused entirely on words that are important to students. The teacher gets to select a word, too.

Vocabulary Self-Collection Strategy. Martha Rapp-Haggard Ruddell (Haggard, 1982, 1986) is the creator of the Vocabulary Self-Collection Strategy (VSS). The process begins with each member of the class, including the teacher, bringing to class a word chosen because "this is a word the class should learn." When VSS is used in content area classes, the words may be chosen from the textbook or related trade books, or from conversation about content area topics. That is, the words may come from what students have read, or what they have heard. In class, students call out their words and the teacher lists them on chartpaper or chalkboard, and students provide, discuss, and elaborate upon, definitions for their words and words suggested by others. The class agrees upon a predetermined number of words that everyone is to learn. These words may be recorded in vocabulary notebooks by the students, or the class may have discussions in which it is everyone's aim to use the words purposefully and correctly. Alternatively, VSS can be used as one weekly assignment for cooperative groups. Each student in the group is expected to propose a word or term related to the current topic of study and to justify its importance to the rest of the group. Group members then discuss and elaborate on definitions, consulting with the teacher if they wish. The group then decides on a way to present their chosen words to the class later in the week. The process of choosing words for everyone to learn should not become competitive. This can be avoided by allowing for individualization of lists, so that everyone learns the agreed upon words plus their own choices.

Writing and Reading

In a print-rich classroom environment, writing and reading can develop successfully together. But

*S*chool can be a caring place, a place where all students come to value and enjoy learning. In school, all students can explore, experience a print-rich environment, and learn together as discussed in Chapter One.

*G*ood teachers are continually learning and devising ways to intervene to help their students learn. Chapters Two, Three, and Four illustrate this point.

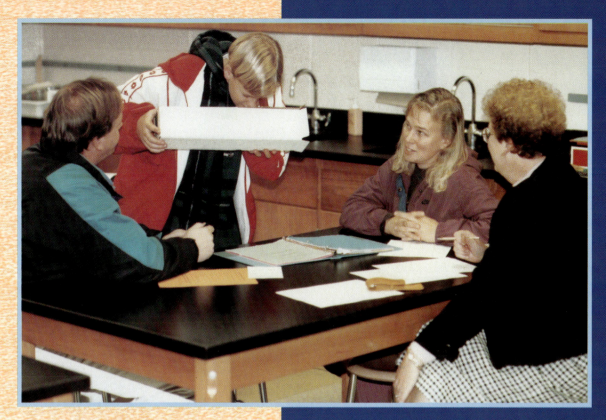

*S*tudent-led conferences (discussed in Chapter Nine) are an innovative method for conducting school-home conferences. Students themselves conduct the conference, explaining to their parents their goals and progress, and showing samples of their work. As many as six conferences can be held simultaneously in separate centers set up in the classroom. This method of school-home communication can accomplish many useful purposes: easing the conference burden for teachers and adding to their pride in students' accomplishments, increasing the percentage of families who attend conferences, and fostering student's sense of responsibility and self-worth.

Conferences held in the science classroom enable family members to see displays and equipment. Here several conferences are being conducted simultaneously. Yanna displays the notebook she used to collect work samples during the fall. Kyle explains the record of his work to the group as he demonstrates a science experiment.

*I*n school, all students can build and develop their knowledge, see how ideas are interrelated, use and apply learning important to them now and in the future, develop feelings of capability and industry, and be encouraged to become lifelong learners. Chapter Twelve discusses planning for the present and the future.

although reading and writing are parallel language processes, writing yields a visible product, which reading does not. (When a student writes, that writing can easily be seen and collected and examined; when a student reads, there is no similar lasting product.) When teachers feel obligated to make writing assignments that are much more detailed than reading assignments and to respond to students' writing with corrections and an evaluation, the result is to make their students reluctant to write. Teachers do well to engage students in writing in ways that encourage, rather than discourage, the process. The Guided Writing Procedure, which involves a cycle of talk, writing and reading, is a strategy that explicitly links reading and writing.

Guided Writing Procedure (GWP). Discussion, writing, and reading are the three elements of the Guided Writing Procedure (Searfoss, Smith, & Bean, 1981). Students who have been studying a content area topic brainstorm information they have acquired, which the teacher records so that it is visually available (on a blackboard, chart, or overhead projector screen). As a class, or in cooperative groups, students then arrange the brainstormed items in a semantic map or an outline. Then, working individually or cooperatively, they write the first draft of an informational paper using the map or outline as a guide. At this midpoint in the writing process, the Guided Writing Procedure makes the link between reading and writing explicit. Rather than moving directly to revision of first drafts, the class now stops to read. Students note places where their writing was not clear because they did not have enough information about their topic; they search texts and related materials to get the additional information they need. Only after this period of further reading do they revise their papers. Teacher-student conferences can be incorporated during the period of reading and writing, which should span several days.

Though the Guided Writing Procedure, particularly when it is used in content area instruction, should be focused primarily on concept development, a teacher may also choose to use a checklist to comment on technical aspects of the writing (e.g., organization, usage) and the students may revise

the writing several times. Conceptually, the important element of the Guided Writing Procedure is the reading that occurs between first and second drafts of the paper. As students write about the topic, they become aware of knowledge gaps, and this gives purpose to their reading.

Today With Support, Tomorrow Independently

A variety of strategies that foster aspects of reading development can be combined with content area reading instruction. The Think-Aloud technique and the Directed Reading-Thinking Activity are a form of scaffolding; they encourage aspects of metacognition and help students develop as strategic readers. Essential Reading is a thoughtful method of engaging students in identifying and using main ideas in text. The QAR strategy was designed to teach students what kinds of questions are likely to be asked about expository text and how to examine text to find answers. Minilessons and FYIs are highly versatile, easily used methods that enable teachers to tailor instruction to the immediate needs of a class or group of students.

Think-Aloud. One way teachers can help students to develop as strategic readers is to model the thinking process of mature readers. The Think-Aloud strategy, developed by Beth Davey (1983) is designed to do this. In the Think-Aloud process the teacher chooses a text passage (often one that students will find difficult) to read aloud to the class. The teacher reads a short but meaningful section of text, and pauses to put into words the thought processes that occur to a knowledgeable and strategic reader; e.g., identifying the purpose for reading, predicting on the basis of what has been read, or discussing how terms are used. Then the think-aloud continues as the teacher reads further and stops again to comment, again giving current understandings and identifying parts of the text that confirm or disconfirm previous predictions. Think-alouds make aspects of strategic reading explicit for students; they provide a way for the teacher to model metacognition.

Directed Reading-Thinking Activity (DR-TA). Like the Think-Aloud strategy, the Directed Reading-

Thinking Activity (Boyle and Peregoy, 1990; Stauffer, 1969), can be seen as a form of scaffolding. In DR-TA, a primary emphasis is on giving students guided practice in making, and verifying or modifying, predictions as they read. Other facets of metacognition that the strategy encourages are setting purposes for reading, and recognizing that rate of reading should vary according to the material being read and the reader's purpose. DR-TA differs from the Think-Aloud strategy because the teacher guides students to engage in metacognitive activities, rather than simulating for them the thought processes of a skilled reader.

Using a piece of unfamiliar text that typically is several pages long, students first predict its topic and main points, after examining the title, pictures, etc. This initial predicting sets a purpose for reading. Students then read (or hear) sections of the text, with the teacher stopping the reading at points where earlier predictions can be discussed, verified or disconfirmed, and new predictions made. During this process, students get practice in varying their rate of reading according to their purpose for reading, with a first reading of the assigned portion at a normal rate of speed, followed by skimming to find support for ideas expressed in discussion. The cycle—predicting, reading, discussing, predicting—continues until the entire text section has been read and discussed.

When DR-TA is used, care must be taken so that an attempt to develop one facet of strategic reading will not result in promoting poor reading and thinking habits. Good predicting consists of thinking of reasonable possibilities that can be supported by evidence from the text: It does not consist of always "being right." Teachers who choose to use the DR-TA strategy need to guard against a tendency, on their students' part and on their own, to classify predictions as "right" and "wrong"; for example, by asking "How many of you were right about your predictions?" In their desire to make correct predictions, some students will look ahead in the text, a practice they may feel guilty about and may even be classified as a form of cheating. If, in the process of teaching students to make predictions, we discourage them from reading to find information, we have done more harm than good. In real-life reading of an exciting story (rather than teacher-directed, in-school reading) predicting, if it occurs, happens with the speed of thought. Rather than pausing, the reader hurries on. Real reading is based on "I wonder what will happen next—let's see!" Moreover, writers who are skilled in their craft deliberately set out to foil their readers' talents for guessing what will happen next. If their aim is to surprise and delight us, they succeed when events fit with what has gone before, yet were beyond our ability to predict.

A further caution about the DR-TA strategy is that students read at different speeds, and the activity needs to be planned so that rapid readers are not made to wait for other classmates to reach the designated stopping points. One useful method is to give students text sections sequentially—by handing out copies, by projecting them on a screen, or even by having the teacher read the text aloud. (Separating the text into four or five sections works best.) Students can begin making notes about their predictions as soon as they have read the text section. There is an added advantage in giving students copies of the text sections: Students can write their predictions directly on the page, and can highlight the section(s) of text that support their predictions. This also provides a practical way to continue a DR-TA over more than one day's lesson, or to give a portion of it for homework. When the DR-TA process is completed, the collected text sections can form the basis for other learning activities; for example, students working in cooperative groups might write questions to share with other groups, create or find illustrations, or turn the text into a Readers' Theater script.

Essential Reading. Another strategy that helps to develop a particular facet of reading is the Essential Reading (ER) strategy, originated by Dorothy Hennings (1991). This method, which may be used with either narrative or expository reading material, focuses students' attention on the main ideas presented in the text. There are three components to ER, which correspond to instruction offered before, during, and after reading. Each can be identified by the acronym TAP. Before reading, students are guided to survey the text and predict what important ideas will be presented. At this point, the TAPping is Targeting A Point. During reading, the TAPping activity is Tracking A Point; that is, comparing what they are learning from the text with their predicted main ideas, and modifying those ideas to match what they are learning. After reading, TAPping consists of Thinking about A Point, through personal reflection, writing, and group discussion. The Essential Reading strategy can be used in combination with many of the other strategies described in this text. For example, students might arrange their Targeting A Point predictions in a semantic map, which they could then use as a form for note-taking while tracking these predicted main ideas. Alternatively, a RESPONSE form could be used for making notes. Thinking about the points could be encouraged by using the Write-Out strategy, or through discussions.

Question-Answer Relationships (QAR). QAR is an instructional activity designed to help students work with a standard feature of school-based reading: answering questions based on a text. The strategy was developed by Taffy Raphael (Raphael, 1982, 1984, 1986; Raphael & Pearson, 1985). The purposes of QAR are to show students that text questions are of different kinds, and to teach them how to recognize and answer four kinds of questions: literal, inferential, interpretive/application, and scriptal. Names that suggest how their answers are to be found are given to each category of question. Raphael suggests teaching students to call literal questions "Right There" questions, because their answers can be found "right there" in the text. The second category, questions that teachers usually call inferential questions, consists of questions that must be answered by thinking analytically and combining information from the text. In the QAR method these questions are called "Think and Search" to describe the two actions that must be taken in order to answer them. A third category, "Author and me" questions, are questions in which the answer is based on a combination of the author's and the student's ideas. By listing the author first, the name of the question indicates that the information and ideas presented in the text are the primary sources of information, to which students' ideas are to be added. Some "Author and me" questions will require students to draw conclusions about an author's point of view based on their own

reasoning; these are interpretive questions. Others will require them to apply information from the text to the solution of a related problem; these are application questions. The fourth category of questions consists of those that students can only answer by drawing on their own prior knowledge or opinions. A technical term for questions that can only be answered on the basis of personal knowledge is *scriptal* questions. The term for these questions in the QAR strategy is *"On My Own."*

The purpose of teaching the relationship between different kinds of questions and the ways to find their answers is, of course, to enable students to become skillful in independently answering questions presented in texts, or posed by teachers based on text passages. Questions presented in texts, then, become the basis for practice of the QAR strategy. (Teachers should be aware that the challenge of doing this will be limited if the questions in the text follow a predictable, repetitive pattern, e.g., three "Right There" questions, and one "Think and Search" question.) Teachers can begin QAR instruction by using questions, either from the text or teacher-written, which are based on very short passages and then gradually increase the length of the selections used. After the strategy has been taught and practiced, it is useful for teachers to make a practice of periodically calling attention to different categories of questions as they appear in texts. An additional reinforcement may be to have children try writing questions in some of the categories. "Right there" (literal) and "On my own" (scriptal) questions are the easiest kinds to prepare.

Mini-lessons and FYIs. Mini-lessons are brief periods of instruction focused on a single topic, presented for students who need the information, when they need it. Teachers can give mini-lessons to a group of students or to the whole class. Part of the rationale behind this useful idea, proposed by Nancie Atwell (1987b), is that people are more receptive to learning specific information at the time when they need to use it. Mini-lessons are a multipurpose strategy; for example, they are often used to teach writing conventions (e.g., the use of quotation marks), but they can also be used to teach or review important items of content information, or they can be used to provide brief introductions to literary concepts. Marie Dionisio (1989) writing about her work with adolescent struggling readers, advocates book talks as a form of mini-lesson, and mini-lesson talks on poetry, accompanied by reading it aloud.

The acronym FYI, which often appears in business correspondence, stands for "For Your Information." In education, the term *FYI* is given (Staab, 1990) to very brief mini-lessons—mini-mini-lessons—that skilled teachers can incorporate throughout the school day. Staab defines FYIs as teacher-supplied information presented briefly at a time when it is relevant to students' needs. FYIs can last as long as a few minutes, or can be accomplished in less than 10 seconds. The teacher can use the FYI strategy with the whole class, a small group, or an individual student. The possible topics are innumerable. These brief pieces of instruction are given at "teachable moments"—points where students see the need for information, and are therefore more likely to use and recall it. In the last item in Figure 6–5, for example, the teacher gives information about affixes. Familiarity with common suffixes and prefixes supports vocabulary growth and enables mature readers to understand words that they have never seen before, but such knowledge is not best acquired from a lengthy sequence of lessons about language rules. Knowledge of language structure is best acquired from wide reading, and from getting brief pieces of information when they are needed.

It is important to notice what mini-lessons and FYIs are and what they are not. They are pieces of useful information that the teacher has, and gives at a time when it suits students' immediate needs—not a discussion, nor a question and answer session. Moreover, their focus is instructional, not procedural. (Reviewing class rules for how to behave with a substitute teacher and stressing the importance of clean desks are not mini-lessons or FYIs.) The kind of very brief, to-the-point teaching provided in mini-lessons or FYIs, which many teachers provide repeatedly whether they have a name for

FIGURE 6–5 Examples of FYIs

During a lesson on rain forests, a teacher might provide these FYIs:

(for the whole class) The teacher points out on a globe the locations of the Lacandona rain forest in Chiapas, Mexico, and the Amazon rain forest in South America.

(for the whole class) The teacher gives a mnemonic for the correct spelling of *environment*: "*Environment* is a word that's often misspelled as" (writing on the board) "*enviornment*. The correct spelling is *environment*, and a way to remember it is to put the mineral *iron* in the envi*ron*ment."

(for a cooperative group, working on a map activity) "You'll need to look at political maps to see where rain forests exist across the boundaries of countries, and physical maps that show rivers and forests. It would also be useful to look at maps that show natural resources. I'll stay with you while you look for the different kinds of maps in these atlases and in our map collection." (Teacher comments and assists as students look for the different kinds of maps.)

(for an individual student, checking a resource text) "I'll write down *Chiapas* for you. It sounds as if there's an *e* in the word, but there isn't. I'm not sure whether the name is a Spanish one or an Indian one. We could look that up."

(for the whole class, when a student has asked about a difficult word in the text that the teacher can use to teach an element of structural analysis) "Stop a minute and look at this interesting word that Affie found." (Teacher writes *irretrievable* on the board.) "The author writes, 'When rain forests are destroyed, losses of plant and animal species are irretrievable.' The basic word there is *retrieve*, meaning *to get back, bring back*. Think of a dog that retrieves a stick you throw. But there's a suffix—able—that means *able to be*, so something that's retrievable is something that we can get back. There's also a prefix, and *ir-, im-,* and *in-* usually mean *not*. So *irretrievable* means *not-get-back-able*. Once a rain forest is destroyed, plants and animals that existed only in that habitat will vanish, and we'll never be able to get them back."

the strategies or not, is a kind of teaching that depends for its effectiveness on brevity, clarity, cheerful repetition of the same or related information when new teachable moments occur, and a positive, straightforward presentation by the teacher.

Reading Develops Through Use

Throughout the wide range of educational views, and across time, there is general agreement that reading development is based on reading. How is it that reading itself can be recommended as a strategy to help students develop as readers? How can struggling readers be expected to read, especially from a variety of sources that are *not* carefully chosen to present limited vocabulary and simple sentence structure? Much of the answer lies not in the structure of the texts, but in the structure of the classroom that the teacher establishes. If it is part of the instructional program that there will be many, varied opportunities to read, from a variety of interesting, attractive, non-trivial materials, in an atmosphere where students and teacher alike accept one another as colearners, then students will be free to read and free to consult with others about their reading. Texts students would be unable to read independently can be read if they may consult freely with classmates and ask for information from the teacher, and are willing to do so.

Learning to read occurs most easily and satisfyingly in a situation where learners feel comfortable, learning is respected, and the environment is print-rich. Lively, thoughtfully conducted content area classrooms provide just such an environment, where, for each student, knowledge building and reading development occur simultaneously and continuously. Effective content area classrooms provide learning environments in which reading to learn and learning to read are interrelated, ongoing processes. Moreover, students in these classrooms, as part of their content learning, have many opportunities to read to accomplish a task, and to experience enjoyment in reading. School experiences such as these produce lifelong benefits.

Reading and More Reading.   The importance of reading is an essential theme of this book, so the topic reappears in chapter after chapter. In this chapter, the strategies of reading aloud, wide reading, and multiple readings, which have been addressed earlier, are reviewed. Additional strategies are presented for engaging students in multiple readings of text, and repeated reading and the paired reading strategy are described. There is no better path to reading development than reading and more reading.

Reading Aloud.   The first experience that most people have of reading is a vicarious one. Long before being able to read, often before being able to talk, children experience reading through someone else, through hearing and watching the reading of someone who is already a reader. The enjoyment and benefit of listening to someone else read is, for many people, a lifelong pleasure. Adults often stop their own reading to read aloud an especially important, or powerful, or hilarious excerpt to someone else. Many commuters listen to books on tape as they travel. As an educational strategy, the importance of reading aloud to students across the grades and throughout the content areas can hardly be overstressed.

Wide Reading.   In addition to reading aloud to students, providing trade books and other materials to encourage wide reading about content area topics is among the most effective ways to enable students to learn new information and concepts in depth. Direct experience of most of the issues and events that students are expected to learn about in their content area studies is impossible. We cannot travel in space, nor transport ourselves in time. Books are the answer.

Multiple Readings.   A strategy of providing opportunities for multiple readings is different from a strategy of encouraging wide reading. As was pointed out in Chapter Four, "In the wide reading strategy, students read from a variety of text materials that are all about the same topic. In multiple readings, the same text section is read repeatedly in a variety of ways." When interesting text is read repeatedly, it is likely that both understanding and fluency will be enhanced. Timothy V. Rasinski (1988, 1990) is among the reading scholars who have provided a rich variety of suggestions for incorporating repeated reading into instruction, including LEA, classroom plays, and reading silently while listening to text being read aloud. He warns that when students are reading aloud, fluency will not develop if teachers insist on accuracy and interrupt to make corrections.

Teachers' choices of instructional strategies may result in students reading important sections of text many times. Or, in some cases, using only one strategy will engage students in multiple readings. Rereading, described later, by definition produces multiple readings. A group of students using a Readers' Theater script will typically read the script over several times before performing for others—and the Readers' Theater performance itself constitutes yet another reading. Students who successfully solve a challenging cloze passage will reread parts of it several times as they test out potential word choices, and conclude with a reading of the whole text to see if the completed passage makes sense in its entirety. When a group uses the A-Qu-A strategy, individual students read parts of a text sequentially, and then during the question and answer portion of the activity the same students read all or part of their individual passage again, to confirm the answer to a text-based question. But though some single strategies produce multiple readings, the more usual way of engaging students in multiple readings is to use several strategies. Among these methods are echo reading and chanting, the repeated reading method, and the paired reading strategy.

Echo Reading.   In this activity an experienced reader, usually the teacher, reads aloud a short, meaningful passage from a text; students then read aloud the same passage from their text, echoing the teacher. Because the first reader is skilled, the passage is read with intonation and pausing that make the text easy to understand (rather than with a slow, laborious, word-by-word rendering). A short, interesting, important piece of text is read together in this way, with each portion read aloud first by the teacher, and then by the students. Echo reading can be used as a remedial method, in a one-to-one setting, but it can also be a whole class activity, and it is that form which is recommended here. To be successful, echo reading has to be brief, purposeful and

enjoyable. In the early grades, where students are beginning to be readers, echo reading is one of a number of activities that a teacher can weave into a daily program. After echo reading is introduced—an easy process because the activity requires minimal directions and is quickly understood—and the class has enjoyed it for a week or two, the teacher may encourage students, or cooperative groups, to choose passages for echo reading, and a list can be posted in the classroom, to which everyone, including the teacher, may add ideas. Choices must be drawn from materials where there are enough copies for everyone, so most selections will come from textbooks. The teacher should include echo reading from content textbooks as students are learning the process, and encourage them to suggest sections from content texts also.

Chanting.   Chanting is rhythmic group recitation. In other times, and in other countries, chanting has been an accepted pedagogical strategy for students of all ages, especially in situations where textbooks are not readily available and students are required to memorize large amounts of material. These conditions (few written materials and much to be memorized) are not a feature of our educational system, so chanting is rarely used; nevertheless it can be a useful strategy for teachers to be aware of, and to use sparingly, if it suits their teaching situation and their teaching preferences. Chanting can be used effectively as one kind of reading opportunity when students are beginning to learn to read. Text is posted on a chart, and the teacher or a student uses a pointer to move across the lines as the class chants the words, which may be a poem, the words of a song, or a short text passage. Because chanting is a memory aid, the passages for chanting should be chosen carefully; there is no point in having a drab, unimportant piece of text impressed upon the mind. Chanting may be used with somewhat older students when it is important that they remember a set of information, particularly in sequence. For example, the teacher might post a map of the solar system, showing the orbits of the planets, and the class might chant the names of the planets in order from the sun.

Paired Reading.   This strategy is a practical alternative to two commonly used methods of in-class reading—"round robin" reading and individual silent reading—neither of which are useful for building a shared knowledge base. Round robin reading is "an encircled group of students reading orally, order of reading determined by the location of the student in the circle [or]… students in groups randomly assigned a page or paragraph to read, or students volunteering to read" (Richardson, Anders, Tidwell & Lloyd, 1991, p. 574). It uses classroom time unproductively and is often harmful (Beach, 1993; Kelly, 1995). Individual silent reading does not contribute to shared knowledge, and prevents readers who are not yet skilled from learning. A variety of options for paired reading can be modeled and explained for students. Whenever many students are reading aloud simultaneously, everyone should use "murmur reading," which is reading in a voice audible to one's partner, but quiet enough not to bother others."Another term for the same concept is "reading in a 12 inch voice"; that is, a voice just loud enough to be heard by someone who is 12 inches away. (Yet another term is "mumble reading." Teachers can decide what names they will give to strategies, but it is a good idea to use neutral or pleasant names. To mumble is speak unclearly, in a way that is hard to understand; to murmur is to speak very softly.)

Younger students will benefit most from reading aloud to a partner. When a classroomful of students all read aloud in pairs, a method called "evens & odds" is useful, because less skilled readers often are enabled to read short passages of text when they are paired with successful readers. In the "evens & odds" method, students choose partners, and then come to the teacher who simply points to one student and says "Evens" and to the other and says "Odds," meaning that one student is to read all the even numbered pages (2, 4, 6, and so on.) and the other is to read the odd numbered pages (1, 3, 5, 7, and so on.). As soon as a pair has their even & odd assignment, they find a comfortable place to settle down and they read. Each time the assignment is given to members of pairs—"You're evens; you're odds," "Odds, evens," "You read odds; you read evens"—the teacher gives the "evens" assign-ment to the better reader in the pair. The reason for this is based on the way books are printed. Open any book and you will see that even numbered pages are on the left and odd numbered pages on the right. Whenever an even numbered page is read, the next page is always in sight. Without ever being told to do so, readers who are not yet adept typically do look carefully at the page of text being read by a skilled reader and use information to help them read their own page (which of course, includes many of the same words, as well as being about the same topic).

The practice of making even and odd assignments in this way can be followed regularly without students being aware of the basis for the teacher's choices: in part because the student pairs will change and someone who is the better reader in one pair will not be in another, and also because in some cases the readers will be very evenly matched and the teacher will make the assignment randomly. On the other hand, children often accept all sorts of differences straightforwardly. For example, they know which classmate to go to for help in drawing, or in buttoning coats, or making decisions, just as they know who (besides the teacher) to go to if they want to hear a favorite book read aloud. So a teacher might encourage student pairs to decide who will be the "helper reader" and read the even numbered pages. As students move through the grades in school, however, they tend to acquire the idea that "being a good reader" is honorable and "being a poor reader" is shameful. (A sensible, caring teacher can do much to minimize the stigma of being not yet skilled in reading and to create an atmosphere in which it is *learning*, rather than *having already learned*, that is most respected.)

As students mature as readers, they will probably prefer to read silently, but the option of reading sections of text aloud alternately should be available to students at every grade level, and interrupting silent reading to share important sections or ideas about the text should be actively encouraged. Paired reading, of course, can be expanded to include reading together in groups of three, or a cooperative group of any size can read an assigned text section together. When this method is used, it is essential for teachers to establish an atmosphere where understanding, enjoyment, and conscientious, capable completion of assignments are the accepted goals for paired reading—not, emphatically *not*, attempting to demonstrate reading superiority by finishing reading first.

Paired reading becomes the basis for multiple readings when it is combined with other methods. Paired reading ought to be preceded by one or more activities that will make it easier for students to read the text; for example, a Teacher Read-Aloud Commentary, a vocabulary building activity, a set of Search Tasks. It is useful also to accompany paired reading with another assignment that focuses students' attention on the essentials of what they are reading; for example, use of a RESPONSE form (which requires the students to identify what is important, what is puzzling, and what is unfamiliar) or completion of a Three-Level-Guide or a Pattern Guide, where questions prepared in advance by the teacher serve to guide students' thinking as they read. Cooperative completion of these activities contributes to the active, social dimension of paired reading. In one way or another, students who are engaged in paired reading and other strategies will read important text sections several times.

Repeated Readings, Rereading.   Repeated reading is, of course, rereading. Rereading is an essential part of reading for those who love to read, and at best an annoying idea to those of any age who dislike it. Samuel Perez (1989, p. 62), quotes the author Vladimir Nabokov: "One cannot read a book: one can only reread it. A good reader, a major reader, an active and creative reader is a rereader." The statement "one cannot read a book: one can only reread it" is an aphorism, an ingenious, crisp way of stating a complex truth. On the surface, the statement is puzzling: Rereading must follow reading, and, of course, reading is reading. But the person who made the statement is stating that important text—text containing information that we need to learn thoroughly, or thoughts that are important in our lives—will mean more to us on a second, third, or even more frequent reading. More than one reading of important text is necessary if we are to read it with depth of understanding.

Many lifelong readers are enthusiastic rereaders. Many inexperienced readers have not been encouraged to reread nor seen the process modeled. And many students, unfortunately, acquire the belief based on the reading instruction they observe and experience that "poor readers" have to reread, whereas "good readers" only have to read once: therefore, they dislike the idea of rereading. But in life, if not in school, we reread. Of course we reread! Imagine receiving an affectionate letter from someone you love dearly. Do you read it once and toss it away? Surely not. Do you read it all the way through from beginning to end and then start again right at the top with the date and go straight through again without skipping a single word? Probably not. We reread to experience again what is important to us. One of the most important gifts teachers can give to their students is an appreciation of the value of rereading. This is *not* achieved by telling students to read a text, and start at the beginning and read it again. Instead rereading can be modeled; for example, by sometimes choosing favorite excerpts to reread during Themed Reading. We can talk about rereading favorite books and encourage (rather than discourage) students who want to borrow a well-loved library book several times. We can recognize and applaud rereading to make sure that content area information is fully understood and we can use strategies that engage students in rereading. (And, by the way, we can remember how often little children ask to have their favorite books read to them and how much they learn from that rereading.)

 ## A Summary

The message of this chapter is that students' ability to read develops and grows while they are learning in active, interesting, language-rich content area classrooms. In these classrooms, the textbooks are teaching tools for the teacher and an important source of information for the students; but they do not control the curriculum, nor are students expected to learn primarily from reading the text and completing text-presented activities. One of the major themes of this chapter, and of this text, is that teachers have the responsibility to teach content area information to all students, and that useful strategies are available to help accomplish this. Teachers are educators, not "sorters" of students.

Visualize…

a group of students in a content area classroom. (What is the grade level and content field of study? You choose.) These students are all set for learning.

Ask: What helped these students reach this point?

Ask: What are some of the many strengths these students can bring to their learning?

Consider: If you were their teacher, what would you do to make the textbook one of your teaching tools, and one important source of information for these students?

Glossary of Reading-Related Terminology

In the following pages, some of the technical terms related to the field of reading education are presented and defined. Education is a complex field in which new ideas and new technical terms are being introduced constantly. The best way to find out about new ideas is to read professional journals. The most efficient way to find out what a new term means is to ask the person who uses it, or a knowledgeable colleague; an alternative is to check the indexes of recent textbooks in the appropriate field.

One advantage of being fairly knowledgeable about terminology in a professional field is that this helps us appreciate important ideas, and also helps protect us from being overly impressed—or even alarmed—when others use technical terms with which we are unfamiliar. For example, imagine being assigned to teach in a classroom where the students have been recently tested and found to be both emmetropic and hyperlexic! Would you a) ask what *emmetropia* and *hyperlexia* mean? or b) quit the job? Unless one already knows the meaning of those terms, the sensible strategy is to ask about them. (*Emmetropia* is normal vision, and *hyperlexia* is the condition of reading better than is expected.)

Reading Ability and Readability

The term *reading ability* refers to people's ability, specifically to the ability of a person to read. Usually the term is used in the context of assessment; that is, on the basis of a test, a person's reading ability is described as above, at, or below what is typical at a particular age or grade, or identified in terms of a percentile score, a grade level, or a level of book in a basal reading series. Thus Rita might be described as "reading above grade level," which is a way of asserting that Rita can, in many circumstances, read with understanding and enjoyment books most children at her grade cannot yet manage. Information about Bill's reading ability might be given as "scoring at the thirtieth percentile." From this information we can conclude that Bill has been given a standardized reading test and that he did not do well on it. If we are also told that Bill is "reading at a 2^2 level" we can conclude that Bill is likely to be a fourth or fifth grader: we know from his low percentile score that typical students in his grade do much better on the test than he did. So if his score is matched with a basal reading book, the book will be for a grade well below his current placement.

Another way of describing a person's reading ability is in terms of three levels: independent, instructional, and frustration. These levels indicate the grade levels of reading material that are likely to be easy for this reader (the independent level); appropriate for this reader in an instructional setting (instructional level); and too difficult for this reader (frustration level). An important fact to keep in mind is that a reading level ranges along a continuum; it is not a characteristic that people either have or do not have. And a reading level given in terms of age or grade is still an oversimplification: A person can read some kinds of materials more easily than others. Moreover, a reading level is not fixed. Students' reading levels are, or should be, continually rising; that is, if instruction is progressing well, students should become better and better at reading, and the same material that was once classified as at their frustration level will eventually be at their instructional level, and finally at their independent level. (For example, people who can read this text would, earlier in their reading development, not have been able to do so.)

It is important for teachers to be able to understand and interpret information about students' reading ability, but it is even more important that

Reading Is for Life

teachers do not give such information too much weight in their planning, except to provide a rich range of reading materials for students to choose from. Test information should not alarm us into thinking that we are incapable of providing useful content instruction for particular students; intelligent teacher intervention can make difficult text accessible. A major theme of this text is that learners can acquire content area information through effective instruction even when they can't read their textbooks independently, and that successful learning in a content area classroom can help students develop as readers. It is *essential* that students not be restricted in their reading experiences on the basis of test scores. Library selections should not be limited to books a librarian or teacher believes are "at the right level" for a student or class. Classroom libraries and collections for Themed Reading should include a wide range of reading material, from which students may choose freely.

Visualize... two images:

a person
We may want to know how capably this person can read.
We ask, "What information is there about this person's reading ability?" (We can also ask, "Where did this information come from?")

a book

We may want to have some information about how difficult this book is to read.

We ask, "What is the readability level of this book?" (We can also ask, "What readability formula was used?")

We should remember that:

...as readers grow, their reading ability increases.

...readability level should not be over-emphasized in choosing books.

The term *readability* refers to text, specifically to a match between reading material and readers. Usually readability level of text is expressed as a grade level; the statement "the readability of this textbook ranges from 4.0 to 5.0" means that the textbook can probably be read successfully by typical fourth graders. Although readability formulas can be misused (as is demonstrated in the following section), they have a benign origin and can provide useful information. (One of the earliest readability formulas, the Dale-Chall formula, was created at the request of people preparing brochures giving health information, who wanted to make sure that as many people as possible could read them.)

Readability is usually determined according to a mathematical formula. To apply such a formula, we must have numbers; therefore, there must be something about text that can be counted. Over time, scholars have explored many possibilities. Text elements that are often used in computing readability include sentence length (because it is generally true that shorter sentences are easier to read than longer sentences) and number of syllables per sentence (because it is generally true that short words are easier to read than long words). When readability formulas were first devised, *people* had to count the number of unfamiliar words, the number of syllables in words, and/or the number of words designated as unfamiliar, if they wanted to calculate a readability level. (You can still do this, of course.) Then along came computers, which count many things very efficiently. Now readability levels are almost always calculated by computers, and the formulas are based on features of text that computers can count, such as the average number of words in sentences (sentence length), the average number of syllables in words, and/or the average number of

letters in words (word length). How can a computer count syllables? Because every syllable contains a vowel sound, a good estimate is obtained by counting vowel and vowel combinations that are separated by consonants; for example, the seven-letter word *stretch* has one syllable and the six-letter word *reader* has two. In calculating the readability level of most text, several samples of approximately 100 words are chosen randomly from throughout the text, the formula is applied to them, and a range of readability levels is reported.

Although it is possible to calculate a readability level for any written text, this is not done for most reading material. The books we buy in typical bookstores, the books we borrow from libraries, and the magazines and newspapers we read—these do not have readability levels provided. It is not needed. We look at books before buying or borrowing them and we are able to judge whether the text looks too difficult for us to read. Moreover, the link between the author and publisher on the one hand, and the reader on the other, is quite direct. Books, magazines, and newspapers need readers who will buy them. If they appear childish (too easy) or incomprehensible (too hard), people will not buy them. But for school textbooks, there are more links in the chain connecting the author and reader. The students who read the textbooks do not get to pick them out. Adults who are already capable readers choose the books, and they must consider how useful the textbook will be for younger, less skillful readers. Information about a textbook's readability, if it is available, may be useful information to consider, but it is by no means the only, or most important, feature of a text to consider. It is important for anyone who takes readability levels into account in evaluating books to have an understanding of readability formulas and their limitations.

Use and Misuse of Readability Formulas. The readability levels of the following five passages have been calculated. The original paragraph appears earlier in this chapter. The last two sentences of the excerpt are a quotation from Don Holdaway (1982, p. 295).

> Like speaking and listening, reading is a form of language, and we know that humans are adept language learners. Young children, unless they have

grave sensory or mental impairments or are terribly abused, learn to speak the language they hear spoken. Language development proceeds in predictable ways, but it is not acquired by learning rules, practicing, and mastering one bit at a time. Like spoken language, reading develops through use and is fostered by a learning environment that is print-rich, full of opportunities to see and hear and use written text. Just as speech develops in an environment which is immensely more rich than the immediate needs of the learner, so the orientation to book language develops in an environment of rich exposure beyond the immediate needs of the learner. In both situations, the learner selects appropriate items from the range.

The word processing program used to prepare text for this book will provide readability information, using two formulas. According to one, the readability level of the paragraph is 12.7 (last year of high school); according to the other, the readability level is 13.6 (first year of college). Sentence length is considered in both formulas. Computers can tell when a sentence ends by checking punctuation marks. What would happen if periods were put in haphazardly, thus making it appear that the passage has shorter sentences?

> Like speaking, and listening, reading is a form. Of language, and we know that humans are adept. Language learners. Young children, unless they have grave. Sensory or mental impairments or are terribly abused, learn. To speak the language they hear spoken language. Development proceeds in predictable. Ways, but it is not acquired by learning rules, practicing, and mastering one. Bit at a time like spoken. Language, reading develops through use, and is. Fostered by a learning environment that is. Print-rich, full of opportunities to see and hear and. Use written text just as speech. Develops in an environment which is immensely more. Rich than the immediate needs of the learner, so. The orientation to book language develops in an. Environment of rich exposure beyond the. Immediate needs of the learner in both. Situations, the learner. Selects appropriate items from the range.

According to both readability formulas, this second passage is easier to read than the first: 8.7 (seventh month of eighth grade), or 6.3 (third month of sixth grade). Notice that this time there is more dif-

ference between the two numbers, perhaps suggesting that there is something unusual about the passage. Of course, the second version of the passage is *not* easier to read than the first. The problem, however, is not with the readability formulas but with the person who put periods where they did not belong. Moreover it is not a serious problem; such a passage would not appear in a school textbook. Books by writers who put periods in crazy places (except to illustrate an idea) do not get published. However, readability formulas can be misused in ways that do present problems for readers, as the following revised passage illustrates:

> Speaking and listening are forms of language. Reading is a form of language. We know that humans are adept language learners. Some young children have grave sensory or mental impairments. Some young children are terribly abused. Most young children learn to speak the language they hear spoken. Language development proceeds in predictable ways. It is not acquired by learning rules. It is not acquired by practicing. It is not acquired by mastering one bit at a time. Reading is like spoken language. It develops through use. It is fostered by a learning environment that is print-rich. Print-rich environments are full of opportunities to see and hear and use written text. Speech develops in an environment that is immensely more rich than the immediate needs of the learner. Orientation to book language develops in an environment of rich exposure beyond the immediate needs of the learner. The learner selects appropriate items from the range.

Now the readability level is 8.8 (near the end of eighth grade) according to one formula and 6.8 (near the end of sixth grade) according to the other. The original passage has been "simplified" by removing words and phrases that link ideas: *like, and, unless, but, just as, so, in both situations.* Taking out those words and phrases makes the sentences shorter, but it also makes the ideas expressed in the paragraph more difficult to grasp. Occasionally, people who prepare textbooks for use in the schools do change text just to lower its readability level. Once again, the readability formulas and their creators are not at fault. An author and editor are at fault because they have not produced a good text. Educators who have the responsibility for selecting textbooks would be even more at fault if they chose books on the basis of their readability level, without examining the quality of the writing. The readability level of the passage was artificially lowered by removing words that connect ideas. Another way to lower readability level artificially is to overuse anaphora. (Remember the definition of anaphora given in Chapter One: words and phrases that can only be understood by referring back to previous text.) In the next version of the paragraph, pronouns have been substituted for some of the nouns and noun phrases in the previous version.

> Reading is like speaking, and listening. It is a form of language. We know that humans are adept language learners. Some young children have grave sensory or mental impairments. Some are terribly abused. Most learn to speak the language they hear spoken. Language development proceeds in predictable ways. It is not acquired by learning rules. It is not acquired by practicing. It is not acquired by mastering one bit at a time. Reading is like spoken language. It develops through use. It is fostered by a learning environment that is print-rich. This is full of opportunities to see and hear and use written text. Speech develops in an environment which is immensely more rich than the immediate needs of the learner. Orientation to book language develops in an environment of rich exposure beyond these needs. The learner selects appropriate items from the range.

According to the readability formulas that have been used, this is the easiest version so far: 8.4 according to one formula, and 6.2 according to the other. Contrast the two former revisions with the final passage that follows, where the ideas expressed in the original paragraph are presented accurately and honestly, but more simply:

> In many ways, reading is like other forms of language, such as speaking and listening. Very young children are good at learning language. They learn to understand what they hear, and they learn to talk. They learn all this without lessons, long before going to school. Children learn to listen and talk by hearing and using language, not by learning rules.
>
> Having many experiences with books helps children learn to read. Homes and classrooms where children see many books and magazines and signs are called "print-rich," because there are many dif-

ferent kinds of writing for children to see. In these homes and classrooms, adults read to children, and children can look at books and draw pictures and try writing alphabet letters. Children don't understand all that they see and hear, of course, but they do pay attention to the written language, and learn from their experiences.

Here the two readability formulas are in close agreement: 8.2 and 8.3. This passage would fit well into a textbook on family living written for use by high school students, or even older middle school students. However, more sophisticated readers might find it annoying to be assigned a textbook written in this style. They might think the author was "writing down" to an unsophisticated audience.

Readability information can provide one potentially useful piece of data to educators who are choosing textbooks for students to use. But information about readability level should be only a minor factor in choosing a text. Text accuracy and text considerateness, discussed in Chapter One, are of primary importance. Prior knowledge and interest strongly affect a person's ability to read material with understanding; for example, texts for courses in car repair, chemistry, computer science, drama, and education may all have the same readability level, but it is unlikely that the same person would be able to read all five texts with equal ease and understanding.

Aliteracy vs. Illiteracy

Although illiteracy is the inability to read and write well enough to meet current standards of a particular culture and time, aliteracy is simply not reading. An aliterate person is one who has no desire to read, and either does not read at all or reads only what is minimally necessary to meet the requirements of work and everyday life. People within and outside the field of education have expressed concern that many students who learn to read in our schools nevertheless leave school without the inclination to be readers (e.g., Cramer & Castle, 1995).

Automaticity

When an action can be taken without conscious thought, it is automatic. Automaticity is a facet of skilled reading. Mature readers have an extensive vocabulary of words that are recognized instantly and can be read and understood more quickly than they can be said aloud. Moreover, mature readers have internalized an understanding of how written language works so that they can come up with a reasonable way of pronouncing words they have never seen or heard before. All reasonable people who think about the reading process agree that automaticity is essential for mature reading; what people have traditionally disagreed about is how best to help developing readers move toward automaticity—by learning rules and drilling, or by reading, writing, listening, and speaking in a print-rich environment. The position espoused in this text is that automaticity of any skill is acquired through its use, and that learning to read develops best when opportunities for reading and reading-related activities are many and satisfying.

Basal Reading Series

A basal series is a sequential set of books and supplementary materials: workbooks, teacher's manuals, and additional components, such as tests and exercises. Books intended to teach reading have been published in America since the late 1700s, and in other (older) countries long before that. Over the past century, basal reading series have come to dominate reading instruction in our schools. (In England and several other countries, the term *reading scheme* is used instead of *basal series*.) A basal series typically consists of a set of books for first grade: preprimers, primer, and 1^2 reader (*primer* rhymes with *swimmer* and 1^2 is read "one-two"); two books each for second and third grades: 2^1, 2^2, 3^1, 3^2; and one book each for grades 4, 5, and 6. Individual books within the series are called basal readers or basals.

Basal reading series are designed to provide virtually everything a teacher might need to teach reading. Critics of basals regard this as an attempt to make the materials "teacher-proof." What does *teacher-proof* mean? Think about the term *waterproof*. A waterproof raincoat protects against water; it does not let water in. Teacher-proof materials protect against bad teaching in a similar way. They try to ensure that the teacher does not get very far into the teaching process. The teacher's manual tells teachers exactly what to say at every step in every reading lesson, and also includes the replies teachers can expect students to give to the questions the teachers are told to ask. (For open-ended questions, the manual tells teachers that "Answers will vary.") All the materials for reading lessons are provided—so many that to use them all would absorb enormous amounts of time. Jeanne Chall surveyed authors of basal readers and reports the comment that in one school "the teachers had followed the teachers' guidebooks and their suggestions for activities so thoroughly, having the children do all the exercises and all the supplementary reading, that the children were still on the first-grade program in the fourth grade" (Chall, 1967, p. 197). Supplementary materials for basal series now typically include tests, several different workbooks, blackline masters (these used to be ditto masters) from which multiple copies of worksheets can be made, and often letters, in both English and Spanish versions, to be sent from the teacher to parents at specified times. (Another word to keep in mind when considering whether it is desirable to invest in teacher-proof materials is *foolproof*. That word describes something that has been made so easy that not even a fool can make it go wrong. In fact, nothing can be made completely foolproof, nor is it possible for any publisher to prepare materials that are proof against incapable or lazy teachers. What we should all look for is materials that are well designed to assist capable teachers in providing useful instruction.)

When basal materials are used rigidly, in a linear fashion, to provide all or most of the reading material used in instruction (as they are presented by the publishers), children's reading development is constrained, their vision of what reading is may become distorted, and the differing rates of individual children's development are ignored. (Children who learn to read easily must still work their way through quantities of simple reading and the accompanying "skills" exercises; children who begin slowly remain forever behind. Both situations have the same cause—directions to teachers indicating that no books in the series are to be skipped, and that every one must be worked through from start to finish.)

Recently, Jane Hansen, a scholar who has studied reading and writing processes and practices extensively, described a series of interviews with children who were asked what they planned to do to become better readers. Invariably, the students explained what they intended to do *at home*—read more, read many books by authors of their choice, and widen their range of reading interests. Her research, showing that these students did not regard school as a place where they had opportunities to become better readers, helped influence the school's principal, who had previously insisted that reading instruction must center on basal readers, to change his opinion. Teachers did change their programs, and reading instruction eventually provided "lots of time for children to read from books of their choice, opportunities for children to talk about books with their classmates, no ability groups, and sessions within which children could plan their growth as readers" (Hansen, 1992c, p. 102).

Case (Upper Case, Lower Case)

THESE ARE UPPER-CASE LETTERS (ALSO CALLED CAPITAL LETTERS)
these are lower-case letters

Before machinery made the process automatic, printers used to "set type" by hand; that is, they put metal pieces, each containing a letter, in rows and clamped them together in lines, from which text was printed. The individual letters were kept in two cases, one above the other, and those on the top were the ones used least; the capital letters were in the upper case. When you prepare materials for your students to use, remember that writing that uses lower-case letters (except for capitals in customary places, such as the beginnings of sentences, of course) is easier to read than text printed entirely in capitals. This is because lower-case letters are more distinctive in height and shape and thus easier to recognize. Another reason for not preparing student materials using only capital letters is that it is more useful for students to see words printed in lower case; the text they see elsewhere is usually printed that way, so their learning is transferable.

Note that in the English language, the upper- and lower-case forms of many letters are quite different.

To experienced readers, the following two words look the same because they *are* the same. But it takes time and much experience with print, before new readers automatically look at the two words and see no important difference. Look carefully to see how different the upper- and lower-case forms of the five letters in the word are.

GRADE and grade

Chunking

Breaking passages and words apart into their tiniest sections is not an effective way to read; working with such bits and pieces is not a useful way to learn to read. Skilled readers naturally separate text into meaningful sections ("chunks") as they read, rather than reading word by word. For developing readers it can be useful to separate text into chunked phrases (Cromer, 1970). The following passage is the first paragraph of this chapter, printed in meaningful chunks of text:

> Reading is the primary way
> of acquiring content area information
> —not the only way, by any means,
> but the major method.
>
> Most content area information
> is available in the form of text:
> in books, magazines, and journals,
> and, increasingly, on computer screens.
>
> The ability to read with understanding
> underlies success in learning.

When teachers read aloud, students hear the text separated into meaningful sections. Students are also encouraged to chunk when strategies, such as echo reading and choral reading, are used.

Cueing Systems, Context

Language has many aspects. Semantics is the study of word meanings. Syntax is the study of grammar. Orthography is the study of the symbol system of a language; the word often refers to correct spelling. Phonology is the study of speech sounds, and graphemics is the study of written symbols used to represent speech sounds. A phoneme is the smallest speech unit that affects meaning (e.g., /b/ because *bit* and *pit* are different words); and a morpheme is the smallest part of a written word that affects meaning (e.g., *-s*, *-ed*, and *-ing*, which are added to create different forms of a verb).

Readers can read words in isolation. Most beginning readers can immediately identify the word *go* when it is printed on a card. Mature readers can read transportation or **transportation** or TRANSPORTATION whenever, and however, they see the written word. Readers develop a vast store of words that they can recognize at sight. When they do so, they are not using context, because there is no context—no meaningful surrounding text. In real life reading, however, there is context. Context enables readers to read and understand text more rapidly, and sometimes also enables readers to figure out the meaning of an unknown word. (Recall, however, discussions in earlier chapters of the fact that the meaning of technical vocabulary in content areas usually cannot be determined solely from context.) When readers do learn the meaning of a word from its context, they are likely to use both semantic and syntactic cues (or clues), with semantic cues being more informative. Consider this statement:

> The krait is highly dangerous because its venom is lethal.

Mature users of the English language know that *krait* is a noun because they recognize *the* as a noun marker (a word that precedes a noun or noun phrase); this is a syntactic cue. The words *dangerous* and *venom* are semantic cues that suggest that a krait is a snake, which it is. Of course, people who already know the meaning of all the words in the statement will be able to understand it immediately because they have all the necessary semantic knowledge to do so.

Semantic and syntactic information helps us to grasp meaning whether language is spoken or written. Other cues, however, are available only from written language. Consider the following contrived set of words:

> we will leave tomorrow we think you should not go to see your friend

If the words were spoken, pauses and stress on certain words would convey the intended meaning.

When the words are written, one needs graphic cues based on the printing conventions of language, such as capitalization and punctuation. Without these cues from language's writing system, there would be at least three ways to interpret these words:

> We will leave tomorrow, we think. You should not go to see your friend.
>
> We will leave. Tomorrow, we think, you should not go to see your friend.
>
> We will leave tomorrow. We think you should not. Go to see your friend.

Another aspect of language is pragmatics. The concern here is with the practical aspects of language that enable us to get along together, for example, by knowing when to use terms such as *hello, thank you, excuse me*. Very young children who are native speakers of a language typically have no difficulty learning the pragmatic aspects of language; however, a person acquiring a new language may find this aspect of language learning difficult. For example, a speaker will learn many forms of greetings—good morning, hi, yo!—and must also learn which to use in different circumstances.

Dyslexia

The word *dyslexia* comes from a Latin prefix, *dys-*, meaning *abnormal, impaired, difficult*, or *bad*, and a Greek word, *lexis*, meaning *speech*. Dyslexia is the term now commonly used to refer to a serious difficulty in learning to read that is not due to sensory or cognitive impairment, or environmental problems. *Alexia, word blindness*, and *strephosymbolia* are among the other terms that have also been used to name this puzzling condition. Many reading scholars now believe that there are different kinds of dyslexia, but that this kind of reading problem has its source in the brain—often the language center of the brain—rather than in the eye. Frank Vellutino, a leading scholar in the field of dyslexia research, has conducted experiments that demonstrate the relationship between language processes and learning problems that are characteristic of dyslexia (e.g., Vellutino, 1977, 1987). We do not yet know the cause of this problem; the best treatment for it is good teaching. Students with this and other reading problems can learn content area information, except in classrooms where the teacher simply assigns students to read the text on their own.

People with this problem often make reversals in reading and writing; for example, reading *saw* for *was*, and writing *d* for *b*. Logical reasoning and observation, as well as research, tell us that this is not because some people see everything backwards. If this were so, they would see all letters and words reversed, and things in the environment would be seen in reverse also: doorknobs would appear to be on the opposite side of doors; cars would be seen in the opposite lane, and so forth. It is most likely that some words and letters are confused because they are similar.

Young children also confuse similar words and letters when they are learning to read, and this is not a sign of dyslexia. It is useful for teachers to consider that one very early thing that people learn while they are still infants is that an object remains the same object even when we see it from different perspectives; its orientation (the way that it is turned) is unimportant. When children learn to recognize and name letters, they are faced with the problem of learning and remembering that orientation *is* important. If we flip a *b* horizontally, it becomes a *d*; if we flip it vertically, it becomes a *p*.

d b

q p

Young children also sometimes use mirror writing, particularly if they pick up a pencil or a piece of chalk in the hand they do not normally use. Some adults can still do this, and use their mirror writing abilities as a trick to entertain others. Parents and teachers should not be alarmed when young readers and writers make reversals.

There are many ways in which people experience difficulties in learning. Often it appears that progress has been made in solving these problems when, in fact, all that has happened is that someone has come up with a new name for the difficulty. Although it is professionally useful for teachers to be aware of new terminology, we should not be deceived into thinking that a new name is, in itself, a cure for students' difficulties.

Eye Movements

A reader's eyes do not follow a line of print at a smooth, even, steady pace. Instead they move along in a series of very rapid jumps. The first person to examine and report on eye movements while reading was a French scholar who called these jumps saccades. (*Saccade* is pronounced *sah-kahd'*.) Between saccades, the eyes stop; these points are called fixations. Fixations last longer than the saccadic movements, and it is during fixations that the mind takes in meaning from the text. Two other eye movements are regressions, a backward movement, and return sweeps, when the eye moves from one line of text to the next. Tracking is a related term; it refers to the process of following lines of print. Technology has allowed researchers to do extensive research on eye movements while reading. One consistent finding of this research is important for teachers to know about, because the information has been misinterpreted and misused. Consider the following facts. (I am using the terms *good readers* and *poor readers* here, although you will rarely see them used elsewhere in this text.)

> The eye movements of good and poor readers are different. For good readers, the saccades cover large chunks of text, fixations are brief, there are few or no regressions, and the return sweeps are smooth. For poor readers, all the movements tend to be irregular and uneven, with short chunks of text covered in the saccadic movements, long fixations, and many regressions. Some poor readers may return to the same line they have read before, or may skip a line, during the return sweep.

These statements are widely accepted as accurate. How shall teachers interpret them? Some people believe that training people to move their eyes more efficiently will make them better readers. (Some people even sell programs that claim to do this.) But the truth lies in the other direction: When people become successful readers, their eye movements become efficient. One way for good readers to test this assertion is to find a very difficult text about a topic you know very little about. Now you will become, temporarily, a struggling reader. You will look back rather than moving smoothly forward and may lose your place on a return sweep. If you hold the book so that a friend can look at your eyes as you read, your friend will notice irregular, short saccades and regressions.

More than fifty years ago, a reading scholar, Ernest Horn, wrote, "The classroom teacher needs to be concerned with movements of the eyes little more than with the movements of the bones of the inner ear" (Horn, 1937, quoted in the International Reading Association's *Dictionary of Reading*, edited by Theodore L. Harris and Richard E. Hodges, 1981, p. 114). The reason the topic is introduced here is to tell content area teachers that we need not be concerned about whether students' eye movements are smooth; instead—as this text stresses repeatedly—we need to teach content effectively, in ways that foster reading development. The best strategy we can use to help students develop as readers is to give opportunities to practice purposeful skimming and scanning. Students may also find it helpful to keep a file card in their texts as a bookmark, and use it as a guide while reading, moving it down line by line as the text is read. (When readers mark text in this way, the card should be placed above the line of text, rather than below it, covering what has been read, rather than what is to be read, in order not to interfere with the return sweep of the eye.)

Another point about eye movements that it is useful to be aware of is that there is nothing built in to the human brain that makes it natural to read a page from top to bottom, in a sequence of lines where each is read from left to right. This is the pattern for our language, and children do learn it—most easily from observing others read and being read to. But there are many languages in which lines of text are printed from right to left, and others in which text is printed in columns. Some ancient languages were written with the lines alternately moving from left to right and then from right to left, so that to follow the text the eye would move in series of S-curves. This method of writing is called boustrophedon, which means *turning as the ox plows*. People who live in places where the printed text moves from right to left learn to follow text as easily as those who learn to read written English do; many people know how to read text in languages that are printed both ways.

Eye-Voice Span (EVS)

When capable readers are reading aloud, they see (and read mentally) text that is ahead of the words they are saying; thus they do not read word-by-word, but in meaningful phrases. The distance between the farthest word seen by the eyes and the word spoken by the voice is the eye-voice span (Clark, 1995; Levin, 1979). The existence of EVS can be easily demonstrated by turning off the lights, or closing a book suddenly, during a read-aloud session. A skilled reader will be able to say a few more words without seeing the text. It can be useful for developing readers to know about the eye-voice span, especially if they have acquired the erroneous idea that good readers do read one word at a time.

Modalities, Modes of Learning, Learning Preferences

Educators are always interested in finding out how best to teach students, and the idea that there are differences among people in the way they learn is hardly disputable. One of the ways in which some learners differ is in a preference for learning through seeing (visually) or in learning through hearing (auditorily). A few learners have impairments so severe that they need to learn through the modes of touch (tactilely) and muscle movement (kinesthetically). Many years ago, Grace Fernald, a reading educator working with people who had severe difficulties in learning to read, devised the multisensory VAKT (visual, auditory, kinesthetic, tactile) method of teaching (Fernald & Keller, 1921). It is useful for teachers to provide instruction that taps many modes of learning, but it is not necessary to invest time and resources in sorting and classifying students according to their preferred learning modality or style. Unless one sensory modality is absent (e.g., a student is blind or deaf), all students learn by seeing and hearing. Moreover everyone needs opportunities to move about, and young children in particular should not be required to spend long periods of time sitting still. The need to move about does not mean that a person is "a kinesthetic learner."

Phonics

The term *phonics* is used to refer to methods of teaching the relationship between the written symbols of the English language and the sounds they typically represent. Translating written symbols (groups of letters) into meaningful words is called decoding, because the process is like solving a code. Learning to use letters to write words is sometimes called encoding. Although people do in fact learn to decode (we can, for example, translate the letters in a nonsense word such as *frupstungle* from written into spoken language) this does not mean that early instruction should concentrate on teaching phonics through rules and workbooks.

Over the years, some people interested in education have become vehement in their views about the value of phonics, to the extent that the issue becomes a matter of good and evil, with people involved in the argument defining whoever agrees with them as good, and whoever does not as not only wrong, but bad. Readers of this text are urged to take a more balanced view. The English language has a fairly regular sound-symbol correspondence; all successful readers of English understand that system without needing to remember any rules; instruction in phonics, which can be accomplished pleasantly and quickly without memorization or writing (see Glass, 1973), can be useful to developing readers, although many people learn to read successfully with no formal phonics instruction at all.

Critics of phonics sometimes point to the irregularities in English spelling. It can be amusing to consider the different ways words in the English language are spelled and pronounced. Early in his career, Theodore Geisel (Dr. Seuss) wrote a book called *The Tough Coughs as He Ploughs the Dough* (reissued in 1987). The book's title is a reminder of the many ways that the letter combination *-ough* is pronounced in English. And you might challenge a friend to pronounce this combination of letters:

ghoti

Surprise your friend by explaining that the word would be pronounced *fish*. (The *GH* is pronounced as in *enouGH*, the *O* as in *wOmen*, and the *TI* as in *acTIon*.) But despite some exceptions, the sound/

symbol relationship in English is generally regular. There is only one word in the English language where no letters have a typical sound. (The word is *of*.) Mature readers of English do have an understanding of how the language works, even though they are usually not conscious of it.

Reading Inventories

Reading ability is often determined on the basis of a reading test; some tests (often called IRIs, Informal Reading Inventories, or SRIs, Standardized Reading Inventories) provide information in the form of reading levels. These reading levels are often given in numbers corresponding to grade levels. Typical reading inventories include a word list and a series of short reading selections of increasing levels of readability, each followed by a series of comprehension questions (questions designed to see whether the student has understood the passage). Working one-to-one with a student, a knowledgeable adult asks the student to read the list of words until a specified number of errors have been made, then to read a series of passages orally and answer questions about them, then to read similar passages silently and respond, orally, to the comprehension questions.

Reading Recovery

It is useful for classroom teachers to be aware of the Reading Recovery program, its background, and its principles. Reading Recovery was devised by the New Zealand educator Marie Clay (now Dame Marie, having been awarded the title—equivalent to a British knighthood—for her contributions to education worldwide). In districts that have established a Reading Recovery program, children who appear at risk of having difficulty in learning to read receive a half-hour of one-to-one assistance, daily, from a qualified Reading Recovery teacher, in addition to participation in their classroom reading program, beginning when they *enter* first grade. One aspect of the program is reading and rereading real books (very short and easy ones to begin with)—at least one per session. The goal of the program is for children to be "discontinued" (i.e., to stop participating in Reading Recovery) during their first-grade year, after such substantial progress that they can read as well as the average for children in their school and district. Children who are discontinued from the program are expected to be reading as well as most of their classmates, whatever the standards and expectations are in the district where they live. Because Reading Recovery begins before children have begun to feel the stigma of being "poor readers," and ends with their reading capably along with their classmates, their reading development is not hampered by feelings of inadequacy.

To become qualified Reading Recovery teachers, experienced teachers, who already hold master's degrees, study fulltime for a full year, and continue to study to maintain and enhance their skills thereafter. These teachers learn a series of techniques to use at each session, and also develop their skill in making quick, effective decisions during lessons, about how best to help the student at that moment. Part of their program of study involves being observed while teaching (behind a one-way mirror) by other Reading Recovery teachers, followed by a group critique and discussion of the lesson and the choices the teacher made. Unlike many well-advertised programs, which come and go, no one makes money from Reading Recovery through workshops or sales of materials. Preparation to offer the program requires a major commitment of time on the part of the teachers who give at least a year to earning credentials and a major commitment on the part of a school district to free teachers for a year of study and then for full- or half-time work as Reading Recovery teachers.

Silent Reading

Just as there is nothing innate about reading lines of print from left to right, reading silently is a custom—longstanding and very useful, but nevertheless not something that humans are naturally programmed to do. Writing toward the end of the fourth century, Aurelius Augustinus, later known as Saint Augustine, described something he had not seen before, a person reading, who did not read aloud: "When he was reading, his eyes ran over the page and his heart perceived the sense, but his voice and tongue were silent…. Very often when we were

there, we saw him silently reading and never otherwise." Musing about this unusual practice, Augustinus suggested possible reasons. Possibly the purpose was to prevent interruptions from others who might want to talk with the man about what he was reading, or might ask him to explain some difficult ideas in the text. Possibly he wanted to keep his voice from getting hoarse. Augustinus was sure the man was a good man: "Whatever motive he had for his habit, this man had a good reason for what he did" (Saint Augustine, *Confessions*, 1991, pp. 92–93). The translator has added a footnote: "In antiquity silent reading was uncommon, not unknown."

Sometimes, in the teaching of reading, it has been accepted practice to urge children who are beginning to read to read silently, and even to use various techniques (such as having them hold a pencil clenched between the teeth) to prevent them from moving their lips while reading. Such methods are unnecessary as well as unpleasant, and can interfere with children's understanding of what they are supposed to be reading, as well as their enjoyment of reading. To read silently is an advantage, because skilled silent reading is much faster than reading aloud. However, the learner's pace of development in learning to read should not be forced into a rigid pattern. Reading development can best be fostered in the classroom through many opportunities to read, write, talk, and listen in a welcoming, print-rich environment.

Skimming, Scanning

Well-developing readers usually spontaneously vary the pace of their reading depending on the kind of material they are reading, and their purposes for reading. Difficult material is usually read more slowly; but a reader looking for recreational reading who pulled a complex book of philosophy from the shelf might read a page or two very rapidly and then replace the book. The reader intended, in this case, to decide whether or not to select this book for thorough reading, and chose to skim the text quickly as a basis for making the decision. If the text had been assigned for a college course, the same reader would probably have read the entire text, but far more slowly than a magazine or book of fiction would have been read, and often would have reread passages repeatedly, sometimes to come to an understanding of a difficult passage, sometimes to make sure of remembering an important point, sometimes to savor ideas particularly well-expressed. Students need to learn, however, that slow reading is not always efficient reading. It is also important for students to understand how and when to scan text. While skimming is rapid glancing through text in order to get an idea of what it is about, scanning is a purposeful kind of skimming—reading rapidly for the purpose of finding specific information. Text hunts and similar activities can encourage students to scan one or two pages of text to find the answer to a literal question, and the skill of scanning is very useful as students begin to use a wide variety of texts. For example, a student looking for information about Rosa Parks would first check the indexes of a variety of books on recent U. S. history, and on the civil rights struggle, noting page numbers where Parks is mentioned. Then the student would scan each page listed, first to find the name *Rosa Parks*, and then to see whether the needed information was given.

Structural Analysis, Word Derivations

The study of word parts is called structural analysis. It can be useful and interesting to learn about word roots, to notice how, in English, the words *structure* and *structural*, *analyze* and *analysis*, *use* and *useful*, *interest* and *interesting*, for example, are related, and how many words can be based on a single root word; for example, *read, reads, reader, reading, readable, unreadable, rereading.* Meaningful word parts that are added to root words to form new words are called affixes, and there are two kinds: prefixes are placed at the beginning of words and suffixes at the end. Familiarity with common prefixes and suffixes contributes to rapid vocabulary growth and enables mature readers to understand words they have never seen before. For example, if I wrote that some concepts are *ungraspable*—a word which I have never used before nor seen used—readers might want to argue (how can there be a concept nobody can grasp?) even though they had not encountered the word *ungraspable*

before either. Most readers understand the meaning of *ungraspable* because they know the meaning of *un-* and *-able* through wide reading rather than because they have had formal instruction about affixes. Unless a person is strongly motivated to learn a list of prefixes and suffixes, information about word structure is likely to be better learned and recalled when information is provided briefly at a time when it is needed (as in the FYI strategy described earlier in this chapter). Many English words are derived from other languages. Knowing the meaning of some Latin and Greek words, which are the roots of English words, can also be useful and interesting. The word derivation boxes included throughout this text provide examples. Teachers who have an interest in word derivations are likely to be able to encourage a similar interest in their students.

Vowels, Consonants

In English, the letters *a, e, i, o,* and *u* represent vowel sounds, which are voiced as air flows freely through the parts of the body that enable us to speak, from the lungs to the mouth. The letters *y* and *w*, though usually consonants, sometimes represent vowel sounds (as in *by* and *how*). The other letters are consonants, representing speech sounds made by altering the flow of air. (Try forming the sound of /t/, for example, and notice the position of your tongue and teeth.) There is extensive terminology to name different kinds of vowel and consonant combinations—*blend, digraph, diphthong, schwa,* for example—and different terms used to classify words with different combinations of vowels and consonants. (For example, cvc words are words that begin with a consonant or combination of consonants, followed by a vowel and then a consonant: *can, pet, shin, hop, hug;* in cvc words the vowel typically has what is called a short vowel sound. Another common pattern is cvce, in which the consonant, vowel, and consonant are followed by a silent e: *cane, Pete, shine, hope, huge;* in these words there is a long vowel sound, in which the vowel sound and the letter name are the same. Teachers in some fields need to know the meaning of this kind of terminology;

however, it is not necessary for all teachers—or for *any* students—to learn the terms, unless they are interested in doing so. (If in doubt about whether a student needs to learn a term or a rule to read, ask yourself if you need to know it. Can you, for example, read this page without being able to circle all the words that contain a schwa? You bet you can!)

Strategic Teachers, Part Four

"We're serious about learning."

This is Rose Spen's ninth year of teaching; she describes her career in education, to date, as divided into before-children and after-children. Although there were many applicants for positions at the time, she was hired as a kindergarten teacher immediately after graduating from college. Three years later she married and moved to a different state where she taught second grade and music in a private school for two years. She stopped teaching when her first child was born, but always looked forward to returning. When her second child was three, Ms. Spen decided to apply to enter a master's program at a local university and prepare over a period of several years to resume teaching. She was pleased to be accepted into the program, though disappointed to discover that the graduate courses were all taught at night except in the summer. She had hoped, with one child in second grade and another in preschool, to take courses in the morning. But she enjoyed her classes, began substituting in the following year, and then found a position as first grade teacher in the same district her children attend. Now her children are 13 and 10; she has a master's degree in reading education, and she is completing her fourth year of teaching first grade.

She loves teaching first grade and is pleased that it sandwiches in so neatly with her prior experience as a kindergarten and then second grade teacher. All of her past experiences have influenced her teaching, and she sees even situations that have been difficult as helping her learn. One particularly influential experience, which she nevertheless wishes had not happened, was that her first child's first grade year was not happy. The child entered school with a love of books and a lively interest in math, loved talking and bubbled with energy—qualities that ebbed away into silence and sometimes belligerence or tears. The first report card indicated less than adequate work ("Needs Improvement") in most subjects; the teacher's comment was that the child was "beginning to learn how first graders behave." In a conference, the teacher explained that her goals were related to behavior: first graders needed to follow rules, work neatly, listen carefully, and remain quiet. Second grade, the teacher pointed out, was tough, and she needed to prepare the children for it. Ms. Spen and her husband still debate whether they made the right decision in sticking out the year, but they did, waiting till June to make an appointment with the principal to ask that their child's second grade teacher be someone with warmth and a love of learning. With normal ups and downs, school has generally been a good experience for the Spen children since that year, and the unhappy first grader has become a vigorous seventh grader who loves to read and is an enthusiastic member of the school's math club. One of Ms. Spen's most firmly held beliefs about teaching is influenced by her child's experience. She believes that it is a teacher's responsibility to make every student's experience, each day, as happy and productive as possible, and never, never to use the idea that school may be harsh in the future as an excuse for making it unpleasant now.

One of the many texts that impressed her during her graduate study was Jean Carew's longitudinal study of eight children during their early years. She found the description of the child called "Sonia" particularly vivid, because of the language-rich environment Sonia's mother provided for her. Carew describes the child as being "bathed in words" (Carew, 1976, p. 94) and Ms. Spen relates this to some of her beliefs about teaching. First, she believes in the metaphor of immersion—in the idea that people learn best when they are fully and comfortably surrounded by events and language related to their learning. Second, she believes that school can and must provide a language-rich environment and that this is good for all students as a satisfying extension of homes where literacy is an important aspect of life for adults and children, and as an expansion of literacy horizons for children whose learning in this area will come primarily from school. Based on these beliefs, she incorporates literacy and oracy activities into every part of her teaching.

How Does She Do It?

Ms. Spen is a teacher who enjoys her own professional learning. She established the habit of reading professional journals regularly during her years of graduate study and intends never to stop. Rather than attending commercially sponsored workshops, she prefers to go to conferences of professional education organizations. Both the International Reading Association (IRA) and the National Association for the Education of Young Children (NAEYC) have active affiliate organizations in her state, and she tries to attend at least one day of each annual state conference. Once a year she attends a conference of a national professional organization. Her school makes a small financial contribution, but most of the cost comes from family savings; however, her family always links the conference with a vacation—pleasant to plan and to do, because the conferences are always held in places the family enjoys visiting.

She brings back both books and ideas from the conferences, often children's books autographed by their authors and illustrators, which she enjoys talking about with her students. Many of the strategies that she uses regularly are ideas she has learned about from her professional reading and from conference attendance, and adapted for her classroom and her students. Several examples give a flavor of her classroom, though by no means a complete description.

Reading. She uses science trade books as one of the major bases for her reading program, incorporating a variety of strategies. Her version of guided imagery is to use books in Joanne Ryder's "Just for a Day" series, such as *White bear, ice bear* (1994) and *Lizard in the sun* (1990), in which readers or listeners are led to imagine themselves as the creature that is the subject of the book. These are favorite read-aloud stories and Ms. Spen often incorporates the Say Something and Do Something strategies into her reading. The text in Ryder's book is chunked into meaningful phrases, which makes if easier for students to read. Ms. Spen has multiple paperback copies, so that children can use them in pairs or groups for a variety of emergent literacy and reading activities, such as retelling the story, listening to a classmate read, paired reading, copying words and phrases of their choice from the pages, creating new illustrations, and writing their own stories.

Each year there are children in Ms. Spen's class who enter as fluent readers. She knows that there are other children in the class who are not readers but will leap ahead during the year. These children enjoy hearing and reading storybooks repetitively; when these books also include an informational Foreword or Afterword, these children enjoy the challenge of reading that and can then serve as resources for their classmates. Lois Ehlert's large print rhyming storybook about a squirrel at her door, *Nuts to you* (1993), is one which all the children can soon read from memory; a few children can also read, and share with others, the information about a squirrel's tail, nest home, and food, which is included at the end of the book.

She has adapted the RESPONSE study strategy for her first graders by combining it with two other strategies: Daily Journal and LEA. After she reads a book aloud—perhaps once, perhaps several times—she scribes students' ideas on a chart, divided into the three sections used on a RESPONSE form: "These are important ideas." "These are our questions." "These are interesting new words." As answers to questions are sought and found (from students' families, from other teachers and classroom guests, and from resource materials ,which Ms. Spen shares using a Reference Source Commentary), these are recorded on the RESPONSE charts. She uses the RESPONSE charts after reading topic-relevant science books, such as Seymour Simon's *Earthquakes* (1991), *Storms* (1989), and *Weather* (1993). Eventually she prepares the information from the RESPONSE chart in the form of a Language Experience Activity (LEA) story.

She also uses read-alouds as a gentle version of Discrepant Events, choosing for this purpose Hana Machotka's "Guess and Learn" series (e.g., *What neat feet* (1991) and *Outstanding outsides* (1993)). For these first graders, the discrepancy that catches their attention is seeing a part—for example in *Breathtaking noses*, 1992, a close-up photograph of an animal's nose—before seeing the whole.

She also uses trade books, and activities based on trade books, as students learn math concepts and computation. Books such as *Ten old pails* (Heller, 1994) are read repeatedly for the cheerful story and for the counting process: one to ten, and then from ten back to one. One of many ways that children learn about geometrical shapes is through Lois Ehlert's *Color farm* (1989) and *Color zoo* (1990). Ms. Spen knows that for some of the children in her class, these and many other books are old familiar favorites, while other

children encounter and enjoy them for the first time. Reading and math and cooking are linked as the class reads and follows directions for making tasty food in *Eating fractions* (MacMillan, 1991). Multiple copies of *Anno's counting house* (Anno, 1982) are available and children use them as the basis for devising math questions and writing simple equations. *Animal numbers* (Kitchen, 1987), links math and science as it matches numbers with animal pictures, asking the question "How many babies in each mother's brood?" The final page gives "Animal Facts" for each of the numerals pictured, e.g., "2. Swan: Swans lay 2–5 eggs which hatch into cygnets. These generally swim in close procession behind their mother." Fourth graders who are engaged in a cross-grade collaboration with her first graders read the books and talk about them, being careful to use mathematical language: "We can *count* the number of people sitting, and the number of people standing, and then we can *add* the numbers to find the *total* number of people."

She uses a rich array of strategies for engaging her students in multiple hearings and readings of text: echo reading, chanting (a class favorite is Verna Aardema's *Bringing the rain to Kapiti plain* (1981), which Ms. Spen has available as a Big Book, along with multiple sets for children), manipulable cloze, and taped readings (readers include parents of students, both Ms. Spen's children, and fourth graders from Mr. Garwin's classroom). Joyce and Daniel McCauley's article (1992) on choral reading inspired her to use this strategy with a wide variety of poetry. Among the poets children enjoy are Eloise Greenfield (1986), Nikki Giovanni (1985), Valerie Worth (1987) and Charlotte Pomerantz (1980, 1989), whose poems integrate several languages. She uses poems from Greenfield's *Honey, I love* as a starting point for long lists (such as lists of things the children love), which she records on charts for chanting. Ms. Spen's favorite collection of poetry for children is *Tomie dePaola's book of poems* (dePaola, 1988).

She and her students love books by Anna Grossnickle Hines (1993, 1994), and also *Galimoto* (Williams, 1990) and *Where are you going Manyoni?* (Stock, 1993), which are about African children their age. After multiple read-alouds, she puts the text on cards for sequence reading. They also love books which illustrate songs, such as Wendy Watson's *Fox went out on a chilly night* (1994). Ms. Spen plays her guitar while a student turns the pages and the whole class sings. Beginning in February, Ms. Spen brings out a variety of Readers' Theater scripts which are adaptations of familiar stories and poems.

In addition to being rich in books, signs, and pictures, Ms. Spen makes her classroom learning-filled and lively by encouraging her students to bring in samples of environmental print, such as labels, logos and stickers, that they can recognize—and therefore read. She knows that many children can recognize words that are a part of their environment, such as stop signs and the names of stores and brand names for food and clothing, well before they come to school, and that this kind of reading through recognition can build confidence as well as reading ability.

Cross-Grade Collaboration. Her resources here are several conference presentations and journal articles (e.g., Morrice and Simmons, 1991). Her first graders enjoy their fourth grade buddies, and are proud to plan events they can share with their friends; for example, performing Readers' Theater scripts for them. A book that both classes enjoy is *Communication*, by Aliki (1993), with its dedication "For all the tellers and the listeners of the world." The fourth graders never tire of reading it and soon the first graders can read sections also. Noticing how much information can be conveyed by a cartoon strip format encourages both groups of students to create and share original captioned cartoons. Another shared activity is a "Seed Stroll" in the spring—an idea Ms. Spen read about in *Foodworks* (Ontario Science Center, 1987, p. 61), a book she bought at a conference held in Canada. For this activity, the two classes take a nature walk on the playground and in a wooded area near the school, first putting on old wool socks over their shoes. Back in the classroom after the walk, the students carefully pull off the seeds that have clung to the socks, and later classify their seed collections. In April, first and fourth graders collaborate in studying the weather.

Classroom Arrangement. After reading Gay Fawcett's "Moving the big desk" (1992), and visiting the classroom of a friend with lively ideas about room arrangement, Ms. Spen rearranged the way her own desk is placed. It is now completely out of the way at one side of the room and set up to be a real adult workstation, which she uses primarily before and after school. (During the school day she moves around the room or sits where she can be close to students, in low chairs beside them, at a low table where she can meet with a group, or in a comfortable chair on the read-aloud rug.) Near the desk there is a file cabinet and a bookshelf and two comfortable adult chairs. (Additional folding chairs are available if needed for conferences and the children are welcome to use the adults' chairs during their "reading choice" time.) On the wall there is a bulletin board, which Ms. Spen uses to post announcements and reminders, and also her favorite quotations. She feels particularly fortunate in having two computers and a printer in her room; these are resources for her students and also for her, because she uses the computer to prepare newsletters and classroom materials, and the computer area is near her desk so that she can easily put the computer on her own desk. Several years ago she began a collection of quotations, which are important to her teaching. (One thing she is meticulous about is being sure she notes down the full source, a practice she developed after a few occasions when she wanted to cite quotations—in a paper for a graduate class, and in a newsletter for parents—and had to spend a lot of time tracking them down.) From time to time she chooses a quotation and makes it into a small poster that she displays by her desk. This month's poster is a quotation from a chapter on teaching science to children, from a British text:

> Teachers need to take children's ideas seriously
>   and avoid making them believe
>   that they have to search for the right
>   answer, hidden
>
> somewhere in the teacher's head.
>
> When teachers are open to children's ideas,
>   all pupils in a class
>   are taken seriously
>   as learners and thinkers.

Adapted from Pamela Wadsworth, 1992, p. 61. "Primary science: Starting from children's ideas." In Tony Booth, Will Swann, Mary Masterton and Patricia Potts (Eds.). *Learning for all 1: Curricula for diversity in education.* London: Routledge.

Challenge to the Reader: Suggest a way to expand the collaboration between the first grade and fourth grade classes.

Choose and Use: If you were to choose one aspect of Ms. Spen's program to use in your own classroom, what would it be? How would

Meeting Needs and Celebrating Strengths: Diversity in the Content Area Classroom

Students differ. So what? This is the question we should be answering.

ROBERT E. SLAVIN, 1993, P. 14.

One of this text's major themes is that good theory, ethics, and practice encourage respect for the worth and talents of all people. Inclusionary education—educational policies and practices that assume the inclusion of a diversity of students in the schools and classrooms—is based on meeting students' varying needs in ways that link students rather than create separations. This text is premised on the idea that inclusionary education is both desirable and possible. In addressing the issue of diversity in education, an important first step is to accept that diversity is unavoidable, then to move on from accepting diversity among students to valuing it. The first section focuses on the fact that there is bound to be diversity among students in the classroom. Subsequent sections discuss the opportunities and challenges this diversity provides.

The chapter does not consist of a series of separate sections about student differences; there are many excellent sources from which teachers can draw upon for such information, including texts and journals about particular student characteristics and situations and relevant articles throughout the professional literature. Instead of focusing on factors that separate them, attention is given to the needs all students share and to the variety of strengths they possess. A major feature of the chapter is the presentation of important educational concepts that have been developed by educators who are working to meet the special needs of particular groups of students. Some of the concepts and instructional interventions that have been developed specifically for students with disabilities or with other special needs can be helpful and practical for other students as well. However, although they can be applied to the teaching of all students, they may be unfamiliar to many teachers because they are usually discussed in literature that is focused on students' special needs or characteristics.

Diversity Is a Fact

Students differ. Over the years, vast amounts of time, thought, and energy have been squandered on efforts to make this untrue, through exclusion and separation. However, in situations where ethnic minorities, girls and women, and people with disabilities have been barred from educational opportunities, those who are admitted as students differ from one another. Even in situations where students are tested, classified, ranked, rated, and differentially placed, within every separate track or group, students differ. Earlier in this text, at the end of Chapter Three, there is an introduction to the sections describing hypothetical strategic teachers that follows Chapters Three through Eleven. There the fact that there are differences among students is described as "a given," that is, as something that is a feature of every teaching situation.

> Their classrooms are the same every year in one important way: every student is different. …There are students who come into the class interested in learning and others who begin the year unhappy and resistant; students with extensive prior knowledge about subject matter they will be learning and students with very little; students who have read (or been read to) extensively and have an excellent command of the English language, others whose primary language is not English, and yet others whose prior experience of books is severely limited. Every year some students enter after school has begun and others move away. Students get sick; some families extend vacation time before and after holidays. Some families set aside a regular time and place for homework as a household routine; in some families no attention is paid to students' assignments, while a few children are punished or heavily rewarded because of what happens in school. There are students from happy homes and homes beset by troubles, and the teachers know that every year between September and June many events—some joyous, some painful—will cause significant changes in students' home lives. …[These] teachers…—like all teachers—have a diversity of students. That's one feature of teaching they don't need to worry about—it's a given.

Seymour Sarason is a scholar whose recent book *You are thinking of teaching?* reflects on his experi-ences as a researcher, clinician, consultant, and teacher educator, spanning 50 years. He explains that his first awareness of the great diversity that exists among any group of students occurred during his first job, in the 1940s, when he was working with children who were institutionalized and classified as being mentally retarded. In a footnote, he remarks that Public Law 94-142—discussed briefly later—gave many teachers the opportunity to learn that "regular and special children did not constitute two nonoverlapping human species" (Sarason, 1993, p. 90). In the quotation below he has chosen to use the word *wildly* to emphasize how much students vary, regardless of how they are grouped or classified:

> …the odds are overwhelming that the children in your class will vary widely and wildly on almost every significant personal, intellectual, and behavioral characteristic. *Of course high school students are different in obvious ways from middle school students, who are different from elementary school children, who are different from preschoolers…*, But in each classroom in each category, the teacher will be confronted with what in principle are identical problems centering around variations [in the characteristics] of students. (Sarason, 1993, p. 91–92)

Attempts to Avoid Diversity

The question quoted at the beginning of this chapter— *Students differ. So what?*—has been, and continues to be, approached in educational settings in four major ways. Three of these approaches, which are all based on attempts to avoid or circumvent the fact that students differ, will be discussed here.

▪ Students differ [but they must be taught in the same way], so differences are the students' problem. *We will ignore, or rule out, differences.*

▪ Students differ [and each one must be taught in a different way], so we will invent ways to find out all about each student and then find instructional packages that will teach each student individually. *We will create a teaching system in which all students are taught separately.*

▪ Students differ [and we cannot teach them all together], so we will identify groups and put students into groups [and then students within the groups will be the same]. *We will create teaching situations in which students do not differ.*

The first approach to avoiding diversity—ignore, or rule out, differences—is now in many cases illegal. Laws have been passed guaranteeing students with characteristics that had previously been grounds for exclusion the right to be educated in environments that are as inclusive (least restrictive) as possible. The second attempt—create a teaching system in which all students are taught separately—is impractical. Efforts to accomplish it isolate students and diminish the teacher's role, although "teacher-proof" programs and packages continue to be advertised, claiming to identify different characteristics for each student and provide sets of materials for students to work through individually. The third approach—create teaching situations in which students do not differ—is impossible, even though methods intended to accomplish this are still widely used.

Inclusion Is a Mandate: IDEA

Education is a need. Government actions have sometimes worked against equal access for everyone to educational opportunities, but far more often they have contributed to gains in this area. (The history of legislative action and judicial decisions relating to public education is itself an interesting and valuable topic of study.) Efforts in the United States to ensure equitable access to education for people whose physical, intellectual, and behavioral characteristics create a need for accommodations to enable them to learn or function within school settings have resulted, in the latter part of the twentieth century, in a series of federal laws, with landmark legislation passed in 1975, when Public Law 94-142 was signed into law.

Through PL 94-142, the Education of All Handicapped Children Act, people of school age with specified handicaps are guaranteed the right to an education that is free, appropriate, and public. Two concepts institutionalized by that act were least restrictive environment (LRE) and mainstreaming. For all students, education must be provided in the least restrictive environment possible. For most stu-

dents, this means placement in regular schools and classrooms for some or all of their program, thus inclusion in the main stream of the educational system. Christine Salisbury and Barbara Smith make a distinction between conceptual and legal meanings of the term least restrictive environment. In practice, placing students in the least restrictive environment means educating people with disabilities so the fewest restrictions are placed on their opportunities to interact with typical agemates. As these authors point out, such placements require collaboration among teachers, paraprofessionals, and other staff. The legal interpretation of the term is that "the law presumes that services will be delivered in the classroom the child would attend were he or she not handicapped" (Salisbury & Smith, 1991, p. 25).

In 1990, the legislation was reauthorized as PL 101-476, the Individuals with Disabilities Education Act, known by its acronym, IDEA. Specific categories of disabling conditions are identified in these laws. One difference between PL 94-142 and PL 101-476 is in the terminology. The word *disabilities* is substituted for *handicaps*, and, in a subtle but important change, the word referring to "people" is placed before words describing conditions: "handicapped people" is changed to "individuals with disabilities." Legislation alone cannot accomplish all that needs to be done so that the needs of diverse students can be met, but the law establishes structure and rules for inclusion. As Kenneth Cushner and his colleagues (Cushner, McClelland, & Safford, 1992, p. 141) note, "…these new provisions extend through force of law the concern of the society for those whose 'difference' has traditionally excluded them from full participation in ordinary life. It is, perhaps, a mark of some maturity that, as a nation, we have come this far." Twenty-five disabling conditions are identified by PL 101-476. Inclusion of students with disabilities in regular classrooms—known as the Regular Education Initiative, or REI—has been a practice in some states for many years. In federal and state agencies, universities and colleges, school districts, communities, schools and individual classrooms, educators, parents, and other concerned citizens continue to seek ways to provide effective, inclusive education. Inclusive education has been the subject of much discussion (e.g., O'Neil, 1993). Successful inclusion requires collaboration among educators and administrators who are themselves diverse in their areas of specialization and who use their combined knowledge and talents to find ways to accommodate diverse students in a shared setting.

Grouping To Exclude Is Harmful

The way in which education is provided affects students' progress as well as their enjoyment of school. Over the past 60 years, a method usually called "ability grouping" has been the framework for providing instruction, especially instruction in reading and language arts, in huge numbers of American classrooms. This method is based on dividing students according to some estimate of their achievement—often based on flimsy data—or a presumption about the rapidity with which they are able to learn. Calling such groups "ability groups" implies two things: first, that there are real and significant similarities in the ability to learn among students within each group, and second, that there are real and significant differences in learning ability between students in different groups. Solid evidence of this does not exist. Evidence that the practice is harmful has been presented for many years. Two decades ago, Kenneth Hadermann (1976, pp. 85 and 89) wrote, "In general, research indicates that ability grouping of pupils not only is unfavorable, but that it actually is deleterious. In effect, ability grouping really is not possible, has negative effects on the learning of pupils assigned to 'low ability' groups, tends to group pupils by socioeconomic class rather than by innate ability, and locks pupils into a pattern of nonachievement." He went on to express the hope that "perhaps, someday, the facts may change the collective mind of the schools."

Though the term "ability grouping" continues to be used in professional literature, it is now often placed in quotation marks (as it is here) to show that authors do not accept its literal meaning. In other words, many people who write about this kind of grouping do not believe that students' "ability" is the basis for grouping.

> [Schools often group] students according to "abilities." …[M]ainstream students tend to be placed in advanced classes while non-mainstream students

find themselves in "remedial" classes or in the "low" groups within heterogeneous classes… [where they] practice subskills in boring exercises characterized by redundancy and irrelevancy; they concentrate on grammar, punctuation, spelling, or decoding exercises and practice simple memory or comprehension tasks rather than reading good literature, writing extended text, or practicing problem solving or critical thinking. …Thus, they are not given the chance to develop the skills that they are penalized for not having. (Lucas & Schecter, 1992, pp. 99–100)

The term "high/middle/low" grouping will be used here (abbreviated sometimes to HML grouping), as a more accurate descriptor than "ability grouping." A high group is a group whose members are identified by the teacher or school as advanced, with the expectation that they will be taught using more challenging materials, and at a more rapid pace, than students in other groups. Conversely, a low group consists of students who are viewed as lagging behind their classmates, and for whom a slow pace of instruction and simple learning materials are used. A middle group consists of students presumed to be too advanced for the low group and not sufficiently capable to be included in the high group. Sometimes teachers form more than three groups in an effort to create greater similarity within groups. Based on classroom studies, Claude Goldenberg (1989) has noted that when there is high/middle/low grouping for reading, the number of groups tends to increase over the year and the newly formed groups are "lower" than the previous "low" group. Such grouping does both immediate and long-term harm. Results of research (e.g., Borko & Eisenhart, 1986) indicate that ability grouping itself is a major causal factor in reading failure for students placed in "low" reading groups. The harmful features of high/middle/low grouping have been widely discussed in the professional literature over the past several decades.

Many factors in high/middle/low grouping make the process a "self-fulfilling prophecy" (Eder, 1981), that is, a prediction that makes itself come true. When students are first placed in HML groups those in the high group have not yet had the opportunity to excel academically; those placed in the low group have not yet failed. Grouping them is a prophecy, a prediction about how these students will progress in the future. What happens to the students as a result of HML grouping, however, makes the prediction come true. Placing students in these categories gives them school experiences that virtually ensure that those in the high group will excel in school-related activities, those in the middle group will perform adequately, and those in the low group will do poorly.

The sequel to HML grouping in the elementary school is tracking in the middle school and high school. Tracking is the assignment of students to different curricula designed to prepare them for different kinds of lives, with their work ranging from professional careers to menial jobs. Here there is no need to use an alternative phrase to describe the practice: students who are "ability grouped" are getting ready to be tracked. There may be more than three groupings in a tracked system, but essentially the high/middle/low distinction is maintained. One track is designed to prepare students for college and professional careers. Another is intended to prepare students for middle level jobs and perhaps attendance at two-year colleges. Another is for students for whom the appropriate vocational goal is deemed to be work in jobs with minimal chance for advancement, students who are not expected to attend college and may not finish high school. Paul George (1993, p. 18) has summarized research findings on HML grouping and tracking, noting that the available research strongly indicates that accurate placement of students into groups is very difficult to accomplish, but that "once placed in a group it appears that students are increasingly unlikely to be moved to a supposedly faster group. It is 'a locked in/locked out situation.'" Richard Allington's research on reading instruction, which spans many years, led him to write, "If one accepts the premise that children are more likely to learn what they are taught and also accepts the preliminary evidence that poor readers are taught quite differently from good readers, then one must accept that poor readers will never become good readers" (Allington, 1983, p. 556).

HML grouping and tracking control and often limit students' opportunities to learn and progress. When high/middle/low grouping is used, students whose academically related development is less advanced than their classmates at an early point in their school careers, are given instruction that *slows them down.* "The pace of instruction is slowed for some learners, incredibly by design, thus ensuring that they will not develop literacy on schedule with their peers, if ever" (Allington, 1991, p. 25). Claude Goldenberg (1989, p. 331) characterizes the content of instruction in low groups as "anemic." He comments that there is "widespread agreement that substantial differences exist in the academic content and learning opportunities offered to children in different academic groups [and] …low group placement restricts the range and level of what students are taught or exposed to." Henry M. Levin advocates acceleration—the use of activities designed to interest and challenge students and to encourage higher level thinking—rather than remediation, for students who need special help. "Acceleration works just as well for at-risk students…[and remedial procedures often] deliberately slow the learning of children who lack educational advantages" (Levin & Hopfenberg, 1991, p. 12).

> There does not have to be a bottom group. …For nearly a century we have had a too limited view of the potential of children and of the power of instruction. (Allington, 1991, pp. 26 and 27)

> *Never* remediate. *Always* enrich. Treat students as if they were all gifted and talented, and they will show you that in some way or in many ways, they are. (Alejandro, 1994, p. 20)

One of the leading journals for high school and middle school language arts teachers is *English Journal*, published by the National Council of Teachers of English (NCTE). One feature is "The Round Table," where a question is posed and in a future issue readers' answers are summarized and selected responses are printed, representing various points of view on the question. Several years ago (The Round Table, 1990), the question addressed was, "What do you think of tracking? If 'basic' students are served well by tracking in your school, what is the key to your success? If not, what alternatives have you found effective?" For the first time in the journal's history there was absolute unanimity among the responses: all replies opposed tracking. As Patricia Kean (1993, p. 34) reminds us, "ultimately, tracking stunts the opportunity for growth, the one area in which all children are naturally gifted." All learners, not just those classified as low or slow, are limited by this kind of grouping, which exerts a heavy influence on students' views of themselves, of each other, and of school-related learning. Elfrieda Hiebert (1983) surveyed research over three decades and noted a consistency in findings that students are aware of their own and each other's status when grouped for reading instruction. Not only do they evaluate themselves positively or negatively, depending on whether their own placement is high or low, their attitude toward classmates is heavily influenced by the classmates' placements, thus students in high groups tend to be admired and sought after as friends and students in low groups tend to be spurned. Most adults can remember throughout life what their position was if they were grouped for instruction in school.

> By the second or third grade. . . children know precisely where they stand on the 'smart or dumb' continuum, and since most children at this age want to succeed in school, this knowledge profoundly affects their self-esteem. …[T]here are millions of adults who carry with them the conviction that they "can't do math" or play an instrument or write well. And it may all be the result of assessments made of them and internalized as children—long before they had any idea of what they wanted from life. Their sense of inadequacy may prevent them from exploring alternative careers or simply narrow their experiences. (Tobias, 1989, p. 57) Reprinted with permission from *Psychology Today*, © 1989 (Sussex Publishers, Inc.)

Clearly, it is harmful to students whose placement is on the "dumb" end of the placement scheme. But do students whose placement informs them and others that they are smart benefit, even though the benefit is at the expense of others? There are disadvantages for these students as well. Besides limiting the time teachers and students, or students and students, work together, such grouping systems also concentrate resources and attention on grouping, rather than on learning and teaching. In the elementary school, the early weeks of school may be focused on testing to form groups; students who enter in the middle of the year cannot be welcomed

fully until their group placement is determined; teachers' time at the end of the year is spent reporting on students' group status to guide next year's teacher. Within the year, teachers try to solve teaching problems by rearranging student placements.

Worst of all, education becomes focused not on learning but on status. Asked about their reading experience in school, elementary students in "high" groups typically report that they are "in the highest book," rather than talking about authors and themes and exciting ideas. As Peter Winograd and Scott Paris write (1988–1989, p. 33), "…use of ability groups teaches children that success in reading is measured not by information gained or pleasure experienced, but rather by group membership." If students placed in advanced groups, across the K–12 span, internalize the idea that their talents will be recognized without effort on their part, they are likely to be at serious disadvantage in higher education and in their careers. Eventually, in many situations, group placement itself comes to be regarded as meeting the needs of advanced students. Although there is ample evidence that very different kinds of instruction are given to high and low groups at the elementary level, by the time students reach high school the classes in different tracks may no longer be differentiated by the instructional methods used. Kimberly Trimble and Robert Sinclair reported on their study of high school classes for high, middle, and low tracks, titling their article "On the wrong track: Ability grouping and the threat to equity." They found a "numbing similarity of practices and content both within and across classes" (Trimble & Sinclair, 1987, p. 20), and concluded that tracking cannot be justified by a need to diversify instruction, since tracking has not resulted in diversification.

Even when teachers accept the research findings that show ability grouping is ineffective in helping students grow as readers and learners, those who use HML grouping are sometimes reluctant to change because they see no other way to arrange a large portion of the school day. High/middle/low grouping for reading instruction is so commonly used in elementary schools that it has become a method of classroom management. In many classrooms, as Richard Allington and his colleagues have pointed out (e.g.,

What Can Individual Teachers Do?

▪ Teachers who can choose whether or not to use HML grouping, or who work in situations where the policy is not to use HML grouping, have the opportunity to use inclusive methods of grouping. They can learn with and from their colleagues and from their own reflections and use strategies described in texts such as this one and in professional journals to teach using whole class and cooperative group structures, working to produce communities of learners.

▪ Teachers who work in situations where HML grouping is still expected can confer with their administrators to explain the instructional methods they would prefer to use, and request the opportunity to try them. If HML grouping is imposed, they can use good learning activities and good literature for all groups, limit the time spent in the assigned groups, and give students many opportunities to work in a variety of groupings, depending on their interests.

▪ Teachers whose specialization is helping students who are identified as having particular learning needs have important opportunities to work toward inclusiveness. They can team with classroom teachers, spend time in classrooms collaborating with teachers there, and work with students in inclusive groups. When teachers work with students outside of the classroom they can work to achieve "curricular congruence" (Allington & Shake, 1986) for students by meshing their teaching with their students' regular classroom curriculum, focusing on shared subject matter and using teaching methods that match the best of the methods used in the regular classroom. They can arrange for students who are drawn out of the classroom to miss as little as possible of enjoyable, enriching parts of the school day.

▪ Teachers who work in settings where their students are tracked can teach with the belief that everyone can learn. They can work to create communities of learners within the groups of students assigned to them, using the precious time available to ensure that students experience excitement in learning and become aware of their own capacities to learn. Teachers can use strategies described in texts such as this one and in professional journals to teach using whole class and cooperative group structures. They can read the professional literature advocating acceleration rather than remediation (e.g., Brandt, 1992; Levin & Hopfenberg, 1991) and describe some of the successes of low-tracked students working with teachers who care about them (e.g., Dillon, 1989; Howard & Liner, 1990; Richards, 1987). Teachers can team with colleagues, formally or informally, and work toward systemic change.

Jachym, Allington, & Broikou, 1989), students spend two-thirds of the time allotted to their language arts instruction doing seatwork (assigned paper and pencil activities, such as workbook pages, to be completed individually). Why is this so? It is entirely due to the grouping system that categorizes students as high, middle, or low, a grouping system students fully understand, whatever names—Bluebirds, Robins and Eagles, or Racers, Swifties, and Speedies—the groups are given. When the high group meets with the teacher, the middle and low groups do seatwork; when the middle group meets with the teacher, the high and low groups do seatwork; when the low group meets with the teacher, the high and middle groups do seatwork. Thus, for the system to work, two-thirds of students' time allotted to this instruction, which frequently consumes the full morning, is spent doing individual workbook-style tasks.

Arthur Combs, writing more than 15 years ago about beliefs that impede educational progress, devoted a chapter to "the myth of the value of grouping," stressing that grouping of this kind is a management system—he called it "an administrative expedient" (Combs, 1979, p. 217). Grouping, he asserted, is done for the convenience of teachers or administrators, or both, and while there is nothing wrong with acting for convenience sake per se, the effects of the practice on students are more important than adults' convenience. Teachers, therefore, need not only an understanding of why HML grouping is harmful, they need to learn about, or devise, alternatives. It is one of the goals of this text to describe methods of teaching and classroom organization and management that do not depend on attempts to avoid diversity.

Diversity Is a Fact To Be Valued

While three approaches to diversity in education—rule out differences, teach students separately, create groups in which students do not differ—treat diversity as a problem to be overcome, there is a fourth approach, one that treats diversity as a fact to be valued: Students differ [and we will accept and use that fact] so we will be interested in each student individually while we find and use instructional strategies that work well for students with a variety of strengths and needs. We will work to create inclusive learning environments, communities of learners in which our diverse students are welcomed and their different interests, experiences, and talents enrich each other's learning.

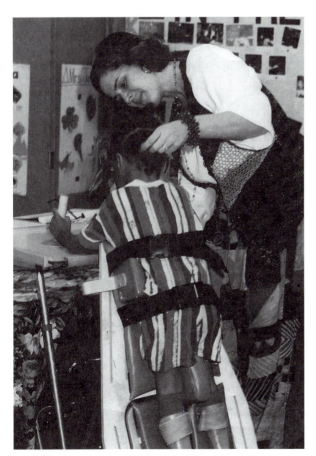

When teachers take a wide view of the way strengths can be demonstrated, they will find many opportunities to recognize and celebrate students' strengths.

This fourth approach is a vision, but the vision is one that more and more teachers and other educators are striving toward and enjoying. Instead of bypassing teachers by relying on people outside of the classroom to determine who can and who cannot participate, or on commercial groups to provide tests and worksheets for students to work on alone, this approach gives teachers a central role. Educational theorists, administrators, community members, parents and students can support and promote the vision, but inclusive, welcoming, effective learning environments depend on teachers who make choices, care for their students, and are themselves actively engaged in learning. In these environments, both the needs and strengths of learners are appreciated and taken seriously.

Strengths and Needs

All people have talents and abilities, strengths that can be used to accomplish and to achieve. The term *strengths* is often contrasted with the term *weaknesses*. But when educators consider students' strengths and weaknesses, there is a tendency to sort or categorize the students themselves as strong or weak, good or poor. These labels lead to the use of differentiated instructional strategies, which research has shown leads in turn to those students who are classified as weak as falling farther and farther behind their classmates. There also are negative effects for students who are classified as strong. If they come to regard themselves as people who learn without effort, they will be unprepared for learning in situations where effort is expected and needed.

It is preferable to consider every student as possessing both strengths and needs and also to realize that these strengths and needs change as the students progress developmentally. A four-year-old child's ability to simulate reading by reciting a favorite story from memory is an important strength. The same child, two years later, may show a different kind of strength in struggling to read the words in the story exactly. Eventually, one of the student's strengths may be the ability and willingness to read the tale aloud to a younger child. Within one classroom, some students' strengths may include the ability to read challenging text-book material with ease; they may need the opportunity to read more widely on content-related topics that interest them. Other students may show strengths in understanding mathematical and spatial concepts quickly and may need opportunities to develop their reading ability by reading with a more advanced buddy or to progress further in math. Older students who need guidance in writing factually sound papers that express an original point of view are likely to bring varying combinations of strengths to the task. Some will have substantial prior knowledge of content topics; some will possess considerable technical skill in writing; some will be quick to develop new ideas and perspectives. At any level, at any time, each student in a class has strengths and needs that an astute, caring teacher can recognize and use when planning appropriate instruction. Moreover, students benefit from thinking of themselves as people who have both strengths and needs, and they can be guided to do so. The concept of strengths and needs is fostered when teachers think of themselves, as well as their students, in this fashion—when the truth that each person has strengths and needs is taken for granted.

As we accept that all students, like all people, have strengths and needs, we need also to understand that it is not our responsibility to test, analyze, and use commercial devices in a futile attempt to determine precisely which students have which strengths or needs in which degree. Edward Kameenui (1993, p. 376) protests against draining the resources of time and energy away from teaching. "…diverse learners face on a daily basis the tyranny of time, in which the educational clock is ticking while they remain at risk of falling further and further behind in their schooling. I maintain that we should not spend any more time and effort determining or assigning fault for why diverse youngsters are failing, or which approach is the 'right' [instructional] approach. …such a search for the 'right' approach… is misguided and takes its greatest toll on students who have diverse learning and curricular needs."

 ## Celebrating Strengths

We have more strengths to celebrate if we take a wide view of the ways strengths can be demonstrated, and of the range of people in whom we are willing to recognize strengths. An advertisement in a professional journal for administrators (*Educational Leadership*, 1994, vol. 51, p. 54) presents this idea vividly. Below the catchy headline, "Spot the bad apple," there are four pictures, each showing part of a golden fruit bowl, lit with a yellow-orange light, each with one piece of fruit against its side. A closer look shows that in the four pictures there are three apples and one orange. The "bad apple" is the orange. This narrow view can be contrasted with the idea that schools are, as James Banks (1994, p. 4) puts it, "*rich* in student diversity."

If acceptability is defined as being like everyone else, many people, including many students, will be seen as unacceptable. When students are seen not as people but as members of groups, those groups are usually ones that are negatively stereotyped. William Ayers describes asking a group of principals whose schools included many students from negatively perceived groups, "What is it, particularly, about the presence of these kids in your school that makes the place wonderful?" He reports that the question was usually received as if it was intended to ridicule; yet, he says, schools cannot be effective learning environments if the adults there find nothing in their students to admire.

> [I]t is virtually impossible to develop a sustained and vital learning project if everything about students is deemed deficient, if everything students bring to school represents (to school people) obstacle and impediment. What experiences, skills, and know-how do kids bring with them to school? How shall we respond to their hopes and dreams? A school organized around the belief that students (and their families and their communities) are unworthy will surely fail…. (Ayers, 1994, p. 61)

Teachers have the doable responsibilities of finding ways to let strengths be shown, recognizing them, and being aware of the many kinds of strengths people may have. Moreover, it should be remembered that possessing an ability, talent, skill, or trait does not mean this characteristic will be shown in all circumstances. A concept that is used in assessment (and discussed in the glossary of assessment-related terminology at the end of the next chapter) is the distinction between competence and performance. Simply put, competence is being able to do something and performance is doing it. In planning instruction we need to choose strategies that will enable students to show us, and perhaps themselves, what they are capable of accomplishing. Mary Poplin (1988) is a scholar who passionately opposes what she calls a "reductionist model" of teaching students identified as having learning disabilities. Reductionist instruction is, and is usually described as, training rather than teaching, and the process is unidirectional, from teacher to student, rather than an interactive, shared learning process in which both teacher and student are involved and influence each other. Marjorie Lipson and Karen Wixson (1986, 1991), writing about students who experience difficulty in learning to read, stress the importance of avoiding unidirectional instruction. Instead they advocate teaching interactively, based on attention to students' competence rather than their perceived weaknesses. They believe the educational response to students should move our attention to the problems students experience "away from simply specifying deficits and toward the specification of the conditions under which a child can and will learn" (Lipson & Wixson, 1991, p. 40).

Careful observation can alert teachers to students' strengths and characteristics that can contribute to their success. In an article titled "Teaching to the distinctive traits of minority students," James Vasquez (1989) advocates combining careful observation with analysis, then using what has been learned to take practical action. His strategy, like many good ideas developed by educators working with one group of students, is widely applicable. Vasquez suggests observing students carefully to identify characteristics relevant to their learning. For example, a teacher might observe that a student prefers to work with others rather than individually, that several students are particularly concerned with pleasing their families, that some students are inhibited when asked questions when they are unsure about the answers, and that some students

understand math concepts more easily when they are related to interactions among people rather than objects. Making these observations is the first step in this observation process. During the second step, the teacher considers questions related to content ("Does any aspect of the trait suggest the kind of material I should be teaching?"), context ("Does any aspect of the trait suggest the physical or psychological setting I should create in the classroom?") and mode ("Does any aspect of the trait suggest the manner in which I should be teaching?"). Vasquez describes students who are strongly family oriented and wish to make their families proud. This is a context-related observation, which teachers can act upon by ensuring that families are aware of students' successes. He describes a student who was adept at mathematical reasoning when the topics were practical ones; the observation relates to mode, and a teacher can act on it by teaching math in relation to practical actions, such as buying and trading. Other observations may lead teachers to honor students' needs for privacy when receiving help with their studies, to encourage students to contribute ideas and information related to their experience and interests, and to give students many opportunities to work together in groups.

Many Ways of Being Bright

Bright is a beautiful word, with many meanings: *colorful, lively, smart, vivid.* Imagine a classroom full of bright students—colorful because they are diverse, with many interests; lively because they are bubbling with ideas; smart in their ability to think, talk, sing, draw, move, make jokes, and understand each other and themselves; and vivid so they will be remembered for years. Students *are* bright in these ways, although it may take brightness on our part to see it and find ways to let students shine.

Teachers need to look at others with a willingness to accept the fact of diversity and a readiness to admire. If they do not, there is a danger that, like the principals interviewed by William Ayers (1994), described earlier in this chapter, they may fall into the habit of thinking of students and groups of students as problems—bundles of deficiencies who contribute nothing, or nothing but trouble, to the school. One action teachers can take to counteract this negative approach to students is to increase the amount of thinking that is devoted to the positive aspects of human nature. It is useful to be aware of the many admirable qualities that people possess and, in the right circumstances, demonstrate. Among many such wonderful characteristics are resilience, willingness to act in prosocial ways, adeptness in language use, humor, and intelligence and talent manifested in a variety of forms. All of these characteristics can be fostered by skillful, caring teachers in the process of providing a sound instructional program. Classroom teachers, who constitute a major audience for this text, have many opportunities to observe these strengths if they look for them.

Inner Strength and Care For Others

Among the quiet strengths that students may possess—often without adults' attention to these qualities—are the ability to remain steady and hopeful in the face of adversity and the desire and ability to be helpful to others. Both of these strengths can be supported by teachers; the latter—the tendency to be helpful and altruistic—can be fostered in the classroom in a variety of ways.

Resilience.   The ability to withstand difficulty is an admirable quality. Over time, some scholars (e.g., Clark, 1983; Garmezy, Masten, & Tellegen, 1984; Pines, 1984; Taylor & Dorsey-Gaines, 1988) have reported on studies of people, particularly children and young adults, who have experienced adversity and have not been overcome by it. These are young people who live in great poverty, or suffer serious illness, or whose parents are so afflicted that they cannot care for their children and instead the children care for them. Originally described as "invulnerables" (literally, those who cannot be wounded), the terminology has now changed because of the recognition that no one is completely impervious to harm, thus the term "resilient" is now used.

Bonnie Benard (1993, p. 44) summarizes the essential qualities of the resilient person as one who "works well, plays well, loves well, and expects well. . . Resilient children usually have four attributes: social competence, problem-solving skills,

autonomy, and a sense of purpose and future." The young people who have been studied are those whose situations are extremely harmful—students who, besides the other difficulties they face, risk being rejected by others as people who are poor, or who have serious physical problems, or who are from dysfunctional families. Most students will not have such serious problems, but all people face some difficulties, and there are ways teachers can help. Having a favorite teacher is a common characteristic of students who can overcome odds. Teachers and others who work with children and youth can, as Emmy Werner puts it, help to "tilt the balance from vulnerability to resiliency" by acting in these ways:

▪ Accept children's temperamental idiosyncrasies and allow them some experiences that challenge, but do not overwhelm, their coping abilities;
▪ Convey to children a sense of responsibility and caring, and, in turn, [show that] helpfulness and cooperation;[are appreciated];
▪ Encourage a child to develop a special interest, hobby, or activity that can serve as a source of gratification and self-esteem;
▪ Model, by example, a conviction that life makes sense despite the inevitable adversities that each of us encounters;
▪ Encourage children to reach out beyond their nuclear family to a beloved relative or friend.
                                    (Werner, 1984, p. 71)

When learning is tough: Kids talk about their learning disabilities (Roby, 1992) is a collection of students' own accounts of their learning difficulties, illustrated with photos of the children with friends, family, and pets, engaged in sports, and working at a computer. The book opens with a Japanese proverb, *"Fall seven times, stand up eight,"* and each recorded interview concludes with a tip for other children:

> Uri's tip: "I want to tell other children with learning problems to do their best and if they don't know something, to ask somebody to help them…"
> Cameron's tip: "I consider my learning problem a challenge. The worst thing you can say is, 'I am disabled and worthless.' The best thing you can be is yourself. You should never try to change that."
> (Roby, 1992, pp. 11 and 35)

Prosocial Actions.   The adjective *antisocial* is an old and familiar word. An opposite term, *prosocial*—meaning helpful, kind, altruistic, caring—was coined several decades ago. The field of prosocial behavior was chosen as a focus of study by psychologists such as Nancy Eisenberg (e.g., Eisenberg, Lennon & Roth, 1983; Eisenberg-Berg & Neal, 1979; Mussen & Eisenberg-Berg, 1977). It is indisputable that people do act in ways that are antisocial and take actions that are harmful, damaging, and cruel. But it is particularly valuable for those in the field of education to be aware that people, including very young children, have the capacity and inclination to be helpful and kind (Solomon, Watson, Delucchi, Schaps, & Battistich, 1988; Wittmer & Honig, 1994). School, where young people spend much of their time and are in contact with others for such long periods is potentially an excellent place for prosocial behavior to be recognized and nurtured. Moreover, acting prosocially is aligned with development of advanced levels of thinking. "[T]he development of perspective-taking—the capacity to imagine how someone else thinks, feels, or sees the world—tends to promote cognitive problem solving generally" (Kohn, 1991, pp. 499–500).

Neither rewards nor punishments are effective ways to promote prosocial actions, unless the concept of reward is defined to include helping people become aware that their actions have been kind and helpful. Even very young children who act altruistically do not attribute their actions to a fear of punishment or to an expectation of praise; they tend to explain their actions as a response to someone else's need (Kohn, 1993; Eisenberg-Berg & Neal, 1979). Adults contribute to students' prosocial development by being caring themselves and by working to establish classrooms that are caring environments (Noddings, 1992; Paley, 1992). Literature can foster prosocial tendencies. Linda Lamme and Linda McKinley (1992) advocate the use of caring themes in literature. They offer lists of suggested children's books in the categories of caring for the sick, for the less fortunate, for special friends, for those who are sad, bitter, or grouchy, for neighbors, siblings, parents, and grandparents, for those in distress, for animals, and for the environment. They observed in a classroom where children made a list of what their

classroom was like, which included, "I think the best part of our classroom is that we're all friends," to which another child added, "Yes, and we turn into nice people, too" (Lamme & McKinley, 1992, p. 65). Charles Smith, writing on "Nurturing kindness through storytelling," lists these messages that stories can convey to students:

▌ Have courage. Difficulty is an intrinsic part of life's struggle. Do not retreat; instead, steadfastly meet unexpected and often unjust hardships. You can overcome obstacles and at the end emerge victorious.

▌ Have hope. Benevolent forces are at work. There are others like you who care.

▌ Take action. You can be one of these benevolent forces; use your power compassionately.

▌ Take responsibility. Never be a passive witness to another's pain.

(Smith, 1986, p. 50)

Adeptness in Language Use

One of the many wonderful things about people is that they are naturally skilled language users who can show this ability in many ways. However, language use is one of the areas of education in which the difference between competence and performance—the difference between what people can do and what they show they can do—is probably most significant. If classrooms are places where teachers are expected to talk and students are expected to listen, teachers have no opportunity to notice the ingenuity of students' language use. If teachers expect that their own language will be understood and responded to as they intend, and students learn to expect that their own written and spoken language will be constrained and corrected, students will mistrust their own abilities and come to believe that interesting language use is out of place in schools. Barbara Flores and her colleagues urge that teaching, for all children, should be based on a recognition of their language capability.

Children are proficient language users and bring many experiences into the classroom. …Children need opportunities to learn language in rich, integrated settings and be successful in regular classroom programs. …[L]anguage development can be effectively monitored by observing their language use in authentic settings across the curriculum. (Flores, Cousin & Diaz, 1991, p. 373)

When these scholars describe children as "proficient language users," they do not refer to high scores on standardized tests of grammar and usage, or a willingness to follow school rules that are not observed in everyday interactions such as, "Always answer in a complete sentence." They mean that the young people in schools use language in a wide variety of ways to communicate, both practically and playfully, and that they are adept in doing so. Kathryn Laframboise and Margie Wynn have reported on their studies of elementary school groups, which were "microcosms of classrooms in many areas. ...The teachers did not speak the languages of all the students, and the students could not always communicate with each other" (Laframboise & Wynn, 1995, p. 96). Observing and participating in language-rich classrooms, they kept field notes and also made videotapes that they watched and analyzed later. They found that the traditional routine of teacher questioning students and students raising their hands and waiting to be called on produced "little connected oral language," while with students who were able to talk freely there was active engagement with the instructional topic.

> When teaching and initially observing the sessions, it seemed to both of us that the students were very noisy and made many call-outs. At times there was a high noise level with many side conversations during the lessons. In observing the tapes, however, we noticed the talk among students was almost all topic-related. At those times when the class followed procedures of handraising and waiting to be called on, there was very little connected oral language in the class except for the teacher's talking. Further examination of the students' oral participation in the discussions revealed a pattern of interaction in which the children participated in the discussions on a variety of levels. Some talked to the teacher, some chose to let others answer questions for them, others talked simultaneously, and others carried on parallel but related talk with students nearby. The many levels of conversation were at first difficult to monitor, but the field notes and videotapes documented the types of language actually occurring in the class. ...We also observed stu-

dents who selected opportunities for Yusef [a child learning English] to participate in group discussions. They would tell us to ask Yusef a particular question when they believed he could answer it correctly. (Laframboise & Wynn, 1995, pp. 101 and 107)

Opening the world of literature to all students is a way to capitalize on their language skills. They can listen; they can hear. They can experience the flow of language when we read to them and with them. The world of books expands their horizons. And all students benefit—not simply those who have demonstrated the abilities that make them good students. Author Katherine Paterson, in a lecture celebrating America's young readers presented at the Library of Congress (1990), tells many stories, some based on her experiences as a visitor to schools. On one occasion, though she had explained her preference for talking with a classroom of students, the junior high school where she was to speak decided that her audience should be the 70-some students in the gifted and talented program. Then, because the special education teacher insisted that her students be there, her audience grew to more than 90 people. She tells how she noticed one student who sat silently but attentively, apart from the others. As students were leaving, he came to her and began asking questions about Gilly Hopkins—what were some stories about her that did not get put in her book? The librarian sent him back to his special education class, but then she talked about 13-year-old Eddy, always a problem, who had never shown interest in any school topic until his teacher began to read aloud *The Great Gilly Hopkins* (Paterson, 1978). Paterson remembered Eddy and sent him a hardback copy of her book, "Even if he won't read it, even if he can't read it, at least, I thought, he'll own a book he likes, and that will be one for our side, won't it?" The letter she received in return (which Eddy gave permission to be quoted) read, "Dear Mrs. Paterson. Thank you for the book, *The Great Gilly Hopkins.* I love the book. I am on page 16. Your friend always, Eddy Young." Eddy went on to read the whole book and reread it, and read others. His story, Paterson concludes (pp. 6 and 7), is about the boy and the book, but also about the teacher. He did not become an academic standout, "but he did become a young reader, because he had a teacher who not only stuck to reality, she stuck to a dream."

Intelligence and Talent in a Variety of Forms

Human thought is a fascinating subject of study. Over the years, some people have focused on human intelligence by looking for evidence that a particular group of people is superior to all others. (Typically, of course, the superior group is the one to which the author of the theory belongs.) On the other hand, some scholars have offered theories, supported by evidence, which emphasize the diversity of human mental abilities.

The concept of *fluid* and *crystallized* forms of intelligence (Cattell, 1971; Horn 1968, 1982) is a useful one for educators to be aware of. "Crystallized intelligence is basically the accumulation of stored information that comes with education and experience. ...[whereas] fluid intelligence reflects one's ability to reason abstractly and is less closely associated with one's stored knowledge" (Myers, 1989, p. 104). As we grow older and our store of information and stock of experiences grow, the kinds of thinking with which we are skillful become closely related to what we have already learned and done. To use Cattell's metaphorical terminology, our knowledge clumps together in the way that crystals are formed. Younger people, however, may be able to apply their intellectual abilities more freely—more fluidly—to new situations.

Multiple Intelligences.   Psychologist and educator Howard Gardner (1983, 1991, 1993b) has developed a theory of multiple intelligences (discussed also in Chapter Two). Defining intelligence "as the capacity to solve problems or fashion products that are valued in one or more cultural settings," he has identified, to date, seven different intelligences: logical-mathematical, linguistic, musical, spatial, bodily kinesthetic, interpersonal, and intrapersonal. According to this theory, everyone (unless they have suffered severe damage to the part of the brain that controls a particular intelligence) possesses all of the intelligences, but in varying degrees. This view takes into account "a wide variety of human cognitive capacities, entail[s] many kinds of symbol systems, and incorporate[s] as well the skills valued in a variety of cultural and historical settings" (Gardner & Hatch, 1989, p. 5). What is true of language ability is equally true of intelligences, as they are conceived by Gardner: that is, unless the classroom environment provides an opportunity for students to use and show their powers in different intelligence areas, their competence will not be recognized nor will it be nurtured and developed by schooling.

Humor.   Sandy Asher (1994) uses the term *fun-Q* to refer to a sense of humor and enjoyment—and laments that a "higher-than-average fun-Q" typically is not recognized in school settings as a valuable characteristic. The ability to enjoy experiences, to see the funny side of events, to cheer others up with a smile, is widely appreciated in life, though it is not always honored in school. Teachers can contribute to a cheerful learning environment through friendly smiles and by allowing humor a place in the classroom and enjoying this talent in their students. Good-tempered, good-humored teachers make their students' lives, as well as their own, more pleasant; yet there have always been those who assert that grimness is necessary for control. Courtney Cazden (1988, p. 168), in discussing her extensive observations of classroom discourse, notes that descriptions of TT (teacher talk) "can be characterized by what they don't include as well as what they do. Just as striking as the prevalence of expressions of control is the absence of expressions of humor and affect. ...For example, the folk advice to beginning teachers, 'Never smile before Christmas,' implies that jokes are part of letting yourself become a person in the eyes of the pupils." Descriptions of effective teachers often show their use of humor and their participation in friendly banter with their students, and the advice sometimes given to novice teachers to avoid smiling for nearly half the year has been the subject of at least one refutational article in the professional literature: "Never smile until Christmas? Casting doubt on an old myth" (Andersen & Andersen, 1987).

Howard Gardner, in his book *Frames of Mind*, refers to humor as a "fascinating and still dimly understood area." In his discussion of multiple intelligences, he links humor with bodily kinesthetic intelligence, because one element of the talent for humor is an ability to mimic. He notes, however, that skill in mimicry is often not appreciated, especially during the school years, as intelligent behavior. "If anything, the ability to mimic, to imitate faithfully, is often considered a kind of arrogance or a failure to understand, rather than the exercise of another form of cognition which can be highly adaptive" (Gardner, 1983, p. 229). Relatively little attention has been given in educational and psychological research to the study of humor. An exception is the work of Paul McGhee (1979), who developed an analysis of children's humor, relating the kinds of things children find funny to Piagetian stages of cognitive development. Those studies have tended to focus on appreciation of humor, rather than a talent for creating humor. At the conclusion of her case study of a preschooler, titled "Learning to make jokes," Dianne Horgan (1988, p. 348) comments on the absence of attention to this talent: "So far most research has concentrated more on what makes children laugh than on what makes some children comedians."

 Meeting Needs

Every person has strengths, and every person has needs. Experience tells us that it is often necessary for needs to be met before strengths become fully apparent. Often, the most pressing need that students have in school is to have their talents and abilities, their strengths, recognized and appreciated by teachers.

Maslow's Theory of a Hierarchy of Needs

The most prominent of psychological theories relating to human needs was developed by psychologist Abraham Maslow (1943, 1968, 1970). A hierarchy is a group of things ranked in an order related to power or importance, from highest or most advanced, at the top of the hierarchy, to lowest or most basic, at the bottom. Maslow analyzed human needs in the form of a hierarchy, making an explicit statement that people seek to satisfy basic needs before higher-level needs (such as the need for achievement and self-fulfillment) can be experienced. Although history and our own observations bring to mind instances when people deny their own

basic needs in order to help and serve others, Maslow's theory is a useful one for teachers to consider and, as pointed out in Chapter Two, many teachers act in accordance with some of Maslow's ideas, without being aware that such a theory exists. Like many hierarchical arrangements, Maslow's categorization of human needs is typically pictured in the form of a triangle, so the base is the largest part and the apex is the smallest part. Such a picture may be misleading, because the number and variety of needs that relate to developing talents and living satisfying, productive lives are virtually infinite. There are seven levels in Maslow's hierarchy, which he divided into two categories: deficiency needs and growth needs. In the first category, deficiency needs, he placed physiological, safety, belongingness and love, and esteem needs. In the second category, growth needs, he placed the need to know and understand, aesthetic and self-actualization needs (Maslow, 1959). A major difference between the two categories is that meeting deficiency needs depends on other people, while meeting growth needs depends primarily on oneself. Another way of classifying these needs is provided by David Myers (1989, p. 353), who identifies three categories: basic needs (physiological needs and the need for safety), psychological needs (needs for love and acceptance), and self-actualization needs (needs for fulfillment of one's highest potential).

Safety and Comfort

While teachers have an obligation to ensure their students' physical safety by observing safety regulations and providing supervision, whether schools are physically safe places depends largely on the efforts and actions of the larger community. Students and teachers need schools that are safe structures, free from toxic substances, where safety regulations are observed, set within communities that are protected from crime and violence. All citizens have an obligation to work toward ensuring that schools are safe places to learn and work.

The establishment of psychologically safe environments, however, depends in large part on teachers' endeavors. A theory originated by Heidi Dulay and Marina Burt (1977) relates students' feelings of safety and comfort to their ability to learn. According to the affective filter hypothesis, there is a strong relationship between **affect** and cognition; that is, feelings and emotions are related to knowing and understanding. Negative feelings, emotions, and past experiences about the subject to be learned or the learning situation form a filter that creates a barrier to learning. What is heard may be understood but will not be internalized and connected to other learning. The affective filter hypothesis was developed to guide teachers who were working with students learning English as a second language and it has become a part of major theories about second language acquisition (Fitzgerald, 1994; Krashen, 1989, 1995; Krashen & Terrell, 1983). Its relevance there can be readily seen. Students who experience a new culture as threatening, or as conflicting with family values, may have difficulty learning the language of that culture. Students whose anxiety level is high are likely to "be thrown so much on the defensive" that [their] learning capacity will be severely impaired" (Stevick, 1976, p. 147). Students who are identified, or who identify themselves, as outside a majority culture also are likely to learn more easily in situations where they are "off the defensive" (e.g., Au, 1993; Fordham & Ogbu, 1986; Ogbu, 1992; Weisner, Gallimore, & Jordan, 1988). Jon Reyhner and Ricardo Garcia (1989, p. 89) stress that teachers should not assume that any difficulties students from minority cultures have in school are due to deficiencies in themselves or in their home situations (i.e., to cognitive or environmental deficits). Instead, the teacher needs to create a classroom environment that promotes learning, characterized by "low anxiety level, good rapport with the teacher, friendly relationships with other students; otherwise acquisition will be hampered. Such an atmosphere is not a luxury but a necessity." Indeed, a psychologically safe and comfortable environment supports learning for all students.

One feature of psychologically safe environments is that they add value, rather than take away what is worthwhile. The issue of additive versus subtractive accommodation to the culture of school affects all students, but particularly those whose primary language is not English and those whose beliefs and family customs are different from most of the school community. An educational practice that has existed often in the past, which unfortunately still persists to some extent today, is the attempt to extirpate the language and culture of students' homes and replace them with mainstream language and customs. "Although they wanted to learn English and American ways," Kathryn Au (1995, p. 94) writes, in commenting on interviews with bilingual high school students, "[they] did not want the process to be a subtractive one, in which their existing language and culture would be supplanted."

One way teachers can make an educational environment safe and nonthreatening for students is remarkably simple—by giving students the information they need to learn. Far from preventing students from becoming independent, teachers who are willing to be thoughtful and sensible resources to their students—by answering students' questions, showing them how to accomplish assignments, providing resources, being willing to repeat and restate directions, expecting to present important information in multiple ways, and telling students what they need to know—make the learning environment safe. Deborah Tegano and her colleagues illustrate this point with an interesting parable to ponder:

---

affect (the verb uh-*fect*, and the noun *aff*-ect)—usually occurs in our language as a verb, meaning to have an influence upon, as in the sentence, "Teachers can affect their students' lives." The word is derived from a Latin prefix *ad-*, meaning *toward,* and the Latin root *facere*, meaning *to do* or *to act*. (Because they look almost the same and sound the same in conversation, the words *affect* and *effect* are sometimes confused when they are used in writing. When the two words have their usual meaning and pronunciation, *affect* is a verb and *effect* is a noun. One useful mnemonic device is to remember the sequence of *A* and *E*: Aff*E*ct is *A* v*E*rb.)

In education and psychology, *affect* is sometimes used as a noun and pronounced with the accent on the first syllable, meaning feeling, emotion, or mood. Earlier in this chapter, the phrase "an absence of expressions of... affect" was used in a quotation describing the view of some teachers, that showing feelings interferes with being "in control" of a class (Cazden, 1988).

A young dancer is sent out on the stage with instructions to improvise a very creative dance routine. As the dancer approaches the stage, a friend whispers that oil was spilled on the stage last night and some places may be very slippery. A second dancer is similarly instructed to perform most creatively; but this dancer is told that oil was spilled on the front right corner of the stage and directed not to use that corner. Who do you think performed more creatively? (Tegano, Sawyers, & Moran, 1989, p. 96)

Sometimes, teachers, and those preparing to become teachers, mistakenly believe that giving students information will harm them by preventing them from learning on their own. More frequently, teachers fail to provide information that students need without realizing they are doing so. A problem that many young students face, which presents continuing difficulties for students whose school and home experiences differ, is that teachers frequently use what Lisa Delpit calls *veiled commands*. A teacher might say to a group of students, "Don't you want the room to look nice?" or, "Put the scissors back in the box." A teacher of older students might say, "I'm waiting" or, "Look and listen. These are the directions for this assignment." All of these are commands, but in each set the first is a veiled command: the teacher's wording conceals the fact that an order has been given. Nevertheless, the teacher expects students to respond as if an order had been given. Some students in the classroom will have experience with language used in this way and will understand and act accordingly. The risk is that other students, despite a wish to please and do what is expected, will not understand such indirect utterances, especially since what the teacher intends as an imperative statement has been phrased as a question. "If veiled commands are ignored, the child will be labeled a behavior problem and possibly officially classified as behavior disordered. In other words, the attempt by the teacher to reduce an exhibition of power by expressing herself in indirect terms may remove the very explicitness that the child needs to understand the rules of the new classroom culture" (Delpit, 1988, p. 289). Delpit's article, subtitled "Power and pedagogy in educating other people's children," has been widely read and discussed

among scholars. One of her messages, applicable to good teaching for all students, is that teachers should make sure they are understood, which can be accomplished without being either rigid or unkind. Giving clear explanations and straightforward directions is an essential part of good teaching.

Belongingness

Motivation is a word frequently used in education; *belongingness*, on the other hand, is not a common term. However, Bernard Weiner (1990), tracing the history of educational research on student motivation, connects the two:

When teachers and parents say that a child is "not motivated," they may refer to a behavioral observation (e.g., the child is not working with intensity or persistence at homework), to inferences about intrinsic interest (e.g., the child is studying only because of extrinsic bribes), or to engagement in activities that are antithetical to the goals of teachers and parents (e.g., the child is interested in sports). Thus, for example, if someone is playing baseball whenever possible and spending time thinking about baseball rather than school-related concerns, then that person is considered by teachers and parents as "not motivated." However, if this same behavior characterized a professional baseball player, then that person would be described as highly motivated [and] would be admired and praised. Motivation therefore is a work-related rather than a play-related concept and must be considered within the context of social values and the goals of the superordinate culture. …[S]chool motivation requires the development and the incorporation of the values of others. Hence, we have to consider frameworks larger than the self, and older motivational constructs, each as "belongingness," must be brought into play when examining school motivation. …[S]chool motivation cannot be divorced from the social fabric in which it is embedded…(Weiner, 1990, p. 621)

Belongingness—the sense that one is a significant member of a group—has both individual and group aspects. People belong by being a part of a community, but their sense of belongingness depends on being an individual whose presence is important to the group. There is one way in which group membership works against the development of a sense of belongingness. This occurs if someone, instead of being perceived by others as a person, is classified and thought of only as part of a group, particularly a group considered different or deficient. This is a special danger in education, where labels for groups abound. Labels serve as a form of shorthand, enabling adults to communicate through speaking and writing by using a word or set of initials rather than describing a person or situation; creating new labels is a way of signifying a change in the way people or situations are perceived. Some adults regard knowledge of the most current labels as an indicator of status; for these people, using labels is a sign of being "in the know." Certainly it can be useful for teachers to know what current terminology is and what the words and phrases mean. (Reading professional journals is an excellent way to keep abreast of current terminology.) Being knowledgeable can enable teachers to explain the meaning of terms to colleagues and parents. It also can be the basis for a healthy skepticism about labeling, because it teaches us that new labels are devised continually and that by giving a problem a label does not mean the problem is solved. To list all of the labels applied to students would take many pages. For example, a student who is learning English might be given one or more of many labels, including ESL, LM, NEP, LEP, or PEP (English as a Sec-

Teachers have the major influence on classroom climate; if they focus on friendly accommodation for students' special needs, this will set a tone for others—students, parents, colleagues—to follow.

How do we use names? Try this:

Observe in a classroom, or think deliberately about your own teaching, to note the placement of students' names when the teacher speaks to them. Either mentally, or by using a 2×2 grid, note where the student's name comes—first or later—when teacher statements spoken loudly enough for the class to hear are positive or negative.

	Positive	Negative
Name first	"Wright, good work."	"<u>Ron, pay attention</u>."
Name later	"<u>Good work, Wright</u>."	"Pay attention, Ron."

The more common pattern in each case has been underlined. Typically, names are used first in a negative statement, and later in a neutral or positive statement. The argument can be made that when a student is misbehaving, the name needs to come first to attract the student's attention. Nevertheless, a consequence of this pattern of using students' names is that students whose names are regularly used in critical statements learn to tune out when they hear their names, because they know what will follow will be unpleasant. Moreover, whenever teachers link students' names with public criticism, the classroom environment suffers. Some students find school aversive. Other students learn to identify certain classmates as "bad." Additionally, some students need attention so intensely that even a negative use of their names is rewarding, thus they will persist in doing whatever the teacher wanted them to stop.

---

ond Language, Language Minority, Non-English Proficient, Limited English Proficient, Potentially English Proficient). In contrast, students not in these categories are FEP (Fluent English Proficient). But a label is not a name. Being known by a label is not being known as a person.

Belonging By Having a Name and a Personality

The people in a successful classroom community are not divided into those with names and those with labels. In a classroom community, each member has a name, and the name is treated with respect. Kenneth Cushner and his colleagues (Cushner, McClelland, & Safford, 1992, p. 11) quote a teacher commenting on the importance of each student being viewed as a person, rather than being characterized by a deficit or difference that belongs to that person: "I came to see a common need in every child. Anything a child feels is different about himself which cannot be referred to casually, naturally, and uncritically by the teacher can become a cause for anxiety and an obstacle to learning."

Because of medical advances, many students with serious chronic illnesses are now able to attend school. Teachers have the major influence on classroom climate; if friendly accommodation for students' special needs is the focus, it will set a tone for others—students, parents, colleagues—to follow. Eleanor Lynch and her colleagues advise reviewing the curriculum to note points where relevant health-related information can be included, inviting guest speakers who have experience with chronic illnesses and providing information through different forms of literature. Families, medical personnel, and especially students can be sources for ideas.

▪ Find out what is the most difficult problem for each child with a chronic illness, and help them through it. Encourage children to talk about, write about, or draw a picture of the problem. Check with their parents to find out what is most troubling to the child…

▪ Work with families and medical personnel to find ways to help children keep up with their school work during absences, and assure them that they will have additional assistance when they return. (Lynch, Lewis, & Murphy, 1993, p. 39)

The attitudes of others can have a strong effect on the way people eventually come to view themselves. Teachers who think of, and speak to, each student as an individual are not only showing care and respect; they are modeling respectful attitudes for all students to observe. Moreover, suggestions given by educators who work with students facing the problems of physical illness or disability can be applied to all students, and indeed to all people.

Don't overdo your efforts to encourage acceptance of children with special needs. If you are accepting of them and relate to them in the same manner you do other children, you will already have provided most of what is needed for successful integration. After that, careful observation and occasional intervention will help you reach the goal of integration. (Chandler, 1994, p. 50)

Just as racism leads to discrimination or prejudice against other races because of the belief in one's racial superiority, handicappism leads to stereotyping of discrimination against the handicapped because of attitudes of superiority of some nonhandicapped individuals. …It is critical to remember that exceptional children are children. Their exceptionality, although having an influence on their lives, is secondary to their needs as children. (Gollnick & Chinn, 1986, pp. 157 and 163)

To compensate for a physical or mental limitation, a pupil with a disability may cope with the environment differently, but different does not mean wrong or abnormal. …[C]alling a child an epileptic or a stutterer, rather than a child *with* epilepsy or a stutter, reduces an entire human being to a label… All people, including those who are disabled, have basic rights—including the right to be different. All differences can be seen both positively and negatively. (Shapiro & Barton, 1993, pp. 55 and 56)

Among many useful books by and about people facing physical challenges, *Special parents, special children* (Bernstein & Fireside, 1991) takes an ingenious approach, with a series of chapters about families in which one or both parents are physically challenged, but their children are not. The biographies include information about blindness, paraplegia, achondroplastic dwarfism and deafness, and extensive quotations from the children, including their straightforward and loving comments: "My dad's not different. Well, he's blind, but he's not disabled." "When we go shopping with Mom and Dad, Stephanie and I reach for things on the shelves." "After a while, my friends forget about my parents not being able to hear." (Bernstein & Fireside, 1991, pp. 7, 37, and 49). The book is extensively illustrated with family photographs, showing parents at work and families at home and in the community. One series of photographs show stages of a paraplegic father moving from his wheelchair into his car, collapsing the wheelchair and putting it in the back seat, all independently.

Belonging By Being Part of a Classroom Community

An essential element of being part of a community is being recognized as a valuable, integral part of that community. When students have, or appear to have, characteristics that may make learning difficult, it is especially harsh to deprive them of the very opportunities that have enabled their classmates to learn easily. Henry M. Levin personalizes the harshness of this approach by calling it "The Villain."

> You can tell where the villain's been. The signs are clear. Students view themselves as failures and slow learners, drop out of school, view school as punishing, use drugs as an escape. …This is the Villain's strategy for at-risk students:

- Identify them.
- Label them as slow learners and make sure everyone knows it.
- Slow down instruction….
- Make school joyless through repetition—"drill and kill."
- Treat parents as part of the problem rather than part of the solution.
- Plan and design programs by remote control for staffs to implement.
- Ignore talent by treating professionals as assembly workers.

> (Levin, cited in *Leadership and Learning Newsletter*, 1990, p. 1)

One aspect of accepting diversity is recognizing that students can be included in the classroom community without attending school every day throughout a full school year. Perfect attendance is desirable, of course, but it is an ideal that is impossible for some students to attain, even though they may earnestly wish they could. Some students are frequently absent because they are ill; other students, occasionally or regularly, move from one community to another during the school year.

Being Part of Class History.   A project that can contribute to students' sense of belonging to a classroom community is the class history wall (Weston, 1988). Each month, the teacher uses a six-foot length of heavy paper to cover a low bulletin board or section of the wall (the correct height for students to reach all parts of the paper panel). During the month, students use the panel to create a collage of class-related memorabilia: for example, book jackets from read-aloud books, important quotations, original poems or poems by favorite authors, items collected on field trips, and photographs. At the end of each month, the class discusses the mounted items, reminisces about class activities, and prepares captions for the items on the panel. Then the paper is mounted high on the wall, to be joined later by future sections of the class history wall. Among many advantages of this process is that the wall presents an opportunity for sharing class history with students who join the class after the year has begun, which enables those students to become part of the class history as soon as they join the group.

Being Visible.   Because this society tends to be a mobile one, a classroom community has members who leave during the school year and others who arrive during the school year. Some mobile students are members of families who travel to help gather crops in different parts of the country. Teachers know when migrant workers will be in the community because their stay is matched with the time of harvest for locally grown crops. Since teachers in these communities know their classes will vary in size and in the complexity of instructional concerns across a school year, and also know when these variations will occur, it is sensible to make this situation part of the annual plan. Cooperative groups can be expanded when new students arrive, and experienced group members can help newcomers get acquainted. If the mobile students are bilingual, this can be a time to learn words from another language, such as terms to use in greetings and in expressing thanks. Such an approach contrasts with practices that ignore students who will only be in the classroom for part of the year. "'Invisibility' is the word migrant educators use to describe the children's plight," Andrew Trotter (1992), tells the school board members who are the audience for his article:

> …language difficulties aside, even the simple act of going to school adds complications for migrant students. The barriers can include different textbooks from district to district, time lost in enrolling and transferring records, and prejudice and ridicule from other students. Many migrant students, in

spite of all these obstacles, are solid achievers. But many others leave little mark in school, moving away before teachers glimpse [their] needs.... (Trotter, 1992, p. 14)

Schools in agricultural areas, urban schools, and schools on military bases may all have substantial numbers of students who transfer in or leave during the school year. In some schools where the school population is generally constant over the course of a year, there are administratively determined transfers during the first month or six weeks of school when students, and sometimes teachers, are moved from one school to another to maintain approximately equal class sizes or to fit the capacity of the various school buildings in the district. In a study of transfer students in elementary schools, Andrea Lash and Sandra Kirkpatrick found a range from 17 percent in a stable suburban school to 50 percent in two schools, one in an agricultural community and one in an urban area. Although the teachers they interviewed were aware of substantial student mobility and believed that moving from one school to another was detrimental to student progress, few took student mobility into account in their planning or adjusted their instruction to accommodate students who were entering or leaving. The teachers they talked with knew that each year their classroom rosters would change and they knew when these changes would occur. Yet few of them took any action to plan for the changes. The researchers quote one teacher's thoughts regarding accommodating incoming students: "Aha, if I'm getting ready for the insect unit in May I'm going to need to incorporate some things that are going to involve new students" (Lash & Kirkpatrick, 1994, p. 830). Schools would be better able to accommodate mobile students, they point out, if the educational financing policy was changed to include mobility as a factor in formulas for allocation of resources, rather than simply basing the amount of funding a school receives on its average enrollment. They also make recommendations to teachers, advising that they "shift their instructional focus from teaching scripted subject matter to more adaptive teaching strategies" (Lash & Kirkpatrick, 1994, p. 840). To read and teach all of their students, teachers should be aware of a wide variety of instructional approaches, plan

thoughtfully to accommodate the particular diversities among their students, communicate with teachers at other schools (phone calls and, increasingly, computer e-mail, make this practical), and work directly with students as they enter, or prior to their leaving, to prepare them and help them cope with change.

In this area, as well as in so many other areas, literature is a means of linking the cognitive and affective domains. In a recent book, *Voices from the fields: Children of migrant farmworkers tell their stories*, photojournalist Beth Atkin presents photographs and records the words of children in migrant families—ranging from young children to mature teenagers. The final entry, with the dual title, "Tú puedes/You can," is by an eighteen-year-old girl who has finished high school and is about to begin college. In a section titled, "Always moving," a twelve-year-old describes a feature of moving and living in different places, sometimes with her mother and sometimes apart from her, which reveals a poignant aspect of her life: waking without a clear memory of where she is.

> When we move, sometimes I don't remember where I am. ...To remember better... I bring special things with me. Usually I only take the clothes and things that I really need. But I always take my teddy bear and a picture of all my family and ones of my cousins. Then I won't forget how they look and act. I have them write something on the back, and then when I come home to the new place, it is like seeing them. Because I miss them when I go. (Atkin, 1993, p. 23)

Other students who are mobile and run the risk of invisibility are students who, with their families, are homeless. The Stewart B. McKinney Act, passed in 1987, guarantees educational opportunity for homeless children. This act mandates that homeless students receive the same free, appropriate and public education as other students in the state. George Pawlas (1994, p. 79) offers suggestions for accommodating some of the educational needs of homeless students, including the idea of providing conveyable resources—that is, inexpensive learning equipment that students can carry back and forth from school. "Provide homeless children with conveyable resources for completing homework. ...Children in shelters may not have any physical space in which to do their homework. Try to provide a 'transportable desk' such as a notebook or clipboard." Other suggestions are also sensible and humane and are applicable to a wider group of students: "Homeless children need play time, too. This may need to be incorporated into the school's program, since space might not be available in a shelter. ...When you know a homeless child is leaving the school, try to bring some degree of ending for the child.... [Allow] time to gather up personal items and to say good-bye to friends and teachers."

The book, *Changing places: A kid's view of shelter living*, is a short work of realistic fiction. Divided into three parts, "Arriving," "Staying," and "Moving On," the authors, all workers at family shelters, present first-person narratives of eight homeless children, ranging in age from Lamont, six, to Wayne, thirteen, woven into a description of shelter living. An introduction addresses multiple audiences: children and parents who are not homeless, those who are, and teachers. "If you are a teacher, you can make the difference between whether school becomes a place for a child to feel ashamed or accepted, alienated, or included. We trust that through the pains and hopes of our friends, you have learned, as we have" (Chalofsky, Finland, & Wallace, 1992, p. 7).

Belonging Through Being Understood

An important characteristic of a community is the shared assumption that the people in it act and communicate in ways that can be understood. Kathryn Au (1993, p. 103) points out that teachers need to assume "that students' actions are inherently logical, even though the logic they are following may be quite different from our own." This is true for *all* students. As we teach, we need to guard against the assumption that although our ideas and ways of expressing them are natural and logical, those of our students, or some of our students, are not.

One illustration of this point comes from Cynthia Lewis (1993), who has written about her own realization that, in following what she had accepted as good teaching practice (i.e., eliciting prior knowledge), she was failing to allow a student to take a point of view different from hers. Her students were

reading Aesop's fables, and she was attempting draw on their prior knowledge and experience to guide them to state the morals. One student was reluctant to offer a moral for "The Stork who Dined with a Fox," a fable in which the fox serves dinner in a shallow dish so the long-billed stork cannot eat it, and is then invited to dinner by the stork who serves dinner in a tall narrow container so the fox must go hungry. Lewis expected the traditional moral, that people will be treated as they treat others, and urged her student to consider how he would feel if he were to invite someone to a dinner they could not eat and then have a similar experience at their house. She also expected her student to take the point of view of the fox at the conclusion of the fable.

> [T]eachers typically advise readers to relate their experiences to what they read. Apparently, this advice will not serve all students equally well in situations where they are obligated to produce responses that match teacher expectation. This seems particularly true when nonmainstream students are expected to respond in ways that conform to the dominant discourse in the classroom. ...[since] students quickly learn that their experience won't help them if these experiences do not fit the 'shared culture' of the classroom. (Lewis, 1993, p. 460)

What she found was that the young man she was trying to guide saw the story as a sad description of people excluding each other unnecessarily. The moral he eventually offered was "Give people a chance." In this situation, the discussion was eventually productive for teacher and student alike, because the teacher was willing to accept, indeed to be impressed by, an interpretation that differed from her own. The issue of prior knowledge, which Lewis raises in her article, is an important one for teachers to consider. An error that is sometimes made is confusing two words that look similar but have different meanings: *accessing* and *assessing*. Bringing out the information and experiences students have about a topic is *accessing* prior knowledge, whereas evaluating and judging the amount and quality of what students know before they have an opportunity to learn in school is *assessing* it. It is not sensible to assess prior knowledge; instead, teachers should expect students to differ in what they know and to work to build a shared knowledge base. Katherine Maria, in an article titled, "Developing disadvantaged children's background knowledge interactively," makes the useful point that even when individual students' knowledge is limited, the knowledge they have as a group, skillfully elicited by a teacher, is likely to be extensive.

> Variation in background knowledge should be expected in any group of children. ...Don't always use the same prereading strategies. ...using the same ones all the time can be boring; combining several is a good idea. ...Choose an interactive strategy [e.g., brainstorming and semantic mapping] and use group discussions. ...When working with disadvantaged children, one cannot ignore the interactive and constructive nature of the [learning] process. (Maria, 1989, pp. 297, 299–300)

Milieu Teaching. Carole Urzúa uses the term *milieu teaching* to describe the interaction between teacher and students, in which they communicate successfully by participating in a shared activity. The method allows students whose ability to use language, or a particular language, is not yet developed to experience conversation with an adept and caring teacher. Its use depends on the teacher and student interacting together in a setting. In the situation Urzúa is referring to in the excerpt that follows, students—who varied in their ability to speak English—were choosing pictures from magazines to create a collage showing things they liked, and she had paused to converse with a student who had already developed some ability to understand English but was not yet speaking the language. She could have demanded that the student speak. (Teacher, pointing to picture: "This is a *cat. What* is this?" Student: "cat.") Instead, she and the student conversed naturally, except that the student responded by pointing, nodding, and smiling.

> The technique involves departing from the stylized, school-culture question-answer-response interchanges and moving to a more conversational tone, where the teacher's language provides the affective bridge between what the child knows cognitively and what the target language linguistically encodes. The result is a patter of language that reflects what the child, or sometimes the teacher, is doing. ...In

milieu teaching I have actually reinforced the underlying assumption that [a student] and I are involved in a conversation, even though [the student] does not use oral language. ...Whenever there is any kind of a response by a child, I assume that is a turn in a conversation and respond as if the child had indeed given a meaningful conversational utterance. (Urzúa, 1989, pp. 22–23)

The concept of milieu teaching can be applied when teachers use their knowledge of their students and the classroom situation to accept and expand on students' ideas in a discussion, rather than criticizing students' comments or the form in which their responses are given. For example, suppose a teacher who intends to start a discussion about the significant events of the American Revolutionary War asks students to suggest events and one student says, "that scary valley." Remembering that she had read aloud to the class about the soldiers' sufferings at Valley Forge, the teacher responds, "Valley Forge, right?" (student nods) "That was a camp here" (points to map). "How was what happened at Valley Forge significant in the war?" That question is addressed to the class, and it is likely that the teacher will get more thorough answers than would have been given if she had been critical of the first student's contribution.

Second language learners can be included in classrooms before they are capable speakers of English, and the oral language of the classroom will enhance their language learning if they have many opportunities to learn through listening, rather than being required to speak. Many educators make the case that content area studies—social studies, science, math—contribute to language learning, when they are well-taught, with teachers taking an active role in presenting information in interesting, comprehensible ways and students engaging together in learning activities. Margaret Early (1990, p. 574) opposes excluding students who are learning English as a second language from content area classes: "ESL learners need not be isolated from their native-English speaking peers or have their cognitive growth, their learning of curricular content, and their learning of academic aspects of English postponed until their social/communicative language is well underway."

Belonging Through Being Able to Understand

When people belong to a community, other members understand them, and they understand what is happening and grasp the meaning of what others say and do. Two useful terms and concepts that have evolved from scholars working with students who are learning English and students who are members of minority populations are *comprehensible input* (Krashen, 1991, 1995; Krashen & Terrell, 1983; Moustafa & Penrose, 1985) and *successive approximations* (Au, 1993; Holdaway, 1979). The two ideas relate to the different modes of language discussed in Chapter One. Comprehensible input is related to receptive language; the concept of comprehensible input reveals that students learn when what they are hearing and reading is challenging but within their range of understanding. The term successive approximations relates to expressive language; the concept of successive approximations is based on the idea of getting closer to a goal through a series of tries. People do not develop their ability to express themselves in a single leap from inability to perfect use. Instead they become more skillful—and more technically correct— in speaking and writing by having many opportunities to use spoken and written language.

Comprehensible Input.   People who are in places where the language is unfamiliar to them will hear that new language spoken and see it written. But hearing and seeing the language will not necessarily result in their learning it. Students who are learning a new language do not simply need exposure to the language, they need "exposure that the learner can and is motivated to make sense of" (Cummins, 1994, p. 45). Stephen Krashen's term, *comprehensible input*, captures the idea that we cannot learn something that is far beyond our present capabilities, and implies also that interest has an important role in learning. This idea can be expanded to apply to content area learning for all students. When what students hear and attempt to read in their content area classes is incomprehensible to them, they will not learn.

The strategies described in this text are designed to help teachers assist their students in understanding and learning. Many of these strategies are ways for students to grasp, use, and remember content area vocabulary. However, to participate in classroom activities and complete assignments, students need not only to understand content area terminology, they also need to understand the wide variety of words and phrases used in giving directions; that is, academic vocabulary, a topic discussed briefly in Chapter One. Although all students may have difficulty understanding teachers' directions occasionally, problems with academic vocabulary cause particular trouble to students whose knowledge of English is still limited. Like the technical terminology of content areas, academic vocabulary is not often used outside of school, thus students do not have opportunities to pick it up in ordinary conversations: *Fill in the blanks. Write up your findings. Provide examples. Elaborate on this point. Draw conclusions. Skim this excerpt. Add your own ideas. Put a check in the correct column. Scan the chapter. Note the page number. Cite the source.* Students who are confronted with written or spoken directions they do not understand may fail to even begin an assignment, so they are at risk of being considered rebellious or lazy, yet another reason to encourage students to help each other and to work in cooperative groups. Problems with academic vocabulary are not likely to arise if students are in situations where what is not yet understood can be quickly explained by classmates.

Successive Approximations.   The term *successive approximation* is one used by Don Holdaway (1979), a scholar-teacher who has been influential in illustrating the ways in which knowledge of how well-developing young children learn in their early years can help provide good instruction in school settings. The term refers to the natural process that is part of developing new capabilities, a process that consists of doing something many times, gradually getting closer to smooth, effortless, automatic use. Much of cognitive as well as physical development occurs in this way. Kathryn Au points out that labeling and separating students can result in a situation where advantaged students are taught in ways that allow them to develop as readers, speakers, and writers naturally, through a process of successive approximation, by using expressive language freely, gradually refining their efforts. However, students whose language use is less well-developed are taught in ways that further stifle their growth, and are required to respond "correctly" to a series of tasks set for them.

> Sometimes teachers assume that becoming literate through a process of successive approximation is a luxury to be allowed only those students for whom they have high expectations. ...When working with students for whom they have low expectations (often, students from diverse backgrounds), teachers are likely to intervene quickly with the correct response, without giving students the chance to come up with answers on their own. (Au, 1993, pp. 37–38)

Talk Story. Many strategies, potentially helpful with all students, come into the field of education from scholars working with students who have pressing needs, such as students who come into an English-speaking educational environment without facility in the English language, such as the students Carole Urzúa works with, or students from particular ethnic or cultural groups. Based on their familiarity with, and study of, Hawaiian culture, Kathryn Au and her colleagues (e.g., Au, 1993; Au & Kawakami, 1985, 1994) have identified a style of teaching patterned after the "talk story" method of recounting events, which is part of Hawaiian culture. When the talk story strategy is used instructionally, the teacher introduces and asks questions about a topic and many students respond. An essential element of the talk story is that talk resembles real talk outside of the classroom—teachers do not choose who will answer questions, and turn-taking occurs naturally as students contribute, with the support of the group. Teachers plan the questions they will ask, but they expect varied responses; that is, they expect to be informed and interested by what students have to say.

> The chief characteristic of talk story is *joint performance,* or the cooperative production of responses by two or more speakers. ...there are very few times during talk story when just one child monopolizes the right to speak. This is because what seems to be important to Hawaiian children in talk story is not *individual performance* in speaking, which is

often important in the classroom, but *group performance* in speaking. Children who are leaders, who are liked and have many friends, are usually those who know how to involve other children in conversation during talk story, not those who speak at length on their own. This value attached to group rather than individual performance seems to be consistent with the importance in Hawaiian culture of contributing to the well-being of one's family or circle of friends, rather than working only for one's personal well-being. (Au & Kawakami, 1985, p. 409)

Balance of Rights. In describing their observations of classrooms, Kathryn Au and Alice Kawakami contrast teachers with two different approaches to classroom talk. Some teachers place effort and attention—whether intentionally or not—on getting children to observe rules about classroom dialogue, rather than on the dialogue itself. Other teachers skillfully create a topic-centered conversation, arranging for perhaps half a dozen students to contribute ideas in a brief period of time, with the teacher guiding the discussion by acknowledging answers without trying to control who should be speaking. Au and her colleagues (Au & Kawakami, 1985; Au & Mason, 1981, 1983) advocate a "balance of rights" in which it is the teacher's right and responsibility to make sure that text and text-related ideas are discussed, while students manage the way turns to contribute are arranged. They note that effective teachers use two practices to maintain this balance of rights.

> First, they allow the children breathing room by seldom calling on individual children and instead letting the children themselves decide exactly when they will participate. Second, teachers give the children equal time to speak. They may occasionally hold the floor so a quieter child will be able to enter the discussion. They are also careful not to take up too much time lecturing the children. In several lessons we studied, the longest utterances came from children and not the teacher. (Au & Kawakami, 1985, p. 410)

Belonging By Being Respected

To belong fully to a community, people must be respected for who they are, and also for their heritage.

Multiculturalism is the term most often applied to the concept of understanding and appreciating the diversity of human cultures, especially as that diversity is manifested in schools. Learning about and learning from the world's diversity is not well-accomplished by assigning such study to discrete bits of the curriculum in isolated times of the year. Janet McCracken writes of the need for teachers to develop "...a daily style of professional practice that is naturally infused with content that values human diversity and democracy" (McCracken, 1993, p. 49). James Banks stresses the *knowledge construction dimension* of multicultural education:

> The knowledge construction dimension of multicultural education is an essential one. Using this concept, content about ethnic groups is not merely added to the curriculum. Rather the curriculum is reconceptualized to help students understand how knowledge is constructed and how it reflects human interests, ideology, and the experiences of the people who create it. Students themselves also create interpretations. They begin to understand why it is essential to look at the nation's experience from diverse ethnic and cultural perspectives to comprehend fully its past and present. (Banks, 1993, p. 37)

Teachers need to guide students, as they learn about diversity, not to think of people in terms of *us* as opposed to *them*. As David Martin points out, when students are learning about people across situations, groups, cultures, and times, teachers need to help them avoid two potential pitfalls. These are quick rejection, as evidenced by statements such as "How awful—how could anyone do that?" and casual acceptance, "Well, we have our ways, and they have theirs." Although what he says applies to all aspects of diversity, Martin is writing about what he terms *classroom ethnocentricism* and is warning against "negative attitudes exhibited toward other cultural groups being studied in the classroom or toward groups represented in the school itself" (Martin, 1987, p. 5); a main focus of his article is the development of inclusive attitudes toward students who are deaf.

To teach well, we must establish a learning environment in which people's differing strengths and needs are recognized, accepted, and built upon. Appreciating diversity in the small setting of the classroom is a basis for sound learning about diversity in the world, and this learning can become cyclical, so that learning about the world can support learning together and valuing one another in the classroom. In this process, it is essential that teachers recognize that a strong knowledge base is essential. Sandra LeSourd (1992, p. 30) has reported that students she observed were "more likely to have a friendly orientation toward foreign people when they were well-informed about the foreigners' way of life. Children who had objective information to use in describing people of other nationalities made fewer evaluative references to their habits and customs." Marilee Rist writes, "Unless you treat the roles of various cultures as part of the whole of history—and unless you see the far-reaching implications of the contributions of each culture—you serve to relegate people to the margin of history and treat them as relatively unimportant...." (Rist, 1991, p. 29). This is a point often made, which continually bears repeating. Jack Weatherford, for example, makes a strong statement in an article titled "Indian season in American schools." He provides information about food, agriculture, and contributions to democratic political thought and deplores the fact that instead of learning and teaching about the many contributions of Native American cultures —"how the Indians of this continent changed the Europeans"—teachers trivialize history, and cultures by continuing to teach as they themselves were taught:

> In the fall of each year, just after school is back into full swing, Indian Season opens throughout the nation's schools. Between Columbus Day on October 12 and Thanksgiving Day at the end of November, teachers and students color pictures of little Spanish ships sailing the ocean blue, make Pilgrim hats and Indian feather bonnets of construction paper for a quick class play, and perhaps stack up a few ears of corn and pumpkins in a corner of the class. (Weatherford, 1991, p. 172)

> Watch out for the signs of a tourist curriculum: trivializing, tokenism, disconnecting cultural diversity from daily classroom life, stereotyping, misrepresenting American ethnic groups." (McCracken, 1993, p. 14)

> To wait for special subjects or times of the year to feature books by and/or about other ethnic or

cultural groups is to minimize or devalue their existence or potential contributions to humanity. (Walker-Dalhouse, 1992, p. 422)

Based on the work of James Banks, Timothy Rasinski and Nancy Padak (1990) discuss four curricular models, arranged in order of their depth and value, for multicultural learning. First is a focus on the *highlights, heroes, and holidays* of a culture. This is a good starting point, but not a place to stop. Next is an *additive approach*, in which information and themes from a culture are added to a set curriculum, but remain separated from it. Greater depth is achieved through a *transformative approach*, in which students are encouraged to explore ideas from the perspective of members of a different culture, and a *decision-making and social action approach*, in which social problems are identified and solutions are sought. Banks (1994, p. 8) offers practical guidance for engaging students in social action: "Action activities and projects should be practical, feasible, and attuned to the developmental levels of students. For instance, students in the primary grades can take action by refusing to laugh at ethnic jokes. Students in the early and middle grades can read about and make friends with people from other racial, ethnic, and cultural groups. Upper-grade students can participate in community projects that help people with special needs."

■■ Celebrating Diversity Through
■■ Literature

A leading scholar in the area of African-American children's literature, Rudine Sims Bishop, uses the powerful metaphor of *mirrors, windows and sliding doors* (Bishop, 1990a) to illustrate the ways in which literature can inform students about themselves and others. Through immersion in literature, doors open that allow our students to enter new worlds, windows are created enabling them to learn about others, and mirrors reflect their own lives and experiences. "Realistic fiction provides both a mirror in which students can see themselves and a window through which they can view the lives and experiences of others. At times the window is also reflective, allowing readers to see the connections

between themselves and the characters in the book, as well as with all humans" (Bishop, 1992, p. 87).

This point is also made by Patricia Ann Romero and Dan Zancanella (1990, p. 27) when they write, "Indigenous literature—that which arises from the students' own culture and locale—allows readers to make powerful connections to works that draw on what they already know and to validate the importance of that knowledge." As significant books are reread, remembered, and discussed, readers may be affected in different ways; a book that has opened a window to unknown places, different people, and unfamiliar ideas may become a mirror in which they see aspects of their own lives and understand themselves more fully. All good literature has this power. Literature that reflects aspects of the diversity that is characteristic of our nation is a powerful resource.

An educational topic frequently addressed in magazines and newspapers, as well as in professional educational journals, is the issue of whether there is a set of literature that all students should read. Such an agreed upon set of texts is called a *canon*; discussions of the issue, often called canon debates, are sometimes bitter. One argument for an accepted canon is that it ensures that every student will be familiar with certain great works of literature. Kathryn Au (1995, p. 95) writes, "the belief in the power of literature is deeply embedded in all levels of American education, and literature is seen as a tool for imparting cultural knowledge and values." Another possible argument in favor of a literary canon is that if all students, across many years, read the same texts there should be a shared knowledge base among all U. S. high school graduates. This argument is seldom made, however, because the process has been tried without these good results. Required study of particular texts has often been an educational pattern in middle and high school English classes, without producing widespread enthusiasm for the texts studied or the desire to revisit and discuss them in later years.

A major difficulty with the concept of a canon concerns the process of selection. What works are to be chosen? What will be the criteria for selection? Who will do the choosing? There is substantial evidence that, with more or less formality, there already exists a common set of literary works that students in U. S. schools read, and also that these shared readings do not represent the diversity of our society. Arthur Applebee (1991) determined that the literary canon for secondary students— defined as the book-length works most frequently taught in U. S. high schools— included only two works by authors of color in the top 50 books, most of which were by male Anglo-Saxon authors. Violet Harris (1990, pp. 540 and 541) argues that a similar selectivity exists in the literature students read across the grades and notes some of the ways this can be harmful. "Canons, or sanctioned lists of works perpetuated by critics, educators, and cultural guardians, constitute the literature many children read. ...[W]hen a tradition is selective or, worse, when it sets up inaccurate and damaging stereotypes, the meanings and knowledge shaped by it become significant because they shape individuals' perceptions of the world and their roles in it."

Informed Choices

Some scholars suggest that a new literary canon is needed, representative of the diversity in our country and world. An alternative—one which is open to classroom teachers and depends upon their knowledge and interest—is to shift away from relying on a group of texts selected by others and to have teachers make their own informed choices. Such choices can vary from year to year as the teacher's knowledge expands and as excellent new books are published. (An established canon is fixed at a point in time, thus new works, however excellent, are necessarily excluded.) One of many advantages of this approach is that rather than expending an extended amount of time on a single text, a process that is likely to become dreary for students and perhaps even for their teachers, many books can become available for study and free reading. Extensive experience with literature, which teachers can provide for their students, has lifelong benefits. Literature, writes Jerry Diakiw (1990, p. 297), is a bridge between our immediate experience and knowledge of a wider world: "Children need the bridge that stories provide in order to link their growing understanding of other cultures to their personal experience and background knowledge."

Using the same bridge metaphor, Cherry A. McGee Banks (1992, p. 8) stresses the importance of the teacher's role in making those connections: "The effective use of multiethnic literature requires that teachers create a bridge between their students and the worlds that multiethnic literature opens up to them." In using literature that presents students with "mirrors, windows, and sliding doors," teachers must choose both wisely and widely. No single book can give a thorough picture of a culture, a group, or a time.

Choosing Wisely and Widely

There are many reasons for seeking out literature that reflects cultural diversity. On the one hand, readers need to be able to make personal connections with literature; on the other hand, all students need to read and learn about the perspectives of others. It also is important for readers to have "experiences with literature reflective of many cultures in order to develop an understanding of the relationship between art and the culture out of which it grows" (Stover, 1991, p. 13). And yet another excellent reason for choosing widely is that the books we need are there, and more and more are being published. The factors that guide wise choices of multicultural literature fall into two categories: cautions about what to avoid, and features to look for. Basic guidance can be based on the Golden Rule. If books were written about us or our families, we would want the authors and illustrators to approach their subject with honesty, knowledge, and respect. What we want for ourselves, we also should expect for others.

When teachers choose books with diversity in mind, media specialists in schools and communities are valuable resources. Colleagues and friends who are members of differing ethnic groups or who have experience with special needs often have excellent suggestions and useful guidance to offer. Support for making wise choices is provided by professional journals, many of which offer articles about using a wide range of literature, reviews of current books for children and young people, and reviews focusing on the literature of particular groups. The professional literature is rich with articles recommending literature for different cultural and ethnic groups and providing suggestions for using multicultural literature. One of the best and most pleasant ways to learn about books is to visit good bookstores and browse. Much of what is currently being published is a treasurehouse of information, imagination, and beauty. Because there are so many excellent books available, teachers can choose widely, making many books available to students in a variety of ways—through classroom libraries, read-alouds, Themed Reading, and by offering students choices about what to read from among a teacher-selected group of books.

A wide range of literature can be enjoyed by all students. Teachers do not need to attempt the impossible, and foolish, task of choosing books to match each student's individual characteristics. Jennifer Altieri (1993) is among the scholars whose research has shown that students enjoy reading about and identify with protagonists of interesting books, regardless of whether these characters are members of the reader's own ethnic group or culture.

> For many years, the teaching of reading…. has proceeded as if the content of the texts being read made no difference…. [A]lthough schools generally have been successful in teaching students how to read, they have not been nearly so successful in engendering an interest in reading or in conveying the idea that reading has some utility outside the classroom and workplace or that it might provide important substance throughout a lifetime. …Recent research and theory, however, has reasserted the importance of story or narrative as a way of knowing, a way of understanding the world. (Bishop, 1990b, p. 561)

Heightened Awareness. Choosing wisely is likely to require a heightened awareness of how groups are sometimes portrayed in harmful or hurtful ways and how stereotypical images in books enter and affect our language. Elizabeth Jones and Louise Derman-Sparks (1992, p. 13) describe a presenter at a professional workshop who spoke of children "running around like wild Indians"—a slur that went unnoticed until a Native American woman in the audience rose to call attention to it. Some kinds and instances of negative stereotyping may be so familiar that they go unnoticed, and this may be particularly true in the case of Native Americans. As

Ginny Kruse (1992, p. 32) writes, "Some cultural blunders are repeated so frequently by society at large that the books containing them escape the notice of almost everyone but the individuals about whose heritage or circumstances the mistakes are made. …Claiming that only American Indian children are apt to notice 'playing Indian,' 'sitting Indian style,' or picture book animals 'dressed up' like Indians does not excuse the basic mistake. Self-esteem is decreased for the affected people, and accurate portrayals are skewed for everyone else." Another important consideration is that literature about groups of people should not be focused solely on problems and disadvantages. Jeanne McGlinn's caution that African American children need to read about positive aspects of African American experience is applicable to teachers' choice of literature about every group, whether or not members of that group are members of the classroom.

> Instead of developing an appreciation for their unique cultures, many children are receiving the message that they are different and somehow inferior to the dominant white culture. Some teachers send this message in spite of their best efforts not to do so, because of lack of understanding of the attitudes and feelings of their students. …Teachers choose books without thinking about the wide range of experience of African-Americans. Not all African-Americans are in crisis; their lives encompass all social and economic strata in American society. …Multicultural literature, like all quality literature, should create a complex view of the individuals who are members of a particular ethnic group, showing their various aspirations, socio-economic levels, occupations, and human characteristics. The problems of poverty and racism do exist, but images of African-Americans enjoying life in the United States should also be available to children. A balanced choice of literature will be a vehicle to convey the history, culture, diversity, and richness of human life. (McGlinn, 1994, pp. 211–212)

Willingness to Change. Choosing wisely may mean abandoning a book that has been a favorite in the past. The ambivalent feelings adults are likely to have when they perceive the bias in a book they greatly enjoyed as a child are captured by the phrase, "much-loved books… [which] contain horrendous stereotypes" (Hirschfelder, 1993, p. 431). With a wide range of good books to choose from, some well-known and even honored books can be left out of the classroom curriculum when teachers realize that the books are outdated and harmful. This is not censorship. It does not mean asking that books be removed from libraries or that people should be prohibited from reading them. Instead, it means choosing books for instruction that do not demean people. It is a mark of "professional maturity" (Kruse, 1992, p. 33) to choose new books for classroom teaching when teachers realize that one or more of their former choices present and perpetuate ideas and information that are hurtful to the people they depict.

Sometimes a well-known but flawed story can be handsomely re-presented in a manner that maintains the original theme with new text and illustrations, thus an old favorite can be used and its subject can be treated with dignity. Mingshui Cai (1994) has given the history of one such situation: "the case of 'the Five Chinese Brothers.' " In the 1930s, a book titled *The Five Chinese Brothers* was published. The story tells of a group of brothers, each with a different special magical power. When one brother is condemned to death, another brother, who cannot be killed by the means prescribed, substitutes for him; when the method of execution is changed, another brother substitutes, and so forth. While the 1938 version of the story (still in print) has objectionable text elements, its illustrations are particularly unpleasant, a fact noted by Albert Schwartz in 1977 in an article titled, "The five Chinese brothers: Time to retire." A few years later, *The Six Chinese Brothers* (Cheng, 1979) appeared, and recently a beautiful and wholly unstereotyped version was published, featuring yet another brother, *The Seven Chinese Brothers* (Mahy, 1990). Unfortunately, not all outdated books that have been popular can be recast in elegant ways.

A Caution Against "Hypersensitivity."   In considering whether a book is marred by stereotyping, it is necessary to be both thoughtful and sensible, especially when teachers are in the position of judging a book about a group they do not belong to. Kathryn Meyer Reimer describes a class of preservice teachers, all Euro-American, who asserted that a book about an African American family excursion should not be used because the food packed for the trip included fried chicken and there was a description of braiding a child's hair. Such a decision is foolish. "A desire to avoid stereotyping can become an excuse not to deal with multiethnic literature—no book will be 'pure' enough," Reimer (1992, p. 19) writes. "Hypersensitivity can… lead to 'watering down' or removing any cultural traits in literature which, in the end, seems to result in devaluing cultural diversity rather than valuing and celebrating it."

Using Multicultural Literature Across the Grades

As students progress through the grades, new realms of literature open up for them. Novels, histories, biographies and autobiographies, poetry, and essays can be read, studied, and compared. Students can hear through their reading the voices of writers from many groups, with a wide variety of experiences and opinions from the past as well as the present. Many important texts are not accessible by younger students, who, even if they are sufficiently advanced to read the material, are not yet ready to grasp the ideas presented. These are doors that will eventually open, as students mature. The reverse of this situation is that as students grow older, many simple kinds of literature they enjoyed, or might have enjoyed in the past, lose their appeal. This is a part of growing up. However, it is sad when doors are closed unnecessarily. It is a typical pattern in schools for books to be classified as grade- or age-appropriate, and some trade books have statements such as "for ages 3 through 6" printed on their back covers. Children learn early that reading "baby books" is something to be scorned. Linda Fielding and Cathy Roller (1992, p. 680), writing on the topic "Making difficult books accessible and easy books acceptable," note that "prejudices against easy books are deeply held" and cite as one reason for this "imagined or real peer pressure to 'keep up' with everyone else."

Because the field of literature for children is currently blooming and because greater attention has been given in recent years to multicultural children's literature, teachers across the grades should seriously consider including texts from the picture-book genre in classroom libraries and as an instructional resource. Many of the books that can entrance young children with story and pictures can also delight and inform older students and adults. One good and beautiful example is *My painted house, my friendly chicken, and me*, (1994), by the poet and novelist Maya Angelou, currently Presidential Poet Laureate, with photographs by Margaret Courtney-Clarke. The protagonist is a young South African girl of the Ndebele people, named Thandi (Hope). In the photographs, she smiles at us; in the text, she addresses the reader directly as "stranger-friend." Readers of all ages will be interested in the language differences, for example, that there is no word in the Ndebele language meaning *beautiful*, and that the word *good* is used instead. Older readers can ponder the effects of language on thought and intercultural understanding. The artistry of painted houses and beaded clothes can be appreciated by all ages; sophisticated readers also can consider the artistry of photography and text design of the book itself.

Books produced collaboratively illustrate diversity. For example, 30 noted authors and illustrators contributed their work to *Home*, edited by Michael J. Rosen. Their works are literally contributions, since all of the illustrators and authors waived their rights to royalties from the book so the proceeds could be used to aid the homeless. The theme of home is common to all times and cultures, and teachers are reminded that books are metaphorical homes for those whose creations live in them. "Every page of this book is a room where a writer and an artist live. In paintings and poems and stories, the thirty people gathered here celebrate favorite spaces, remembered places. In all kinds of houses, in every kind of room, we are all, in our own way, celebrating the sense of home" (Rosen, 1992, bookcover). Other books that emphasize diversity are collections that show commonalties across cultures and languages. In *Hopscotch around the world*, Mary Lankford (1992) has given detailed directions for hopscotch games from around the world and has told something about the countries where they are played, while Karen Milone has drawn the game patterns and shown the children at play. Hank deZutter's ingenious *Who says a dog goes bow-wow?*

(1993) is a compilation of the many ways people have translated animals' noises into their languages. *If I had a paka*, by Charlotte Pomerantz (1993), weaves other languages into English, choosing the words based on rhyme and alliteration in the non-English language. *Magla* (fog) and *vlaga* (mist) are spun into a fairytale about the King of Magla and Vlaga and his doomed love for the Queen of Vetar and Sunce (wind and sun). The similar sound of the words *lulu* and *lilo*, (owl and *secret* in the Samoan language) are the inspiration for the light-hearted poem, "Lulu, lulu, I've a lilo." Students may use the book as an inspiration for creating their own poems by searching through words in other languages to combine.

Riddle collections are fun in themselves and also increase awareness of the world's multiple cultures. What is the solution to this riddle from the Philippines? *I run, I run. When I arrive I bend down and let fall all my white hairs.* The Philippines is an island country, surrounded by water, and the answer is *a wave*—because a wave rushes toward the shore and crests in a fall of white water. The riddle is one of many collected in *A basket full of white eggs* (1988, p. 22) by Brian Swann. John Bierhorst, whose field of scholarship is Native American folklore, introduces a riddle collection titled *Lightning Inside You* with a chapter on "Native riddling in the Americas." These two riddles, devised by people far removed from each other, are related in meaning: *Riddle me: I make something touch far away* (a Native America Koyukon riddle from Alaska). *What is it? A little mirror in a house made of fir branches* (an Aztec riddle from Mexico). The answer to the first of these riddles is *eyesight*; the second answer is *the eye and eye lashes* (Bierhorst, 1992, p. 38). Several of the things Bierhorst relates about the courtesies of riddling are applicable to good teaching. It is fair to know an answer in advance. He writes, "I have now given away two of the riddles in this book. But in fact the ability to remember answers to riddles that one has heard before is another important 'trick' in riddling. Remembering is not cheating." Even more important, responses are to be honored. "If someone came up with an answer that made sense, though it was not the answer the riddler was thinking of, the riddler would say, 'Haku,' meaning 'very good,' or 'almost right'" (Bierhorst, 1992, pp. 3 and 1).

We are at the threshold of being able to offer all of our students a wealth of fine literature and art representing a diversity of cultures and people, thereby opening new doors for our students and ourselves. Marie Frankson (1990, p. 30) notes the importance for students, now and in their future lives, of seeing themselves included in the panorama of literature presented to them in school. "To develop a positive image of their roles as valuable members of society, minority youth need to see themselves represented in good literature, both in their classrooms and on the library shelves." Our choices can, in Violet Harris's phrase, affect "individuals' perceptions of the world *and their roles in it*" (Harris, 1990, p. 541) by illustrating for our students the rich array of contributions already made by real people and fictional characters with whom they can identify and suggesting for them the wide range of possible roles that are open.

◼◼ Accepting the Challenges and
◼◼ Opportunities of Diversity

Earlier in this chapter an approach to diversity was set forth as a vision toward which to strive: *Students differ [and we will accept and use that fact] so we will be interested in each student individually while we find and use instructional strategies that work well for students with a variety of strengths and needs. We will create inclusive learning environments —communities of learners in which our diverse students are welcomed, and their different interests, experiences and talents enrich each other's learning.* One of the challenges of diversity is to seek common ground while recognizing the individuality of each of our students as well as our own uniqueness. Sandy Alber and Adnan Salhi, describing their work in promoting intercultural development and learning in schools and in the community, have used the metaphor of "maintaining the individual voice as the choir sings." They write, "[C]hoirs bring us together, creating an appreciation for our sameness and providing the power for change…. Yet it is the individual voice that adds beauty and strength to the whole. Occasionally,

a single voice must rise above the choir. …Parents, teachers, and children can and do learn to value and use united and single voices" (Alber & Salhi, 1995, pp. 1 and 4).

Doable Tasks

In seeking to celebrate students' many strengths and meet their many needs, it is comforting to remember that the challenges we face are not insuperable. The tasks we undertake are doable, worthwhile, and important, for us as well as for our students. Evidence that this is so comes to us repeatedly from many sources, as we read the professional literature, observe talented colleagues, and reflect on the successes we experience in our own teaching. An impossible task is, logically, not doable; on the other hand, a task that has been accomplished by others is something that we see can be done. One indication that teaching diverse students well is doable is that it does not depend upon impossibilities. Some of the supposed barriers to teaching diverse groups of students, when looked at clearly, are flimsy. We can teach successfully without having the same language skills as our students, experiencing the same problems, or coming from the same backgrounds. For example, we do not need to be multilingual, or even bilingual. (And no teachers could speak the languages of all the students who might enter their classrooms.) Maria de la Luz Reyes (1992, p. 443) tells us that it is useful for a variety of reasons—including enhancing opportunities for employment—for teachers to be able to speak several languages. But she is vehement in stating that it is not necessary to be bilingual in order to teach students who speak languages other than English. "More important than bilingualism is the teacher's conviction about the value of diversity—namely, that differences in language and culture are not deficits—and the teacher's courage to teach out of that conviction."

We do not need to try to match the classroom environment as exactly as possible to the cultures from which our students come. Thomas Weisner and his colleagues use the term *selective accommodation* to refer to thoughtful teacher choices about incorporating aspects of students' home environments into their classroom programs. Selective accommodation means choosing how to adapt instruction and the classroom environment to produce a good match between students' homes and the school. It is the teacher's responsibility to make these choices wisely, on the basis of care for students and for a thoughtful, growing understanding of their personal strengths and needs and cultural characteristics. "Schools are places to learn *new* skills and behaviors. What a child brings to home from the natal culture is a foundation on which to build. Culture is a tool of adaptation. ...culture can aid adaptation to the unfamiliar by providing options to resolve discontinuities between home and classroom" (Weisner, Gallimore, & Jordan, 1988, p. 345).

We do not need to know everything that would be useful to know about the disparate characteristics of our students before we begin to teach them if we respect and appreciate differences, recognize similarities, and are ready to learn. Cynthia Ballenger has written about her experiences teaching in a predominantly Haitian community and learning from her students, their families, and her fellow teachers. "The process of gaining multicultural understanding in education must, in my opinion, be a dual one. On the one hand, cultural behavior [of others] that at first seems strange and inexplicable should become familiar; on the other hand, one's own familiar values and practices should become at least temporarily strange, subject to examination" (Ballenger, 1991, p. 207). The title of her article, "Because you like us: The language of control," is related to her realization that there are cultural differences in the ways adults use to control students' behavior. Whereas she habitually stressed consequences of misbehavior, her colleagues and her students' families stressed acting in accordance with custom and caring: "We don't do that. Your family would not like that." When Ballenger asked her students, "Do you know why I want you to wait for me?" (rather than crossing street without a teacher), they replied, "Yes. Because you like us."

It is not easy to consider ideas and practices which we have never before questioned. "Challenged to examine our biases, many of us become defensive, especially if we have always seen ourselves as unbiased and fair to everyone. Disequilibrium is never comfortable, but as Piaget has made clear, it's a necessary condition for constructing new ways of thinking and doing. Colleagues need to nurture each other through this process, just as they do children. It's OK not to be perfect, to be a learner" (Jones and Derman-Sparks, 1992, p. 14). Reminding ourselves that teaching inclusively does not require the impossible—we do not need to be bilingual, or create a classroom that matches students' home environments, or be fully knowledgeable about the characteristics of our students—is one indicator that our responsibilities can be met.

The other form of evidence that diverse students can learn successfully in inclusive classrooms is that this is occurring. Increasingly, teachers are enjoying opportunities to experience and observe successes. Reports by scholar-educators are presented in newspapers and magazines, on television, at professional conferences, and in professional journals. In a recent article, Thomas Scruggs and Margo Mastropieri (1994, p. 806), experts in the area of special education, have reported on their detailed, year-long study of successful mainstreaming in science classes in which some of the students had moderate to severe physical disabilities and some had problems in learning or were not fluent in English. They tell us that the classroom teachers they observed "promoted student-centered learning and appeared to take a very personal interest in their students. They all regarded diversity in their classrooms as an asset, rather than a burden, and remained open to new suggestions or ideas for improving their practices." The authors comment on the fact that "disability-specific interventions," such as providing a wide variety of ways to enhance vocabulary learning, providing multiple explanations of difficult concepts, adapting activities to students' special needs, "can have positive applications with other students" (p. 802). Their comment echoes one of the major themes of this chapter and this text: teachers can choose methods and strategies that meet students' special needs *and which simultaneously improve the educational experiences of all students.*

Worthwhile Opportunities

It benefits our students and us if we strive to make our classrooms places where all students succeed. Theresa McCormick (1984, p. 96) refers to such striving as exhilarating, compared to the feeling of excelling at a vigorous sport or attaining a significant goal: "Educators can gain strength (and perhaps exhilaration) from being involved in a process of education which seeks to enable all students to become contributing members of our changing society." Working to meet the challenge of diversity is healthy for teachers as well as for students.

> The very fact that one initiates action and makes an attempt to work at the pernicious problems the schools encounter is crucial to the mental health of teachers, the progress of students, and community support for the schools. When nothing is done to eradicate the academic failure of a particular group of students, the effect on everyone involved is to make them feel hopeless, helpless, and depressed. In a school setting, such feelings among teachers and students promote lack of effort and a desire to escape from the environment that produces these destructive feelings. The players in this school drama do indeed escape—teachers through absenteeism, requests for transfers, and retirement; and students through lack of attention, daydreaming, truancy, and dropping out of school. (Samuels, 1986, p. 11)

> The strongest argument for inclusive education may be a moral one. Sorting students on the basis of ability will always participate in the broader and more destructive practice of sorting students on the basis of gender, class, and race. Diversity is a reality in American and Canadian society and should not be seen as a threat to effective education. Classrooms which recognize, celebrate, and accommodate student diversity will play an important role in the creation of a more equitable and just society in which all people have an equal opportunity. (Dudley-Marling, 1994, p. 485)

> *You* may be the only person who sees, listens to, thinks about, believes in this child. Many of our children are lonely and deprived of attention. Many of our children feel alienated, disconnected. There are many more children missing in America than those featured on airport posters or milk cartons. Some of our missing kids sit before us each day—untapped, untouched, unknown. *You* may not even realize that your basic warmth and interest may be sustaining the life and spirit of a child. *You* may not even realize that you make the difference between life and death of self-image, of confidence, of feelings of well-being and self-worth in the lives of your students. (Chenfeld, 1989, p. 424)

Important Challenges

Accommodating diversity gives teachers opportunities to learn and grow, and although this is not always easy or comfortable, it is potentially enriching. Courtney Cazden (1988, p. 1980) writes, "The challenge to every teacher is to find a personal style that [contributes] to a strong and positive sense of community with each year's group of learners." This chapter opened with a brief quotation from an article by Robert Slavin (1993): "Students differ. So what? This is the question we should be answering." The same question is raised by Becky Howard and Tom Liner (1990, p. 52), who wrote about students who had a history of school failure. "A teacher sees each class as 'special,' and we have described our students to you because we care about them and they are special to us. But the class we describe is a normal part of the school's day, the students a sizable minority within its population. …"After recounting their students' successes, they ask, "So what? What difference does it make?" and conclude, "[I]t makes some difference to us, to re-learn some things we knew about teaching kids in a caring way and how that hurts sometimes because caring about people can hurt, but how we don't win anything without risking ourselves."

Students Differ. So What?

As she writes about the students she works with, Carole Urzúa (1989, p. 37) describes her hope that eventually all students will cease to be viewed in terms of labels or characteristics that set them apart, and instead that all teachers will see their students as individuals who are in their care and who are respected: "A respect born of understanding. A respect born of knowledge. A respect of knowing what it is like to view the world from a child's perspective…." For a significant part of their lives, and ours, the students in our classrooms are ours to teach, care for, learn from, and prepare for the future. We have the power—and are given the opportunity—to be their advocates. Perhaps the best answer to the questions raised about student differences is that since diversity is a given, we can remember that *what is given is a gift.*

STRATEGIC TEACHERS, PART FIVE

"I had to make a lot of decisions."

Like most teachers, Connie Pennocc Scott thinks and talks of "years" that run from September through June. Last year was memorable, although it started out in a typical way. Both Mr. and Mrs. Scott were at work after a pleasant family vacation, the three Scott teenagers were glad to be back with their friends at school, involved as usual with classes, music, and sports, and Mrs. Scott was enrolled in a graduate class on content area teaching. Just like the past six years she had taught in the district, Mrs. Scott's assignment was to teach seventh and eighth grade social studies. Although the middle school where she worked does not formally track students, many of her classes included a disproportionate number of students who were experiencing difficulties. The principal had noticed that Mrs. Scott could reach and teach students that some other teachers were angered by or ignored.

By mid-September, Mrs. Scott was enjoying the year, but working even harder than usual. As always, she liked her students and was a quiet advocate for some of them. She has observed over the years that when teachers begin to talk about a student as a problem, they often swap unpleasant anecdotes about the child and the child's family. She has discovered the value of contributing something positive—"I like him. He has a great sense of humor." "Her mother's still learning English, but we managed to have a good talk. We're making a map and postcard display showing everybody's birthplace, and she's sending in a big map of Russia with the place names in the Russian alphabet." At first, particularly when Mrs. Scott was new to the district, it took courage to say something that ran counter to the way her colleagues were talking, but she found that only a

brief comment would often turn the conversation around and sometimes another teacher would think of something good to say. Now colleagues sometimes come to her for suggestions about how to help a student they find hard to reach, or simply to talk about how to search for and appreciate a difficult student's strengths.

Mrs. Scott liked her graduate class, which met one evening a week, although she found the workload substantial and it was not easy to teach all day and have a long class in the evening. At the first class session, with desks arranged in a wide semicircle, the instructor asked students to introduce themselves and to talk briefly about a teaching concern they would like to find an answer to during the course, saying that she would suggest ideas and that students should plan to give suggestions to each other during the course. Mrs. Scott said she was looking for ways to help cooperative learning groups work together more effectively. Another classmate, a sixth-grade teacher, said, "I know journals are a good idea, but I'm having trouble keeping my students interested in them. I can see that I'm going to be trying out a lot of new things this semester—is there an alternative to journals that wouldn't be very time consuming for me, and that would interest my students, even those who don't like to write?" The instructor jotted notes as each of the students talked, and afterwards suggested to many of them that they look ahead to various points in the text, to read about a strategy that might fit their needs. Toward the end of the class, with a nod to the sixth-grade teacher, she described memos as an alternative or supplement to journaling and promised to bring several copies of an article by Michael Soderlund (1993) to the next session, for interested students. The class immediately used the strategy to write memos to the instructor and the option of memoing was available to students throughout the rest of the course; Mrs. Scott was one of the students who wrote memos fairly frequently. The instructor usually responded to students' memos and returned them at the next class session, but occasionally mailed a response to communicate more quickly.

Many of the new ideas Mrs. Scott learned intrigued her. At the first class session, the class formed cooperative groups and tried several strategies the instructor advocated for cooperative work across the grades. Mrs. Scott was particularly impressed with Concept Connections. She taught her students how to use it and was pleased that even reluctant writers worked willingly and collaboratively. She was even more pleased after she used it repeatedly and saw proof that her students, including those who rarely contributed ideas in class, had the ability to see connections among important concepts and to express their ideas in sentences and short paragraphs. She found that Concept Connection papers also provided a good method of documenting students' learning, and she decided to set times when she would keep copies of everyone's work, using her planbook as a reminder by starring these dates. She also suggested to students that they put a note to her on Concept Connection papers that they thought were particularly good. She then made copies of those papers. As Mrs. Scott read about other strategies, she increased her use of Teacher Read-Aloud Commentaries, which she had always used informally, although without having a name for the method, and began looking for places in the textbooks to use an A-Qu-A. She also was interested in ideas for structuring discussions and tried both the Discussion Web and U Debate strategies, finding that both were effective in encouraging a wider range of students to contribute their ideas.

She also began taking photographs of students at work in their cooperative groups. This served a double purpose. First, it promoted collaboration because, although Mrs. Scott was too sensible to talk about using the picture-taking as a reward, it was apparent that as she moved from group to group she used the camera when students were actively and productively involved together. She made it a practice, before she posted pictures on a bulletin board, to ask the cooperative group to choose those they liked best and to write captions describing what they were working on when the pictures were taken. Mrs. Scott's second purpose was to use the pictures for a class history wall. She planned to introduce the idea in mid-October, because she knew students from migrant families would be arriving at that time and she wanted to use this strategy as one of many ways to welcome them and support inclusiveness in her classes. Therefore, she intended to have some photographs ready for the wall panel and to combine them with others in which the new students were included, so the first panel could be displayed soon after the new students arrived. She intended to introduce the class history wall strategy to all of the students at the same time.

One concern Mrs. Scott had was about the long-term assignment for her graduate class. This was to be a project incorporating several of the strategies discussed in class or described in the text, which each student chose and worked on individually during the term and which would be shared through poster sessions at the next to the last class meeting. A problem for many students was that it was difficult to decide on a long-term project early in the term. The instructor also recognized this difficulty and explained that students should propose a tentative plan and discuss it with her, and that the plan could then be modified as necessary. When Mrs. Scott proposed using Concept Connections regularly and examining how students' work developed, and also creating several A-Qu-As, the instructor agreed that this was the basis for an excellent project.

Until the first week of October, Mrs. Scott's year was, aside from being a little busier than usual, an ordinary start for the school year. Many of the "difficult" students who had been assigned to her classes were responding well—their attendance was regular, their behavior in her classes was generally good, and there were some instances of other teachers commenting on these students' willingness to work in their classes as well. Mrs. Scott had introduced the memos strategy, and she was pleased to read memos from a number of students saying that they thought they would like school this year. Several times in her graduate class the instructor explained and used writing strategies. When the Write-Out strategy was demonstrated, the instructor gave the writing prompt, "Write out something that you believe about teaching." Mrs. Scott titled her paper "No student is expendable" and wrote about her belief that the educational system should never treat any students as if they were not going to succeed and as if it did not matter whether they liked school and whether or not they dropped out. The instructor praised the paper; Mrs. Scott was grateful for the chance to explain why she liked working with the students who had been assigned to her.

On a Friday afternoon at the end of the first week in October, the principal called Mrs. Scott to a meeting. They were joined by the principal of the high school; the purpose of the meeting was to tell Mrs. Scott that the district was reorganizing some teaching assignments and she was being transferred. Because high school enrollment was higher than had been anticipated, she would be moving to the high school; a new teacher had been hired to teach her current classes. She would have the next week to wind up her work at the middle school, and if she wished, she could use one day to visit the high school, talk with teachers there, and set up her new room. The high school principal had brought the textbooks for the courses Mrs. Scott would be teaching. She welcomed Mrs. Scott to her faculty and said she hoped she would agree to be one of the chaperons for a senior class trip to Washington, D. C., during the first week in December. Mrs. Scott was shaken by the news. She spent some time trying to persuade the principals that she was needed where she was, but her requests to stay were ineffective: the decision had been made

by the superintendent, and the teacher who would replace her was not qualified to teach at the high school level and had already been hired.

During the weekend, Mrs. Scott and her husband talked about what to do, but it was always clear that resigning was not an option. With three children to send through college, the Scotts needed two incomes; moreover, Mrs. Scott loved teaching. By Saturday afternoon, she was busy with the textbooks and jotting notes about decisions she needed to make. The immediate problem was leaving the students that she still thought of as her own. A more complex problem would be to move into a new, unfamiliar situation. She would be teaching civics and Twentieth Century American History, and although much of the subject matter was familiar she had not taught high school before except for student teaching, many years ago, and the textbooks and the curriculum requirements were new to her. She would be taking over intact civics classes (that teacher was reassigned) but the students in her history classes would be drawn from many different classes; her reassignment to the high school had been made because class sizes had exceeded the district-set limit. A third problem, although minor compared to the others, was what to do about the graduate class; given that she would be even busier than usual, her term project could not be completed as planned, and if she went on the trip to Washington she would miss the session when class projects were to be presented.

How Did She Do It?

Mrs. Scott made the move to high school teaching, and she likes her new school, new colleagues, and new assignment. She hopes, however, never to have another year like that one. Last summer, when the school year was over, Mrs. Scott took another graduate course. (Although she completed the fall course, she did not follow through with her original plan to take another course in the winter semester.) This time the major course assignment was to prepare a paper, which could be written in an innovative format, reflecting on an experience in teaching or learning. Mrs. Scott chose to write about her recollections of the transition between middle school and high school. After struggling to find a practical way to organize her ideas, and conferring with the instructor, she decided to base the paper on thoughts and planning immediately after she learned she would be reassigned, as they related to her last week at the middle school and first week at the high school and prepare the paper in the form of a chart with three columns, listing the questions that arose, the factors to be considered, and the decisions she made at the time. The instructor had helped her work out the format and said the paper could be a good basis for a discussion of decision making. As she worked on this process of organizing her memories, it occurred to her that it was similar in some ways to the Think-aloud strategy that she uses periodically with her students, except that in this case, instead of talking about what she was thinking about during her reading of a piece of difficult text, she was now writing what she recalled about her thoughts during a difficult experience. She made this point in the introduction to her paper, which she called "Recollect-it-down: A Think-aloud in writing."

FIRST WEEK: LEAVING THE MIDDLE SCHOOL

QUESTION	FACTORS TO CONSIDER	DECISION
How can I make the transition as easy as possible for my students?	If I show I'm angry or sad, it's going to harm them.	I'll go on being myself —the teacher they're used to.
	I want them to know I care for them, but I don't want to encourage them to miss me. Some of these students are at risk of dropping out, and I have to do whatever I can to make sure this change doesn't influence them to dislike school.	I'll use the last few minutes of each period for talking together about the high school as a place that they're preparing for. I can talk about the senior class trip as something they have to look forward to. I wonder if any of my students have brothers or sisters at the high school?
	We have to be busy all week, and I can't turn the week into a party.	We'll use some familiar strategies so they'll be very capable at using them if the new teacher decides to continue with them, as I hope he will.

QUESTION	FACTORS TO CONSIDER	DECISION
Thinking ahead, am I going to agree to help chaperone the trip?	It means missing an important session of the grad class. If I'm going to do it I need to tell the instructor right away. (If I decide to do it, I'm going to tell, not ask, and take a penalty on my grade if there is one.) I could put off making the decision, but it's better to decide yes/no right away. The high school principal needs to know, and I need to plan. I'd like to visit D. C.; the trip ties in beautifully with my new courses; it will give me a chance to get to know some of the other teachers better. And it's a good idea to say yes to the principal's request if I can.	Yes, I will be a chaperone. (I wonder if I can do some souvenir shopping for holiday presents?)
What shall I do to prepare for the new teacher?	The class is running well and I keep reasonable plans, so he can see what we've done so far. I've already done most of the planning for October and noted some ideas for the rest of the year. He'll want to make changes, of course. There is no point in my spending time on detailed planning; we will be in the same district, so he can get in touch with me any time.	The best thing I can do is to help the students want to welcome him. I'll call him, and he can decide whether he wants to meet now. I'd be glad to meet after school this week, or to have him visit and meet the students. He'll have my planbook and I'll leave descriptions of some strategies: Concept Connections, TRAC, Discussion Web, and Terminology Trade.
Should I take one day off to work at the high school, as the principals offered to let me do?	Pro: I want to see my new room, meet the teachers, get some of my own things in the room. Con: I want this week with the kids that are *still mine* to be as good and untroubled as it can be.	No, I won't take the day. I can go in to the high school on Saturday—the whole family will help— and I'll do a quick set-up then and we'll all go out for a pizza and then I'll relax (or try to).

QUESTION	FACTORS TO CONSIDER	DECISION
What about the big ideas I had for middle school projects?	My own time now is precious, so I'm not going to put effort into anything extra. The new teacher will have his own ideas. I'd planned on doing the class history wall and on having some guest speakers, but I haven't talked with the students about either project. As it turns out, that's fortunate.	Scrap the class history wall idea, but I can use the pictures already taken. I have every student in at least one group picture, so we'll do a labeled bulletin board to greet the new teacher . Everybody can make a good-sized name card for themselves, and we'll use tacks and yarn to match the people in the pictures with their names. They can write a greeting to the new teacher on their name card too. And we can do a simulation about how to make the new students feel welcome when they arrive later in October.
When shall I tell them they'll have a new teacher?	They're almost certain to hear about it—maybe they'll know by the time they come to school. I was told there are eight transfers. There may be an article about it in the local newspaper.	Clearly, I need to tell each class at their first session on Monday. Okay, I want to practice strategies anyway, and this will be a good opportunity for a Discussion Web. If there's a newspaper article, I can do a TRAC.
So what are my plans for the last week?	This is a time to remember the "CARES for ME" idea: Cheerfulness Appropriate pace Respect Enthusiasm Structure will keep us all Maximally Engaged— and that's the way to handle the week.	We'll keep the things we do regularly—read-alouds and one current events discussion. To a large extent, I can do similar things in every class session on a given day, since I've decided to review the strategies and make the bulletin board. It also will be useful for students to choose a sample of their best work, and I'll compile class sets for the new teacher.

QUESTION	FACTORS TO CONSIDER	DECISION
And what about the grad course?	Well, I won't quit. That's out. I paid for it, and I need the credits, and also I like it. So I need to change my term project. Or can I revise it? And I need to make arrangements with the instructor to present my project at a different time. Oops, that means doing it a week earlier because the last session is the exam. This is a helpful class; I can get support and ideas from the people in my cooperative group as well as from the instructor. I think there are six people in the class who are high school teachers and everybody is friendly and helpful. Those Tuesday classes are going to be more of a help than a problem.	I don't need to change my term project much. I can use the Concept Connections idea, because I already have several from each of my middle school students, and I can use it at the high school too, so there are even more comparisons that I can make. I can certainly talk about the strategies I'll be using to cope with the transition. Since I know right now that I'll be presenting the last Tuesday in November, I can plan on that, and I can use some of the Thanksgiving weekend to get ready. Aha! If I teach my high school students the Concept Connections strategy right away, we can use it at the first class session, and it will give me a chance to move around the class and see how the students work together, and I can also work on learning students' names.

Second Week: Starting at the High School

How am I going to manage the first day? …in American History? …in civics?	I'm teaching three sections of Twentieth Century American History and two sections of civics, so I only have two preparations. I may want to run the different sections of the two courses a little different eventually, but not at first. That means that the afternoon sessions may go better, at least for a while, because I'll learn from teaching the morning classes and modify what I do for the afternoon.	

QUESTION	FACTORS TO CONSIDER	DECISION
How am I going to manage the first day?	Introducing myself should be done quickly, but I want to get the students doing some writing at the first session, because that helps me get to know them and learn their names.	I can introduce myself and tell them that I'm a student too— and that's a way to tell them about memos. Memos are easy to explain and quick to write, so I'll ask for a memo from everybody in which they tell me something about themselves. I can't respond to everyone overnight, so I'll choose one or two sections to respond to each night, and that way I'll get all the memos returned by Thursday.
…in American History?	In American History classes the students don't know each other. The class is as new to them as it is to me.	I'll use cooperative learning in the history classes from the first day. I'll begin by explaining Concept Connections and we'll brainstorm terms from what they've learned so far. Then they can work on CC in groups, and I can go from group to group and observe.
…in civics?	These classes are intact. That's an advantage.	I can follow the plans that are there and gradually incorporate my own strategies.
Can I get a Resource Center going right away?	I'll use *The Timetables of History* (Grun, 1991). I can bring in several dictionaries, an atlas, and an almanac.	Yes. I'm going to use the *Timetables of History* to give me some ideas for read-alouds and also for music to play, maybe, but I won't start that right away.

QUESTION	FACTORS TO CONSIDER	DECISION
What am I going to read aloud?	I know I'm going to read aloud, and I have to get started right away, because there will always be a reason not to. For American History, check *The Timetables of History* — good! O. Henry published his collections of short stories in the early years of the twentieth century.	No problem in civics— at least for a while I'll choose newspaper and magazine articles. American History: I'll choose several O. Henry stories, and we can do some talking and writing about what we learn about the times from stories that were popular. Then I will get students thinking about the people who aren't represented in lists of famous authors, and we'll find what they were writing during this time.
What discussion strategy shall I use?	I want to get the students used to structured discussions. I'm comfortable with Discussion Web and U Debate. Discussion Web is less confrontational for students; they don't have to take a position.U Debate lets me face the students the whole time, because I don't have to record, and I can ask for contributions without knowing students' names yet.	Because it gives me a better chance to get to know students, I'm going to use U Debate, but on a noncontroversial topic— the *Timetables of History* helps again: "1900: Ray C. Ewry wins eight Olympic gold medals." We'll discuss the Olympic Games and I'll work up a discussion topic.

Challenge to the Reader and Choose and Use: Analyze what Mrs. Scott did in response to a career change that she did not choose and did not want. If you were to select one of the actions she took to be an inspiration to you, what would it be and how could you apply that inspiration to your own professional career?

Assessment for Learning and Teaching: Attention, Investigation, Documentation, and Evaluation

If we view evaluation as a type of social interaction, then we must begin to think about how the relationship develops between the people involved. Urie Bronfenbrenner (1979) reckons that when two people start paying attention to each other's behavior, they are likely to become engaged in the same activity together. You may start by watching each other, but you tend to become involved in the same activity as a consequence. Such a relationship between a teacher and a student has an effect on the student's development. The extent of this effect is determined by the extent to which the relationship involves positive feelings towards each other and the extent to which there is a gradual shift in the balance of power in the relationship in favor of the student. ...Implicit in this relationship is a valuing of [the student, and the student's] responses.

PETER H. JOHNSTON, 1992, P. 21.

Assessment—considering and making judgments about what has been accomplished—has many forms. All educational assessment should be directed toward building learning and improving teaching, toward increasing, rather than limiting, opportunities. Assessment in the content area classroom can often be accomplished in ways that enhance learning without consuming instructional time and also can inform teachers without burdening them. In effective learning environments, teaching and assessment are complementary: one supports the other.

---

assessment—like so many other longer English words, assessment is derived from Latin, composed of the prefix *ad-*, meaning *toward* or *beside*, the root word *sidere*, meaning *to sit*, and the suffix *-ment*, which turns the verb *assess* into a noun. The words from which *consider* are derived mean *to sit with*, and the idea behind *assess* is *to sit beside*.

FIGURE 8–1   Some of the Many Aspects of Assessment

Who is doing the assessment?
What is being assessed?

▮ A student says, "I'm no good at writing."
▮ A student's essay receives honorable mention in a community competition.
▮ A teacher reads learning logs and decides to reteach a topic using different strategies.
▮ In a school-home conference, parents, student, and teacher discuss goals and progress.

▮ Parents return students' report cards with comments.
▮ Several students decide they want to take advanced math classes.
▮ Students are tested using a national achievement test.
▮ Students in a cooperative group edit one another's work.
▮ Teachers complete district-mandated report cards.
▮ Teachers confer about a student who appears uninterested in school.

When a teacher sees evidence of students' talents, this is assessment. When a student recognizes an area of personal strength, this is assessment. When a teacher identifies topics that need reteaching, this is assessment. When parents set goals for school achievement with their children, this is assessment. When students examine their written work, completed over a period of months to choose examples that show growth, this is assessment. When a teacher greets students on arrival, thinks about how ready individual students are to participate in class as they come in, and considers what might be done to increase their comfort as learners, this is assessment. When one student thinks of a way to help a friend get better grades, this is assessment. When a teacher compares students' work across time, this is assessment. In the field of education, assessment is collecting information about the processes and results of learning and teaching, as well as making decisions about how to act on that information.

Think of the idea of sitting beside someone to find ways to guide and help, noting what that person is capable of doing and is in the process of learning. This is a benign way to consider assessment and, fortunately, this kind of assessment is what the classroom teacher can do, and has more opportunity to do, than testing experts who rarely enter the classroom. Teachers can look at their students, and their students' products, with attention. Through this thoughtful observation, they can do their best to investigate students' strengths and needs as learners.

They can use record-keeping systems and collections of student work that document students' talents and growth. They can, throughout the learning and teaching process, evaluate in ways that guide their students toward greater success and shape their own teaching to enable students to learn more effectively. Figure 8–1 illustrates some of the many aspects of assessment.

Assessment, like other aspects of teaching addressed in this text, presents teachers with the daunting challenge of how we can find the time and energy to do this, on top of all the other things we are obliged to do and wish to do. But in this case, as in other facets of teaching that have already been discussed, the good news is that effective assessment can be accomplished along with teaching, rather than being separated from it. Moreover, teachers need not be—indeed, should not be—the only people who are engaged in assessment. Students, who are the major stakeholders in the assessment process, can be involved in the assessment of their own learning, and colleagues can cooperate with one another.

▮▮ AIDE: Assessment in the Service ▮▮ of Learning

It is important to remember that in well-managed classrooms (and in schools, districts, and states) the purpose of all assessment is to contribute, either directly or indirectly, to learning. Just as a capable classroom aide, working with a sensible job description, can be a valuable help to a teacher and students, good assessment can aid teaching and learning. The acronym AIDE provides a way to remember four important and interrelated aspects of assessment: attention, investigation, documentation, and evaluation. This chapter is built around those four themes. In the first section on attention, the concept of zones of proximal development is applied to the assessment process. Observation of students and student products and self-observation by students and teachers are considered forms of assessment, and an assessment method based on interactive, reflective observation is described. Next, the section on investigation stresses ways to look at students in terms of strengths and needs. Practical ways to assess students' progress in the classroom—cloze, analysis of oral reading, holistic scoring, and teacher-developed criterion-referenced tests—are described. New models of assessment— dynamic, responsive, and authentic assessment—are discussed. The section on documentation focuses on ways to record and demonstrate student learning and progress, including contracts, checklists, rubrics, work sampling, and portfolios. The final major section of the chapter, devoted to evaluation, includes a discussion of grading and testing and the concepts of formative and summative evaluation. Examples are given of ways in which teaching and learning strategies can be used as assessment tools. Guidelines are given for teachers as they engage in informed classroom assessment. At the end of the chapter, a glossary of assessment-related terminology is provided.

■■ Attention: Looking With Care

Much of the best in current thinking about useful assessment processes is based on the constructivist learning theory of Lev Vygotsky (1962, 1978), in particular, the concept of the zone of proximal development, sometimes referred to as ZPD. As pointed out in Chapter Two, Vygotsky brought to the attention of educators and psychologists concepts which, like many important ideas, seem simple and self-evident. One such idea is that learning is not a "nothing or all" situation. People usually do not

move suddenly from being incapable to being proficient. In terms of assessment, then, rather than determining which students have learned something and which have not, it is far more sensible to look to see what it is that a student currently is learning or has the capability to learn soon. Considered in this way, instruction and assessment are complementary and cyclical. Instruction gives opportunities for students to attempt new learning. Assessment gives the teacher and student information about a student's capability in this learning area and suggests ideas about how to structure the learning environment to provide support to the student in developing new abilities and powers. If each person's current cognitive development is thought of in terms of *now*, and *later-if-all-goes-well*, the space near to *now*, between those two points, is the zone of proximal development.

Observations of Students

Careful, caring **attention** to students is a form of assessment in which teachers have the power to become the experts. Good teachers are constantly observing their students and modifying their teaching in accordance with what they see. Young children who are becoming restless during a lesson may need a change of pace, such as the opportunity to stretch and bend to music, then to gather around the teacher to listen to a story. Older students who do not immediately start on an assignment may need the opportunity to brainstorm ideas with a friend, or may simply need the answer to a question, an encouraging smile, and a chance to progress at their own pace. Blank or puzzled faces mean a new idea should be explained in a clearer or more vivid way.

Besides these spontaneous, unwritten observations that are built into every teaching situation, an important part of assessment is for teachers to observe their students in a variety of thoughtful

---

attention—like assessment, is derived from Latin and begins with the same prefix *ad-*, meaning *toward*. Here the root word is *tendere*, which means *to stretch*. Attention can be thought of as a way of stretching, or reaching out, toward something or someone.

ways and to record these observations. Observing students, as Lynn Rhodes and Curt Dudley-Marling (1988, p. 37) point out, "isn't just a matter of waiting for certain behaviors to occur so that they can be recorded. Observation is a skill, one that teachers must practice frequently over an extended period of time." And it is a skill that benefits students. "Keeping anecdotal records helped teachers look at the positive, at what the children *could* do. They looked at their children with different eyes, and they saw far more than they had previously about how individual children learned. ...[O]bservational record keeping helped teachers observe things that before had gone unnoticed" (Lamme & Hysmith, 1991, p. 634). There is no single best way to record observations. It is sensible to try different methods and find one that seems practical. Making notes during conferences with students or while sitting in on a cooperative group session is a practical, straightforward observation method. Clifford Clark and Marvin Nelson (1993) describe students working in cooperative groups in mathematics while the teacher circulates, putting a dot on problems where students have reached an incorrect solution. This promotes student consultation as they recheck their work to find out where and how an error has occurred. During this observation process, the teacher can determine which students, if any, need a mini-lesson reteaching a particular math concept.

Some teachers record their reflections about teaching in a journal at the end of the day, whereas some keep impromptu notes on file cards or post-it notes that they carry in a pocket and simply collect in a file folder for later examination. These are anecdotal observations, brief accounts that provide a glimpse of a student at a particular time. One technique is to keep a file of brief observations of individual students written during part of the time that students are working independently. (During most of this time, of course, teachers should be actively engaged in conferring or working with students, individually or in small groups.) These observations should be written using neutral language, which means that neither negative terms (e.g., whined, fidgeted, yelled) nor trivial compliments (e.g., sweet, cute) should be used, and they should be explicit; that is, the teacher should list what the student does

rather giving a summary comment. Contrast these pairs of observations:

3/12, 10:00–10:05 A.M.: Liz got pencil/study guide fr. desk; opened soc st book; read/wrote alternately; pt. 1 of guide completed in 5 min.

3/12, Liz: good work; good behavior

3/14, 10:00–10:05 A.M.: Ted opened sci text; turned pgs rapidly; looked at map, p 124, traced places w. finger; looked through papers in desk; asked Maura if she had extra copy of study guide; came to desk for extra copy of st. guide; wrote name; got up to sharpen pencil

3/14, Ted wasted his time

In each case, of course, the first observation of the pair is more useful. Besides documenting Ted's difficulty, the observation, coupled with others, will enable a teacher to develop some hypotheses about how to help Ted make a change. Looking back at the notes of the detailed, nonevaluative observations months later, or referring to them in a conference, the teacher will be able to provide documentation that, at the time of these observations, Liz tended to be task-oriented and conscientious, while Ted tended to have difficulty settling down to work on assignments. Current observations will then show whether there have been changes, or whether the same characteristics continue to be shown.

An exercise for teachers

Think about one class of students you teach. Take a sheet of paper and write numbers in a column, from 1 to the number of students in the class. Now list the names of all the students in the class. When most teachers try this, they have no difficulty filling in the first part of the list—students' names readily come to mind. But toward the end of the list, teachers have problems. "I've got 28 students; I know them all," they say, "but who are those last two? Who have I forgotten?" Students who have been left off the list will probably not be those who are succeeding in class in outstanding ways, and these students probably do not create difficulties. Teachers might decide to look carefully at these students to become aware of what is special and memorable about them.

Anecdotal records, when analyzed thoughtfully by teachers, are a useful source of ideas for tailoring instruction to students' needs. Lynn Rhodes and Sally Nathenson-Meija (1992, p. 505) advocate preparing an observation guide as a basis for focusing anecdotal observations, then periodically reviewing and analyzing the observations made about each student. The observation guide is a list of what the teacher wants to notice; for example, "insightful or interesting things students say; …plans students make and whether/how plans are amended; how, where, and with whom students work; what students are interested in; …how students generate and solve problems." Notice that the items on this list imply a classroom environment in which students have choices, work in a variety of settings, and generate ideas that are treated with respect. They would be useful items for observation in the Triple Lists observation strategy, described later in this chapter. Bertille Gallicchio (1992), writing for high school teachers, suggests a less complicated system, which she calls a "kid log." This can be a notebook, or annotations in a grade record book or planbook, where the teacher jots down notes (which may be as brief as "soccer") that may be useful clues in matching schoolwork with students' interests and concerns. Students themselves are important sources of information. One useful observation strategy is to talk with students about the processes they are using and about their estimates of their own progress.

> The quickest and richest source of process information is simply to watch students as they perform a task and, in appropriate circumstances, interrupt individuals from time to time to ask: What did you do to get to this point? Why did you do that? What might you do next? We can even ask students to record in journals their reflections about their work in progress; or. …we might hold debriefing or in-progress conferences with students and then summarize results in our anecdotal records. (Herman, Aschbacher, & Winters, 1992, p. 116, The National Center of Research on Evaluation, Standards and Student Testing (CRESST). *A Practical Guide to Alternative Assessment*. Alexandria, VA: ASCD. Copyright © 1992 by The Regents of the University of California and supported under the Office of Educational Research and Improvement (OERI), U. S. Department of Education.)

Advancing Learning Through Reflective Assessment: STAIR.   Assessment based on the concept of the zone of proximal development suggests a rising progression. Learners are always in position to be able to develop further. When they do, a new and more advanced ZPD is before them. Peter Afflerbach (1993) suggests an assessment process named STAIR: System for Teaching and Assessing Interactively and Reflectively, based on teacher observation. In this process, teachers observe students as they are engaged in learning and develop a hypothesis about what kind of instruction is likely to be useful, given students' current level of development, strengths, and needs. They then plan and conduct instruction, observe further, think about their observations, and update the hypothesis. Afflerbach gives the example of a teacher who observes and notes what a student is interested in, and therefore supplies reading material about that topic and links it to classroom instruction. Further observation, however, reveals that the student's interest does not simply depend on the topic, but on the opportunity to share ideas about it with other knowledgeable classmates. The teacher then uses the student's talent for interaction and leadership in small groups to foster learning in other areas. This example illustrates that the hypotheses teachers generate—like all hypotheses—are subject to modification and may be changed or even discarded based on further observation.

It is important in the STAIR method, as the teacher learns about students' strengths, to share and discuss observations with students themselves and with their parents. It also is an essential part of STAIR to document two aspects of learning: processes—learning methods that work—and progress. The strategy is similar to the thoughtful method of observation suggested by James Vasquez (1989), described in Chapter Seven. The five steps in the STAIR method are 1) observation (what strengths and needs are seen); 2) hypothesis development (how can teaching be adjusted to make use of this information?); 3) teaching; 4) observation of teaching; 5) reflection (what part of the teaching worked? what other student strengths are there? what part of the teaching should be revised?). As Afflerbach points out, good teachers habitually do these things (even if they have never heard of STAIR).

> [STAIR includes actions] that the best teachers do on a regular basis. Teachers' hypotheses and students' needs establish a running record of attention to these needs and students' accomplishments. STAIR provides a means for teachers to reflect on their knowledge of students and to continue their updating of understandings and instructional methods and procedures. Further, STAIR can help communicate increased understandings of students and students' accomplishments. (Afflerbach, 1993, p. 263)

Triple Lists.   One systematic yet flexible method of observation has been suggested by Charlotte Keefe (1993), who asserts that the richest source of information teachers have is the observation of learners within their learning environment. To prepare for observing through Triple Lists, the teacher first develops a Things I Want to Know List, with predetermined categories, such as "How does the student approach a task?" "What does the student enjoy?" This is the most detailed of the three observation lists. Some or all of the items may have subcategories, so the list can function as a checklist teachers can annotate as they observe. Suppose one of the things a teacher wants to know is how students respond to tasks they perceive as difficult. Figure 8–2 shows how that one item on a "want to know"

list, with predetermined subcategories, might be annotated over several weeks for two students. Note that the list does not contain negative items, as they are not necessary. When C. N. crumpled and threw away several first attempts, for example, the teacher could note the evidence of early discouragement in the context (working alone) where it occurred.

In the Triple List format, the second list—the Aha! List—is not prepared in advance. Aha!s are things the teacher does not know before the observation that come as a revelation or surprise. When they observe using their Things I Want to Know Lists, teachers are sensibly focusing on aspects of learning and teaching that are important to them and that they have thought about in advance. The Aha! List provides a way for teachers to note ways and kinds of learning that they had not anticipated, such as a student choosing a particular book, responding to or offering help in a productive way, or coming up with an ingenious idea. The third list—a CAN DO List—is created after reflection about observations made on the other two lists. This is a list of what students are currently able to do, and what they can build on as they progress further. The CAN DO List can be the basis for conferences with students, and students themselves can contribute to it. The three parts of Triple Lists observations can be kept on the same form, especially if the teacher makes multiple copies of the I Want to Know list and

FIGURE 8–2   Example of Single Item From What I Want to Know List, Annotated with Observations of Two Students, Over Several Weeks

Student: C. N.
How does the student work on a challenging assignment?
- makes a plan √ 10/3—*Yes! (brief semantic map)*
- works through parts in linear fashion   √ *9/20*
- divides work; chooses where to begin √ *10/4*
- asks for teacher assistance
- confers with peers √ *10/3;* √ *10/4*
- works alone √ 9/20; *discouraged—crumpled and discarded, two tries*

Student: D. O.
How does the student work on a challenging assignment?
- makes a plan √ 9/30 —*interested in planning methods taught; tried map* √ *10/3, tried checklist*
- works through parts in linear fashion
- divides work; chooses where to begin √ *10/4; using checklist*
- asks for teacher assistance √ *10/3, with Q.Y. from group*
- confers with peers √ *9/27,* √ *9/30,* √ *10/3*
- works alone

keeps one form for each student. Figure 8–3 shows how an I Want to Know list for a particular student can be annotated, over time, by a teacher so that Aha!s are added as the teacher observes and items are added to a CAN DO list in a section at the end.

Cautions About Observations

Observers are not infallible. The tendency for observers to show systematic bias has been documented repeatedly by psychologists, as Walter MacGinitie (1993) has noted. A common kind of bias, called "the halo effect," refers to the tendency for people to assume that what they see is evidence of judgments they have already made—like looking at people through a halo-like cloud of previous impressions. When we have a favorable view of a person (or group), we are likely to interpret actions in a way that supports our opinion. Looking for the best in people is usually a good idea; however the halo effect can also bias an observer to see the actions of a person (or group) as proof of their inadequacy. If students are experiencing problems either academically or socially, it may be particularly difficult for teachers not to see their actions negatively. In such situations, observing the student in a variety of settings (e.g., lunchroom, outdoors, and in special area classes) can often provide information that will lead to more positive impressions and suggest ideas for ways to help. Conferring with other school personnel who view the student positively is also valuable.

FIGURE 8–3   Example of Triple Lists Format with What I Want to Know List, Annotated With Observations of One Student, Aha!s Added, and CAN DO List at End

Student: C. N.

How does the student work on a challenging assignment?
▪ makes a plan √ *10/3—Yes! (brief semantic map)—maps also on 10/11, 10/13*
▪ works through parts in linear fashion   √ *9/20*
▪ divides work; chooses where to begin √ *10/4, 10/11 —(coop group is helping)*
▪ asks for teacher assistance—*10/13, asked me to read intro to paper and comment—aha! this comes after he's been working with coop group. He went back to group and conferred with them about what I'd said.*
▪ confers with peers √ *10/3; √ 10/4, 10/11 aha! Ada advised trying the semantic map, which worked well.*
▪ works alone √ *9/20; discouraged—crumpled and discarded, two tries*

Working choices: where? ...with whom?
    9/20 aloof from group
    10/3 Ada offers help, C. N. responds
    10/4 moves into group quickly, sits somewhat apart —(aha?—needs/wants personal space? doesn't like to get too close? Idea: make sure coop group has ample working space.)

Interests
▪ books absorbed by the Russell Freedman read aloud
▪ topics 10/4 Themed Reading—choosing books on the basis of illustrations? 10/11 "Can I take all these to look at?" —(books illustrated by Dillons)
▪ people/members of group, Cooper especially
▪ outside of school/community choir (just found out)— maybe a guest speaker from choir could come to class?

Interesting/ insightful comments by student:
    Asked to look at photographs in read-aloud book. Found Leo/Diane Dillon illustrations in Ashanti to Zulu and Aida, same as Many Thousand Gone. Asked about medal on cover of A. to Zulu (Caldecott)—got group interested

CAN DO notes, 10/20
▪ Can/does work well with others and learns from their suggestions; this is a helpful coop group
▪ Showing interest in arts—check with art/music teachers
▪ Let's try a coop group assignment on Caldecott winners—compare/contrast; what information do we learn from the illustrations. ...(See media specialist)

Problems with observations also occur if teachers attempt to diagnose and identify physical, mental and emotional difficulties without the advanced study and credentials that qualify them to do so. New teachers may notice colleagues saying that students have conditions such as "attention deficit disorder" or "dyslexia," even though these conditions have not been diagnosed by pediatricians or psychologists, and identifying students as being "hyperactive," having "poor visual memory," or being "kinesthetic learners"—and be tempted to talk in the same way themselves. Casual use of labels and terms is extremely common. A second grader's journal entry, for example, notes that a fish leapt out of its tank because it was "high per," but it is improper for teachers, who are in positions of authority and respect, to make diagnostic classifications casually and, among knowledgeable listeners, it will make the speaker seem foolish. Teachers should use their knowledge and good sense to describe what they see without jargon. "Vivi is active—needs opportunities to move around, and shouldn't be required to sit still for long periods" is a sound and sensible statement. "Vivi is a kinesthetic learner" is not clear and may very well not be true. Good teachers observe their students carefully and caringly, describe what they see accurately, and analyze their observations as they look for ways to tap strengths and meet needs.

Encouraging Students To Observe Their Own Learning

Important topics addressed in this section on attention—the zone of proximal development, observations, STAIR, Triple Lists—can all be adapted in ways that encourage students to attend to their own learning. The zone of proximal development is an important part of learning theory for teachers to understand and use, but it also is possible for students to grasp important features of the theory: they can learn, what they know now will help them learn more, and they can learn from classmates and help classmates learn. Students can observe their own learning. A journal is a tool students can use to record what they have learned and to reflect on their approaches to learning. The STAIR process is one older students

would probably enjoy learning about and could benefit from using. Steps in the STAIR method, adapted for students' use, are 1) observation (what strengths can I apply in this learning situation? What do I need?); 2) hypothesis development (how can I use my strengths and accommodate my needs as I learn?); 3) learning; 4) observation about the learning process; 5) reflection (what parts of my strategy worked? what other strengths have I shown? what part of my learning strategy should be revised?). The Triple Lists method of observation can be explained to students, who might enjoy and benefit from recording their thoughts about what they are learning, noting Aha!s when they discover a surprising talent or ability, and compiling their list of Can Do's.

 ## Investigation: Gathering Data

In this chapter, attention was considered the first element in assessment. The next aspect of assessment to consider is **investigation**—gathering information that will help improve learning and teaching and increase opportunities to learn and grow.

Strengths and Needs

Every student has strengths and needs, and focusing on those strengths is an important element of assessment. Investigating to identify students' strengths means looking to see what they have learned and what they can do. It also means recognizing what they are in position now to learn and what characteristics they possess that can foster future accomplishments. This assessment is set in a classroom context. In terms of what we expect our students to have accomplished and to be able to do when they leave our classes at the end of the year or semester, where are they now and what are they poised to do? In terms of what we know about their

---

investigation—is a word with a vivid derivation. The root word, in Latin, is *vestigium*, which means a footprint, or trace. Investigation is looking for evidence, for data—for "footprints" that give us information.

learning, accomplishments, and capabilities when we began to teach them, what has their progress been like? What hypotheses do teachers have about how to teach now in ways that will best help students learn and enjoy learning?

The term *need* is not another way of saying *weakness*, a fact stressed in Chapter Seven and throughout this text. All people need food and rest; they become weak if their need is not met, but it is not a weakness to have the need to eat and sleep. Sometimes, when we lapse into thinking in terms of strengths and weaknesses, we divide classes into a group of students who are bundles of strengths (so they should not need much attention), a group of students who are bundles of weaknesses (so they need to be fixed, probably by someone else who knows more than we do about fixing students), and a group of students who have no strengths or weaknesses (so they will just be in class and we will teach them the way we always do). Of course, this is not

productive, and moving away from this way of thinking can be enjoyable as well as useful.

Sometimes strengths and needs are linked. Willingness to work hard is a strength; some hard workers need to develop the habit of prioritizing, so that they give the most attention and effort to work that will produce the most benefit. Having an intense desire to succeed is a need; those who have this need often possess the strengths of energy and task commitment.

- What needs do all students have that a teacher can help meet?
- What strengths do all students have that a teacher can recognize and build on?

Since everyone has strengths and needs, it follows that teachers do. When teaching strategies are considered, the following are important questions to raise: How can I adapt this teaching strategy to meet my students' strengths and needs in a way that suits

---

FIGURE 8–4   Strengths and Needs; Needs and Strengths

The following descriptions of imaginary students include only teachers' notes about strengths. Choose one or more and add to the description by listing some needs that a student with that set of strengths might have.

- Natalya takes the lead in her cooperative group; eagerly contributes to class discussions; art teacher comments on her talent.
- Evan, at the beginning of the year, wrote only a line or two in his learning log. He responded to the double entry journal strategy only by drawing, then by labeling drawings. Now the labels for his drawings are becoming very detailed.
- Esther is consistent in completing all assignments on time; she works quietly in class.
- Danita - Aha! I didn't realize how well she understood what we're studying till I heard her explaining it to Fred.
- Sam had such a good grasp of subject matter when the year began that he probably could have met ending course goals then.

For the next list of imaginary students, only teachers' notes relating to some of their needs are listed.

Choose one or more and add to the description by listing some strengths that a student with those needs might have.

- Sherry sets goals she can't yet meet.
- Ted worked best in the afternoon until I began having paper cups of dry cereal available for snacking during the read-aloud time at the start of class.
- Ricky gets discouraged easily.
- Ellie talks a lot—except during class discussions.
- Nadja prefers to work alone.
- Glenn often arrives after class has started because his bus is late, so he needs help getting into class activities.
- Tran is just beginning to learn English.
- Hakeem has arranged with the librarian and me to borrow books twice a week, rather than once a week.
- Sereno sometimes falls asleep when I'm reading aloud, though he will write and talk about the parts of the read-alouds he hears.

Choose one student and develop an idea for adjusting teaching to make use of the information given.

my own pattern of strengths and needs? Similar questions should be asked in the area of assessment. How can classroom assessment be accomplished in ways that meet my students' strengths and needs? How can I manage assessment in ways that suit my own pattern of strengths and needs? Then, going a step further, How can I assess my own teaching so that I can use my characteristics to become more effective in my profession? Figure 8–4 discusses teachers' notes about imaginary students' strengths and needs.

Classroom Methods To Investigate Students' Progress

There are questions that teachers may want to find answers to as they seek to identify students' strengths and needs and adapt classroom instruction accordingly: Can my students read assigned and free-choice material with understanding and reasonable fluency? How are my students progressing in writing development? Can students meet a standard in their content area learning that I believe is necessary for all my students? To answer these questions, there are practical methods of assessment, well-adapted to classroom use, that teachers can use in a manageable amount of time with no cost for materials. Among these methods are cloze, analysis of oral reading, holistic scoring, and teacher-developed criterion-referenced tests.

Can Students Read Assigned and Free-Choice Material With Understanding and Reasonable Fluency?
Two methods of getting this information can be easily meshed with regular instruction: cloze, and listening, briefly and occasionally, to students as they read aloud. Cloze, which can be used as a whole class activity, is a practical way of investigating students' ability to read a textbook (or other material) independently. Listening analytically to oral reading requires attending to one student, but it can be a quick way for a knowledgeable teacher to obtain information about how a student's reading is progressing.

Cloze. As a written task in which students are expected to fill in missing words in a piece of text, cloze is a useful group language development activity. It also can be used to investigate the match

between students and their texts. Cloze is well-suited for classroom assessment for many reasons. Cloze passages are easily prepared by teachers, using materials that are part of the curriculum. Teachers can create passages that vary in difficulty by changing the frequency with which words are omitted. Cloze passages can be given to an entire class simultaneously, then quickly evaluated. To use cloze in this way, select a passage from an assigned textbook, and type it, double-spaced, replacing some of the words with blanks, following directions for standard cloze (provided in Chapter Six). Completed cloze passages can be evaluated holistically by reading the student's completed passage and determining whether it makes sense. Alternatively, a passage may be scored by counting as correct only those items where the student has written the exact word from the original passage (even if it is misspelled). According to this method, a score between 44 percent and 57 percent indicates that the student shows adequate comprehension of the material, and a score above 57 percent shows good comprehension. These guidelines were devised by John Bormuth (1968) on the basis of extensive research on the use of cloze and are based on cloze passages of approximately 300 words in which every fifth word is omitted.

Investigation of the match between students and text can readily be accomplished by giving a cloze passage (or a series of cloze passages of graduated difficulty over a period of days) to the whole class. When cloze is used in this way, students' completion time will vary substantially. Ample time should be allowed for all students to finish. (Thus, it is a good idea to ensure that students have independent reading to do if they finish ahead of the others.) Besides the information to be gained from each student's completed cloze paper, additional indications of individual students' strengths and needs can be obtained by noting the time each student takes to complete a cloze passage. This can be accomplished simply. Cloze passages are given out to the whole class at the same time; the teacher notes the exact time. As students finish the cloze, they bring their papers to the teacher. Each time a paper is handed in, the teacher notes the time on that paper. Most results will fall into one of four categories: 1) work completed successfully and quickly; 2) work completed successfully and slowly; 3) work completed unsuccessfully and quickly; 4) work completed unsuccessfully and slowly.

Examining and Using Results.

As in every form of testing, successful results provide more reliable information than does lack of success. Students who complete the cloze passage accurately and quickly are capable of reading and understanding a text from which the cloze passage is a representative sample. Students who complete the cloze passage accurately, but take a rather long time to do so, also understand the text. They may have taken longer because the passage is not as easy for them as for the students whose work is in the first category—or they may be more deliberate workers, who approach tasks with care and like to check their work. Inaccurate work completed quickly may be due to many factors: inability to understand the text, confusion, lack of task commitment, and so forth. It is likely that the passage is really too difficult for the student who works for a long time without success, but other factors may also have affected this result. The completed cloze passages provide some evidence of students' strengths and needs and can aid the teacher in instructional decision-making. For example, if the text reading proves too difficult for many students, the teacher could decide to take one or more of these actions: supplement the text with many tradebooks; use Teacher Read-Aloud Commentaries to introduce each text section; tape important text sections for students to listen to; use five minutes of class time for group creation of Language Experience Approach style summaries of what has been learned, and make copies for each student of the LEA summaries. Because cloze requires students to write, students' cloze passages provide some indication of their spelling development. Teachers might decide, on the basis of cloze results, to use one or more strategies that integrate spelling instruction with content area learning.

Analyzing Oral Reading.

It is not a good use of instructional time for the class to read textbooks aloud, taking turns in "round robin" fashion. Peter Johnston (1992) notes that oral reading has value primarily in performance activities, such as choral reading or Readers' Theater. However, a knowledgeable teacher can learn a good deal about how well a student is able to read assigned texts by occasionally listening to the student read a short selection orally. This can be done during a teacher-student conference, or more informally by observing students during paired reading sessions.

When analyzing oral reading to determine how well a student can read a particular piece of reading material—and whether a student is using effective strategies in reading—the concept of *miscue analysis* is a useful one for teachers to be aware of. A miscue is a deviation from an expected response (Goodman & Burke, 1972), that is, a miscue occurs whenever what a student reads aloud differs in any way from the written text. The principle underlying miscue analysis is that all readers make changes in the text as they read, but that the kinds of changes differ according to whether the text is easy or difficult for the reader. (In a few cases, miscues occur because a reader makes unnecessary corrections.) When the changes a reader makes do not interfere with the understanding of the text, then the reader is managing successfully. When the changes distort meaning, the reader may need assistance in using that text. When a reader strives for absolute accuracy and self-corrects changes that do not affect meaning (e.g., going back to reread a part of the sentence when *a* has been substituted for *the*), then the reader needs guidance in understanding how to relax and read for meaning and pleasure. Although there are methods and materials teachers can use to prepare in-depth analyses of readers' miscues, classroom teachers who understand the two major categories of miscues— those that do not affect meaning and those that do—can make judgments simply by listening to oral reading.

Another method of analyzing oral reading is to use shorthand-style symbols to keep a written record of changes in the text made by the reader. All textbooks on reading diagnosis include a set of these symbols, which provide quick methods of noting insertions, omissions, substitutions, and repetitions of words or phrases. If teachers use this procedure, it is useful to make a copy of the text the student will be reading and record text changes directly on this copy.

The *running record* is a method of notetaking devised by Marie Clay that enables a teacher to keep a record of a student's oral reading. She provides a clear description of conventions to use in taking a running record (Clay, 1985, p. 17–22) and a summary form in an appendix. Running records include a check for each word correctly read, positioned as the words are placed on the page (e.g., a line of text including eight words would be represented by a line of eight check marks if all words were accurately read). Through symbols, the running record also takes into account departures from the text: words omitted, substituted, added, self-corrections, and repetitions.

> The first step is a matter of action. [S]et yourself the task of recording everything that a child says and does as he tries to read the book . ...after about two hours of initial practice, no matter how much you might be missing, you have made a good start. It is not a case of knowing everything first and then applying it. Try yourself out and you will begin to notice a few things that you have not noticed before. Practice some more and you will notice more. [With practice] your records will become more and more reliable. (Clay, 1985, p. 17)

Examining and Using Results. Like cloze based on a textbook section, records of oral reading from the textbook provide evidence of how well students can read it, and teachers can choose instructional strategies based on the information. Teachers who listen thoughtfully and look carefully at records of oral reading will note different ways that students cope with difficult text and can then give useful guidance to individual students. For example, if a student halts at unknown words, the teacher may suggest going on with the reading, to see if the word can be learned through context. The symbols used in running records are not difficult to understand, and students may benefit from seeing and conferring about them, and setting personal goals to develop their reading further.

How Are Students Progressing in Writing Development? Investigating this question can be part of a regular classroom program, if a teacher chooses. Holistic scoring is designed to be accomplished quickly, and it is a practical way of assessing many

similar products. Teachers who wish to investigate their students' writing progress can plan to give short writing assignments to all students three or four times during the school year and score the writings holistically.

Rating Students' Work Holistically. Holistic scoring consists of giving a rating to a product, based on an overall view of its characteristics (Breland, Camp, Jones, Morris, & Rock, 1987; Cooper, 1977). The method is most frequently used to score many pieces of writing done in response to the same assignment. "The chief assumption that underlines holistic scoring," Hunter Breland and his colleagues assert, "...is that the whole text or composition is more than the sum of its parts" (Breland et al., 1987, p. 18). When teachers need to evaluate the ability of many students to produce a good product of a particular kind (e.g., a piece of writing in a particular style, such as an essay on a set topic) holistic scoring is a useful technique. In this method, a very narrow range of scores or ratings are given and raters read and rate each product quickly, without making any notes or comments on the paper. A score range from 1 (low) to 4 (high) is common. This limited range of scores makes it likely that raters will agree. Two people looking at the same product are more likely to give it the same score if the possible scores are 4, 3, 2, or 1, than if they have to decide whether the product is worth 100, 99, 98, 97... 3, 2, 1, or 0 points.

In preparation for holistic scoring, it is useful for teachers to identify what aspects of the product they will consider—for a writing task these might be clarity, interest, and technical accuracy—even though these factors will not be considered or rated separately. Ideally, teachers will have identified, using an earlier set of students' writings, examples of an excellent product (rated 4), a good product (rated 3), a barely adequate product (rated 2), and a poor product (rated 1). It is useful and informative if two teachers work together on the task, with a third person available to be called in if there is disagreement among the raters. However, a single teacher can rate a group of products holistically, working alone, and without preestablished standards. The whole product is read quickly but thoughtfully, and a rating is written on a separate scoring sheet. A score of zero is given if the student has done nothing at all, or if the product is wholly unrelated to the assigned task. No more than two minutes is spent reading and rating each piece.

If several products by the same student are being rated by a single teacher, the student's score is the total of the numbers assigned to each product. If two teachers score a set of student products holistically, they each rate every piece, without consultation. Then they compare ratings, and if their ratings of the same product are identical, or differ by only one point, the student's score for that piece is the total of both teachers' ratings. If scores differ by more than a point, a third rater is asked to rate the piece independently. When this happens, the two closest ratings are added to obtain the student's score for that product, unless the ratings consist of three numbers in sequence, in which case the middle rating is counted twice. For example, if a piece of writing is rated 3 by one rater and 1 by another, and 3 by the third rater, then the rating of 1 is discarded and the student's score is 6 (3 + 3); if the third rating is 4, then the rating of 1 is discarded and the student's score is 7 (3 + 4). However if the original ratings are 3 and 1 and the third rating is 2, then the middle rating is counted twice and the student's score is 4 (2 + 2). (In practice, disagreements of more than one point are rare in holistic scoring, because the range of scores is narrow. It is essential in recording and reporting holistic scores to note what the maximum and minimum scores are. If a single teacher rates two products for each student, then the maximum score for students who have completed the task is 8 (4 for each piece of writing) and the minimum score is 2. If two teachers have rated each rated two pieces, then scores can range from 16 to 4. A wide variety of student work can be rated holistically but holistic scoring is most frequently used to assess writing samples. This method can be a powerful alternative to the use of standardized, multiple-choice tests to evaluate writing development—one that encourages attention to real writing, rather than to isolated technical aspects of writing (Haney & Madaus, 1989; Suhor, 1985).

Examining and Using Results.   Extensive writing is a valuable part of learning, so teachers do well to include writing in content area study whether their students' scores on holistically rated writing samples are high or low. However, low scores give a strong signal that many opportunities for brief, purposeful, ungraded writing are needed, thus teachers might choose to take one or more of the following actions: use Confer and Write as an opening class activity, use Write-Out as a concluding activity, incorporate journals, assign QUiP or SAIL papers often for pairs or small groups.

Can Students Meet a Teacher-Set Standard for the Class?   Questions about reading and writing are questions about how well students are progressing in acquiring tools for learning and work. This question focuses on single aspects of learning that a teacher believes are especially important. The question can be answered by developing and using a criterion-referenced test.

Criterion-Referenced Testing.   A criterion is a standard to be met. Teachers can decide to assess students' progress against a criterion; when they do, teachers decide what that criterion is. To determine whether students have met important standards, teachers can develop an assessment measure and establish a standard, a criterion, that shows sufficient mastery. For example, if being able to name the 50 U. S. states and identify their locations on a map is an important classroom goal, the teacher might set it as a criterion that a student be able to label 47 states correctly on a U. S. map. Students who can meet the criterion have met this curriculum goal. Because setting the criterion is the teacher's decision, rather than a criterion of 47/50, the teacher might set it at 42/50, or might require a perfect score of 50/50. Some tasks, such as simple arithmetic computations, require both accuracy and speed. When this is the case, the criteria for success on the test will incorporate both speed and accuracy. These are other examples of criterion-referenced tests that a teacher might use:

The student completes a Focused Cloze using content-related vocabulary with 100 percent accuracy.

Given a list of 15 major events during the American Civil War, the student arranges them in chronological order with 80 percent accuracy.

Given 12 mounted postcards of the works of 4 artists studied in class, the student can identify the artist who produced each work for at least two-thirds of the postcards.

The student states safety rules for lab work with 100 percent accuracy.

It is possible—indeed it is a desired outcome—for all students to pass criterion-referenced tests. Their performance is judged against an agreed-upon standard, rather than by comparison with the work of other students, as is done in norm-referenced testing (discussed later in this chapter). This assessment method can be adapted for use with cooperative groups, by assigning members of cooperative learning groups to work together to ensure that each member has mastered content area information, with success attained when all group members meet the established criterion. A criterion-referenced test provides teachers with a useful method of determining if a topic needs reteaching, either as a whole class activity or in mini-lessons for a selected group. Not all learning is appropriately measured by criterion-referenced tests, however, and teachers should avoid commercial programs that offer packaged tests of many small subskills, because they consume instructional time and focus attention on small, unconnected aspects of learning. Nevertheless, the concept of measurement against a standard is a useful one for teachers to consider as an element of informed classroom assessment.

Alternative Models of Assessment

Assessment has too often been assumed to consist solely or primarily of testing, using commercially produced or state-developed tests. This assumption disempowers classroom teachers, whose role then is to administer tests devised by others, following directions supplied to them. Sometimes such testing is called formal assessment and, in contrast, assessment done by classroom teachers is called informal. Kenneth Wolf suggests using the term *informed assessment,* rather than informal assessment, to describe teachers' involvement in the assessment process.

[Informed assessment] is a label that conveys respect for the kinds of everyday assessments knowledgeable teachers carry out in their class-

rooms and that recognizes that teachers' assessments provide the most accurate and useful information about student achievement. When teachers have meaningful goals for instruction and clear purposes for assessment, and when they use a variety of strategies to observe and document their students' performances across diverse contexts and over time, these teachers are practicing not informal but *informed* assessment. (Wolf, 1993, p. 519)

In recent years, new conceptions of assessment have been devised, and the importance of assessment by thoughtful teachers has been recognized by scholars. "An enlightened teacher is the best evaluator of students' growth in process learnings. Teachers can directly observe and collect evidence of student performance in situations that demand application and transfer of knowledge as well as cooperativeness, persistence, and creativity" (Costa, 1989, p. 2). New models encourage moving away from assessment processes that rank students in comparison to one another, or categorize them as above or below average. Rather than depending on results of standardized testing, informed assessment by classroom teachers can play a major role in the assessment process. *Dynamic assessment* is a new testing procedure. *Responsive assessment* is based on interactions between the assessor and those assessed. *Authentic assessment* focuses on students' products. The three models of assessment are not exclusive, that is, teachers may find ways to use all three methods in their classrooms.

Dynamic Assessment. Unlike typical testing methods, dynamic assessment integrates teaching and testing. The method of testing with which most people are familiar consists of a series of questions to answer, or tasks to perform. Regardless of whether the test is given to a single individual or to large groups, each person works alone, without assistance, and the test results are based on the number of correct responses the person gives. Because the test itself, and the conditions of testing, are the same for everyone, test scores can be compared and people can be ranked or categorized on the basis of those scores. In a testing situation, people cannot be helped by the examiner or by others, because that would mean that test results would not be comparable. Dynamic assessment, on the other hand, is not focused on ensuring comparability in test administration and test results. Instead of every testing situation being the same, every dynamic testing situation should be unique.

Dynamic assessment is based on the principle that the proper purpose of testing is to determine ways to advance learning. Therefore, testing becomes an attempt to examine students at some point in a zone of proximal development—engaging in a task that is neither already mastered, nor beyond their current capabilities.

> As a teacher, at what point are you interested in assessment? Probably it is pointless to try to measure this thing if the child has not yet started to learn it. Probably it is equally silly to take time out to assess it if the child can already complete the task perfectly. That leaves the period in between as a time that might be very interesting to the teacher. It could be the time when support or a hint about direction to move next might have the most effect. So, for the purposes of teaching we might want to be able to capture the half-right, half-wrong responding of our students and gain the maximum information on how to guide their next attempts or what opportunities we might provide to help them. (Clay, 1990, p. 295)

Clearly, dynamic assessment does not yield statistically determined test scores, nor is it intended for large group use. For these very reasons, it is a form of testing that a classroom teacher can learn to use and that is well-suited to the classroom environment. Dynamic assessment, as Victor Delclos and his colleagues point out, is "based on the assumption that the best estimate of an individual's learning ability comes from direct observation of that individual in a learning situation rather than from a test of what has been learned in the past" (Delclos, Burns, & Kulewicz, 1987, p. 325). In dynamic assessment, the teacher gives a student a task that is new and somewhat challenging and observes how the student approaches the task. For example, the task might be to solve an unfamiliar math problem, plan a science experiment, or compare events in different historical periods. As the student works independently, the teacher observes the strategies the student uses and notes what the student is able to

accomplish. Based on these observations, the teacher provides teaching in the form of a "mediated mini-lesson" (Kletzien & Bednar, 1990, p. 531). This is a supportive, collaborative process in which the teacher points out the strengths the student has shown in approaching the task and teaches the student a way to work more effectively. The student then has the opportunity to work on the problem further, and the teacher notes how much the student can accomplish after the mini-lesson.

Research indicates that using dynamic assessment or watching videotapes of students in a dynamic assessment session tends to raise teachers' estimations of what students can accomplish (Delclos et al., 1987). Although the technique is not suitable for use with large groups of students (because it would be impossible to observe each individual's strategy use), classroom teachers can adapt dynamic assessment for use with cooperative groups, by giving groups a challenging task, sitting quietly to observe members of one group at work, providing a mini-lesson for the whole class, and then returning to observe how members of the group being observed modify their approach to the task. Dynamic assessment is a method with an established procedure: give task, observe student's methods of working on task, teach useful strategy, observe student's progress after instruction, and make a judgment concerning the quality of work. It is also useful for classroom teachers to keep in mind the reasoning that underlies this procedure—that teachers need to know what students are capable of doing with assistance (either from students or from classmates), because that is an indicator of what they will be able to do later independently, if the learning environment is effective in helping them learn.

Responsive Assessment. The concept of responsive assessment comes from a system devised for the evaluation of programs, called responsive evaluation (Guba & Lincoln, 1981; Stake, 1975). This method emphasizes the value of interaction between people in learning about progress, rather than the development and use of tests for decision-making purposes. Brian Cambourne and Jan Turbill (1990) are among the educators who suggest the use of responsive assessment in working with individuals. They encourage teachers to engage in persistent, prolonged observation, choose which data to collect and record, find multiple ways of looking at students' work and progress, and consult with colleagues and with students themselves as they interpret the data they have compiled.

> Responsive evaluation. ...rejects the assumption that assessor-assessee interaction needs to be carefully controlled through standardization of procedures or the imposition of a standard instrument. Rather, it is based on the assumption that the 'human-as-instrument' is as effective and valid as the 'test-as-instrument' when assessing human behaviors. ...Essentially, responsive evaluation is an approach that aims at the study of behavioral phenomena within the context of the situation. (Cambourne & Turbill, 1990, p. 340)

Responsive assessment can be an ongoing part of the instructional program, based on observing, collecting, and analyzing students' work, engaging with students in mutual inquiry about their strengths, needs, and progress, and asking good questions and listening carefully to answers. Essential to responsive assessment is interest in, and respect for, students on the teacher's part.

Authentic Assessment. A major purpose of educational assessment is to investigate and then document what students have learned. Everyone is familiar with the method of accomplishing this through testing: investigate by giving a test; document by recording the test score. The assumption that underlies this method is that the test stands for learning. In authentic assessment, on the other hand, real products are the indicators of real learning. If students create a diagram listing the similarities and differences between plant and animal cells accurately, clearly, and thoroughly, that product shows that they know how plant and animal cells are similar and how they differ. If students create and solve original problems involving rate, time, and distance, these products demonstrate that they understand the necessary mathematical concepts and processes. What students have done successfully is proof of what they have learned. Authentic assessment is based on linking learning activities directly to investigation and documentation. Although some writers on assessment make a distinction between authentic assessment and performance assessment, others (e.g., Reed, 1993; Wiggins, 1989) treat the terms as equivalent, as this text does.

> Performance-based assessments require students to demonstrate specific skills or competencies in an open-ended situation, such as writing an essay, delivering a speech, explaining the steps taken to solve a mathematics problem, demonstrating scientific method during an experiment, or engaging in some other application of high-order thinking. Performance-based assessments require the student to know more than just the one right answer. They represent a synergism in learning: the total effect is greater and more fluid than the sum of the discrete parts that compose it. (Reed, 1993, p. 12)

When authentic assessment is used, teachers assess their students' learning by looking at what they can do and by examining evidence of progress over time as demonstrated by changes in students' products. Learners' achievement is not measured by tests but by "activities that represent ...behavior of the community and workplace, and that reflect the actual learning and instructional activities of the classroom and out-of-school worlds" (Valencia, Hiebert, & Afflerbach, 1994, p. 11). When we think about this definition, we see that there is one basic requirement teachers must meet before engaging in authentic assessment: they must create classrooms that are productive learning environments. If students do little besides reading the text, answering questions from a teacher's manual, writing answers to questions in the text, and then taking a test, it is not possible for the classroom teacher to use authentic assessment, since there is nothing authentic to assess. It would be possible, however, for teachers who decide to move away from ineffective teaching methods to plan a changed classroom and changed assessment methods simultaneously—indeed, that would be a sensible change strategy.

Using authentic assessment requires thoughtful planning, and takes time. But one of the striking features of well-planned and conducted authentic assessment is that it can be enjoyable and satisfying, in fact, fun, for teachers as well as students.

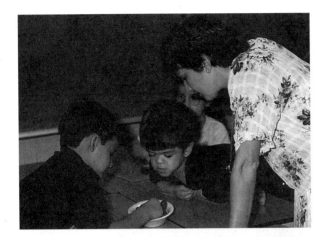

Some of the Many Aspects of Assessment

Moreover, it provides an effective way of informing students about their learning and teachers about their teaching. Learning portfolios, described in the next section of this chapter, can be used effectively in authentic assessment. Thomas Barone (1991) describes the culmination of a local history curriculum in the form of an exposition, with dramatic productions, media presentations, and students reading their own stories and essays. Tynette Hills suggests basing assessment on games, interviews, contracts, and directed assignments, such as creating an illustration to show a math problem and its solution.

> Appropriate assessment enhances the professional role of teachers, lifting them far above the "meter reader" metaphor that captures the misgivings many have felt as they scored daily worksheets, end-of-unit tests in basal texts, and standardized tests. ...Authentic assessment. ...forms a basis for teachers to evaluate their own efforts as dedicated professionals, fitting comfortably with their implicit theories about what is significant for children to learn and do. (Hills, 1992, p. 61)

Collecting Information Across Settings and Times

If only one piece of information about a student's achievement has been collected, for example, a test score, then it is impossible to be sure that the information gives an accurate picture. One reason why teacher assessment is so useful is that teachers have the opportunity to observe and collect data over time, in many situations. The term used to refer to the planned collection of assessment information from multiple sources is *triangulation* (Mathison, 1988). "What is sought in triangulation is an interpretation of the phenomenon at hand that illuminates and reveals the subject matter in a thickly contextualized manner" (Denzin, 1988, p. 512). To get a thorough and accurate picture of what something is like, it is necessary to look at it from more than one angle. The process of triangulation is getting multiple pieces of information, at least three, about the person or event being investigated. Information may be collected in different ways (e.g., teacher observations, completed assign-

ments and journal entries, tests); at different times (e.g., across a time period and at different times of the day); in different settings (e.g., during cooperative group work, in a formal testing situation, while working independently); and from different sources (e.g., the student, a previous year's teacher, a special area teacher).

Encouraging Students To Gather Data

Aspects of the investigative component of assessment that are especially appropriate for student involvement are identification of personal strengths and needs, developing self-established achievement criteria, and selecting and collecting work as part of the authentic assessment process. In a classroom environment where strengths and needs are recognized both as important and subject to development and change, students are more likely to value themselves and their classmates as learners than they would in an environment where strengths are contrasted with weaknesses. The concept of setting and meeting a criterion that indicates successful learning is one that students can readily understand, and by encouraging students to decide what criteria they will aim to meet in their own learning helps them develop independence. Making students a part of the decision-making process about what categories of work to include and what work samples to choose for analysis and display enhances authentic assessment.

Documentation: Keeping and Analyzing a Record of Learning

The different aspects of assessment are interrelated. Attention leads to investigation, and the results of observations and data gathering need to be recorded and examined thoughtfully. **Documentation** is keeping a record—compiling and analyzing materials that provide evidence of students' status and progress. Some methods of documentation, such as contracts, checklists, and rubrics, can be made an integral part of instruction. Other methods, such as work sampling and portfolios, are based on collecting products of instruction.

Integrating Documentation and Instruction

Contracts, checklists, and rubrics are methods that can be used to guide students' work on projects and other assignments by specifying clearly what the characteristics of satisfactory work are. Besides providing useful direction to students, these teacher-prepared materials, when well-constructed, are an excellent source for documentation of student progress and achievement.

Contracts.   A learning contract is a written agreement between student and teacher that clearly identifies required and optional learning activities and specifies the benefits to be obtained on satisfactory completion of the contract. Contracts are a useful method of tracking and documenting progress for students in middle school and high school (e.g., Greenwood, 1985), and can be adapted for use with younger students. Because contracts will vary among students, they "enable the teacher to raise levels of expectation, to provide individual attention, and to personalize the educational experience" (White & Greenwood, 1992, p. 17), and they can encourage students to take responsibility for their own learning. Figure 8–5 provides the generic basis for a contract that can be adapted across grade levels and topics.

Checklists.   A checklist is a list of items, prepared by the teacher, to be checked off as they are accomplished by students. Checklists are useful when students are engaged in long-term projects. These checklists will be specific to the project. Advance preparation will help the teacher in planning, and checklist use is a practical method of recording and dating progress. Checklists also can be devised for use in units of study throughout the year. To prepare a checklist, the teacher lists, in advance of providing instruction on a topic, what students will be expected to accomplish. (This is a place where objectives are useful—they can readily be translated into a checklist.) Once prepared, a copy of the checklist will be needed for each student. A practical way to keep checklists up-to-date and readily available is to keep them in a looseleaf notebook. Figure 8–6 gives an example of a checklist for elementary students; Figure 8–7 gives excerpts from paired checklists prepared by middle school science and language arts teachers for a shared project.

Rubrics.   While detailed checklists give students clear information about the requirements for an assignment, rubrics (Farr, 1992; Herman, Aschbacher, & Winters, 1992; O'Neil 1994) set forth the characteristics of products of differing quality. "A rubric is a scaled set of criteria that clearly defines for the student and teacher what a range of acceptable and unacceptable performance looks like" (Pate, Homestead, & McGinnis, 1993, p. 25). Rubrics are usually teacher-developed, but teachers may decide to involve students in developing rubrics for a particular assignment. Daniel Pearce provides a rubric for grading papers on the topic of approaches to civil rights in the United States during the 1960s. His rubric lists the characteristics of papers in each of four categories: high quality, medium quality, lower quality, and lowest quality. According to his rubric, the highest quality papers have the following characteristics:

- An overview of civil rights or their lack during the 1960s, with three specific examples
- A statement defining civil disobedience, with three examples of how it was used and Martin Luther King's role
- At least one other approach to civil rights, with specific examples, and a comparison of this approach with King's civil disobedience that illustrates the differences or similarities in at least two ways
- Good organization, well-developed arguments, few mechanical errors

(Pearce, 1983, p. 215)

Rubrics serve a double purpose. They provide a structure for teachers who are using a holistic rating process to evaluate multiple products. They

---

documentation—in Latin, means *an official paper*. The root word is the verb *docere*, meaning *to teach*. Documentation is the process of keeping records, and these records should be those which give us useful information on which to base sound decisions.

FIGURE 8–5   Sample of Generic Contract

Name: _____ Topic: _____
Contract # _____ Dates: _____ to _____

I will complete the following required activities:
▮   ▮
▮   ▮

I will select and complete the two activities I have chosen from this list:
▮   ▮
▮   ▮

I will demonstrate what I have learned by:

Successful completion of this contract will earn: (to be specified by teacher)

Signatures: _____ (*student*)   _____ (*teacher*)

Formative evaluation conference(s) _____ _____   Comments:

Summative evaluation conference: _____   Comments:

FIGURE 8–6   Example of Project-Focused Checklist For Elementary School

Checklist: Study of Communities   Name: _____

▮ Reading
  ☐ Participates in buddy reading of text
     (partners: _____)
  ☐ Contributes to group RESPONSE chart on text
     chapter
  ☐ Reads trade books (_____)
  ☐ Participates in *Say Something* and *Discussion Web*
     discussions
▮ Other learning activities
  ☐ Completes *Typical to Technical Meaning* on map
     words with buddy
  ☐ Completes *Focused Cloze* in group (during
     instruction)
  ☐ Contributes to (urban/suburban/rural) mural

▮ Guest speaker
  ☐ Suggests question (in advance)
  ☐ Thank-you letter
▮ Achievement
  ☐ Can explain terms: *urban, suburban, rural*
  ☐ Writes at least four Learning Log entries during
     period of study
  ☐ Identifies locations on maps: North America,
     USA, state, town, home street
  ☐ Completes Focused Cloze individually (after
     instruction) Score: ____
▮ Additions
  ☐ Photo of mural
  ☐ Copy of student-chosen Learning Log entry

FIGURE 8–7   Paired Checklists (Science and English) For Research Project

SCIENCE

Student: _____   Hour: _____

Peer evaluator: Student: _____

	Self		Peer		Teacher	
	Y	**I**	**Y**	**I**	**Y**	**I**
Preparation						
Thesis questions/predicted answers	☐	☐	☐	☐	☐	☐
Three sources—only 1 encyclopedia	☐	☐	☐	☐	☐	☐
Note sheets—5 minimum	☐	☐	☐	☐	☐	☐
Picture/graphic	☐	☐	☐	☐	☐	☐
Research time used productively	☐	☐	☐	☐	☐	☐
Content						
A. Characteristics—what it looks like						
scientific name	☐	☐	☐	☐	☐	☐
physical description	☐	☐	☐	☐	☐	☐
color	☐	☐	☐	☐	☐	☐
weight	☐	☐	☐	☐	☐	☐
height	☐	☐	☐	☐	☐	☐
outer body covering	☐	☐	☐	☐	☐	☐
B. Habitat—where it lives						
location	☐	☐	☐	☐	☐	☐
description of location	☐	☐	☐	☐	☐	☐
climate	☐	☐	☐	☐	☐	☐
C. Niche—role it plays in the environment						
predator-prey relationships	☐	☐	☐	☐	☐	☐
food requirements (what kind,						
how much, how often)	☐	☐	☐	☐	☐	☐
D. Life cycle						
reproduction	☐	☐	☐	☐	☐	☐
courtship	☐	☐	☐	☐	☐	☐
mating (including length of pregnancy)	☐	☐	☐	☐	☐	☐
care of young (where are they raised?)	☐	☐	☐	☐	☐	☐
E. Relationship to people						
effect people have on it	☐	☐	☐	☐	☐	☐
effect it has on people	☐	☐	☐	☐	☐	☐
is it endangered?	☐	☐	☐	☐	☐	☐
why? why not?						
how would its loss affect the ecosystem?						
how is this animal used by people?	☐	☐	☐	☐	☐	☐

Comments

FIGURE 8–7 Continued

ENGLISH

Student: _____ Hour: _____

Peer evaluator: Student: _____

	Self Y	Self I	Peer Y	Peer I	Teacher Y	Teacher I
A. Title page						
Title capitalized and spelled correctly	☐	☐	☐	☐	☐	☐
Title attracts the reader's interest	☐	☐	☐	☐	☐	☐
Student's name and date in right-hand corner	☐	☐	☐	☐	☐	☐
B. Introduction						
Lead that catches reader's attention	☐	☐	☐	☐	☐	☐
One or two paragraphs that introduce animal	☐	☐	☐	☐	☐	☐
…and tell why student chose animal	☐	☐	☐	☐	☐	☐
C. Report (body)						
Follows outline developed by the student	☐	☐	☐	☐	☐	☐
Does not plagiarize—uses own words/quotes	☐	☐	☐	☐	☐	☐
Includes factual information	☐	☐	☐	☐	☐	☐
Includes interesting details	☐	☐	☐	☐	☐	☐
Arranged in a logical order	☐	☐	☐	☐	☐	☐
Uses transitions between paragraphs/sections	☐	☐	☐	☐	☐	☐
Written in formal style (no slang)	☐	☐	☐	☐	☐	☐
D. Conclusion						
At least one paragraph	☐	☐	☐	☐	☐	☐
Tells what student learned	☐	☐	☐	☐	☐	☐
Expresses student's attitude toward animal	☐	☐	☐	☐	☐	☐
Explains if/how student's attitude/behavior toward animal has changed	☐	☐	☐	☐	☐	☐
Identifies what student still wants to learn	☐	☐	☐	☐	☐	☐

Comments

Notes: Each of three evaluators (student, peer evaluator, teacher) rates each item by checking either Y (Yes—the item is complete) or I (Incomplete).

These checklists were developed by Kathy Cook and John Kleis; some adaptations have been made for this text.

also are designed to be given to students, to inform them about what grade they will receive or rating a product with specified characteristics. Like contracts, rubrics open the possibility for students to elect to work toward a B or C grade, or to aim at producing a paper of medium quality or even lower quality. Although students may sometimes benefit from encouragement to set their sights higher, their decisions should be respected. If teachers believe that it is unwise to offer students a choice about goals, then they should not use processes that allow this kind of goal setting.

Collecting Materials Thoughtfully

The essential part of documentation is thoughtful compilation of data and materials that demonstrate what students have learned and achieved. Samples of students' work provide evidence of their progress. Work sampling is the collection of materials based on thoughtful decisions about what, how often, and when examples of students' work should be kept. The use of portfolios—collections of a wide variety of evidence showing what has been achieved—is an assessment method used for students as well as for adults.

Work Sampling.   Keeping a file of students' work, in selected categories, done at different times of the year, provides evidence, or documentation, of their achievement, effort, and progress. Using work sampling in the assessment process requires decision-making, analysis, and reflection. Teachers who decide to use work sampling begin by deciding what kinds of work to collect. The student products chosen for sampling should be based on learning activities that are used repeatedly (so development over time can be investigated) and related to important course learning. Teachers then need to decide how frequently samples should be collected and how they will be kept. It is useful for students to have opportunities to choose their best work. The collected samples provide an opportunity for students and teachers to collaborate in examining progress over time, and work samples can be one component of student portfolios.

Portfolios.   Portfolios are an organized, diverse, displayable collection of students' work, collected thoughtfully over time. Samuel Meisels defines portfolios as "a purposeful collection of [students'] work that illustrates their efforts, progress, and achievements and potentially provides a rich documentation of each [student's] experience throughout the year. …[and enables them] to become involved with the process of selecting and judging the quality of their own work" (Meisels, 1993, p. 37). Roger Farr, who refers to portfolios as "the flagship of performance assessment," describes them as "a shifting, growing repository of developing processes and ideas—a

rather personal melting pot" (Farr, 1992, p. 35). Although portfolio use is time-consuming, the time spent is potentially a valuable part of a lively instructional program. Moreover, as Elfrieda Hiebert and Robert Calfee have noted, "portfolios of students' work can also create links between instruction at different grade levels. Last year's student projects can guide teachers' decisions" (Hiebert & Calfee, 1989, p. 54). Portfolios should present an accurate picture of students' progress and talents. It is not their purpose to present a balance of successes and failures, or to document lack of achievement. As Grant Wiggins (1989, p. 711) writes, authentic assessments "ferret out and identify (perhaps hidden) strengths. The aim is to enable the students to show off what they can do."

Angelo Collins identifies three categories of portfolio contents: productions, reproductions, and attestations. *Productions* are documents such as samples of finished work and work in progress— papers, drafts, journal entries, drawings, photographs, audiotapes and videotapes, computer disks, all of which are the student's work—intended for inclusion in the portfolio. Each production should be captioned by the student to provide a context for the work, as it relates to the goal of the portfolio. *Reproductions* are "documents about typical events in the work of the person developing the portfolio, but events which are usually not captured," for example, photographs of a student preparing a display as well as of the display itself. *Attestations* are "documents about the work of the person prepared by someone other than the portfolio developer," for example, comments on a student's work by an expert other than the teacher, or a letter of thanks for participation in a community project.

> [P]urposefulness is the] feature common to all portfolios that distinguishes them from scrapbooks filled with pretty mementos and manila folders randomly stuffed with paper. A portfolio is a container of collected evidence with a purpose. Evidence is documentation that can be used by one person or group of persons to infer another person's knowledge, skill, and/or disposition. The requirement that the evidence in a portfolio be focused on a purpose is key both to designing and to developing one. (Collins, 1992, pp. 452–453)

The use of portfolios in assessment is increasing for groups over a wide age range. In some college programs, students preparing to become teachers develop portfolios, collecting materials over a period of several years that demonstrate their knowledge of development, their proficiency in writing, their ingenuity in creating learning materials, and their successes in working with students. Besides written materials, these portfolios are likely to include videotapes and photographs. Portfolios also are an assessment instrument that can be used by professionals, including teachers and administrators. More than any other form of assessment, portfolios are student-centered. Portfolios are a form of assessment done *by* the student, not *to* the student. Their use should be integrated with teaching and designed to help students learning about their own learning. Time for a series of conferences about portfolio development should be scheduled in advance. Some of the conferences may be held in small groups, so students share ideas. The collection of work in portfolios is ongoing, thus one decision teachers who plan to use portfolios need to make is how materials are to be kept, so they can be stored efficiently and accessed easily. Dennis Adams and Mary Hamm (1992) suggest using stackable boxes for younger students and, for older students, either artists' folders or three-ring binders with items hole-punched or placed in plastic envelopes. Care should be taken so that items are not simply stored without thought and attention. Each item should be dated, with a short description or caption written at the time it is placed in the portfolio collection. A completed portfolio should include an itemized Table of Contents and a letter by its creator. For younger students, these materials can be teacher-prepared forms to which students have added their own thoughts, in writing or by dictation.

Encouraging Students To Document and Analyze Their Learning

Some methods of documentation, such as checklists and contracts, can be made an integral part of instruction. Other methods, such as work sampling and portfolios, are based on collecting products of instruction. Portfolios are ideal for encouraging students to document their learning and engage in self-assessment. Dennie Wolf (1989) stresses the value of portfolios in developing students' sense of responsibility for their own learning. Student-led conferences (Little & Allan, 1989) in which students join regular school conferences between teacher and adult family members and conduct a portion of the conference are frequently based on student explanation of their work as demonstrated in portfolios. (This newly introduced style for conferences is discussed in Chapter Nine.)

Jane Hansen (1992b) advocates portfolio use from elementary through high school, suggesting that teachers model portfolio development for their students by creating and sharing their own portfolios, including their teaching goals. She notes that students may need to begin by creating very personalized, individual portfolios based on their interests and experiences, and she quotes a teacher's rationale for emphasizing student choice: "My students have such shaky self-concepts that they first need a portfolio that shows who they are. Then, later, when they've gained some confidence in themselves, they can assess who they want to be as students" (Hansen, 1992a, p. 607). Thinking in terms of strengths or needs, then, it is useful to remember that it is only the most secure people who are comfortable in focusing immediately on personal needs and goals. Others *need* to have their strengths recognized first.

■■ Evaluation: Weighing Evidence and ■■ Making Decisions

Three of the components of assessment discussed in this chapter—attention, investigation, and documentation—extend over time. Teachers look with care at students; gather data about students' strengths, needs, and progress; record and analyze evidence of students' accomplishments. These activities occur throughout the period of time—a year, a semester—that students and teachers are working together. **Evaluation,** however, occurs at selected times; it represents a decision about students' progress, based on evidence obtained through the other aspects of the assessment process.

Formative vs. Summative Evaluation

Ongoing assessment of progress is especially useful when it provides evaluative information that increases the likelihood of a good final evaluation. A final evaluation of a person's work, a product's value, or a program's success, is called *summative evaluation*—a summing up that occurs at an endpoint. For students, summative evaluation is typically provided by a final course grade. While program requirements make such summative evaluation necessary, it is more useful to provide evaluative information about progress before a final summing up, while the information can be used to make changes that will help in achieving eventual success. Evaluation given for the purpose of providing information and direction during the course of a program of study is called *formative evaluation*—information that helps to form future endeavors along even more productive lines. The distinction between formative and summative evaluation is a useful one for teachers to keep in mind. Evaluation aimed at helping students become successful during a course of study is more valuable than evaluation that rates students at a concluding point. An important aspect of planning good classroom assessment is to establish times when students' progress and accomplishment will be examined, so both teacher and students are informed and changes can be made.

The Role of Testing in Evaluation

In our educational system, a major element of assessment and of the evaluative component of assessment is testing. Scholar and educator Samuel Meisels (1993, p. 34) points out how powerful the influence of testing can be. "Tests have the power to change teachers' and children's perceptions of themselves and their view of the entire educational process." There is currently little likelihood that the extent of testing in our schools will substantially decrease.

> By 1990, it was conservatively estimated that each year elementary and secondary students take 127 million separate tests as part of standardized test batteries mandated by states and districts. ...At some grade levels, a student might have to sit for 7 to 12 such tests a year. ...[N]ot only has the volume of testing increased, but testing has become a high-stakes policy tool looming ominously over the lives of many educators and children, influencing what is taught and how, and what is learned and how. (Madaus & Tan, 1993, pp. 60 and 65)

Overreliance on test results puts a substantial number of students at risk of being classified as failures. Moreover, it is likely to give all students a distorted view of learning by encouraging the idea that learning is not an enjoyable, ongoing process, but something that must be done in order to pass a test. Overemphasis on testing draws time away from instruction and may mislead those who set educational policy into thinking that learning can be accomplished through testing. Several years ago, the delegate assembly of the International Reading Association voted unanimously to oppose the proliferation of standardized testing. "Probably the most incisive comment on the current emphasis on mandated, extensive, continuing testing came from Heather Fehring, IRA delegate from Australia: 'As any wise old farmer can tell you,' she said, 'you don't fatten your lambs simply by weighing them'" (Fehring, quoted in *IRA News*, 1990). It is the responsibility of each classroom teacher to minimize the amount of time testing draws away from teaching and to use test results sensibly to help students.

Testing can be a useful part of assessment, but there are two ways in which teaching and testing do not mix. First, teaching time should not be focused on preparation for a test. When teachers know in advance what items will be on a test that their students and others will take, it is improper to teach them the answers to these items. It also is wrong to

---

evaluation—a word that was developed in English because a term was needed to express an idea in business. Its first known written use was in 1755, in relation to insurance. ("When a certain evaluation is admitted in the policy no premium can be demanded back.") The word is based on Latin, where the root word is *valere*, meaning *to be strong* or *to have worth*. Evaluation is a process of determining worth, or value, thus is a decision-making process.

concentrate instruction on subjects that will be tested to the neglect of other important topics, or to spend extensive amounts of class time teaching students how to take tests. Second, teaching should be teaching, not a subtle form of testing. To consume instructional time in asking questions to check students' recall from their reading is testing, not teaching. To give assignments with no teacher intervention except for a final grade is testing, not teaching. Effective teachers keep in mind the difference between teaching and testing and use assessment to help students.

Classroom Tests.   Most classroom tests are teacher-chosen but not teacher-developed. These tests are provided by text publishers or other sources as part of a package of commercial educational materials. In some teaching situations, teachers are required to give these tests, but in many cases whether or not to use them is a teacher's decision. That decision should be made thoughtfully, on the basis of what is best for students and for the instructional program the teacher has planned. Teacher-made tests are a valuable alternative to commercial tests, if they are thoughtfully, carefully prepared. Criterion-referenced tests, discussed earlier in this chapter, are one form of test teachers can readily create. Classroom tests devised to assess students' grasp of a topic that has been studied can incorporate student-created questions; in fact, students' ability to generate good questions can be used in itself as a method of assessment. Teacher-prepared tests are potentially excellent assessment measures, because teachers can focus the test directly on the most important aspects of what has been taught. Although this can be done, and certainly should be done, it is not always accomplished. David Lohman has commented vividly on the shortcomings of some classroom tests:

> I am not so much concerned here with nationally constructed tests as with the daily, weekly, and course tests that teachers construct, or, increasingly, take from a teacher's manual. Here is an example of what I mean. Several years ago we celebrated the 200th anniversary of the U. S. Constitution. Children in schools studied special units on the Constitution. I was working with a class of fifth-

grade students at the time and was shown their mastery test of multiple choice and true-false questions on this unit. The first thing I noticed was that nowhere on the test was there a question like 'What is a constitution?' or 'Why do we need a constitution?' Thus, it was possible for children to come away from this test thinking they knew something about the U. S. Constitution without having the foggiest notion of what a constitution is or why a government might need one. Questions on the test ranged from reasonable to absurd. One of the latter was, 'Who was the signer of the constitution who had six children?' Answer: Thomas Jefferson. There are many things one might want to know about Thomas Jefferson, but surely the fact that he had six children is not one of the most important. Yet this was the only question about Thomas Jefferson on the test. (Lohman, 1993, p. 19)

Using Teaching Strategies As Tests.   As Joan Herman (1992, p. 75) notes, "[t]he tasks selected to measure a given content domain should themselves be worthy of the time and efforts of students and raters." One practical and time-effective way to link teaching and assessment is to have frequently used teaching strategies serve a double purpose—both as learning activities and as assessment measures. The products of activities themselves can provide evidence of students' achievement, or a familiar instructional strategy can be used toward the end of study of a topic, as a test. If a teaching strategy assignment is treated as a test, students must have used the strategy often as part of classroom instruction and thus be fully familiar with how to use it. (This prior use has an additional advantage, because it enables teachers to observe whether their students work well with a particular strategy. If they do not, that strategy should not be used in testing.) Also, students must be told when an activity is being used as a test. Figure 8–8 gives examples of some of the many ways teaching strategies can be used as tests, after a period of study.

Encouraging Students To Make Decisions

Many scholars and educators advocate engaging students in the process of self-evaluation. Linda Rief (1990, p. 27) makes a useful distinction about the dual roles that are appropriate for students and teachers in the evaluation process. She suggests that students are the best evaluators of their own work, but teachers are the best evaluators of student growth. "As teachers we must listen first to the perceptions our students have of themselves—and address what they think they can and cannot do." Student self-evaluation is most useful when it is formative, that is, when it occurs during the time students and teacher are working together, rather than at the end of this time. Teachers of older students, however, may decide to include student self-evaluation as a part of summative evaluation. For example, students can write letters evaluating their own progress, which teachers respond to with a short written evaluation and grade.

■■ Guidelines for Informed Classroom
■■ Assessment

When teachers incorporate assessment into their instructional program, evaluation need not be based solely on test results. Documentation of student achievement, effort, and progress through teacher-selected methods provides the basis for evaluation and evidence to support evaluation decisions. Formative evaluation can occur through conferences or exchanges of written messages before summative evaluation is made in the form of a grade or final progress report that becomes a part of the record. It is useful for teachers who decide to take responsibility for classroom assessment to keep three points in

FIGURE 8–8   Examples of Instructional Strategies Used As Individual Tests of Learning

Note that students must be accustomed to using the strategy as a learning activity, before it is used as an assessment

STRATEGY	EXAMPLE
▪ Concept Connections (Chapter Four)	After studying the polar regions, students are given a list of terms —*adaptations, glaciers, icecap, meltwater, permafrost, plates, tabular icebergs, treeline, tundra*—with the assignment to place the nine terms in a grid and write two paragraphs, each showing the connection among three terms. (Assessment to be done individually, in class, without using notes or text.)
▪ Concept of Definition (Chapter Four)	After completing a unit of study on the fifty U. S. states, students are given a list of ten states and are assigned to prepare Concept of Definition maps for four states of their choice. (Assessment to be done individually, in class, with the opportunity to use the text as a resource.)
▪ Focused Cloze (Chapter Four)	After completing study of the purchase of the Louisiana territory, students are assigned to complete a Focused Cloze passage with 20 omissions. (Assessment to be done individually, in class, without using notes or text.)
▪ Semantic Feature Analysis (Chapter Five)	After studying the noble gases, students are given an SFA grid listing only features. Their assignment is to list the elements that are noble gases and complete the grid by marking plus or minus for each, for each feature. (Assessment to be done individually, in class, without using notes or text.)

mind: 1) informed assessment is a teacher's responsibility 2) effective assessment depends on teacher decision-making and 3) the main purpose of assessment is to increase opportunities for students.

Rely on Yourself, Your Students, and Your Colleagues. Informed assessment depends on teacher knowledge. The best classroom assessment is a shared process in which students are active participants and colleagues share ideas. However, the teacher's role in the assessment process is central. Attention and investigation are ongoing teacher responsibilities, and it is the teacher who documents and evaluates students' achievement. Do not give aides, paraprofessionals, or volunteers the task of examining or grading students' work unless you work alongside them and confer, because this removes opportunities for you to learn about students' strengths, needs, and progress. (If there is a huge amount of paperwork to be evaluated, rethink the assignments you give. If there are time periods when many papers must be submitted at once, consider working with colleagues to use a holistic scoring process.) Do not surrender authority for decision-making to tests. Use what you learn from mandated tests as one kind of information in planning ways to meet students' needs and build on their strengths.

Do What You Can. Do not reject new ideas because they seem overwhelming. Choose some small steps and start there. One way for teachers to change assessment practices is to apply the AIDE acronym to the change process. *Attention* comes first. Teachers can look with care at new ideas about assessment and compare them with what they are already doing. What good ideas are already in place, or easy to put in place? *Investigation* comes next. Each teacher has a unique set of strengths and needs. What assessment practices fit best with those characteristics? What ideas would be most useful, practical, and interesting to adopt? These are the ideas to try out, to investigate. *Documentation* is the next step. Without a large expenditure of time, some records should be kept; for example, jotted notes about how new processes work and samples of students' work. *Evaluation*, formative evaluation, is the last step. How have the changes worked so far? How

could the ideas that are being tried be adapted to be a better fit in our own teaching situation? What new ideas can be added?

> Don't try to do it all at once. Pick one assessment idea, such as portfolios or observations, and try it for a while. Revise and try again. Find ways to make the idea simpler, such as random sampling or looking for only one characteristic on a set of papers. Try to include one simple assessment technique in each lesson. For example, ask students to spend the last ten minutes of class writing what they learned... (Stenmark, 1991, p. 1)

Use Assessment to Open Doors. The purpose of all assessment should be to enhance students' learning, either directly or indirectly. Wise teachers regard all students as capable of learning and as possessing unique and interesting combinations of learning strengths and needs.

> We should stop thinking of assessment as a way of making categories and start thinking of assessment as a way of making opportunities. If our assessment tells us that a student needs help with some school task, that is an opportunity for us to help and for the student to grow. If our assessment tells us that a student has reached some remarkable level, that is an opportunity for us to share the joy and for the student to explore new paths to fulfillment. (MacGinitie, 1993, p. 559)

■■ Glossary of Assessment-Related
■■ Terminology

Teachers are expected to be able to understand and interpret test results, thus it is important for them to be knowledgeable about basic testing terminology and test-related concepts. Often, it is a teacher's responsibility to explain standardized test scores and the meaning of test terminology to parents and students.

Types of Tests

There are many different kinds of tests, and there also are different ways in which tests are classified. One category of tests is those that are mandated. A *mandated test* is any test that is required. (*Mandate* and *command* are derived from the same Latin word.) In some states, there are state-prepared, state-mandated tests that must be given to all students in the state at specified times (e.g., in third, sixth, and ninth grades). In many school districts, commercial tests that have been chosen by a district testing committee are mandated for administration at specified grade levels, at specified times of the year. All such mandated tests are accompanied by a set of directions giving precise directions to teachers about how the tests are to be administered, and it is the teacher's responsibility to follow the directions exactly. Tests are mandated by school, district, or state-wide decisions, so whether a particular test is mandated will vary from place to place, and across time. Teachers who are interested in participating in the decision-making process for their district may want to look into the possibility of volunteering to serve on their district's testing committee.

> American students are the most tested and least examined students in the world. When things go badly, we just add another test—as if taking the temperature more often would heal the patient. (Howard Gardner, quoted in Fernie, 1992, p. 226)

Most mandated tests are *achievement tests*. The purpose of the test is to ascertain what students have learned, or achieved, in a specified area. In some schools, commercial *aptitude tests* are required also. These are tests intended to determine a person's ability to learn; some are called group IQ tests. (*IQ* stands for *Intelligence Quotient*; originally, tests of this sort had scores based on a mathematical formula that yielded a quotient.) The value and propriety of such tests have been increasingly questioned on the basis of test validity—are they truly accurate measures of innate capacity to learn?—and on the uses to which test results are put (e.g., Gould, 1981).

Strong performance on assessment measures indicates a student's strengths. Poor performance on any assessment measure, however, may not be due to a student's current inability to fulfill the task, but to such task-irrelevant factors as illness, lack of interest, misunderstanding, carelessness, or fear. Scholars use the term *competence vs. performance* to refer to the distinction between possessing a capability (competence) and showing that capability (performance). For example, a young child may know the names of letters but, out of reluctance or puzzlement about directions, may not give the names in a testing situation. An older student may have a good understanding of the subject being tested, but may rank very low on a standardized test because of marking an answer sheet incorrectly. Teachers should not use a test score as the basis for deciding that a student is unteachable. (Indeed, teachers should not decide that students are unteachable—period.)

Mandated tests are almost always *standardized tests*—published tests, for which uniform test conditions have been set and norms established. They are thus *norm-referenced tests*, and this means that while the tests are being developed they are tried out by groups of people similar to those who will eventually take the published test. Test scores from people in these groups are used by the test developers to set the meaning of scores achieved on the published tests, in terms of percentile rank scores, stanine scores, and other standardized scores (described below). Teachers have an obligation to administer standardized tests following test guidelines. The test manual should be read carefully, well in advance of administering the test. It will tell exactly what directions the teacher should give and, when there are time limits, how much time is allotted for each test. One way to classify tests is on the basis of whether or not there are time limits…timed. *Timed tests* measure how many correct answers students can give in a predetermined amount of time, often based on a careful estimate of how much time students who have sound aptitude or achievement in the subject will need. Timed tests make it possible to compare people's scores because everyone is given the same amount of time to work on the test. *Power tests*, on the other hand, either are completely untimed or give very generous time allowances, thus students have as much time as they need to complete the test. Usually, power tests are given when the purpose of testing is to focus on students who are most in need of remedial help. Removing time limits makes it more likely that students who have very low scores really are unable to perform the tasks set by the test and are not simply those who work slowly.

Although in most cases teachers are familiar with the content of the standardized tests they give, under no circumstances should they give students information about test answers. To do so is grounds for dismissal from a teaching position. Giving students answers to test questions is extremely rare, but "teaching to the test" is, unfortunately, a fairly common misuse of instructional time. Spending class time giving students extensive practice in responding to the type of questions used on required tests (e.g., multiple choice questions) wastes time intended for useful learning. Repeated review of topics that appear on required tests causes other important content area topics to be ignored. One criticism of the widespread use of standardized tests (e.g., Fredericksen, 1984; Lohman, 1993) is that test content biases instruction. As David Lohman (1993, p. 15) puts it, "unmeasured outcomes often go untaught." It is useful to give students brief directions about how to take standardized tests sensibly: *Listen to the directions. Read each item carefully. If one item is difficult or puzzling, skip it and return to it later. If all items are completed and there is still time left, go back and read each item and check each answer.* This kind of test preparation can be quickly and calmly accomplished. Other than this, the best preparation teachers can give their students to enable them to do well on present and future tests is to help them develop a thorough understanding of what they are studying and an interest in learning more.

Types of Test Scores

A *raw score* is the number of test items answered correctly. Raw scores are not informative, unless we know how many items were on the test. (For example, a raw score of 7 is a perfect score on a test with 7 items and a very low score on a test with 30 items.) In a teacher-developed test, the raw score is often translated into a *percent score*, which is based on 100 as a perfect score. A score of 80, or 80%, is thus considered a fairly good score, whether 4 out of 5 items, or 40 out of 50, or 80 out of 100, were answered correctly.

The results of standardized, norm-referenced tests are often given in the form of percentile rank scores, normal curve equivalent scores, stanine scores, or grade equivalent scores. These scores enable a student's score to be compared to the scores of a norming group, typically a large group of students drawn from around the country at the same grade level, who took the test while it was being prepared for publication, and on whose scores the national norms for the test are based.

Percentile Rank Scores.   Percentile rank scores are represented by numbers ranging from 1 (low) to 99 (high). A student's percentile rank score indicates what proportion of students in the norming group this student surpassed. Thus, a percentile rank score of 65, using national norms, is an above-average score, indicating that the student scored better than 65% of students in a national sample. Percentile rank scores are based on the concept of a normal, or bell-shaped, curve. The *bell curve* is a mathematical illustration of the expected distribution of a large number of measures of the same factor. For example, suppose the entire adult population of a town was measured for height and the measurements were graphed by listing the various heights, from shortest to tallest, along a line, with each person's measurement indicated by a dot placed above the point on the line marking their height. There would be a few dots at the low end of the range and a few at the high end—these are the "tails" of the distribution—but most of the dots would be at or near the middle, and the result would be a symmetrical distribution, shaped like the outline of a bell.

A graph of classroom grades should *not* have the pattern of a bell curve. The practice of "grading on a curve" is, fortunately, becoming increasingly rare. Those who do grade in this way—with most students receiving a "C" grade or its equivalent, with equal numbers of "B" and "D" grades, and a few "A" grades matched by the same number of failing grades—misunderstand the bell curve concept. Jean Stenmark is among those who have stressed that a statistical concept that often applies in large populations is inapplicable in very small samples such as a classroom, where grading on a curve, she points out, "is both illogical and statistically invalid"

(Stenmark, 1991, p. 6). Moreover, if teachers fulfill their responsibility to teach effectively, at the end of a period of study (when grading occurs) students' ratings should cluster near the top of the distribution rather than in the middle. An additional reason why such a grading practice should not be used is that it makes each person's success or failure dependent upon the performance of others:

> Telling students you are grading on a curve suggests to them that it's enough to be better than someone else, that whoever is in the lower third is second rate, regardless of their efforts and yours, and that absolute standards of what constitutes acceptable or excellent work are not important. (Herman, Aschbacher, & Winters, 1992, p. 110, The National Center of Research on Evaluation, Standards and Student Testing (CRESST). *A Practical Guide to Alternative Assessment*. Alexandria, VA: ASCD. Copyright © 1992 by The Regents of the University of California and supported under the Office of Educational Research and Improvement (OERI), U. S. Department of Education.)

Normal Curve Equivalent (NCE) Score. Normal Curve Equivalent (NCE) scores have the same range as percentile rank scores, but the intervals between scores are equivalent, whereas the intervals between percentile rank scores are not.

Stanine Scores. Stanine scores are scores ranging from 1 (low) to 9 (high). (The term *stanine* is an abbreviation for *standard nine*.) Test scores in the top three stanines (7–9) show strong performance on the test, scores in the middle three stanines (4–6) are indicative of average performance, and scores in the lower three stanines (1–3) are often considered an indication that the student needs special help in the area tested.

Grade Equivalent Scores. Grade equivalent (G. E.) scores are complex, and often misunderstood. These scores appear as two numbers separated by a decimal, with the first number indicating a grade and the second number indicating a month (0=September; 9=June). Thus, a G. E. score of 4.7 is translated as fourth grade, seventh month. Clearly, a second grader with a 4.7 G. E. score did well on the test, and a seventh grader with the same score did not. Surprisingly, however, a G. E. score of 4.7 does *not* mean that the student with that score should be instructed using texts typically used in fourth grades during the month of April. It means that the student's score is approximately the same as the score that would be expected, statistically, from an average fourth grader, if that hypothetical fourth-grade student had taken the same test during April. Put simply, if typical fourth, fifth, and sixth graders took a test designed for second graders, they would be expected to have high scores. Turning this fact around, it is possible to say that second graders who have a range of high scores on a second grade test have scores like those that the fourth, fifth, or sixth graders would get. Saying that a student's test score is similar to the test score a student in another grade would be likely to get, however, is not the same as saying that the student who took the test ought to be considered as learning in the same ways, at the same pace, and using the same materials, as a student who is dissimilar in age and grade.

In 1981, the major professional organization in the field of reading, the International Reading Association, formally stated its opposition to the use of grade equivalent scores. Nevertheless, they continue to be used, thus it continues to be the teacher's responsibility to understand and explain what such scores mean. Parents whose children attain above-average grade equivalent scores (and whose percentile rank scores and stanine scores are therefore also high) have reason to be pleased with their child's progress and to expect that their child should be studying interesting and challenging material. Parents whose children's test scores are low have reason to be concerned, reason to expect that information from the test should be compared with other sources of data, and reason to expect that their child should be receiving attentive, sensible instruction in an interesting, effective, welcoming learning environment. Teachers need to not only be able to explain the meaning of grade equivalent scores, but, more importantly, demonstrate that their classroom program is a good one, suited to each of their students' strengths and needs.

STRATEGIC TEACHERS, PART SIX

"It's exciting to think about teaching."

When Andrew Criefton was in college (the first time) he was undecided about his career choice. A lot of possibilities looked promising. After graduating, he held several jobs before deciding that he wanted to teach. As he studied to obtain teaching credentials, he switched to a part-time job in the evenings so he could be available for substitute teaching, which he found he enjoyed very much. He preferred subbing in the grade range from fourth through tenth, and indicated this and his interest in science to school districts where he signed up to substitute. Soon after he began substituting, he was being called regularly, particularly for middle school classes. He is now certified to teach elementary school and grades 7-12 science; he also has a middle school endorsement.

One of the reasons he did not originally consider teaching as a career is that he disliked a lot of his own school experiences. He recognizes now that he was not easy to teach. Although he grasped ideas quickly, he was negligent about getting work done. He was apt to talk in class and make others laugh. He believes that one of the reasons he bothered teachers was that he didn't become a conscientious student even when they tried hard to help him. He tries now to find ways to reach and teach all of his students, including those who remind him of his younger self. At this point in his career he has had some successes and some failures, but, learning from his own experiences, he has committed himself not to become angry with students who don't respond to his teaching. Instead, he stays concerned for them and hopes that some future teacher will be more successful. Therefore, he is careful not to get into the habit of talking negatively about students. Sometimes, though, he *needs* to talk freely

about a student who's irritating him. He and an English teacher in the same school often plan together and talk about all aspects of their work, including the funny, annoying, or foolish things their students do. They can talk freely back and forth, without worrying that what they say will be told elsewhere. What's even better is that because several of their classes are paired, with the same group of students together for a section of English and a section of science, the two teachers have opportunities to integrate their teaching.

Now, in his fourth year of teaching seventh-grade science, and in the first year of a graduate program, he is enthusiastic about his career choice and believes that he could not have found any other profession that could have provided him with so many interesting ideas—and people—to think about. Although he recognizes that his tendency to get excited about new ideas needs to be balanced by sensible self-pacing, he intends never to lose his enthusiasm.

How Does He Do It?

In his teaching, he uses the assigned science textbooks as a curriculum guide and resource, but does not rely on them as a primary instructional source, and he limits the amount of textbook reading he assigns. While he was substituting, he discovered that some topics he thought he understood became fuzzy as he tried to teach them, so before he ever heard the term *concept statements* he began writing summaries of the information he needed to teach. This showed him that understanding something could mean being familiar enough with it to talk about it in conversation and to read more about it, but that a more thorough, better-organized understanding was needed in order to summarize the topic in a clear piece of writing. Even though it is hard to do, in fact, *because* it is hard to do, he has continued to prepare for teaching important topics by writing a summary of what he expects students to learn. By now he has a large file of these summaries, and he uses them extensively in his teaching. Because he prepares them on a computer he can add to them or revise them easily, and he can also easily turn them into teaching activities such as Focused Cloze, Detection and A-Qu-A. Often he provides them to students to be included in their science notebooks, and students use them to create Semantic Maps or as the basis for a RESPONSE.

He has continued to use many of the strategies he used as a substitute. In one of his education courses, he gave a presentation on practical strategies for substitute teachers; later, the professor asked him if he would give the presentation again as a guest lecture. Mr. Criefton was delighted and has since given the talk several times. He is now thinking of writing a proposal to present it at a professional conference. These are the strategies he suggests:

- *Teacher Read-Aloud Commentary.* A typical assignment for a substitute teacher is to "have the class read" a textbook selection. Mr. Criefton found it worked well to begin by reading the most important part of the textbook assignment aloud to the class and commenting on it. He kept the students' attention because he was talking to them as he read, and he established himself as a person who knew the subject he was teaching. (Of course, he would not have used TRAC if he was substituting in a class where he did not understand the textbook; fortunately this did not happen. When he was unfamiliar with something in the text, he asked the students or commented that this was something he would need to find out.) In his own teaching, he uses TRAC at least once a week.

- *Discrepant Events.* Introducing a topic with an experiment or other experience that catches students' attention and makes them want to know more is an effective way to begin a lesson. The plans left for him when he substituted in science classes often suggested that he conduct an experiment while students watched. Mr. Criefton tried to structure the observed exper-

iment so that students would perceive what happened as surprising, then he encouraged students to talk and write about what they had observed. In his own teaching, he introduces many topics through the Discrepant Events strategy, but most of these are experiments the students do themselves.

- *Confer and Write.* This is a strategy Mr. Criefton thinks is useful across all subjects. In many of the classes where he substituted, the students were unfamiliar with the strategy, but they caught on quickly and enjoyed giving him a writing assignment. He found that students remembered the strategy and would ask to use it again if he returned to substitute in their class. In his own teaching, the class uses Confer and Write once or twice a week, often as a follow-up to a Discrepant Events experiment.

- *Concept Connections.* When the assignment for the class where he was substituting was to study a list of vocabulary terms, Mr. Criefton taught the students the Concept Connections strategy and then walked around the classroom giving help and advice as students worked in pairs. Of course, he used this as an "open book" strategy. The students were able to look up the terms in textbooks or other resources as well as to consult with each other and ask him questions. In his own teaching, the whole class scans a textbook section and often the teacher-prepared concept statement, to identify and list important technical terms. Then the preparation of a specified number of Concept Connection paragraphs is a weekly assignment for cooperative groups.

- *U Debate.* When he first read about this strategy, Mr. Criefton loved it right away. As a substitute teacher, he could run an active discussion without knowing the names of students, because he could call for ideas from people with different points of view that they had signaled by the place in the "U" where they chose to sit. In his own teaching, he uses the strategy about twice a month. Sometimes a cooperative group has the assignment of choosing a topic for U Debate.

■ *Reading aloud.* He got into the habit of bringing along some tradebooks in a colorful canvas carryall whenever he substituted. He and the students would work on getting the assignments for the day completed with enough time to spare for a read-aloud at the end of the day. After a while, he found that students expected to see the carryall and were enthusiastically curious about what books Mr. Criefton would pull from it. In his own teaching, he reads aloud at impromptu times and also schedules a regular 15-20 minute read-aloud period once a week.

One of the many pleasures of teaching, for Mr. Criefton, is the opportunity to share ideas and collaborate with colleagues. Last year, he and his friend, an English teacher, were discussing whether book reports should be required. Mr. Criefton remembers hating them; the English teacher rather liked doing them, but her students generally do not. She was taking a graduate course in which she needed to select a commonly given assignment for students and find suggestions from least three different professional journals giving practical strategies to enliven the assignment. (The course instructor made a point of requiring that the articles come from professional journals, rather than from teacher magazines. She explained that the articles that appear in professional journals are published by professional organizations, universities, or publishers of scholarly materials and that these journals are *juried*—that is, each published article has been read and evaluated by several experts in the field before it is accepted.)

The English teacher chose the topic of book reports, and she and Mr. Criefton both got interested. They consulted with the school's media specialist, who suggested Shrinklits (from Teri Lesesne's 1991 article in the *ALAN Review*). Mr. Criefton suggested that *RAFT* (based on Kathy Dueck's 1986 article in the Kappa Delta Pi Record) could be adapted for a book report format, with a student taking the Role (R) of a character

in the book writing to an audience (A) of another character, or the role of a book reviewer writing to an audience of teenage readers. The English teacher found a suggestion that students write book reports in the form of *acrostics* (by Emily Long, writing in a 1993 issue of *The Reading Teacher*) and the ingenious idea of *book report floats*—having a parade of book reports prepared as small sculptures on an array of wheeled toys (a 1989 suggestion by Barbara Mumma, in *Reading Horizons*).

With their usual enthusiasm, the two teachers decided to work together to try all of the ideas with the students they teach in science and English. In English class, the teacher demonstrated RAFT and acrostics and the whole class prepared several; then her students wrote a book report using the format of their choice. Then Mr. Criefton began Themed Reading twice a week, using a collection of science trade books he chose for their interest, accuracy, and detail. Many books in his collection are not difficult to read; many are beautifully illustrated. Because it looked like fun, both teachers demonstrated the Shrinklit strategy, in which the plot of a book is summarized in rhymed couplets (as in Figure 8–9). For the next round of book reports, students could use a traditional format, or RAFT, or prepare an acrostic or a Shrinklit. The teachers kept a tally of students' choices; acrostics were most popular, and only two students used the traditional format.

For the third round of book reports, students continued reading science tradebooks and used the Book Report Float strategy. Each student brought in a small wheeled toy (such as a skateboard, little wagon, or even an old-style roller skate) and built a three-dimensional display on it, illustrating the book they had read. During science class, the students incorporated their study of electricity by building battery-powered motors for their floats. Each cooperative group was in charge of preparing a narrative script describing their floats, and eventually the parade of books was taken to visit other classrooms. For the rest of the year, students continued the once-a-month book report assignment, but they were allowed to choose one of these book report formats or suggest an idea of their own.

Mr. Criefton also is eagerly thinking and talking about a new enthusiasm he expects to pursue throughout his teaching career: the concept of "teacher as researcher," which he has learned about through several of his graduate courses, one of them a course on ethnographic research. He has begun collecting excerpts about the topic of teacher research in their own classrooms in preparation for writing a paper for one of his graduate classes:

Ethnographic research consists essentially of a description of events that occur within the life of a group... In ethnography the researcher participates in some part of the normal life of the group and uses [what is learned] from that participation to produce the research findings. ...In ethnographic studies no generalization can be treated as final, only as a working hypothesis for further studies... (Taft, 1988, pp. 59 and 62)

I believe that teachers are masters of the complexity of their tasks; they have a good, if intuitive, grasp of the changes that occur in pupils over time, and they understand a great deal about the interaction between teachers and pupils, which is, after all, the essence of teaching. (Clay, 1989, p. 30)

FIGURE 8–9   Two Examples of Shrinklits

Shrinklit for
Wanna bet? Science challenges to fool you
Vicki Cobb and Kathy Darling (1993)

Wanna bet you can use your ears to
get rid of a red nose?
Read all about it in the book I chose.
Wanna bet parallel lines can intersect?
(See page 116. I checked.)
Wanna bet you can make sugar glow in the dark?
It's caused by piezoelectricity;
87 is the page to mark.
Wanna bet a wire remembers its shape?
You can trust *me*.
Nitinol (from nickel and aluminum),
used in braces,
is described on pages 62 and 63.

Shrinklit for
Backyard birds of winter
Carol Lerner (1994)

Black-capped chickadees, this book tells readers
Usually don't migrate and are
"snatch-and-grab" feeders.
For a bright red cardinal and his brownish mate
A feeder with sunflower seeds is great.
Flickers feed on insects. Cowbirds eat grains.
Robins eat fruits and berries in the
East and the Central Plains.
Jays store food, like acorns and seeds.
Cracked corn meets a towhee's needs.
Grosbeaks' bills are strong enough to
crack a cherry pit.
The mourning dove has a craw
and can store food in it.
Thrushes and mockingbirds are
some birds that like suet.
When there's a birdfeeder with peanut butter,
wrens fly right to it.

Teacher researchers ...undertake research in order to get a better understanding of events in their particular educational environments. ...Putting findings into practice is essential to the teacher researcher. Simply stated, teacher researchers use research to do a better job.

...Teacher researchers tend to give a great deal of attention to why they think the way they do. They are more apt to know what others believe about a subject and to relate that knowledge to their own thinking. They are acutely aware of the questions that still need answers for them. (Strickland, 1988, pp. 756 and 763)

Mr. Criefton has never liked the idea of experiments in which one group of people is treated one way and another group is treated differently. He believes that his teaching, including his collaboration with another colleague, opens a wealth of possibilities for small research studies using the ethnographic method—that is, observing, collecting, and interpreting data about real teaching.

Challenge to the Reader: Suppose you were asked to participate in a U Debate on this topic: *A factor that contributes strongly to Mr. Criefton's success as a teacher is his lack of success as a student in grade school, middle school, and high school.* Where, in the U-shaped distribution of seats—strongly agree, agree, neutral, disagree, strongly disagree—would you choose to sit? If you were asked to give reasons for your position, what would you say?

Choose and Use: If you were to choose one aspect of Mr. Criefton's program to use in your own classroom, what would it be and how would you begin?

Case Study 3

Rae Serrech is a middle school English teacher. This is her third year of teaching. Her closest colleague, Andrew Criefton, is enthusiastic about the idea of teachers doing research in their own classrooms, and they have decided to try it out in collaboration. They have been talking about what to do and how to do it. First they decided they were interested in strategies, then they settled on two that they both have been using and like: Confer and Write and U Debate. The next things to do are harder. They have two possible subjects for research, but to what questions do they want answers? ("Is this a good strategy?" is too fuzzy a question to test.) What will they look at? Are they interested in changes in students' work over time? Do they want to vary the way they use a strategy and make comparisons? They are working on making and refining a list of possibilities:

- In Confer and Write, students talk together first about the writing topic before they write. *How, and how much, does conferring help students' writing? Does it interfere with originality? Does it let some students "coast"?*
- *How do students' Confer and Write papers change over time? Are there differences in the changes in English and Science papers?*
- Mr. Criefton encourages students to draw diagrams and graphs as part of their papers. *When students' papers include drawings, how does this affect the quality of the writing, if at all? Do any students incorporate drawings in their English papers, even though Ms. Serrech does not suggest it?*
- In Confer and Write, while students are writing on a topic set by the teacher, the teacher writes on a topic set by one or more students. *What topics do the students ask the teachers to write about? What are similarities/differences between the tasks set for Ms. Serrech and for Mr. Criefton? Are the differences attributable to subject matter differences, or teacher differences?*
- In U Debate, chairs are arranged in a U and students who have the strongest feelings (for or against a position) sit at the two ends of the U, while sitting toward the middle indicates a neutral point of view. *Are students consistent, across time, in taking strong or neutral positions? …consistent regardless of whether the debate is in English or in science?*
- *How do students' contributions to U Debate discussions change over time?*
- About half of the time it is part of one cooperative group's weekly assignment to set a discussion topic for the U Debate at the end of the week. *What topics do cooperative groups suggest? How do they differ from teacher-suggested topics, if they do? How are discussions of student-chosen topics different from discussion where the teacher sets the topic, if they are?*
- Although they have not tried this yet, they are wondering what would happen if the U Debate topic was announced ahead of time. *How would U Debate discussions differ, if the position to be debated was announced when study of the general topic was introduced?*

Decide:	Choose one of the research questions for the teachers to investigate, or add one of your own. Can a related question be studied simultaneously?
Make a plan:	What can the teachers do to get answers to their question(s)? Revise and refine the question(s), if necessary.
Evaluate:	What features of the plan make it doable and worthwhile?

CHAPTER NINE

Communication and Collaboration: Linking School and Home

Making a positive difference in the lives of our children, while they are in school, is the challenge at hand for all teachers… Commitment, collaboration… hard work, and the courage to change [make] a significant difference in children's lives at school.

(FLORES, COUSIN, & DIAZ, 1991, P. 377)

…and the third group [besides students and teachers] we found consistently underrated were parents. Quite frankly, the schools we went to looked at parents as a negative influence—they don't participate; they don't care about the kid's education—and yet, again, we saw some exceptional things being done by people with a fifth-grade education.

LEVIN, QUOTED IN BRANDT, 1992, P. 20.

 ## School-Home Relationships

Examining the various aspects of teaching provides opportunities to explore educational, psychological, and sociological theories that are the foundation for good practice. An important theory to consider regarding the relationship between school and home is the systems approach developed by Urie Bronfenbrenner and James Garbarino (Bronfenbrenner, 1976, 1979; Comer & Haynes, 1991; Garbarino, 1982, 1985) to illuminate the various features of the environment that affect people. These scholars point out that each individual is influenced by aspects of the world (systems) that affect the individual's life either directly or indirectly, either closely or from a distance. The systems themselves are linked, and action in one system affects other systems. Bronfenbrenner and Garbarino identify four levels of environmental influence on individuals: microsystems, mesosystems, exosystems, and macrosystems.

Microsystems are the set of influences nearest the individual. This includes people (family, friends, school personnel, neighbors, employers); places where the individual spends extensive time (for example, for students, home, school, recreational settings); things (objects that are necessary or important in a person's life); and events (ordinary and unusual life occurrences in a person's life). Beyond these direct influences are exosystems, influences that affect the individual and people within the microsystems, but which most individuals have very little effect upon. Examples of exosystems are workplaces of other family members and agencies that plan, make decisions, and set rules that affect the daily lives of individuals within a community. In this environmental model, macrosystems, shared beliefs and ways of behaving, common language and history, and views about what the world is like, influence all the other systems that affect an individual's life. Macrosystems are a set of cultural understandings about the nature of the world "as it is *and as it might be*" (Garbarino, 1985, p. 61). Lisa Delpit (1988, p. 297) expresses the effect of macrosystems on our thinking and perceptions of the world when she writes, "We do not really see through our eyes or hear through our ears, but through our beliefs."

Exosystem effects on the lives of children aged 0-17 are illustrated in a recent report by Donald Hernandez, who provided information about economic living conditions for children between 1830 and 1930 and from that time to the near present (1988). Earlier exosystem forces affecting children included a shift away from farm life, reduced family size, and extension of the years spent in school. More recent influences include the increased number of women in the workforce and a rise in single-parent homes. "A fundamental force driving these seemingly disparate changes," Hernandez writes, "has been and continues to be parents' desires to improve, maintain, or regain their relative social and economic status in the face of changing, often uncertain, or precarious social and economic conditions" (Hernandez, 1994, pp. 1–2). An analysis of the economic living conditions—categorized as luxury, middle-class comfort, near-poor frugality, and relative poverty—for children between 1939 (toward the end of the Great Depression) and 1988 shows that at the beginning of that time span, the

percentage of children whose economic status was at either extreme (luxury or poverty) began to decline, with a corresponding expansion of those living in comfortable or frugal conditions, but that this trend began to reverse in 1980 (Hernandez, 1994, p. 13). If this new trend continues, an increasing number of students in the schools will live in conditions of economic poverty. Another group that will increase will be the students whose economic situation is one of affluence.

Microsystems, exosystems, and macrosystems can be visualized as a set of concentric circles, surrounding an individual or a connected group of individuals. We can think of these concentric systems with an individual student at the center, a classroomful of students at the center, or ourselves at the center. In each case, the person or group is affected both closely and from a distance by people, events, conditions, and beliefs.

The Importance of Links Between School and Home

Another kind of system in this model is the *mesosystem*, a term derived from a Greek word, *mesos*, meaning *in the middle*, or *intermediate*. Mesosystems are connections that link different microsystems, for example, the connections between a person's family and others in the neighborhood, or the connections between students' homes and their school. Garbarino writes of the importance of strong mesosystems in students' lives:

> Mesosystems are relationships between microsystems. The links themselves form a system. We measure the richness of mesosystems by the number and quality of connections. …Is there only a single link between home and school—the [student's] participation in both? If there is only a single link, the mesosystem is weak and this may place the [student] at risk, particularly if there is little cultural agreement between home and school. …The central principle here is that the stronger and more diverse the links between settings, the more powerful the resulting mesosystem will be as an influence on development. (Garbarino, 1985, pp. 56–57)

There is much discussion, in the media and in personal conversations, about the importance of the home in students' school success. It is indisputable that home environment has a powerful influence on people. But it is unproductive for school personnel to attribute students' actions and attitudes solely to their environment outside the school. Moreover, it is actively harmful if students are stigmatized in school by what is known or assumed about their home life. Teachers and other school personnel have the responsibility for making students' school experiences productive and satisfying. They also can take a major role in developing and fostering linkages between school and home. The idea that strong, satisfying, and varied connections between school and home are advantageous to students is an important concept for teachers to keep in mind.

Communication and collaboration between school and home are the major themes of this chapter, which is premised on the belief that students' learning in school is likely to be enhanced when there are multiple linkages between school and home, and that teachers should accept major responsibility for ensuring that these connections are positive. As in other chapters, a variety of strategies will be presented, along with explanations of theory and principles that stress the importance for students of school-home relationships. Readers may notice that the words *child* and *children* occur more frequently in this chapter than in others where the

word *student* is used, because the information presented applies to students across grade levels. The reason for the change in terminology is that this chapter focuses on families. A teacher's students—from prekindergarten through high school—remain the children of their parents.

Respecting Students' Families

One of the important elements of a sound educational program is the maintenance of positive relationships between students' homes and their school. An earlier chapter in this text was introduced with a brief quotation that began, "Students differ. So what?" The response to that question is that we have an obligation to teach students, all of whom differ from one another, by meeting their strengths and needs in inclusive ways. Families also differ. And again the question can be posed: Our students' families differ. So what?

This is a different question from the earlier one and should receive a different answer. Because our students are, during a part of their lives, ours to teach, care for, learn from, and prepare for the future, we have a straightforward obligation to them. Because we are teachers, we will affect their lives directly. If we are successful in our teaching, we will change them in helpful ways. We do not have this kind of relationship with our students' families. We are not required to alter them or judge them.

> As educators, we talk about 'the changing family,' but the language we use has changed little. The institutional view of nonparticipating parents remains based on a deficit model. 'Those who need to come, don't come,' a teacher explains, revealing an assumption that one of the main reasons for involving parents is to remediate them. It is assumed that involved parents bring a body of knowledge about the purposes of schooling to match institutional knowledge. Unless they bring such knowledge to the school, they themselves are thought to need education in becoming legitimate participants. (Finders & Lewis, 1994, pp. 50–51)

When family members do not come to conferences and school events, school personnel usually cannot know for certain their reason or combination of reasons for not being there and should avoid

The attitude of respect for families has its basis in respect and care for students and in a more general respect for all people.

assuming motives that reflect negatively on the family. Time constraints and child care responsibilities may make it difficult for adults to come to school, even when conferences are scheduled in the evening. Entering a situation where others are more socially comfortable, language-proficient, and affluent can create feelings of anxiety. For many parents, their own personal school experiences are obstacles to involvement. It requires a good deal of courage to enter a place that is full of unhappy memories.

Margaret Finders and Cynthia Lewis (1994), writing on the question of "Why some parents don't come to school," describe a father's reluctance to go to school to discuss his son. The father says he has heard the same thing each year. "They just tell me my kid is bad." This is what the father's teachers said about him, years before. Many aspects of situations such as this are tragic: the father's experiences as a child and as a young man before he dropped out of school; the son's similar difficulties; and the teachers' (past and present) lack of success in reaching and teaching hard-to-teach students. It also is disheartening to realize that the parent who does not attend a conference, anticipating painful news, might miss a conference that would be helpful and provide positive insights.

Teachers usually are in a position to know a good deal about students' families, often more than we expect to know about close neighbors, and often far more than we would want our neighbors to know about us. It is temptingly easy to "sort" students, that is, to classify them as likely or unlikely to have attributes that will lead to school success according to what is known about their home situations. This does nothing to help students. Writing in a publication of the National Middle School Association, J. Howard Johnston (1990, p. 7) discusses the wide variety of family structures from which students come and asserts that attributing all of a student's behavior to the family structure in which the student lives "does a great disservice to that child and undermines the school's authority to educate... [All students] come to the school from the only family [they have]. Judging it as the 'right' or 'wrong' family structure does little to advance the child's success or that of the school."

A practice once taken for granted in educational research was that the SES, or socioeconomic status,

of children and young people who were studied would always be specified when the results of the research were reported. Many scholars and educators no longer regard this practice as necessary or useful. Despite vast differences in economic situations among families, there are many similarities across economic divisions and many differences within groups that are economically similar. Shirley Brice Heath urges us to recognize the falseness of the idea that "all those of the middle class socialize children in one way while the socialization practices of other classes may be lumped into one 'other' set of practices" (Heath, 1993, p. 176). Barbara Flores and her colleagues vigorously dispute the idea that students are at risk because they come from nonmainstream backgrounds, noting that there is "extensive research that documents the intense interest that parents of minority students have in the education of their children" (Flores, Cousin, & Diaz, 1991, p. 373). Reginald Clark (1983, p. 210), summarizing results of his extensive study of economically disadvantaged African American families, notes his agreement with other scholars who "have correctly maintained that there is no such thing as a best way to raise children" and asserts that "a universal formula for academic grooming, equally effective for all developing persons, does not exist. Children are different, families are different, and societies are different. The parents in each family will use their authority to create family life-styles and to encourage the child's intellectual development as well as they can."

> [Families] provided, or tried to provide, the necessary material comforts to support the home learning environment. Low socioeconomic conditions limited the parents' material resources, but did not detract from parental discipline, scheduling time for schoolwork and bedtime, and organizing their lives around a familiar routine. ...The error of relying on overly simplistic explanations about the learning environment.... such as the cultural deficit explanation, is that they deflect attention away from the schools' responsibility to develop effective programs for students from unrepresented groups. (Delgado-Gaitan, 1992, p. 512–513)

Just as teachers are not required to change students' families or judge them, we also are not obligated to find out as much as possible about the families of our students. The attitude of respect for families has in its basis respect and care for students, and, more generally, respect for all people. Just as teachers do well in the classroom to move away from thinking of students in terms of deficits (what is wrong with this student?) and differences (how is this student different from society's mainstream?), we do well to avoid this kind of thinking about students' families. Respecting diversity, then looking for similarities that unite us, helps establish a foundation of regard and discretion that supports useful communication and collaboration linking school with students' homes.

Communication: Sharing Information in Helpful Ways

In all schools, some **communication** between school and home is mandated. This communication is both written and oral and serves multiple purposes. In many schools there are two situations in which teachers are required to meet with parents or guardians of their students: one or more individual conferences and one group meeting. Teachers' major responsibility, in terms of formal communication with the home, is to prepare regular reports about students' work in school—report cards. Although the format for this kind of communication varies widely, the information is always provided in written form. The document that is prepared is thus a permanent one, a record of a teacher's judgment about a student's work, of which both parties, the teacher who gives information and the family members who receive it, have copies. Putting the information in writing (so it can be mailed) makes it likely that the report will reach the adult or adults who are responsible for every student, whether or not they are in personal contact with the school. The

primary reason for putting these reports in written form, however, is to create a permanent record of students' progress.

Permanent School Records

Schools have the responsibility to keep records of the students who attend. These records are typically filed in the school office, often in a cumulative folder, a file folder holding whatever forms are required by the state and school district, with essential information about the student, for example, date of birth, family address, necessary health information, and attendance records. Copies of the student's report cards during the time the student has attended the school also are kept in the folder. Among many reasons why it is important for teachers to thoughtfully and accurately prepare such reports and other records for the permanent file is that others—administrators and the student's future teachers—will read them. If there are harsh or trivial comments, or comments that contain misspellings and errors in grammar, future readers' opinions of the teacher who has written them will be lowered.

Guidelines about permanent records vary from one situation to another, and teachers have the responsibility to be aware of the rules in their school setting. Teachers have access to the cumulative folders of their students, although in most schools the folders may not be removed from the place where they are stored without administrative permission. Typically, only administrators may remove items from the cumulative folders. Placing items other than those which are required or expected into a student's folder should be done only after consultation with an administrator. However, with an administrator's agreement, it is useful to keep records of school-home contact, especially in situations where there are ongoing concerns or difficulties.

It is virtually always the case that teachers can look through the cumulative records of their students, and often, particularly in the elementary school, administrators expect that teachers will prepare for each new school year by reading these records for the students assigned to their class. To do so is time-consuming—it may take several hours to scan the cumulative folders of 30 students—and

---

communication—has a Latin derivation. It comes from the Latin verb *communicare*, meaning *to make common to many people, to share*, and *to impart*. The word *communicare* is derived from another Latin word, *communis*, meaning common. The English word *community* comes from the same root.

not all teachers take advantage of this opportunity. Sometimes teachers assert that it is right not to look at students' records, on the grounds that by *not* looking at them they avoid being prejudiced by negative comments made by previous teachers. This is a weak argument. Every person who teaches should be strong enough not to be swayed toward disliking, disapproving, or underrating students by the comments of someone else. The cumulative records give an impression of a student's previous school experiences that may be helpful in getting the year off to a good start. In addition to report cards, included in the records will be attendance reports and, if a student has a health condition about which teachers need to be aware, the cumulative folder may provide the teacher's first information about it. If there is an indication that a student's progress has been hampered by frequent moves and many absences, or if a previous teacher recorded only negative information, the new teacher can begin the year with the resolve to find ways to reach and teach a student who has not yet found school to be a helpful, welcoming place.

Report Cards

The basic method of school-home communication is through report cards. The timing and format of these reports are set by the school district. They must be completed at specified times, and whatever the method of summative evaluation is, letter grades, percents, symbols (e.g., O=Outstanding, or + = good), or checkmarks on a checklist, that method has been established in advance. Formal summaries of students' achievement, through report cards, give parents information and form a record of students' progress for the school to keep. Ideally, the information can encourage students to strive to improve. For students whose grades indicate areas of excellence, this confirmation of their strengths can encourage them toward advanced study and help them choose and prepare for a career.

It is difficult to summarize a student's achievement and progress by using a single mark. It also is difficult to move from the task of teaching and caring for students to the task of informing others about the student. Nel Noddings (1984, p. 194)

states this distinction clearly: "The teacher does not grade to inform the student. She has far better, more personal ways to do this. She grades to inform others about the student's progress. Others establish standards, explicitly or implicitly, and they charge her to report faithfully in observance of these standards." In a recent study, Peter Afflerbach and Peter Johnston (1993) studied the reporting process in action, and their findings are thought-provoking. They observed teachers, all of whom volunteered to participate in the study, as they prepared report cards. The teachers were asked to talk about their thoughts as they did so. By expressing their thoughts to a researcher who recorded them, the teachers followed a process similar to the Think-Aloud strategy described in Chapter Six. The teachers' comments frequently related to concerns that the reports might harm their students. In some cases, they regretted giving a low grade in relation to established standards, even though the student was trying hard and beginning to find success. They commented that some students would find their grades discouraging, and in some cases they believed families would respond to a report card by punishing the child.

It is difficult to promote a good balance—in our own thinking and teaching and in the attitudes of students and families—between summative evaluation and the ongoing school program, yet establishing such a balance is an important aspect of good teaching. Teachers have many opportunities to say and show that, while grades are a part of school, working, learning, and developing a lasting interest in learning are more important. We also need to examine our teaching to see whether our actions create a harmful imbalance between summative evaluation and learning. For teachers to obtain attention or to keep order by reminding students that they risk getting a low grade, for example, makes grades a threat, and, what is worse, guides students to think that learning only occurs in response to threats.

Almost all report cards have a section for teachers' comments. Writing comments that are brief, helpful, and specific to the student is a skill teachers should work to develop. Cliché comments that can be written without thought or preparation (e.g.,

"Good work!" or "Must pay better attention") are not useful. Even praise such as "A joy to teach!" provides little information when this is the only comment given. Instead, comments should make it clear that the teacher knows and cares for the student:

- Adrienne is beginning to turn in homework regularly (five out of six assignments in the last two weeks). Her classwork has improved as a result. Encourage her to keep it up.
- Alan's report on astronomers was very well done. He is a responsible contributor to cooperative group work.
- Ardis is reading widely and has shared her interest in folktales. She is working with classmates on a bulletin board based on *The People Could Fly.*

As computer use becomes more sophisticated, teachers will be able to prepare comments for students at personal computers, which will require less effort and time than handwriting comments and will convey more information than choosing several items from a number of stock comments. Writing thoughtful, individualized comments is easier when teachers have one class (as elementary teachers typically do) rather than many classes (as middle and high school teachers typically do). One method of writing report card comments at the upper grade levels is for teachers who work with the same students to divide the responsibility, so if four teachers are teaming together, each teacher writes comments for one-fourth of the group. When this method is used, teachers either work in a group, discussing students during the comment-writing process, or supply each other with information. An example of a comment prepared by this method might be the following:

> Stu is an enthusiastic problem solver in math; his journal entries are detailed and insightful; quiz scores are consistently high. For English, two commentaries on short stories have not been submitted; in general, his writing is improving and he is more willing to share ideas. His group's science/social studies presentation on vaccination was very well done and the charts he contributed were excellent.

Such comments supplement the section of the report card that gives grades, and of course the comments and grades should not give conflicting information. From these comments, we can draw several inferences. We can infer that the student has a high grade in math and that there are no problems in science or social studies. If there are problems, these should be mentioned in the comments. We can conclude that the student's English grade, although perhaps higher than last time, is not yet on a par with other grades.

Although assessment and reporting should not control teaching, it is sensible for teachers to build the school's reporting system into their planning, so progress checks will precede the required progress reports to the home and samples of students' work will be available to illustrate strengths and needs when conferences are held. Documenting students' work through methods described in Chapter Eight (e.g., checklists, contracts, and work sampling) is a useful preparation for writing report cards, providing evidence of the best work that individual students produced up until this point. Samples of students' work and observations of students also provide the basis for supplementing grades with comments about students' strengths and interests.

Group Meetings

In addition to providing report cards, school districts often require teachers to engage in two other forms of school-home communication: individual conferences and group meetings. Individual conferences are typically held once or twice a year, when report cards are written and information about standardized tests is available. Group meetings usually occur once, toward the beginning of the school year, when parents or guardians are invited to school to meet teachers and hear a brief overview of the instructional program planned for the year. Sequentially, then, a group meeting is often the first mandated link between school and home. Later, report cards are prepared to be sent home, and one or several reporting periods may coincide with scheduled individual conferences. Many schools schedule a Meet the Teacher Night or Back to School Night during early fall. These meetings are designed to acquaint parents with the school and with school personnel. There may be tours of the school building and short talks by the principal and chairperson of the school's organization that links families and schools, such as a Family School Organization (Myers & Monson, 1992). Teacher-led meetings in individual classrooms are typically the major feature of the evening.

While writing report cards is a difficult task, meeting with and speaking to a group of adults from students' families presents another kind of challenge. Many teachers who have no qualms whatever about talking to a classroom full of students experience anxiety annually as they anticipate these meetings—that is, they suffer from a mild form of communication apprehension. This problem, which Hilary Taylor Holbrook (1987) defines as "a pattern of anxiety…. which can profoundly affect…. oral communication, social skills, and self-esteem," is described in Chapter Ten, as it affects students. An effective way for teachers to cope with anxiety about group meetings with parents is to plan a brief presentation and have displays of students' work in the room. These displays will capture parents' attention and illustrate important aspects of the year's curriculum. Describing the displays gives the teacher an opportunity to move from place to place and creates a situation where listeners' attention is focused on different points around the room. Both these strategies—avoiding the situation of standing motionless before a group and arranging to have listeners look at different points of interest—are likely to reduce anxiety about speaking to a group, and the displays are, of course, important in themselves. As Elfrieda Hiebert and Robert Calfee write (1989, p. 54), "…back-to-school nights, where samples of classroom activities can be directly examined, give parents concrete evidence of their children's progress…". The power of displays to interest family members is one indication of their care for their children.

Many professional organizations, such as the International Reading Association (IRA), the National Association for the Education of Young Children (NAEYC), and the National Middle School Association (NMSA) offer booklets and brochures focused on school-home relationships. John Myers and Luetta Monson (1992) include a chapter on communication with the home in a NMSA publication.

Their suggestions are primarily for school-wide use, although some can be implemented by individual teachers. They advocate planning ahead for the fall back-to-school night by issuing the first invitation to it during the previous year. By setting this date well in advance, it is easy to alert news media, and an invitation can be given, in person and through a flyer, when new families register children for school.

> It is what parents do rather than their status that accounts for the learning development of their children. (Benjamin S. Bloom, 1981, p. 92)

> The child must experience the school as an extension, not a rejection, of home and community. (Thomas Sobol, 1990, p. 28)

> Parents have a strong emotional investment in their children. Work *with* it, not *against* it. (Elizabeth Morgan, 1989, p. 56)

Conferences

Conferences strengthen the connections between school and home by providing an opportunity for one or more family members to visit the school, talk with the teacher, see what the classroom is like, and learn about their child's progress in school. In order to establish school-home contact through conferences, the conference schedule must be established with family members' needs and constraints in mind. Two factors to be considered are families' work schedules and child care needs. Adults need a conference time that does not conflict with their job, and some will need to bring their children with them when they come to the conference. In many schools, a time for individual conferences is scheduled shortly after the Back to School Night. This arrangement is sensible for several reasons. First, the group meeting provides general information, freeing time in conferences for sharing information that is unique to particular students. Second, questions raised by family members at the group meeting about their own child's progress can be deferred till the upcoming conference.

Guidelines for Conferences.   The rich array of articles about conferencing in professional journals yields advice that centers on the interrelated themes of establishing a comfortable environment for the conference, showing care for students, as well as knowledge of the curriculum, conveying information clearly, and conducting the conference wisely. These guidelines are discussed below.

- *Be welcoming.* The school is, as Gail Bjorklund and Christine Burger (1987) note, "teacher territory." Therefore, it is the teacher's responsibility, as host, to help family members feel comfortable and wanted there. Planning the physical arrangements of the conference area in the room and the waiting area, which should be outside of the room to ensure privacy for the conference, increases visitors' comfort and promotes a positive atmosphere. It often happens that a conference will run slightly overtime and that some family members will arrive early, so it is sensible to think of ways to make waiting time comfortable and interesting. Minimally there should be adult-sized chairs and some informational reading material about the school or classroom program placed in the hall outside of the classroom. A wall display of some informal photographs of the class will be of interest, as will a thoughtfully prepared display of students' work. One ingenious method of making waiting time profitable, which, however, requires time and effort to implement, is to conduct a classroom project, some time before the conferences, culminating in student presentations that are videotaped. The videotape can then be kept running outside of the classroom during conference time. (When this technique is used, extra seating in the waiting area may be needed. Family members sometimes return to the waiting area after the conference so they will not miss seeing their child or to watch him or her a second time.)

An important part of ensuring that parents are welcomed and that the conference is effective is the inclusion of an interpreter if family members are not English-speaking and if the teacher is not fluent in the family's language. It is essential, however, as Kelt Cooper and María Gonzalez (1993) note, for the teacher not to turn the conference over to the interpreter, but to conduct the conference, remaining attentive while the interpreter speaks. It also is useful for the teacher to learn and use conversational phrases in the family's language, to express greetings, thank-yous, and farewells.

- *Be knowledgeable and caring.* Family members need to be confident that their child's teacher knows the curriculum all students are to learn and cares about their child as an individual. The organization of the room, the learning materials and projects that are displayed, and the samples of the individual student's work that will be shown during the conference are all potential indicators of teacher knowledge and competence.

Teacher care for each individual student also needs to be clearly shown. J. Howard Johnston (1990) advises teachers to identify at least one significant characteristic about the student that they particularly enjoy and to share information about this feature. In cases—and these should be very rare—when a classroom teacher has not yet been able to relate positively to a student, the teacher should seek out colleagues (well before conferences are held) who *do* enjoy the student and recognize the student's strengths. These may be teachers who have worked with the student in the previous year, or teachers in special areas such as physical education, art, music, or the media center. Not only can these colleagues give advice about ways to reach and teach the student, they also may be able to sit in on the conference where the teacher can ask them to contribute positive information. Remembering to think in terms of strengths and needs, and focusing first on strengths, sets the tone for a productive conference.

> The practice of describing children in terms of their strengths in lieu of deficits has made me a better teacher, especially during conference time. As teachers, we tend to forget how anxiety-provoking a place school can be for some of our parents. By letting them know immediately that I have a positive view of their child, despite their past school experiences, the conference and the year get off to a good start. Once parents have heard me list their child's strengths, they see that I view their child the way they do. Then trust is established. (Fournier, 1993, p. 180)

- *Be clear.* The ability to give important information without ambiguity is an important skill for teachers to develop. Both good and bad news should be delivered with clarity, but because describing problems is not pleasant there is more likelihood that miscommunication will occur when discussing problems. Johnston (1990, p. 32) makes the point that although kindness and tact are important, the conference will not be successful if the teacher wants so much not to cause distress that necessary information is not conveyed. He writes, "It is not a kindness to hedge or be wishy-washy when the outline of the problem is very clear to you. If you are not direct about your message, parents may look back later and insist that you never told them what was happening." Another aspect of communicating clearly is avoiding overstatement, especially about problems. Most statements beginning *Your child is...* or *Your child can't...* are better expressed by describing what has happened, rather than by giving a label or final judgment. "Hassim has not been turning in homework. I send work three nights a week to do at home, but Hassim does not bring it back" starts a dialogue that can lead to a solution; "Hassim is lazy" does not. "Isabel is a problem in class" tells nothing except that the teacher is dissatisfied with Isabel. To say that "Candace can't do the work" or "Candace can't get on with classmates" establishes a hopeless situation. On the other hand, describing a problem, explaining how it is being addressed, and asking for other suggestions set the stage for improvement.

It is important to keep in mind that messages cannot be clear if they include unfamiliar terms. One recommendation that recurs consistently when educators give advice about teacher conferences is that teachers should avoid jargon (Fredericks & Rasinski, 1990; Margolis & Brannigan, 1986; Reis, 1988). Every profession has its own technical terminology and the educational field is rich with acronyms and names of people, programs, and theories with which parents have no reason to be familiar. When it is necessary to use technical terminology in a conference, teachers should explain it. "Scott scored in the sixth stanine on the CAT reading test" may be well understood by family members who are familiar with the school and its testing practices, but may be a baffling statement to others, who need to have the information clearly expressed: "Our school gives achievement tests in reading and math in the fall. We use the California Achievement Tests and they're called 'the CAT.' On the reading test, Scott's score was in the sixth stanine. That's within the average range, but at the higher end of that range. What the test shows corresponds with what I see in class. Scott can read the textbook with understanding, and he enjoys magazines about science."

■ *Listen.* In reflecting on good ways to conduct parent conferences, Tedd Levy describes a lesson he learned from a middle school student: "Some time ago, I complimented a developmentally handicapped student who seemed to have a particularly caring and effective way of helping his fellow students. 'You're a fine teacher, Tom,' I told him. 'I know,' he said without hesitation. 'I don't tell 'em. I ask questions'" (Levy, 1992, p. 49). Levy relates this to helping parents by not doing all the telling, but by standing back and letting others talk. "It is important that the problem statement not be the solution," advise Howard Margolis and Gary Brannigan (1987). Their point is that teachers should not give their preconceived solutions to problems without first listening to ideas family members have to contribute.

A conference is a time for sharing information and ideas, and both parties benefit from listening with care to the other person's point of view. Professional organizations publish useful brochures for parents that can be purchased inexpensively in bulk and distributed to them. Many of these also are available in Spanish versions. A pamphlet written by Nancy Roser and published by the International Reading Association, "Helping your child become a reader," includes a section that gives advice to parents about what to tell, and what to ask, in a conference. Although Roser's suggestions are focused on reading and on the early years of school, they are applicable to school conferences generally. (Although written for parents, they can be used by teachers as a reminder of useful information to give.)

Tell the teacher what you think is most important to know about your child. Then ask some specific questions and really listen to the answers. Ask how the teacher thinks you can best encourage your child's [learning] and what the teacher sees as your child's greatest strengths. You may want to know what the teacher's hopes and expectations are for your child and how the teacher is working to achieve those goals.

You may also want to know what is expected in your child's responses to homework assignments, how frequently homework is assigned, and how the… program is organized. Your conversation should focus in a positive manner on attributes, strengths, and actions—of children, parents, and teachers. (Roser, 1989, p. 16)

■ *Be aware of what can—and cannot—be accomplished.* When thinking of individual students' strengths and needs in planning for conferences, it is important to focus on strengths and also on practical needs in areas where changes can be made. Finding a way to work toward improvement in one aspect of a student's schooling is a productive, useful conference result, but radical changes in the student's ways of thinking and acting cannot be achieved through the conference. What surely cannot be accomplished, and ought not to be attempted, is to change the student's family. As Howard Margolis and Gary Brannigan (1986) caution, "Accept parents as they are and do not try to induce fundamental changes."

■ *Give one doable suggestion.* The essential purpose of conferences is to foster students' success in school. Teachers, who know the school program and their students, can help by suggesting one practical idea that can be used at home to contribute to a student's progress. Giving suggestions, such as those listed below, during a conference is, of course, much less time-consuming than writing them on a report card.

Adrienne's responsibility about completing homework is something to be proud of, and I'm glad to hear that you've established a time and place for her to work. As you know, I give homework three nights a week. We're starting to study rocks and minerals, and on homework nights she'll bring home a page of information reviewing what we've studied. Her task will be to study the page and list several important facts. Ask her to tell you some things she's learned before she begins to write. It will help her think through her ideas before she writes.

After the report on astronomers, Alan's zeroing in on William Herschel. He's listing information on file cards and working on ways to organize it. It will be helpful if you encourage him to arrange the cards in the mapping strategy I showed you—he knows how to do this—and then explain the arrangement to you. He'll keep on adding cards for about a week, and it's a good idea for him to try arranging the facts in different ways before he begins to write the report.

I want to encourage Ardis to extend her reading of factual material. Because she was so interested in *The People Could Fly*, I suggested she borrow another book by Virginia Hamilton from the school library, *Many Thousand Gone*, which is a series of short historical accounts about events related to slavery in this country. Several classmates are reading from the same book, and they plan to make a time and place map, like the one you saw in the hall about inventions, to show when and where events occurred. Ask her to talk with you about the project.

What characterizes doable suggestions that come from school to home? A doable suggestion is clear and purposeful, not a nebulous direction about how to fix a difficult problem. It asks adults to do something that will both support students' learning and interest family members. Usually a doable suggestion is repeatable; it is most helpful for family members to learn about a simple strategy that can be used often. Finally, a doable suggestion is practical. When the teacher has explained the suggestion, no further resources are necessary—no expense, no reference books, no trips to the library, not even an extensive outlay of time. Subject matter expertise is irrelevant. In the first example, it might be the case that one of Adrienne's parents is a geologist, or it might be that neither of her parents finished high school. In either case, the suggestion can be followed.

Student-led Conferences.   An innovative format for school-home conferences has been devised by Nancy Little and John Allan (1989). These are conferences in which students themselves, rather than not being present, as is customary in parent-teacher conferences, conduct the conference, explaining to their parents their goals and progress and showing samples of their work. In explaining how student-led conferences work, these educators make a point which upon the first reading seems startling: "With this method of conferencing, between four to six families can be seen comfortably during one half-hour time slot" (Little & Allan, 1989, p. 213). Such efficiency is possible not by having each conference last a few minutes, but by holding as many as six conferences simultaneously, in separate centers that have been set up in the classroom to accommodate small family groups. Simultaneity of conferences has the added advantage of ensuring that the conferences will truly be led by students, since the teacher cannot be everywhere at once.

> [T]he teacher joins each family group and gives encouragement and support to the child who leads the conference. The students proceed through the plan for the interview showing, explaining, and demonstrating what they have learned.... The teacher's role changes from the moment the parents arrive... to a facilitator for the student, ...wandering about the class and joining each family unit for approximately 5 to 10 minutes. ...If necessary, the teacher redirects questions for students to answer. Being aware of the overcritical parent, the teacher intervenes, if necessary, to change the direction of the interview and to strengthen the child's position. The role of the teacher is to enrich the emerging leadership skills of the child.... (Little & Allan, 1989, pp. 213–214)

Preparation for student-led conferences begins with administrative and teacher acceptance of the idea, followed by careful planning. Minilessons for teachers, conducted by teachers or counselors who are familiar with the concept, are recommended by Jane Guyton and Lynda Fielstein (1989). Preparation by teachers and students is woven into the classroom program of teaching, learning, and assessment, through student goal-setting, portfolio planning, and collection of documents. Through role playing prior to the conference, students can simulate conducting their conferences. This form of school-home communication can accomplish many useful purposes: easing the conferencing burden for teachers and adding to their pride in students' accomplish-

ments, increasing the percentage of families who attend conferences, and fostering students' sense of responsibility and self-worth.

Responding to, and Sending, Messages

Unlike communication through report cards, group meetings and conferences, for which dates are set in advance, another obligation in the area of school-home communication occurs at unscheduled times. This is the obligation to respond to notes and phone calls from students' homes, or to contact an adult family member about a school-related concern. Some teachers prefer to telephone, others to send notes. What is essential is that written communications not only be clear but technically accurate (i.e., using correct standards of written and spoken language) and that communication be straightforward and calm. Besides the obligation to respond to parent calls or letters, it is important to anticipate concerns by a call to the home if an incident in school is serious or surprising enough that family members need to be aware of it. In addition to their function as planning documents, teachers' planbooks can serve as a record, for teacher use, home-school, and school-home contact. For example, if a parent calls the school and asks that a teacher return the phone call, this can be noted on the date in the planbook and a checkmark can show that the call was returned, thus documenting the call and response. Notes from home can be clipped to planbook pages, with a checkmark to indicate if a reply to the message was sent.

Many schools supply students' families with a bulletin or handbook that provides necessary information about the school, its programs and policies. All teachers should have a copy of the parent handbook, if one exists, and be familiar with its contents. Such a handbook is likely to have information about communication between school and home that will be useful to teachers. The handbooks may state school policies about unscheduled home-school communication, for example, they may inform parents that telephone messages for teachers should come to the school rather than to teachers' homes.

Complicating Factors in School-Home Communication

School-home communication is not always simple. There may be language barriers because family members and the teacher do not share a common language. In this case, the teacher and the parents or guardians will need to rely on an interpreter when they talk together. The interpreter may be a community volunteer or someone who is employed by the school, a family member, or perhaps an older sibling of the student who can communicate well in English. Written communications should be translated and both the translation and the original message sent home. Language also is a barrier if adult family members have limited ability to read. One way teachers can ameliorate this problem is to avoid using complicated phrases in written communication when simpler ones are available. Susan Davis and Sheila Diaz (1994, p. 322) provide a list of terms that may be difficult for families to understand, with suggested replacements:

Child care provided	Do you need a baby sitter?
Transportation requested	Do you need a ride?
2:00 dismissal	Students go home at 2:00
Spring recess	No school
Assessment week	Testing this week
Registration	Sign up for…
Vision screening	Eye testing
Remediation needed in…	Needs extra help in…

More challenging problems in school-home communication arise when family members are angry or belligerent. "[N]o one will ever learn to be entirely comfortable meeting with angry parents," Robert Ciscell advises (1990, p. 47). "Some conflict is an inevitable fact of a teacher's professional life. While it is unreasonable to expect miracles, it is within our control to establish a constructive dialogue designed to build trust and cooperation even with parents whose initial approach reflects anger." Suggestions for managing such conferences (Ciscell, 1990; Kurtz, 1988; Oppenheim, 1985) emphasize that teachers should seek to support the family members who have requested the conference. Thus, teachers should listen with care to family members'

concerns and try to understand their point of view. It also is important for teachers to arrange the conference situation so they themselves have support. The meeting should be scheduled at a time and place where other school personnel are nearby, and an administrator should be apprised of the conference and be invited to attend. One method of handling a difficult conference is to establish an ending time in advance, with an opportunity to schedule another meeting later. It is important for the teacher to record the major points of such conferences as soon as possible afterwards. This information can be used to set an agenda for a future meeting and serves as the basis for informing the school administrator about unresolved difficulties.

It sometimes happens that reactions from the student's home to problems at school exacerbate problems rather than help solve them. Ben Piltch (1991, p. 58) suggests in-house (i.e., in school) assistance for students in the rare cases when parents tell the school not to involve them and in situations where the family's reaction to negative reports from the school is to punish the student harshly. In-house attention to the problem may take the form of a teacher-administrator team setting up and using a plan for improvement with the student. "Time and energy formerly spent in defensive and fruitless discussion with uncooperative parents have been freed to work on positive and constructive activities for students," Piltch writes. This kind of intelligent help is likely to produce successes, and eventually good news can be shared with the family.

Communication to Help Students Away From the Classroom

Some families move frequently. The result is that children in these families may attend several schools during a single year. Often there are periods of time when these students are not enrolled in any school, having been withdrawn from one and not yet enrolled in another. Teachers who take their role as educators seriously will think carefully about ways to welcome these students, make their time together productive and pleasant, and send students on their way as well-equipped as possible for their next learning situation.

For a variety of reasons, some students frequently are absent. This is a concern that should be shared with the building administrator. Frequent absences occur for many reasons, and it is important for an administrator, sometimes working with an attendance officer, to find out why a student is missing school and to provide help as needed. The teacher's role should be to help students who are frequently absent to feel welcome when they are in the classroom and to make it as easy as possible for them to keep learning. Figure 9–1 illustrates an assignment form for the student who will be absent due to family travels. Page numbers from the texts can quickly be filled in. Copies of the classroom texts should be supplied.

Most schools have extra copies of textbooks. Rather than expecting books to be carried back and forth from school, it is helpful to provide frequently absent students with a set of textbooks to be kept at home. It is a part of good content area teaching to teach the entire class some strategies that do not require many materials and that students can learn to use on their own, for example, writing about assigned readings, keeping a learning log, completing RESPONSE forms, answering end-of-chapter questions using the QAR strategy, and brainstorming and semantic mapping. When frequently absent students have learned these strategies, they can be encouraged to use them when they are studying at home. If the work done at home is seen by both the teacher and student as an opportunity to share ideas, then the student may become eager to bring in work done at home. On the other hand, if having home assignments becomes a reason for questioning and scolding and teacher displeasure, then the process will be unsuccessful. Figure 9–2 shows an assignment form for students who are absent due to illness or injury. Page numbers from the texts can quickly be filled in. Copies of the classroom texts should be supplied.

FIGURE 9-1   Assignment Form For Student Who Will Be Absent While Family Travels

Assignments for: *Levi Grant*   Date: *2/15*
Length of absence: *2 weeks*
From: *Ms. Harctee*

Language arts: (Approximately 45 minutes, 5 times a week) 1) Keep a journal, a combined travel diary, and learning log, and write in it each school day, Mondays through Fridays. 2) Read at least one trade book of your choice. (The book may be borrowed from the class library.) Write about your reading in your journal several times, as done in the class literature logs. 3) If you have time early in your trip, send the class a postcard showing where you are, and what you're doing.

Math: (Approximately 30 minutes, 3 times a week) 1) Do the even-numbered computation exercises on pages _____ in your text, and ask a family member to check your work; then correct any errors you made. 2) Create several word problems about your trip and write them in your journal. 3) Bring back a map of the place(s) you traveled to, with your route marked on it.

Social studies and science: (Approximately 30 minutes, 5 times a week. A session should be either social studies or science.) 1) Read pages _____ in your social studies text and complete a RESPONSE form. 2) Read pages _____ in your science text and complete a RESPONSE form. 3) Choose a topic from either science or social studies; brainstorm information about it, and make a semantic map. Family members may join in the brainstorming and mapping with you, but you should draw the final semantic map. 4) (Optional) Make a semantic map about your trip.

Checklist of items to be brought to school when you return:
- ☐ journal
- ☐ trade book(s) you read
- ☐ math work completed, checked, corrected
- ☐ map, showing your travel route
- ☐ social studies RESPONSE form
- ☐ science RESPONSE form
- ☐ social studies or science web
- ☐ math text
- ☐ social studies text
- ☐ science text

FIGURE 9–2 Assignment Form For Student Absent Due To Illness or Injury

Assignments for: *Jed Nuri*   Date: *4/11*
From: *Mr. Charete*

We miss you! Here are some plans for school work to use when you feel well enough.

Until you feel better, we'll keep most of the heavy textbooks in school and send along only the social studies and science books, with some paperback trade books and a math exercise book.

Language arts: 1) Keep a journal, which can be a personal diary, a learning log, or a literature journal—or any combination of these. 2) Read trade books and keep a record of your reading. 3) Write to us—we'll write to you.

Math: 1) Practice computation using the exercise book. Ask a grown-up to check your work; then correct any errors you made. 2) Create some word problems and write them in your journal, with their solutions.

3) Choose something that you can observe and make a graph or chart to share with us when you come back.

Social studies and science: 1) Read in your social studies text beginning at page ____ and complete one RESPONSE form. 2) Read in your science text beginning at page ____ and complete one RESPONSE form. 3) Choose a topic from either science or social studies. Brainstorm information about it and make a web. Family members may join in the brainstorming and webbing with you, but you should draw the final web. 4) (Optional) Make a web about something that interests you.

Enclosures: Math exercise book, __ paperback book(s), science and social studies texts, (notebook for journal)

Frequently absent students usually are coping with difficult problems, and may, quite reasonably, regard completion of homework—especially workbook pages and assignments that have no meaning for them—as unimportant. Students with frequent, short absences may be suffering from a chronic illness, in which case their energy and enthusiasm may be low not only during the time they are absent but also when they return to school. Students who are kept out of school because they are needed at home, for example, to care for a younger sibling, are likely to be tired and under stress. It is unkind as well as useless for teachers to blame these young people for their absences. The teacher who creates pleasant associations for school, who shares good literature with students and helps them become enthusiastic readers, is not only serving the current generation of students but is making life better for their future children as well.

When an extended single absence is due to injury or illness, some school systems provide the services of visiting teachers, who visit the home or hospital to provide individual tutoring. When this service is provided, teachers should cooperate by giving the tutor or visiting teacher thorough infor-

mation about what topics are being studied and what materials are being used. Sometimes students are absent for an extended period because they are traveling. These absences usually are known in advance, and families often notify the school and request assignments. It may be useful to be prepared with information for families so they can help their children keep up with school assignments during an extended absence and give generic assignments, that is, those that apply regardless of when the absence occurs.

Additional Opportunities to Communicate

Well-prepared displays of students' work, newsletters, personal letters from students to their families, and celebrations of learning to which family members are invited are methods of sharing information about the school program that have the additional advantage of contributing to content area and language arts programs. The effectiveness of these optional forms of school-home communication depends on teacher thought and effort, but some of the preparation can provide practical opportunities for students to organize and present information, thus enhancing their learning.

Displays. Well-organized, up-to-date displays of student projects are an indication to visitors that schools and classrooms are active and interesting learning environments. Linda Leonard Lamme (1989, p. 65), reminding us that "a school that values writing and artwork displays it everywhere," advises teachers to place bulletin boards at eye level and display students' work on readily seen areas such as the classroom door, which she calls "door decor." Gill Potter (1989) notes the value of lively, well-labeled bulletin boards placed outside of the classroom. He suggests including a timetable of events that parents may attend or want to be made aware of. Several versions of the poster-style announcements can be prepared using the different languages of the community. Impromptu photographs of class activities add color and interest to displays. If snapshots are used, students should help select them and should have the right to veto the use of those photographs of themselves they do not like.

A map and postcard display—one or more maps with postcards or small pictures of important sites (and sights) can be prepared about places the class is studying or can be used to illustrate class history. Another use for this strategy is world, national, and state maps marked to show students' birthplaces, which has the advantage of demonstrating the importance of scale in cartography. Students can be invited to bring in postcards or pictures of the places they were born; through newsletters, families may be invited to send contributions for the display. When a map and postcard display is used for this purpose, teachers need to ensure that no student is excluded. If some students do not bring in contributions for the map, the teacher can set out materials from which they can cut out appropriate illustrations.

The interest and usefulness of bulletin boards and showcases are increased if they include information about student products that are displayed. Susan Hepler is among the educators who remind us that school visitors probably do not know what the assignment was that resulted in the displayed products or what the assignment was intended to teach. Teachers, or teachers and students collaboratively, should prepare a description of the assignment, and the rationale for it, and add this to the display. "'I see so many *inert* displays,' she commented.

'Displays that are explained give parents an understanding of the theory behind the instruction given. When we really educate parents about what we are doing, they really understand' " (Hepler, quoted in Jacobson, 1990b, p. 169).

Many teaching strategies described in this text can result in displays that communicate information about students' learning to family members and other visitors to the school. Displaying students' products outside of the classroom is a form of publication—making the work public—and published work requires editing. This means work chosen for display by agreement between teacher and students needs to be checked for factual accuracy, technical correctness, and attractiveness. Some written work can be most clearly and attractively prepared for presentation by using a computer, but it still is necessary to check for accuracy and correctness, since there are some errors a computer spellcheck cannot catch. In planning displays, it is useful to consider how much time must be committed and how students will be involved in ways that contribute to their learning. Some of the many strategies that yield products that can form the basis of displays are listed in Figure 9-3, with examples of some of the ways they might be used and a sample of informative statements that might be added to the display.

Newsletters. Newsletters sent from school to home are a lively and practical way of sharing information with families about their children's educational program. Typical newsletters are single-sided sheets that contain a series of short articles giving information about current and future activities. Newsletters can include information about upcoming topics of study. Families may be asked to send in relevant items, such as maps, labeled photographs, and postcards if the class is studying a particular area of the country or world. Jean Stenmark (1991) recommends newsletters from math class that include some information about math teaching methods, then samples of students' work on problem-solving activities in current topics of study.

Preparation of newsletters can be an effective method of integrating content area learning and language arts. Students of all ages can dictate or write articles and older students can format the newsletter

FIGURE 9–3   Using Products of Learning Strategies in Displays

Labeled Semantic Maps (See Chapter Four)

Example: As a class project linking language arts and social studies, students select people who have made important contributions benefiting others and then read several biographies. Individually, or in pairs or groups, they next prepare labeled semantic maps (such as the one about Sojourner Truth, shown in Chapter Four) to organize information about the person they have chosen. A colorful 5 x 8 file card can include the signatures of the students who created the map and their statement about the significance of the person's life. Book jackets from the biographies, displayed with the maps, can be used to add color to the display, and if the display is in a recessed, glass cabinet, some of the books themselves also can be displayed.

Sample statement: "Semantic Mapping is a way of organizing information to show the relationship among ideas. In our class we use semantic mapping often. This display shows maps that students have made during a project in which they read several biographies of an admired person."

Concept of Definition (See Chapter Four)

Example: While studying the hydrosphere, students in an earth science class in which this strategy is used regularly prepare definitions for the technical terms in Concept of Definition style. The display consists of a map of the earth, showing the hydrosphere, and definitions of terms (in CD style) that have been written neatly or prepared by using a computer. Bright-colored tacks connected by yarn are used to link a section on the map with the definition of a matching term.

Sample statement: "We have been studying about the part of the earth that is made up of water, the hydrosphere, and learning about saltwater and freshwater and water-covered areas of the earth. Our class uses a strategy called Concept of Definition to define important concepts. For every term we define we answer a series of questions: "What is it?" (we list its category and another term in that category); "What is it like?" (we give characteristics); and "What are some examples?"

RAFT (See Chapter Five)

Example: As one of the culminating activities in a study of inventors and inventions, students use the RAFT strategy to take the role of an inventor, writing to an audience of people who will use the invention in the future.

Sample statement: "One way of showing that we have learned about other people is to try to see things from their point of view. In our class we have used RAFT writing, taking the point of view of an inventor we studied. RAFT is a writing strategy and its name comes from the initials of the directions for writing. *R* stands for Role; each of us took the role of an inventor. *A* stands for Audience; we wrote to the people who would use our inventions. *F* stands for Form; each of us chose the form we would use, but most of us wrote letters. *T* stands for Theme; as inventors, we wanted to give advice about how to use our inventions wisely and safely in years to come."

Time and Place Maps (See Chapter Five)

Example: In a class study of state history, students choose areas of the state for special study, labeling a map of their area with important events in its history and color coding the labels to indicate the time periods in which the events occurred. The individual maps can be displayed around a large outline map of the entire state. If students follow up the map activity by writing short papers analyzing one aspect of the connections between time and place, several of the papers also could be selected for display.

Sample statement: "Most maps give information about places. Time and Place Maps also give information about events that have happened in the place shown on the map, across time. Each map has a color code showing the colors that represent different time periods, and the events are labeled according to this system. When you look at all the events labeled in the same color, this tells you that they all occurred in the same time period."

using computer word processing or publishing software. Personalized newsletters can be produced by printing informational articles in three of four sections of a regular-sized sheet of paper, leaving the lower right section blank. Students then use the blank section to write a message or create a drawing, especially for their own families. This kind of personalization increases the likelihood that students will deliver newsletters and that family members will read them. A sample of this kind of newsletter is shown in Figure 9–4, where an art teacher has used a quarterly newsletter to give information about the fall art program, leaving a section for students to complete individually, with a design of their choice related to one of the themes.

FIGURE 9–4 Newsletter With Space For Personalization

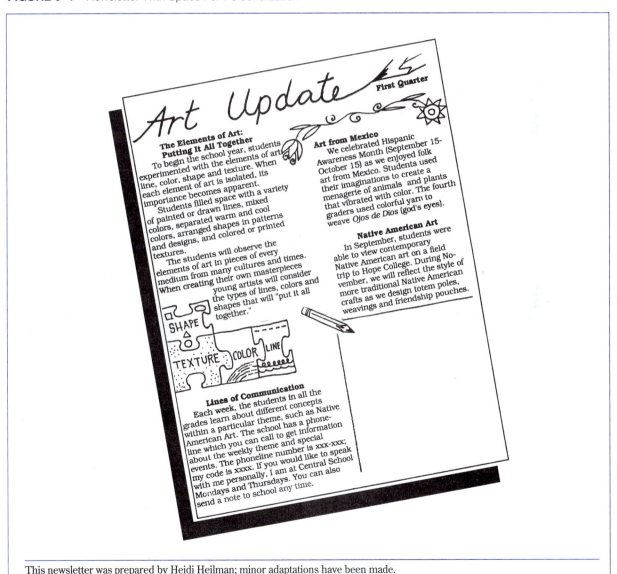

This newsletter was prepared by Heidi Heilman; minor adaptations have been made.

FIGURE 9–5 Newsletter For a Vocational Education Class

✳ ✳

BUILDING TRADE NEWS for APRIL
THE SPECIAL ED/VOCATIONAL ED BUILDING TRADES CLASS

✳ ✳

OPEN HOUSE: MAY 11, 7:00-8:30 P.M.

You are invited to view the Building Trades House and meet some of the students who helped construct it.

"CONSTRUCTIVE" INFORMATION

The class completed the baseball dugout roof construction project. New rafters, fascia decking, and end trim were installed. Then drip edge was attached and roll roofing was secured to the low pitch roof. The students worked hard on some rather chilly days so the dugout would be ready for baseball season.

The family room at the building trades house is looking very nice. The students have been doing the trimming work: hanging doors, casing, and attaching base trim. The class will also be helping finish the electrical work. Then, with just a little bit of touch-up work, the room will be ready for floor covering.

The students have also been working on a wall mock-up. This mock-up provided review of many of the skills and it will also help us finish the plumbing and electrical units. During the coming weeks we will also be doing more work on the mock-up and quite a bit of concrete flat work. We will also help build a deck on the house.

OUT AND ABOUT

Just prior to spring break our class visited a custom built home that was in the trimming-out stage. We were able to see many of the aspects of finished carpentry work. Soon we will be visiting a company that pretreats lumber for decks and other outdoor projects.

QUESTIONS AND ANSWERS

Q: In plastering and dry wall what is a "hawk" and what is it used for?

A: A hawk is a flat board with a handle, used to hold the compound or "mud."

"NAILING IT DOWN" — (ADULTS AT HOME)

Please discuss the following question with your student. Then sign below and have your student return this portion. WHAT ARE THE THREE PARTS OF A STAIRWAY CALLED?

_____

Adult family member signature:

Please include any questions about our program. Additional comments are also welcome.

This newsletter was prepared by Jim Bird; minor adaptations have been made.

In terms of providing information to parents, building or class newsletters are usually more interesting to students' families than are district-wide informational reports. A recent study (Jaeger, 1994) showed, in fact, that school district officials may not have a good understanding of what kinds of information parents most want to receive. In some districts, students' families are kept informed through "school report cards"—reports providing information about the characteristics of the school, such as school environment, facilities, finances, program offerings, staffing, standardized testing information, and student services. Jaeger surveyed parents to determine what kinds of information they were most interested in receiving and surveyed superintendents and school public relations officials as well to find out what they thought parents were most interested in. As a group, parents indicated that they most wanted to be informed about school environment, such as statistics on school safety and the extent of parental and community involvement in the schools, while school superintendents rated this kind of information the least important to report to parents.

A newsletter may take the form of a letter from the teacher to the family. This kind of school-to-home communication is particularly useful when a teacher plans an extensive learning project. When such projects are a regular part of a teacher's program from year to year, it is especially practical to prepare an informative description of the project to send home with students. Keith Wilhelmi (1988, p. 14) refers to this kind of communication as a means to "*educate* as well as communicate." He advocates describing a major assignment (his example is assigning middle school students to create an extensive leaf collection as part of a science unit), explaining what activities the students will be engaging in and how family members can contribute and giving a rationale for the assignment that includes developmental theory to explain why it is appropriate for students at this time in their learning.

The newsletter shown in Figure 9–5 is an example of a monthly newsletter for a high school special education and vocational education class, where students are bused in to the program. Because most of the students' homes are a substantial distance from the class site, it is especially difficult for families to have direct contact with the teachers, except during open houses at the beginning and end of the school year. The newsletter is prepared collaboratively with a computer class, where a student puts information supplied by the teachers into a format that is the same for each newsletter (general information; "Constructive" Information, describing current building projects and units of study; Out and About, telling about field trips; Questions and Answers, and Nailing it Down, in which an interesting question is asked that the students know the answer to and the answer to the previous month's question is given; and a space for a family member to sign. An added advantage for the teachers of the class is that sending a copy of the newsletter serves as a thank-you letter when businesses host field trips—and often is used by those businesses as part of a wall display.

Personal Letters From Students to Their Families.

The semantic mapping strategy can be used to prepare students for writing letters to give information about class activities. As a teacher-led, whole class activity, students brainstorm things they want to include and create a semantic map. Then each student writes home using ideas and organization from the map. Janet Johnston (1989) suggests linking mini-lessons in communications to writing home in this style. The teacher writes the different parts of the map in various colors to make organization of ideas especially clear. Because the map is displayed as students write, they have available the correct spelling of significant words. In Johnston's fourth-grade classroom, students write letters home which parents sign, often adding a message, and return. These letters are kept in student folders and are eventually bound and returned to students as a diary of the year. Madeline Brick (1993) has described using student letters as a means of sending mid-term progress reports when working with middle school students. As a communications lesson, she worked with students to express negatives and positives clearly, accentuating the positive and stressing strengths. After each student had written a letter, the teacher wrote a cover letter to parents and mailed the letters from school. She reports that parents responded with letters of their own, some in their native languages, and that one parent sent a tape recording in Spanish. Students were involved in monitoring their own progress and interested in improving their study habits and work.

Celebrations of Learning.

Inviting family members to the school can be a warm and memorable culmination of a learning project. Kathy Bakst and Eva Essa (1990, p. 150) describe the creation of an anthology of the class's written works, followed by a community party. "To top off each semester, a gala 'Authors and Artists' party—to which parents, guests and the media are invited— provides an opportunity for one of each of the children's stories to be read aloud by a local actor." Learning also can be celebrated through gifts. Rose Reissman (1993, p. 76) describes a project in which students prepared gift books for their families. Students can be made aware of the many kinds of beautiful books through a field trip to a bookstore or a teacher-prepared display of gift books. Then students prepare a planning sheet on which they list the intended recipient's name, age, relationship, and interests, and next, ideas for the style of book they plan, such as a series of quotations from literature, original poetry, or captioned photographs. Although students may work in pairs or groups, each prepares an individual gift book, with the classroom teacher and art teacher collaborating on the project. Reissman suggests a party at school for family members to receive their gifts. "We held it on a weekend morning so parents and family members who worked could come."

■■ Collaboration: When School and ■■ Home Work Together

Although there are substantial differences among families regarding the extent of home-school interactions, **collaboration** exists whenever young people attend school. The first and most basic collaboration consists of families fulfilling their obligation to enroll their children in school, enabling them to attend by providing for their health and safety needs. (Epstein, 1988; Epstein & Dauber, 1991). Teachers also have a basic obligation to collaborate with the home —an obligation that is met by educating students and informing families of students' progress. Beyond this basic collaboration, teachers have the opportunity to encourage families' involvement in school programs as well.

Creating and maintaining fruitful, nontrivial opportunities to work together is a challenge for adults who care for children at school and home. School personnel and family members have many demands on their time and energy, both in their work and leisure time. Teachers who take the initiative in arranging collaborative activities add to their own professional obligations and may draw time away from their own family responsibilities. Family members who make time to collaborate on school activities must balance these desirable uses of time with other demands and family and career responsibilities. In our complex society, collaboration is both important and difficult.

---

collaboration—the Latin words from which *collaboration* is derived mean exactly what the modern word means, although the order of the parts is different. To collaborate is to work with, and the word is derived from *com-*, a prefix meaning *with*, and *laborare*, a verb meaning *to work*.

Teachers should accept major responsibility for ensuring that the connections between school and home are positive.

Complicating Factors in School-Home Collaboration

At the same time that influential people, both within and outside the field of education, are urging greater collaboration between school and home, there also are educators who caution that effective, enduring collaboration is not easily developed or maintained. One factor that inhibits collaboration is language disparity between school and home, a disparity that occurs in two forms. In some families, parents and other family members have limited ability to use the English language, although they may be adept in speaking and reading in one or more other languages. Methods of accommodating language diversity when communicating with students' families have been addressed earlier in this chapter: an interpreter—a bilingual adult or possibly a child in the family who has become bilingual—is needed for conferences; written materials sent home can be translated; posted displays in a school are enhanced when information is given in the many languages spoken in students' homes. But while school-home communication is usually managed one-to-one, through a report from the school sent to a family or a teacher meeting with one or more adults from a family, collaborative activities often involve groups of parents. Such situations can become friendly interactions even when the participants are limited in their ability to speak each other's languages fluently.

A different kind of language disparity exists when one or more adult members of a student's family are unable to read and write English capably, even though English is the only language they speak. Illiteracy may cause family members to believe that they cannot help their children with schoolwork and to feel reluctant to participate in school activities (Davis & Diaz, 1994). However, as Pamela Farris and Mary Denner write, "Illiterate parents can cultivate literacy in their children if teachers are willing to devote the time and patience to assist such parents. Teacher-parent interactions require that the teacher be sensitive, understanding, and responsive to the needs not only of the children but of the parents as well" (Farris & Denner, 1991, p. 65). In an article titled, "Parents who can't read: What the schools can do," Marycarolyn France and Jane Meeks (1987) list a series of actions all parents can take to contribute to their children's academic success, actions that do not require that the parents be literate. Parents can emphasize good work habits. They can encourage children to talk about what they are learning in school. They can plan leisure time activities that foster learning, for example, trips to the library, museum, or park. They can establish a place and time where the child is expected to work on homework each school night. And parents can show their children that they expect them to succeed in school.

Another problem in collaboration is more widespread than difficulties that arise from language disparity. This problem can be thought of as one of status disparity, where one group is perceived as knowledgeable (and therefore superior) and the other is perceived as lacking in knowledge (therefore, with inferior status). Timothy Rasinski (1989), describing problems that may arise when schools initiate programs to link the home with the school, speaks out against rigid, didactic programs in which parents are told the correct way (as determined by school personnel) to help their children. Such one-way directives may cause parents to worry about their capacity to help their children, particularly when "the correct way" changes from year to year.

> For interaction to be successful, it depends very largely upon the attitudes and skills of teachers and administrators. It is a complex process because chil-

dren bring to school with them, attitudes, beliefs, values, and behavior which sometimes are incongruent with the school. Teachers must take care not to set objectives for children which may be unattainable simply because of the values at home. Should there be a gap between teacher values and parent values, then great will be the task of reconciliation. It is not a challenge to be taken lightly. Children will have many teachers in their lives, but only one family. (Potter, 1989, p. 28)

It also can be troubling that the pendulum of educational practice swings back and forth on the issue of whether family members should help their children at home with schoolwork. At present, there is a general expectation that parents should work with their children at home to review and reinforce what is being taught in school. However, there was recently a time when teachers and administrators admonished parents *not* to attempt to help their students at home, based on the assumption that only school personnel understood content and correct teaching methodology. It is conceivable that this attitude may prevail at some future time. Either of these directives—*you must help* and *you mustn't help*—can be anxiety-producing. Opportunities for collaboration typically originate from the school. Teachers, therefore, must work to avoid a built-in inequality that puts parents in an inferior position.

Opportunities For Doable Collaboration

Unlike communication, which is essentially the delivery or exchange of information, collaboration can develop partnerships. Collaboration is the more demanding and also potentially more rewarding opportunity for adults from the school and the home. Successful school-home collaboration among adults can have a powerful influence on students' school success. In terms of systems theory, as discussed at the beginning of this chapter, such collaboration can contribute to a strong, supportive mesosystem by building connections between the two elements of students' microsystem, home and school, which are most important to students and where most of their time is spent.

Earlier in this chapter, a discussion about school-home communication through conferences made the point that it is a useful element of a conference for a teacher to "give one doable suggestion." The characteristics of suggestions that describe something helpful that families can undertake (and are therefore *doable*) were listed: besides being clearly expressed, doable suggestions are purposeful, interesting, repeatable, and practical. Doable methods of home-school collaboration have similar characteristics. The plan and management of the collaboration are practical. The time and skills required of both teacher and family members are within their capacity. The collaboration is, or has the potential to be, more lasting than participation in a single event. The collaborative activity has a sensible purpose and is interesting for all of the adults involved and for students as well.

Practical, Ongoing, Purposeful, Interesting Opportunities

For shared school-home activities to be practical, three criteria need to be met. First, administrator awareness and approval are essential. Then the collaborative activities need to be appropriate for students' ages and grades. Finally, the collaboration should not demand time commitments that participants—teacher and family members—will find difficult to meet, or skills that are beyond their capacities. It should be structured to be pleasant and nonstressful for everyone involved.

Getting Approval.   Appropriately, school-home collaborations often are planned and managed at the district or school level. When this is the case, individual teachers may serve on planning committees, and they may decide to participate actively in the events that are planned. In this chapter, however, the focus is primarily on school-home collaborations, planned by a classroom teacher or a team of teachers. For such collaborations to succeed, the first element of practicality is for teachers to ensure that their building principals are consulted during the planning stage and kept informed as the collaboration occurs.

Choosing Grade-Appropriate Ideas.   Many of the suggestions for collaborative activities that appear in professional journals are focused on the elementary school years. This is a time when family members are particularly concerned about their young children's school success. However, what is particularly influential in making a wide range of collaborative activities succeed at this point in students' school careers is that young children typically welcome family members' active participation. It usually is a mark of prestige for young children when family members come into their classes to help. They welcome such visits with joyful enthusiasm. That enthusiasm for family members' presence in the classroom is not typical of middle school or high school students. Jay Heath (1992), writing about his experiences as a principal moving from an elementary school to a middle school, notes the great difference he observed, not in family members' willingness to help at school, but in the kinds of help they were willing to provide, given their children's strong desire to appear independent. It can be useful for teachers of older students to read about the kinds of school-home collaboration that have worked at the elementary school level, because they may have elements that can be adapted for middle school and high school. However, successful collaborations at middle school and high school are likely to be those that focus on the special skills, talents, and interests of students in these grades. Such activities include intergenerational after-school programs focused on content and study skills, family collaboration to assist with special projects, mentoring that parents provide for students with whom they share special interests and talents, and activities in which students and family members cooperate in a variety of school improvement activities.

Arranging Nonstressful Collaboration.   School-home collaboration requires mutual respect. (It is important to remember that in every human relationship, we can treat others with respect, without first waiting to see whether we are being respected.) Teacher thought and thoughtfulness are essential in arranging plans that are reinforcing to parents. Thoughtful, detailed planning should focus on large-scale issues such as how much teacher time and family time will be needed, and whether special facilities and materials will be needed. Small factors, however, may make a large difference in determining whether shared activities are practical and pleasant, including, for example, as Carol Seefeldt (1987, p. 16) points out, whether the seating arrangements provided for older visitors to the school is comfortable for them. She notes the importance, in school-home collaborations that involve students directly, of "protecting the prestige of elders as well as children… planning for interaction that has integrity and is functional for both groups [and] ensuring that contact between old and young is rewarding and pleasant for both groups."

Ongoing Collaboration.

Lasting collaboration between school and home is promoted when parents engage in activities that they can use to support their children's learning across the school years, such as reading together and establishing regular, uninterrupted times when children will do homework and adults will be nearby, also engaging in reading and writing activities. Professional organizations and journals often supply brochures that teachers can make available to families, giving practical suggestions for this kind of home support for the school (e.g., Erickson, undated; Resh & Wilson, 1990). All successful collaborations provide the potential for promoting a relationship between home and school that is solid and satisfying, a situation that is beneficial to students across their school careers.

Purposeful, Interesting Collaboration.

The professional literature contains descriptions of a wide variety of collaborative activities that teachers have devised and used successfully across the grade range. While most require family members to come to the school, either regularly over a period of time or for specified occasions, some lively, productive collaborations can occur without the adults needing to come to school.

When Family Members Come to School

Workshops, help with special projects, and engagement in assessment activities are three forms collaboration can take. Among the most successful workshop activities are those that engage adults and children together, including those where grandparents participate. As the world-famous anthropologist Margaret Mead (1970, p. 3) wrote, "the continuity of all culture depends on the living presence of at least three generations."

Workshops.

The extent and variety of workshops that can be provided for parents seems almost limitless, given teachers' energy and ingenuity. Anne Giordano (1992) describes a series of evening meetings she holds monthly to discuss school-related topics with family members. The first meeting is set by the teacher-coordinator, and the topic is helping students with homework. Other topics are suggested by parents (e.g., math instruction, children's social and emotional needs, writing, understanding test scores). Susan O'Connell (1992) writes about a workshop program that paired elementary school students and family members to work on problem-solving methods and activities and on ways to encourage hypothesizing and risk-taking. Teachers prepared weekly problem sets, based on school and local activities, for the workshop sessions.

One way families can assist students is by encouraging them to use study strategies taught in the schools—if they know about them. Jennifer Allen and Kimberly Freitag (1988, p. 923) describe a two-session workshop on studying, offered in the early evening, for parent-student teams to learn and practice study strategies together. For students, the learning is a review of what has been taught in school, in an atmosphere that encourages them to apply their learning and explain it to family members. "The parent-student workshop gave parents specific tools and the confidence to support the school's efforts. Schools must work to involve all families—not just those who tend to be 'education oriented' or 'upwardly mobile.' " Elizabeth Quintero, writing with Ana Huerta-Macias (1990) and Cristina Velarde (1990) describes workshop sessions, with a special emphasis on bilingual and bicultural families, that engage students and family members in working together on special projects and in using the Language Experience Approach to record their activities. They quote a parent who said, "I want to help my kids so they don't have go through what I did" (Quintero & Velarde, 1990, p. 14), and note the benefit to parents of observing their children's learning at school and becoming aware that the school culture values the child's contributions (rather than expecting the child to be silent in the presence of adults).

Help With Special Projects. When parents have time to come to school regularly, even over a short period of time, there are many projects with which they can assist. In an article titled, "Give the home volunteers something interesting to do!" Julie Jensen and Nancy Roser (1990) describe a publishing project in which parents serve as consultants, as students decide which major pieces of their writing should be published, help with revisions, and plan and carry out publication of the writing in the form of a homemade book or a collection of writings.

Collaboration in Assessment. With the current emphasis on authentic assessment, many scholars and practitioners in the field of education have suggested ways to engage family members in interacting with their children, as the students document their school achievements. James Flood and Diane Lapp (1989, p. 514) advocate student participation in creating portfolios that will be shared with their families. "The preparation of a parent portfolio should not become an overwhelming task.... materials can be accumulated during the school year.... [and students] can share in the preparation of portfolios. In this way, a portfolio becomes a joint project for the teacher and the student—there will be two voices capable of and willing to explain progress." Ray Levi (1990) invites parents' comments on students' portfolios by including a questionnaire that provides a structure enabling them to respond thoughtfully to what they have observed about their children's learning.

When Family Members Help Without Leaving Home

Some collaborative activities that are lively and involving do not require family members to come to school. Oral history activities, described in an earlier chapter, can provide strong and appealing links between home and school. Reading aloud is a possibility for all families, even those with language disparities. Take-home packs, primarily for younger children, and class history records, suitable for older students, are both ways of involving families

without adults coming to school. Collections of "family folklore"—recipes, sayings, documents—add to students' understanding and appreciation of each other's families, as well as their own.

Reading Aloud. The benefits of reading aloud are well-documented, a theme discussed in Chapter Four. Encouragement for reading at home need not exclude parents who are not fluent in English, nor parents who cannot read. It is useful for parents who cannot read English well to be assured that it is desirable for them to read to their children from books in the language, or languages, in which they are fluent. Besides the intrinsic enjoyment of being read to, children benefit from the closeness that family reading aloud provides, from recognizing that their family values books and reading and from developing a sense of story structure and literacy language across languages and cultures. Whether parents can or cannot read to their children, children can read to their parents.

> Researchers found that children who read to their parents made significantly greater progress in reading than those who were given additional reading instruction...—particularly so for children who, at the beginning of the project, were experiencing difficulty in learning to read.... Most parents expressed great satisfaction at being involved in this way by the schools, and teachers reported that the children showed an increased interest in school learning and were better behaved. Lack of literacy or English fluency did not detract from parents' willingness to collaborate with the school, nor did it prevent improvement in... children's reading. (Cummins, 1994, p. 54)

Take-Home packs. Methods of engaging students and their families in school-related activities by sending interesting and useful packs of materials home with students on a rotating basis have often been described in professional journals. Teachers, or teachers and students working together, can put together a set of materials to be sent home with a student and shared with the family, to form the basis for something to be created and brought back to school. Family Theme Bags (Helm, 1994) are sent home over a weekend with a journal to record weekend events, a book to share, and art supplies that may be used to produce a collaborative family creation. Helm gives the useful advice that materials in take-home packs should not be new and shiny, since they are meant to be used. Traveling Tales (Reutzel & Fawson, 1990) is a project in which writing supplies are packaged in an inexpensive but sturdy backpack, that also includes writing guidelines—emphasizing the importance of writing about something of interest, rather than focusing on technical correctness—in the form of a letter to parents. Student and family members collaborate in writing—perhaps a group story, or separate stories from different family members. Kimberly Rodriguez (1991) describes two styles of take-home packs. One or more inexpensive carrying cases are equipped with supplies for writing and artwork and students take turns bringing them home as Writing Briefcases. The products prepared there may be shared later at school. A Traveling Suitcase is a small overnight suitcase with stickers and tags from various countries and states. In addition to writing supplies, the suitcase can contain maps and students write descriptions of real or imaginary journeys. Projects such as these are enjoyable and inclusive. Even though sending materials home may be a special boon to families who would find it difficult to provide them, the activity is used by all students.

Class History Records.   Creating class history records, a strategy suggested by Lynda Weston (1988), is a way of recording, organizing, and sharing the history of a particular class of students during a year. The strategy requires an inexpensive camera and film for classroom use. On a rotating basis, one student each week is assigned the role of class historian, with the responsibility for taking one picture each day. After a lapse of time—Weston suggests two weeks—the current class historian mounts the pictures in an album and asks classmates to write captions for them, which are mounted with the pictures in the album. When there are bilingual students in the classroom, pictures may have captions in several languages. The captioning of pictures taken earlier encourages students to recall and reminisce about the events shown. Preparation of the album can make students more aware of the importance of inclusiveness, with those in the role of historian checking to ensure that all classmates are

featured in interesting ways. After two months, the album will have a substantial record of class activities. At this point, the teacher can arrange for students to take turns bringing the album home to share with their families. Family collaboration comes from engaging with children in learning and talking about the children's school experience. Both take-home packs and the class history album present the potential problem that the materials sent home may be lost or damaged. Take-home packs should be inexpensively prepared, and there should be several in use, so a loss need not be a cause for scolding or abandoning the project. The class album, on the other hand, is one-of-a-kind, and teachers may choose to send copied pages for students to share at home, rather than the entire book.

Family Folklore.   School-home collaboration also can be based on developing collections to which families contribute. Sigrid Renner and JoAnn Carter (1991, p. 604) offer a variety of suggestions, including recipe collections. Each of their students contributed one special family recipe "with an accompanying story or commentary on its origin or special meaning. Students found that many of the recipes had never been recorded. They had to talk to the cook, write directions, and test their recipes." Another possibility is a compilation of proverbs that are important to families, a project also recommended by Janet McCracken (1993). Background for such a project can be provided by examining a collection of proverbs such as *Poor Richard's Almanac.*

Renner and Carter also describe a project in which the class compiles copies of documents that are part of their families' history, for example, old letters, deeds, certificates of birth or marriage. The guidelines they suggest for the project are that the documents must be at least 30 years old and that students must talk to some adult in the family who knows about the document firsthand or who has received information handed down through the family. Students summarize these interview notes and write a brief statement explaining the significance of the document to their families. The documents and the background information can be studied and discussed as evidence of the times in which they originated. Older students can write brief analyses.

Teaching Strategies That Encourage Collaboration

Many teaching strategies and processes described in this text can be adapted to encourage collaboration between home and school. Annual overviews—visually displayable summaries of the learning plan for the year—provide one of several ways to link school and home. An annual overview can be posted in the classroom as a bulletin board display, and smaller versions of the overview can be prepared and shared with students' families. Family members may be invited to visit school and contribute to classroom learning at times when their interests and talents match a particular topic of study, and they may be invited to assist with class activities at regular intervals or occasional special events. Sharing an annual overview opens a way for family members to learn how they can collaborate with the school by sharing knowledge, or by sharing their time.

Sharing Knowledge. The saying, "None of us is as smart as all of us," is a clever way of expressing an important truth. A community consisting of a teacher, students, and students' families has traveled more widely, is qualified to do more kinds of work, can speak more languages, and has a wider range of experience than any one member of that group. Family members are experts about their own experiences and therefore potential resources when classes engage in oral history projects. An interview with an adult family member with knowledge and experiences relevant to a SAIL project is ideal for inclusion as a source of information when this research strategy is used. When different parts of the country or the world are studied, family members may be able to lend photographs, postcards, maps, and artifacts, or to contribute recipes that are typical of regional or national cuisine. All of these are ways in which knowledge may be shared without family members having to take time to come to school.

Methods of knowledge sharing by family members that require one-time visits to school include serving as a guest speaker (perhaps in a class that uses the RESPONSE to speakers strategy or where the guest's presentation serves as the Experience

Activity for the LEAD strategy). Family members with special talents in the arts may be willing to be visiting artists for a day.

Sharing Time. Family members who can arrange to come to school on a fairly regular basis can read aloud, listen to readers, help writers working in groups or individually to publish their products, and work with students who are preparing presentations or displays. Bilingual or multilingual family members can translate or interpret. Students' talents and interests may be matched with those of adults, who can serve as mentors.

There also are ways in which family members who cannot easily come to school can contribute by sharing their time. Some may be fluent oral readers who have access to a tape recorder and who may be interested in taping stories or textbook chapters if blank tapes are provided. Some may have word-processing capabilities that they can use to prepare final copies of students' writing for publication, teacher-developed materials (such as cloze, Focused Cloze, three-level guides, and so forth), or newsletters.

Reaching Out: School To Home

Throughout this chapter, when the words *school* and *home* have been placed together, *school* has almost always been placed first. This deliberate placement is not intended to indicate that teachers and school experiences are more important or more influential for children and young people than are their families and homes. Emphasizing the importance of school, in this text, is a reminder to readers of the text—who are primarily teachers or those planning a career in teaching—that our sphere of responsibility is the school and that we can contribute to school-home relationships by actions that are within our control—by regarding students' families with respect and discretion, communicating in helpful ways, and encouraging practical methods of collaboration.

The relationship that exists today between school and home is a relatively recent phenomenon, as James Coleman has written:

> For most of society's children and youth, formal schooling hardly existed until this century. Children

grew up in the context of the household and the neighborhood. All the activities and facilities for training that would prepare them for adulthood took place within the household or in easy distance from it. A child, as it grew, would slowly move into those activities, with training being almost wholly confined to "on-the-job training," and the job being closely linked to household activities. (Coleman, 1987, p. 32)

Our situation is vastly different from those that Coleman describes. Formal schooling over a lengthy period of time is not only expected in our society, it is required. Young people must attend school at least until they reach a legally determined age, and the expectation that students will remain in school is clear in the term *dropout*, used to name a person who is of the age to have graduated from high school but who does not have a diploma or its equivalent, or a person who no longer attends school even though age-mates do. (Note that the word conveys the idea of moving down, as well as away. To drop is to fall below one's previous place.)

The value of formal education in our society comes in two forms: evidence and results. Credentials providing evidence of education, such as a high school diploma, a college degree, or an advanced degree in a professional field, are needed for most kinds of employment. Results of education, such as literacy and mathematical capability, content area knowledge, and habits of learning that make it possible to learn more are a significant part of the foundation for a productive, satisfying life.

Although we can question why it should be so, it is unfortunately often the case that teachers, when they perceive a student's parents as uncaring and unsupportive, think and speak of that student as a person who is difficult to help and unlikely to succeed. Such an attitude is easily communicated to students and is likely to influence their school careers and their adult lives. Teachers can take responsibility to protect their own students from this kind of misfortune in the present and future, as they work with students and as they relate to students' families.

The most important help, of course, is given directly to the students, by teaching them well, awakening their interests and fostering their talents, caring for them, and avoiding speaking negatively

about them. Surprisingly, the ideas cited earlier in this chapter about ways that illiterate parents can help their children succeed in school (France & Meeks, 1987) contribute to this kind of help. Teachers can emphasize good work habits. They can encourage children to talk about what they are learning. They can plan direct and vicarious activities that foster learning. They can provide some structured time during the school day for students to work on assignments and never give major assignments in which students' success is dependent on what their families can provide and do for them. And teachers can demonstrate their belief that their students will succeed in school.

The second thing teachers can do to protect their students in the present and future is even more challenging. If teachers can reach their students' families and engage them in collaborative activities that family members enjoy, and in which they feel successful, then family members may begin to think of the school as a welcoming place and regard themselves as people who help. If this kind of linkage between school and home develops, the chances of a student being well-regarded by future teachers is improved.

In our society, the learning that will be important in students' future lives is extensive, specialized, and changing, and the major responsibility for providing this learning rests with the schools. There is ample evidence, however, that home support fosters school success. Across family situations—those in which one or more adult family members are committed to home-school cooperation and collaboration, and those in which there is little or no connection between the two settings— most adults believe that good school-home relationships are a key to students' success. In some families, this expectation leads adults to be assured that their children will succeed in school. In other families, the same belief in the importance of home-school cooperation leads adults to a despondent conviction that their children are likely to fail. Finding inclusive ways to help every family become confident in supporting their children's schooling promotes educational success for students now, and is likely to help future generations of students as well.

Looking Ahead

Because education is such a complex field, linkages of many sorts are essential if teaching is to be effective and learning is to be worthwhile. The two chapters in Part One, "Characteristics of Content Area Learning and Teaching," stressed the importance of integrating sound educational theory with good pedagogy. In Part Two, "Before, During, and After: Strategies for Content Area Learning and Teaching," strategies selected for their usefulness in introducing content area topics, developing understanding, and enhancing learning were discussed. That section stressed the importance of integrating instruction throughout a period of study. Part Three, "Building Strengths, Meeting Needs, and Making Connections," focused on important teacher responsibilities—enabling students to progress as readers, teaching inclusively, assessing progress, and fostering linkages between school and home. An important message in these four chapters is that the responsibilities are best met when they are integrated with content area teaching, rather than added as an extra burden.

Part Four, "Extending Content Area Learning," is the final section of the text. Two of the three chapters focus on educational theory that supports aspects of integration and add to the array of teaching strategies from which teachers can choose. Chapter Ten, "Integration of Listening, Speaking, Reading, and Writing in Content Area Study," presents strategies that encourage the development of oracy (listening and speaking) and literacy (reading and writing) in content area learning. Chapter Eleven, "Integration of the Arts With Content Area Learning," provides a rationale and strategies for incorporating the arts in content area programs. Although literature for young adults and children is cited and described throughout the text, this is the chapter that offers the richest array of examples. In Chapter Twelve, "Planning For the Present and Future," two aspects of teaching that relate to life-long learning are discussed: influential experience—school learning as an influence on students' futures—and optimal experience—learning that provides deep and enduring value. Topics from chapters that relate to planning are revisited through simulations of teachers' planning for different purposes, featuring the hypothetical teachers who are described at the end of Chapters Three through Eleven.

STRATEGIC TEACHERS, PART SEVEN

"I know more ways to teach this. . ."

Dave Lusolo is a middle school teacher who teaches sections of seventh and eighth grade math and is a member of a five-person team. He has ten years of experience and completed a master's degree several years ago. One teacher he particularly admires is a professor in a graduate course on statistics—a required part of the master's program. Mr. Lusolo loves math and grasps mathematical concepts easily, but many of his classmates were unsure of their ability to learn statistics. "Don't worry," the professor told the class at its first session. "I have more ways of teaching this than you have of not learning it." Mr. Lusolo was impressed with what she said and has adopted her comment as a favorite saying. One of his goals, each year, is for all his students to think of themselves as math-capable and math-interested, and he chooses teaching strategies with this goal in mind.

He and his wife teach in the same district— Mrs. Lusolo teaches art at the high school. They have two children, a first grader and a third grader. The Lusolos like to travel, and they take a carefully planned family trip each summer. They are enthusiastic teachers, but they have decided to arrange their lives to minimize the work they bring home during the school year. Instead, they prepare teaching materials during the summer, in a leisurely way. When they're traveling, the parents alternate occasionally in taking sole care of the children, leaving the other one free to work on planning and preparation for teaching. The strategies Mr. Lusolo uses, therefore, fall into two categories: those that require little or no time for preparation and follow-up, and those that depend on previously prepared materials, but don't require a lot of work to review or correct.

In the first category Mr. Lusolo uses these strategies: Solve Aloud, for the entire class, to start the day; LEAD, for the entire class, when a new topic is suitable; math journals, with a current events component, individually and in cooperative groups (bringing in current events articles is a homework assignment); transmediation activities, including word posters, individually and in cooperative groups (making the posters is usually a homework assignment); RESPONSE to speakers, for the whole class, when there is a guest speaker; thinking challenges in math and logic, at workstations—he likes to prepare his own, and some are student-created, although he also uses some carefully chosen commercial materials; computer math, graphing, and LOGO, at a workstation; and reading aloud, for the whole class.

In the second category Mr. Lusolo uses these strategies: Text Hunts, once, at the first class session; Search Tasks, for the entire class to introduce text sections; Typical to Technical Meaning, at workstations; Graphic Information Lessons (GIL), for the whole class and cooperative groups; No-Travel Trips, for the whole class and workstations. Periodically, he sends newsletters describing the math program to students' families.

In his planning, he reorders text chapters so that review and new learning are spaced out over the first part of the year. Geometrical concepts are studied throughout the year—often through workstation activities—and graphing, statistics, and probability are ongoing topics. Tests occur several days before he plans to start a new topic and are followed by reteaching, if that is needed. He makes a point of teaching each topic in multiple ways and of ensuring that students are commended for asking questions and seeking help from him and from classmates until they have fully understood concepts and processes. (He explains his favorite saying, "I have more ways of teaching this than you have of not learning it," to his classes early in the year.) After a few weeks of school, Mr. Lusolo's room is decorated with students' work, and the bulletin board outside his room is used to display word posters, students' work in graphing and tessellations, student-created problems based on trade books (the cover of the trade book makes an attractive addition to the display), and teacher- and student-created graphics from Graphic Information Lessons. Graphic Information Lessons are often linked with social studies topics, and Mr. Lusolo collaborates with colleagues on these. When GIL work is displayed, an explanation of the strategy and its purpose, and of the individual graphics, also is posted.

He uses cooperative learning extensively, for multiple purposes. First, it encourages students to talk about math. In their small groups, students solve math problems together, ask each other questions, check each other's work, and create ways to illustrate math concepts—and they can't do that silently. Learning math also is easier when students review and study together. Other purposes are practical. Groups collect and organize their homework and check at least one person's work. Group members help each other understand how to use workstation activities; after Mr. Lusolo has explained and given directions once, he finds that students can usually answer each other's questions about what to do and get started efficiently. (There's never a temptation for a student to use up class time with repeated questions about procedures.) Colleagues who haven't yet gotten started with cooperative learning are surprised when Mr. Lusolo tells them that members of his cooperative groups keep each other on task.

Of the four categories of cooperative group work—immediate assignments, regular assignments, long-term assignments, and special assignments—he uses only the first two. The Text Hunts that groups work on together are an immediate assignment as soon as groups are formed. Thereafter, there are a variety of regular assignments that groups work on daily or weekly. He believes that, in his classes, adding special extended projects involving long-term and special assignments would draw time away from his students' learning mathematics. He does not spend time assessing cooperative group work. He sees what occurs daily, and if there are problems he works them out with the students right away. Students know that they are responsible for their own homework and their own learning; tests are given individually. Cooperative group work is graded as done or not done (and Mr. Lusolo would not let a "not done" slide by him), with frequent verbal or written commendations for thoroughness, ingenuity, and raising good questions.

How Does He Do It?

Class sessions follow either an "as usual" or "something special" plan. Students know that Tuesday through Friday classes will be as usual and that Mondays are often for something special. Mr. Lusolo gets the plan for usual days organized and into action within the first week of school: Solve Aloud, cooperative group work, closing lecture. Because he has multiple class sections and needs to keep track of activities in each, he keeps a stock of colored file cards and matching colored post-it notes and assigns a different color for each of his classes. (For example, his first eighth-grade math class is "blue," and the students' names are on blue file cards, and he uses blue post-it notes to write on-the-spot observations and keep track of what he is reading and has read to that class.) At the first class session he introduces himself, then gets students rapidly and randomly into cooperative groups. He plans on groups of four or five, with six groups per class.

▌**Getting started with cooperative groups.** His usual method for forming groups is an easy one: for each class section he runs off six copies of a page with a favorite saying printed on it. (To avoid mix-ups, he uses a different color paper for each class.) He cuts each page into five sections like a jigsaw puzzle and puts one piece of each page aside. (Each page is cut differently.) He mixes up the remaining pieces, so he has a pile of 24 puzzle pieces. This is the number he will need if he has a class of 24 students, six groups of four each; typical class size is between 24 and 30. When it is time to form cooperative groups—about ten minutes into the first class session—he gives each student a puzzle piece, adding more from the pile he has set aside if the class has more than 24 students. Then he tells the students to move around and find their cooperative groups, by putting the puzzle pieces together to form a saying. He puts any remaining puzzle pieces on his desk; groups with only four students will complete their puzzle with one of these pieces.

None of us is as smart as all of us.

Two assignments for groups to work on as soon as they find the other members of their group are written on the board:

1. Everyone: Take a file card and write your name on it.
2. Get Text Hunts from my desk; divide up the questions and get going. I'll bring around the textbooks as soon as I see you sitting in a group.

While the students work on the Text Hunt, Mr. Lusolo moves from group to group and collects the file cards, matching students with their names and making sure he can pronounce all of the names correctly. He keeps the cards for each cooperative group together, because it is easier for him to learn students' names in groups. He tries to use students' names as often

as possible, to associate names and faces. Ten or fifteen minutes before the session ends, he calls a halt to the Text Hunt work. He has made the hunt long enough so that groups won't be quite finished and discusses answers with the class, calling attention to important and useful text features students have discovered. Class ends promptly. During this first session, then, the students have met Mr. Lusolo and have had their first taste of working together in their cooperative groups. They have become somewhat familiar with the texts they'll be using and have learned a strategy they'll use again in the form of Search Tasks, throughout the year. They know math class will move quickly and be interesting. Mr. Lusolo has started to learn students' names. He aims to know everyone after a week.

Usual class sessions begin promptly with a Solve Aloud that typically takes about seven minutes. Students then move immediately into their groups to work on assigned problems. Each group is required to use transmediation by creating a drawing or chart to illustrate a math problem or group of problems. Students also work on math journal entries during cooperative group time. Groups are responsible for collecting and discussing homework and turning it in before the end of the period, clipped together with a record form.

During cooperative group time Mr. Lusolo usually works with one group at each session,

---

Date: _____   Coop group initials: _____

Homework assignment
☐ Everyone's work is here, and complete.
☐ All done except for _____
   absent?   if not, explain (briefly)

Questions/comments about homework:

Whose paper(s) did the group check?
   Comments:

working cyclically throughout the class, although he does not always maintain the same order with the cycles. The group he works with meets near his desk, and for the first fifteen minutes he checks homework or math journals while listening to the group at work. (He is also attuned to the group talk throughout the room and is a good judge of whether a group is off task.) He then meets for about fifteen minutes with the group that has worked near him to consult and check their work. (This group is expected to have worked efficiently for fifteen minutes, but not to have completed the full assignment. Mr. Lusolo and the group solve some of the problems together, and he works with them on an illustration of a problem.) About ten minutes before the period ends, Mr. Lusolo brings the whole class back together. Students from one of the groups display and explain their illustration, and Mr. Lusolo winds up with a brief summary of the day's lesson. He makes it a practice to restate and discuss, for the entire class, a question or difficulty expressed by someone in the group he met with, commending the student or students who raised the point.

Getting his program started at the beginning of the year, Mr. Lusolo uses Solve Aloud and introduces group work at the second class session, assigns homework beginning with the third session, and by the second week of school, students are working capably in this routine. Four days a week the students have a math assignment for homework: on two of these days they have additional practice problems to solve. The other two assignments are to make a word poster illustrating a math term or concept and to find a math-related item in a magazine, newspaper, or similar publication, and write a brief explanation for their math journal about its relationship to a math concept the class has studied. When he introduces math journals he models a variety of entries, then includes journaling as an activity to be done in cooperative groups. During the next several weeks he introduces activities that will be available at workstations, beginning with computer activities, Typical to Technical Meaning, and math and logic challenges. From this point on, he has several workstations going during cooperative learning time. The stations are set up at the sides of the room, arranged so there is enough room for a cooperative group to work at each, in pairs or triads. In addition to the workstations, there is a desk that serves as a classroom research center, with reference books: atlases, an almanac, a dictionary, and several copies of a trade book by Mary Blocksma, *Reading the numbers: A survival guide to the measurements, numbers, and sizes encountered in everyday life* (1989). Students refer to these resource books during journal writing and when they are creating math problems.

▌**Linking math and literature.** He gives no homework on weekends, and every Friday he has a short read-aloud period at the end of class instead of the lecture. He keeps an accordion file of clippings (poems, essays, columns) as well as a bookrack on his desk. He often reads short items and excerpts because he knows students would have difficulty remembering and attending to a long story divided into many short read-aloud sessions over many weeks. He sometimes links his reading aloud to what some or all of the students in a class are studying in another class; for example, he reads from Russell Freedman's *Immigrant kids* (1995) when students are studying immigration in American history, and *Childtimes: A three-generation memoir* by Eloise Greenfield and Lessie Jones Little (1993) as an example of family histories, as a link to the events over the last century, and as part of African-American history. He has had a lot of practice in reading aloud, and he knows that he almost always keeps students' interested, but he also relies on one simple technique that helps avoid distraction: when he reads aloud he stands at the opposite side of the room from the wall where the clock is. That way he can always judge the time, so that he can end class promptly, but students are looking at him and never at the clock.

Soon after he begins reading aloud to the class, he sets up another workstation—"the bookstation"—where there are always half a dozen trade books, including those he has recently used for read-alouds. Students use these as models for creating original math-related books; making graphs, charts, and time-lines; and devising story-based math problems. Sometimes read-aloud time and bookstation books are linked to a theme. For example, during the study of measurement, he invites an architect and a construction engineer as guest speakers; he reads aloud excerpts from *Homemade houses: Traditional homes from many lands* (Nicholson, 1993) and *Round buildings, square buildings, & buildings that wiggle like a fish* (Isaacson, 1988), and places these and other books related to architecture at the bookstation.

Of course, he also treats the bookstation as an opportunity for his students to enlarge their awareness and love of books. He and his wife often suggest books to each other, and he puts beautifully illustrated children's books and books about art there for his students to use as the basis for the word problems. Favorite books include *Spirals, curves, fanshapes and lines*, a wordless book of color photographs by Tana Hoban (1992), and Lucy Micklethwait's *I spy two eyes: Numbers in art* (1992), in which the numbers from 1 to 20 are matched with beautiful paintings. He finds that books with easy text are good resources for writing challenging math problems, and he believes it also is important for students who may not have encountered much good children's literature when they were younger to have the opportunity to use such books now, in a way that does not make their use seem demeaning. Do some students reject the math activities at the bookstation because they want to read and reread

the books? Of course. And that's "a problem" only because his students need to be capable and enthusiastic mathematicians as well as readers. One part of the solution is that cooperative groups are assigned to the bookstation on a rotating basis, about once every two weeks. The more powerful part of the solution is that Mr. Lusolo makes a point of noticing which students are particularly absorbed in the books. He then arranges with individual students for a book to be borrowed, with a special assignment to complete book-related math activities as homework.

■ **Something special.** Special activities in Mr. Lusolo's classes usually occur on Mondays—there is no homework over the weekend, thus one part of cooperative group work is unnecessary. Special activities early in the year include introducing and modeling a new strategy, which then becomes part of cooperative group work or a workstation activity. Search tasks, which introduce new units or chapters that have many new features, are always scheduled on Mondays. LEAD-style discussions using math vocabulary are another special activity that uses an entire class session. When Mr. Lusolo uses the Graphic Information Lesson strategy, which he does about three times a year, he devotes an entire class session to it, follows up with cooperative group work, and concludes with another whole class session at which students' work is shared and discussed. The exception to Monday specials is when another day is more convenient for a guest speaker. Guest speakers are people from the community, including family members, who have agreed to come to class to talk about the ways that math relates to their work. During these talks/demonstrations, students take notes using a RESPONSE form, and afterwards they have the opportunity to ask the speaker to respond to some of their questions. They have a homework assignment to summarize the speaker's main points, based on their RESPONSE notes. They keep the RESPONSE forms in their math journals and draw upon them for ideas when each cooperative group prepares a thank-you note for the speaker.

Over the summer, Mr. Lusolo reviews, revises, and extends his plans and materials for the year. He enjoys writing new math and logic puzzles; some of these are based on trade books. Other summer preparation includes working on materials for the Graphic Information Lesson strategy, because he has only used it for a few years and wants to continue to add to his teacher-created pseudographics. Otherwise, he occasionally reviews or adds to materials, but those he has created are usable year after year. For example, since mathematical terminology doesn't differ from textbook to textbook, ideas for LEAD discussions and Typical to Technical Meaning materials do not change. The kind of planning done over the summer changes every six years, however, when the district changes its math textbook series. This has happened twice during Mr. Lusolo's career, and in the two summers before new texts were introduced, he spent most of his time creating textbook-related activities—a Text Hunt and a series of Search Tasks for each textbook—and annotating the textbook for places to use Graphic Information Lessons and deciding where Solve Alouds would be most important.

One of the aspects of planning that the whole family enjoys is the collection of materials for vicarious field trips—a strategy devised by Mr. Lusolo, which he calls No-Travel Trips. He likes this strategy not only because it draws on his ingenuity and that of his students, but because it does not require him to spend time on things he finds tedious, such as getting administrative approval for a trip, collecting money and permission slips, arranging transportation, and supervising students while traveling, and it doesn't take time away from his math program or cause students to miss other classes. A No-Travel Trip is a two- or three-week imaginary excursion to another place (for practical reasons, usually a place that the Lusolos have visited). It begins with a short slide show followed by a brainstorming session in which students contribute as many different answers as they can to the question, "How does this relate to math?" Students become very adept at giving answers: "Compare the height of the office buildings," "Figure out the cost of getting there by train, car, and plane," "Graph the population compared to other cities in the state." Then several workstations are set up with maps of the area; postcards; historical information; statistics about population, education, industry, agriculture, and tourism; information from organizations for travelers giving prices for transportation, housing, meals, and admission to places of interest. Each cooperative group plans a trip, estimates day-by-day costs, and computes the total cost of their trip. They also prepare a trip-related project of their choice, such as a timeline of historical events, a brochure giving statistics about the area, or a set of math challenges inspired by postcards or maps. When Mr. Lusolo thought of this idea six years ago, he began with one No-Travel Trip and has since expanded his repertoire substantially. In addition to trips based on his family's travels, he now has materials for trips to other countries that have been supplied by student' families, and he recently added a shorter version: No-Travel Trips Around Town. These begin with a visit from the owner of a local business, for example, a bookstore or restaurant, who gives a guest lecture and leaves materials, such as posters and newsletters about books or restaurant menus. Students then plan shopping trips or excursions within a specified budget.

▌**Newsletters.** Mr. Lusolo prepares and sends home newsletters, describing the math program, about six times a year. One thing he has learned is not to commit himself to a set number of newsletters or an established time, such as once a month, so the heading is always something like *Eighth Grade Math News* and a date. He uses the same newsletter format for all classes, but prepares different newsletters for seventh and eighth grades and sometimes individualizes them for classes, if, for example, a guest speaker comes to one class but not to another. He uses the personalized newsletter style, with three-fourths of a page printed with information and the remaining quarter of a page left for students to write a message to their families. When students' families are not fluent in English, he asks the students to work with him, using a word processing program on the computer to write a translation that summarizes the news, if they can do so, and if the family's native language uses the English alphabet. Sometimes a student who is learning English works with a classmate on the translation; sometimes a parent volunteer prepares the translation and discusses it with the student. For several years now, he has used the same article, shown on this page, as part of the first newsletter sent home to all classes.

Challenge to the Reader: Draft a plan for a newsletter about Mr. Lusolo's program, choosing topics for articles and deciding on a format.

Choose and Use: If you were to choose one aspect of Mr. Lusolo's program to use in your own classroom, what would it be and how would you begin?

Family Members Can Be Part of Our Math Program

If you can come to school...

- Would you be able to come to math class once during the year to talk to a class about the ways mathematics is important in your work? We welcome guest speakers. Talks last about 20-30 minutes, with time afterward for students to ask questions.

- Are you able to be a math mentor for a student who has shown strong talent and interest in mathematics? Mentors need to be able to commit time to meet with their students during the school day, either once or twice a month.

If you can help us from your home...

- Are you a fluent reader, in English or in another language spoken by students in our school, who would be willing to tape record (or translate and tape record) excerpts from our math textbook?

- Do you have word processing capability from your home that you could use to prepare final copies of student-written materials for publication or for bulletin board displays?

- Do you enjoy solving math problems? One of the many math assignments students have is to create and solve original math problems. Each year students are so productive that I have a hard time keeping up with them. It's very useful if one or several family members volunteer to read, check, and edit students' work. I will supply guidelines.

If you would like to volunteer for one of these opportunities, please send a note to the school, or leave a message for me at the the school office: XXX-XXXX.

PART FOUR

Extending Content Area Learning

CHAPTER TEN

Integration of Listening, Speaking, Reading, and Writing in Content Area Study

Human beings are gifted and talented in naming the objects and inhabitants of their world. They are also brilliant symbolizers— inventing metaphors and similes, imagery and symbols to enrich the naming. They are askers of questions and explorers searching for answers. They are playful, making jokes and riddles and puns. …They give words to their deepest dreams and try to find words to comfort them through darkest times. I think of language as being at the core of our thinking, learning, and living.

MIMI BRODSKY CHENFELD, 1987A, P. 75.

Teaching and learning in the content areas depend on language, so language in all of its aspects is an inseparable part of content area study. Language is not confined to English classes; listening and reading, speaking and writing are essential elements of learning mathematics, science and social studies, and every branch of study in middle and high school, and literacy and oracy are necessary for careers and satisfying lives in our society. The *effective* **integration** of content area study and listening, speaking, reading, and writing is based on teachers' knowledge and teachers' decisions.

With thought, ingenuity, and the ongoing professional development that keeps us aware of new ideas, we can create classrooms in which the different facets of language—speaking as well as listening, writing as well as reading—enhance learning about content area topics. With attention and care, we can create classroom environments that are language-rich, language-comfortable places to learn. Not only is sensible attention to aspects of what is termed language arts a way to enhance content area

---

integration—is derived, like many other English words, from Latin. It comes from *integratus*, a form of the verb *integrare*, meaning *to renew*, or to *make whole*. That Latin word is the combination of a prefix, *in-*, meaning *not*, and another verb, *tangere*, meaning *to touch*. Something that is untouched is whole; the word *integer*, meaning a whole number, has the same Latin root. So does the word *integrity*, referring to the quality of wholeness, of having sound principles for living.

study, the converse is also true: content area topics are interesting and challenging to read, write, talk, and hear about. Each of the strategies presented throughout this book emphasizes one or more language modes, so choosing and using a variety of strategies integrates language arts and content area study. When strategies are thoughtfully combined, the modes of language—reading, writing, listening, and speaking—are not added to content study, they are an integral part of it.

Language can be classified as receptive or expressive, depending on whether it is used to receive information (through listening and reading) or to express information (through speaking and writing). Modes of language also can be classified as oral (listening and speaking) or as written (reading and writing). It is this second method of classification that is commonly used in education. Because this is a literate society, in which we expect that a great deal of knowledge will be transmitted through written text, we emphasize the importance of literacy and distinguish between literate and illiterate people on the basis of the ability to read and write.

Developmentally, the oral modes of language precede the written modes. Except for people with severe sensory impairments, skill in listening and speaking begins to develop rapidly at birth, and the later development of the ability to read and write is built upon already acquired skillful use of oral language modes. In recent years, scholars and educators have stressed the importance of oral as well as written language in learning. The term *oracy* was originated about 30 years ago as a parallel for *literacy* by the British scholar Andrew Wilkinson (1965), who defined oracy as general ability in the skills of speaking and listening. The strategies described in this chapter are designed to engage students as active language users during content area study. The first focus is on oracy, engaging students in content area learning through activities that emphasize listening and speaking and that link oral and written language. A second section of the chapter focuses on literacy, particularly on ways to use writing in content area learning. The chapter concludes with a section stressing the importance of creating classrooms that are language-rich, language-respectful, language-pleasant places to learn.

■■ Oracy: Speaking and Listening in ■■ Content Area Learning

One difference between oral and written language is that speaking and listening usually are closely linked in time and space. In the classroom, speaker and listener(s) are in the same place (an exception is when students listen to audio or audiovisual materials) and engaged in thinking about the same topic (an exception is when a speaker does not have the attention of others). This closeness makes interaction easy. Speakers can become listeners and listeners can become speakers, and each person's knowledge of a topic can grow as information is exchanged, considered, and clarified.

For students to learn effectively from listening and speaking, they need many opportunities to do both. It is a sad truth that in many classrooms listening is the major activity expected of students: teachers talk; students listen. In such classrooms, students often are differentiated on the basis of how attentively and effectively they listen. In such classrooms "good students" are those who are able to be (or appear to be) attentive for long periods of time and who grasp directions quickly, even from teachers who threaten, "Listen carefully, because I'm only going to say this once." Many students acquire the belief that listening is a form of good behavior, rather than a method of getting information, during their early years in school. In an article titled, "Children's beliefs about listening: Is it enough to be still and quiet?" researchers reported the results of structured interviews with elementary children. Students, particularly those in the early grades, typically did not connect listening with any purpose, but thought of it as a form of required self-control. One child defined "a good listener" as someone who "doesn't play with her pencils" (McDevitt, Spivey, Sheehan, Lennon, & Story, 1990, p. 715). The phrase often used in directions—*pay attention!*—implies that, in school, listening is an obligation—attention is owed and must be paid—rather than an opportunity to learn.

Learning through listening is most effective when both purposes exist: to listen out of respect to the speaker and to listen to add to a store of knowledge—to discover something we are interested in knowing. (Think of the phrase that is often used, outside of school, by a speaker to attract the attention of listeners: *"You know what?"*) Listening to find out is the more important purpose, but learning through listening is fostered in an environment where it is expected that speakers will be heard with attention. The process is cyclical. When what listeners hear is interesting and positive, they are likely to attend and learn. Learning through listening then becomes habitual, not because of scolding and admonitions to attend, but because what is heard is valued.

Teachers need to be good listeners. It is particularly important to model attentive listening when endeavoring to promote good listening habits directly. Rebecca Brent and Patricia Anderson (1993) compare two classrooms in which students shared their writing by reading it aloud to classmates. In one classroom, students were cautioned, "remember to be good listeners" and constantly admonished if they were not attending. In the other, the teacher prepared students for the activity by a minilesson on listening strategies, (watching the speaker, setting a purpose for listening, thinking of questions while listening, blocking distractions), and then herself followed these guidelines by giving her complete attention to the student who was speaking. In that classroom, teacher and students were interested in and attentive to the speakers, whereas in the other classroom the teacher was the most inattentive of all, since she was fully involved in watching the group for signs of misbehavior and giving reprimands.

Engaging Students Actively As Listeners

Several of the strategies that have been presented in earlier chapters are based on students listening to their teacher. Teachers speak to give information directly to students in Teacher Read-Aloud Commentaries, Solve Alouds, Reference Source Commentaries, and Previews. Instructional talking is the essence of mini-lessons and the SAY-IT and FYI strategies, and an essential part of Refutational Teaching. In the Guided Imagery strategy, teachers' descriptions make a topic come alive. In all of these strategies, teacher talk is topic-focused, relatively

brief, and usually followed by opportunities for students to talk together in learning groups. Other strategies, described below, are based on active listening by students: the Structured Listening Activity, RESPONSE to speakers, and Collaborative Listening-Viewing Guide.

Structured Listening Activity (SLA). The Structured Listening Activity (Choate & Rakes, 1987) is designed to engage students as listeners who learn, while giving them guided experience in listening. That experience will then be transferable to other situations in which they will be expected to acquire and organize information gained from a lecture style of instruction or from hearing text read aloud. The strategy is useful over a wide age range. Jeanne Swafford and Tamara Paulos (1993) have described a Structured Listening Activity, based on Joanna Cole's The magic school bus at the waterworks (1986) as a component of second-grade science study of the water cycle. Figure 10–1 gives an example of an SLA suitable for middle or high school students. The strategy has five components. The first step consists of concept building, engaging students in activities that will provide a shared knowledge base about what they will hear. If a Structured Listening Activity will be used toward the beginning of a topic of study, a strategy that develops conceptual vocabulary, such as LEAD (described in Chapter Three), might be used. Next, the teacher sets purposes for listening, telling students what information to listen for and perhaps also providing a visual aid in the form of a chart with questions that will be answered through listening. The third step in an SLA process—reading aloud or giving a lecture—is interwoven with the fourth component, in which the speaker gives listeners the opportunity to answer literal, interpretive, and critical questions about what they have been hearing. The final step consists of teacher-led group summarization. For younger students, this might include arranging pictures in sequence and creating a group Language Experience Activity story that retells what has been learned, while older students might brainstorm and organize main points before working in pairs to summarize what has been learned and to do further reading.

FIGURE 10–1   Structured Listening Activity Based on *Lincoln: A Photobiography,* by Russell Freedman

Background: As part of an American History course, this class uses biographies extensively. Reading three or more biographies (in whole or part) of a single historical figure is the basis for short reports; the teacher reads aloud regularly from biographies and oral histories; cooperative groups base class presentations and murals on their study of people who have influenced, or are influencing, the country's history. Teacher and students particularly enjoy Russell Freedman's photobiographies and later in the year the class will read *Kids at work: Lewis Hine and the crusade against child labor* (Freedman, 1994) and the teacher will read aloud excerpts from Studs Terkel's *Hard times: An oral history of the great depression* (1970) and *American dreams: Lost and found* (1980).

The teacher uses this Structured Listening Activity early in the year for multiple purposes: to engage students in active listening through a strategy that will be used periodically throughout the course, to prepare students for learning through listening to teacher read-alouds, and, most important, to introduce a concept that will be stressed throughout the course:

Not only is each person complex (so that it is difficult to acquire an accurate picture, even with much study), but also those who comment upon the person do so from personal perspectives, which cannot be wholly complete and accurate, and which may change over time. Nevertheless, historians and biographers who write after extensive study, and who do not try to sensationalize their subjects, give us our knowledge of people and of times.

Depending on the time available, the SLA described below may extend over two or three days, exclusive of the time given to follow-up activities. If time permits, the first three steps, and part of the fourth, can occur on the first day, and the SLA can be completed on the second day.

Structured Listening Activity: The five steps

▮ For concept building, because students do have prior knowledge about Lincoln, the teacher uses the List-Group-Label strategy. As a whole class activity, students brainstorm items of information about Lincoln, then decide how the items should be grouped into categories. Listing the items and marking the categories is done on the board by the teacher, and cooperative groups will later transfer the items to charts.

▮ The teacher, who is using this activity to develop students' understanding of a sophisticated concept, sets the purpose for listening, "Listen to learn about what people thought of Lincoln, during his life and after his death," and displays this concept statement on a chart that is visible during the remainder of the SLA:

All people are complex, and no one can know everything about them. Sometimes biographers have a great deal of material to use in learning about a person; sometimes they have very limited resources.

Each person who tells or writes about another person does so from a personal perspective, and the full picture we are given of the person they describe cannot be entirely complete or accurate. Others may present a very different impression of the same person. Moreover, the way people are viewed may change over time, during their lifetimes and afterwards.

Good biographers, like all good historians, collect information widely, and analyze and interpret the information they have. "Having read the volumes concerned and in large part studied the evidence on which these works are based, I make my own interpretation and shall stand by it" (Catherine Drinker Bowen, 1966, xiii). When we read biographies, we analyze and interpret what we read. *

▮ The teacher reads aloud "The Mysterious Mr. Lincoln," the first chapter of *Lincoln: A photobiography,* using the *Teacher-Read Aloud Commentary* strategy.

▮ Calling attention to the concept statement that is displayed, the teacher elicits instances from the chapter that illustrate alternative and changing views of Lincoln, in his own time, and across the years since. As students contribute ideas, the teacher probes for reasons for the disparities; for example, Why do you think that for a period during his presidency Lincoln was so unpopular? What reasons can you think of that might have caused Frederick Douglass's views about Lincoln to change?

▮ The teacher leads the group in summarizing the information gained and the ideas shared. Then cooperative groups prepare semantic maps about Lincoln, incorporating items from the List-Group-Label activity used at the beginning of SLA. The remaining six chapters of the book are divided among cooperative groups who will use a jigsaw strategy to share information. The concept statement will be a point of reference for the class throughout the course, and the semantic maps will be revised as students learn more.

**The quotation in this passage is from *Miracle at Philadelphia: The story of the constitutional convention May to September 1787* by the historian Catherine Drinker Bowen. The book was first published in Boston by Little Brown in 1966.*

RESPONSE to Speakers.   The RESPONSE strategy, described in Chapter Four, is typically used for structured note-taking while reading; however, students also can use RESPONSE forms to take notes during a presentation, such as a talk by a guest speaker, thus prepare themselves to ask good questions afterwards. In the RESPONSE strategy, students use a sheet of paper divided into sections to take notes in three categories: important points, questions, and new terms. Students should be familiar with the strategy before using it as part of a listening activity, particularly when it is used while listening to a guest speaker. In this case, the speaker also should know in advance that students will be taking notes during the presentation. The questions jotted down on the RESPONSE form will provide the basis for an active question-and-answer period after the lecture. Forms collected after the talk by the teacher serve as a record of students' grasp of important ideas and as a reminder of students' questions that remain to be answered.

Collaborative Listening-Viewing Guide.   Excellent videotapes often are available to teachers through media centers or central libraries. Supplementing classroom instruction with well-chosen tapes can be useful, and many tapes are available captioned for students with hearing impairments. The Collaborative Listening-Viewing Guide strategy (Wood, 1990) is intended as a notetaking strategy when videotapes are used instructionally. As in the Structured Listening Activity, there are five components. First, as a whole class activity, the teacher previews the information that is to be learned if the video is used at the beginning of learning about a topic, or reviews through brainstorming, if it is a concluding activity. Then students record their notes, individually, during their viewing. Notes must be brief, but they also must be made in sequence, so they will be more easily understood later. The remaining three steps occur after viewing. In small groups, students share their notes and elaborate and extend them. Then as a whole class, the group synthesizes their learning in discussion. Finally, students work in pairs on a teacher-assigned culminating activity, such as Concept Connections, to use important terminology, or

transmediation, to present information in the form of a poster, poem, or skit.

Linking Listening and Speaking

Strategies presented in earlier chapters that engage students in listening and speaking include brainstorming, idea-sharing, and discussion-based strategies such as Semantic Mapping and List-Group-Label, the Significant Sayings and Experience-Text-Relationship strategies, LEAD and Terminology Trade, and roundtable and poster session presentations of research findings. Additionally, every strategy with a cooperative learning component necessarily involves oral language. Listening and speaking are combined when students are actively engaged in discussions and debates and when they participate in impromptu and more formal dramatic activities. Storytelling, discussed in Chapter Eleven, is an ideal method of linking the oral language modes. Andrew Wilkinson (1991) makes an interesting distinction between opportunities for student talk, based on whether speakers are expected to take short turns, as in discussions, or long turns, as in storytelling.

In all content areas students may be given the regular assignment of bringing to class a relevant newspaper or magazine article to summarize for the class. (This procedure is particularly easy to incorporate in health, civics, and science classes.) Current events sharing can be built into the instructional program at times when students are both relaxed and prepared to listen actively, for example, as the concluding activity in a high school class once a week, or in the elementary school when everyone is settled quietly for snacktime or has listened quietly to a short read-aloud after returning from an active recess or gym period. Discussions can be used to introduce topics in every content area—activating, building upon, and enhancing students' prior knowledge. In math and science, students can brainstorm ways in which mathematical processes and scientific information are important in daily living. After working on problem solving, students can share ideas about alternate ways to reach correct solutions. Social studies learning is enhanced when students discuss similarities and differences between the present and past, especially when such discussions are founded on a strong knowledge base. Debates and simulations are a more formal kind of discussion, which should be presented only after research and careful preparation so the information shared is thorough and sound.

Communication Apprehension

In classrooms where there is little opportunity for student talk, it is often customary for students to be required to speak to the class as an occasional assignment. The instructional purpose for making students engage in this kind of public speaking is typically to help them develop communication skills. Instead, many students develop communication apprehension. This fear of speaking in front of others, which may have a lifelong impact, has been defined as "a pattern of anxiety, established often in the elementary grades, which can profoundly affect much or all of a student's oral communication, social skills, and self-esteem" (Holbrook, 1987, p. 554). Communication apprehension may be prevented or counteracted when teachers establish a comfortable classroom environment in which students can get to know one another early in the year and have many opportunities to work together, and in which idea sharing is constantly occurring, rather than being confined to a limited number of formal speaking assignments that are long anticipated and formally evaluated. Drama and role-playing, speaking in groups or panels composed of self-chosen classmates, and speaking from their seats rather than when standing before a group are ways of increasing students' comfort in speaking. Perhaps the most important factor in whether students talk readily in a classroom setting is whether there are interesting ideas to talk about.

Engaging Students Actively As Speakers

When teachers speak and students listen, there is no problem in arranging how talk time will be shared, because there is one speaker with many listeners. When teachers plan to share talk time by using discussion as an instructional strategy, prob-

lems of two kinds may arise. One problem arises when students enjoy the opportunity to speak in a group so much that it is difficult for everyone to have equal opportunity for turns to talk. Two methods of structuring shared talk are Talking Chips (Baloche, Mauger, Willis, Filinuk, & Michalsky, 1993), and Paraphrase Passport (Kagan, 1989/1990). The Talking Chips technique involves giving each student three plastic chips. As students contribute to the discussion, they give up a chip, thus each student is limited to three turns. The Paraphrase Passport method is a useful way to encourage students to listen carefully. Each speaker, as a "ticket for talking," must begin by giving a brief restatement of what the previous speaker has said. These strategies should be used occasionally rather than consistently in an atmosphere where students enjoy and are interested by the strategy as well as the discussion. They should not be imposed by the teacher to correct students. It is important for teachers to find ways for students to have opportunities to share ideas freely. The Talk Story method, described in Chapter Seven, serves this purpose. Working in cooperative groups multiplies the opportunities for talk time because conversations are occurring simultaneously in each group. Another form of idea sharing is through writing, because everyone can write at once. Journals (discussed below) enable students to express their ideas at length, if they choose, and several types of journals are a written form of conversation with one or more participants.

A different problem occurs when students, rather than wanting to talk more, are reluctant to talk in a classroom group. Donna Alvermann and David Hayes (1989, pp. 330–331) suggest, on the basis of their observations of content area classroom discussions, that these activities "generally resembled recitation rather than give-and-take dialogue between teacher and students" and that it was difficult to get teachers to change their pattern of simply asking questions and calling on students to answer. Under these circumstances, students' reluctance to participate is understandable. Strategies that provide structure and support for sharing ideas and that help the teacher find a way to step out of the role of questioner encourage students to overcome their reluctance to share ideas.

Say Something.   One gentle, easily used strategy, suggested by Barbara Lindberg, provides a relaxed setting and alleviates students' anxiety about having nothing to say. The class arranges their desks in a circle and the teacher reads aloud, stopping occasionally. Whenever the teacher stops reading, a designated student says something, which gives the strategy its name: Say Something. It is a feature of the strategy that comments are not judged. "Anything a person says is acceptable and deserves a serious response" (Lindberg, 1988, p. 733). Shelley Lindauer (1988, p. 139) makes a similar comment when she writes, "It is not the teacher's role to suggest what [students] should look for or see." When the strategy is first used, the teacher models the commenting process by noting an interesting word or phrase, raising a question, or giving a personal opinion. When a student has commented, others may add their contributions freely. There is no hand-raising or waiting to be called upon. Then the teacher resumes reading, pauses again at a good stopping point, and the next student takes the responsibility to "say something." During the Say Something reading, the teacher's "serious response" that Lindberg refers to is best given as a nod, a smile, a look of approval. If teachers respond in words to what students say during the reading, the flow of the story will be lost.

The possibilities for books to use during Say Something are endless, but learning is increased if the reading material is connected to class interests and study topics. The brief example below showing how a Say Something might begin is based on *The tree of life: The world of the African baobab,* by Barbara Bash (1989). The book describes the life cycle of the world's longest-lived trees and the support it gives to other life forms, interwoven with views of the African savannah. There also is a brief pourquoi story explaining the tree's unusual appearance. *Pourquoi stories*—the name comes from the French word that means *why*—are common to all cultures. (The word *pourquoi* is pronounced *poor-kwah*.) These stories provide imaginative answers to explain events in the natural world that are not yet understood scientifically.)

In the oldest times, as the !Kung Bushmen of Africa tell the story, the Great Spirit gave each animal a tree to plant. Hyena arrived late and was given the very last tree, the baobab.

Sheela: That's the hyena by the tree. I saw hyenas at the zoo.

Being a careless creature, he planted it upside down—and that is why its branches look like gnarled roots.

Alan: We planted seeds upside down once, to see what happened.

The baobab grows on the dry savannahs of Africa. Reaching crookedly into the air, it stands silent and ancient.

Yael: I wonder why the grass is yellow.

Notice what is, and what is not, a part of Say Something. There are dozens of points where the teacher could stop to comment and explain, but this is never done. Reading and pausing to explain is part of the Teacher Read-Aloud Commentary strategy, described in Chapter Three, where the purpose is to develop a pre-reading knowledge base. That strategy can be accomplished quickly because only the teacher comments and only a short portion of text is used. In Say Something there is a longer text, a book or a chapter, and students' comments are an integral part of the strategy. The strategy does not take an excessive amount of time because the process is solely a cycle of read-aloud, comment, read-aloud, comment. Group discussion and finding the answers to questions can be added when the Say Something read-aloud is over. Particularly for younger students, some stories may call for actions rather than words; in this case, the teacher may change the strategy to *Do Something*, pausing periodically in the reading to invite children (as many who wish to participate) to do something in response to the story or its illustrations.

When the Say Something strategy is blended with re-reading a favorite book, students' understanding is enhanced and deepened. In this case, Say Something is used after a book has been read and enjoyed repeatedly. One of a wide range of possibilities is *Shortcut*, written and illustrated by noted artist Donald Crews (1992), an exciting picture book conveying an important safety message—don't walk on the train tracks!—as Crews retells a true story from his own childhood. (Older students engaged in oral history projects may be interested in the book as an example of a remembered event being presented in book form.) Dramatic but limited text—on several pages the only words are the "klak-klakity-klak" as the long train passes—is likely to evoke elaborated responses from listeners.

Language development can be fostered through the Say Something strategy in a variety of ways, depending on the choice of books. Typically, the strategy is used with picture books and the teacher reads holding up the book while moving it so that students can see. (Teachers reading picture books need to develop the skill of reading while looking at a book from the side, holding it up, and moving it smoothly so all students have a chance to see the pictures. This will eliminate cries of "I can't see." Having a read-aloud book available for students to look at singly or with a partner later also is helpful.) However, the Say Something strategy can be used with books written for older students and adults as well, so a teacher's pauses for students' comments need not come at the end of a page since there are usually no pictures to show. When a whole class of students is reading the same book, beginning a session with a Say Something based on a portion of text is a useful way to precede cooperative group reading. The circular seating arrangement is not necessary, nor is turn-taking. Students can make their comments in Talk Story fashion, without being called on, thus multiple comments may be made when a teacher pauses.

Just as Say Something can be used with books that have no pictures, it also can be used with books that have nothing but pictures. The genre of wordless picture books has become a rich field, and the constraints of telling a story without words requires thoughtful sequencing by the illustrator-author. "The fact that wordless books do not have text to serve as cues for the story line has motivated the most gifted and perceptive authors/illustrators to sequence their tales beautifully through detailed illustration" (Lindauer, 1988, p. 137). These books are an excellent resource for comments by prereaders as well as readers and by students who are in the process of learning English.

Some books that rely on pictures to provide their stories are conceptually very challenging. The stories they evoke will be different, depending on the sophistication of the tellers. An almost-wordless example in the realm of fantasy is *The Mysteries of Harris Burdick* by Chris Van Allsburg (1984), which purports to be a collection of captioned pictures, submitted to a publisher by an author who never returned to claim them. The wit and humor of *Tuesday*, David Wiesner's (1991) Caldecott-award winner, is in the illustrations; its few words simply tell the time—"Tuesday evening, around eight," "11:21 P.M.," "4:38 A.M.," "next Tuesday, 7:58 P.M."—when frogs, and later other animals, will be flying through the air. Jeannie Baker's *Window* (1991) illustrates ecological risk by a series of pictures in which we see the outdoors through a window in a house, often as if we were standing behind someone. In the first picture, a mother holding a red-haired baby looks out over spacious wilderness. In subsequent pictures, the growth of the child to manhood gives us information about the passage of time as we see the area around the house become increasingly crowded and polluted; in the final picture, a red-haired man, looking out another window, again holds a child. The book is wordless until the final author's note, which discusses environmental dangers.

Several publishing houses are now producing children's books translated into languages other than English—the same format, the same bright illustrations as the English version, but with text solely in another language. Most of these books in translation are Spanish versions. In a classroom that includes Spanish-speaking students, they can be used with the Say Something strategy, with or without the teacher reading the text. Among many examples are *¡Salta, Ranita, Salta!* (Kalan, 1994) and *Llaman a la puerta* (Hutchins, 1994). Because the books were originally written for prereaders and beginning readers, the text is repetitive, the story line is easy to follow, and the large, colorful illustrations help tell the tale. In *Llaman a la puerta*, a plateful of mama's cookies disappears as more and more friends come to share them, until the day is saved by one more person at the door, *Abuela*, grandmother, bringing a huge tray of cookies, enough for all. In *¡Salta, Ranita, Salta!* a frog is threatened by a fish, a snake, a turtle, and children who wish to capture it. What advice will we give to the frog? *¡Salta, ranita, salta!*—jump, frog, jump! A teacher who speaks Spanish can read the book aloud; students can comment in English, and those whose primary language is Spanish can be a resource for their classmates. A teacher who does not speak Spanish can treat the book as a wordless picture book and invite students to tell the story. Students can also, as in the Daily Journal strategy described later in this chapter, pick out words and phrases they can understand. The strategy also can be used in introductory language courses for middle school and high school students. Its use is an application of the whole language principle that speaking and reading are best learned in language-rich, print-rich environments, where people are actively engaged with books. The concept of comprehensible input—that students learn when what they are hearing and reading is challenging but within their range of understanding—also is relevant.

One of the usual features of Say Something is a circular seating arrangement. This enables all of the students to see one another and signals that the obligation to talk will rotate. When there is difficulty getting a good discussion started and keeping it going, altering seating arrangements away from a standard desks-in-rows pattern is likely to be useful. Several educators have suggested ways to structure discussions by organizing the placement of people within the group. Both the U Debate strategy, discussed in Chapter Five, and Fishbowl Discussions, discussed below, have unique seating arrangements. The Fishbowl Discussion strategy also has a metacognitive component: the strategy encourages students to consider the constructive features of the discussion as it is occurring.

Fishbowl Discussions. Another way to organize and support discussion through a seating structure is to arrange seats in two concentric circles—the inner circle for discussants (fish) and the outer circle (the bowl) for their observers. The discussion relates to a topic the class has been studying, so there is a sound knowledge base. Lynda Baloche and her colleagues (Baloche et al., 1993) recommend having an equal number of seats in each circle. The

teacher assigns students to either the inner or outer circle, or students may choose their role by choosing where to sit. Those in the inner circle have seven or eight minutes to discuss an assigned topic. In the outer circle, each student focuses on one student in inner circle (their "fish"). Using a worksheet, they tally that student's contributions to the discussion, counting the number of times the person contributes a new idea, paraphrases another student's ideas, supports or accepts the ideas of others, encourages others to contribute, summarizes, focuses or refocuses the discussion, or relieves tension by joking. After the discussion, observers commend the students they watched on the basis of the tally they have kept. Calling attention to positive ways of discussing ideas encourages students to use these tactics. An alternative way to use a fishbowl strategy (Priles, 1993) is to have a smaller ring of discussants and a larger outer ring of observers, recorders, and affirmers. In this arrangement, two additional seats are placed opposite one another, slightly outside of the inner circle but still a part of it, so observers who wish to can move into the discussion, contribute, and then withdraw.

Bringing Closure to a Discussion. Adept teachers keep the time in mind. Rather than have a discussion ended by the close of a class period, it is useful to allow about five minutes for wind-up activities. A minor but helpful management technique for teachers to use toward the end of class is to stand opposite to the wall clock. In this way, the teacher, who has the clock in view, can pace the concluding instruction so that class is sure to end on time; the students, on the other hand, are facing the teacher and are not distracted by watching the clock. Teachers may end a discussion by giving a quick summary, or they may engage students in sharing concluding thoughts. The following are some possible organizing ideas: What conclusion did we reach? If we continue the discussion, what question should we start with? What are one or two ideas raised in discussion that you hadn't thought of before? Younger students may give their responses orally, while the teacher makes a written record. For older students, the last few minutes of class may be allotted for quick, written responses to one of these questions, with papers to be handed in at the end of class. The written responses give information to the teacher about students' learning from the discussion; credit may be given for doing the assignment and turning in a paper, but the responses should not be corrected or graded.

Responding To What Students Say

Later in this chapter is a section titled "Responding to students' writing." Teachers are familiar with that phrase and with the idea that they have a responsibility to comment helpfully on students' written work. Ways of responding to what students *say*, when their task is to contribute orally during classroom instruction, are less often considered. Jane Schaffer, in an article titled "Improving discussion questions: Is anyone out there listening?" points out the importance of acknowledging students' contributions in a straightforward manner.

> I asked my students what teachers do when some-one gives an inaccurate or incomplete response to a question. Most said that the teacher ignores the answer, pretends it hasn't been said, and moves on to another student.
>
> I asked what they would like teachers to do instead. They said they wanted to be recognized as having spoken, and if they were wrong, to be told so in a kind or humane way. They did not want to be ignored or dismissed; it made them feel like a nonentity. (Schaffer, 1989, p. 42)

One of the talents teachers should strive to develop is the ability to see what is reasonable and relevant in students' comments. Often, when we have a solid knowledge base about a topic we will be able to see that an incorrect answer is the result of a reasonable, intelligent misunderstanding, something that we can explain and clarify on the spot. Suppose, in a discussion of influential figures in history, a student names Benjamin Franklin as an important person in the seventeenth century. A teacher can recognize the response as being reasonable, although incorrect: "Franklin is surely an influential figure in history. He was born in the early 1700s and died in the late 1700s—but that means he lived entirely in the *eighteenth* century,

just as we, toward the end of the 1990s, are living in the twentieth century. Good suggestion, but we'll list Franklin in the column for the eighteenth century." Being able to understand a student's idea even when it is incorrect or unexpected, finding the intelligent thinking that underlies the idea, and responding in a way that clarifies the student's contribution and incorporates it into a class discussion, these are among the talents of adept, knowledgeable teachers. Teachers can cultivate the talent of seeing the sensible reasoning behind an incorrect response. Examples abound. A student learning English as a second language writes *vacachen* and *nachenal* for *vacation* and *national*; an insightful teacher sees the misspellings as logical because the student, in speaking, gives both /sh/ and /ch/ the sound of /sh/. For the student, learning the /tion/ cluster becomes easier because the teacher can link the student's inventive spelling to standard spelling. A preschooler, asked how long it takes a baby to be born, answers briskly, "Two weeks!"—and she is correct, because her new brother or sister is expected in just two weeks. The math teacher described in Chapter Two who allowed class time for discussion after some students had asserted that rectangles have only two right angles eventually understood why the students had a good reason for giving that answer.

The responses teachers give to students can be categorized as *terminal feedback* or *sustaining feedback*. Jeanne Martin and her colleagues (Martin, Veldman, & Anderson, 1980) define terminal feedback as criticism or immediate correction of a student's answer by the teacher giving the desired answer or calling on another student to do so. Examples of sustaining feedback, on the other hand, include restating questions, giving guidance and clues, and allowing ample time for students to respond. Research shows that higher achievement is related to sustaining feedback and that lack of achievement is related to terminal feedback.

Allowing Adequate Wait Time

An important factor in treating students with respect involves giving them time to reflect before being expected to speak; that is, allowing adequate wait time. The term *wait time* refers to the interval allowed by a teacher between asking a question and either receiving a response or repeating the question for someone else to answer. (The person who waits is the teacher; the wait time is intended to give students the opportunity to think about a question or direction and respond to it.) Often, wait time is very short, as brief as a second or less (Rowe, 1974, 1986). Visualize a classroom where the teacher is using questioning and answering as an instructional strategy, with a short wait time.

> What kind of damage would you expect from an earthquake measuring 6.0 on the Richter scale? (one-second pause) …Ora?" (Ora looks up, hesitatingly; teacher waits one second.) "Lee?" (Lee looks down and gives no response. After about a second the teacher repeats the question for another student.) "Okay, Starr, you tell us. Suppose there's an earthquake measuring 6.0 on the Richter scale. What kind of damage would an earthquake of that magnitude cause?" (Starr gives an accurate answer. The teacher says, "Good" and asks another question, using the same style of questioning.)

In this situation, how much time is there for students to consider and answer the question? Is it the case that each student has one second, and that the third student called on answers before that second elapses? Consider this. The teacher asks a question and waits briefly to call on a student. There is an interval of about one second between the time Ora finds out that is her responsibility to answer and the time the teacher moves on to Lee, who also fails to respond within one second. The time interval between asking the question and the end of the time allowed for a response is approximately one second for Ora and two seconds for Lee, but it may be that neither student can use even the brief wait time productively. Both were called on after the question was asked, and it is possible they did not understand it, or were not listening, or that fright hampered their ability to respond. It is likely that the teacher, on the third attempt, calls on a student who can be relied upon to respond correctly, but the teacher has taken two actions that, in addition to the longer wait time, contribute to the third student's success. When Starr is called on she is identified as the person to answer *before* the question is asked, and the teacher restates, rather than repeats, the question for her.

Mary Budd Rowe is a scholar who has investigated wait time extensively. In summarizing her findings, she notes that when teachers wait three seconds or more for a response, rather than the usual one second or less, there are a number of important benefits: the length and quality of students' responses to the questions increases, students ask questions and interact with others, a wider range of students voluntarily contribute to discussions, and the quality of students' subsequent written work related to the questioning is enhanced. Some teachers believe that rapid-fire questioning and waiting to name the student who will answer a question until after the question will force all students to be attentive. But learning and threat do not mesh well. If the teacher phrases questions so students are alerted that they will be called upon (by naming the student before the question is asked), and if the teacher makes it a practice to restate questions as necessary, then not only will students be helped to respond without anxiety, but class time will be spent hearing useful information (rather than on unproductive pauses). Among the effects on students that Rowe has noted when wait time increases is a decrease in the need for disciplinary actions.

> Students maintained on a rapid recitation pattern show signs of restlessness and inattentiveness sooner than do students on the longer wait time treatment plan. At first this seems counter-intuitive to teachers. It appears that fast paced teacher questioning is a device for maintaining control of behavior. In fact it not only inhibits the kind of thinking teachers seek to encourage but it can also increase the need to discipline. …[I]t may not be apparent why increased wait time should be a factor for improved classroom discipline. The explanation may lie in a remark by a fifth grader to his mother about his teacher who was experimenting with 3-second wait times: "It's the first time in all my years in school that anybody cared about what I really thought—not just what I am supposed to say." Protracted wait time appears to influence motivation, and that in turn may be a factor in attention and cooperation. (Rowe, 1986, p. 44) Reprinted by permission. Copyright by the American Association of Colleges for Teacher Education

Jane Schaffer (1989, p. 41) has suggested some interesting variants on wait time: announcing an interesting and different amount of wait time at each session (e.g., 48 seconds, or one minute, three seconds) and using the pauses for students to jot down ideas. She writes, "…the quantity and quality of response goes up geometrically with every second when everyone has time to think and jot down some possible responses. There is a reward for thoughtful reflection on the question at hand. This procedure also reinforces the value of writing as an act of discovery and the value of talking about ideas after they have been formulated in writing."

Linking Oral and Written Language Modes

Listening and reading combine a wealth of interesting and useful strategies. *Paired reading, chanting*, and *echo reading* are described in Chapter Six. Another strategy that pairs listening and reading is *sequence reading*. Speaking and reading are linked when students present information to their classmates about reading they have done, or make informative presentations about content area topics. In *choral reading* and *Readers' Theater* (described in Chapter Eleven), students not only listen for their cues and read their lines, but listen critically to their own readings and to those of their classmates, with the purpose of becoming more effective speaker-readers or actor-readers. Listening and writing are integrated when listening events, such as a guest speaker, a literature selection read aloud, or an evocative piece of music, are used as the inspiration for writing. Listening, speaking, and writing are integrally related when students engage in discussing and editing their own and their classmates' writing. Multiple modes of language are used in many strategies that can become regular elements of a classroom program, across the grade levels. When *themed reading* is followed by the sharing of ideas, students read, speak, and listen. The *confer and write* strategy, described later in this chapter, enables students to prepare for writing through group discussion and brainstorming, and when the activity is followed by opportunities for students to read from their work, all four modes of language are used. Cooperative learning itself is a strategy that produces active learning while all the modes of language come into play. All of the language modes— listening, reading, writing, speaking—can be combined through two strategies that focus attention on text: *text impressions*, used before a text is read (pretelling), and *retelling*, used afterwards. Three of these linking strategies, sequence reading, text impressions, and retelling, are described next.

Sequence Reading.   One way to engage a large group of students in reading an important piece of text is to use sequence reading. (The A-Qu-A strategy, described in Chapter Four, is sequence reading with a question component added.) In sequence reading, the text is separated into sections and each section is placed on a separate card. (A copy of the printed text can simply be cut apart and the sections taped to file cards.) Then, at the top of every card except the first, the last sentence or phrase from the previous card is printed to serve as a cue. The cards are distributed randomly, and the student who has a card with no cue reads first. The student whose card has the cue heard at the end of that reading is the next reader, and so forth. Readers across the grade span can understand and use the strategy easily and experience shared pride in the success of the group reading. Often students ask for the cards to be redistributed and for the reading to be done again. During sequence reading the teacher needs to be attentive, willing to wait or to help if there is a pause or a problem, and never critical of individuals or the group. (This is true of other strategies described here as well.) Figure 10–2 presents a passage from an earlier chapter, prepared for a sequence reading. The separate inner boxes represent different text cards. The italicized text in small print, on all cards but the first, is the cue for which readers listen. As the text is divided, it forms a sequence reading for 10 readers. The same text could be divided in other ways, to provide a sequence reading for fewer or more readers. (Note, however, that to accommodate more readers it would be better to look for a longer text.)

When preparing a sequence reading, it is important to choose good cues. They should not be too long, but they should not be so short that listening for them becomes difficult, as would be the case with two- or three-word cues. Moreover, although the cues need not always be complete sentences, they should make sense in terms of the whole text. Although students will not read aloud the cues on their cards, they will see them and therefore read them silently, and teachers should be careful that the cues give some accurate information, especially when the sequence readings are based on content area informational text. In Figure 10–2, for example, the cue chosen for one of the cards is… *not ready to go through the front door.* In context, that cue makes better sense than a cue of… *ready to go through the front door.*

FIGURE 10–2 Sequence Reading

Entering into learning: A parable

Let us imagine a beautiful, well-furnished house. There is a handsome front door and an entry way, a living room, a dining room, a kitchen, enough bedrooms for each family member, one or more bathrooms, a laundry room, and a family recreation room. In each of the rooms there is everything we need to be comfortable there.

…everything we need to be comfortable there.

There are plenty of books in the living room, recreation room, and bedroom; there are lots of cooking utensils in the kitchen; the bedrooms have ample bureaus and closets. The house is ours—all we have to do is to show that we know how to live there.

…show that we know how to live there.

Our guide opens the front door and welcomes us in. We can explore the rooms, and the guide is ready to anticipate our needs and answer our questions about how things work. Some of the kitchen and laundry equipment is new to us, so we need to experiment before we can work with it; our guide demonstrates, watches while we try things out, gives us some "How to do it" booklets.

…some "How to do it" booklets.

It takes us a little while to find our way around the house—but only a little while; everything is interesting, and we can soon see how the various rooms are connected. The house is ours!

The house is ours!

There is another way to enter the house. Suppose when we approached it, our guide looked at us and decided we were not ready to go through the front door.

…not ready to go through the front door.

First, we need to learn "house basics": living room, kitchen, bedroom. Our guide takes us into a cellar area where, if we look up, we can see most of the living room through its clear plastic floor. First we need to learn which chairs are most comfortable. (The guide has a list for us to memorize.)

(The guide has a list for us to memorize.)

Then we must learn how to open the windows. (The guide has something that looks like a little window that we can practice on.) Finally, we need to know what places in the house all the doors out of the living room lead to. (The doors are closed so we can't see what lies beyond, but our guide will tell us and then test us to see if we get it right. The testing is a little scary.)

The testing is a little scary.

When we can prove to the guide that we know enough about the living room, we can move on to the area beneath the kitchen. Learning about the kitchen will be even harder than learning about the living room. We will need to learn lots of new words and match them with pictures of things that are in the real kitchen up above our heads.

…in the real kitchen up above our heads.

Our guide is kind, but sometimes gets discouraged with us because we are so slow to understand. We make mistakes, and often after we have learned something we forget it later.

…after we have learned something we forget it later.

We are discouraged too. The house must be a fine one. All that we can see of it looks very nice, but being down here underneath is unpleasant and tiresome. Perhaps the best thing to do is to give up.

Text Impressions. The text impressions strategy is based on story impressions (Bligh, 1995; McGinley & Denner, 1987) and renamed here because it can be used effectively with expository as well as narrative text. William McGinley and Peter Denner, who devised the original strategy, describe story impressions as "story fragments in the form of clue words and phrases that, when assembled, enable the reader to form an overall impression of how characters and events interact in the story" (1987, p. 249). They give the example of 14 clue words and phrases drawn from Edgar Allan Poe's famous horror story, "The Telltale Heart"; for example, *house; old man; young man; hatred; ugly eye; death; tub; blood; knife.* The terms are chosen by the teacher from the text and presented to students in the form of a sequential list, such as the list shown in Figure 10–3. Effective use of the text impressions strategy depends on thoughtful choice of terms by the teacher, with the selection made so that words and phrases are likely to be familiar to students and suggest a probable sequence of events on which to base a pretelling. The words and phrases are *not* chosen on the basis of the undesirable technique of giving students a list of unrelated vocabulary words to learn before reading a story. (If that system of choice were used for the book the terms in Figure 10–3 are taken from, a list would include *atop, nestled, cattails, rhythm, pelts, trespass, disrupted, grist, mourned, petitions, greenway*—not a sound basis for creating a connected piece of writing, although all of the words do appear, in that order, in the book.)

When this strategy is used in content area study, it is important to select topics that students can relate to their own knowledge and experience. To minimize differences in prior knowledge among students and to maximize thoughtful interaction, the strategy works best when students tell or write their text impression passage working in pairs, triads, or cooperative groups after thinking together about the clues to create meaning from them. Discussion of the passages students have created should precede reading the book and can be revisited afterwards, although there should never be a focus on "right" and "wrong" pretellings. The 11 terms listed in Figure 10–3 are taken from an illustrated history of the Nashua River, a beautifully illustrated trade book by

FIGURE 10–3 Terms for a text impressions activity, based on *A River Ran Wild,* written and illustrated by Lynne Cherry (1992).

long ago a river
beavers, turtles, and schools of fish
native people
clear water
trading post
sawmills
paper mills
factories
murky water
vision
once again the river

Lynne Cherry, giving a factual account of the river's renewal after decades of industrial pollution. The book could be used for reading aloud or as a resource text, with a wide age range of students during a study of ecology. For this text impressions activity, the terms come sequentially from throughout the book, although for a longer text the terms could be chosen from the first section or any part the teacher decided would be useful for a pretelling. Although the terms are given in the order in which they appear in the text, students do not need to use the terms in that order when they create their text impression. Sensible and ingenious text impressions are what is wanted; it would be a mistake to treat the task evaluatively by checking to see that all terms have been used exactly.

Retelling. In their book titled *Read and Retell*, Australian educators Hazel Brown and Brian Cambourne (1990) advocate retellings as a strategy that can be used with a wide variety of important texts, which can help students develop their understanding both of particular texts and different genres. Nonfiction text for retelling, for example, may include many forms of expository text, as well as charts, diagrams, and maps. The authors give the example of a diagram showing the life cycle of an insect as an appropriate text for retelling. They identify formats in which retelling of text can occur: hearing a text read aloud may be followed by oral retelling or written retelling (through writings or drawings); or reading a text may be followed by oral retelling or retelling in writing or through drawings. They recommend multiple readings prior to retelling, with the first reading done by the teacher. "It is important that the children receive demonstrations of how the text sounds when read by an expert reader" (Brown & Cambourne, 1990, p. 33). Students may reread the text or portions of it as often as they want to before retelling. As the authors point out, retelling is easy when we understand meaning, but difficult if we must recall a text using rote memory.

For retelling to be useful and interesting, rather than a boring or threatening activity, both the classroom environment and the retelling process need to be well-organized. In particular, participants must "feel safe about taking part in the activities in the setting without fear of being hurt, ridiculed, denigrated, or demeaned if they make mistakes" (Brown & Cambourne, 1990, p. 30). Purposes for retelling vary, and whatever purposes are set for a particular retelling must be clear; for example, teachers might ask students to retell for one of the following three purposes: retell the main ideas only, *or* retell for someone so that they will enjoy the story as much as you did, *or* retell so that the important details are clear and in correct sequence. Whole class brainstorming is a useful preparation for retelling, and vocabulary terms listed during the brainstorming process should be displayed while students prepare their retellings individually. A quiet atmosphere is needed for the retelling process. The authors suggest (pp. 33–34) that partners share and compare their retellings (oral, written, or drawn), by questioning one another about how their retellings differ, why items were included or omitted, and whether the meaning of the passage has been distorted: "Have I muddled-up, changed, or omitted anything that alters meaning?" They also suggest the partners ask each other, "Did you use any words or phrases that are different from those in the story but still mean the same thing?" Finally, they suggest a "borrow a bit" process in which partners ask each other, "If you could borrow a bit of my retelling and include it in yours, which bit would you take?"

Peer editing and discussions support the writing process.

◼◼ Literacy: Writing and Reading in
◼◼ Content Area Learning

Writing and reading are the written parallels of speaking and listening. In writing, ideas are expressed to a reader, who receives them, just as a speaker expresses ideas to a listener. The writing-reading manner of giving and getting information differs from the speaking-listening method in ways that affect how widely a message can be shared and how effectively it can be transmitted. Potentially, a writer's audience is vastly greater than a speaker's. Many books, newspapers, and magazines are read nationally or even internationally, and the works of many authors continue to be read hundreds or even thousands of years after they have died. On the other hand, writer and reader are typically separated by space and time; interaction is usually impossible. Speakers can adjust what they are saying while they are speaking, based on clues from listeners' interpolated questions or body language that indicate how well the intended message is being understood. Writers, once their work is published, do not have this opportunity to adjust their message in response to readers.

Writing is, however, a powerful learning tool. Writers who have a personal concern for expressing their ideas in writing are their own audience—and they can and do adjust their message in response to their own rereading of what they have written. In recent years, there has been a strong emphasis in the professional literature on writing to learn, and many teachers have altered their ways of teaching to include much more writing and to stress writing that enables students to learn both about what they are studying and also about the process of writing itself. Professional journals provide a wealth of suggestions for incorporating writing into content area instruction. When students are engaged as writers to express ideas (rather than to be evaluated on the extent of their understanding or the quality of their writing), reading and writing are linked. Students are readers of their own writing as they revise a writing in process or read a finished piece of work with pride. When collaboration in the writing process is encouraged, they also read and respond to the writing of fellow students. The term *process writing* is

used to refer to writing that focuses on more than a final product. Process writing emphasizes the author's ownership of writing and the value of writing for members of an audience (who then acquire, in a sense, a shared ownership in the process). The focus, sequentially, is on fluency first, then clarity, and finally correctness; that is, beginning by expressing ideas freely, then revising to convey meaning clearly, and finally editing to produce a technically accurate piece of writing. Process writing belongs not only within the language arts program, but within all of content area learning. Students develop as writers and build their understanding of what they have learned when they and their classmates engage together in the writing process—sharing, editing, revising, and discussing what has been written.

> One of the keys to using writing as an instructional tool involves understanding the difference between form and content. Form can be thought of as the mechanics of writing, such as spelling, capitalization, sentence structure, and elements of grammar…. Form is obviously important in writing, but it is only one component.
>
> The other major component of writing is content: the concepts and facts presented and their organization within a paper. If writing is to serve as a catalyst for gaining more insight into course material, content—not form—needs to be emphasized. Once the content of a paper is appropriate, logical, and organized, then its form can be improved, but the opposite is not necessarily true. If a paper has poor content, then no amount of correcting the elements of form will transform it into a good piece of writing. …[I]n order to use writing as an instructional tool and not be overwhelmed by the paper work, teachers need to develop a perspective that lets them view elements of form as just one component of writing. …Furthermore, teachers should be aware that errors in form are a normal occurrence as writers venture into new areas of semantic and syntactic usage. (Pearce, 1983, pp. 213–214)

Writing Apprehension

Like speaking, writing is an expressive form of language. Just as some people develop oral communication apprehension, people also may develop writing apprehension. This fear of writing is learned, usually in school, and it has harmful effects. "An individual's predisposition toward writing—positive or negative—is extremely important and one that educators need to be concerned about. No matter how skilled or capable students are in writing, if they believe they will do poorly or if they choose to avoid writing situations, their skills or capabilities matter little" (Kaywell, Johnston, & Markle, 1991, p. 55). The term *writing apprehension* was coined by John Daly and Michael Miller (1975), who devised a self-rating scale to measure the trait.

> Individuals with high apprehension of writing… fear evaluation of their writing…[and believe] they will be negatively rated on it. Thus they avoid writing when possible and when forced to write exhibit high levels of anxiety. They expect to fail in writing, and logically they should since they seldom engage in it. In classroom situations [they are] the individuals who consistently fail to turn in compositions, who do not attend class when writing is required, and who seldom enroll voluntarily in courses where writing is known to be demanded. …They will seek occupations they view as requiring little writing… (Daly & Miller, 1975, p. 244)

When Kathleen Block (1991, p. 211) asked college students in their first composition course to create illustrations showing their writing process, stress and procrastination were dominant themes. One student captioned a series of drawings to show the writing sequence: "Step 1: Wait patiently. Step 2: Get hit by lightning bolt of inspiration. Step 3: Write wonderful paper. Step 4: Get picked apart by cruel teacher." College students, of course, are the group of students who have been most successful throughout the K–12 school years, therefore presumably have had better, happier experiences in writing instruction than many of their classmates. Consider the analysis of the writing process given by Block's students. Of course it is humorous, but many people, recalling their own school experiences, are likely to find it realistic also. The four-step sequence—wait, get struck by inspiration, write, get negative comments—neatly conveys the roles of student and teacher in an ineffective pattern of writing instruction where the emphasis is solely on product.

As a method of instruction, this pattern is an obvious failure, since there is no instruction, except

Teacher's Role	Student's Role
• Give assignment	• Get assignment
	• Produce a finished piece of writing
• Evaluate product	• Feel disappointed (or, if given a high grade, pleased)

insofar as a grade and marginal comments provided by the teacher will influence the student's future writing. Nevertheless, the pattern has been a common one. Many teachers themselves have had similar experiences in writing when they were in school—experiences that made them feel incompetent as writers, and apprehensive about writing. Reed Larson uses the metaphor of an airplane's capacity to maneuver when discussing the problems students face in fulfilling writing assignments. The range of what an aircraft is capable of doing is called its "performance envelope." To push beyond what the plane's structure permits it to do will cause it to crash. On the other hand, the machine is underused if it is consistently used for tasks that could be accomplished by a less sophisticated craft.

> Young writers, unfortunately, spend a lot of time outside of their performance envelopes. They put themselves in situations they cannot handle. Debilitating emotions result; their thinking becomes fragmented and directionless; and their work tumbles out of control. Often these situations result from challenges they have set that are beyond their abilities, tasks that are too large or undefined for them to deal with. In these cases experience takes the form of anxiety. Other times it is absence of genuine challenge that creates the problem. They are unable or unwilling to find anything engaging within their writing, and boredom ensues. (Larson, 1988, pp. 170–171)

How can content area teachers be expected to teach writing? Recall the problem discussed in Chapter Six, where the question addressed was, How can content area teachers be expected to teach reading? A quotation from that chapter follows, changed to refer to writing: *…how will a teacher with limited background in writing education* *know how to teach writing? And how can an extensive and demanding curriculum be taught if time is taken from subject matter instruction to include writing?* Just as there is good news for content area teachers about reading instruction, there is similar good news about writing. Again, sections from Chapter Six— the "good news bulletins"—can be changed to refer to writing. Reading and writing can go hand in hand. What students can do today, with support, they will be able to do later independently. The skill of writing, like other skills, develops through use. The decision to incorporate writing as part of content area programs and wise choices of writing strategies to use are the major contributions content area teachers can make to their students' writing development.

Engaging Students Actively As Writers

Several of the strategies that have been presented in earlier chapters are based on students' writing. In Concept Connections, students create a short written passage showing the relationship among concept-related terms. In the Guided Writing Procedure, students alternate reading and writing as they prepare short informational papers. SAIL, RAFT, QUiP, QUAD, and the Structured Research Process (all discussed in Chapter Five) provide ways of guiding students as they write about what they are learning. Each of these strategies emphasizes both content learning and the process of writing, but, in each, content learning has greater weight. They are content area instructional methods that incorporate writing. The strategies described in this chapter, on the other hand, also have a dual emphasis, but the writing aspect has greater weight. Methods of engaging students in writing that can be used effectively in content area instruction include **journal** writing, correspondence, and prompted writing.

Journal Writing and Correspondence

In recent years, journals have become widely used throughout the grades, and in college and university programs. The journal has always been a writer's tool—used as a daily record of events, as memoranda of ideas for writing projects, and as notebooks in which to draft and redraft pieces of writing. One aspect of whole language learning has been to encourage all learners, both children and adults, to write freely and for a variety of audiences, including the private audience of self. Although the words *journal* and *diary* have the same derivation and are sometimes used synonymously, in educational settings, journal writing typically is shared and often is required, in contrast to diaries, which are personal, private, and not used in schools.

Journal writing encourages an approach to writing that emphasizes fluency and deemphasizes correctness in the mechanics of written text. The lack of emphasis on producing neat, technically accurate written pieces is one of the elements that promotes writing fluency. Accuracy in spelling, the use of standard grammar, and an attractive format are important when writing is to be widely shared, but concentrating on these features when beginning to create a piece of writing interferes with expression of ideas. Professional writers focus their attention on conveying ideas; writing instruction in schools should give students a similar focus. John Mayher and his colleagues (Mayher, Lester, & Pradl, 1983) are among those who advocate the sequence of fluency first, then clarity, and finally correctness, and also note that journals encourage fluency. When a piece of writing is to be done once (as in journal writing and,

---

journal—a diary. The words *journal* and *diary* come from the Latin word *diurnalis*, meaning *daily*; the root of that word is *dies*, Latin for *day*. Journals and diaries are day books, personal accounts of events and thoughts written each day. *Diary* comes into English directly from Latin, but *journal* is a French word (derived from Latin) that became part of the English language. *Journalism* and *adjourn* are related words. The French word *jour* is sometimes found in restaurant menus, where *soup du jour* means *soup of the day*. The Latin word *dies* occurs in legal language. A court or other group that has been meeting regularly may adjourn *sine die* (without a day). *Adjourn* ("to the day") originally referred to ending a meeting by setting a time for the next one. A court, or other group, that adjourns *sine die* does not intend to meet again, thus stops without setting a day for the next meeting.

usually, in prompted writing) the writer's purpose should be to generate and express ideas. When a piece of writing is chosen for revision, the writer's purpose should be to express ideas as clearly and compellingly as possible. When that piece of writing is intended for publication, or for submission as an important assignment to be evaluated, the final revision should give careful attention to correctness. Journal entries, which are typically written once and not revised, provide writers with the experience to express their ideas freely and fluently.

Categories of journals include *personal journals*, whose primary or sole audience is the writer; *dialogue journals*, in which two or more people engage in a written conversation for an agreed-upon purpose; *learning log journals*, used for teaching and study; and *group journals*, which provide an opportunity for written exchanges among many people. These categories are flexible rather than fixed; for example, dialogue journals and learning logs can be readily combined. In educational settings, journals have several purposes: to share ideas, create and maintain a record of events, and promote fluency in writing. The third purpose—writing development—is typically a teacher's goal for students; many students will not consider this a purpose of their own. Sharing ideas and recording events, however, can become important to students. Some forms of group journals, such as weather and snapshot journals, are primarily records of events, and learning logs provide a record of responses to what is studied. The *Our-Search group journal*, described in Chapter Five, is a record of the real events occurring in a class-wide search for information. Dialogue journals are, by definition, a method of sharing ideas, and in some forms of dialogue journals and group journals, such as the buddy, group, and APA journals, the sharing is student-to-student, rather than student-to-teacher. These journals are a form of correspondence, but other forms of correspondence that can be used educationally are not journals. These include *Opinion and Comment*, *Letters to the Author*, *pen pals*, and *Partnership Stories*.

Personal Journals. When personal journals are used in a school setting, the teacher sets aside a regular time for writing, and all members of the class, the teacher as well as students, write for an agreed-upon length of time. Typically the students' journals are kept at school until the end of the year or term, then are returned to them. The decision about whether the teacher will read and comment on entries is made by each student individually, according to an agreed-upon system; for example, the student may clip a note to the front of the journal to ask the teacher to read and comment on entries. Entries that are not supposed to be read may be folded over or stapled together. Of all of the forms of journaling, personal journals are most similar to diaries. A problem with using personal journals as a class assignment is that the privacy that this sort of writing should be accorded is difficult to ensure in a school setting. Probably personal journals are most appropriately used as a component of a writing course. In all content areas, there is a wealth of options from which teachers can choose if they decide to include journal writing in their classes.

A version of the personal journal suitable for prereaders or beginning readers is the *scrapbook journal* (Kelly, 1990). This is an individual journal designed to record events in a way that makes them both personal and useful for showing and sharing, thus privacy is not a concern. A journal page begins with a piece of memorabilia—a drawing, photograph, memento from a party, or leaf brought back from a leaf walk. This item is pasted or taped into the scrapbook journal, and the writer prepares an entry about it by using invented spelling, dictating to an adult, or drawing. It is useful to have a second version of entries that are written in invented spelling in which an adult confers with the writer and then transcribes the entry using "dictionary spelling." The illustrative items on each journal page help the writer later recall, and read or retell, the journal entries. Elementary teachers who decide to link writing with science instruction can adapt the scrapbook journal as a learning log. For each science activity, students can choose small items to be taped into the journal (e.g., a chip of wood and a pebble to illustrate things that float and things that do not; different kinds of seeds to illustrate how seeds travel), or they can create pictures showing a process they have learned about. Their own accounts, in invented spelling, of what they learned can be supplemented with a copy of a group Language Experience Activity (LEA) account.

Dialogue Journals.   Notebooks in which two or more people, often a teacher and a student, engage in a written conversation over an extended period of time are called *dialogue journals* (Atwell, 1987a, 1987b). Jana Staton (1988, p. 198) describes them as "functional, interactive, mostly about self-generated topics and deeply embedded in the continuing life of the classroom." *Reading journals or literature logs* (Danielson, 1992; Newton, 1991) are a form of dialogue journal in which students express their ideas about what they are reading, or what the teacher is reading aloud to the class. *Reading response journals* (Simpson, 1986) can be used when teachers read aloud, with the reading aloud followed first by group brainstorming, then by five minutes during which teacher and students write, and concluding with voluntary sharing of writing. Pamela Farris (1989) describes *story journals*, which are students' elaborated responses to read-alouds, including drawings, retellings, critiques, and the creation of new, original episodes in the style of the text being read aloud.

Dialogue journals provide not only writing opportunities, but reading material for students who have a wide range of reading abilities and language backgrounds. Teachers' comments become reading text for students. Because mature writers usually adapt their writing style to their audience, the likelihood is that students will be able to read their teachers' comments. Martha Dolly (1990, p. 361) writes, "Dialogue journal writing ensures that each students' reading text will be roughly tuned to. . . reading ability [since] teachers modify their sentence structure and vocabulary according to the perceived language proficiency of the student." The teacher need not be the correspondent in dialogue journals, however. *Buddy journals* (Bromley, 1989) are written, student-to-student exchanges. Correspondents may be students in different grades (e.g., fifth graders paired with second graders), or students within the same class who either select each other as writing partners or are randomly paired by the teacher. When buddy journals are used within a class, the writers may write side by side, trading

journals back and forth. Within a single writing period, three or four exchanges may be made, and extensive idea sharing may be accomplished in a relaxed and enjoyable way. Joanne Gillespie (1993) advocates *buddy book journals*, a form of literature log. Students select partners, and the partners agree on a book they will simultaneously read. (Ideally, two copies of the book are available; if not, students can trade the book back and forth or use paired reading.) Gillespie suggests that each student write six entries in the journal while reading the book, with each partner originating three of the entries and using the other three to respond to the partner's entries. All entries should be dated and signed. This kind of journal also can be used for cross-age buddying and parent buddying about shared books.

Michael Soderlund suggests using *memos* as a supplement or alternative to dialogue journals and learning logs. Memos are brief messages from student to teacher, usually written weekly, commenting on some significant aspect of the class during the previous week. Memos have a clear audience—the teacher—and require less time to respond to than journals because they are briefer, and also because, as Soderlund (1993, p. 57) suggests, "memos are shorter than the reflective writing usually found in student journals [and] the content of the memo is more specific and cogent. My responses are then more specific. I can read and respond *authentically* to a set of memos in approximately one-fourth the time it takes me to read and respond to a set of journals." Students who resist journal writing often find it easy to use the memo format because they are in no doubt about what to write and because brevity is acceptable (although some students choose to write long memos).

Learning Logs.   Learning logs are journals in which students write about what they are learning in a content area subject. The writing may be accounts of observations or experiments in journals such as science lab books, or step-by-step descriptions of solutions for math problems. Students also may be assigned to restate important points from lectures or assigned readings. Creative and analytical writing also can be a part of every subject. In math, students can prepare original word problems;

in social studies, they can write imaginatively from the perspective of another's situation in another time period; in science, they can propose ways to investigate questions and explore new ideas. While most learning log assignments focus on what is being studied, some teachers use learning logs to encourage students to think about their own learning progress and processes. Wendy Weiner (1986, p. 73) describes an assignment in which students in her English class were asked to write about a course with which they were having the most trouble. She suggests using the following questions as prompts for writing: "What course will you focus on? What is giving you trouble in the course right now? What content is the class focused on? What kinds of tests are given? What grade did you get on the last test? What did you do right on the last test? What gave you trouble? When is the next test?" Donald Graves (1989c, p. 49) advocates using learning logs for students to write about learning problems they have solved. "Write a short entry on any learning problems you've solved lately, something you didn't know how to do but do now" he suggests, commenting that "this is one way for children to be more specifically aware of their learning successes and histories."

Those who think of math as unrelated to language may be surprised to find that *math journals* are recommended across the age and grade span and that an extensive variety of suggestions for their use are published. Very young children can use journals for pictures and drawings illustrating math learning, such as those that show their understanding of fractions (Wilde, 1991). Students in elementary school can be guided to use the journals to develop strategies for solving math problems by drawing a picture or working out a simpler problem (Wadlington, Bitner, Partridge, & Austin, 1992). Across all grades, journal use involves students using math vocabulary repeatedly and, as David Schleper and Sandra Paradis (1990) point out, students learn that writing about a puzzling problem helps them reason their way to a solution. Leah Richards (1990) gives an extensive list of the kinds of writing that can be used in math journals: summaries of findings, translations of mathematical equations into words, definitions, reports, personal

writing, labels for math-related drawings, captions for math-related illustrations, step-by-step instructions for problem solving, descriptions, predictions, explanations, and arguments.

Cynthia Nahrgang and Brice Petersen substituted journal-writing sessions for quizzes in math classes, with assignments that required students to develop and describe a real-life, nonmathematical analogy to a mathematical formula or rule. Students' work was given 2, 1 or 0 points credit (no effort = no credit), and the teachers wrote brief comments and corrected all mathematical errors. They specify two major functions of journals. "First, they allow students to proceed at their own rate and to converge on an understanding of mathematical concepts using their own experiences. Second, they provide teachers a unique diagnostic tool: the writings of students immediately reveal areas of confusion and expose misunderstandings of mathematical concepts" (Nahrgang & Petersen, 1986, p. 463). The diagnostic advantages of math journals also have been noted by Christine Gordon and Dorothy MacInnis (1993, p. 42), who used prompted and free writing in math journals. "In essence, the journal was the private interview or the hotline between a student and teacher." These teachers did not use the journals for extensive explanation; instead, they noted what needed to be explained and retaught the topic in class, partnered students to work together, and responded to journal entries by writing brief pieces of relevant information (e.g., "Remember the number in the tenths place always determines which decimal number is larger"). Current events can be linked to math journals as one type of entry. Students find a newspaper article, feature, or advertisement that can be related to math—of course, with thought and imagination everything can be related to math—and write a brief explanation of the math connection. As an added activity, students can create and solve one or more math problems based on the current events item. This can be a weekly homework assignment or one that can be worked on in class if the teacher supplies newspapers. The current events math pages can be included as an entry in individual students' journals or can be compiled into journals for cooperative groups or the entire class.

Lab books—journals in which students summarize the materials, procedures, and results of an experiment and describe their observations—are a common form of learning log in science classes, but other kinds of journal writing may be incorporated in lab books, or may supplement or substitute for them. Denise Levine (1985, p. 46) describes using *science journals* in middle school science classes that require students to write about what they have learned, observed, and done. She noted that students produced their best writing when they wrote about lab work, hands-on activities, rather than about class lectures or assigned readings, when they had some choice of topics and when the audience for their writing was their classmates rather than their teacher. She suggests reading aloud journal excerpts as a basis for class discussion and review. In evaluating this use of science journals, students expressed enthusiasm; for example, they wrote, "When you write, it reinforces it in your mind and can help you to study. Sometimes when you write it, you can understand it more clearly," and "It helps you to realize what you don't understand."

Science journaling can be used to relate science to other courses, and the pairing can be particularly worthwhile if teachers of different courses share in the process of writing journal comments. Frances Smith and Cheryl Hausafus (1993) suggest pairing science and home economics for presentations, followed by journaling, on stain removal, food additives, textile fibers, and the chemistry of household cleaning. Learning activities such as those recommended by Valerie Bristor (1993)—student-constructed semantic maps, Venn diagrams, compare and contrast charts—provide structure for science learning logs. James Scarnati and Cyril Weller (1992) advocate writing as a part of science classes in four styles: narration, description, explanation, and persuasion. These four types of writing can be the basis for regular assignments, done in class or as homework. Students can write about current or historical scientific events in narrative style and can describe scientific instruments in accurate detail or write a sensory description about the results of an experiment—what was seen? ...heard? ...smelled? Concepts that are being studied can be explained; persuasive writing can be based on logic and can be accompanied by graphs and charts.

Social studies journals are another form of learning log. William Brozo (1988) suggests adapting questions that are typically used to prompt students to write about narrative text to apply to expository writing, particularly in the social studies area. Learning log entries can be based on questions such as, In this reading, what ideas do you feel strongly about? How do your own experiences relate to what you have read about? Randy Mills (1988) notes the importance of giving students, particularly older students, a rationale for journal writing, one that encourages them to make connections between what they are learning and their own ideas and beliefs. For example, students might be given this rationale: Keeping a personal journal will help you make connections between your own views about a topic we discuss in class and policies that have been decided on in the past and are being debated in the present. This will help give you a picture of how decisions are made in a democracy. Mills advocates the use of journals to promote student-teacher dialogue, which then can be used as the basis for class discussions. *Current events response journals* (Galda, Cullinan, & Strickland, 1993) can become the basis for discussion or further writing. As a regular homework assignment, students read or listen to a news report or commentary from a newspaper, radio, or television program. The following day, they write a journal entry about the news item, offering their comments and interpretations. The assignment can be more fruitful if the original source accompanies the writing, so teachers may require that the entries be based on written or graphic material from current newspapers—news articles, columns, editorials, captioned pictures, cartoons—that can be mounted in the journal.

One way of setting up a learning log is to use *double entry journals*, or DEJs (Vaughan, 1990). With this format, students keep a spiral bound notebook in which they use the left-hand pages for graphics and notes such as drawings and sketches, diagrams, ideas, and observations, and the right-hand pages for putting those ideas into written form. Vaughan's students kept journals in both science and social studies. As part of a lesson about electricity, students experimented with batteries, illustrated the concept of circuits on the left page, and stated what they had learned on the facing page. When younger students use double entry journals, the drawing process can be followed by a Language Experience Activity story on the theme of "what I learned." Copies of the LEA stories can then be taped into students' journals. Double entry journals also can be used to stress the learning process by using the left side for goal setting and the right side for brainstormed strategies for ways to achieve those goals.

Dialectical journals (Edwards, 1991/1992) are learning logs structured to encourage logical thinking and writing. Dialectical teaching is a method of instruction that emphasizes the logical analysis of ideas by asking and answering a series of questions. In dialectical journals, entries consist of a short statement quoted from a text or lecture, followed by a two- or three-part comment in response to patterned questions. For example, a journal entry in social studies might begin with a textbook definition of migration, followed by "What it means" (the student's restatement of the definition) and "What it means to me" (the student's application of the concept to personal experience or observations). A problem-solution journal entry in science, beginning with a quotation from the text about animals' need for water, would be followed by a restatement ("What it means"), then sections on "What it means to me" and "What it means to the world," calling for personal application and also a grasp of the general meaning of the concept. The pattern for journal writing is set in advance: a technical term or brief quotation, followed by writing about that topic in two or three columns (what it means, what it means to me, what it means to the world).

Group Journals. For younger students, group journals in the classroom can be established for a variety of purposes. A *weather journal* may be placed by a window for the daily recording of weather news, by as many students who choose to contribute. A *classroom science journal* will contain daily entries about the progress of science experiments, such as growing plants. A *guest journal* placed near the door will provide an opportunity for classroom visitors to leave written messages for the class. These journals,

kept in the classroom for reading by future classes, will eventually constitute a useful historical record. A group variation of the scrapbook journal, described earlier, is a *snapshot journal* (DeYoung, 1994), in which a series of snapshots of a class activity are mounted, along with student-written captions. A central section of the page is used for a short student-written description of the activity pictured. These journals provide a record of class events that family members and other classroom visitors will enjoy browsing through, which students can enjoy during the year. Class snapshot journals prepared annually provide a record of class events that can be kept and examined in future years.

With younger students or students with limited English proficiency, group journals can provide a variety of emergent literacy experiences. The *daily journal* (Strickland & Morrow, 1990) can be a regular part of the teaching process. Group members dictate an account of a shared experience and a scribe, the teacher, or an aide, writes from the dictation, thinking aloud and modeling during the process by repeating what is being written and, if necessary, crossing out errors and revising. The scribe pauses often so class members who choose to do so can predict the next letter or word. When the journal entry is completed, students are encouraged to read it chorally with the adult(s), as the scribe tracks the writing from left to right, showing the return sweep from line to line. Students are then invited to share thoughts and comments about whatever print elements of the entry they find interesting (e.g., "There's a *J*," "That's a capital letter," "The word *school* is on the top line"), but it is a rule that no student is ever asked to read all or part of the entry individually. The session may conclude with a final choral or echo reading. Completed charts are posted around the room for a time. A series of charts with a common theme may be collected to form a Big Book, or students may take turns choosing which chart, rolled up like a scroll, to take home for family reading. The Daily Journal strategy differs from some methods of using chart stories in the early grades. In a Daily Journal, the teacher invites the class to contribute information; the teacher does *not* ask specific questions. The teacher provides children with the opportunity to respond by asking the whole class a question such as, "What can you tell me about today's journal?"—and all of the children have the opportunity to comment and be correct and pleased with themselves. When a teacher asks questions such as, "How many times did I write *The*?" or "Who can find the word *school*?" many children will compete to answer a question and only one will be chosen. Moreover, the process may degenerate into fussing about hand-raising and turn-taking, and opportunities for literacy learning and enjoyment will be lost.

For older students, a *group journal* (Jacobson, 1989b) may be placed in an easily accessible setting, with all members of the class, including the teacher, encouraged to contribute. For college students, the journal may be put on reserve in the library. A good strategy for keeping a group journal is to have the right-hand pages of the journal used for original contributions and the facing pages kept for comments on those entries. The first page of the journal may contain a list of all those who will be using the journal; thereafter, entries need only be initialed. It is important to establish in advance the rule that the group journal may not be used to express negative opinions about any person or group of people. The *traveling journal* provides a way for adults who live at a distance but share common interests to communicate. The names and addresses of the people who agree to participate are recorded on the first page, and the journal then rotates among the group, by mail. Commitment to participation in a traveling journal means agreeing to write in it and send it along within an agreed-upon time, usually a maximum of two weeks.

A group journal variation that links correspondence and publication is the *APA journal*. When used in education, APA—pronounced like the first two syllables in *appe-tite*—stands for *Amateur Publishing Association* (Jacobson & Kinnucan-Welsch, 1993). An APA is an ongoing correspondence among a group of people—a type of huge letter from everyone to everyone. The first round of an APA consists of each participant writing a letter, typically about personal interests and ideas. (Part of the fun of an APA is that participants may choose to write using a pseudonym, for example, Sting, Knight Girl.) Letters must be written in dark pencil or blue or black ink on stan-

dard-sized typing paper, leaving about a one-inch margin on all four sides so that they can be copied. For students who have access to computers, the letters can be written using a word processing program and then printed. Many writers like to add illustrations. A coordinator, usually a teacher or an aide, collects the letters, makes copies, collates the collection of letters, adds a Table of Contents, listing the APA participants and giving the date of publication, and distributes copies to each participant. After this introductory round of letters, each person's contribution consists of two elements: a new letter and comments (e.g., questions, shared information) to the other correspondents about their previous letters. The comments make an APA journal unique. Participants have three kinds of reading material: their own letter, which is always interesting to see published; the letters of others; and the comments about their previous letter, which others have written to them. APA correspondents can live a distance from one another. In APA journals focused on content area learning, members of cooperative groups in different schools who are engaged in similar research projects can correspond, or a group of high school students can form an APA with a group of elementary students to write about what younger students are learning in social studies, math, or science.

Correspondence.   The APA journal strategy is a method of communication among people or groups who are separated from one another; other strategies also encourage such communication, but do not involve an exchange of ideas through journals. Of the four strategies described here—Opinion and Comment, Letters to the Author, pen pals, and Partnership Stories—correspondence in the first strategy is often between students in the same school district, although in different schools, or different teams or grades within the same school. For the strategies to be practical, sending materials needs to be simple and inexpensive; an in-district interschool mail system accomplishes this. The other two strategies are typically long-distance forms of correspondence, especially Partnership Stories, which were originated as a means of linking students from different cultures to different parts of the world.

The Opinion and Comment strategy can be used when some of the writing done by students is in the form of essays that express a point of view or propose a solution to a problem about situations that affect students' lives, for example, "We need music in the lunchroom," "Why the high school library should be open one evening a week," "Petting zoos in the mall are cruel," "Ban tobacco advertising at sports events." A batch of essays written and prepared for publication (i.e., sharing with others) by students in one classroom are sent to another class, where students read and discuss them, choose one or several to respond to, and write comments that are then sent to the essay writers. Letters to the Author is a similar strategy, except that the writing shared and commented on is typically literary, such as stories or poems.

The pen pals strategy is a long-standing method of linking people in different areas or different countries through the exchange of letters. Ideally, pen pal correspondence continues over an extended period of time. The basis for an effective pen pal arrangement begins with a linkage between teachers who agree to this long-distance collaboration. Matching pen pal pairs in the two locations can be done randomly or on the basis of students' mutual interests. One group writes first; thereafter, time is provided to write replies after letters are received, and teachers take responsibility for mailing the batches of letters that go back and forth. Pen pals projects in which college students in teacher education programs correspond with younger students (e.g., Rankin, 1992) have several potential advantages. In addition to learning about the interests and ideas of their young correspondents, education students can draw inferences about the process of writing development by studying the letters they receive. The younger students receive letters that are technically correct—college students should do peer editing to ensure this—which makes the letters easier to read. Also, such an exchange of letters encourages students to think about the possibilities of college education for themselves.

Kenneth Cushner (1992, pp. 45–46) proposes a strategy called *Partnership Stories*, in which a group of students compose the first part of a story, then send it to students in another area or country to complete. As a variation, students could create an entire story, but send it without its conclusion. Later, students in both groups could compare the ending they wrote with the conclusion developed by the others. Cushner describes a linkage between fourth graders in the United States and India, in which the U. S. students began a fairy tale they titled "A Jungle Adventure" and invited the students in the school in India to devise an ending. He writes,". . . significant learning might also occur by having children within one country complete a Partnership Story. Improved understanding, interactions, and relationships could be developed between diverse groups in the United States through such an effort. For example, how might stories develop between children in inner-city schools and those in nearby suburbs? Between children on reservations and in nearby areas?"

Responding To Journals

When students use journals for which the teacher is the sole or primary reader, it is likely that considerable time will elapse between the student's writing and the teacher's comment. Therefore, the journal conversation is likely to be a series of unrelated exchanges in which the student writes on a topic and the teacher responds, then the student introduces a new idea. This form of one-way exchange is particularly likely to be true for younger writers, who will start a new topic unrelated to their previous entry. Although the teacher's comments will be enjoyed and perhaps even shared with others, the child often does not write in response to what the teacher has written. Journal advocates agree that grading journals interferes with their use and that teachers should contribute to dialogue journals by sharing ideas rather than making corrections or commenting on the quality of what students have written, either with criticism or praise. Journal writing may be credited toward a course grade by giving full credit for all who participate within the preset guidelines for journal writing. (The guidelines should be understood in advance; for example, the purpose of writing in learning logs is to express ideas related to a content area topic, rather than just to share personal concerns.)

We cannot overestimate the importance of responding to written work. Writing is a private affair, but anyone engaged in it ultimately craves a response, something which indicates whether or not they have communicated an idea with clarity or force. The problem is that we, as teachers, have been conditioned to think response means correction, evaluation, and grading. …Evaluation impedes experimentation. Students will not take risks if a grade hangs over them. They'll give you what they think you want… and generally produce hackneyed, lifeless essays. However, if we aim for original thought and an occasional flash of brilliance, then we must give students an opportunity to write without inhibition, without fear of failure, without the terror of grades. The response they seek is not a numeral or a single letter but an intellectual reaction to their ideas: a dialogue. (Burniske, 1994, p. 85)

Teachers who use journals in their programs need to establish, in advance, a workable plan for responding to students so they will not be overburdened. One method is to allot one or two hours a week to commenting, working through the journals in order; another is to divide the number of journals by three and respond to one-third each week. It is not necessary for teachers to respond to everything students write. "The amount of writing done by students should never be limited by the time available for the teacher (or even other pupils) to respond to students' writing" (Searle & Dillon, 1980, p. 780). Students themselves can determine which journal portions they want teachers to comment on, if teacher and students establish a simple coding system; for example, students mark sections for the teacher to respond to by putting an arrow at the beginning of the section and a line at the end. The teacher and students may agree that the pages that are folded over or stapled together will not be read by the teacher. (The possibility of such an agreement should not be introduced by teachers unless they are committed to honoring students' privacy.) Or, the students may mark confidential passages that they want the teacher to read with special care. "This allows for privacy or cries for help, as they choose. They know I am legally required to refer any concerns I might have about serious problems to outside professionals, but they also know this will occur only after I have a conference with the student" (Van Ausdall, 1994, p. 34).

Written comments teachers can use in responding to students' journal entries are of three kinds: evaluations, corrections, and substantive comments. Substantive comments are those that have meaningful substance or convey ideas related to the topics the student has written about. Consider these two journal entries and the three possible comments following them.

Student's entry: When I read that each of the major tektonic plates touches at least two other ones, that helped me realize how complicated movement of the plates can be and how many ways these movements can affect us. I'm glad you're reading aloud to us from the book while we're studying this. (I forget the title.) It makes reading the textbook easier and not so dull.

▪ Possible comment: good!
▪ Possible comment: tectonic
▪ Possible comment: Remind me that we should have a class discussion about the major tectonic plates having multiple points where they touch, and how the movement of one affects at least two others. The book is *Our Patchwork Planet* by Sattler and Maestro. I think it's terrific.

Student's entry: I couldn't consentrat on the book today becuse my brother was in a car aksident but keep on reading, I like it.

▪ Possible comment: I'm sorry. Try to concentrate, though, and remember you need to write longer entries.
▪ Possible comment: *concentrate, because, accident.* Watch out for run-on sentences. I'm sorry about your brother.
▪ Possible comment: I'm sorry about your brother's accident. I'll talk with you about it tomorrow, so you'll probably read this after we talk. You're right that it's hard to think about anything else when we're worried about someone we love. Yes, I'll keep on reading, and I'll go back over the part you missed, about the movement of tectonic plates.

Although it is more time-consuming to comment substantively than it is to write an evaluative comment such as "Good work!", students respond better to those comments that show the teacher's interest in their ideas. "Teachers who assume information-gathering stances and become a receptive and trusted audience for writers can enhance the writing process" (Soto, 1989, p. 149). Although it may be difficult for teachers to refrain from correcting errors in students' journals, it is important to develop and exercise that restraint. Curtis Hayes and Robert Bahruth, in describing journal interactions with their students who are children of families engaged in migrant labor, point out that writing substantive comments is, in fact, a way of providing instruction:

> By writing, we demonstrated the importance of writing in both their lives and our lives.... We provided accurate spellings, structures, and forms [when we wrote our replies]. ...Teachers are worried over errors, and we were no exception. Our children exhibited a number of them but we seldom had errors which obscured meaning. ...[Students] will make errors, but as they become more proficient, as their production increases, as they read and write more, the number of errors will decrease. But they will not disappear overnight. If children did not make errors they would not be learning. (Hayes & Bahruth, 1985, pp. 100–102)

Prompted Writing

One way to make writing a regular part of content area instruction is to plan one or more short sessions each week, when students write in response to a "prompt"—a short assignment that gets them past the "I don't know what to write" barrier, while still allowing them freedom to match the writing task to their own ideas and interests. Writing prompts can be format-based, as in the Write-Out strategy, or topical, as in Confer and Write. Prompted writing can be linked to journal writing by using prompts, periodically, when time is assigned for students to write in their journals. One method of incorporating prompted writing as a content area class assignment is to use it as an introductory activity at the beginning of class. "Exemplary teachers do not waste class time," Diane Miller points out. "They begin as soon as students enter the room by engaging them in a constructive activity." One of the prompts Miller suggests for repeated use in a math class is, "Suppose a friend asks you to check the answers to some homework problems. Would you mark the following problem correct or incorrect? Explain why it is correct or incorrect" (Miller, 1992, p. 354).

Katharine Breece (1988, p. 15) suggests a series of open-ended, generic writing prompt formats that can be used in all content areas. *Write out what you know about* [a topic being studied]. *Write out what you remember about* [the topic]. *Write out what you discovered about* [the topic]. *Write out what you think about* [the topic]. The Write-out strategy differs from the Confer and Write strategy because the teacher does not write while the students do. In Write-out, the teacher interacts with students while they are writing, moving briskly among students to encourage them. Breece describes the teacher as reading over a student's shoulder, "prompting, asking questions when the student's writing is unclear, listening to students' responses, and showing students that oral responses can be written."

Just as Themed Reading (described in Chapter One) focuses sustained reading on content area topics, the Confer and Write strategy is a method of incorporating sustained writing in content area study. In both strategies, the component of structure ensures content focus. In traditional sustained silent reading activities, students read whatever they wish, and in typical sustained writing activities, students have free choice of topics. The activities suggested in this text allow student choice within the structure of a content area topic. During Themed Reading, both students and teacher read trade books, resource texts, and other materials about what they are learning.

During Confer and Write, both students and teacher write about a content-related topic. The teacher presents a topic for in-class, open book, expository writing—one that is related to course content. Students have five minutes to confer about the topic in cooperative groups before they begin to write. The writing is then done individually and silently. Conferring—group talk preceding individual writing— reduces students' anxiety about writing and enhances the quality of their written product. In Confer and Write, all writing is open book, open notebook. This rule makes the writing more realistic and transferable; ordinarily a writer is not required to base informational writing solely on memory. Because students have access to their books and notes and can consult one another before they write, they are unlikely to produce trivial, superficial pieces of writing. A feature of the Confer and Write strategy is that writers do not know the writing topic in advance. Because the topic is related to what the class has been studying, all students should have a knowledge base for writing, and the group conversation that precedes writing helps each student come up with pertinent ideas. Nevertheless, the writing task is an impromptu one for which students cannot directly prepare. Therefore, since the teacher's writing task should resemble the students', the teacher cannot write about the teacher-assigned topic. Just as the teacher assigns the students a topic to write about, students assign a topic for the teacher. Figure 10–4 describes the steps in the Confer and Write process.

At each Confer and Write session, one of the groups is in charge. One of the group's responsibilities is to decide when to end the writing session by calling time; the other responsibility is to give the teacher a topic to write about. After the teacher has given the students their writing assignment, during the talk time that precedes writing members of this group give a writing assignment to the teacher. The assignment should be content- or class-related; the teacher may decline the assignment and ask for another on one of two grounds: "I don't know enough about that topic to write about

it," or "That calls for personal information." During the time the students write, the teacher also writes. The group that set the teacher's topic gets the teacher's writing, which serves as a model of draft writing. Typically, the paper is not neat and often is unfinished. (Confer and Write provides a good opportunity to teach students about the punctuation mark called an ellipsis, three dots (…) that signal something has been omitted or that a passage is unfinished.)

Responding To Students' Writing

The decisions teachers make about how they will respond to students' writing are important ones, which should be made thoughtfully in the context of the decision-making factors—subject, students, situation, self—which are stressed throughout this text. A teacher's subject area is likely to have an influence on the amount of writing done in the classroom and on the teacher's responsibilities to ensure students' writing progress. Additionally, for students to develop as people who communicate effectively in writing and who are not apprehensive about writing, teachers must consider their students' strengths and needs as they respond to their writing. They also should think deliberately about their own situations, abilities, and attitudes toward writing as they make decisions.

FIGURE 10–4   Steps in the Confer and Write Process

1. The teacher proposes the expository writing assignment—either a single assignment that requires choice of topic (e.g., choose two of the biomes we have studied so far and compare and contrast them) or two similar assignments from which students can choose (e.g., discuss animal adaptations in biomes with variable climates or choose one animal and describe ways in which it is adapted to its habitat).

2. Students confer to discuss ideas and, as necessary, ask classmates for suggestions, in their cooperative learning groups, for approximately five minutes. Students begin writing whenever they are ready.

3. During the period for conferring, one group or person assigns a writing topic to the teacher.

4. Everyone writes.

5. The group that made the assignment to the teacher calls time after approximately ten to fifteen minutes.

6. Students may share excerpts from their writing—not talking about the writing process, but reading some portion of what they have written.

7. The teacher's writing is given to the group that set the topic.

8. Students hand in Confer and Write papers for teacher comments or include them in their learning logs.

When responding to students' writing, the teacher has four roles from which to choose: recorder, summative evaluator, formative evaluator, and friend or colleague. (An additional role, which can be called "ignorer," is illustrated by Nancie Atwell's anecdote, quoted in Chapter Five, regarding a situation in which a teacher assigned a major writing assignment and then apparently avoided looking at the piles of paper until the night before the last day of school.) Of these four roles, that of recorder is the most limited and least time-consuming; it consists of noting whether or not an assignment has been done. This is useful if materials are not returned, or if, as in the case with some journal entries, students have requested that their writing not be read; it is not helpful or encouraging, however, for students to have returned to them significant written work with nothing but a checkmark indicating that the teacher noted the assignment was done. Summative evaluation is assigning a grade, which may or may not be accompanied by comments. Formative evaluation is more varied, extensive, time-consuming, and useful. Teachers who fulfill the role of formative evaluator effectively give comments about students' writing that help students progress as writers. Finally, teachers can respond to students' writing much as a friend would—by expressing interest in students' ideas and sharing ideas of their own. (As was noted earlier in this chapter, when suggestions were given about responding to students' journal entries, responses that consist entirely of superficial comments such as "Good!" "Tell me more" or "Wow!" are not useful. In fact, responding in this way is simply an expansion of the recorder's role—a way of indicating that the student's writing has been seen by the teacher.)

Considering these four possible roles serves as a reminder to teachers that they do have options and that they do not have to teach as they were taught. If writing in school as they experienced or observed it was unpleasant and unproductive they do not need to repeat that kind of instruction in their own classrooms. Additionally, teachers can choose different roles for different kinds of writing assignments. Although they should not choose the recorder role in response to all of the writing students do, it can sometimes be a sensible approach to take; for example, a

teacher could decide to respond substantively each week to one-fourth of students' prompted writing and simply record that the other papers were done. (The Strategic Teachers section at the end of this chapter describes a teacher whose students write extensively and the ways in which the teacher organizes this aspect of her teaching.)

For teachers whose subject area is English and language arts, the subject factor probably will be primary when they decide how to respond to students' writing, since these teachers have a major professional obligation to help their students develop as effective writers. Much of teachers' response to students' writing should be in the category of formative evaluation. However, because these teachers will—or certainly should—plan their teaching so students write extensively, it is wise for them to choose a variety of ways to respond to writing assignments. Teachers with other subject area assignments also should consider thoughtfully the roles they will take in responding to students' writing. (It is a theme of this text, and this chapter in particular, that all teachers can and should incorporate all of the language modes, especially writing, in their content area teaching, and that doing so will enhance their teaching and their students' learning.) All roles—recorder, grader, teacher, friend—are open to all teachers who include writing in their programs. For all teachers, a major part of their role as formative evaluators of students' writing will relate to content. (Recall Daniel Pearce's comment, quoted earlier in this chapter: "If a paper has poor content, then no amount of correcting the elements of form will transform it into a good piece of writing."). But it is important for all teachers to recognize that they need not yield to the English teacher the role of formative evaluator in regard to the mechanics of writing. In addition to their comments and advice about content, teachers can give their students suggestions about how to improve the clarity of their writing and provide information about one or two aspects of writing mechanics (e.g., how to spell several words or what punctuation to use). This kind of guidance is particularly helpful when it comes from a content area teacher, because it demonstrates to students that good writing is expected everywhere.

The two roles teachers most frequently take in the writing process correspond to the formative versus summative distinction in evaluation, discussed in Chapter Eight. Formative evaluation occurs during a process, while the process and product can be shaped, altered, and revised. Summative evaluation occurs at the end of a process and expresses a final decision. When teachers are an audience for student writing, when they confer with students or give written comments that are part of an ongoing dialogue, they are responders and the process is formative. When teachers judge a final written product, they are graders, and the process is summative. Alan Weber (1992, p. 24) notes that "grading a paper and giving written or oral feedback are two different personalities of evaluation." Useful formative evaluation focuses on teaching a limited amount of information, clearly and directly. Judith Dobler and William Amoriell (1988, p. 222) report research showing that comments about students' writing "worked best when they kept the writer's attention on the task and focused on the specific prose feature being taught—over several comments, not just one." Repeatedly, writing scholars and practitioners note the importance of teachers focusing on the formative role of commenter and adviser. Moreover, they emphasize that most comments should relate to content, to ideas, and not to technical elements of students' writing. Dennis Searle and David Dillon propose a hypothetical conversation to illustrate this point:

Teacher: (answering door) Hi.

Friend: I'm sorry I'm late, but a funny thing happened to me on the way to your house this evening.

Teacher: That's an awfully trite way to begin your conversation. Try to be more original.

Friend: I was driving along when I heard this high-pitched, whining, abrasive screech from the engine.

Teacher: Those are good descriptive words!

Friend: Just then I come to a service station.

Teacher: You "came" to a service station.

Friend: Worried to death about my car, the service station attendant told me it wasn't serious.

Teacher: You misplaced your modifier.

(Searle & Dillon, 1980, p. 775)

Providing Support For Writing

In some situations, teachers may decide to include Writer's Workshop (Atwell, 1987b; Wentworth, 1990) as an element of their programs. In the elementary grades, workshops can be built into language arts time; in middle school and high school, teachers may incorporate workshop time as one activity for cooperative groups, during parts of the year when students are heavily engaged in writing assignments. During Writer's Workshop, students have the opportunity to meet during one or more half-hour sessions a week to confer in small groups about writing in progress. Mary Heller (1991) provides guidelines for Writers' Workshops, suggesting that the groups be limited to three or four members (in addition to the teacher, if needed) and that students themselves decide when a first or second draft is ready for discussion. Another addition to the classroom writing program that teachers may choose to put into place—literally—is an Author's Chair (Graves & Hansen, 1983). This is a chair that is set aside for students when they wish to read portions of their work aloud, then invite comments and suggestions from classmates. Moving to the author's chair is a signal that a student wants to share a writing in progress; students who wish to participate then gather around.

What About the Mechanics?

Surely, the mechanics of writing—accurate spelling, correct punctuation, standard grammar—are important. But just as surely it is not the primary role of content area teachers to teach spelling, punctuation, and grammar. Here again are good-news messages for content area teachers. Of the six items listed below, the first three have been addressed in earlier chapters. The additional ideas—a developmental progression in acquiring written language conventions, methods of engaging students in revising their writing, and strategies that integrate learning the mechanics of writing with content area study—are discussed later.

- When teachers read aloud, students build their knowledge of standard grammar by listening to the author's language.

■ When students read widely, and when they see teachers' writing that is technically accurate, they have models of correct spelling, punctuation, and usage.

■ When teachers use mini-lessons and FYIs, they can give quick instruction about the technical aspects of writing.

■ When students revise their writing, then technical correctness becomes a focus. (Remember the three-step progression—fluency, clarity, and correctness—discussed earlier in this chapter.)

■ There are useful, lively strategies that integrate learning about conventions of written language with content area learning.

Language Development in Talking and Writing

Those who observe and think about young children's language development are aware that there is a developmental progression in the way children talk. Very young children use single words to communicate, then progress to short sentences that are different from adult speech in omitting certain kinds of words ("e.g., I go store"), and later in using certain language conventions consistently (e.g., adding -ed in all past tense forms: "I goed to the store"). Except in unusual circumstances, children progress, without instruction, through various stages of oral language use and become adept speakers of their language. Written language also develops through successive approximations (Au, 1993; Holdaway, 1979). As with spoken language, beginning writers are apt to overgeneralize what they have learned. For example, once children begin to observe the combination of *apostrophe*+s, used to indicate possession, they often begin inserting apostrophes whenever a word concludes with *s*, so that they form plurals by adding *'s*, instead of *s*. Skillful teachers will see the reason for the error, commend students for their developing understanding, and take the opportunity for a whole class or small group mini-lesson about apostrophes. They also will not expect immediate and perfect use of the new information. Successful progression is helped, rather than hindered, when teachers encourage writing without insisting that all writing be error-free. Doris Blough (1992, p. 56)

uses a gardening metaphor to caution teachers. "Unfortunately, [we often] don't give kids enough time. We leap onto every error—sometimes with glee. Why? Surely we aren't in competition with children eight or ten or twelve years old! …we have an obligation to help each student achieve literacy, to give each one a chance to grow before we start pruning."

Scholars point out that it is a mistake to attempt to teach all aspects of technical correctness in language use at once, and to teach them by means of memorizing rules. "Worthless rules, added to the waste of time, cause frustration," Ed Vavra writes, and adds that, "If we taught students how sentences work, students would eventually learn to fix their errors themselves. One of the problems with traditional grammar, in fact, is that it has focused too much on error and not enough on the norm"(Vavra, 1993, pp. 82 and 83) In an article titled "Grammar and syntax: The student's perspective" (Vavra, 1987), he advocates integrating grammar instruction with students' own writing, focusing on what students show that they are learning and have learned with the texts they are reading. In a similar vein, Lucy Calkins (1980) describes her research showing that students who write frequently and whose questions about writing are answered and discussed, learn and remember the conventions of punctuation much more readily and thoroughly than do students who are drilled about punctuation rules.

Janet Norris (1989, pp. 106–107) asserts strongly that spelling is developmental, thus when students are forced away from a developmental progression, they are left to depend on rote memorization or the application of seemingly arbitrary rules that appear to have more exceptions than regularities. "Unable to recreate the adult system without progressing through the qualitatively different stages of developmental spelling, many will remain poor spellers, or may spell words correctly on weekly tests while misspelling the same words when writing contextually." These and other educators and scholars, however, are united in the view that teachers should have a solid understanding about the technical conventions of the language and be models for students in their writing and speaking. One of the most important and effective kinds of modeling is to be, demonstrably, a learner—a person who checks spelling, consults with colleagues about questions of correct usage, and acknowledges and corrects errors.

Revising As Part of the Writing Process

Students should not be expected to revise all, or even most, of what they write, especially in content area classes. "There is only one good reason for revising," writes author Marion Bauer (1993, p. 134), "and that is to create a piece that will communicate more effectively. If everything a student writes must be laboriously revised, then most students will simply learn, again, to hate writing." Writing assignments that will be evaluated by the teacher for content accuracy, clarity of expression, responsiveness to assignment guidelines, and technical correctness have an important audience: the teacher/evaluator. These writings should be revised before final submission, and peer editing is a productive method to use. Lynn Havens (1989) suggests peer conferences, using a checklist, before writing assignments are turned in, to check technical aspects of the writing: Does the writing fit the assigned topic? Do the format and length of the writing match assignment guidelines? Is the spelling correct? Additionally, she suggests that the peer conference should address one rule of sentence structure or grammar. One of many valuable features of peer editing conferences (Jacobson, 1988) is the potential for disagreements among students about issues of technical accuracy, which can have the effect of making learning a new rule of usage more memorable than if a teacher had simply made a marginal correction.

When students' writings are to be shared with classmates, or with a wider audience, revision becomes an essential part of the writing process. Bill Lyons (1987) suggests his PQP—Praise, Question, Polish—process, discussed in Chapter Five, as a way of engaging students in discussion about issues of technical accuracy, without using time for isolated skill lessons and drills. Peer editing during the revision process also helps writers to see which of their ideas need clarification. Because writers are familiar with their subject and know what they mean to say, they may not fully explain their ideas. What they meant to write may not be in accordance with what their readers grasp: then the message sent and the message received are different. Jill Fitzgerald (1989, p. 45) notes that peer editing and discussions among the writer and readers can resolve these differences, a process she describes as "dissonance-resolution." Julie Jensen and Nancy Roser (1990, p. 8) describe a schoolwide program in which students publish their own writings in book form, with the help of volunteer aides. "Once the decision [to publish] is made, the revision and polishing procedures of that particular classroom kick in, whether it be self-polishing, peer editing, conference, group discussion, or a combination of these. Of course, there is less revision in the kindergarten than in the 5th grade, but even so, every author is convinced of the importance of making the piece as appealing as possible to the 'real" readers in the library." A useful adjunct to the peer editing process is to learn and use professional proofreading symbols (Madraso, 1993; Vallecorsa, Ledford, & Parnell, 1991).

Integrating Mechanics of Writing With Content Area Learning

For content area teachers who wish to teach correct punctuation and standard usage directly and quickly as part of the content area program, the Correct It strategy is useful. It is an adaptation of a technique called "sentence lifting," which is flawed—and which students actively dislike—because it consists of using students' own errors in writing as examples for the whole class to discuss and correct. Even when the incorrect passages are presented anonymously, the student whose work is being displayed is aware and feels ashamed. The same learning can be produced with enjoyment, rather than pain, if students' *correctly* written passages are chosen by the teacher, who deliberately alters them to include some errors that the class, including the student whose writing is used, is invited to find and correct. The Correct It strategy is similar to Detection, discussed in Chapter Five. In the Correct It strategy, however, the focus is on the technical aspects of writing—punctuation, usage, and spelling—rather than on concepts and facts. Also, students are given only the incorrect version of a paper, rather than both correct and incorrect versions. An advantage of using students' writing as the basis for instruction in the mechanics of writing is that the text passages are appropriately matched with students' developmental level of language use. Figure 10–5 describes a Correct It Challenge exercise.

Directed Spelling Thinking Activity. Jerry Zutell, who originated the Directed Spelling Thinking Activity, or DSTA, writes, "In spelling, quantity of correct spellings and quality of attempts grow in mutually supportive ways" (1993, p. 185). In the DSTA strategy, students develop spelling concepts through a compare-contrast method. Like more traditional spelling activities, the DSTA process includes a series of sessions over a period of several days. To prepare, the teacher chooses a series of words that have some patterns in common. In a DSTA linked with social studies, for example, the words, taken from a reading assignment about the American Revolution, might include *action, adventure, bridge, capture, dislodge, edge, militia, revolution,* and *pastures.* The first DSTA

session consists of spelling predictions. The process resembles a spelling pretest, but is nonthreatening and encourages students to reason about how words might be spelled. The teacher reads the words, and the students write them. ("This is the way I guess these words would be spelled.") Of course, some students, particularly those who are wide readers, will know in advance what the correct spelling of the words is, but the subsequent discussion and analysis of the spelling predictions is not a matter of finding out who is right, but of identifying the various reasons for spelling parts of words in particular ways. The spellings are discussed, word by word, and students give rationales. Then, after a word has been discussed, the teacher gives the correct spelling, "complimenting students on the reasonableness (and sometimes ingenuity) of their guesses and pointing out parts of the word that cause particular difficulty" (Zutell, 1993, p. 189). At the second session, all of the words, correctly spelled, are shown on

FIGURE 10–5 Correct It Challenge

On the nose!

Were we disappointed in the quality of the papers this class produced about animal adaptations? A loud chorus of noes! This Correct It exercise is based on papers about the sense of smell, written by Graham, Murray, and Cybella, each of whom nose a lot about the mechanics of writing.* All *six errors in the text below* were not in their papers originally, and have been deliberately placed there for you to nose out. Remember that all the facts are accurate, so there's interesting information to be learned. (Note: when correcting one error requires making two changes, the error is counted only once. Some of these errors are easy, but one is a really tough challenge.)

Many insects have legs and antennas that are covered with bristles, some of the bristles are hollow. And have holes in them. Odors in the air go into the holes and threw the bristles and reach cells that are sensitive to the odors. The odors help the insects find food. They also help them find mates.

The ways some sea creatures have to detect the animals they eat is like the human sense of smell exsept that sea creatures are sensitive to chemicals in water instead of in the air. Starfish have sense cells at the end of each of their tentacles. Fish have sense cells in their heads and some fish can smell using parts of their skin and tails. Salmon and sea turtles use their sense of smell to find their way back to the places were they were born. They go back to these places to lay their eggs.

1)

2)

3)

4)

5)

6)

Okay, you've been waiting to point out the error in the introduction. Go ahead!

* The major source of information for their papers was *Smell, the subtle sense,* by Alvin, Virginia, and Robert Silverstein, published in 1992 by William Morrow and Company.

a chart, and the students identify common features. (In the example, the features are the *-dge* spelling of the */j/* sound in *bridge*, *dislodge* and *edge*; the *-ture* cluster in *adventure*, *capture*, and *pastures*; and the use of *-ti* to spell the */sh/* sound in *action*, *militia*, and *revolution*.) The students suggest other words that share these patterns, and over the next several days they add words to the chart that they find in their reading or hear used. Students are encouraged to test each other on the words in the original list. In the final session, there is a spelling test in which students not only write the words but separate them into categories, according to their salient features.

Integrated Spelling Lessons. Fran Salyers (1992) describes a spelling program based on important texts and documents, using a spelling lesson based on the words to "The Star Spangled Banner," for which the spelling words were *banner, bursting, dawn, gallantly, glare, gleaming, hailed, perilous, ramparts, spangled, streaming, through*, and *twilight*. The lesson, which spanned several days, included a writing assignment which explained the song to someone from another country who heard it for the first time. Integrated Spelling Lessons are ideal for content area learning when a single teacher is responsible for all content areas, or when teachers with different content area classes agree to incorporate this kind of teaming as part of language arts instruction. A spelling test concludes the lesson, but preparation time, which can be a cooperative group activity, is used not only for studying words but for working on several challenging activities relating to the words and text from which they are taken. One noteworthy point is that if spelling lessons are based on real texts, frequently used words (such as *through*) that are difficult to spell can, because they occur often in text, be used repeatedly as spelling words. Content area and language arts teachers can take turns creating spelling lessons that are related to different content areas. There is much more opportunity for learning through such an activity than there is in memorizing the spelling of a list of unrelated words. An example of an Integrated Spelling Activity is shown in Figure 10–6. The text for the lesson is an actual exchange of letters written in the seventeenth century. The lesson materials consist of text, spelling words chosen from the text, a content-related writing activity (for this lesson, "Thinking scientifically"), tasks focused on word meanings and grammar, and another writing activity linking the lesson with one from the previous week.

■■ Language-Rich, Language-Respectful ■■ Classrooms

All people's use of language should be valued. Language itself should be protected from trivialization through superficial teaching. In some classrooms, it is an instructional pattern for students to be expected to use receptive language to learn and expressive language to prove that they have learned. Students listen, then respond orally to teachers' questions. Students read, then write answers to questions about their reading, complete other written assignments, and take written tests. In such situations, language becomes a form of self-incrimination for many students who must speak in response to a question and write to fulfill an assignment, but these uses of language are evaluative, not instructional. Such experiences teach students not about a topic of study, but about how they are rated and ranked as learners in a school setting. They also teach students that this kind of learning belongs in school and is to be avoided when school is over, for the day or for a lifetime. One goal for teachers should be to establish classroom environments where language is a delight. *Responsive language* is the term Janet Stone (1993, p. 13) uses to refer to language that shows students that they and their ideas and feelings are valued, contrasting responsive language with restrictive language, which is characterized by speaking to lecture, control, and assert power. "Responsive language encourages verbal give-and-take and independent thought, implies alternatives and choices, and includes other-oriented induction, in which reasons and explanations are provided." Language-rich, language-respectful, language-pleasant classrooms offer students school experiences that promote learning and the love of learning. In these classrooms, teachers value language and learning and value students and the ideas they express. Speaking and listening, writing and reading, are pervasive. Each person is recognized as a contributor and a learner.

FIGURE 10–6 Integrated Spelling Lesson

Blaise Pascal (1623–1662) to Florin Périer, his brother-in-law, November 15, 1647:

I am taking the liberty of interrupting you in your daily professional labors, and of bothering you with questions of physics, because I know that they provide rest and recreation for your moments of leisure. . . The question concerns the well-known experiment carried out with a tube containing mercury, first at the foot and then at the top of a mountain, and repeated several times on the same day, in order to ascertain whether the height of the column of mercury is the same or differs in the two cases. . . For it is certain that at the foot of the mountain the air is much heavier than at the top.*

Florin Périer to Blaise Pascal, September 22, 1648:

I have at last carried out the experiment which you have so long desired... On top of the Puy-de-Dôme... we found that there were 23.2 inches of mercury in the tube, whereas in the cloister gardens the tube showed 26.35 inches. There was thus a difference of 3.15 inches between the levels of the mercury in the tube in the two cases. This filled us with wonder and admiration.*

▌ *Spelling words:* admiration, certain, difference, experiment, heavier, height, levels, mercury, physics, professional, question, repeated.

▌ *Thinking scientifically:* What questions do you have about the experiment? (Think of at least two.)

▌ *Thinking about word meanings:* Choose two words and write a clear, useful definition for each one, based on the word's meaning in this week's spelling text. If you quote from the dictionary, use quotation marks and tell which dictionary you used. If you consult with other people, give them credit.

▌ *Thinking about grammar:* Find a word that can be used as two different parts of speech (as a noun and a verb, as a noun and an adjective, or as a verb and an adjective) and write a one-paragraph story in which the word is used both ways.

Last week's spelling assignment was based on the poem, "The Road Not Taken," by Robert Frost. This is Gareth DeRigh's grammar story, using *sigh* as a noun and a verb.

"Don't make a sound!" Dave the Detective said to his partner Ann. Ann was happy that the case was nearly over, and she gave a small sigh of relief. "Don't even sigh!" Dave shouted. "Even though we aren't in sight, a sigh could give a sign to the criminals and they could get away!" But the criminals did detect that Dave the Detective was on their trail, and they got away. Was it Ann's fault, or Dave's?

▌ *Thinking analytically:* The word *difference* was in the spelling text last week and it's used again this week:

"Two roads diverged in a wood, and I—I took the one less traveled by, and that has made all the difference."

"There was thus a difference of 3.15 inches between the levels of the mercury in the tube in the two cases."

Does *difference* have the same meaning in both of these statements, or a different one? Give a short explanation of your answer, and be prepared to discuss.

Reprinted with the permission of Simon and Schuster from *A Treasury of The World's Great Letters*, edited by M. Lincoln Schuster. Copyright © 1940 by Simon and Schuster.

STRATEGIC TEACHERS, PART EIGHT

"Everyone writes!"

Gloria Glenns teaches several different high school courses in history and economics and has the opportunity once a year to teach an advanced placement course. In a typical semester, she teaches five periods in a six-period day and has either two or three different preparations. She is active in a community theater organization, and during the spring she is one of several teachers who helps out with the school's major drama production. While she was in college, she was inspired by reading some of Donald Graves' books and articles on writing (Graves, 1979, 1989a, 1989b, 1989c) and she tries to structure her life to provide a regular time for her own writing, in addition to the writing she does with her students. Several of her poems have been printed in programs for theater productions, and she has published an article in a professional journal. She has been teaching for six years, all at the same high school, and several of her colleagues have become close friends. In all of her classes, she emphasizes writing (including writing as a mode of student-to-student communication), reading, and listening/speaking.

Glenns has three categories for the strategies she uses regularly:

- *"Moving along and making it live!"* These strategies are Experience-Text-Relationship (ETR), storytelling, teacher reading aloud from the text and related materials, and students' reading together and conferring about the text.
- *"Everyone writes!"* These strategies are Learning logs, Confer and Write, Write-Out, Concept Connections and SAIL. She also has a box on her desk for memos.
- *"Everyone shares!"* These strategies are EVOKER, creative drama, and roundtable and poster sessions.

Additional strategies aid her planning. Ms. Glenns uses her own personal version of the Annual Overview and prioritizes her curriculum. She uses mini-lessons for multiple purposes: to teach and reteach content ("Okay, everybody, two minutes of quiet for a mini-lesson to review supply and demand curves"), to teach process ("Today you're going to learn how to do Concept Connections. Listen up."), and to teach writing conventions ("The spelling demons of the day are *occasion*—2 c's, and *accommodate*—2 c's, 2 m's. I estimate these two words accounted for more than a dozen misspellings that grated on my eyes last week. This is the occasion *to seize* to get them right.")

Ms. Glenns is beginning a collection of *Significant Sayings* and plans to try out this strategy the next time she teaches an advanced placement course, with the intention of eventually using the strategy occasionally in all classes. Although she does not use paper and pencil *Pattern Guides*, she is aware of the strategy and of the value of recognizing text patterns, and teaches students to recognize and use patterns. She accomplishes this by marking in her copies of the various textbooks she uses sections and passages that follow particular patterns; when the class reaches these points, she usually does a brief *Think-Aloud* and follows it up by asking questions that encourage thinking in terms of the pattern (e.g., "What problem was Roosevelt addressing when he declared the bank moratorium? ...Did his action help to solve the problem?") She has posted a chart of symbols for the most common text patterns (see Figure 1–3 in Chapter One) and periodically requires students to write following a pattern as a prompted Learning Log assignment.

Ms. Glenns intends for her classes to move rapidly, and she wants class time spent efficiently. Classes begin exactly on time, with Ms. Glenns reading from the text, telling stories to illustrate concepts, or using her style of ETR to link her students' experiences with ideas in the reading. Students then usually read from the text to follow up the ideas she presented; they may read in pairs or groups if they wish, with murmur-level conversation. Because Ms. Glenns prioritizes (emphasizing some text sections and deemphasizing others), students do not read every section of the text. She speeds up the study of some topics by using a longer period of teacher presentation, with opportunities for student questions and discussion, followed directly by writing. In this way, some sections in a history text or a chapter in the economics text are a class focus for only one or two days, which allows time for the class to study other topics in depth.

The strong content emphasis is possible because Ms. Glenns thinks about procedures in advance so almost no class time is spent on them. Students know class activities typically follow the same sequence—Learning about… Read… Write… Share—and the assigned reading pages and the day's writing activity are listed on the board when students enter the class. Necessary materials are always ready and in the same place. When students will be using materials other than their texts and logs, they know that copies of these (e.g., poems for EVOKER) will be in a large envelope labeled "Take one," posted by the door. Although her special interests are in drama and writing, Ms. Glenns uses a sports analogy to structure her class sessions. Her own lively presentations of content help get students focused and can be viewed as a warm-up. Each session concludes with a cool-down period during which students share, for five minutes daily, ideas from their writing.

Several times during a semester the class format changes to allow for a more extensive sharing of ideas. Two or three consecutive days are set aside for cooperative groups and individual students both to present to the class papers or their analyses of course topics using roundtable and poster sessions or creative drama. Assessment is integrated with the total class program. At preplanned intervals, a regular writing assignment (Concept Connections or an essay based on Write-Out and Confer and Write papers) is used as a test. Grades are based on the sharing sessions, learning logs, two SAIL papers, and tests. Ms. Glenns expects her students to get good grades—and they do. If anyone were to question her students' high grades, she has ample documentation of their work.

How Does She Do It?

Ms. Glenns has two major challenges: to teach extensive content efficiently and to structure a way to read and comment on students' writing. Her first group of chosen strategies (reading aloud, storytelling, and ETR, plus mini-lessons) provides ways to help her meet the first challenge. By using them, she not only makes historical events and concepts in economics come alive for her students, she sets a rapid pace that leaves time later on for students to engage in writing and sharing their ideas. In other words, her strategies do not slow her down but are ways of progressing through the curriculum at a lively speed and of making efficient use of class time. As a reader, storyteller, and guide who links students' experiences to text ideas, and as a conductor of mini-lessons, Ms. Glenns controls the instructional pace for a part of each class session. During this time, students are listeners, and in Ms. Glenns' classes, listening is interesting.

Ms. Glenns second way of managing to teach extensive content efficiently is through planning. She creates her own version of an Annual Overview with one column for each of her courses and another for "The Rest of the World." This allows her to arrange topics and space out assignments for her different classes so it is manageable for her. She also can note in the final column what is happening in the world outside of her classroom that is relevant to her planning (e.g., vacations, school play, community theater responsibilities, special family events). Ms.

Glenns drafts her overview in August and keeps one copy at school and another at home, adding and revising as necessary throughout the year. The overview is for her own use, so she does not need to be detailed, neat, or clear to anyone but herself. Additionally, she annotates her own copies of the texts, preferring to work from a student textbook rather than a teacher's manual. Besides noting patterns in the writing, Ms. Glenns marks sections she intends to read aloud to the class, stars places where she intends to use storytelling, notes sections to be moved through rapidly, clips in notes for mini-lessons at appropriate points, and lists ideas for linking her students' experiences with text concepts. She also uses her history texts as a place to store copies of poems for EVOKER.

Meeting her second challenge—arranging a way to use a lot of writing without driving herself crazy—took quite a bit of thought; she is proud of the results and she is ready to share them in detail.

■ *Step One: Teach the writing processes efficiently.* To make the writing strategies manageable Ms. Glenns first plots out the semester on her annual overview. She introduces her five major writing strategies sequentially—learning logs, Confer and Write, Write-Out, Concept Connections, and SAIL, in that order. She marks her Annual Overview with the times when she is going to introduce each one. The introductions occur simultaneously in all of her courses, which is a timesaver for her. Several years ago, she drafted a concise set of guidelines for each type of writing; a friend who enjoys calligraphy made five posters for her, which she puts up as each new strategy is introduced, then leaves on display.

■ *Step Two: You have to read the writing; decide when, in advance.* Next, Ms. Glenns marks on the overview timeline points for two SAIL papers she assigns in her history classes each semester—select topic, draft 1, draft 2, paper due. With these times and all of her "Rest of the World" events in mind, she marks her "Checkpoints"—weeks when she is going to use her planning periods (and sometimes after school time as well) to read and react to Learning Logs. She reads each student's log twice, once fairly early in the semester and once later on. The Learning Logs, as Ms. Glenns uses them, are not dialogue journals; that is, their purpose is to engage students in using writing as a method of learning, rather than to provide a way for the students and the teacher to interact. (For this reason, she keeps a box for memos on her desk, which she checks daily. Students know that they can leave her notes and that she will respond to them at the next class session, usually in brief conversations.)

Each semester Ms. Glenns has two sections of one history course and two sections of another, in addition to either an economics or advanced placement course. For the purpose of reading the logs, she treats the two sections of the history course as a unit, thus she has three batches of logs and needs six checkpoints. She puts the checkpoints for the history courses after the first draft of each content-related paper so commenting on the draft is combined with reading the log. Except for this constraint, she can set her checkpoints at times that suit her schedule. Checking logs for an economics or an AP course can always be accomplished in school, over the week during her planning time, but there are four weeks during the semester when she needs more than the planning time so she takes a batch of logs home each evening. (Note that Ms. Glenns looks at the logs once more at the end of the semester, but only makes a summary comment at that time—at that point, she and her students are no longer interacting through their writing.)

■ *Step Three: Recognize that you can not do everything.* To make the writing strategies practical, Ms. Glenns has made a series of decisions that involve trade-offs: to accomplish a major goal, she is willing to risk or give up something else.

Here are her decisions.

a) *Read and comment on each log twice.* (Critic: Twice? How can you call yourself a teacher when you only look at their writing twice? Ms. Glenns: Some of the items in the log I've already read and commented on: homework, the second drafts, and final versions of the papers. The alternatives to reading the logs twice are to do it more often—I can't! I won't! I have a life of my own!—or not to use them. Would I be a better teacher if my students didn't write often? Nope.)

b) *Use students as readers and commenters.* After every session of Confer and Write or Concept Connections, students read each other's papers and write initialed comments; they also comment on drafts of SAIL papers. When she checks logs, Ms. Glenns notes a plus for students whose comments are interesting and useful and a minus for any student whose comments are not helpful. She gives occasional mini-lessons to describe useful ways to comment. (Critic: Surely students' comments aren't as useful as yours! You're a qualified teacher; they're not. Ms. Glenns: My comments are good, but students' comments are often remarkably perceptive. They learn a lot about writing, too, from reading each other's work.)

c) *Put it all together.* All of a student's writing goes into a single log. Ms. Glenns has a batch of three-ring notebooks students can use, or they can bring in their own at the beginning of the semester. (Critic: Gotcha! Some kids are going to goof off and then do all of the writing just before the checkpoint, and you'll never know. Ms. Glenns: I doubt it. They'd have to be pretty slick and there'd have to be a conspiracy. Students number the pages in their logs, date their writing, and other students date their comments. I write when they write during Confer and Write, but for the other writing activities I'm moving around the room and looking over students' shoulders. I'd notice if a student wasn't writing. Besides, what would be the point? Students enjoy the writing and sharing activities, and they'd rather write in school than do a huge pile of homework.)

d) *The logs stay in school.* (Critic: So they're never going to write for homework? Ms. Glenns: Remember my three-ring binders. When I assign writing for homework, students put it in their logs after I've read it.)

■ *Step Four: Work on saying yes to students' ideas.* Although she has thought through her procedures carefully, Ms. Glenns makes it a habit to accept students' ideas for variations whenever possible. ("Ms. Glenns, can I do my Write-Out today while I'm reading the text, instead of afterwards, sort of like making notes?" "Sure. Try it and tell me if you think you learn as much that way." "Can we all do Concept Connections together, with a recorder, and then just tell you whose log to look in?" "Okay, but remember there'll be Concept Connections on the test, so everybody's got to be good at it." "Can we use one recorder for Confer and Write and do it as a group?" "No, remember that all of us write in Confer and Write and afterwards we pass the papers around and write comments." "Ms. Glenns, it's time to turn in our logs next week. Can we take some time to read each other's logs in cooperative groups?" "Great idea! We'll do it.")

■ *Step Five: Simplify the commenting.* Except for SAIL papers, Ms. Glenns comments only on content—not because she thinks issues of spelling and usage belong only in English classes, but because she wants the students to focus on getting their ideas across in writing, so she focuses on their ideas too. She often begins the writing portion of class with two-minute mini-lessons on some aspect of grammar, spelling, punctuation, and usage that her students need to be taught or retaught, and she often gives information about technical points when she is moving around the room during writing sessions (unless the assignment is Confer and Write, when she also is writing).

She needs to know where to start reading when she starts the second round of checking, and when she gives the logs a last look at the end of the course. So after each of the two checkpoints, she inserts a brightly colored page in the log, noting on it the number of pages to date and writing a summary comment.

Using students' suggestions as well as her own ideas, Ms. Glenns has developed symbols or abbreviations that represent comments, which she uses as she reads; for example, an exclamation point means "Exciting!" She also has originated what she calls "The Guidelines, Gripping, and Grandma Rules": "1. We do several different kinds of writing and the guidelines for each are posted; follow them. 2. You write a lot; I read *a lot*—make it interesting. 3. My grandma is a feisty woman with a good sense of humor—but she objects to some words and phrases. I sometimes share your papers with her; *don't annoy Grandma*." If necessary, she uses G1, G2, or G3 as a marginal comment when she is reading students' writing. (She uses the G2 comment sparingly because she realizes, as a writer herself, that a helpful reader makes an effort to be interested.)

▐ *Step Six: Make sure the writing gets used.* In Ms. Glenns' classes, students use their writing as the basis for the daily sharing of ideas, major papers, poster or roundtable sessions, creative drama productions, and open book tests.

Challenge to the Reader: Make a rough, partial draft of an Annual Overview in Ms. Glenns' style: columns for several subjects or courses you teach or plan to teach; rows for time periods (months). Include a column for "The Rest of the World" and begin by jotting down some events in that column—some things you plan to do apart from teaching that will affect how you would want to schedule students' assignments.

Choose and Use: If you were to choose one aspect of Ms. Glenns' program to use in your own classroom, what would it be, and how would you begin?

Integration of the Arts With Content Area Learning

...Discovery occurs as students learn through adventures in the arts something of the possibilities of human experience. The journeys they take through the patterned sound we call music, through the visual forms we call painting, and through the metaphorical discourse we call poetry and literature are means... [to] help students find their individual capacity to feel and imagine.... [T]hrough the arts students can learn how to discover not only the possibilities the world offers but also their own possibilities. Expression and discovery are two major contributions the arts make to human development.

ELLIOT EISNER, 1992, P. 595.

Schooling is a preparation for life. Yet so much of young people's lives are spent in school—approximately 15,000 hours over a period of thirteen years, from kindergarten through high school—that the life they spend in school ought to be valuable and satisfying in itself, rather than something to be endured for its potential future usefulness. (In fact, research and our own observations tell us that students who find school most difficult to endure are frequently those whose schooling is not a useful preparation for a productive, enjoyable life.) Elliot Eisner's commentary reminds us that engaging students in the arts—with "the patterned sound we call music... the visual forms we call painting... the metaphorical discourse we call poetry and literature"—has the potential to enrich our students' lives, both in the future and in the present.

Engaging in the arts and expanding awareness of the arts are ways of making school *lifelike*. Music, painting, sculpture, drama, dance, poetry, and tales of what is, what was, and what might be, have been parts of human life since before human history was recorded. Through the expression of their own artistic ideas, exercise of their artistic talents, and discovery of the beauty and power of the creations of others, new horizons open to students. The arts are learning; they promote learning; they mesh with other learnings. When our students paint, draw, sculpt, sing, play a musical instrument, act, dance, tell stories, or write, they express themselves as artists. But each artist learns from and depends upon the work of others, so artists are themselves discoverers. Becoming absorbed in the work of artists—seeing visual art, hearing music, watching drama and dance, reading or hearing literature—is discovery. But the new worlds that open through art become a part of our understanding and affect the way we think and express ourselves. Expression and discovery in the arts are linked.

Just as this book is not a textbook about human development, theories of education, or ethical principles, it also is not a textbook about cultural diversity, the family, or the arts. But a principle on which this book is based is that content area learning is best accomplished when the various subject areas are not treated narrowly and in isolation, and that content teaching is most effective and joyous when it is integrated and enriched. This is a book about content area learning and teaching; therefore, the arts are deliberately treated in relation to their integration with content area subjects. Each of many topics addressed in this text—for example, diversity among people, connections between school and students' families, reflective practice in one's professional life—is worthy of book-length treatment in itself and is indeed the subject of many books. To devote only one chapter to the arts—or any of these other topics—does not diminish their major importance in the field of education or in all of life. Because the topic of this book is content area learning and teaching, the arts, including literature, are considered as they mesh with and promote content area learning—with the recognition, of course, that these arts are valuable in themselves.

■■ The Arts in Content Area Learning:
■■ Decision-Making

Decision-making is a part of good teaching. In Chapter Two, decision-making was discussed in terms of four factors to consider when choosing teaching strategies. It is useful to think about the same factors when making other educational decisions as well. In the Decision Chart shown in Chapter Two (Figure 2–7), the factors are presented as parts of a circle—we can begin our decision-making at any point and can choose to give the greatest weight to any of the factors: *self, subject matter, students, situation.* In deciding whether, and how, to integrate the arts with other parts of the curriculum,

many teachers will start with the factor of self; for example, *self, situation, students, subject matter,* or they may choose to reverse or rearrange the order of factors: *self, subject matter, students, situation* or *self, students, subject matter, situation.* It is sensible for teachers to consider first their own interests, talents, experiences, and strengths.

Factors in Decision-Making

Self.   Professional education journals often include articles focused on teaching practice, including articles written by teachers describing how they have chosen to use the arts. Ann Alejandro has written about her teaching, in which her students are deeply engaged in creating their own drawings and in seeing and thinking about paintings of great artists. In the article from which this quotation is taken, she describes the conditions in which her students learn and live, which are very difficult, and what they achieve, which is impressive. What she has written also gives us information, based on inference, about the writer herself: that she is artistically talented and knowledgeable and that she uses her interests, skills, and background of information to enrich her teaching. Most of us who read this short article will be moved by it, but will not see ourselves as able to teach as she does, because we are not similarly talented.

> I believe that most writing is visually dependent, I am convinced of the parallels between teaching children how to draw and teaching them how to read and write. In all cases, students need to learn how to see, to interpret data from the world, the canvas, and the page. We see whole texts in painting, in the scenes of life around us, and in the books we read. I believe children can understand thematic wholes as they look back on the events of books, the composition of paintings, and the unfolding autobiographies of their own lives.
>
> …I believe that immersion in art can parallel and enhance the same critical thinking and decision-making brain power that we use when we paint or respond to paintings. Probably the same comparisons among musical, sculptural, and printed compositions can be made… (Alejandro, 1994, pp. 13–14)

Consider the phrase, "not *similarly* talented." Like all students, all teachers are diverse in their talents, strengths, and needs. Although we may not be similarly talented when we compare ourselves to a teacher whose work we admire, we can still learn from that person, and use part of what we learn in our own teaching. We can adopt elements of another person's teaching that suit us and fit well with what we teach, with our students, and with our situation. Looking back at what Alejandro wrote, we can see that her emphasis on drawing and painting is a decision based on her own interests and talents. We also are reminded that in-depth attention can be given to some—but not all—worthwhile subjects for learning. In her comment, "Probably the same comparisons among musical, sculptural, and printed compositions can be made," she is listing some of the many forms of art that she did not stress in her teaching. By including some aspects of the arts in their instruction, teachers can share their own interests, talents, and knowledge and expand their students' horizons. When this happens, the teachers' learning is cyclical: teachers develop their talents and build their knowledge as they prepare, teach, reflect, and gain new insights from their students, thus they have even more to share in the future.

Situation. Every teacher's situation is unique, but everyone is likely to face constraints relating to work requirements, professional growth, and personal life. In their work, teachers are obliged to follow established curricula and to meet district-specified requirements (e.g., administering required tests and following a format and schedule for reporting students' progress). Beginning teachers are learning many new things at once. Experienced teachers may have building and district responsibilities in addition to their teaching. Many teachers are engaged in their own professional development through graduate study. Apart from school, teachers have responsibilities and pleasures related to family, friends, community activities, and recreational interests.

As teachers make decisions about how they will teach, it is sensible to consider the relation of new plans to existing responsibilities. What is not sensible is to decide quickly that nothing new can be done because the workload is already burdensome. Adding something new, separately, on top of every-

thing else, may be more trouble than it is worth, but integrating a lively new idea—building it into an existing program in ways that enhance what is already required and being done—can make teaching and learning more pleasant and profitable. Many of the ideas suggested in these chapters can be fit into pieces of time that might otherwise not be well-used. Many can be incorporated as regular or long-term activities for cooperative groups. Some form the basis for projects at the culmination of a unit of study; some yield lively bulletin board displays. Many give students the opportunity to be physically active as an interlude in otherwise sedentary days. All of the strategies described give students opportunities to relate their own talents to their academic learning. Yet another advantage is the opportunity for classroom teachers and special area teachers to interact and, if they choose, to plan and teach collaboratively.

Students. Students' strengths and needs should be considered in planning—especially in areas such as integration of the arts, where there is a wealth of possible ideas from which to choose. Students' individual interests and preferences also should be taken into account as particular strategies are used, so instruction does not err in expecting every student to enjoy what most students do. For example, many students welcome the opportunity to draw and to create three-dimensional art, but an equal degree of enthusiasm and willingness to try should not be demanded of every student. Teachers need to provide alternative options, in addition to encouraging students to participate.

Subject. Integration of the arts in content area teaching, by definition, requires that content subject matter be considered in planning. Teachers need to consider how a particular form of art, or a strategy for engaging students in the arts, will fit with the content area and topic they are teaching. Many of the strategies described in this chapter can be used in any content area by an enthusiastic and skilled teacher; some fit readily with one content area and require thoughtful adaptation if they are linked with other subjects. Storytelling, for example, probably meshes more readily with social studies than with science or math, although teachers who are dedicated storytellers can find ways to make the integration work across subjects. Artists' Workshop can be linked effectively with an elementary science program and can be adapted for older students by an adept teacher or team of teachers; teachers in other content areas who find the strategy interesting and valuable can find ways to adapt and use it.

Serious, Joyous Engagement in the Arts

Incorporating the arts should enrich and enhance students' learning and school experience. Arts engagement should often be a time for fun and laughter. The arts can serve, in Sandy Asher's words, as "teaching tools that delight as well as entertain" (Asher, 1994, p. 5). Serious attention to the arts can produce joyousness or playfulness—what is incompatible with seriousness is the refusal to regard the arts as important. When the arts are unimportant in a classroom, artwork is treated as a sort of cute decoration to the school program, often, indeed, turning classroom "art" into the making of holiday decorations, while music, drama, literature, and real art are ignored. Writing from her perspective as president of the National Association for the Education of Young Children, Lilian Katz laments time spent on "frivolous, trivial, sometimes amusing, and sometimes boring activities—particularly in the arts and crafts."

> Despite the enormous social, historical, economic, cultural, and geographic diversity of our great country, from north to south, east to west, young children spend too much of the first quarter of the year cutting construction paper, making identical collages featuring snowflakes and snowmen and making valentines and shamrocks! What can we do to prevent such widespread waste of children's minds? (Katz, 1994, p. 2)

The opposite of joyous attention is an approach to the arts that equates "art" with following directions to create a neat product, treats memorization of notation systems as "music," regards putting on an annual class play in which there are a few starring and many minor parts and students must memorize their lines as "drama," and requires students to complete worksheets and identify correct interpretations and calls this "literature study." A handbook prepared by the National Art Education Association (*Visual Arts Education Reform Handbook*, 1995, p. 2) stresses the importance of a substantive focus, one which treats the arts as an essential part of life and learning, rather than as unimportant, inconsequential, and trivial. The handbook poses these questions for teachers to consider in evaluating the quality of art activities: "1) Is the focus on student art learning rather than special events, teaching techniques, exhibits, art media, or resources? 2) Is the focus on art education, not on art enrichment, exposure, or entertainment? 3) Is the focus on art content, instead of special projects, activities, contests, or processes?"

It is essential, if integration is to be useful and sound, that neither the subject matter nor the art form be trivialized. Subject matter is trivialized when important topics are linked with pointless assignments. Writing a limerick about a historical event, doing math assignments on paper cut into the shape of George Washington's profile, or paraphrasing a popular song to incorporate science terms is easy and superficial. The learning that results is, at best, minimal. Both subject matter and art are demeaned when the study of art is constricted and twisted into a curriculum in which students are required to memorize terminology, facts, and dates and to learn a series of expected answers, a method that would no doubt amuse or infuriate the artists chosen as subjects.

Expressive art can be trivialized in at least three ways: when teachers grade and rate students' productions as if each creation were a test, when teachers' expectations convey the idea that originality and excellence are immediately attainable, and when teachers give students the impression that the creation of art is a simple matter. Unless teachers are absolutely required to give a grade to artistic products, they should not do so. The ill effects of grading include giving many students the idea that they "aren't good at" something which, with encouragement and time, they might come to enjoy; inculcating the attitude that works of art should be approached as items to be evaluated; and conveying to students that the teacher is the final authority on artistic quality.

Art also is trivialized when students are immediately expected to produce something excellent or original. (The error of expecting excellence is related to the tendency to grade art work.) Janet McCracken (1993) quotes Jo Miles Schuman: "It is not to be expected that students will be able to create pieces of art as fine as the examples shown them, which are usually the result of years of training and tradition." It also is a mistake to demand originality. The paintings and clay productions of very young students often are original because young children usually approach art materials with a sense of joy and freedom and because the very fact that they are young, inexperienced, and not fully developed, physically and cognitively, results in productions which do not look like copies of something else. However, as people grow older, they learn from observing what has already been done, or is being done, by others. When students enjoy the work of a particular author, painter, or musician, it is both reasonable and desirable for them to work in the style of the admired artist. It is typical for artists, as they are learning their craft, to copy the work of others before they develop their own unique style. Writers are inspired by the work of others. Mem Fox (1993) makes this point forcefully when she says she could not have written in the style she used in *Feathers and Fools* (1989a), a children's picture book with an anti-nuclear war message, if she had not read the Bible, the stories of Hans Christian Andersen and Rudyard Kipling, and the poetry of John Keats.

Nancie Atwell shows her understanding of the importance of allowing students to work in the patterns of creative people whose work they admire when she writes of her pride in a student who became an enthusiastic reader and writer after years of failure: "In December, Daniel was reading S. E. Hinton *and writing* S. E. Hinton." (Atwell, 1984, p. 245). Rather than criticizing her student for failing to be original, she was rejoicing that he had found an author he loved, was reading all of her books he could find, and copying her style in his writing. Experienced writers, such as the poet Paul Fleischman, advise that imitation is a route to finding one's own voice, and that the choice of whose work to imitate should be a personal one:

> Don't be afraid to imitate other writers. I was a great imitator when I was younger. Just as art students copy famous paintings in museums, I copied the

style of Edward Lear's limericks when I was younger. I also liked Mark Twain and got to the point where I could imitate his style almost exactly. I also imitated Dylan Thomas and my father. Have fun with this imitation. Learn from it. Everybody imitates a different set of writers and has a different experience of life so that the voice that finally emerges is unique. (Paul Fleischman, quoted in Copeland & Copeland, 1994, p. 39)

Another kind of trivialization of art occurs when students are taught rules or specifications for producing a particular art form but are not given opportunities to examine great works of art in that form or to learn about artists who use it. An example of this is teaching students rules to follow in creating a classic form of poetry, such as haiku, then assigning "write a haiku" in the same way that "write about your summer vacation" is assigned. Students can indeed learn to write haiku, but their writing should not be done in an atmosphere that suggests that the process of creation is a simple one. Their learning should be accompanied by reading and thinking about haiku which has been written over the centuries by poets who have devoted themselves to the art form.

Guest Artists

One way for students to become aware of the importance and timeliness of the arts is to observe artists at work or in performance. Arrangements can sometimes be made for those engaged in the arts as professionals or gifted amateurs to visit schools. Some schools regularly arrange to have students observe the work of artists such as potters, weavers, or painters by engaging them to spend a day working in a public area of the school. For example, a weaver may set up a loom in a hall area near the school's entrance and work there, while teachers, following a time schedule, bring their classes to observe the weaver at work, then to ask questions. Some parent-teacher-student organizations raise funds for musicians, storytellers, or artists to spend a day in the schools visiting classrooms. In areas where there are repertory theaters, arrangements may be made for students to attend a theater production and to go backstage afterwards to talk with the actors and production crew. Sometimes theater companies offer opportunities for theater personnel to teach one-session classes at the theater or at a school.

Storytellers who are guest artists may perform at an assembly for the whole school, or for individual classrooms or several classrooms grouped together. Part of the fun can be for several classes to gather together in a single room, sit on the floor or on desks, and use all sorts of classroom spaces to settle in with friends. Such an occasion can be a delight or a disaster, depending in large part on teachers' skills in preparation. Stern warnings, lists of rules about behavior, and threats from the teacher are counterproductive, but talking over good ways to manage and deciding on a few rules of courtesy and good sense that each person will take responsibility for observing is a useful class activity.

For the visits of guest artists to influence and enhance classroom learning, two related criteria are essential. First, the students must be there. This means that exclusion and threats of exclusion from special events must not be used as a means of punishing students for infractions of school rules. Engagement with the arts is an opportunity that should be afforded to all students. To turn it into a means of classroom management trivializes the arts, distracts those students who are permitted to attend, and may deprive students who are not permitted to attend of an event that could open their horizons and alter their lives. Second, *teachers must be there.* Teachers who treat the appearance of a guest artist (or any other guest to the classroom) as an opportunity to leave the class are erring in a number of serious ways. Besides being discourteous they are failing to fulfill their responsibility of ensuring that their classes are adequately supervised. An additional reason why it is essential for teachers to remain is that if they do not they cannot learn along with their students and incorporate the learning into their programs. Folksinger and songwriter Victor Cockburn (1991, p. 73) has expressed this idea, writing from the artist's point of view: "[S]ometimes, when students and I are sitting together, singing and swapping songs, the teacher leaves. It is difficult for a guest artist to proceed when the teacher is absent from the class, and it is

also disheartening to realize that the teacher is not likely to use my techniques when I have left the classroom."

There are many advantages in meeting artists personally. One somewhat surprising benefit is illustrated by the experience of author and illustrator Keith Baker, who describes it in an article titled "Have you been dead?"—a question a child asked him when he visited a kindergarten class. Baker said he had not, and moved rather quickly to the next question, but when the question and answer time was over, he asked the child why he had raised that question. The child replied, "Well, whenever we talk about authors, they're dead" (Baker, 1993, p. 373). It is useful for students of all ages to have vivid proof not only that the work of great artists lives on after their deaths, but also that there are always many living artists who are producing work that can be enjoyed now as well as in future years.

Choosing From a Wealth of Possibilities

The ideas that are suggested in this chapter have been chosen because they have the potential to enhance students' understanding and interest in content area learning, to engage them actively in enjoying and participating in the arts, so they become more widely and deeply aware of the artistic richness that will always be available to them. Making choices requires a knowledge base. As teachers, we need to be aware of possibilities. It is the purpose of this chapter to provide a wide array of ideas, ranging from those which allow teachers and students to engage in art-related activities in depth to those which can be incorporated very simply and easily. The ideas presented—which provide only a selection from many opportunities—can be supplemented by further reading in the professional literature, where new practices are regularly described and discussed, and by attention to the arts themselves, taking advantage of opportunities to view visual art, hear music, attend dramatic performances, and read widely. Making choices also requires a willingness to act. Our knowledge base does not—cannot—include all there is to know about the arts, or an aspect of the arts; however, with awareness of some of the possibilities open to us, we can consider self, situation, students, and subject—and make our choices. And within the structure of the decisions we have made, we need to provide opportunities for students to make their own choices as they engage in the arts.

Four aspects of the arts—visual, music, drama and dance, and oral and written literature—are discussed in this chapter in relation to content area studies. (The four classifications are not distinct, of course; oral literature and drama are linked in story-telling; song and slide shows combine music and graphic art; all of the arts can be combined in dramatic activities.) In every aspect of the arts, students benefit from immersion in the rich world of art, which has been and continues to be created. They also benefit from opportunities to become creators themselves. Here as throughout this text, many more ideas are described than any one teacher can use; the aim is to provide a rich array of good choices. The classroom observation shown in Figure 11–1 demonstrates the serious engagement in the arts of which very young children are capable, with the guidance of an adept teacher.

■■ Visual Arts: "To Create a Piece
■■ of the Future"

Repeatedly, those who stress the importance of the arts as an integral part of education point to the impressiveness of students' observed work and the promise that talents fostered will benefit the world. After the death of the poet Langston Hughes in 1967, his unpublished papers were donated to Yale University. An editor of children's books found a set of alphabet poems among them, which has since been published as *The sweet and sour animal book* (Hughes, 1994). All of the illustrations for the book were created by students, mostly from the primary grades, at the Harlem School of the Arts. Actor Ben Vereen concludes his introduction to the book:

> The children who created the illustrations have used their brushes and paints and clay and scissors to create a piece of the future. I believe that children come to this planet with a special gift that they will give in their time. This book gives me a powerful sense of the possibilities that await all of us. (Ben Vereen, in Hughes, 1994, unpaginated)

Engaging in Art That Enhances Learning

Drawing is a highly accessible art form. For many students, a pencil stub, a scrap of paper, and a guess that the teacher is not looking are all that is required. Many students enjoy drawing and choose to draw rather than write when they have an option. Journals that incorporate drawings were discussed in the previous chapter. Helen Caldwell and Blaine Moore conducted a research study in which drawing was contrasted with discussion as a prewriting activity. When students' first drafts were rated on a seven-point anchored scale (i.e., a scale in which characteristics were given for each of seven possible ratings), the writing of the students who prepared for writing by drawing was significantly better than that of the students who prepared by discussion. These authors recommend drawing as a planning activity that "has the potential to act as a simple, effective strategy for increasing students' motivation to write and enhances the quality of the resultant writing" (Caldwell & Moore, 1991, p. 219). Of course, talking about a topic and creating drawings can both be used in preparation for writing, and combining both is likely to be better than using either in isolation.

The drawing, painting, and creation of three-dimensional art works can be linked with writing

Through expression of their own artistic ideas, new horizons open to students.

FIGURE 11–1   Integration of the Arts in Teaching

Observation (20 minutes) of a First-Grade Class

Background: The children have been introduced to the "word of the day" (artist), which is the focus of the day's teaching. (Artists' creations are an ongoing focus.) At this point in the day, the children are on their group rug where many of their activities take place.

Teacher (T): I want you to sit with your eyes closed and picture in your head a haystack. Do you see it?

Children: Yes.

T: Do you see a pitchfork in the haystack?

Children: (some say yes; some say no)

T: Is it day or night?

Children: (different responses)

T: Is the pitchfork old-fashioned or rounded?

Ana: What's old-fashioned?

T: Open your eyes. This is a picture of a haystack with a pitchfork.

Rick: The pitchfork in the picture is old-fashioned. And it was painted by an artist.

T: Wonderful! You knew that without my telling you, Rick. Ana, old-fashioned pitchforks are squared like this (she uses her hand and fingers to illustrate). More recent pitchforks are kind of rounded at the top. This artist paints similar pictures, but at different times of the day. His name is Monet.

Teresa: Your shirt says *Monet*.

T: Aha! I wondered how long it would take someone to notice that. The front of my shirt has a painting by Monet on it. Let's look at some of the books I've set out by different authors and illustrators.

Isaac: Illustrators are artists too.

T: Isaac, you remembered! I'm so proud of you! Illustrators are artists, and you know what? Authors are special kinds of artists. They use words to make pictures in our minds. Who can tell me the title and author of this book?

Su-Lee: *A Snowy Day* and I know the author too—Ezzer Keats.

T: Yes, it is *The Snowy Day*, by Ezra Jack Keats. Thank you, Su-Lee. The way an artist makes pictures is the artist's style. Do you remember what style Ezra Jack Keats uses?

Tim: He uses wallpaper.

T: That's right. He uses different colors and shapes of wallpaper to make his illustrations.

Jan Brett's style is to draw pictures around the edges of the page. Let's make a nice big circle, and while we're doing that let's say our numbers in French.

(Children make a circle, counting in French from one to ten. As they do so, the teacher is randomly placing postcards of different artists' works on the rug.)

T: We are going to play a matching game. All of these postcards were painted by famous artists. Let's see if we can find two postcards that use the same artistic style. I'll go first. These are both paintings of haystacks. Do you remember this artist's name?

Children: Monet!

T: Yes! You all are learning so much. Roman, you've been sitting so quietly. Would you like to go next?

Roman: Yes. *(He hesitates to pick any.)*

T: Remember, it's okay to be wrong. We're all wrong sometimes and we're all each other's helpers in this room too.

(Roman selects two pictures.)

T: Very good, Roman! These two *are* by the same artist. His name is Picasso. Yolanda, would you like to take a risk?

Yolanda: Sure.

(The children are picked to choose pairs of postcards and the teacher then asks them to go back to their seats quietly. She tells them she would like them to use the artistic styles they have seen, or a combination of them, to make their own artistic creations.)

T: Any questions?

(The children are already involved in their projects.)

Comments: This day was an absolute joy to observe. The teacher's cooperative group approach to whole language instruction was an interesting and positive learning experience for me. On several occasions throughout the day, the teacher used positive reinforcement to establish good behavior. Her students are extremely well-behaved, and in instances where they were not she handled them quietly yet firmly. She has a creative approach to her instruction which includes reading instruction using books from the classroom library and "word of the day" for spelling. She then incorporates this word into the day's curriculum. She uses learning centers and portfolios in the children's daily schedule, as well as for individual assessment.

This observation was written by Terri Blake, who was at the time an undergraduate student. Minor changes have been made.

throughout subject matter areas and also can engage students in applying their knowledge by illustrating what they have learned. Beth Smout (1990) lists printmaking, rubbings, and collages among the more unusual art forms that students can learn to create, and she suggests that books illustrated in these media be displayed, read, and discussed as particular art forms are used. Rubbings are replicas of tablets that are cast in metal or carved in stone, such as commemorative plaques and markers in historical buildings, or gravestones. They are made by placing paper over the tablet and carefully rubbing a soft chalk, crayon, or pencil across the paper, so the incised words and decorations appear as white space surrounded by the darkened area that is formed when the chalk is rubbed across a flat surface. Using a variety of art forms, students can illustrate their own writing or the works of others. Making and illustrating a collection of quotations can be an individual, group, or class project. Individually made collections can be made into giftbooks, described in Chapter Nine. Text and illustrations may be the student's own or may be quotations selected by the student (credited, of course, to the original author and source), with original illustrations by the student. Looking at some of the many books that match art works and quotations from literature can be a voyage of discovery for students. Isabelle Brent's *All creatures great and small* (1994) is a beautiful, recent example of a book where the creator is the illustrator; here, the illustrator has chosen a series of whimsical poems about animals and created elaborate illustrations for them in the style of an illuminated manuscript.

Lois Daniel, commenting that art is "an excellent motivational tool for social studies teaching because it can provide evidence," describes the creation by sixth graders of two-dimensional replicas of Greek pottery and ancient mosaics, including the Alexander Mosaic that was found in the ruins of Pompeii.

> The art component does not become a craftsy side activity, but a learning experience in itself, enhancing the goals of the social studies and the arts. Social studies classes are too often reading-based and textbook-bound. The minutes allotted to elementary social studies are often swallowed by other subjects. Time needs to be used meaningfully and relevantly. If students can have visual and hands on experiences, the impact can be far more lasting. …Art can enhance and develop the social studies unit. It also provides a common denominator for success for students of varying abilities. (Daniel, 1989, pp. 3 and 5)

The mosaic art form—an image composed by combining many individual pieces—can be used to create a collaborative artwork that illustrates the beauty of human diversity. Just as each individual person is part of a larger group—classroom, school, community, nation, world—so these groups can be thought of as mosaics created from many individual pieces. "The beauty of the mosaic as a whole outshines any of its individual components," writes Mark Gura (1994, p. 40), who describes an art project, The Human Mosaic, which he uses in his classes to promote intergroup relationships. Using two-inch squares of tagboard, students create a piece of the mosaic, a tile, by drawing a person on one of the squares. Students may create as many tiles as they wish; Gura notes that, in his experience, most produce at least half a dozen. The finished tiles are glued onto a large sheet of cardboard that holds approximately 250 tiles, forming the mosaic that can eventually become a panel in a larger mosaic.

Art can be incorporated into the classroom program systematically by establishing an Artists' Workshop, as Karen Ernst (1994) suggests. Artists' Workshop is a visual arts parallel to Writers' Workshop, a strategy in which an extended time (half an hour or more) is provided several times a week for students to write—brainstorming, drafting, revising, and choosing work to finish for publication. In an Artists' Workshop, students draw or paint in notebooks, then write about what they have drawn. They may go on, individually or collaboratively, to create larger art works based on the drawing and writing. The process is recursive. That is, drawing leads to writing and writing may lead to a return to the drawing to elaborate on it. Ernst describes a student who painted trees and a pond, then when she wrote about her painting she took the displayed painting down to add the reflection of the trees in the pond, because her writing recalled this part of the image to her. Choice is an essential aspect of Artists' Workshop—choice of topic, materials, and style. For students to

Art can be linked with every area subject

be able to exercise choice, they need a knowledge base, thus workshop sessions frequently begin with mini-lessons introducing art materials or techniques so students will be aware of the possibilities that are open to them, a method also used by Ann Alejandro (1994). Inclusion of Artists' Workshop in content area study can serve as the basis for a fruitful collaboration between art and content area teachers.

Creating Artwork That Demonstrates Learning

Nancie Atwell (1990) suggests murals and mobiles as ways of presenting information. The creation of a mural—a large artwork covering all or part of a wall—to illustrate what is being studied is a useful long-term assignment for cooperative groups. The process involves decision-making about what should be shown and how space should be used, as well as creation of an artwork. Montages made by superimposing drawings and pictures cut from magazines and collages, created by applying separate drawings and paper sculptures, enhance the mural and also make the creation process more practical, since students can work on parts of the mural without clustering around a wall space.

Like murals, mobiles—three-dimensional artworks that have moving parts—can be created as a cooperative group project, or they may be prepared by individual students. Whereas the creation of a mural, whatever its topic, has components that relate to mathematics through measurement, estimation, and perspective, creating mobiles can teach students about elements of physics. A book in the Boston Children's Museum Activity Book series, *Mobiles: Building and experimenting with balancing toys* (Zubrowski, 1993), is one resource for teachers who choose to link topic-based mobiles with scientific learning. Biographies are one of many themes that can be the basis for mobiles. Students can brainstorm significant facts that they have learned about an important historical figure, then decide how to arrange concisely presented information on figures cut into shapes that relate to elements in the person's life. These can then be hung, in balance, from the main balancing beam. For example, all of the information about Amelia Earhart might be put on cutouts of airplanes, while information about Thomas Edison might be placed on a series of different cutouts representing his major inventions.

While mobiles, by definition, have elements that move, stabiles are nonmovable sculptures. An adaptation of the stabile form, suitable for a visual display of content information, can be created by cutting and fastening heavy paper into three different cylindrical shapes, the tallest being the smallest in diameter and the shortest being the largest in diameter. Thus, the three cylinders can be arranged together, with the tallest on the inside to form a background and the shortest on the outside to form a foreground. Such sculptures are an excellent basis for visual displays of the habitats of land and sea animals, with the animals themselves shown on the middle circle and elements of their environment shown in the background and foreground. The sculpture is placed on a table or stand, thus is stable, but any of the three cylinders can be turned, so that many different views are possible. All of these creations—murals, mobiles, and stabiles—display information, therefore, should be positioned so students and visitors to the classroom can examine and learn from them.

The strategy called *storyboarding*—a "systematic visual development that portrays or summarizes ideas through a combination of words, pictures, diagrams, or slides" (Sinatra, Beaudry, Stahl-Gemake & Guastello, 1990, p. 615)—is a structure for illustrating a sequence of ideas visually. Originally designed, as the title implies, as a way of showing the sequence of events in a story, storyboarding is a versatile method of analyzing and presenting information and ideas. In its simplest form, a storyboard can be created by folding a sheet of paper into sections, onto which students make drawings of a sequence of events that they recall from a text to that has been read or predict on the basis of evidence about a text that will be read. Simple storyboards also can be used by students as an aid when they write; in this case, students use the panels for sketches of events that they plan to write about, and the storyboard becomes a method of remembering ideas and a plan for organization. Elaborate storyboards, using drawings, collages, computerized art, or photographs, can be prepared by students to illustrate a sequence of events in a story, novel, or poem; in a period of history; or in a scientific experiment. Storyboarding also can be part of long-term cooperative assignments in content areas. Richard Sinatra and his colleagues describe a middle school study of neighborhoods in which students, working in pairs, planned, took photographs of neighborhood areas, prepared storyboards using the photographs, and captioned photographs to create visual essays.

Diane Wildman (1990) calls the process that she and her students use to combine history and art *picture research*. As her students research a topic, they select pictures to illustrate events and concepts and work in teams to take slides of the pictures. They organize their slides into a slide presentation, create an audiotape, and present their research to other classes. Wildman describes the careful process used in creating a slide show about a topic of her students' choice—the Wright brothers first flight at Kitty Hawk. The first component was examining hundreds of pictures from books, slides, old newspapers, and brochures. When pictures were tentatively chosen, it was then necessary to obtain permission to use those which were protected by copyright. Wildman had a copy stand on which a camera was mounted, loaded with slide film, which students used to create the slides. In preparation for making the audiotape, students practiced reading, remembering to pause long enough for the slide to be viewed before recording a bell sound to signal the projectionist to move to the next slide. Students also selected music to be played in the background of the audiotape and prepared their bibliography to be displayed on a poster.

Photography is one of the many forms of artistic expression that is open to students. Joanne Kiaune (1992) describes using photographs taken by students as the center of semantic maps, then using the maps as the basis for descriptive writing. Picture essays can be created by collecting and arranging photographs and other visual images from printed sources. A wide variety of literature for children and young adults uses photographs as the sole or primary illustrations. Vicki Cobb has produced a series of books that explain scientific phenomena through photographs, accompanied by explanatory text; for example, in *Natural wonders: Stories science photos tell* (Cobb, 1990), a series of photographs show a drop of rain as it falls into a pond, demonstrating that the drop is spherical rather than teardrop-shaped; a photograph in *Fun and games: Stories science photos tell* (Cobb, 1991), shows the effect of a tennis ball on a racket and a racket on a tennis ball at the moment of impact. The photobiographies of Russell Freedman may be studied and enjoyed for the photography as well as for the information they impart. One of his books, *Kids at work: Lewis Hine and the crusade against child labor* (1994), also is the biography of a photographer who used his talents to expose the abuses of child labor.

Books To Delight the Eye

A beautiful use of photographs is exemplified in Walter Dean Myers' *Brown angels,* where the author has created verses to accompany a collection of African American children's photographs acquired from antique shops, markets, and auctions over the years. "These pictures speak to me of hardworking people—of tenant farmers, porters, and teachers of the 'colored' schools—who celebrated the lives of their babies as have all people before them and since. And they did so despite the difficulties of their own lives," Myers writes in an introduction (Myers, 1993, unpaginated). Students who become immersed in the book, perhaps during a study of family history, might wish to create a family giftbook by combining photographs with original text in verse or prose.

Books that bring art into the classroom are of several kinds. There are books that engage students in art by giving examples and directions. Interesting examples in this category include *Origami animals* by Hector Rojas (1993) and *Origami safari* by Steve and Megumi Biddle (1994). Rojas includes detailed family and species descriptions of animals, birds, and insects; the Biddles give information about animal habitats. Both books describe and teach an art form and are models of careful directions for completing tasks with multiple steps. Other books describe the process artists and craftsworkers follow in creating works of art; recent examples range from beautiful photographs and text that show the creation of a huge building (*Cutters, carvers & the cathedral,* by George Ancona, 1995) to photographs of a wood-carver father and his daughter and the step-by-step construction of a wooden toy (*Puddle jumper: How a toy is made,* by Ann Morris, 1993).

Books that bring art into the classroom include collections of prints or photographs of artwork. Several current series present artwork in ways that intrigue and instruct students over a wide age range. Lucy Micklethwait's *I Spy* series—*I spy: An alphabet in art* (1992a), *I spy two eyes: Numbers in art* (1992b), and *I spy a lion: Animals in art* (1994)—each consist of many full-color reproductions of paintings from across the centuries and around the world. In every full-page spread, the painting is on the right and the facing page contains only the repetitive "I spy…" and the name of the artist and title of the painting. Finding the "I spy…" items is a challenge: it requires a careful look to find two tigers among the multitude of animals in Edward Hicks's "Noah's ark;" it takes clever eyes to find the mouse in Jan van Os's "Fruit and flowers in a terracotta vase," because it is hidden in floral profusion. At the end of the books, brief information is given about each artist, along with the date of the painting and its current location.

In a series prepared by Gladys Blizzard, which includes *Come look with me: Exploring landscape art with children* (1992), *Come look with me: Enjoying art with children* (1993a), and *Come look with me: World of play* (1993b), the beautifully produced photographs of the artwork are always on the left-hand page, while the right-hand page is for text. Questions for readers to think about are followed by a vividly written short biographical piece and discussion of the artwork. The questions are well-designed to generate careful viewing and thoughtful answers. For Diego Rivera's painting "Pinata," one question asks, "Which child looks the most eager to gather the falling fruits and candies? How did the artist show that?" For Elaine de Kooning's "Baseball players," readers are told, "Pretend you have a paintbrush in your hand. Select one color in the painting and make the kind of brush strokes you think the artist used to put that color on her canvas. What kind of brush strokes would you use in your own painting of a baseball game?" (Blizzard, 1993b, pp. 27 and 29). Many of the biographies provide information about how events in the artists' childhood shaped their careers. We learn that Joseph Whiting Stock was given art lessons to keep him busy after he was paralyzed in a childhood accident, and that a doctor, impressed by his paintings, designed and built a wheelchair that enabled him to move about; that Picasso could draw before he could talk (Blizzard, 1993a pp. 15 and 29); and that, as a child, Horace Pippin "won six crayons, a box of watercolors, and two brushes" by entering a drawing in a magazine contest, had to leave school to work when he was fourteen, was wounded in World War I by a bullet that paralyzed his right hand but continued to paint, right-handed, "by using his left hand to guide the hand that held the brush" (Blizzard, 1993b, p. 25).

Art-related books for the classroom also include biographies of artists, which can be rich additions to a study of the biography genre or can add to knowledge about the time period in which an artist lived and worked. (A genre—pronounced *zhan'-ruh*—is a form or style, and the term is most commonly used in connection with written literature; novels, essays, plays, and short stories are examples of different genres.) In any genre, some publications are accurate, well-written, and beautifully designed, while others are cheaply and carelessly prepared. Not all biographies are worthy of students' attention, and teachers need to take care in choosing books that will contribute to the print-rich environment of their classrooms. Biographies of artists need careful presentation so the text will not trivialize the artist's life or work, and so the examples of artwork that are shown will be well-chosen and carefully reproduced. Robyn Montana Turner's biography of Georgia O'Keeffe (1991) is an example of a powerful though simply written text, which is accompanied by photographs of the artist as well as full-color reproductions of O'Keefe's paintings. Another biography by Turner (1991) is about the nineteenth century French artist Rosa Bonheur, whose specialty was drawings and paintings of animals. Books in the "First Impressions" series, for example, *Mary Cassatt* (Meyer, 1990), *Marc Chagall* (Greenfield, 1989), are longer books with multiple chapters, lists of illustrations, and indexes. The handsome reproductions of the artists' works have detailed captions. Some are shown in double-page and fold-out spreads, while other illustrations show details of a painting.

Beautifully designed, printed and illustrated books are themselves a form of art that is worthy of attention and study (Goldenberg, 1993; Stewig, 1995), a study that Linda Leonard Lamme (1989) calls *illustratorship*. Books showing various art forms can be placed at a workstation with resource books that enable students to prepare short informational reports based on artworks and artists. The styles of different artists can be compared, and for some artists, such as Chris Van Allsburg, the varying styles they have chosen to use can be contrasted. John Stewig (1995) suggests as another contrast the works of artist and author John Steptoe—the bright, broad-brush paintings in *Stevie* (1969), published

when Steptoe was nineteen, and the elaborately detailed, sumptuously designed artwork in *Mufaro's beautiful daughters: An African tale* (1987), published near the end of his tragically short life.

Some books include detailed descriptions about the processes artists have used to create illustrations. "A note about the art" describes the multiple steps Tom Feelings used to create the illustrations for *Jambo means hello: Swahili alphabet book* (Feelings, 1974, unpaginated) and the methods the printer employed to accurately reproduce the illustrations. In an "Illustrator's Note" at the conclusion of *Dance me a story* (1993, p. 125), Jane Rosenberg specifies exactly what kind of paper, paints, and brushes she uses, as well as the steps she uses in producing the drawings and paintings in the text. David Wisniewski creates and illustrates original folktales based on legends of ancient cultures: from the Mayas, *Rain player* (1991), from Mali in West Africa, *Sundiata, Lion King of Mali* (1992), and from Scandinavia, *Elfwyn's saga* (1990). In each of the tales, the protagonist is a child who eventually grows and triumphs, despite difficulties. The heroine of *Elfwyn's saga*, a folktale based on the history and legends of Iceland, is a child whose blindness and bravery protect her from a sorcerer's magic crystal into which others stare and become lost. In an "Author's Note," Wisniewski discusses the history that underlies his story and tells how he prepared the intricate cut-paper illustrations for the book.

> The illustrations are cut [the] same size from ChromaRama colored papers and adhered with double-stick photo mountings. They are first sketched on layout paper, with a final drawing made on tracing paper. The drawing is then transferred to the back of the colored papers and cut out. An X-Acto knife and over one thousand very sharp blades were used to produce the illustrations for this book. And because I paid attention, I didn't cut myself once. (Wisniewski, 1990, unpaginated)

Increasingly, illustrations that enhance the beauty and informational content of books are being used in ingenious ways. For example, the endpapers of books—the spreads at the front and back of a book consisting of the inside of the covers and the facing pages—are no longer always blank or printed with simple patterns. Some endpapers are artworks in themselves. For Catherine Stock's *Where are you going Manyoni?*, which is set in Zimbabwe, the endpapers are watercolor copies of "cave paintings made by indigenous people who lived in the area thousands of years ago," the author and illustrator writes. "The land and its inhabitants probably appeared very much to them as it did to me" (Stock, 1993, unpaginated: Author's Note). In other books, such as *Around the world in a hundred years: From Henry the Navigator to Magellan* (Fritz, 1994) and *The Great St. Lawrence Seaway* (Gibbons, 1992) the endpapers are labeled maps; in Jean Fritz's book, the routes that explorers traveled are marked. In *Communication* (1993), author-artist Aliki uses endpapers to show English upper- and lower-case alphabets and the alphabet in sign language and Braille. Many of Seymour Simon's science trade books use the endpapers for full-color illustrations to which readers can refer for information. In *Weather* (1993), there are labeled pictures of different forms of clouds. *Mountains* (1994) shows the highest of the mountains on each of the continents and at the poles and in Oceania. *Our solar system* (1992) has a chart that provides information about each of the planets. The elaborate endpapers at the front and back of Steven Kellogg's retelling of *Jack and the beanstalk* (1991)—a picture book that delights and instructs readers of all ages—provide, solely through pictures, the author-illustrator's conception of a prequel and sequel (i.e., new stories that precede and follow a known story) to the familiar tale. The first painting is particularly ingenious. It shows the bags of gold, the magic harp, and the hen that can lay golden eggs all as part of loot taken by a pirate ship, while the cowering pirates are attacked by the giant ogre. Thus, readers may decide to absolve Jack of the crime of stealing when he cleverly brings back treasures from the ogre's lair at the top of the beanstalk, because they are not the rightful property of the ogre, nor even of those from whom the ogre stole them.

Music: "The Ordering of Sound in Ways That Please the Ear"

"Musical classrooms are joyful places, classrooms that invite children to relax and participate," Linda Lamme writes (1990, p. 299). Of all the arts apart from literature, music is the one whose richness and diversity can be most readily brought into the classroom. Audiotapes and compact disks enable teachers to play classical or modern music and music representative of various cultures and times to entertain, inform, invigorate, inspire, soothe, and delight. Through all of its variations, music remains a universal language. "In every known culture, the ordering of sound in ways that please the ear has been used extensively to improve the quality of life" (Csikszentmihalyi, 1991, p. 108).

Making Music

When a painter or sculptor has created a work of art, that product is complete, waiting only for people to view it with wonder and appreciation. When a writer has completed a work of literature, it is ready for readers. Those who display art and publish literature, who themselves may be gifted in their craft, are the only link needed between the creators and their audience. But for music, drama, and dance, a combination of artists is needed to present the art to its audience. Mozart's music exists because he composed it; it enters our lives through the artists who perform it. Students in our classrooms can compose music and would probably do so more readily if this

Performing music is a collaborative activity. Musical classrooms provide opportunities for students to participate as singers or players.

aspect of the art were encouraged. It is unusual, but not unknown, for classrooms to be furnished with pianos or equipped with autoharps, recorders, and other musical instruments. Songwriting, however, can be done in classrooms where the only musical instruments are human voices. Author and educator Mem Fox (1993) describes visiting a third-grade classroom and being welcomed with an original song based on her book Koala Lou (1989b), written by a child in the class who conducted its performance with the whole class as a choir.

While composing music is often an independent process and sometimes a solitary one, performing music—in the sense of *doing* music—is collaborative. Describing the joy that musical participation can bring to adults, Mihalyi Csikszentmihalyi (1991, p. 112) describes singing as part of a choir or playing an instrument in an amateur musical ensemble as among "the most exhilarating ways to experience the blending of one's skills with those of others." For students in classrooms, there need not be a choir or an ensemble. What is needed instead are opportunities to participate in music as singers or players, and teachers are wise to encourage enthusiastic participation rather than aiming for perfection in performance. Singing is a part of learning in many classrooms for young students; charts with the lyrics of familiar songs are an excellent form of reading material for emergent readers. Although music permeates the lives of teenagers—Gail Farrell (1991) writes that "young adolescents live a world of song"—singing for older students, in a school setting, is typically only for those who are members of school choirs. Spurred by a teacher who cares for music, or inspired by a guest artist, everyone can sing. Folk music, for example, is a way of linking music, storytelling, and history. "Folk songs," writes Victor Cockburn (1991, p. 72) "are intended for off-key singers, amateur musicians, whistlers, hand clappers, and folks who love a good song enough to want to join in."

Musical Accompaniments to Learning

Just as well-written text is appreciated more fully when it is read many times, good music is more deeply felt and understood when it is heard repetitively. Some teachers choose to incorporate a period of listening to music into the school day. Nancy Cecil and Phyllis Lauritzen (1994) discuss selecting major pieces of music that are played repeatedly over a period of a month, when students first come to class in the morning and at other times during the day. When timing and selections are planned with care, music can enhance learning by accompanying other classroom activities. Themed Listening is a strategy that consists of students' hearing teacher-selected recordings related to what they are learning. Often, the music is played while students are quietly working on group projects. For very young students, Themed Listening may involve a teacher playing a guitar or other instrument, while the children rest. Music chosen to supplement learning may include instrumental music characteristic of other times and cultures. "Just the tunes from around the world give children a sense of other cultures. Learning to sing songs in other languages and what those songs mean expands their awareness of the world" (Epeneter & Chang, 1992, p. 66). Folk songs and other music from particular historical time periods, such as the American Revolution, the Civil War, or the Great Depression, are ideal for Themed Listening. An alternative use of Themed Reading is to play related music as a background for reading aloud. Kathy Short and Junardi Armstrong (1993) describe reading aloud informational text about the desert while Navajo flute music is played in the background, then continuing the music during a brainstorming session.

Students who have become familiar with music from a time period or culture they have studied can use their knowledge in a strategy parallel to the picture research strategy discussed earlier—a student-created slide show that emphasizes music. An entertainment form known as the illustrated *song and slide show* was originated in the middle of the nineteenth century, became widely popular by the turn of the century, and faded a few decades later. George Chilcoat (1991) describes the process his middle school students use to create song and slide shows based on historical events, using slides with original drawings and student-written captions, accompanied by music from the time period. To prepare a song and slide show, students collect information from multiple sources and plan and prepare a series of slides: an introduction, a buildup of incidents dramatizing interrelationships among individuals with roles in the events, showing causes and effects, a climax, and a conclusion. Slides with written captions can provide information, or narration, and music can accompany the slides.

Music can be an inspiration for journal entries and other writing. Music response journals provide an opportunity for students to write about music they love, react to new music that they have heard, and contrast two pieces of music that are by the same composer or similar in theme. Imaginative writing can be done in response to music listened to before writing and played while students write. Students can select musical compositions to accompany choral readings or Readers' Theater, or they may choose musical passages that would be appropriate themes for characters in a story, poem, or history. Many people, when they have the option, choose to listen to music while studying and working on projects; classroom music, rather than being a distraction, may contribute to a productive work environment for cooperative groups.

Words and Music

Collections of songs are often sources for information about history and culture, and many are beautifully illustrated. One example of a book that links literature, song, and visual art is *From sea to shining sea: A treasury of American folklore and folk songs*, compiled by Amy Cohn (1993). Cohn has classified the works in the anthology according to ethnic and religious groups, geographical regions, story and song types; the songs are ballads, call-and-response songs, chants, comic ballads, cumulative songs, hand claps, hymns, jump songs, laments, lullabies, nonsense songs, popular songs, rounds, sea shanties, spirituals, wake-up songs, and work songs. Each section of the book is illustrated by an artist or artist pair who have been honored with a Caldecott award. David Weisner is the illustrator for a section titled, "I've been working on the railroad," stories and songs from the time when workers, many of them immigrants, labored to construct the railroad tracks that would connect the eastern and western parts of this country. One of the songs is a ballad that jokes about the hard-working conditions: "Drill,

ye tarriers, drill!" These were times when workers who were injured at work lost their jobs or lost pay for missed time, as two verses of the ballad tell us:

The new foreman was Jean McCann;
By gosh, he was a blamed mean man!
Last week a premature blast went off
And a mile in the air went big Jim Goff.
(chorus: Drill, ye tarriers, drill!)

When next payday it came around,
Jim Goff a dollar short was found;
When he asked what for, came this reply,
"You were docked for the time you were up
in the sky!"

Another folk song in this section, titled, "A gust of fall wind," is not widely known; it was sung by the Chinese workers who built much of the lines coming from the west toward the east, working far away from their country and families. "This lament, sung by the Chinese in America," Cohn explains (1993, p. 168), "uses the image of the coming winter as a metaphor for loneliness and sorrow." Besides the words and the music for the song, and Weisner's powerful illustration, the song is shown in Chinese characters and their transliteration into English sounds.

Collections of songs can bring music into the classroom. Jane Yolen, a prolific author of books for children and young adults, has edited books of music (1972, 1977, 1986, 1992) including compilations of lullabies and rounds. Each piece of music is annotated with information about its history and could be an interesting challenge to match the most familiar songs with the facts given about them. For example, Yolen gives this information about a song in *The fireside song book of birds and beasts* (1972): "Often called the 'best-known round in the world,' this grisly little song is a popular nursery rhyme. There is a version of it to be found in Thomas Ravenscraft's *Deuteromedia, or the seconde part of Musick's melodie*, printed in 1609." Thus, readers find that there is always something new and interesting to learn, even about something as familiar as "Three blind mice." Many books feature a single song in a detailed and exciting way. Peter Spier's books *The Erie Canal* (1970) and *The Star Spangled Banner* (1973) present the music—a folk song and the U. S. national anthem—in the context of the history of the building of the canal and the history of the War of 1812, during which *The Star Spangled Banner* was written. In *Abiyoyo* (1986), folksinger Pete Seeger recounts the South African folktale that was the basis for one of the most popular songs in his repertoire. The book includes music for the song, as well as memorable illustrations of the leaping giant Abiyoyo. Cultural folklore is sometimes transmitted through lyrical, rhythmical words. *Did you hear wind sing your name? An Oneida song of spring* (Orie, 1995), shares a Native American song of the Oneida people. The book is written by an artist and a teacher who grew up on the Oneida Nation Reservation in Oneida, Wisconsin, and who is now principal of a school there; the illustrator has decorated introductory pages and borders with paintings of the beadwork, which is the traditional form of art and expression for the Oneida people.

Opera is an art form linking music and drama, rich with sound and spectacle. Becoming familiar with the exciting stories that operas dramatize is a way to widen students' horizons, and when the stories are known, operatic arias can be set in context and made a part of music played in the classroom. *Sing me a story* (Rosenberg, 1989) is a handsomely illustrated collection of stories that recounts the plots of famous operas, among them *Carmen, The Magic Flute*, and *Porgy and Bess*; the introduction is by the world-famous tenor Luciano Pavarotti:

> Sometimes it is a problem that opera is sung in so many foreign languages—but believe me, even opera sung in English can sound like a different language. …[L]earn the story of the opera, …listen to recordings, …watch videocassettes [and] your appreciation will grow as you recognize your favorite moments and feel the extraordinary power of grand opera. The more you know about opera, the more you will love it. And then—you will want to go to a live performance.…The next time I am on the stage I will look for you in the audience. (Luciano Pavarotti, in Rosenberg, 1989, p. 6)

Other books tell the stories of a single opera. *Turandot* (Mayer, 1995) is a handsomely illustrated retelling of the folktale that is the basis for a famous opera by Puccini. Music and drama, art and biography, are combined in *Aïda* (1990), majestically illustrated by Leo and Diane Dillon and retold by famed soprano Leontyne Price, who concludes with a "Storyteller's Note" in which she describes her own experiences in the title role:

> Aïda as a heroine—and Aïda as an opera—has been meaningful, poignant, and personal for me. In many ways, I believe Aïda is a portrait of my inner self. She was my best friend operatically and was a natural for me because my skin was my costume. This …allowed me a freedom of expression, of movement and of interpretation that other operatic heroines I performed did not. I always felt, while performing Aïda, that I was expressing all of myself—as an American, as a woman, and as a human being. (Price, 1990, unpaginated)

■■ Drama and Dance

"The unique contribution of classroom drama lies, not only in the way it can help children to learn knowledge, but …in its power to enable them to understand more deeply *what they already know*" (Edmiston, Encisco, & King, 1987, p. 222). In this perceptive comment about drama in the classroom, Brian Edmiston and his colleagues relate that engaging in drama in the classroom links the cognitive and affective domains. Taking on another's role in a dramatized action awakens understanding of that person and those with whom the person interacts. Improvising a dramatization of episodes deepens awareness and understanding of events that have been known but have never come alive in our minds. Among the benefits for students when drama is incorporated intro teaching is that engagement in dramatic improvisation gives them protection to express their ideas and emotions.

> I am proposing the reintegration of drama into the curriculum in the light of the special contributions the drama process can make to children's learning. Drama has the power to place children in a position to take risks in their learning without fear of penalty, to face and deal with human issues and problems, again without penalty, as well as to reflect on the implications of choices and decisions they have made in the dramatic context. (Verriour, 1989, p. 285)

While visual art, music, and literature created by others can readily be brought into the classroom, when the arts of drama and dance become a part of classroom life they are usually provided by the students themselves. Describing classroom drama as "a far cry from the class play," Stephen Yaffe notes that when it is part of the classroom program "...drama can effectively address and hone thinking skills, greatly enhance and increase comprehension of subject matter, substantially decrease the distance between the written word and the reader." Students who talk about what they are learning and then play out their ideas about it through improvisational drama develop a basis from which to write their ideas. "At-risk students were captured first through their oral skills, which were vastly superior to their written ones. Only after they realized that improvisation is writing on your feet were the pens put in their hands" (Yaffe, 1989, pp. 32 and 11).

> Do not think of drama as theatre. Drama for learning is concerned with the experience of the participants. It is not meant to be rehearsed and performed for an audience. No sets, costumes, or props are needed, although sometimes a costume piece (such as a hat, glasses, apron, or cape) or a hand prop (such as a quill pen, book, telephone, or piece of paper) can help a student take on a role. ...Often the most significant learning occurs, not during the drama itself, but during the discussion that follows. (Flynn, 1989, p. 81)

Enhancing Understanding Through Creative Drama

The American Alliance for Theatre and Education defines creative drama as "an improvisational, nonexhibitional, process-centered form of drama in which participants are guided by a leader to imagine, enact, and reflect upon human experiences." The range of possibilities for creative drama, writes Ruth Heinig (1988), is wide, including moving to music, drama and movement games, pantomime, impromptu acting out of stories, improvisations, and group-planned dramatizations. However, even when students' actions are spontaneous, creative drama is not a wholly impromptu process. Rosalind Flynn and Gail Carr (1994, p. 41) provide a suggested structure for teachers who decide to incorporate drama into their teaching. "Planning allows the students to create within a specified framework... [and] ensures that we all know where the drama is going." The first step is

the teacher's rereading of literature that the class will study or has studied, looking for passages that include possibilities for drama. Examples are a turning point in the story, an intriguing but briefly mentioned event that could be elaborated on, a character who could step out of the text to advise other characters about what to do or what is coming next, or a point at which a new character could be created to interact with those who are a part of the story. After deciding the point at which the drama will occur and what form it will take (using one of the examples listed above or inventing another), the teacher tells or reads the story briefly up to the point of the improvised drama, explains the format, and encourages students to think of things to do and say when the action begins. Figure 11–2 gives an example of this process. As the illustration shows, fables are a useful genre for creative drama. Even though many fables have only one or two characters, a chorus of animals can be added to comment on or intervene in the action.

Two Sides.   Traditional stories and myths provide an excellent basis for linking storytelling with creative drama. For example, the story of Prometheus giving fire to humans can be dramatized with half of the students taking the role of immortals and the other half the role of humans. (An advantage of the Two Sides strategy is that there is no difficulty about finding enough parts for everyone to participate.) The teacher tells, slowly and with frequent pauses, the beginning of the story with which the students are already familiar through their reading.

> No one knows who first discovered how to make fire. Long ago, people told a story to explain how this wonderful thing happened. They said: Once upon a time, long, long, long ago, there were immortals—gods and Titans—who had fire. But people had no fire, and did not know how to create it. The winters were cold and the people suffered. Then Prometheus, one of the Titans, looked down and took pity on the people.

At this point, each group clusters together to discuss their situation (immortals on one side, humans on another) and make some decisions about how to act out their roles. At various points in the story, the narrator describes more, while the actors pause to listen. When students are familiar with this kind of

FIGURE 11–2 Example of Planning and Beginning Creative Drama

▮ (Preparation) *Teacher chooses event or story for dramatization:* Choice: "Belling the cat," one of Aesop's fables. Plot: Mice who have been terrorized by a cat debate what to do. When one mouse suggests that a bell be tied around the cat's neck to alert the mice to the cat's approach everyone is enthusiastic—but the plan fails because no one will take on the task of belling the cat.

▮ (Preparation) *Teacher identifies possible point(s) for dramatization:*
— Elaborate on parts of the story:
   Mice describe aggressive acts by the cat
   Mice debate how to solve their problem
— Invent new character(s) to interact with those in story:
   Possibly a chorus of other animals to react to ideas of mice, during their debate—this could be an opportunity for cooperative group planning, if groups or individuals take on appropriate characteristics and roles of other animals; for example, dog might be scornful of cat; fox might have suggestions for trickery
— Character steps out of role:
   Someone (the cat?) takes on the role of Aesop and gives a moral, which students could

develop. Issue to consider: Avoid putting a student (or students) in villainous roles or roles that stigmatize them. Teacher could be the cat or cat could be offstage sound effects (that's a good idea!), and the character who steps out of role could be a particularly wise mouse or a member of the animal chorus.

▮ *Setting the stage:* Teacher prepares students for elaboration of the beginning of the fable by reading opening passage of fable, then steps into a role in the story by addressing students: "Mice! Are you frightened? Angry? Worried? What has the cat done to make you feel this way?"

▮ *Dramatic action:* Student improvisation of mice, justifying their fear of the cat. The teacher may interrupt while remaining in the role, whispering, "Group meeting! Talk softly! What are we going to do to protect ourselves?"

▮ *Next steps:* The improvisation may suggest what should happen next. The action may flow easily into the rest of the story, or the teacher may stop to read further or suggest new possibilities. Students may move to cooperative groups to prepare for a second round of improvisation.

dramatization, the process can be made more complex by having the groups switch roles; in this case, the students playing gods would become humans, and the humans would take on the roles of the immortals. The Two Sides strategy can be used to link drama and debate and can be compared to the discussion strategy called Structured Controversy (Johnson & Johnson, 1979, 1988); (Maruyama, Knechel, & Petersen, 1995), described in Chapter Five. It is a component of Structured Controversy that after arguing for one position, groups change sides and argue for the contrary idea. Patrick Verriour (1989) describes a drama in which the two sides are members of a Native American tribe and pioneer settlers, with the groups changing their roles midway through the drama, then eventually seeking solutions.

Tableaux. A tableau is a staged grouping of people who are arranged in a way that conveys a

comprehensible idea or theme. (Both singular and plural forms of the word *tableau* and *tableaux*, are pronounced *tab-lo'*.) While the tableau is on view, the people in it usually do not move, although in an elaborate tableau variation, characters may, in turn, step out of the group and explain their roles. Traditionally, tableaux often involve elaborate costumes and scenery, but it can be a creative thinking opportunity to decide how to present a scene effectively but simply. Eleanor Albert (1994) and Rosalind Flynn (1989) suggest the use of tableaux—or, to use a more modern term, *freeze frames*—to engage middle school and high school students. Cooperative groups might each create a tableau for a presentation illustrating a series of myths, or several events relating to a single mythological figure, such as the labors of Hercules. Another possibility would be to choose an author and create a series of tableaux based on different works by that author. Biographies or oral history can be dramatized through tableaux, using a simple stage with a curtained area and a desk and chair where a narrator sits. The narrator pauses at set times, and the curtain is drawn to reveal a person or group of people posed to illustrate the event being described. Flynn suggests chronological tableaux illustrating, for example, women's fight for the right to vote, or imaginary twists on history, such as the discovery of Europe by people who have crossed the sea from the "North American" continent. She also suggests *What if...* dramas (what if a given person had acted differently at a crucial period in history?); imaginary interactions between a fictional character and historical figure; and dream sequences, which involve students in creating an exaggeratedly optimistic rendition of how a current problem might be solved, or how changes in past events might have led to good outcomes.

Eleanor Albert advocates using drama work groups as a form of cooperative learning in the middle school. In their groups, students work on storytelling and pantomime, which they may enhance with drawings and music and may later combine, or use separately, in presentations for the class. "Unlike the school play format, there are no stars, no chorus, no tech crew," she writes. "[I]n using storytelling and pantomime, [students] are using the two components of characterization, in isolation. In storytelling the reader relies only on voice to depict character, and in pantomime the actor uses only movement. These techniques require more of both actor and audience" (Albert, 1994, pp. 21 and 22). Albert also suggests the groups prepare monologues written from the points of view of different people—real or fictional—and then form a tableau from which the different characters in turn come forward to read or speak their monologues. Tableaux combined with monologues can be based on historical events. For example, a teacher may choose to enhance the study of the American Revolution by reading aloud excerpts from Barbara Tuchman's *The first salute* (1988), a history of the Revolution focused on the events surrounding November 16, 1776, when, for the first time, a ship flying the flag of the American Continental Congress received the cannon salute on entering another nation's harbor that recognized it as the ship of a sovereign nation. Students might prepare monologues for the governor who bravely ordered

the salute (thus defying the British) for the captain of the ship, for King George III, and for members of the Continental Congress.

Sequence Drama.   Ruth Heinig presents *sequence drama* as a drama game. The teacher analyzes a text or story and divides it into a series of many brief, connected events, then decides how each event can be presented dramatically through an action, words, or both. Event cards are then prepared, instructing the student who is holding the card what to do. The cards are given sequentially to students who are seated in a circle. Sitting cross-legged works better than does using a circle of desks and chairs. In Heinig's example of a sequence drama for sixth graders about exploration in the new world, these are the first four cards:

- You begin the game. Stand up and say, "The time is the late 1400s. The place is Europe. Curtain going up!" Sit.
- You stand, walk around the circle, and call out, "For sale, for sale, our latest shipment of spices, silks, perfumes, and gems! For sale, directly from the Indies. Come and get it while it lasts!" Return to your seat.
- You stand and say (shaking your head sadly), "Too bad we can't have more." Sit.
- You jump up and say excitedly, "Ah, but we could if we had a sailing route to the Indies." Sit.

(Heinig, 1988, p. 180)

Simulation Drama.   An alternative to sequence drama is simulation drama, in which the teacher and students take on roles of characters in a real or fictional situation, discuss together or in groups how the action should proceed, then interact to dramatize the situation. An example of a simulation drama is given in Figure 5–17, an observation of a simulation in an eighth-grade history class of some of the events leading up to the Revolutionary War. The observation presents a portion of a dramatization that spanned several days.

Enhancing Learning Through Dance and Creative Movement

Every art has its advocates among teachers who have experienced or observed the way in which that method of artistic expression—visual art, music, drama, literature, dance—has the power to delight and inform. Peggy Schwartz (1991, p. 46), discussing the effect of dance in promoting intercultural understanding and appreciation, writes, "We can study dance in the doorway through which we step to learn more about ourselves and others. . . Through art and dance, students of different cultural and ethnic backgrounds can better understand themselves and each other, a critical aspect of social stability and civility at this time in history." Dance is one of the ways in which bodily kinesthetic intelligence—one of seven human intelligences identified by Howard Gardner (1993b)—is manifested. There are benefits for students, in terms of learning, enjoyment, and health, if physical action is integrated with learning, and those with special talents are recognized. Patricia Lee (1994, p. 83) describes her experience in allowing a student to demonstrate understanding of a topic of study through creation and performance of a dance. "I didn't want to know how 'smart' Janet was according to some predetermined standard," she writes, "I wanted to know *how Janet was smart.*"

Guided kinesthetic imagery, a parallel to guided visual imagery, can be created by using movement. Susan Griss (1994) offers several examples about how students' learning of science concepts can be supported through movement and dance. She suggests that the movement of sound waves through air, water, or a solid can be demonstrated by students forming three lines that simulate different molecule arrangements—closest together as a solid and furthest apart as a gas. A shoulder tap passed along the formation will be transmitted most rapidly along the "solid" group. She also suggests creating a dance to simulate the movement of planets around the sun, with Venus the only planet rotating counterclockwise. When creative movement and dance are used in the classroom, the teacher's role is to plan, to create purpose, and to arrange a welcoming and secure environment. It is the students who use their energy and bodily kinesthetic intelligence in physical action. Griss advises teachers who are concerned that students' energy can turn a movement and dance activity into uncontrolled action and noise that a combination of freedom and restraint is necessary. Students, as well as teachers, need the security of structure, which can be provided by establishing routines that will regularly be used to begin and end a period of creative movement, and a signal, which means everyone must freeze into silence and stillness to wait for further direction from the teacher. Setting a clear theme for improvisation also provides structure; music, simple props, and beautifully illustrated children's books can support the theme.

> For teachers who may feel intimidated or overwhelmed by the idea of using movement and creative improvisation as a teaching tool, remember that *you do not have to do the movement yourselves.* The children will supply all the physicality needed for a successful lesson. Your job is to supply the direction, the guided imagery, the permission to be physical, and an encouraging gleam in your eye. The idea is not to have the children imitate your movements, but to discover their own physical language. (Griss, 1994, p. 80)

Stories of Drama and Dance

Creative drama and movement can be stimulated by important text and intriguing, beautiful illustrations, so books themselves open almost infinite possibilities for engaging in these forms of art. Videotapes can bring classical and modern drama and dance into the classroom. There are many opportunities for students of all ages to see how books are dramatized, to compare text and videotape versions, and to see theater and dance performances of well-known stories. The plays of William Shakespeare are timeless classics, but reading them is not the way to encounter them for the first time. Although many repertory theaters present the plays vividly, most students do not have access to live productions. Fortunately there are wonderful videotape presentations, such as Franco Zeffirelli's *Romeo and Juliet* and *The Taming of the Shrew* and Kenneth Branagh's *Much Ado About Nothing*, which can be enjoyed in the classroom. Knowing the stories the plays present increases familiarity and understanding, and many children in previous generations enjoyed reading Shakespearean stories as told by Charles and Mary Lamb. Their *Tales from Shakespeare*, first published in 1807, has become outdated in style, thus difficult to read, but a two-volume, gorgeously illustrated set has recently been published as *Shakespeare stories* and *Shakespeare stories II*

(Garfield, 1985, 1994), with the stories vividly retold. This excerpt is the beginning of *Hamlet*:

> It happened in Denmark, long ago. High up on the battlements of the castle at Elsinore, two sentinels, their cloaks snapping in the whipping dark, met at the limit of their watch, the one ending, the other beginning. Their faces, seen faintly by the light of a thin seeding of stars, were white as bone. It was midnight. (Garfield, 1985, p. 169)

For some classics of the theater, however, the stories are not well-known, and familiarity with those plots can lead to enjoyment of dramatic performances that might otherwise be a blur of color and noise, with little meaning. Just as there are books that tell the stories of famous operas, there are books that present the plots of ballets and plays. As a companion volume to *Sing me a story*, Jane Rosenberg's *Dance me a story* (1993) illustrates the retellings of ballets such as *Firebird*, *The Nutcracker*, *The Sleeping Beauty*, *Swan Lake*, *Cinderella*, *Romeo and Juliet*, and *Coppélia*, with full-page paintings based on real productions. The stories are told in a way that creates a view of the stage: "Set among the brightly painted wooden houses of a charming old village square is a dark, stone workshop where mysterious Dr. Coppélius and his shy daughter, Coppélia, live."

> Unlike a ballet in live performance, when the myriad details and the action flash by, defying the quickest eye, here the text and the pictures stand still, allowing time for reverie and review. Later, when one enters the reality of the theater, it will be with a keener eye and clearer understanding, and the result, quite simply, will be greater appreciation and pleasure. (Merrill Ashley, in Rosenberg, 1993, p. 7)

■■ Oral and Written Literature: ■■ To Surprise and Delight

Literature is the art that should be most widespread and welcome in classrooms. "Expect that you and your students will surprise and delight yourselves," Maryann Eeds and Ralph Peterson (1991, p. 126) tell us, as they describe ways of engaging with literature. This is exciting advice. There are ways we can choose to teach that will result in our students' enjoy-

ment as they learn and also will give us pleasure in our own insights about the literature we are reading with our students. In contrast, there are methods of teaching that create a lifelong dislike of reading and of books that are in any way seen as classics; most adults have experienced such teaching at some point in their education. Many scholar-educators have described ways to change the way readers of literature, and literature itself, are treated in many classrooms.

Do Not Dissuade Students From Reading

In the field of medicine, a guiding principle is *primum non nocere*: first of all, do no harm. This maxim is based on the recognition that actions taken for the purpose of helping may not, in fact, be helpful and may actually cause injury. The principle *first of all, do no harm* applies to teaching as well. The primary basis for ensuring that our students acquire experiences and attitudes that will lead them to enjoy reading all of their lives is *not* to teach in ways that discourage literacy. Joseph Sanacore puts it this way: "Avoid conditions that dissuade students from reading" (1990, p. 416). That statement is a reminder that methods used now to **persuade** students to read may **dissuade** them from reading later in life, after their teachers can no longer control what they do.

Avoid "Motivating" Students to Read. When people's desire to act in certain ways comes from within themselves, that is intrinsic motivation, and it is likely to be lasting and strong. People can also, in many instances, be controlled from the outside, through extrinsic motivation that may be applied

---

persuade and **dissuade**—have the same Latin root: *suadere*, meaning *to urge*, or *to advise*. The prefix *per-* in this case is used to intensify the meaning, so *persuadere*, in Latin, means to advise strongly. In English, to persuade someone is to cause that person to act in a certain way, usually through gentle means. In the Latin word *dissuadere*, the prefix *dis-* reverses the meaning of the root word. To dissuade someone is to keep that person from taking an action, usually by reasoning rather than by force.

It is an educational paradox that efforts to persuade students to read may have the effect of causing them to dislike and avoid reading.

through punishment or through rewards, but extrinsic motivation usually ceases to be effective when it is withdrawn. Students who read during their school years in order to receive good grades or escape penalties no longer have those motives when they leave school. In a recent book, *Punished by rewards: The trouble with gold stars, incentive plans, A's, praise, and other bribes* (1993), Alfie Kohn argues cogently against controlling students' behavior by doling out prizes and privileges, because doing so turns students' attention away from the rewarding nature of the activity itself and focuses their attention on the reward. It is often difficult for teachers to stop using a reward system, however, for several reasons. First of all, we are accustomed to it. Extrinsic rewards for reading, such as colorful teacher-made displays showing how many gold stars each student has "earned" by writing book reports, were traditional parts of the grade school classrooms that many of us attended. Moreover, making those attractive displays and giving rewards to our students is satisfying to teachers—contributing to our sense that we are creative and kind people.

There is a danger, however, in treating students—and books—as if a teacher's attention and effort is necessary in order to make students read or make books worthy of being read. Our own personal reading is not controlled from outside, and the books that we relish are enjoyed for themselves, not because someone else has found creative ways to entice us to read them. When we have finished a book we read for pleasure we set it aside or return to reread favorite parts of it. We may join a discussion group or talk to friends about a good book, but we do not follow our reading by writing a report, playing a game, or answering questions. Nobody comes between us and our reading. And when we do intervene, even from the best of motives, we may prevent a love affair between reader and book from occurring. As Katherine Paterson puts it (1990, p. 14), "Books can delight us and console us and even change us, but not without our permission."

There are many times, particularly in working with a required textbook, when teacher intervention is necessary to help students learn from their reading. However, such mediation is often not needed when books are read for their literary value. Wendy

Saul (1993) draws a distinction between mediated and unmediated books. Unmediated books are those students come to directly, which they select and read independently or in groups with other students. Mediated books are those teachers choose, thus teachers control the ways in which students will use them. The mediation that Saul describes is not a feature of books—any book can be mediated or unmediated—but of teachers' decisions about whether the link will be between a reader and a book, or whether the teacher will be in the middle, coming between the reader and the book. It is important for students to believe that reading books is rewarding in itself and for their teachers to act in ways that do not interfere with this belief.

> The preservice teachers in my University methods classes seem fairly confident about their goals vis á vis reading. That is, they want to go into schools and "motivate" children to read. Sometimes they see this motivation as a system of external rewards. What can we give to children who "try hard"— grades? stickers? smiley faces? These teachers-in-training want learning to be fun and often contrive puzzles and games to sugar-coat ideas and information found in books. Many are oblivious to the hidden curriculum of their message, that the ideas and information are uninteresting and unpalatable unless they are sugar-coated.
>
> Those more familiar with literary ideas seek activities in which motivation is more intrinsic— "What can we do with this book? is a question frequently asked. When I answer honestly—"What did you do with the last book *you* read?"—some think that I am being a bit sarcastic. It is difficult for them to imagine a classroom where children are not listening to or following a teacher's directions; they seek to hold their students spellbound. ...Teachers believe that their skill ultimately is gauged by what they can do with a book. (Saul, 1993, pp. 174–175)

Authors have an interest—often passionately expressed—in the direct link between their books and readers. Mem Fox (1993, p. 128) writes, "If literature in the classroom is to be effective teachers must learn to trust the book to do its own teaching. ...Let the story fight back!" She describes a time when she was autographing her books at an educational conference and overheard one teacher's enthusiastic comment:

"Oh, isn't this book just darling? I can use it to teach the five senses." ...I felt my heart contract in sorrow. What's so sinful about reading a book for reading's sake? ...What's wrong with happiness as an outcome of reading? Is it too cheap? Too vulgar? What's wrong with laughter as an outcome? Or fright? Or enchantment? Or sadness? (Fox, 1993, p. 129)

Avoid Treating Reading Like a Package of "Skills."
The opposite of using literature to surprise and delight is using time allotted to the study of literature to teach skills, as if a love of written and spoken words in all of the glorious combinations that people have created and continue to devise could be produced by learning labels and facts. The tepid, drab actions of naming, labeling, and memorizing are a contrast to life's intensity. Writers have used this opposition for a theme, as in a poem written during World War II, whose first stanza begins by contrasting routine training to learning the parts of guns with, on one hand, the implied horrors of war, and on the other, the beauties of flowering shrubs in springtime.

> Today we have naming of parts. Yesterday,
> We had daily cleaning. And tomorrow morning,
> We shall have what to do after firing. But today,
> Today we have naming of parts. Japonica
> Glistens like coral in all of the neighboring gardens,
>   And today we have naming of parts.
> (Henry Reed, in Allison, Barrows, Blake, Carr, Eastman & English, 1975)

Elizabeth Nelms alludes to Reed's poem as she cautions English teachers to "Beware the naming of parts":

> One of the dangers we face as teachers of English is that we dedicate our time to 'covering the material' and repeat, year in and year out, similar bits of information prescribed in curriculum guides.
>
> Too often we assign short stories just so we can introduce the fictional elements of character, plot, setting, and theme. We underline, circle, and isolate the eight parts of speech, whether the language really fits the tight traditional description or not.
>
> This repetition in presentation, elementary school through high school, can ruin the students' enjoyment of a good story or hinder the true appreciation of a carefully crafted sentence. Somewhere

in the teaching of new terms and the intricacies of the curriculum guide, we must be careful that in the naming of parts we not lose sight of the whole. (Nelms, 1992, p. 83)

A false idea, often fostered by prescribed curricula and the way it is taught, is that life, and literature, are without ambiguity—there are no puzzles, no in-betweens, only right and wrong answers. For example, many textbooks and workbooks, in grade after grade, provide exercises that teach students to distinguish fact from opinion. Of course, it is important in life to recognize that not everything that is written or spoken is unbiased; however this piece of common sense is not best acquired by sorting statements into two categories. Textbook exercises are, in a sense, unambiguous, because they are accompanied by a Teacher's Guide that provides the correct answers. However, when three middle school students decided to go to a higher authority to settle their fact versus opinion argument, they wrote to the National Council of Teachers of English. Editors there sent the students' question to the president of NCTE and five other authorities, including the director of a university graduate school writing project. The results were interesting. When teachers' manuals tell teachers what questions to ask, they also supply the right answers; when a question does not have a single correct answer, the manuals say, "Answers will vary." Despite the fact that, according to the teachers' manual, there was only one correct answer, the experts' answers varied.

The task set for students, in a seventh-grade English textbook, published in 1990, was to analyze a letter written several years earlier to the editor of the *Boston Globe* to determine whether sentences within that letter stated a fact or an opinion. The letter was written by the brother of young man killed in an automobile accident while riding in the back of a sports car which had no seatbelts for the rear seats. The letter writer was supporting a proposed law to require seatbelts. The sentence in question was, "The tragedy of a needless death causes tremendous pain and suffering for the family and friends." Most students in the class said the statement expressed an opinion. A few said it stated a fact, and they held to their position. Perhaps because the sentence communicates a powerful and moving idea, students were concerned enough to make serious efforts to find out who was right. Letters from six scholars, many of them presenting lengthy analyses filled with technical language, were published in the June 1994 issue of *The Council Chronicle*, an NCTE publication. Editors of *The Council Chronicle* presented the letter from the head of a university English department last. He drew a parallel with a Saturday Night Live sketch that parodied a commercial, in which the announcer proclaimed the correctness of both panelists' decisions about an imaginary product called "New Shimmer": "You're both right! It's a floor wax *and* a dessert topping."

> ...Maybe the editors of your book think that the sentence "The tragedy of a needless death causes tremendous pain and suffering for the family and friends" is an opinion because it is an assertion without proof. But any sensitive reader knows it is a fact.
>
> ...It is important, when you are reading, to test the truth and value of what you are being told. Perhaps instead of worrying about whether a particular sentence is one thing or another, a floor wax or a dessert topping, you should test the truth and value of an exercise that forces you to label a sentence as fact or opinion when you should be considering the much more important question of how it works in the context of an essay.
>
> And that's a fact. (Dennis Baron, 1994, p. 17)

Avoid "Inquisitions." In describing classroom discussions of literature, Bryant Fillion (1981, p. 40) wrote that the style of talk resembled an inquisition—a prolonged series of questions in a situation where those questioned are not at ease. A too-common pattern of classroom talk consists of teachers asking questions to which they believe they know the answers and students attempting to give the expected answers based on memory, extended experience in giving "correct" answers, or skill in using teacher-provided cues. Becky Reimer (1989, p. 38) uses another metaphor, "the machine gun model of teacher/student discourse." She describes the pattern this way: "Teacher fires a question at students and students fire back with 'right' answers; teacher fires another question, and students return fire again." This long-standing questioning practice, discussed in Chapter Two, persists primarily because it *is* widespread and long-standing. It is the

pattern of classroom talk that most teachers experienced throughout their years as students and observed as a common practice during their teaching careers. There are other reasons why the practice persists. First, it places the teacher firmly in a role of authority—the person who controls what questions will be asked and determines what answers will be accepted. There is little or no chance that the teachers' knowledge of the subject will be challenged. Additionally, it is a system of classroom management and control. The time allotted for instruction will be used up; students' eyes will be on the teacher and they will be at least apparently attentive; there will be no risk of unnecessary noise; the subject matter will be "covered." To change this flawed practice, teachers need to have other ideas about what to do and need to be willing to risk changing.

Some teachers believe they are obligated to question students about what they have read. If asked why they must question, these teachers are likely to answer that if they do not, students will not read. The teachers probably recognize that they are assuming that students will not read literature, even if they are assigned to do so, without some kind of threat. Another assumption goes unrecognized, however. This is the assumption that, of two competing risks—first, that some students will not read what they are assigned to read; second, that the method used to make students read will cause them to dislike reading—the first risk is more dangerous. But which is worse, for students to shirk an assignment, or for students to hate to read? . . . for a high school student not to read a poem, or for that student never to read another poem after graduating from high school? "Teaching literature" in ways that cause a lifelong avoidance of serious reading is a far more terrible thing than skipped assignments. That this kind of teaching occurs is doubly tragic when there are so many exciting ways to engage students with good literature.

Experiencing Literature Without Reading

Sometimes teachers are reluctant to include non-print materials in instruction for fear that doing so will interfere with students' development as readers.

It is interesting to note that centuries ago, when the invention of printing began to make books readily available, some teachers of that time bemoaned this novelty, on the grounds that using books would interfere with students' ability to learn from professors' lectures. Peter Shaheen makes this point as he muses about whether he is harming or helping his students by encouraging them to listen to literary works on audiotapes.

> Scholars living in the early days of print wondered openly about what would happen if print became dominant over vocal discussions. Their concern was about the degradation of reasoning power due to writing. …Books on tape are just another stage in the marriage between reason and technology. Books on tape will have an impact on the relationship, but it will not divorce them. In fact there is an argument to be made suggesting that books on tape will enhance the relationship as other technologies have. (Shaheen, 1992, p. 83)

Sometimes teachers decide that only students identified as needy in some way should be allowed or encouraged to use non-print media such as audiotapes, even though many capable adults enjoy books on tape (Aron, 1992). Any opportunity can be turned into a burden if it is provided in ways that stigmatize those who use it. Students should not have to qualify for educational opportunities in their classrooms, either by proving that they are capable or by being identified as lacking in some way. Listening to audiotapes is a form of support for students who are learning to read, or learning from materials that are difficult to read, but the opportunity to use audiotapes should be available for any student. Susan Neuman is among the scholars who have studied students' learning when different media are used. Her research, showing that students' understanding and thinking processes were similar when different instructional media—videotapes as well as books—were used, provides evidence that the use of videotapes and other video-related formats in instruction will not hamper students' understanding or interfere with their ability to learn from printed materials. She concluded that reading and viewing, used together, may enhance learning.

> …the medium per se may have little direct influence in cognition and learning… Instead of limiting learning, different media may act synergistically, affording children opportunities to activate and practice skills necessary for subsequent phases of mental elaboration in higher levels of learning. This potential for synergy should encourage educators to adopt creative uses of video-related and print technologies to support students' engagement in active learning and thinking. (Neuman, 1992, pp. 133–134)

Noting that "videotape has become a pervasive visual medium," John Stewig (1995, pp. 133–134) advises that "[w]hen teachers choose a media version of a book, they need to consider fidelity to the original. Fidelity does not mean complete correspondence with the original version, which is impossible, but rather a sensitive adaptation of it to a new mode. …[Changes should be] sympathetic to the book content and should not overshadow the original concept." He contrasts the different advantages of books and videotapes as ways of engaging with literature. Readers have greater control of books. They can choose to read slowly to experience the beauty of language, or rapidly to find out what will happen next. They can skip pages, go back to check details, and return again and again to reread favorite parts. On the other hand, videotapes provide the enhancement of visual images and music, and moreover, they more naturally provide opportunity for a shared group experience. On videotape, the story unfolds for all of the viewers together, whereas even when the same book is read by members of a group, each reader moves through text at an individual pace. Diana Green (1989) suggests that teachers take advantage of what the technology enables them to do when videotapes are used. The capacity to pause, rewind, and fast forward tapes provides opportunities to pause for discussion and to select excerpts for viewing and reviewing.

One of the themes of this text is that teachers have the responsibility—and delight—of opening doors, and that they should never succumb to forces that encourage them to shut students out. Leslie McClain-Ruelle and Richard Telfer (1990) make this point strongly, citing Grant Wiggins, who asks, "Why should students who are less able or motivated have to 'earn' the right to engage in interesting work?" An instance of deprivation which they describe is the separation of students at the high school level into those who are allowed to read Charles Dickens' *A Tale of Two Cities*, and those who must read an adapted version in which much of the famous and exciting language of the original book has been removed to produce a so-called "high interest, low vocabulary" version. ("High interest, low vocabulary" is the term applied to writing that is designed to be interesting, often because it is about currently popular topics in sports and entertainment, but which uses a limited number of easy-to-read words. One problem in using such materials is that the vocabulary *is* limited—readers do not expand their vocabulary because the same core of basic vocabulary is used repeatedly.) *A Tale of Two Cities* is probably the novel which combines the most famous opening and closing passages in English literature: *It was the best of times; it was the worst of times…* and *It is a far, far better thing that I do than I have ever done; it is a far, far better rest that I go to than I have ever known.* To deprive students of the story and its language is not only a tragedy, but an unnecessary tragedy. Many splendid versions of the Dickens novel are available on videotapes, which can be supplemented by the teacher's reading aloud selections from the text. Viewing these dramatizations combined with reading the text is preferable for capable readers as well, and learning is further enhanced if students have the opportunity to see and compare multiple videotape versions and to compare film and text.

Taking a Stand

Literature has value, in and of itself. Although our understanding of ourselves, others, and the world is made stronger and deeper by novels, plays, poems, histories, and essays, the purpose of literature is not to develop comprehension—and it is most emphatically not the purpose of literature to provide opportunities for comprehension to be "checked." Although our vocabularies expand dramatically if we are wide readers, the purpose of literature is not to teach vocabulary. Some people understand the first premise—that wide reading increases vocabulary—but do not grasp or accept the idea that vocabulary development is not the

purpose for reading widely and that stories and poems do not exist in order to teach the words they contain. Patricia Kelly and Nancy Farnan describe Katherine Paterson's refusal to allow an excerpt from her Newbery-medal winning book about friendship and death, *Bridge to Terebithia* (1977), to be "blanded out" by publishers of a basal series who said the adaptation would be perfect for a section on "Expanding Your Vocabulary." Kelly and Farnan (1994, p. 180) point out that "a primary value of literature lies within the work itself, our appreciation of it, and the connections we make to it. If we always use literature as a vehicle for teaching something else, children will miss out on enjoyment of it as a work of art, and they will miss out on the personal connections that can enrich their lives."

In classrooms where books and students are valued and trusted, literature is not treated as something bland but mildly nutritional, which students must be spoon-fed or force-fed. Instead, the coming together of students and books can be described in lively, forceful metaphors: students need to come to grips with the reading; stories must be allowed to fight back; readers need to take a stand. The concept of stance—of taking a stand in relation to our reading—has been widely discussed in the professional literature, inspired by Louise Rosenblatt's (1978) identification of two approaches to reading: *efferent* and *aesthetic*. When readers take an efferent stance, they approach the text intending to learn; they are looking for information that can be taken from it. When they read aesthetically they attend to feelings, perceptions and ideas that the text inspires in them. Rosenblatt pointed out that often students are taught only to take the efferent stance and urged that greater attention be given to aesthetic response. Her work has been the impetus for useful research and important changes in practice. Sometimes, however, her ideas have been oversimplified and the two stances have been seen as polar opposites, and even identified as good (the aesthetic stance) and bad (the efferent stance). Rosenblatt herself has sought to correct these misapprehensions.

> Instead of thinking of the *text* as either literary or informative, efferent or aesthetic, we should think of it as written for a particular *predominant* attitude or stance, efferent or aesthetic, on the part of the

reader. We read for information, but we are also conscious of emotions… and feel pleasure when the words we call up arouse vivid images and are rhythmic to the inner ear. Or we experience a poem but are conscious of acquiring some information …[W]e can read aesthetically something written mainly to inform or read efferently something written mainly to communicate experience. (Rosenblatt, 1991, p. 445)

It can be useful for students to think about the concept of stance. All students can understand that books can give us information, excitement, laughter, and a sense of the beauty and power of language. The concept is readily acquired if teachers and students talk seriously together about books. It is learned from wide experiences with reading, but not, emphatically *not*, from learning terms such as *aesthetic* and *efferent* and sorting books or statements into two categories. Teachers can guide students to adopt a particular stance in discussions about literature by using prompts. A *prompt* is a question or brief direction used to encourage and focus a response. Chapter Ten gives examples of prompted writing. For example, a teacher might include short writing sessions in content area classes by giving students one of these four prompts: *Write out what you know about* [a topic being studied], *Write out what you remember about* [the topic], *Write out what you discovered about* [the topic], or *Write out what you think about* [the topic] (Breece, 1988). The directions are clear and brief. They can be given repeatedly because the topic is different for each writing session, so what students write will be different. Thus, the teacher has no need to invent a new writing assignment, and the students are not confronted with complicated directions. Questions teachers can use to prompt students to respond aesthetically to what they have read include: *what did you notice? how did you feel about it? how does it relate to your own experiences?* Prompts such as *what did you learn?* and *what is a passage that you think is memorable?* can also be used. Such prompts are predominantly efferent, but they might evoke a response about the reader's feelings, just as the aesthetically focused prompt *what did you notice?* might receive an answer related to interesting new information a student learned.

In considering what questions to use in guiding discussions about literature, it is important to distinguish between prompts such as *how did [this piece of writing] make you feel?* and inferential questions such as *how would you feel if…?* Both questions are about feelings, but responses to the first question are likely to be more thoughtful and honest because readers are asked to describe their own feelings, rather than to imagine how they would feel in a situation which may not affect them deeply or which they may not fully understand. (Phrasing questions in the second style is described in Chapter Four as a common error teachers should avoid when writing inferential questions about content area topics.) Judith Langer (1990), Elizabeth Close (1990), and Violet Harris (1993) are among the scholars who have conceptualized and discussed a different aspect of stance. They describe four stances that readers may take, sequentially and recursively, as they read: being out and stepping in, being in and moving through, being in and stepping out, stepping out to reflect and solidify the experience. At first, readers and text are separated, but then each reader enters into the text, carrying a personal set of ideas, experiences, and values. Then readers are absorbed in the text. The slang phrase "really into it" is apt. Then this stance—being in and moving through— may alternate with another—being in and stepping out—as the reader periodically pauses to think about the text and reread portions of it. Finally, the reader steps away from the text, and if the reading has been important enough to have influence, it will become part of that reader's ideas, experiences, and values which will be brought to future reading.

Engaging in Grand Conversations

Instead of "gentle inquisitions," Maryann Eeds and Deborah Wells write, discussions of literature can be "grand conversations" (Eeds & Wells, 1989, p. 27). A *grand* conversation—one which is grand in the sense of *important, impressive, splendid, superb*, and in the more informal sense of *great, wonderful, sensational, outstanding* can be characterized by its results. People who have been part of an important, wonderful conversation are pleased with their own participation. If they have talked, they are generally pleased with what they have said and with the ways others have responded to their ideas; if they have listened without speaking, this has been their own choice, which they, and others, are comfortable with. They have heard new ideas—insights that they would never have thought of on their own, which have already begun to influence their thinking. At the end of the conversation, they are even more interested in what they have been talking about than they were at the beginning. When classrooms are settings for grand conversations, teacher and students are co-participants, and the teacher's experience resembles that of the students. The teacher, thinking about the discussion afterwards, is satisfied at having shared interesting ideas or listened thoughtfully without speaking. Students' ideas have been illuminated and the teacher has been interested, in fact, surprised and delighted.

Creating a classroom environment in which wonderful, important conversations occur is not a simple matter, in part because there is often incongruity between such discussions and students' prior experiences of what talk is like in a school setting. Conversations—grand or otherwise—do not consist of interchanges where A speaks and B speaks to A; A speaks and C speaks to A; A speaks and D speaks to A, and so forth, through an entire alphabet of students from B to Z, each directing whatever they have to say to the powerful "A" who is the teacher. Therefore, one way for teachers to work toward grand conversations is to sit, look, listen, and talk in ways that place them *in* the discussion, not apart from it or above it. Sitting is important—to stand provides the opportunity to look down from a height and also makes it possible to move easily and walk around, which is not a privilege students ordinarily have. Looking and listening are important—in a conversation, attention is usually on the speaker; attentive listening makes it possible to be informed and impressed by what is said.

It is especially important for teachers to consider their options about talking. Teachers always have both the power to do most of the talking and good reasons to do so—they are older and know more. Conversations, one aspect of classroom talk, are not enhanced if the teacher is the primary and most influential talker, thus it may be wise for teachers

to talk less, not only less than they do in other kinds of classroom talk, but less than students do, which might mean not talking at all. On the other hand, teachers may choose to be active in conducting discussions, following the practices suggested for developing Instructional Conversations (described in Chapter Five), by adding information, restating students' ideas, and making connections among different contributions. Another decision that is useful for teachers to consider is whether to contribute to discussions by asking questions or making statements. Even when teachers avoid question-and-answer sessions, it is typical for them to use questions when they do speak. But students' experience may lead them to interpret teacher's questions in a way that discourages them from thinking and talking freely and instead focuses their attention on trying to figure out "what the teacher wants." It contributes to good conversation if teachers express their ideas as statements, which they would do in ordinary conversations, and usually ask questions not to produce a desired effect, such as setting the purpose for a discussion or drawing a quiet student into the conversation but in the hope of receiving informative, interesting ideas about something they wonder about.

> [T]rust the books, trust the students, and trust yourself. Wonderful books offer innumerable opportunities for talking about an author's work. When something is important in a book, you can be sure that [students] will talk about it and that you will notice it as well—if not one day, then another. Expect that you and your students will surprise and delight yourselves with your knowledge. (Eeds & Peterson, 1991, pp. 125–126)

Read-Aloud, Read, Create, and Discuss. Talking together in-depth about reading depends on a shared topic. This sharing can occur with the whole class or with several small groups within the class. It also depends on opportunities for students to read, think, and talk together before they are asked to share ideas in a larger discussion. When the basis for discussion is a literary work which the entire class reads, *Read-Aloud, Read, Create, and Discuss* is a method that provides structure and good pacing. This four-step strategy is designed as a structure for whole class reading of a text, usually a text that is long enough and important enough to use two or three weeks to read and savor.

The teacher plans by dividing a text, such as a chapter book (a book with multiple chapters) into sections, each of which will be the basis for a two-day Read-aloud, Read, Create, and Discuss session. The session begins with the teacher reading aloud a short portion of the text that has been chosen for its importance and also as an illustration of the author's skillful use of language. After the read-aloud, the teacher gives brief guidance for reading and students move directly to cooperative groups to read the text or an assigned portion of it, making notes or talking quietly together about the reading as they wish. Reading together enables students to make choices and learn from one another: to ask about the meaning of words, to share exciting passages, even to ask an adept reader in the group to read aloud. This period of reading together is followed by a strategy in which students apply the ideas they have acquired to create something collaboratively, for example, by retelling, making a semantic map, drafting a storyboard sequence, or illustrating a significant event through creative drama or any of a variety of transmediation activities. Following the period of reading with a period of active creation serves a double purpose. First,

students are engaged in working productively when the reading assignment is completed, even though groups, and individuals within groups, finish at different times. Second, applying the ideas from their reading engages students in thinking about the reading and gives them ideas to share in the discussion, which is the final step in Read-aloud, Read, Create, and Discuss.

Typically the four steps span two days, although the discussion can be continued on a third day. The two-day arrangement is purposeful; to stretch out the process by putting each step on a separate day would diminish its effectiveness by eliminating the connections among the four components. The Read-aloud and Read steps occur on the first day and are followed by the Create step, which is continued on the second day, followed by the Discussion. Continuing the third step from one day to the next provides a period of incubation—a thinking time—between beginning a creation and finishing it, and during this time students may generate more ideas about how to enhance their product. The Discussion step, which follows immediately, is enhanced because students have been engaged in thinking about the reading and applying their ideas immediately before talking together. An example of a Read-aloud, Read, Create, and Discuss session is given in Figure 11–3.

FIGURE 11–3   Example of Read-Aloud, Read, Create, and Discuss

Background: The whole class is reading *The house of Dies Drear* (Hamilton, 1968). The teacher has selected the book to tie in with a study of the pre-Civil War period, particularly the Underground Railroad. Also, mystery is one of the genres the class is using for free reading and in literature circles, and this book received the Mystery Writers of America "Edgar" award.

Over the year, the teacher alternates whole class reading using Read-aloud, Read, Create, and Discuss (RRCD), with literature circles in which each small group reads something different. For RRCD, students work in their regular cooperative groups; for literature circles, students have different groups based on interest.

The house of Dies Drear has nineteen chapters; the

teacher has planned the reading so the class reads one, two, or three chapters at a time, and reading the book will take two weeks. For the strategies in the Create steps, the teacher has chosen retelling and storyboarding; the latter will culminate in a bulletin board display. The class is familiar with both strategies. One of the groups, rather than making a storyboard, has elected to choose music to match the story.

The teacher has made it clear to the class that the style of reading used for Read-aloud, Read, Create, and Discuss is different from ordinary reading because everyone stops at the same point. It is important for students to understand that ordinarily readers read as far as they want to before stopping, and in a book as

FIGURE 11–3 Continued

exciting as this, they might read it all at once. However, it is part of this strategy for everyone to read together, stopping at the same point. To accomplish this, every student uses a bookmark which is the same size as a full page in the book or slightly larger. Before beginning the reading assignment, students put their bookmarks at the end of the assignment, thus they do not read beyond that point, and if the ending page is on the left, the page on the right which starts the next reading is covered.

The teacher has chosen the stopping points to emphasize that the book is a mystery, so Chapters 1 and 2 were read in the first RRCD session, ending with "But what is it? What is the answer?" and Chapter 3 in the second session, ending with "Coming forth now was the strangest sight he'd seen in all his life."

Step 1, Read-aloud: The teacher reads the last sentence of Chapter 3, pauses, and then reads aloud the first three paragraphs of Chapter 4, describing the sight Thomas has seen: a huge black horse whose rider is a tiny barefoot girl. After the brief read-aloud, the teacher gives directions for the Read and Create steps. These are also written on a chart, so students have the information both auditorily and visually and can refer to the chart for guidance:

"The reading assignment is chapters 4, 5, and 6, so put your bookmark after page 82.

The author is clever. She describes mysterious happenings and then shows how they are not so mysterious after all. Look for the strange events and for the ways the author explains them.

After your group has read, retell. Each group member should retell one short part of the story, for example, the part where Thomas hears the strange sound. Talk about your retellings first, so you can put them in the order they happened.

Decide how the events in these chapters should be shown on a storyboard. How many panels will you need? Sketch the panels. You may decide to do some sketches for homework."

Step 2, Read: After the teacher has read aloud and given the directions quickly, students receive their copies of the book and move immediately into cooperative groups for reading. A few students want to read by themselves; other members of their cooperative groups

know this and do not interrupt them; most students stop occasionally to talk quietly or point out something. All the students use post-it notes to mark important places in the text and to make notes. As individual students finish, they begin to plan their retellings, or they may join with another member of the group as a resource. This is one of the longer reading sessions, so the teacher has allowed some extra time. During this step, the teacher visits several of the groups, sitting quietly, observing, and making notes. The students are used to this pattern. Occasionally, a student will ask about a word—either how to read it or what it means—and the teacher gives the information.

Step 3, Create: Students talk about what they want to retell and arrange the retellings in sequential order. If several students want to retell the same incident, the students know this is fine, as long as each retelling is complete (without comments like "well, it was just like he said"). Some students begin sketching storyboard panels during the retellings.

After the retellings, students debate the number of storyboard panels, make decisions, and may begin to draft them; they also may decide to prepare drafts overnight and bring them to school the next day. During this time, the teacher also visits several groups as before. The teacher aims to end the session with each group having made their decisions about the storyboard panels; some will have progressed further.

The teacher starts the session by commending some of yesterday's good work and sets a time when the work on storyboard panels will stop and the discussion will start. The teacher also sets a general topic for the discussion, because this will guide the students as they continue working on the storyboard panels, which the students may choose to display and talk about during the discussion:

"Yesterday as I listened to some of your retellings, I heard about the children—Pesty and Mac—and about how Thomas fell through the floor, and about how he was chased by someone or something called Mr. Pluto.

Those are all mysterious happenings. That's our discussion topic—the many little mysteries Virginia Hamilton shows us, and then the ways that she explains some of them to us so that they don't seem so strange."

FIGURE 11–3   Continued

Step 4, Discussion: At the time set for stopping work on the storyboard panels, students and teacher arrange themselves comfortably for the discussion, and the teacher waits for students to begin talking (keeping in mind the importance of allowing wait time). If necessary, the teacher starts the discussion: "Let's begin with Pesty riding up on the big horse, with Mac walking along beside. I'd like to hear your ideas about what made that event seem mysterious when you first read about it." Students share ideas without raising hands, and the teacher is attentive to each speaker, working toward discussions in which students talk to each other, rather than addressing their comments to the teacher. Occasionally the teacher enters the discussion to restate a point or to focus on a new idea. Throughout the discussion, the students have their books to refer to, and they sometimes show their drawings for the storyboard to illustrate a point.

The discussion time ends with the teacher restating an idea that will lead into the next reading, perhaps, "You picked out something to talk about today that I hadn't thought about—how Thomas felt *uneasy* when he was in the narrow, dark tunnel where he'd never been before. You're right—*uneasy* is such a simple little word but when you think about it, it's frightening. The author makes us feel what Thomas is feeling. We'll go on with that discussion next time we talk about the book." Students put their books away and store the storyboard panels in their cooperative group's file box.

Literature Circles.   An alternative to whole class discussions of literature is the use of literature circles, in which the class divides into small groups, each studying a different shared reading. Kathy Short and Charlene Klassen (1993, p. 74) suggest organizing the circle experience beginning with book talks to introduce books students may choose, after which students have an opportunity to browse through the books before making their selections. Student groups are formed based on their book choices, and groups meet regularly to read or write in journals. "They are not expected to write summaries, answer specific questions, or analyze literary elements, but simply to share their enjoyment of the book." These authors emphasize student choice, not only in selecting a book, but in determining whether they will discuss as they read or wait till they have finished the entire book (which Short and Klassen suggest should be done in a week), how long the discussions will be (they suggest the possibility of extending discussions over a period of several weeks), whether they will prepare a culminating project, such as a mural or dramatization, and whether they will start another literature circle immediately or have an interval of independent reading.

In the literature circles described by researcher Anne Simpson and sixth-grade teacher Paula Willson, students identify their first and second choices from among five books, then groups are formed and meet daily to read together. As they read, students use post-it notes to record "interesting descriptions, words or events they did not understand, questions they have, predictions, things they wondered about, how they felt, what they thought was funny, sad, exciting, etc.," putting the notes in the book to mark the passages they have commented on. Each day the teacher meets for discussion with one of the groups; students are encouraged to base some of their contributions to the discussion on the comments they have written. Afterwards, students tape the notes into their journals and use them as the basis for further writing. Willson, the classroom teacher, writes about her part in the discussions: "My role in the group is to guide and listen. I tell the students to imagine that the group is in a car and that they are in control of the direction in which we go. I sit in the back seat and occasionally offer some suggestions on steering and braking, when necessary" (Simpson & Willson, 1993, pp. 136–137).

Katherine Samway and her co-authors (1991) have described the use of literature circles in a combination fifth- and sixth-grade multilingual classroom. One interesting aspect of their article, published in a major professional journal, is that the first two authors are adult collaborators—a university professor and a classroom teacher—but the remaining four were former or present students in the teacher's classroom: at the time of publication, three were seventh graders and one was a sixth grader. The teacher, Gail Whang, uses literature study circles, and students read and discuss one book a week—a rapid pace that is made possible by allowing extensive time to read and by eliminating interventions such as question-answer sessions and teacher-designed "comprehension" or "enrichment" assignments. Each week she begins with a book talk session in which she describes four or five books she has selected for students' reading that week and for which five or six copies are available. Students choose the book they want to read. There is a lottery if there are not enough copies of a particular book to go around and students are given large blocks of time to read, which increase during the year from twenty minutes to one hour. Assignments are tailored to the books and ideas students have shared in discussions, for example, students may be asked to notice, as they read, how an author shows changes in characters over time. During the week, students read and discuss; the teacher sits in on discussions on a rotating basis. After one year's experience with literature circles, students were interviewed about their views of this method of studying literature and other methods they had experienced before. "Over and over again we noticed the presence of four themes. The students commented on the importance of reading complete books, talking about books, being given some choice over which books they would read, and having plenty of time to read" (Samway, Whang, Cade, Gamil, Lubandina, & Phommachanh, 1991, p. 202).

Reading and discussing books in literature circles usually depends on having multiple copies of each of the books that students will read in groups. An alternative is to use *text sets* (Bishop. 1990b; Harste, Burke, & Short, 1988; Hartman & Hartman, 1993). In a text set, each book (or other literary material) is different, but all are related. They may be by the same author, have the same illustrator, share a common theme, or provide different perspectives on the same event, person, or idea. There are often more items in a text set than there are group members. Members of a literature circle may read one, several, or all of the texts, and discussions may include retellings and reading excerpts.

> While shared book discussions involve an intensive look at one book, text set discussions include more retelling and focus on broad connections and comparisons across literature. With text sets, readers begin to see pieces of literature as part of a larger whole and become aware of diverse perspectives on similar topics in their search for connections among the books circle members have read. (Short & Klassen, 1993, p. 71)

Using Learning Strategies to Spark Discussion. Wonderful discussions of literature can occur spontaneously or be guided by a planned discussion topic. Working together on a challenging text-focused activity can be a source of interesting insights, and this also can inspire discussion. Many of the strategies described in this text can be used for this purpose, among them Concept Connections, which is described in Chapter Four. The juxtaposition of terms in a Concept Connections grid will often suggest new ideas that can be expressed in writing or during a discussion. For example, these are connections based on a grid in which characters from *Romeo and Juliet* have been selected and placed:

Juliet	Friar Lawrence	Tybalt
the nurse	Romeo	Paris
Lady Capulet	Balthasar	Mercutio

The play is so sad because it's full of what if's. Balthasar disobeyed Romeo just enough to stay outside the tomb when he'd been ordered to go away. What if he had disobeyed even more and gone inside? He might have delayed Romeo's suicide just long enough for Juliet to wake. What if Friar Lawrence had come earlier to the tomb? He would have found Romeo and been able to explain that Juliet was only asleep. (terms from middle column)

The nurse is trying to help Juliet when she tells her to give up Romeo and marry Paris. She may not believe what she's saying, but she tells her, "I think you are happy in this second match, for it excels your first; or if it did not, your first is dead; or 'twere as good he were." Instead she makes Juliet despair, because her parents and her nurse are all against her, and there is no one at home to help her. (terms from middle row)

For children in the early grades, making connections among three terms is challenging. Concept Connections terms can be combined in sentences, rather than paragraphs, and children may connect only two terms, or make connections among four or more. It is useful for children to talk over their ideas and for someone—a teacher, an aide, a visiting student from an upper grade, or an adept writer within the group—to serve as a scribe. The examples below are based on *Princess Furball*, as retold by Charlotte Huck (1989).

first cook	the nurse	Ogre
second cook	Furball	hunters
Princess	King-father	Young King

The Princess turned into Furball because she didn't want to marry the Ogre. (diagonal)

One cook was kind to the princess, but the other cook was mean to Furball until she turned into a princess again. (left column, plus another term)

The nurse took better care of Furball than her father did. (center column)

Linda DeGroff and Lee Galda (1992) suggest the strategy of *Graphing a Book*. The process involves listing, in sequence, the major events in which a character is involved, rating each on an 11-point scale from +5 (good news) to –5 (bad news), then creating an annotated graph. Their example is "the rise and fall of Wilbur's fortunes" based on E. B. White's classic *Charlotte's Web* (1952)—from a low of –5—"Mr. Arable gets the ax"—to a concluding high of +5—"Wilbur meets Joy, Aranca, and Nellie" (DeGroff & Galda, 1992, p. 130). A more complex graph can show a rating scale on the vertical axis and a timeline on the horizontal axis and can use different lines to graph events from the points of view of different characters. Because literature frequently recounts the vicissitudes—the ups and downs—of life, narrative tales (and indeed factual historical accounts) can be analyzed in this good news-bad news format. Moreover, the inter-

est in judging and rating ("I'll give that a 10!") is strong in our society, and middle and high school students may find Graphing a Book an appealing way to create a graphic to serve as the basis for discussions. The strategy also could be used to analyze historical situations and events in the lives of famous people.

Another strategy in which the creation of a graphic can become the basis for discussion is not widely known but can guide older students to think analytically. This is the *Johari Window*, a concept used in personnel relations (Luft, 1969), then adapted for the study of characterization in literature. Luethel Kormanski (1988) uses the method to analyze a fictional character perceived by others as enviably handsome and rich but whose view of his own life causes him to despair, from Edward Arlington Robinson's poem, "Richard Cory." The Johari Window is a graphic like an actual window, with four panes arranged in a 2×2 format. One dimension views a person being observed (for example, a character in a story) from that person's own perspective; the other dimension views the person from the perspective of an observer (the reader). Thus, the four sections of the window, known as the open pane, the closed pane, the hidden pane, and the mystery pane, each show a different aspect of the person being viewed. The open pane of the window shows what is known to the person being observed, and to the observer. The closed pane of the window shows what is not known to the person being observed, though it is known to the observer. The hidden pane of the window shows what is known to the person being observed, but is concealed from the observer and other characters in the story, though the reader may be able to infer this information. The mystery pane of the window contains what is unknown to both the person being observed and the observer, though, again, this information may be inferred by a thoughtful reader. The strategy can link content area study with literature when historical fiction is used as a read-aloud for the class. Figures 11–4 and 11–5 show the format for a Johari Window, then an application of the strategy to a short story about Daniel Webster, a famous U. S. senator in the time immediately preceding the American Civil War.

FIGURE 11–4   Johari Window, Showing Format

K N O W N to O T H E R S		KNOWN to SELF	
		YES	**NO**
	Y E S	*the __open__ pane of the window* This information is public—known to the person (character being studied), to others, and to the reader.	*the __closed__ pane of the window* This information is not known to the person (character being studied), but it is known by other characters and the reader.
	N O	*the __hidden__ pane of the window* This information is known only to the person (character being studied). Other characters and the reader can only infer it.	*the __mystery__ pane of the window* This information is not known by anyone, although it can be inferred by the reader and is usually revealed at the end.

FIGURE 11–5   Johari Window, Applied to "The Devil and Daniel Webster," by Stephen Vincent Benét (1942)

Character: Daniel Webster

K N O W N to O T H E R S		KNOWN to SELF	
		YES	**NO**
	Y E S	the __open__ pane of the window Daniel Webster is a national figure, a highly respected United States senator, admired by fellow New Hampshire citizens, a great orator, a prosperous farmer.	the __closed__ pane of the window Webster does not realize that he is in danger of being overpowered by his own anger and his desire to win at any cost, however, the Devil knows this.
	N O	*the __hidden__ pane of the window* No one but Webster, not even the Devil, knows how intense his commitment is to maintaining the Union.	*the __mystery__ pane of the window* ▪ within the story: Can Daniel Webster defeat the Devil in a trial in which judge and jury come from the ranks of the damned? ▪ in story and history: Which of Webster's ambitions and hopes were achieved? ▪ in history across time: What were the differing perceptions of Webster in his own time? How is he perceived today, or has he been forgotten?

Delighting in Sounds and Stories

Literature can be read and treasured in silence, whenever readers are ready to do so—from emergent reading, based on recalling heard stories and imagining the meanings of illustrations, to meditative reading and rereading of texts that have become important in our lives. Literature can be enjoyed through hearing the reading of others, or hearing and seeing dramatizations. Readers also can share in bringing literature to life, as their voices join with those of others. Choral reading and Readers' Theater are two methods for performing literature, and either strategy can be adapted for use over the complete age range, from young children through adults.

Choral Reading.   In choral reading, an important, well-written piece of text is prepared by separating it into parts, which groups or individuals are assigned to read. Everyone has a copy of the text and people read their parts in chorus. In the simplest form of choral reading, a class of students is divided in two groups—left side of the room, right side of the room—and the groups read stanzas of a poem alternately, with everyone joining in the chorus. For more elaborate readings, teacher or students plan in advance how the text can best be divided for the reading. The meaning of portions of text and the sounds of the language provide the basis for choosing how combinations of voices and contrasts in style—loud and soft, slow and fast— should be used. Multiple copies of the text are then prepared, with each group's or individual's parts highlighted on their copies. Choral reading has many benefits, both aesthetic and practical. "The pleasure of interpreting a favorite poem orally is one of the rewards... Another is the sense of group participation toward an artistic effort" (Sutherland & Arbuthnot, 1991, p. 600). Andrew Johnson (1995, p. 438) describes it as "a safe, effective method for improving reading fluency. Readers have multiple cue systems happening all around them in the form of other students and the teacher. Through repetition, and by stressing the expressive and affective elements, readers begin to get a feel for the piece as a whole and bring new meaning to the text."

Joyce and Daniel McCauley advocate choral reading because it engages students in active reading and rereading in a situation that creates interest and reduces anxiety. Readings provide comprehensible input, because the text and the method combine to create a situation where students are reading and thinking about something intricate, which is nevertheless within their capacity to understand. The McCauleys (1992, p. 529) relate choral reading to another important theoretical concept, the zone of proximal development, because the method provides support for students to accomplish reading and interpretation that is beyond their current ability to manage independently. "Children hear the poem read properly by a model language user, usually the teacher. The children read what they can at first and, through the process of repeated reading and teacher/peer modeling, are led to new words, new concepts, and language growth." Planning and practicing choral readings are useful cooperative group activities, and well-prepared choral readings provide excellent opportunities for whole class or group performances for visitors or assemblies. Choral readings based on texts related to content areas enrich and extend content area learning and are one way to provide students with long-lasting memories of important text without requiring memorization. Kathy Danielson and Susan Dauer (1990) recommend choral reading as a form of creative drama. Among the resources they suggest is the work of Paul Fleischman, who creates poems designed, in topic and in format, to be read by two voices, which can readily be adapted to be performed by two choruses of readers. Fleischman's poems are a strong addition to content area programs because they combine great beauty with effective presentation of information. *I am phoenix: Poems for two voices* (1985) is a collection of poems in which birds such as the now-extinct passenger pigeon tell their stories: "We were counted not in thousands nor millions but in billions..." In *Joyful noise: Poems for two voices* (1988), the voices are those of insects—grasshoppers, water striders, mayflies, fireflies, and crickets.

Readers' Theater.   Engaging in the performance of literary works without the cost and complication of preparing stage settings or the anxiety of memorizing parts is open to students and teachers through a popular strategy called Readers' Theater. The history of this activity has been traced back to 1806 (Groff, 1978, p. 16) and in the course of its use across places and times the name of the activity has been spelled in a variety of ways, for example, *Reader's Theater, Readers Theatre.* The spelling *Readers' Theater* has been chosen for use in this text because several readers are involved in Readers' Theater and because *theater* is the more common spelling of the word in this country; however, when other authors are quoted directly, their spelling of the term is used. In Readers' Theater, a text is prepared in play script form, usually with parts for a narrator or narrators as well as for characters. As many copies of the text as there are parts are needed. It is useful to keep the scripts in a file folder or envelope labeled with the name of the play and the number of parts. As an assigned activity or during free choice time, students select a play, choose parts, and read the script together, practicing it in different ways. Eventually the group may wish to perform for other classmates. Readers' Theater can be used effectively in all of the content areas; for example, brief Readers' Theater scripts can be developed to dramatize math word problems. Terrell Young and Sylvia Vardell (1993) encourage its use as a way of bringing nonfiction into the curriculum, giving an example of a Readers' Theater script about Sojourner Truth based on a biography and citing examples of science trade books to adapt. Among the advantages of this strategy are its effectiveness in concept and vocabulary development and in language and social development for students as they work together on aspects of Readers' Theater. Audiences also benefit from and take pleasure in the process. Beverly Busching writes of the readiness of elementary students to become engaged in the drama of Readers' Theater, but her comments may apply to older students as well.

> To the surprise of many teachers, elementary school audiences become as deeply involved with a well staged Readers Theatre presentation as with an acted play. Perhaps they are not distracted by shaky props or sagging costumes, or by the novice actors' efforts to manage stage maneuvers …[T]he audience can enter directly into the world of the play, letting the words they hear intertwine with their imagination. (Busching, 1981, p. 331–332)

Kathy Latrobe (1993) advocates using Readers' Theater for high school students, noting that school media specialists may be interested and skilled in the preparation of scripts. She suggests basing Readers' Theater on an excerpt from a longer text, such as *Huckleberry Finn.* When sections of a longer text are used as Readers' Theater scripts, the narrator's part can be written to provide background in an introduction and follow-up—a glimpse of what is to come—in a conclusion. A narrator, or multiple narrators, can be used in versatile ways when a book or story is translated into a Readers' Theater format, and the use of several narrators adds characters, so more students can be involved as actor-readers. Among a wealth of texts appropriate for Readers' Theater is *Ahyoka and the talking leaves* by Peter and Connie Roop. The story tells about a fascinating and important event in the history of human language development: the creation, completed in 1821, of a written language for the Cherokee nation, based on a syllabary with eighty-six characters. The man who devised this system of written language for his people was called Sequoyah. (The great sequoia trees in the western forests were named in his honor by a British naturalist.) A scholar who talked with Sequoyah through translators wrote that he accomplished his great work "by the aid of his daughter, who seemed to enter into the genius of his labors" (Roop & Roop, 1992, p. 57). In addition to the major characters of Sequoyah and his daughter Ahyoka, a Readers' Theater script can include two narrators, one who reads the narrative which relates to the daughter and one who reads the narrative which relates to the father.

Tales "told newly, told memorably, told again"

Storytelling is an age-old, worldwide method of bringing literature to life. "The old tales inspire not only the obvious reactions of laughter or tears, but also the deeper sense of a story linking us to human lives over the ages, a story that has been told time and time again in many parts of the world" (Sutherland & Arbuthnot, 1991, p. 565). In her book *Storytelling,* Eileen Colwell recounts her own memorable experiences as a storyteller and advises teachers about how to develop their abilities in this art. She quotes John Masefield, a storyteller as well as a poet, who said that the world was longing for stories—"told newly, told memorably, told again."

> Storytelling is still a living tradition in many countries where education and books are not readily and widely available. In Morocco storytellers are found in market places, and in Egypt Bedouins listen to professional storytellers with loud clapping of hands. In Java the honoured dalang chants tales from the Ramayana, moving puppets against a screen. And in Nigeria villagers welcome traveling storytellers whose tales play an important part in educating children in tribal customs and tradition. Sometimes what is sacred or precious is given a reverence by the human voice that cannot be conveyed on the printed page. (Colwell, 1991, pp. 13–14)

Teachers As Storytellers.   Many references in the professional literature give teachers guidance for storytelling. (Information also is available from NAPPS, the National Association for the Preservation and Perpetuation of Storytelling, P. O. Box 309, Jonesborough, Tennessee, 37679.) In his advice for teachers who wish to become storytellers, Robert Cooter (1991, p. 73) puts choosing a story that seems "just right" as the first step. Then, he suggests, teachers should prepare by rereading the story, forming mental pictures of the events and describing them. He cautions against using overly dramatic voice changes for different characters, particularly male storytellers using falsetto voices for female characters. Cooter advocates storytelling using the book from which the story comes as a prop and mixing reading with telling: "When sharing [a story] from the book, two subtle, but powerful, messages are being sent: a) that books contain great stories, and b) if students enjoyed this story then [others can be found] in their school or community library." *Story nets* can be used as a backdrop for a storytelling area. Sandra Imdieke (1990, 1991) describes nets on which many little objects are hung, used by West African minstrels. Passers-by may choose one of the objects and pay to hear a story told about it. In a classroom, similar nets can be hung with miniatures that suggest a story, or paperback books can be attached to the net and used for a combined reading and storytelling.

Teachers can use storytelling to bring information to life and make it memorable. Kathleen Martin and Etta Miller (1988), discussing the use of storytelling in science education, mention an instance where students disagreed about the number of moons circling the planet Mars. Rather than giving the correct information or telling students to look it up, their teacher told a story from mythology. Martin and Miller do not provide the story, but it is one among many in which the myths of ancient times were used by scientists when choosing names for newly discovered bodies in space. Such a story can be told briefly:

> Since ancient times, people have been able to see some of the nearer planets in the night sky. One of those planets appears reddish—and red is the color of blood, so the planet was named Mars, for the Roman god of war. Ancient people believed that wherever people fought, Mars (whom the Greeks called Ares) was there. The god of war rode through the battlefield in a chariot drawn by horses with golden bands around their heads. He wore bronze armor and carried a huge spear, and with him rode his two sons, Deimos and Phobos, whose names meant Terror and Panic.
>
> See if you can tell from this story how many moons circle the planet Mars, and what their names are.
>
> (Note for storytellers: Deimos is pronounced *day-mos'*, with the accent on the second syllable; Ares is pronounces *ah'-reez*.)

Students and Storytelling.   Storytellers depend on their listeners, so students' participation is necessary if teachers' storytelling is to be successful. Such participation can be as simple as students chanting lines in the story that are used repetitively. Barbara Reed (1987, p. 36) advocates the use of improvised drama after storytelling, as well as retellings by students. Letting students interpret stories in their own way provides time for reflection and avoids "trying to elicit reactions by questions about what the story 'means,' or what characters should have done." Teachers also can choose from a variety of strategies to encourage students themselves to be storytellers. In *Story Theater*, teacher and students participate together; Tellers' Theater provides an opportunity for groups to storytell on a shared theme. *Yarn-in-a-box* and *Catch a character* provide comfortable structure for shared storytelling. Two storytelling strategies that are particularly suitable for older students are *"No you didn't"* and *Another point of view*, which links storytelling and writing.

Story Theater. Drama and storytelling are combined in a technique called Story Theater (Heinig, 1988). The teacher tells a familiar story, or reads it slowly, pausing for students to pantomime the action. Roles in the story can be chosen by students in advance, or students can step into the roles of characters spontaneously as they appear in the story. Sebesta notes that when students are accustomed to participating in Story Theater they may even take on the role of an important piece of scenery. One of many genres well-suited to story theater is that of poems which tell a story. An example is Nancy Winslow Parker's (1985) presentation of Longfellow's famous poem "Paul Revere's Ride," which sets the stirring, quasi-historical poem into accurate historical context. Once familiar with Parker's introduction, students can act out the roles of Paul Revere, colonial families, and British soldiers, John Pulling, the sexton of the Old North Church, and Dr. Samuel Prescott (unmentioned by Longfellow), who escaped when Paul Revere and his comrades were captured by British militia and completed the task of carrying news of the British advance to the American colonists. Here is a poem where scenery has a crucial role: a student can act the part of the belfry tower where the number of lanterns signal to Paul Revere, waiting across the river to ride with his warning, how the British will travel to attack the colonists: "One, if by land, and two, if by sea."

Tellers' Theater. In this group method of storytelling, suggested by Martha Combs and John Beach (1994) the participants practice telling a story before sharing it through a performance. As long as the original story line is maintained, improvisation is encouraged. Related stories can be combined, retellings can be polished and presented, or anecdotes about a shared class experience can be the basis for the storytelling. Combs and Beach suggest that stories based on text sets used in literature circles can be shared through Tellers' Theater.

Yarn-In-A-Box. This turn-taking method of group storytelling is fun for a variety of reasons. Its name is a pun, to begin with, since a yarn is a slang name for a good story. Some simple preparation must begin before the storytelling, which students themselves may enjoy. The necessary props are a ball of yarn and a closed box. Another name for the strategy is *Story Box* (Wendelin, 1991). As the yarn is wound into a ball, knots are tied into it at irregular intervals. The box needs a small hole in the top; the ball of yarn goes inside, and one end comes out through the hole. One person starts to tell the story, while pulling on the yarn. When a knot appears, the box is given to another person, who continues telling, and pulling, until the next knot, when another teller takes a turn with the box, the yarn, and the story. Members of the group will soon see that they can have some control over the length of their turns, even though they cannot see when a knot will pop out of the box, by taking long, rapid pulls if they want a short turn, or pulling very slowly if they have a lot to say—and, of course, any way that the tale teller chooses to pull the yarn is fine.

Catch a Character. Group storytelling also can be organized around an array of characters who are introduced by chance (Cliatt & Shaw, 1988). This activity requires a story box that contains a large collection of small figures of people and animals. One student reaches in, "catches" a character, and begins a story. Then the first storyteller passes the box to a classmate, who, without looking into the box, pulls out another character and weaves it into the story, and so forth. Students may pass the box back and forth, rather than adding extra characters to the story. Miniature characters for this activity can be purchased or stuffed figures may be made by parents or created as a crafts project. This storytelling method can be used across a wide age range. When story boxes are prepared for traditional stories that are familiar to all the tellers, the strategy is a reminder that there are many ways to tell a familiar story. For the Red Riding Hood story, for example, the story box will contain figures of Red Riding Hood, the grandmother, mother, wolf, and hunter. As the story is usually told, the hunter appears on the scene last, but if that figure is pulled from the box first, then the story must begin with the hunter, who might say, "Each day as I go through the woods, I see a friendly old lady tending her garden. But for a week now, I have not seen her. I wonder if she has gone visiting her family on the other side of the woods." The story box will then be handed to another teller. The telling will differ, depending on which character is drawn next, although the overall plot of the story will remain the same. The strategy also can be used with stories that are familiar because they have been read by the whole class, and the assignment to create the puppet figures could rotate among cooperative groups.

"No, you didn't!"   This activity, based on a suggestion by David Dynak (1993), is a form of creative drama and storytelling with a special twist. It can serve as a way of helping students who have difficulty expressing or experiencing disagreement, but it is primarily an intriguing method of telling a tale. Students pair up, and one begins a story. The listener, instead of simply absorbing the tale and nodding in agreement, must stop the storyteller at some point and deny what has been told, saying "No, it wasn't like that!" or, in the words of the strategy's name, "No, you didn't." The storyteller must agree— "You're right. This is really what happened…"—and continue the story in a new direction. After a time, either partner can signal for the other to continue the story—"Now this is where you came in. You tell about it" or "Now this is where I came in, so I'll tell…" The partner continues the story, which, in turn, is eventually contradicted. Flat denial of what another person is saying is rude in ordinary circumstances, so this apparently simple strategy requires a thoughtful introduction. A key to maintaining good humor and ensuring ingenuity is built into the strategy, because the same narrator continues the story after being contradicted. So the interjection of "No, you didn't!" is not a way of getting a turn; it is a signal that the teller must now display cleverness in moving the story in a new direction. In introducing the strategy, the teacher can be the storyteller who is interrupted periodically by students. Students can try out different ways of saying "No, you didn't"—sadly, quietly, in a scary manner, or as if they were very surprised; like a judge, referee, or someone making a

joke. This style of storytelling can be occasionally included in a teacher's repertoire and after students are familiar with it, they can try it in pairs and then use it in groups as a form of creative drama.

The "No, you didn't!" pattern can be applied to retellings of folktales and other simple, familiar stories. Pairs of students can choose the roles of two characters in the story and retell it, either making slight changes or taking the story down an entirely new path. If the activity is popular, cooperative groups can adapt a story so each member has a role, and they can work toward creating a drama in which the contradictions and changes of the narrator are effectively combined. Alternatively, the storytelling can be based on historical or classroom events that can be told humorously through opposing views of what really happened. Reading the book *That's exactly the way it wasn't* (Stevenson, 1991) is a hilarious way to introduce or follow up the strategy; it tells of a series of adventures through conversation and cartoons from the points of view of two people who never agreed about anything, including whether they are or are not falling off a cliff.

Another Point of View.   Bonnie Warawa (1989) suggests using storytelling in high school English classes. After reading a classic story, poem, or drama, students choose a character who plays a major role but who lacks a voice within the story as it was originally told. One of the examples Warawa gives is retelling Robert Browning's chilling poem *Porphyria's lover*, in which the only voice is that of the anonymous lover-murderer, from the point of view of the beautiful and doomed Porphyria. In some cases, responding to a classic from another point of view can enable present-day readers to express the words and passions of characters whose roles were diminished because of their gender, culture, or class.

The World of Books

In the first chapter of this text, features of textbooks were discussed—both those that make them useful resources for learning and those that create difficulty for student readers. That chapter also provided a definition of trade books—"books produced for a general audience and sold in bookstores to people who are interested in their subject matter… [which] can be read and enjoyed by readers with a fairly wide range of ages and reading skill"—and contrasted them with textbooks—"[which] are assigned to their readers, rather than chosen by them, and [whose] topics may not be intrinsically interesting to the reader."

Why Trade Books?

Teachers, not textbooks, must be the providers of instruction so students can learn well. One way teachers can intervene to support and supplement students' learning from textbooks is by using well-chosen trade books in their instructional programs, a practice that is widely advocated (e.g., Fuhler, 1991; Kliman, 1993). Barbara Moss (1991), urging the use of nonfiction trade books in content area instruction, contrasts the disadvantages of textbooks with the advantages of trade books. Textbooks are often difficult reading for the students at the grade level for which they are intended and include a heavy load of abstract technical vocabulary, teaching about many topics in a general way. Good trade books, on the other hand, provide in-depth information organized in a logical way, are thoughtfully and attractively illustrated, and are published frequently, so they are not as likely as textbooks to be outdated.

> Texts… assume that students know unrealistic amounts of background information, and inadequately explain background events and their relationships. …texts rarely guide students step-by-stop through the process of understanding new content. Before students have time to reflect on an idea, let alone command it, the text has moved on to another concept. …[B]y contrast, tradebooks provide causal relationships between concepts to help students grasp those ideas. (McGowan & Guzzetti, 1991, p. 17)

While Tom McGowan and Barbara Guzzetti (1991, p. 19) agree wholeheartedly that high quality trade books are more intriguing and easier to read than textbooks, they also point out that relying on textbooks permits teachers to avoid decision-making

and effort. The well-planned use of trade books is likely to lead to better learning for students and greater enjoyment for both students and teacher, but, they caution, "the instructional utility of a literary work depends largely on the classroom teacher's ingenuity and resourcefulness." Besides the need to plan how to use trade books effectively as resources, the decision to use them requires teachers to exercise thought in choosing them. Writing about the power of histories and historical fiction to make the past come to life, Linda Levstik (1993, p. 12) emphasizes the significance of teacher choice. "The power of a literary interpretation of history places a burden on the classroom teacher to select the finest books available for children. A good story does not compensate for bad history, nor does good history justify a poorly written text."

One example of wise trade book use is given by Patricia Crook, who describes a fifth-grade teacher's use of *Charley Skedaddle* (Beatty, 1987) as her students were learning about the Civil War. This trade book received the Scott O'Dell Award for Historical Fiction, an award established to honor outstanding books of historical fiction written for children or young adults. The teacher began by reading about the experience of Union soldiers lost in the forests and swamps of Virginia before the battle (that became known as the Battle of the Wilderness) was fought. Over a period of several weeks, the teacher read the entire text aloud while students discussed, created semantic maps, and wrote extensively in response to the reading. Crook (1990, p. 492) points out that the teacher "has not, in her planning, changed the curriculum. She has merely altered the emphasis. Using children's literature has enabled her to move away from the social studies textbook as the primary source for studying curricular concepts." In this class, most students were capable of reading the text independently; however, the teacher's reading enabled her to comment, and she shared the text with all students without demeaning the few who were not yet sufficiently skilled to read it on their own. It is useful to remember that when poems and short stories are used as introductions to topics in the content areas, they almost certainly must be read aloud by the teacher, rather than assigned as independent reading by students, who may find many unfamiliar words, read too slowly to grasp the meaning, and perhaps protest that the assignment is irrelevant and unnecessary.

Trade books spark discussion and can offer opportunities for students to think about ways to solve problems in hypothetical situations. Because problem solutions are offered in a group setting, students see that there can be many reasonable ideas and that good plans can be improved by others who point out flaws or suggest additions. Ted Riecken and Michelle Miller (1990, p. 60) advocate developing students' problem-solving skills using literature, rather than teaching predetermined step-by-step methods, because real-life decision making is "rarely as straightforward a process as the frameworks imply."

> In addition to containing topics that students can easily identify with, children's literature can contain problematic situations that reflect the complexities of real life. For instance, one character's solution to a problem may become another character's problem. ...[Moreover], children's stories often have strong moral components in them. Teachers can use these aspects of children's literature to help students reflect on morals and values. (Riecken & Miller, 1990, p. 63)

Well-written, wisely used trade books can create a thirst for knowledge and a love of reading. School textbooks are unlikely to turn students into passionate readers. "Rarely," Betty Carter and Richard Abrahamson observe, "do young adults refer to textbooks as the catalysts that propelled them into any lifelong interests. Helpful adults, the popular media, trade books, and life experiences perform these functions. Textbooks do not" (Carter & Abrahamson, 1990, p. 175). Isabel Beck and Margaret McKeown (1991, p. 486) advocate trade books as a supplement or substitute for textbooks, noting that "the point of teaching [historical] topics should not merely be to develop a catalog of events and characters. Rather, it is to help students come to understand why events occurred, why one thing led to another, and how the culmination of a sequence of events affected people's lives." Linda Levstik (1990, p. 849) writes, "[i]n a historical novel the author holds a magnifying glass up to a piece of history, providing humanizing details often left out of broad survey history texts.

The reader finds out how people felt about history, how they lived their daily lives, what they wore, how they spoke." Jean Fritz, now an author of many acclaimed trade books for children, has written about her own experiences of entering an American elementary school for the first time and receiving a social studies textbook. The first chapter was titled "From forest to farmland":

> Since both my mother's and father's family had helped to settle Washington County, I was interested to see how they and other pioneers had fared. I skimmed through the pages but I couldn't find any mention of people at all. There was talk about dates and square miles and cultivation and population growth and immigration and the Western movement, but it was [as] if the forests had lain down and given way to farmland without anyone being brave or scared or tired or sad, without babies being born, without people dying. Well, I thought, maybe that would come later. (Fritz, 1982, p. 153)

Folklore and Poetry

It is worthwhile for students to have opportunities to read and hear many different forms of literature, and there are many ways for content area teachers to integrate different genres into their programs. Folklore and poetry are two rich genres. Including them as a part of school learning may provide the only opportunity for students to encounter them. Both forms of literature provide rich meanings concisely, so they can be included without extensive use of time; moreover, teachers have a wealth of examples from which to choose.

Collections of folklore from many countries and cultures are now being published in increasing numbers, in formats that provide extensive background information and handsome, authentic illustrations. One recent example, *The golden carp and other tales from Vietnam* (1993), compiled by Lynette Dyer Vuong, includes an extensive and informative introduction, annotations about each of the stories, and a guide to pronunciation of Vietnamese names. *Dreamtime* (1994) is a two-part collection of stories from Australia, written and transcribed by Oodgeroo. The first section contains family tales from the childhood of Kath Walker, the third child in an Aboriginal family, some of them heart-wrenching accounts of her school experiences. In her middle years, she collected the folklore—dreamtime stories—of her people and wrote stories in the dreamtime style; these comprise the second half of her book. Kath Walker gave up the name white people had given her, and the final story recounts how she was given the name *Oodgeroo*, which means *paperbark tree*, because she wrote the stories about her tribe on bark: "In the new Dreamtime there lived a woman, an Aborigine, who longed for her lost tribe and for the stories that belonged to her people; for she could remember only the happenings of her own Dreamtime. But the old Dreamtime had stolen the stories and hidden them. The woman knew that she must search for the old stories—and through them she might find her tribe again" (Oodgeroo, 1994, p. 80).

Many forms of folklore have been told across the ages. Pourquoi stories, discussed briefly in Chapter Ten, are tales created to answer the ever-recurring question, Why... ? "These stories explain a natural phenomenon, like the color of a bird's feathers, or a cultural manifestation, like a ritual dance. People all over the world at one time or another have told these stories to explain the world around them" (Zarillo, 1994, p. 59). Children and adults delight in good pourquoi stories, and older students can be drawn into the enjoyment by a teacher who arranges the lessons so students do not feel stigmatized by reading something they regard as babyish. One justification for reading pourquoi stories is to consider how people explained natural phenomena before they possessed scientific knowledge. Much of mythology has this basis; for example, the Greek myth that tells of the daughter of the harvest goddess being forced to live part of each year in the underworld is an explanation of why fruits and flowers cease to grow during the winter. Questions asked in pourquoi stories, and answers given, tell much about particular cultures and provide a vision of different world views. From reading and hearing these stories, students can move to writing them. Pourquoi stories provide a theme, in the form of a why question, and encourage imaginative answers.

Rudyard Kipling's *Just so stories* (1978) are pourquoi stories—tales for children telling how the elephant got a long trunk, the camel a hump, the rhinoceros a wrinkly skin, the armadillo its stickly prickliness and its ability to swim. Many of Kipling's stories are classics; their humor and vivid language continues to delight child listeners and adult readers across the years. The author used the pourquoi story genre to invent stories to amuse children and wrote as if the storyteller was speaking directly to a child, who is addressed throughout the stories with the phrase, "O best beloved." *The first dog*, a pourquoi story by Jan Brett (1988) begins, "Long, long ago in the great days of the Pleistocene..." and tells the story of how a paleowolf came to be the first dog. (The story might be compared with Kipling's "The cat that walked by himself," which imagines how dog, horse, and cow came to be domesticated and how cat agreed to be *a little tame*.)

Most pourquoi stories published in recent years, however, are retellings of tales handed down within a culture. In the best of these, the author gives evidence of their authenticity by discussing the sources for the tales and setting the stories in historical, cultural, and sometimes geographical context. *Soft child: How rattlesnake got its fangs* (1993) is a Native American folktale retold by Joe Hayes and illustrated with beautiful, accurate drawings of the wildlife and vegetation of the Southwestern United States. The tale of how a defenseless "soft child" is bullied by other animals before being gifted with a rattle and fangs is from the Tohono O'odham (Pápago) people; an endnote gives information about their history and current way of life. *The girl who loved coyotes: Stories of the Southwest* (Wood, 1995), a recent collection of folktales from the American Southwest, includes many pourquoi stories. "How the eagle learned to see" answers two questions: *Why is it that the eagle can see from such far distances?* and—a question wondered about in all early cultures—*How did people come to have fire?* Although the colorful illustrations and flowing language of books such as this one will interest young children, the books are equally well-designed to interest and inform students in middle and high school, and many of the stories have a romantic interest. Here, a glossary of terms derived from Spanish is included. The preface is a historical account of the three cultures that are part of the Southwest, beginning with "the Anasazi, or the Old Ones [who] came from the southwest about two thousand years ago…" and continuing with a description of the ways the descendants of that ancient culture have both adapted to and resisted the influences of Spanish invaders and then "the soldiers, cowboys, trailblazers, railroad builders, fur trappers, and homesteaders" (Wood, 1995, pp. 7–8). A history such as this could supplement (and be contrasted with) bland or biased presentations in other sources.

Another ancient form of story is the fable, "a short story devised to convey some useful moral lesson, but often carrying with it associations of the marvelous or the mythical, and frequently employing animals as characters" (Drabble, 1985, p. 335). The fable genre is one that can be effectively used in inclusive classrooms, and text sets based on fables are easy to compile. Aesop's fables are the most famous, and many editions, ancient and modern, present the same moral stories in varying forms. Folksinger Tom Paxton (1991, 1993) has created a series of rhymed retellings of these fables, which Robert Rayevsky's illustrations place in an urban landscape where the animals are dressed as teenagers, complete with sneakers, jeans, and boomboxes. Frances and Rowan Barnes-Murphy (1994) present an extensive, ingeniously illustrated collection of Aesop's fables without including a moral at the end of each; the introduction notes that, "In some collections each fable is capped with a moral epigram. But these morals are thought to be later additions to the fables, probably dating from medieval times. …I have elected to tell the stories as Aesop would have, leaving readers to discover for themselves the universal truths they contain."

Misoso: Once upon a time tales from Africa, retold by Verna Aardema, is an elegant book which would be a good source for classroom read-alouds. Aardema explains that *misoso* (pronounced *me-saw'-saw*), a word from the Mbundu tribe of Angola, refers to tales told mostly for entertainment. "The stories in this collection were selected with that in mind; if they teach a lesson, or illuminate the culture of a people, that is a plus" (Aardema, 1994, p. iv). Nevertheless, these entertaining tales do inform, illuminate, and provoke thought. The stories can be read aloud, without introduction or follow-up; they can be discussed in the manner of grand conversations;

FIGURE 11–6   Terms for a Text Impressions Activity, taken from "The Hen and the Dove: An Ashanti Fable," in *Misoso: Once Upon a Time Tales from Africa,* retold by Verna Aardema and illustrated by Reynold Ruffins (1994).

	fable	
Akoko the hen		Aturukuku the dove
village of men		tall grass country
tied to a tree		
fusses over me and brings me food		scratch and search to find any food
cooking pot		
	better to be free	

students can illustrate or replay them using visual art, music, or drama; the Text Impressions strategy, described in Chapter Ten, can be used to inspire pretellings. Figure 11–6 provides an example, using ten terms taken from an Ashanti fable, "recorded during the period when the Gold Coast was a British colony and the Ashanti were not free in their own land" (Aardema, 1994, p. 35). Although the terms are given in the order in which they appear in the text, students do not need to use the terms in that order when they write their text impression, and indeed do not need to use the exact terms. Like all of the tales in this beautifully illustrated collection, the fable of "The hen and the dove" begins with a short glossary explaining the unfamiliar terms in the story and concludes with an afterword, explaining the story's place in tribal history.

Poetry is a genre that crosses cultures and times. It is older than the written word, and some of the poetry in libraries, books, and minds today is there because poets, many thousands of years ago, told grand stories in patterned language that was remembered and retold over centuries, until a written language was devised. Poetry is for reading and savoring, for laughter, tears, and excitement, for learning through ear and eye and heart and mind. Naomi Shihab Nye has compiled an anthology, *This same sky: A collection of poems from around the world,* its endpapers a collage of stamps and envelopes and poet's signatures. The voices of the poets have the power to fill us—teachers and students alike—with wonder. She writes, "I think of a house with a thousand glittering windows. I think of poets over the ages sending their voices out into the sky, leaving quiet indelible trails" (Nye, 1992, p. xii). There is such richness in a single poem, and such a wealth of poetry to share, that it is a shame to exclude it from our teaching. It also is a shame to present only rhyming jingles to children and to teach older students that poetry is difficult and confusing by requiring them to interpret the meaning of poems, line by separate line, as if significant poems have one and only one interpretation and the meaning of the whole is a collection of many little meanings. Guidelines given earlier in this chapter about methods to avoid in teaching literature apply strongly to poetry. Poetry itself has needs: it needs to reach listeners and readers directly, and it needs to be protected from being turned into a tool to teach skills or to be used as the basis for an inquisition.

Poetry needs a human voice. Sometimes that voice is in the mind of a reader for whom the poet's words resound, echo, and repeat. Often, however, a teacher's skillful reading is one of the best ways to bring poetry into the classroom. Bill Moyers (1995) writes that he did not begin to love and understand poetry until he was taught by teachers who read it aloud. Students' voices can bring poems alive in choral reading; their actions can bring it to life through creative drama. Poetry also deserves conversations. Too often the process used to study a poem is a question-and-answer session in which the teacher asks about the meaning of each line and students' answers are judged as right or wrong. An alternative to this inquisitional pattern is the EVOKER strategy. Originally developed by Walter Pauk (1974) for use in studying literature independently, the strategy can be adapted for poetry study by whole class and cooperative groups across a wide age range. The strategy's title is an acronym, standing for Exploration, Vocabulary study, Oral reading, Key ideas, Evaluation, Recapitulation. The process that is described here is effective when poetry, famous speeches, or similar texts are incorporated in content area study. While poetry should usually be enjoyed simply through extensive listening and reading, the EVOKER strategy is useful in providing teachers with a way to engage a whole class in an organized discussion of a poem.

When EVOKER is used as a group activity, the first three steps (Exploration, Vocabulary study, and Oral reading) are completed as a whole-class, teacher-led process; then cooperative groups complete the next two steps (Key Ideas and Evaluation); finally there is a return to whole class discussion for the final step (Recapitulation). Figure 11–7 describes the steps in the EVOKER process. This method allows groups of students to discuss and support their interpretations of the whole poem, and the teacher does not risk stifling the discussion by imposing an interpretation before students have developed their ideas. It also is a useful strategy for language courses, where the teacher can read aloud a poem in the language being learned and share the text with the students who read and savor the lilt of the poem's language, but discuss its meaning in English. This method, an alternative to the traditional *explication du texte*, produces richer discussions and a deeper understanding than those where students must use only the limited vocabulary available to them in the new language they are studying.

> The themes and styles of poetry derived from such diverse cultures as Inuit, Native American, African, Japanese, Chinese, Latin American, Middle Eastern, Russian, and Celtic can help students perceive how heritage and language influence thought and expression while common themes such as family, environment, memories, and dreams connect cultures and the experiences of our students. Growing numbers of our students come from backgrounds where poetry is an integral part of the culture. …where poetry is held in esteem and poetic thinking is as valued as logical thinking, [and] we must be sure to respect and build on these values. (Steinberg, 1991, p. 57)

Poetry written far away or long ago reaches us in translation. In the introduction to *This same sky*, Naomi Shihab Nye (1992, xiii) expresses appreciation to the poets and also to their translators. "Deep appreciation to the dedicated translators who labored on all horizons to make these border-crossings possible. Whenever someone suggests 'how

FIGURE 11–7   Steps in the EVOKER Process

▌**Exploration:** Students have copies of the poem (or other text) and read through it silently one or more times. If students are beginning readers, the teacher reads aloud. During this reading students may note unfamiliar words or phrases.

"Take time to explore the poem. Read it and see whether you find words you don't know, or words used in an unusual way. Later we'll talk about them."

▌**Vocabulary study:** Students share any words or terms that are unfamiliar to them, or words used in an unusual way. This is a group-share process, without questioning or hand-raising. Students say the words; the teacher lists them. It is useful to have several good dictionaries available so students can begin looking up definitions. Recall, from Chapter One, that "the category of unfamiliar words is unique, because whether a term is familiar or not depends not on the word itself, but on the match between the word and each individual reader." If there are students in the classroom who are unfamiliar with words that are known to others, this can lead to a richer discussion; poets choose words with care, and the discussion of a familiar word may call attention to the fact that it is used for a particular purpose. When words are listed, students share ideas—often we have an impression about a word even if we cannot define it—and read dictionary definitions. The teacher commends, clarifies, and briefly explains the meaning within the context of the poem.

"What are some words that are new to you, or that the writer has used in usual ways? Call them out and I'll list them…"

▌**Oral reading:** Unless the poem is unusually long, take time to read it aloud several times. (If the poem is long, read it once and then suggest that students read aloud some portions that seem especially intriguing or powerful.) In a group, different readers take turns—again, without hand-raising or being called upon; the reader just begins to read. The teacher should decide whether to read first as a model. A first reading by the teacher may help student readers with pronunciation of words not discussed during the previous phase and demonstrate that poems should ordinarily not be read with a pause at the end of each line. Younger students may be eager to read; if two or more students start at once, they can be encouraged to read in chorus. With older students, it may be necessary to allow plenty of wait time in order for someone to be courageous enough to read.

"We're going to read the poem aloud several times, so we can all listen to the sounds of the language. Anyone who wants to can read. I won't call on you; just begin."

▌**Key ideas:** The previous steps were for the whole class. This step and the next one are done in cooperative groups. In this step, students brainstorm a list of important ideas or phrases that seem important, perhaps working stanza by stanza.

▌**Evaluation:** After the group has identified key ideas, they use this information and impressions gained during all of the previous steps to discuss imagery, evocative use of language in the poem, and the sense of the poem. The evaluation is a weighing of ideas to get an impression of the poem's meaning, *not* a rating of the poem as good/bad, interesting/uninteresting.

During these two steps, the teacher moves from group to group, listening.

"In your groups look for key ideas in the poem. Brainstorm a list of important ideas and vivid language. Then go on to evaluate your ideas—see if you can put them together to get a sense of the meaning of the whole poem."

▌**Recapitulation:** At this point, groups come together for a whole class discussion, sharing their thoughts about the poem and discussing or arguing about its meaning. Occasionally the teacher will need to step into the discussion with information if a group has misunderstood a word or phrase in a way that distorts the poem. Usually this step is rewarding for the teacher, who is likely to be surprised and delighted by students' insights and may be led to deeper personal understanding by what students have seen. The teacher summarizes the groups' understanding of the poem, and the process concludes with another oral reading of the entire poem, perhaps a choral reading in which everyone who wishes to do so joins in.

much is lost in translation!' I want to say, 'Perhaps— but how much is gained?' A new world of readers, for one thing." Poetry in translation can bring special strength to content area learning because it enables readers to be touched by ideas that would otherwise never reach them. Translations of poetry also can demonstrate vividly that the same thoughts can be interpreted in many, rich ways.

Earlier in this chapter, there was discussion about making art trivial by teaching the rules for a particular art form and assigning students to produce it. The example given was teaching students the apparently simple format for haiku, a traditional form of Japanese poetry, then assigning them to write in that form—without opportunities to hear, read, discuss, and think about famous haiku and without the options to write their poetry in another way or to express their ideas in prose. One reason this assignment is given is that the haiku form makes evaluation easy. Haiku have seventeen syllables, so the teacher only needs to count syllables to ensure that the assignment has been correctly done. Such a process cheapens this form of poetry and puts students at risk in believing that writing poetry is a tedious exercise. A wise and enriching way of engaging students with haiku has been described by Gary DeCoker (1989), who uses haiku in social studies teaching. His method of using *poetry in translation* begins with reading and displaying a single haiku in transliterated Japanese, so students can hear the sound of the poem in its own language. (Transliteration is the translation of one language into the sounds of another, and it is needed when languages do not use the same symbol system for writing. For example, because Spanish and English are written using the same alphabet, people who speak English but not Spanish can look at the phrase *una docena de deliciosas galletitas*, and pronounce it, although the accent will not be correct. They can decode the written text, although they may not realize they are saying "a dozen delicious cookies." People who do not know the Japanese system of writing cannot look at Japanese characters and pronounce their sounds; for this to happen, someone who knows both languages must write the English letters that represent the sounds of Japanese words—this is transliteration.)

In the process of studying haiku that DeCoker suggests, after students hear the transliterated haiku, they are given a literal, word-by-word translation. Then some of the many translations of the haiku are shared and discussed, and finally students create their own translations of the poem. In DeCoker's teaching, he chose a poem by the most famous Japanese writer of haiku, Basho, who lived from 1644 to 1694. (A beautiful source of haiku is a collection arranged according to the four seasons, by Demi, 1992: *In the eyes of the cat: Japanese poetry for all seasons*.) Students who learn from this translation strategy, DeCoker writes, are able to grasp two profound concepts: that the same thing is perceived differently by different people, and that people's perceptions are affected by which version of an idea they encounter.

> Given the same original poem, …translators have created vastly different English translations… [giving] students a concrete example of an important social studies objective—understanding differences in perspectives. …Our understanding of [the original poem] depends on which translation we read. If we limit ourselves to only one translation, [we limit] our perception. …The same is true for anything that we learn from others. If we accept the first interpretation that we come across, our understanding will be limited. When we seek more information and begin to make our own interpretations, we gain more personal insights. (DeCoker, 1989, p. 223)

Award-Winning Books

Of the many awards now given to honor books written for children and young adults, the two oldest and most prestigious are the Newbery Medal, for an author, and the Caldecott Medal, for an illustrator. The Newbery Medal is awarded to the author of the most distinguished contribution to literature published in the United States during the preceding year (with the stipulation that the author must be a U. S. citizen or resident). It was donated by an American publisher, Frederic G. Melcher, who named it in honor of the eighteenth century English publisher John Newbery, who was the first to publish children's books in English. The award was first given in 1922 to Hendrik Willem Van Loon for *The story of mankind.*

Not all award-winning books can stand the test of time; some books that were honored years ago now appear biased and outdated. However, many Newbery award-winning books continue across the years to be widely known, read with pleasure, and used in teaching. Because of their Newbery award status, as well as their literary quality, many remain in print; (that is, they can be purchased in stores or ordered from their publisher, whereas books that are out of print are no longer available from publishers, although they may be found in bookstores that sell used books, and in libraries). The Caldecott award, also the conception of Frederic Melcher, was first given in 1938; the award bears the name of an English illustrator *Randolph Caldecott: "Lord of the nursery"* (Engen, 1988), who recounts the artist's short life and includes an extensive, annotated selection of his work. The National Council of Teachers of English now produces a Caldecott Calendar, which features illustrations from award-winning and honor books and provides a complete list of the artists honored.

Although the Newbery medal is given for a distinguished contribution to literature for children, many Newbery books reach out to older readers as well. The winners in 1988 and 1989—*Lincoln: A photobiography* (Freedman, 1987) and *Joyful noise: Poems for two voices* (Fleischman, (1988)—are examples of books that older students and adults, as well as children, can read for information and aesthetic enjoyment. However, because visual images are less age-specific than written text, the Caldecott winning picture books have the potential to delight and educate even more widely. Between the early 1920s, when the Newbery award was first given, writing styles have changed far less dramatically than the blossoming of new styles in illustration since the first Caldecott award in the late 1930s, and a comparison of the illustrations in a series of Caldecott winners is a worthwhile subject for study. Many recent Caldecott medal books focus on complex, thought-provoking themes. Allen Say's *Grandfather's journey* (1993) is an account of family history that illustrates the tensions felt by those who take up

a new life in a new land—the nostalgia felt for a place left behind, even though returning is impossible. The award for *Smoky night* (1994), written by Eve Bunting and illustrated by David Diaz, raised controversy because the book's subject is urban riots with their accompanying vandalism and looting. The story, which is both realistic and touching, can answer younger students' questions, and the book's theme and intricate illustrations—acrylic paintings on collage backgrounds—can inspire discussion among high school and middle school students. The recent and growing interest in works of nonfiction has been demonstrated by the creation of an award established by the National Council of Teachers of English, the Orbis Pictus Award for Outstanding Nonfiction for Children. The name commemorates a work by Johannes Amos Comenius in 1657, considered the first book planned for children, *Orbis Pitus, The world in pictures*. Figure 11–8 shows books that received the award during the years 1990 to 1995 and the books that received an honorable mention— the honor books—for those years. Each of the books listed was published in the year preceding the year in which the award was made.

Discovery and Expression

Including the arts in our classrooms can be as simple as displaying poetry, significant quotations, and prints of great art works on classroom walls; playing music softly while students work together; providing a wide array of beautiful books for students to read and browse through; reading aloud from literature that delights us as well as our students. Other choices may lead to classrooms glowing with students' art, lively with students' drama, storytelling, and song. We can bring the world into our classrooms for our students to discover and permit time for personal discoveries to be made. Although we cannot control the content or timing of our students' discoveries, we can provide, share, guide, open doors, and plan ingeniously and wisely.

FIGURE 11–8 Orbis Pictus Awards, 1990–1995

1995 *Safari beneath the sea: The wonder world of the North Pacific coast* by Diane Swanson (Sierra Club).

Honor books: *Wildlife rescue: The work of Dr. Kathleen Ramsay* by Jennifer Owings Dewey (Boyds Mills Press); *Kids at work: Lewis Hine and the crusade against child labor* by Russell Freedman (Clarion); and *Christmas in the Big House, Christmas in the quarters* by Patricia C. McKissack & Fredrick L. McKissack (Scholastic).

1994 *Across America on an emigrant train* by Jim Murphy (Clarion).

Honor books: *To the top of the world: Adventures with Arctic wolves* by Jim Brandenburg (Walker) and *Making sense: Animal perception and communication* by Bruce Brooks (Farrar, Straus & Giroux).

1993 *Children of the dust bowl: The true story of the school at Weedpatch Camp* by Jerry Stanley (Crown).

Honor books: *Talking with artists* by Pat Cummings (Bradbury) and *Come back, salmon* by Molly Cone (Sierra Club).

1992 *Flight: The journey of Charles Lindbergh* by Robert Burleigh and Mike Wimmer (Philomel).

Honor books: *Now is your time! The African American struggle for freedom* by Walter Dean Myers (Harper-Collins) and *Prairie vision: The life and times of Solomon Butcher* by Pam Conrad (HarperCollins).

1991 *Franklin Delano Roosevelt* by Russell Freedman (Clarion).

Honor books: *Arctic memories* by Normee Ekoomiak (Holt) and *Seeing earth from space* by Patricia Lauber (Orchard).

1990 *The great little Madison* by Jean Fritz (Putnam).

Honor books: *The great American gold rush* by Rhoda Blumberg (Bradbury) and *The news about dinosaurs* by Patricia Lauber (Bradbury).

STRATEGIC TEACHERS, PART NINE:

"There are so many stories."

Dr. Lilyet Strong has been teaching for more than thirty years. Not surprisingly, one of her favorite articles from the professional literature is Mimi Brodsky Chenfeld's inspirational essay, "The first 30 years are the hardest" (1987b). Her professional experience includes teaching sixth grade in an elementary school, teaching high school English and Spanish, working as a media specialist, and serving as an assistant principal. She has worked in her current district for twelve years and has been district curriculum coordinator for the past five years. She believes education is the most important and exciting profession she could have chosen and that every position she has held, including the present one, is *teaching*. One of her major responsibilities is to coordinate staff development for the district, a task she never ceases to find interesting and challenging. The phrase *to coordinate staff development for the district* has structured her planning, which she bases on her beliefs about development, coordination, staff, and also about the effects of staff development on her district's educational system.

Development is an ongoing process throughout one's life. Dr. Strong believes, and encourages others to believe, that professional development must be ongoing throughout each educator's career. This belief has several important implications for her work. First, while there are certainly "quick fixes" for some problems—wise, effective solutions to special needs that can readily be put into place—there is no such thing as a "permanent fix." There is no program, booklet, or policy that teachers and administrators can use, read, or apply that will be so comprehensive and powerful that they will never need to learn any more about their profession. Not to develop is to decline. Second, development needs support. Dr. Strong is ingenious, not only in devising low-cost and no-cost learning opportunities within the district, but also in encouraging arrangements for teachers to have time to plan and work together and in helping find ways to provide financial support for staff who attend professional conferences.

The most important part of taking the idea of professional development seriously, Dr. Strong believes, is to recognize that *development happens*—teachers do grow, improve, learn new ideas, and acquire important information and insights from professional reading and professional conferences. Since becoming a district administrator, she has put this belief into action. The district now depends primarily on its own staff, particularly teachers, to provide professional development opportunities, and this new policy has proved practical, rewarding, and economically sound. Among the benefits are that a wide variety of in-service opportunities can be provided, at convenient times, and that most staff development activities include multiple sessions so participants have the chance to try out new ideas, then come together again to discuss them. Moreover, if questions arise after the sessions are over, it is easy to consult with the session leaders, since they are colleagues working in the district. The district has saved money that would have been spent hiring outside experts, while expanding the number of staff development opportunities and increasing the number of staff who take advantage of them.

Coordination comes from the Latin verb *coordinare*, meaning *to arrange together*, and this is what Dr. Strong believes in doing. In her first year as curriculum coordinator, she established a large and ongoing Professional Development Council (PDC), whose purpose is to discuss and plan staff development. There are twenty-six teachers as members, two from each of the district's six elementary schools, four from each of the two middle schools, and six from the high school. Except for the first year, when one- and two-year terms for representatives from each school were determined by lot, each member serves two years, thus schools always have both new and experienced representatives on the council. In the first year, council members brainstormed a list of teacher characteristics that should be represented on the council. Thereafter, faculties of each of the schools have been asked to consider the council's continuing membership—the thirteen representatives who will be serving a second term—and keep the desired mix of characteristics in mind when choosing new members. Through this informal method, the council has achieved a good degree of diversity. The council meets four times a year, twice in the early fall and again in January and April, and subcommittees meet at self-set times. The fall and April meetings are supper meetings, sponsored by the district; the January meeting is a full day meeting for which the district provides substitute teachers for members' classes.

Toward the end of each school year Dr. Strong sends a brief, optional questionnaire to all district staff, asking for opinions about staff development opportunities in the current year and ideas for topics or programs for the coming year. She summarizes the information and sends it to members of the Professional Development Council before the group's first fall meeting. At that session, the council prepares a list of possible topics for faculty meetings and other building and district professional development activities. Council members share the list with the faculties of their buildings. At the second PDC meeting, based on interest expressed at the various schools, the council sets a schedule for the year. Some programs will be offered more than once and in more than one building; some programs on the original list of suggestions will not be offered because of lack of interest. What follows are excerpts from last year's list:

- *Responsive language.* (Two 75-minute sessions). A panel of three elementary teachers will talk about the difference between responsive and restrictive language and engage participants in exercises to translate restrictive statements to responsive statements. At the second session, participants will share reflections on changes. If building faculties wish, a half-hour preliminary session can be given at a faculty meeting.
- Reading: Stone, Janet. (1993). Caregiver and teacher language—Responsive or restrictive? *Young Children, 48,* 12–18. (Copies will be provided.)
- *Tell/ask questions.* (Three brown bag lunch sessions). One or more teachers from your building will discuss questions that begin by giving information and how/when this form of questioning is useful. Group members will collaborate in creating and critiquing tell/ask questions and will share observations and materials.
- *Social studies simulations.* (Three sessions, after school or evenings; two to three hours per session). Designed for middle and high school teachers, led by faculty who are experienced simulators. Videotapes, guidelines (getting started, winding up, stepping in and out of role), and improvising simulations. Participants will be asked to provide background knowledge about social studies topics that are appropriate for simulations to other group members, as needed, and to suggest readings.
- Readings: As the basis for a first simulation, all participants are asked to read Levine, Ellen. (1993). *...if your name was changed at Ellis Island*, NY: Scholastic, and the first section, "Coming Over," from Freedman, Russell. (1995). *Immigrant kids.* NY: Puffin. (Books are in media centers.) Participants are invited to share relevant family history.
- *Nature walks.* (Three sessions: fall, winter, spring). Faculty and high school student guides will identify flora and habitats of fauna in schoolyards and areas within easy walking distance. Dress appropriately; bring cameras. Wind-up discussions will be held following the walks, with seasonal refreshments provided (cider, hot cocoa, lemonade).
- *Reading groups* (Ongoing meetings, with times set by groups). A number of groups are already established, some reading and discussing professional articles, others enjoying and sharing personal reading. See a PDC representative if you are interested in joining a current group or setting up a new group—or join and/or organize on your own.

Readings: to be chosen by groups.

Additional suggestions: Cardarelli, Aldo F. (1992). Teachers under cover: Promoting the personal reading of teachers. *The Reading Teacher, 45,* 664–668; Jongsma, Kathleen Stumpf. (1992). Just say know! *The Reading Teacher, 45,* 546–548; and excerpts from Routman, Regie. (1988). *Transitions.* Portsmouth, NH: Heinemann. (Copies of the articles will be provided on request; copies of the book, with excerpts marked, are in media centers.)

Staff, in Dr. Strong's view, means everyone who is employed in the school district. Although members of the PDC are all faculty members, the council's assignment is to plan inclusively. All professional development opportunities are open to administrators as well as faculty, and many programs are open to other school personnel as well: aides, bus drivers, custodians, lunch room personnel, nurses, paraprofessionals, secretaries, and people who are regularly called as substitutes. (Of the programs in the partial list above, all except the programs about preparing tell/ask questions and simulations were open to all staff members. In the elementary schools, special efforts were made to encourage wide participation in the sessions about using responsive language, and several school bus drivers were among those attending.)

After reading Barbara Steele's article on "The micro-shop," Dr. Strong suggested to building administrators that they include this as a component of staff development. Micro-shops are fifteen- or twenty-minute single sessions usually held just before or after school, about topics in which one staff member is an expert and in which others are interested. Topics given as examples in Steele's article (1992, p. 40) include "making electrical circuit boards, making or using an abacus, setting up a salt-water aquarium, identifying trees on the school grounds, using alternative ways to teach long division." In Dr. Strong's district, the micro-shop idea has caught on and, as an additional advantage, it has proven to be a good way for faculty and other staff members to get to know one another. Micro-shops on the topics of "Playground first aid," "Getting cars started in cold weather," "Building a birdhouse," and "Veggie desserts: carrot cookies and sauerkraut cake" have been offered by non-teaching personnel, and micro-shops offered by faculty on topics such as *Brown angels* and other books by Walter Dean Myers" and "MULTIPASS: a study strategy for school and home" have been attended by both teachers and non-teaching personnel, many of whom have school-age children they want to read to and help at home.

Telling the Stories of Teaching

Dr. Strong works to ensure that a rich variety of useful staff development opportunities are provided in ways that make it likely that what is learned will be well-used. She also knows it is important to share information about educational challenges, insights, and successes in the community. She is known as a powerful speaker and is a good teller of stories. She is often invited to speak to community organizations. Besides the stories that come from her own professional experiences and from her heart, Dr. Strong has many stories from the professional literature in her repertoire. She combines reading with telling during prepared talks, or she storytells in response to an unexpected opportunity to talk about an important idea. When issues of ability grouping and tracking arise, one of the stories she tells is based on an article written by a friend who achieved her dream of becoming a teacher—in spite of tracking.

> School had been so easy for her, filled with successes throughout her elementary years. The teachers all had said that she had a lot of "potential." In fact, she dreamed of someday being a teacher herself. However, when she reached high school the classes were divided according to an in-district system of tracking. She was tracked in with the academically lower, non-college bound students. No one had discussed this with her or her parents. Her family was large and poor, her parents drop-outs. College was not considered an option for her by the faculty or advisors. Scholarships were never mentioned.
>
> Tired of the mediocre educational system in which she was trapped and the aimless direction in which it was taking her, she dropped out of school after her junior year, got a job in a factory and was married that fall. Two years later she became a mother. The years that followed were happy busy ones… She was happy with her life, her family, her friends. Yet her husband knew.
>
> She wanted to teach.
>
> (Wickey, 1992, pp. 420–421)

One of the read-alouds Dr. Strong has shared at faculty meetings is a brief article by Daniel Meier (1986), titled "Learning in small moments." The opening paragraph, in which the author tells about morals first graders have suggested for Aesop's fables, always starts a group off smiling, especially a first grader's moral for "The tortoise and the hare": *Don't ever take a nap.* Dr. Strong tells much of the article, but she reads its conclusion:

> …small moments of learning… are incidents and situations that cannot be predicted or planned. They will pop up as a surprise, as a treat… And often, when these moments arise,

they come quietly and subtly. ...They are the odd and quirky moments that spin off from a teacher's love of the moment and willingness to improvise, to go on a hunch, to take a risk, to deviate a little, to go with one's teaching intuition. For the students, such moments are like the morals to fables. ...They are quickly absorbed and, being pocket-sized, are easily carried away. (Meier, 1986, p. 300)

As part of her role in the district, Dr. Strong collaborates with the Family-School Organization, which now funds visits to the school by guest artists. She works closely with the superintendent of schools and other district administrators and with the school board. A part of each monthly board meeting is a presentation by teachers, often assisted by students, other staff members, or parents and other community members. Dr. Strong has been a storyteller throughout her career, and she thinks of these monthly sessions as opportunities to tell some of the many stories that illustrate the educational life of the district. Presentations given this year provide a flavor of how Dr. Strong helps the community notice and understand aspects of professional development:

▪ At the September meeting, four teachers and students from two cooperative groups, one from a high school science class and one from a middle school math class, talked about getting started in cooperative learning. Both groups of students had prepared for the presentation in consultation with classmates, and the teachers and Dr. Strong had prepared a two-page informational handout for board members.

▪ In October, a panel of eight teachers, representing the many teachers who received district support for attending professional conferences in the previous year, each gave a precisely timed three-minute description about how one of the conference sessions they attended was influencing their teaching. Copies of the convention programs—all color-

ful, handsome, magazine-like publications—were displayed, and board members were invited to browse through them. With the help of students in a middle school general math class and a computer class, Dr. Strong compiled statistics about staff attendance at professional conferences. These were displayed at the meeting, with copies distributed to board members.

▪ The presentation at the November meeting was made by three second-grade students who were members of a class piloting student-led conferences, a practice the district is considering adopting. Their teacher attended, along with their family members. As was done for September's meeting, students prepared with the help of all of their classmates. The classroom teacher arranged a display of photographs taken during conference time, captioned with parent and student comments about this style of conferencing.

Dr. Strong never loses sight of the purpose of staff development, which is to enhance and promote the district's educational system, nor of the proper aim for that educational system, which is to ensure that all students are welcomed and well-taught and that there are high expectations for every student. She believes the correct goal for the school system is to have every adult working to make every day happy and productive for every student. Many of the stories she draws from her long career in education are joyous. One in particular is not, but for her it illustrates an important belief. It is a story which, for Dr. Strong, has no known ending. She has come to terms with the sorrow she still feels about a single troubled, lost child through her conviction that the only way that *each child* can be safe and happy in our schools is for *all children* to be safe and happy. She resolves to work toward that unattainable goal just as hard and long as she can:

I remember Angela. I met her before she was six years old. She was beautiful, but not easy to reach—and no wonder. In the year that I knew her she lived with her mother, her grandfather, two foster families and then her mother again. I kept track of her as she moved through three different schools, and after that I don't know where she was taken. Her teacher in the last of these three schools was particularly energetic and kind, and she loved Angela. She talked to me about Angela's progress and how she was beginning to read and to be able to be friendly. But before the end of the school year Angela was gone. Her teacher had been in the classroom while the children were at the library, when an aide rushed in to say that Angela's mother had come to take her out of school. And the aide said, 'If you want to say goodby to Angela, *run!*'

I think about Angela still. Wouldn't it be a wonderful miracle if Angela's other teachers gave her the care she needed? She would have needed all the teachers, because she had so many. Angela is a teenager now—perhaps a young mother. There need to be teachers who care for Angela's children, and are kind and welcoming to Angela too.

Because of Angela, I know that if we want to help a child we can't put it off. We have to seize every opportunity. We have to *run!*

Challenge to the Reader: Brainstorm a list of ways Dr. Strong's district is making professional development appealing. What additional idea would you suggest?

Choose: If you were to attend one of the staff development programs listed above, which would it be?

Tell: What is one of your stories about teaching?

Case Study 4

In January, after five and a half years of teaching, all in the same school and at the same grade level—years that have been, on the whole, satisfying and successful—C. H. Anges is reflecting on that teaching career.

Last summer, Anges enrolled in a master's program at a nearby university and was able to apply some credits from workshops taken over the past several years, so the projected date for graduation from the program is two years from this semester. The classes so far have been exciting and useful. Family members are supportive of Anges' career, and at holiday time family members gave Anges a promise of subscriptions to two professional journals (choices still to be made).

A new principal came to Anges' school in September, when the previous principal retired after twenty years in that position. The observation-evaluation system used by the former principal was always a relaxed process, consisting generally of a friendly visit by the principal to a class session, followed by a meeting at which a brief written account of the visit was signed. Included was general conversation about a variety of topics, for example, the high school's sports record. The new principal, with district approval, has instituted a different evaluation process, which includes short-term and long-term goal setting. Some of the goals have been established by the district; for example, increased breadth and depth of parent inclusion in the reporting and evaluation process. Teachers have been asked to set their individual goals for the next year, with principal guidance. One suggestion that the principal has given is to enliven classroom and hall displays through the use of student work.

Anges looks ahead to the immediate future—rounding out another successful teaching year, supporting the students' school experiences, taking graduate classes this term and in the spring, enjoying a family trip in the summer—and to the long-term aspects of a career in education.

Preparation for discussion: As you can see, care has been taken in writing this case study to avoid giving a full description of Anges. Describe Anges further, perhaps making the description like yourself. (Feel free to change the name, too.)

Analysis: Make a two-column list—one of features in Anges' situation that are forces for change, and the other of features that work against change at this time.

Decision points: Note several points at which changes should be made, and/or should not be made.

Choices: Make two decisions for Anges

Possible results: For one or both decisions, list possible outcomes.

Follow-up: Create a scenario based on the decisions you have made.

Planning For the Present and Future

When we're teaching in the content areas, our purposes are:

- *to help all our students build and develop their store of knowledge;*
- *to help all our students organize their knowledge so they see how ideas are interrelated;*
- *to help all our students use, apply, and remember learnings which are important to them now and will be in the future;*
- *to foster in all students feelings of capability and industry;*
- *to encourage lifelong learning—for all our students, and ourselves.*

CONTENT AREA LEARNING AND TEACHING: INTEGRATION
WITH THE LANGUAGE ARTS, CHAPTER ONE

The major aim of the common enterprise in which we are engaged... has to do with the improvement of educational practice so that the lives of those who teach and learn are themselves enhanced.

ELLIOT EISNER, 1993, P. 10.

You should expect the world of your students.

MEM FOX, 1993, P. 185.

The aim of education is to change the lives of students for the better. The word *education* comes from the Latin words meaning *to lead out*, and the proper function of the school is to be a place where students are led to develop knowledge and capabilities that will enable their lives to be productive, happy, and worthwhile. That this aim for education is not met for all students—and almost certainly will not be achieved for all students in the lifetimes of the writer and readers of this text—does not mean that the goal is impossible. Within the classrooms of many readers who will be teachers, the goal will be met for their students. Within the classrooms of many readers who are teachers now, the goal is already being met for their students. Failures may make the roads to success harder, but they do not close off those roads, and every success contributes to future good.

Students' experiences in school are influential; they also can be exciting and memorable. This final chapter begins with a discussion of influential learning and optimal learning—educational experiences that have a strong and beneficial impact on students' lives and those events in the learning process that are remembered as being the best. The main portion of this chapter is devoted to a discussion of the planning teachers do to contribute to students' education now and in their future. To illustrate some of the many aspects and purposes of planning, the nine "strategic teachers" whose work has been described at the end of previous chapters are recalled. The conclusion of the chapter and of this text is, appropriately, a discussion of lifelong learning for ourselves as well as for our students.

▪▪ Influential Experience

School affects students. How could it not do so? How could any person be untouched by near-daily experiences that continue for years? How could any person's self-opinion not be shaped by hundreds of age-mates and adults who express their attitudes openly or implicitly? At its most tragic, education influences students by implanting and confirming a sense of failure, creating and building anger and despair. "Where is school along the path to prison?"

Hill Walker and Robert Sylvester ask, and they answer their own question: for some students, school is "merely a way station"—though this need not be so if there are teachers and peers "who take an active interest in the antisocial, at-risk student's school success" (Walker & Sylvester, 1991, pp. 14 and 16).

Each Teacher Can Make a Difference

At its best, the education that students experience is provided by the action and interaction of many teachers who devote their minds and hearts to teaching, expect the world of their students, and care for each student. But one teacher alone can change students' lives. Some years ago, Eigil Pedersen and his colleagues set out to investigate a question that interested them: what changes, if any, occur in students' IQ scores during their school years? The site for their research was an inner-city school in an impoverished neighborhood; the researchers were given access to students' test scores and records kept by the school system, including teachers' ratings of students' effort, leadership, and initiative, given annually in grades one through seven. As they studied these data they found a different topic that interested them more: the effects of a single teacher on the lives of her students. A first-grade teacher whom they called in their report "Miss A" had taught in the same school for thirty-four years. Consistently, the students in her classes had higher ratings for effort, leadership, and initiative than did other first graders. Of course, this is easily explained: Miss A was the rater; she gave high ratings. But the high ratings continued. The students from her first-grade class went to different second-grade teachers, were again mixed with other students in third grade, and so on. But across the years, students from Miss A's first-grade classes were rated, on average, more highly than others were when they were second, third, fourth, fifth, sixth, and seventh graders. Moreover, when the status of graduates of the school system was examined, based on variables such as educational attainment, occupational prestige, and characteristics of their housing, the difference between Miss A's first graders and other students continued to be apparent. Men and women interviewed twenty-five years after she had taught them could name Miss A as their first-grade teacher and recalled that she never lost her temper, but kept attention and control through her energy and the affection they knew she felt for them.

> We do not dispute the fact that, regardless of teacher quality, children from privileged backgrounds are more likely to achieve high adult status than children from disadvantaged backgrounds. But our research does show that the teacher can make a difference, not only to pupils' lives in schools but to their future as well. ...[T]eachers currently at work should not accept too readily the frequent assertion that their efforts make no long-term difference to the future success of their pupils. ...[We should] not dismiss the likelihood that teachers' best efforts may have positive long-range results. (Pedersen, Faucher, & Eaton, 1978, p. 30)

All Teachers Do Make a Difference

"What can I possibly do as one teacher to make a difference?" Edward Kameenui quotes some teachers as asking. Sometimes a similar question—"What can I do as one teacher to make a difference?"—is asked seriously, with a straightforward intention. In this case, asking the question is a sign of an intelligent desire to teach well. Each of us needs to ask ourselves, and learn from others, how we, individually, can influence students' lives for the better. When the question is rhetorical and is intended as a statement—"I cannot make a difference"—Kameenui (1993, p. 380) calls it an example of "pedagogical paralysis, which is in part reflected in a teacher's lack of personal teaching efficacy." In fact, all teachers do affect their students' lives, and it is our choice whether the difference will, on balance, contribute to learning or failure to learn, enjoyment and satisfaction or boredom and distress, lives that are better or worse than they might have been.

The work of Erik Erikson illustrates the tapestry of human life, the eight life stages which Erikson described and which his wife, Joan Erikson, illustrated through her weavings (Erikson & Erikson, 1981; Hall, 1983). In our society, within the varied tapestries of people's lives, the school years are a significant part of life's fabric, and the threads from those years extend into the later stages of people's lives. If the time spent in school during the elementary school years is productive, Erikson writes, "the child develops a sense of industriousness... [and] can become an eager and absorbed member of that productive situation called 'school.'" As a result of their experiences in this period of life, heavily influenced by their life in school, these students develop competence: "the free exercise... of dexterity and intelligence in the completion of serious tasks [that] is the basis of cooperative participation in some segment of the culture" (Erikson, 1982, p. 8). There are dangers inherent in this stage as well as possibilities for future growth. Some children become overcompliant; their school experiences merely teach them to do as they are told. Others despair of their ability to learn or to be well-accepted by others and become discouraged from further learning. It is important to remember that if a favorable outcome is not achieved in one stage of life, other life stages may still be productive and, though it is more difficult, the positive outcome of an earlier stage may be attained later. For example, a student whose elementary school years have been unsuccessful and unhappy, may, with effort and support, become an industrious, competent person later on.

During the years spent in middle school and high school, students have time to learn further and make choices that will determine their future lifestyles and careers. Ideally, in this period of identity development, students have the opportunity to develop and understand their own interests, talents, strengths, and needs more fully before they commit themselves to major decisions about how and with whom they will spend their future lives. In our society the length of adolescence—which means *growing to be an adult*—varies widely from person to person, depending primarily on the length of time spent in school. For students who move from high school to college, decisions about careers and life partners usually are postponed until they are in their twenties. Students who do not choose to go to college or for whom it is not an option usually have a much shorter time to discover interests and capabilities and consider possibilities. Teachers can provide occasions and encouragement. The quality of students' middle school and high school education strongly affects the outcome of this stage in the lives of all students.

Optimal Experience

The possibilities which scholars have found for interesting research within the field of education are virtually limitless. One intriguing field of study is the learning events that are most intense, memorable, and highly valued, and the conditions—and teachers—that promote and produce these superlative experiences. An unsurprising finding that emerges from this research is that such events are rare, and a major impetus that underlies the research is to make optimal—best—learning experiences more accessible to all students.

Flow

Mihaly Csikszentmihalyi is among the best-known and most prolific of all of the scholars who have studied human talent and creativity (Csikszentmihalyi, 1990, 1991; Csikszentmihalyi, Rathunde, & Whalen, 1993). (Note that the Author Index of this text provides information about the pronunciation of several scholars' names, including *Csikszentmihalyi*.) The topic that currently absorbs Csikszentmihalyi and toward which his studies over the past twenty-five years have led him, is an experience he calls *flow*, which he defines as "the state in which people are so involved in an activity that nothing else seems to matter" (Csikszentmihalyi, 1991, p. 4). Edward Miller (1994, p. 3), in discussing Csikszentmihalyi's work, describes flow in a way that relates it to the zone of proximal development: "Flow usually begins when one takes on challenges that are just at or above one's skills. When challenges and skills are in balance, the activity becomes its own reward." Education is one of the fields in which scholars have conducted research on the flow experience, finding, for example, high school students' enjoyment of a course to be a better predictor of their final grades than are measures of general aptitude or achievement and student attentiveness to be related to the amount of enjoyment their teachers get from teaching (Csikszentmihalyi & Csikszentmihalyi, 1988, pp. 11–12).

Jeanne Nakamura (1988) has analyzed typical responses to educational situations that present

FIGURE 12–1   The Conditions Necessary for Flow

	High Challenge	Low Challenge
high skill	*flow*	boredom
low skill	anxiety	apathy

challenges to students' skills. To be confronted with a challenging task that is far beyond one's capacity to accomplish is frightening; the result is anxiety. Assignments or activities that are too easy are boring for students who are past masters of the skills required, and they arouse no interest in students with a low level of skill in that area, resulting in an apathetic, "who cares?" attitude. Only when students have a task worthy of their skills and talents will they experience flow. The chart shown in Figure 12–1 shows conditions that lead to various responses. It is not a classification system for people, and the terms "high skill" and "low skill" refer to people's capabilities in relation to a particular challenge, not to people themselves. All students can, under the right conditions, experience the joy of flow; anyone can be faced with a task that will produce, in that individual, anxiety, boredom, or apathy. Teachers' actions can support the development of students' talents and encourage flow:

First, teachers should never stop nurturing their own interests. They should spend time outside class pursuing the practice of writing, music, math, or whatever attracted them to the field. Second, good teachers pay attention to conditions that help students experience intrinsic rewards...—they minimize the impact of competition, grades, prizes, scholarships, needless rules, and bureaucratic procedures that tend to undermine students' inherent enjoyment of learning. Finally, successful teachers [see] the shifting needs of learners. ...Good teachers move between moments of intervention and withdrawal, critique and encouragement, always gauging the effects of their attention on each student. (Miller, 1994, p. 3)

Peak Learning Experiences

Based on the work of Abraham Maslow (1968), Benjamin Bloom explored the concept of peak learning experiences in education—times that stand out in students' memories as the high points of their years in school. When an interviewee described a particular class session in vivid detail, Bloom was sometimes able to find and interview other students who had been in that same class. Although these people did not know why they had been chosen to be interviewed, often they also described the same classroom event, in similarly glowing terms.

> Imagine a classroom learning session which is so powerful that many students have almost total memory of it twenty years later. When these students begin to recall this session, it becomes quite vivid, and they actually appear to be reliving it. This one experience forms a landmark in their school recollections. For a few of these students the session becomes a turning point in their educational careers, and they trace major decisions, new interests, and the formation of particular attitudes and values to this single hour. (Bloom, 1981, p. 193)

Bloom's approach to education is upbeat, as the title of the book from which the quotation is taken implies: *All our children learning*. He asserts that teachers can plan in ways that make it likely that all students will share in peak learning experiences, sev-eral times during a year. He identifies the conditions which, taken together, are necessary for peak learning experiences to occur. It is essential for the teacher to be respected by the students and capable of inspiring them to believe that the subject they are learning about is important and worthwhile. The learning experience is an insight, a discovery of an important truth or new way of seeing the world, and there is likely to be an element of surprise, a contrast with what is already known and understood. There also is a lack of closure, a sense that this new learning opens the door to further learning that must be pursued before the new idea is fully grasped. That aspect of the peak learning experience is similar to the conditions of challenge that produce flow: learning that is too difficult will be rejected or glossed over; learning that is too simple will not be memorable; learning in which challenge is met by capability is likely to be exciting and memorable.

Influential Teachers

Robert Ruddell (1990) has studied teachers who add significant value to their students' educational experience. He speaks of *flow* in a different sense from Mihaly Csikszentmihalyi's use of the word. In Ruddell's terms, "instructional flow" is part of a metaphor based on the progress of rivers and streams as they flow toward the ocean. Figure 12–2

FIGURE 12–2   Alternate Streams in Education: Instructional Flow in the Classrooms of Non-Influential and Influential Teachers

The instructional flow in the classrooms of non-influential teachers may be described as being like a straight, yet shallow, river, whose waters are held close to a precharted course, unable to veer from the laborious goal of reaching the ocean, or as a river whose banks wind toward the sea but whose rocky bed causes the waters to splash aimlessly in all directions, easily losing sight of its elusive goal of also reaching the sea.

By contrast the instructional flow in classrooms of the influential teacher is similar to a deep full river meandering to the sea following a clear course. While bubbling waters from entering streams may gurgle excitedly as they join the river they are easily assimilated, adding a richness and complexity to the river. Even a casual observer could follow the river's flow as it reaches its destination.

Robert B. Ruddell, speaking at the annual conference of the International Reading Association, May 7, 1990. Reprinted from *Reading Horizons,* 31, 1990, p. 74.

presents that metaphor, which captures vividly many important educational concepts. Authoritarian and laissez-faire teaching are illustrated through the image of two rivers, one straight and shallow where progress is laborious, another where aimless splashing means that the final goal may never be attained. Authoritative teaching is envisioned as a deep river enriched by many tributary streams that enter it, a river whose clear path to the ocean is made more interesting and beautiful because of its turnings and variations. The bubbling waters of entering streams are analogous to the diversity of students, enriching classrooms where diversity is welcomed. The sound-image of the excited gurgling of these streams evokes a vision of classrooms full of interested, active, excited learners.

Planning Embedded in Teaching

Planning is an exciting part of teaching, because teaching itself is exciting. One of the pleasures for teachers who enjoy their profession is thinking about teaching. Teachers plan on the way to school and on the way home; they plan while mowing the lawn, doing the laundry, jogging, and sitting in meetings that do not interest them. Sometimes colleagues call each other up in the evening to confer. Does this planning for these teachers mean preparing written plans? Clearly it does not. Although teachers are expected to keep written plans, the styles and methods of their planning differ widely. In practice, it is far more effective to plan by thinking than to plan by writing detailed plans following an elaborate format. Preparing thorough, written plans is valuable in teacher preparation programs in that it simulates some of the kinds of thinking teachers need to do. In addition, written plans are a way to assess ability to make sensible educational decisions and to write with technical correctness. However, a plan for a lesson does not comprise all aspects of teachers' planning, and some educational scholars believe elaborate lesson plans are potentially misleading. Dona Kagan and Deborah Tippins describe reliance on the traditional lesson plan format as "counterproductive," because it gives insufficient emphasis to linking important learning across a

series of lessons and across subjects, overemphasizes evaluation, "masks the importance of improvisation," and requires unnecessary writing.

> Objectives and materials are often self-evident or already [listed] in texts; requiring that they be included in lesson plans seems gratuitous. …Apparently teachers—even those with only a few years of classroom experience—find that detailed lesson plans are not functional in classrooms. Planning for most lessons appears to occur mentally, without committing anything to paper. At most, a teacher may jot down an outline… using a cryptic shorthand. This outline will not reflect the complexity of the teacher's plan, which will probably exist as an image of a particular flow of activities. (Kagan & Tippins, 1992, pp. 487 and 478)

Skillful teachers think about their teaching cyclically, making choices and preparing in advance, then adapting their plans as they teach and later reflecting on the process and deciding what modifications would be useful in the future. They know before they begin instruction what they intend their students to learn. They know their subject matter well enough to think about teaching as they are engaged in it, so they can make the most of spontaneous opportunities. They think afterwards about what they have discovered and consider what changes will make their teaching more effective.

Planning Formats

Assignments to prepare written lesson plans are one way to engage students enrolled in teacher education programs in thinking about the aspects of planning, however, they are not a complete simulation of real planning. It would be impossible to plan in writing all of the actions and events of an effective teaching and learning session, because so many elements are interwoven. Observing talented teachers is like watching ice skaters whose skill makes their artistry appear almost effortless. Linda DeGroff and Lee Galda (1992, p. 136) call teachers "the ultimate jugglers." The resemblance between skilled teaching and a demonstration of physical skill goes beyond the smooth performance; there also is similarity in feeling and attitude. Despite times of discouragement and exhaustion, talented teachers

All of these teachers are engaged in planning.

experience feelings of exhilaration. For many teachers, teaching is often a flow activity where high challenge is met by high skill. Teaching and thinking about teaching are rewarding and inseparable.

While the methods used by practicing teachers in preparing their plans vary widely, it is useful to consider several methods and levels of planning. Two forms of planning have been discussed earlier in this text: concept statements, a form of microlevel planning, and the Annual Overview, a form of macrolevel planning. Through the preparation of concept statements, teachers specify the information they plan to teach about a topic. Preparation of an Annual Overview provides a graphic summary of plans for the year, within and across subject matter areas. Creation and use of an Annual Overview also helps teachers focus on what will be studied, even many months ahead, and on what has been studied; perceive opportunities for integration within and across content areas; and present instruction within previously set guidelines for timing. An attractively prepared Annual Overview posted in the classroom enables students to observe curricular progress and anticipate future topics of study; it also serves to inform students' families about what will be learned. While concept statements and the Annual Overview are practical methods of planning about content, two other methods encourage teachers to consider pedagogy as well as content. Both of these methods are simulations of planning—exercises in stating explicitly some of the many considerations that experienced, skillful teachers are able to keep in mind (usually with little or no written preparation) as they teach a topic over a series of several days or several weeks. The Session-by-Session Plan provides a structure for planning how to teach a topic over a series of days; the Content Area Planning Sketch is a method of planning at the topic or unit level.

Session-by-Session Plan.   Teachers whose classes progress smoothly and productively have considered many aspects of their lessons as they plan to teach a topic over a series of days. Their planning is based on experience and often may be so swiftly accomplished that they are not really aware of it, but over time they have thought about the pieces of a lesson. Necessary materials are ready. The lesson begins efficiently; it ends purposefully and on time. Students have work to do, and the work is planned so students or groups who finish at different times remain productively engaged. One session is linked to the next. The Session-by-Session Plan format shown in Figure 12–3 provides a way to make this kind of planning explicit. In later sections of this chapter, Figure 12–6 gives an example of the Session-by-Session plan focused on pedagogy; that is, on an aspect of how to teach skillfully. The Session-by-Session plan, shown later in Figure 12–12, incorporates a concept statement and focuses primarily on content, on planning what to teach as well as how to teach it. Experienced teachers can, if they choose, use this format as the basis for a written plan, or as an organized way to jot planning notes. It can be useful for preservice teachers to practice this kind of planning by preparing a Session-by-Session Plan, focused on content, for three or four sequential lessons. (Of course, planning with a pedagogical focus is also useful, but that tends to be easier than content-focused planning, and a challenging assignment is usually a better preparation for teaching than a simple one.)

FIGURE 12–3   Session-by-Session Plan Format

Topic:

Session 1:
- Materials needed:
- Lesson opens with:
- Student assignment:
- While students work:
- Assignment for those who finish early:
- Lesson ends with:
- Homework assignment (if any):
- Preparation for next session:

Session 2, 3, 4... as above, with each day linked to the one before.

Lesson components can be added, removed, or adapted, but all lessons should begin and end in ways that promote learning, and student assignments always need to be thought through.

Content Area Planning Sketch.   A Content Area Planning Sketch is based on both a microlevel curriculum focus (i.e., teacher knowledge about each topic to be taught, without which teaching is bound to be trivial) and a macrolevel curriculum focus (i.e., thoughtful teacher planning of an integrated, year-long program). The method simulates the kinds of thinking skilled and knowledgeable teachers do and the many factors they consider when devoting several weeks to teaching an important topic. Teachers need to be able to specify the concepts (not simply the labels for concepts) they intend to teach and to know which concepts are likely to be difficult for students to grasp. Determining the important concepts leads into thinking about which instructional strategies will be most useful. Teaching for lasting value is supported when teachers consider how to make connections with what has been previously studied and what will be studied later, how linkages can be made with other content area subjects, and what opportunities there will be to revisit the topic. Teachers who think purposefully about their own professional growth organize and extend their own knowledge base about a topic each time they teach it; they see their teaching as an opportunity for building both content and pedagogical knowledge.

The Content Area Planning Sketch (CAPS), whose format is shown in Figure 12–4, incorporates all of these elements and ends with a day-by-day, week-by-week listing of planned events. Later in this

---

FIGURE 12–4   Content Area Planning Sketch Format

Topic:
Relevant features of teaching philosophy:
Major concepts:
What concepts are likely to be difficult for students to grasp?
Surrounding topics:
    …and possibilities for connections:
Time devoted to the topic (approximately)
    …how many weeks?   …sessions per week?
    other time constraints/considerations:
Time of year:
How will I teach the vocabulary related to this topic?
How will textbook reading be accomplished?
How will I incorporate direct instruction?

What familiar instructional strategies will be used?
Will new strategies be introduced?
    How?
Before strategies:
During strategies:
After strategies:
What books and other resources will be useful?
How will I incorporate writing?
What connections can I make with concurrent content area learning?
What connections can I make with special classes, special programs, etc.?

What connections can I make with literature and the arts?
How will I observe student learning?
    …document student learning?
Will there be evaluation?
Will I need outside resources (e.g., speakers, films, trip)?
Will assistance be necessary at any point?
Are there opportunities for interaction with other teachers/grades?

What are some possibilities for returning to this topic later?
What is there in this plan that builds students' transferable knowledge?
What is there in this plan that builds my own knowledge base
    …about content?
    …about teaching?
What is my day-by-day sketch of the instructional plan, over the planned period of teaching? (List activities by week and day: 1–1, 1–2, 1–3, 2–1, etc. Session 1–1 is first week, first day; 1–2 is first week, second day; 2–1 is second week, first day, and so forth.)
Preliminary activities (if any)
1–1
1–2
etc.

chapter, Figure 12–9 gives an example of a completed plan using this format; the example is more complex than a CAPS usually is, because it is a preparation for cross-grade collaboration, so the activities for two grades are listed. Preparing a Content Area Planning Sketch gives preservice teachers an exercise in integrating many aspects of planning. Examining the components of the sketch serves to remind experienced teachers about important factors in planning. A day-by-day, week-by-week outline can be used by itself for draft planning. For example, if a field trip is planned, on which day should this be scheduled? For the trip to be an effective learning experience, what kind of preparation is needed and when should that occur? How and when will the event be followed up to ensure that that learning is sound and lasting? If student learning will be evaluated through some form of testing, what kind of assessment will be used and when will it be scheduled? Clearly this must be placed toward the end of the period of study, but to schedule a test at the last session is a poor decision because assessment should contribute to learning. Brief, interesting revisiting of concepts which students have shown they understand will consolidate learning and reteaching of other concepts may be necessary. Time is needed for these follow-up processes.

Many Factors To Consider

The Decision Chart shown at the end of Chapter Two, titled "Factors to consider in making instructional decisions," illustrates the fact that self, subject, students, and situation affect teachers' decisions about their teaching. Following Chapters Three through Eleven are sections describing some of the many facets of good teaching. The imagined teachers in these examples have all made sound decisions, but there is immense variation in how they teach. Their instructional decisions are bound to be different because the subjects they teach differ and their students are at different developmental stages and educational levels. Also, because these teachers are not automatons, their teaching decisions are shaped by situational factors, such as their years of teaching experience and aspects of their personal lives, and by what they are like as individuals—their strengths,

needs, talents, and preferences. For each of the teachers described, as for all effective teachers, planning is integrated with teaching rather than isolated as a separate process. Thinking closely and purposefully about how best to accomplish their goals produces unique results because it is based on the factors of self, situation, subject, and students, and each of these factors is multifaceted. Decision-making is an essential part of planning and the Decision Chart, shown again in Figure 12–5, is a useful planning device.

Planning About Organization

Good teaching depends, in part, on sensible organization. If there is no structure for sessions or days and the procedures for each activity need explanation, teachers' and students' time will be focused almost wholly on process and behavior rather than on content. Such a situation does not contribute to lifelong learning. In contrast, sensible planning about how to begin and end classes, organize group work, give directions, and make transitions minimizes the time spent on procedures and maximizes the time spent on content learning. Thoughtful arrangements for organizing materials and keeping records produce an orderly learning environment. Planning for a series of lessons and for a semester or a year has the advantage of minimizing the total time spent on this kind of thinking, since a group of related decisions, which can of course be changed or adapted to suit new circumstances, can be made simultaneously instead of in piecemeal fashion.

Planning About Keeping Plans. One of the aspects of *self* that is sensible for teachers to consider in their planning is whether they like to write plans. One of the aspects of *situation* they are obliged to consider is whether they are required to maintain up-to-date written plans. Cinde Otte, like a sizable number of her colleagues, does not enjoy spending time writing plans and she must keep a planbook. However, she does not spend her valuable time complaining and has devised a system that works well for her. She uses the planbook that is standard in her district. Her written plans, prepared monthly, are brief and simple: topics, page numbers of text sections, and lab

FIGURE 12–5   Decision Chart: Factors To Consider in Planning

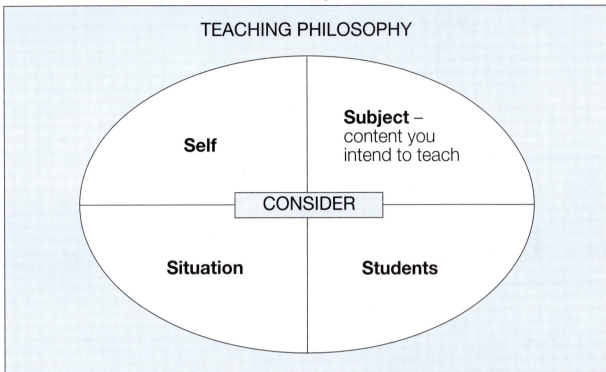

information. She also uses her planbook to document home-school contacts, such as a note from a parent or a phone call to a student's family.

Mrs. Otte supplements the planbook in two ways. She annotates the teacher's copies of the textbooks she uses, highlighting, crossing out, adding notes, and clipping in relevant read-aloud material. She uses an orange highlighter to mark sections where refutational teaching is needed and concepts that are difficult for students to grasp, and she pencils in information about ways of explaining and strategies that students have found helpful. The annotated textbook is a useful resource for her, as well as for a substitute teacher; the information in it has been accumulated over several years and new ideas can be added quickly. The other supplement is a substitute's handbook, a thin, three-ring notebook with information about how the class is run and what cooperative groups should do. She also includes a map of the school, showing the teachers'

meeting room and information that might be needed, such as fire drill procedures. Mrs. Otte prepared the notebook years ago, when a principal asked her to make her plans more detailed. The notebook was a good solution for her, since she dislikes writing extensive plans and especially dislikes writing the same thing repeatedly. The principal liked the idea, and it has worked well for her. Each semester she adds new class lists and removes old ones. When she adds a new strategy to her teaching repertoire, she prepares a one-page description for the substitute's handbook; since the description is on a computer disk, she can also run off copies as informational handouts for students' families if she wishes. She reviews the handbook annually and makes occasional additions; otherwise, it requires none of her time. Although teaching is an absorbing interest, she devotes very little time to writing about it. Her written plans are efficient but minimal, and even though she admires her colleagues who keep reflective journals, she does not ever intend to do so herself.

Using the Session-by-Session Plan to Focus on How to Teach. Although Mrs. Otte minimizes the time she spends in writing plans, thinking about what she is teaching and how to teach it is important to her. The Session-by-Session format resembles her thought pattern. She would never take the time to write such a plan, except that demonstrating a use for it fulfilled an assignment about planning and giving directions for a graduate class she took last fall. Mrs. Otte tape recorded one of her eleventh-grade chemistry sections over three sessions and made a transcription, in the format of a Session-by-Session plan, which is shown in Figure 12–6. The focus for Mrs. Otte's planning was on pedagogy rather than content. What she was thinking about and what she

FIGURE 12–6 Session-by-Session Plan Focused on Pedagogy

Mrs. Otte introduces four teaching strategies in a high school class at the beginning of the school year

Background: I don't rely on the chemistry textbook as the major provider of instruction, but I do plan my teaching so that my students will read and learn from the assigned text. I see this is as a tool and process for learning in the present, and as a preparation for reading science textbooks in college.

Four of the strategies that I use regularly link together neatly for my purposes: Teacher Read-Aloud Commentary, RESPONSE, SAY-IT and Terminology Trade. I introduce them in the first week of school, before beginning lab work, and I expect students to use them efficiently thereafter. I believe it's never sensible to separate strategy from content, so my students learn how to use a strategy by learning information using that strategy.

At this beginning point in the school year students are learning about the periodic table of elements and the structure of atoms; although in the textbook these topics are discussed in separate chapters, I integrate them.

Students have already received their textbooks, and cooperative groups have already been formed. In the Session-by-Session Plan below, *T* stands for *teacher* and *S* for any *student*. I am the teacher. At a few points I've included what might happen and what I would do in that case, in addition to what did happen.

Session 1

▪ Materials needed: projector and transparency of RESPONSE form
▪ Lesson opens with: brief description of TRAC. "One of the learning strategies we use in this class is called a Teacher Read-Aloud Commentary—or TRAC. The commentaries take about five minutes. I'll read a short, important excerpt from the textbook, stopping to explain parts of it. While I read, you should have your textbook open so that you can follow along if you wish. But whether you listen and read, or just listen, is up to you. Today I'm going to read from the top of page 7, under the heading, 'Structure of the Atom,' so turn to page 7."

—*T* reads and comments (TRAC)—

T turns on projector, showing RESPONSE form. "This is the format for another strategy, called RESPONSE. You'll be using it in groups while you read assigned sections of the text. Notice that there are three parts: Important points, Questions, New terms. A RESPONSE form isn't complete unless each of those three parts has been sensibly used.

"Ordinarily I won't repeat a Teacher Read-Aloud Commentary, but I'm going to do that today to show you how to use a RESPONSE form. As you listen, if I come to a piece of information that you think is important, stop me, and I'll record it. If you have a question, stop me, and I'll write it on the form. If I use a word or phrase that's new to you, tell me, and I'll list it under New terms.

"In this class, unless I tell you otherwise, I don't want you to raise your hands and wait to be called on. When you have something to say—and I expect you to do a lot of talking about what you're learning—just say it. If two people start to talk at once, I'll expect one of you to continue and then the other one to talk immediately afterwards—just as you would if you were at the dinner table at home."

T rereads text section, pausing and recording students' ideas. When (as usually happens) a student

FIGURE 12–6   Continued

names a topic rather than giving an important statement about the topic, this is an opportunity to show how to use the form correctly.

S: Electrons and protons.

T: Two new terms, okay. (lists them in New terms section)

S: But that's also an important point.

T: Important points give information; they don't just name something. Tell me something you've learned about electrons.

S: Electrons are negatively charged particles.

T: Good point. (records it in the Important points section) Somebody give me an important piece of information about protons.

S: Protons are positively charged particles.

T: Yes, that can be recorded all together: Electrons are negatively charged particles, and protons are positively charged particles.

T continues filling out the form based on student responses. If a student raises a question, teacher commends and records it. Every question is accepted, even those many students know the answer to. T restates, or rephrases, negotiating meaning to make sure it's what S wants to ask and commends S. T may decide to answer a question in some detail, giving information that other students are not likely to know already as a way of encouraging question-raising.

Near end of class period, T comments quickly on the RESPONSE form entries which have been recorded, commending students' understanding of the strategy.

▌ Student assignment: None this day.

▌ Lesson ends with: "Give me five"—a process for learning names. T points to student; that student points to self and says name. Another student (anyone) points to self and says name and points to and names previous student. Another student (anyone) points to self and says name and points to and names the two previous students—and so forth, until five students have been named. T points to another student to start the next chain of five. (Because T selects the person to start the chain, there is little risk that the same students will name each other repeatedly.)

▌ Preparation for next session: Choose section for TRAC; have RESPONSE forms available.

Session 2

▌ Materials needed: RESPONSE forms

▌ Lesson opens with: TRAC. "The TRAC today is on page 9, the section headed 'How electrons are organized into orbitals.' Turn to page 9. You decide whether to listen, or listen and read."

　　—TRAC—

　　"Get together in your cooperative groups and read pages 7–10. As you read, find important points, raise questions, list new terms. I expect one RESPONSE form from each group; you decide whether you're going to take turns making entries on the form, or choose one member of the group to record all your ideas."

▌ Student assignment: (as directed)

▌ While students work: T moves from group to group, observing, commending, giving guidance on using the RESPONSE form if necessary. T is looking for one or two good questions, and also for any spontaneous uses of SAY-IT—which is simply one student asking for content-related information and someone else supplying it.

▌ Assignment for those who finish early: Not likely to happen—if it does, T directs students to scan the assigned section again with the goal of picking out *all* the new terms that will be listed by any group—a comprehensive set of new terms.

▌ Lesson continues with: T calls a stop to group work, and gives some brief praise.

T: Now we've used three strategies. Name one.

S: RESPONSE.

T: Good. Name another.

S: TRAC.

T: "Good. The name of the third strategy is SAY-IT, and I saw several people using it. When Wanda asked what the difference is between an orbital and a shell, Ansel explained. (Now, if you want to know that information you can check with Wanda or Ansel.) That's exactly what I want you to do—ask when you need information about what we're studying; answer each other's questions when you can, or call on me as a resource. That's the SAY-IT strategy, and we'll all use it, except when there's a quiz or a test, and then each person will work independently and save questions till later.

"Back to the RESPONSE forms—you're doing good work there. This group has written a sensible question, in the form of a comment: "We're not sure what the difference is between molecules and atoms." (T answers.)

FIGURE 12–6   Continued

■ Lesson ends with: another round of Give me five.

■ Preparation for next session: Prepare cards for Terminology Trade. (Later in the semester, cooperative groups take responsibility for this.)

Session 3

■ Materials needed: cards for Terminology Trade

■ Lesson opens with: explanation of Terminology Trade: "I've put the words you listed on your RESPONSE forms as new terms on these file cards. Some of those terms you already understand from your reading; some you don't. Terminology Trade is a strategy for learning technical vocabulary—there's a lot of that in chemistry. I'm giving each group five cards, each with a different term. You have five minutes, in your group, to sort the cards into those with terms you can define, and those you're not sure of. You can all use your textbooks to find information. When five minutes is up, I'll point to one group, and that group will define one term, give me a term to define, and hand one term to the next group. Then that group will define a term they've chosen, give me one to define, and hand one on, and so forth, until each group has had a turn. Then you'll have a minute or two to work with the cards you have, and we'll do another round.

■ Student assignment: In groups, students have five minutes to sort terms and find definitions for some.
— Two rounds of Terminology Trade, with a two-minute interval between rounds—

■ Lesson ends with: quick commendations. *T* tries to use as many students' names as possible as they leave—noticing those she doesn't know yet and planning to learn those names during cooperative group work in the following days.

■ Preparation for future sessions: Plan for another round of TRAC, RESPONSE, and Terminology Trade, then incorporate lab work, begin homework assignments, and, schedule first quiz.

Challenge to the Reader: The "Assignment for those who finish early" is a component of Session-by-Session style planning, needed in some, though not all, sessions. Check the Strategy Glossary following this chapter and identify several strategies in which students or student groups are likely to finish an in-class assignment at different times. Then identify a grade level and subject matter topic for which one of the strategies would be useful and plan an assignment, related to the subject matter topic, for students who finish early.

Choose and Use: If you were to choose one facet of Mrs. Otte's planning to use in your own classroom, what would it be? How would it suit the factor of *subject* or the factor of *students*?

described for her instructor and the colleagues in her graduate class was a way to introduce a number of strategies quickly and effectively.

Planning About Routines.   Among the ways teachers can minimize the time spent on routine aspects of teaching and make the time that is spent productive is by planning thoughtfully and ingeniously in advance. Giving directions and making transitions from one activity to another are two worthwhile subjects for attention, as shown in Figure 12–7. Figure 12–8 illustrates some of the many ways that the scheduling problems which face teachers can be managed advantageously.

FIGURE 12–7   Planning About Giving Directions and Making Transitions

Mr. Garwin makes the most of teaching moments

When Mr. Garwin was growing up, dinner table conversations were often about teaching. Both of his parents were experts on the subject because they were teachers, and Eddie and his older brother and younger sister were experts because they sat in classrooms all day and observed teachers. Sometimes they joked about what they called "blank directions": *"Does everyone have the blue book? Today we're going to do lesson 2 in chapter 7. Turn to page 125. Everyone look at the title."* Surely the book and the instruction fit somewhere into a curriculum, but it is impossible to tell where. Students who hear these instructions learn to follow directions, but they also receive a subtle message: what they are doing is not about anything important. Mr. Garwin makes a point of using directions to reinforce content area learning:

"Social studies time; take out Regions and People, *and sit with a partner. You remember that we've started to study about what* archeology *tells us about the way people lived in the past - there's the word* archeology *on our List of Terms.*

Good—a lot of you have already figured out where I'm going to start reading—yes, page 57, and the topic is artifacts. *After I've read and you've read in groups I'll show you some artifacts I brought in that are hundreds of years old, and maybe you can show me some artifacts you have in your pockets."*

Mr. Garwin also recognizes that teaching time is maximized if transitions—between one activity and another, one subject and another, or one class and another—are crisp and content-focused, rather than blank. *"Math time is over; hurry up and get ready for science,"* or worse, muddled and time-consuming.

He ensures that transitions serve multiple purposes. The students are usually physically in motion, which is good for them, and sometimes as they move they accomplish the organizational task of putting papers where Mr. Garwin needs them. (He has three boxes for students' folders, separated alphabetically, spaced along one wall to avoid congestion.) In the example below, there is noise, but purposeful noise, as students respond to math fact questions in chorus. Students will have an opportunity to talk socially when they are in their cooperative learning groups, which provides an impetus for moving quickly.

Cooperative group tasks are listed on a chart or on the board. Mr. Garwin tells or reads them, so students receive directions both visually and auditorily.

"We're going to move from math to science—put your math papers in your math folders as you get into cooperative learning groups.

Let's have a math chorus as you're getting set: OKAY! 28 divided by 4 is…; 56 divided by 7 is…; 5 times 7 is…. SO 35 divided by 7 is… AND 35 divided by 5 is …(and so forth).

Good. We've been practicing division facts in math, and now we're going to be thinking about dividing in another way. Scientists think about a different kind of division. They create taxonomies, systems of classifying things in nature. I'm putting a box of minerals on each of your tables. Your task is to decide on a way to divide them into groups. Do this first without your textbooks and make a record or chart of your classifications. After we talk about your decisions we'll begin reading about the features of minerals that scientists use in their classifications."

Challenge to the Reader: Even in brief moments, teachers' actions can be based on some of the features of good teaching, summarized in the CARES for ME acronym below:

C: Challenge, Clarity and Cheerfulness
A: Appropriateness and Acceptance of Ambiguity
R: Respect—also Repetition, Revisiting, and Re-viewing
E: Enthusiasm and Expertise
S: Safety and Structure
for ME: Maximized Engagement

Identify ways that Mr. Garwin's methods of giving directions and making transitions show some of these features. Practice applying features of good teaching by describing a way to translate a set of blank directions or a blank transition (which you create based on experience, observation, or recollection) into a brief but learning-packed teaching moment.

Choose and Use: If you were to choose one facet of Mr. Garwin's planning to use in your own classroom, what would it be? How would it suit the factor of *situation* or the factor of *students*?

FIGURE 12–8   *Planning to Fit Scheduling Constraints*

Mr. Criefton and Ms. Spen turn scheduling problems into teaching opportunities

Like all teachers, Ms. Spen and Mr. Criefton know their plans will be affected by circumstances they do not control. However, like the effective teachers that they are, they know they can adapt to constraints and even use them productively. In the words of the folk saying, give them lemons, and they will make lemonade.

During the winter months, there may be a dozen days when a third of the students in Mr. Criefton's first period science class are late because of bus slowdowns on icy roads. Although he cannot predict in advance when—or even whether—his first period class will be affected in this way, he does know several things. First, it's always happened before—he's never known a winter to pass without some delayed buses. Second, he can easily find out which students will be affected. Moreover, he can predict bus delays, with reasonable accuracy, at least one day ahead because he watches the weather forecast.

He can't do anything about the weather, but he can do something about his class. Here's his strategy. He changes the membership of cooperative groups in January, because winter weather is worst from January through mid-March, so he makes this combination work for him. In January, instead of grouping on a wholly random basis, Mr. Criefton divides the students who ride the buses that may be delayed, so each cooperative group has a nucleus of one or two students. Then he randomly divides the rest. (This year, he came into school after the holidays with six bags of popcorn, each dyed a different color, and gave a bag to each nucleus student or student pair. He handed out cards of the six different colors to the other students, who then matched up with their color group; then the class had a popcorn party while Mr. Criefton explained the plan for bus-delay days.) This was the plan: Bad days *always* start off right on time with Mr. Criefton teaching something new and important. (If there was a special activity planned, of course it's postponed due to the weather.) Cooperative groups then *instantly* go into action to decide how to teach the information to the people who will be arriving late. Sensibly, they've conferred earlier and the potential latecomers get to tell what helps them

learn, such as a quickly made poster; the opportunity to be told information and to ask questions; or written information that they can take with them. The next day (weather permitting) there's a quick quiz, and the day after there's popcorn for all students if quiz scores are 90 percent or better across all groups.

Ms. Spen has two organizational problems that are just as inevitable as bad weather, although these problems have a good origin. It is a great advantage to have teachers in her school who specialize in the arts, media, and physical education, who are Reading Recovery teachers, and who have studied to meet the needs of students with disabilities. The problem is she needs to plan her schedule keeping in mind that students are in and out of the class.

Every year Ms. Spen's schedule varies; sometimes her class has one "special" each day; sometimes there will be one day with two special classes and one day with none. She has described her dream schedule for the principal: she would like one special class each day, with music and art right after lunch, library Friday mornings, and physical education before lunch on Tuesdays and Thursdays. However, she and the principal both understand that it is unlikely that the dream will ever be fully realized, since other teachers' wishes are similar. This year, some parts of the schedule suit her very well. Library time is Friday, which gives students the opportunity to read their new books over the weekend with their families. Ms. Spen encourages bringing the books back to school for in-class reading on Wednesday and Thursday; so even with some forgetfulness it's common for each child to be ready on Friday to return last week's book.

The rest of the schedule isn't hard to accommodate, except for a fifteen-minute interval between physical education and lunch on Monday. This is Ms. Spen's solution. Gym class is exciting; children need to be calmed down before lunch. Ms. Spen meets her students at the gym door and says a few quiet tempting words about a story, for example, "The story is about a boy who makes a *galimoto*." As they walk back to class, she follows her usual sensible system of walking in the middle of her group, rather than at the head of a line (where she can't see any of the students) or at the end (where she's far away from the first students). Students

FIGURE 12–8   Continued

learn this routine early and easily. They also know there will always be a story at this time, and they always put their lunch boxes on their desks before they leave for gym. Now Ms. Spen reads, with her first graders settled around her on the reading rug, where they can sit or lie down as they please. The reading session is not hurried or abruptly ended, because after lunch everyone goes straight back to the reading rug and Ms. Spen picks up right where she stopped. Ms. Spen is aware that her students haven't had time in class to talk about several interesting parts of their day, but they are learning that writing and drawing are ways to express and shared ideas. When the book is finished, it's writing time, and students know there are three possibilities for their writing: they can write or draw about the story they just heard; they can write or draw about gym class—still vivid in the minds of several; or they can write and draw about something else that interests them. Writing is not a silent or an isolated act, and students are active in conferring, consulting, and sharing with one another. One or two family member volunteers (often grandparents) come in Monday afternoons, and during writing time Ms. Spen and the other adults walk around the room, observing and talking with students and, if a student asks, they transcribe a story into "dictionary spelling" or write out a word if a student doesn't want to use invented spelling. Often the family members speak languages other than English, and students enjoy finding out about how to write an important word or phrase in two languages.

Another scheduling constraint is produced by the departures and returns of Ms. Spen's first graders, who leave the classroom at different times for physical therapy sessions or Reading Recovery lessons. Other special education teachers come into the classroom, and Ms. Spen regards their presence and collaboration as a plus for her and the class. To adapt a schedule so that no child leaving the classroom would miss anything important could only be accomplished by providing a drab and neutral program, which Ms. Spen has no intention of doing, so she solves the problem simply. Each month, each of the students who has a special class outside the classroom picks two buddies. The buddies have the responsibility of saying "good-bye" quietly when their friends leave and catching them up on what's been going on when they come back. Students can pick the same buddies month after month or choose new ones, although Ms. Spen occasionally suggests a student she thinks would like the opportunity to be a buddy. The simple solution works well. If the number of students with out-of-class opportunities increases, then more buddies are chosen (including buddies who themselves leave for special lessons). When students are successful enough to be discontinued from Reading Recovery, their buddies-of-the-month are retired.

Challenge to the Reader: In the profession of teaching, the work teachers do is sometimes impacted by factors they cannot control. Benjamin Bloom (1981) calls these *static variables*, that is, features of an educational situation which may vary but which the teacher can't change, such as in the one example above, the weather, and in the other example, scheduling decisions made by others. Bloom points out that teachers can examine situations where static variables cause problems and discover *alterable variables*—features of the situation that they can change to improve educational opportunities for students. Based on your own teaching situation, one you've observed, or one of the teaching situations described in this text, identify a constraint that is beyond a teacher's power to change, and look for a way to turn the problem into an advantage.

Choose and Use: If you were to choose one facet of either Mr. Criefton's or Ms. Spen's planning to use in your own classroom, what would it be? How would your choice suit the factor of *self* or the factor of *students*, or both?

Collaborative Planning

Most teachers work cooperatively with colleagues, sharing ideas and working together on projects; now, teaching that involves collaboration among two or more teachers is increasingly being advocated. Besides being advantageous for teachers themselves, there are many benefits for students. One of the many advantages is that teachers who work together model professional collaboration for students, who are likely to need the ability to work well with others in their future careers. Teacher collaboration in content area instruction also demonstrates that learning is interrelated. When education consists of a collection of subjects, each taught in its own time period by a single teacher in a closed room, a silent but powerful message is given: what is learned in school is not connected to other learning. Figure 12–9 and Figure 12–10 illustrate planning for two major types of collaborative teaching: cross-grade collaboration and themed teaching.

FIGURE 12–9 Content Area Planning Sketch

Ms. Spen and Mr. Garwin plan for cross-grade collaboration

Topic: first grade: weather changes
fourth grade: measuring weather conditions

Relevant features of our teaching philosophies:

Students teach and learn from each other when teachers arrange the conditions for cooperative learning and cross-grade collaboration.

Observation and question-generating are important parts of scientific inquiry.

Students learn from direct instruction, reading, writing, talking, and listening, and from observing, collecting, and analyzing data.

Young children can grasp important ideas.

Trade books are excellent resources.

Curriculum should not isolate and limit the teaching of important concepts. We intend to continue to collaborate; therefore, many of these first graders will study weather using some of the same materials when they are in fourth grade. We hope they will remember and learn more from being the older buddies then.

Major concepts:

Earth's weather is affected by the sun, the earth itself (shape, rotation), earth's atmosphere, and physical features of the earth, such as oceans and mountains.

Weather conditions differ and change. At any one time, the weather is different in different places; over time, the weather in one place will vary.

The temperature of the air above the earth varies. Air masses are sections in which the air is similar in temperature and in the amount of moisture. A *front* is the boundary of an air mass; weather changes occur along fronts. Air masses advance and move back; a cold front occurs when a mass of cold air pushes a mass of warmer air. As these air masses with different temperatures collide, the colder air pushes the warmer air up. As it rises, the warm air mass cools and condenses into clouds; often rain and storms follow.

Studying the weather is a science *(meteorology)*. Scientists have developed instruments that enable people to make predictions about the weather, although it is not possible to predict weather conditions with absolute accuracy.

What concepts are likely to be difficult for students to grasp?

The concept of *front* is a difficult one, because the idea of forces colliding suggests that we should be able to see the collision, rather than just the effects.

We all talk about "good weather" and "bad weather," and many students equate good weather with sunshine and bad weather with rain. We need to teach that precipitation is essential (and also that snow, like rain, meets our needs for water).

Surrounding topics and possibilities for connections:

We will connect the topic with measurement in math.

In science, the topic is linked with the study of the sun, earth's rotation around the sun, geophysical features of earth, and the water cycle.

We have considered whether it would be useful to expand on the idea of change. This would be a good time for students in both grades to look at changes in themselves across the year—but we will give attention to this without trying to link these with changes in the weather

FIGURE 12–9   Continued

(especially since weather changes are cyclical and changes in students are developmental and result in progress). Perhaps some students may come up with an analogy between weather and other kinds of changes.

Time devoted to the topic (approximately)

...how many weeks? Our programs have been moving along well and this is an important topic. Four weeks.

...sessions per week? four sessions for fourth graders; three or four for first graders; art classes in weeks 2 and 3. Sessions will vary in length, and fourth graders will work on some activities during language arts time or free time.

other time constraints/considerations: none

Time of year: April. In our climate the weather is very changeable during this month, and there are significant changes from the beginning of the month to the end. Also, students are accustomed to buddying and are settled into school routines. They will enjoy having a guest speaker.

How will we teach the vocabulary related to this topic?

For fourth graders, List-Group-Label. For both groups, RESPONSE. We will do a Terminology Trade with mixed groups of first and fourth graders. We will do lots of talking, reading, and writing.

How will textbook reading be accomplished?

We will use textbooks at both grade levels. First graders have not been using science texts, but they are available; by April, the children are readers. Reading this section of the first-grade science text with their fourth grade buddies will help familiarize students with textbooks. We will be doing more of this at the end of the school year in preparation for second grade. Fourth graders will use List-Group-Label, reading in cooperative groups, and Teacher Read-Aloud Commentary—all strategies they are familiar with.

How will we incorporate direct instruction?

As usual. Introducing lessons by telling students important information at both grade levels; Teacher Read-Aloud Commentaries (TRAC); and answering students' content-related questions (SAY-IT). The guest speaker's talk also provides direct instruction.

What familiar instructional strategies will be used? Will new strategies be introduced? How?

This is a good time to use strategies familiar to one grade but not to another. (See below.) This will be the first time students have used a bibliography list, which will be posted in the classroom as a chart.

Before strategies: Read-aloud, storytell, TRAC.

During strategies: RESPONSE (new to fourth graders). Vicarious experience: observing two experiments illustrating fronts. These are "The cold front" and "The occluded front," from *Weather in the lab*, pp. 61–67, and require only equipment and materials we have (aquarium, sand bags, beaker).

After strategies: Manipulable Cloze for first graders, based on "Weather Facts" booklets prepared by fourth graders. (Fourth graders are familiar with cloze, but not manipulable cloze.) Terminology Trade (new to first graders).

What books and other resources will be useful?

Guest speaker, TV meteorologist

Books: *Weather in the lab*, Baker, 1993; *Weather forecasting*, Gibbons, 1987; *Weather*, Simon, 1993 (also *Storms*, 1989, as a resource); *When the wind stops*, Zolotow, 1995.

Also, we (Rose and Eddie) will read the sections on weather from all of the textbooks, grades 1–6, to see how the topic is treated across the grades.

We need two copies of *When the wind stops* and six copies each of *Weather* and *Weather Forecasting*. Rose needs to be familiar enough with *Weather* to be able to storytell the information, page by page, reading only the first and last pages.

How will we incorporate writing?

Fourth graders will prepare RESPONSE forms in cooperative groups; first and fourth graders will collaborate to create "Weather Facts" booklets. First graders will use the Daily Journal to write a group thank-you letter to the guest speaker, and fourth graders will collaborate so there will be a letter from each cooperative group.

What connections can we make with concurrent content area learning?

Language arts and math connections are listed above.

What connections can we make with special classes, special programs, etc.? We will not attempt this.

FIGURE 12–9 Continued

What connections can we make with literature and the arts?

1) *Choral reading.* We will adapt Charlotte Zolotow's *When the wind stops* so the "little boy" part is read by first graders and the "mother" part by fourth graders:

First graders: *Where does the rain go when the storm is over?*

Fourth graders: *Into clouds to make other storms.*

First graders: *And where do clouds go when they move across the sky?*

Fourth graders: *To make shade somewhere else.*

2) *Weather Mosaic.* In art classes, students will use 4 × 4 oaktag "tiles" to create illustrations of different weather conditions. First and fourth graders will group to decide how sets of tiles should be arranged, then glue them to a panel to make a mosaic. (Note: tiles need to be this large for students this age; we will produce a mosaic-mural about 4′ × 6′ if each student creates four tiles.)

How will we observe student learning?

As usual. We both use post-it notes for anecdotal observations. We are both good observers of our own students, but it is very helpful when we have both classes together, because there are times when Rose observes something about a fourth grader, or Eddie about a first grader, that we have missed seeing in our own students.

...document student learning?

photographs, RESPONSE forms, Weather Facts booklets.

Will there be evaluation?

Only informally. We will have many opportunities to observe students engaged in a variety of activities. RESPONSE forms and discussions will show us whether there are misunderstandings; if so, we will reteach.

Will we need outside resources; e.g., speakers, films, trip?

The meteorologist from the local TV station has agreed to talk to our classes jointly.

Will assistance be necessary at any point?

Family School Organization subcommittee will supply refreshments for guest speaker's visit. Classroom volunteer will prepare Big Book.

Are there opportunities for interaction with other teachers/grades?

Art class

What are some possibilities for returning to this topic later?

We may want to keep collecting weather data. In our separate classes, we will have opportunities to review during current events discussions, because weather events are often in the news.

What is there in this plan that builds students' transferable knowledge?

We expect students to understand and to be able to explain weather concepts, and this knowledge is useful in everyday life.

What is there in this plan that builds our own knowledge base ...about content?

Reading the texts across grade levels; listening to the guest speaker. As we have questions (as has already happened while we have been drafting this plan) we will turn to resource texts for answers.

...about teaching?

Rose has not tried conducting this kind of science lab for students before; she intends to practice, because she will be leading off. Eddie hasn't tried choral reading, nor has he tried adapting a text for choral reading with his students. And we continue to learn about collaboration.

Day-by-day sketch of the instructional plan, over the planned period of teaching: *(Note: sessions in boldface are times when classes meet together. Except for 3-2, joint sessions are held in the first-grade classroom, which is larger.)*

Preliminary activities: On the first day of April, fourth graders begin collecting weather-related magazine and newspaper articles for bulletin board display (follow up later with current events discussions, mounting selected articles in looseleaf scrapbook). First graders begin cutting and mounting daily weather reports from newspapers brought in by teacher. This continues throughout the month.

1–1 grade 4: List-Group-Label; TRAC based on science textbook; cooperative reading of text.

FIGURE 12–9   Continued

grade 1: Teacher storytells about weather changes, using *Weather*, showing the illustrations and telling selected information through pages explaining *fronts* (book is unpaginated).

both grades: Begin recording weather conditions and temperature outside of classroom windows at the beginning and end of school day. (Eventually we will chart data and also compare data from two sets of measurements and discuss reasons for discrepancies, if any.)

1–2 grade 4: Teacher read-aloud of *Weather*, through pages explaining *fronts*. Distribute copies of *Weather* to cooperative groups and copies of first-grade science textbooks. Students compare and contrast, talk over what they have learned, and discuss concepts to explain to first-grade buddies.

grade 1: Distribute, examine, discuss science textbooks; find and mark (with a paper clip) chapter about weather. Discuss in *Talk story* style what has been learned, yesterday and today.

1–3 Fourth- and first-grade buddies read section on weather from first-grade science textbook and discuss.

1–4 grade 4: Teacher explains plan for Weather Facts booklets. Using resources (textbook, trade books) students begin to write weather facts. Sources must be cited; quotations must be used if sources are quoted. Teacher has posted bibliography list so citing sources is easy. Students peer-edit each other's work, working toward factual accuracy, clarity, appropriateness for first-grade audience, and technical correctness. no science lesson in grade 1 this day.

In second week, begin *Weather Mosaic* in art class; students also may work on tiles outside class; limit = four finished tiles per student. Illustrations in trade books and textbooks can be used as resources.

2–1 Teachers explain/students talk about concept of *front* and purpose of laboratory demonstrations (both classes, separately). In grade 4, teacher demonstrates use of RESPONSE form.

2–2 "Cold front" experiment: (Rose conducting, Eddie assisting). Students contribute ideas for RESPONSE, using chart, first-grade style, with Rose recording.

2–3 "Occluded front" experiment: (Eddie conducting, Rose assisting). Students complete standard RESPONSE forms in pairs with fourth-grade

buddies recording for first graders.

During lunch or after school, teachers meet to look over RESPONSE forms, determine whether there are misconceptions, and identify questions to be answered.

2–4 Classes meet separately. Further discussion of fronts and experiments. Teachers provide instruction that will correct misconceptions, if any. Class discussion during which student-raised questions are answered, either by other students with teachers restating information, or teachers explaining answers. Fourth graders continue to work on Weather Facts.

During third week, in art class, complete work on tiles for Weather Mosaic. During this week and next, when weather permits, first and fourth graders will go outside for joint recess activities; informal discussion of weather. In math, students begin analyzing weather data collected so far. In language arts, teachers read aloud *When the wind stops*. Fourth graders work on adapting the text for choral reading. (Classroom volunteer, working at home, then prepares an adapted version as a Big Book, which will be traded back and forth as students practice reading their parts chorally.)

3–1 grade 4: Distribute copies of *Weather forecasting* to cooperative groups. Students read aloud to one another and discuss concepts to talk about with first-grade buddies; continue work on Weather Facts.

grade 1: Teacher reads and storytells *Weather Forecasting*; class discusses.

3–2 Fourth graders go to first-grade classroom to bring first-grade buddies back to their classroom (fourth graders carrying first graders' chairs). Teachers announce planned visit of TV meteorologist on 4-2. First graders meet with fourth-grade cooperative groups for read-aloud (by fourth graders) and discussion of Weather forecasting. Students complete standard RESPONSE forms in pairs with fourth-grade buddies recording for first graders. Selected questions from RESPONSE forms will be shared with guest meteorologist in advance.

During lunch or after school, teachers meet to look over RESPONSE forms to determine whether there are misconceptions. If necessary, explanations will be given through mini-lessons in separate classrooms. Teachers also choose questions for the guest meteorologist and, by prearrangement, fax them to the TV station.

FIGURE 12–9 Continued

3–3 Fourth graders share their Weather Facts papers with first-grade buddies. (Several buddy pairs may group together.) First graders may dictate more Weather Facts.

Fourth graders do a final round of editing. Teacher approves, explains concept of manipulable cloze; fourth graders choose four or five significant terms from each Weather Fact page to omit for the cloze activity, print terms neatly on 3 x 5 cards cut in half, lengthwise, and paper clip the cards to their pages.

3–4 By this time, both grades have had their weekly art class. Teachers distribute tiles to groups formed by several buddy pairs; each group decides how to arrange their tiles and glues them to a panel; panels will be combined to form a large mosaic. The group session winds up with shared choral readings of the "When the wind stops" Big Book.

Art teacher oversees finishing of mosaic panels (checking that tiles are securely glued, weighting panels over the weekend) and discusses with custodians how the panels will be mounted in the hall, prior permission having been obtained from the principal.

Over the weekend, Rose (with the help of her own children) uses a computer to prepare manipulable cloze from student-written Weather Facts pages. Cloze pages are printed in large type on regular-sized paper with widely spaced lines and spaces for the omitted words; the cards with the missing terms are paper clipped to their pages. These cloze pages are not designed to be long-lasting; they can be reproduced because they're saved on the computer. If teachers wish, the cloze can be prepared later in sturdier fashion (perhaps by family volunteers working at home). Weather Facts pages are returned to fourth graders for collection into Weather Facts booklets, to be shared between first- and fourth-grade class libraries.

In the fourth week, recess and math activities from previous week are continued.

4–1 grade 4: In cooperative groups, prepare for meteorologist's visit by reviewing textbook and trade books; whole class discussion of what we know.

grade 1: Students try out some of the manipulable cloze pages; whole class discussion of what we know.

both classes: Discuss ways of being polite and respectful to guests. In the afternoon, (by prearrangement with principal) students from both classes sit in hall to watch custodian mount the Weather Mosaic on hall wall.

4–2 Long session, with refreshments. TV meteorologist visits. Weather Facts booklets, manipulable cloze pages, RESPONSE charts, and trade books are on display. Students explain Weather Mosaic. Meteorologist talks to group, followed by a question-and-answer period. Students do choral reading for the guest. The Big Book will be displayed, but students will have copies of the text from which to read. (The TV station may send a photographer to record the visit.)

4–3 both classes: Discuss guest speaker's visit and what we learned. (Quick praise for students' good manners, but concentrate on *content*.)

grade 4: Terminology Trade. Cooperative groups prepare thank-you letters.

grade 1: Class prepares thank-you to guest speaker through Daily Journal entry; students work on manipulable cloze pages.

4–4 Group wind-up session with first graders joining fourth-grade buddies in their cooperative groups for a Terminology Trade. Group sharing of what we have learned from each other. Outdoor play together if weather permits.

Challenge to the Reader: When teachers plan instruction, it is useful to keep in mind Margaret McKeown's and Sandra McCormick's *ME/MC* concept: students learn best when they have *multiple encounters* with important information in *multiple contexts*. Working independently or with colleagues, make a quick listing of the ways in which this plan puts the ME/MC idea into practice. Then create an imaginary student with a particular set of strengths and needs and tell how the planned activities tap those strengths and meet those needs.

Choose and Use: If you were to choose one facet of this collaborative planning to use in your own classroom, what would it be? How would your choice suit the factor of *situation* or the factor of *subject*?

FIGURE 12–10   Collaborative Planning For Themed Teaching

Mr. Lusolo records team members' ideas and decisions

Notes from Meeting 1

Present: Team members: Inga (English), Si (Science), Sasha (Social Studies), Yoli (Spanish), and Dave (Math). Recorder = Dave. Guests: Mi-Ja (Media Specialist)

Background: Both teachers and administrators are interested in the idea of using themes; our middle school team is going to try themed teaching on a pilot basis. We have decided to develop one theme that will tie in with others if we decide to continue, but can stand alone if we decide to stop or pause after one try. We prepared for this meeting by reading two articles and a section on themes from a booklet published by the National Middle School Association: "Topics and themes in interdisciplinary curriculum," Cook & Martinello, 1994; "Second thoughts about interdisciplinary studies," Roth, 1994; *A Middle School Curriculum: From Rhetoric to Reality,* Beane, 1990.

Notes on our readings:

Beane strongly believes in using themes for middle school teaching. He suggests organizing middle school curriculum around themes that promote reflective thinking, critical ethics ("identifying and judging the morality in problem situations"), and problem-solving. He believes themes should relate to early adolescent concerns and also to social concerns, such as a "transitions" theme, which would encourage students to understand personal changes and discuss living in a changing world.

Roth has concerns about using themes. It isn't enough just to integrate different content areas. She discusses trivial themes (clearly for younger students than ours though), such as a color, or teddy bears. A quote: "The children read stories about teddy bears, everything they did in writing class was written on paper cut in the shape of a teddy bear, they wrote their own teddy bear stories, brought in teddy bears from home, did math problems with 'Gummy Bear' candy, explored different kinds of 'real' bears in science, and on and on. Thoughtful decisions about curriculum content and goals were superseded by one central command: How well something fit with the theme" (Roth, 1994, p. 44). Roth and her colleagues decided on a year-long unit integrating social studies and science on a "1492" theme, for fifth graders. Problem: important science topics weren't taught because they didn't link with the theme.

Cook and Martinello's article was the most useful for us. They say it's good for teachers to do extensive planning, especially if they're new to themed teaching, as we are, but it's also important to involve students in the planning. They give criteria for deciding whether a theme—a "big idea"—is important enough to study: 1) Is the big idea true over space and time? 2) Does it broaden students' understanding of the world? 3) Is the big idea interdisciplinary? 4) Does it relate to students' genuine interests? 5) Does it lead to student inquiry? They suggest using artifacts—real things—related to the theme that students can look at and examine: "One of the most effective ways to develop theme studies with students is to start with an object or artifact," and they say a good basis for choosing a theme is teachers' interests and expertise: "Teachers know that their own enthusiasm for a topic or subject of study can develop the interest of their students" (Cook & Martinello, 1992, p. 43).

Our thoughts: We already decided to try a theme, and we're doing it without committing ourselves to more than one. We aren't about to make some of the mistakes we read about (making the theme silly) and we also think it would be mistake to try a year-long theme. So we want a theme that's interesting, worthwhile, and one we (teachers) already are somewhat knowledgeable about, although we expect to expand our own knowledge as we prepare to teach and as we use the theme. The connections are not going to be contrived or silly, and we are not going to try to force everything we do into the theme. We also think we will do better with a theme that's more concrete than some of the ideas we've read about.

Decisions: After brainstorming, we decided to use Australia as a theme. Advantages: it's a district goal to teach geography more thoroughly (and if we go on to other themes, they could be about other countries or areas of the world). Australia gets us into hemispheres that are opposite to ours—Eastern and Southern—so not only are the time zones almost opposite, the seasons are the reverse of ours—but the language is the same so we'll have easy access to more reading and there won't be a language difficulty if we organize a pen pals

FIGURE 12–10 Continued

project. Inga spent time at a conference and brought back books and brochures; there's a teacher on staff who has family in Australia; Si suggests we all read a book about Australian history, which he will bring to the next meeting. We can make connections between our history and some of our current problems and theirs. We think that together we've got a lot of information and ideas to pool. Although we don't think we'd want to use this theme again next year, we could use it as a pattern for themed units about other places. And if we do link up with an Australian school (for pen pals) we could continue that after the theme is completed.

Assignments for next time:

Mi-Ja, Inga, and Dave: look for and bring in books that we can use, including children's literature. Mi-Ja will also look for maps.

Sasha and Yoli: do a computer search for articles in the professional literature.

Si: bring in Robert Hughes's *The fatal shore*, a book about the European settlement of Australia as a penal colony for convicts transported from England.

Dave will continue to keep notes on the laptop computer; Yoli has agreed to put together a bibliography and collection of materials. We want to invite other teachers (art, music, physical education) to plan with us; Si will contact them.

Everybody: Think about how Australia fits the criteria suggested by Cook and Martinello.

Next meeting is after school, with a brown bag supper; Inga volunteers to bring cookies.

Notes from Meeting 2

Present: Inga, Si, Sasha, Yoli, Dave. Guests: Artie (Art), Coe (Physical Education), Coral (Music), Mi-Ja.

Review: We did some readings about themes (Yoli has copies for anyone who wants them). We have chosen Australia as a theme; we brought in materials to share. We do not intend to force the theme into content areas but we want to be inclusive; we've asked Artie, Coe, and Coral to help us plan.

Discussion: We started to discuss Australia as a "big idea" for a theme but we only came up with generalities:

1. *Is the big idea true over space and time?* Is this applicable? Australia *exists* in space and across

time; it has a history (with a lot of parallels to ours).

2. *Does it broaden students' understanding of the world?* Yes.

3. *Is the big idea interdisciplinary?* We already have lots of ideas.

4. *Does it relate to students' genuine interests?* We're not sure whether students will start off interested (although the Australian theme in movies is popular). We're confident interest will be roused.

5. *Does it lead to student inquiry?* It will be our responsibility to see that it does; there are lots of possibilities.

Then we realized that although Australia is our topic, we need to think about important ideas related to Australia, so we'll come back to this later.

Question: When do we want to begin? *Decision:* January—there isn't an outdoor component to the theme, and the seasonal differences will be dramatic. Waiting till January will give us time to gather materials and also to set up a pen pal project—our letters will be about snow and theirs may be about how hot it is. We want to talk with students beforehand so they can be thinking and maybe reading about Australia over the holiday, then they can brainstorm questions and ideas that will give us all something to think about.

Sharing:

▌Mi-Ja brought a *National Geographic* map celebrating Australia's bicentennial (1788–1988), "A Traveler's Look at Australia" (1988). The map is backed with maps of "Australia's Continental Odyssey," showing how this area of the world may have looked 120, 85, and 45 million years ago. She also brought a copy of *Our patchwork planet* (Sattler & Maestro, 1995) which shows the possible position of Australia linked with Antarctica 25 to 350 million years from now. *Si took the book to examine for his program. We want to see about getting multiple copies of the map.*

▌Inga brought in copies of an Australian paperback text on grammar, *English essentials* by Mem Fox and Lyn Wilkinson (1993), that she was planning to use anyway with cooperative groups. It's a good grammar resource (down-to-earth, clear) and the examples are funny—and Australian. Inga tried a brainstorming activity with us that she will use: "What can you learn about Australia from this example?" (In the

FIGURE 12–10   Continued

text, it teaches about pronouns.) *Who would think that Tran, whose parents came from Vietnam in 1974, was a native-born Aussie? He doesn't look like the stereotypical …freckled ocker yob who hangs around pubs, sportsfields, and beaches. His accent, which is true-blue Aussie, surprises those who meet him for the first time. It still surprises his parents, for whom it's a mixed blessing since they hope he won't forget his cultural background. Tran himself now identifies with Australians as much as he does with the Vietnamese community, [where] he is a favourite because of his sense of humour, which is side-splitting* (Fox & Wilkinson, 1993, p. 60). We were stellar at brainstorming—we expect the students may be even better. (But we have questions too; Coe explained *yob*, which is backwards slang—boy = yob—and means a tough young man, but we need to find out what *ocker* means.)

▮ Sasha and Yoli brought in these articles and gave us brief summaries: "Students as cartographers," Beaupré, 1992; "Creating cross-cultural understanding through internationally cooperative story writing," Cushner, 1992; "Designing curriculum materials for multicultural education: Lessons from an Australian development project," Kennedy & McDonald, 1986; "Global perspectives through children's games," Nickell & Kennedy, 1987; "Studying Australia—Beyond the textbook approach," Tomlinson, 1988. They also checked a dictionary of quotations and came up with this one about Australia: *"Earth is here so kind, that just tickle her with a hoe and she laughs with a harvest"*—from an essay by Douglas Jerrold, titled "A Land of Plenty," listed in *The Penguin Dictionary of Quotations,* (Cohen & Cohen, 1976, p. 205). Again, we can use this for brainstorming—what does it tell us about Australia? *Si claims it for science because he plans a two-pronged focus: ecology and climate/ land features. Inga wants it too, as a metaphor and as an example of why collections of quotations are useful and interesting, so Si will tell her when he's planning to use it.*

Decision: As we find and share ideas and materials, we can "claim" them for our own teaching, and ideally, because we are collaborating on a theme, more than one of us will claim them. Then those teachers will do a kind of mini-teaming, so they use the material/idea/

strategy at the same time. This will move students away from thinking, for example, that science and English have nothing to do with one another—minimally, by showing that we know what's going on in each other's classrooms—and getting away from subject matter separation is a major purpose for using a theme.

Ideas from the articles:

▮ An article by Carl Tomlinson lists similarities and differences between Australia and the United States—in the land, cities, economy, climate, people, language, history, and schools. He gives a bibliography of Australian children's books and lists some concepts and generalizations: "Geography, climate, natural resources influence the lives of a country's inhabitants. The culture of a nation is formed in part by its people, their origins, languages, and customs. The cultures of Australia and the United States are similar in many ways. This accounts, in part, for our friendly relationship" (Tomlinson, 1988, p. 33). *This will be useful for us in many ways; Mi-Ja made copies for everyone.*

▮ "Kotaut Mina Mieta" is a game adapted from Australian aborigine culture. Equipment: tetherball (detached from pole) and playground balls. Students form two parallel lines about ten yards apart; one player pulls the tetherball between the two lines; students attempt to hit the tetherball with balls (points may be deducted if the puller is hit); balls may be retrieved and thrown again, but from behind the line. Puller starts slow and on each pass speeds up. The game mimics hunting skills. Students can consider what sort of hunting is imitated and also whether the hunter is dominant over nature, or nature is dominant over the hunter (Nickell & Kennedy, 1987). *Coe and Sasha claim this; Si wants to consider it also. Dave sees a possibility of math activities: statistics on number of hits at different speeds. Coe notes that it's a game where students who are in wheelchairs aren't at a disadvantage—and with motorized wheelchairs they can be the runners too.*

▮ "Partnership stories" are stories begun by students in one place and finished by students who live at a distance. The first group can write the whole story and send half to the other group for completion, then the two endings can be compared or they can

FIGURE 12–10   Continued

write only half. Then brainstorming can occur about what the two parts of the stories tell us about ourselves and the other group (Cushner, 1992). *Inga likes the idea; Sasha wants to get in on the brainstorming. Artie would like to collaborate on production and illustration. Yoli wants to consider a spin-off (unrelated to the theme, but another use of the strategy) where the story written by one group is written in English and finished elsewhere in Spanish, and vice versa. Dave will consider whether the idea could be adapted to fit with any of the problem-creating his students do in math.*

▪ Australian teachers developed a unit called "An Indian Ocean People," which "sought to portray the family life styles of ethnic groups whose country of origin was in the Indian Ocean region but who were now resident in Western Australia." The curriculum materials were descriptions of real families. "The problem of stereotyping ethnic groups was avoided by using real families rather than abstract 'average' families." The unit was developed in response to immigration to Australia from nations in the Indian ocean region— Burmese, Indians, Christmas Islanders, Timorese, and Mauritians—and it also took into account other groups that have emigrated to Australia from Pakistan, Sri Lanka, Malaysia, and Singapore" (Kennedy & McDonald, 1986, p. 317). *Creating materials like this would be beyond us, but Mi-Ja will inquire to see whether copies of the materials could still be obtained. We agree that immigration is one of the important facets of our theme. One important question is what makes Australia and the United States places where people from other countries want to go? What is it about conditions elsewhere that make people want/need to leave the countries where they were born?*

▪ Students in grades 8–12 began a themed unit by making a wall map after a lesson on cartography. The project was originally planned for two days (this was a summer school program so they were full days) but it took two weeks, linked with other activities, and it was an effective cooperative project (Beaupré, 1992). *We agree this is a good idea. Dave claims it for math; Artie wants to be involved and we might be able to schedule some double periods for math and art classes. A large wall map of Australia could be drawn and then copies could be made so that maps could be in all our team classrooms, elaborated for dif-*

ferent purposes (political, geographical, climatological, historic).

Wind-up: At this point, we decided to move quickly and delay some of the things we had planned to do till next time—especially the book display/discussion. Dave lent Si the two books by Jeannie Baker he had brought in: *Window* and *The story of rosy dock* as possibilities for the study of ecology. We did a round of comments from everyone and wound up with Si reading aloud from *The fatal shore.* Sasha borrowed his copy and Mi-Ja will see about getting several more copies for us through an inter-library loan. The rest of us did not know the relationship between the American Revolution and English settlement of Australia. England is a small country, which in the eighteenth century had severe penalties for many crimes. It did not have enough room for its convicts and had been sending them to the American colonies. When the American colonists rebelled against England, a new place to send convicted criminals was necessary, and after debate, Australia, about which the English knew little, was decided upon. (Lots to think about there, and it relates to current concerns about how to house a large prison population.)

Comments:

Yoli: I'm not going to force connections between the theme and Spanish language classes, but I do want to plan a project in which students create simulated travel brochures, in Spanish, about places in Australia for tourists who are Spanish-speaking.

Coral: I haven't contributed much but I'd like to come back next time with some folk songs about Australia. Right now all I could do for you is hum some of "Waltzing Matilda."

Artie: There are a lot of possibilities for links with art; Mi-Ja, can you help me find some resources about Australian art? *Mi-Ja:* Yes, and some of the picture books we'll share next time will be useful there. Make a list of suggestions about materials, and I'll get to work. And I'd can link with Yoli when she works on the travel brochure project.

Inga: I see a lot of links for my classes—many ideas

FIGURE 12–10 Continued

already and more will come. I've remembered that the happy ending for a lot of the characters in Dickens' novel *David Copperfield* is to emigrate to Australia after they've been unsuccessful or miserable in England. When Sasha is talking about the European settlement of Australia, I can do a talk-through and read-aloud of that excerpt.

Dave: I think it would be a good idea for Sasha and Si to coordinate the theme with most of the important ideas linked to social studies and science, and the rest of us linking through the activities we use. *Sasha:* I think that would work well. *Si:* Agreed.

Inga: Good idea, but I want English classes to be very involved in this. There's some wonderful writing—educational articles as well as children's books—coming out of Australia. I'm thinking about a "big idea" related to language—I'll work on it and bring it in next time. And I'd be pleased to run the pen pals project through English classes, especially if I can get some help on this from Coe. The Partnership Story idea can be part of the pen pals project after that gets started. *Coe:* I'll write to my cousins and see about getting some copies of Australian newspapers too.

Assignments for next time:
Mi-Ja will do a read-aloud from a book of Australian folktales. Coral will bring in folk music tapes. We'll have a book display/discussion. The main activity will be considering the important ideas we want to stress and deciding when/how to involve the students in our planning.

Excerpt from the read-aloud—imagining what it was like for the original inhabitants of what is now Australia to see the first convict ships arrive: *Take away this territory and they were deprived, not of "property," but of their embodied history... their "dreaming." ...[condemned] to spiritual death—a destruction of their past, their future. ...[N]one of them could have imagined this, as they had never before been invaded. And so they must have stood in curiosity and apprehension but without real fear, watching from the headlands as the enormous canoes with their sails like stained clouds moved up the harbor to Sydney Cove, and the anchors splashed, and the outcasts of Mother England were disgorged upon this ancestral territory to build their own prison.* (Hughes, 1986, p. 17)

Notes from Meeting 3
Present: Inga, Si, Sasha, Yoli, Dave, Artie, Coe, Coral, Mi-Ja
Read aloud: Mi-Ja read two selections from *Dreamtime: Aboriginal Stories:* "Stradbroke," about a beautiful island and its destruction by "civilization and man's greed," and "Oodgeroo," which is the author's own story of her return to her aboriginal heritage. We're impressed with this book as a read-aloud that we would all share. Our students can learn a lot from it, and we think they will be particularly interested in the author's stories about her own—largely unhappy—school experiences.

Coral played a tape of folk songs with an Australian theme, and we took time to browse through the book display set up by Mi-Ja, Inga, and Dave:

Koala Lou and *Possum magic*, Mem Fox, 1989b, 1990
Fairy tales for young Australians, Wade, 1992 (including "The Three Koalas," "Poss in Boots," and "The Three Kangaroos Gruff")
Window, Where the forest meets the sea and *The story of rosy dock*, Jeannie Baker, 1991, 1994, 1995
When the city stopped, Joan Phipson, 1978
Fire in the stone, Colin Thiele, 1974
The nargun and the stars, Patricia Wrightson, 1974
Books for teachers by Australian educators:
Read and retell, Brown and Cambourne, 1990 (ideas applicable to middle school)
Radical reflections: Passionate opinions on teaching, learning and living, Fox, 1993 (We will set up a schedule for borrowing this so each of us can read it.)
The writing process; One writing classroom, Hill, 1984 (A book about beginning writing, which our students might be interested in reading.)

Coe also brought in some Australian newspapers, which would be useful for compare/contrast analyses. We think newspapers might be the "artifacts" we could use as we begin the theme.

FIGURE 12–10 Continued

Decisions:

Inga is borrowing the books by Phipson, Thiele, and Wrightson; some have sequels; the Wrightson book is science fiction with an ecological message. When she's made choices, Mi-Ja will investigate the possibility of buying or borrowing multiple copies for literature circles. Library funds are available to purchase several copies of Mem Fox's children's books for trade book centers in classrooms. Dave will lend his copy of Jan Wade's book. Jeannie Baker's books will be used in science and art; Si and Mi-Ja will discuss needs/funds for multiple copies. We will also get copies of the animated films made from *Where the forest meets the sea* and *The story of rosy dock.*

We can use the music Coral brought in for *Themed Listening.* Students also can brainstorm about one of our ongoing activities: "What can you learn about Australia from this?" We think the kind of analytical and creative thinking that will be produced will develop students' higher-level thinking. Coral is interested in the possibility that students—perhaps as an optional project chosen because of their interest in music—could select instrumental music that suggests the different landforms of the Australian continent.

All of us on the team will read *The fatal shore*, and Sasha will use it for excerpted read-alouds (like the passage Si read last time we met). The book is written for adults, not transescents and adolescents, and much of the history that's recounted is horrifying, but valuable for us to understand in terms of Australian history.

Discussion: During the rest of the meeting we talked over the important ideas we want to teach through the theme. We don't know enough yet to put all of our major topics into statement form, and doing this will be a process we'll work on with our students as the theme progresses. At this point, these are our theme topics:

▮ Similarities/differences in the prehistory and history of the original inhabitants, the settlement of the countries by Europeans, the arrival of immigrants from many countries, and the resulting conflicts and problem solutions up to and including present times.
▮ Similarities/differences in geography, climate, resources, ecological problems.

▮ Similarities/differences in language, with attention to the rapid changes in a language resulting from our use of slang.
▮ Tourism between the two countries; monetary differences.

Plan: We'll meet again in three weeks; Si and Sasha will have mapped out a timeline, which we'll all add to. We'll discuss then how to involve the students in generating ideas during December. Mi-Ja will update us on search for resources; we may be able to view one of the Jeannie Baker films. The principal will join us at the end of that meeting.

Challenge to the Reader: Themed teaching in which a group of teachers collaborate is likely to provide students with a variety of what Howard Gardner calls *entry points* to learning. "My own belief," he writes, "is that any rich, nourishing topic—any concept worth teaching—can be approached in at least five different ways" (Gardner, 1991, p. 245). Using the ideas listed above, and adding your own if you wish, identify some features of the plan that would draw upon students' differing interests, talents, and intelligences to interest and then immerse them in learning.

Choose and Use: If you were to choose one facet of this theme-related planning to use in your own classroom, what would it be? How would your choice suit the factor of *self* or the factor of *situation*?

Planning As Problem-Solving

Education is full of problem situations. Teaching is improved when sensible attention is given to thinking about them in preparation for doing something about them. In terms of the four factors that relate to educational decision-making and planning—self, subject, students, situation—it is a mistake to think of any factor except the last as *a problem*. We may cause problems for ourselves or others, but we do not say "I am a problem." We may have difficulties getting information, collecting resources, or learning all we need to know about a subject we teach, but it is not sensible to say, for example, that "science is a problem." Some teachers, unfortunately, do talk carelessly about students. "Fern *is* a problem. Ilse *is* a problem. Xavier *is* a problem," but this kind of thinking and talking is harmful rather than helpful. It leads to the idea that the way to fix educational problems is by getting rid of Fern, Ilse, and Xavier. But recognizing that a particular *situation* is a problem or presents a problem can be the first step in doing something constructive.

It is useful to think of two categories of educational problem-solving. There are situations where something might go wrong or has gone wrong and need to be fixed. There also are situations that present a complex or difficult challenge, and although we may not speak of these situations as problems, planning to face the challenges is a form of problem-solving. Additionally, two ways to act when solving problems—proactively and reflectively—can be considered. We can plan ahead to fix or face a problem before it arises, or we can think afterward about what to do. (Spontaneous, on-the-spot problem-solving is the result of reflective planning, which is so rapid it can be acted upon instantly.)

Proactive problem-solving—anticipating possible problems and structuring situations so problems will not arise, or arranging to meet the challenges inherent in a situation—is part of good teaching. Often this kind of thinking tends to be rapid and cyclical: *We need to do this* or *that would be a good thing to do... but it might not work because... but we can prevent that problem by...*, and so forth. Figure 12–11 provides examples of this kind of rapid, proactive planning to avoid problems that

FIGURE 12–11   Cyclical Thinking for Proactive Problem-Solving

▌ **Mrs. Scott decides how to introduce a strategy in a school with mobile students.**

▌ **Dr. Strong thinks about scheduling meetings of a planning group, and arranging a student presentation for the Board of Education.**

▌ **Ms. Glenns finds ways to encourage high school students to use children's books for learning and pleasure.**

▌ **Ms. Spen and Mr. Garwin consider students' needs as they plan classroom arrangements for a guest speaker.**

Mrs. Scott thinks:

It would be a good thing: to try out the Class History Wall idea.

But it might not work: We'll just get started and there'll be an influx of students from migrant families.

Here's what I can do: We won't start the wall till all the students are here—I won't even talk about it till we're all together. The photographs I'll take of cooperative groups at work can become part of the first wall panel and will be a way for students to get to know one another; I'll save some other memorabilia from the first weeks too. Making the first big panel can be a cooperative group and whole class activity, and putting it together will be a great way for new students to get to know those who are already here.

Dr. Strong thinks:

We need: to have meetings of the Professional Development Committee.

But it might not work: The meetings might be burdensome, and if they're held during the school day they'll take too much time away from teaching.

Here's what we can do: Limit the meetings to four a year, with subcommittee meetings when it's convenient for subcommittee members. Have supper meetings, with the district furnishing the meal; that's a

FIGURE 12–11 Continued

nice benefit to show appreciation, and we can talk and work during the meal and afterwards. We'll need to meet twice in the fall; good times for the other meetings would be January and April.

But it might not work: Winter is really cold around here; nobody will want to come back for an evening meeting any time between December and March, even though we do need a meeting in that time.

Here's what we can do: The January meeting can be our one day-long meeting. The district can fund substitutes once, and we'll only be taking one day in the year away from teaching. And nobody will have to drive on icy roads at night.

It would be a good thing: to have a presentation for Board of Education members about student-led conferences.

But it might not work: Teachers who are trying the method can talk about it, but some of the board members won't believe what they're hearing, because this is a startling idea.

Here is what we can do: The presentation can be by students.

But it might not work: What students? We're piloting it across the range of grades, but seeing high school or middle school students conduct a conference won't convince anyone that elementary school students can do it. And little ones shouldn't be up late.

Here's what we can do: The meetings start at 7:30 and the reason the presentations are always first is partly to get the meetings off to a great start, but also so that students can take part in the presentations or come to observe them. Student-led conferences are working beautifully even in the kindergarten (but there's a risk that the adults would just focus on how "cute" kindergartners are). If the presenters are second graders, the Board will see the strategy works. Teacher and parents will be there with the children.

But it might not work: We can only have a few presenters (three?) and the children not selected may be disappointed.

Here's what we can do: The whole class can coach the presenters and help them prepare; the whole class and their parents can be invited to attend the first part of the Board meeting (we're always trying to get more members of the public there). We can use a photo display that will include everyone and which can go back to the classroom for a wall display.

Ms. Glenns thinks:

We need: to have a wide variety of reading material available for students because they need opportunities to read history and, at present it's very difficult for some students to read the textbook. I'll arrange to have lots of trade books (including books that depend heavily on illustrations) available for Themed Reading and as resources for finding information.

But it might not work: The students who aren't skilled readers are very sensitive. I'm afraid they won't even touch a book that looks like it's for children. (One good thing is that better-quality, recently published children's books don't have those awful labels on the back, like "For ages 3–6"—as if nobody older than six could enjoy them.)

Here's what I can do: I can think of three things to do. First, I'm going to read aloud and storytell from trade books and give some brainstorming assignments: "What can you learn about American history from this book?" I'll get enough copies of Walter Dean Myers' *Brown angels: An album of pictures and verse* for each cooperative group, and start with that. Because of the photographs, taken over time, it's wonderful for this purpose.

Second, I'm going to give a straightforward talk to my students about the value of children's books as resources for learning. Another benefit of the talk is that a lot of my students will be parents in a few years' time and they should be familiar with good books for children so they don't just buy cheap stuff from the supermarket checkout counter. It's pointless for me to try to get important information across subtly, when I can tell my students something I think they need to know.

Third, I'm going ask for 20 to 30 minutes of time in a teachers' meeting. I'll get together with other colleagues who know how valuable good trade books are; we'll collect books, and at the meeting we'll talk briefly about our reasons for using children's trade books. Then we'll spread out an array of gorgeous children's books and let teachers browse and share. If teachers are willing, I'll take a lot of photographs, and we'll make a bulletin board display—then students can see their teachers enjoying children's books.

Ms. Spen and Mr. Garwin think:

We need: to fit both our classes into the first-grade classroom for the guest speaker's visit. And displays… And refreshments…

But it might not work: Well, it won't work if we try to

FIGURE 12–11   Continued

pack everybody and everything in, especially since it's going to be a long session.

Here's what we can do: The Weather Mosaic will already be up in the hall. Everything displayed in the first-grade class, except the Big Book, will be posted on the walls, and we can clear everything else away to make room. Student greeters can take the guest to the fourth grade classroom, where we'll have a display of books and Weather Facts. This will make the guest's visit a little longer for fourth graders than for first graders, which is good. When the fourth graders, plus guest, come to the first-grade room, fourth graders will carry their chairs and sit beside their first-grade buddies.

Obviously, the refreshments don't come in until we're ready for them. The volunteers who'll provide and organize this know how to manage; they'll prepare refreshments in the kitchen, on carts, to wheel in when we're ready.

But there's more to consider: In both of our classrooms, there are students with physical disabilities and students who have difficulty managing themselves in unusual or crowded situations.

Here's what we can do: It's worked well in the past to ask students for planning ideas; we'll do it again. And here are some of the results:

▌ (First grade) Pete says, "I'd like Lee and André to team up with me. In a crowded place kids sometimes bump my wheelchair or trip over me, and they're good at helping keep a space around me without making people mad. We can be over by the windows."

▌ (Fourth grade) Nell says, "Can Nedra and her aide be at the side and near the front? A lot of us like to see the signing, and it helps us pick up more sign language ourselves."

▌ (First grade) Ms. Spen says, "I know you don't like to be crowded, Ellie, and I've got an idea to make sure you have some room when our guest is here. Why don't you and Dale welcome the fourth graders to our class. Then when everyone's here, you and a friend will be right by the door where it won't be too packed."

Challenge to the Reader: Trying new instructional strategies is easier if teachers anticipate possible problems and plan proactively to avoid them. Refer to the Strategy Glossary and text descriptions of strategies to choose a teaching idea that appeals to you but one that is unlike the methods you typically use or are observed being used. Follow the cyclical proactive problem-solving process, shown in the examples above. *It would be a good thing* to use that strategy. *But it might not work* because... Don't abandon the plan to use the strategy because of the potential problem. Do some proactive problem-solving to decide *here's what I can do* to make the strategy work for my students.

Choose and Use: If you were to choose the kind of planning done by one of these teachers to use in your own classroom, what would it be? How would your choice suit the factor of *situation* or the factor of *self*?

need to be fixed. Thoughtful planning about how to provide content instruction is one example of proactive problem-solving about challenges that need to be faced. An illustration is provided in Figure 12–12. Reflective problem-solving is thinking back about what has occurred in order to make changes in the future, based on what we have done, observed, studied, and learned. Both proactive and reflective problem-solving are components of *reflective teaching*, defined in Chapter Two as "the ability—and habit—of

capable teachers to think about their own teaching before they teach, while they are teaching, and after they have taught." The two remaining illustrations in this section illustrate reflective problem-solving: Figure 12–13 illustrates a teacher's thinking over time about how to fix one feature of a good program; Figure 12–14 is an example of a teacher's reflections about her teaching philosophy. These examples, as well as all of the other illustrations provided in this chapter, demonstrate aspects of reflective teaching.

FIGURE 12–12 Session-by-Session Plan Focused on Content

Mr. Criefton's planning includes a summary of what he intends his students to learn and a plan for coordinating lessons across several days.

Topic: The ocean floor

    Concept statement: Although the earth, like all of the planets in our solar system, is shaped roughly like a sphere, the surface of the earth is not smooth. The land surface of the earth has hills and plains and valleys, deep canyons and high mountain ranges, which we see when we travel over land or when we look down from an airplane. Oceans cover more than two-thirds of the earth's surface. If we travel on the ocean, all we see is the flat surface of the water, but the features of the earth beneath the ocean—on the *ocean floor*—are like those on land: hills and plains and valleys, mountain ranges called *ridges* and deep valleys called *trenches*. In some places, the mountains below the ocean are so high that they rise above sea level and form islands. Like the landforms on the land surface, the ocean floor has been shaped by the movement of tectonic plates, by volcanic eruptions, and by erosion. Over the years, oceanographers have produced increasingly detailed maps of the ocean floor.

Resources (besides text):
- The World: Physical Map (1994), National Geographic Society. (Six laminated copies are available, one for each cooperative group.)
- Living on the edge. (1995). National Geographic Society. (Displayed on the wall by the classroom research center.)
- *The oceans: A book of questions and answers*, by Don Groves (1989). (Available in the classroom research center.)
- *Our patchwork planet*, by Helen Roney Sattler and Giulio Maestro (1995). (This is an ongoing read-aloud, and several copies are available in the classroom research center.)
- news article 10/95: *Recently declassified military data has helped confirm the theory that giant plates are slowly moving the continents around the globe and shed light on other mysteries of the ocean floor. A new map that is 30 times more detailed than anything available before shows that giant ridges and deep valleys scar the earth at the bottom of the oceans, said scientists at the Scripps Institution of Oceanography in LaJolla,*

California. Also, previously unknown shoals and banks give promise of new fishing grounds while sediments may help geologists locate new oil and gas fields. Scientists were excited over the new information. "This is a day of celebration," Scripps researcher David T. Sandwell said Monday. "We're having a data feast." (Six copies, one for each cooperative group)

Note: T = Teacher
Session 1
- Materials needed: 1) profile map of a section of ocean floor, beginning with continental shelf, drawn on blackboard or bulletin board, 2) terminology cards backed with magnets (if blackboard is magnetic), or cards and tacks for bulletin board. Cards needed: *shoreline, continental shelf, continental slope, continental rise, continental margin, ocean basin abyssal plain, trench, ridge, rift valley, seamount, guyot, island*, 3) List of terms (one per student), and 4) Adapted RESPONSE forms for each cooperative group with question substituted for "Important points" section:
    How are the surface of the land and the surface of the ocean floor alike?
    Your questions: (Star those for which you need answers.)
    New terms: (Star those you need to have explained.)

- Lesson opens with Teacher Read-Aloud Commentary from text section on the topography of the ocean floor. As TRAC progresses, T arranges terms on profile map to create a visual map of the ocean floor (display will be used for several sessions).
    TRAC is followed by question-generating session, in which T asks for and listens to students' ideas, comments, or questions. (*No* hand-raising). T then raises the question: How are the surfaces of the land and ocean floor alike?
- Student assignment: Cooperative groups read textbook, making notes as they find information that contributes to answering the question. Text reading and RESPONSE will carry over to next session.
- While students work: T circulates among groups, giving help and guidance as needed, commending work. T takes note of one or two points to comment on at the end of the lesson.

FIGURE 12–12   Continued

■ Assignment for those who finish early: not needed
■ Lesson ends with T commenting on students' ideas or responding to one or two students' questions. T collects RESPONSE forms to look over before next session.
■ Homework assignment: Check terminology list; attempt to write definitions.
■ Preparation for next session: Make sure materials are available for cooperative group use.

Session 2
■ Materials needed: laminated maps; copies of news article. Ocean floor display remains up, but terminology cards are taken down.
■ Lesson opens with: continuation of text reading/RESPONSE form (15 minutes).
■ T calls time, distributes maps, and copy of news article. Students write questions for which answers can be learned or inferred from map or reading materials (and also write answers for their own questions). Materials from research center may be used for clarification and confirmation.

   During this time, one group has the opportunity to place terminology cards on the outline map; if the placement is not accurate, T corrects, shows students. Time permitting, other groups have the same opportunity. (If any placements are not accurate, students in that group collaborate in preparing a clear definition of the terms that were not correctly placed and suggest a way of remembering them.)
■ Assignment for those who finish early: not needed
■ Lesson ends with: T inviting groups to pose questions for one another to answer.
■ Preparation for next session: T checks students questions, chooses six (several similar questions may be combined) that relate to intended learning, and prepares a page of questions on the computer, then prints out copies for each cooperative group.

Session 3
■ Materials needed: Question pages and T-prepared plan for assessment. This is the plan: In group, compose answer to one of six questions. Individually, students 1) label an outline map of ocean floor; and 2) write two Concept Connections passages about similarities between the land surface and ocean floor.

Students will choose their own terms for Concept Connections.
■ Lesson opens with: T explains assessment, planned for session 4.
■ Student assignment: Student groups work on making notes for answers to questions, reviewing for assessment session.

   The rest of the groups have the opportunity, in turn, to place terminology cards on the outline map.
■ While students work: T circulates, giving information on request (SAY-IT), or seeing that questions are answered capably by other students.
■ Assignment for those who finish early: not needed
■ Lesson ends with: Student opportunity to ask T questions about *content* (*not* about process, e.g., what will quiz be like). T answers/explains.
■ Homework assignment: preparation for assessment. (Within cooperative groups, it is customary for students to confer by phone in the evening; Mr. Criefton encourages this.)
■ Preparation for next session: Take down ocean floor display.

Session 4
■ Materials needed: T has prepared copies of unlabeled profile map of ocean floor—the map is not identical to the one that has been displayed (shoreline reversed, different placement of ridges, plains, guyots, etc.).
■ Lesson opens with Terminology Trade (15 minutes)
■ Student assignment: Assessment, beginning with 10 minutes for groups to make notes that answer the teacher-selected question, followed by individual tasks.
■ Lesson ends with end of class.
■ Preparation for next session: T checks assessment; plans how to confirm students' understandings and how to reteach concepts as needed.

Session 5
■ Materials needed: students' papers, with comments
■ Lesson opens (if all has gone as expected) with T commendations to whole class on assessment results and confirmation/reteaching.
■ Whole class activity: Discussion, focused on how features of the ocean floor provide resources and need ecological protection.

FIGURE 12–12 Continued

▌Lesson ends with: Five minutes during which T returns papers; students can review them and, if they wish, share. If there is a student who has not done well, T decides how best to prevent discouragement and to promote success the next time.

Challenge to the Reader: Dolores Durkin (1990, p. 476) opposes a teaching style that she calls *mentioning:* "saying just enough about a topic to allow for doing an exercise related to it." Howard Gardner (1993a) is highly critical of a teaching practice in which students read an assignment and then are tested with questions that can be answered by repeating what they have read. When teachers and students tacitly agree that this is proof that students have learned well and teachers have taught well, they have settled for what Gardner calls *the correct answer compromise.* Brainstorm a list of ways that Mr. Criefton's teaching goes beyond mentioning and the assessment for his students does *not* represent a correct answer compromise.

Choose and Use: If you were to choose one facet of Mr. Criefton's planning to use in your own classroom, what would it be? How would your choice suit the factor of *students* or the factor of *subject*?

Planning how best to provide instruction is a problem—a challenge—that teachers face. It would be extraordinarily stressful, of course, to pursue a career in which each new day of teaching loomed as a complex problem—what will I teach, what will I do, how will I manage? Fortunately, many such questions are already answered. A curriculum is in place; educational materials are available; school-wide routines that give structure to the school day are established. Within this framework, however, there are teachers who take no further responsibility for planning. Trite teaching strategies fill the time; decision-making is surrendered to the textbook and teacher's manual. There are also, though more rarely, teachers who overplan down to each detail of what they will "have the students" do, then rely on some form of behavior control to manage a classroom in which there is no place for student spontaneity or teacher improvisation. Between these two extremes, styles of teacher planning are diverse and wide-ranging, and most teachers change their planning methods and styles over time. A significant change is often an attitudinal one—a change from planning that is primarily worrying, to planning as an enjoyable form of mental gymnastics. Time spent in planning, as well as time spent in classroom teaching, can be exhilarating. Two features of effective lesson planning are having a clear understanding of what we intend to teach, and planning a series of interrelated learning sessions (rather than treating each day in isolation). Some teachers accomplish this kind of planning with little or no writing; others write plans in some detail. Figure 12–2 is an example of a detailed written plan, combining the Session-by-Session plan format with a concept statement.

Figures 12–13 and 12–14, presented sequentially, illustrate some of the many ways in which good teachers seek to make their teaching better. In the first instance, a teacher striving toward one of her instructional goals is able to reach many of her students, but she is unwilling to consider her teaching successful if some students remain unreached; therefore, she considers ways to draw in everyone. In the second example, a teacher takes time to consider her teaching philosophy, to ensure that her teaching will promote the educational principles in which she believes.

FIGURE 12–13   Reflective Thinking to Solve a Problem

Ms. Glenns considers the problem of writing reluctance

Gloria Glenns describes a significant aspect of her teaching with the brief but impressive claim, "Everyone writes!" Is it true? *Well, almost...* It is surely not the case that all of her students write well or willingly from the moment they enter her classroom door. Occasionally, though rarely, a student will refuse to write at all; some other students write, but briefly. Ms. Glenns herself loves to write (much of the time), but she can understand some of the feelings of her students who hate and resist writing, because she knows how hard it can be to get started, how easy it is to lose the threads of her ideas, and how painful deadlines can be. Her interest in writing, however, helps her approach her work with knowledge and energy. Her knowledge comes not only from her own experience but from books, journal articles, and conference presentations about writing. Her energy is high because using writing in her teaching is her choice, not a burden imposed upon her. Because writing and thinking are so closely linked for her, she enjoys keeping a reflective journal in which she usually makes entries twice a week, in the evenings. Several years ago, she began to reflect on the theme of how to make "Everybody writes" a reality. Some journal excerpts follow:

The semester's nearly over; I really am doing pretty well with the writing. A lot of students aren't willing writers when they first come into my classes. (Why is it so easy—apparently—to squash students' confidence and enthusiasm?) But it works to use a collection of strategies that aren't tough to understand (and cooperative groups are wonderful because the students answer each other's questions about directions and help each other get started). The posters with directions are a good idea—bless Callie's heart for making them. I don't hear "What does she want?"—which *I hate*—any more.

But pretty well isn't where I want to be. There's a lot less of "I can't" than there used to be, but there are still students leaning in that direction. And each semester, so far, I've had a few real resisters. They say, "This is boring" but I believe they're saying, "I can't. I won't"—and I don't think getting into a contest of wills helps them or me.

Mac and several other students switched over from reluctance to real eagerness when they used computers. So many students hate (despise, dislike intensely, abhor, have an aversion to) writing because they define writing as picking up a pen and moving it around on paper. Word processing, editing, spellchecking, and printing out—that's a joy.

I believe I'm doing the right thing when I don't allot equal time for computer use. Students all have computer lab, so they have equal time there. (I do stress the importance of being computer-literate, and I keep an eye out for gender differences—girls thinking computers are not for them. Fortunately, I see a lot less of that now than I saw when I was in school.) In my class, there's one computer for each cooperative group—I'm working on getting more—and the students themselves are good at recognizing that Mac, for example, *writes* when he's at the computer and is still so troubled by his handwriting that pencil and paper writing is hard. Now it's better, because when he can't use the computer he jots notes. The notes are fine for Learning Log entries and I allow them for a Write-Out. He used computer lab time to translate notes into a well-written SAIL paper. Mac's problems with writing are conquerable because he is a reader, he has something to say, and he can organize his ideas.

New semester. Will, in fifth-period history, won't write at all. The learning log is blank. That's clever, on his part, because whatever his problem is, he can keep it a secret from me and the other students. If he's not writing because he can't read, the strategies I use—reading aloud, storytelling, ETR, and students talking together about what we're learning—will help him; the information he needs to learn won't be locked away in a textbook. I need to check his school records to see if there's information there.

FIGURE 12–13 Continued

Will's records are sparse, partly because he's moved a lot —"discipline" problems beginning in middle school, poor but passing grades. I've talked with the guidance counselor and Booker, who's the new reading specialist. What a joy it is that they both are so knowledgeable and caring. Booker's going to block out time to come to my fifth-period class several days a week for a while. He says it will be useful for him to get a sense of the reading/writing demands in an American history course, and he's interested in some of the strategies I use. He'll sit in on all of the cooperative groups and observe and participate.

I have an idea about the Learning Log—sort of an environmental print idea—a little time-consuming but I'm only going to try it with the fifth-period class (unless it works like a charm). I'm going to clip cartoons and current events headlines that have some relation to what we're studying—the past does repeat itself—and tape them into some of the logs (Will's, of course, but a sprinkling of other people's too), so when they open the log to write, there will already be something there for them to see and react to.

post script: Things are better. Will wrote a line or two and also wrote me a memo. Booker has a wonderful way with students, and he's going to work with Will. Reading is the problem—or at least part of it—but we've got ways to work on that. For one thing, I'm building a big collection of trade books about history, and most of them are so beautiful that everyone wants to look at and read them. When students who always get high grades are clearly interested, then it's no shame for others to be looking at "easy" books.

Nona and Nietta are pretty much in the "I won't" category when it comes to writing—so far, anyway. Learning log entries and Write-Outs are sparse and what they write doesn't interest them or me. No memos to me, which is not surprising; they're both taciturn—so far. (They both smile sometimes though, a delight to see.) Confer and Write is working for Nietta; she will write what her group has talked about and members are writing really helpful comments *about ideas*—not

technical corrections. She's writing enough now so I can plan some mini-lessons around what she needs to know.

Concept Connections—yes! Of course, there's a wide range of writing, but everybody, even the hitherto "I won't" people, produced interesting sentences, paragraphs, and even what are really drafts of short essays when I used it for the first time as a test. (Fortunately, I never, never mark "on the curve" or a few people would drive down everybody else's grade because what they turned out is so spectacular.) I think the Concept Connections format puts students on the road to success because the act of arranging the terms gives them the ideas they're going to write about.

Why didn't I think of this sooner? *I* read a lot about writing and I enjoy it and learn from it. Some wonderful pieces are aimed at elementary teachers (good! get off to the right start, and my high school students won't be coming in carrying a load of reasons why they hate writing), but a lot of the ideas are applicable to me as a writer so they cross the age barrier and I'm going to share them. I'm going to start off by reading Shelley Harwayne's article, "Chutzpah and the nonfiction writer." It will start us off on the road to using SAIL, which I'm going to begin in three weeks.

They've liked it. I read the whole thing—half on Monday, half on Tuesday—very quickly. Incidental benefits: Reed went to the library and borrowed the collected works of Ring Lardner and has been sharing witticisms that he likes; one cooperative group got started talking about favorite books by Jane Yolen—what a versatile writer she is. (Idea: wouldn't it be a good idea to do research reports about writers in American history?) Two big messages from Harwayne's article, which a lot of students took hold of when we did a Write Out, were that it's good to take a "wanna make something out of it" attitude toward the facts, and also that she winds up telling teachers what *they* ought to do about *their*

FIGURE 12–13   Continued

writing. And the opening section was a winner, especially since it let all of my students feel sophisticated, because they know about fiction and non-fiction.

> …a kindergarten teacher …approached one of the five-year-olds in her class and asked, "What are you writing?"
>
> "I'm writing about infection."
>
> "Oh really," [the teacher] responded, highly impressed. "You mean germs and viruses?"
>
> "No, infection. You know—real stuff, true stuff. Like this book about ghosts—that's fection. But this book about different kinds of houses—that's infection." (Harwayne, 1993, p. 19)

I'm putting together a collection of articles about writing to share with cooperative groups. They won't be required to read from it, but I think with the occasional mini-lesson and read-alouds I'm doing, they'll be interested. One item I'm including is Katharine Auld Breece's 1988 article about Write-Out; it's good for students to know that ideas come from somewhere (usually ideas that are written). I'm including Don Graves' paperback book on *Investigate nonfiction* (1989b) and marking the section on Learning Journals (pp. 48–49). An added bonus for my students is that these articles and books—written for teachers—are much easier to read than their textbooks and the typeface is larger. I hadn't thought about that before, but it's interesting to consider.

I'm still working on overcoming writing reluctance. Taping in clipped items from newspapers works well; I'm also going to try drawing. It's not one of my talents, but when I do the first round of comments, I'm going to use a lot of labeled drawings and I'll talk about drawing as an alternative or supplement to writing.

One wonderful surprise, and some other good reactions to my drawings (including "I'm going to draw for you—I can do it better"). Drew created three detailed pictures about events leading up to America's entry into WWII in the time spent on a Write-Out. I've copied them (with his permission) and we'll use them as the basis for a Confer and Write.

More to be pleased about. "Guest lecturers"—including reluctant-but-eventually-they-got-going writers who are now high school graduates. Being able to do this is an advantage of teaching in the same high school for six years. So far, I've arranged for visitors to come back to all of the classes—history and economics—to talk for a little while about "yes, I need to write now that I'm a graduate" and then join the class for the rest of the period. The fourth-period guests stayed and had lunch with a group of students, including Nona.

Summarizing: here are some ideas that have worked to reduce writing reluctance (in addition to my main writing plan, and affection and praise):

▌ Computers are wonderful.

▌ Strategies that encourage thinking and talking together before writing—such as Concept Connections and Write-Out—work well.

▌ Many students respond when I put something—a cartoon, headline, short news article—into their Learning Logs ahead of time (rather than commenting afterwards).

▌ Sharing professional articles with students is a good idea.

▌ Some students will draw without reluctance when they won't write, and I need to do more with this and begin earlier in the semester. What about linking drawing with labeling? Maybe by having groups work together to add labels to illustrations from text, newspapers, or drawings by other students.

▌ Talking with recent graduates has a wealth of advantages.

▌ When students won't write or write very little there are many possible reasons. Colleagues are good resources for me, but patience and attention are my best allies. I can always teach my subject so students can become interested and reasonably well-informed.

Challenge to the Reader: Negative feelings can interfere with learning. This important educational concept is illustrated by the metaphor of an *affective filter*—a barrier of

FIGURE 12–13   Continued

emotions that can be raised or lowered. Students in a learning environment that is safe and comfortable for them are not distracted by tensions, but when students are fearful or angry an emotional barrier is raised which may keep them from learning. Many teachers who have not heard of the affective filter theory nevertheless act in accordance with it by trying to minimize situations that produce tension and anxiety. Analyze Ms. Glenns' actions to identify those that contribute to a learning environment in which instruction is not filtered through a barrier of negative emotions.

Choose and Use: If you were to choose one facet of Ms. Glenns' planning to use in your own classroom, what would it be? How would your choice suit the factor of *students* or the factor of *self,* or both?

FIGURE 12–14   Reflective Thinking To Face a Challenge

Miss Ditmers considers the importance of "a level playing field"

As is true for all teachers, Miss Ditmers' students are diverse. Many aspects of this diversity are a delight. She enjoys her students' wit and humor; she loves to see the aha! of new insights; she values the ways students find to help and care for each other; she knows from experience that each student, given opportunities, has ways to sparkle. She thinks middle school students are the most vivid, exciting, annoying, lively, ingenious, and challenging age group to teach, and she wouldn't trade with anyone. But she is grateful for the fact that teachers are diverse too, especially when she hears other teachers claim that *their* students are most rewarding to teach—a claim she has heard from teachers of pre-kindergartners through high school and from teachers who work with students of every variety of special need, including those who are incarcerated. Some differences among her students make her thoughtful. For some of her students, school is a place where they are successful and home is a place where they are secure. The future is full of opportunity, and Miss Ditmers knows that, apart from unpredictable misfortunes, these students will have productive careers and that future teachers will enjoy teaching their children. For other students, the past and present seem to predict a difficult future. Miss Ditmers knows she cannot change

the past, so she will not waste time deciding where to place blame. She is not so foolish as to think that she is the only influence on her students' present lives. Moreover, she knows her own actions are not always wise; she can look back on some of her past teaching that may have harmed students rather than helped them, and she knows she will make mistakes in the future. But she has resolved that throughout her teaching career she will do what she can do to help her students. She will never become hopeless about a student. She will always work to make her classroom a place where students experience genuine success and joy in learning.

As Miss Ditmers thought about her teaching philosophy, she has found a metaphor that appeals to her. She is not an avid sports fan, although she often attends athletic events when her students are team members, but in recent years she has devoted considerable thought to the idea of a level playing field as an educational goal. In her view, a level playing field is not a highly competitive area, a place for playing "zero sum games" where one person's gain is another person's loss. Instead, it is a place for the active, enjoyable exercise of skills and development of talents. Also, it is not a place where *people* are all the same; it is not produced by insisting that all of the people on the field must somehow be forced to be alike. Instead it is a place with level ground. Rather than an exercise field that is smooth and well-tended for

FIGURE 12–14   Continued

some people and rocky and dangerous for others, the ideal playing field provides a solid, safe foundation for everyone to use. All of her planning and teaching has the aim of making school, for her students, a place where they are successful and secure. A major source of inspiration is her students themselves; other encouragement and inspiration comes from colleagues and from her readings in the professional literature.

Miss Ditmers knows that particularly for students who come to her without expecting school to be interesting and worthwhile, what she teaches needs to be related to their interests and lives. She keeps in mind Alfie Kohn's caution (1993, p. 219), "When things are taught in isolation, they are harder to understand and harder to care about. Thus, our question is not merely, 'What's the task?' but 'How does the task connect to the world that the students actually inhabit?'" She is impressed with Lilian Katz's idea (1988, p. 16) that what students do and learn in school must have horizontal as well as vertical validity for them. The vertical dimension of education prepares students for the future; the horizontal dimension is important *now*—"that is, it should teach them something that will be useful, perhaps, on the way home or in some familiar aspect of community life." Two of her favorite quotations are clipped inside her planbook, as a reminder that school, like a fortunate family setting, can be a caring place, a place where students come to see the riches of learning:

> Just as books pervade and permeate some homes… so are some classrooms book-based and others not.

[T]his emphasis invariably and inevitably depends on the personality and taste of individual teachers. …The richest classroom may well be the poorest, in material terms. Schools are like households; it's the quality of the people rather than the furnishings which makes the difference from the child's point of view. Give me teachers of strong and loving heart, good humor, and imagination every time. These teachers will have faith in books and in their capacity to enrich [their students'] lives. (Butler, 1982, p. 312)

As teachers, we must become more like parents who are engaged in the task of raising a huge heterogeneous family. (Noddings, 1992, p. 177)

Challenge to the Reader: The educational principle that underlies the idea of *Matthew effects*, a concept discussed in Chapter Six, is that students who would otherwise fail can succeed with thoughtful, effective, caring teacher intervention. What do you see as being of value for teachers of making a strong effort to intervene to help their students?

Choose and Use: If you were to adopt one of the ideas which is important to Miss Ditmers as a principle to guide your own teaching, what would it be?

Planning For Professional Growth

Teachers, like students, need to grow and learn. The resources available to everyone for ongoing learning—colleagues, reading and viewing, travel—are even richer for teachers, who can have the benefits of professional literature and professional meetings. Figures 12–15 and 12–16 provide examples of

how continuing learning can be planned and structured. The scenarios presented in Figure 12–16 are based on real events, annual meetings of two professional organizations in which educators from around the country and world came together, as they do each year, to share ideas and to enjoy learning more about their chosen profession.

FIGURE 12–15 Planning To Learn More About the Topics We Teach

With other teachers, Dr. Strong develops the "target a topic" approach

Often during her career, Dr. Strong has served on district-wide committees focusing on in-service education for teachers. When she became curriculum coordinator for her district, she established a Professional Development Council (PDC) to arrange and coordinate staff development opportunities. The Council is co-sponsored by the Teachers' Association and the superintendent of schools, who specified when the Council was established that a major goal would be to help new teachers at the elementary school level develop subject matter expertise, particularly in science and math, so students did not have teachers who themselves disliked or feared subjects that were their responsibility to teach. In its first year, the committee arranged meetings, all of which were optional and open, at which experienced faculty members spoke briefly, shared professional materials, and answered questions. The committee also prepared a set of suggestions for ongoing learning, called "Target a Topic."

* * * * * * * * * * * * * * * * *

TARGET A TOPIC

The decision to target topics for personal study enables teachers to move beyond dependence on a textbook as their sole instructional resource. Our knowledge base becomes stronger and more sound. Moreover, by becoming learners ourselves we can appreciate some of the difficulties students have in understanding these topics. There are seven steps in the Target a Topic approach, all of which can be followed individually or with colleagues.

▪ Begin by listing the major topics that are part of the content area curricula in the courses or subjects you teach. (These usually appear in the form of units in textbooks or curriculum guides.) Elementary teachers list topics in each of the three major content areas—math, science, social studies. Middle school and high school teachers list the curriculum topics in the courses they teach. Then choose one, two, or—as a maximum—three topics as a focus for personal learning, over a period of a year.

▪ Keep the targeted topic(s) in mind when reading magazines, deciding which TV specials to watch, visiting bookstores and libraries. When traveling, look for museums, art galleries, nature preserves, and sites of historical and cultural interest.

▪ Raise questions about aspects of your topic that you don't know, or don't understand. In a style that suits you, keep notes and list your sources of information. As your knowledge grows, the number of questions you have also will grow. Talk with knowledgeable people—they usually will enjoy answering your questions.

▪ Read widely. Reading material may be self-selected or suggested by knowledgeable colleagues. Professional journals also can be useful resources. Besides reading expository text about chosen topics, read widely in other genres—fiction, biographies, and essays—related to your topic of study. Look for primary sources such as speeches, newspaper columns and editorials, diaries, and other documents from earlier time periods.

▪ Start a wish list of books you'd like to own or periodicals to which you'd like to subscribe. When birthdays and holidays come round, suggest items from your list as gifts you'd like to receive. Give yourself a birthday gift from your own wish list.

▪ Collect materials that will be useful for teaching. (Be sure to label them so you will always know their source.) Use an accordion file or other organizational system to store them efficiently.

▪ Next year, choose another set of topics for a personal learning focus. Since the world's store of knowledge continues to expand, this process of knowledge-building can be a continuous cycle; by the time many curriculum topics have been studied in-depth, it will be reasonable to begin studying them again.

The program has proven to be helpful. The meetings with experts continue, and Target a Topic suggestions are included in materials distributed to teachers. There have been two important spin-offs. First, several groups of new and experienced teachers formed across the three school levels—elementary, middle, and high school—because of mutual interest in a subject matter field. Usually these teachers meet after school or for an evening about once a month, and they are in contact more often informally to answer each other's questions about content and teaching strategies and sometimes

FIGURE 12–15   Continued

about students who have particular needs and strengths as students progress through the grades. Increasingly, members of these groups have made it a practice to attend local, state, or national professional conferences together. Second, both new and experienced teachers with common responsibilities and interests have paired or grouped to follow the Target a Topic style of learning together. Enthusiasm for this mutual learning has spread.

Challenge to the Reader: Elliot Eisner (1993), who was quoted at the beginning of this chapter,

wrote about the importance of structuring teaching so "the lives of those who teach and learn are themselves enhanced." Good teachers are learners as well as teachers. Think of a teacher you admire and list the ways in which that person is both learner and teacher.

Choose and Use: If you were to choose one facet of this kind of planning as part of a professional development plan, what would it be? How would your choice suit the factor of *self* or the factor of *subject*, or both?

FIGURE 12–16   Planning For Professional Development

Ms. Spen and Mr. Lusolo plan to attend professional conferences

In 1995, Ms. Spen attended the 40th annual convention of the International Reading Association (IRA) in Anaheim, California. Her district allows teachers five days to attend district-approved professional conferences and meetings and provides a small amount of funding. She and her family left after school on Friday, April 28, and returned home late on Sunday, May 7. For Mr. Spen and the children, the time was wholly a vacation; Ms. Spen swam and went sightseeing the Saturday before the convention, spent lunchtimes and evenings with her family, and enjoyed a mini-vacation beginning Friday at noon. She is an enthusiastic and experienced conference-goer and is happy to describe her preparations and planning.

Because she is an IRA member, she receives a preliminary program many months before the convention—nearly 200 pages of information about the planned events. She studies it immediately and consults with her husband because she knows the importance of preregistering and making housing reservations early. Preregistering means that when she arrives she goes right to the long tables where convention packets and badges for people who have preregistered are ready, in alphabetized sections (A-C, D-F, etc.). She has saved money—on-site registration is double the

cost for preregistration—and she saves time standing in line. Also, some of the sessions she wants to attend have limited enrollment; if she delays, they may be filled. Housing is important too; the preliminary program lists hotels—sixteen of them—with their prices. She and her husband choose the hotel they prefer immediately and mail the housing form, knowing that waiting is likely to mean that a first-choice hotel will be filled. As an IRA member, registration costs her $100, and she adds $40 for an all-day institute on Sunday and $25 for the Book and Author luncheon. Then she checks the program, which is arranged by day and time periods, to make her choices—from a rich array of possibilities—about what to attend:

Sunday: all-day institute. Out of twenty-two possibilities, she chooses "The arts and literacy." It's limited to 150 participants, another reason to register early.

Monday: Two "Featured Author" sessions: Jan Brett, followed by Joanna Cole and Bruce Degen. Then a visit to the poster sessions, with special attention to "Ecological literacy through children's picture books" and "Using intergenerational literature in the elementary classroom." Then from 3:00-5:45, a symposium in which two of the presenters are speaking on "The science museum in the classroom; first graders write to learn science, and middle graders read, write, and talk about science." Afterwards she goes quickly to the

FIGURE 12–16 Continued

exhibitors' displays, which are open till 6:00, and notes some booths she wants to visit on subsequent days. Like other convention-goers, she collects materials to take back to the classroom, such as free posters about children's books. She plans to visit booths at times when some of her favorite children's authors are autographing their books and to buy autographed books for her classroom and to save for holiday gift-giving.

Tuesday: a very hard choice among eleven microworkshops, including "Poetry packages for linking science and literature," "Teaching children through the magic of song: Integrating music into the curriculum," and "Buddy reading: Cross-age tutoring in a multicultural/multilingual elementary school context." She chooses the third, in part because two of the presenters are Katherine Samway and Gail Whang, and an article they wrote (1991) is part of the professional article collection she maintains. In the afternoon, she attends a symposium on "The Caldecott awards: Multiple views."

Wednesday: Special Interest Group (SIG) meetings are open to all. SIGs are organizations within a major professional organization; there are more than forty SIGs in the IRA, and members communicate throughout the year via newsletters and schedule one half-day meeting at each convention. Ms. Spen is thinking of joining one or more SIGs and plans to sample two at this convention. "Teaching History Through Literature" has an emphasis on trade books and also on women's place in history; another tempting feature is the closing activity, "raffling off free history trade books." In the afternoon, she attends a symposium on "The joys of diversity in the inclusionary classroom," chaired by Richard Allington, whose writing she admires.

Thursday: Hard choices again, but the decision is an all-morning micro-workshop, "From Anansi to Zomo: A celebration of folk literature in the classroom," then a Book and Author luncheon, and in the afternoon, the "Reading Excellence through the Arts" Special Interest Group session.

Friday: School visitations are in the morning, with a $10 fee which covers transportation: Ms. Spen chooses the Writers Workshop, elementary level: "Observe a mini-lesson, status of the class check, dyads and triads sharing and responding, individual students conferencing, composing, and appreciating during author's chair." An exciting convention!

A few weeks before Ms. Spen and her family flew to Anaheim, Mr. and Mrs. Lusolo's children welcomed their grandparents as babysitters while their parents headed out for four days in Boston, where Mr. Lusolo attended the 73rd annual meeting of the National Council of Teachers of Mathematics (NCTM). The district where the Lusolos teach allows four conference days; the NCTM meeting runs from Thursday through Saturday, so the Lusolos only miss two teaching days. Although Mr. Lusolo has been a member of NCTM for many years, this is the first time he has attended an annual meeting. He knows, however, that it is important to preregister early, so he begins planning as soon as the preliminary program—which is sent to all members—arrives, and preregisters by phone, using NCTM's 800 number.

The 160-page booklet is thoroughly organized and extremely detailed, with a color- and symbol-coded key to indicate the level and strand of each presentation. Many of the sessions are listed as "Admission by ticket." Conferees can attend up to two ticketed sessions, if they preregister for them. After careful reading, the Lusolos decide that rather than take two personal days, Mrs. Lusolo will use one conference day and one personal day, and spend Thursday at the conference, where a number of the presentations can be linked with art. Costs: $65 for the full conference for Mr. Lusolo (NCTM member); $63 for one day for Mrs. Lusolo (nonmember). The Lusolos also sign up for a Boston Pops concert on Friday ($45 each) and a Twilight Mystery Tour ($27 each) on Saturday.

Thursday: Mr. Lusolo begins with a welcoming session for people attending their first NCTM meeting. Then his first ticketed session, "Using knowledge of plane and solid geometry, students will create box kites," followed by "Is less really more? What do students gain when we don't cover the curriculum?" The Lusolos meet for lunch. Then "Color separations using paper chromatography: Mathematics and science meet in a low-cost lab," "I've given them an open-ended question—now what? Scoring and using OEQs," and finally his second ticketed session, "I hate math! So why do I love your class? Capture the unmotivated student's interest."

During her one day at the conference, Mrs. Lusolo attends a ticketed session on "A study of Amish quilts: An

FIGURE 12–16 Continued

interdisciplinary approach to mathematics, reading, and art," followed by "Interdisciplinary projects, transformation T-shirts—Congressperson for a day." (Lunch.) "Tessellations in the high school classroom," and (for senior high-college) "Using cartoons, birthday cards, and mind-reader tricks to introduce word problems."

Friday: "Musically enhanced learning—how music improves the teaching and learning of mathematics," "Mathematics in the middle grades through multicultural linkages," "Lessons from the classroom: Teachers collaborating for change," "Was Rapunzel worth the climb? Help your students answer unexpected questions," and finally, "Who is Monet, and why is he hanging around my math class? Proportion in art" (in which he takes notes and collects handouts for Mrs. Lusolo). In the evening, a Boston Pops Concert.

Saturday: Morning begins at 8:00 with poster sessions, with special attention to two: "Exploring geometry through tessellations—Empowering all students" and "Golden fractals: Using phi and Fibonacci numbers to create self-similar patterns." Then a research strand session, "Helping students become more reflective about their mathematics activities." Then "Tackling percent, variables, and integers with Hypercard (Bring a blank disk)," followed by "Weather data analysis: An integrating theme for mathematics, science, geography, and language arts." In the evening, a Twilight Mystery Tour.

Sunday: Sessions are only in the morning; Mr. Lusolo plans to attend one, from 9:00 to 10:00: "Problem solving with spreadsheets in the middle school mathematics classroom." The Lusolos plan to check out, leave their baggage at the hotel, walk the Freedom Trail, and then have an elegant dinner before leaving for home.

Challenge to the Reader: When Kathleen Jongsma wrote "Just say know!" (1992), she stressed to teachers the importance of reading professional literature. She noted that teachers who do read the professional literature say they find it invaluable. Those who do not, she reports, give two reasons: they have no time and they are unaware that professional journals exist. Readers of this text know that professional journals exist—over 100 are cited or quoted, and listed in the References section. Reading the professional literature is made easy for people who subscribe to a journal or who have a membership in a professional organization that includes a journal subscription with membership, because the journals arrive in the mail regularly with an interesting array of articles. It also is valuable for teachers to be aware of the benefits of attending professional conferences. Step back in time to April 1995. Which of the two conferences described above would you choose to attend and which of the presentations listed would have been of most interest to you?

Choose and Use: How would further professional development—through reading and conference attendance—be useful to you in terms of *self, subject, students,* and *situation*?

Planning For the Present and Future

In many ways, protecting our students' futures protects our own. Learning with our students and caring for them sensibly is interesting and enriching and promotes our own continuing development. In Erikson's eight stages of life development, the longest, when people live out a full life span, are the last two stages: maturity and old age. Erik and Joan Erikson lived long and productive lives. Erik Erikson died in 1994, shortly before his ninety-second birthday; toward the end of his life, he wrote and spoke about human development in maturity and in old age, when the developmental achievement is wisdom (Erikson & Erikson, 1981; Hall, 1983). Throughout most or all of our careers, teachers are in the life stage of maturity, and in this time the developmental crisis is between generativity—continuing growth and a concern for guiding the next generation—and stagnation. The favorable outcome of this life stage is care. Teaching is clearly a profession that has the potential to provide a rewarding maturity; it is the responsibility of teachers to act in ways that protect themselves and their colleagues from stagnation. The profession of teaching is designed to guide the next generation; teaching gives us the opportunity to care, and the professional literature in the field of education is rich with ideas and inspiration. In one of the immense array of articles written by educators, for educators, Lorri Neilsen (1992, p. 643) raises two questions that are useful for teachers to ask them-

Visualize... a person at the same point in a teaching career as you are now. (Perhaps you will visualize yourself.)

Reflect: What influenced this person to reach this point?

Visualize... Several satisfying and productive future points in this person's teaching career.

Consider: What steps might be taken to reach the most significant of these future attainments?

selves at the beginning of their careers and throughout their years of teaching: "How can I help human beings grow and learn in this world, now and for tomorrow? And what kind of person do I provide as an example?"

Strategy Glossary

KEY

Learning strategies are used by students to accomplish some aspect of learning; for example, *Focused Cloze* is a strategy used in learning technical vocabulary. Learning strategies are listed in **boldface** type. Several items included in the list below are underlined to indicate that they are solely or primarily instructional materials, or methods used by teachers. The four categories are:

Structures for providing instruction, e.g., *Direct experiences* and *Vicarious experiences*
Materials, e.g., *conveyable resources, Big Books*
Methods and materials for assessment, e.g., *Triple Lists, holistic scoring, checklists*
Planning methods, e.g., *Concept statements, Annual Overview, Session-by-Session Plan*

The category of learning strategies is broadly inclusive, although all learning strategies also are teaching strategies because teachers choose, introduce, guide, and monitor them. In some learning strategies, such as *Reading aloud, Guided Imagery,* and *Reference Source Commentaries,* the teacher has the major role throughout strategy use. Some learning strategies listed here, such as *Bibliography Lists* and *Fact Finding Charts,* are teacher-made materials which students use. *Cooperative learning, the Structured Research Process,* and *Cross-grade collaboration* are classified as learning strategies even though they also are structures for providing instruction. *Portfolios* and *contracts* are classified as learning strategies because they are assessment methods in which students are participants. People, (e.g., *Guest speakers*), and aspects of room arrangement, (e.g., *Author's Chair* and *displays*) also are classified as learning strategies.

In some cases, the names of learning strategies are preceded by two letters used as symbols:

Di   (Directions) indicates that special attention to directions is more likely to be needed for this strategy than for others.

Om   (Organization of materials) indicates that special attention must be given to organizing or collecting materials, or to making special arrangements.

Pm   (Preparation of materials) indicates that teachers will need to give substantial time and attention to preparing original materials that students will use.

Ru   (Rules) indicates that the strategy requires that the students learn rules and terminology related to the strategy (rather than to content).

Pm **A-Qu-A:** a comprehension strategy emphasizing listening in which sequence reading about a content topic is followed by an oral question-and-answer process. *Described in chapter 4, on pages 115–120.*

Accordion fold: a method of eliciting ideas for questions about a topic which a student-researcher might investigate. Students list their topics at the top of papers which are passed around; other students write questions about the topic at the bottom of the paper and fold it so their questions are not visible before passing the paper on for other questions to be added. *Described in chapter 5, on page 191.*

Acrostics: method of presenting research findings or preparing a book report by giving a series of facts, each of which begins with a letter in the topic's name, in acrostic fashion. *Described in chapter 5, on page 208, and discussed in the Strategic Teachers section following chapter 8.*

Alternate Uses: a divergent thinking activity— "Tell me all the uses you can think of for…" *Described in chapter 5, on page 174.*

Annual Overview: a planning method that provides an overview of an entire year, enabling integration of topics across subjects and over time. *Described in chapter 2, on pages 57–58, in chapter 12, on page 486, and also in the Strategic Teachers section following chapter 10.*

Another point of view: storytelling based on a literary work in which a different or parallel story is created from the point of view of a major character the author has kept voiceless. *Described in chapter 11, on page 463.*

Di, Om **APA (Amateur Publishing Association) journal:** a journal format in which writers' work is collected and published in a series of journal issues. In each issue after the first, writers include comments to other journal contributors about their writing published in the previous issue. *Described in chapter 10, on page 407.*

Om **Artifact kits:** collections of documents, tools, memorabilia, and so on, from a time period studied, prepared as a way of demonstrating learnings. *Described in chapter 5, on pages 207–208.*

Artists' Workshop: an extended time provided regularly for students to draw or paint in note-

books, then write about what they have drawn. They may go on, individually or collaboratively, to create larger art works based on the drawing and writing. *Described in chapter 11, on pages 432–433.*

Audiotapes: Recorded literature or music for students to listen to as a supplement or an accompaniment to learning. *Discussed in chapter 11, on page 449.*

Author's Chair: a chair set aside for students when they wish to read portions of their work aloud and invite comments and suggestions from classmates. Moving to the author's chair is a signal that a student wants to share some writing in progress; students who wish to participate then gather round. *Described in chapter 10, on page 413.*

Pm **Bibliography List:** a list of the reference materials available for students during research projects, in which each is identified by initials (e.g., World Book Encyclopedia=WB). This enables students to note their sources of information quickly as they obtain information from reference sources. *Described in chapter 5, on page 200.*

Big Books: books with large pages, and extra-large print and illustrations, useful in the Shared Book Experience. *Described in chapter 4, on pages 132–133.*

Om **Book report floats:** a parade of book reports prepared as small sculptures on an array of wheeled toys. *Described in the Strategic Teachers section following chapter 8 on page 342*

Bookends: a cooperative learning strategy for partners who study together before and after a learning activity. *Described on chapter 4, on page 155.*

Books about Books: topical annotated bibliographies prepared as a group research project. *Described in chapter 5, on page 209.*

Books as Reports: presenting content area information in the form of short, illustrated books, which may be placed in a classroom library or given to students in earlier grades. *Described briefly in the Stratetic Teachers section following Chapter 3, on pages 108–109.*

Books in translation: children's books translated into languages other than English, often in Spanish versions. They can be used with the Say Something strategy, with or without the teacher reading the text. The process can be useful in language courses. *Described in chapter 10, on pages 391–392.*

Bookstation: a classroom workstation where trade books, including those chosen for the beauty and information of their illustrations, are placed for student browsing or for their use in content-related assignments. *Described in the Strategic Teachers section following chapter 9.*

Brainstorming: generating many ideas on a topic after a short period of quiet thought (incubation). While ideas are being generated, no evaluative comments—positive or negative—are made. *Described in chapter 4, on page 138, and referred to throughout the text.*

Buddy book journals: partners—who may be classmates, buddies from different grades, or parent and child—agree on a book they will both read, then exchange comments through a shared journal. *Described in chapter 10, on page 403.*

Buddy journals: journals in which two or more people write to one another to exchange ideas. The partners in writing may be classmates or students in other classes or grades. *Described in chapter 10, on page 403.*

Om **Catch a character:** a group storytelling strategy in which miniature characters from a story are placed in a box. As tellers take turns drawing out a character they tell a part of the story from the point of view of that character. The sequence of the story told depends on the random order in which characters are "caught." *Described in chapter 11, on pages 462–463.*

Chanting: reading together, rhythmically, especially from a posted chart. *Described in chapter 6, on page 244.*

Checklists: a list of items, prepared by the teacher, to be checked off as they are accomplished by students, as a method of documenting progress. *Described in chapter 8, on page 327–330.*

Choral reading: a form of group reading aloud in which different groups of readers read different portions of a text, such as a long poem. The reading may be as simple as dividing readers into two groups based on their seating arrangement (right side of the room, left side of the room) or it may be elaborate, with some readers reading individually and others in chorus, each reader having a copy of the text with the portions to be read aloud highlighted. *Described in chapter 11, on page 459, and in the Strategic Teachers section following chapter 6.*

Om **Class history album:** a method of recording, organizing, and sharing class history in which students acting as class historians take one photograph a day to be captioned and mounted in an album. Captions may be multilingual, and when students serve as historians they are responsible for ensuring that all classmates are featured in interesting ways. *Described in chapter 9, on page 371.*

Om **Class history records:** an album of photographs taken to record class activities. Photographs are taken by students, acting in turn as class historian, and are then captioned by students. *Described in chapter 7, on page 285 and in Chapter 9 on page 371..*

Om **Class history wall:** a student-created display of classroom memorabilia, prepared in monthly panels. *Described in chapter 7, on page 285.*

Classroom science journal: a group journal placed near an ongoing classroom science project in which students make daily entries about the progress of the experiments. *Described in chapter 10, on page 406.*

Cloze (standard cloze): a language development activity in which students complete a meaningful text passage from which words have been systematically omitted. (Cloze also can be used in assessment.) *Described in chapter 6 on pages 234–236, and chapter 8, on pages 318–319. See also cloze variations: Cloze-Plus-Questions Guides, Focused Cloze, and Manipulable Cloze.*

Pm **Cloze-Plus-Questions Guides:** teacher-prepared materials that begin with a short passage presenting an important content topic in standard cloze format, followed by a series of questions based on the passage. *Described in chapter 4, on pages 142–143.*

Collaborative Listening-Viewing Guide: note-taking method, with whole class, small group, and individual components, for use during videotapes and filmstrips. *Described in chapter 10, on page 388.*

Collage: artwork composed by arranging objects and materials and attaching them to a surface. *Described in chapter 11, on page 433.*

Computation Challenge: *See Computation Minute.*

Computation Minute: a math activity in which students work for a minute on computation exercises in math areas in which they are approaching mastery. The score is the number correct before the first error, so both accuracy and speed are emphasized. *Described in chapter 4, on pages 122–123.*

Concept Connections: a strategy in which students arrange technical terms in a grid and write short passages which link three terms; also known as Structural Indexing. *Described in chapter 4 , on pages 147–148, and discussed further in chapter 11, on pages 456–457.*

Concept Mapping: *See Semantic Mapping.*

Concept of Definition: a vocabulary development activity in which a word is defined by its category, examples, and features. *Described in chapter 4, on pages 148–149.*

Concept statements: an aspect of planning for teaching important topics in which teachers state the essential information they expect their students to learn. Concept statements can be used as the basis for teacher-prepared activities, such as Cloze-Plus-Questions Guides, Focused Cloze, and Detection. *Described in chapter 2, on pages 52–57. There are additional examples in chapters 4, 10, and 12.*

Concept-Text-Application (CTA): *See Experience-Text-Relationship.*

Confer and Write: a whole-class, open-book writing activity in which the teacher sets the topic and students confer, sharing ideas, before writing individually. During the time students are conferring, a student suggests a topic for the teacher to write about. *Described in chapter 10, on pages 410–411.*

Confronting concept overload: prioritizing concepts when textbook sections present so many new ideas that learning them all would be very difficult and arranging to focus on the most important while giving some attention to others. *Described in chapter 3, on pages 80–82.*

Content Area Planning Sketch: planning format that simulates aspects of experienced teachers' planning and the many factors they consider, when several weeks will be devoted to teaching an important topic. The format incorporates a day-by-day, week-by-week listing of planned events. *Described in chapter 12, examples on pages 487–488 and 496–500.*

Contracts: a written agreement between student and teacher identifying required and optional learning activities - a method of documenting progress. *Described in chapter 8, on pages 327 and 328.*

Conveyable resources: inexpensive learning equipment which students can carry back and forth from school. *Described in chapter 7, on page 286.*

Cooperative learning: a widely used instructional method in which students work together collaboratively in groups. *Discussed in chapter 4, on pages 149–158 and in Chapter 5 on pages 191–192.*

Pm **Correct It:** a strategy—somewhat similar to Detection—to teach the mechanics of writing. A well-written passage from students' work is deliberately altered by the teacher to include some common technical errors (spelling, punctuation, grammar) which students are challenged to identify and correct. *Described in chapter 10, on pages 415–416.*

Creative drama: dramatic activities that are, to varying degrees, created spontaneously; they are "nonexhibitional"—that is, participants engage in the drama for their own pleasure and learning, rather than for the purpose of preparing to perform for others. *Described in chapter 11, on pages 96, 98–99.*

Pm **Creative Reasoning Guides:** teacher-prepared materials designed to encourage anticipatory thinking and allow opportunity for divergent thinking. *Described in chapter 3, on page X.*

Om **Cross-grade collaboration:** older students working with younger ones—a technique which, when well-conducted, benefits both age groups. *Described in chapter 2, on pages 60–61, and in the Strategic Teachers sections following chapters 3 and 6.*

Current events math journals: journals or journal entries in which students relate a current event to math. *Described in chapter 10, on page 404.*

Current events response journals: Group or individual journals based on written comments about news items. *Described in chapter 10, on page 404.*

Daily journal: a group strategy recommended for beginning readers, in which students decide on a topic, and contribute ideas about it, which the adult writes on a chart (preferably a large piece of lined paper). When the day's journal entry is completed, teacher and students read it in chorus, and the teacher asks anyone who wishes to do so to tell something about it (e.g., "I see a J" or "that word is the same as this word" or "I can find the word school.") No student is ever asked or invited to read the whole entry; thus all, whatever their stage of emergent literacy, can contribute useful information. Students respond as they choose, rather than answering teachers' questions. *Described in chapter 10, on pages 406–407.*

Pm **Detection:** an activity designed to develop analytic thinking in which students read two versions— one accurate and one deliberately falsified—of a short fact-packed passage and identify the errors. *Described in chapter 5, on pages 168–171*

Dialectical journals: journals in which entries consist of a short statement quoted from a text or lecture, followed by a two- or three-part comment in response to patterned questions. *Described in chapter 10, on page 406.*

Dialogue journals: notebooks in which two or more people, often a teacher and student, engage in a written conversation over an extended period of time. *Described in chapter 10, on page 403.*

Dictionary Commentary: a version of Reference Source Commentary in which the teacher reads and comments on one or more dictionary entries (derivation as well as definition). *Described in chapter 5, on pages 185–187.*

Direct experiences: bringing the part of the world that is being studied into the classroom or the school, or taking students out of school to experience that part of the world. *Described in chapter 4, on page 121.*

Directed Reading-Thinking Activity (DR-TA): a strategy emphasizing making and verifying predictions while reading. *Described in chapter 6, on pages 239–240.*

Directed Spelling Thinking Activity: a method of teaching spelling based on the idea that "quantity of correct spellings and quality of attempts grow in mutually supportive ways." The DSTA strategy extends over several days, and the words—chosen from material being studied—have some patterns in common and are studied using a compare-contrast method. *Described in chapter 10, on pages 416–417.*

Pm **Discrepant Events:** an introductory strategy designed to rouse students' attention and curiosity about a topic by providing an experience that contradicts their experience or does not fit with what they expect. *Described in chapter 3, on pages 91–92.*

Discussion Web: teacher-guided discussion of opposing points of view, using a graphic. *Described in chapter 5, on pages 178–179.*

Om **Displays:** exhibits on bulletin boards, walls, and doors that can contribute to student learning and provide information about classroom and school programs. *Displays are described or mentioned in each chapter; displays as means of school-home communication are discussed in chapter 9, on page 361.*

Divergent thinking: thinking characterized by fluency, flexibility, elaboration, and originality; linked to creativity. *Described in chapter 5, on pages 173–174, and in chapter 3, on page 96.*

Do Something: a version of the Say Something strategy in which students respond when the teacher pauses during a read-aloud by miming an action related to the story. *Described in chapter 10, on page 390.*

Om **"Door decor":** displays of students' work on classroom doors—by extension, displays of students' work at their eye level on available surfaces inside and outside of the classroom. *Mentioned in chapter 9, on page 361.*

Double-entry journals: journals in which the left-hand pages are used for drawings, notes, and so on, and the right-hand pages are used for putting those ideas into written form. Alternatively, left-hand pages can be used for goal-setting and right-hand pages for brainstorming ways to achieve the goals. *Described in chapter 10, on pages 405–406.*

Draw-a-problem: *See Transform-a-problem.*

Dream sequences: improvisational dramas based on exaggeratedly optimistic renditions of how a current problem might be solved, or how changes in past events might have led to good outcomes. *Described in chapter 11, on page 443.*

Echo reading: a strategy in which one reader (usually the teacher) reads a short portion of text that is then repeated by a student or group of students. *Described in chapter 6, on page 244.*

Essential Reading: a three-step strategy that focuses on understanding main ideas in text. *Described in chapter 6, on pages 240–241.*

Estimating: an aspect of analytical thinking that involves making an educated guess about a question (usually mathematical) based on known information and a judgment about what answer would be reasonable. *Described in chapter 5, on pages 165–166.*

EVOKER: a strategy for studying poetry or other genres in which the text is fairly brief, meanings are rich and complex, and language patterns may be unfamiliar (for example, a speech or other historical document). The strategy name is an acronym referring to steps in the process (Exploration, Vocabulary, Oral Reading, Key Ideas, Evaluation, Recapitulation); it works well for steps 1-3 and 5-6 to be whole class activities, and for cooperative groups to work together on identifying the key ideas and evaluating their relationship to find meaning. *Described in chapter 11, on pages 468–469.*

Excerpting: choosing vivid, important portions of a written text to read aloud, rather than reading the text in its entirety. Besides making reading aloud more exciting, excerpting demonstrates to students that good reading does not always mean starting at the beginning and reading straight through to the end. *Described in chapter 4, on page 133.*

Experience-Text-Relationship (ETR): a method of linking students' prior knowledge with unfamiliar text concepts. *Described in chapter 6, on page 237.*

Fact and Fable: a research follow-up activity in which students write and illustrate one false and one true statement about their topic. The pages can be collected in a Fact and Fable booklet. *Described in chapter 5, on page 208.*

Fact-Finding Chart: a grid containing questions to be answered for a research project with spaces for noting relevant information. *Described in chapter 5, on pages 200 and 203.*

Fact Storm: a cooperative learning strategy that incorporates planning about how to accomplish a study assignment. *Described in chapter 4, on page 155.*

Om Family folklore: a method of school-home collaboration in which families contribute to collections; (e.g., recipe collections, compilations of proverbs) or share copies of documents that are part of their family's history. *Described in chapter 9, on page 371.*

Om Family Theme Bags: take-home packs, sent home over a weekend, which include a journal to record weekend events, a book to share, and art supplies that may be used to produce a collaborative family creation. *Described in chapter 9, on pages 370–371.*

Fishbowl discussions: discussion strategy in which discussants sit in an inner circle and observers, who use checklists to record aspects of discussion, sit in an outer circle. *Described in chapter 10, on page 392.*

Focused Cloze: a teacher-prepared cloze activity in which the omitted words are related to important text concepts. *Described in chapter 3, on pages 87–88.*

FYI ("For Your Information"): very brief mini-lessons in which a teacher gives information to a student, a group, or the class, at the time the information is needed. *Described in chapter 6, on pages 242–243.*

Om Giftbooks: elegant books planned and created by students as a gift for a family member or friend. The topic of the books can be chosen to demonstrate learning. *Described in chapter 9, on pages 365–366, and referred to in chapter 11, on page 432.*

"Give me five": a strategy enabling the teacher to learn students' names and students to learn each other's names, for use early in the school year. *Described in chapter 12, on page 492.*

"Giving credit where credit is due:" the practice of crediting sources—a method of combating plagiarism. *Described in chapter 5, pages 183–184.*

"Grand conversations": Active, absorbing discussions in which students interact with one another about topics of mutual interest, as opposed to question-and-answer sessions controlled by the teacher. It is characteristic of grand conversations that at the end of the conversation, participants are even more interested in what they've been talking about than they were at the beginning. *Described in chapter 11, on pages 451–452.*

Pm **Graphic Information Lesson:** a post-reading strategy in which the teacher leads students to interpret and categorize text graphics and devise original "pseudographics." *Described in chapter 5, on pages 172–173.*

Graphing a Book: preparation of a graphic showing the ups and downs of the events experienced by a character or historical figure. *Described in chapter 11, on page 457.*

Group journal: a journal placed in an accessible setting where members of a group can make entries. A useful method is to have the right-hand pages of the journal used for original contributions and the facing pages kept for comments on these entries. The first page of the journal may contain a list of all those who will be using the journal; thereafter, entries need only be initialed. *Described in chapter 10, on page 407.*

Group journals: journals which are written by large numbers of people, for example, students in a classroom, or groups of colleagues. *Described in chapter 10, on pages 406–407.*

Group reading with RESPONSE: A method of using the RESPONSE study strategy in cooperative groups. *Described in chapter 4, on page 125.*

Guest journal: a journal kept open in the classroom in which visitors to the classroom are invited to write entries. *Described in chapter 10, on page 406.*

Om **Guest speakers, guest artists:** people with special talents, expertise, or experiences who are invited to share these in a class or school. *Described in chapter 11, on pages 428–429 with an example given in chapter 3, on page 86.*

Guided Imagery: a method of providing vicarious experience by guiding students to visualize a situation. *Described in chapter 4, on pages 121–122.*

Guided kinesthetic imagery: a parallel to guided visual imagery, created by using movement. *Described in chapter 11, on page 444.*

Om **Guided Writing Procedure (GWP):** a strategy linking reading and writing in which students pause in the process of writing about a content area topic to do further reading. *Described in chapter 6, on page 239.*

Holistic rating: giving a rating to a product, based on an overall view of its characteristics; most frequently used to score many pieces of writing done in response to the same assignment. *Described in chapter 8, on pages 320–321.*

the Human Mosaic: an art project that emphasizes human diversity. Students use small squares of tagboard to create tiles for the mosaic, each with a drawing of a person; tiles are glued onto a large sheet of cardboard forming a mosaic. *Described in chapter 11, on page 432.*

Pm **Identity Creation (I See):** teacher-prepared materials that provide historically accurate descriptions of simulated people in different time periods, for students to elaborate upon after studying a time period. *Described in chapter 5, on pages 174–175.*

I-Search a Word: a research assignment in which students search reference materials and prepare a paper on the derivation of a word of their choice. *Described in chapter 5, on page 190.*

I-Search papers: research papers describing the search for answers to a question of the student's choice (as opposed to papers that focus on findings alone). *Described in chapter 5, on page 190.*

Pm **Illustratorship:** the study of book illustrations as works of art. *Described in chapter 11, on page 436.*

Instances: a divergent thinking activity—"Tell me all the different things you can think of that…" *Described in chapter 5, on page 174.*

Instructional Conversations: teacher-guided discussions in which the teacher contributes by making connections among ideas expressed by students, establishing a "challenging, but non-threatening, atmosphere," and encouraging wide participation by students through self-selected turn-taking (rather than requiring students to wait to be called upon). *Described in chapter 5, on page 178.*

Pm **Integrated Spelling Lessons.** a spelling program in which the words are chosen from important content-related texts and documents. *Described in chapter 10, on pages 417–418.*

Jigsaw: a cooperative learning strategy in which each member of a group becomes an expert in an aspect of the topic being studied, then returns to share information with the group. *Described in chapter 4, on page 155.*

Ru **Johari Window:** a strategy for the study of characterization in literature that also can be applied to history, based on a 2 x 2 graphic formed like a window with four panes: open pane, closed pane, hidden pane, and mystery pane, each showing a different aspect of the person being viewed. *Described in chapter 11, on pages 457–458.*

Journals: an approach to writing which emphasizes fluency. Journals can be used for many purposes; e.g., records of events, expression of opinions, accounts of what has been learned, memoranda of ideas for writing projects, and drafts of writing. *Described in chapter 10, on pages 401–407.*

K-W-L: a study strategy in which students identify what they know and what they want to know, and later, what they have learned. *Described in chapter 4, on page 128.*

K-W-L Plus: an adaptation of the K-W-L study strategy used as a preparation for writing a research report in which items on the "L" list (What I Have Learned) are categorized and arranged in a semantic map, which then becomes the basis for a written report. *Described in chapter 5, on page 192.*

Lab books: science journals in which students summarize the materials, procedures, and results of an experiment and describe their observations. *Described in chapter 10, on page 405.*

Language Experience Approach (LEA): a process in which students dictate an experience story that is transcribed by a teacher or tutor, then

used as reading material. *Described in chapter 6, on page 234.*

LEAD: a three-step method of learning terminology through direct or vicarious experience. The strategy's name indicates the three steps: L=Listing; EA=Experience Activity; D=Discussion. It is a feature of LEAD discussions, that all contributions must include one or more of the technical vocabulary terms that have been listed. *Described in chapter 3, on pages 84–87.*

Learning centers: *See Workstations.*

Learning logs: journals in which students write about what they are learning in a content area subject. *Described in chapter 10, on pages 403–406.*

Letters to the Author: Comments written by students in response to written work published or shared by other students in a different class or school. *Described in chapter 10, on page 408.*

List-Group-Label (L-G-L): a method of building conceptual vocabulary through categorizing and labeling terminology. *Described in chapter 4, on pages 137–138.*

Literature circles: An alternative to whole class discussions of literature in which the class divides into small groups, each studying a different shared reading. Student groups are formed based on their book choices and meet regularly to read, or write in journals. *Described in chapter 11, on pages 455–456.*

Literature logs: journals in which students write about what they are reading or what is being read aloud to them. *Described in chapter 10, on page 403.*

Lookbacks: brief purposeful rereading of text to find information that supports an idea, or to confirm an answer. *Described in chapter 4, on page 131.*

Pm **Manipulable cloze:** a cloze passage prepared in such a way that students can move words around to test where they are best suited. This can be accomplished by writing the text on posterboard and backing the cards with omitted words with velcro; it is a useful cloze activity for younger learners. *Described in chapter 6, on page 236.*

Om **Map and postcard display:** one or more maps with postcards or small pictures showing places being studied, or topics related to class or family history. *Described in chapter 9, on page 361.*

Math journals: learning logs for math, which can be used across a wide age range. *Described in chapter 10, on page 404.*

Memos: a supplement or alternative to dialogue journals and learning logs consisting of brief messages from student to teacher (to which the teacher responds), usually written weekly, commenting on some significant aspect of the class during the previous week. *Described in chapter 10, on page 403, and referred to in the Strategic Teachers section following chapter 7.*

Milieu teaching: interaction between teacher and students in which they communicate successfully by participating together in a shared activity, even if the student does not communicate in words. *Described in chapter 7, on page 288.*

Mini-lessons: brief lessons that are focused on a single topic which small groups of students or the whole class need to know at a particular time. *Described in chapter 6, on pages 241–242, and referred to throughout the text.*

Mobiles: three-dimensional artworks with moving parts; one of many forms of transmediation that students can use to demonstrate their learning. *Described in chapter 11, on page 433.*

Montage: artwork created by combining superimposed pictures. *Described in chapter 11, on page 433.*

Ru **MULTIPASS:** a study strategy designed to encourage strategic reading in which students make three "passes" through instructional text, to Survey, Size Up, and Sort Out information. *Described in chapter 4, on page 128.*

Multiple readings: combining strategies to provide many opportunities to read text in different ways. *Described in chapter 4, on pages 129–132, and in Chapter 6, on pages 243–244.*

Pm **Multi-text hunt:** a text hunt prepared over more than one text; for example, a hunt tht engages intermediate grade students in exploring text features of the science, social studies, and math texts they will be using. *Described in chapter 1, on page 16.*

Mural: a large artwork covering all or part of a wall, which can be created by students to illustrate what is being studied—a useful, long-term assignment for cooperative groups. *Described in chapter 11, on page 433.*

Music response journals: journals in which students respond to music, for example, writing about music they love or contrasting two pieces of music. *Described in chapter 11, on page 439.*

Pm **Newsletters:** a method of sharing information with families about their children's educational program; typically, they are single-sided sheets that contain a series of short articles giving information about current and future activities. *Described in chapter 9, on pages 361, 363–365 and page 381.*

"No, you didn't!": turn-taking storytelling in pairs in which the story changes direction when the listener contradicts what the teller has said. *Described in chapter 11, on page 463.*

No-Travel Trips: an imaginary excursion to another place, typically beginning with a short slide show or a guest speaker. Students may prepare a trip-related project of their choice, such as a timeline of historical events, a brochure giving statistics about the area, or a set of thinking challenges inspired by postcards or maps. *Described in the Strategic Teachers section following chapter 9.*

Om **Opinion and Comment:** essays expressing opinions or proposing problem solutions written by students and shared with students in another class or school who comment in response, then return their comments to the original authors. *Described in chapter 10, on page 408.*

Om **Oral history projects:** collecting information through interviews, especially from older people in the family or community who recall important events of the past. *Described in chapter 5, on page 189, and referred to in chapter 4, on page 132.*

Oral text hunts: Teacher-guided Text Hunts for younger students or inexperienced readers. *Described in chapter 1, on page 16.*

Our-Search group journal: an adaptation of I-Search papers in which the teacher is the scribe for a group journal describing the process of a class research activity. *Described in chapter 5, on page 190.*

Paired Reading: a method of reading text in which two readers read passages aloud alternately. *Described in chapter 6, on pages 245–246, and also in chapter 4, on page 130.*

Paraphrase Passport: a turn-taking method in which a prerequisite for contributing to a discussion is giving a brief summary of the ideas of the previous speaker. *Described in chapter 10, on page 389.*

Om **Partnership Stories:** Creation of a story by students in one school to be completed by students elsewhere—in another country or different area of the country. *Described in chapter 10, on page 408.*

Pattern Graphics: visual representations—such as timelines and Venn diagrams—that show relationships among ideas. *Described in chapter 4, on pages 145–146.*

Pm **Pattern Guides:** teacher-prepared materials that identify the pattern or patterns used in the text (e.g., compare-contrast; chronological sequence) and present a series of questions that lead students to understand the text topic based on a grasp of the text pattern. *Described in chapter 4, on pages 143–145.*

Om **Pen pals:** ongoing, planned correspondence between students and students in another grade, school, college, or country. *Described in chapter 10, on page 408 and referred to in chapter 12, on page 502, and the Strategic Teachers section following chapter 3.*

Personal journals: journals in which all members of the class—the teacher as well as students—write for an agreed-upon length of time. Typically the students' journals are kept at school until the end of the year or term, when they are returned to them. *Described in chapter 10, on pages 402–403.*

Photography: a form of artistic expression students can use to demonstrate or expand their learning. Photographs taken by students can be used as the center of semantic maps, as the basis for descriptive writing, or as part of picture essays created by collecting and arranging photographs and other visual images from printed sources. *Discussed in chapter 11, on page 434.*

Om **Picture research:** a strategy to follow up research in which students choose pictures to illustrate information they have learned, make slides from the pictures, and create a slide presentation accompanied by an audiotaped narrative. *Described in chapter 11, on page 434.*

Om **Poetry in translation:** a strategy that explores various translations of poetry originally written in other languages and teaches that the same thing is perceived differently by different people and that one's own perception is affected by which version of the idea that is encountered. *Described in chapter 11, on pages 467–468.*

Om **Portfolios:** an organized, displayable collection of students' work, collected over time according to a plan. *Described in chapter 8, on pages 331–332.*

Poster Sessions: a method of sharing research results or project information, similar to presentations used at professional conferences, in which several presenters display highlights of their information on posters and talk about their work with those who stop to inquire. *Described in chapter 5, on page 209.*

PQP (Praise, Question, Polish): a structure for peer-editing of writing in which one or more colleagues responds to a piece of writing by offering praise, asking a question, and giving a suggestion for improvement. *Described in chapter 5, on pages 193, 195, and also in chapter 10, on page 415.*

PReP (Pre-Reading Plan): an introductory strategy in which students brainstorm about the topic they will be studying and evaluate their ideas. *Described in chapter 6, on pages 237–238.*

Pm **Previews:** an introductory strategy in which the teacher presents an analogy between a familiar concept and the concept to be studied. *Described in chapter 3, on pages 72–74.*

Ru **QAR (Question-Answer Relationships):** a strategy designed to enable students to identify and answer the types of questions frequently asked in school: literal, inferential, application, and scriptal. *Described in chapter 6, on page 241.*

QUAD (QUestions, Answers, Details): a grid-based method of organizing information that is being collected for a research project. *Described in chapter 5, on pages 192–193, 194.*

Quick Draw: a transmediation strategy in which student teams present a drawing illustrating a concept, challenging their classmates to identify it. *Described in chapter 5, on page 176.*

QuIP (Questions Into Paragraphs): a grid-based method of collecting information that provides the structure for a short research report. *Described in chapter 5, on page 192.*

Quotation collections: student-selected and student-illustrated quotations, which may be compiled into booklets or giftbooks. *Described in chapter 11, on page 432.*

RAFT (Role, Audience, Form, Theme): a strategy that provides structure for a writing assignment in which the writer writes from the perspective of another character or thing. *Described in chapter 5, on pages 206–207, and referred to in the Strategic Teachers section following chapter 8.*

Read-aloud, Read, Create, and Discuss: a four-step strategy to provide a structure for whole class reading of a text over two or three weeks. The teacher divides the text into sections, each of which will be the focus for a two-day session. On the first day a teacher read-aloud is followed by a small group reading and the creation of a text-based product; the creation step is continued on the next day, followed by a discussion. *Described in chapter 11, on pages 452–455.*

Readers' Theater: an activity in which text is presented in the form of a play to be read aloud by several readers taking different parts. Expository as well as narrative text can be revised into playscript form to become a Readers' Theater script. Readers' Theater is designed primarily for the enjoyment of the readers—not intended to be a fully developed major production for an audience. There is no memorization, since, by definition, the readers read from scripts. *Described in chapter 11, on pages 459–460.*

Reading aloud (Read-alouds): a widely recommended instructional activity, useful throughout subjects and across grades, which consists of teachers reading to their students. *Described in chapter 4, on pages 132–137, and in Chapter 6, on page 243, and in Chapter 9 on page 370, and referred to throughout the text. Each Strategic Teachers section includes the topic.*

Reading and More Reading: a term referring to the many ways to engage students in produc-

tive and enjoyable reading. *Described in chapter 6, on page 243.*

Reading journals: a form of dialogue journal in which students express their ideas about what they are reading or what the teacher is reading aloud to the class. *Described in chapter 10, on page 403.*

Reading response journals: journals used when teachers read aloud, with the reading aloud followed first by group brainstorming, then by five minutes during which the teacher and students write, and concluding with voluntary sharing of writing. *Described in chapter 10, on page 403.*

Reading Road Map: a teacher-prepared guide given to students before a reading assignment from a difficult text, providing information about what parts to give special attention to and which to skim or scan. *Described in chapter 4, on page 123–124.*

Recollect-it-down: A reflective, written version of Think-Aloud. *Described in the Strategic Teachers section following chapter 7.*

Reference Source Commentary: a version of Teacher Read Aloud Commentary in which the teacher comments on selections from resource texts, for example, encyclopedia, atlas, or almanac. *Described in chapter 5, on pages 185–186.*

Refutational teaching: an introductory teaching strategy to be used when it is likely that students have prior incorrect information about a topic. *Described in chapter 3, on pages 92–94.*

Repeated readings (see also rereading and multiple readings): reading text or hearing text read aloud more than once—a useful way to deepen understanding and extend enjoyment. *Described in chapter 6, on page 246, and referred to throughout the text.*

Rereading: (see also repeated readings and multiple readings) reading text again, choosing portions to read several times for enjoyment or better understanding. *Discussed in chapter 4, on page 130, and chapter 6, on page 246, and referred to throughout the text.*

Research At Your Service: a research project in which students who are experienced in using media center resources conduct searches to provide information requested by others; for example, teachers in the school may request an annotated bibliography on a topic. *Described in chapter 5, on page 209.*

RESPONSE: an interactive study strategy in which students categorize their notes, which enables the teacher to respond to students' questions. *Described in chapter 4, on pages 124–127.*

RESPONSE to speakers: an adaptation of the RESPONSE study strategy in which students use a RESPONSE form to take notes during a guest speaker's presentation. The process enables students to raise pertinent questions after the talk; the forms serve as a record for the teacher of students' grasp of important ideas and as a reminder of students' questions which remain to be answered. *Described in chapter 10, on page 388.*

Retelling: a strategy which can be used with a wide variety of important texts; hearing a text read aloud may be followed by oral retelling or written retelling (through writings or drawings); or reading a text may be followed by oral retelling, or retelling in writing or through drawings. Purposes for retelling include retelling the main ideas only, retelling for someone so they will enjoy the story as much, or retelling so the important details are clear and in the correct sequence. *Described in chapter 10, on pages 397–398.*

Roundtable sessions: a method of presenting research findings in which students who have done research on related topics present their findings together to an audience of peers. *Described in chapter 5, on page 209.*

Pm   **Rubrics:** a method of guiding students as they complete an assignment and guiding teachers as they evaluate products. Rubrics set forth the characteristics of products of differing quality. *Described in chapter 8, on pages 327 and 330.*

Om   **SAIL:** a method for structuring a research report in a way that introduces students to appropriate resources while minimizing the likelihood of plagiarism. The title of the strategy is an acronym, standing for Sources, Audience, Information, and Length. The teacher (perhaps with student input) specifies or provides three to five sources for the report, identifies an audience, states the information to be provided, and sug-

gests the length for the report. *Described in chapter 5, on pages 195–199.*

SAY-IT: giving students content-related information briefly when they ask. (The strategy's name is an acronym, standing for Share And You Instruct Time-efficiently.) *Described in chapter 4, on pages 112–113.*

Say Something: a strategy to encourage oracy in which students respond with comments (unguided, self-chosen) when the teacher pauses in reading. *Described in chapter 10, on pages 390–391.*

Scaffolding: providing appropriate guidance and support—including giving information directly—for students who are in the process of learning something new, based on the concept of a zone of proximal development, which is an area in which learners can accomplish, with the help of adults or more capable peers, what they will later be able to do independently. *Described in chapter 6, on pages 229–231.*

SCAMPER: a method of thinking divergently about objects or ideas by Substituting, Combining, Adapting, Modifying, Putting to other uses, Eliminating, or Rearranging their features. *Described in chapter 5, on page 174.*

Science journals: learning logs for use in science classes, which may include descriptions and discussions of lab activities, semantic maps and diagrams, or responses to readings. *Described in chapter 10, on page 405.*

Om   **Scrapbook journals:** journals in which the entries are responses to something mounted in the journal (e.g., photograph, pressed flower, or memorabilia); a useful journal style for beginning writers. *Described in chapter 10, on pages 402–403.*

Pm   **Search Tasks:** teacher-prepared materials designed to acquaint students with a new chapter or section of text. *Described in chapter 3, on pages 76–80.*

Seed Stroll: a nature walk in which thick socks are worn over shoes to pick up seeds. *Described in the Strategic Teachers section following chapter 6, on page 264.*

Pm   **Semantic Feature Analysis:** an analytic, grid-based strategy in which the features that do or do not characterize related concepts are displayed. *Described in chapter 5, on pages 166–168.*

Semantic Mapping: organizing terminology graphically to show relationships among topics. *Described in chapter 4, on pages 132–141.*

Pm **Sequence drama:** drama in which students, sequentially, speak and mime what is written on their cards; the cards, taken together, provide an account of a historical or fictional event. *Described in chapter 11, on page 443.*

Pm **Sequence reading:** a group method of reading a text in which text sections are distributed randomly, with all but the first section preceded by a cue consisting of the last sentence or phrase from the previous reading. Readers listen for their cues and read in turn. *Described in chapter 10, on pages 395–396.*

Session-by-Session Plan: planning format that simulates experienced teachers' thinking about how to organize and link instructional sessions over a series of days. *Described in chapter 12, on pages 486 with examples on pages 490–492 and 510–512.*

Shared book experience: a method by which a classroom teacher can simulate for all children the experience many children have of being read aloud to at home. *Described in chapter 4, on pages 132–133.*

Shrinklits: book report format in which the plot of a book is summarized in rhymed couplets. *Described in the Strategic Teachers section following chapter 8, on pages 342–343.*

Pm **Significant Sayings:** an introductory strategy to encourage anticipatory thinking and reasoning based on quotations from text-related sources. *Described in chapter 3, on pages 96 and 97.*

Similarities: a divergent thinking activity—"Tell me all the ways you can think of that …and …are alike." *Described in chapter 5, on page 174.*

Simulation drama: improvisational drama in which teacher and students take on the roles of characters in a real or fictional situation, discuss together or in groups how the action should proceed, then interact to dramatize the situation. *Described in chapter 11, on page 443; an example is given in the Strategic Teachers section that follows chapter 5, in Figure 5–17 .*

Sketch to Stretch: a transmediation strategy in which students illustrate concepts and share and explain their products in a group. *Described in chapter 5, on page 176.*

Om **Snapshot journal:** a version of the scrapbook journal in which a series of snapshots of a class activity are mounted with student-written captions. A central section of the page is used for a short student-written description of the activity pictured. *Described in chapter 10, on page 406.*

Social studies journals: learning logs for social studies in which students' writing may be prompted by questions such as *In this reading, what ideas do you feel strongly about? How do your own experiences relate to what you have read about?* Student-teacher dialogue through the journals can be used as the basis for class discussions. *Described in chapter 10, on page 405.*

Solve Aloud: a form of Teacher Read Aloud Commentary focused on math, for repetitive use, in which the teacher talks through the solution to a problem. *Described in chapter 4, on page 113–115.*

Om **Song and slide shows:** a strategy in which students demonstrate their learning about a historical time period by matching appropriate music with informative slides. *Described in chapter 11, on pages 438–439.*

Ru **SQ3R:** a study strategy with five steps (referred to in the title): Survey the text, raise Questions, Read to find answers, Recite (state findings aloud), Review. *Described in chapter 4, on pages 127–128.*

Ru **SQRQCQ:** a six-step study strategy for math (Survey, Question, Read, Question, Compute, Question) *Described in chapter 4, on pages 114–115.*

Stabiles: nonmovable three-dimensional art works (as opposed to mobiles, which are movable), one form of which provides an effective way to illustrate animal habitats. *Described in chapter 11, on page 433–434.*

STAIR: a method for linking teaching and assessment in which the steps are observation, hypothesis development, teaching, observation, and reflection. (The acronym stands for System for Teaching and Assessing Interactively and Reflectively.) *Described in chapter 8, on pages 313–314.*

Story Box: *See Yarn-in-a-Box.*

Story journals: journals in which students write elaborated responses to read alouds, including drawings, retellings, critiques, and the creation of new, original episodes in the style of the text being read aloud. *Described in chapter 10, on page 403.*

Om   **Story nets:** wide-meshed nets from which items used as props in storytelling are hung; used as a backdrop for a storytelling area. *Described in chapter 11, on page 461.*

Story Theater: creative drama strategy in which students pantomime roles as the teacher reads aloud a familiar story or poem. *Described in chapter 11, on page 462.*

Storyboarding: illustrating a sequence of ideas visually so the events of a fictional story or factual situation are shown on a chart. *Described in chapter 11, on page 434.*

Storytelling: sharing stories with others using voice and gestures to enhance interest; an art form that exists across cultures and throughout recorded time. *Described in chapter 11, on pages 460–463.*

Ru   **Structured Controversy:** a multiple session discussion strategy in which teams argue for opposing points of view, confer, argue for the position they previously opposed, then seek some consensus. *Described in chapter 5, on page 179.*

Structured Listening Activity: a five-step strategy to guide students as they learn important information by listening to a read-aloud or brief lecture. *Described in chapter 10, on pages 386–387.*

Om   **Structured Research Process:** a method of organizing student research in which the roles of the teacher and the students are specified over a period of weeks, including advanced preparation and follow up. *Described in chapter 5, on pages 199–205.*

Om, Ru **Student-led conferences:** individual conferences to inform family members about students' progress which, as the name indicates, are led by the students themselves. *Described in chapter 9, on pages 456–357.*

Tableaux: staged groupings of people arranged to illustrate an event, idea, or theme. While the tableau is on view, the people in it usually do not move. *Described in chapter 11, on pages 442–443.*

Om   **Take-home packs:** materials related to school learning packaged for students to take home to

use with their families and then return. *Described in chapter 9, on pages 370–371.*

Talk story: a style of teaching patterned after the method of recounting events which is part of Hawaiian culture. When the talk story strategy is used instructionally, the teacher introduces and asks questions about a topic and many students respond. Teachers do not choose who will answer questions, and turn-taking occurs naturally as students contribute, with the support of the group. Teachers plan the questions they will ask, but they expect varied responses. *Described in chapter 7, on page 290.*

Talking Chips: a strategy that teachers may choose to use occasionally to encourage distribution of talk time in a discussion. Each student is given three plastic chips; as they contribute to the discussion, they give up a chip, thus each student is limited to three turns. *Described in chapter 10, on page 389.*

Om   **Taped readings:** teacher-prepared audiotapes for students to listen to while following along in a book. *Described in chapter 4, on page 130. See also the discussion of audiotapes in chapter 11, on page 449.*

Teacher Read-Aloud Commentary: a strategy in which the teacher reads aloud a short portion of the text, interjecting comments and explanations. *Described in chapter 3, on pages 68–72.*

Tellers' Theater: group storytelling in which multiple stories may be linked. *Described in chapter 11, on page 462.*

Terminology Trade: a vocabulary instruction strategy in which student groups select content area terms to define and give others to the teacher for definition; the teacher has the opportunity to expand upon or correct students' definitions. *Described in chapter 4, on pages 128–129.*

Pm   **Text Hunts:** teacher-prepared materials that engage students in activities through which they use and learn about basic features of a textbook, for example, Table of Contents, Glossary, Index. *Described in chapter 1, on pages 12–16. See also Oral text hunts and Multi-text hunts.*

Text Impressions: a strategy in which students construct an imagined or predicted text based upon selected words and phrases from a text, which are presented before the text is read. *Described in chapter 10, on page 397; additional example given in Chapter 11, on page 467.*

Text scans: purposeful skimming of text that has not yet been read to find a specific piece of information. *Described in chapter 4, on page 131.*

Om **Text sets:** collections of books or other literary material in which every item is different, but all are related, for example, by the same author or illustrator, with a common theme, or providing different perspectives on the same event, person, or idea. For use in literature circles as an alternative to all students reading the same text. *Described in chapter 11, on page 456.*

Om **Themed Listening:** listening to music related to a time, place, or culture that is being studied. *Described in chapter 11, on page 438.*

Om **Themed Reading:** a version of Sustained Silent Reading, also called Structured Sustained Silent Reading, in which everyone reads at the same time, and readers choose their reading from a pre-selected set of materials related to what is being studied. *Described in chapter 2, on pages 37–38.*

Om **Then and now displays:** displays contrasting present and past information and views of a location or place (such as the school itself). The display can be supplemented with transcriptions of oral history in the form of recollections by long-time residents in the area. *Described in chapter 5, on page 169.*

Think-aloud: a strategy in which teachers model the thinking processes of strategic readers by commenting about their own thoughts while reading aloud a short portion of text. *Described in chapter 6, on page 239.*

Thinking challenges: puzzles and problems that engage students in logical, mathematical and creative reasoning. *Examples are given on pages 149–151.*

Pm **Three-level Guides:** teacher-prepared materials that develop students' understanding of a topic through literal, inferential, and application questions. *Described in chapter 4, on pages 141–142.*

Di **Time and Place Maps:** maps that show the location of a series of events and, through a system of color-coding, classify time periods in which they occurred. *Described in chapter 5, on pages 171–172.*

Transform-a-problem: a transmediation strategy in which the structure and solution of a problem is presented through art, graphing, drama, and so on. *Described in chapter 5, on page 176.*

Transmediation: transferring information from one form to another, as, for example, when ideas that have been learned from text and classroom study are presented through drama or art. *Described in chapter 5, on pages 175–177, and referred to throughout the text.*

Traveling journal: a shared journaling method for adults who live at a distance. *Described in chapter 10, on page 407.*

Om **Traveling Suitcase:** a take-home pack in the form of a small overnight suitcase with stickers and tags from various countries and states. In addition to writing supplies, the suitcase can contain maps, and students can write descriptions of real or imaginary journeys. *Described in chapter 9, on page 371.*

Om **Traveling Tales:** a take-home pack project in which writing supplies are packaged in an inexpensive but sturdy backpack. Child and family members collaborate in writing—perhaps through a group story or separate stories from different family members. *Described in chapter 9, on page 371.*

Triple Lists: an assessment method based on observations in which the teacher prepares a checklist of things to observe, supplements it with notes about unanticipated findings, then prepares a list of students' strengths ("CAN DO" list). *Described in chapter 8, on pages 314–315.*

Two Sides: improvisational drama in which half of the participants take on the role of the members of one group, and the other half act as members of another group; groups may switch roles at midpoint in the drama. *Described in chapter 11, on pages 441–442.*

Pm **Typical to Technical Meaning:** a vocabulary development activity designed to build students' understanding of specialized vocabulary. *Described in chapter 3, on pages 88–91.*

U debate: a discussion strategy in which participants choose seats, arranged in a U-shape, according to their views (agree, neutral, disagree) with a point of view being debated. *Described in chapter 5, on page 179.*

Venn diagrams: a pattern graphic of overlapping circles used in comparing and contrasting information. *Described in chapter 4, on page 146.*

<u>Vicarious</u> <u>experiences:</u> experiences, such as listening to a guest speaker or watching a videotape, which substitute for direct experiences. *Described in chapter 4, on pages 121–122.*

Videotapes: Productions of classic works of literature or other aspects of the arts, biographies, or presentations on science and history, which students view as a means of learning. *Discussed in chapter 11, on pages 449–450.*

Vocabulary Connections: a vocabulary development strategy in which the teacher defines a word and students look for examples of its use. *Described in chapter 3, on pages 101, 103.*

Vocabulary Self-Collection Strategy (VSS): a vocabulary development activity in which it is the responsibility of each learner (including the teacher) to choose a term for the class to learn. *Described in chapter 6, on page 238.*

Weather journal: a group journal in which the day's weather is recorded and commented on. *Described in chapter 10, on page 406.*

Om **Weather mosaic:** a mosaic whose tiles illustrate different weather conditions; possible cross-grade collaboration activity when weather is studied. *Described in chapter 12, on pages 499–500.*

We-Search: a strategy for conducting a whole-class research project with younger students. *Described in chapter 5, on page 190.*

What if...: improvisational drama based on what might have happened if a crucial event in history or fiction had been different. *Described in chapter 11, on page 443.*

Om **Wide reading:** building knowledge by reading about a topic from several sources. *Described in chapter 3, on pages 99–103, and in chapter 6, on page 243.*

Word posters: student-prepared posters illustrating a content-related term. The strategy is a form of transmediation. *Described in chapter 5, on pages 176–177.*

Wordless books: books in which the story is conveyed only through pictures. Wordless books can be used in the Say Something strategy. *Described in chapter 10, on page 391.*

<u>Work</u> <u>sampling:</u> keeping a file of students' work, in selected categories, done at different times of the year, as a method of documentation. *Described in chapter 8, on page 331.*

Pm <u>Workstations:</u> locations in the classroom where materials and equipment are available for students' use. Workstations for ongoing assignments can be set up for use by cooperative groups. *Described in the Strategic Teachers section following chapter 9.*

Write-out: a prompted writing strategy in which students write what they know, remember, discovered, or think about a topic. *Described in chapter 10, on page 410.*

Writers' Workshop: sessions of class time set aside for students to confer in small groups about writings in progress. *Described in chapter 10, on page 413.*

Om **Writing Briefcase:** a take-home pack consisting of inexpensive carrying cases equipped with supplies for writing and artwork that students take turns bringing home. The products prepared there may be shared later at school. *Described in chapter 9, on page 371.*

Writing Suitcase: *See Writing Briefcase.*

"Yarn-in-a-box" storytelling: in preparation for this method, yarn is rolled into a ball with knots tied at irregular intervals. The ball of yarn is put into a box; tellers put on the yarn and tell a part of a story until they reach a knot; the yarn and the opportunity to continue the story then passes to the next teller. *Described in chapter 11, on page 462.*

Solutions

CHAPTER 3

Figure 3-11: Completed Focused Cloze

There are **three** classifications of **rocks**, and the names for them are based on how the rocks were formed. Some rocks were formed when molten lava, which is rock material that is so hot that it is a liquid, was pushed up from far below the earth. The center of the earth is very **hot**, but when lava reaches the earth's surface it cools, hardens, and eventually breaks apart into rocks. The term **igneous** rock comes from a Latin word, *ignis*, which means *fire*. It is related to the more familiar words, *ignite* and *ignition*.

Other rocks are called **sedimentary** rocks. Have you ever mixed a powdered drink and found that some bits of the powder didn't dissolve? This material that settles at the bottom of the glass is called *sediment*, from a Latin word meaning *to settle*. Some rocks were formed when small fragments of minerals were pressed together so intensely that they formed into rocks, and these are the **sedimentary** rocks.

Sometimes both **igneous** and **sedimentary*** rocks become changed by heat, pressure, or other causes. The name for the kind of rocks that are produced when other rocks are changed comes from two Greek words: *meta*, which means *change*, and *morphe*, which means *form*. **Metamorphic** rocks are changed in form. Marble is a **metamorphic** rock which is a harder form of the sedimentary rock, limestone.

* (or sedimentary and igneous)

Figure 3-13: Solution of the Discrepancy

The discrepant event is that a king, even though pleased that a task had been well accomplished, said that the results caused him great loss. That's unexpected. How can it be accounted for?

The underlying cause for the discrepancy is that the sum of human knowledge grows and changes over time, and at various points in time there's a narrow range in which knowledge expands suddenly. The task successfully accomplished was creation of an accurate map; the loss was that the map showed the country to be much smaller than previous maps showed.

The king was Louis XIV of France. The person he employed was Giovanni Domenico Cassini, a surveyor and astronomer who came from Italy to France in 1669 to work at the Royal Academy of Sciences, established by the king. The task he was given was to prepare an accurate map of France, and he was able to invent ways to accomplish this, even though the science of cartography was not yet well developed. Previous mapmakers tended to exaggerate the size of a country as a way of pleasing the country's rulers by showing them how great their territory was. The accurate map that Cassini produced showed that France was much smaller than the king expected.

Source: Wilford, John Noble. (1981). *The mapmakers*. NY: Knopf, p. 114.

Notes on Figure 3-16: Creative Reasoning Guide

Among the reasons why France and America ceased to be allies during Adams' presidency:

- The most important reason was that France changed. There was a revolution in which the government was overthrown.
- France declared war on Britain, and America did not support France. Although America and France had signed a treaty promising mutual assistance, the new American nation was not strong enough to wage war. President Washington issued a proclamation of neutrality.
- Toward the end of Adams' term as president, America signed a treaty with Britain.

The most significant reasons why the people were and are known as X, Y, and Z:

- They were engaged in secret negotiations.
- They were following orders from an important person, but they were not well known.
- What they were doing was dishonorable.

President Adams sent a commission (Elbridge Gerry, Charles Pinckney, John Marshall) to France to negotiate a treaty in order to avert war. The French minister of foreign affairs sent three men to meet with them; when the Americans sent messages about their meetings they referred to these men as X, Y, and Z. As the price for negotiating, X, Y, and Z demanded a $10 million dollar loan to France from the American government, and they also asked for $250,000 for themselves. (The Americans refused.) Added note: the French negotiators who were referred to as X, Y, and Z were named Bellamy, Hauteval, and Hottinguer (Tuleja, 1992, p. 48).

The major reason why electing the president was so complicated in 1800 was that the candidates for president and vice president ran separately; either of a party's two candidates could be elected president. At this time in our history, the presidental election was held in the Senate; if the Senate failed to decide the election was decided in the House of Representatives. When the Senate voted, Thomas Jefferson and Aaron Burr were tied; therefore, President Adams was defeated, but the Senate had not selected a president. The election moved to the House of Representatives, where thirty-six ballots were held, with Jefferson and Burr tied each time until Jefferson was elected on the thirty-sixth.

 CHAPTER 4

Completed Text of Cloze Passage in Figure 4-11

Historians of the 1830s were struck by the many changes in industry that had occurred between 1760 and 1790 in Western Europe and America. Before 1750, most goods had been produced by hand, and **most** people had been farmers. There was a shift from **farming** to manufacturing when machines replaced hand tools, and new **sources** of power (steam and electricity) replaced human and animal **power**. Industry was taken from the home into factories; handwork **was** replaced by machinery. The scholars of the 1800s who **studied** these changes saw that the changes had dramatically altered **the** way people lived.

J. A. Blanqui, a French political economist, first **coined** the phrase "Industrial Revolution" when writing about these changes. **The** word *revolution* suggests a sudden, drastic, rapid change, but **we** now know that these changes were the result of **long**, gradual, evolutionary developments. It is interesting to note that **Blanqui** and other scholars thought that the Industrial Revolution would **soon** come to an end and that any future changes **would** come gradually. We now know that the possibilities for **new** inventions are manifold, and that new inventions can be **rapidly** created and put to use. It is amusing to note that in the late 1800s, it was seriously proposed that the United States Patent Office should be closed because everything possible had already been invented.

■ Note about the follow-up questions: The war that we now call World War I was, at the time of the fighting, often called the war to end all wars. People would have been horrified to know it would be called World War I, because that name clearly implies a World War II in the future.

Solutions to thinking challenges in Figure 4–15 through 4–17
Math Thinking Challenge: FIND THREE, Figure 4–15

1. 12, 13, 14   **2.** 8, 9, 10   **3.** 16, 17, 18   **4.** 9, 10, 11
5. 9, 10, 11   **6.** 23, 24, 25   **7.** 18, 19, 20   **8.** 1, 2, 3

Logic Challenges, Figure 4-16

Lon Gago puzzle: The second statement is the false one; the events Lon is reading about occurred during the seventeenth century. (Of the four combinations of one False and three True answers-NYYY, YNYY, YYNY, and YYYN—every combination except the second leads to a contradiction. The events occurred during or after the seventeenth century, therefore, in the seventeenth or eighteenth; they occurred after the fifteenth century, and before the eighteenth. Therefore, they occurred in the seventeenth century.)

Lon Gago and Farah Weihe puzzle: Last week Lon and Farah each borrowed 7 books. This week Farah borrowed 4 and Lon borrowed 2, for a total of 20 books. (It is obviously not possible for both statements in the last pair to be true. Neither is it possible for both statements in the first pair of statements to be true, because that would lead to more than 20 books being borrowed. If it is true that Lon borrowed more than 6 books last week, then he could have borrowed 7, 8, or 9. Farah borrowed the same number, so if this statement is true, together they borrowed 14, 16, or 18. But if both statements in the first pair are true, Lon borrowed more than 6 books this week—and 14 plus more-than-6 is more than 20. Therefore, it is the middle pair of statements that are both true. Farah borrowed 4 books this week and Lon borrowed 3, 2, or 1. Therefore, in the first pair of statements, what Lon says is a fib; therefore, what Farah says is true. Last week, Lon and Farah together borrowed 14, 16, or 18 books. Lon is telling the truth in the final pair of statements.)

1796 Crossnumber, Figure 4-17

A is 204.	B is 487.	C is 94.
D across is 54.	D down is 56.	
E across is 1796.	E down is 18.	F is 934.
G across is 38.	G down is 36.	H is 449.

 CHAPTER 5

The solution to the Semantic Feature Analysis grid in Figure 5-1 is Neptune, Earth, Saturn, Pluto, Jupiter, Mars, Uranus, Venus, and Mercury.

Figure 5-2

The solution to the Semantic Feature Analysis chart in Figure 5-2, column-by-column is:

Erie: No, no, yes, yes   Huron: Yes, no, no, no

Michigan: No, yes, no, yes   Ontario: No, no, yes, no
Superior: Yes, yes, yes, yes

Note that the correct answer to the question "Is Lake Michigan larger than Lake Michigan?" is *No*. (If the question were "Is Lake Michigan smaller than Lake Michigan?" the correct answer would also be *No*.)

Figure 5–3

In the Detection activity shown in Figure 5-3, version 1 is correct. The nine errors in version 2 are:

1) President Johnson (not Lincoln) appointed Marshall. 2) He was born in Baltimore Maryland (not Delaware) 3) …in 1908. 4 and 5) The beginning and ending years of his service as NAACP chief counsel are reversed. 6) He served on the Supreme Court for more than 20 years. 7) John Marshall was the fourth, not the twenty-fourth Chief Justice. 8) and he was appointed by President John Adams. 9) The Thurgood Marshall scholarship was named, of course, for Thurgood Marshall.

 CHAPTER 6

Translation of the passage shown in Figure 6–3

"In the early days, most of the Hawaiian people lived in areas by the sea. They were able to fish. The housing compounds were close to the taro patches in the midland areas. Sometimes, the people went to the upland areas for the gathering of fruit and firewood. The upland areas are far from the seashore." (Snakenberg, 1988, p. 100)

 CHAPTER 10

Solution to Correct It challenge in Figure 10-5

Many insects have legs and antennas that are covered with bristles, 1) some of the bristles are hollow. 2) And have holes in them. Odors in the air go into the holes and 3) threw the bristles and reach cells that are sensitive to the odors. The odors help the insects find food. They also help them find mates. The 4) ways some sea creatures have to detect the animals they eat is like the human sense of smell 5) exsept that sea creatures are sensitive to chemicals in water instead of in the air. Starfish have sense cells at the end of each of their tentacles. Fish have sense cells in their heads and some fish can smell using parts of their skin and tails. Salmon and sea turtles use their sense of smell to find their way back to the places were they were born. They go back to these places to lay their eggs.

1) A period is needed instead of a comma, because these are two sentences. (When this change is made Some needs to be capitalized.) 2) This is not a sentence because there is no subject. The phrase can be combined with the previous sentence. 3) The word should be spelled through. 4) This is the tough one. Ways… are is correct, rather than ways …is. 5) The word is spelled except. 6) The word should be spelled where. The error in the introduction was put there for fun: each of whom nose a lot, should be, of course, each of whom knows a lot…

References

Aardema, Verna. (1981). *Bringing the rain to Kapiti plain.* New York: Dial. Illustrated by Beatriz Vidal.

Aardema, Verna. (1994). *Misoso: Once upon a time tales from Africa.* New York: Apple Soup. Illustrated by Reynold Ruffins.

Aaron, Ira E., Chall, Jeanne S., Clymer, Theodore, Durkin, Dolores, Early, Margaret J., Farr, Roger, & Robinson, H. Alan. (1992). Reflections on the past: Memorable *Reading Teacher* articles. *The Reading Teacher, 45,* 386–392.

Adams, Dennis M., & Hamm, Mary E. (1992). Portfolio assessment and social studies: Collecting, selecting, and reflecting on what is significant. *Social Education, 56,* 103–105.

Adams, Marilyn Jager. (1990). *Beginning to read: Thinking and learning about print.* Cambridge, MA: M.I.T. Press.

Afflerbach, Peter. (1993). STAIR: A system for recording and using what we observe and know about our students. *The Reading Teacher, 47,* 260–263.

Afflerbach, Peter, & Johnston, Peter H. (1993). Writing language arts report cards: Eleven teachers' conflicts of knowing and communicating. *Elementary School Journal, 94,* 73–86.

Alber, Sandy, & Salhi, Adnan. (1995). Maintaining the individual voice as the choir sings. Paper presented at the Second International Congress on Challenges to Education, Cancun, Mexico, July 1995.

Albert, Eleanor. (1994). Drama in the classroom. *Middle School Journal, 25,* 20–24.

Alejandro, Ann. (1994). Like happy dreams—Integrating visual arts, writing, and reading. *Language Arts, 71,* 12–21.

Alexander, Patricia A., Jetton, Tamara L., Kulikowich, Jonna M., & Woehler, Carol A. (1994). Contrasting instructional and structural importance: The seductive effect of teacher questions. *Journal of Reading Behavior, 26,* 19–45.

Aliki. (1993). *Communication.* New York: Greenwillow.

Allen, Jennifer M., & Freitag, Kimberly Koehler. (1988). Parents and students as cooperative learners: A workshop for parents. *The Reading Teacher, 41,* 922–925.

Allington, Richard L. (1977). If they don't read much, how they ever gonna get good? *Journal of Reading, 21,* 57–61.

Allington, Richard L. (1983). The reading instruction provided readers of differing reading abilities. *Elementary School Journal, 83,* 548–559.

Allington, Richard L. (1991). The legacy of "slow it down and make it more concrete." In Jerome Zutell (Ed.) *National Reading Conference Yearbook: Issues in Literacy Research and Instruction.* Chicago, IL: National Reading Conference.

Allington, Richard L. (1992). Reconsidering instructional groupings. *Reading Horizons, 32,* 349–355.

Allington, Richard L., & Shake, Mary C. (1986). Remedial reading: Achieving curricular congruence in classroom and clinic. *The Reading Teacher, 39,* 648–654.

Allison, Alexander W., Barrows, Herbert, Blake, Caesar R., Carr, Arthur J., Eastman, Arthur M., & English, Hubert M, Jr. (Eds.). (1975). *The Norton anthology of poetry, Revised.* New York: Norton.

Allison, Linda. (1975). *The reasons for seasons: The great cosmic megagalactic trip without moving from your chair.* Covelo, CA: Yolla Bolly Press.

Altieri, Jennifer L. (1993). African-American stories and literary responses: Does a child's ethnicity affect the focus of a response? *Reading Horizons, 33,* 236–244.

Alvermann, Donna E. (1991). The Discussion Web: A graphic aid for learning across the curriculum. *The Reading Teacher, 45,* 92–99.

Alvermann, Donna E., & Hayes, David A. (1989). Classroom discussion of content area reading assignments: An intervention study. *Reading Research Quarterly, 24,* 305–335.

Ancona, George. (1995). *Cutters, carvers & the cathedral.* New York: Lothrop, Lee & Shepard.

Anders, Patricia, & Bos, Candace. (1986). Semantic feature analysis: An interactive strategy for vocabulary development and text comprehension. *Journal of Reading, 29,* 610–616.

Andersen, Janis F., & Andersen, Peter A. (1987). Never smile until Christmas? Casting doubt on an old myth. *Journal of Thought, 22,* 57–61.

Anderson, Gaylyn Karle. (1990). "I -Search a word": Reclaiming the library's reference section. *English Journal, 79,* 53–57.

Anderson, Richard C., Hiebert, Elfrieda H., Scott, Judith A., & Wilkinson, Ian A. G. (1986). *Becoming a nation of readers.* Washington, DC: The National Institute of Education.

Angelou, Maya. (1994). *My painted house, my friendly chicken, and me.* New York: Clarkson Potter. Photographs by Margaret Courtney-Clarke.

Anno, Mitsumasa. (1982). *Anno's counting house.* New York: Philomel.

Applebee, Arthur. (1991). Literature: Whose heritage? In Elfrieda H. Hiebert (Ed.), *Literacy for a diverse society: Perspectives, practices, and policies.* New York: Teachers College Press.

Armbruster, Bonnie B., & Anderson, Thomas H. (1984). *Producing considerate expository text (Reading Education Report No. 46)* Urbana, IL: University of Illinois, Center for the Study of Reading.

Aron, Helen. (1992). Bookworms become tapeworms: A profile of listeners to books on audiocassette. *Journal of Reading, 36,* 208–212.

Aronson, Elliott N. (1978). *The jigsaw classroom.* Beverly Hills, CA: Sage.

Artzt, Alice. (1994). Integrating writing and cooperative learning in the mathematics class. *Mathematics Teacher, 87,* 80–85.

Ash, Barbara Hoetker. (1990). Reading assigned literature in a reading workshop. *English Journal, 79,* 77–79.

Asher, Sandy. (1994). Life, live theater, and the lively classroom. *ALAN Review, 21,* 2–8.

Asimov, Isaac. (1993). *Isaac Asimov's guide to earth and space.* New York: Ballantine.

Athanases, Steven. (1988). Developing a classroom community of interpreters. *English Journal, 77,* 45–48.

Atkin, S. Beth. (1993). *Voices from the fields: Children of migrant farmworkers tell their stories.* Boston: Little, Brown.

Atwell, Nancie. (1984). Writing and reading literature from the inside out. *Language Arts, 61,* 240–252.

Atwell, Nancie. (1987a). Building a dining room table: Dialogue journals about reading. In Toby Fulwiler (Ed.) *The journal book.* Portsmouth, NH: Heinemann.

Atwell, Nancie. (1987b). *In the middle: Writing, reading and learning with adolescents.* Upper Montclair, NJ: Boynton/Cook.

Atwell, Nancie (Ed.). (1990). *Coming to know: Writing to learn in the intermediate grades.* Portsmouth, NH: Heinemann.

Au, Kathryn Hu-Pei. (1979). Using the experience-text-relationship method with minority children. *The Reading Teacher, 32,* 677–679.

Au, Kathryn Hu-Pei. (1980). Participation structures in a reading lesson with Hawaiian children: Analysis of a culturally appropriate instructional event. *Anthropology and Education Quarterly, 11,* 91–115.

Au, Kathryn H. (1993). *Literacy instruction in multicultural settings.* Fort Worth, TX: Harcourt Brace.

Au, Kathryn Hu-Pei. (1995). Multicultural perspectives on literacy research. *Journal of Reading Behavior, 27,* 85–100.

Au, Kathryn Hu-Pei, & Kawakami, Alice J. (1985). Research currents: Talk story and learning to read. *Language Arts, 62,* 406–411.

Au, Kathryn Hu-Pei, & Kawakami, Alice J. (1994). Cultural congruence in instruction. In Etta R. Hollins, Joyce E. King, & Warren C. Haymon (Eds.), *Teaching diverse populations: Formulating a knowledge base.* Albany, NY: SUNY Press.

Au, Kathryn Hu-Pei, & Mason, Jana M. (1981). Social organizational factors in learning to read: The balance of rights hypothesis. *Reading Research Quarterly, 17,* 115–152.

Au, Kathryn Hu-Pei, & Mason, Jana M. (1983). Cultural congruence in classroom participation structures: Achieving a balance of rights. *Discourse Processes, 6,* 145–167.

Ayers, William. (1994). Can city schools be saved? *Educational Leadership, 51,* 60–63.

Baker, Jeannie. (1991). *Window.* New York: Greenwillow.

Baker, Jeannie. (1994). *Where the forest meets the sea.* New York: Greenwillow.

Baker, Jeannie. (1995). *The story of rosy dock.* New York: Greenwillow.

Baker, Keith. (1993). "Have you been dead?" Questions and letters from children. *The Reading Teacher, 46,* 372–373.

Baker, Thomas Richard. (1993). *Weather in the lab.* Summit, PA: McGraw-Hill.

Bakst, Kathy, & Essa, Eva L. (1990). The writing table: Emergent writers and editors. *Childhood Education, 66,* 145–150.

Ballenger, Cynthia. (1991). Because you like us: The language of control. *Harvard Educational Review, 62,* 199–208.

Baloche, Lynda, Mauger, Marilyn Lee, Willis, Therese M., Filinuk, Joseph R., & Michalsky, Barbara V. (1993). Fishbowls, creative controversy, talking chips: Exploring literature cooperatively. *English Journal, 82,* 43–48.

Banks, Cherry A. McGee. (1992). Shattering stereotypes and reducing prejudice with multiethnic literature. *Social Studies and the Young Learner, 5,* 6–8.

Banks, James A. (1987). The social studies, ethnic diversity, and social change. *Elementary School Journal, 87,* 531–543.

Banks, James A. (1993). Multicultural education: Historical development, dimensions, and practice. In Linda Darling-Hammond (Ed.), *Review of Research in Education.* Washington, DC: American Educational Research Association.

Banks, James A. (1994). Transforming the mainstream curriculum. *Educational Leadership, 51,* 4–8.

Barclay, Kathy Dulaney. (1990). Constructing meaning: An integrated approach to teaching reading. *Intervention in School and Clinic, 26,* 84–91.

Barnes-Murphy, Frances. (1994). *The fables of Aesop.* New York: Lothrop, Lee & Shepard. Illustrated by Rowan Barnes-Murphy.

Baron, Dennis. (1994). Fact versus opinion: Three middle school students ask NCTE to settle a debate. *The Council Chronicle: The National Council of Teachers of English, 3,* 16–17.

Barone, Thomas. (1991). Assessment as theater: Staging an exposition. *Educational Leadership, 48,* 57–59.

Barron, Ronald. (1991). What I wish I had known about peer-response groups but didn't. *English Journal, 80,* 24–25.

Bartolome, Lilia I. (1994). Beyond the methods fetish: Toward a humanizing pedagogy. *Harvard Educational Review, 64,* 173–194.

Bash, Barbara. (1989). *The tree of life: The world of the African baobab.* San Francisco, CA: Sierra Club.

Bauer, Marion Dane. (1993). Have students revise only their best writing. *Journal of Reading, 37,* 134–135.

Baumann, James F. (1988). Direct instruction reconsidered. *Journal of Reading, 31,* 712–718.

Beach, Sara Ann. (1993). Oral reading instruction: Retiring the bird in the round. *Reading Psychology, 14,* 333–338.

Beane, James A. (1990). *A middle school curriculum: From rhetoric to reality.* Columbus, OH: National Middle School Association

Beatty, Patricia. (1987). *Charley Skedaddle.* New York: Morrow.

Beaupré, Daniel J. (1992). Students as cartographers. *The Social Studies, 83,* 83–84.

Beck, Isabel L., & McKeown, Margaret G. (1991). Social studies texts are hard to understand: Mediating some of the difficulties. *Language Arts, 68,* 482–490.

Benard, Bonnie. (1993). Fostering resiliency in kids. *Educational Leadership, 51,* 44–48.

Benét, Stephen Vincent. (1942). The devil and Daniel Webster. In *The Selected Works of Stephen Vincent Benét, Volume Two: Prose.* New York: Farrar & Rinehart.

Berlyne, David E. (1965). Curiosity and education. In J. D. Krumholtz (Ed.), *Learning and the educational process.* Chicago: Rand McNally.

Bernstein, Joanne E., & Fireside, Bryna J. (1991). *Special parents, special children.* Morton Grove, IL: Albert Whitman. Photographs by Michael J. Bernstein.

Berthoff, Ann E. (1982). *Forming thinking writing.* Upper Montclair, NJ: Boynton/Cook.

Biddle, Steve, & Biddle, Megumi. (1994). *Origami safari.* New York: Tupelo.

Bierhorst, John (Ed.). (1992). *Lightning inside you.* New York: William Morrow. Illustrated by Louise Brierley.

Binet, Alfred, & Simon, Theophilus. (1916). *The development of intelligence in children.* Baltimore, MD: Williams & Wilkins.

Bishop, Rudine Sims. (1990a). Mirrors, windows and sliding glass doors. *perspectives, 6,* ix–xi.

Bishop, Rudine Sims. (1990b). Walk tall in the world: African American literature for today's children. *Journal of Negro Education, 59,* 556–565.

Bishop, Rudine Sims. (1992). Extending multicultural understanding. In Bernice E. Cullinan (Ed.). *Invitation to read: More children's literature in the reading program.* Newark, DE: International Reading Association.

Bjorklund, Gail, & Burger, Christine. (1987). Making conferences work for parents, teachers, and children. *Young Children, 42,* 26–31.

Bligh, Tanya. (1995). Using story impressions to improve reading comprehension. *Reading Horizons, 35,* 287–298.

Blizzard, Gladys S. (1992). *Come look with me: Exploring landscape art with children.* Charlottesville, VA: Thomasson-Grant.

Blizzard, Gladys S. (1993a). *Come look with me: Enjoying art with children.* Charlottesville, VA: Thomasson-Grant.

Blizzard, Gladys S. (1993b). *Come look with me: World of play.* Charlottesville, VA: Thomasson-Grant.

Block, Kathleen. (1991). How students see their writing: A visual representation of literacy. *Journal of Reading, 35,* 204–214.

Blocksma, Mary. (1989). *Reading the numbers: A survival*

guide to the measurements, numbers, and sizes encountered in everyday life. New York: Penguin.

Bloom, Benjamin S. (Ed.) (1956). *Taxonomy of educational objectives: Cognitive domain.* New York: David McKay.

Bloom, Benjamin S. (1981). *All our children learning.* New York: McGraw-Hill.

Blough, Doris B. (1992). How language arts teachers help produce dropouts. *Principal, 71,* 53–56.

Blount, H. Parker. (1992). Making history live for secondary students: Infusing people into the narrative. *The Social Studies, 83,* 220–223.

Boardman, David J. (1976). Graphicacy in the classroom. *Educational Review, 28,* 118–125.

Booth, David, & Thornley-Hall, Carol. (1991). *The talk curriculum.* Carlton, Victoria, Australia: Australian Reading Association.

Borenson, Henry. (1986). Teaching students to think in mathematics and to make conjectures. In Mark Driscoll & Jere Confrey (Eds.). *Teaching mathematics: Strategies that work.* Portsmouth, NH: Heinemann.

Borko, Hilda, & Eisenhart, Margaret. (1986). Students' conceptions of reading and their reading experiences in school. *Elementary School Journal, 86,* 589–611.

Bormuth, John R. (1968). Cloze test reliability: Criterion reference scores. *Journal of Educational Measurement, 5,* 189–196.

Bowen, Catherine Drinker. (1966). *Miracle at Philadelphia: The story of the constitutional convention May to September 1787.* Boston, MA: Little, Brown.

Boyle, Owen F., & Peregoy, Suzanne F. (1990). Literacy scaffolds: Strategies for first- and second-language readers and writers. *The Reading Teacher, 44,* 194–200.

Brandt, Ron. (1992). On building learning communities: A conversation with Hank Levin. *Educational Leadership, 50,* 19–23.

Brandt, Ron. (1993). On teaching for understanding: A conversation with Howard Gardner. *Educational Leadership, 50,* 4–7.

Breece, Katharine Auld. (1988). Write-Out: A way to teach content and writing too. *Middle School Journal, 20,* 14–15.

Breland, Hunter M., Camp, Roberta, Jones, Robert J., Morris, Margaret M., & Rock, Donald A. (1987). *Assessing writing skill.* New York: College Board Publications.

Brent, Isabelle (Illustrator). (1994). *All creatures great and small.* Boston, MA: Little, Brown.

Brent, Rebecca, & Anderson, Patricia. (1993). Developing children's classroom listening strategies. *The Reading Teacher, 47,* 122–126.

Brett, Jan. (1988). *The first dog.* San Diego, CA: Harcourt Brace Jovanovich.

Brick, Madeline. (1993). When students write home. *Edu-cational Leadership, 50,* 62–63.

Brierley, John. (1990). Using winds and ocean currents in teaching human movement. *Journal of Geography, 89,* 165–169.

Bristor, Valerie J. (1993). Enhancing instruction by integrating reading and writing with science. *Journal of Reading Education, 18,* 20–30.

Bromley, Karen D'Angelo. (1989). Buddy journals make the reading-writing connection. *The Reading Teacher, 43,* 122–129.

Bronfenbrenner, Urie. (1976). The experimental ecology of education. *Teachers College Record, 78,* 157–204.

Bronfenbrenner, Urie. (1979). *The ecology of human development: Experiments by nature and design.* Cambridge, MA: Harvard University Press.

Brown, Ann L. (1994). The advancement of learning. *Educational Researcher, 23,* 4–12.

Brown, David L., & Briggs, L. D. (1989). Success in reading: Four characteristics of strategic readers. *Reading Horizons, 30,* 30–38.

Brown, Hazel, & Cambourne, Brian. (1990). *Read and retell.* Portsmouth, NH: Heinemann.

Brown, John Seely, Collins, Allan, & Duguid, Paul. (1989). Situated cognition and the culture of learning. *Educational Researcher, 18,* 32–42.

Brown, Roger. (1973a). *A first language.* Cambridge, MA: Harvard University Press.

Brown, Roger. (1973b). Development of the first language in the human species. *American Psychologist, 28,* 97–106.

Brozo, William G. (1988). Applying a reader response heuristic to expository text. *Journal of Reading, 32,* 140–145.

Bruner, Jerome S. (1965). *The process of education.* Cambridge, MA: Harvard University Press.

Bruner, Jerome. (1975). The ontogenesis of speech acts. *Journal of Child Language, 2,* 1–40.

Bucher, Katherine T., & Fravel, Mark, Jr. (1991). Local history comes alive with postcards. *Social Studies and the Young Learner, 3,* 18–20.

Bunting, Eve. (1994). *Smoky night.* San Diego, CA: Harcourt Brace. Illustrated by David Diaz.

Burniske, R. W. (1994). Creating dialogue: Teacher response to journal writing. *English Journal, 83,* 84–87.

Busching, Beverly A. (1981). Readers theatre: An education for language and life. *Language Arts, 58,* 330–338.

Butler, Dorothy. (1982). Reading begins at home. *Theory into Practice, 21,* 308–314.

Cai, Mingshui. (1994). Images of Chinese and Chinese Americans mirrored in picture books. *Children's Literature in Education, 25,* 169–191.

Caldwell, Helen, & Moore, Blaine H. (1991). The art of writing: Drawing as preparation for narrative writing in the primary grades. *Studies in Art Education, 32,* 207–219.

Calkins, Lucy McCormick. (1980). When children want to punctuate: Basic skills belong in context. *Language Arts, 57,* 567–573.

Cambourne, Brian, & Turbill, Jan. (1990). Assessment in whole-language classrooms: Theory into practice. *Elementary School Journal, 90,* 337–349.

Cardarelli, Aldo F. (1992). Teachers under cover: Promoting the personal reading of teachers. *The Reading Teacher, 45,* 664–668.

Carew, Jean V. (1976). *Observing intelligence in young children: Eight case studies.* Englewood Cliffs, NJ: Prentice-Hall.

Carr, Eileen, & Ogle, Donna M. (1987). K-W-L Plus: A strategy for comprehension and summarization. *Journal of Reading, 30,* 626–631.

Carter, Betty, & Abrahamson, Richard F. (1990). *Nonfiction for young adults: From delight to wisdom.* Phoenix, AZ: Oryx Press.

Carter, Betty, & Abrahamson, Richard F. (1991). Nonfiction in a read-aloud program. *Journal of Reading, 34,* 638–642.

Cattell, Raymond B. (1971). *Abilities: Their structure, growth, and action.* Boston, MA: Houghton-Mifflin.

Cazden, Courtney B. (1972). *Child language and education.* New York: Holt, Rinehart & Winston.

Cazden, Courtney B. (1988). *Classroom discourse: The language of teaching and learning.* Portsmouth, NH: Heinemann.

Cecil, Nancy Lee, & Lauritzen, Phyllis. (1994). *Literacy and the arts for the integrated classroom: Alternative ways of knowing.* New York: Longman.

Chall, Jeanne S. (1967). *Learning to read: The great debate.* New York: McGraw-Hill.

Chall, Jeanne S. (1983). *Stages of reading development.* New York: McGraw-Hill.

Chalofsky, Margie, Finland, Glen, & Wallace, Judy. (1992). *Changing places: A kid's view of shelter living.* Mt. Rainier, MD: Gryphon House.

Chandler, Phyllis A. (1994). *A Place for Me.* Washington, DC: National Association for the Education of Young Children.

Charles, Jim. (1991). Celebrating the diversity of American Indian literature. *ALAN Review, 18,* 4–8.

Chenfeld, Mimi Brodsky. (1987a). *Teaching Language Arts Creatively, 2nd ed.* San Diego, CA: Harcourt Brace Jovanovich.

Chenfeld, Mimi Brodsky. (1987b). The first 30 years are the hardest: Notes from the Yellow Brick Road. *Young Children, 42,* 28–32.

Chenfeld, Mimi Brodsky. (1989). "What has two legs and loves you?": Four-letter words in the classroom. *Language Arts, 66,* 423–428.

Cheng, Hou-tien. (1979). *The six Chinese brothers.* New York: Holt.

Cherry, Lynne. (1992). *A river ran wild.* San Diego, CA: Harcourt Brace Jovanovich.

Chilcoat, George W. (1991). The illustrated song slide show as a middle school history activity. *The Social Studies, 82,* 188–190.

Chinn, Clark A., & Brewer, William F. (1993). The role of anomalous data in knowledge acquisition: A theoretical framework and implications for science instruction. *Review of Educational Research, 63,* 1–49.

Choate, Joyce S., & Rakes, Thomas A. (1987). The structured listening activity: A model for improving listening comprehension. *The Reading Teacher, 41,* 194–200.

Cianciolo, Patricia J. (1989). No small challenge: Literature for the transitional readers. *Language Arts, 66,* 72–81.

Ciscell, Robert E. (1990). How to prepare for a conference with angry parents. *Middle School Journal, 21,* 46–47.

Clark, Charles H. (1995). Teaching students about reading: A fluency example. *Reading Horizons, 35,* 251–266.

Clark, H. Clifford, & Nelson, Marvin N. (1993). Improving mathematics evaluation through cooperative learning strategies. *Middle School Journal, 24,* 15–18.

Clark, Reginald. (1983). *Family life and school achievement: Why poor black children succeed or fail.* Chicago, IL: University of Chicago Press.

Clarke, John, Martell, Kevin, & Willey, Carol. (1994). Sequencing graphic organizers to guide historical research. *The Social Studies, 85,* 70–75.

Clay, Marie M. (1966). *Emergent reading behavior.* Unpublished doctoral dissertation. University of Auckland Library. Auckland, New Zealand.

Clay, Marie M. (1979). *Reading: The patterning of complex behavior.* Auckland, New Zealand: Heinemann.

Clay, Marie M., Clay, Marie. (1985). *The early detection of reading difficulties, 3rd ed.* Portsmouth, NH: Heinemann-Boynton/Cook.

Clay, Marie. (1989). Involving teachers in classroom research. In Gay Su Pinnell & Myna L. Matlin (Eds.) *Teachers and research.* Newark, DE: International Reading Association.

Clay, Marie. (1990). Research currents: What is and what might be in evaluation. *Language Arts, 67,* 288–298.

Cleary, Beverly. (1968). *Ramona the Pest.* New York: Morrow.

Clement, Rod. (1991). *Counting on Frank*. New York: Gareth Stevens.

Clewell, Suzanne F., & Haidemos, Julie. (1983). Organizational strategies to increase comprehension. *Reading World, 22,* 314–321.

Cliatt, Mary Jo Puckett, & Shaw, Jean M. (1988). The storytime exchange: Ways to enhance it. *Childhood Education, 65,* 293–298.

Close, Elizabeth. (1990). Seventh graders sharing literature: How did we get here? *Language Arts, 67,* 817–823.

Cobb, Vicki. (1990). *Natural wonders: Stories science photos tell.* New York: Lothrop, Lee & Shepard.

Cobb, Vicki. (1991). *Fun and games: Stories science photos tell.* New York: Lothrop, Lee & Shepard.

Cobb, Vicki, & Darling, Kathy. (1993). *Wanna bet? Science challenges to fool you.* New York: Lothrop, Lee & Shepard.

Cockburn, Victor. (1991). The uses of folk music and songwriting in the classroom. *Harvard Educational Review, 61,* 71–79.

Coffey, Kathy. (1989). Playing the accordion and framing the research question. *English Journal, 78,* 45.

Cohen, Elizabeth G. (1994). Restructuring the classroom: Conditions for productive small groups. *Review of Educational Research, 64,* 1–35.

Cohen, J. M., & Cohen, M. J. (1976). *The Penguin dictionary of quotations.* Baltimore, MD: Penguin.

Cohn, Amy (Compiler). (1993). *From sea to shining sea: A treasury of American folklore and folk songs.* New York: Scholastic.

Cole, Joanna. (1986). *The magic school bus at the waterworks.* New York: Scholastic.

Coleman, James S. (1987). Families and schools. *Educational Researcher, 16,* 32–38.

Collins, Angelo. (1992). Portfolios for science education: Issues of purpose, structure, and authenticity. *Science Education, 76,* 451–463.

Colwell, Eileen. (1991). *Storytelling,* Oxford, England: Thimble Press

Combs, Arthur. (1979). *Myths in education: Beliefs that hinder progress and their alternatives.* Boston: Allyn & Bacon.

Combs, Martha, & Beach, John D. (1994). Stories and storytelling: Personalizing the social studies. *The Reading Teacher, 47,* 464–471.

Comer, James P., & Haynes, Norris M. (1991). Parent involvement in schools: An ecological approach. *Elementary School Journal, 91,* 271–277.

Cook, Gillian E., & Martinello, Marian L. (1994). Topics and themes in interdisciplinary curriculum. *Middle School Journal, 25,* 40–44.

Cooper, Charles R. (1977). Holistic evaluation of writing. In Charles R. Cooper & Lee Odell (Eds.) *Evaluating writing: Describing, measuring, judging.* Urbana, IL: National Council of Teachers of English.

Cooper, Kelt, & Gonzalez, María Luisa. (1993). Communicating with parents when you don't speak their language. *Principal, 73,* 45–46.

Coote, Edmund. (1596). The English school-maister, teaching all his scholars, of what age soever, the most easie, short, and perfect order of distinct reading, and true writing our English tongue that hath ever yet been knowne and published by any. (Cited in Wade, Barrie. (1991). Tests and texts: The state of reading. *Educational Review, 43,* 213–223.)

Cooter, Robert B., Jr. (1991). Storytelling in the language arts classroom. *Reading Research and Instruction, 30,* 71–76.

Copeland, Jeffrey S., & Copeland, Vicky L. (1994). *Speaking of poets 2: More interviews with poets who write for children and young adults.* Urbana, IL: National Council of Teachers of English.

Corno, Lyn, (1986). The metacognitive control components of self-regulated learning. *Contemporary Educational Psychology, 11,* 333–346.

Costa, Arthur L. (1989). Re-assessing assessment. *Educational Leadership, 46,* 2.

Cox, Beth. (1991). A picture is worth a thousand worksheets. *Journal of Reading, 35,* 244–245.

Crafton, Linda K. (1983). Learning from reading: What happens when students generate their own background information? *Journal of Reading, 26,* 586–592.

Cramer, Eugene H., & Castle, Marrietta (Eds.). (1995). *Fostering the love of reading: The affective domain in reading education.* Newark, DE: International Reading Association.

Crews, Donald. (1992). *Shortcut.* New York: Greenwillow.

Cromer, Ward. (1970). The difference model: A new explanation of some reading difficulties. *Journal of Educational Psychology, 61,* 471–483.

Crook, Patricia R. (1990). Children confront civil war issues: Using literature as an integral part of the social studies curriculum. *Academic Therapy, 25,* 489–503.

Csikszentmihalyi, Mihaly. (1990). Literature and intrinsic motivation. *Daedalus: Journal of the American Academy of Arts and Sciences, 119,* 115–116.

Csikszentmihalyi, Mihaly. (1991). *Flow: The psychology of optimal experience.* New York: HarperPerennial.

Csikszentmihalyi, Mihaly, & Csikszentmihalyi, Isabella Selega. (Eds.). (1988). *Optimal experience: Psychological studies of flow in consciousness.* New York: Cambridge University Press.

Csikszentmihalyi, Mihaly, Rathunde, Kevin, & Whalen, Samuel. (1993). *Talented teenagers: The roots of success and failure.* New York: Cambridge University Press.

Cudd, Evelyn T. (1989). Research and report writing in the elementary grades. *The Reading Teacher, 43,* 268–269.

Cummins, Jim. (1994). The acquisition of English as a second language. In Karen Spangenberg-Urbschat & Robert Pritchard (Eds.). *Kids come in all languages: Reading instruction of ESL students.* Newark, DE: International Reading Association.

Cushner, Kenneth. (1992). Creating cross-cultural understanding through internationally cooperative story writing. *Social Education, 56,* 43–46.

Cushner, Kenneth, McClelland, Averil, & Safford, Philip. (1992). *Human diversity in education: An integrative approach.* New York: McGraw-Hill.

Daly, John A., & Miller, Michael D. (1975). The empirical development of an instrument to measure writing apprehension. *Research in the Teaching of English, 9,* 242–248.

Daniel, Lois W. (1989). Art and architecture. *Social studies and the young learner, 1,* 3–7.

Danielson, Kathy Everts. (1992). Literature groups and literature logs: Responding to literature in a community of readers. *Reading Horizons, 32,* 372–382.

Danielson, Kathy Everts, & Dauer, Susan Crites. (1990). Celebrate poetry through creative drama. *Reading Horizons, 31,* 138–148.

Davey, Beth. (1983). Think-aloud—modeling the cognitive processes of reading comprehension. *Journal of Reading, 27,* 44–47.

Davey, Beth. (1988). The nature of response errors for good and poor readers when permitted to reinspect text during question-answering. *American Educational Research Journal, 25,* 399–414.

Davis, Susan, & Diaz, Sheila. (1994). Identifying and educating low-literate adults. *Reading Horizons, 34,* 315–323.

Davis, Susan J. (1994). Teaching practices that encourage or eliminate student plagiarism. *Middle School Journal, 25,* 55–58.

Davis, Suzanne F. (1993). Can good become better?: The progression of an exemplary teacher. *Reading Horizons, 33,* 441–448.

Day, David. (1989). *Vanished Species.* New York: Gallery Books.

DeCoker, Gary. (1989). Bringing foreign languages into the social studies classroom. *The Social Studies, 80,* 219–224.

DeGroff, Linda, & Galda, Lee. (1992). Responding to literature: Activities for exploring books. In Bernice E. Cullinan (Ed.), *Invitation to read: More children's literature in the reading program.* Newark, DE: International Reading Association.

Delclos, Victor R., Burns, M. Susan, & Kulewicz, Stanley J. (1987). Effects of dynamic assessment on teachers' expectations of handicapped children. *American Educational Research Journal, 24,* 325–336.

Delgado-Gaitan, Concha. (1992). School matters in the Mexican-American home. Socializing children to education. *American Educational Research Journal, 29,* 495–513.

Dellinger, Dixie G. (1989). Alternatives to clip and stitch: Real writing in the classroom. *English Journal, 78,* 31–38.

Delpit, Lisa. (1988). The silenced dialogue: Power and pedagogy in educating other people's children. *Harvard Educational Review, 58,* 280–298.

Demi. (1992). *In the eyes of the cat: Japanese poetry for all seasons.* New York: Henry Holt.

Denzin, N. K. (1988). Triangulation. In John P. Keeves (Ed.), *Educational research, methodology, and measurement: An international handbook.* Oxford, England: Pergamon.

dePaola, Tomie. (1988). *Tomie dePaola's book of poems.* New York: G. P. Putnam's Sons.

Deutsch, Morton. (1949). A theory of cooperation and competition. *Human Relations, 2,* 129–152.

Deutsch, Morton. (1962). *Cooperation and trust: Some theoretical notes.* In Marshall R. Jones (Ed.), *Nebraska Symposium on Motivation.* Lincoln, NE: University of Nebraska.

Deutsch. Morton. (1985). *Distributive justice: A social-psychological perspective.* New Haven, CT: Yale University Press.

Dewey, John. (1913). *Interest and effort in education.* Boston, MA: Houghton Mifflin.

Dewey, John. (1933). *How we think.* Lexington, MA: Heath.

DeYoung, Kimberly. (1994). *Personal communication.*

deZutter, Hank. (1993). *Who says a dog goes bow-wow?* New York: Doubleday. Illustrated by Suse MacDonald.

Diakiw, Jerry Y. (1990). Children's literature and global education: Understanding the developing world. *The Reading Teacher, 44,* 296–300.

Dillon, Deborah R. (1989). Showing them that I want them to learn and that I care about who they are: A microethnography of the social organization of a secondary low-track English-reading classroom. *American Educational Research Journal, 26,* 227–259.

Dillon, J. T. (1982). The multidisciplinary study of questioning. *Journal of Educational Psychology, 74,* 147–164.

Dillon, J. T. (1984). Research on questioning and discussion. *Educational Leadership, 42,* 50–56.

Dionisio, Marie. (1989). Filling empty pockets: Remedial readers make meaning. *English Journal, 78,* 33–37.

Dobler, Judith M., & Amoriell, William J. (1988). Comments on writing: Features that affect student performance. *Journal of Reading, 32,* 214–223.

Doiron, Ray. (1994). Using nonfiction in a read-aloud program: Letting the facts speak for themselves. *The Reading Teacher, 47,* 616–624.

Dolch, Edward W. (1931). *The psychology and teaching of reading.* Boston, MA: Girard.

Dole, Janice A., Valencia, Sheila W., Gregg, Eunice Ann, & Wardrop, James L. (1991). Effects of two types of prereading instruction on the comprehension of narrative and expository text. *Reading Research Quarterly, 26,* 142–159.

Dolly, Martha R. (1990). Integrating ESL reading and writing through authentic discourse. *Journal of Reading, 33, 360–365.*

Donaldson, Margaret. (1978). *Children's minds.* London: Fontana/Collins.

Drabble, Margaret (Ed.). (1985). *The Oxford companion to English literature, 5th ed.* New York: Oxford University Press.

Dreher, Mariam Jean. (1992). Searching for information in textbooks. *Journal of Reading, 35,* 364–371.

Dreher, Mariam Jean, & Guthrie, John T. (1990). Cognitive processes in textbook chapter search tasks. *Reading Research Quarterly, 25,* 323–339.

Dreher, Mariam Jean, & Singer, Harry. (1989). Friendly texts and text-friendly teachers. *Theory into Practice, 28,* 98–104.

Dudley-Marling, Curt. (1994). Struggling readers in the regular classroom: A personal reflection. *Reading Horizons, 34,* 465–487.

Dudley-Marling, Curt, & Dippo, Don. (1991). The language of whole language. *Language Arts, 68,* 548–554.

Dueck, Kathy. (1986). RAFT: Writing. *Kappa Delta Pi Record, 22,* 64.

Dulay, Heidi C., & Burt, Marina K. (1977). Remarks on creativity in second language acquisition. In Marina K. Burt, Heidi C. Dulay & Mary Finnochiaro (Eds.) *Viewpoints on English as a second language.* New York: Regents.

Durkin, Dolores. (1989). *Teaching them to read, 5th ed.* Boston, MA: Allyn & Bacon.

Durkin, Dolores. (1990). Dolores Durkin speaks on instruction. *The Reading Teacher, 43,* 472–476.

Duthie, James. (1986). The web: A powerful tool for the teaching and evaluation of the expository essay. *History and Social Science Teacher, 21,* 232–236.

Dynak, David. (1993). *Personal communication.*

Dyson, Anne Haas. (1990). Weaving possibilities: Rethinking metaphors for early literacy development. *The Reading Teacher, 44,* 202–213.

Early, Margaret. (1990). Enabling first and second language learners in the classroom. *Language Arts, 67,* 567–575.

Ecroyd, Catherine Ann. (1991). Motivating students through reading aloud. *English Journal, 80,* 76–78.

Eder, Donna. (1981). Ability grouping as a self-fulfilling prophecy: A micro-analysis of teacher-student interaction. *Sociology of Education, 54,* 151–162.

Edmiston, Brian, Encisco, Pat, & King, Martha L. (1987). Empowering readers and writers through drama: Narrative Theater. *Language Arts, 64,* 219–228.

Edwards, Phyllis R. (1991/1992). Using dialectical journals to teach thinking skills. *Journal of Reading, 35,* 312–316.

Eeds, Maryann, & Peterson, Ralph. (1991). Teacher as curator: Learning to talk about literature. *The Reading Teacher, 45,* 118–126.

Eeds, Maryann, & Wells, Deborah. (1989). Grand conversations: An exploration of meaning construction in literature study groups. *Research in the Teaching of English, 23,* 4–29.

Ehlert, Lois. (1989). *Color farm.* New York: Lippincott.

Ehlert, Lois. (1990). *Color zoo.* New York: Lippincott.

Ehlert, Lois. (1993). *Nuts to you.* San Diego, CA: Harcourt Brace Jovanovich.

Eisenberg, Nancy, Lennon, Randy, & Roth, Karlsson. (1983). Prosocial development: A longitudinal study. *Developmental Psychology, 19,* 846–855.

Eisenberg-Berg, Nancy, & Neal, Cynthia. (1979). Children's moral reasoning about their own spontaneous prosocial behavior. *Developmental Psychology, 15,* 228–229.

Eisner, Elliot W. (1992). The misunderstood role of the arts in human development. *Phi Delta Kappan, 73,* 591–595.

Eisner, Elliot W. (1993). Forms of understanding and the future of educational research. *Educational Researcher, 22,* 5–11.

Elley, Warwick B. (1989). Vocabulary acquisition from listening to stories. *Reading Research Quarterly, 24,* 174–187.

Elley, Warwick B., & Mangubhai, Francis. (1983). The impact of reading on second language learning. *Reading Research Quarterly, 19,* 53–67.

Ellsworth, Peter C., & Sidt, Vincent G. (1994). Helping "aha" to happen: The contributions of Irving Sigel. *Educational Leadership, 51,* 40–44.

Engen, Rodney K. (1988). *Randolph Caldecott: "Lord of the nursery."* London, England: Bloomsbury Books.

Epeneter, Susan, & Chang, Candace. (1992). Exploring diversity through the arts. In Bonnie Neugebauer (Ed.) *Alike and different: Exploring our humanity with young children.* Washington, DC: National Association for the Education of Young Children.

Epstein, Joyce L. (1988). How do we improve programs for parent involvement? *Educational Horizons, 66,* 58–59.

Epstein, Joyce L., & Dauber, Susan L. (1991). School programs and teacher practices of parent involvement in inner-city elementary and middle schools. *Elementary School Journal, 91,* 289–305.

Erickson, Ann. (undated). *Studying: A key to success. . . ways parents can help.* Newark, DE: International Reading Association.

Erickson, Frederick. (1982). *Classroom discourse as improvisation: Relationships between academic task structure and social participation structure in lessons.* In L. C. Wilkinson (Ed.) Communicating in classrooms. New York: Academic Press.

Erikson, Erik H. (1963). *Childhood and society, 2nd ed.* New York: Norton.

Erikson, Erik H. (1968). *Identity, youth and crisis.* New York: Norton.

Erikson, Erik H, & Erikson, Joan M. (1981). On generativity and identity: From a conversation with Erik and Joan Erikson. *Harvard Educational Review, 51,* 249–269.

Erikson, Erik. (1982). Life cycle. In Judith Krieger Gardner (Ed.), *Readings in developmental psychology, 2nd ed.* Boston, MA: Little, Brown.

Ernst, Karen. (1994). Writing pictures, painting words: Writing in an Artists' Workshop. *Language Arts, 71,* 44–52.

Farr, Roger. (1992). Putting it all together: Solving the reading assessment puzzle. *The Reading Teacher, 46,* 26–37.

Farrell, Gail E. (1991). Drawbridges and moats: The arts and the middle school classroom. *Middle School Journal, 22,* 28–29.

Farris, Pamela J. (1989). Story time and story journals: Linking literature and writing. *New Advocate, 2,* 179–185.

Farris, Pamela J., & Denner, Mary. (1991). Guiding illiterate parents in assisting their children in emergent literacy. *Reading Horizons, 32,* 63–72.

Farris, Pamela J., Fuhler, Carol, & Ginejko, Mary Louise. (1991). Reading, writing and discussing: An interactive approach to teaching in the content areas. *Reading Horizons, 31,* 261–271.

Fawcett, Gay. (1992). Moving the big desk. *Language Arts, 69,* 183–185.

Fay, Leo. (1965). Reading study skills: Math and science. In J. Allen Figurel (Ed.), *Reading and Inquiry.* Newark, DE: International Reading Association.

Feelings, Muriel. (1974). *Jambo means hello: Swahili alphabet book.* New York: Puffin. Illustrated by Tom Feelings.

Fernald, Grace M., & Keller, Helen. (1921). The effect of kinesthetic factors in development of word recognition in the case of nonreaders. *Journal of Educational Research, 4,* 357–377.

Fernie, David E. (1992). Profile: Howard Gardner. *Language Arts, 69,* 220–227.

Fielding, Linda, & Roller, Cathy. (1992). Making difficult books accessible and easy books acceptable. *The Reading Teacher, 45,* 678–685.

Fillion, Bryant. (1981). Reading as inquiry: An approach to literature learning. *English Journal, 70,* 39–45.

Finders, Margaret, & Lewis, Cynthia. (1994). Why some parents don't come to school. *Educational Leadership, 51,* 50–54.

Findley, Maureen J., & Cooper, Harris M. (1983). Locus of control and academic achievement: A literature review. *Journal of Personality and Social Psychology, 44,* 419–427.

Fitzgerald, Jill. (1989). Enhancing two related thought processes: Revision in writing and critical reading. *The Reading Teacher, 43,* 42–48.

Fitzgerald, Jill. (1994). Crossing boundaries: What do second-language-learning theories say to reading and writing teachers of English-as-a-second-language learners? *Reading Horizons, 34,* 339–355.

Flavell, John H. (1976). Metacognitive aspects of problem solving. In Lauren Resnick (Ed.), *The nature of intelligence.* Hillsdale, NJ: Erlbaum.

Fleischman, Paul. (1985). *I am phoenix: Poems for two voices.* New York: HarperCollins. Illustrated by Ken Nutt.

Fleischman, Paul. (1988). *Joyful noise: Poems for two voices.* New York: HarperCollins. Illustrated by Eric Beddows.

Flood, James, & Lapp, Diane. (1987). Forms of discourse in basal readers. *Elementary School Journal, 87,* 299–306.

Flood, James, & Lapp, Diane. (1989). Reporting reading progress: A comparison portfolio for parents. *The Reading Teacher, 42,* 509–514.

Flores, Barbara M., Cousin, Patricia Tefft, & Diaz, Esteban. (1991). Transforming deficit myths about learning, language, and culture. *Language Arts, 68,* 369–379.

Flynn, Rosalind M. (1989). English and history via drama: Ways and means. *The Clearing House, 63,* 79–81.

Flynn, Rosalind M., & Carr, Gail A. (1994). Exploring classroom literature through drama: A specialist and a teacher collaborate. *Language Arts, 71,* 38–43.

Fordham, Signithia, & Ogbu, John U. (1986). Black students' school success: Coping with the "burden of acting white." *Urban Review, 18,* 176–206.

Fournier, Julia M. (1993). Seeing with new eyes: Becoming a better teacher of bilingual children. *Language Arts, 70,* 177–181.

Fox, Mem. (1989a). *Feathers and fools.* Melbourne, Australia: Ashwood House.

Fox, Mem. (1989b). *Koala Lou.* San Diego, CA: Harcourt Brace Jovanovich.

Fox, Mem. (1990). *Possum magic.* San Diego, CA: Harcourt Brace Jovanovich.

Fox, Mem. (1993). *Radical reflections: Passionate opinions on teaching, learning and living.* Sydney, Australia: Harcourt Brace.

Fox, Mem, & Wilkinson, Lyn. (1993). *English essentials.* South Melbourne, Australia: Macmillan.

Frager, Alan, & Vanterpool, Maureen. (1993). Point-counterpoint: Value of school textbooks. *Reading Horizons, 33,* 300–312.

France, Marycarolyn G. & Meeks, Jane Warren. (1987). Parents who can't read: What the schools can do. *Journal of Reading, 31,* 222–227.

Frankson, Marie Stewart. (1990). Chicano literature for young adults: An annotated bibliography. *English Journal, 79,* 30–35.

Fredericks, Anthony D., & Rasinski, Timothy V. (1990). Conferencing with parents: Successful approaches. *The Reading Teacher, 44,* 174–176.

Fredericksen, Norman. (1984). The real test bias: Influences of testing on teaching and learning. *American Psychologist, 39,* 193–202.

Freedman, Glenn, & Reynolds, Elizabeth G. (1980). Enriching basal reader lessons with semantic webbing. *The Reading Teacher, 33,* 677–684.

Freedman, Russell. (1987). *Lincoln: A photobiography.* New York: Clarion.

Freedman, Russell. (1994). *Kids at work: Lewis Hine and the crusade against child labor.* New York: Clarion.

Freedman, Russell. (1995). *Immigrant kids.* New York: Puffin. (First published in 1980 by Dutton.)

Friedl, Alfred E. (1995). *Teaching science to children, 3rd ed.* New York: McGraw-Hill.

Fritz, Jean. (1982). *Homesick.* New York: G. P. Putnam's Sons. Illustrated by Margot Tomes.

Fritz, Jean. (1994). *Around the world in a hundred years: From Henry the Navigator to Magellan.* New York: G. P. Putnam's Sons. Illustrated by Anthony Bacon Venti.

Fuhler, Carol J. (1991). Add spark and sizzle to middle school social studies: Use trade books to enhance instruction. *The Social Studies, 82,* 234–237.

Galda, Lee, Cullinan, Bernice E., & Strickland, Dorothy S. (1993). *Language, literacy and the child.* Fort Worth, TX: Harcourt Brace Jovanovich.

Gallicchio, Bertille C. (1992). Tracking again: Bringing the center into focus. *English Journal, 81,* 75–76.

Gambrell, Linda, Kapinus, Barbara A., & Wilson R. M. (1987). Using mental imagery and summarization to achieve independence in comprehension. *Journal of Reading, 30,* 216–220.

Ganyard, Nancy T. (1986). Guide for parents on writing their child's first term paper: A letter. *English Journal, 75,* 62–67.

Garbarino, James. (1982). *Children and families in the social environment.* New York: Aldine.

Garbarino, James. (1985). *Adolescent development: An ecological perspective.* Columbus, OH: Merrill.

Gardner, Howard. (1982). *Developmental psychology, 2nd ed.* Boston, MA: Little, Brown.

Gardner, Howard. (1983). *Frames of mind: The theory of multiple intelligences.* New York: Basic Books.

Gardner, Howard. (1991). *The unschooled mind: How children think and how schools should teach.* New York: Basic Books.

Gardner, Howard. (1993a). Educating for understanding. *American School Board Journal, 180,* 20–24.

Gardner, Howard. (1993b). *Multiple intelligences: The theory into practice.* New York: Basic Books.

Gardner, Howard, & Hatch, Thomas. (1989). Multiple intelligences go to school: Educational implications of the theory of multiple intelligences. *Educational Researcher, 18,* 4–9.

Garfield, Leon. (1985). *Shakespeare stories.* Boston, MA: Houghton Mifflin. Illustrated by Michael Foreman.

Garfield, Leon. (1994). *Shakespeare stories II.* Boston, MA: Houghton Mifflin.

Garmezy, Norman, Masten, Ann S., & Tellegen, Auke. (1984). The study of stress and competence in children: Building blocks for developmental psychopathology. *Child Development, 55,* 97–111.

Garner, Ruth, Alexander, Patricia A., Gillingham, Mark G.,

Kulikowich, Jonna M., & Brown, Rachel. (1991). Interest and learning from text. *American Educational Research Journal, 28,* 643–659.

Gaskins, Irene W., Anderson, Richard C., Pressley, Michael, Cunicelli, Elizabeth A., & Satlow, Eric. (1993). Six teachers' dialogue during cognitive process instruction. *Elementary School Journal, 93,* 277–304.

George, Diana. (1984). Creating contexts: Using the research paper to teach critical thinking. *English Journal, 73,* 27–32.

George, Paul S. (1993). Tracking and ability grouping in the middle school: Ten tentative truths. *Middle School Journal, 24,* 17–24.

Gibbons, Gail. (1987). *Weather forecasting.* New York: Morrow.

Gibbons, Gail. (1992). *The Great St. Lawrence Seaway.* New York: Morrow.

Gillespie, Cindy S. (1993). Reading graphic displays: What teachers should know. *Journal of Reading, 36,* 350–354.

Gillespie, Joanne S. (1993). Buddy book journals: Responding to literature. *English Journal, 82,* 64–68.

Gillis, M. K. (1994). Attention Deficit Disorder: Just another label. *Reading and Writing Quarterly, 10,* 119–124.

Giordano, Anne. (1992). Strengthening the home-school connection. *Principal, 71,* 38–39.

Giovanni, Nikki. (1985). *Spin a soft black song.* New York: Hill and Wang.

Glass, Gerald G. (1973). *Teaching decoding as separate from reading.* Garden City, New York: Adelphi University Press.

Goldenberg, Claude. (1989). Parents' effects on academic grouping for reading: Three case studies. *American Educational Research Journal, 26,* 329–352.

Goldenberg, Claude. (1992/1993). Instructional conversations: Promoting comprehension through discussion. *The Reading Teacher, 46,* 316–326.

Goldenberg, Claude. (1993). The design and typography of children's books. *Horn Book Magazine, 69,* 559–567.

Golick, Margie. (1987). *Playing with words.* Markham, Ontario, Canada: Pembroke.

Gollnick, Donna M., & Chinn, Philip C. (1986). *Multicultural education in a pluralistic society, 2nd ed.* Columbus, OH: Merrill.

Good, Thomas L., Slavings, Ricky L., Harel, Kathleen Hobson, & Emerson, Hugh. (1987). Student passivity: A study of question asking in K-12 classrooms. *Sociology of Education, 60,* 181–199.

Goodman, Kenneth S. (1970). Behind the eye: What happens in reading. In Kenneth S. Goodman & Olive S. Niles (Eds.), *Reading: Process and program.* Urbana, IL: National Council of Teachers of English.

Goodman, Kenneth S., & Goodman, Yetta M. (1977). *A whole language comprehension-centered reading program.* Occasional paper #1. Tucson AZ: University of Arizona.

Goodman, Yetta, & Burke, Carolyn. (1972). *Reading miscue inventory manual: Procedure for diagnosis and evaluation.* New York: Macmillan.

Gordon, Christine J., & MacInnis, Dorothy. (1993). Using journals as a window on students' thinking in mathematics. *Language Arts, 70,* 37–43.

Gould, Stephen J. (1981). *The mismeasure of man.* New York: Norton.

Graves, Donald H. (1979). Andrea learns to make writing hard. *Language Arts, 56,* 569–576.

Graves, Donald H. (1989a). *A researcher learns to write.* Portsmouth, NH: Heinemann.

Graves, Donald H. (1989b). *Investigate fiction.* Portsmouth, NH: Heinemann.

Graves, Donald H. (1989c). *Investigate nonfiction.* Portsmouth, NH: Heinemann.

Graves, Donald H., & Hansen, Jane. (1983). The author's chair. *Language Arts, 60,* 176–183.

Graves, Michael F. (1986). Vocabulary learning and instruction. In Ernst Rothkopf (Ed.), *Review of Research in Education.* Washington, DC: American Educational Research Association.

Graves, Michael F., & Prenn, Maureen. (1984). Effects of previewing expository passages on junior high school students' comprehension and attitudes. In Jerome A. Niles & Larry A. Harris (Eds.). *Changing perspectives on research in reading/language processing and instruction: Thirty-third Yearbook of the National Reading Conference.* Rochester, NY: National Reading Conference.

Green, Diana Huss. (1989). Beyond books: Literature on the small screen. In Masha Kabakow Rudman, Ed., *Children's Literature: Resource for the classroom.* Boston, MA: Christopher-Gordon.

Greenfield, Eloise. (1986). *Honey, I love.* New York: HarperTrophy. Illustrated by Diane and Leo Dillon.

Greenfield, Eloise, & Little, Lessie Jones. (1993). *Childtimes: A three-generation memoir.* New York: HarperTrophy. Illustrated by Jerry Pinkney.

Greenfield, Howard. (1989). *Marc Chagall.* New York: Abrams.

Greenwood, Scott C. (1985). Use contracts to motivate and manage your secondary reading class. *Journal of Reading, 28,* 487–491.

Griss, Susan. (1994). Creative movement: A language for learning. *Educational Leadership, 51,* 78–80.

Groff, Patrick. (1978). Readers Theatre by children. *Elementary School Journal, 79,* 15–22.

Groves, Don. (1989). *The oceans: A book of questions and answers.* New York: John Wiley.

Grun, Bernard. (1991). *The timetables of history, 3rd ed.* New York: Simon & Schuster.

Guba, Egon., & Lincoln, Yvonna S. (1981). *Effective evaluation: Improving the usefulness of evaluation results through responsive and naturalistic approaches.* San Francisco, CA: Jossey-Bass.

Guilford, J. Paul. (1950). Creativity. *American Psychologist, 5,* 444–454.

Gura, Mark. (1994). The human mosaic project. *Educational Leadership, 51,* 40–41.

Guskey, Thomas R., & Passaro, Perry D. (1994). Teacher efficacy: A study of construct dimensions. *American Educational Research Journal, 31,* 627–643.

Guthrie, John T., & Kirsch, Irwin S. (1987). Distinctions between reading comprehension and locating information in text. *Journal of Educational Psychology, 79,* 220–227.

Guyton, Jane M., & Fielstein, Lynda L. (1989). Student-led parent conferences: A model for teaching responsibility. *Elementary School Guidance and Counseling, 24,* 169–172.

Guzzetti, Barbara J. (1990). Effects of textual and instructional manipulations on concept acquisition. *Reading Psychology, 11,* 49–62.

Guzzetti, Barbara J., Snyder, Tonja E., Glass, Gene V. (1992). Promoting conceptual change in science: Can texts be used effectively? *Journal of Reading, 35,* 642–649.

Hadermann, Kenneth F. (1976). Ability grouping—Its effect on learners. *NASSP Bulletin, 60,* 85–89.

Haggard, Martha R. (1986). The Vocabulary Self-Collection Strategy: Using student interest and world knowledge to enhance vocabulary growth. *Journal of Reading, 29,* 634–642.

Hahn, Deborah. (1991). *The Swineherd by Hans Christian Andersen (narrated by himself and acted by his favorite friends and relations).* New York: Lothrop, Lee & Shepard.

Hall, Elizabeth. (1983). A conversation with Erik Erikson. *Psychology Today, 17,* 22–30.

Haller, Eileen P., Child, David A., & Walberg, Herbert J. (1988). Can comprehension be taught? A quantitative synthesis of "metacognitive" studies. *Educational Researcher, 17,* 5–8.

Hamilton, Virginia. (1968). *The house of Dies Drear.* New York:. Collier. (Reissued 1984).

Hamilton, Virginia. (1985). *The people could fly: American Black folktales.* New York: Alfred A. Knopf.

Hamilton, Virginia. (1993). *Many thousand gone: African Americans from Slavery to Freedom.* New York: Alfred A. Knopf.

Haney, Walter, & Madaus, George. (1989). Searching for alternatives to standardized tests: Whys, whats and whithers. *Phi Delta Kappan, 70,* 683–687.

Hansen, Jane. (1992a). Literacy portfolios emerge. *The Reading Teacher, 45,* 604–607.

Hansen, Jane. (1992b). Literacy portfolios: Helping students know themselves. *Educational Leadership, 49,* 66–68.

Hansen, Jane. (1992c). Students' evaluations bring reading and writing together. *The Reading Teacher, 46,* 100–105.

Hare, Virginia Chou, & Smith, Douglas C. (1982). Reading to remember: Studies of metacognitive reading skills in elementary school-aged children. *Journal of Educational Research, 75,* 157–164.

Harris, Violet J. (1990). African American children's literature: The first one hundred years. *Journal of Negro Education, 59,* 540–555.

Harris, Violet J. (1993). Literature-based approaches to reading instruction. In Linda Darling-Hammond (Ed.), *Review of Research in Education,* Vol. 19. Washington, DC: American Educational Research Association.

Harste, Jerome, Burke, Carolyn, & Short, Kathy. (1988). *Creating classrooms for authors.* Portsmouth, NH: Heinemann.

Harte, Sandra W., & Glover, Matthew J. (1993). Estimation is mathematical thinking. *Arithmetic Teacher, 41,* 75–77.

Hartman, Douglas K., and Hartman, Jeanette A. (1993). Reading across texts: Expanding the role of the teacher. *The Reading Teacher, 47,* 202–211.

Harwayne, Shelley. (1993). Chutzpah and the nonfiction writer. In Bernice E. Cullinan (Ed.), *Pen in hand: Children become writers.* Newark, DE: International Reading Association.

Hatcher, Barbara A. (1990). Who's in the kitchen with Dinah? History! *The Social Studies., 81,* 101–105.

Hatcher, Barbara A. (1992). History in my hand—Making artifact kits in the intermediate grades. *The Social Studies, 83,* 267–271.

Havens, Lynn. (1989). Writing to enhance learning in general mathematics. *Mathematics Teacher, 82,* 551–554.

Hayes, Curtis W., & Bahruth, Robert. (1985). *Querer es poder.* In Jane Hansen, Thomas Newkirk, & Donald Graves (Eds.), *Breaking ground: Teachers relate reading and writing in the elementary school.* Portsmouth, NH: Heinemann.

Hayes, Joe. (1993). *Soft child: How rattlesnake got its fangs.* Tucson, AZ: Harbinger House. Illustrated by Kay Sather.

Heacock, Grace Anne. (1990). The We-Search process. *Social Studies and the Young Learner, 2,* 9–11.

Heath, Jay A. (1992). When an elementary school principal moves to junior high school. *Principal, 71,* 39–40.

Heath, Shirley Brice. (1993). The study of cultural activity: Moving toward multiple approaches in research on child development. In Barbara Rogoff, Jayanthu Mistry, Artin Göncü, & Christine Mosier, (Eds.). *Guided participation in cultural activity by toddlers and caregivers.* Chicago, IL: Society for Research in Child Development.

Hedlund, Dalva E., Furst, Tanis C., & Foley, Kathryn T. (1989). A dialogue with self: The journal as an educational tool. *Journal of Humanistic Education and Development, 27,* 105–113.

Heinig, Ruth Beall. (1988). *Creative drama for the classroom teacher.* Englewood Cliffs, NJ: Prentice Hall.

Heller, Mary F. (1988). Comprehending and composing through language experience. *The Reading Teacher, 42,* 130–135.

Heller, Mary F. (1991). *Reading-writing connections: From theory to practice.* White Plains, NY: Longman.

Heller, Nicholas. (1994). *Ten old pails.* New York: Greenwillow. Illustrated by Yossi Abolafia.

Helm, Jeanne. (1994). Family theme bags: An innovative approach to family involvement in the school. *Young Children, 49,* 48–52.

Hennings, Dorothy Grant. (1991). Essential reading: Targeting, tracking, and thinking about main ideas. *Journal of Reading, 34,* 346–353.

Hennings, Dorothy Grant. (1993). On knowing and reading history. *Journal of Reading, 36,* 362–370.

Herber, Harold L. (1978). *Teaching reading in content areas, 2nd ed.* Englewood Cliffs, NJ: Prentice-Hall.

Herman, Joan L. (1992). What research tells us about good assessment. *Educational Leadership, 49,* 74–78.

Herman, Joan L., Aschbacher, Pamela R., & Winters, Lynn. (1992). *A practical guide to alternative assessment.* Alexandria, VA: Association for Supervision and Curriculum Development.

Hernandez, Donald J. (1994). *Children's changing access to resources: A historical perspective.* Chicago, IL: Society for Research in Child Development.

Hiebert, Elfrieda H. (1980). Peers as reading teachers. *Language Arts, 57,* 877–881.

Hiebert, Elfrieda H. (1983). An examination of ability grouping for reading instruction. *Reading Research Quarterly, 18,* 231–255.

Hiebert, Elfrieda H., & Calfee, Robert. (1989). Advancing academic literacy through teachers' assessments. *Educational Leadership, 46,* 50–54.

Hill, Kathleen J. (1984). *The writing process; One writing classroom.* Melbourne, Australia: Thomas Nelson.

Hills, Tynette W. (1992). Reaching potentials through appropriate assessment. In Bredekamp, Sue, & Rosegrant, Teresa (Eds.), *Reaching potentials: Appropriate curriculum and assessment for young children, Vol. 1.* Washington, DC: National Association for the Education of Young Children.

Hines, Anna Grossnickle. (1993). *Gramma's walk.* New York: Greenwillow.

Hines, Anna Grossnickle. (1994). *What Joe saw.* New York: Greenwillow.

Hirschfelder, Arlene B. (1993). Native American literature for children and young adults. *Library Trends, 41,* 414–436.

Hoban, Tana. (1992). *Spirals, curves, fanshapes and lines.* New York: Greenwillow.

Holbrook, Hilary Taylor. (1987). The quiet student in your classroom. *Language Arts, 64,* 554–557.

Holdaway, Don. (1979). *The foundations of literacy.* Sydney: Ashton-Scholastic.

Holdaway, Don. (1982). Shared book experience: Teaching reading using favorite books. *Theory into Practice, 21,* 293–300.

Holubec, Edythe Johnson. (1992). How do you get there from here? Getting started with cooperative learning. *Contemporary Education, 63,* 181–184.

Horgan, Dianne. (1988). Learning to tell jokes: A case study of metalinguistic abilities. In Margery B. Franklin & Sybil S. Barten (Eds.), *Child language.* New York: Oxford University Press.

Horn, Ernest. (1937). *Methods of instruction in the social studies.* New York: Scribner's.

Horn, John L., (1968). Organization of abilities and the development of intelligence. *Psychological Review, 75,* 242–259.

Horn, John L., (1982). The aging of human abilities. In J. Wolman (Ed.), *Handbook of developmental psychology.* Englewood Cliffs, NJ: Prentice-Hall.

Howard, Becky, & Liner, Tom. (1990). Ninth grade, low level, fifth period: A kind of case study. *English Journal, 79,* 47–52.

Hoyt, Linda. (1992). Many ways of knowing: Using drama, oral interactions, and the visual arts to enhance reading comprehension. *The Reading Teacher, 45,* 580–584.

Huck, Charlotte. (1989). *Princess Furball.* New York: Greenwillow. Illustrated by Anita Lobel.

Huey, Edmund. (1968). *The psychology and pedagogy of*

reading. Cambridge, MA: The M. I. T. Press. (First published in 1908.)

Hughes, Langston. (1994). *The sweet and sour animal book.* New York: Oxford University Press.

Hughes, Robert. (1986). *The fatal shore.* New York: Vintage Books.

Hunt, Lyman. (1970). The effect of self selection, interest and motivation upon independent, instructional and frustration level. *The Reading Teacher, 24,* 416.

Hutchins, Pat. (1994). *Llaman a la puerta.* New York: Mulberry.

Hynd, Cynthia R., & Alvermann, Donna E. (1986). The role of refutation text in overcoming difficulty with science concepts. *Journal of Reading, 29,* 440–446.

Hynd, Cynthia R., & Alvermann, Donna E. (1989). Overcoming misconceptions in science: An on-line study of prior knowledge activation. *Reading Research and Instruction, 28,* 12–26.

Hynd, Cynthia R., Qian, Gaoyin, Ridgeway, Victoria G., Pickle, Michael. (1991). Promoting conceptual change with science texts and discussion. *Journal of Reading, 34,* 596–601.

Imdieke, Sandra J. (1990). Sharing stories: Multicultural traditions. *ERIC Document: 320–146.*

Imdieke, Sandra J. (1991). Using traditional storytellers' props. *The Reading Teacher, 45,* 329–330.

IRA News: Delegates speak out on assessment. (1990). *Reading Horizons, 30,* 319.

Isaacson, Philip M. (1988). *Round buildings, square buildings, & buildings that wiggle like a fish.* New York: Knopf.

Iwicki, Ann L. (1992). Vocabulary connections. *The Reading Teacher, 45,* 736.

Jachym, Nora K., Allington, Richard L., & Broikou, Kathleen A. (1989). Estimating the cost of seatwork. *The Reading Teacher, 43,* 30–35.

Jacobs, Janis E., & Paris, Scott G. (1987). Children's metacognition about reading: Issues in definition, measurement, and instruction. *Educational Psychologist, 22,* 255–278.

Jacobson, Jeanne M. (1988). How are we supposed to learn that? *Syntax in the Schools, 5,* 1, 3.

Jacobson, Jeanne M. (1989a). RESPONSE: An interactive study technique. *Reading Horizons, 29,* 85–92.

Jacobson, Jeanne M. (1989b).Writing a Conversation: Journals in the College Classroom. *ERIC Document: ED 311 462.*

Jacobson, Jeanne M. (1990a). Group vs. individual completion of a cloze passage. *Journal of Reading, 33,* 244–250.

Jacobson, Jeanne M. (1990b). Reading: The Conferences. *Reading Horizons, 31,* 168–171.

Jacobson, Jeanne M. (1992/1993). Engaging preservice teachers in reading the professional literature through Structured Sustained Silent Reading. *Journal of Reading Education, 18,* 61–67.

Jacobson, Jeanne M. (1995). Collaborative learning as a component of inclusive strategies for literacy development. Paper presented at the Second International Congress on Challenges to Education, Cancun, Mexico, July 1995.

Jacobson, Jeanne M., & Kinnucan-Welsch, Kathryn. (1993). The Amateur Publishing Association: A strategy for engaging clinic students in authentic reading and writing. *The Reading Professor, 16,* 29–36.

Jaeger, Richard M. (1994). What parents want to know about schools: A report on school report cards. *Evaluation Perspectives, 4,* 2–4.

Jensen, Julie M., & Roser, Nancy L. (1990). Are there really 3 R's? *Educational Leadership, 47,* 7–12.

Johnson, Andrew. (1995). I was a less able reader: What concert choir taught me about reading instruction. *Reading Horizons, 35,* 430–441.

Johnson, Dale D., & Pearson, P. David. (1984). *Teaching reading vocabulary, 2nd ed.* New York: Holt, Rinehart & Winston.

Johnson, Dale D., Pittelman, Susan D., & Heimlich, Joan E. (1986). Semantic mapping. *The Reading Teacher, 39,* 778–783.

Johnson, David W., & Johnson, Roger T. (1978). Cooperative, competitive and individualistic learning. *Journal of Research and Development in Education, 12,* 3–15.

Johnson, David W., & Johnson, Roger T. (1979). Conflict in the classroom: Controversy and learning. *Review of Educational Research, 49,* 51–70.

Johnson, David W., & Johnson, Roger T. (1988). Critical thinking through structured controversy. *Educational Leadership, 45,* 58–64.

Johnson, David W., & Johnson, Roger T. (1989). Cooperative learning: What special education teachers need to know. *The Pointer, 33,* 5–10.

Johnson, David W., & Johnson, Roger T. (1994). *Learning together and alone: Cooperative, competitive and individualistic learning, 4th ed.* Boston MA: Allyn & Bacon.

Johnson, Roger T., & Johnson, David W. (1985). Student-student interaction: Ignored but powerful. *Journal of Teacher Education, 36,* 23–26.

Johnson, Scott D., & Thomas, Ruth. (1992). Technology education and the cognitive revolution. *Technology Teacher, 51,* 7–12.

Johnston, J. Howard. (1990). *The new American family and the school.* Columbus, OH: National Middle School Association.

Johnston, Janet Speer. (1989). Personal newsletters for parents. *The Reading Teacher, 42,* 737–739.

Johnston, Peter H. (1992). *Constructive evaluation of literate activity.* New York: Longman.

Johnston, Peter H., & Allington, Richard L. (1984). Remediation. In Rebecca Barr, M. I. Kamil, Peter Mosenthal, & P. David Pearson (Eds.), *Handbook of reading research, Vol. 2.* New York: Longman.

Jones, Elizabeth, & Derman-Sparks, Louise. (1992). Meeting the challenge of diversity. *Young Children, 47,* 12–18.

Jongsma, Kathleen Stumpf. (1992). Just say know! *The Reading Teacher, 45,* 546–548.

Jorgensen-Esmaili, Karen. (1990). Making the reading, writing, social studies connection. *Social Studies and the Young Learner, 2,* 20–22.

Juel, Connie. (1991). Cross-age tutoring between student athletes and at-risk children. *The Reading Teacher, 45,* 178–186.

Kagan, Dona M., & Tippins, Deborah J. (1992). The evolution of lesson plans among twelve elementary and secondary student teachers. *Elementary School Journal, 92,* 477–489.

Kagan, Spencer. (1989/1990). The structural approach to cooperative learning. *Educational Leadership, 47,* 12–15.

Kalan, Robert. (1994). *¡Salta, Ranita, Salta!* New York: Mulberry. Illustrated by Byron Barton.

Kameenui, Edward J. (1993). Diverse learners and the tyranny of time: Don't fix blame; fix the leaky roof. *The Reading Teacher, 46,* 376–383.

Katz, Lilian G. (1988). The disposition to learn. *Principal, 68,* 14–17.

Katz, Lilian G. (1994). Let's not waste children's minds! *Young Children, 49,* 2.

Kaywell, Joan F., Johnston, J. Howard, & Markle, Glenn C. (1991). Writing apprehension. *Middle School Journal, 22,* 52–56.

Kean, Patricia. (1993). Blowing up the tracks. *Washington Monthly, 25,* 31–34.

Keefe, Charlotte Hendrick. (1993). Responsive assessment for special learners. *Reading and Writing Quarterly, 9,* 215–226.

Keller, Holly. (1994). *Grandfather's dream.* New York: Greenwillow.

Kellogg, Steven. (1991). *Jack and the beanstalk.* New York: Morrow.

Kelly, Cynthia. (1990). Preschool scrapbook journals. *Reading Horizons, 30,* 78.

Kelly, Patricia R. (1995). Round robin reading: Considering alternative instructional practices that make more sense. *Reading Horizons, 36,* 99–115.

Kelly, Patricia R., & Farnan, Nancy. (1994). Literature: The ART in language arts. *New Advocate, 7,* 169–183.

Kennedy, Kerry J., & McDonald, Gilbert. (1986). Designing curriculum materials for multicultural education: Lessons from an Australian development project. *Curriculum Inquiry, 16,* 311–326.

Kiaune, Jo Ann. (1992). "Phoetry" in the middle school. *English Journal, 81,* 70–71.

Kipling, Rudyard. (1978). *Just so stories.* New York: Weathervane. (A reprint of the first edition, published in 1902.)

Kirsch, Irwin S., & Mosenthal, Peter B. (1990). Exploring document literacy: Variables underlying the performance of young adults. *Reading Research Quarterly, 25,* 5–30.

Kitchen, Bert. (1987). *Animal numbers.* New York: Dial.

Klasky, Charles. (1979). The history mystery. *The Social Studies, 70,* 41–43.

Klemp, Ronald M., Hon, Jeanne E., & Short, Abbe A. (1993). Cooperative literacy in the middle school: An example of a learning-strategy based approach. *Middle School Journal, 24,* 19–27.

Klesius, Janell P., & Klesius, Stephen E. (1989). Vocabulary on the playground. *Reading Horizons, 29,* 197–204.

Kletzien, Sharon B., & Bednar, Maryanne R. (1990). Dynamic assessment for at-risk readers. *Journal of Reading, 33,* 528–533.

Kliman, Marlene. (1993). Integrating mathematics and literature in the elementary classroom. *Arithmetic Teacher, 40,* 318–321.

Kohn, Alfie. (1991). Caring kids: The role of the schools. *Phi Delta Kappan, 72,* 496–508.

Kohn, Alfie. (1993). *Punished by rewards: The trouble with gold stars, incentive plans, A's, praise, and other bribes.* Boston, MA: Houghton Mifflin.

Kormanski, Luethel, M. (1988). Using the Johari Window to study characterization. *Journal of Reading, 32,* 146–152.

Kounin, Jacob S. (1970). *Discipline and group management in classrooms.* New York: Holt, Rinehart & Winston.

Krashen, Stephen. (1989). *Language acquisition and language education.* Englewood Cliffs, NJ: Prentice-Hall.

Krashen, Stephen. (1991). Bilingual education: A focus on current research. (Focus occasional papers in Bilingual Education Number 3). Washington, DC: The

George Washington University and Center for Applied Linguistics.

Krashen, Stephen. (1995). Bilingual education and second language acquisition theory. In Diane Bennett Durkin (Ed.), *Language issues*. White Plains, NY: Longman.

Krashen, Stephen, & Terrell, Tracy D. (1983). *The natural approach. Language acquisition in the classroom*. Hayward, CA: Alemany.

Kruse, Ginny Moore. (1992). No single season: Multicultural literature for all children. *Wilson Library Bulletin, 66*, 30–33, 122.

Kurtz, William H. (1988). Succeeding in confrontational conferences—An operational model. *NASSP Bulletin, 72*, 26–33.

Laframboise, Kathryn, & Wynn, Margie. (1995). Oral participation in shared reading and writing by Limited English Proficient students in a multiethnic class setting. *Reading Horizons, 35,* 95–109.

Laminack, Lester L. (1990). "Possibilities, Daddy, I think it says possibilities": A father's journal of the emergence of literacy. *The Reading Teacher, 42*, 536–540.

Lamme, Linda Leonard. (1989). Illustratorship: A key facet of whole language instruction. *Childhood Education, 66*, 83–86.

Lamme, Linda Leonard. (1990). Exploring the world of music through picture books. *The Reading Teacher, 44*, 294–300.

Lamme, Linda Leonard, & Hysmith, Cecilia. (1991). One school's adventure into portfolio assessment. *Language Arts, 68*, 629–640.

Lamme, Linda Leonard, & McKinley, Linda. (1992). Creating a caring classroom with children's literature. *Young Children, 47*, 65–71.

Lamott, Anne. (1995). *Bird by bird: Some instructions on writing and life*. New York: Pantheon.

Langer, Judith A. (1981). From theory to practice: A prereading plan. *Journal of Reading, 25*, 2.

Langer, Judith A. (1983/1984). Examining background knowledge and text comprehension. *Reading Research Quarterly, 19*, 468–481.

Langer, Judith A. (1990). Understanding literature. *Language Arts, 67*, 812–816.

Lankford, Mary D. (1992). *Hopscotch around the world*. New York: Morrow. Illustrated by Karen Milone.

Lapp, Diane, & Flood, James. (1993). Literature in the science program. In Bernice E. Cullinan (Ed.), *Fact and fiction: Literature across the curriculum*. Newark, DE: International Reading Association.

Larson, Reed. (1988). Flow and writing. In Mihaly Csikszentmihalyi & Isabella Selega Csikszentmihalyi (Eds.), *Optimal experience: Psychological studies of flow in consciousness*. New York: Cambridge University Press.

Lash, Andrea A., & Kirkpatrick, Sandra L. (1994). Interrupted lessons: Teacher views of transfer education. *American Educational Research Journal, 31*, 813–843.

Latrobe, Kathy. (1993). Readers Theatre as a way of learning. *ALAN Review, 20*, 46–50.

Lee, D. M., & VanAllen, Roach. (1963). *Learning to read through experience*. New York: Appleton-Century-Crofts.

Lee, Nancy G., & Neal, Judith C. (1992/1993). Reading Rescue: Intervention for a student "at promise." *Journal of Reading, 36*, 276–287.

Lee, Patricia A. (1994). To dance one's understanding. *Educational Leadership, 51*, 81–83.

Leinhardt, Gaea. (1992). What research on learning tells us about teaching. *Educational Researcher, 49*, 20–25.

Leland, Christine, & Fitzpatrick, Ruth. (1993/1994). Cross-age interaction builds enthusiasm for reading and writing. *The Reading Teacher, 47*, 292–301.

Lerner, Carol. (1994). *Backyard birds of winter*. New York: Morrow.

Lesesne, Teri S. (1991). Shrinklits: An alternative to traditional book reporting. *ALAN Review, 18*, 17–19.

LeSourd, Sandra J. (1992). A review of methodologies for cross-cultural education. *The Social Studies, 83*, 30–35.

Levi, Ray. (1990). Assessment and educational vision: Engaging learners and parents. *Language Arts, 67*, 269–273.

Levin, Henry. (1979). *The eye-voice span*. Cambridge, MA: M. I. T. Press.

Levin, Henry M. (1990). The villain's strategy for at-risk students. In *Leadership and Learning Newsletter, 2* National Center for School Leadership, University of Illinois at Urbana-Champaign University High School Laboratory School.

Levin, Henry M., & Hopfenberg, Wendy S. (1991). Don't remediate: Accelerate! *Principal, 70*, 11–13.

Levine, Denise Stavis. (1985). The biggest thing I learned but it really doesn't have to do with science… *Language Arts, 62*, 43–47.

Levine, Ellen. (1993). *…if your name was changed at Ellis Island*. New York: Scholastic.

Levstik, Linda S. (1990). Mediating content through literary texts. *Language Arts, 67*, 848–853.

Levstik, Linda S. (1993). Making the past come to life. In Bernice E. Cullinan (Ed.), *Fact and fiction; Literature across the curriculum*. Newark, DE: International Reading Association.

Levy, Tedd. (1992). Planning for more effective parent conferences. *Middle School Journal, 24*, 49–51.

Lewin, Kurt. (1935). *A dynamic theory of personality.* New York: McGraw-Hill.

Lewin, Kurt. (1948). *Resolving social conflicts.* New York: Harper.

Lewis, Cynthia, (1993). "Give people a chance": Acknowledging social differences in reading. *Language Arts, 70,* 454–461.

Lim, Hwa-Ja Lee, & Watson, Dorothy J. (1993). Whole language content classes for second-language learners. *The Reading Teacher, 46,* 384–393.

Lindauer, Shelley L. Knudsen. (1988). Wordless books: An approach to visual literacy. *Children's Literature in Education, 19,* 136–142.

Lindberg, Barbara. (1988). Teaching literature: The process approach. *Journal of Reading, 31,* 732–735.

Lipson, Marjorie Y., & Wixson, Karen K. (1986). Reading disability research: An interactionist perspective. *Review of Educational Research, 56,* 111–136.

Lipson, Marjorie Y., & Wixson, Karen K. (1991). *Assessment and instruction of reading disability: An interactive approach.* New York: HarperCollins.

Little, A. W. (Nancy), & Allan, John. (1989). Student-led parent-teacher conferences. *Elementary School Guidance and Counseling, 23,* 210–218.

Lloyd, Carol V., & Mitchell, Judy Nichols. (1989). Coping with too many concepts in science texts. *Journal of Reading, 32,* 542–545.

Lohman, David F. (1993). Teaching and testing to develop fluid abilities. *Educational Researcher, 22,* 12–23.

Long, Emily. (1993). Using acrostic poems for research reporting. *The Reading Teacher, 46,* 447–448.

Lucas, Tamara, & Schecter, Sandra R. (1992). Literacy education and diversity: Toward equity in the teaching of reading and writing. *Urban Review, 24,* 85–104.

Luft, Joseph. (1969). *Of human interaction.* Palo Alto, CA: National Press Books.

Lynch, Eleanor W., Lewis, Rena B., & Murphy, Diane S. (1993). Improving education for children with chronic illnesses. *Principal, 73,* 38–40.

Lyons, Bill. (1981). The PQP method of responding to writing. *English Journal, 70,* 42–43.

Lyons, Bill. (1987). Integrating mechanics with literature and writing. *English Journal, 76,* 51–52..

MacGinitie, Walter H. (1993). Some limits of assessment. *Journal of Reading, 36,* 556–565.

Machotka, Hana. (1991). *What neat feet!* New York: Morrow.

Machotka, Hana. (1992). *Breathtaking noses.* New York: Morrow.

Machotka, Hana. (1993). *Outstanding outsides.* New York: Morrow.

Mackey, Barbara J. (1990). Cross-age tutoring: Students teaching students. *Middle School Journal, 22,* 24–26.

MacMillan, Bruce. (1991). *Eating fractions.* New York: Scholastic.

The Macmillan Visual Dictionary. (1992). New York: Macmillan.

Macrorie, Ken. (1984). *Searching writing.* Upper Montclair, NJ: Boynton/Cook.

Madaus, George F., & Tan, Ann G. A. (1993). The growth of assessment. In Gordon Cawelti (Ed.) *Challenges and achievements of American education.* Alexandria, VA: Association for Supervision and Curriculum Development.

Madraso, Jan. (1993). Proofreading: The skill we've neglected to teach. *English Journal, 82,* 32–41.

Mahy, Margaret Jean. (1990). *The seven Chinese brothers.* New York: Scholastic. Illustrated by Mou-sien Tseng.

Makler, Andrea. (1987). Recounting the narrative. *Social Education, 51,* 180–185.

Mallow, Jeffry V. (1991). Reading science. *Journal of Reading, 34,* 324–338.

Margolis, Howard, & Brannigan, Gary G. (1986). Building trust with parents. *Academic Therapy, 22,* 71–74.

Margolis, Howard, & Brannigan, Gary G. (1987). Problem solving with parents. *Academic Therapy, 22,* 423–425.

Margolis, Howard, & Freund, Lisa A. (1991). Implementing cooperative learning with mildly handicapped students in regular classrooms. *International Journal of Disability, Development and Education, 38,* 117–133.

Margolis, Howard, & Schwartz, Elliot. (1988–1989). Facilitating mainstreaming through cooperative learning. *High School Journal, 71,* 83–88.

Maria, Katherine. (1989). Developing disadvantaged children's background knowledge interactively. *The Reading Teacher, 42,* 296–300.

Maria, Katherine, & MacGinitie, Walter. (1987). Learning from texts that refute the reader's prior knowledge. *Reading Research and Instruction, 26,* 222–238.

Martin, David S. (1987). Reducing ethnocentrism. *Teaching Exceptional Children, 19,* 5–8.

Martin, Jeanne, Veldman, Donald, & Anderson, Linda M. (1980). Within-class relationships between student achievement and teacher behaviors. *American Educational Research Journal, 17,* 479–490.

Martin, Kathleen, & Miller, Etta. (1988). Storytelling and science. *Language Arts, 65,* 255–259.

Maruyama, Geoffrey M., Knechel, Sharon, & Petersen, Renee. (1995). The impacts of role reversal and minority empowerment strategies on decision making in numerically unbalanced cooperative groups. In Rachel Hertz-Lazarowitz & Norman Miller (Eds.), *Interaction in cooperative groups: The theoretical anatomy of group learning.* Cambridge MA: Cambridge University Press.

Maslow, Abraham H. (1943). A theory of human motivation. *Psychological Review, 50,* 394–395.

Maslow, Abraham H. (1959). Cognition of being in the peak experience. *Journal of Genetic Psychology, 94,* 43–66.

Maslow, Abraham H. (1968). *Toward a psychology of being, 2nd ed.* New York: Van Nostrand.

Maslow, Abraham H. (1970). *Motivation and personality, 2nd ed.* New York: Harper & Row.

Mathison, Sandra. (1988). Why triangulate? *Educational Researcher, 17,* 13–17.

Mayer, Marianna. (1995). *Turandot.* New York: Morrow. Illustrated by Winslow Pels.

Mayher, John S., Lester, Nancy, & Pradl, Gordon M. (1983). *Learning to write/Writing to learn.* Upper Montclair, NJ: Boynton/Cook.

McCarthy, Cameron. (1990). Multicultural education, minority identities, textbooks, and the challenge of curriculum reform. *Journal of Education, 172,* 118–129.

McCauley, Joyce K., & McCauley, Daniel S. (1992). Using choral reading to promote language learning for ESL students. *The Reading Teacher, 45,* 526–533.

McClain-Ruelle, Leslie, & Telfer, Richard. (1990). Using quality literature with "at-risk" secondary students. *Reading Horizons, 30,* 169–179.

McCormick, Sandra. (1989). Effects of previews on more skilled and less skilled readers' comprehension of expository text. *Journal of Reading Behavior, 21,* 219–239.

McCormick, Sandra. (1994). A nonreader becomes a reader: A case study of literacy acquisition by a severely disabled reader. *Reading Research Quarterly, 29,* 157–176.

McCormick, Theresa E. (1984). Multiculturalism: Some principles and issues. *Theory Into Practice, 23,* 93–97.

McCracken, Janet Brown. (1993). *Valuing diversity: The primary years.* Washington, DC: National Association for the Education of Young Children.

McCracken, Robert A. (1971). Initiating Sustained Silent Reading (1971). *Journal of Reading, 14,* 521–524, 582–583.

McCracken, Robert A., & McCracken, Marlene J. (1978). Modeling is the key to sustained silent reading. *The Reading Teacher, 31,* 406–408.

McDevitt, Teresa M., Spivey, Norm, Sheehan, Eugene P., Lennon, Randy, & Story, Rita. (1990). Children's beliefs about listening: Is it enough to be still and quiet? *Child Development, 61,* 713–730.

McGhee, Paul. (1979). *Humor: Its origin and development.* San Francisco, CA: Freeman.

McGill-Franzen, Anne, & Allington, Richard L. (1991). Every child's right: Literacy. *The Reading Teacher, 45,* 86–89.

McGinley, William J., & Denner, Peter R. (1987). Story impressions; A prereading/writing activity. *Journal of Reading, 31,* 248–253.

McGlinn, Jeanne. (1994). Their own story: Literature for African-American children, *Reading Horizons, 34,* 208–212.

McGowan, Tom, & Guzzetti, Barbara. (1991). Promoting social studies understanding through literature-based instruction. *The Social Studies, 82,* 16–21.

McKenna, Michael C., & Robinson, Richard D. (1990). Content literacy: A definition and implications. *Journal of Reading, 34,* 184–186.

McKeown, Margaret G. (1993). Creating effective definitions for young word learners. *Reading Research Quarterly, 28,* 16–30.

McLaughlin, Elaine M. (1987). QuIP: A writing strategy to improve comprehension of expository text structure. *The Reading Teacher, 40,* 650–654.

Mead, Margaret. (1970). *Culture and commitment.* New York: Natural History Press Doubleday.

Meier, Daniel. (1986). Learning in small moments. *Harvard Educational Review, 56,* 298–300.

Meisels, Samuel J. (1993). Remaking classroom assessment with the work sampling system. *Young Children, 48,* 34–40.

Memory, David M. (1990). Teaching technical vocabulary: Before, during, or after the reading assignment? *Journal of Reading Behavior, 22,* 39–53.

Merrill, Jean. (1964). *The pushcart war.* New York: Dell.

Meyer, Debra. (1993). What is scaffolded instruction? Definitions, distinguishing features, and misnomers. In Donald Leu & Charles K. Kinzer (Eds.), *Examining central issues in literacy research, theory, and practice.* Chicago, IL: National Reading Conference.

Meyer, Linda A. (1991). Are science textbooks considerate? In *Science learning: Processes and applications.* In Carol Minnick Santa & Donna E. Alvermann (Eds.). Newark, DE: International Reading Association.

Meyer, Susan E. (1990). *Mary Cassatt.* New York: Abrams.

Micklethwait, Lucy. (1992a). *I spy: An alphabet in art.* New York: Greenwillow.

Micklethwait, Lucy. (1992b). *I spy two eyes: Numbers in art.* New York: Greenwillow.

Micklethwait, Lucy. (1994). *I spy a lion: Animals in art.* New York: Greenwillow.

Miller, Edward. (1994). Letting talent flow: How schools can promote learning for the sheer love of it. *Harvard Education Letter, 10,* 1–3, 8.

Miller, George A., & Gildea, Patricia M. (1987). How children learn words. *Scientific American, 257,* 94–99.

Miller, L. Diane. (1992). Begin mathematics class with writing. *Mathematics Teacher, 85,* 354–355.

Miller, L. Diane. (1993). Making the connection with language. *Arithmetic Teacher, 40,* 311–316.

Mills, Heidi, & Clyde, Jean Anne. (1991). Children's success as readers and writers: It's the teacher's beliefs that make the difference. *Young Children, 46,* 54–59.

Mills, Randy. (1988). Personal journals for the social studies. *Social Education, 52,* 425–426.

Moniuszko, Linda K. (1992). Motivation: Reaching reluctant readers age 14–17. *Journal of Reading, 36,* 32–34.

Morgan, Elizabeth L. (1989). Talking with parents when concerns come up. *Young Children, 44,* 52–56.

Morrice, Connie, & Simmons, Maureen. (1991). Beyond reading buddies: A whole language cross-age program. *The Reading Teacher, 44,* 572–577.

Morris, Ann. (1993). *Puddle jumper: How a toy is made.* New York: Lothrop, Lee & Shepard. Photographs by Ken Heyman.

Moss, Barbara. (1991). Children's nonfiction trade books: A complement to content area texts. *The Reading Teacher, 45,* 26–32.

Moustafa, Margaret, & Penrose, Joyce. (1985). Comprehensible input plus the Language Experience Approach: Reading instruction for limited English speaking students. *The Reading Teacher, 38,* 640–647.

Moyers, Bill. (1995). *The language of life: A festival of poets.* New York: Doubleday.

Mumma, Barbara. (1989). Book report floats. *Reading Horizons, 30,* 22.

Mussen, Paul H., & Eisenberg-Berg, Nancy. (1977). *Roots of caring: The development of prosocial behavior in children.* San Francisco, CA: Freeman.

Muth, Denise K. (1993). The thinking-out-loud procedure: A diagnostic tool for middle school mathematics teachers. *Middle School Journal, 24,* 61–65.

Myers, David G. (1989). *Psychology, 2nd ed.* New York: Worth.

Myers, John, & Monson, Luetta. (1992). *Involving families in middle level education.* Columbus, OH: National Middle School Association.

Myers, Walter Dean. (1993). *Brown angels: An album of pictures and verse.* New York: HarperCollins.

Nahrgang, Cynthia L., & Petersen, Brice T. (1986). Using writing to learn mathematics. *Mathematics Teacher, 79,* 461–465.

Nakamura, Jeanne. (1988). Optimal experiences and uses of talent. In Mihaly Csikszentmihalyi & Isabella Selega Csikszentmihalyi (Eds.), *Optimal experience: Psychological studies of flow in consciousness.* New York: Cambridge University Press.

National Geographic Society. (1988) *A traveler's look at Australia* (map). Washington, DC.

National Geographic Society. (1994). *The world: Physical map.* Washington, DC.

National Geographic Society. (1995). *Living on the edge* (map). Washington, DC.

Nattiv, Amalya. (1994). Helping behaviors and math achievement gain of students using cooperative learning. *Elementary School Journal, 94,* 285–297.

Neilsen, Lorri. (1992). Eternity's sunrise and other multiple choice questions. *The Reading Teacher, 45,* 642–643.

Nelms, Elizabeth D. (1992). The middle view: Beware the naming of parts. *English Journal, 81,* 83.

Nelson-Herber, Joan. (1986). Expanding and refining vocabulary in content areas. *Journal of Reading, 29,* 626–633.

Neuman, Susan B. (1992). Is learning from media distinctive? Examining children's inferencing strategies. *American Educational Research Journal, 29,* 119–140.

Newman, Judith M. (1991). Whole language: A changed universe. *Contemporary Education, 62,* 70–75.

Newman, Judith M., & Church, Susan M. (1990). Myths of whole language. *The Reading Teacher, 44,* 20–26.

Newton, Evangeline V. (1991). Developing metacognitive awareness: The response journal in college composition. *Journal of Reading, 34,* 476–478.

Nicholson, John. (1993). *Homemade houses: Traditional homes from many lands.* St. Leonards NSW, Australia: Allen & Unwin.

Nickell, Pat, & Kennedy, Mike. (1987). Global perspectives through children's games. *Social Education, 51,* 1–8.

Noddings, Nel. (1984). *Caring: A feminine approach to ethics and moral education.* Berkeley, CA: University of California Press.

Noddings, Nel. (1992). *The challenge to care in schools: An alternative approach to education.* New York: Teachers College Press.

Noddings, Nel, & Shore, Paul J. (1984). *Awakening the inner eye: Intuition in education.* New York: Teachers College Press.

Norris, Janet A. (1989). Facilitating developmental changes in spelling. *Academic Therapy, 25,* 97–109.

Novak, Joseph. (1991). Clarify with concept maps. *Science Teacher, 58,* 45–49.

Novak, Joseph D., & Gowin, D. B. (1984). *Learning how to learn.* Ithaca, NY: Cornell University Press.

Nye, Naomi Shihab. (1992). *This same sky: A collection of poems from around the world.* New York: Four Winds.

O'Connell, Susan R. (1992). Math pairs—parents as partners. *Arithmetic Teacher, 40,* 10–13.

Ogbu, John U. (1992). Understanding cultural diversity and learning. *Educational Researcher, 21,* 5–14.

Ogle, Donna M. (1986). KWL: A teaching model that develops active reading of expository text. *The Reading Teacher, 39,* 64–70.

Olson, Mary W., & Gee, Thomas. (1989). Discovering roots. *Middle School Journal, 20,* 29–31.

Olson, Mary W., & Gee, Thomas. (1991). Content reading instruction in the primary grades: Perceptions and strategies. *The Reading Teacher, 45,* 298–307.

Olson, Mary W., & Longnion, Bonnie. (1982). Pattern guides: A workable alternative for content teachers. *Journal of Reading, 25,* 736–741.

O'Neil, John. (1993). 'Inclusive' education gains adherents. *ASCD Update, 35,* 1, 3–4.

O'Neil, John. (1994). Making assessment meaningful: 'Rubrics' clarify expectations, yield better feedback. *ASCD Update, 36,* 1, 4–5.

Ontario Science Center. (1987). *Foodworks.* Reading, MA: Addison-Wesley.

Oodgeroo. (1994). *Dreamtime: Aboriginal stories.* New York: Lothrop, Lee & Shepard. Illustrated by Bronwyn Bancroft.

Oppenheim, Kenneth. (1985). The parent *what!?!* or How an elementary teacher can cope with parent conferences. *Kappa Delta Pi Record, 21,* 89–91.

Orie, Sandra deCoteau. (1995). *Did you hear wind sing your name?: An Oneida song of spring.* New York: Walker. Illustrated by Christopher Canyon.

Osborne, Alex. (1963). *Applied imaginations.* New York: Scribner's.

Ostrow, William, & Ostrow, Vivian. (1989). *All about asthma.* Niles, IL: Albert Whitman. Illustrated by Blanche Sims.

Owsley, Vicki. (1989). Quick draw. *The Reading Teacher, 43,* 269–270.

Paley, Vivian Gussin. (1992). *You can't say you can't play.* Cambridge, MA: Harvard University Press.

Palincsar, Annemarie S., & Brown, Ann L. (1984). Reciprocal teaching of comprehension-fostering and monitoring activities. *Cognition and Instruction, 1,* 117–175.

Pappas, Christine C. (1993). Is narrative "primary"? Some insights from kindergarteners' pretend readings of stories and information books. *Journal of Reading Behavior, 25,* 97–129.

Pardo, Laura S., & Raphael, Taffy E. (1991). Classroom organization for instruction in content areas. *The Reading Teacher, 44,* 556–565.

Parker, Nancy Winslow (Illustrator). (1985). *Paul Revere's ride, by Henry Wadsworth Longfellow.* New York: Mulberry.

Parker, Nancy Winslow (Illustrator). (1992). *Barbara Frietchie, by John Greenleaf Whittier.* New York: Greenwillow.

Pate, P. Elizabeth, Homestead, Elaine, & McGinnis, Karen. (1993). Designing rubrics for authentic assessment. *Middle School Journal, 25,* 25–27.

Paterson, Katherine. (1977). *Bridge to Terebithia.* New York: Thomas Crowell.

Paterson, Katherine. (1978). *The Great Gilly Hopkins.* New York: Thomas Crowell.

Paterson, Katherine. (1990). *Stick to reality and a dream.* Washington DC: Children's Literature Center, Library of Congress.

Pauk, Walter, (1974). *How to study in college, 2nd ed.* New York: Houghton Mifflin.

Paul, Peter V., & O'Rourke, Joseph P. (1988). Multimeaning words and reading comprehension: Implications for special education students. *Remedial and Special Education, 9,* 42–52.

Pawlas, George E. (1994). Homeless students at the school door. *Educational Leadership, 51,* 79–82.

Paxton, Tom. (1991). *Androcles and the lion and other Aesop's fables.* New York: Morrow.

Paxton, Tom. (1993). *Birds of a feather and other Aesop's fables.* New York: Morrow.

Pearce, Daniel L. (1983). Guidelines for the use and evaluation of writing in content classrooms. *Journal of Reading, 17,* 212–218.

Pedersen, Eigil, Faucher, Thérése Annette, & Eaton, William. (1978). A new perspective on the effects of first-grade teachers on children's subsequent adult status. *Harvard Educational Review, 48,* 1–31.

Perez, Samuel A. (1989). Rereading to enhance text understanding in the secondary classroom. *Reading Horizons, 30,* 62–66.

Perrin, Robert. (1987). Myths about research. *English Journal, 76,* 50–53.

Phipson, Joan. (1978). *When the city stopped.* New York: Atheneum.

Piaget, Jean. (1929). *The child's conception of the world.* New York: Harcourt Brace.

Piaget, Jean. (1932). *The moral judgment of the child.* New York: Harcourt Brace.

Piaget, Jean. (1955). *The language and thought of the child.* New York: Harcourt Brace.

Piaget, Jean, & Inhelder, Barbel. (1968). *The psychology of the child.* New York: Basic Books.

Piaget, Jean, & Inhelder, Barbel. (1973). *Memory and intelligence.* New York: Basic Books.

Piltch, Ben. (1991). When parent involvement is not possible—or desirable. *Principal, 71,* 58.

Pines, Maya. (1984). Michael Rutter: Resilient children. *Psychology Today, 18,* 60, 62, 64–65.

Pittelman, Susan D., Heimlich, Joan E., Berglund, Roberta L., & French, Michael P. (1991). *Semantic Feature Analysis: Classroom applications.* Newark, DE: International Reading Association.

Pomerantz, Charlotte. (1980). *The Tamarindo puppy.* New York: Greenwillow.

Pomerantz, Charlotte. (1993). *If I had a paka: Poems in eleven languages.* New York: Greenwillow. Illustrated by Nancy Tafuri.

Poplin, Mary S. (1988). The reductionistic fallacy in learning disabilities: Replicating the past by reducing the present. *Journal of Learning Disabilities, 21,* 389–400.

Potter, Gill. (1989). Parent participation in the language arts program. *Language Arts, 66,* 21–28.

Power, Brenda Miller. (1989). Beyond "Geddinagrupe": A case study of three first grade collaborators. *Language Arts, 66,* 767–774.

Prawat, Richard S. (1991). The value of ideas: The immersion approach to the development of thinking. *Educational Researcher, 20,* 3–10.

Price, Leontyne. (1990). *Aïda.* San Diego, CA: Gulliver. Illustrated by Leo and Diane Dillon.

Priles, Maria A. (1993). The fishbowl discussion: A strategy for large honors classes. *English Journal, 82,* 49–50.

Quintero, Elizabeth, & Huerta-Macias, Ana. (1990). All in the family: Bilingualism and biliteracy. *The Reading Teacher, 44,* 306–312.

Quintero, Elizabeth, & Velarde, M. Cristina. (1990). Intergenerational literacy: A developmental, bilingual approach. *Young Children, 45,* 10–15.

Rankin, Joan L. (1992). Connecting literacy learners: A pen pal project. *The Reading Teacher, 46,* 204–214.

Raphael, Taffy E. (1982). Question-answering strategies for children. *The Reading Teacher, 36,* 186–190.

Raphael, Taffy E. (1986). Teaching question answer relationships, revisited. *The Reading Teacher, 40,* 516–522.

Raphael, Taffy E., & Pearson, P. David. (1985). Increasing students' awareness of sources of information for answering questions. *American Educational Research Journal, 22,* 217–235.

Rasinski, Timothy V. (1988). Making repeated readings a functional part of classroom reading instruction. *Reading Horizons, 29,* 250–254.

Rasinski, Timothy V. (1989). Reading and the empowerment of parents. *The Reading Teacher, 43,* 226–231.

Rasinski, Timothy V. (1990). Making a place for fluency instruction in the regular reading curriculum. *Reading Research and Instruction, 29,* 85–91.

Rasinski, Timothy V. (1991). Inertia and reading: Stimulating interest in books and reading. *Middle School Journal, 22,* 30–33.

Rasinski, Timothy V., & Padak, Nancy D. (1990). Multicultural learning through children's literature. *Language Arts, 67,* 576–580.

Reed, Barbara. (1987). Storytelling: What it can teach. *School Library Journal, 34,* 35–39.

Reed, Lorrie C. (1993). Achieving the aims and purposes of schooling through authentic assessment. *Middle School Journal, 25,* 11–13.

Reimer, Becky L. (1989). Helping teachers remain learners: Becoming experts on a topic. *Journal of Reading Education, 14,* 36–52.

Reimer, Kathryn Meyer. (1992). Multiethnic literature: Holding fast to dreams. *Language Arts, 69,* 14–21.

Reinking, David. (1986). Integrating graphic aids into content area instruction: The graphic information lesson. *Journal of Reading, 30,* 146–151.

Reis, Elizabeth M. (1988). Conference skills: Working with parents. *Clearing House, 62,* 81–83.

Reissman, Rose C. (1993). Give the gift of family literacy—Student-designed gift books. *English Journal, 82,* 74–76.

Renner, Sigrid M., & Carter, JoAnn M. (1991). Comprehending text— appreciating diversity through folklore. *Journal of Reading, 34,* 602–604.

Resh, Celeste A. & Marilyn J. Wilson. (1990). The teacher-parent partnership: Helping children become good readers. *Reading Horizons, 30,* 51–56.

Reutzel, D. Ray, & Fawson, Parker C. (1990). Traveling tales: Connecting parents and children through writing. *The Reading Teacher, 44,* 222–227.

Reutzel, D. Ray, & Hollingsworth, Paul M. (1991). Reading comprehension skills: Testing the distinctiveness hypothesis. *Reading Research and Instruction, 30,* 32–46.

Reyes, María de la Luz. (1992). Challenging venerable assumptions: Literacy instruction for linguistically different students. *Harvard Educational Review, 62,* 427–446.

Reyes, María de la Luz, & Molner, Linda A. (1991). Instructional strategies for second-language learners in the content areas. *Journal of Reading, 35,* 96–103.

Reyhner, Jon, & Garcia, Ricardo L. (1989). Helping minorities read better: Problems and promises. *Reading Research and Instruction, 28,* 84–91.

Rhodes, Lynn K. (1989). Comprehension instruction as sharing and extending. *The Reading Teacher, 42,* 496–500.

Rhodes, Lynn K., & Dudley-Marling, Curt. (1988). *Readers and writers with a difference: A holistic approach to teaching learning disabled and remedial students.* Portsmouth, NH: Heinemann.

Rhodes, Lynn K., & Nathenson-Meija, Sally. (1992). Anecdotal records: A powerful tool for ongoing literacy assessment. *The Reading Teacher, 45,* 502–509.

Richards, Leah. (1990). Measuring things in words: Language for learning mathematics. *Language Arts, 67,* 14–25.

Richards, Monica. (1987). A teacher's action research study: The 'bums' of 8H. *Peabody Journal of Education, 64,* 65–70.

Richardson, Judy S. (1995). Coordinating teacher readalouds with content instruction in secondary classrooms. In Eugene H. Cramer & Marrietta Castle (Eds.), *Fostering the love of reading: The affective domain in reading education.* Newark, DE: International Reading Association.

Richardson, Virginia, Anders, Patricia, Tidwell, Deborah, & Lloyd, Carol. (1991). The relationship between teachers' beliefs and practices in reading comprehension instruction. *American Educational Research Journal, 28,* 559–586.

Riecken, Ted J., & Miller, Michelle R. (1990). Introduce children to problem solving and decision making by using children's literature. *The Social Studies, 81,* 59–64.

Rief, Linda. (1990). Finding the value in evaluation: Self-assessment in a middle school classroom. *Educational Leadership, 47,* 24–29.

Rigg, Pat. (1989). Language Experience Approach: Reading naturally. In Pat Rigg & Virginia G. Allen (Eds.), *When they don't all speak English: Integrating the ESL student into the regular classroom.* Urbana, IL: National Council of Teachers of English.

Rist, Marilee C. (1991). Ethnocentric education. *American School Board Journal, 178,* 26–39.

Robinson, Francis, (1961). *Effective study, revised edition.* New York: Harper & Row.

Roby, Cynthia. (1992). *When learning is tough: Kids talk about their learning disabilities.* Morton Grove, IL: Albert Whitman. Photographs by Elena Dorfman.

Rodriguez, Kimberly Miller. (1991). Home writing activities: The Writing Briefcase and the Traveling Suitcase. *The Reading Teacher, 45,* 160.

Rojas, Hector. (1993). *Origami animals.* New York: Sterling.

Romero, Patricia Ann, & Zancanella, Dan. (1990). Expanding the circle: Hispanic voices in American literature. *English Journal, 79,* 24–29.

Roop, Peter, & Roop, Connie. (1992). *Ahyoka and the talking leaves.* New York: Lothrop, Lee & Shepard. Illustrated by Yoshi Miyake.

Rosen, Michael J. (Ed.). (1992). *Home.* New York: HarperCollins.

Rosenberg, Jane. (1989). *Sing me a story: The Metropolitan Opera's book of opera stories for children.* New York: Thames & Hudson.

Rosenberg, Jane. (1993). *Dance me a story: Twelve tales from the classic ballets.* New York: Thames & Hudson.

Rosenblatt, Louise M. (1978). *The reader, the text, the poem.: The transactional theory of the literary work.* Carbondale, IL: Southern Illinois University Press.

Rosenblatt, Louise M. (1991). Literature—S.O.S.! *Language Arts, 68,* 444–448.

Roser, Nancy L. (1989). *Helping your child become a reader.* Newark, DE: International Reading Association.

Rosow, LaVergne. (1988). Adult illiterates offer unexpected cues into the reading process. *Journal of Reading, 32,* 120–124.

Roth, Kathleen. (1987). Learning to be comfortable in the neighborhood of science. An analysis of three approaches to elementary science teaching. In Wendy Saul & Sybille A. Jagusch (Eds.), *Children, Science, and Books.* Washington, DC: Library of Congress.

Roth, Kathleen J. (1994). Second thoughts about interdisciplinary studies. *American Educator, 18,* 44–48.

Roth, Wolff-Michael, & Roychoudhury, Anita. (1992). The social construction of scientific concepts or the concept map as conscription device and tool for social thinking in high school science. *Science Education, 76,* 531–557.

Rotter, Julian B. (1966). Generalized expectations for internal versus external control. *Psychological Monographs, 80 (Whole N. 609).*

The Round Table (1990). Tracking: What do you think? *English Journal, 79,* 74–76.

Routman, Regie. (1988). *Transitions.* Portsmouth, NH: Heinemann.

Rowe, Mary Budd. (1974). Wait time and rewards as instructional variables, their influences on language, logic, and fate control: Part One—Wait time. *Journal of Research in Science Teaching, 11,* 81–94.

Rowe, Mary Budd. (1986). Wait time: Slowing down may be a way of speeding up! *Journal of Teacher Education, 37,* 43–50.

Ruddell, Robert B. (1990). Alternate streams in education: Instructional flow in the classrooms of influential and noninfluential teachers. *Reading Horizons, 31,* 74.

Ryder, Joanne. (1990). *Lizard in the sun.* New York: Mulberry. Illustrated by Michael Rothman.

Ryder, Joanne. (1994). *White bear, ice bear.* New York: Mulberry. Illustrated by Michael Rothman.

Saint Augustine. (1991). *Confessions.* Translated by Henry Chadwick. New York: Oxford University Press.

Salisbury, Christine L., & Smith, Barbara J. (1991). The least restrictive environment: Understanding the options. *Principal, 71,* 24–27.

Salyers, Fran. (1992). Spelling with the curriculum. *Middle School Journal, 23,* 24–26.

Samuels, S. Jay. (1986). Why children fail to learn and what to do about it. *Exceptional Children, 53,* 7–16.

Samway, Katharine Davies, Whang, Gail, Cade, Carol, Gamil, Melindevic, Lubandina, Mary Ann, Phommachanh, Kansone. (1991). Reading the skeleton, the heart, and the brain of a book: Students' perspectives on literature study circles. *The Reading Teacher, 45,* 196–205.

Sanacore, Joseph. (1990). Creating the lifetime reading habit in social studies. *Journal of Reading, 33,* 414–418.

Santa, Carol Minnick, & Alvermann, Donna E. (1991). *Science learning: Processes and applications.* Newark, DE: International Reading Association.

Sarason, Seymour B. (1993). *You are thinking of teaching?: Opportunities, problems, realities.* San Francisco, CA: Jossey-Bass.

Sattler, Helen Roney. (1990). *The new illustrated dinosaur dictionary.* New York: Lothrop, Lee & Shepard. Illustrated by Joyce Powzyk.

Sattler, Helen Roney, & Maestro, Giulio. (1995). *Our patchwork planet.* New York: Lothrop, Lee & Shepard.

Saul, Wendy E. (1993). Mediated vs. unmediated texts: Books in the library and the classroom. *New Advocate, 6,* 171–181.

Saunders, William, Goldenberg, Claude, & Hamann, Janet. (1992). Instructional conversations beget instructional conversations. *Teaching and Teacher Education, 8,* 199–218.

Say, Allen. (1993). *Grandfather's journey.* Boston, MA: Houghton Mifflin.

Scarnati, James F., & Weller, Cyril J. (1992). The write stuff. *Science and Children, 29,* 28–29.

Schack, Gina D. (1993). Involving students in authentic research. *Educational Leadership, 50,* 29–31.

Schaffer, Jane C. (1989). Improving discussion questions: Is anyone out there listening? *English Journal, 78,* 40–42.

Schatz, Elinore Kress, & Baldwin, R. Scott. (1986). Context clues are unreliable predictors of word meaning. *Reading Research Quarterly, 21,* 439–453.

Schleper, David R. & Paradis, Sandra J. (1990). Learning logs for math: Thinking through writing. *Perspectives, 9,* 14–24.

Schug, Mark C., & Baumann, Eddie. (1991). Strategies to correct high school students' misunderstanding of economics. *The Social Studies, 82,* 62–66.

Schumaker, Jean, Deshler, Donald, Alley, Gordon, Warner, Michael, & Denton, Pegi. (1982). MULTIPASS: A learning strategy for improving reading comprehension. *Learning Disabilities Quarterly, 5,* 295–304.

Schuster, M. Lincoln (Ed.). (1940). *A treasury of the world's great letters.* New York: Simon & Schuster.

Schwartz, Albert V. (1977). The five Chinese brothers: Time to retire. *Interracial Books for Children Bulletin 8,* 3–7.

Schwartz, Peggy. (1991). Multicultural dance education in today's curriculum. *Journal of Physical Education, Recreation and Dance, 62,* 45–48.

Schwartz, Robert M. (1988). Learning to learn vocabulary in content area textbooks. *Journal of Reading, 32,* 109–117.

Schwartz, Robert M., & Raphael, Taffy E. (1985). Concept of definition: A key to improving students' vocabulary. *The Reading Teacher, 39,* 198–205.

Scriven, Michael. (1991). *Evaluation thesaurus, 4th ed.* Newbury Park, CA: Sage.

Scruggs, Thomas E., & Mastropieri, Margo A. (1994). Successful mainstreaming in elementary science classes: A qualitative study of three reputational cases. *American Educational Research Journal, 31,* 785–811.

Searfoss, Lynn W., Smith, C. C., & Bean, Thomas W. (1981). An integrated language strategy for second language learners. *TESOL Quarterly, 15,* 383–389.

Searle, Dennis, & Dillon, David. (1980). Responding to student writing: What is said or how it is said. *Language Arts, 57,* 773–781.

Seefeldt, Carol. (1987). Intergenerational programs: Making them work. *Childhood Education, 64,* 14–19.

Seeger, Pete. (1986). *Abiyoyo.* New York: Macmillan.

Seigel, Marjorie. (1984). Sketch to stretch. In Orin Cochrane, Donna Cochrane, Sharon Scalena, & Ethel Buchanan (Eds.), *Reading, writing and caring.* New York: Richard C. Owen.

Seuss, Dr. (Theodore Geisel). (1987). *The tough coughs as he ploughs the dough.* New York: Morrow.

Shaheen, Peter. (1992). To look or to listen? A dumb question. *English Journal, 81,* 82–83.

Shanks, Marlene. (1988). The research paper: Two more alternatives. *English Journal, 77,* 81–82.

Shapiro, Arthur, & Barton, Elizabeth. (1993). Disabilities are *not* handicaps. *Principal, 72,* 54–55.

Sharp, Peggy Agostino. (1984). Teaching with picture books throughout the curriculum. *The Reading Teacher, 38,* 132–137.

Sharp, Sidney J. (1989). Using content subject matter with LEA in middle school. *Journal of Reading, 33,* 108–112.

Sheingold, Karen. (1987). Keeping children's knowledge alive through inquiry. *School Library Media Quarterly, 15,* 80–85.

Short, Kathy G., & Armstrong, Junardi. (1993). Moving toward inquiry: Integrating literature into the science curriculum. *New Advocate, 6,* 183–193.

Short, Kathy G., & Klassen, Charlene. (1993). Literature circles: Hearing children's voices. In Bernice E. Cullinan (Ed.), *Children's voices: Talk in the classroom.* Newark, DE: International Reading Association.

Silverstein, Alvin, Silverstein, Virginia, & Silverstein, Robert. (1992). *Smell, the subtle sense.* New York: William Morrow. Illustrated by Ann Neumann.

Simon, Seymour. (1989). *Storms.* New York: Morrow.

Simon, Seymour. (1991). *Earthquakes.* New York: Morrow.

Simon, Seymour. (1992). *Our solar system.* New York: Morrow.

Simon, Seymour. (1993). *Weather,* New York: Morrow.

Simon, Seymour. (1994). *Mountains.* New York: Morrow.

Simpson, Anne, & Willson, Paula. (1993). Literature circles: Children talking and writing about their reading. In *Literacy for the new millennium.* Carlton, Victoria, Australia: Australian Reading Association.

Simpson, Mary K. (1986). A teacher's gift: Oral reading and the reading response journal. *Journal of Reading, 30,* 45–50.

Sinatra, Richard, Beaudry, Jeffrey S., Stahl-Gemake, Josephine, & Guastello, E. Francine. (1990). Combining visual literacy, text understanding and writing for culturally diverse students. *Journal of Reading, 33,* 612–619.

Slavin, Robert E. (1990). *Cooperative learning: Theory, research, and practice.* Englewood Cliffs, NJ: Prentice-Hall.

Slavin, Robert E. (1992). When and why does cooperative learning increase achievement? Theoretical and empirical perspectives. In Rachel Hertz-Lazarowitz & Norman Miller (Eds.) *Interaction in cooperative groups: The theoretical anatomy of group learning.* Cambridge, MA: Cambridge University Press.

Slavin, Robert E. (1993). Students differ: So what? *Educational Researcher, 22,* 13–14.

Smith, Charles A. (1986). Nurturing kindness through storytelling. *Young Children, 41,* 46–51.

Smith, Charlotte T. (1978). Evaluating answers to comprehension questions. *The Reading Teacher, 31,* 896–900.

Smith, Frances M., & Hausafus, Cheryl O. (1993). An academic/vocational curriculum partnership: Home economics and science. *Middle School Journal, 24,* 48–51.

Smith, Patricia L., & Tompkins, Gail E. (1988). Structured notetaking: A new strategy for content area readers.

Journal of Reading, 33, 46–53.

Smith, Walter S., & Burrichter, Cindy. (1993). Look who's teaching science today! Cross-age tutoring makes the grade. *Science and Children, 30,* 20–23.

Smout, Beth. (1990). Reading, writing, and art. *The Reading Teacher, 43,* 430–431.

Snakenberg, Robert Lokomaika'iokalani. (1988). *The Hawaiian sentence book.* Honolulu, HI: Bess Press.

Snow, Catherine. (1972). Mothers' speech to children learning language. *Child Development, 43,* 549–565.

Sobol, Thomas. (1990). Understanding diversity. *Educational Leadership, 48,* 27–30.

Soderlund, Michael D. (1993). Classroom memos: Creating purposeful dialogue. *English Journal, 82,* 55–57.

Solomon, Daniel, Watson, Marilyn S., Delucchi, Kevin L., Schaps, Eric, & Battistich, Victor. (1988). Enhancing children's prosocial behavior in the classroom. *American Educational Research Journal, 25,* 527–554.

Sosniak, Lauren A., & Stodolsky, Susan S. (1993). Teachers and textbooks: Materials use in four fourth-grade classrooms. *Elementary School Journal, 93,* 249–275.

Soto, Lourdes Diaz. (1989). Enhancing the written medium for culturally diverse learners via reciprocal interaction. *Urban Review, 21,* 145–149.

Spiegel, Dixie Lee. (1990). Content bias in reference and study skills. *The Reading Teacher, 44,* 64–65.

Spier, Peter. (1970). *The Erie Canal.* Garden City, NY: Doubleday.

Spier, Peter. (1973). *The Star Spangled Banner,* Garden City, NY: Doubleday.

Spires, Hiller. (1990). Metacognition and reading: Implications for instruction. *Reading, 24,* 151–156.

Staab, Claire F. (1990). Teacher mediation in one Whole Literacy classroom. *The Reading Teacher, 43,* 548–552.

Stake, Robert E. (1975). *Evaluating the arts in education: A responsive approach.* Columbus, OH: Merrill.

Stanish, Bob. (1989). *Mindglow: Classroom encounters with creative thinking.* Carthage, IL: Good Apple.

Stanovich, Keith E. (1986). Matthew effects in reading: Some consequences of individual differences in the acquisition of literacy. *Reading Research Quarterly, 21,* 360–407.

Stanovich, Keith E. (1993/1994). Romance and reality. *The Reading Teacher, 47,* 280–291.

Staton, Jana. (1988). ERIC/RCS report: Dialogue journals. *Language Arts, 65,* 198–201.

Stauffer, Russell G. (1969). *Directing the reading-thinking process.* New York: Harper & Row.

Stauffer, Russell G. (1970). *The language experience approach to the teaching of reading.* New York: Harper & Row.

Steele, Barbara. (1992). The micro-shop. *Principal, 72,* 40–41.

Steinberg, Judith Wolinsky. (1991). To arrive in another world: Poetry, language development, and culture. *Harvard Educational Review, 61,* 51–70.

Stenmark, Jean. (Ed.). (1991). *Mathematics assessment: Myths, models, good questions, and practical suggestions.* Reston, VA: National Council of Teachers of Mathematics.

Steptoe, John. (1969). *Stevie.* New York: HarperCollins.

Steptoe, John. (1987). *Mufaro's beautiful daughters: An African tale.* New York: HarperCollins.

Stevens, Romiett. (1912). *The question as a measure of efficiency in instruction: A critical study of classroom practice.* New York: Teachers College, Columbia University.

Stevenson, James. (1991). *That's exactly the way it wasn't.* New York: Greenwillow.

Stevick, Earl W. (1976). *Memory, meaning, and method.* Rowley, MA: Newbury House.

Stewig, John Warren. (1995). *Looking at picture books.* Fort Atkinson, WI: Highsmith.

Stock, Catherine. (1993). *Where are you going Manyoni?* New York: Morrow.

Stone, Janet. (1993). Caregiver and teacher language—Responsive or restrictive? *Young Children, 48,* 12–18.

Stover, Lois. (1991). Exploring and celebrating cultural diversity and similarity through young adult novels. *ALAN Review, 18,* 12–15.

Strickland, Dorothy S. (1988). The teacher as researcher: Toward the extended professional. *Language Arts, 65,* 754–764.

Strickland, Dorothy S., & Morrow, Lesley Mandel. (1990). The daily journal: Using language experience strategies in an emergent literacy curriculum. *The Reading Teacher, 43,* 422–423.

Suhor, Charles. (1985). Objective tests and writing samples: How do they affect instruction in composition? *Phi Delta Kappan, 66,* 635–639.

Sutherland, Zena, & Arbuthnot, May Hill. (1991). *Children and books, 8th ed.* New York: HarperCollins.

Swaby, Barbara. (1984). FAN out your facts on the board. *The Reading Teacher, 37,* 914–916.

Swafford, Jeanne, & Paulos, Tamara N. (1993). Creating experiences for listening and learning. *Reading Horizons, 33,* 401–417.

Swann, Brian. (1988). *A. basket full of white eggs.* New York: Orchard.

Taba, Hilda. (1967). *Teacher's handbook for elementary social studies.* Reading, MA: Addison-Wesley.

Taft, R. (1988). Ethnographic research methods. In John P. Keeves (Ed.), *Educational research, methodology, and measurement: An international handbook.* Oxford, England: Pergamon.

Taylor, Barbara M., Frye, Barbara J., & Gaetz, Thomas M. (1990). Reducing the number of reading skill activities in the elementary classroom. *Journal of Reading Behavior, 22,* 167–179.

Taylor, Denny, & Dorsey-Gaines, Catherine. (1988). *Growing up literate: Learning from inner-city families.* Portsmouth, NH: Heinemann.

Taylor, Wilson. (1953). "Cloze procedure": A new tool for measuring readability. *Journalism Quarterly, 30,* 415–433.

Taylor, Wilson. (1956). Recent developments in the use of the cloze procedure. *Journalism Quarterly, 33,* 42–48, 99.

Tegano, Deborah W., Sawyers, Janet K., & Moran, James D., III. (1989). Problem finding and solving in play: The teacher's role. *Childhood Education, 66,* 92–97.

Terkel, Studs. (1970). *Hard times: An oral history of the Great Depression.* New York: Pantheon.

Terkel, Studs. (1980). *American dreams: Lost and found.* New York: Pantheon.

Thelen, Judith N. (1986). Vocabulary instruction and meaningful learning. *Journal of Reading, 29,* 603–609.

Thiele, Colin. (1974). *Fire in the stone.* New York: Harper.

Thomas, Sharon K., & Wilson, Marilyn. (1993). Idiosyncratic interpretations: Negotiating meaning in expository prose. *English Journal, 82,* 58–64.

Thorndike, Edward L. (1917). Reading as reasoning: A study of mistakes in paragraph reading. *Journal of Educational Psychology, 8,* 323–332.

Tobias, Sheila. (1989). Tracked to fail. *Psychology Today, 23,* 54–58, 60.

Tomecek, Steve. (1995). *Bouncing and bending light.* New York: W. H. Freeman.

Tomlinson, Carl M. (1988). Studying Australia—Beyond the textbook approach. *The Social Studies, 79,* 32–36.

Tone, Bruce. (1988). Guiding students through research papers. *Journal of Reading, 32,* 76–79.

Totten, Samuel. (1989). Using oral histories to address social issues in the social studies classroom. *Social Education, 53,* 114–116, 125.

Trafton, Paul R. (1984). Toward more effective and efficient instruction in mathematics. *Elementary School Journal, 84,* 514–528.

Trelease, Jim. (1989). *The new read-aloud handbook.* New York: Penguin.

Trimble, Kimberly D., & Sinclair, Robert L. (1987). On the wrong track: Ability grouping and the threat to equity. *Equity and Excellence, 23,* 15–23.

Trotter, Andrew. (1992). Harvest of dreams. *American School Board Journal, 179,* 14–18.

Tuchman, Barbara W. (1988). *The first salute: A view of the American Revolution.* New York: Ballantine.

Tuleja, Tad. (1992). *American history in 100 nutshells.* NY: Fawcett Columbine.

Turner, Robyn Montana. (1991). *Georgia O'Keeffe.* Boston, MA: Little, Brown.

Turner, Robyn Montana. (1991). *Rosa Bonheur.* Boston, MA: Little, Brown.

Urzúa, Carole. (1989). "I grow for a living." In Pat Rigg & Virginia G. Allen (Eds.), *When they don't all speak English: Integrating the ESL student into the regular classroom.* Urbana, IL: National Council of Teachers of English.

Valencia, Sheila W., Hiebert, Elfrieda H., & Afflerbach, Peter. (1994). *Authentic reading assessment: Practices and possibilities.* Newark, DE: International Reading Association.

Vallecorsa, Ada L., Ledford, Rita Rice, & Parnell, Ginger G. (1991). Strategies for teaching composition skills to students with learning disabilities. *Teaching Exceptional Children, 23,* 52–55.

Van Allsburg, Chris. (1984). *The mysteries of Harris Burdick.* Boston, MA: Houghton Mifflin.

Van Ausdall, Barbara Wass. (1994). Books offer entry into understanding other cultures. *Educational Leadership, 51,* 32–35.

Vasquez, James. (1989). Teaching to the distinctive traits of minority students. *The Clearing House, 63,* 299–304.

Vaughan, Charlene Loughlin. (1990). Knitting writing: The double-entry journal. In Nancie Atwell, (Ed), *Coming to know: Writing to learn in the intermediate grades.* Portsmouth, NH: Heinemann.

Vavra, Ed. (1987). Grammar and syntax: The student's perspective. *English Journal, 76,* 42–48.

Vavra, Ed. (1993). Welcome to the shoe store? *English Journal, 82,* 81–84.

Vellutino, Frank R. (1977). Alternative conceptualizations of dyslexia: Evidence in support of a verbal deficit hypothesis. *Harvard Educational Review, 47,* 334–354.

Vellutino, Frank R. (1987). Dyslexia. *Scientific American, 256,* 34–41.

Vermette, Paul. (1994). The right start for cooperative learning. *High School Journal, 77,* 255–260.

Verriour, Patrick. (1989). "This is drama": The play beyond the play. *Language Arts, 66,* 276–286.

Visual Arts Education Reform Handbook. (1995). Reston, VA: National Art Education Association.

Voss, Margaret M. (1988). "Make way for applesauce": The literate world of a three year old. *Language Arts,* 65, 272–278.

Vuong, Lynette Dyer. (1993). *The golden carp and other tales from Vietnam.* New York: Lothrop, Lee & Shepard. Illustrated by Manabu Saito.

Vygotsky, Lev. (1962). *Thought and language.* (E. Haufmann and G. Vakar, Trans.). Cambridge, MA: M.I.T. Press.

Vygotsky, Lev . (1978). *Mind in society: The development of higher psychological process.* (E. Haufmann and G. Vakar, Trans.). Cambridge, MA: Harvard University Press.

Vygotsky, Lev. (1982). Play and its role in the mental development of the child. In Judith Krieger Gardner (Ed.), *Readings in developmental psychology,* 2nd ed. Boston, MA: Little, Brown.

Wade, Jan. (1992). *Fairy tales for young Australians.* Sydney, Australia: Weldon.

Wadlington, Elizabeth, Bitner, Joe, Partridge Elizabeth, & Austin, Sue. (1992). Have a problem? Make the writing-mathematics connection! *Arithmetic Teacher, 40,* 207–209.

Wadsworth, Pamela. (1992). Primary science: Starting from children's ideas. In Tony Booth, Will Swann, Mary Masterton & Patricia Potts (Eds.), *Learning for all 1: Curricula for diversity in education.* London: Routledge.

Walker, Barbara J., & Wilson, Paul T. (1991). Using guided imagery to teach science concepts. In Carol Minnick Santa & Donna E. Alvermann (Eds.), *Science learning: Processes and applications.* Newark, DE: International Reading Association.

Walker, Hill, & Sylvester, Robert. (1991). Where is school along the path to prison? *Educational Leadership, 49,* 14–16.

Walker, Jim. (1989). Getting them unstuck: Some strategies for the teaching of reading in science. *School Science and Mathematics, 89,* 130–135.

Walker-Dalhouse, Doris. (1992). Using African-American literature to increase ethnic understanding. *The Reading Teacher, 45,* 416–422.

Wallach, Michael A., & Kogan, Nathan. (1965). *Modes of thinking in young children: A study of the creativity-intelligence distinction.* New York: Holt, Rinehart & Winston.

Warawa, Bonnie. (1989). Write me the story: Responding to literature through storytelling. *English Journal, 78,* 48–50.

Watson, Becky. (1995). Relinquishing the lectern: Cooperative learning in teacher education. *Journal of Teacher Education, 46,* 209–211.

Watson, Dorothy. (1989). Defining and describing whole language. *Elementary School Journal, 90,* 129–141.

Watson, Wendy. (1994). *Fox went out on a chilly night.* New York: Lothrop, Lee & Shepard.

Weatherford, Jack. (1991). Indian season in American schools. *The Social Studies, 82,* 172–178.

Webb, Noreen M. (1993). Collaborative group versus individual assessment in mathematics: Processes and outcomes. *Educational Assessment, 1,* 131–152.

Webb, Noreen M. (1995). Group collaboration in assessment: Multiple objectives, processes, and outcomes. *Educational Evaluation and Policy Analysis, 17,* 239–261.

Weber, Alan. (1992). Evaluating the writing of middle school students. *Middle School Journal, 24,* 24–27.

Weiner, Bernard. (1990). History of motivational research in education. *Journal of Educational Psychology, 82,* 616–622.

Weiner, Wendy F. (1986). When the process of writing becomes a tool for learning. *English Journal, 75,* 73–75.

Weisner, Thomas S., Gallimore, Ronald, & Jordan, Cathie. (1988). Unpackaging cultural effects on classroom learning: Native Hawaiian peer assistance and child-generating activity. *Anthropology and Education Quarterly, 19,* 327–353.

Welker, William A. (1987). Going from typical to technical meaning. *Journal of Reading, 31,* 275–276.

Wells, Gordon. (1986). *The meaning makers: Children learning language and using language to learn.* Portsmouth, NH: Heinemann.

Wells, Robert E. (1993). *Is a blue whale the biggest thing there is?* Morton Grove, IL: Albert Whitman.

Wells, Robert E. (1995). *What's smaller than a pygmy shrew?* Morton Grove, IL: Albert Whitman.

Wendelin, Karla Hawkins. (1991). Students as storytellers in the classroom. *Reading Horizons, 31,* 181–188.

Wentworth, Julie Welch. (1990). "A whole lot" of learning going on in an urban environment. *English Journal, 79,* 74–76.

Werner, Emmy E. (1984). Resilient children. *Young Children, 39,* 68–72.

Weston, Lynda. (1988). Class history records. *The Reading Teacher, 42,* 176.

White E. B. (1952). *Charlotte's web.* New York: HarperCollins.

White, George P., & Greenwood, Scott C. (1992). Empowering middle level students through the use of learning contracts. *Middle School Journal, 23,* 15–20.

Whitin, David J. (1992). Explore mathematics through children's literature. *School Library Journal, 38,* 24–28.

Wickey, Brenda J. (1992). The non-traditional student. *Reading Horizons, 32,* 420–421.

Wiesendanger, Katherine D. (1986). Durkin revisited. *Reading Horizons, 26,* 89–98.

Wiesner, David. (1991). *Tuesday.* New York: Clarion.

Wiggins, Grant. (1989). A true test: Toward more equitable and authentic assessment. *Phi Delta Kappan, 70,* 703–713.

Wilde, Sandra. (1991). Learning to write about mathematics. *Arithmetic Teacher, 39,* 38–43.

Wildman, Diane. (1990). Researching with pictures. *English Journal, 79,* 55–58.

Wilford, John Noble. (1982). *The mapmakers.* New York: Knapf.

Wilhelmi, Keith. (1988). Enhancing communication with parents. *Middle School Journal, 19,* 14–15.

Wilkinson, Andrew. (1965). *Spoken English.* Birmingham, UK: University of Birmingham.

Wilkinson, Andrew. (1991). Talking sense: The assessment of talk. In David Booth, & Carol Thornley-Hall *The talk curriculum.* Carlton, Victoria, Australia: Australian Reading Association.

Williams, Karen Lynn. (1990). *Galimoto.* New York: Lothrop, Lee & Shepard.

Williams, Kipling, Harkins, Stephen, & Latané, Bibb. (1981). Identifiability as a deterrent to social loafing: Two cheerful experiments. *Journal of Personality and Social Psychology, 40,* 303–311.

Winograd, Peter, & Paris, Scott G. (1988–1989). A cognitive and motivational agenda for reading instruction. *Educational Leadership, 46,* 30–36.

Wisniewski, David. (1990). *Elfwyn's saga.* New York: Lothrop, Lee & Shepard.

Wisniewski, David. (1991). *Rain player.* New York: Clarion.

Wisniewski, David. (1992). *Sundiata: Lion King of Mali.* New York: Clarion.

Wittmer, Donna Sasse, & Honig, Alice Sterling. (1994). Encouraging positive social development in young children. *Young Children, 49,* 4–12.

Wolf, Dennie Palmer. (1989). Portfolio assessment: Sampling student work. *Educational Leadership, 46,* 35–39.

Wolf, Kenneth P. (1993). From informal to informed assessment: Recognizing the role of the classroom teacher. *Journal of Reading, 36,* 518–523.

Wong, Jo Ann, & Au, Kathryn Hu-Pei. (1985). The concept-text-application approach: Helping elementary students comprehend expository text. *The Reading Teacher, 38,* 612–618.

Wood, Karen D. (1987a). Fostering cooperative learning in middle and secondary school classrooms. *Journal of Reading, 31,* 10–18.

Wood, Karen D. (1987). Teaching vocabulary in the subject areas. *Middle School Journal, 19*, 11–13.

Wood, Karen D. (1988). A guide to reading subject area material. *Middle School Journal, 19*, 24–26.

Wood, Karen D. (1990). The Collaborative Listening-Viewing Guide: An aid for notetaking. *Middle School Journal, 22*, 53–56.

Wood, Nancy. (1995). *The girl who loved coyotes: Stories of the Southwest*. New York: Morrow. Illustrated by Diana Bryer.

Worth, Valerie. (1987). *all the small poems*. New York: Farrar, Straus & Giroux. Illustrated by Natalie Babbitt.

Wrightson, Patricia. (1974). *The nargun and the stars*. New York: Atheneum.

Wyatt, Flora. (1988). Rethinking the research project through cooperative learning. *Middle School Journal, 19*, 6–7.

Yolen, Jane. (1977). *Rounds about rounds*. NY: Franklin Watts.

Yolen, Jane. (1986). *The lullaby songbook*. Fort Worth TX: Harcourt Brace Jovanovich.

Yaffe, Stephen H. (1989). Drama as a teaching tool. *Educational Leadership, 46*, 29–32.

Yager, Robert E. (1983). The importance of terminology in teaching K–12 science. *Journal of Research in Science Teaching, 20*, 577–588.

Yolen, Jane. (1972). *The fireside song book of birds and beasts*. New York: Simon and Schuster.

Yolen, Jane. (1992). *Street rhymes around the world*. Honesdale, PA: Wordsong.

Yore, Larry D. (1991). Secondary science teachers' attitudes toward and beliefs about science reading and science textbooks. *Journal of Research in Science Teaching, 28*, 55–72.

Young, Petey, Ruck, Carolyn, & Crocker, Betty. (1991). Reading science: It's not quite *Jack and the Beanstalk. Science Teacher, 58,* 46–49.

Young, Terrell, & Vardell, Sylvia. (1993). Weaving Readers Theatre and nonfiction into the curriculum. *The Reading Teacher, 46*, 396–406.

Zabrucky, Karen, & Ratner, Hilary Horn. (1992). Effects of passage type on comprehension monitoring and recall in good and poor readers. *Journal of Reading Behavior, 24*, 373–391.

Zarillo, James. (1994). *Multicultural literature, multicultural teaching*. Fort Worth, TX: Harcourt Brace Jovanovich.

Zarnowski, Myra. (1991). Wait!...before you throw out that outdated textbook. *Social Studies and the Young Learner, 3*, 3–5.

Zolotow, Charlotte. (1995). *When the wind stops*. New York: HarperCollins. Illustrated by Stefano Vitale.

Zubrowski, Bernie. (1992). *Mirrors: Finding out about the properties of light*. New York: Morrow. Illustrated by Roy Doty.

Zubrowski, Bernie. (1993). *Mobiles: Building and experimenting with balancing toys*. New York: Morrow. Illustrated by Roy Doty.

Zutell, Jerry. (1993). The Directed Spelling Thinking Activity (DSTA). In *Literacy for the new millennium*. Carlton, Victoria, Australia: Australian Reading Association.

Subject Index

Author Index

Strickland, Dorothy S., 234, 344, 405, 406, 551, 566
Suhor, Charles, 321, 566
Sutherland, Zena, 459, 460, 566
Swaby, Barbara, 138, 566
Swafford, Jeanne, 386, 566
Swann, Brian, 296, 566
Sylvester, Robert, 480, 568

Taba, Hilda, 137, 566
Taft, R., 343, 566
Tan, Ann G. A., 333, 558
Taylor, Barbara M., 223, 566
Taylor, Denny, 226, 276, 566
Taylor, Wilson, 87, 566
Tegano, Deborah W., 281-282, 566
Telfer, Richard, 449, 559
Tellegen, Auke, 276, 551-552
Terkel, Studs, 132, 387, 566-567
Terrell, Tracy D., 281, 289, 557
Thelen, Judith N., 83, 567
Thiele, Colin, 505, 567
Thomas, Ruth, 140, 556
Thomas, Sharon K., 176, 567
Thorndike, Edward L., 227, 567
Thornley-Hall, Carol, 59, 545
Tidwell, Deborah, xv, 245, 563
Tippins, Deborah J., 484, 556
Tobias, Sheila, 271, 567
Tomecek, Steve, 92, 567
Tomlinson, Carl M., 503, 567
Tompkins, Gail E., 17, 565
Tone, Bruce, 191, 567
Totten, Samuel, 189, 567
Trafton Paul R., 28, 567
Trelease, Jim, 132, 134, 567
Trimble, Kimberly D., 271, 567
Trotter, Andrew, 285-286, 567
Tuchman, Barbara W., 443, 567
Tuleja, Tad, 540, 567
Turbill, Jan, 32, 323-324, 546
Turner, Robyn Montana, 436, 567

Urzúa, Carole, 288, 290, 299, 567

Valencia, Sheila W., 74, 324, 549, 567
Vallecorsa, Ada L., 415, 567
VanAllen, Roach, 234, 557
Van Allsburg, Chris, 391, 436, 567
Van Ausdall, Barbara Wass, 136-137, 409, 567
Vanterpool, Maureen, 8, 551
Vardell, Sylvia, 460, 569

Vasquez, James, 275, 313, 567
Vaughan, Charlene Loughlin, 405, 567
Vavra, Ed, 414, 567
Velarde, M. Cristina, 369, 562
Veldman, Donald, 393, 559
Vellutino, Frank R., 255, 567, pronunciation: vella-tee'-no
Vermette, Paul, 150, 152, 567
Verriour, Patrick, 440, 442, 567
Voss, Margaret M., 227, 567
Vuong, Lynette Dyer, 465, 567
Vygotsky, Lev, 3, 33-34, 152, 229, 311, 567

Wade, Barrie, 48
Wade, Jan, 505, 567
Wadlington, Elizabeth, 404, 567
Wadsworth, Pamela, 176, 265, 567-568
Walberg, Herbert J., 227, 553
Walker, Barbara, J., 121, 568
Walker, Hill, 480, 568
Walker, Jim, 166, 568
Walker-Dalhouse, Doris, 291-292, 568
Wallace, Judy, 287, 546
Wallach, Michael A., 174, 568
Warawa, Bonnie, 463, 568
Wardrop, James L., 74, 549
Warner, Michael, 128, 564
Watson, Becky, 150, 568
Watson, Dorothy, 224, 230, 558, 568
Watson, Marilyn S., 277, 565
Watson, Wendy, 264, 568
Weatherford, Jack, 291, 568
Webb, Noreen M., 157, 158, 568
Weber, Alan, 413, 568
Weiner, Bernard, 282, 568
Weiner, Wendy F., 404, 568
Weisner, Thomas, 281, 297-298, 568
Welker, William A., 89, 568
Weller, Cyril J., 405, 564
Wells, Deborah, 451, 568
Wells, Gordon, 132, 568
Wells, Robert E., 183, 568
Wendelin, Karla Hawkins, 462, 568
Wentworth, Julie Welch, 413, 568
Werner, Emmy, 276, 568
Weston, Lynda, 285, 371, 568
Whalen, Samuel, 482, 548
Whang, Gail, 456, 520, 564
White, E. B., 457, 568
White, George P., 327, 568
Whitin, David, J., 165, 568
Wickey, Brenda J., 475, 568

Wiesendanger, Katherine D., 47, 568
Wiesner, David, 391, 568
Wiggins, Grant, 59, 324, 331, 568
Wilde, Sandra, 404, 568
Wildman, Diane, 434, 568
Wilford, John Noble, 92, 196, 539, 568
Wilhelmi, Keith, 365, 568
Wilkinson, Andrew, 385, 388, 568
Wilkinson, Ian A. G., 63, 132, 218, 543. 565
Wilkinson, Lyn, 502-503, 551
Willey, Carol, 146, 546
Williams, Karen Lynn, 264, 568
Williams, Kipling, 157, 569
Willis, Therese M., 389, 544
Willson, Paula, 455, 565
Wilson, Paul T., 121, 568
Wilson, Marilyn, 176, 567
Wilson, Marilyn J., 369, 563
Wilson, R. M., 121, 551
Winograd, Peter, 271, 569
Winters, Lynn, 313, 327, 339, 554
Wisniewski, David, 436, 569
Wittmer, Donna Sasse, 277, 569
Wixson, Karen K., 275, 558
Woehler, Carol A., 51, 542
Wolf, Dennie Palmer, 332, 569
Wolf, Kenneth P., 322, 569
Wong, Jo Ann, 237, 569
Wood, Karen D., 83, 123, 138, 150, 388, 569
Wood, Nancy, 466-467, 569
Worth, Valerie, 263, 569
Wrightson, Patricia, 505, 569
Wyatt, Flora, 191-192, 569
Wynn, Margie, 278, 557

Yaffe, Stephen H., 441, 569
Yager, Robert E., 19, 569
Yolen, Jane, 439, 514, 569
Yore, Larry D., 36, 569
Young, Petey, 133, 569
Young, Terrell A., 351, 460, 569

Zabrucky, Karen, 10, 569
Zancanella, Dan, 292, 563
Zarillo, James, 466, 569
Zarnowski, Myra, 24, 569
Zolotow, Charlotte, 497, 498, 569
Zubrowski, Bernie, 92, 433, 569
Zutell, Jerry, 416, 569